REDHOUSE'S TURKISH DICTIONARY,

In Two Parts,

ENGLISH AND TURKISH,
AND
TURKISH AND ENGLISH

REDHOUSE'S TURKISH DICTIONARY,

In Two Parts,

ENGLISH AND TURKISH,
AND
TURKISH AND ENGLISH

IN WHICH THE TURKISH WORDS ARE REPRESENTED IN THE ORIENTAL CHARACTER, AS WELL AS THEIR CORRECT PRONUNCIATION AND ACCENTUATION SHOWN IN ENGLISH LETTERS.

BY J. W. REDHOUSE, M.R.A.S.

BY

CHARLES WELLS, Ph. D. (Leipsic)

GYAN

Published by

GYAN

Gyan Publishing House
5, Ansari Road
Daryaganj, New Delhi-110002
Phone: 011-47034999, 9811692060
E-mail: books@gyanbooks.com

Distribution Network
gyanbooks.com
India, USA, Canada, UK, Australia

ISBN: 978-81-212-8406-6 (HB)
First Published, 1856

2nd Impression 2024

Printed at: Gyan Press, Delhi.

REDHOUSE'S TURKISH DICTIONARY, IN TWO PARTS, ENGLISH AND TURKISH, AND TURKISH AND ENGLISH
Author: J. W. REDHOUSE, CHARLES WELLS

تركجه انكليزجه لغت كتابى

تأليف ردحاوص الانكليزى

REDHOUSE'S TURKISH DICTIONARY,

In Two Parts,

ENGLISH AND TURKISH,

AND

TURKISH AND ENGLISH.

ترکجه انکلیزجه لغت کتابی
تألیف ردحاوص الانکلیزی

REDHOUSE'S TURKISH DICTIONARY,

In Two Parts,

ENGLISH AND TURKISH,

AND

TURKISH AND ENGLISH.

IN WHICH THE TURKISH WORDS ARE REPRESENTED IN THE ORIENTAL CHARACTER, AS WELL AS THEIR CORRECT PRONUNCIATION AND ACCENTUATION SHOWN IN ENGLISH LETTERS.

BY J. W. REDHOUSE, M.R.A.S.

MEMBER OF THE IMPERIAL ACADEMY OF SCIENCE OF CONSTANTINOPLE, ETC.

Second Edition, Revised and Enlarged

BY

CHARLES WELLS, Ph.D. (Leipsic),

Formerly Professor at the Imperial Naval College, Constantinople, Author of علم تدبیر ملك *(An Essay on Political Economy in Turkish), of "Mehemet the Kurd and other Tales from Eastern Sources." Late Private Secretary to Lieut.-General Sir Arnold Kemball on the Turco-Persian Frontier Commission, Turkish Prizeman of King's College, London, &c.*

لوندره شهرنده پیکادیلی صوقاغنده کتابجی قواریچ افندینك
دکاننده فروخت اولنور

LONDON:

BERNARD QUARITCH, 15 PICCADILLY.

1880.

INTRODUCTION TO THE SECOND EDITION.

It is an extraordinary and lamentable fact that the language of the Turks has hitherto received little or no attention in England, although it is spoken by millions of people belonging to a vast empire with which we are closely connected by mutual vital interests, and is more or less used, in official circles, from Tunis in Africa to the walls of China. It is the Court language of Persia, and in many provinces of that country is spoken as much as Persian. It is difficult to account for the absolute neglect of the study of such an important language, considering that it is used by a people who once influenced half the world, who overturned and established empires, who have possessed the thrones of Persia, Syria, Greece, and Arabia, whose power was once dreaded by Italy, Germany and France, and to whom our proud Queen Elizabeth applied for aid against the Spanish Armada. The Turkish language has always been of the greatest consequence to us, owing to the importance of our political and commercial relations with the Ottoman Empire, and the complete ignorance of it on the part of our countrymen has greatly impeded proper communication and intercourse between the two nations and given rise to most serious misunderstandings and difficulties, both in the diplomatic and commercial world. Hitherto, the only means of communication between the two peoples has been the employment of Levantine interpreters, who seldom or never know either English or Turkish properly, and speak the latter unidiomatically and with a vulgar accent peculiarly distasteful to the educated Osmanlis. Recent events in the East, by which we have become in one sense identified with the Turkish Empire through having undertaken the Protectorate of Asia Minor and the administration of Cyprus, now render the acquisition of the Turkish language by English officials and commercial men more urgent than ever, and indeed it is absolutely indispensable if we wish to fulfil our task efficiently and avoid endless complications with the natives and the Turkish Government. We may therefore hope that this subject will at last receive the attention it deserves on the part of the Government and the nation, that proper facilities will be afforded for the acquisition of the language by a Professorship of Turkish being founded at one of our Universities, and encouragement and reward being offered to those who devote themselves to this arduous study. Persons wishing to become student-interpreters, or officials in any part of Turkey, in Asia Minor, or in Cyprus, should be required to possess, at least, some knowledge of Turkish before being appointed and before leaving England, as they will find the want of proper teachers in Turkey an insuperable barrier against beginning its study in that country. The only persons who teach Turkish in the East are Greeks and Armenians, most of whom appear physically incapable of pronouncing Turkish correctly, and possess in general little or no knowledge of the literary language. As we have in English nearly every sound existing in Turkish, an Englishman, if properly taught, can pronounce far better than a Greek or an Armenian. For the same reason, as I found from experience in instructing the students at the Imperial Naval College of Constantinople, Turks can pronounce our language far more purely than the Christian races under their government. A good dictionary is indispensable for acquiring any language, and Mr. REDHOUSE rendered a national service when he produced his excellent work, which I hesitate not to say is incomparably the most correct and trustworthy Turkish lexicon in any European language. The original edition having been exhausted, I willingly consented to Mr. QUARITCH's proposal that I should edit a second issue, as all students of the language would find such a book most necessary, and the learned author sanctioned my undertaking. While preserving all the valuable matter contained in the first edition, I have attempted to increase its usefulness by the addition of a considerable number of words omitted originally for want of space, or which have been coined by the Turks during the last twenty years to meet the requirements of their advancing civilisation. Amongst other things, the names of countries, towns, rivers, mountains, and other geographical words were entirely left out of the English-Turkish part, and nearly completely omitted in the other part. These I have supplied, giving special attention to names of places in the East. The English-Turkish portion being scarcely copious enough to enable a Turk to read an English book, or an Englishman to write or speak on all subjects in Turkish, I have introduced a large number of fresh words into it, and I have also, to some extent, augmented the Turkish-English part. Thus, the present edition will be found to contain several thousand more words than the original work published twenty-five years ago, which, however, was far more correct and copious than any other European Turkish lexicon.

It is a strange fact that the number of Englishmen who can read and write Turkish is so small that they can be counted on the fingers of one hand. The English public, and what is more astonishing, the English residents in Turkey, know scarcely anything of this curious and interesting tongue, and rarely succeed even in speaking a few words properly; yet to understand a nation rightly a knowledge of its language is most essential. As I once remarked in an article in the *Gentleman's Magazine* published some years ago, the physical features of the East, the length and breadth of its rivers, the height of its mountains, and the costumes of its peoples, have been ascertained and described by enterprising European travellers; but the spirit of the East, which only can be comprehended by a thorough acquaintance with its language and familiar intercourse with the natives, has remained a sealed book to Europe. Indeed many works which have been written for the purpose of enlightening us with regard to the East, have, with rare exceptions, only misrepresented and burlesqued it, although, I admit, that the writers did this in all sincerity and unconsciousness. If Europeans ever learn what the inner life of the East is, they will find that their ideas have been wonderfully narrow and one-sided; that many things they believed to be universally true are, under certain circumstances and in certain places, absolutely false; and they will discover much that is good and valuable in the institutions, and much that is admirable in the manners and customs of the Turks, as well as some things which we might with advantage imitate.

A lengthy discourse on the language and literature of the Osmanlis would be somewhat out of place here, but a brief account of them may be interesting to the general reader and, especially, to those about to commence the study of Turkish. The Turkish language is of Tartar origin, as the Turks came from Central Asia, and is consequently quite distinct from Arabic and Persian; although it is true that in modern times the Arabic characters have been adopted for all three languages, and that the Constantinople dialect is half filled with Arabic and Persian words, but these have been incorporated without affecting the nature or framework of the Turkish, which is as different from Arabic and Persian as Anglo-Saxon from Latin and Greek. The original Turkish tongue was somewhat barbarous, but extremely forcible and concise when spoken. Very often, in colloquial language, a whole sentence in a European language can be expressed by one or two words in Turkish. For example, the phrase "The book which I have written," can be expressed in Turkish in two words, viz., *yazdighim kitab*. In fact, Turkish is a language in which pronouns personal and relative, conjunctions, and other parts of speech constantly recurring in European languages are almost entirely dispensed with, by the help of certain peculiar inflections of which the verb is capable. Unfortunately, this superiority in Turkish has been more than counterbalanced by the cumbersome and inflated style which has become prevalent in writing, especially in official documents, sentence on sentence being strung together into one, until the reader is at a complete loss to catch the writer's meaning. Another mistake the Turks have made is in adopting Arabic and Persian words *ad libitum;* so that to understand their language it is absolutely necessary to be acquainted with nearly all the words in the other two, and something of their grammars. Thus in reality to comprehend written Turkish you have to acquire three languages, in great part, instead of one. This fact, no doubt, is one great reason why so few Europeans have succeeded in mastering Turkish; and a Turk must study his own language many years before he can either read or write it properly. There are almost always in Turkish three names for everything—the original Turkish, the Arabic, and the Persian—and thus the student has a triple vocabulary to acquire. Had Persian and Arabic words been taken only when there was no Turkish word to express what was required, Turkish would have become an extremely rich and powerful language; but words having been adopted indiscriminately has led to a redundancy which is only embarrassing both to the native and the foreigner, while thousands of abstract but most useful words are still non-existent in Turkish. Notwithstanding, therefore, the enormous number of words to be found in a Turkish dictionary, it is an extremely difficult thing to express one's self in Turkish on any civilised subject, or to translate any ordinary European work into it. Great progress, however, has been made during the last twenty years in simplifying the Turkish style, and in coining words to express scientific ideas. Ali Pasha and Fuad Pasha took the initiative in this matter, and they have since had many worthy imitators, such as Ali* Suavi Effendi, Kemal Bey, and Zia Bey. The Imperial Military and Naval Colleges have also been most useful laboratories for the production of new words, the necessity for which was found in instructing the students in European arts and sciences, and in translating French and English works for them. A great number of very useful books have been prepared by the professors of those excellent institutions, and although generally not original, they are very creditable, and have done much good in shaping and improving modern Turkish. Some enlightened and unprejudiced officials, such as Saïd Pasha, who was Minister of Marine in 1878, and formerly Governor of the Naval College,

* Ali Suavi Effendi, a well-known Turkish *savant* and a very able writer, was the editor of a Turkish newspaper, called the "*Mukhbir*" (مخبر), published some years ago in London, to which I myself contributed, which aimed at introducing not merely political reforms into Turkey, such as parliamentary government, financial control, &c., but also recommended and inaugurated a reform of Turkish composition, orthography, &c., and the introduction of a clear and simple style similar to that approved of in most European languages.

have also lately set the example of writing Turkish in a simple and practical style, and encouraged and promoted this improvement. This able statesman (Saïd Pasha) is a striking illustration of what I have stated above, that Turks and Englishmen can acquire each other's language with remarkable purity, as he speaks and writes English like an Englishman.

Yet, notwithstanding the cumbrousness I have above complained of, the language of the Turks possesses a great and interesting literature; works on almost all subjects known to Orientals: history, geography, astronomy, mathematics, logic, theology, geometry, arithmetic, &c., were to be found in Turkish hundreds of years ago—in manuscripts only, of course. Indeed, books on those subjects had been written at so remote a period as a century prior to the conquest of Constantinople, and some historical, astronomical, and poetical works by celebrated writers of that day are still in existence. It is also to the credit of the Turks that they always had in ancient times, and still have, a deep reverence for learning and literary men, while their sovereigns have been great patrons of literature, and have treated authors and *savans* with the most liberal favour and munificence. It is reported that the last words of Sultan Othman to his son Orkhan were, "Be the upholder of the faith and the protector of science;" and no sooner had the crescent been planted on the walls of Broussa than Orkhan gave orders for the erection of a royal college. This example was followed by his successors, who have vied with each other in the protection and encouragement of letters.

The Turkish writers excel particularly in historical composition. They have many valuable works of history, written by private individuals, and a regular series of public annals from the most remote times to the present, compiled by the official historiographers of the empire.

Among their most celebrated historians are Sead-u-din, the historiographer of Murad the Third, the author of "*Taj-u-Tevarikh*," ("The Crown of Histories,") Jelal Zadé, the author of "*Tarikhi Jelal Zadé*," the Annals of the reign of Suleiman I. and Selaniki, whose works are only to be found in manuscript, and Rashid Effendi, Sami, Shagir, and Subhi, whose works have been printed by the Imperial press. Amongst historians also must not be forgotten the learned Haji Khalifé, who wrote several historical and geographical books, and a work on Oriental bibliography, a universal history in Arabic, and also the History of the Maritime Wars of the Turks, the History of Constantinople, and the celebrated Oriental geography called "*Jihan Numa*," ("The World-Shewer").

The Turks have always cultivated poetry with the greatest zeal and considerable success. Poets have ever been greatly honoured and munificently rewarded by them. Their poetry, it is true, is somewhat wild and extravagant, but full of power and imagination. Amongst others, Fazli's version of the *Gul-u-Bulbul* ("The Rose and the Nightingale") is a really beautiful poem, and a mere list of Turkish poets of respectable ability would fill pages.

In conclusion, the Turkish language, in the simplicity and regularity of its original framework and mechanism, is only equalled among European languages by the Spanish, in the attention it pays to euphony by no European language, except perhaps Hungarian, and in the richness of its resources, if it would make but proper use of them, it might rank with any language of Europe or Asia.

To cement the alliance and the friendship which have existed for so many years between England and Turkey, and to promote the interest of both nations, nothing is more indispensable than that they should acquire each other's language. The Turks have made great efforts and spared no expense to this end. Hundreds of young Turkish officers studied English under me, after my appointment by the Turkish Government as Professor of the English Language at Constantinople, and nearly all of them displayed the greatest zeal and ability. It is to be hoped now that the same ardour will be shown and the same attention given, on the part of the British Government and people, in promoting the study of the Turkish language in England.

Having had great experience in connection with the acquisition of Turkish and other Oriental languages, I venture to call the attention of the Government and the public to the fact that sending out gentlemen to Turkey who have merely given proof of possessing an ordinarily good European education, and who have evinced no special aptitude for acquiring Eastern languages, is not the best method they could have adopted for obtaining a body of Oriental scholars who would be really useful to them. Facilities should be afforded for studying Turkish in England, and then only those who gave proof of capability to master Turkish—a feat by no means in everybody's power—should be appointed student-interpreters. Austrian and Russian officials in the East learn Turkish at their respective universities before going to Turkey, and Russia and Austria have consequently had for many years good Turkish scholars in their service. We shall never have good Oriental scholars in ours until we adopt the same system. No one can learn to speak and write Turkish by mere residence in the country, as is proved by English and other European residents in Turkey not being conversant with the language who have lived there for twenty and thirty years.

But any one who goes to Turkey, having already studied the language successfully, will speedily become thorough master of it. He will find plenty of opportunities for practising his knowledge of Turkish, if he have any; but if he have none, he will never pick the language up, as it is called, by merely breathing the air of Constantinople. Without study, Turkish, as written and spoken for diplomatic purposes, can never be mastered, and facilities for this study at first, at least, are best found in England. Moreover, it is far better that the government should only help those who have given proof of their ability, and this could be tested by establishing a Turkish Professorship here, and sending out only those who should have passed an examination in Turkish—the plan already adopted, I believe, in the case of Chinese students.

CHARLES WELLS.

LONDON, *December*, 1879.

CONTENTS.

NOTICE.

The abbreviations ا *and* او *in the Turkish character, and* et *and* òl *in the English, used in both parts of this Dictionary, stand respectively for the auxiliary verbs* ایتمك *and* اولمق*, and their pronunciations* ètmek *and* òlmak.

REDHOUSE'S TURKISH DICTIONARY.

PREFACE TO THE FIRST EDITION.

In the spring of 1855, on the occasion of the formation of the Turkish Legion, the author of the present work published a "Vade-Mecum of Ottoman Colloquial Language," in the Preface of which he promised to prepare, "for the information of those who may wish afterwards to penetrate deeper into the arcana of this really beautiful tongue, a series of more complete and scientific works."

The following pages are a first instalment towards the redemption of the pledge then given. From the size of this volume, the reader must at once perceive that it has not the pretension of being a complete dictionary of the two languages, which it would require several years of constant labour to bring into existence. But as there does not exist in English any similar work, it has been judged that a book which shall contain the more usual terms of the two languages, and explain the more striking modifications of their meanings—which shall give, not only the orthography of the Turkish words (whether of Arabic, Persian, or Turkish origin), but also their *correct* pronunciation *and accentuation*—two things never achieved, and the latter never attempted, even in the best dictionaries published on the continent—could not fail of being acceptable to the very great number of our countrymen now interested in obtaining quickly a competent knowledge of the language of our Eastern allies; and the author has therefore undertaken to provide them with as good a dictionary as could be prepared within a reasonable space of time.

For the materials of this book he is indebted to no one, even of the continental authors, unless in so far as he has used two dictionaries to arrive without loss of time at the alphabetical arrangement and selection of the words contained in either part of this publication. He does not pretend to be absolutely and entirely free from mistakes of any kind; but he confidently appeals to all capable of judging, to pronounce whether the great number of errors to be traced in every page of the more voluminous continental works, ancient or modern, is not a circumstance which greatly deteriorates the value of their productions, although, at the same time, the greatest credit is due to the authors for the immense labours they have undertaken in preparing their works for the use of the public. They have done their best, and the thanks of a host of students have been, and will continue to be, their just meed. Neither is it in any spirit of detraction that the author here notices these defects of his precursors; but, on the contrary, by alluding to them, he desires to stir up their authors, or others, to investigate the subject with renewed zeal and acumen, under the conviction that the greater the facilities afforded for an interchange of ideas between the East and West, the more rapidly will be effaced those invidious distinctions of caste or class, or nationality, or religious denomination, which ignorance and intolerance set up in bygone times, but which in England have generally given place to the more becoming rule and feeling of respecting in all the conscientious dictates of faith and taste, even as we ourselves wish to have respect and consideration shown to our own by all.

As above noticed, the publication of a complete Turkish and English Dictionary, if ever undertaken, will be a work of considerable expense, and will require years for its performance. Hitherto the number of those who might have occasion for such a book has been too limited by far to induce any one to make the attempt. These circumstances appear now likely to be changed, through the attention drawn to Turkey by the recent aggressions of Russia, and also by the vitality so unexpectedly discovered in the Ottoman Empire—the "sick man" of the aggressor. The author would be proud to answer this change, if effective, by an energetic attempt to fill up the void in English literature left by the want of such a work. The Turkish language is, in itself, well worthy of the labour; and, whatever the ideas on the subject hitherto current in England, as in the rest of Europe generally, there exists in that language a literature, mostly in manuscript as yet, it is true, as varied and as refined as that which is known to be found in the Persian tongue, though it does not embrace those periods of time, the middle ages, which render the study of Arabic and Persian doubly interesting. In a political and in a commercial view, the tongue of the Osmanli merits as great attention as any, since its use, or that of its congeners, among natives of every sect and nationality, or among official people, is spread from Tunis in Africa, throughout the Turkish Empire, the northern half of Persia, Khorassan, to Independent, Chinese, and Russian Tartary. But it is as true, as it will appear singular, that whether from apathy, or from the fatal delivering themselves up into the hands of *double sets* of interpreters (one set consisting of Greeks, Armenians, Jews, or Levantines, who explain verbally between Europeans and Turks, and the other of Turkish writers, who reduce these verbal expressions into written forms of their own), the greater part of our merchants and consuls living in Turkey, some for periods of fifty years, are unable, with a few rare exceptions, to read a word of the language, or perhaps to understand it when read to them; and many are even incapable of uttering a single phrase in common conversation. The fact, however, of servants, working engineers, and others picking up Turkish in a short time, without books or aids of any kind, is sufficient to indicate that there is nothing peculiarly difficult in the language itself; while the mere mechanical difficulty of the handwriting, as is known to all students, is equally easy to be got over with a little practice.

Hoping, therefore, that a taste for this useful language may spread, and that the occasion will thence arise for the preparation of more extensive works on the subject, to which he engages to respond to the best of his abilities, the author now offers the present work to the public, in the trust that it will be found as useful in its sphere as he could wish or expect.

LONDON, 1856.

ON THE SYSTEM OF ORTHOGRAPHY EMPLOYED TO REPRESENT THE TURKISH WORDS, AND ON THE POWERS OF THE TURKISH LETTERS AND ORTHOGRAPHICAL SIGNS.

IN representing the sounds of one language with the characters of another, we find that all or many of those characters generally possess more than one value in their original language. We observe, further, that the authors of pronouncing dictionaries are obliged to have recourse to various systems of orthography, in order to represent to the mind, through the eye, in a way freed from doubt, the sound of every letter in each separate word; and that a considerable difference exists between the current orthography and the results of each such system. The reasons of this divergence, in respect to the English language, may be reduced to three: 1st, Many words of foreign origin have preserved their original orthography and pronunciation (this latter more or less vitiated), which do not follow the same rules as the words of our own language; 2ndly, Many other words of foreign origin, though they have more or less been submitted to a process of adaptation to our pronunciation and orthography, still retain so many traces of their origin as to require explanation on the former, and authority for the latter, inasmuch as the two do not agree together with sufficient simplicity, or according to our received ideas of the fundamental values of their component letters; 3rdly, The difference of pronunciation of even indigenous words in different parts of the country, whereby an orthography more or less in consonance with the pronunciation of one part, at a certain period of time, was adopted by some one or other of the early English writers, and has since become (either with or without modification) generally or universally current, although it does not accord with the usual pronunciation now in use among the educated classes in the greater part of the kingdom.

Causes analogous to these have also affected the orthography and pronunciation of the Turkish language, the present alphabet and orthographical system of which are originally Arabic. In the pure Arabic the simple short vowels are never written, being merely marked over or under the consonant affected by them, and are but three in number—*a*, *i*, and *u* (Latin). When these are long, they are represented by separate letters, which have still their special values as consonants, viz. ا, و, and ی. Of these, the ا represents the sound of *ā*, the و of *ū* (*oo* English), the ی of *ī* (*ee* English). This system of the Arabic language (common also to the other Semitic dialects) was next adopted by the Persians when they embraced the religion of Muhammed; and although four consonants (پ, چ, ژ, گ) were added to the twenty-eight of the Arabians, nothing was done to extend the number of vowel-letters, or of the vowel-points, beyond the original three, excepting the definite adoption of a fourth consonant (ه) to represent the terminal broad *e* or surd *a* found in so many Persian words. The three original vowel-letters received also a second value each in addition to the Arabic one, viz. ا was made to represent the broad *a* of the English, the و the *o* of European languages, and the ی the *e* of the same as heard in our word *there*. The Turkish nation, coming from the eastern parts of Central Asia, first encountered the Arabian system of writing, under its modified form, in Persia. Adopting this, and, by their chief and early conquests in Greece and Asia Minor, escaping from the direct influence of the Arabians, they in their turn gave a new value to one consonant (ڭ) by making it represent a nasal *n* in addition to its Arabic value of *k*, and its Persian value of *g hard* (*gh*, or *gu*), and they also greatly extended the use occasionally made by the Persians of the three long vowels as representatives of their cognate short vowels.

Passing over, therefore, the consideration of the true number of different vowel-sounds which may exist in Arabic or in Persian, or of the number which may exist in any uncultivated Turkish or Tartar dialects, we may now proceed to observe that there are eleven distinct vowel-sounds in the cultivated Ottoman Turkish language, besides the modifications of certain of them by mere prolongation of sound; whereas there are still but three vowel-signs, and but four vowel-letters to represent them. This necessarily causes great confusion and difficulty, especially to learners; and to it, in great measure, I attribute the prevalent use of Arabic and Persian words (in writing, much more than in speaking) in preference to many of their most common Turkish equivalents. In all three of these languages a combination of two, three, or four letters, may often be read several different ways, the signification varying with each modification of sound.

and there is no system in use among the nations speaking them whereby the true vowel-pronunciation of each word can be depicted to the intelligence through the medium of the eye, in a manner entirely free from doubt. The Persians have adopted two terms whereby they describe the different values of the vowel و as representing *u* and *o*, also of ى as representing *e* and *i*; but further they have not gone, and these terms have no equivalent mark in writing; so that the number of vowel-letters remains but four, and of the vowel-points but three, to represent the eleven vowels existing in Turkish. At the beginning of words they employ two combinations (او and اى) of these vowel-letters, which have been looked upon as diphthongs; but this is not really so: they represent no separate vowel-sound; they are merely used, or rather the و and the ى are introduced to define the value of the ا, which in Arabic takes the three vowel-sounds indifferently, in the same way as the other consonants. These, then, are no true addition to the number of Turkish vowel-letters, and او is read *u* the same as قو is read *ku*, and اى *i* as قى is *ki*.*

The eleven Turkish vowel-sounds are the following:—

1st,	*of*	a	*in*	all.	7th,	*of*	i	*in*	girl.
2nd,	..	a	..	far.	8th,	..	o	..	go.
3rd,	..	a	..	about.	9th,	..	u in the French *tu*.		
4th,	..	a	..	pan.	10th,	..	u	..	full.
5th,	..	e	..	pen.	11th,	..	u	..	fun.
6th,	..	i	..	pin.					

Our system of orthography in this book for representing the pronunciation of the Turkish words is founded upon the two following axioms:—First, *No character shall have two values;* and second, *No value shall be represented by more than one special character.*

In applying these two rules to the eleven vowel-sounds, we have been led to

* There exists even at the beginning of some Turkish words the combination اوى, which may have been considered in like manner a triphthong; but in this case, as in that of the two combinations, اى and وى at the ends of some words and syllables, the ى is a true consonant, and therefore we are justified in totally denying the existence of diphthongs or triphthongs in the Turkish language.

adopt the following eleven characters to represent them, all of which are well known modifications in form of our own five vowels :—

1st,	a *as in* wall,	*thus* A		7th,	i *as in* girl.	*thus* *i*
2nd,	a . . . far,	. . . a		8th,	o . . . go,	. . . o
3rd,	a . . . about,	. . . *a*		9th,	u . . . *tu* French	. . u
4th,	a . . . pan,	. . . E		10th,	u . . . full,	. . . U
5th,	e . . . pen,	. . . e		11th,	u . . . fun,	. . . *u*
6th,	i . . . pin,	. . . i				

By the use of these modified vowels the learner can see at once what particular value is attached to each, and, at the same time, he will not be obliged to make the distinction, unless he prefers doing it, in making notes himself of words he may meet with in reading or in conversation. This book is essentially a pronouncing dictionary; and were the European character ever to be adopted in Turkey, for the purpose of writing the Ottoman language, there is no reason why the *a*, the *e*, the *i*, and the *u* should not bear several values as they do with us; whereas, in printing, and, if necessary, even in writing, the difference could be pointed out by one or two strokes under them, thereby leaving the upper part free for the introduction of special signs to distinguish the long from the short vowels, and the accentuated from the unaccentuated syllables.

We have adopted these characters in preference to others, because they are to be found at the printers', and because every one knows them. True it is that their special value here has to be learnt and remembered, but so would that of any signs we might have invented. Our special reason for not adopting Sir William Jones's "*dashed vowels*" is because, their dash being over them, it would have interfered with the introduction of the signs of syllabic accent and vowel quantity. We have further felt obliged to abstain from and condemn the diphthongs *ai* and *au* of that great philosopher and most distinguished writer, by reason that the idea which caused him to employ them is fundamentally erroneous in conception; and we have been grieved to observe that these errors have been already too extensively adopted by other writers of distinction, and by the numerous body of missionaries in India and the South Seas. It is singular that an Englishman should have fallen into the error of calling these combinations diphthongs, when his own language contains the true solutions to the problem. Sir William Jones appears to have been led away in this matter by the study of French or Latin, in neither of which languages does the consonant *w* exist, neither is the letter *y* regarded in their grammars as a consonant.

English grammarians have laid it down as a rule that *w* and *y* are consonants at the beginning of words or syllables, but vowels at the end or in the middle. It must be conceded that *y* standing alone in the middle of a syllable is a vowel; but *w* is never so used in English. As the second letters of diphthongs in the middle of syllables they may be considered either as vowels or consonants, without much practical inconvenience resulting from the error in either case; and *y*, at the end of syllables, when immediately preceded by a consonant, may certainly be considered a true vowel. There remains then to be considered the case of these two letters when they terminate a syllable and are preceded by a vowel. In this case Oriental grammarians have justly regarded them as consonants; nor would it be difficult to establish that the practice of the English tongue fully confirms that decision, as regards the letter *y*, and also as regards the *w* if preceded by an *o*. Take for instance the words *flow* and *flay*: now, in forming from them the participles *flowing* and *flaying*, we can perceive that *w* and *y* are as much consonants as though the division of the two words into separate syllables was *flo-wing* and *fla-ying*, when, even by the admitted rules of our grammarians, these letters would be consonants. This being established, more as a means of comparison between certain conditions of our language and the elements of the Turkish, we may now state that we consider the letters *w* any *y* as consonants in all cases where we use them in our system of orthography as here adopted for representing the sound of the Turkish language; and, to complete our system of syllabic formation, we have but to follow out the series of vowels preceding or following these two letters in the same manner as for the other consonants; thus:—

Ab	ab	*ab*	eb	Eb	ib	*ib*	ob	ub	Ub	*ub*
bA	ba	*ba*	bé	bÉ	bi	*bi*	bo	bu	bU	*bu*
AW	aw	*aw*	ew	EW	iw	*iw*	ow	uw	UW	*uw*
WA	wa	*wa*	wé	WÉ	wi	*wi*	wo	wu	WU	*wu*
Ay	ay	*ay*	ey	Ey	iy	*iy*	oy	uy	Uy	*uy*
yA	ya	*ya*	yé	yÉ	yi	*yi*	yo	yu	yU	*yu*

Several of the combinations contained in the third, and nearly all those in the fifth of these lines, will be met with in the following pages. The learner must then merely take heed not to give to the combination the sound of a diphthong, as he would have to do were he reading English, but to keep the sound of the vowel pure in the same way as when read before any other consonant. Thus:—Kaw will sound as our English *cow*, and y*i*w analogously;

pay will read like *pie*, rey like *ray*, soy exactly as in English, and kıy, as also muy, will each be readily understood, though we have no similar combination in our language. It will thus become apparent that these are not diphthongs composed of two consecutive or combined vowel-sounds, but, on the contrary, a pure and simple vowel, followed by a simple consonant.

The foregoing remarks are of more consequence than appears at first sight: not only is a correct appreciation of any subject a great desideratum in itself, but this particular bears also in no slight degree upon the question of reduplicated consonants, since we frequently meet with both the و and the ى reduplicated, and this could not be unless they were true consonants. It has also a very great grammatical influence upon the words, and roots of words, which have these terminations, as it will be seen throughout the Turkish Grammar that affixes and inflexions vary, according as they are joined on to a word ending with a vowel, or to one ending with a consonant; and it will be found that in all these cases the doctrine here laid down agrees with the principle upon which that language moves. It has the further advantage, too, of confining the letters *w* and *y* to one sole value, instead of using them sometimes as vowels, sometimes as consonants.

Proceeding, now, to a consideration of the Turkish characters in themselves, and of their values, as also of the mode of transcription here adopted for the consonants, we first observe that the Turkish alphabet consists of twenty-eight simple and primitive characters of Arabic origin, the ordinary names and primary forms of which are as follows :—

ا èlif, ب ب bè, ت ت tè, ث ث sè, ج ج jìm, ح ح hà, خ خ khì, د د dàl, ذ ذ zèl, ر ر rì, ز ز zè, س س sìn, ش ش shìn, ص ص sàd, ض ض dàd, ط ط tì, ظ ظ zì, ع ع "àyn, غ غ ghàyn, ف ف fè, ق ق kàf, ك ك kèf, ل ل làm, م م mìm, ن ن nùn, و و wòw, ى ى yè.

To these original Arabic letters are to be added the three following, received from the Persian, which have a special form, distinguished from the originals whence they are derived by the number of dots under or over them, viz.—

پ پ pè,	*derived from*	ب ب bè.
چ chìm,	. . . .	ج jìm.
ژ zhè (French j)	. . . .	ز zè,

The additional dots of these letters of Persian origin are often to be found in written, and even in printed, books. The last of them is only used in a very few (five or six at most) words of Persian origin.

The fourth letter added by the Persians, namely, the ڭ, is generally left without its distinguishing points, and these, even when added, are sometimes used as marking, not the Persian value of the character, but a third use to which this letter is universally applied by the Turks, that of a nasal *n*, equivalent to our English *ng* at the end of *sing, ring,* &c., but softened down to a common *n* in the pronunciation of the capital, and of people of refined manners in many of the provinces. A second method is also in use, by which to distinguish the Persian value of this letter: it consists in giving it a double dash in all its positions, whether initial, medial, or final; whereas, in the case of the Arabic value, the dash is single in the two first positions, and totally wanting in the last-named one. It results, therefore, that in printing, and in common or official writing, the one character ك has three distinct values, for which no discriminating signs are employed; and it is only in some manuscript books, generally when the whole of the vowel-points and other diacritical marks are inserted, that any distinction is made of the three values of this letter.

There is also a compound character in use, which is always to be found inserted in alphabets, and which, for that reason, cannot be passed over in silence. It is the character لا, called *làm-èlif,* being, in fact, nothing more than ل *làm* joined calligraphically to a following ا *èlif,* in a similar manner to that whereby our printers continue to join the *f* and *l* in fl, or the *f and i* in fi, &c.

Of these thirty-one (or thirty-two or thirty-three) Turkish letters, the ا (èlif), in its various uses, requires the greatest amount of explanation.

This letter is sometimes a vowel, and sometimes a consonant; the latter in some words of Arabic origin only, and even then only in the middle or at the end of these words, never as an initial. To denote this consonant value of the ا, it is always surmounted by the diacritical mark ء, named hèmzé, so that no confusion can occur between the vowel ا and the consonant. This rule of the hèmzé never affecting an initial ا, is a practical rule of Turkish, and does not apply to the Arabic language, which we are not here considering.

The consonant أ, then, we proceed to say, follows the same rules as do the other consonants in point of being followed or not by a vowel in the same syllable, and we need not dwell upon that subject here: we shall only remark that its power is that of a *slight* hiatus, or catch in the breath, and that we have represented it in this work, as in our little "Vade-Mecum of Ottoman Colloquial Language," by an inverted apostrophe, thus (ʻ). The sign hèmzé represents in Arabic, I apprehend, the transition from the natural state of the organs of speech when in perfect repose and closed against the passage of vocalized breath: it represents, also, *vice versâ*, the stop applied, when speaking, to cut off suddenly the emission of this vocalized breath; and the action it represents differs, therefore, altogether from that whereby a vowel-sound is made to follow the formation of any definite consonant, or whereby that sound is cut off by such a formation following it, or whereby it is simply allowed to cease itself from being emitted without any change of position in the organs of speech. This view of the value of the hèmzé is, as before stated, altogether overlooked, however, in Turkish, at the beginning of words; and the ا (élif) is then regarded always as a simple vowel.

As a vowel at the beginning of words the ا may represent every vowel-sound found in the language, in the same manner that any consonant may be followed by every such sound. Nor does it differ from the consonants in the modes of determining the vowel-sound to be given to it; and, as those modes are general, we proceed to state them here.

It has already been noticed that there are three signs of Arabic origin, used in Turkish to indicate the vowel which is *to follow* a letter. These are named حركه hàréké (motion, *or* movement), and the first, consisting of an oblique straight stroke marked above the letter from right towards the left in descending (thus ´), is called اوستون ùsstun and فتحه fètha (t-h.) It indicates that the letter over which it is placed is to be followed in pronunciation by one of the vowels, A, a, *a*, E, *or* é, which, it will be perceived, form a series of vocal sounds of a cognate character, varying merely in breadth, and capable of infinite sub-modifications of tone. In fact, these five vowels do not correctly and fully express all the modulations which an experienced ear can detect in Turkish pronunciation, which may be truly compared, in its nicety of differentiation, to a violin, in which the notes are left to be formed by the player, rather than to any instrument in which the notes or half-notes are absolutely fixed. Therefore, although we have deemed it useful and very necessary to indicate, to the extent we have done, the different vowel-sounds of Turkish words, we admit that a still greater variety exists, which we leave to practice and experience to indicate to learners, believing that the extent to which we have pushed the subject will be found sufficient for all practical purposes.

The second vowel-sign consists in a precisely similar stroke placed under the letter, and is called اسره èsséré, *or* كسره késsré. It indicates that the letter is to be followed by one of the vowels i or *i*. The third is a small character something of the shape of the figure 9, or of the Turkish letter و, placed over the letter it affects, where the ùsstun would otherwise be. This sign is called اوتوری ùturu (and rarely ضمه dàmma *or* zàmma), and indicates that the letter affected is to be followed by one of the vowels o, u, ᴜ, or *u*, which it will be perceived are of a kindred kind.

According to what is stated above, the letter ا, when it bears the mark ùsstun, is equivalent to any one or other of the same five vowels indicated by the sign itself, and it may thence be correctly inferred that of itself, and at the beginning of words, it has no real value. It is in fact, in that position, a mere representative of the hèmzÉ, which is itself never introduced into Turkish writings at the beginning of words, though in Arabic it is figured over or under the ا, and in ancient manuscripts, and even common African writings, is sometimes made to precede that letter.

It may now be readily inferred that according as the ا is affected by one of the remaining vowel-points èsséré *or* ùturu, it takes the value of either i *or i*, or of o, u, ᴜ, *or u*. Thus اَ is read A, a, *a*, É, *or* é ; اِ is read i *or i* ; and اُ is read o, u, ᴜ, *or u*.

Not to have to repeat what is thus explained, we here shortly mention that the same rule applies generally to the whole of the remaining letters, the vowel following, but never preceding them. Thus, بَ is either bA, ba, b*a*, bÉ, *or* bé ; بِ is either bi *or* b*i* ; and بُ is either bo, bu, bᴜ, *or* b*u* ; and so throughout. It may not be amiss to notice particularly the case of the two letters و and ی, and to remark that, as with their English representatives *w* and *y*, they are always consonants at the beginning of words, and consequently وَ is to be read, vA (*or* wA, &c.), va, v*a*, vÉ, *or* vé ; وِ as vi *or* v*i* ; وُ as vo, vu, vᴜ, *or* v*u* ; while یَ is read, yA, ya, y*a*, yÉ, *or yé* ; یِ as yi *or* y*i* ; and یُ as yo, yu, yᴜ, *or* y*u*.

To make certain of these vowels long (the others never being prolonged in Turkish), the letter bearing the vowel-point is followed up by that one of the three letters ا, و, *or* ی, which is homologous with that vowel-point ; namely, by ا when the vowel-point is ùsstun, by ی when it is èsséré, and by و when it is ùturu. To avoid the repetition of the ا itself in following out this rule the sign ~, named مد mèdd, *or* مده méddÉ, is placed over the first ا in lieu of the ùsstun, and the second ا is suppressed. Thus آ is read Ā *or* ā, اِی ī *or* ī, and اُو ū ; بَا is read bĀ *or* bā, بِی bī *or* bī ; and بُو bū ; &c. The combination وِو is not to be met with in Turkish. The ى final, as a vowel in some Arabic words, after a consonant marked with ùsstun, takes the value of a or A, and the same word, adopted into Turkish, is very frequently written with ا instead of the ى, in consequence; as, for instauce, اولا ūlà *for* اولى, اقصا Aksà *for* اقصى, &c.

As, however, these vowel-points are never marked in common writing or printing, the three Arabic letters of prolongation, ا, و, and ى, have, according to what has already been remarked, come to be very frequently used in Turkish, as in Persian, as short vowels; and the mèdd over the ا is sometimes indicative of the short sound of A, when, without it, this letter is more frequently read with one of the four remaining values. To obviate the almost insurmountable difficulty which hence may seem to arise in relation with the distinction of long and short vowels in Turkish words, a very simple and seldom varying rule may here be noticed. It is, that in words of purely Turkish origin there are scarcely any long vowels (European authors generally state that there are none), whereas in words of Arabic or Persian origin these letters are generally esteemed to be long vowels.

There remains now to be noticed the use of the letter ه as a vowel. It has been seen that ا, as a vowel after a consonant, represents one of our vowels A or a. The other three vowels, of which the vowel-point ùsstun is the representative, are therefore left without an equivalent. But even in the original Arabic, the final ه, in the case of feminine nouns, has always been sounded as a vowel of the fètha class, when the word is final in its sentence; though it is changed into the value of ت (*t*) on other occasions, and although this letter, in the case of other words, even when final, preserves its value as an aspirated *h*. This value of the ه was accordingly adopted by the Persians to represent the *a* or É wherewith so many of their words are terminated; and the Ottomans, finding it so used, have extended its sphere of utility by introducing it, in certain determinate cases, into the middle of words, but always at the end of a syllable, with the same vowel value of *a*, É, *or* é; as, for example, into the future active participle, into the second gerund, sometimes into the first and second persons (as well as the third, where it is final) of the conditional aorist, into the root and entire conjugation of the impotential verb, and at the end of the roots of various verbs. It is sometimes to be seen introduced into the very body of nouns at the end of some syllable; but these are generally words of foreign origin, and the example is never to be followed without good and sufficient authority. This circumstance of the ه vowel never being used unless as the final vowel of a syllable establishes a marked difference between itself and the three letters,

ا, و, and ى, which are commonly to be found in the middle of syllables, though, again, ا alone is ever used as an initial vowel.

Into whatever part of a word this letter ه is introduced with a vowel value, the greatest care should be taken by the student of Turkish (as by those of the Persian, Arabic, and cognate languages) never to transcribe it by using our English letter *h*, as this practice, more or less followed, has the very great inconvenience of incapacitating us from properly distinguishing it from the aspirate consonant value of that letter, and of its cognate, though stronger aspirate, the letter ح. This incorrect and incommodious practice may be seen, and will be felt in use, in almost every English author who has yet written on the subject; and even the French are by no means free from the defect, as is noticed and reprehended by Bianchi in a note at the foot of p. xxviii of the first volume, second edition, of his "Dictionnaire Turc-Français."

Of the mere consonants the letter ب has the value of the English letter b, by which it is also represented in our system of transcription; although sometimes, at the end of words, and when preceded by certain sharp-sounding letters, such as t, ch, or sh, it acquires the sound of p.

پ has always the sound of p, ت of t (but is sometimes changed orthographically into د d), and ث of s sharp or double, never degenerating into z under any circumstances. This remark is equally applicable to the other two letters which we are forced to represent by our s: they must never be degraded into z; and to avoid the tendency, so strongly pronounced in Englishmen, to give to all final letters s, as well as to those placed between two vowels, the sound of z, we have thought it better to double that letter on all occasions, when it is not the first letter of a syllable. Theoretically, we are wrong to do so, but in this instance we reluctantly sacrifice consistency to the practical object of trying to prevent the malpronunciation of whole classes of words of which the well-known *Kars* and *fez* are instances. In both these words the final letter is *s;* and if they were written according to our system *Kàrss* and *fèss* respectively, every one would pronounce them right; whereas, in the latter word, French delicacy has even changed the orthography, and our travelling countrymen have adopted it, so corrupted, from the writers of our gallant allies. The letter ث is equivalent in Arabic to our *th* in *think*, but that value is not known in Turkish.

ج has the value of our English j, by which we invariably represent it, to the exclusion of our equivocal *g*, which is sometimes hard, as in gat, get, gird, got, gully, and sometimes soft, as in gem, gin, gymnastics.

چ is our *ch* in *church*, and the addition of a t before these letters, as is often done, is of no use in English, though necessary in French.

ح has the sound of h, as has also the letter ه when a consonant. We have not thought it necessary to establish any difference between these two letters in our mode of transcribing them, as there is no difference, perceptible to English ears, in the mode of pronouncing them; and, besides this, the Turkish orthography being at hand, no error is likely to occur, and our transcription is a system of guidance to pronunciation, not to orthography.

خ is transcribed, according to general custom, by the letters kh: its power is equivalent to that of the combination ch in German and in Scotch. This can only be learnt by practice; but, until the true value of this consonant be acquired, we recommend the learner never to sound it as a k, but always as a strongly aspirated h. Thus the word khan must be sounded hȂn, and not kȇn.

د is a d, sometimes, after sharp letters, acquiring the sound of t; ذ is a z (its Arabic value being that of our *th* in *though;* but it is never so used in Turkish), ر an r, and ز another z; ژ is equivalent to the French j, and of the letter *s* in *pleasure*. We have represented it, in the very few words where it occurs, by the combination zh.

س is the true Arabic s, ش is equivalent to our sh, and ص is also a pure s in Turkish. Of the difference between the س and the ص we shall have occasion to speak further in treating of the hard and soft letters. ض is generally a z, but in some few Arabic words has the value of d.

ط is generally a t, though, as an initial in some few words of purely Turkish origin, it takes the sound of d. ظ is another z. We may here remark, that, in a few words, one of the letters t (ت *or* ط) is followed by one of the letters h (ح *or* ه) forming the succession th in our transcription. When this does occur, the t and the h are to be kept separate in pronunciation, as the t is generally the last letter of one syllable, and the h the first letter of the following syllable.

ع is a letter that has generally been considered and treated as a vowel by European writers, always excepting the learned De Sacy, and a few scholars of his stamp. Nothing can be conceived more erroneous, since, in the mouth of an Arab, no consonant exists having greater claims to the appellation. It is pronounced in the deepest part of the throat, with an effort that must be learned in infancy, or which can never afterwards be attained. In Turkish, however, the letter becomes silent at the beginning and end of words, but is indicated by a kind of hiatus in the middle. We have mentioned the hiatus of the hèmzé, in treating of the ا; and we may here notice that the letter ع and the hèmzé have the same relation to each other that س and ص, and that ت and ط, as also that ق and ك, and ز and ض or ظ, have to each other; namely, the one is hard and the other soft in pronunciation, as is to be hereafter noticed. Of the two, the ع is the hard hiatus, and we have therefore represented it with a double inverted apostrophe (") in this work; and we repeat that, at the beginning and end of words, it is generally quite or almost silent, after the fashion of our *silent h*, but it is never a vowel.

غ is a hard g, taking sometimes a gliding sound, of which we have no example in English. The French in Algeria have taken it to be the equivalent of their *r grasséyé*, or r pronounced, as by some people, like a *w*. From this they have formed the now so well-known word "razzia," which is the Arabic *gazya* (a military expedition against infidels, a crusade). In the present work we have uniformly transcribed this letter by gh, instead of using a single g, on account of the double value of this letter, our sole, though amply sufficient reason, for rejecting it in a pronouncing dictionary. This letter is sometimes softened down to the value of *w* when preceded or followed by o or ʊ, and even by *i*; at other times it becomes almost imperceptible in the pronunciation. This we have designated by putting the *gh* in italics.

ف is our f (it would be mere folly and pedantry to represent it by *ph*). ق and ك are both simple k, as far as the first or Arabic value of the latter letter is concerned. We see no advantage to be gained in a pronouncing dictionary by using the letter *q* for ق, as is sometimes done, and it is a further violation of the special rule which requires the letter q to be followed by a u. The letter c is sometimes used for ق and for ك, but it has the disadvantage of a double value, being sometimes equivalent to k, and sometimes to s.

In its second, or Persian value, ك is a hard g, somewhat like غ, and we represent it, equally with that letter, by gh in all cases, though with this distinction; namely, the Persian value of ك is susceptible in Turkish of being softened down to a value approaching that of *y*, as the غ does that of *w*, and at other times becomes imperceptible also. As with the غ, so with the ك, we designate this by placing the *gh* in italics. To render this quality of the two letters better appreciable by our readers, we here point out that the very same thing obtains in our own language in the case of the combination gh. For example, in the word *throughout*, that combination is sounded as *w*, and in *sighing* it is pronounced as *y;* so, in Turkish, صوغان sò*gh*ᴀn (onion) is pronounced sòwᴀn, and دكل dì*gh*il is pronounced dìyil. In both these values of ك, the letter, when followed by any of the vowels a, o, u, ᴜ, *u*, takes before the vowel a short and incipient sound of y, which we have denoted by introducing after the ك, and before the vowel, a letter *y* in italics. This is often heard in English, as in the words *cure, pure,* &c., some persons using it also before an *a* in the same manner.

The third, or purely Turkish value of ك, when it is called surd kᴇ̀f (صاغركاف), and even surd nòn (صاغرنون), is that of our *ng* at the end of *sing, ring,* &c. It is never to be found elsewhere than at the ends of words or syllables, and consequently never can be initial. At Constantinople, and generally among the educated classes, it loses, almost constantly and entirely, the influence of the final *g*, and is sounded like a common *n*. This also we indicate by placing the *g* in italics, showing that by some people it is sounded, though dropped by others. In the two words, اكلامق and دكلەمك, where the ك is followed by ل, the sound of the ل is lost; and the first is generally pronounced ànn*a*m*a*k, the second dìnᴇ́mek, instead of ànglam*a*k and dìnglᴇ́mek, their true original, and even now their provincial sounds. When followed by other letters, whether vowels or consonants, the g of this combination is never to be sounded as a separate letter; but the English words *singer, ringer,* are to be imitated, while those of *anger* and *finger* are the models to be avoided, the division of syllables being different in the two classes; as, *sing-er, ring-er; an-ger, fin-ger*.

ل is our l, م is our m, and ن our n. The only remark necessary here, is, that when the ن is followed by a غ, or a ك with its Persian value, forming, in the transcription, the combination ngh, it is to be understood that the combination is not solvable into ng-h, but only into n-gh. Also, as remarked above, the sound of the ل is entirely suppressed, in the ordinary pronunciation of Constantinople, in the words اكلامق ànglam*a*k, and دكلەمك dìnglᴇ́mek (pronounced respectively ànnam*a*k, dìnᴇ́mek).

The letter و requires more particular remark, as it has three distinct proper values as a consonant, besides one other incidental. It is sometimes a pure v, sometimes, though not frequently, a pure w, and more generally a combination of the two, its pronunciation beginning as a v, and ending as a w. In its value as a pure v, it may be classed as a soft consonant, since it takes this sound before the soft vowels é, ᴇ́, i, and u; whereas, before ᴀ, a, *a*, o, and ᴜ, it is sounded as a combined v and w. At the end of syllables, the same rules occur with regard to the preceding vowel, to which we may add that it is a pure v after *i* and *u*.

In its incidental value as a consonant, the letter و is always surmounted by the sign hèmzé, before mentioned, thus ؤ; and it is necessarily and constantly a consonant when so surmounted, whether it be placed at the end of a syllable, or whether it begins one. In the former case the vowel preceding it, and in the latter case its own vowel, must be an ùturu (and confined to the two branches of that class u or ʊ, to the exclusion of o and *u*); and this is the reason why the letter و is then selected as the recipient of the hèmzé, as is the ا when the vowel-point is ùsstun; and, it may now be added, as is the ى when the vowel-point is èsséré, this letter also being then always a consonant. Whenever the hèmzé is used, the letter over which it is placed may be considered merely in the light of a support, the hèmzé itself being the real and true consonant letter, which in Arabic is capable even of reduplication in the same way with every other consonant. We have therefore always represented it with the inverted apostrophe; but we do not recollect many instances of the employment in Turkish of those Arabic words in which its reduplication occurs.

The ه, as a consonant, is an aspirated h: in fact, the idea of a *silent h* has never occurred to an oriental; and whether the ه consonant or the ح be at the beginning, or at the end of a word or syllable, it must be equally and fully aspirated as a rule of grammar and language, whatever degradation it may occasionally be subjected to in the tongue of the common people, and of every-day intercourse. It is, in this respect, something like our English letter r at the end of words and syllables, which we so generally omit in pronunciation, but which no grammarian has ever held up to notice and imitation as a silent letter. The two letters ه and ح are, however, generally sounded, the omission being quite the exception, even at the end of words.

It may be as well to notice here the circumstance of the use of the hèmzé, placed over the letter ه, when used as a vowel at the end of words. It only occurs in the case of nouns, substantive or adjective, which are connected with the following word in the sentence by the Persian rule of construction, which governs the relation of a noun with its qualifying term. The ه, then, performs its proper function of final vowel in the word where it occurs, and the hèmzé takes as its own separate vowel the èsseré, which may always, in these cases, be represented by the letter i, as in the terms, بندهٔ خدا bèndé'i-khùdā رتبهٔ ثانیه rùtbé'i-sāniyyé, &c.

The ى consonant is our English y, both at the beginning and at the end of words or syllables, being in the latter case always preceded by a vowel. It is really a sad mistake for us, who possess this useful consonant, and are aware of its nature, to adopt the lame expedient to which other languages are forced to have recourse, namely, the use of the vowel i, with or without the diæresis over it. Take, for instance, the word تربيه, where the consonant ى is reduplicated, and compare the lame and erroneous transcription by an eminent French author, terbïiè, which is at variance even with the French rules of diæresis, with the plain method rendered possible by our estimation and use of y, as a consonant equivalent to the oriental ى consonant, namely, tèrbìyyé, in which the syllables are tèr-bìy-yé, precisely as in the original, the reduplication being merely what we sometimes practise ourselves by placing a dash over m or n, when we have omitted a second one, as in the word com̃on. This was very frequently practised in manuscripts before the invention of printing. French authors have an excuse for not using the y in this, to us, natural manner, because they do not recognise it as a consonant in their own language; but for us to adopt their imperfect substitute is to abandon gratuitously an advantage of no mean character.

When the hèmzé is placed over a ى in the middle of words, the two dots which usually distinguish the letter are omitted. But it is frequently the case, that whereas, in an original Arabic word, a ى with a hèmzé is correctly used, the same word, on passing into Turkish, loses its hèmzé, and the ى becomes a long vowel, resuming its suppressed dots. Thus the Arabic word استئذان (ìsstì'zān) becomes generally in Turkish استيذان (ìsstīzān).

To finish what we have to note respecting the various uses of the hèmzé, we may here say, that at the end of a very few words it is found without any letter to support it, though sometimes a و is added under it to those words.—Ex. جزء (*or* جزؤ) jùz', بدء (*or* بدؤ) bèd'. In this case, if the word be alone, or at the end of a phrase, it is very common to add to it, in pronouncing, a vowel homologous to the one in the word, and جزء is then uttered jùz'u, بدء as bèd'i, and so forth. In a kind of imitation of this rule, a certain number of nouns ending in ا (but which, in the original Arabic, have a hèmzé after that letter) assume a hèmzé after them, with èsséré as its vowel-point, when they are in Persian construction with a following noun. Thus the word ايفا īfā (originally ايفاء īfā'), in construction with the word دين dèyn, becomes ايفاءدين īfā'i-dèyn. It is, however, more usual nowadays to use a supplemental ى instead of the hèmzé in this case, so that the same two words would be written ايفاىدين īfāyi-dèyn.

Having had occasion to mention the distinction of the Turkish letters as *hard* and *soft*, we may here elucidate the meaning of the terms, as the subject has a very great part to play in the euphony of the language. Any Englishman can appreciate the distinction between the value of *a* in *wall, call, tall*, &c., and of the same letter in *father, arm, part*, &c.; and perceive that the first value is broad, hard, and masculine; whereas the latter is soft and feminine. So to an ear accustomed to French is the difference between the vowels of *bulle* and *boule*. We do not, however, carry our distinctions any farther than the vowels; whereas the Easterns, as the alphabet shows, not having vowel letters by which to paint their distinctions, have introduced them into the consonants instead. We will not contend that this is the correct view of the case; for my practical knowledge of spoken Arabic, in its purest dialect, is not sufficient to enable me to judge of the shape into which the organs of speech have to be thrown, when pronouncing respectively ت and ط, ح and ه, س and ص, ز and ظ, ق and ك, for instance. We believe they are really the representatives of effectively different modes of utterance in the original language; but we are also convinced that it would be impossible to convey to an English, or to any European mind, a just appreciation of the differences. Nor, as far as the Turkish is concerned, is this necessary; and, for all practical purposes, we are convinced that by throwing upon the vowels alone the effect of the distinction of the letters into hard and soft, we have adopted the most effective method of rendering the subject clear and easy to our readers. We will therefore simply observe that ح, خ, ص, ض, ط, ظ, ع, and ق are the hard letters, generally followed by the hard vowels A, *a*, *i*, O, U; whereas ت, ز, س, ك, ه, and HÈMZÉ, are the soft consonants, generally followed by the soft vowels a *é*, *or* É, i, u, or *u*; and that the remaining letters may be considered neutral, both because they are not ranged in pairs, and because they are followed by vowels, sometimes of the one class, sometimes of the other, though far more frequently by those of the soft class. It is, indeed, one great characteristic of this beautiful language, to soften and embellish every word it adopts.

Reduplication of a letter in Turkish is not the mere matter of orthography that it is in English. On the contrary, when a letter is doubled in writing, it must be doubled in pronouncing, as we do with the letter *d* in *mid-day*, with *l* in *full long*, with *n* in *thin nose*, with *s* in *less smoke*, or with *t* in *fat turkey*. In Turkish there are two modes of reduplicating a letter: the first is, as with ourselves, by simply writing the two one after the other, as in the word قوللانمق (kŭllAnm*a*k), where the *l* is doubled, in the word اوممق (ŭmm*a*k), where the *m* is repeated, and in many cases where the locative preposition ده (dĕ or da) follows a word ending in *d*. The second method is of Arabic origin, and is confined in use to Arabic words mostly, with a few Persian exceptions. By this method the letter to be sounded double, that is once at the end of a syllable, and again at the beginning of the next following syllable of the same word, is only written once; but in manuscripts where the diacritical marks are used there is a sign, called تشدید (tèshdīd), and figured thus ـّ, which is placed over the letter written, just as the dash is sometimes employed in our old manuscripts to indicate that the letter over which it is placed should have been repeated in writing: the difference is, that the Arabian sign indicates that the letter must be repeated in pronunciation, *or so dwelt upon as to be equivalent to two letters*. This Arabian rule of reduplication is carried still further; for in cases where a noun, preceded by the definite article ال, commences with any one of the letters ت, ث, د, ذ, ر, ز, س, ش, ص, ض, ط, ظ, *or* ن, then, in pronunciation, the ل of the article is omitted, and the first letter of the noun is doubled. As this rule is of pretty frequent application in compound proper names and adverbial expressions, adopted bodily into Turkish, we have represented this suppression or conversion of the ل, by using our own common apostrophe, followed by the letter the sound of which takes the place of the original one of the ل; being further moved to the adoption of this method by the consideration that, in these compound expressions, the ا of the Arabic article is also suppressed in the utterance, and its place taken by the vowel which, theoretically and grammatically, always terminates ordinary Arabic nouns. Thus the proper name عبدالرحیم is figured by us, as it is pronounced, "Abdu-'r-Ràhīm, &c. In further illustration of this subject, we may explain that in Arabic اله (for الاه) ìlāh means *a god*, and this word, with the article ال, forms by contraction الله Allāh, the God, the true and very God; from which again, by composition and suppression, is formed the proper name "Abdu-'llāh," generally written erroneously Abdalla, or Abdallah.

We now come to the consideration of the Turkish consonants when they follow a vowel in a syllable. This may be divided into three branches:—First, when the vowel begins a syllable, having no other consonant before it (and we may here remark that in Turkish a vowel can never begin a syllable which is not the first of a word); secondly, when the vowel has another consonant before it in the syllable; and thirdly, when the consonant under consideration is followed by another consonant in the same syllable.

As to the first case, it follows, from what we have already explained, that ا is the only vowel that can commence a Turkish word, either followed immediately by a consonant or with a و or a ى intervening; thus ات is either ăt or èt, اوت is òt or ŭt, ايت is ìt; or, as in the last example, the intervening vowel may be long, and the word read īt, and the sole ا may itself be long, as in آل āl, آن ān, &c.

With respect to the second case, the syllable is composed of two consonants, the first of which bears (or would bear, if marked) the vowel-point, and may be or not followed by one of the three vowel letters ا, و, or ي, and these again may be either long or short. Ex. لب lèb, دل dìl, ذل zùll; باش băsh, قول kòl, قيز kìz; حاج hājj, زور zūr, تيز tīz.

In the third case, the final consonant follows the preceding one in exactly the same manner as in similar words of our own language, but with this difference, that with us the preceding consonant is limited to a small class (except in cases of orthographical reduplication or composition, such as ll, ss, ch, sh, ph, th, ck, &c.) called liquids, namely l, n, r, with s, and sometimes p, if followed by t; whereas in Turkish every consonant is capable of being followed by every other. Thus we have the words دخل dàkhl, عفو ʻʻăfv, عزو ʻʻàzv, امر èmr, قتل kătl, وجه vèjh, رهن rèhn, &c., which must appear quite unnatural to English eyes and ears, and which, we may explain, are generally Arabic words of two syllables originally, from which the final vowel has been dropt. These words are, however, not in perfect keeping with the spirit of the Turkish, for in that language we meet with a less combination of consonants than even in English or any of those derived from Latin. The consequence is, that the Turks very frequently intercalate a vowel between the two following consonants, when a vowel does not follow the word; and we generally hear them say èmir for èmr, hùk*y*um for hùkm, &c., in the first case; though they correct this when the opportunity offers, and say èmr*i*-ʻālī, hùkmu-shèrīf, &c.

This quality of a consonant, viz. its not being followed by a vowel, is called its *quiescent state* (سكون sùk*y*ūn), and is denoted in manuscripts by the sign ـْـ placed over it. The sign is called جزم jèzm.

We must here add a remark as to two circumstances which will be noticed in the body of the dictionary, by our readers, as seeming incongruities, but which are only the necessary and regular consequences of two leading bases of the Turkish language, its euphony and its euphuism. We have already touched upon the sequence of hard vowels with hard consonants, and soft vowels with soft consonants; but the first of the circumstances to which we now allude is, that in words or inflexions and affixes of Turkish origin, if the syllables bearing the vowel-point èsséré (or value of i, *i*) be immediately preceded, in the same word, by a syllable having the vowel-point ùturu (o, u, ʊ, *u*), then the syllable or syllables having the èsséré are influenced by the preceding ùturu, and all are sounded as though they bore that vowel-point. The word ùturu is itself an instance: its orthography is أُوتُرِى, but the last syllable is affected by the vowel of the preceding one. The rule is, that when the value of the preceding ùturu is one of the hard vowels o or ʊ, then the èsséré takes the sound of ʊ; and when the preceding vowel is either of the soft sounds u or *u*, it takes the value of u. Ex. حُكْمِنِى hùkmunu, عُذْرِيمِى "ùzrumu; قُولُكِزِى kòlunguzu, *or* kùlunguzu. These latter syllables are always short and unaccented. Attention to this rule, and freedom from obtrusiveness in the pronunciation of the affected syllables, constitutes one of the niceties of the Turkish language; and I may add, that after the first affected syllable, the sound is again slightly modified in both cases *towards*, but not *to*, the value of *u* or *i* respectively, according as the tone is of the hard or soft class.

The second of these two circumstances may be said to be the very reverse of the former, inasmuch as it consists in the pronunciation as i or *i*, of the vowel-point ùturu accompanied by a vowel و. Its occurrence is limited to one syllable of a few classes of words, viz. the last syllable of the aorist indicative and aorist active participle, of such verbs as form them in ور, which is then pronounced ir or *i*r accordingly as the tone of the word is soft or hard. Ex. كلور is pronounced ghèlir, صالالانور is pronounced sàllanir. The last syllable of the first gerund is also affected in this way when the tone of the verb is not that of ùturu. Ex. كيدوب ghìdip, كلوب ghèlip, باقوب bàkip, &c. Purists, however, pronounce all these words as they are written. Again, the syllable لو which ends so many adjectives, is pronounced li or l*i* in a general way.

To conclude these remarks, we have now only to add that, as in all languages, there are in Turkish a few words of every-day use which have an accepted pronunciation more or less at variance with their orthography. We have pointed these out in parenthesis, by the side of the correct pronunciation (when this is also used by persons of education), or by itself (when everybody

uses the incongruous pronunciation alone). We shall not do aṃiss to notice, also, that, in ordinary conversation, a few words are used as Turkish singulars, which are, in reality, Arabic plurals; but this is not correct in writing. Such are the words اولاد èvlād (children) child; رجال rijāl (men) a state functionary; كبار kìbār (great. men) a grandee, &c. Even in writing, the Arabic singulars of these words are not used, but the phrase is turned; as, *one of the children, one of the state functionaries, &c.*

REDHOUSE'S DICTIONARY.

PART I.—ENGLISH AND TURKISH.

A, An, *art.* بر bìr.

Abaft, *ad.* and *pr.* كيروده ghèrìda, قيچ طرفنده kìch-tàrafìnda.

Abandon, *v.a.* براقمق bràkmak, ترك‌ا tèrk-et, وازكچمك vàz-ghèchmek; چيقمق chìkmak; قاچمق kàchmak; —ed, *p.p.* متروك mètrūk; عارسز "ārsiz, چاپقين chàpkin.

Abash, *v.a.* اوطاندرمق ùtàndirmak, قيرمق kìrmak, محجوب‌ا màhjūb-et.

Abate, *v.a.* ازالتمق àzàltmak, قيرمق kìrmak, تنزيل‌ا tènzil-et, اشاغى وارمق àshàghi-vàrmak; —, *v.n.* ازالمق àzàlmak.

Abbey, *s.* مناستر mànastir.

Abbot, *s.* مناستر بشى mànastir-bàshi.

Abbreviate, *v.a.* قصالتمق kìssaltmak, اختصارا ìkhtissār-et; —ed, *p.p.* قصه kìssa, مختصر mùkhtassàr.

Abbreviation, *s.* اختصار ìkhtissār; مختصر mùkhtassàr.

Abdicate, *v.n.* ترك سلطنت‌ا tèrki-sàltanàt-et, سلطنتدن چكلمك sàltanàt-dan-chèkilmek.

Abdomen, *s.* قارن kàrn.

Abed, *ad.* يتاقده yàtakda.

Abet, *v.a.* يوز ويرمك yùz-vèrmek; ياردم‌ا yàrdim-et.

Abhor, *v.a.* هيچ سومامك hìch-sévma-mek, منفور طوتمق mènfūr-tùtmak.

Abhorrence, *s.* تنفر tènèffur.

Abide, *v.a.* اوطورمق òturmak, قالمق kàlmak, ساكن او sākin-òl.

Ability, *s.* اقتدار ìktidàr, قدرت kùdret; هنر hùner, قابليت kābilìyyèt.

Abject, *a.* مسكين mìsskin; مسكين كبى mìsskin-ghìbi.

Abjure, *v.a.* يمين ايدوب براقمق yèmin-èdup-bràkmak, ترك‌ا tèrk-et.

Ablative, *s.* or *a.* مفعول عنه mèfūlun"ành.

Ablaze, *ad.* مشتعل mùshtà"il.

Able, *a.* قادر kādir, الندن كلور èlindan-ghèlir, مقتدر mùktèdir.

Able-bodied, *a.* صاغ sàgh, صاغلم sàgh-làm. [ghùssl.

Ablution, *s.* ابدست àbdèsst, غسل

Aboard, *ad.* كمى ايچنده ghèmi ìchinda.

Abode, *s.* او èv, ير yèr, مسكن mèsskèn.

Abolish, *v.a.* قالدرمق kAldirmak, لغوا làghv-et فسخا fèsskh-et.

Abominable, *a.* فنا fēna, مردار mùrdàr (mùn-), منفور mènfūr.

Abominate, *v.a. v.* abhor.

Abomination, *s.* نفرت nèfrèt; بوق bòk, منفورشی mènfūr-shèy.

Aborigines, *s.pl.* اصل یرلولر Assl-yèrliler.

Abortion, *s.* دوشوك dùshuk.

Abortive, *a.* بوش bòsh, نافله nàfila, بیهوده bihūdé.

Abound, *v.n.* چوق‌او chòk-òl, چوق بولنمق chòk-bùlunmak.

About, *pr.* اطرافنه ètràfina, اطرافنده ètràfinda; دائر dā'ir; تقریبا tākrība, تخمینا tàkhmīna; جوارنده jèwàrinda, یقینلرنده yàkinlarinda; اوستنده ùss-tunda; صره‌لرده siralarda, صولرنده sùlarinda; —, *ad.* اوته‌برو ùté-bèri; اشاغی یوقاری Ashàghi-yùkàri; محیطاً mùhītan; طولاشمسیله برابر dòlàsh-massìla-bèrābér; to go *or* set about, *v.a.* باشلامق bAshlamak; ایتمك ètmek, یاپمق yàpmak, یول طوتمق yòl-tùtmak.

Above, *pr.* یوقاریسنه yùkàrissina, یوقاریسنده yùkàrissinda; فوقنه fèv-kina, فوقنده fèvkinda; دن زیاده dàn-zìyādé; —, *ad.* یوقاری yùkàri, یوقاریده yùkàrida.

Abrade, *v.n.* اشنمق Ashinmak; —, *v.a.* اشندرمق Ashindirmak.

Abreast, *ad.* یان یانه yàn-yàna.

Abridge, *v.a. v.* abbreviate.

Abroad, *ad.* طشره tAshra (dìshàri), طشره‌ده tAshrada (dìshàrda).

Abrogate, *v.a. v.* abolish.

Abrupt, *a.* دیك dik, باش اشاغی bAsh-Ashàghi; ترس tèrss.

Abscess, *s.* چبان chìban.

Abscond, *v.n.* قاچمق kAchmak; کیزلنمك ghìzlenmek, صاقلنمق sàk-lanmak. [ghàybūbèt.

Absence, *s.* یوقلق yòkluk, غیبوبت

Absent, *a.* یوق yòk, غایب ghā'ib; دالغین dAlghin; — one's self, *v.a.* کتمك ghìtmek, غایب‌او ghā'ib-òl, صاوشمق sàwushmak.

Absinth, *s.* پلین‌اوتی pèlin-òtu.

Absolute, *a.* مطلق mùtlAk, مستقل mùsstAkill.

Absolutely, *ad.* مطلقا mùtlAka.

Absorb, *v.a.* ایچمك ìchmek, چکمك chèkmek, المق Almak.

Abstain, *v.n.* پرهیزا pèrhīz-et, صاقنمق sàkinmak, چکنمك chèkinmek.

Abstemious, *a.* پرهیزکار pèrhīzkyār.

Abstinence, *s.* پرهیز pèrhīz.

Absurd, *a.* مسخره‌لق mAsskharalik; محال mùhāl (impossible).

Abundance, *s.* بوللق bòlluk, چوقلق chòkluk, کثرت kèssrèt.

Abundant, *a.* بول bòl, چوق chòk.

Abuse, *s.* فساد fèssAd; یولسزلق yòl-suzluk; یولسزقوللانش yòlsuz-kùl-lAnish; کفر kyùfr, سوکوب‌صایمه sù-ghub-sàyma; —, *v.a.* یولسزقوللانمق yòlsuz-kùllAnmak; سوکمك sùgh-mek.

Abut, *v.n.* طیانمق dàyanmak; وارمق vàrmak.

Abyss, *s.* وارطه vàrta, حفره hùfré.

Academy, *s.* مکتب mèktɛb; مدرسه mèdréssé.

Accede, *v.n.* قائل‌اول kā'il-òl, موافقت‌ا mùwāfakʌt-et.

Accelerate, *v.a.* تسریعا tèssrī''-et, تعجیلا tà''jīl-et, حیزلاندرمق hìzlandɪrmak. [būl-et; اخذا àkhz-et.

Accept, *v.a.* المق ʌlmak; قبولا kʌ-

Acceptance, *s.* اخذ àkhz; قبول kʌbūl.

Acceptation, Acception, *s.* معنا mà''nà.

Access, *s.* دخول dùkhūl.

Accident, *s.* قضا kʌzā; عرض ''ʌraz.

Accidental, *a.* اتفاقی ìttifākī, تصادفی tèssādufī; عرضی ''ʌrazī.

Accidentally, *ad.* ازقضا èz-kʌzā, قضارا kʌzārā, اتفاقا ìttifākā, قضاایله kʌzā-

Acclivity, *s.* یوقش yòkush. [ila.

Accommodate, *v.a.* یرویرمك yèr-vèrmek; ایشنی کورمك ìshini-ghyùrmek.

Accommodation, *s.* یر yèr; ایشك کوریلمسی ishing-ghyùrulmassi.

Accompany, *v.a.* برابرکتمك bèrābèr-ghìtmek, رفاقتا rèfākʌt-et.

Accomplice, *s.* قباحت‌ارقه‌داشی kʌbāhat-àrkadashi, ارقه‌داش ārkadash, معاون mu''avin.

Accomplish, *v.a.* بجرمك bèjɛrmek, باشارمق bʌshàrmak, حصوله‌کتورمك hùssūla-ghètirmek; تماما tʌmʌm-et, اتماما ìtmām-et, اکمالا ìkmāl-et, تکمیلا tèkmīl-et.

Accord, *s.* اتفاق ìttifʌk, اتحاد ìttihàd; —, *v.a.* ویرمك, vèrmek, احسانا ìh-sàn-et, انعاما in''àm-et.

Accordance, *s.* مطابقت mùtābakʌt, وفق wèfk.

According (to *or* as), *pr.* ئه‌کوره -é-ghyùré; اوزره ùzéré; —ly, *ad.* اکاکوره ʌnga-ghyùré.

Accouchement, *s.* وضع‌حمل vwàz'i-hʌml.

Accoucheur, *s.* ابه هکیم èbé-hèkīm.

Account, *s.* حساب hìssʌb: — *v.a.* صایمق sàymak, طوتمق tùtmak, عدا ''àdd-et, اعتبارا ì''tibàr-et; — for, *v.a.* دیمك dèmek; جواب‌ویرمك jè-wʌb-vèrmek; سببنی کوسترمك sèbè-bini-ghyùsstermek, حکمتنی اکلامق hìkmètini-ànglamak; — book, *s.* دفتر dèftɛr.

Accountable, *a.* مسئول mèss'ūl.

Accumulate, *v.a.* برکمك bìrikmek, طوپلانمق tòplànmak; —, *v.a.* برکدرمك bìrikdirmek, طوپلامق tòp-lamak, جمعا jèm''-et.

Accumulation, *s.* برکدرش bìrikdirish; طوپلانش tòplànish; یغین yìghin.

Accuracy, *s.* طوغریلق dòghruluk, صحت sìhhʌt.

Accurate, *a.* طوغری dòghru, صحیح sàhih.

Accursed, *a.* ملعون mèl''ūn.

Accusation, *s.* شکایت shìkyàyet, اسناد issnàd, اتهام ìthām.

Accuse, *v.a.* حقنده‌شکایتا hʌkkinda-shìkyàyet-e-, اتهاما ìthām-et.

Accused, *s.* مدعی علیه mùddà''a-''àlèyh.

Accuser, *s.* مدعی mùddà''i.

Accustom, *v.a.* آلشدرمق Alishdirmak; — one's self, *v.n.* آلشمق Alishmak, عادت‌ایدنمك 'ādet-èdinmek; اعتیاد‌ا i''tiyAd-et. [mè'lūf.

Accustomed, *a.* آلشق Alishik, مألوف

Ache, *s.* آغری Aghri, صانجی sAnji, سزی sìzi, وجع vèja'', درد dèrd; —, *v.n.* آغریمق Aghrimak, سزلمك sìzlémek.

Achieve, *v.a.* یاپمق yàpmak, فعله کتورمك fi''lÉ-ghètirmek.

Acid, *a.* اکشی èkshi: sub-acid, *a.* مایخوش màykhòsh. [hùmūzAt.

Acidity, *s.* اکشیلك èkshilik, حموضت

Acknowledge, *v.a.* اقرارا ìkràr-et, اعترافا i''tirAf-et, تسلیما tèsslīm-et, بلمك bìlmek, طانیمق tAnimak.

Acknowledgment, *s.* سند sèned; تشکر tèshèkkyur; اقرار ìkràr.

Acme, *s.* اوج evj.

Aconite, *s.* خانق الذئب khAnik-u'zzīb.

Acorn, *s.* پلاموط pAlamut. [vèrmek.

Acquaint, *v.a.* خبرویرمك khAbEr-

Acquaintance, *s.* خبر khAbEr, معلومات mà''lūmāt; بلدك bìldik; الفت ùlfèt.

Acquainted, *a.* خبردار khAbErdàr, بلور bìlir, خبری‌اولان khAbéri-òlAn.

Acquiesce, *v.n.* راضی‌او rAzi-òl, قائل‌او kA'il-òl, موافقتا mùwAfakAt-et.

Acquiescence, *s.* رضا rìzā, موافقت mùwAfakAt.

Acquire, *v.a.* آلمق Almak, الە کتورمك ÈlÉ-ghètirmek, پیداا pèydā-et, کسبا kèssb-et, تحصیلا tàhsīl-et, استحصالا isstìhsAl-et.

Acquit, *v.a.* تبریەا tèbriyyé-et; — one's self, *v.n.* تبریە‌ٔ ذمتا tèbriyyè-i-zìmmèt-et.

Acquittal, *s.* تبریە‌معناسندە‌حکم tèbrìyyé-mà''nàssinda-hùkm.

Acquittance, *s.* مقبوض‌سندی mAkbūz-sènédi, ابراسندی ìbrā-sènédi.

Acre, *s.* دونم dùnum.

Acrid, *a.* آجی Aji, سرت sèrt.

Across, *pr.* بریانندن‌اولبریاننە bìr-yànindan-ò-bir-yànina, حاچواری‌اولەرق hAchwàri-òlarak, آرقوری àrkiri (àykiri).

Act, *s.* ایش ìsh, فعل fi''l, عمل ''AmEl; فصل fAssl; —, *v.n.* ایشلمك ìshlÉ-mek, ایتمك ètmek, یاپمق yàpmak, حرکتا hàrékÈt-et.

Action, *s.* ایش ìsh, فعل fi''l, عمل ''AmEl; دعوی dà''wà; غوغا ghàwgha (kàwgha), جنك jènk, محاربە mùhārébÉ, دوکش dùghush.

Active, *a.* ایشکذار ìshghyuzàr; کسکین kèsskin, سرت sèrt; *verb active*, فعل‌معلوم‌متعدی fi''li-mà''lūmi-mùta''àddī.

Actor, *s.* اویونجی òyunju, مقلد mùkAllìd.

Actress, *s.* اوینجیوی‌قاری òyunju-kAri.

Actual, *a.* اصل Assl, ذات zāt.

Actually, *ad.* حالا hāla, شمدی shìmdi, الان èl-ān; بالفعل bì-'l-fi''l, حقیقتا hAkīkAtan, فی الحقیقە fī-'l-hAkīka.

Acute, *a.* سیوری sìvri; اینجە ìnja; عقللو ''Aklli, درایتلو dìrāyetli; (disease) یکی‌ظهورایتمش yèngi-zùhūr-ètmish; — angle, زاویە‌ٔ حادە zāviyyè-i-hāddÉ.

Acuteness, *s.* درايت dìrāyèt, فراست fèrāssèt, عقل "ākl.

Adamant, *s.* پولاد pūlād.

Adapt, *v.a.* اويدرمق ùydurmak.

Adapted, *a.* اويغون ùyghun, مناسب mùnāssib, موافق mùwāfik.

Add, *v.a.* قاتمق kātmak, علاوه ا "ìlāvé-et, ضم ا zàmm-et; —up, *v.a.* يكون ا yèkyun-et, طوپلامق tòplamak, جمع ا jèm"-et.

Adder, *s.* انكرك ènghérèk, افعى èf"à.

Addict one's self, *v.n.* آلشمق ālishmak, عادت ايدنمك "ādet-èdinmek.

Addicted, *a.* مبتلا mùbtélā.

Addition, *s.* علاوه "ìlāvé, ضم zàmm; (arith.) جمع jèm", قره جمله kāra-jùmlé.

Additional, *s.* قاتمه kātma, علاوه "ìlāvé, زائد zā'id; يدك yèdek. [chùruk.

Addle, Addled, *a.* جلق jìlk, چوروك

Address, *v.a.* سويلمك sùwèylémek, خطاب ا khìtāb-et; كوندرمك ghyùndermek; (a letter) مكتوبك اوستنى يازمق mèktubung-ùsstunu-yàzmak; —, *s.* هنر hùner, معرفت mà"rifèt, چابكلك chàbukluk; مكتوبك اوستى mèktubang-ùsstu; سمت sèmt, ير yèr, ادرس àdrèss.

Adduce, *v.a.* ايراد ا īrād-et. (ùsstāz.

Adept, *s.* اوستا ùssta, استاد ùsstād, استاذ

Adequate, *a.* الويرر èlvèrir, يتشور yèti-shir, كافى kyāfi, وافى wāfi.

Adhere, *v.n.* ياپشمق yàpishmak, طوتمق tùtmak; ملازمت ا mùlāzémèt-et.

Adherent, *s.* تابع tābi", طرفدار tàrafdàr.

Adhesion, *s.* لسوق lùssūk, ياپشمه yà-pishma.

Adhesive, *a.* ياپشقان yàpishkān, لزوجيتلو lùzūjiyyètli.

Adieu, *int.* اي والله èy-vā-'llàh, اللهه اصمارلدق āllāha-ìssmàrladik; اوغوراوله òghur-òla, اوغورلراوله òghurlar-òla; صفا كلدك sāfā-ghèlding, خوش كلدك khòsh-ghèlding; سلامتله sèlāmètla; الدعا èd-du"ā; والسلام wè-'ss-sèlām.

Adjacent, *a.* يقين yàkin, جوار jìwār, همجوار hèmjìwàr; بتشك bìtishik, ملاصق mùlāssik, متصل mùttāssil.

Adjective, *s.* صفت sìfāt. [tèrfīk-et.

Adjoin, *v.a.* قاتمق kātmak, ترفيق ا

Adjourn, *v.a.* بشقه وقته براقمق bàshka-wākta-bràkmak; —, *v.n.* بشقه وقت طوپلانمق اوزره مجلس شمديلك طاغلمق bàshka-wākit-tòplanmak-ùzéré-mèjliss-shìmdilik-dàghilmak.

Adjournment, *s.* بشقه وقته احاله bàshka-wākta-ìhālé.

Adjudicate, *v.n.* دعوى فصل ا dà"wà-fāssl-et; —, *v.a.* حكم ا hùkm-et.

Adjunct, *s.* تتمه tètìmmé, ضميمه zā-mīmé; ياردمجى yàrdimji.

Adjure, *v.a.* يالوارمق yālvàrmak, رجا ا rìjā-et, نيازا nìyàz-et.

Adjust, *v.a.* اويدرمق ùydurmak, طوغريلتمق dòghrultmak, تصحيح ا tāsshīh-et.

Adjustment, *s.* تصحيح tāsshīh.

Adjutant, *s.* آلاى امينى ālay-èmini.

Admeasurement, *s.* مساحه mèssāhè.

Administer, *v.a.* باقمق bākmak, رؤيت ا

rŭʻyèt-et, اداره ا ìdārɛ́-et ; ويرمك vèrmek, يدرمك yèdirmek, ايچورمك ìchirmek, تناول ايتدرمك tènāvul-èttirmek.

Administration, *s.* اداره ìdārɛ́ ; وكلاى طاقمى vùkèlā-tàkimi.

Admirable, *a.* كوزل ghyùzèl, شايان تحسين shāyAni-tàhsīn.

Admirably, *ad.* پك اعلا pɛ̀k-à-ʻʻlà.

Admiral, *s.* بحريه پاشاسى bàhrìyyɛ́-pàshassi, اميرال àmiràl ; قپودانه پاشا kApudàna-pàsha ; lord-high —, قپودان پاشا kApudAn-pàsha (kAptAn-pAsha), قپودان دريا kApudAni-dɛ̀ryā ; vice — of the fleet, بحريه فريقى bàhrìyyɛ́-fèrìki ; vice —, پطرونه پاشا pAtrūna-pàsha ; rear —, رياله پاشا ìriyàla-pàsha ; — superintendant, ليمان رأيسى پاشا līmAn-rèʻyissi-pàsha ; —'s ship, پاشا كميسى pàsha-ghè-missi, سنجاق كميسى sAnjak-ghɛ̀missi.

Admiralty, *s.* بحريه قپوسى bàhrìyyɛ́-kApissi ; (at Constantinople) ديوانخانه diwAnkhānɛ ; first lord of the —, بحريه ناظرى bàhrìyyɛ́-nāziri.

Admiration, *s.* بكنش bèghɛ́nish, تحسين tàhsīn, مستحسن mùsstàhsɛ̀n.

Admire, *v.a.* بكنمك bèghɛnmek, تحسين ا tàhsīn-et. [mèrAkli.

Admirer, *s.* عاشق ʻʻAshik, مراقلو

Admission, *s.* اخذ àkhz, قبول kAbūl ; كيرش ghìrish, دخول dùkhūl ; تسليم tèsslīm, قبول kAbūl.

Admit, *v.a.* المق Almak, اخذ ا àkhz-et, ايچرو قوسق ìchèri-kòmak, صوقمق sòkmak, قبول kAbūl-et, تسليم ا tèss-līm-et, اذن ويرمك ìzin-vɛ̀rmek.

Admittance, *s.* دخول dùkhūl.

Admixture, *s.* قاتما kAtma, قارشدرلمه kArishdirilma, علاوه ʻʻìlāvɛ́.

Admonish, *v.a.* نصيحت ويرمك nAssī-hàt-vɛ̀rmek, تنبيه ا tènbīh-et.

Admonition, *s.* نصيحت nAssīhàt, تنبيه tènbīh.

Adolescence, *s.* كنجلك ghènjlik.

Adopt, *v.a.* طوتمق tùtmak ; اويمق ùymak, امتثال ا imtissàl-et ; قبول ا kAbūl-et ; اولادلغه قبول ا èvlàdligha-kAbūl-et.

Adoption, *s.* قبول وامتثال kAbūl-u-ìmtissāl ; اخذ وقبول àkhz-u-kAbūl.

Adoptive, *a.* اخرتلك àkhirètlik.

Adorable, *a.* طاپنلور tApinilir, سجده وعبادته شايان sèjdɛ́-vé-ʻʻìbādètɛ́-shāyAn. [ʻʻìbādèt.

Adoration, *s.* سجده sèjdɛ́, عبادت

Adore, *v.a.* سجده ا sèjdɛ́-e-, عبادت ا ʻʻìbādet-e-, پرستش ا pèrèstish-e-, طاپنمق tApinmak.

Adorn, *v.a.* زينتلندرمك zīnetlɛndirmek, تزيين ا tèzyīn-et.

Adrianople, *s.* ادرنه èdìrnɛ́. [fezi.

Adriatic, *s.* وندك كورفزى Vènédik-kyùr-

Adrift, *ad.* يالكز صويك اقنديسيله كتمك اوزره yàlngiz-sùyung-Akindissīla-ghìt-mek-ùzèrɛ́.

Adroit, *a.* چابك chābuk, تتك tètik, هنرلو hùnɛrli, معرفتلو màʻʻrifètli.

Adroitness, *s.* چابكلك chābuklik, هنر hùnɛr, معرفت màʻʻrifèt.

Adulation, *s.* مداهنه mùdāhané.

Adult, *a.* and *s.* بیوك biyuk, عقله بالغ "àkla-bālìgh.

Adulterate, *v.a.* صافلغنی بوزمق sàfli-ghini-bòzmak, ایچنه شی قاتمق ìchina-shèy-kàtmak.

Adulterer, *s.* زانی zānī, زناكار zìnākyār, زنپاره zènpāré (zàmpàra).

Adulteress, *s.* زانیه zānìyyé, روسپی ròsspi (òrosspò), فاحشه fāhishé.

Adulterous, *a.* زناكار zìnākyār, زنائی zìnā'ī.

Adultery, *s.* زنا zìnā, زنپاره‌لك zènpā-rélik (zàmparalik), روسپیلك ròss-pilik (òrosspòluk).

Advance, *v.n.* ایلروكلمك ìléri-ghèlmek, ایلرولمك ìlérilémek; —, *v.a.* ایلرولتمك ìlérilètmek, ایلروكتورمك ìléri-ghètirmek, ایلروچكمك ìléri-chèkmek, ایلروسورمك ìléri-sùrmek; درپیش ا dèr-pīsh-et, ایراد ا īrād-et, سویلمك sùwèylémek, ایلرودن ویرمك ìléridan-vèrmek: —, *s.* ایلرولیش ìlèriléyish, ایلرودن ویرش ìléridan-vèrish.

Advancement, *s.* ایلرولیش ìlèriléyish; ایلرولدش ìlérilédish.

Advantage, *s.* كار kyār, فائده fā'idé, نفع nèf", منفعت mènfa"àt; to take —, فرصتی قوللانمق fùrsati-kūllanmak.

Advantageous, *a.* كارلو kyārli, فائده‌لو fā'idéli.

Advent, *s.* قدوم kùdūm.

Adventure, *s.* ماجرا mājérā, سركذشت sèrghyuzèsht, سرمایهٔ تجارت حصه‌سی sèrmāyè'i-tìjārèt-hìsséssi; —, *v.n.* جسارت ا jèssāret-et; —, *v.a.* قومق kòmak.

Adventurer, *s.* سرسری sèrsèrī, بختنه كوكنور مجهول الاصل كمسنه bàkhtina-ghyùghènir-mèjhūlu-'l-àssl-kìmèssné.

Adversary, *s.* خصم khàssm, دشمن dùshmèn.

Adverse, *a.* ترس tèrss, مخالف mù-khālif.

Adversity, *s.* بختسزلك bàkhtsizlik, دوشكونلك dùshkyunluk, نكبت nìkbèt, فلاكت fèlākèt.

Advert, *v.n.* ایما ا īmā-et, اكدرمق àng-dirmak.

Advertise, *v.a.* اعلان ا ì"lān-et; خبرویرمك khàber-vèrmek.

Advertisement, *s.* اعلان ì"lān.

Advice, *s.* خبر khàber; نصیحت nàs-sīhāt; تدبیر tèdbīr.

Advisable, *a.* مناسب mùnāssib.

Advise, *v.a.* نصیحت ویرمك nàssihàt-vèrmek; اخطار ا ìkhtār-et; تدبیر ا tèdbīr-et; —, *v.n.* استشاره ا ìssti-shāré-et, دانشمق dànishmak. Ill-advised, عقلسز "àklsiz.

Advocacy, *s.* التزام ìltizām, صحابت sàhābet.

Advocate, *s.* صحابت ایدن sàhābet-èden; دعوی وكیلی dà"wà-vèkīli; —, *v.a.* صاحب چیقمق sāhib-chìk-mak (sā'ab), صحابت ا sàhābet-et, تعصب ا tàssàhhub-et.

Æra, *s.* تاریخ tārīkh; مبدأ تعداد اوقات mèbdè'i-tà"dādi-èvkāt.

Aerial, *a.* هوائی hàwā"ī.

Æsthetics, *s. pl.* علم جمالات "ilmi-jèmālat.

Afar, *ad.* اوزاق ūzăk, اوزاقده ūzăkda.

Affability, *s.* چلبيلك chèlébilik, تلطف tàlàttuf, تلطيف tăltīf, نوازش nù-wāzish.

Affable, *a.* چلبى chèlébi, تلطيفجى tăl-tifji; to be affable with, *v.a.* تلطيف ا tăltīf-et.

Affair, *s.* ايش ìsh, مصلحت măsslāhat; جنك jènk, محاربه mŭhārébé; وقعه wàk"à.

Affect, *v.a.* تأثيرا tè'sīr-et.

Affectation, *s.* بوقدن نزاكت bòkdan-nèzākèt.

Affected, *a.* متأثر mùté'èssir; ياپمه yàpma.

Affecting, *a.* مؤثر mù'èssir, دوقنور dòkunur.

Affection, *s.* حس قلبى hèssi-kălbī; محبت màhàbbèt, خلوص khùlūss, خصوص khùssūss; علت "ìllèt, مرض màraz.

Affectionate, *a.* محبت مشمول màhàb-bèt-mèshmūl.

Affiance, *s.* اعتماد ī"timād, توكل tè-vèkkyul; —, *v.a.* نكاح ا nìkyāh-et, عقد ا "àkd-et.

Affidavit, *s.* يمين تحتنده ويرلن تقرير و بيان yèmīn-tāhtinda-vérilān-tàkrīr-ū-bèyān.

Affinity, *s.* تزوجدن حاصل اولان قرابت tezèvvujdan - hāssil - òlan - kàrābèt, صهريت sìhrìyyèt; مناسبت mùnāssé-bèt.

Affirm, *v.a.* تصديق ا tăssdīk-et, اثبات ا issbāt-et, ادعا ا ìddi"ā-et, سويلمك sùwèylémek.

Affirmation, *s.* تصديق tăssdīk, اثبات ìssbāt; ادعا ìddi"ā.

Affirmative, *a.* تصديقى tăssdīkī, ثبوتى sùbūtī.

Afflict, *v.a.* كدرويرمك kèdεr-vèrmek; دوچارقيلمق dūchār-kìlmak.

Affliction, *s.* كدر kèdεr; مصيبت mùs-sībèt, بلا bèlā.

Affluence, *s.* زنكينلك zènghinlik.

Affluent, *a.* زنكين zènghin.

Afford, *v.a.* ويرمك vèrmek, كتورمك ghètirmek, ايرات ا īrāss-et; تحمل ا tàhàmmul-et.

Affranchise, *v.a.* ازاد ا āzād-et.

Affray, *s.* غوغا kàwgha.

Affront, *s.* معامله غيرلايقه mū"āmélè'i-ghàyri-lāyīka, بدمعامله bèd-mù-"āmélé; —, *v.a.* قارشوقومق kàrshi-kòmak; كوجندرمك ghyùjèndirmek, دارلتمق dărìltmak.

Afghan, *a.* افغان àfghān.

Afghanistan, *s.* افغانستان àfghānìsstān.

Afire, *ad.* يانيور yānìòr.

Afloat, *ad.* يوزيور yùziyor.

Afoot, *ad.* اياقده àyakda.

Afore-mentioned, afore-named, afore-said, *a.* مذكور mèzkyūr, مزبور mèzbūr, مسفور mèssfūr, مومى اليه mùmà-ìlèyh, مشاراليه mùshārun-ìlèyh.

Afraid (to be), *v.n.* قورقمق kòrkmak, خوف ا khàvf-et.

Afresh, *ad.* يكيدن yèngidan, مجدداً mùjèddédan; مكرراً mùkεrrεran.

Africa, *s.* افريقه àfrìka.

African, *a.* افريقه لو àfrìkalu.

Afront, *ad.* برابر bèrābèr, برحذاده bìr-hìzāda.

Aft, *ad.* كيرو ghèri, كيرويه ghèriya, كيروده ghèrida, قيچه‌طوغرى kìcha-dòghru.

After, *pr.* دنصكره dan-sòngra, بعد bà"da; —, *ad.* صكره sòngra, بعده bà"dahù; —, *a.* (mar.) كيروكى ghèriki, كيروده‌كى ghèridèki.

Afterbirth, *s.* صوك sòng.

Afternoon, *s.* ايكندى‌وقتلرى ìkindi-wakitlari. [bà"dahù.

Afterwards, *ad.* صكره sòngra, بعده

Again, *ad.* ينه yìné (ghèné), تكرار tèkrār, تكراراً tèkrāran, بردها bìr-dàhà.

Against, *pr.* ئه a; ئه‌قارشو a-kàrshi; قارشيسنه kàrshissina; قارشيسنده kàrshissinda; عليهنه "àlèyhina, عليهنده "alèyhinda; خلافنه khìlā-fina, خلافنده khìlāfinda.

Agate, *s.* سليمانى sùlèymānī. (?)

Age, *s.* ياش yàsh, سن sinn; عصر "àssr, دور dèvr, قرن kārn; of age, *a.* بالغ bāligh, عقله‌بالغ "àkla-bāligh; under age, *a.* صبى sābī.

Aged, *a.* كونلك ghyùnluk; ايلق àylik; ياشنده yàshinda; اختيار ìkhtiyàr, قوجه kòja, مسن mùssinn.

Agency, *s.* واسطه wāssita, وساطت wèss-ātèt, معرفت mà"rifèt.

Agent, *s.* وكيل vèkīl, واسطه wāssita, ادم ādem (àdam). [ètmeklik.

Agglomeration, *s.* طوپ ايتمكلك tòp

Aggrandizement, *s.* بيوتمكلك bìyut-meklik.

Aggravate, *v.a.* دهافنا dàhà-fèna, et, دهابترا dàhà-bèter-et; قيزدرمق kìz-dirmak, دارلتمق dàriltmak.

Aggravation, *s.* اغضاب ìgzāb.

Aggregate, *a.* & *s.* مجموع mèjmū".

Aggression, *s.* تجاوز tèjāvuz, تخطى tàkhàttì.

Aggressor, *s.* تجاوزوتخطى برله نزاعه سبب اولان tèjāvuz-vè-takhàtti-bìrla-nìzā"a-sèbeb-òlan.

Aggrieved, *a.* مظلوم màzlūm, مغدور màghdūr, ستمديده sìtemdīdé.

Agility, *s.* چابكلك chàbukluk.

Agio, *s.* باش bàsh.

Agitate, *v.a.* چالقامق chàlkamak; اضطراب‌ويرمك ìztirāb-vèrmek, مضطربا mùztàrib-et; قارشدرمق kàrishdirmak.

Agitation, *s.* چالقانش chàlkànish; اضطراب ìztirāb; تلاطم tèlātum, تموج tèmèvvuj.

Ago, *ad.* بوندن‌مقدم bùndan-mùkàd-dem, بوندن‌اول bùndan-èvvel.

Agony, *s.* عظيم اضطراب "àzīm-iztàrāb; حالة‌النزع hālétu-'n-nèz"i.

Agree, *v.n.* قولا kàvl-et, مقاوله‌ا mù-kàvélé-et; قرارويرمك kàrār-vèrmek; راضى‌او rāzi-òl, موافقتا mùwāfàkàt-et; ايوكلمك īyi-ghèlmek, اويمق ùymak, اويغون‌كلمك ùyghun-ghèl-mek, موافق‌كلمك mùwāfik-ghèlmek; مطابق‌او mùtābik-òl, توفقا tàwàffuk-et; — together, *v.n.* اويوشمق ùyushmak.

Agreeable, *a.* طاتلو tàtli, كوزل ghyùzèl, خوش khòsh, شيرين shīrīn, لطيف làtīf.

Agreeably to (*or* with), *ad.* تطبيقاً tàtbīkan, توفيقاً tèvfīkan. [mùkàvélé.

Agreement, *s.* قول kàvl, سوز suz, مقاوله

Agriculture, *s.* زراعت zìrā"àt, حراست *and* حراثت hìrāssèt, فلاحت fèlāhàt.

Agriculturist, *s.* اهل زراعت èhli-zìrā"àt.

Aground, *ad.* قرهيه اوطورمش kàraya-òturmush.

Ague, *s.* سته sìtma, ايسته ìssìtma.

Ah, *int.* آه àh, واه wàh, ايواه èywàh, حيف hàyf, دريغ dìrīgh.

Ahead, *ad.* ايلرو ìléri.

Ahoy! *int.* اى èy.

Aid, *s.* ياردم yàrdam, اعانه ì"ānè, امداد ìmdād, معاونت mù"āvénèt; —, *v.a.* ياردم ا yàrdam-et, اعانه ا ì"ānè-et, معاونت ا mù"āvénèt-et.

Aide-de-camp, *s.* ياور yāvèr, ياور حرب yāvèri-hàrb.

Ail, *v.n.* what ails me? نه م وار nèm-vàr; — thee? نه لث وار nèng-vàr; — him, her, it? نه سى وار nèssi-vàr; — us? نه مز وار nèmiz-vàr; — you? نه كز وار nèngiz-vàr; — them? نلرى وار nèléri-vàr.

Ailing, *a.* كيفسز kèyfsiz, خسته khàssta, مزاجسز mìzājsiz, نامزاج nāmizāj.

Ailment, *s.* كيفسزلك kèyfsizlik, خسته لق khàsstalik; علت "ìllèt; درد dèrd.

Aim, *v.n.* نشان المق nìshàn-àlmak; قورمق kùrmak, امل ا èmel-et; —, *s.* قصد kàssd, امل èmel, مرام mèrām, مقصود màksūd; نشان الش nìshàn-àlish.

Air, *s.* هوا hèwā (hàwa); نفس nèfess; طور tàwr; —, *v.a.* اتشه كوسترمك àtèsha-ghyùsstermek, كونشه سرمك ghyùnèsha-sèrmek, هوايه سرمك hàwaya-sèrmek, هواويرمك hàva-vèrmek; to give one's self airs, اطوار صاتمق àtwār sàtmak.

Air-balloon, *s.* بالون bàlon. [(tùfèghi).

Air-gun, *s.* يل تفنكى yèl-tùfènghi

Air-hole, *s.* نفسلك nèfesslik, نفس دلیکی

Airy, *a.* هوادار hàwadār. [nèfess-dèlighi.

Ajar, *a.* اچق àchik.

Akin, *a.* خصم khìssm.

Alabaster, *s.* اق مرمر àk-mèrmer.

Alacrity, *s.* مسارعت mùssāra"àt, ممنونيت mèmnūnìyyèt.

Alarm, *s.* قورقو kòrku, خوف khàvf, دهشت dèhshet; خبر khàber; —, *v.a.* قورقتمق kòrkutmak, قورقو ويرمك kòrku-vèrmek, تخويف ا tàkhwīf-et, اخافه ا ìkhāfé-et.

Alas, *int.* اى ày, واى wày, واه wàh, حيف hàyf, دريغ dìrīgh.

Albania, *s.* ارناود ولايتى àrnàwd-vìlāyèti.

Albanian, *s.* and *a.* ارناود àrnàwd.

Albeit, *c.* هرنقدر hèr-nàkadar, ايسه ده ìssada.

Alchymist, *s.* كيمياكر kìmiyā-ghèr.

Alchymy, *s.* علم كيميا "ìlmi-kìmiyā.

Alcohol, *s.* روح rūh.

Alcove, *s.* حجره hùjré. [àghaji.

Alder-tree, *s.* مرورا غاجى mùrvèr-

Alderman, *s.* اعيان a"yān.

Ale, *s.* بياض ارپه صويى bèyAz-àrpa-sùyu.
Alembic, *s.* انبيق ìnbik.
Alert (to be on the), *v.n.* اويانق او ùyànik-òl, دورت كوز او dùrt-ghyùz-ò, كوز قولاق او ghyùz-kùlAk-òl.
Algebra, *s.* جبر jèbr.
Algiers, *s.* جزاير Jézā'ir.
Alias, *ad.* نام ديكر nAmi-dīghèr.
Alien, *s.* اجنبى èjnébi; يبانجى yàbAnji.
Alienate, *v.a.* اخره تمليك ا àkhàra-tèmlīk-et, تبريد ا tèbrīd-et.
Alight, *v.n.* انمك ènmek, قونمق kònmak.
Alike, *a.* بكزر bèngzèr, مشابه mùshābih, بر bìr.
Aliment, *s.* غذا ghìdā, ييه جك yèyéjek, بسليه جك bèssléyéjek, يمك yèmek.
Alimony, *s.* نفقه nàfaka.
Alive, *a.* ديرى dìri, صاغ sàgh, برحيات bèr-hàyāt, حياتده hàyātda.
Alkali, *s.* القلى àlkali.
All, *a.* هپ hèp, بتون bìtun, جميع jèmī", جمله jùmlé; above —, خصوصا khùsūsA; after —, خلاصهٔ كلام khùlāsé-'i kélām.
Allay, *v.a.* تسكين ا tèsskīn-et.
Allegation, *s.* دعوى dà"wà, قضيه kAziyyé.
Allege, *v.a.* ايراد ا īrād-e.
Allegiance, *s.* تبعيت tèba"ìyyèt; صداقت sAdākAt.
Alleviate, *v.a.* خفيفلتمك khAfifletmek, تخفيف ا tàkhfīf-et.
Alley, *s.* دار صوقاق dàr-sòkAk, چيقمز صوقاق chìkmàz-sòkAk.
Alliance, *s.* اتفاق ìttifAk.
Allied, *a.* متفق mùttèfik.
Alligator, *s.* تمساح tìmsāh.
Allocution, *s.* نطق nùtk.
Allot, *v.a.* تخصيص ا tàkhsīss-et.
Allotment, *s.* حصه hìssé.
Allow, *v.a.* براقمق bràkmak, قومق kòmak, اذن ويرمك ìzin-vèrmek, رخصت ويرمك rùkhsAt-vèrmek, جوازويرمك jèwāz-vèrmek, ويرمك vèrmek, تعيين ا tà"yīn-et, تخصيص ا tàkhsīss-et; — of, قبول ا kAbūl-et; — for, حساب ا hissAb-et; —, *v.n.* تسليم ا tèsslīm-et, اعتراف ا ì"tirAf-et.
Allowable, *a.* جائز jā'iz.
Allowance, *s.* ايلق àylik, كونده لك ghyùndélik, يللق yìllik, تعيين tà"yīn, تعيينات tà"yīnAt; to make — for, *v.a.* نظر ا nAzar-et, حسابه داخل ا hìssAba-dākhil-et.
Alloy, *s.* التونه كومشه قاتلان باقر Altina-ghyùmisha-kAtilAn-bAkir; عيار "àyār.
Allude to, *v.a.* ايما ا īmā-et, اكدرمق Angdirmak.
Allure, *v.a.* جزب ا jèzb-et.
Allurement, *s.* جاذبه jāzibé.
Alluring, *a.* جاذب jāzib.
Allusion, *s.* ايما īmā, اكدرش āngdirish.
Ally, *v.a.* رابطهٔ واحده تحتنه ادخال ا rAbità'i-wāhidé-tàhtina-idkhāl-et; —, *s.* متفق mùttèfik.
Almanack, *s.* تقويم tàkwīm, سالنامه sālnāmé.
Almighty, *a.* قدير kAdir.
Almond, *s.* بادم bàdem.
Almoner, *s.* امام ìmAm.

Almost, *ad.* همان hèmAn (hèmEn), ازقالدی Az-kAldi.

Alms, *s.* صدقه sAdaka.

Aloes, *s.* صبر sAbr; wood of —, عوداغاجی "ud-Aghaji.

Aloft, *ad.* یوقاری yùkàri, یوقاریده yù-kàrida (yùkàrda).

Alone, *a.* یالکز yAlngiz, تنها tènhā, باشلوباشنه bAshli-bAshina; all —, یاپه یالکز yàpa-yAlngiz.

Along, *ad.* بوینجه bòyunja; come along! کل باقالم ghèl-bAkAlim; go along, کیت بقالم ghit-bAkAlim, ایشکه کیت ìshinga-ghit, هایدی سکدر hàydi-sìktir.

Alongside, *ad.* یاننه yànina, یاننده yà-ninda; — one another, قارن قارنه kàrn-kàrna, بورده بورده یه bòrda-bòr-daya.

Aloof, *ad.* اوزاقده ùzAkda, الارغه ده àlàr-ghada.

Aloud, *ad.* پك pèk, جهراً jèhran, صوت بلند ایله sAvti-bùlènd-ila.

Alphabet, *s.* الفبا èlif-bā (èlif-bE).

Alphabetically, *ad.* حروف هجا ترتیبی اوزره hùrūfu-hèjā-tèrtībi-ùzérE.

Already, *ad.* شمدی بیله shimdi-bilE, اول وقته قالمیه رق òl-wAkta-kAlmaya-rak.

Also, *c.* کذلك kèzālik, وکذلك vè-kèzālik, ده dE, دخی dàkhi, ودخی vE-dàkhi, وهمدخی vè-hèm-dàkhi, وبرده vè-bìr-dE, وهمده vè-hèm-dE, همده hèm-dE.

Altar, *s.* مذبح mèzbàh.

Alter, *v.a.* دیکشدرمك dìghishdirmek, بشقه هیئته قومق bAshka-hèy'èta-kò-mak, تبدیل ا tèbdīl-et, محوواثبات ا màhv-u-ìssbAt-et; —, *v.n.* دیکشمك dìghishmek, تغیرا tàghàyyur-et.

Alteration, *s.* تبدیل tèbdīl; محوواثبات màhv-u-ìssbAt.

Altercation, *s.* نزاع nìzā", منازعه mù-nāza"à, غوغا ghàwgha (kàwgha).

Alternate, *a.* متبادل mùtébādil, متناوب mùténāvib; on alternate days, *ad.* کون اشوری ghyùn-Ashiri.

Alternate, *v.n.* نوبتلشمك nùbetleshmek.

Alternately, *ad.* نوبتله nùbètla, متناوبة mùténāvibétEn, علی المناوبه "àlE-'l--mùnāvébE.

Alternative, *s.* چاره chārE, بشقه یول bAshka-yòl, طریق اخر tàrīki-àkhàr.

Although, *c.* هرنقدر hèr-nàkAdar, ایسه ده issada.

Altitude, *s.* ارتفاع ìrtifā".

Altogether, *ad.* بتون بتون bìtun-bitun.

Alum, *s.* شاب shAb.

Alluminium, } *s.* بردرلو معدن bìr-dùrlu
Alluminum, } -ma"den.

Always, *ad.* دائما dā'ima, هرزمان hèr-zàmAn, هروقت hèr-wAkit.

Amanuensis, *s.* کاتب kyātib.

Amass, *v.a.* طوپلامق tòplamak, برکدرمك bìrikdirmek, جمع ا jèm"-et.

Amateur, *s.* هوسلو hàvèssli.

Amaze, *v.a.* تعجب ایتدرمك tà"àjjub--èttirmek; amazed, *a.* متعجب mù-ta"àjjib, حیران hàyrAn; to be

—, تعجب ا tà"àjjub-et, شاشمق shàshmak, حيران قالمق hàyrān-kālmak, قالمق kālmak, باقه قالمق bàka-kālmak.

Amazing, a. عجيب "ājīb (ājà'ib), غريب ghàrīb ; —ly, ad. چوق chòk.

Ambassador, s. ايلچى èlchi, سفير sèfīr.

Amber, s. كهربا kèhrubā (kèhlibàr).

Ambergrease, Ambergris, s. عنبر "ànbèr.

Ambiguous, a. قپانق kāpānik, مغلق mūghlāk.

Ambiguity, s. مغلقلق mùghlàklik.

Ambition, s. حرص الشان hìrssu-'sh-shān, حرص حكومت hìrssi-hùkyū-mèt. [-'sh-shān.

Ambitious, a. حريص الشان hàrīssu-

Amble, s. راهوان ràhwān, اشكين èsh-kin ; —, v.n. اشمك èshmek, اشكين كتمك èshkin-ghìtmek, راهوان كتمك ràhwān-ghìtmek,

Ambler, Ambling-horse, s. راهوان ràhwān, اشكين باركير èshkin-bārghīr (bèghir).

Ambuscade, Ambush, s. پوصو pùssu ; to lay an ambush, پوصى قورمق pūssu kūrmak ; to fall into an ambush, پوصى يه طوتلمق pūssūyyè tùtul-

Amen, int. امين āmīn. [mak.

Amenable, a. مسئول mèss'ūl.

Amend, v.a. طوغرلتمق dòghrultmak, تصحيح ا tàsshīh-et-, اصلاح ا ìsslāh-et- ; —, v.n. برازايواو bìr-āz-īyi-òl, ايواولمغه يول طوتمق īyi-òlmagha-yòl-

Amendment, s. فرق fàrk. [-tūtmak.

Amends, to make, v.n. تضمين ا tāz-mīn-et, ترضيه ويرمك tarzìyyé-vèr-mek ; اجيسنى چيقارمق ājissini-chì-kàrmak.

America, s. امريقا Amérika.

American, s. and a. امريقالو Amérikalì.

Amethyst, s. جبلقوم jèbélòkum.

Amiable, a. كوزل خويلو ghyùzèl-khūylu, طاتلو tātli. [dòsstānè.

Amicable, a. Amicably, ad. دوستانه

Amidst, pr. اورته سنده òrtassinda, اراسنده àrassinda.

Amidships, ad. اورته يرلرينه طوغرى òrta-yèrlérina-dòghru.

Amiss, a. فنا fèna, سقط sàkat.

Amity, s. دوستلق dòsstluk, دوستى dòssti, محبت màhàbbèt, مخادنت mūkhādénèt.

Ammonia, s. نشادر nìshādir.

Ammoniac, s. نشادر nìshādir.

Ammunition, s. باروت bārut, جبخانه jèbkhānè.

Amnesty, s. عفو عام "àfvi-"āmm.

Among, Amongst, pr. اراسنه àras-sina, اراسنده àrassinda.

Amorous, a. عاشقانه "āshikānè.

Amount, s. مبلغ mèblàgh ; طوپ tòp, يكون yèkyūn ; —, v.n. بالغ اولو bā-ligh-òl.

Amphibious, a. هم صوده هم قره ده ياشار hèm-sūda-hèm-kàrada-yàshar.

Ample, a. بول bòl, كنش ghènish.

Amplitude, s. سعهٔ مشرق sì"à'i-mèshrik.

Amputate, v.a. كسمك kèssmek, قطع ا kāt"-et. [kāt".

Amputation, s. كسلمه kèssilmè, قطع

Amulet, *s.* نسخه nùsskh*a* (m*à*ssk*a*).
Amuse, *v.a.* اكلندرمك è*gh*l*e*ndirmek ; — one's self, *v.n.* اكلنمك è*gh*l*e*n-mek.
An, *art.* بر bìr.
Analogous, *a.* مشابه mùshābih, مقيس m*à*kīss. قياس kìyāss.
Analogy, *s.* مشابهت mùshābéhèt ;
Analysis, *s.* حل hàll.
Analyze, *v.n.* حل‌ا hàll-et.
Anarchy, *s.* فساد fèssād, اختلال ìkhtilāl.
Anathema, *s.* لعنت là"nèt, بددعا bèd-dù"ā, افوروز àforòz.
Anatomize, *v.a.* تشريح‌ا tèshrīh-et.
Anatomy, *s.* تشريح tèshrīh.
Ancestor, *s.* جد jèdd (pl. اجداد èjdād.)
Ancestry, *s.* اجداد èjdād ; نسب nèsseb.
Anchor, *s.* تيمور tīmūr (dèmir), لنكر lènghèr ; —, *v.a.* تيمورلمك dèmir-lémek ; —, *v.n.* تيمورلمك dèmirlé-mek, تيموراتمق dèmir-àtm*a*k ; at —, تيمورلو dèmirli ; to cast —, دمير اتمق dèmir-àtmak ; to weigh —, دميرى قالدرمق démiri-kàldirm*a*k.
Anchorage, *s.* تيموريرى dèmir-yèri, تيمورليه‌جك‌ير dèmirléyéjek-yèr.
Anchored, *a.* تيمورلو dèmirli.
Anchovy, *s.* سارده sārdèl*a*.
Ancient, *a.* اسكى èsski, قديم kàdīm, كارقديم kyāri-kàdīm.
Ancients, *s. pl.* متقدمين mùt*a*kàd-dimīn, اسكى زمان ادملرى èsski-z*à*-màn-àd*a*ml*a*ri.
And, *c.* و vè, ده dè, دخى dàkhi.
Anecdote, *s.* فقره fìkra, منقبه mànk*a*bé.
Anemone, *s.* مانسه mànissa.

Angel, *s.* ملك mèlek, ملائكه mèlā'iké.
Angelic, *a.* ملكى mèlekī.
Anger, *s.* دارغينلق dàrgh*i*nl*i*k, قيزغينلق k*i*zgh*i*nl*i*k, غضب ghàzab.
Angina, *s.* خناق علتى khŭnnāk-"ìllèti.
Angina pectoris, *s.* بر نوع ضيق الصدر bìr-nèv-"i-zìku-sàdr.
Angle, *s.* كوشه kyùshé, زاويه zāvìyyé ; —, *v.n.* اولته ايله بالق اولامق òlt*a*-il*a*-bàl*i*k-àwlam*a*k.
Angry, *a.* دارغين dàrgh*i*n ; to be —, *v.n.* دارلمق dàr*i*lmak, قيزمق k*i*zm*a*k, كوجنمك ghy*ù*jènmek, غضبه كلمك ghàzab*a*-ghèlmek, حدتلنمك hìd-dètl*e*nmek.
Anguish, *s.* عظيم درد "àzīm-dèrd, عظيم كدر "àzīm-kèder.
Angular, *a.* كوشه‌لو ky*ù*shéli.
Animal, *s.* حيوان hàywān ; —, *a.* حيوانى hàywānī.
Animalcule, *s.* حيوانجق hàywānj*i*k.
Animate, *v.a.* جان ويرمك jàn-vèrmek, جانلندرمق jànl*a*ndirm*a*k, احيا‌ا ìhyā-et.
Animated, *a.* بشاشتلو bèshāshètli.
Animation, *s.* بشاشت bèshāshèt.
Animosity, *s.* عداوت "àdāvèt, كين kīn, كنيه kīné.
Aniseed, *s.* اناسون ànassòn.
Ankle, *s.* طوپوق tòpuk.
Annalist, *s.* مورخ mùvèrrikh, وقعه نويس wàk"à-nùwīss.
Annals, *s. pl.* تاريخ tārīkh (pl. تواريخ tàwārīkh).
Annex, *v.a.* الحاق‌ا ilhàk-et, ضم‌ا zàmm-et.

Annihilate, *v.a.* وجودینی قالدرمق vùjūd*i*n*i*-kÀld*i*rmak, یوق ا yòk-et, افنا ا ìfnā-et.

Anniversary, *s.* کون ghyùn.

Announce, *v.a.* خبرویرمك khÀbER-vÈrmek, تبلیغ ا tèblīgh-et, افاده ا ìfādÉ-et.

Annoy, *v.a.* تعجیز ا tā''jīz-et, صقندی ویرمك s*ì*k*i*nt*i*-vÈrmek, اذیت ویرمك èzìyyèt-vÈrmek, راحتسز ا rāh*a*tsiz-et; کوجندرمك ghyùjÈndirmek, کوجنه کتمك ghyùjun*a*-ghìtmek.

Annoyance, *s.* اذیت èzìyyèt, صقندی s*ì*k*i*nt*i*.

Annoying, *a.* ادمك کوجنه کیدر ÀdAm*i*ng-ghyùjun*a*-ghìdER.

Annual, *a.* سنوی sÈnÉvī.

Annuity, *s.* سهیم sèhīm, ایراد īrād.

Annul, *v.a.* فسخ ا fèsskh-et, ابطال ا ìbtāl-et, بطال ا bÀttāl-et.

Annular, *s.* حلقه رسمنده hÀlk*a*-rèss-minda.

Annum, *s.* سنه sènÉ; per annum, ییلده y*ì*lda, سنوی sÈnÉvī.

Anoint, *v.a.* یاغ سورمك yāg*h*-sùrmek, تدهین ا tèdhīn-et.

Anointed, *a.* مسیح mèssīh, مدهن mù-dèhhèn.

Anomalous, *a.* **Anomaly,** *s.* خلاف العاده kh*ì*lÀfu-'l-''ĀdÉ.

Anonymous, *a.* امضاسز ìmzāssiz.

Another, *a.* بشقه بر bÀshk*a*-bìr, دیکربر dìghER-bìr.

Answer, *s.* جواب jÈwĀb; —, *v.a.* جواب ویرمك jÈwĀb-vèrmek; —, *v.n.* اولمق òlm*a*k, اویمق ùym*a*k; — for, کفیل او kèfīl-ol; مسئول او mèss'ūl-ol.

Answerable, *a.* مسئول mèss'ūl.

Ant, *s.* قارنجه kÀr*i*nj*a*.

Antagonist, *s.* خصم khÀss*i*m.

Antarctic, *a.* جنوبی jènūbī.

Antecedent, *a.* سالف sālif, سابق sāb*i*k, مقدم mùkÀddEm; —, *s.* مقدم mù-kÀddEm, موصول به mèvsūl*u*n-bìh.

Antechamber, *s.* دیوانخانه dīwAnkhānÉ.

Antediluvian, *a.* طوفاندن اول tūfĀnd*a*n-ÈvvEl.

Antelope, *s.* جیران jèyrĀn (jèylĀn), اهو āhū.

Antemeridian, *a.* اویله دن اول *u*ylÉden èvvel.

Anterior, *a.* سالف sālif, سابق sāb*i*k, مقدم mùkÀddEm.

Anthropophagi, *s. pl.* یامیام yàmyàm.

Antichrist, *s.* دجال dèjjāl.

Anticipate, *v.a.* اومق ùmm*a*k, مأمول ا mÈ'mūl-et; اول طورانمق ÈvvEl-dāw-r*a*nmak; طلب اولنمزدن اول حس ایدوب ویرمك یاخود یاپمق tÀleb-òl*u*nm*a*zd*a*n-ÈvvEl-hìss-èd*u*p-vÈrmek-yākhud-yàpm*a*k.

Antics, *s. pl.* مسخره لق mÀsskharal*i*k.

Antidote, *s.* علاج ''ìlāj.

Antimony, *s.* تیموربوزان tīmūr-bòzAn (dèmir-bòzAn).

Antipathy, *s.* نفرت nèfrèt; عداوت ''àdāvèt, خصومت khùssūmèt.

Antique, *s.* عنتقه ''àntik*a*; —, *a.* اسکی èsski, عتیق ''àtīk, قدیم kÀdīm, کارقدیم ky*ā*r*i*-kÀdīm.

Antiquity, *s.* عنتقه ''àntik*a*; اسکی زمان èsski-z*à*mAn.

Antler, *s.* بوينوز bòynuz.
Anus, *s.* مقعد màk''àd.
Anvil, *s.* اورس àrss.
Anxiety, *s.* قصاوت kàssāvèt; تلاشی tèlāshī (tèlàsh).
Any, *pro.* بر bìr, برآز bīr-àz, بعض bà''zi; هیچ hìch, هیچ بر hìch-bìr.
Anybody, *pro.* کمسنه kìmèssné (kìmssé).
Anyhow, *ad.* نصل اولورسه nàssl-òlursa; هیچ بر درلو hìch-bìr-dùrlu.
Apace, *ad.* چابك chàbuk.
Apart, *ad.* ایری àyri.
Apartment, *s.* اوطه òda; دائره dā'iré.
Apathy, *s.* قیدسزلق kàydsizlik, عدم تقید ''àdémi-tàkàyyud.
Ape, *s.* میمون màymūn, شبك shèbek; —, *v.a.* تقلید ا tàklīd-et.
Aperient, *a.* مسهل mùsshil (ss-h).
Aperture, *s.* دلیك dèlik, ارالق àralik, اچقلق àchiklik, نفسلك nèfesslik.
Apex, *s.* رأس rè'ss, ذروه zìrvé.
Aphelion, *s.* حضیض hàdīd.
Apiece, *ad.* بهرینه bèhèrina.
Apocryphal, *a.* مشکوك mèshkyūk.
Apogee, *s.* حضیض hàdīd. [lémek.
Apologize, *v.n.* عذردیله مك ''ùzr-dì-
Apology, *s.* عذرنامه ''ùzrnāmé; عذربیانی ''ùzr-bèyāni.
Apoplexy, *s.* طمله dàmla, نزول nùzūl.
Apostasy, *s.* ارتداد ìrtidād.
Apostate, *s.* مرتد mùrtèdd (mùrtàd), دونمه dùnma.
Apostatize, *v.n.* دینندن دونمك dīnin-dan-dùnmek.
Apostle, *s.* رسول rèssūl, مرسل mùrsèl; the apostles of Christ, حواریون hàwāriyyūn. [ìsspènchiyàr.
Apothecary, *s.* اجزاجی èjzāji, اسپنچیار
Appal, *v.a.* قورقتمق kòrkutmak, تخویف ا tàkhwīf-et.
Appanage, *s.* ارپه لق àrpalik, باشمقلق bàshmaklik.
Apparatus, *s.* طاقم tàkim, الات ادوات ālāt-èdawāt.
Apparel, *s.* اثواب èsswāb (èssbàb), لباس libàss, البسه èlbissé.
Apparent, *a.* ظاهر zāhir, بدیدار bèdīdār, هویدا hùwèydā, آشکار āshikyār.
Apparently, *ad.* غالبا ghāliba; ظاهرا zāhira. [yālé.
Apparition, *s.* ظهور zùhūr; خیاله khà-
Appeal, *v.n.* دوشمك dùshmek, صیغنمق sìghinmak; مراجعت ا mùrāja''àt-et.
Appear, *v.n.* کورنمك ghyùrunmek, کوزکمك ghyùzikmek, ظهورا zùhūr-et; it appears, *v. imp.* غالبا ghāliba; کلور ghèlir, کورنیور ghyù-runiyor.
Appearance, *s.* صورت sūrèt, هیئت hèy'èt; کورنش ghyùrunush; ظهور zùhūr.
Appease, *v.a.* تسکین ا tèsskīn-et.
Append, *v.a.* ضم ا zàmm-et, علاوه ا ''ìlāvé-et.
Appendage, **Appendix**, *s.* تتمه tè-timmé, ضمیمه zàmīmé, علاوه ''ìlāvé.
Appertain, *v.n.* راجع او rāji''ol, منوطاو mènūt-ol, متعلق او mùta''àllik-ol.
Appetite, *s.* اشتها ìshtihā (ìshtàh.)

Applaud, *v.a.* ستايش ا sìtāyish-et.
Applause, *s.* ستايش sìtāyish.
Apple, *s.* الما èlma.
Applicable, *a.* دوقنور dòkunur ; مناسبتالور mùnāssébèt-Alir.
Application, *s.* دوقندرش dòkundu-rush, ياپشدرش yàpishdirish ; دوشش dùshush, باش اورش bAsh-ùrush (wùrush), مراجعت mùrājaʻʻàt ; چالشش chAlishish, سعى وغيرت sàʻʻy-u-ghàyrèt, صرف ذهن sàrfi-zìhn, جد و جهد jìdd-u-jèhd.
Apply, *v.a.* دوقندرمق dòkundurmak, ياپشدرمق yàpishdirmak ; سورمك sùrmek ; تطبيق ا tàtbik-et ; طلا ا tìlā-et ; —, *v.n.* باش اورمق bAsh-wùrmak, دوشمك dùshmek, مراجعت mùrājaʻʻàt-et ; — for, استمك ìssté-mek, استدعا ا ìsstìdʻʻā-et, مطالبه ا mùtālébé-et, مطلوب ا mAtlūb-et ; —, one's self, چالشمق chAlishmak, سعى ا sàʻʻy-et, سعى وغيرت ا sàʻʻy-u-ghàyrèt-et.
Appoint, *v.a.* تعيين ا tàʻʻyīn-et, نصب ا nAssb-et, تخصيص ا tàkhsīss-et.
Appointment, *s.* مأموريت mèʻmū-rìyyèt ; ايش ìsh.
Apportion, *v.a.* حصه حصه تقسيم ا hìsssé-hìsssé-tàksīm-et. [nāssib.
Apposite, *a.* يوللو yòllu, مناسب mù-
Appraise, *v.a.* قيمت تقديرا kīmèt-tAkdīr-et, بها بچمك bàhà-bìchmek (pAhà).
Appreciate, *v.a.* تقديرا tAkdīr-et, قدرينى بلمك kAdrini-bìlmek.

Apprehend, *v.a.* طوتمق tùtmak, يقالمق yàkalamak, اخذ و كرفت ا àkhz-u-ghìrìft-et ; اكلامق ànglamak (ànnamak), درك ا dèrk-et ; قورقمق kòrkmak.
Apprehension, *s.* اخذ و كرفت àkhz-u-ghìrìft ; فهم و ادراك fèhm-u-ìdrāk ; قورقو kòrku. [kussu-òlAn.
Apprehensive, *a.* قورقوسى اولان kòr-
Apprentice, *s.* شاكرد shāghird ; —, *v.a.* شاكردلكه ويرمك shāghirdlighé-vèrmek.
Apprenticeship, *s.* شاكردلك shā-ghirdlik. [mek.
Apprize, *v.a.* خبر ويرمك khAber-vèr-
Approach, *s.* يول yòl ; تقرب tàkàr-rub ; —, *v.a.* & *n.* تقرب ا tàkàr-rub-et, يقينلاشمق yàkinlashmak, يقين وارمق yàkin-vàrmak. [ìsstìhsān.
Approbation, *s.* تحسين tàhsīn, استحسان
Appropriate, *v.a.* تخصيص ا tàkhsīss-et ; —, *a.* مناسب mùnāssib.
Approval, *s.* استحسان ìsstìhsān ; on —, *ad.* مخير mùkhAyyèr.
Approximate, *a.* تقريبى tAkrībī, تخمينى tàkhmīnī ; —, *v.n.* تقرب ا tàkàr-rub-et. [tàkhmīna.
Approximately, *ad.* تقريبا tAkrība, تخمينا
Approximation, *s.* تقرب tàkàrrub ; تخمين tàkhmīn.
Apricot, *s.* قيسى kàyssi, زردالو zèrdāli.
April, *s.* نيسان nīssān.
Apron, *s.* پشتمال pèshtamAl.
Apropos, *a.* & *ad.* مناسب mùnāsib.
Apt, *a.* مستعد mùsstāʻʻidd. [vwèjilé.
Aptly, *ad.* مناسبتى وجهله mùn-āsibéti-

Aptitude, Aptness, *s.* استعداد **ìss-tì"dād.**

Aquafortis, *s.* تیزاب **tīzāb,** كذاب صويى [**kèzab-suyu.**

Aqueduct, *s.* صويولى **sù-yòlu,** كمر **kèmer,** كمرلر **kémerler.**

Arab, *s.* عرب **"àrab.**

Arabia, *s.* عربستان **"àrabistan.**

Arabic, *s.* عربجه **"àrabj*a*.**

Arable, *a.* اكلوربچلور **èkilir-bìchilir,** مزروع **mèzrū"**; —, **land,** *s.* مزرعه **mèzr*a*"*à*,** طرلا **tàrla.**

Ararat, Mt., *s.* اغرى طاغى **Aghr*i*-dAghi.**

Arbiter, Arbitrator, حكم **hàkem.**

Arbitrate, *v.n.* ايرد ا **àyrd-et.**

Arc, *s.* قوس **kàvss.**

Arch, *s.* كمر **kèmer.**

Archer, *s.* كمانكش **kèmankèsh.**

Archery, *s.* كمانكشلك **kèmankèshlik.**

Architect, *s.* معمار **mì"màr,** قالفه **kAlf*a*.**

Architecture, *s.* فن معمارى **fènni-mi"-màrī**; بنا **bìnā**; بنالر **bìnāl*a*r.**

Archives, *s. pl.* قيودات **kùyùdAt,** دفترخانه **dèfterkhāné,** اوراق مخزنى **èvrAk-màkhzéni.**

Arctic, *a.* شمالى **shìmālī.**

Ardent, *a.* اتشلو **àtèshli**; يانار **y*à*nar.**

Ardour, *s.* گرميت **ghèrmìyyèt.**

Arduous, *a.* كوچ **ghy*ù*ch,** چتين **chètin,** متعسر **mùt*a*"*à*ssir.**

Area, *s.* سطح **sAth** (t-h.)

Argue, *v.n.* لقردى ا **làk*i*rd*i*-et,** مباحثه ا **mùbāhéssé-et**; چكه يارشى ا **chèn*g*é-yār*i*sh*i*-et.**

Argument, *s.* لقردى **làk*i*rd*i*,** كلام **kèlām,** سوز **sùz.**

Arid, *a.* قورو **kùru,** چول **ch*ù*l.**

Arise, *v.n.* قالقمق **kAlkm*a*k**; طوغمق **dò*gh*m*a*k,** طلوع ا **tùlū"et**; نشئت ا **nèsh'èt-et,** لازم كلمك **lāz*i*m-ghèlmek.**

Aristocracy, *s.* كبار **kìbār.**

Aristocrat, *s.* كبار دن بری **kìbār-den-bìri.**

Arithmetic, *s.* علم حساب **"ìlmi-hìssAb** (**hès-**). ["**ìlmi hìssāb.**

Arithmetician, *s.* اهل علم حساب **èhli-**

Ark, *s.* **Noah's** —, نوح كميسى **nūh-ghèmissi**; — **of the covenant,** تابوت سكينه **tābūti-sèkīné.**

Arm, *s.* قول **kòl**; سلاح **sìlāh**; —, *v.n.* سلاحلنمق **sìlāhl*a*nm*a*k**; —, *v.a.* سلاح ويرمك **sìlāh-vèrmek**; دوناتمق **dòn*a*tm*a*k.**

Armada, *s.* دونما **dònanmā.**

Arm-chair, *s.* قولتقلى **kòltuklu,** قولتقلى صندالیه **kòltuklu-sāndālìyyé.**

Armenia, *s.* ارمنستان **èrmènisstān.**

Armenian, *a.* ارمنى **èrmènī**; —, *s.* ارمنى **èrmènī**; ارمنيجه **èrmènījé.**

Armfull, *s.* قوجاق **kùjAk,** قوجاق طولوسى **kùjAk-dòlussu.**

Armillary sphere, *s.* كرهٔ مشبكه **ky*ù*ré-'i-mùshèbbéké.**

Armistice, *s.* متاركه **mùtāréké.**

Armlet, *s.* بازوبند **bAzūbènd.**

Armorer, قلجى **kìlìjji,** تفنكجى **tù-fènkji,** چاقمقجى **ch*à*km*a*kj*i*.**

Armory, *s.* جبه خانه **jèbé-khāné.**

Armour, *s.* زره **zìrh**; سلاح **sìlāh.**

Armpit, *s.* قولتق **kòltuk.**

Army, *s.* اردو **òrdu,** عسكر **"Assker.**

Aromatic, *a.* قوقولو **kòkulu.**

Around, *ad.* and *pr.* اطرافه ètrāfa, اطرافده ètrāfda.

Arouse, *v.a.* قالديرمق kàldirmak, اویاندیرمق ŭyàndirmak.

Arrange, *v.a.* دیزمك dìzmek, ترتيب ا tèrtìb-et, تنظيم ا tànzīm-et, نظامه قومق nìzāma-kòmak; قرارلاشدیرمق kārār-lashdirmak.

Arrangement, *s.* ترتيب tèrtīb, نظام nìzām; قرار kāràr. [صف sāff.

Array, *s.* ترتيب tèrtīb, نظام nīzam,

Arrayed, *a.* كييلو ghìyili, ملبس mù-lèbbèss. [bākāyā.

Arrears, *s. pl.* مانده māndé, بقايا

Arrest, *s.* حبس hābss; —, *v.a.* اخذوكرفت ا àkhz-u-ghìrìft-et; توقيف ا tèvkīf-et.

Arrival, *s.* قدوم kŭdūm, كلش ghèlish; وصول vùssūl, وارش vàrish.

Arrive, *v.n.* كلمك ghèlmek, وارمق vàr-mak, واصل او wāssil-òl, وصول بولمق wùssūl-bùlmak. [tèkèbbur.

Arrogance, *s.* تعظم tà''àzzum, تكبر

Arrogant, *a.* متكبر mùtékèbbir.

Arrogate to one's self, *v.a.* قالقشمق kālkishmak, اوزرينه المق ùzériné-àlmak.

Arrow, *s.* اوق òk, تير tīr, سهم sèhm.

Arse, *s.* كوت ghyùt, دبر dùbr, كون kyùn.

Arsenal, *s.* طوبخانه tòp-khāné.

Arsenic, *s.* سيچان اوتی sìchan-òtu.

Arson, *s.* خانه ياقمق khāné-yàkmak.

Art, *s.* صنعت sàn''àt; فن fènn; معرفت mà''rifèt; حيله hīlé.

Artery, *s.* شاهطمر shāh-dāmar.

Artful, *a.* شيطان shèytān, حيله باز hīlébāz.

Artfulness, *s.* حيله بازلك hīlébāzlik.

Artfully, *adv.* حيله ايله hīlé-ìlé.

Artichoke, *s.* انكنار ìnghinār; Jerusalem —, يرالماسی yèr-èlmassi.

Article, *s.* متاع màtā'', مال māl; بند bend, فقره fìkra; definite —, حرف تعريف hàrfi-tà''rīf; indefinite —, ادات تبهيم èdāti-tébhīm.

Artifice, *s.* حيله hīlé.

Artificer, *s.* اصناف èssnàf, اهل صنعت èhli-sàn''àt.

Artificial, *a.* صنعی sùn''ī, مصنع mù-sànnà'', ياپمه yàpma, تقليد tāklīd.

Artillery, *s.* طوبلر tòplar, طوبجی عسکری tòpji-''àsskèri; — man, *s.* طوبجی tòpji. [èhli-sàn''àt.

Artisan, *s.* اصناف èssnàf, اهل صنعت

Artist, *s.* رسام rèssām.

Artless, *a.* صافدرون sāfdérūn; حيله سز hīléssiz.

As, *c.* چونكه chùnku, چون chūn; *ad.* ايكن ìkèn; as . . . as . . ., قدر kādr; as soon as, ديغی كبی -dighi-ghìbi; as it were, as though, صانكه sànki; as for, as to, كلنجه ghèlinjé; as much, بوقدر bū-kādr, اولقدر òl-kādr (ò-); as much as . . ., قدر kādr; as well as, كبی ghìbi, قدر kādr.

Ascend, *v.a.* and *n.* چيقمق chìkmak, صعود ا sù''ūd-et.

Ascendency, *s.* نفوذ nùfūz, اعتبار ì''tibār, حكم hùkm.

Ascension, *s.* صعود sù''ūd.

Ascent, *s.* صعود sū"ūd ; يوقش yòkush.

Ascertain, *v.a.* تحقيق ا tàhkīk-et.

Ascribe, *v.a.* اسناد ا ìssnād-et.

Ash, Ashes, *s.* كول kyùl ; ash-tree, ديش بوداق اغاجى dìsh-bùdàk-àghàji.

Ashamed, *a.* محجوب màhjūb ; to be —, *v.n.* اوطانمق ùtànmak.

Ashore, *ad.* قرەيه kàraya, قرەده kàrada.

Asia, *s.* اسيا àssia.

Asiatic, *a.* اسيالو àssiali.

Aside, *ad.* بريانه bìr-yàna, برطرفه bìr-tàrafa ; بريانده bìr-yànda, برطرفده bìr-tàrafda ; ايرى àyri.

Ask, *v.a.* صورمق sòrmak, سؤال ا sù'āl-et ; استمك ìsstémek.

Askew, Aslant, *ad.* ارقورى àrkuri (àykiri), چارپق chàrpik.

Asleep, *a.* اويويور ùyuyor, اويومش ùyumush, اويقوده ùykuda.

Asparagus, *s.* قوش قونمز kùsh-kònmàz.

Aspect, *s.* منظره mànzara ; باقش bàkish ; هيئت hèy'èt ; نظارت nèzārèt.

Aspire, *v.n.* كوز ديكمك ghyùz-dìkmek, امل ا èmel-et.

Ass, *s.* اشك èshek, حمار hìmār, خر khàr.

Ass-colt, *s.* صيپه sìpa.

Assail, *v.a.* هجوم ا hùjūm-et.

Assailant, *s.* هجومجى hùjūmju, هجوم ايدن hùjūm-èden.

Assassin, *s.* قانلو kànli, قاتل kātil.

Assassinate, *v.a.* اولدرمك ùldurmek, قتل ا kàtl-et, تلف ا tèlef-et.

Assassination, *s.* قتل kàtl.

Assault, *s.* يورويش yùruyush, هجوم hùjūm ; اوزرينه يوريمك ùzériné-yùrumek, يورويش ا yùruyush-et, هجوم ا hùjūm-et.

Assay, *v.a.* محكه طوتمق màhèkké-tùtmak (mèhènké), عيارينه باقمق "àyàrina-bàkmak.

Assayer, *s.* عيارجى "àyyārji.

Assemble, *v.a.* طوپلامق tòplamak, جمع ا jèm"-et ; —, *v.n.* طوپلانمق tòplanmak, جمع او jèm"-ol, تجمع ا tèjèmmu"-et.

Assembly, *s.* جمعيت jèm"ìyyèt.

Assent, *s.* رضا rìzā, موافقت mùwāfakàt ; —, *v.n.* رضا ويرمك rìzā-vèrmek, موافقت ا mùwāfakàt-et.

Assert, *v.a.* ادعا ا ìddi"ā-et, ديمك dèmek.

Assertion, *s.* لاقردى làkirdi, سوز sùz, قول kàvl, ادعا ìddi"ā.

Assess, *v.a.* تعيين ويركو ايچون كشف ا tà"yīni-vèrgū-ìchin-kèshf-et.

Assets, *s. pl.* مال ايله اقچه māl-ila-àkcha.

Asseveration, *s.* يمين yèmīn.

Assiduity, *s.* اقدام īkdām.

Assiduous, *a.* مقدم mùkdim, چالشقان chàlishkàn.

Assign, *v.a.* تعيين ا tà"yīn-et, تخصيص ا tàkhsī-s-et ; حواله ا hàwālé-et.

Assignee, *s.* وكيل vèkīl.

Assist, *v.a.* ياردم ا yàrdim-et, معاونت ا mù"āvénèt-et, امداد ا ìmdād-et ; —, *v.n.* بولنمق bùlunmak, كلمك ghèlmek, حاضر او hāzir-ol.

Assistance, *s.* ياردم yàrdim, امداد ìmdād, اعانه ì"āné, معاونت mù"āvénèt.

Assistant, *s.* ياردمجى yàrdimji, معاون mù"āvin, يماق yàmak.

Associate, *s.* ارقه‌داش àrk*a*d*a*sh, رفیق rèfik, قرین kArīn ; —, *v.n.* قوکشمق kòn*g*ushm*a*k, کورشمك ghy*ù*rush-mek, ارقه‌داشلق ا àrk*a*-d*a*shl*i*k-et, اختلاط ا ìkhtilāt-et, الفت ا ùlfèt-et.

Association, *s.* شرکت shìrkèt, قومپانیا kòmpànya.

Assuage, *v.a.* تسکین ا tèsskīn-et.

Assume, *v.a.* المق Alm*a*k, قبول ا kAbūl-et ; اوزرته‌المق ùzérìné-Alm*a*k ; کیرمك ghìrmek.

Assurance, *s.* سوز sùz, تأمینات tè'mināt (pl.) ; یمین yèmīn ; اعتماد ì"timAd, ثبات sèbāt ; عارسزلق "àrs*i*zl*i*k ; سیغورته sìghūrt*a*.

Assure, *v.a.* تأمین ا tè'mīn-et ; یمین ا yèmīn-et ; امین ا èmīn-et.

Asterisk, *s.* اشارت (*) اشبو

Astern, *ad.* ارقه‌سنه àrk*a*ssin*a*, ارقه‌سنده àrk*a*ss*i*nd*a* ; اردینه àrd*i*n*a*, اردنده àrd*i*nd*a*.

Asthma, *s.* ضیق‌النفس zīku-'n-nèfess, ضیق‌الصدر zīku-'ss-sAdr.

Astonish, *v.a.* تعجب‌ایتدرمك tà-"àj-jub-ètdirmek.

Astonished, *a.* متعجب mùt*a*"àjjib ; to be —, *v.n.* تعجب ا tà"àjjub-et, شاشمق shàshm*a*k.

Astonishment, *s.* تعجب tà-"àjjub, حیرت hàyrèt.

Astound, *v.a.* حیرته صالمق hàyrèt*a*-sAlm*a*k.

Astray, *ad.*, to go astray, *v.n.* یاکلش یول طوتمق yànglish-yòl-tūtm*a*k (yānish).

Astringent, *a.* صیقیجی sìk*i*j*i*.

Astrologer, *s.* منجم mùnèjjim.

Astrology, *s.* علم‌نجوم "ìlmi-nùjūm.

Astronomer, *s.* اهل‌هیئت èhli-hèy'èt.

Astronomy, *s.* علم‌هیئت "ìlmi-hèy'èt.

Asunder, *ad.* ایکی‌پارچه ìki-pàrch*a* ; ایری àyri, منفصل mùnfAssil.

Asylum, *s.* صیغنه‌جق یر s*i*gh*i*n*a*j*a*k-yèr, ملجا mèljā.

At, *pr.* ئه è, *a* ; ده dé, d*a*.

Atheism, *s.* انکار بالله inky*ā*r-bì-llàh.

Atheist, *s.* منکر بالله mùnkir-bì-'llāh.

Athens, *s.* اتینا Atinà.

Athletic, *a.* قوی kàwī, قوتلو kòvvètli.

Atlantic, *s.* بحر محیط غربی bàhri-mūhīt-ghàrbī.

Atmosphere, *s.* کرهٔ هوا ky*ù*ré'i-hàwā ; هوا hàwā.

Atom, *s.* ذره zèrré.

Atone, *v.n.* کفارت ا kèfārèt-et.

Atonement, *s.* کفارت kèfārèt.

Atrocious, *a.* شنیع shènī", اشنع èshnà". [shènā"*à*t.

Atrociousness, Atrocity, *s.* شناعت

Attach, *v.a.* باغلامق bAghlamak, ربط ا rAbt-et, بند ا bènd-et ; — one's self, *v.n.* باغلانمق bAghlanmak, علاقه ا "àlāk*a*-et.

Attaché, *s.* (French) معیت مأموری mà"iyyèt-mémūri. [m*à*h*à*bbèt.

Attachment, s. علاقه "àlāk*a*, محبت

Attack, *s.* هجوم hùjūm ; نوبت nùbèt, ظهور zùhūr, اصابت ìssābèt ; —, *v.a.* هجوم ا hùjūm-et ; علیهنه چیقشمق "àlèyhin*a*-chìk*i*shm*a*k ; اصابت ا ìssā-bèt-et, ظهور ا zùhūr-et.

Attain, *v.a.* واصل او wāss*i*l-ol ; بالغ او

bāligh-òl ; نائل او nā'il-òl ; مظفر او mùzàffer-òl, موفق او mùwàffak-òl ; تحصيل ا tàhsīl-et, كسب ا kèssb-et.

Attainment, *s.* تحصيل tàhsīl.

Attar, *s.* (Arabic) عطر "ìtr ; — of roses, كل ياغى gyùl-yàghi, عطر ياغى "ìtr-yàghi.

Attempt, *s.* قالقشش kàlkishish ; —, *v.n.* قالقشمق kàlkishmak.

Attend, *v.a.* بكلمك bèklémek ; رفاقت ا rèfākàt-et ; باقمق bàkmak, خدمت ا khìdmèt-et (hìzmet).

Attendance, *s.* رفاقت rèfākàt ; خدمت khìdmèt (hìzmet) ; اتباع طاقمى ètbā"-takimi. [اتباع ètbā".

Attendant, *s.* رفيق rèfīk ; attendants,

Attention, *s.* دقت dìkkàt, تقيد tàkày-yud, اهتمام ìhtimām ; to pay —, دقت ا dìkkàt-et ; to call — to, دقت جلب ا dìkkàt-jèlb-et.

Attentive, *a.* مقيد mùkàyyèd ; to be —, *v.n.* دقت ا dìkkàt-et.

Attest, *v.a.* يمين ويرمك yèmīn-vèrmek ; —, *v.n.* يمين ا yèmīn-et, شهادت ا shàhādèt-et. [shàhādèt.

Attestation, *s.* يمين yèmīn ; شهادت

Attic, *s.* طوان اراسى tàwàn-àrassi.

Attire, *s.* البسه èlbìssé, زى zìy, قياق kìlik, كسوت kìssvèt ; —, *v.a.* كيندرمك ghìyindirmek.

Attitude, *s.* دورش dùrush, وضع wàz"i (pl. اوضاع èvzā") ; هيئت hèy'èt.

Attorney, *s.* وكيل vèkīl, دعوا وكيلى dà"-wà-vèkīli ; power of —, وكالتنامه vèkyālet-nāmé.

Attract, *v.a.* جذب ا jèzb-et, چكمك chèkmek. [-jāzibé.

Attraction, *s.* قوت جاذبه kùvvèti-

Attractive, *a.* جاذب jāzib.

Attribute, *s.* صفت sìfàt ; —, *v.a.* ويرمك vèrmek, عزوا "àzv-et, اسناد ا ìssnād-et.

Auburn, *a.* لپسقه lìpìsska.

Auction, *s.* مزاد mèzād (mèzàt), مزايده mùzāyédé. [dèllāl (tèllàl).

Auctioneer, *s.* مزادجى mèzādji, دلال

Audacious, *a.* جسور jèssūr ; عارسز "ārsiz.

Audacity, *s.* جسارت jèssārèt ; عارسزلق "ārsizlik.

Audible, *a.* ايشديلور ìshìdilir.

Audience, *s.* ملاقات mùlākàt (interview) ; جماعت jèmā"àt, سامعين sāmi"īn ; to hold an —, ديوان قورمق diwan-kùrmak.

Audit, *v.a.* حساب يوقلامق hìssāb-yòk-lamak, محاسبه ا mùhāssébé-et ; — office, *s.* محاسبه قلمى mùhāssébé-kàlemi.

Auditor, *s.* دكليان dìngléyen (dīnèyen), سامع sāmi" ; محاسبه جى mùhāssébéji.

Auger, *s.* بورغى bùrghu.

Aught, *s.* برشى bìr-shèy ; هيچ برشى hìch-bìr-shèy.

Augment, *v.n.* ارتمق àrtmak, ازدياد بولمق ìzdiyād-bùlmak, ترقى ا tèràk-ki-et ; —, *v.a.* ارترمق àrtirmak, تكثير ا tèksīr-et.

Augmentation, *s.* ازدياد ìzdiyād, تزايد tèzāyud, ترقى tèràkki.

Augur, *s.* كاهن kyāhin, فالجى fàlji.

Augury, *s.* فال fÂl.

August, *s.* اغستوس àghosstoss; —, *a.* عالی "ālī, سامی sāmī.

Aunt, *s.* (paternal) خاله hÂla; (maternal) تیزه tèyzÉ; (uncle's wife) ینکه yènghé. [sā"adÉ.

Auspices, *s. pl.* سایه sāyÉ, مساعده mùs-

Auspicious, *a.* مساعد mùssā"id.

Austere, *a.* سرت‌طبیعتلو sert-tÂbī"àtli; ریاضتلو rìyāzàtli.

Austerity, *s.* ریاضت rìyāzàt.

Australia, *s.* اوستراليا Àvstrālia.

Austria, *s.* اوستريا Àvstria. [bèr.

Authentic, *a.* صحیح sàhīh, معتبر mù"té-

Authenticity, *s.* صحت sìhhàt.

Author, *s.* باعث bā"iss, بادی bādī, صانع sÂni"; مؤلف mù'èllif, مصنف mùssānnif.

Authoritative, *a.* امرانه āmirānÉ.

Authority, *s.* حکم kùkm, امر èmr; حاکم hakim, آمر āmir, ضابط zābit; اذن ìzn, رخصت rùkhsÂt; مأذونیت mè'zūnìyyèt; سند sèned, برهان bùrhān.

Authorization, *s.* اذن ìzn, رخصت rukhsÂt; مأذونیت mè'zūnìyyèt.

Authorize, *v.a.* اذن ویرمك ìzn-vèrmek, ترخیص ا tèrkhīss-et.

Autumn, *s.* کوز ghyùz, صوك‌بهار sòng--bàhār, فصل‌خریف fÂssli-khàrīf.

Autumnal, *a.* خریفی khàrīfī.

Auxiliary, *s.* یاردمجی yàrdimji.

Avail, *v.n.* فائده‌ا fā'idÉ-et; — one's self of, *v.n.* قبول ا kÂbūl-et. [الده ÈldÉ.

Available, *a.* حاضر hÂzir, موجود mèvjūd,

Avalanche, *s.* (French) چیغ chìgh.

Avarice, *s.* خست khìsssèt, خسیسلك khÂssīsslik.

Avaricious, *a.* خسیس khÂssīss.

Avenge, *v.a.* انتقامنی‌المق ìntikÂmini-Âlmak; — one's self, *v.n.* انتقام‌المق ìntikām-Âlmak.

Average, *a.* وسط wÂssAt, اورته òrta; on an —, بربری‌اوستنه bìr-bìri-ùsstuna.

Averse, *a.* راضی‌دکل rāzi-dìghil.

Aversion, *s.* عدم‌رضا "àdÉmi-rìzā; نفرت nèfrèt.

Avoid, *v.a.* قاچنمق kÂchinmak. صاقنمق sàkinmak, چکنمك chèkinmek.

Avow, *v.a.* اقرارا ìkrār-et, اعترافا ì"ti-rÂf-et.

Awake, *a.* اویانق ùyànik; —, *v.a.* اویانمق ùyànmak; —, *v.a.* اویاندرمق ùyàndirmak.

Award, *s.* حکم hùkm, قرار kÂrār.

Aware (to be), *v.n.* خبری‌او khÂbÉri-òl; (to become), خبر‌المق khÂber-Âlmak.

Away, *ad.* اوزاغه ùzÂgha, اوزاقده ùzÂkda; to do — with, قالدرمق kàldirmak.

Awful, *a.* قورقنجلو kòrkunjlu.

Awhile, *ad.* بروقت bìr-wÂkìt, براز bìr-Âz.

Awkward, *a.* یاقشمز yàkishmaz, یاقشقسز [yàkishiksiz.

Awl, *s.* بیز bīz.

Awning, *s.* تنته tènta.

Awry, *a.* چارپق chàrpik.

Axe, *s.* بالطه bÂlta.

Axis, *s.* محور mìhver.

Axle, *s.* دنکل dìnghil.

Azure, *a.* اچق‌مائی àchik-mā'ī (màvi), کوك‌مائیسی ghyùk-mā'īssi (māvissi).

B.

Babbler, *s.* کوزه ghèvézé, بوش بوغاز bòsh-bòghàz.

Babe, *s.* چوجق chòjuk, ببك bèbek.

Baboon, *s.* میمون màymūn.

Baby, *s.* چوجق chòjuk, ببك bèbek.

Babylon, *s.* بابل شهری Bàbèl-shèhiri.

Bachelor, *s.* بیکار bīkyār (bèykyār).

Back, *s.* ارد àrd ; ارقه àrka ; صرت sìrt ; ظهر zàhr ; ترس tèrss ; کیرو ghèri ; ورا vèrā ; —, *ad.* کیرو ghèri, کیرویه ghèriya, کیروده ghèrida ; —, *v.a.* and *n.* (a boat in rowing) سیه ا sīyé-et.

Backgammon, *s.* طاوله اویونی tàwla-òyunu.

Backwards, *ad.* ترسنه tèrssina, ترس tèrss, کیرو کیرو ghèri-ghèri, قیچین قیچین kìchin-kìchin.

Bacon, *s.* طوکز پاصدرمه سی dònguz (dò-muz) pàssdirmàssi.

Bad, *a.* فنا fèna ; بوزق bòzuk ; قالپ kàlp ; کوتی kyùtu, ایش یوق ìsh-yòk.

Bag, *s.* توربه tòrba, کیسه kèyssé.

Baggage, *s.* اشیا èshyā, یوك yùk, پرتی [pìrti.

Bail, *s.* کفیل kèfil.

Bait, *s.* یم yèm ; —, *v.a.* یم ویرمك yèm-vèrmek ; یملمك yèmlémek.

Bake, *v.a.* فرونده پشرمك fìrinda-pìshir-mek ; —, *v.n.* فرونده پشمك fìrinda-pìshmek.

Bake-house, *s.* فرون fìrin,

Baker, *s.* اتمکجی ètmekji (èkmekji) ; فرونجی fìrinji. [kyāni.

Bakery, *s.* اتمکجی دکانی ètmekji-dùk-

Balance, *s.* ترازو tèrāzi ; فضله fàzla ; باقی قالان مبلغ bākī-kàlàn-mèblagh ; محاسبه دفتری mùhàssébé-dèfteri.

Balanced, *a.* دنك dènk.

Balcony, *s.* شاهنشین shāhnishīn.

Bald, *a.* باشی طاس bàshi-tàss ; كل kèl.

Bale, *s.* دنك dènk.

Ball, *s.* طوپ tòp ; یومق yùmak ; کله ghyùllé ; قورشون kùrshun ; بالو bàlo.

Ballad, *s.* ترکی tùrkyu.

Ballast, *s.* صفره sàfra.

Balloon, *s.* بالون, bàlon, چادر chàdir.

Ballot, *s.* قرعه kùr"à, پیانقو pìyànko.

Bamboo, *s.* قامش kàmish.

Band, *s.* باغ bàgh ; طاقم tàkim, بولك bùluk ; موزیقه mùzika.

Bandage, *s.* صارغی sàrghi.

Banish, *v.a.* سورمك sùrmek, سورکون ا sùrghyun-et, نفی ا nèfy-et ; دفع ا dèf"-et.

Banishment, *s.* سورکون sùrghyun, نفی nèfy.

Bank, *s.* صو کناری sù-kènàri ; سد sèdd ; بانقه bànka.

Banker, *s.* صراف sàrrāf (sàraf).

Bankrupt, *s.* مفلس mùfliss.

Bankruptcy, *s.* مفلسلك mùflisslik.

Banner, *s.* بیراق bāyrak, سنجاق sànjak, باندره bàndara.

Banquet, *s.* ضیافت ziyāfèt.

Baptize, *v.a.* وافتیز ا wàftiz-et.

Bar, *s.* قول kòl ; صیرق sìrik ; قومسال kùmsàl ; مانع mānì" ; —, *v.a.* منع ا mèn"-et, مانع او mānì-òl.

Barb, *s.* عرب اتی "àrab-àtì.

Barbarian, *s.* ترك tùrk, وحشى ادم vàhshi-ʌdʌm.
Barbarity, *s.* انسانيتسزلك ìnsānìyyèt-sizlik.
Barbarous, *a.* انسانيتسز ìnsānìyyètsiz; قبا kʌba, تربيهسز tèrbìyyéssiz.
Barber, *s.* بربر bèrbɛr.
Barberries, *s.* عنبربارس ‘‘ànbèrbāriss.
Bard, *s.* شاعر shā‘‘ir.
Bare, *a.* چپلاق chìplʌk; اچق àchik; قورو kùru; —, *v.a.* اچمق àchmak.
Barefoot, *ad.* يالين اياق yʌlin-āyak.
Barely, *ad.* كوچ بلا ghyùch-bèla.
Bargain, *s.* پازارلق pàzarlik; —, *v.n.* پازارلق ا pàzarlik-et.
Barge, *s.* ماغونه màghona; صندال sʌndʌl, فلوقه fìlika.
Bark, *s.* اغاج قبوغى ʌghʌj-kʌbughu; ناوى nàvi; —, *v.n.* حاولامق hàw-lamak; —, *v.a.* قبوغنى صويمق kʌ-bughunu-sòymak.
Barley, *s.* ارپه àrpa.
Barn, *s.* انبار ànbar.
Barometer, *s.* هوا ترازوسى hàwa-tèrāzissi.
Baron, *s.* بر لقب bìr-làkb.
Baronet, *s.* بر لقب bìr-làkb.
Barracks, *s.* قشلا kìshla, قشلاغ kìshlāgh.
Barrel, *s.* فوچى fìchi, واريل vàril; gun-barrel, تفنكك تيمورى tùfèghing--dèmiri; double-barrel gun, چفته تفنك chìfté-tùfék.
Barren, *a.* قسر kìssr; چول chùl, محصولسز màhsūlsiz; خيرسز khàyrsiz.
Barricade, *s.* برنوع مانع ديوار bir-nev’i-māni‘‘-dùwàr.
Barrier, *s.* قپو kʌpi.
Barrow, *s.* ال عربهسى ɛl-‘‘ʌrabassi.

Barter, *s.* ترانپه trànpa, ديكش dìghish; *v.a.* and *n.* ترانپه ا trànpa-et, ديكش ا dìghish-et.
Base, *s.* كرسى kyùrsi; قاعده kā‘‘idɛ; —, *a.* الچق ʌlchàk.
Base-line, *s.* ضلع معلوم dìl‘‘i-mà‘‘lūm.
Bashful, *a.* محجوب màhjūb, اوطانغاج ùtʌnghʌch.
Bashfulness, *s.* حجاب hìjāb.
Basin, *s.* كاسه kyāssɛ, چناق chànak; حوض hàwz.
Basis, *s.* اساس èssāss.
Basket, *s.* سپد sèped, كوفه kyùfɛ.
Bason, *s.* لكن lèghɛn.
Bassora, *s.* بصره bàssra.
Bastard, *s.* and *a.* پيچ pìch.
Bastinado, *s.* طياق dàyak.
Bastion, *s.* طابيه tʌbiya.
Bat, *s.* چومق chòmak; يراسه yèrassa.
Bath, *s.* حمام hʌmmām (hʌmʌm).
Bathe, *v.n.* صويه كيرمك sùya-ghìrmek; يقانمق yìkanmak; —, *v.a.* يقامق yìkamak.
Battalion, *s.* طابور tʌbur.
Batter, *v.a.* دوكمك dùghmek.
Battery, *s.* طابيه tʌbiya.
Battle, *s.* جنك jènk, غوغا (kàwgha), محاربه mùhārébɛ.
Bawl, *v.n.* حيقرمق hàykirmak, باغرمق bàghirmak.
Bay, *s.* (gulf) كورفز kyùrfez; (tree) دفنه dèfnɛ; (colour) دورو dòru.
Bayonet, *s.* سوبكى sùnghyu.
Be, *v.n.* اولمق òlmak; بولنمق bùlun-mak, موجود او mèvjūd-òl.
Beach, *s.* يالى كنارى yʌli-kènāri.
Beacon, *s.* نشان nìshʌn, علامت ‘‘àlāmèt.

Bead, *s.* تسبیح دانه‌سی tèssbīh-dānéssi; **beads**, *s. pl.* تسبیح tèssbīh.

Beak, *s.* بورون bùrun, غاغه ghàgha; امزك èmzik.

Beam, *s.* (of wood) كرش kìrish; (of light) شعاع shù"ā", پرتو pèrtèv.

Bean, *s.* (broad) باقله bàkla; (kidney) فصولیه fàssūlya.

Bear, *s.* آیو àyi; —, *v.a.* قالدرمق káldirmak; طیانمق dàyanmak, چكمك chèkmek, تحمل ا tàhàm-mul-et; (fruit, &c.) ویرمك vèr-mek; (children) طوغرمق dòghur-mak; to bear in mind, درخاطر ا dèr khātir-et.

Beard, *s.* صقال sàkal.

Bearer, *s.* حامل hāmil, دارنده dārendé.

Bearing, *s.* (direction) جهت jihèt, كرته kérté; (armorial) ارمه àrma.

Beast, *s.* حیوان hàywān.

Beastliness, *s.* مردارلق mùrdārlik.

Beastly, *a.* مردار mùrdār.

Beat, *v.a.* دوكمك dùghmek; (over-come) بوزمق bòzmak, الت ا àlt-et.

Beating, *s.* طیاق dàyak.

Beautiful, *a.* كوزل ghyùzel, دلبر dìlbèr.

Beauty, *s.* كوزللك ghyùzèllik; حسن hùssn.

Beaver, *s.* قوندوز kùnduz.

Becalmed, *a.* (to be) روزكارسز یاتمق rūzghyārsiz yàtmak.

Because, *c.* زیرا zīrā, چونكه chùnku, شوسببدنكه shū-sèbebdàn-ki.

Beckon, *v.n.* اشارت ا ìshāret-et.

Become, *v.n.* اولمق òlmak; (suit) یاقشمق yàkishmak.

Bed, *s.* یتاق yàtak, دوشك dùshek; (stratum) طبقه tàbaka; (of flowers) تخته tàkhta.

Bedridden, *a.* كوترم kyuturum.

Bedroom, *s.* یتاق اوطه‌سی yàtak òdassi.

Bedstead, *s.* كره‌وت kèrévet.

Bee, *s.* اری àri, بال اریسی bàl-àrissi.

Beech, *s.* كولكن ghyùlghèn.

Beef, *s.* صیغراتی sìghir-èti.

Beehive, *s.* اری قوانی àri-kòwàni.

Beer, *s.* اریه‌صویی àrpa-sùyu, بیره bìra.

Bees'-wax, *s.* بالمومی bàl-mumu.

Beet, Beetroot, *s.* پانجار pànjàr.

Beetle, *s.* (insect) بوجك bùjèk; (fullers', &c.) دیبك الی dībèk-èli.

Before, *pr.* (in front) اوكننه ùnguna, اوكنده ùngunda; (in time) دن اول dan-èvvel; —, *ad.* اول èvvel, مقدم mùkàddem, مقدما mùkàd-démā; ایلرو ìléri.

Beg, *v.a.* استمك ìsstémek, دیله‌مك dìlémek; —, *v.n.* دیلنمك dìlenmek.

Beget, *v.a.* حاصل ا hàssil-et, ایراث īrāss-et; (procreate) یاپمق yàp-mak, پیدا ا pèydā-et.

Beggar, *s.* دیلنجی dìlènji.

Begin, *v.a.* and *n.* باشلامق bàshlamak.

Beginning, *s.* باش bàsh; باشلانغج bàshlanghij; ابتدا ìbtidā, اول èvvel.

Behaviour, *s.* طور و حركت tàwr-u-hàrékèt, اطوار àtwàr, حركت hà-rékèt.

Behead, *v.a.* باشنی كسمك bàshini-kèssmek, بویوننی اورمق bòyununu-wùrmak.

Behind, *pv.* اردینه àrdina, ارده

àrdinda; ارقەسنە àrkassina, ارقەسندە àrkassinda; كيروسنە ghèrissina; كيروسندە ghèrissinda; —, *ad.* كيرو ghèri, كيرودە ghèrida, ورادە vĕrāda.

Behindhand, *ad.* كچ ghèch; to be —, *v.n.* كچ كلمق ghèch-kàlmak; يتشەمامك yètishémamek.

Behold, *v.a.* باقمق bàkmak, كورمك ghyürmek; —, *int.* اشتە ìshta, نا nā.

Being, *s.* (thing) شى shèy; كائن kyā'in, موجود mèvjūd, واراولان vàr-òlan; (existence) وارلق vàrlik, وجود vùjūd, موجوديت mèvjūdìyyèt, كون kèvn, كينونت kèynūnèt.

Being, the Supreme, الله Allāh.

Belabour, *v.a.* دوكمك dùghmek.

Belch, *v.n.* ككرمك ghéghirmek, كيرمك ghèyirmek; —, *s.* ككرمە ghèghirma, كيرمە ghèyirma.

Beleaguer, *v.a.* محاصرەا mùhàssera-et.

Belgian, *a.* بلجيقالو Bèljikali.

Belgium, *s.* بلجيقا Béljika.

Belief, *s.* اعتقاد ì''tikād; ايمان ìmān.

Believe, *v.a.* اينانمق ìnànmak, قولاق ويرمك kùlàk-vèrmek; اعتقادا ì''tikàd-et; ايمانا ìmān-et.

Believer, *s.* مؤمن mù'min, مسلم musslim.

Bell, *s.* (large) چاك chàng; (small) چنغراق chìngharàk; (of a time-piece) زل zil.

Bell-hanger, *s.* چنغراق اصان اهل صنعت chìngaràk-àsān-èhli-sàn''àt.

Belligerent, *a.* and *s.* محارب mùhārib.

Bell-man, *s.* دلال tèllāl.

Bell-metal, *s.* توج *or* طوج tùj (tùnch).

Bellows, *s.* كورك kyùruk.

Belly, *s.* قارن karn.

Belong, *v.n.* مخصوص او màkhsūss-òl; متعلق او mùta''àllik-òl; منسوب او mènsūb-òl.

Beloved, *a.* عزيز ''Azīz; سوكيلو sèvghili; (mas.) معشوق mà''shūk; (fem.) معشوقە mà''shūka.

Below, *pr.* التنە Altina, التندە Altinda; التيانە Alt-yànina, التياندە Alt-yànìnda; تحتنە tàhtina, تحتندە tàhtinda; زيرينە zīrina, زيرندە zīrinda; —, *ad.* التە Alta, التدە Altda; الت يانە Alt-yàna, التياندە Alt-yànda; زيردە zīrda; اشاغى Ashàghi, اشاغيدە Ashàghida.

Belt, *s.* (strap) قايش kàyish; (waist-band) كمر kèmer, قوشاق kùshàk.

Bench, *s.* صرە sìra, پيكە pèyké; (carpenter's, &c.) دستكاه dèsstghyāh (tèzghyàh).

Bend, *v.a.* اكمك èghmek; —, *v.n.* اكلمك èghilmek, چارپلمق chàrpil-mak; bend down, *v.a.* ياترمق yàtir-mak; — —, *v.n.* ياتمق yàtmak.

Beneath, *pr.* التنە Altina, التندە Altinda; مادوننندە mā-dùnunda; — one's notice, دكمز dèghmàz; — one, ياقشمز yàkishmàz. [vèlī-nì''mèt.

Benefactor, *s.* افندى èfèndi, ولى نعمت

Beneficence, *s.* احسان ìhsān.

Beneficent, *a.* كريم kèrīm.

Beneficial, *a.* يارار yàràr; to be —, *v.n.* يارامق yàramak.

Benefit, *s.* خير khàyr, ايولك īyilik, منفعت mènfa''àt; احسان ìhsān, نعمت nì''mèt; —, *v.a.* يرامق yàramak, فائده ا fā'idé-et; — by, *v.n.* فائده كورمك fā'idé-ghyùrmek.

Benevolence, *s.* خيرانديشلك khàyr-èndìshlik. [-èndìsh.

Benevolent, *a.* خيرانديش khàyr-

Benign, *a.* خيرلو khàyrli.

Benignity, *s.* شفقت shafakat.

Benumbed, *a.* اويوشمش ùyushmush, اويوشق ùyushuk; to be —, *v.n.* اويوشمق ùyushmak; (with cold) طوكمك dòngmak.

Bequeath, *v.a.* وصيت ا vwàssìyet-et.

Bequest, *s.* وصيت vwàssìyet.

Bereft, *a.* محروم màhrūm.

Berry, *s.* يمش yèmish, دانه dānè (tānè).

Berth, *s.* ير yér; (employ) خدمت khìdmèt (hìzmet).

Beseech, *v.a.* يالوارمق yàlvarmak, رجا ا rìjā-et, نياز ا nìyāz-et.

Beset, *v.a.* اطرافنى المق ètrāfini-àlmak, قوشاتمق kùshàtmak, هجوم ا hùjūm-et.

Beside, *pr.* يانته yànina, يانده yàninda, يانى باشنده yàni-bàshinda.

Besides, *pr.* دن بشقه dan-bàshka, دن ماعدا dan-mā''adā, دن فضله dan-fàzla; —, *ad.* اندن بشقه àndan-bàshka, بوندن بشقه bùndan-bàshka,

Besiege, *v.a.* محاصره ا mùhàssara-et. [&c.

Bespeak, *v.a.* اصمارلمق ìssmàrlamak, سپارش ا sìpàrish-et.

Bessarabia, *s.* بوجاق būjàk.

Best, *a.* الك ايو èng-īyi, الك اعلا èng-à''là.

Bestow, *v.a.* ويرمك vèrmek, انعام ا in''ām-et. [بحث ا bàhss-et.

Bet, *s.* بحث bàhss; —, *v.a.* and *n.*

Betray, *v.a.* خائنلق ا khā'inlik-et, خيانت ا khìyānèt-et. [kyāh-et.

Betroth, *v.a.* عقد ا ''àkd-et, نكاح ا nì-

Better, *a.* دها ايو dàhà-īyi, دها كوزل dàhà-ghyùzèl, دها اعلا dàhà-à''là.

Between, Betwixt, *pr.* اراسنه àrassina, اراسنده àrassinda; بيننه bèynina, بيننده bèyninda; مابيننه mābèynina, مابيننده màbèyninda; —, *ad.* ارايه àraya, اراده àrada; مابينده mābèynda.

Bevel, *s.* **Beveled,** *a.* شيو shèv.

Beware, *int.* صاقن sàkin; —, *v.n.* صاقنمق sàkinmak.

Bewilder, *v.a.* شاشرتمق shashirtmàk.

Beyond, *pr.* اوتهسنه ùtéssiné, اوتهسنده ùtéssindé; —, *ad.* اوته ùté, اوتهيه ùtéyé, اوتهده ùtédé; اشورى àshiri.

Bias, *s.* عدول ''ùdūl; ميل mèyl.

Bible, *s.* كتاب الله kìtābu-'llāh (God's book. [ويرمك vèrmek.

Bid, *v.a.* امر ا èmr-et; (at a sale)

Bier, *s.* تابوت tàbut.

Big, *a.* بيوك bìyuk, ابرى ìri, قوجهمان kòjamān; (— with child) كبه ghèbè.

Bight, *s.* كورفز kyùrfez, قوى kòy.

Bigot, *s.* **Bigoted,** *a.* متعصب mùta-

Bigotry, *s.* تعصب tà''àssub. [''àssib.

Bile, *s.* صفرا sàfrā (sàfra).

Bilge, *s.* سنتينه sèntina; bilge-water, سنتينه صويى sèntina-sùyu.

Bilious, *a.* صفراوى sAfrāvī; صفراسى قبارمش sAfrassi-kAbarmish.

Bill, *s.* (account) دفتر dèftɛr, پوصله pùssla; (for advertising) يافته yAfta; (bird's —) غاغه ghàgha; (for cutting) ساطور sAtir; — of exchange, تحويل tAhvīl; (cheque) حواله hàwālé; — of parcels, پوصله pùssla; exchequer —, خزينه‌تحويلى khàzīné-tàhvīli.

Bill-broker, *s.* تحويل سمسارى tAhvīl-sìmsāri.

Billet, *s.* (note) پوصله pùssla, تذكره tèzkéré; كوتك *or* كوتك kyùtuk; (soldier's —) قوناق kònak; —, *v.a.* قوناق ا kònak-et.

Billet-doux, *s.* (French) عشقنامه "Ashk-nāma.

Bin, *s.* انبار ànbar.

Bind, *v.a.* باغلامق bàghlamak; (— books) جلدلمك jìldlémek; قابلامق kAblamak.

Binding (of a book), *s.* جلد jìld, قاب kAb.

Birch-tree, *s.* قاين‌اغاجى kàyn-Aghaji.

Bird, *s.* قوش kùsh.

Birdlime, *s.* اوكسه ùksé.

Birth, *s.* طوغش dòghush, ولادت vè-lādèt.

Birthday, *s.* ولادت كونى vèlādèt-ghyùnu.

Biscuit, *s.* پكسمات pèksémèt, كورك ghèvrèk, قاليته kàlyèta.

Bisect, *v.a.* تنصيف ا tànsīf-et.

Bissextile, *s.* كبيسه kèbīssa.

Bit, *s.* (piece) پارچه pàrcha; (— of a bridle) كم ghèm, قنطارمه kAntàrma.

Bitch, *s.* قانجق kAnjik.

Bite, *v.a.* اصرمق ìssirmak.

Bitter, *a.* اجى Aji.

Blab, *s.* بوش‌بوغاز bòsh-bòghAz; —, *v.n.* بوش‌بوغازلق ا bòsh-bòghAzlik-et.

Black, *a.* قره kAra, سياه sìyah; —, *s.* (negro) عرب "àrab.

Blackamoor, *s.* عرب "àrab.

Blackberry, *s.* بوكرتلن bùghurtlɛn.

Blackbird, *s.* قره‌طاوق kàra-tàwuk.

Blackboard, *s.* درس تخته‌سى dèrss-tàhtassi.

Blackguard, *s.* چاپقين chApkin, كولخنى kyùlkhāni.

Blackguardism, *s.* چاپقينلق chApkinlik.

Blacking, *s.* قوندره‌بوياسى kùndura-bòyassi.

Blacksmith, *s.* تيمورجى *or* دميرجى dèmirji.

Bladder, *s.* سديك‌قاوغى sìdik-kàwu-ghu; (gall —) عود "ūd.

Blade, *s.* (sword —) نامـلو nAmli; (knife —) اغز Aghz; (shoulder —) كورك kyùrèk; (grass —) يپراق yàprAk.

Blame, *s.* (fault) قباحت kAbāhat; (censure) ازار Azàr; —, *v.a.* قباحت بولمق kAbāhat-bùlmak, ازارلمق Azàr-lamak, تعييب ا tà"yīb-et.

Blank, *a*, بوش bòsh; (without ball) قورشونسز kùrshunsuz; point-blank, تام‌منزل tAmm-menzil; to fire with blank cartridge, قورو صيقى‌يه اتمق kùru-sìkiya-Atmak; —, *s.* (space) بوش‌ير bòsh-yɛr.

Blanket, *s*, فانله‌يورغان fānèla-yùrghAn.

Blaspheme, *v.a.* سب ا sèbb-èt.

Blasphemy, *s.* كفر kyùfr.

Blaze, *s.* علو "àlev; — *v.n.* علولنمك "àlevlɛnmek.

Bleach, *v.n.* اغارمق Agharmak, بياضلنمق

bèyAzlanmak; — *v.a.* أغارتمق Aghart-mak.

Bleacher, *s.* چرپيجى chìrpiji.

Bleed, *v.n.* قانامق kAnamak; —, *v.a.* قان‌المق kAn-Almak. [لكه lèkè.

Blemish, *s.* سقط sàkAt, عيب "àyb,

Bless, *v.a.* (man to man) خيردعا khàyri-dù"ā-et; (man to God) شكرا shùkr-et; (God to man) خيرنصيب ايملك khàyr-nAssīb-èylémek.

Blessing, *s.* (prayer) خير دعا khàyri-dù"ā; (fruits of God's goodness) بركت bèrékèt.

Blind, *a.* كور kyùr, اعمى à"mà; —, *v.a.* كورا kyùr-et.

Blister, *s.* (of the skin) قبارجق kAbarjik; (vesicatory) ياقى yàki; —, *v.n.* قبارمق kAbarmak, ; — *v.a.* قبارتمق kAbart-mak.

Block, *s.* (block of stone) طاش tAsh; (of wood) كتوك kyùtuk; (mould) قالب (kAlip); — *v.n.* قپامق kApamak, طيقامق tìkamak.

Blockade, *s.* ابلوقه àbloka, محاصره mù-hāssara; —, *v.a.* ابلوقها àbloka-et.

Blockhead, *s.* اشك èshek.

Blood, *s.* قان kAn.

Blood-horse, *s.* جنس‌ات jìnss-àt.

Bloodshed, *s.* سفك دما sèfki-dèma.

Blood-vessel, *s.* طمر dAmar.

Bloody, *a.* قانلو kAnli.

Bloom, Blossom *s.* چيچك chìchek; —, *v.n.* چيچك‌اچمق chìchek-àchmak.

Blot, *v.a.* مركب طملاتمق mùrèkkèb-dAmlatmak; —up, قوروتمق kùrut-mak; — out, چيزمك chìzmek, بوزمق bòzmak, ترقين‌ا tèrkīn-et.

Blow, *s.* اورش (wūrush), چالش chAlish; — of the fist, مشته mùshta; (mis-fortune) فلاكت fèlākèt; (injury) ضرر zàrar; تكمه tèkmé.

Blow, *v.n.* (wind) اسمك èssmek; (mouth or bellows) اوفلمق ùflémek; (flower) اچمق àchmak; — one's nose, بورنني سلمك bùrnunu-sìlmek; سومكورمك sùmkyurmek.

Blow up, *v.n.* پاتلامق pAtlamak.

Bludgeon, *s.* صوپه sòpa.

Blue, *a.* (light) مائى mā'ī (māvi), كوك ghyùk, كوك مائيسى ghyùk-mā'īssi (māvissi); (deep) لاجورد lājivèrd.

Blunder, s. ياكلش yàngilish (yānish), سهو sèhv, خطا khātā; make a —, ياكلمق yàngilmak (yàngilmak).

Blunderbuss, *s.* قره‌بينه kārabīna.

Blunt, *a.* كور kyùr, كسمز kèssmàz; (plain spoken) لاقرديسنى صاقنمز làkirdissini-sàkinmàz.

Blush, *v.n.* قزارمق kìzarmak.

Boar, *s.* اركك طوكز èrkek-dònguz (dò-muz), ازولى طوكز Azili-dòmuz.

Board, *s.* تخته tàkhta; (food) يمك yèmèk, ييه جك yèyéjek; on board, *ad.* and *pr.* كمى يه ghèmiyé, كميده ghè-midé.

Boast, *v.n.* اوكنمك ùghènmek.

Boat, *s.* قايق kàyik; فلوقه fìlika, صندال sAndAl.

Boat-hook, *s.* قانجه kAnja.

Boatswain, *s.* پورصون pòrsun.

Body, *s.* (man's living —) وجود vùjūd, بدن bèden, كوده ghyùwdé; (dead or alive) جسد jèssed; (substance) جسم jìssm; (troop) طاقم tàkìm, سوری sùru, کومه kyùmé.

Bog, *s.* بتاق bàtak, بتاقلق bàtaklik.

Bohemia, *s.* چه ché.

Bohemian, *s.* and *a.* چه‌لو chéli.

Boil, *s.* چبان chìbàn; —, *v.n.* قاینامق kàynamak; صوده پسمك sùda-pìshmek; —, *v.a.* قایناتمق kàynat-mak; حاشلامق hàshlamak, صوده پشورمك sùda-pìshirmek.

Boiled meat, *s.* صویش sùyush.

Boiler, *s.* قزغان kàzghàn (kàzan).

Boiler-maker, *s.* قزغانجی kazganji.

Boisterous, *a.* شماته‌لو shàmatali, فرطونه‌لو fìrtìnali. [shàmata.

Boisterousness, *s.* سرتلك sèrtlik, شماته

Bold, *a.* جسور jèssūr, جسارتلو jèssārètli, یکیت yīghit.

Boldness, *s.* جسارت jèssārèt.

Bolster, *s.* یاصدق yàssdìk.

Bolt, *s.* سورکی sùrghu, سورمه sùrmé; (large nail) انکسر ènkser, جواته jìwàta, پرنو pèrno.

Bomb, *s.* خمبر khùmbara (kùmbara).

Bombard, *v.a.* اوزرینه طوپ اتمق ùzériné-tòp-àtmak.

Bombardier, *s.* خمبره‌جی (kùmbaraji).

Bombardment, *s.* طوپ و خمبره ایله اورمقلق tòp-vé-khùmbara-ìla-wùr-maklik. [gèchmaz.

Bomb-proof, *a.* خمبره کچمز khùmbara-

Bomb-shell, *s.* خمبره khùmbara.

Bond, *s.* تحویل tàhvīl, تمسك tèmèssuk; ایپ ìp, صارغی sàrghi, زنجیر zìnjir.

Bone, *s.* کموك kèmik.

Bone-setter, *s.* جراح jèrrèh, چیققجی chìkìkji, قیرقجی kìrìkji.

Book, *s.* کتاب kìtàb.

Bookbinder, *s.* مجلد mùjèllid.

Bookseller, *s.* کتابجی kìtābji; (of Corans) صحاف sàhhāf.

Boom, *s.* سرن sèren.

Boot, *s.* چزمه chìzma; —, *v.a.*; what boots it? نه فائده‌سی وار nà-faidassi-[vàr.

Bootmaker, *s.* پاپوچجی pàpuchji.

Booty, *s.* یغما yàghma, غنیمت ghànī-mèt.

Border, *s.* کنار kènàr; (frontier) سرحد sèr-hàdd, سنورباشی sìnirbàshi.

Bore, *s.* (of a gun) چاپ chàp, دلیك dèlik, اغز àghz; (troublesome fellow) ثقیل حریف sàkīl-hèrif; —, *v. a.* دلمك dèlmèk; (trouble) صقندی ویرمك sìkìndi-vèrmek.

Born, *a.* طوغمش dòghmush; to be —, *v.n.* طوغمق dòghmak.

Borrow, *v.a.* اودنج المق ùdunj-àlmak, استقراض ا isstikrāz-et.

Borrower, *s.* اودنج الان ùdunj-àlàn.

Bosnia, *s.* بوسنه Bòssna.

Bosnian, *a.* and *s.* بوسنه‌لو Bòssnali.

Bosom, *s.* کوکس ghyukss, قوین kòyn, سینه sīné. [kàléssi.

Bosphorus, *s.* چناق قلعه‌سی chànak-

Botany, *s.* علم نباتات 'ìlmi-nèbātāt.

Botch, *v.a.* بوزمق bòzmak.

Both, *pr.* ایکیسی ìkissi; —, *c.* هم ... وهم ... hèm ... vè-hèm.

Bother, *s.* صیقندی sìkìndi; —, *v.a.*

صیقندی ویرمك sìkindi-vèrmek, تعجیزا tà''jīz-et. [pùtkal.

Bottle, *s.* شیشه shìshé; wine —, پوتقال

Bottom, *s.* دیب dìb; (fundy) گوت [ghyùt.

Bough, *s.* دال dàl.

Bounce, *v.n.* صیچرامق sìchramak.

Bound, *s.* حد hàdd, پایان pàyān, صوك sòng, اوج ùj, بوجاق bùjak.

Boundary, *s.* حدود hùdūd, سنور sìnir.

Bounteous, Bountiful, *a.* بول bòl, برکتلو bèrékètli; جومرد jùmèrd, الی اچیق èli-àchik, سخی sàkhī, سخاوتلو sàkhā-vètli.

Bounty, *s.* احسان ìhsān, انعام ìn''ām; سخا sàkhā, سخاوت sàkhāvèt.

Bouquet, *s.* (French) چیچك دستی chìchek-dèméti.

Bow, *s.* (in reverence) باش اکمه bàsh-éghmé, باش کسمه bàsh-késsmé; (weapon) یای yày; (of a ship) باش bàsh; —, *v.n.* باش اکمك bàsh-éghmek; باش کسمك bàsh-kèss-mek; — down and worship, سجده‌ا séjdé-et.

Bowels, *s. pl.* بغرصق bàghirsak.

Bower, *s.* مهتابیه mèhtābìyyé.

Bowie-knife, *s.* بچاق bìchàk.

Bowl, *s.* کاسه kyāssé, طاس tàss, چناق chànak; (wooden) قواته kàwata; (of a pipe) لوله lùlé.

Bowline, *s.* بولینه bòlina, بورینه bòrina.

Bowsprit, *s.* جوادره jìwàdira.

Bowstring, *s.* کرش kìrish, زه zìh.

Box, *s.* (chest) صندق sànkik; (desk) چکمجه chékméjé; (small) قوتی kùtu; (on the ear) شمار shàmar, سیلی sīlì (sìlé); (wood) چمشیر chìmshir; (of instruments) استج ùsstuj (ùsstunj). [ghàssi.

Boxing, *s.* مشته غوغاسی mùshta-kàw-

Boy, *s.* اوغلان òghlàn, چوجق chòjuk.

Boyhood, *s.* چوجقلق chòjuklùk.

Boyish, *a.* چوجق کبی chòjuk-ghìbi.

Brace, *s.* (pair) چفت chìft; (tie) باغ bàgh, قوشاق kùshàk; (of a yard) براصه bràssa; braces (for trousers) اصقی àsski.

Bracelet, *s.* بلازك bìlézik.

Braid, *s.* شرید shèrid; خرج khàrj; —, *v.a.* اورمك ùrmek.

Brain, *s.* بین béyn, دماغ dìmàgh.

Bramble, *s.* چالی chàli.

Bran, *s.* كپك kèpek.

Branch, *s.* دال dàl; (of a road, &c.) قول kòl; (of a family, science, &c.) شعبه shù''bé, فرع fèr''.

Brandy, *s.* راقی ràki.

Brasier, *s.* باقرجی bàkirji; منقال màn-ghal.

Brass, *s.* پرنج pìrinj.

Brassfounder, *s.* دوکیجی dùkuju.

Brave, *a.* یکیت yìghit, جسور jèssūr.

Bravo, *int.* افرین āférīn (àférim).

Bray, *v.n.* اکرمق àngirmak. [maz.

Brazen, پرنجدن pìrinjden; اوتانمز ùtān-

Brazier, *s.* باقرجی bàkirji, قزغانجی (kàzanji).

Brazilwood, *s.* بقام bàkkàm.

Bread, *s.* اتمك (èkmek), نان عزیز nāni-''àzīz. [''àrz.

Breadth, *s.* ان en, انلولك ènlīlik, عرض

Break, *v.a.* قیرمق kìrmak; — off,

قوپارمق kòparmak; — a promise, خلف ا khùlf-et; — a treaty, نقض ا nAkz-et; —, *v.n.* قیرلمق kìrìlmak, قوپمق kòpmak, كسلمك kèssilmek.

Breakfast, *s.* قهوالتی kàhwAltì.

Breast, *s.* كوكش ghyùkss, سینه sīnÉ; (teat) ممه mèmÉ.

Breastwork, *s.* سپر sìpEr.

Breath, *s.* صولوق sòluk, نفس nèfess.

Breathe, *v.n.* صولومق sòlumak, نفس المق nèfess-Almak, تنفس ا tènèffuss-et.

Breathing, *s.* صولومقلق sòlumakluk.

Breeches, *s.* شلوار shAlwàr, پوطور pòtur.

Breed, *s.* صوی sòy, جنس jìnss; —, *v.a.* یاوری ویرملك yàvri-vÈrmek; توره‌ملك tùrÉmek; —, *v.a.* تورتملك tùrEtmek, حاصل ا hāssīl-et, یتشدرملك yètishdirmek; well-bred, *a.* تربیه‌لو tÈr-bìyyàli; good breeding, *s.* تربیه tÈrbiyyà.

Breeze, *s.* روزكار rùzghyār; (light —) خفیف روزكار khAfīf-rùzghyār; (fresh —) صیقی روزكار sìki-rùzghyār.

Brethren, *s. pl.* اخوان ìkhwAn.

Brevet, *s.* برات bèrāt.

Brevity, *s.* قصه‌لق kìssalik.

Brew, *v.a.* اربه‌صویی یاپمقلق àrpa-sūyū-yApmaklik.

Brewer, *s.* بیراجی bìrāji.

Brewery, *s.* اربه‌صویی فابریقاسی àrpa-sūyū-fàbrikassi.

Bribe, *s.* رشوت rìshvèt; —, *v.a.* رشوت ویرملك rìshvèt-vÈrmek.

Brick, *s.* طوغله tùghla.

Bricklayer, *s.* یاپیجی yàpìji, دیوارجی dìwàrji.

Bride, *s.* كلین ghèlin, عروس "àrūss.

Bridegroom, *s.* كویكی ghyùwèghi.

Bridge, *s.* كوپری kyùpru.

Bridle, *s.* باشلق bAshlik; —, *v.a.* كم اورمق ghèm-wùrmak.

Brig, Brigantine, ابریق ìbrìk.

Brigade, *s.* لوا lìwā.

Brigadier, *s.* میرلوا mīri-lìwā.

Brigand, *s.* خرسز khìrsiz, ایزباندوت ìzbàndut.

Bright, *a.* (light) اچیق àchik; (shining) پارلاق pàrlàk; (polished) جلالو jìlāli.

Brighten, *v.n.* اچلمق àchilmak.

Brilliant, *a.* پارلاق pàrlàk; —, *s.* پرلانطه pìrlànta.

Brim, *s.* كنار kÈnar; اغز Aghz.

Brimstone, *s.* كبریت kìbrit, كوكورد kyùkyurd.

Brine, *s.* صالموره sAlamùra.

Bring, *v.a.* كتورملك ghètirmek.

Brink, *s.* كنار kènar.

Bristle, *s.* قیل kìl, طوكز قیلی (dòmuz)-kìli.

Brittle, *a.* پك كورك pèk-ghèvrèk, پك قولای قیریلور pèk-kòlay-kìrìlir.

Broad, *a.* انلو ènli, كنش ghènish, عریض "àrīz.

Broadside, *s.* (ship's) بورده bòrda; (of guns fired) الاباندا àlabànda.

Broil, *v.a.* قزارتمق kìzàrtmak, اسقره ا ìsskàra-et.

Broken, *a.* قیرق kìrìk.

Broker, *s.* دلال dèllāl (tèllAl), سمسار sìmsār.

Brook, *s.* چای chày, صو sū, دره dÈrÉ; —, *v.a.* چكملك chèkmek, قبول ا kAbūl-et.

Broom, *s.* سپورگه sùpurghÉ.

Broth, *s.* ات صویی èt-sūyu, چوربا chòrba.

Brother, *s.* قرنداش kàrndàsh (kàrdash), برادر bìrādER.
Brotherhood, *s.* قرنداشلق kàrndàshlik.
Brother-in-law, *s.* (wife's brother) قاين kàyn; (sister's husband) انشته ènishtÉ; (wife's sister's husband) باجناق bÀjanak, باجناخ bÀjanakh.
Brown, *a.* اسمر èssmER, قهوه رنكى kāhwÉ-rènghi; — sugar, خام شكر khÀm-shèkER.
Bruise, *s.* بره bèrÉ, چوروك chùruk; —, *v.a.* دوكمك dùghmek; چوروتمك chùrutmek, بره لتمك bèrÉlEtmek.
Bruised, *a.* بره لنمش bèrÉlEnmish, بره لى bèrÉli; چوروك chùruk; to become —, *v.n.* بره لنمك bèrÉlEnmek.
Brush, *s.* فرچه fìrcha; (fine — for painting) قلم kàlEm; —, *v.a.* سپورمك sùpurmek.
Brutal, *a.* انسانيتسز insānìyyètsiz.
Brutality, *s.* انسانيتسزلك insānìyyètsizlik.
Brute, *s.* حيوان hàywĀn.
Bubble, *s.* كپوك kyùpuk, كپوك دانه سى kyùpuk-tānÉssi, حباب hàbĀb.
Bucket, *s.* قوغه kògha.
Buckle, *s.* طوقه tòka.
Bud, *s.* طمروق tòmruk; —, *v.n.* طمرقلنمق tòmruklanmak.
Buffalo, *s.* ماندە mÀnda, صو صيغرى sū-sìghiri, جاموس jàmūss (jÀmish).
Buffoon, *s.* دالقاوق dÀlkàwuk, مسخره mÀsskhara (mÀsskara).
Bug, *s.* تخته بتى tàkhta-bìti, تخته كهله سى tàkhta-kèhlÉssi, تخته قوروسى tàkhta-kùrussu.
Bugle, *s.* بورى bòru.

Build, *v.a.* ياپمق yàpmak, ياپدرمق yàpdirmak, بنا ا bìnā-et, انشا ا ìnshā-et.
Builder, *s.* (founder) بانى bānī; (working —) قالفه kÀlfa.
Building, *s.* ياپى yàpi, بنا bìnā.
Bulb, *s.* صوغان sòghAn. [جرم jùrm.
Bulk, *s.* بيوكلك biyukluk, حجم hÀjm,
Bulkhead, *s.* بولمه bùlmÉ.
Bull, *s.* بوغا bòghĀ.
Bullet, *s.* قورشون kùrshun, دانه dānÉ.
Bullock, *s.* اوكوز ùkyuz.
Bump, *s.* شيش shìsh, يومرى yùmru; — against, *v.n.* چاتمق chàtmak.
Bunch, *s.* صالقم sÀlkim; دمت dèmet.
Bundle, *s.* بوغچه bòghcha; طوپ tòp.
Bung, *s.* منطار mÀntàr.
Buoy, *s.* شماندره shàmÀndara; — up, *v.a.* قالدرمق kÀldirmak, طوتمق tùtmak. [صقندى sìkindi.
Burden, *s.* يوك yùk, حموله hàmūlÉ;
Burglar, *s.* خرسز khìrsiz.
Burglary, *s.* خرسزلك khìrsizlik.
Burial, *s.* جنازه الايى jènāzÉ-Àlayi; تدفين tèdfīn.
Burn, *v.n.* يانمق yànmak; *v.a.* ياقمق yàkmak.
Burning-glass, *s.* پرتوسوز pèrtèvsūz (pèrtevsìz).
Burnish, *v.a.* اچمق àchmak, مصقله ا mÀsskAla-et, جلا ويرمك jìlā-vèrmek.
Burnisher, *s.* (tool) مصقله mÀsskAla.
Burst, *v.n.* پاتلامق pÀtlamak; —, *v.a.* پاتلاتمق pÀtlatmak.
Bury, *v.a.* كومك ghyùmmek, دفن ا dèfn-et.
Burying-ground, *s.* مزارلق mèzarlik.
Bush, *s.* اغاج Àghaj, چالى chÀli.

Bushel, *s.* كيله kilé.

Business, *s.* ايش ìsh, ايش كوچ ìsh-ghyùch; مصلحت màsslāhat; مشغوليت mèshghūlìyyèt.

Bustard, *s.* (greater) طوى tòy; (smaller) مزملدك mèzmèldèk.

Bustle, *s.* تلاش tèlàsh, عجله "àjélé.

Busy, *a.* مشغول mèshghūl.

But, *c.* لكن làkin, اما àmmà, ولكن vè-làkin, فقط fàkat; —, *pr.* دن بشقه dan-bàshka, دن فضله dan-fàzla, دن ماعدا dan-mā"àdā; all but, همان همان (hèmen-hèmen), ازقالدى àz-kàldi.

Butcher, *s.* قصاب kàsssàb (kàssàp).

Butchery, *s.* قصابلق kàssàblik; سفك دما sèfki-dìmā.

Butt, *s.* نشان nìshān, هدف hèdef; —, *v.a.* and *n.* توس اورمق tòss-wùrmak.

Butt-end, *s.* دیبجك dìbjik; صاپ sàp.

Butter, *s.* ياغ yàgh; (fresh) تره ياغ tèré-yàgh, تره ياغى tèré-yàghi; (clarified) صاى ياغى (sày-yàghi), روغن ساده rūghàni-sādé.

Butterfly, *s.* كله بك kèlébèk.

Buttock, *s.* بوط bùt; قايناق kàynak, قايناق يرى kàynak-yèri.

Button, *s.* دوكمه dùghmé (dùymé); —, *v.a.* دوكمه لمك dùymélémek, ايلكلمك iliklémek; —*v.n.* دوكمه لنمك dùymélenmek, ايلكلنمك iliklenmek.

Buttress, *s.* پاينده pàyèndé, اياق àyak.

Buy, *v.a.* المق àlmak, صاتون المق sà-tin-àlmak, اشترا ìshtirā-et, مبايعه mùbāya"à-et.

Buyer, *s.* الان àlan, اليجى àlìji, مشترى mùshtèrī.

Buzz, *v.n.* وزلامق wìzzlamak, جزلامق [jìzzlamak.

By, *pr.* دن dan; ايله ìlé; يانده yànina, يانده yànìnda, ياندن yànìndan; — bye, good-bye, *int.* اللهه اصمارلدق àllàha-ìssmàrladik; اوغورلر اوله òghur-lar-òla.

Bye-and-bye, *ad.* برازدن bìr-àzdan, برازدن صكره bìr-àzdan-sòngra, براز وقتلردن صكره bìr-àz-wàkitlardan-sòngra.

Bye-law, *s.* نظام nìzàm.

Bye-word, *s.* ضرب مثل zàrbi-mèssèl.

Bygone, *a.* كچمش gèchmish.

C.

Cab, *s.* عربه àraba.

Cabbage, *s.* لحنه làhana; —, *v.a.* چالمق chàlmak. [قامره kàmara.

Cabin, *s.* (hut) قلبه kùlubé; (ship's)

Cabin-boy, *s.* ميچو mìcho.

Cabinet, *s.* (private room), اوطه òda, خلوت khàlvèt; (chest) چكمجه chèkméjé, صندق sàndik; (cupboard) طولاب dòlap; (— of ministers) وكلا طاقمى wùkélā-tàkimi; — council, مجلس خاص mèjlissi-khàsss.

Cabinet-maker, *s.* طاوشان tàwshàn.

Cable, *s.* غومنه ghòmana; chain —, زنجير zìnjir.

Cadet, *s.* شاكرد shāghird.

Cage, *s.* قفس kàfess.

Cake, *s.* (pastry) قورابيه kùrābiyyé; (moulded form) قالپ kàlip.

Calamity, *s.* قضا kāzā, بلا bèlā.

Calcine, *v.a.* یاقمق yàkmak; —ed, *a.* یانمش yànmish.

Calculate, *v.a.* حساب ا hìssāb-et.

Calculus, *s.* طاش tāsh; حساب hìssāb.

Caldron, *s.* قزغان kàzghān (kāzan).

Calender, *s.* تقویم tākwīm, روزنامه rūz-nāmé. [بالدر bāldir.

Calf, *s.* دانه dāna; — of the leg,

Calibre, *s.* چاپ chāp.

Calico, *s.* قالنقوت kàlinkòt, بز bèz.

Caligraphist, *s.* خطاط khāttat.

Caligraphy, *s.* خطاطلق khāttātlik; حسن خط hùssnu-khātt.

Caliph, *s.* خلیفه khālīfé.

Caliphate, *s.* خلافت khìlāfèt.

Call, *s.* چاغرش chàghirish, چاغرمه chàghirma, دعوت dà''vét; —, *v.n.* اوغرامق òghramak; —, *v.a.* and *n.* چاغرمق chaghirmak; — at, اوغرامق òghramak; on *or* upon, (invite) دعوت ا dà''vèt-et; (visit) اوغرامق òghramak.; — for, استمك isstémek; — in, (visit) اوغرامق òghramak; (collect again) کیرو المق ghèri-āl-mak; کیرو چاغرمق ghèri-chàghirmak; طوپلامق tòplamak; — out, *v.n.* باغرمق bàghirmak; —, *v.a.* دوکشمکه دعوت ا dùghushméghé-dà''vèt-et; — over, یوقلامق yòklamak; اوقومق òkumak; —together, طوپلامق tòplamak; — up, دعوت ا dà''vèt-et; وجوده کتورمك vùjūda-ghètirmek.

Calling, *s.* صنعت sàn''àt, حرفت hìr-fèt, مشغولیت mèshghūlìyyèt.

Callipers, *s.* چاپ پرکاری chāp-pèr-ghyāri (pèrghèli).

Callous, *a.* دویمز dùymaz.

Calm, *s.* and *a.* (wind or water) لیمانلق līmānlik; —, *a.* (morally) اسوده āssūdé, راحت rāhat; —, *s.* راحت rāhat, اسایش āssāyish.

Calmly, *ad.* یواش yawāsh. [yish.

Calmness, *s.* راحت rāhat, اسایش āssā-

Calomel, *s.* طاتلو سولمن tātli-sùlumèn.

Calumniate, *v.a.* افترا ا īftirā-et.

Calumny, *s.* افترا īftirā, بهتان bùhtān.

Cambric, *s.* دلبند dùlbènd (tùlbènt); [باتسته bàtìsta.

Camel, *s.* دوه dèvé.

Camelopard, *s.* زرافه zùrāfé (zùrāfā).

Camlet, *s.* شالی shāli, صوف sòf.

Camomile, *s.* پاپادیه pāpādiyé.

Camp, *s.* اردو òrdu; —, *v.n.* اردو قورمق [òrdu-kùrmak.

Campaign, *s.* سفر sèfer.

Camphor, *s.* کافور kyāfūr.

Can, *s.* تنکه tènéké; مشربه (māshraba).

Canal, *s.* بوغاز bòghāz (strait), خندق (hèndek) (ditch); قازمه نهر kāzma--nèhir.

Canary-bird, *s.* قناریه kànàriya.

Cancel, *v.a.* بوزمق bòzmak, ترقین ا tèrkīn-et, بطال ا bāttāl-et.

Cancer, *s.* (sore) ییان علتی yèyen-''ìlleti, اکله ākilé. [sùwèyler.

Candid, *a.* (truthful) طوغری سویلر dòghru-

Candle, *s.* موم mùm. [(shàmdan).

Candlestick, *s.* شمعدان shèm''à-dān

Cane, *s.* قامش kāmish, هزارن hèzārèn; —, *v.a.* دوکمك dùghmek, طیاق اتمق dàyak-ātmak.

Canister, *s.* تنکه tènékÉ.

Cannibal, *s.* یامیام yàmyàm, مردمخوار mÈrdumkhōr.

Cannibalism, *s.* مردمخوارلق mÈrdum-

Cannon, *s.* طوپ tòp. [khōrlik.

Cannonade, *s.* طوپ آتشی tòp-Atèshi; —, *v.a.* طوپ ایله دوکمك tòp-il*a*-dùg*h*mek.

Canon, *s.* قانون kānūn, قاعده kā''idÉ.

Canopy, *s.* شمسیه shèmsìyyÉ, سایه بان sāyébAn, طاق tAk.

Canter, *s.* طرس tàr*i*ss; —, *v.n.* طرس کتمك tàr*i*ss-ghìtmek. [jèg*h*i.

Cantharides, *s.* قندوزبوجکی kùnduz-bù-

Cantle (of a saddle), *s.* قاش kAsh.

Canvass, *s.* یلکن بزی yèlkèn-bèzi.

Cap, *s.* فس fèss; شپاقه shApk*a*; قلپاق kAlpAk; percussion-cap, اجزا èjzā; — of a mast, دستهموره dèsst*a*mòr*a*.

Capability, *s.* قابلیت kābilìyyèt.

Capable, *a.* قادر kādir, مقتدر mùktèdir.

Capacious, *a.* کنش ghènish, واسع wāssi'', بیوك bìyuk.

Capacity, *s.* (size) بیوکلك bìyukluk; (capaciousness) وسعت vùss''àt; (intelligence) عقل ''Akl, ذکا zèky*ā*, استعداد ìsstì''dād; (quality) صفت sìfAt. [cloak) یقا y*à*ka.

Cape, *s.* (headland) بورون bùrun; (of a

Capital, *a.* (good) اعلا à''là; (great) بیوك bìyuk, عظیم ''Azīm, کبیر kèbīr; (principal) باش bAsh; —, *s.* (city) پایتخت pày*i*tàkht; (of a column) باش bAsh, باشلق bAshl*i*k. [māyÉ.

Capitalist, *s.* صاحب سرمایه sāhibi-sèr-

Capitulate, *v.n.* رای استمك rày-ìssté-mek; رای ایله تسلیم او rày-il*a*-tèsslīm-òl; ویره ویرمك vÈr*a*-vÈrmek.

Capitulation, *s.* رای rày; ویره vÈr*a*.

Capon, *s.* ابلق ìbl*i*k (ìml*i*k).

Capricious, *a.* عجیب طبیعتلو ''Ajàyb-tAbi''àtl*i*, میمون اشتهالو màymun-ìsht*a*hāl*i*; بردالده دورمز bìr-dAld*a*-dùrm*à*z.

Capricorn (tropic of), *s.* جدی jèdi, مدار جدی mèdāri-jèdi.

Captain, *s.* (warrior) جنکجی jènkji; (army) یوزباشی yùz-bAsh*i*; (navy) سواری sùwAri, قپودان kApucAn (kAptAn); (merchant) رئیس rè'īss; (European) قپودان kApudAn (kAptAn).

Captive, *s.* اسیر èssīr (yèssir).

Captivity, *s.* اسیرلك èssīrlik.

Capture, *v.a.* المق Alm*a*k, طوتمق tùtm*a*k, ضبط zAbt-et; اسیرا èssīr-et.

Carat, *s.* قیراط kīrAt.

Caravan, *s.* کروان kÈrwAn, قافله kAfil*a*.

Caravanserai, *s.* خان khAn.

Caraway, *s.* کراویه kÈrāvìyyÉ.

Carbine, *s.* قرابینه kàrabìn*a*.

Carbuncle, *s.* (disease) شیرپنچه shīr-pènchÉ; (stone) لعل là''l.

Carcase, *s.* کوده ghy*ù*wdÉ, جسد jèssed; لاشه lāshÉ (lèsh); (of war) یاغلو پچاوره yàg*h*l*i*-pàchàvr*a*.

Card, *s.* کاغد ky*ā*g*h*id; مقوا mùkAwwa; (comb) طراق tàr*a*k; —, *v.a.* طرامق tàram*a*k, اتمق àtm*a*k.

Cardamum, *s.* قاقله kākulÉ.

Carder, *s.* حلاج hAllAj (hAlAj).

Care, *s.* (attention) دقت dìkkAt; (anxiety) درد dèrd, كدر kèdEr; —, *v.n.* وظيفه ايدنمك wAzīfé-èdinmek; — for, باقمق bàkmak; صايمق sàymak; take care, *v.n.* كوزينى اچمق ghyùzunu-àchmak, دقت ا dìkkAt-et, صاقنمق sàkinmak; (take pains) اوزنمك ùzènmek; take care of, باقمق bàkmak, صاقلامق sàklamak.

Careen, *v.a.* قلفاطه ياترمق kàlafAta-yàtirmak; —, *v.n.* ياتمق yàtmak.

Careful, *a.* مقيد mùkàyyed; to be —, *v.n.* دقت ا dìkkAt-et, مقيد او mùkAyyed-òl.

Carefulness, *s.* دقت dìkkAt.

Careless, *a.* دقتسز dìkkAtsiz.

Carelessness, *s.* دقتسزلق dìkkAtsizlik.

Caress, *v.a.* اوخشامق òkhshamak; —, *s.* اوخشامه òkhshama.

Cargo, *s.* يوك yùk, حموله hàmūlé.

Caricature, *s.* هجو رسمى hìjv-rèssmi.

Carmine, *s.* لعل là''l.

Carpenter, *s.* (house) دولكر dùlghEr; (joiner) دوغرامه جى dòghramaji; (ship's) مرانقوز màrankoz (màranghoss).

Carpet, *s.* قالى kālī (hàli), كليم kìlim, كچه kèché; prayer —, سجاده sèjjādé.

Carpet-bag, *s.* چانطه chànta.

Carriage, *s.* (vehicle) عربه ''àraba, حنطو hìntò, تاليقه tàlika, فايطون fàytòn; gun —, (field) عربه ''àraba, (ship's) قونداق kùndAk; (act of carrying) نقل nAkl, طاشيمه tAshima; (— hire) نقليه nAklìyyé.

Carrier, *s.* حمال hàmmAl; قاطرجى kAtirji.

Carrion, *s.* لاشه lāshé (lèsh).

Carronade, *s.* قلومبر kùlumbìr.

Carrot, *s.* هاوج hàwuj.

Carroty, *a.* صارى sAri.

Carry, *v.a.* طاشيمق tAshimak; كوترمك ghyùturmek; (a gun, &c.) سورمك sùrmek; (by assault) ضبط ا zAbt-et; — away *or* off, الوب كوترمك Alìp-ghyùturmek; — on, ياپمق yàpmak, ايتمك ètmek, اويدرمق ùydurmak, بجرمك bèjErmek; — the day, اوسته چيقمق ùssta-chikmak, غالب او ghālib-òl, قزانمق kAzAnmak.

Cart, *s.* عربه ''àraba.

Cartilage, *s.* قيقرداق kìkirdAk.

Cartridge, *s.* (small arms) فشنك fìshènk (fìshèk); (cannon) حارطوج hàrtuj.

Cartridge-box, *s.* پلاسقه pAlAsska.

Carve, *v.a.* (meat, &c.) دوغرامق dòghramak; (wood, &c.) اويمق òymak.

Carver, *s.* (in wood) اويمه جى òymaji.

Cascade, *s.* چاغليان chàghlayAn.

Case, *s.* (box) صندق sAndik; محفظه màhfaza; قوتى kòtu, قاب kAb; (sheath) قين kìn; (condition) حال hāl; (matter) ماده màddé, خصوص khùssūss, امر èmir; —, *v.a.* قابلامق kàblamak (kàplamak).

Case-shot, *s.* مسكت mìsskèt.

Cash, *s.* نقد nAkd, پاره pārè (pàra).

Cashier, *s.* صندقدار sAndikdàr, وزنه دار vèznédàr, خزينه دار khAzīnédàr (khAznadàr); —, *v.a.* رتبه سنى المق rùtbéssini-Almak, خدمتدن قوغمق khìdmetdan-kòghmak.

Cask, *s.* فوچی fìchi, واریل vàril.

Casket, *s.* چکمجه chèkmÉjÉ, صندق sÀndik.

Cassia, *s.* خیارشنبه khìyarshènbÉ.

Cast, *a.* دوکمه dùkmÉ; —, *s.* اتم Àtim, اتش Àtish; (in the eye) شاشیلق shàshilik; —, *v.a.* (throw) اتمق Àtmak; (metal) دوکمك dùkmek; — down, قیرمق kìrmak, اوزمك ùzmek, کدر ویرمك kèdEr-vèrmek; — up, (accounts) یکون ا yèkyūn-et, جمع ا jèm''-et, طوپلامق tòplamak; (vomit) قوصمق kùssmak; — off, اتیویرمك Àtivèrmek, دفع ا dèf''-et, طرد ا tàrd-et; صالیویرمك sÀlivèrmek, قاپوب صالیویرمك kÀpip-sÀlivèrmek; — out, قوغمق kòghmak, دفع ا dèf''-et, طرد ا tard-et.

Castle, *s.* قلعه kàl''a (kàyla).

Castor-oil, *s.* هند یاغی hìnd-yàghi.

Casual, *a.* تصادفی tèssÀdufī, اتفاقی [ìttifÀkī.

Casualty, *s.* قضا kÀzā.

Cat, *s.* کدی kèdi.

Catalogue, *s.* دفتر dèftEr.

Cataplasm, *s.* لاپه lÀpa.

Cataract, *s.* صولرك اوچمسی sùlaring-ùchmassi, جندل jèndèl. [nèwāzil.

Catarrh, *s.* زکام zùkkyām, نزله nèzlÉ, نوازل

Catch, *v.a.* طوتمق tùtmak, یقالمق yàkalamak; اله کتورمك Èla-ghètirmek; — cold, صوغوق المق sòghuk-Àlmak.

Catching, *a.* ساری sārī, بولاشر bùlàshir.

Catechise, *v.a.* استنطاق ا ìsstintÀk-et, امتحان ا ìmtihān-et.

Categorical, *a.* قطعی kÀt''ī.

Category, *s.* مقوله màkūlÉ.

Caterpillar, *s.* قورت kùrt.

Catgut, *s.* کرش kìrish. [poss-kèlīssassi.

Cathedral, *s.* پسقپوس کلیساسی pìsska-

Cattle, *s.* حیوانات hàywÀnÀt.

Caucasus, *s.* چرکسستان chèrkèssìsstān.

Caulk, *v.a.* قلفاط ا kÀlafÀt-et.

Caulker, *s.* قلفاط kÀlafÀt.

Cauliflower, *s.* قرنابت kàrnabìt.

Cause, *s.* باعث bā''iss, علت ''ìllèt, سبب sèbeb; دعوی dà''wà; —, *v.a.* باعث او bā''iss-òl, سبب او sèbeb-ol, ایراث ا īrāss-et.

Causeway, *s.* قالدرم kÀldirim.

Caustic (lunar), *s.* جهنم طاشی jìhènnem-tÀshi (jìhànnam). [یاقمق yàkmak.

Cauterize, *v.a.* داغلامق dāghlamak,

Cautery, *s.* یاقی yàki, داغ dàgh.

Caution, *s.* بصیرت bÀssīrèt, تأنی tÈ'ènnī, حذر hàzEr; —, *v.a.* خبر ویرمك khÀber-vèrmek.

Cautious (to be), *v.n.* احترازا ìhtirāz-et, احتذارا ìhtizār-et, صاقنمق sàkinmak.

Cavalry, *s.* سواری عسکری sùwāri-''àss-kEri, اتلو Àtli.

Cave, Cavern, *s.* مغاره màghara.

Cavity, *s.* چقور chùkur.

Cease, *v.n.* کسلمك kèssilmek, منقطع او mùnkÀti''-òl.

Cedar, *s.* سرو ازاد sÈrvi-āzād.

Cede, *v.a.* ترك ا tÈrk-et, ویرمك vÈrmek.

Ceiling, *s.* طوان tÀwAn.

Celebrate, *v.a.* اجرا ا ìjrā-et.

Celebrated, *a.* مشهور mèshhūr.

Celery, *s.* کرویز kèréviz.
Celestial, *a.* سماوی sèmāvī.
Cell, *s.* حجره hùjré; خانه khānè, کوز [ghyùz.
Cellar, *s.* مخزن màkhzèn.
Cement, *s.* الجی Alchi, معجون mà''jūn; —, *v.a.* یاپشدرمق yàpishdirmak, طوتدرمق tùtdurmak.
Cemetery, *s.* مزارلق mèzarlik, قبرستان kAbristān, مقبره mAkbéré.
Censer, *s.* بخوردان būkhūrdān (bū-khurdanlik).
Censure, *s.* ازار àzār; —, *v.a.* تعییب ا tà''yīb-et, ذم ا zèmm-et, لوم ا lèvm-et.
Census, *s.* تعداد نفوس tà''dādi-nùfūss.
Cent. (per cent.), *ad.* یوزده yùzdé.
Central, *a.* مرکزی mèrkezi. [wAssAt.
Centre, *s.* مرکز mèrkez, اورطه òrta, وسط
Centurion, *s.* یوز باشی yùz-bAshi.
Century, *s.* مائه mì'é. یوز ییل yùz-yìl, یوز سنه yùz-sèné, عصر ''Assr.
Cerecloth, *s.* مشمع mùshèmma'' (mù-shàmba). [tèklīf; تکلف tèkèlluf.
Ceremony, *s.* رسم rèssm (rèssim); تکلیف
Certain, *a.* معلوم mà''lūm, صحیح sàhīh, شبهه‌سز shùbhéssiz; فلان filAn; بعض bA''zi, بر طاقم bìr-tàkim.
Certainly, *ad.* البته èlbètté, شبهه‌سز shùb-[héssiz.
Certificate, *s.* سند sèned.
Certificated, *a.* سندلو sènedli.
Cessation, *s.* انقطاع ìnkitā'', کسلمه kèssilmé.
Cession, *s.* ترك tèrk, فراغت fèrāghAt.
Chafe, *v.a.* اشنمق Ashinmak.
Chaff, *s.* صمان sàmAn. [ghAl).
Chafing-dish, *s.* منقال mAnkAl (mAn-

Chagrin, *s.* (grief) تأسف tè'èssuf; (kind of skin) کلر kèlèr.
Chain, *s.* زنجیر zènjir (zìnjir); —, *v.a.* زنجیر ایله باغلامق zìnjir-ila-bàghlamak.
Chair, *s.* صندالیه sAndālìyyé; arm —, قولتقلو kòltuklu.
Chairman, *s.* رئیس مجلس rè'īssi-mèjliss.
Chalk, *s.* تباشیر tèbāshīr (tAbèshir).
Challenge, *v.a.* میدان اوقومق mèydAn-òkumak.
Chamber, *s.* اوطه òda; (of a mine, gun, &c.) خزینه khAzīné (hAzna).
Chamberlain, *s.* قپوجی باشی kApiji-bAshi.
Chance, *s.* تصادف tèssAduf, اتفاق ìtti-fAk, بخت bàkht; by —, راست‌کله rAsst-ghèlé; —, *v.a.* بخته حواله ا bàkhta-hàwālé-et.
Chancellor of the Exchequer, *s.* مالیه ناظری mālìyyé-nāziri.
Chandelier, *s.* اویزه āvīzé.
Chandler, *s.* بقال bAkkāl.
Change, *s.* دکش dìghish, دکشش dì-ghishish, دکشمه dìghishma, تبدل tèbèddul, تبدیل tèbdīl, انقلاب ìnki-lāb; —, *v.n.* دکشمك dìghishmek, دونمك dùnmek; —, *v.a.* دکشدرمك dìghishdirmek; چویرمك chèvirmek; تبدیل ا tèbdīl-et; بوزمك bòzmak.
Changeable, *a.* قرارسز kArarsiz, اویناق òynak.
Channel, *s.* یول yòl; بوغاز bòghAz; یتاق yàtak, مجرا mèjrā.
Chap, *s.* چاتلاق chàtlAk; حریف hèrif.
Chaplain, *s.* امام ìmām; پاپاس pApass
Chaplet, *s.* تسبیح tèssbīh. [(pApAz).

Chapman, *s.* مدراباز mAdrabAz, قولتقجى kòltukju.

Chapter, *s.* باب bāb, فصل fAssl.

Character, *s.* (moral) طبيعت tAbi''àt, جبلت jìbillèt, خوى khùy; (writing) يازى yàzi, خط khAtt; (letter) حرف hàrf (pl. حروفات hùrūfAt).

Charcoal, *s.* كومر *or* كمور kyùmur.

Charge, *s.* (employ) خدمت (khìzmet), مأموريت mè'mūrìyyèt, ايش ìsh; (command) امر èmir, تنبيه tènbīh; (of powder) اتم Atim; (attack) يورويش yùruyush, هجوم hùjūm; (thing confided) امانت èmānèt; —, *v.a.* (fill) طولدرمق dòldurmak; (attack) هجوم ا hù-jūm-et; (command) امرا èmr-et, تنبيه ا tènbīh-et; (accuse) اسناد ا ìssnād-et.

Charity, *s.* (alms) صدقه sAdaka; (humane consideration) انسانيت ìnsAnìyyèt, انصاف ìnsAf.

Charm, *s.* (spell) بويو bùyu, سحر sìhr; charms, *s. pl.* حسن hùssn, كوزللك ghyùzèllik.

Charmer, *s.* بويوجى bùyuju, سحرباز sìhrbAz; (beloved) معشوقه mà''-shūka; فتنه‌كار fìtnèkyār, دلبر dìlbèr.

Charming, *a.* كوزل ghyùzèl, دلبر dìlbèr, لطيف làtif.

Chart, *s.* خريطه khàrīta.

Charter, *s.* فرمان fèrmAn, برات bèrāt; —, *v.a.* نوله طوتمق nèvla-tùtmak (nàvluna), كراايله‌طوتمق kirā-ila-tùtmak.

Chase, *s.* آو Av, شكار shìkyār; —, give chase to, *v.a.* قوغالمق kòghalamak; — away, قوغمق kòghmak.

Chasm, *s.* بيوك يارق bìyuk-yàrik.

Chaste, *s.* عفيف ''àfīf, (woman) عفيفه ''àfīfè; (simply elegant) ساده كوزل sādè-ghyùzèl.

Chasten, **Chastise**, *v.a.* تربيه ويرمك tèrbìyyè-vèrmek, تربيه ا tèrbìyyè-et.

Chastisement, *s.* تربيه tèrbìyyè, طياق dàyak. [mèt.

Chastity, *s.* عفت ''ìffèt, عصمت ''ìss-

Chat, *s.* لاف lAf, لقردى làkirdi; —, *v.n.* لاف ا lAf-et, قونوشمق kònushmak.

Cheap, *a.* اوجوز ūjùz.

Cheapness, *s.* اوجوزلق ūjùzluk.

Cheat, *s.* (fraud) حيله hīlè; (knave) حيله‌كار hīlèkyār; —, *v.n.* حيله ا hīlè-et.

Check, *s.* (pattern) شطرنج shAtrènj (sAntrànch); (in accounts) ميزان mīzAn; (upon conduct) كم ghèm; (slight defeat) شمار shàmar, (banker's) حواله hàwAlè; —, *v.a.* ضبط ا zAbt-et, اليقومق Alikomak, دوردرتمق dùrdurt-mak; (defeat) بوزمق bòzmak; (the king at chess) كش ا kìsh-et.

Checkmate, *v.a.* مات ا mAt-et.

Cheek, *s.* يناق yànak.

Cheer, *v.a.* شنلندرمك shènlèndirmek, فراحلندرمق fèrāhlandirmak.

Cheerful, *a.* شن shèn, فراح fèrāh; [مفرح mùfèrrih.

Cheese, *s.* پنير pènir.

Cheesemonger, *s.* بقال bAkAl.

Chemist, *s.* كيمياكر kìmiyàghèr; أجزاجى èjzājì, اسپنچيار ìsspènchiyàr.

Chemistry, *s.* علم كيمياى جديد "ìlmi-kìmiyàyi-jèdīd.

Cherish, *v.a.* عزيز طوتمق "àzīz-tùtmak; بسلمك bèsslémek. [vìshna.

Cherry, *s.* كراز kìrāz; morella —, وشنه

Chess, *s.* شطرنج shàtrànj (sàntrànch); — board شطرنج تختەسى sàntrànch-tàkhtassi.

Chest, *s.* (box) صندق sàndìk; (bosom) كوكس ghyùkss, صدر sàdr, سينه sīné; — of drawers, چكمجه chèkméjé.

Chestnut, *s.* كستانه kèsstāné.

Chew, *v.a.* چينەمك chìnémek.

Chick, Chicken, *s.* پلیج pìlij.

Chickpea, *s.* نخود nòkhud.

Chide, *v.a.* ازارلمق àzarlamak.

Chief, *a.* and *s.* بيوك bìyuk, باش bàsh.

Chiefly, *ad.* خصوصا khùssūssā; اكثريا èksérìyyā.

Child, *s.* چوجق chòjuk; children and family, چولق چوجق chòluk-chòjuk; with child, كبه ghèbé, حامله hāmilé. [صوغوق sòghuk.

Chill, *v.a.* اوشوتمك ùshutmek; —, *s.*

Chilly, *a.* صوغوق sòghuk; to feel —, *v.n.* اوشومك ùshumek.

Chimney, *s.* اوجاق òjak, باجه bàja.

Chin, *s.* چكه chèngé (chèné).

China, *s.* (old) اسكى معدن èsski-mà"dɐn; (new) فغفور fàghfūr; (stone) چينى chìni.

Chink, *s.* يارق yàrìk, چاتلق chàtlàk; —, *v.n.* اوتمك ùtmek.

Chintz, *s.* چيت chìt, باصمه bàssma.

Chip, *s.* يونغه yòngha; —, *v.n.* فرلامق fìrlamak; —, *v.a.* فرلاتمق fìrlatmak.

Chisel, *s.* قلم kàlɐm.

Chocolate, *s.* چقولاطه chìkolàta.

Choice, *s.* اختيار ìkhtiyār, انتخاب ìntìkhāb; —, *a.* سچمه sèchma, منتخب mùntakhàb, مختار mòkhtār, كزيده ghyùzīdé.

Choke, *v.a.* بوغمق bòghmak; — up, *v.a.* طيقامق tìkamak; —, *v.n.* طيقانمق tìkanmak.

Choose, *v.a.* سچمك sèchmek, ايرمق àyrmak, انتخاب ا ìntìkhāb-et, اختيارا ìkhtiyār-et.

Chop (mutton), *s.* بريزوليه brìzòlya; —, *v.a.* كسمك kèssmek; — up, *v.a.* (small) قيمق kìymak, (large) طوغرامق dòghramak; (wood) يارمق [yàrmak.

Chopper, *s.* ساطور sàtìr.

Chopping-block, *s.* كتوك kyùtuk.

Chopping-knife, *s.* ساطور (sàtìr).

Chord, *s.* وتر vèter.

Christ, *s.* حضرت عيسى Hàzréti-"Issà.

Christen, *v.a.* وافتيزا wàftiz-et, اد قومق àd-kòmak, اد ويرمق àd-vèrmek.

Christening, *s.* وافتيز wàftiz.

Christian, *s.* خريستيان khrìsstiyàn; —, *a.* عيسوى "ìssévī, مسيحى mèssīhī.

Christianity, *s.* خريستيانلق khrìsstiyànlìk. [-pàsskàlya.

Christmas, *s.* كچوك پاسقاليه kùchuk

Chronicle, *s.* تاريخ tārīkh.

Chronology, *s.* علم تقويم التواريخ "ìlmi-tàkvim-u-tèwārīkh.

Chronogram, *s.* تاریخ tārīkh.

Chronometer, *s.* طول ساعتی tūl-sā''*ati*.

Church, *s.* کلیسه kìlīssé.

Churchyard, *s.* مزارلق mèzarl*i*k.

Chyle, *s.* کیلوس kèylūss.

Chyme, *s.* کیموس kèymūss.

Cicatrize, *v.n.* قپانمق kApAnm*a*k, قبوقلنمق kAbuklanm*a*k. [kyùmur.

Cinder, *s.* سونمش کمور sùnmush-

Cinnamon, *s.* دارچین dàrchin (tàrchin).

Cipher, *s.* (zero) صفر sìfr; (secret writing) جفره jìfr*a*; (initials) طغرا tūg*h*ra (for the Sultan), صح sàhh (for a high officer), امضا ìmzā (for any individual). N.B.—These are not initials in Turkish, but each a kind of signature.

Circle, *s.* دائره dā'iré; —, *v.a.* قوشاتمق kūshAtm*a*k, احاطه ا ìhāt*a*-et.

Circuit, *s.* قضا kAzā, دائرۀ حکومت dā'iré'i-hùk*y*ūmèt; to make a —, طولاشمق dòl*a*shm*a*k.

Circuitous, *a.* طولاشق dòlàsh*i*k.

Circular, *a.* مدور mùdèvvèr, دکرمی dè*gh*irmi.

Circulate, *v.n.* دوران ا dèvérān-et; (as money) تداول ا tèdāvul-et; —, *v.a.* اداره ا ìdāré-et; نشر ا nèshr-et.

Circulation, *s.* دوران dèvérān; (of money, books, &c.) تداول tèdāvul.

Circumcise, *v.a.* سنت ا sùnnèt-et, ختان ا khìtān-et. [khìtān.

Circumcision, *s.* سنت sùnnèt, ختان

Circumference, *s.* چوره chèvré, محیط mùhīt.

Circumlocution, *s.* طولاشقلو لاقیردی dò-l*a*shikli-làk*i*rd*i*.

Circumnavigate, *v.a.* کمی ایله اطرافنی طولاشمق ghèmi-ìlé-ètrāfini-dòlashm*a*k.

Circumstance, *s.* خصوص khùssūss, ماده mAddé, کیفیت kèyfìyyèt.

Cistern, *s.* صارنج sàrnij, خزینه (khAzn*a*).

Citadel, *s.* ایچ قلعه ìch-kàl''à.

Cite, *v.a.* ذکر ا zìkr-et; دعوت ا dà''vet-et.

Citron, *s.* اغاج قاونی A*gh*Aj-kàwunu.

City, *s.* شهر shèhr, مملکت mèmlékèt.

Civil, *a.* طاتلو tAtl*i*, ادبلو èdèbli, چلبی chèlébi; (not military) غیر عسکری ghàyr*i*-''Asskérī.

Civilian, *s.* باشی بوزوق bAsh*i*-bòzuk, عسکریدن اولمیان ''Asskérīd*a*n-òl-mayAn.

Civility, *s.* طاتلیلق tAtl*i*l*i*k, اغز طاتلیلغی à*gh*z-tAtl*i*l*i*g*hi*.

Civilization, *s.* تربیه tèrbìyyé.

Civilize, *v.a.* تربیه ا tèrbìyyé-et.

Claim, *s.* دعوی dà''wà, استدعا ìsstid''ā; مطلوب mAtlūb; —, *v.a.* دعوی ا dà-''wà-et, استدعا ا ìsstìd''ā-et, مطلوب ا màtlūb-et, مطالبه ا mùtAlébé-et.

Claimant, *s.* دعواجی dà''wàj*i*, مدعی [mùddà''ī.

Clamp, *s.* کنت kìnèt.

Clandestine, *a.* ال التنده Èl-Alt*i*nd*a*, کیزلو ghìzli, صاقلو sàkl*i*, خفی khàfī.

Clap, *s.* (disease) بل صوغوغی bèl-sò*gh*u-*gh*u; —hands, *v.n.* ال چالمق Èl-chAl-m*a*k, القشلمق Alk*i*shlam*a*k.

Clarify, *v.a.* تصفیه ا tAssfìyyé-et.

Clasp, *s.* قوپچه kòpch*a*; —, *v.a.* قوجاقلمق kùjAklam*a*k.

Class, *s.* صنف sìnf; —, *v.a.* ترتیب ا tèrtīb-et, تنظیم ا tànzīm-et.
Clatter, *s.* چاتردی chàtirdi, طاقردی tàkirdi, پاطردی pAtirdi.
Clause, *s.* بند bènd, فقره fikra.
Claw, *s.* طرناق tìrnak; پنچه pènché; —, *v.a.* طرمالمق tìrmalamak.
Clay, *s.* بالچق bAlchik, اوزلو طپراق ùzlu-tòprak, لوله جی چاموری lùléji-chàmuru.
Clean, *a.* تمیز tèmiz, پاك pāk, طاهر tāhir; —, cleanse, *v.a.* تمیزلمك tèmizlémek.
Clear, *a.* تمیز tèmiz, براق bèrrAk; (free) اچق àchik; — up, *v.n.* اچلمق àchilmak. [یاپشمق yàpishmak.
Cleave, *v.a.* یارمق yàrmak; — to, *v.n.*
Cleaver, *s.* ساطور sAtir.
Clemency, *s.* مرحمت mèrhàmet.
Clergyman, *s.* پاپاس pàpass.
Clerk, *s.* كاتب kyātib, یازیجی yàziji.
Clever, *a.* هنرلو hùnèrli.
Cliff, *s.* یار yàr, اوچروم ùchurum.
Climate, *s.* هوا hàwā. [sù''ūd-et.
Climb, *v.n.* چیقمق chìkmak, صعودا
Clinch, *v.a.* پرچین ا pèrchin-et.
Cling, *v.n.* صارلمق sArilmak. [kèssmek.
Clip, *v.a.* قرقمق kìrkmak, كسمك
Cloak, *s.* شنل shìnèl, قپوط kApud.
Clock, *s.* میدان ساعتی mèydan-sā''ati.
Clog, *s.* نعلین (nAlin); —, *v.a.* طولدرمق dòldurmak, طیقامق tìkamak.
Close, *a.* صیق sìk; صیقی sìki; صیقندیلو sèkintili; قپالو kApali; یقین yàkin; —, *v.a.* قپامق kApamak; —, *v.n.* قپانمق kApanmak; — in, *v.a.* چویرمك chèvirmek; —, *v.n.* صیقلاشمق sìklashmak, یقینلاشمق yàkinlashmak; (the evening) اخشام تیز اولمق Akhsham-(tèz)-òlmak; — up, *v.a.* قپامق kApamak; —, *v.n.* قپانمق kApanmak; — with, *v.a.* (in agreement) اویوشمق ùyushmak; (in fight) صارلمق sArilmak.
Closet, *s.* (room) اوطه جق òdajik; (cupboard) طولاب dòlap.
Cloth, *s.* (broad) چوقه (chòha); (cotton) بز bèz; (table —) صفره بزی sòfra-bèzi.
Clothe, *v.a.* روبا یاپمق rùba-yàpmak, روباكیدرمك rùba-ghidirmek, روبا ویرمك rùba-vèrmek, الباس ا ilbāss-et, اكسا ا iksā-et; اورتمك ùrtmek.
Clothes, Clothing, *s.* روبا rùba (ùrùba), اثواب èsswāb (èssbab), البسه èlbissé.
Cloud, *s.* بلوط bùlut, سحاب sihāb.
Clout, *s.* پچاوره pàchàvra.
Clove, *s.* قرنفل kArenfil.
Cloven, *a.* چتال chàtAl.
Clover, *s.* یونجه yònja.
Club, *s.* چوماق chòmak; by way of clubbing together, عارفانه ''ārifāné.
Clue, *s.* ایپ اوجی ip-ùju.
Clumsy, *a.* (person) یاقشمز yàkishmàz; (thing) حنطال hAntAl.
Cluster, *s.* كومه kyùmé, طوپ tòp.
Coach, *s.* عربه ''àraba, حنطو hìntò, فایطون fàytòn.
Coagulate, *v.n.* طوكمق dòngmak; كسلمك kèssilmek; پكشمك pèkishmek.
Coal, *s.* كمور kyùmur, معدن كموری mā''den-kyùmuru

Coal-hole, Coal-house, *s.* کومورلك kyù-murluk. [kyùmur-màdèni.

Coal-mine, Coal-pit, *s.* کومور معدنی

Coarse, *a.* قبا kàba; ایری ìri.

Coast, *s.* ساحل sāhil, دکز کناری dèngiz--kènàri; یقا yàka, قیی kàyi.

Coat, *s.* ستری sètri, صورطو surtu; صورطیقو sùrtiko; خرقه khìrka; (of a horse) طون dòn. [-tòkhmu.

Cocoa, *s.* چیقولاته تخمی chìkolāta-

Cocoa-nut, *s.* بیوك هندستان جوزی bìyuk-hìndòstān-jèvizi.

Cobbler, *s.* پاپوشجی pàpushju (pàpujju), اسکیجی èsskiji.

Cobweb, *s.* اورمجك اغی ùrumjek-àghi, تار عنکبوت tāri-‘‘ànkébūt.

Cochineal, *s.* قرمز kàrmiz.

Cock, *s.* (bird) خروس khòross; (tap) مصلق mùssluk; (of a gun) خروس khòross; (penis) سك sìk; — a gun, *v.a.* اوست تتکه المق ùsst-tètighé-àlmak. [-ìbighi.

Cock's-comb, *s.* خروس ابکی khòross-

Cocoon, *s.* قوزه kòza, قوزه لق kòzalàk.

Cod, *s.* (fish) مورینه بالغی mòrina-bàlighi; (of beans) قبوق kàbuk; (scrotum) طاشاق توربه سی tàshak-tòrbassi.

Coffee, *s.* قهوه kàhwé.

Coffee-pot, *s.* جزوه jèzwé; (large) کوکم ghyùghyum, ابریق ìbrik.

Coffer, *s.* صندق sàndik.

Coffin, *s.* تابوت tàbut.

Cog, *s.* دیش dìsh.

Cogent, *a.* مهم mùhìmm, معتنا mù‘‘téná, مبرم mùbrìm (mùbrèm).

Coil, *s.* قنغال kànghàl; —, *v.a.* قنغال ا kànghàl-et.

Coin, *s.* سکه sìkké; پاره pàra, اقچه àkcha; (of a gun) سیل sīl; —, *v.a.* ضرب ا dàrb-et, کسمك kèssmek, باصمق bàssmak.

Coincide, *v.n.* مطابق او mùtābik-òl.

Coition, *s.* سکش sìkish, جماع jìmā‘‘.

Cold, *a.* and *s.* صوغوق sòghuk; (in the head) نوازل nèwāzil, نزله nèzlé, زکام zùkkyām. [-àghrissi.

Colic, *s.* صانجی sànji, قارن اغریسی kàrn-

Collar, *s.* یقا yàka; (horse —) حموط hàmut; —, *v.a.* یقالمق yàkalamak.

Collate, *v.a.* مقابله ا mùkābélé-et.

Colleague, *s.* رفیق rèfìk, ارقه داش àrka-dash. [tòplamak.

Collect, *v.a.* جمع ا jèm‘‘-et, طوپلامق

Collection, *s.* جمع jèm‘‘; مجمعه mèj-ma‘‘a; طاقم tàkim; صره sìra. [dressé.

College, *s.* مکتب mèktèb; مدرسه mè-

Collier, *s.* کومور قایغی kyùmur-kàyighi; کومور معدنی ایشجیسی kyùmur-mà‘‘-deni-ìshjissi. [déni.

Colliery, *s.* کمورمعدنی kyùmur-mà‘‘-

Collision, *s.* چاتشمه chàtishma, تصادم tàssàdum; to come into —, *v.n.* چاتشمق chàtishmak, تصادم ا tàs-sàdum-et. [عین ìghmāzi-‘‘àyn.

Collusion, *s.* مسامحه mùssāmaha, اغماض

Colonel, *s.* میرالای mīr-àlày; lieutenant- —, *s.* قائممقام kā'im-màkàm (kày-

Colony, *s.* اوجاق òjak. [makàm).

Colour, *s.* رنك rènk.

Colt, *s.* طای tày; (of an ass) صیپا sìpa.

Column, *s.* دیرك dìrèk, عمود "àmūd, ستون sùtūn; (of soldiers) طابور tabur, قول kòl. [tàramak.

Comb, *s.* طراق tàrak; —, *v.a.* طرامق

Combat, *s.* دوكش dùghush; —, *v.a.* بوزمغه چالشمق bòzmagha-chalishmak.

Combination, *s.* تركيب tèrkīb; اتفاق ìttifak.

Combine, *v.a.* تركيب ا tèrkīb-et, مزج ا mèzj-et; —, *v.n.* اتفاق ا ìttifak-et; امتزاج ا ìmtizāj-et.

Combustible, *a.* یانار *or* ینار yànar; —, *s.* یاقه جق yàkajak.

Combustion, *s.* یانش yànish, یانمه yànma.

Come, *v.n.* كلمك ghèlmek; — along, كلیویرمك ghèlivermek; — asunder, قوپمق kòpmak, ایرلمق àyrilmak; — at, یتشمك yètishmek, یاننه وارمق yanina-vàrmak; — away, براقوب كلمك bràkip-ghèlmek; — back, كیرو كلمك ghèri-ghèlmek; — back again, ینه كلمك *or* بردها bìr-dàha *or* yìné (ghèné)-ghèlmek; — between, ارایه كیرمك àraya-ghìrmek; — by, *v.n.* كچمك ghèchmek; — —, *v.a.* پیدا ا pèydā-et, بولمق bùlmak; — off, اولمق olmak; قوپمق kòpmak; چیقمق chìkmak; — on, طوتمق tùtmak; باشلامق bashlamak; كلیویرمك ghèlivermek; — out, چیقمق chìkmak; — short, اكسك كلمك èksik-ghèlmak; — to, ایتمك ètmek, بالغ اول bāligh-òl; — together, طوپلانمق tòplanmak, بر یره كلمك bìr-yèra-ghèlmek, بولشمق bùlushmak, بر لشمك bìrleshmek; — to light, میدانه چیقمق mèydana-chìkmak, بللو اول bèlli-ol; — up, چیقمق chìkmak; سورمك sùrmek; — upon, باصمق bassmak, طوتمق tùtmak, یقالمق yàkalamak; —, *int.* دی dèy, دی بقالم dèy-bakalim, دی امدی dèy-imdi (dèyindi).

Comet, *s.* قویرقلو یلدز kùyruklu-yìldiz, ذو ذوابه zū-zèwābè. [kerlémé.

Comfit, *s.* شكر sheker, شكرلمه shè-

Comfort, *s.* (ease) راحت rāhat; (consolation) تسلی tèssèlli; —, *v.a.* تسلی ویرمك tèssèlli-vèrmek.

Comfortable, *a.* راحت rāhat.

Command, *s.* امر èmr (èmir), فرمان fèrman, تنبیه tènbīh; (military) قومانده kòmànda; —, *v.a.* امر ا èmr-et, تنبیه ا tènbīh-et, فرمان ا fèrman-et, بیورمق bùyurmak; قوماندا ا kòmànda-et; (as a gun) سپورمك sùpurmek; (as a fort) دوكمك dùghmek; محافظه ا mùhafaza-et, قپامق kapamak.

Commander, *s.* آمر āmir, ضابط zābit, بیوك bìyuk; سرعسكر sèr-"assker; (navy) ملازم قپودان mùlāzim-kapudan (kaptan), ایكنجی ìkinji.

Commence, *v.a.* and *n.* باشلامق bashlamak, اغازا aghāz-et, بدءا bèd'-et.

Commencement, *s.* اول èvvel, باش bash, ابتدا ìbtidā, بدء bèd'i, باشلانغج bashlanghij.

Commend, *v.a.* مدح ا mèdh-et, ثنا ا sènā-et; توصیه ا tàvsìyyé-et.

Comment, *s.* شرح shèrh, حاشیه hA-shìyyé; لقردی làkirdi, دیه‌جك dè-yéjek; —, *v.a.* شرح‌ا shèrh-et; — upon, *v.n.* مطالعه بیان‌ا mùtāla''a-bèyān-et.

Commentary, *s.* شرح shèrh.

Commentator, *s.* شارح shārih.

Commerce, *s.* تجارت tìjārèt, الش‌ویرش Alish-vèrish, بازرکانلق bAzir-ghyānlik.

Commercial, *a.* تجارته‌متعلق tìjārèta-mùta''àllik. [tàràhhum-et.

Commiserate, *v.a.* اجیمق Ajimak, ترحم‌ا

Commissariat, *s.* نزل امانتی nùzal-èmānèti; ذخیره zàkhīré.

Commissary, *s.* نزل‌امینی nùzul-èmīni.

Commission, *s.* سپارش sìpārish; خدمت khìdmet, مأموریت mè'mūrìyyèt; مأمورین mè'mūrīn, مأمورلر mè'mūr-lar; فرمان fèrmān, بیورلدی bùyu-ruldu; قومیسیون kòmīssion.

Commissioner, *s.* مأمور mè'mūr.

Commit, *v.a.* یاپمق yàpmak, ایتمك ètmek, ارتکاب‌ا ìrtikyāb-et; تسلیم‌ا tèsslīm-et, سپارش‌ا sìpārish-et, توديع‌ا tèvdī''-et.

Committee, *s.* ایریجه‌ومخصوص‌اولان‌مجلس àyrija-vé-màkhsūss-òlan-mèjliss.

Commodious, *a.* راحت rāhat, قوللانلشلو kùllAnilishli, قولایلقلو kòlaylikli.

Commodity, *s.* متعه mAt''à, مال mAl; راحت rāhat. [boghu.

Commodore, *s.* فیلو باشبوغی filobAsh-

Common, *a.* عادی ''ādī, بیاغی bàyà-ghi; مشترك mùshtérèk; —, *s.* چایرلق chàyrlik, مرعه mèr''à.

Commonly, *ad.* اکثریا èksèrìyyā.

Commons, the House of Commons, *s.* مبعوثان ملت مجلسی mèbūssāni-mìllèt-mèjlissi.

Commotion, *s.* تلاشی tèlāshī, تلاش tèlàsh.

Communicate, *v.a.* افاده‌ا ìfādé-et, تبلیغ‌ا tèblīgh-et; — with, *v.n.* خبرلشمك khAbèrleshmek, مخابره‌ا mùkhābéré-et; متصل‌او mùttAssil-ol.

Communication, *s.* افاده ìfādé, تبلیغات tèblīghAt; مخابره mùkhābéré; یول yòl. [mìllèt, جماعت jèmā''àt.

Community, *s.* اشتراك ìshtirāk; ملت

Compact, *s.* مقاوله mùkAvélé, قول kAvl; —, *a.* صیق sìk, صیقی sìki.

Companion, *s.* رفیق rèfik, ارقه‌داش àrkadash; اش èsh.

Company, *s.* (set) طاقم tàkim; (set of guests) مسافرلر mùssāfirlèr; (people present) حضار hùzzār, حاضرین hAzirīn; (public) قومپانیه kòm-pànya; (companionship) ارقه‌داشلق àrkadashlik; رفاقت rèfākAt; (of soldiers) بلوك bùluk; to keep —, *v.n.* قوكشمق kòngushmak, كورشمك ghyùrushmek.

Comparable, *a.* مقیس màkīss, قیاس‌اولنور kìyāss-òlunur, تشبیه‌اولنور tèshbīh-òlunur.

Comparatively, *ad.* قیاسله kìyāssla.

Compare, *v.a.* یان‌یانه‌قومق yàn-yàna-kòmak, مقابله‌ا mùkābélé-et, مقایسه‌ا mùkāyéssé-et, قیاس‌ا kìyāss-et, تشبیه‌ا tèshbīh-et.

Comparison, *s.* قياس kìyāss, تشبيه tèshbīh. [bùlmé.

Compartment, *s.* خانه khānÉ, بولمه

Compass, *s.* حد hàdd, اندازه Èndāzé; دائره dā'iré; (mariner's) پوصله pùssla; to fetch a —, *v.n.* طولاشمق dòlashmak; —, *v.a.* قوشاتمق kùsh-Atmak; — one's ends, *v.n.* اويدورمق ùydurmak, مرامنه نائل او mèrāmina-nā'il-òl. [(pèrghèl).

Compasses (pair of) *s.* پركار pèrghyār

Compassion, *s.* مرحمت mèrhàmet.

Compatriot, *s.* همشهری hèmshèhrī.

Compeer, *s.* كفو kyùfv, اقران Akrān.

Compel, *v.a.* جبرا jèbr-et, اجبارا ìjbār-et.

Compendious, *a.* قصه kìssa, مختصر mùkhtAssàr, مجمل mùjmèl.

Compensate, *v.a.* تضمينا tAzmīn-et; —, *v.n.* قارشيلق او kàrshilik-ol.

Compensation, *s.* تضمين tAzmīn, تضمينات tAzmīnAt; قارشيلق kàr-shilik.

Compile, *v.a.* تصنيفا tAssnīf-et, جمعا jèm''-et, تأليفا tè'līf-et.

Complain, *v.a.* شكايتا shìkyāyet-et, تشكيا tèshèkki-et, اشتكاا ìshtikyā-et.

Complaint, *s.* شكايت shìkyāyet, شكوی shèkwà; مرض màraz, علت ''illèt, درد dErd. [kim; تتمه tètìmmé.

Complement, *s.* ترتيب tèrtīb, طاقم tà-

Complete, *a.* تكميل tèkmīl, مكمل mùkèmmèl, تام tAmm, تمام tAmām; — *v.a.* تكميلا tèkmīl-et, تماملمق tAmAmlamak, بترمك bìtirmek.

Complexion, *s.* رنك rènk, لون lèvn.

Complicate, *v.a.* قارشدرمق kàrish-dirmak, قارشقا kArishik-et.

Compliment, *s.* سلام sèlām; استحسان افادەسی ìsstìhsān-ìfādéssi.

Comply, *v.n.* امتثالا ìmtissāl-et; موافقتا mùwAfakAt-et.

Compose, *v.a.* ترتيبا tèrtīb-et, تركيبا tèrkīb-et; يازمق yàzmak, قلمه المق kàléma-Almak; سويلمك sùwèylé-mek, نظما nAzm-et; تركيبنه داخل او tèrkībina-dākhil-òl, اجزای مركبه سی او èjzāyi - mùrèkkibéssi - òl, اعضاسی او à''zāssi - òl; — one's self, *v.n.* ياتشمق yàtishmak.

Composition, *s.* تركيب tèrkīb; ترتيب tèrtīb; اجزا èjzā; معجون mà''jūn; كتابت kìtābet, شعر shì''r.

Compost, *s.* كوبره ghyùbré.

Compound, *a.* مركب mùrèkkèb; —, *v.a.* تركيبا tèrkīb-et.

Comprehend, *v.a.* احاطها ìhāta-et, شامل او shāmil-ol, شمولی او shù-mūli-òl; اكلامق ànglamak (ànna-mak), ادراكا ìdrāk-et.

Compress, *s.* صارغی sàrghi.

Comprise, *v.a.* شامل او shāmil-ol.

Compromise, *s.* صلح sùlh, اوزلاشمه ùz-lashma; —, *v.a.* قارشدرمق kArish-dirmak; مسئولا mèss'ūl-et; اوزلاشمق ùzlashmak, صلح او sùlh-òl.

Compulsion, *s.* مجبوريت mèjbūrìyyèt, اجبار ìjbār, اضطرار ìztirār.

Compunction, *s.* ندامت nèdāmèt, پشيمانلق (pìshmAnlik).

Compute, *v.a.* حسابا hìssāb-et.

Comrade, *s.* ارقه‌داش àrk*a*d*a*sh, يولداش yòld*a*sh.

Concave, *a.* مقعر mŭkà‘‘‘àr, چقور chŭkur.

Conceal, *v.a.* صاقلامق sàkl*a*m*a*k, كيزلمك ghìzlémek.

Concede, *v.a.* تسليم ا tèsslīm-et.

Conceivable, *a.* متصور mùt*a*ssÀvvèr, عقله‌صيغار ‘‘Àkl*a*-sìghàr.

Conceive, *v.a.* تصورا tàssÀvvur-et, عقلا ‘‘Àkl-et; —, *v.n.* كبه‌قالمق ghèbé-kÀlm*a*k, حامله او hāmilé-òl.

Concentrate, *v.a.* طوپلامق tòpl*a*m*a*k; خلاصه ا khŭlāss*a*-et.

Conception, *s.* تصور tàssÀvvur, تخيل tàkhàyyul, حامله اولمقلق hāmilé-òlm*a*klik.

Concern, *s.* ماده màddé, ايش ìsh, مصلحت mÀsslāh*a*t; قساوت kÀssā-vet, كدر kèder; —, *v.a.* دوقونمق dòkunm*a*k; — one's self, *v.n.* قساوتا kÀssàvet-et.

Concert, *s.* اتفاق ìttifĀk, اتحاد ittihād; چالغی‌مجلسی chÀlghi-mèjlissi; — together, *v.n.* اتفاقا ìttifĀk-et, قرار ويرمك kÀrar-vèrmek.

Conciliate, *v.a.* جلب ا jèlb-et.

Concise, *a.* مختصر mùkhtÀssàr, قصه kìss*a*.

Conciseness, *s.* قصه‌لق kìssalik.

Conclude, *v.a.* بترمك bìtirmek; عقدا ‘‘àkd-et: —, *v.n.* بتمك bìtmek; اكلامق ànglam*a*k (ànnam*a*k), استخراجا ìsstikhràj-et, معنا ويرمك mà‘‘nà-vèrmek.

Conclusion, *s.* صوك sòng, اخر ākhir; عقد ‘‘àkd; قرار kÀrār; اكلايش àng-layish (ànnayish), استخراج ìsstikhrāj.

Conclusive, *a.* قطعی kÀt‘‘ī, مقنع mŭkni‘‘.

Concord, *s.* وفاق wìfĀk, مخادنت mŭ-khādénèt. [(kÀl*a*bÀlik.

Concourse, *s.* ازدحام izdihām, غلبه‌لق

Concubine, *s.* اوطه‌لق òdalik.

Concur, *v.n.* برابر او bèrābèr-òl.

Concussion, *s.* صارصش sàrsish, صارصلش sàrsilish, صدمه sÀdAm*a*.

Condemn, *v.a.* قباحت‌بولمق kÀbāh*a*t-bŭlm*a*k; قباحتلوبولمق kÀbāh*a*tli-bùlm*a*k; جزاسنه حكما jèzāssin*a*-hùkm-et; يرامز ديو قرار ويرمك yàra-m*a*z-dèy*u*-kÀrār-vèrmek.

Condensation, *s.* تكثف tèkèssuf.

Condense, *v.a.* تكثيفا tèksīf-et; —, *v.a.* تكثف ا tèkèssuf-et.

Condescend, *v.n.* تنزلا tènèzzul-et.

Condescension, *s.* تنزل tènèzzul.

Condign, *a.* مستحق‌اولديغی mùsst*a*-hÀkk-òld*u*ghu.

Condiment, *s.* چرز chèrez, قاتق kÀtik.

Condition, *s.* حال hāl; پرسه pèréssé; شرط shàrt.

Condole, *v.n.* تعزيه‌ا tà‘‘zìyyé-et.

Condolence, *s.* تعزيه tà‘‘zìyyé.

Conduce, *v.n.* منتج‌او mùntij-ol, مورث‌او mŭriss-ol, موجب‌او mŭjib-ol.

Conduct, *s.* حركت hàrékèt; —, *v.a.* كوترمك ghyùturmek.

Conduit, *s.* صويولی sù-yòlu.

Cone, *s.* مخروط màkhrūt.

Confectioner, *s.* شكرجی shèkerji.

Confectionery, *s.* شكر shèker.

Confederacy, *s.* اتفاق ìttifĀk; متفقين mùt-
Confederate, *s.* متفق mùttèfik. [tèfikīn.
Confederation, *s.* اتفاق ìttifĀk ; متفقين mùttèfikīn. [قونفرانس kònferānss.
Conference, *s.* مكالمه mùkyālémé ;
Confess, *v.a.* اقرار ا ìkrār-et, اعتراف ا i"tirāf-et..
Confession, *s.* اقرار ìkrār, اعتراف i"tirāf.
Confide, *v.a.* تسليم ا tèsslīm-et, توديع ا tèvdī"-et ; —, *v.n.* امنيت ا èmnìyyèt-et. [i"timād.
Confidence, *s.* امنيت èmnìyyèt, اعتماد
Confident (to be), *v.n.* هيچ شبههسى اولمامق hìch-shùbhéssi-òlmamak.
Confine, *v.a.* حبس ا hAbss-et, قپاتمق kApAtmak ; حصر ا hAssr-et ; to be confined, *v.n.* طوغرمق dòghurmak ; — — — to one's room, طشره چيقمامق tAshra (dìshāri) chìkmamak ; — — — (one's bowels) انقباضى او ìnkibAzi-ol.
Confinement, *s.* ايچرويه قپانمقلق ìchéri-ya-kApAnmaklik, طيشارى چيقمامقلق dìshāri-chìkmamaklik ; حبس hàbss ; چوجق طوغرمقلق chòjuk-dòghurmak-
Confines, *s. pl.* حدود hùdūd. [lik.
Confirm, *v.a.* (ratify) تصديق ا tàssdīk-et ; (in office) ابقا ا ìbkA-et.
Confiscate, *v.a.* ضبط ا zAbt-et, مصادره ا mùssAdara-et. [hàrīk.
Conflagration, *s.* يانغين yànghin, حريق
Conflict, *s.* تصادم tàssAdum ; جنك jènk ; چكشمه chèkishma, منازعه mùnāza"à.
Conform, *v.n.* امتثال ا ìmtissāl-et, اقتفا ا ìktifā-et, مماثلت ا mùmāssélèt-et, اويمق ùymak.
Conformable, *a.* مماثل mùmāssil.
Conformably, *ad.* امتثالاً ìmtissālan ; تطبيقاً tAtbīkan.
Conformity, *s.* مماثلت mùmāssélèt.
Confound, *v.a.* مبهوت قيلمق mèbhūt-kìlmak, اسكات ا ìsskyāt-et ; قارشدرمق kArishdirmak, تخليط ا tàkhlīt-et.
Confuse, *v.a.* شاشرتمق shAshirtmak ; قارشدرمق kArishdirmak.
Confused, *a.* (things) قارشق kArishik ; to become — (a person), *v.n.* شاشرمق shàshirmak.
Confusion, *s.* قارشقلق kArishiklik.
Congeal, *v.n.* طوكمق dòngmak, منجمد او mùnjèmid-ol ; —, *v.a.* طوكدرمق dòngdurmak.
Congelation, *s.* انجماد ìnjimAd.
Congestion, *s.* سده sùddé.
Congratulate, *v.a.* تبريك ا tèbrīk-et, تهنيه ا tèhnìyyé-et ; I — you ! كوزك ايدين ghyùzung-àydin. [tèhnìyyé.
Congratulation, *s.* تبريك tèbrīk, تهنيه
Congregate, *v.n.* طوپلانمق tòplanmak, تجمع ا tèjèmmu"-et, مجتمع ا mùjtèmi"-òl. [جمعيت jèm"ìyyèt.
Congregation, *s.* جماعت jèmā"àt,
Congress, *s.* مجلس مشورت mèjlissi-mèshvérèt.
Conic, Conical, *a.* سوبى sùbu, مخروطى màkhrūti ; conics, *s. pl.* مخروطيات màkhrūtìyyAt.
Conjecture, *s.* ظن zànn ; تخمين tàkh-.

mīn ; —, *v.n.* ظن ا zAnn-et ; تخمين ا tàkhmīn-et.

Conjointly, *ad.* مشتركاً mùshtĕrékEn.

Conjugal, *a.* زوجى zèvjī, ازدواجه متعلق ìzdìvAj*a*-mùt*a*''*à*llik.

Conjugate, *a.* مزدوج mùzdèvij ; —, *v.a.* تصريف ا tAssrīf-et, صيغەسنى چكمك sīgh*a*ss*i*n*i*-chèkmek.

Conjugation, *s.* صيغه sīgh*a*.

Conjunction, *s.* حرف عطف hàrf*i*-''Atf.

Conjuncture, *s.* وقت wAk*i*t, حال hāl.

Conjure, *v.a.* يلك رجا ا pèk-rìjā-et, پك نياز ا pèk-nìyāz-et, پك يالوارمق pèk-yAlvarm*a*k ; —, *v.n.* سحر ا sìhr-et.

Conjurer, *s.* سحرباز sìhrbAz.

Connect, *v.a.* بتشدرمك bìtishdirmek, اولاشدرمق ùlashd*i*rm*a*k ; باغلامق bA*gh*lam*a*k.

Connexion, *s.* مناسبت mùnāssébèt, ارتباط ìrtibAt, علاقه ''àlāk*a* ; خصم khìssm, اقربا Akrabā.

Connivance, *s.* مسامحه mùssām*a*h*a*, اغماض عين ìghmAz*i*-''àyn.

Connive, *v.n.* كورمميويرمك ghy*ù*rmÉyi-vErmek, اغماض عين ا ìghmAz*i*-''àyn-et.

Conquer, *v.a.* (men) مغلوب ا màghlūb-et ; (places) فتح ا fèth-et, ضبط ا zAbt-et, تسخير ا tèsskhīr-et.

Conqueror, *s.* فاتح fāt*i*h ; غالب ghālib.

Conquest, *s.* فتح fèth, تسخير tèsskhīr ; مملكت مفتوحه mèmlékèti-mèftūh*a*.

Conscience, *s.* قلب kAlb, ضمير zàmīr ; انصاف ìnsAf. [mùnsif.

Conscientious, *a.* انصافلو ìnsAfl*i*, منصف

Conscious (to be), *v.n.* دويمق dùym*a*k, حس ا hìsss-et ; خبرى اول khAbÉri-ol. واقف اول wAk*i*f-òl ; —, *a.* واقف wAk*i*f.

Consciousness, *s.* خبر khAbEr, وقوف wùkūf ; حس hìsss.

Consecrate, *v.a.* تقديس ا tAkdīss-et ; تخصيص ا tàkhs*i*ss-et.

Consecrated, *a.* مخصوص màkhs*ū*ss, مخصص mùkhAsssèss ; مقدس mù-kAddèss.

Consecutive, *a.* متوالى mùtévālī, متتالى mùtétālī, متعاقب mùt*a*''āk*i*b.

Consecutively, *ad.* متعاقباً muta''āk*i*b*a*n, متواليه mùtévālìyyétEn.

Consent, *s.* رضا rìzā ; —, *v.n.* رضا ويرمك rìzā-vErmek, راضى اول rāzī-òl.

Consequence, *s.* نتيجه nètījÉ, ثمره sèmÉrÉ ; of —, خاطرى صايلور khAt*i*ri-sày*i*l*i*r ; of no —, صايلمز sàyìlmàz ; that is of no —, ضررى يوق zàrāri-yòk.

Consequent, *s.* تالى tālī ; —, *a.* تابع tāb*i*'', منوط mènūt, مربوط mÈrbūt ; (in word and act) ايشى واقوالى بربرينه مطابق اولان ìshi-vÉ-AkwAl*i*-bìrbirinÉ-mùtA-b*i*k-òlAn.

Consequently, *ad.* بناء عليه binā'*an*-''àlèyh, بناء على ذلك bìnā'*an*-''àlà-zāl*i*kÉ, بنابرين bìnābÉrīn, بوكابناء bùn*g*a-bìnā'*an*, بوكا مبنى bùn*g*a-mèbnī.

Conserve, *s.* رچل rèchel ; — of roses, كل بشكر ghyùl-bé-shèkEr.

Consider, *v.a.* (a thing) مطالعه ا mùtāla''à-et, ملاحظه ا múlāh*a*z*a*-et, دوشنمك dùshunmek ; (a person)

صایمق sàymak; — as, عدّ ا "àdd-et, اعتبار ا ì"tibār-et, صایمق sàymak.

Considerable, *a.* بیوك bìyuk, جسیم jèssīm; كلی kyùllī, عظیم "ʌzīm.

Consideration, *s.* ملاحظه mùlāhaza, مطالعه mùtāla"à, تأمل tè'èmmul, صایغی sàyghi; اعتبار ì"tibār; قارشیلق kàrshilìk.

Consign, *v.a.* تسلیم ا tèsslīm-et, تودیع ا tèvdī"-et; سپارش ا sìpārish-et.

Consist, *v.n.* عبارت او "ìbāret-òl, مترتب او mùtérèttib-ol. [tèsslìyyèt.

Consolation, *s.* تسلی tèssèllī, تسلیت

Console, *v.a.* تسلی ویرمك tèssèllī-vèrmek, تسلیت ا tèsslìyyèt-et.

Consolidate, *v.a.* تقویت ا tʌkvìyyèt-et, تقویت ویرمك tʌkvìyyèt-vèrmek, تأكید ا tè'kīd-et. [mùtʌbik.

Consonant, *s.* حرف hàrf; —, *a.* مطابق

Consort, *s.* زوج zèvj; زوجه zèvjé; ارقه داش àrkadash, رفیق rèfīk; —, *v.n.* قوكشمق kòngushmak, اختلاط ا ìkhtilʌt-et. [-ùngunda, میداننده mèydʌnda.

Conspicuous, *a.* كوز اوكنده ghyùz-

Conspiracy, *s.* كیزلو فساد ghìzli-fèssād, فتنه

Conspirator, *s.* فتنه كار fitné-kyàr. [fitné.

Constancy, *s.* ثبات sèbāt, رسوخ rùsūkh, صداقت sʌdākʌt.

Constant, *a.* ثابتقدم sābitkʌdem, راسخ rāsikh, صادق sʌdik; دائم dā'im, دائمی dā'imī, ثابت sābit, مستمر mùsstémèrr.

Constantinople, *s.* استانبول ìsstànbòl; در سعادت dèri-sà"ādet (the Gate of Felicity).

Constantly, *ad.* دائما dā'imā, بردوزیه bìr-dùziyé, لاینقطع lā-yànkʌti".

Constipation, *s.* انقباض ìnkibʌz.

Constitute, *v.a.* ایتمك ètmek; نصب ا nʌssb-et; اولمق òlmak, حاصل ا hʌssil-et.

Constitution, *s.* (man's) وجود vùjūd, بنیان bùnyʌn, مزاج mizāj; (state's) اساس قانون èssāssi-kānūn.

Constitutional, *a.* خلقی khilkī, طوغشدن اولان dòghushdan-òlʌn; اساس قوانینه مطابق اولان èssāssi-kàwānīna-mùtʌbik-òlʌn; مشروط mèshrūt; مقید mùkàyyèd.

Constrain, *v.a.* جبر ا jèbr-et, زورلامق zòrlamak, اجبار ا ìjbār-et.

Constraint, *s.* صیقی siki; صیقندی sikindi; جبر jèbr; حبس hʌbss.

Construct, *v.a.* اعمال ا ì"māl-et, انشا ا ìnshā-et, بنا ا binā-et, یاپمق yàpmak.

Construction, *s.* اعمال "ìmāl, انشا ìnshā; بنا binā, یاپی yàpi.

Consul, *s.* قونسلوس kònsoloss.

Consult, *v.a.* دانشمق dʌnishmak, استشاره ا ìsstishāré-et; — together, *v.n.* مشاوره ا mùshāvéré-et, مشورت ا mèshvérèt-et; (doctors) قونسولتو ا kònsùlto-et.

Consultation, *s.* استشاره ìsstishāré; مشاوره mùshāvéré; مشورت mèshvérèt; قونسولتو kònsùlto.

Consume, *v.a.* بترمك bìtirmek, دوكتمك dùkètmek, یمك yèmek; —, *v.n.* بتمك bìtmek, تلف او tèlef-òl, كتمك ghìtmek.

Consummate, *v.a.* اتمام ا تكميل tèkmīl-et, اتمام ا ìtmĀm-et; —, *a.* مكمل mùkèmmèl.

Consumption, *s.* خرج khàrj; (disease) ورم vÈrEm.

Consumptive, *a.* ورملو vÈrEmli.

Contact, *s.* تماس tèmÀsss, تلاقى tèlākī, اتصال ìttissĀl.

Contagion, *s.* سرايت sìrāyet, بولاشمه bùlàshma, كچمه ghèchma; علت سارية "ìllèti-sārìyyÉ.

Contagious, *a.* سارى sārī, بولاشور bùlàshir, كچر ghèchEr, سرايت ايدر sìrāyet-èdEr.

Contain, *v.a.* المق Àlmak; حاوى او hāvī-òl, شامل او shāmil-òl, مشتمل او mùshtèmīl-òl; ضبط ا zÀbt-et; — one's self, طيانمق dàyanmak.

Contaminate, *v.a.* بوزمق bòzmak, افساد ا ìfsād-et, بولاشدرمق bùlàshdirmak, تلويث ا tèlvīss-et.

Contaminated, *a.* بوزق bòzuk, فاسد fāssid; بولاشق bùlàshik, ملوث mù-lèvvèss. [ìfsād; تلويث tèlvīss.

Contamination, *s.* سرايت sìrāyet; افساد

Contemn, *v.a.* صايمامق sàymamak, استخفاف ا ìsstìkhfāf-et, استحقار ا ìss-tìhkĀr-et. [mùlāhaza-et.

Contemplate, *v.a.* نظر ا nÀzar-et, ملاحظه ا

Contemporary, *s.* and *a.* معاصر mù"Āssir.

Contempt, *s.* استحقار isstìhkĀr; استخفاف ìsstìkhfāf; عدم رعايت "àdÉmi-rì"-āyèt, عدم حرمت "àdÉmi-hùrmèt.

Contemptible, *a.* (person) مستحقر mùss-tàhkàr, ذليل zèlīl, رذيل rèzīl; (thing) لاشى مقوله سى lā-shèy-màkūlÉssi, جزئى jùz'ī.

Contend, *v.n.* نزاع ا nìzā"-et, منازعه ا mùnāza"à-et; ادعا ا ìddi"ā-et.

Content, *a.* راضى rāzī, خشنود khòshnud; قانع kĀni"; —, *v.a.* راضى ا rāzi-et; خشنود ا khòshnud-et, اقناع ا ìknā"-et.

Contention, *s.* نزاع nìzā", منازعه mù-nāza"à, غوغا (kàwgha).

Contentment, *s.* قناعت kĀnā"at.

Contest, *s.* مجادله mùjādélé, مباحثه mùbāhassÉ; —, *v.a.* عناد ا "ìnād-et.

Context, *s.* سياق سباق sìyĀk-sìbĀk.

Contiguous, *a.* متصل mùttÀssil, ملاصق mùlāssik, بتشك bìtishik.

Continence, *s.* عصمت "ìssmèt.

Continent, *s.* قره kĀra, بر bèrr; قطعه kìt"à.

Contingent, *a.* اتفاقى ìttifĀkī, مشكوك mèshkyūk; —, *s.* حصه hìssÉ.

Continual, *a.* متمادى mùtémādī; —ly, *ad.* بلا فاصله bìlā-fĀssila, لا ينقطع lā-yànkÀti".

Continuance, *s.* دوام dèwām, بقا bĀkĀ, استمرار ìsstimrār.

Continue, *v.n.* دوام ا dèwām-et; دائم او dā'im-òl; تكرر ا tèkèrrur-et; —, *v.a.* ابقا ا ìbkā-et; تكرار ا tèkrār-et; الت يانني سويلمك Àlt-yànini-sùwèy-lémek; ينه ياپمق yìnÉ (ghènÉ) yàp-mak.

Contortion, *s.* پيچ وتاب pīch-u-tĀb.

Contraband, *a.* يصاق yàssĀk, ممنوع mèmnū"; كمركدن قاچرمه ghyùm-rukdan-kĀchirma.

Contract, *s.* كوترى پازارلق ghyùturu-pàzarlik, تعهد tà"àhhud; قونطراطو

kònturàto; مقاوله mùkĀvélĖ; —, *v.n.* تعهد ا tà‘‘àhhud-et; كوترى المق ghyù-turu-Ālmak; كوترى ويرمك ghyù-turu-vÈrmek; بوزلمك bùzulmek, چكلمك chèkilmek; دارالمق dĀrĀl-mak, ازالمق ĀzĀlmak; —, *v.a.* الشمق Ālishmak; ايدنمك èdinmek, پيدا ا pèydā-et; عقد ا ‘‘Ākd-et; قاصمق kĀssmak; دارالتمق dàrĀltmak, ازالتمق ĀzĀltmak.

Contraction, *s.* قصالش kìssAlish, چكلش chèkilish, بوزولش bùzulush.

Contractor, *s.* متعهد mùta‘‘àhhid, ملتزم mùltèzim, كوترى الان ghyùturu-ĀlAn.

Contradict, *v.a.* تكذيب ا tèkzīb-et.

Contrariety, *s.* خلاف khìlĀf, عكسيلك ‘‘àksīlik, ترسلك tÈrsslik.

Contrary, *a.* ترس tÈrss, عكسى ‘‘àksī, مخالف mùkhālif, ضد zìdd.

Contrast, *s.* فرق fàrk.

Contravene, *v.a.* خلافنه حركت ا khìlĀ-fina-hàrékÈt-et.

Contribute, *v.n.* ياردم ا yàrdim-et, اعانه ا ì‘‘Ānè-et; —, *v.a.* ويرمك vÈrmek, اعانه ا ì‘‘ānÉ-et. [vīrghyù (vÈrghi).

Contribution, *s.* اعانه ì‘‘ānÉ, ويركو

Contrition, *s.* ندامت nèdāmèt, پشيمانلق pèchīmĀnlik (pìshmĀnlik).

Contrivance, *s.* يول yòl, قولاى kòlay, چاره chārÉ, معرفت mà‘‘rifèt, ايجاد ījād; حيله hīlÉ.

Contrive, *v.a.* ايجاد ا ījād-et, بولمق bùlmak; —, *v.n.* اويدرمق ùydurmak, يولنى بولمق yòlunu-bùlmak, قولاينى بولمق kòlayini-bùlmak.

Control, *s.* امر èmr; ضبط zAbt; اداره ìdārÉ; نظارت nAzārèt; —, *v.a.* ضبط ا zAbt-et; قوللانمق kùllAnmak; اداره ا ìdārÉ-et, نظارت ا nAzārèt-et.

Controversy, *s.* مباحثه mùbāhÉssÉ; مجادله mùjādÉlÉ; منازعه mùnāza‘‘à.

Controvert, *v.a.* تكذيب ا tèkzīb-et.

Contumacious, *a.* متمرد mùtémÈrrid, غير مطيع ghāyri-mùtī‘‘, عاصى ‘‘Āssī.

Contuse, *v.a.* برهلمك bèrÉlemek.

Contusion, *s.* بره bèrÉ.

Convalescence, *s.* افاقت ìfākAt.

Convene, *v.a.* جمع ا jèm‘‘-et, طوپلامق tòplamak.

Convenience, *s.* راحت rāhat, قولايلق kòlaylik; ممشا mèmshà, ابدستخانه àbdesstkhānÉ.

Convenient, *a.* راحت rāhat; قولاى kòlay; قولايلقلو kòlaylikli.

Convent, *s.* قيز مناسطيرى kìz-mĀnàsstīri.

Convention, *s.* عهد ‘‘àhd, معاهده mù-‘‘āhÉdÉ, مقاوله mùkāvélÉ.

Converge, *v.n.* طوپلانمق tòplanmak, برلشمك bìrleshmek, يقينلشمق yà-kinlashmak.

Conversation, *s.* صحبت sòhbet, لقردى làkirdi, لاف lĀf.

Converse, *v.n.* صحبت ا sòhbet-et, لقردى ا làkirdi-et, لاف ا làf-et, سويلشمك sùwèylEshmek; —, *s.* عكس ‘‘àkss, ترس tÈrss.

Convert, *s.* مهتدى mùhtédī; —, *v.a.* اهتدايه كتورمك ìhtidāyÉ-ghètirmek; چويرمك chèvirmek, دوندرمك dùn-dErmek.

Convex, *a.* محدب mŭhàddèb, تومسك tùmsèk, قبه وارى kŭbbĕvārī.

Convey, *v.a.* (carry) نقل ا nÂkl-et; كتورمك ghètirmek; كوترمك ghyù-turmek; (communicate) تبليغ ا tè-blīgh-et; (a meaning) افاده ا ìfādé-et, قالدرمق kÂldirmak.

Convict, *s.* پرانغه لو prànghali; —, *v.a.* جنحه سنى اثبات ا jŭnhàssini-ìssbÂt-et.

Conviction, *s.* جزم jèzm, علم اليقين "ìlmŭ-'l-yàkīn; اثبات جنحه ìssbÂti--jŭnhà.

Convince, *v.a.* قاندرمق kàndirmak, الزام ا ìlzām-et, اسكات ا ìsskyāt-et, اقناع ا ìknā"-et. [-jèm"-et.

Convoke, *v.a.* دعوتله جمع ا dà"vètla-

Convoy, *v.a.* قونبوى ا convoy-et; رفاقت ا rèfākÂt-et; —, *s.* قونبوى كميسى convoy-ghèmissi.

Convulsion, *s.* تشنج tèshènnuj.

Cook, *s.* اشجى Âshji; —, *v.n.* پشمك pìshmek; —, *v.a.* پشورمك pìshirmek.

Cool, *a.* سرين sèrin; (brave) جسور jèssūr; (impudent) عارسز "ārsiz; —, *s.* سرينلك sèrinlik; —, *v.n.* صوغومق sò-ghumak; —, *v.a.* صوغوتمق sòghutmak.

Coolness, *s.* سرينلك sèrinlik; جسارت jèssārèt; عارسزلق "ārsizlik; (want of affection) برودت bŭrūdèt.

Coop, *s.* كومس kyùmèss.

Cooper, *s.* فوچيلجى fìchiji.

Co-operate, *v.n.* برلكده ايش كورمك bìrlikdé-ìsh-ghyùrmek.

Co-operation, *s.* معاونت mŭ"āvénèt.

Copal, *s.* صندروس sÂndaròss.

Copious, *a.* بول bòl, بركتلو bèrékÈtli.

Copper, *s.* (metal) باقر bÂkir; (boiler) قزغان kÂzghĀn (kÂzan).

Copperas, *s.* (blue) كوزطاشى ghyùz-tÂ-shi; (green) زاج قبريس zĀji-kìbriss.

Copt, *s.* قبطى kìbtī.

Coptic, *a.* قبطى لسانى kìbtī-lìssāni.

Copulate, *v.n.* سكشمك sìkishmek, جماع ا jìmā"-et, چفتلشمك chìftlishmek.

Copy, *s.* (model of writing) مشق mèshk; (writing - exercise) قره لمه kÂralama; (sample of scholar's wri-ting) تعليم tà"līm; (of a book) نسخه nŭsskha; (of a writing) صورت sūrÈt; (of a drawing) عين "àyn, اورنك ùrnèk; —, *v.a.* (imitate) تقليد ا tÂk-līd-et; (a writing) يازمق *or* چيقارمق *or* صورتنى المق sūrÈtini-Âlmak, *or* chìkàrmak, *or* yàzmak; (a drawing, &c.) عيننى المق "àynini - Âlmak, اورنكنى المق ùrnèghini-Âlmak.

Coral, *s.* مرجان mÈrjĀn.

Cord, *s.* ايپ ìp. [ìksīr.

Cordial, *a.* صميمى sàmīmī; —, *s.* اكسير

Cordovan, *s.* تلاتين tèlātīn.

Core, *s.* ايچ ìch.

Corfu, *s.* كورفز kyurfez; قورفه kòrfa.

Coriander, *s.* كشنش kìshnish.

Cork, *s.* منطار mÀntàr; (stopper) طپا tÂpa. [tÂpa-àchajak.

Corkscrew, *s.* بورغى bŭrghu, طپا اچه جق

Corn, *s.* بوغداى bòghday, حنطه hìnta, ذخيره zàkhīré; (for horses) اريه àrpa; (on the foot) نصر nÂssir; (grain) دانه dāné (tāné).

Cornel-berry, *s.* قزلجق kìzìljìk.
Cornelian, *s.* عقيق "àkīk.
Corner, *s.* كوشه kyùshé.
Cornice, *s.* پرواز pèrwàz.
Corollary, *s.* نتيجه nètījé.
Coronation, *s.* تتويج tètwīj, تتوج tè-[tèvvùj.
Coronet, *s.* تاج tāj.
Corporal, *s.* اونباشی ònbàshi; —, *a.* جسمانی jìssmānī; — punishment, طياق dàyak.
Corporation, *s.* اهالی àhālī; مجلس mèj-liss, شوری shūrà; اصناف èssnāf.
Corporeal, *a.* جسمانی jìssmānī.
Corps, *s.* بلوك bùluk; طابور tàbur; الای àlay; لوا lìwā; طاقم tàkim.
Corpse, *s.* جنازه jènāzé, جسد jèssed.
Corpulent, *a.* ششمان shìshmàn, ملحم mùlàhhàm.
Correct, *a.* طوغری dòghru, صحيح sàhīh, تام tàmm, تمام tàmām; —, *v.a.* طوغرلتمق dòghrultmak, تصحيح ا tàsshīh-et.
Correspond, *v.n.* (by letter) مكتوبلشمك mèktublèshmek, مخابره ا mùkhābéré-et, مكاتبه ا mùkyātébé-et; (in quality) اويمق ùymak, مطابق كلمك mùtābik-ghèlmek.
Correspondence, *s.* مكاتبه mùkyātébé; مطابقت mùtābakàt. [mùkhbir.
Correspondent, *s.* مخابر mūkhābir, مخبر
Corroborate, *v.a.* تصديق ا tàssdīk-et; تقويت ا tàkvìyyèt-et, تأكيد ا tè'kīd-[-et.
Corroboration, *s.* تصديق tassdik.
Corroborative, *a.* مصدق mùssàddik; مقوی mùkàvvī.
Corrode, *v.a.* يمك yèmek, چوروتمك chùrutmek, پاصلاندرمق pàsslan-dìr-mak.
Corrupt, *a.* (bad) فاسد fāssid, بوزق bòzuk; (mercenary) رشوت ير rìshvèt-yèr; —, *v.a.* بوزمق bòzmak, افساد ا ìfsād-et; (with money) رشوت ويرمك rìshvèt-vèrmek, پاره يدرمك pāré (pàra)-yèdirmek.
Corruption, *s.* بوزمقلق bòzmaklik, چوروتمكلك chùrutmeklik.
Corsair, *s.* دكز خرسزی dèngiz-khìrsizi.
Corselet, *s.* كوكسلك زره ghyùksslik-zìrh.
Corset, *s.* قورسته kórseté.
Cortege, *s.* الای àlay.
Corvette, *s.* قوروت kùrvèt.
Cosecant, *s.* تمام قاطع tàmāmi-kāti".
Cosey, *a.* راحت rāhat.
Cosine, *s.* تمام جيب tàmāmi-jèyb.
Cossack, *s.* قزاق kìzāk.
Coss-lettuce, *s.* مارول mārul.
Cost, *s.* بها bàhā (pàha); مصرف màssràf; —, *v.a.* اولمق òlmak.
Costiveness, *s.* انقباض ìnkìbàz.
Costly, *a.* بهالو pàhali; مكلف mùkèllìf.
Costume, *s.* قيافت kìyāfèt.
Cot, *s.* قلبه kùlubé, اوجكز èvjèghiz.
Cotangent, *s.* تمام مماس tàmāmi-mùmàsss.
Cotemporary, *s* and *a.* معاصر mù"àssir.
Cottage, *s.* كوی اوی kyùy-èvi.
Cotton, *s.* پاموق pàmuk (pàmbuk), پنبه pènbé.
Couch, *s.* مندر mìnder; قناپه kànapé; دوشك dùshèk, يتاق yàtak.

Cough, *s.* اوكسرك ùksuruk ; —, *v.n.* اوكسرمك ùksurmek.

Council, *s.* مجلس mèjliss.

Councillor, *s.* اعضاى مجلسدن اولان à"zāyi-mèjlissdan-òlan ; مستشار mùsstéshār.

Counsel, *s.* نصيحت nàssīhàt, اوكوت ùghut ; —, *v.a.* عقل اوكرتمك "àkl-ùghrètmek, نصيحت ا nàssīhàt-et.

Count, *s.* رتبهٔ ثالثه بكى rùtbé'i-sālissé-bèghi ; —, *v.a.* صايمق sāymak ; —, *v.n.* صايلمق sàyilmak.

Countenance, *s.* يوز yùz, چهره chèhré, منظر mànzar, سيما sīmā.

Counter, *s.* پول pùl ; (of a shop) پيشتخته pèshtàkhta ; (who counts) صاييجى sàyiji ; (opposite) قارشى kàrshi. [چاره بولمق charé-bùlmak.

Counteract, *v.a.* بوزمق bòzmak, چاره

Counterbalance, *v.a.* قارشيلق او kàrshilik-òl.

Counterfeit, *a.* قالپ kàlp, ساخته sākhté ; —, *s.* تقليد tàklīd ; —, *v.a.* تقليد ا tàklīd-et.

Counterfeiter, *s.* قالپزن kàlpazàn, ساخته كار sākhtékyār.

Countermand, *v.a.* امرينى كيرو المق èmrini-ghèri-àlmak, ياپلمسون ديو تنبيه ا yàpilmassin-dèyu-tènbīh-et.

Countermarch, *s.* كيرو دونش ghèri-dùnush.

Counterpane, *s.* يورغان yùrghan.

Counterpart, *s.* عين "àyn.

Counterpoise, *s.* قارشيلق kàrshilik.

Countersign, *v.a.* شهادت ايچون امضا قومق shàdādet-ìchun-ìmzā-kòmak ; —, *s.* پاروله pārola. [ghaza.

Counting-house, *s.* اوطه òda, مغازه mà-

Country, *s.* (native) وطن wàtan, ولايت wìlāyèt (wìlā'at) ; (territory) مملكت mèmlékèt, الكا ùlkyā (ùlké) ; (out of town) كوى kyùy ; چفتلك chìftlik ; (open —) صحرا sàhrā, قير kìr.

Countryman, *s.* كويلو kyùylu ; (fellow —) همشهرى hèmshèhri.

County, *s.* سنجاق sànjak, لوا lìwā.

Couple, *s.* چفت chìft.

Couplet, *s.* بيت bèyt. [yìghitlik.

Courage, *s.* جسارت jèssārèt, يكيتلك

Courageous, *a.* يكيت yìghit, جسور jèssūr. [kùriyèl.

Courier, *s.* تتار tàtār, منزل mènzil, قوريل

Course, *s.* (whole time) مدت mùddèt ; (of studies) صره درسلر sìra-dèrssler ; of —, البته èlbètté.

Court, *s.* (royal) سراى sàray, مابين mābèyn ; ديوان dīwān, ركاب rìkyāb, بينش bīnish ; (of justice) محكمه mèhkémé ; (martial) ديوان حرب dīwān-i-hàrb ; — plaster, جانفس ياقيسى jàmfèss-yàkissi ; — yard, حولى hàvli ; to pay —, *v.n.* عرض عبوديت ا "àrzi-"ùbūdìyyèt-et, ال اوپمك èl-ùpmek, اياق اوپمك àyak-ùpmek, اتك اوپمك ètek-ùpmek.

Courteous, *a.* نوازشلو nùwāzishli, خاطر نواز khātir-nùwāz.

Courtesy, *s.* خاطر نوازلق khātir-nùwāzlik.

Cousin, *s.* عموجه اوغلى "àmuja-òghlu, داى اوغلى day-òghlu, &c.

Cove, *s.* کورفز kyùrfez, قوی kòy.
Covenant, *s.* عهد "àhd, قول kàvl, مقاوله mùkāvélé.
Cover, *s.* اورتی ùrtu; (case) قاپ kāp; (lid) قپاق kāpak; (shelter) بارینه‌جق‌یر bàrinajak-yèr; —, *v.a.* اورتمك ùrtmek; قاپلامق kāplamak; قپامق kāpamak.
Covering, *s.* اورتی àrtu.
Coverlet, *s.* یورغان yùrghan.
Covert, *a.* ال التنده Èl-altinda, کیزلو ghìzli, صاقلو sàkli, خفی khāfī.
Covet, *v.a.* کوز دیکمك ghyùz-dìkmek, طمع ا tāmà"-et.
Covetous, *a.* طمعکار tāmà"kyār, حریص hàrīss, اچ کوزلو àj-ghyùzlu.
Covetousness, *s.* طمعکارلك tāma"kyārlik.
Cow, *s.* اینك īnek; —, *v.a.* قورقوتمق kòrkutmak.
Coward, *s.* قورقاق kòrkàk.
Cowkeeper, *s.* صوتجی sūtji.
Cowl, *s.* قپوط باشلغی kāput-bāshlighi, باشلق bāshlik.
Crab, *s.* ینکچ yènghèch, چغانوس chàghanòss; یبانی الما yàbānī-èlma.
Crack, *s.* چاتلاق chàtlāk, یارق yàrik; پاتلایش pātlayish; اورش wùrush; —, *v.n.* چاتلامق chàtlamak, یاریلمق yàrīlmak, پاتلامق pātlamak; —, *v.a.* چاتلاتمق chàtlatmak, یارمق yàrmak, پاتلاتمق pātlatmak.
Cracked, *a.* چاتلاق chàtlāk, یارق yàrik; (mad) چالق chālik, قاچق kāchik.
Cracker, *s.* پاتلانغیچ pātlanghìch.
Cradle, *s.* بشك bèshik.
Craft, *s.* (trade) صنعت sàn"àt; (cunning) حیله hīlé; (shipping) تکنه tèkné, قایق kàyik.
Crafty, *a.* حیله‌کار hīlékyār, شیطان shèytān, دوباره‌جی dūbāraji.
Cram, *v.a.* صیقی طولدرمق sìki-dòldurmak.
Cramp, *s.* سکیرلر طوتلمسی sìngirler-tùtulmassi; —, *v.a.* صیقمق sìkmak.
Cramp-iron, *s.* کینت kìnèt.
Crane, *s.* (bird) طورنه tùrna; (machine) ماچونه màchūna.
Crank, *s.* ال Èl, قول kòl, دیرسك dìrsèk; —, *a.* قولای دوریلور kòlay-dèvrilir.
Crape, *s.* بورنجك bùrunjuk.
Cravat, *s.* بویون باغی bòyun-bāghi.
Crawfish, Crayfish, *s.* بوجك bùjek.
Crawl, *v.n.* یره سورینه‌رك یوریمك yèra-sùrunérek-yùrumek; اغر یوریمك àghir-yùrumek.
Crazy, *a.* (mad) قاچق kāchik; (tumble-down) یقله‌جق yìkilajak, (ship) باته‌جق bātajak.
Creak, *v.n.* چاتردامق chàtirdamak, غجردامق ghìjirdamak.
Cream, *s.* سود یوزی sùd-yùzu; (clotted —) قایمق kàymak.
Crease, *v.a.* قیرمق kìrmak; —, *s.* قیرم kìrim, قیرمه kìrma.
Create, *v.a.* یراتمق yàrātmak, وارا vàr-et, خلق ا khàlk-et; (appoint to a rank or office) نصب ا nāssb-et, ایتمك ètmek.
Creation, *s.* (act of) یرادش yàrādish, خلق khàlk; (being created) یرادیلش yàrādilish, خلقت khàlkat,

آفرينش āférīnish ; (thing created) مخلوق màkhlūk ; (all creation) عالم "ālem ; (of officers) نصب nàssb.

Creator, *s.* يراديجى yàràdiji, خالق khālik, بارى bārī, آفريننده àférī-nendé, آفرين āférīn.

Creature, *s.* مخلوق màkhlūk. [ì"tibār.

Credence, *s.* اعتماد ì"timād, اعتبار

Credentials, *s. pl.* اعتمادنامه ì"timād--nāmé. [ويرهسيه vèréssiyé.

Credit, *s.* اعتبار ì"tibār ; on —,

Creditable, *a.* Creditably, *ad.* ايو īyi, كوزل ghyùzel, اعلا à"là.

Creditor, *s.* الهجقلو àlajakli.

Creed, *s.* ايمن īmān ; آمنت āmèntù.

Creek, *s.* بوغاز bòghàz, اغز àghz ; چاى chày, دره dèré. [rek-yùrumek.

Creep, *v.n.* سورينهرك يوريمك sùruné-

Cremation, *s.* احراق ìhrāk.

Creole, *s.* ملز mèlez.

Crescent, *s.* (new moon) هلال hilāl ; (decoration) اى ày ; (placed on spires, &c.) علم "àlem. [صو ترهسى sù-tèréssi.

Cress, *s.* تره اوتى tèré-òtu ; water —,

Crest, *s.* (ridge) صرت sìrt.

Cretan, *s.* and *a.* كريدلو Ghìrìdli.

Crete, *s.* كريد Ghìrìd.

Crevice, *s.* ارالق àralìk, چاتلاق chàt-

Crew, *s.* طائفه tā'ifé. [làk, يارق yàrìk.

Cricket, *s.* (insect) چكركه chèkirghé.

Crier, *s.* دلال dèllāl, منادى mùnādi.

Crime, *s.* قباحت kàbāhat, جنحه jùnhà, جرم jùrm, صوچ sùch.

Criminal, *s.* قباحتلو kàbāhatli, قباحت صاحبى kàbāhat-sāhibi, مجرم mùjrim ; —, *a.* (wrong) قبيح kàbīh, خبيث khàbīss. [قرمزى kìrmizi.

Crimson, *a.* آل àl, كوس ghùwèss,

Cripple, *s.* سقط sàkat ; —, *v.a.* قولنى قناديني قيرمق kòlunu-kànadini-kìrmak.

Crisis, *s.* (of disease) بحران bùhrān ; (of events) نازك وقت nāzik-wàkit.

Crisp, *a.* كورك ghèvrèk.

Criterion, *s.* معيار mì"yār, محك mà-

Criticise, *v.a.* جرح ا jèrh-et. [hèkk.

Criticism, *s.* جرح jèrh. [-mèmlékèti.

Croatia, *s.* خروات مملكتى Khìrvāt-

Croatian, *s.* and *a.* خروات Khìrvāt.

Crockery, *s.* چناق چوملك chànak-

Crocodile, *s.* تمساح tìmsāh. [chùmlek.

Crocus, *s.* (flower) چيك دم chìgh-dèm.

Crooked, *a.* اكرى èghri, چارپق chàrpìk.

Crop, *s.* (produce) محصول màhsūl, حاصلات hāssìlāt ; (bird's) قورصاق kùrsàk ; —, *v.a.* كسمك kèssmek, بچمك bìchmek, قرقمق kìrkmak ; (trees) بودامق bùdamak.

Cross, *s.* حاچ hàch, چارميخ chàrmìkh ; —, *a.* تتيز tìtiz, ترس tèrss, ارغين dàrghin ; —, *v.a.* كچمك ghèchmek.

Crossbow, *s.* تاتار اوقى tàtar-òku.

Crosslegged, *ad.* to sit —, باغداش قورمق bàghdash-kùrmak.

Crosspatch, *s.* ترس و خويسز دارغين كمسه tèrss-vé-khūysiz-dàrghìn-kìmsé.

Crosstree, *s.* قورجته kùrchèta.

Crossway, *s.* صاپه يول sàpa-yòl.

Crotchet, *s.* (fancy) مراق mèràk.

Crow, *s.* قارغه kàrgha ; cock's —,

خروس أوتمسی khòross-ùtméssi ; —, *v.n.* أوتمك ùtmek.

Crowbar, *s.* تیمور قول (dèmir)-kòl.

Crowd, *s.* قلبالق *or* غلبه‌لق (kālabālik), أزدحام ìzdihām ; —, *v.a.* صیق قومق sìk-kòmak ; —, *v.n.* صیقشمق sì-kishmak.

Crown, *s.* (regal) تاج tāj ; (of head) دپه (tèpé) ; —, *v.a.* (king) تتویج ا tètvīj-et, تاج کیدرمك tāj-ghìdirmek ; (heights) دپه یه عسکر چیقمق (tèpéyé)-"āsskɛr-chìkmak.

Crucible, *s.* پوته pūtā.

Crucifix, *s.* حاچ hāch.

Crucifixion, *s.* حاچه کرلمسی hāché-ghè-relmassi.

Crucify, *v.a.* حاچه‌کرمك hācha-ghèr-mek, چارمیخه‌کرمك chàrmìkha-ghèr-mek.

Crude, *a.* خام khām.

Cruel, *a.* مرحمتسز mèrhàmetsiz, انسانیتسز ìnsānìyyètsiz, جفاکار jèfākyār.

Cruise, *s.* (at sea) سفر sèfɛr, وولته vòlta ; —, *v.n.* وولته‌اورمق vòlta-wūrmak.

Cruiser, *s.* کمی ghèmi.

Crumb, *s.* (not crust) اتمك ایچی (èkmek)-ìchi ; —, (fragment) اتمك اوفاغی èkmek-ūfāghi.

Crumple, *v.a.* بوروشدرمق būrushdurmak, أزمك èzmek.

Crupper, *s.* صغری sàghri.

Crush, *v.a.* ازمك èzmek.

Crust, *s.* قابوق kābuk.

Crutch, *s.* قولتق دینکی kòltuk-dèynéghi.

Cry, *s.* سس sèss, صدا sādā ; ندا nìdā, باغرمه bàghirma ; —, *v.n.* ندا ا nìdā-et, حیقرمق hàykirmak, باغرمق bà-ghirmak, چاغرمق chàghirmak ; (weep) اغلامق àghlamak ; — out, حیقرمق hàykirmak, باغرمق bàghirmak ; — aloud, ندا ا nìdā-et, باغرمق bàghirmak, چاغرمق chàghirmak ; — up, مدح ا mèdh-et, ثنا ا sènā-et.

Crypt, *s.* بدروم bòdurum, یرالتی کمرلر yèr-ālti-kèmɛrlɛr.

Crystal, *s.* بللور bīllūr ; (of salts) ایکنه ìghné.

Cube, *s.* مکعب mùkyà""āb.

Cuckold, *s.* پزونك pèzéwènk, کراته kèrātà.

Cuckoo, *s.* قوغوق قوشی kūghuk-kùshu.

Cucumber, *s.* خیار khìyār.

Cud, *s.* کو ghèv ; to chew the —, *v.n.* کو کتورمك ghèv-ghètirmek.

Cuddle, *v.a.* صارلمق sārìlmak.

Cudgel, *s.* صوپه sòpa.

Cue, *s.* ایپ اوجی ìp-ūju.

Culpable, *a.* (person) صوچلو sùchlu, قباحتلو kābāhatli ; (act) فنا fēna, کریه kèrīh.

Culprit, *s.* صوچلو sùchlu, قباحتلو kābā-hatli, مجرم mùjrim.

Cultivate, *v.a.* (sow) اکمك èkmek ; (plant) دکمك dìkmek ; (the ground) حراست ا hìrāssèt-et, زراعت ا zìrā"at-et ; (science, &c.) اشتغال ا ìshtighāl-et, مشغول او mèshghūl-ol, چالشمق chālishmak.

Cultivation, *s.* زراعت zìrā"at ; اشتغال ìshtigāl.

Cumbersome, Cumbrous, *a.* حنطال hāntāl.

Cummin, *s.* کمون kèmmūn (kìmiyòn).

Cunning, *a.* شیطان shèytān, اورستپوللو òrosstopòllu; —, *s.* شیطانلق shèytānlik.

Cunt, *s.* ام ām, فرج fèrj, کس kyùss.

Cup, *s.* فنجان fìnjān (filjān); —, *v.a.* حجامت ا hājāmèt-et (hājāmat).

Cupbearer, *s.* ساقی sākī.

Cupboard, *s.* طولاب dòlab.

Cupid, *s.* عشق "āshk.

Cupidity, *s.* طمع tāmà", حرص hìrss.

Cupola, *s.* قبه kùbbé.

Cupper, *s.* حجامتجی (hājāmātji).

Cupping-glass, *s.* حجامت جامی (hājamāt)-jàmi; — horn, بوینوز bòynuz.

Curaçoa, *s.* کراسوا kèrasòa.

Curb, *v.a.* ضبط ا zābt-et, اغزینه‌کم اورمق āghzina-ghèm-wùrmak.

Curdle, *v.n.* کسلمك kèssilmek.

Cure, *v.a.* ایوا īyi-et; اصلاح ا ìsslāh-et.

Curiosity, *s.* (rare thing) تحاف شی tùhāf-shèy; عنتیقه "àntīka; (inquisitiveness) مراق mèrāk.

Curious, *a.* (surprising) عجیب "ājīb ("ājā'ib), غریب ghàrīb; (rare) تحاف tùhāf; (inquisitive) مراقلو mèrākli, هرشی‌صورار hèr-shèy-sòrar.

Curl, *s.* (of hair) زلف zùlf; (general) قیوریم kìvrim, بوکلم bùklum; —, *v.a.* قیویرمق kìvirmak, بوکمك bukmek; —, *v.n.* قیوریلمق kìvrilmak, بوکلمك bùkulmek.

Currant, *s.* (fresh) فرنك اوزومی firènk-ùzumu; (dried) قوش اوزومی kùsh-ùzumu. [rā'ij, متداول mùtédāvèl.

Current, *s.* اقندی ākindi; —, *a.* رائج

Curry, *v.a.* (comb) تیمار ا tīmār-et; — favour, *v.n.* یلتاقلنمق yāltāklanmak.

Currycomb, *s.* طراق tàrak, ات طراغی àt-tàràghi.

Curse, *s.* لعنت là"nèt, بددعا bèd-dù"ā; —, *v.a.* لعنت ا là"nèt-et, لعنت اوقومق là"nèt-òkumàk.

Cursed, *a.* ملعون mèl"ūn.

Cursory, *a.* مختصر mùkhtāssàr.

Curtail, *v.a.* قصالتمق kìssaltmak.

Curtain, *s.* پرده pèrdé.

Curve, *a.* منحنی mùnhànī; curve-line, خط منحنی khātti-mùnhànī.

Cushion, *s.* یاصدق yàssdik, (cylindrical) بالین bàlin; (seat) مندر mìnder.

Custom, *s.* عادت "ādèt.

Customer, *s.* مشتری mùshtèri.

Custom-house, *s.* کمرك ghyùmruk; — duty, کمرك ghyùmruk, رسم کمرك rèss-mi-ghyùmruk; — officer, کمرکجی ghyùmrukju, دیده‌بان dīdébān.

Cut, *v.a.* کسمك kèssmek, قطع ا kāt"-et; —, *s.* (wound) یاره yàra; (shape) بچم bìchim.

Cutlass, *s.* قلج kìlij. [بچم bìchim.

Cutler, *s.* (knife) بچاقجی bìchākji; (penknife) قلمتراشجی kālemtràshji; (sword) قلججی kìlìjji.

Cutter, *s.* (who cuts) دوغرایجی dòghrayìji; (knife) بچاق bìchāk; (ship) قوتره kòtra.

Cut-throat, *s.* قاتل kātil; قانلو قاتل [kānli-kātil.

Cycle, *s.* دائره dā'iré.

Cylinder, *s.* اسطوانه ùsstuwāné.

Cypress, *s.* سلوی sèlvi, سرو sèrv.

Cyprus, *s.* قبرس Kìbrìs.

D.

Dab down, *v.a.* أتمق atmak, اتيويرمك ativermek, براقيويرمك brakivermek.

Dabble, *v.n.* اوينامق oynamak; قارشمق karishmak.

Dad, Daddy, *s.* باباجق babajik.

Daffodil, *s.* التون طوب altin-top.

Dagger, *s.* خنجر khanjer (khanchar).

Daily, *a.* هر كونكى her-ghunki, يومى yuvmi; —, *ad.* كونده بر ghyundé-bir; هركون her-ghyun.

Dalmatia, *s.* دالمچيا Dalmachia.

Dam, *s.* (mother) انا ana; (of earth) سد sedd; —, *v.a.* سد ايله ضبط ا sedd-ila-zabt-et. [خسارت khassaret.

Damage, *s.* ضرر zarar, زيان ziyan,

Damages, *s. pl.* تضمينات tazminat.

Damascus, *s.* دمشق Damashk.

Damask, *s.* داماسقو damassko; — rose, مورگل mor-ghyul.

Damn, *v.a.* جهنمه كوندرمك jihennéma-ghyundermek; damn you, جهنم اول jihennem-ol.

Damned, *a.* جهنملك jihennemlik.

Damp, *a.* and *s.* نم nem; *a.* نمناك nem-nak (nemlak), رطوبتلو rutubetli; —, *s.* رطوبت rutubet; —, *v.a.* نملتمك nemletmek, اصلاتمق isslatmak;

Damsel, *s.* قيز kiz. [صوغوتمق soghutmak.

Damson, *s.* موردم اريكى murdum-erighi.

Dance, *s.* حوره hora; —, *v.n.* حوره تپمك hora-tepmek, رقص ا rakss-et.

Dandelion, *s.* هندبا hindiba.

Dane, *s.* دانيمارقه لو Danimarkali.

Danger, *s.* تهلكه tehliké, قورقو korku, مخاطره mukhatara.

Dangerous, *a.* قورقولو korkulu, تهلكه لو tehlikeli, مخاطره لو mukhatarali.

Dangle, *v.n.* صارقمق sarkmak.

Danube, *s.* طونا Tuna.

Dapple-grey, *a.* بقله قيرى bakla-kiri.

Dardanelles, *s.* چناق قلعه سى Chanak-kalessi.

Dare, *v.n.* جسارت ا jessaret-et, جرئت ا jur'et-et; —, *v.a.* ياپه مزسين ديو قيزدرمق yapamazsin-deyu-kizdirmak.

Daring, *a.* جسور jessur, يكيت yighit; —, *s.* جسارت jessaret, يكيتلك yighitlik.

Dark, *a.* قرانلق karanlik; — lantern, خرسز فنارى khirsiz-feneri. [zulmet.

Darkness, *s.* قرانلق karanlik, ظلمت

Darling, *s.* ايكى كوز iki-ghyuz, نورعين nuri-"ayn, جكركوشه jigher-kyushé.

Darn, *v.a.* اورمك urmek.

Dart, *s.* جريد jirid; —, *v.a.* اتمق atmak; —, *v.n.* اتلمق atilmak.

Dash, *v.a.* پارچه پارچه ا parcha-parcha-et; چالمق chalmak, چارپمق charpmak, اورمق wurmak.

Dastard, *s.* قورقاق korkak.

Date, *s.* (fruit) خرما khurma; (epoch) تاريخ tarikh; —, *v.a.* تاريخ قومق tarikh-komak.

Daub, *v.a.* بولاشدرمق bulashdirmak.

Daughter, *s.* قيز kiz, كريمه kerimé; — in-law, كلين ghelin.

Daunt, *v.a.* قورقوتمق korkutmak.

Dawn, *s.* شفق shafak, اورطه لق اغرمسى

òrtalìk-ȧgharmassi, فجر fèjir; —, v.n. اغرمغه باشلامق ȧgharmagha-bȧshlamak; سچلمکه باشلامق sèchil-meghé-bȧshlamak.
Day, s. كون ghyùn, يوم yùvm, روز rūz; — before yesterday, اولسی كون èvvèlsi-ghyùn; — after to-morrow, اوبركون ò-bìr-ghyùn.
Daybreak, s. v. Dawn. [dèlikji.
Day-labourer, s. كوندهلكجى ghyùn-
Daylight, s. ايدينلق àydìnlìk, كوندوزايدينلغى ghyùnduz-àydìnlìghi.
Daytime, s. كوندوز ghyùnduz.
Dazzle, v.a. كوز قماشدرمق ghyùz-kà-mȧshdìrmak, كوز المق ghyùz-ȧlmak.
Dead, a. اولو ùlu, اولمش ùlmush, مرد mùrd, مرده mùrdé, متوفا mùtéwèffà.
Deadly, a. مهلك mùhlìk, اولدرمه درجه سنده مضر ùldurma-dèréjéssinda-mùzìrr.
Deaf, a. صاغر sàghìr, ايشتمز ìshitmàz.
Deafness, s. صاغرلق sàghìrlìk.
Deal, s. چوق chòk; (wood) چام chȧm; —, v.a. طاغتمق dȧghìtmak; — in, v.n. صاتمق sȧtmak, تجارتنى ا tìjā-rètini-et. [ghyàn.
Dealer, s. صاتيجى sȧtìji, بازركان bȧzìr-
Dear, a. (in price) بهالو (pȧhalì); (in affection) عزيز ''ȧzīz.
Dear me! int. عجائب ''ȧjāib.
Dearth, s. بهالولق pȧhalìlìk, قيتلق kìtlìk, قحط kàht, غلا ghìlā.
Death, s. اولم ùlum, موت mèvt, وفات wèfāt, مرك mèrgh, هلاك hèlāk.
Debark, v.n. كميدن چيقمق ghèmìdan-chìkmak; —, v.a. كميدن چيقارمق ghèmìdan-chìkarmak, قره يه دوكمك kȧraya-dùkmek.
Debate, s. مشورت mèshvérèt; —, v.a. مشاوره ا mùshāvéré-et, لقرديسنى ا làkìrdìssìnì-et, مباحثه ا mùbāhéssé-et.
Debauch, s. عياشلق ''àyyāshlìk; —, v.a. ايارتمق àyartmak, افساد ا ìfsād-et.
Debauchery, s. عياشلق ''àyyāshlìk, چاپقينلق chȧpkìnlìk.
Debilitate, v.a. ضعيف ا zà''īf-et, ضعيفلتمق zà''īflatmak. [zà''īflik.
Debility, s. ضعف zà''f, ضعيفلق
Debt, s. بورج bòrj, دين dèyn.
Debtor, s. بورجلو bòrjlu, مديون mèdyūn.
Decadence, s. زوال zèwāl.
Decamp, v.n. صاوشمق sàwushmak, قاچمق kȧchmak, فرار ا fìrār-et.
Decanter, s. صراحى sùrāhī.
Decapitate, v.a. بويوننى اورمق bòyunu-nu-wùrmak, باشنى كسمك bȧshìni-kèssmek.
Decay, s. زوال zèwāl; فساد fèssȧd; —, v.n. بوزلمق bòzulmak, چورومك chùrumek, زوال بولمق zèwāl-bùlmak.
Decease, s. وفات wèfāt; —, v.n. اولمك ùlmek, وفات ا wèfāt-et.
Deceased, a. متوفا mùtéwèffà, مرحوم mèrhūm. [kìzb.
Deceit, s. يلانجيلق yàlȧnjìlìk, كذب
Deceitful, a. يلانجى yàlȧnjì, كاذب kyāzib; ايكى يوزلو ìki-yùzlu.
Deceive, v.a. الداتمق ȧldatmak, اويون ا òyun-et, حيله ا hìlé-et.
December, s. كانون اول kyānūni-èvvel.

Decency, *s.* ادب èdeb, حيا hàyā.

Decent, *a.* تميز tèmiz ; ادبلو èdebli.

Deception, *s.* حيله hīlé, اويون òyun ; الدادش aldàdish ; الدانش aldànish.

Deceptive, *a.* ادمی الدادر adami-aldàdir.

Decide, *v.a.* فصل ا fassl-et, قرارلشدرمق kararlashdirmak ; —, *v.n.* قرار ويرمك karar-vèrmek.

Decimal, *a.* اعشاری à''shārī.

Decipher, *v.a.* چيقارمق chìkàrmak, اوقومق òkumak, سوكمك sùkmek.

Decision, *s.* قرار karar ; متانت mètānèt.

Decisive, *a.* قطعی kat''ī, بترر bìtirir.

Deck, *s.* كوكرته ghyùghèrté ; —, *v.a.* دوناتمق dònatmak, تزيين ا tèzyīn-et, بزه‌مك bèzémek.

Decker, two-decker, *s.* قپاق kàpak ; three-decker, *s.* اوچ انبارلی ùch-ànbàrli. [افاده ìfādé.

Declaration, *s.* تقرير takrīr ; بيان bèyān,

Declare, *v.a.* بيان ا bèyān-et, افاده ا ìfādé-et ; تقرير ا takrīr-et, سويلمك sùwèylé-mek. [the needle) انحطاط ìnhitāt.

Declination, *s.* (astr.) ميل mèyl ; (of

Decline, *s.* زوال zèwāl ; انحراف ìn-hirāf ; *v.a.* قبول ايتمامك kabūl-ètmamek, رد ا rèdd-et ; كيرشمامك ghìrishmamek ; —, *v.n.* زوال بولمق zèwāl-būlmak ; منحرف او mùn-hàrif-ol, بوزلمق bòzulmak, مختل او mŭkhtèll-òl. [باير bàyir.

Declivity, *s.* انش ènish, يوقش yòkush,

Decoction, *s.* شربت shèrbèt, صو sù.

Decompose, *v.a.* حل ا hàll-et; چوروتمك chùrutmek ; *v.n.* چورومك chùrumek.

Decorate, *v.a.* تزيين ا tèzyīn-et, بزه‌مك bèzémek. [nìshān.

Decoration, *s.* تزيين tèzyīn ; نشان

Decoy, *s.* طوزاق tùzak ; —, *v.a.* طوزاغه دوشرمك tùzagha-dùshurmek.

Decrease, *s.* اكسلش èksilish ; —, *v.n.* اكسلمك èksilmek, ازالمق azalmak ; —, *v.a.* اكسلتمك èksiltmek, ازالتمق azaltmak, كسمك kèssmek.

Decree, *s.* اراده ìrādé ; —, *v.n.* & *a.* اراده ا ìrādé-et, فرمان ا fèrmān-et, بيورمق bùyurmak, امر ا èmr-et, حكم ا hùkm-et.

Decrepit, *a.* بونامش bùnamish ; عته كتورمش ''ùtūh-ghètirmish.

Decrepitude, *s.* عتوه ''àtūh.

Dedicate, *v.a.* تخصيص ا tàkhsīss-et ; برينك نامنه يازمق bìrining-nāmina--yàzmak ; — one's self, عمرينی صرف ا ''ùmrunu-sàrf-et.

Deduce, *v.a.* اڭلامق ànglamak (ànna-mak), استنتاج ا ìsstintāj-et.

Deduct, *v.a.* تنزيل ا tènzīl-et, اشاغی وارمق ashàghi-vàrmak, قيرمق kìrmak.

Deduction, *s.* استنتاج ìsstintāj ; نتيجه nètījé ; تنزيل tènzīl.

Deed, *s.* ايش ìsh, فعل fì''l, عمل ''amel, كار kyār ; سند sèned, حجت hùjjèt.

Deem, *v.a.* صايمق sàymak, صانمق sànmak, عد ا ''àdd-et, ظن ا zànn-et.

Deep, *a.* درين dèrin, عميق ''àmīk ; (crafty) شيطان shèytan ; —, *s.* دكز dèngiz.

Deer, *s.* كيك ghèyik ; قراجه kàraja.

Deface, *v.a.* بوزمق bòzmak.

Defamation, *s.* افترا ìftirā, بهتان bùhtān.

Defame, *v.a.* افترا ا ìftirā-et.

Defaulter, *s.* بورجنی ویرمیان bòrjunu-vèrméyen ; خدمتدن قاچان khìdmetdan-kàchan (hìz).

Defeat, *s.* بوزغون bòzghun, بوزغونلق bòzghunluk ; —, *v.a.* بوزمق bòzmak, مغلوب ا màghlūb-et.

Defect, *s.* عیب "àyb, قصور kùssūr, خلل khàlel, اکسك èksik, نقصان nòksān, سقطلق sàkatlìk.

Defective, *a.* سقط sàkat ; اکسك èksik, ناقص nākiss, نقصان nòksān.

Defence, *s.* محافظه mùhāfaza, صیانت sìyānèt, وقایه vìkāyé ; جواب jèwàb.

Defend, *v.a.* قوریمق kòrumak, محافظه ا mùhāfaza-et, صیانت ا sìyānèt-et, وقایه ا vìkāyé-et ; تصحب ا tàssàhhub-et, صاحب چیقمق sāhib-chìkmak, حمایه ا hìmāyé-et.

Defendant, *s.* مدعی علیه mùdda"à-"àlèyh.

Defender, *s.* حامی hāmī.

Defensive, *a.* تدافعی tèdāfu"ī ; offensive and defensive, تجاوزی وتدافعی tèjāvuzī-vé-tèdāfu"ī ; — armour, زره zìrh.

Defer, *v.a.* تأخیر ا tà'khīr-et ; —, *v.n.* بویون اکمك bòyun-èghmek.

Deficiency, *s.* **Deficient**, *a.* اکسك èksik, نقصان nòksān.

Defile, *s.* بوغاز bòghàz, کچید ghèchid, دربند dèrbènd (dèvrènt) ; —, *v.a.* صیچمق sìchmak, مردار ا mùrdār-et (mùndàr), تنجیس ا tènjīss-et.

Define, *v.n.* تحدید ا tàhdīd-et ; (explain) تعریف ا tà"rīf-et.

Definite, *a.* محدود māhdūd ; (fixed) معین mù"àyyèn, معلوم mà"lūm, بللو bèlli.

Definition, *s.* حد hàdd ; تعریف tà"rīf.

Definitive, *a.* اصل àssl, قطعی kàt"ī.

Deform, *v.a.* بوزمق bòzmak, چرکین ا chìrkin-et.

Deformed, *a.* اعضاسی اندامندن خارج اولان à"zāssi-èndàmindan-khārij-òlan ; قانبور kànbur, باجقسز bàjaksiz, جوجه jùjé, اغساق àghsàk.

Deformity, *s.* چرکینلك chìrkinlik.

Defraud, *v.a.* طولاندرمق dòlàndirmak.

Defray, *v.a.* ویرمك vèrmek, کورمك ghyùrmek, اودهمك ùdémek.

Defunct, *a.* متوفا mùtéwèffà, مرحوم mèrhūm.

Defy, *v.a.* میدان اوقومق mèydān-òkumak ; قارشی قومق kàrshi-kòmak.

Degenerate, *a.* بوزق bòzuk, بوزلمش bòzulmush ; —, *v.n.* بوزلمق bòzulmak.

Degradation, *s.* تنزیل رتبه tènzīl-i-rùtbé ; رذالت rèzālèt.

Degrade, *v.a.* رذیل ا rèzīl-et ; عیب او "àyb-òl ; رتبه‌سنی المق rùtbéssini-àlmak.

Degree, *s.* درجه dèréjé, مرتبه mèrtébé, منزله mènzilé, کرته kèrté, پرسه pèrèssé.

Deign, *v.n.* لطف ا lùtf-et, کرم ا kèrem-et, عنایت ا "ìnāyèt-et, تنزل ا tènèzzul-et.

Deity, *s.* اله ìlāh, الله àllāh, معبود mà"būd.

Deject, *v.a.* محزون ا màhzūn-et.

Dejection, *s.* دوشنمه dùshunma, تکسر tèkèssur, غم ghàm, کدر kèder.

Delay, *s.* تاخير tà'khīr, تأخر tè'èkhkhur; دورمه dūrma, قالمه kālma, بكلمه bèklémé; مهلت mūhlèt, وقت wākit; —, *v.n.* دورمق dūrmak, قالمق kālmak, بكلمك bèklémek; تأخرا tè'èkhkhur-et, كچ قالمق ghèch-kālmak, كيرو قالمق ghèri-kālmak; —, *v.a.* تأخيرا tà''khīr-et; اليقومق ālikòmak.

Delegate, *s.* وكيل vèkīl; مأمور mè'mūr; مبعوث mèb''ūss; —, *v.a.* وكيلا vèkīl-et; حوالها hàwālé-et; مأمورا mè'mūr-et.

Deleterious, *a.* ضررلو zàrarli, مضر mūzirr.

Deliberate, *a.* قصدى kāssdī, عمدى ''àmdī; —, *v.n.* دوشنمك dùshunmek; مشاورها mùshāvéré-et.

Deliberation, *s.* تأنى tè'ènnī; مشاوره [mùshāvéré.

Delicate, *a.* نازك nāzik.

Delicious, *a.* طاتلو tātli, لذيذ lèzīz.

Delight, *s.* سونج sèvinj, ممنونيت mèmnūnìyyèt, سرور sùrūr; —, *v.a.* سوندرمك sèvindirmek, مسرورا mèssrūr-et; —, *v.n.* حظا hàzz-et, تلذذا tèlèzzuz-et; سونمك sèvinmek, ممنون او mèmnūn-òl.

Delighted, *a.* محظوظ màhzūz.

Delightful, *a.* كوزل ghyùzèl, لطيف làtīf.

Delinquency, *s.* قباحت kābāhat.

Delinquent, *s.* صوچلو sūchlu, قباحتلو kābāhatli.

Delirious, *a.* چلغين chìlghin. [jùnūn.

Delirium, *s.* چلغينلق chìlghinlik, جنون

Deliver, *v.a.* قورتارمق kūrtarmak, تخليصا tàkhlīss-et, خلاصا khàlāss-et; تسليما tèsslīm-et, ويرمك vèrmek.

Deliverance, *s.* قورتارش kùrtàrish; قورتلش kùrtulush, خلاص khàlāss.

Delivery, *s.* قورتلش kùrtulush, خلاص khàlāss; تسليم tèsslīm.

Delude, *v.a.* الداتمق āldatmak.

Deluge, *s.* طوفان tufān; (flood) سيل sèyl (sèl).

Delusion, *s.* مراق mèrāk, قورنتى kòruntu.

Demand, *s.* استدعا ìsstìd''ā; استدك ìsstèdik; دعوى dà''wà; —, *v.a.* صورمق sòrmak; استمك ìsstémek.

Demi, *a.* يارم yārim.

Democracy, *s.* جمهوريت jùmhūriyyèt.

Demolish, *v.a.* بوزمق bòzmak, يقمق yìkmak, هدما hèdm-et.

Demolishment, Demolition, *s.* هدم hèdm.

Demon, *s.* شيطان shèytān, زبانى zàbānī.

Demonstrate, *v.a.* اثباتا ìssbāt-et.

Demur, *v.n.* ترددا tèrèddud-et, باقنمق bākinmak.

Den, *s.* اين īn, مغاره màghara.

Denial, *s.* انكار ìnkyār; (refusal) عدم انجاز ''àdémi-ìnjāz.

Denmark, *s.* دانيمارقا Danimarka.

Denominate, *v.a.* تسميها tèssmìyyé-et.

Denomination, *s.* اد àd, اسم ìssm, تسميه tèssmìyyé; (sect) ملت millèt, فرقه fìrka.

Denote, *v.a.* علامت او ''àlāmèt-olmek. دلالتا dèlālèt-et. [mek.

Denounce, *v.a.* خبر ويرمك khāber-vèr-

Dense, *a.* قويى kòyu; صيق sìk, كثيف kèssīf, غليظ ghàlīz.

Dentifrice, *s.* ديش توزى dìsh-tòzu.

Dentist, *s.* ديشجى dìshji.

Dentistry, *s.* دیشجیلك dìshjilik.

Denude, *v.a.* صویمق sòymak.

Deny, *v.a.* انكار ا ìnkyār-et; (refuse) انجاز ایتمامك ìnjāz-ètmamek, رد ا rèdd-et.

Depart, *s.* چیقش chìkish; —, *v.n.* چیقمق chìkmak, كتمك ghìtmek.

Department, *s.* (branch) قول kòl, فرع fèr''; (of state) نظارت nAzārèt; (business) وظیفه wAzīfÉ, عهده ''ùhdÉ.

Departure, *s.* كیدش ghìdish, قیام kìyām, عزیمت ''àzīmèt.

Depend, *v.n.* باقمق bAkmak; تابع او tābi''òl; مربوط او mèrbūt-òl, منوط او mènūt-òl; كوكنمك ghyùghEnmek, اعتماد ا ì''timAd-et, ربط قلب ا rAbti-kAlb-et.

Deplorable, *a.* اجنه جق Ajìnajak, فنا fèna, پریشان pèrīshAn.

Deplore, *v.a.* اغلامق Aghlamak.

Depopulate, *v.a.* اهالیدن خالی قیلمق àhālīdan-khālī-kìlmak.

Deportment, *s.* اطوار Atwār, اوضاع èvzā''.

Depose, *v.n.* تقریر ا tAkrīr-et; —, *v.a.* خلع khàl''-et, تختدن اندرمك tàkht-dan-èndirmek.

Deposit, *s.* امانت èmānèt; پی pèy; طورطی tòrtu; پوصه pòssa; —, *v.a.* امانت ویرمك èmānèt-vèrmek, تسلیم ا tèsslīm-et; قمق kòmak, وضع ا wAz''-et; براقمق bràkmak.

Depositary, *s.* امانتدار èmānètdār.

Depreciate, *v.a.* قیمتنی ازالتمق kīmètini-AzAltmak; قدرینی انكار ا kAdrini-ìnkyār-et.

Depredation, *s.* خسارت khAssārèt, زیانكارلق zìyānkyārlik; خرسزلق khìr-sizlik.

Depress, *v.a.* فقیر ا fàkīr-et; محتاج ا mùhtAj-et; مكدر ا mùkÈddEr-et; كساد ویرمك kèssād-vÈrmek.

Depression (of spirits), *s.* كدورت kèdūrèt; (of market) كساد kèssād; (of ground) چقور chùkUr.

Deprive, *v.a.* محروم ا màhrūm-et, خالی براقمق khālī-bràkmak.

Depth, *s.* درینلك dèrinlik, عمق ''ùmk; — of winter, قره قیش kAra-kìsh, زمهریر zèmhérīr, اربعین èrba''īn.

Deputation, *s.* وكیللر vèkīllEr, مبعوثلر mèb''ūsslEr.

Depute, *v.a.* وكیل ا vèkīl-et.

Deputy, *s.* وكیل vèkīl; — judge, نائب nā'ib; — governor, قائممقام kA'im-makAm.

Deride, *v.a.* استهزا ا ìsstìhzā-et.

Derision, *s.* استهزا ìsstìhzā.

Derivation, *s.* (source) اصل Assl; (of words) اشتقاق ìshtikAk.

Derive, *v.a.* بولمق bùlmak, استخراج ا ìsstikhrāj-et, استحصال ا ìsstìhsAl-et.

Derived, *a.* مشتق mùshtàkk.

Descend, *v.n.* انمك ènmek, نازل او nāzil-òl, ساقط او sākit-ol, هبوط ا hùbūt-et; اولادندن او èvlādindan-òl.

Descendant, *s.* اولادندن اولان èvlādindan-òlAn; descendants, آل واحفاد āl-U-àhfād.

Descent, *s.* انش ènish, نزول nùzūl, سقوط sùkūt, هبوط hùbūt; (relationship) انتساب ìntissāb; (degree of

—) درجه dèréjé, بطن bàtn, قرن kàrn; (attack) هجوم kùjūm.

Describe, *v.a.* تعريف ا tà''rīf-et; (a circle) رسم ا rèssm-et.

Description, *s.* تعريف tà''rīf; (sort) درلو dùrlu, صوى sòy, جنس jìnss, نوع nèv''.

Descry, *v.a.* اوزاقدن كورمك ùzākden-gyùrmak.

Desert, *s.* چول chūl, باديه bādìyyé; —, *a.* خراب khàrāb, خالى khālī, اسسز ìsssiz; —, *v.n.* قاچمق kàchmak, فرار ا firār-et; —, *v.a.* براقمق bràkmak, متروك قومق mètrūk-kòmak, ترك ا tèrk-et; deserts, *s. pl.* استحقاق ìsstìhkāk.

Deserter, *s.* فرارى fìrārī, قاچقين kàchkin.

Desertion, *s.* فرار fìrār.

Deserve, *v.a.* مستحق او mùsstahàkk-òl.

Deserving, *a.* مستحق mùsstahàkk; سزا sèzā, شايسته shāyèssté, شايان shāyān.

Design, *s.* نيت nìyyèt, مرام mèrām, قصد kàssd, مقصد màksàd, مقصود màksūd, قوردق kùrduk; (drawing) رسم rèssim; —, *v.a.* نيت ا nìyyèt-et, قورمق kùrmak; قصد ا kàssd-et; (plan) ترتيب ا tèrtīb-et; (draw) رسم ا rèssm-et.

Designate, *v.a.* تعيين ا tà''yīn-et, اسمنى سويلمك ìssmini-sùwèylémek.

Designation, *s.* تسميه ايتمكلك tèssmìyyé-ètmeklik.

Desirable, *a.* استنلور ìsstènilir, ارزو اولنور àrzu-òlunur, مرغوب mèrghūb.

Desire, *s.* استك ìsstèk, ارزو àrzu, رغبت ràghbet; (strong) حرص hìrss; (yearning) اشتياق ìshtiyāk; (concupiscence) شهوت shèhvèt; (thing desired) استدك ìsstèdik, مطلوب màtlub; —, *v.a.* استمك ìsstémek, ارزو ا àrzu-et, ارامق àramak, امل ا èmel-et, طلب ا tàleb-et; امرا èmr-et, تنبيه ا tènbīh-et.

Desirous, *a.* ارزومند àrzumènd.

Desist, *v.n.* وازگچمك vāz-ghèchmek.

Desk, *s.* چكمجه chèkméjé.

Desolate, *a.* (person) كمسسز kìmséssiz; منكوب mènkyūb; خراب khàrāb; (place) ويران vīrān, خراب و يباب khàrāb-u-yèbāb, خالية خاوى khālìyyétun-khāvī; —, *v.a.* خراب ا khàrāb-et, ويران ا vīrān-et.

Desolation, *s.* خراب khàrāb, خرابيت khàrābìyyèt; (desolate place) خالية خاوى khālìyyétun-khāvī.

Despair, *s.* يأس yè'ss, اميدسزلك ùmīd-sizlik; —, *v.n.* مأيوس او mè'yūss-òl, قطع اميد ا kàt''i-ùmīd-et.

Despatch, *s.* تحريرات tàhrīràt, كاغد kyāghid.

Desperate, *a.* اميدسز ùmīdsiz, مأيوس mè'yūss.

Despicable, *a.* (person) الچق àlchàk, رذيل rèzīl, ذليل zèlīl; — thing, رذالت rèzālèt.

Despise, *v.a.* صايمامق sàymamak; (a man) ادم يرينه قومامق àdam-yèrina-kòmamak.

Despite, *s.* in despite, عناديه ''ìnādina; in despite of, هيچ باقميه رق hìch-bàk-mayarak.

Despond, *v.n.* مأيوس او mè'yūss-òl, كنديني براقمق kèndini-bràkmak.

Despondency, *s.* يأس yè'ss.

Despondent, *a.* مایوس mèʻyūss.

Despot, *s.* (tyrant) ظالم zālim; (absolute ruler) حاکم مطلق hākimi-mŭtlăk.

Despotism, *s.* حکومت مطلقه hùkyūmèt-mŭtlăka, ظلم zŭlm.

Destine, *v.a.* تخصیص ا tàkhsīss-et; نامزد ا nāmzèd-et; مقدر ا mŭkădder-et.

Destiny, *s.* قدر kăder, قسمت kìssmèt, طالع tāli", بخت băkht.

Destitute, *a.* فقیر و بیکس fàkīr-u-bīkèss.

Destroy, *v.a.* یوق ا yòk-et, محو ا māhv-et, افنا ا ìfnā-et, وجودینی قالدرمق vùjū-dini-kăldirmak; خراب ا khàrāb-et, پرشان ا pèrīshān-et; یقمق yìkmak, بوزمق bòzmak; اولدرمك ùldurmek, جاننی المق jànini-ălmak, قهر ا kàhr-et.

Destruction, *s.* خراب khàrāb; تخریب tàkhrīb, خرابیت khàrābìyyèt; محو mahv, افنا ìfnā.

Destructive, *a.* باعث خراب bā"iss-i-khàrāb; مهلك mùhlik.

Detach, *v.a.* چوزمك ckùzmek; صالیویرمك sălivèrmek; قوپارمق kòparmak; ایرمق àyrmak.

Detachment, *s.* طاقم tàkim, بلوك bùluk, الای ălay, فرقه fìrka.

Detail, *s.* تفصیل tàfsīl; in detail, تفصیلاً tăfsīlan; (one by one) بربربر bìrer-bìrer; details, تفصیلات tàfsīlāt; —, *v.a.* تفصیل ا tàfsīl-et, تفصیلاً نقل ا tăfsīlan-năkl-et.

Detain, *v.a.* الیقومق ălikòmak.

Detect, *v.a.* طوتمق tùtmak; بولمق bùlmak.

Detective, *s.* کیزلو ضبطیه نفری ghìzli-zăbtìyyé-nèfèri. [hàbss.

Detention, *s.* توقیف tèvkīf; حبس

Deter, *v.a.* مانع اولمق māni-"òlmak.

Deteriorate, *v.n.* فنالشمك fènāleshmek; بوزمقلق bòzmaklik.

Determination, *s.* تصمیم tăssmīm, نیت nìyyèt; قرار kărar; ثبات sèbāt; عناد "ìnād; میل mèyl.

Determine, *v.n.* قرار ویرمك kărar-vèrmek; تصمیم ا tăssmīm-et, نیت ا nìyyèt-et, قورمق kùrmak; —, *v.a.* تصمیمه سبب او tăssmīma-sèbeb-òl; میل ایتدرمك mèyl-ètdirmek.

Detest, *v.a.* منفور طوتمق mènfūr-tùtmak, هیچ سومامك hìch-sèvmamek.

Dethrone, *v.a.* خلع ا khàl"-et, تختدن اندرمك tàkhtdan-èndirmek.

Detonation, *s.* باروت سسی bārut-sèssi.

Detract from one's merits, *v.n.* استحقاقنی انکار ا ìsstìhkăkini-ìnkyār-et.

Detriment, *s.* ضرر zàrar.

Deuce, *s.* دو dù; شیطان shèytăn; the deuce! *int.* اللهه سن ăllăha-sèn; یوغندی yòghundu.

Devastation, *s.* خراب khàrāb.

Develop, *v.a.* متفرعاتنی میدانه چیقارمق mùtéfèrri"ātini-mèydana-chìkàrmak.

Device, *s.* حیله hīlé; صنعت sàn"àt; رسم rèssim, شکل shèkil.

Devil, *s.* شیطان shèytān, ابلیس ìblīss; (imp) زبانی zàbānī.

Devious, *a.* اکری بوکری èghri-bùghri, صاپق طولاشق săpik-dòlàshik.

Devise, *v.a.* (bequeath) وصیت ا wăssiyyèt-et; (invent) بولمق bùlmak, دوشنمك dùshunmek.

Devoid, *a.* خالى khālī.

Devolve, *v.n.* دوشمق dùshmek, اصابت ا ìssābet-et, انتقال ا ìntikāl-et.

Devote, *v.a.* تخصيص ا tàkhsīss-et, فدا ا fèdā-et.

Devotion, *s.* اختصاص ìkhtissāss; تخصيص tākhsīss; فداكارلق fèdākyār-lik; عبوديت "ùbūdìyyèt; ديانت dìyānèt; devotions, نماز nāmaz, عبادت "ìbādèt, دعا dù"ā.

Devour, *v.a.* يمك yèmek, بترمك bìtirmek, يوتمق yūtmak.

Devout, *a.* صوفى sòfu, ديندار dīndār, متقى mùttàki, اهل تقوا èhli-tākwā.

Dew, *s.* چيك chīgh, شبنم shèbnèm.

Dexterity, *s.* ال چابكلكى ēl-chàbiklighi; هنر hùner.

Dexterous, *a.* الى چابك éli-chàbik.

Diadem, *s.* تاج tāj.

Diagonal line, *s.* وتر vètēr.

Diagram, *s.* شكل shèkil,

Dial, *s.* (sun) كونش ساعتى ghyùnesh-sā"ati; — plate, ساعت تختهسى sā"at-tàkhtassi. [zàbān.

Dialect, *s.* دل dil, لسان lìssān, زبان

Dialogue, *s.* ايكى كيشى بيننده اولان لقردى ìki-kìshi-bèyninda-òlan-làkirdi.

Diameter, *s.* قطر kùtr.

Diamond, *s.* الماس ēlmass.

Diarrhœa, *s.* اسهال ìsshāl, قارن سورمسى kàrn-sùrméssi.

Diary, *s.* روزنامه rùznāmé (jùznāmé), مجمعه mèjma"à, ژورنال zhūrnāl.

Dice (pl. of die), *s.* طاوله زارلرى tàwla-zàrlari.

Dictate, *v.a.* تقرير ايدوب يازدرمق tàkrīr-èdup-yàzdirmak; جبراً قبول ايتدرمك jèbran-kābūl-ètdirmek; — *v.n.* آمر او āmir-ol, باشنه ضابط كسلمك bāshina-zābit-kèssilmek. [lùghāt-kìtābi.

Dictionary, *s.* لغات lùghāt, لغات كتابى

Die, *s.* طاوله زارى tàwla-zāri; (for stamping) قالب kālip, (for coining) سكه sìkké; —, *v.n.* اولمك ùlmek, كوچمك ghyùchmek, وفات ا wèfāt-et; (a beast) كبرمك ghèbērmek; (a plant) قورومق kùrūmak.

Diet, *s.* پرهيز يمكى pèrhīz-yèmèghi; حميه hìmyé, پرهيز pèrhīz.

Differ, *v.n.* درلو درلو او (tùrlu-tùrlu)-òl, مختلف او mùkhtèlif-òl; برى برينه اويمامق bìri-bìrina-ùymamak.

Difference, *s.* فرق fàrk; اختلاف ìkhtilāf, مغايرت mùghāyérèt; نزاع nìzā".

Different, *a.* بشقه bāshka, ديكر dīghēr, اخر àkhàr; بشقه بشقه bāshka-bāshka, مختلف mùkhtèlif, كوناكون ghyūnā-ghyūn.

Difficult, *a.* كوچ ghyùch, چتين chètin, صعوبتلو sù"ūbètli, عسرتلو "ùssrètli.

Difficulty, *s.* كوچلك ghyùchluk, چتينلك chètinlik, صعوبت sù"ūbèt, عسرت "ùssrèt.

Diffidence, *s.* محجوبيت màhjūbiyyèt.

Diffident, *a.* محجوب màhjūb, جسارتسز jèssārètsiz.

Dig, *v.a.* قازمق kāzmak, حفر ا hùfr-et; بللمك bèllémek; — up, *v.a.* (ground)

بللمك bèllémek; (plants) سوكمك sùkmek, چيقارمق chìkàrmak; (find by digging) بولمق bùlmak.

Digest, *v.a.* هضم ا hàzm-et.

Digestible, *a.* خفيف و تيز هضم khàfif-vé-tèz-hàzm.

Digestion, *s.* هضم hàzm.

Dignified, *a.* وقارتلو wàkārètli, تمكينلو tèmkīnli, اغر àghr.

Dignitary, *s.* رجال كباردن اولان rìjāli-kībārdan-òlan, اصحاب مناصبدن اولان àsshābi-mànāssibdan-òlan.

Dignity, *s.* تمكين temkin, وقار wàkār; اغر àghr; رتبه rùtbé.

Dike, *s.* سد sèdd; خندق hèndek.

Dilapidation, *s.* خراب kharāb.

Dilemma, *s.* مشكل mùshkil.

Diligence, *s.* چالشقانلق chàlishkànlik, اقدام ìkdām, سعى وغيرت sà''y-u-ghàyrèt; سرعت sùr''àt.

Diligent, *a.* چالشقان chàlishkhàn, مقدم mùkdim.

Dilute, *v.a.* صو قاتمق sù-kàtmak, صولو ا sùlu-et.

Dim, *a.* دومانلو dùmànli, دومان ايچنده كبى dùmàn-ìchinda-ghibi; قرانلق kàranlik.

Dimension, *s.* بيوكلك bìyuklik; the three dimensions, ابعاد ثلثه èb''ādi-sèlāssé.

Diminish, *v.n.* ازالمق àzàlmak; كچولمك kùchulmek, اوفالمق ùfàlmak; —, *v.a.* ازالتمق àzàltmak, كسمك kèssmek, كچولتمك kùchultmek, اوفاتمق ùfàtmak.

Diminution, *s.* ازالمه àzàlma, ازالتمه àzàltma, ازالدلمه àzàldìlma; اكسلمه èksilma; اوفالمه ùfàlma, اوفالتمه ùfàltma, اوفالدلمه ùfàldìlma, تقليل tàklīl; تصغير tàssghīr.

Diminutive, *a.* اوفاق ùfàk, اوفاجق ùfàjìk, كچوك kùchuk, كچوجك kùchujuk; —, *s.* اسم تصغير ìssmi-tàssghīr.

Dimple, *s.* چقور chùkur, چاه chāh.

Dine, *v.n.* يمك يمك yèmèk-yèmek, طعام ا tà''ām-et.

Dinner, *s.* يمك yèmèk, طعام tà''ām, اخشام يمكى àkhsham-yèmèghi.

Diploma, *s.* فرمان fèrmàn, برات bèrāt, رؤس rù'ūss, جائزه jā'izé.

Diplomacy, *s.* آداب سفرات ādāb-i-sùférāt.

Diplomatist, *s.* صاحب آداب سفرات sāhib-i-ādāb-i-sùférāt; ديپلومات dì-plòmāt.

Direct, *a.* طوغرى dòghru, طوغريدن طوغرى dòghrudan-dòghru; بلاواسطه bìlā-wàssita, ذاتى zātī, كندو kèndi; —, *v.a.* (on the road) صاغلق ويرمك sàghlik-vèrmek; (manage) اداره ا ìdāré-et, نظارت ا nàzārèt-et; (point) طوغريلتمق dòghrultmak, عطف ا ''àtf-et, توجيه ا tèvjīh-et, صرف ا sàrf-et; (a letter) اوستنى يازمق ùsstunu-yàzmak; (order) امر ا èmr-et, تنبيه ا tènbīh-et.

Direction, *s.* طرف tàraf, يان yàn, جهت jìhèt; نظارت nàzārèt, اداره ìdāré; امر èmr, تنبيه tènbīh, تعليمات tà''līmāt; مكتوب اوستى mèktūb-ùsstu; صاغلق sàghlik, عدرس ''adrèss.

Directly, *ad.* شمدى shìmdi; اول ساعت òl-sā''at, همان دم hèmāndèm; طوغريدن

طوغری dòghrudan-dòghru, بلا واسطه bilā-wāssita, ذاتاً zātan.

Director, *s.* مدیر mùdīr, دیرکتور direktor.

Dirt, *s.* کیر kìr, پسلك pìsslik, مردارلق mŭrdàrlik.

Dirtiness, *s.* کیرلولك kirlilik.

Dirty, *a.* کیرلو kìrli, پس pìss, مردار mŭrdàr, ملوث mùlèvvèss.

Disable, *v.a.* سقط ا sàkat-et.

Disadvantage, *s.* ضرر zàrar; مانع māni'', سکته sèkté.

Disagree, *v.n.* بوزشمق bòzushmak; (food) معده‌یی بوزمق mì''déyi-bòzmak. [کریه kèrīh.

Disagreeable, *a.* طاتسز tàtsiz, بد bèd,

Disagreement, *s.* اختلاف ìkhtilàf; نزاع nìzā.

Disappoint, *v.a.* الداتمق àldatmak; ایشنی بوزمق ìshini-bòzmak, قازق صوقمق kàzik-sòkmak.

Disapprove, *v.a.* بکنمامك bèghenmamek, تقبیح ا tàkbīh-et.

Disarm, *v.a.* صویمق sòymak; سلاحنی المق silāhini-àlmak; —, *v.n.* سلاح صوینمق silāh-sòyunmak.

Disarmament, *s.* ترك سلاح tèrk-i-silāh; تدارکات حربیه برطرف ایتمکلك tèdārukyāt-hàrbiyyé-bèr-tàraf-ètmeklik.

Disaster, *s.* قضا kàzā, بلا bèlā, فلاکت felākèt.

Disband, *v.a.* طاغتمق dàghitmak; —, *v.n.* طاغلمق dàghilmak.

Disbelief, *s.* عدم اعتقاد ''àdémi-ì''tikàd.

Disbelieve, *v.a.* اینانمامق ìnànmamak.

Disburse, *v.a.* خرج ا khàrj-et, صرف ا sàrf-et, مصرف ا màssràf-et.

Discard, *v.a.* طرد ا tàrd-et, قوغمق kòghmak, دفع ا dèf''-et.

Discern, *v.a.* چیقارمق chìkàrmak, سچمك sèchmek, کورمك ghyùrmek.

Discharge, *s.* اذن ìzin, رخصت rùkhsàt; تبریه tèbrìyyé; اتش àtèsh; اتمه àtma, اتلمه àtìlma, انداخت èndākht; جراحت jèrāhàt; —, *v.a.* اذن ویرمك ìzin-vèrmek, خدمتدن چیقارمق khìdmetdan-chìkàrmak; صالیویرمك sàlivèrmek, حبسدن چیقارمق hàbssdan-chìkàrmak; بوشالتمق bòshàltmak; اتمق àtmak, انداخت ا èndākht-et, اتش ا àtèsh-et; ایفا ا īfā-et, استیفا ا ìsstīfā-et, ویرمك vèrmek; اجرا ا ìjrā-et; —, *v.n.* یوکنی بوشالتمق yùkunu-bòshàltmak; اقمق àkmak.

Disciple, *s.* شاکرد shāghird, تلمیذ tèlmīz; حواریون hàwārìyyūn.

Discipline, *s.* نظام وانتظام nìzām-u-ìntizām.

Disclaim, *v.a.* انکار ا ìnkyār-et.

Disclose, *v.a.* کوسترمك ghyùstermek, میدانه قومق mèydāna-kòmak, کشف ا kèshf-et, سویلمك sùwèylémek, فاش ا fàsh-et. [صیقندی sìkindi.

Discomfort, *s.* راحتسزلق rāhatsizlik,

Discommode, *v.a.* راحتسز ا rāhatsiz-et.

Disconsolate, *a.* تسلی قبول ایتمز tèsèlli-kàbūl-ètmàz.

Discontent, *s.* خشنودسزلق khòshnudsuzluk, عدم رضا ''àdémi-rìzā.

Discontented, *a.* سویلنیور sùwèyléniyor, خشنودسز khòshnudsuz.

Discontinuance, *s.* قطع kʌt''.
Discontinue, *v.a.* كسمك kèssmek; —, *v.n.* كسلمك kèssilmek.
Discord, *s.* نفاق nìfāk.
Discount, *s.* باش bʌsh, فائض fā'iz; —, *v.a.* باشلەالمق bʌshla-ʌlmak, قيرمق kìrmak.
Discountenance, *v.a.* يوز ويرممك yùz-vèrmemek.
Discourage, *v.a.* قورقوتمق kòrkutmak; يوز ويرمامك yùz-vèrmamek.
Discourse, *s.* كلام kèlām, لقردى làkirdi; —, *v.n.* بسط كلام ا bʌssti-kèlām-et.
Discourteous, *a.* رعايتسز rì''āyetsiz.
Discourtesy, *s.* رعايتسزلك rì''āyetsizlik.
Discover, *v.a.* بولمق bùlmak, كشف ا kèshf-et, ميدانه چيقارمق mèydāna-chìkàrmak; كوسترمك ghyùsstermek.
Discovery, *s.* كشف kèshf.
Discreet, *a.* عقللو ''ʌklli, عاقل ''ʌkìl; كتوم kètūm; بصيرتلو bʌssīrètli.
Discretion, *s.* عقل ''ʌkl, تدبير tèdbīr, بصيرت bʌssīrèt, حزم hʌzm; انصاف ìnsāf; to arrive at years of —, عقله بالغ او ''ʌkla-bālìgh-òl; to surrender at —, ويره ويرمك vèra-vèrmek, شرطسز تسليم او shàrtsiz-tèsslīm-òl, امان ديمك ʌmān-dèmek; امان طلب ا āmān-tʌleb-et.
Discriminate, *v.a.* تفريق ا tèfrīk-et.
Discuss, *v.a.* سويلشمك sùwèylìshmek, مباحثه ا mùbāhéssé-et.
Discussion, *s.* مباحثه mùbāhéssé.
Disdain, *s.* استكبار ìsstikbār, استخفاف ìsstikhfāf; —, *v.a.* استخفاف ا ìsstikh-fāf-et; تنزل ايتمامك tènèzzul-ètmamek.
Disdainful, *a.* كبرلو kìbrli.
Disdainfulness, *s.* كبر kìbr.
Disease, *s.* مرض màraz, علت ''ìllèt, درد dèrd, كيفسزلك kèyfsizlik.
Disembark, *v.n.* كميدن قره يه چيقمق ghè-miden-kʌrayé-chìkmak.
Disembarkation, *s.* كميدن قره يه چيقمقلق ghèmiden-kʌrayé-chìkmaklik.
Disengaged, *a.* بوش bòsh, بوشده bòshda, خالى khālī, وقتى خالى اولان wʌktī-khālī-òlʌn.
Disentangle, *v.a.* چوزمك chùzmek, اچمق àchmak.
Disfigure, *v.a.* بوزمق bòzmak; چركين او chìrkin-òl, ياقشمامق yàkishmamak.
Disgrace, *s.* عيب ''àyb, رذالت rèzālèt; نكبت nìkbèt, دوشكونلك dùsh-kyunluk; —, *v.a.* عيب او ''àyb-òl; رذيل ا rèzīl-et.
Disgraceful, *a.* عيب ''àyb, ياقشقسز yàkishiksiz, كريه kèrīh, چركين chìrkin.
Disguise, *s.* تبديل قيافت tèbdīli-kìyāfèt; —, *v.a.* قيافت تبديل ا kìyāfèt-tèbdīl-et; ديكشدرمك dìghishdirmek.
Dish, *s.* صحن sahn, طباق tʌbʌk.
Dishonest, *a.* خرسز khìrsiz; خائن khā'in.
Dishonour, *s.* رذالت rèzālèt, رسوايلق rùssvàylik; —, *v.a.* رذيل ا rèzīl-et; — a bill, قبول ايتمامك kʌbul-ètmamek, اتيويرمك ʌtivèrmek.
Disinherit, *v.a.* ميراثدن محروم ا mīrāss-dan-màhrūm-et.

Disinterested, *a.* غرض وعوضدن خالی اولان ghàraz-vé-"ìvèzdan-khālī-òlan.

Disjoin, *v.a.* ایرمق ayrmak, تفریق ا tèfrīk-et.

Dislike, *v.a.* سومامك sèvmamek.

Dislocate, *v.a.* چیقارمق chìkàrmak.

Dismal, *a.* صیقندیلو sìkindili.

Dismay, *s.* قورقو kòrku, دهشت dèhshèt.

Dismember, *v.a.* تقسیم ا tàksīm-et.

Dismemberment, *s.* تقسیم tàksīm.

Dismiss, *v.a.* اذن ویرمك ìzin-vèrmek; قوغمق kòghmak; صاومق sàwmak.

Disobedience, *s.* عدم اطاعت "àdémi-ìtā"at, اطاعتسزلق ìtā"atsizlik.

Disobey, *v.a.* دکله مامك dìnglémamek, اطاعت ایتمامك ìtā"at-ètmamek.

Disoblige, *v.a.* خاطرینی صایمامق khātirini-sàymamak, خاطرینی قیرمق khātirini-kìrmak.

Disobliging, *a.* مروتسز mùrùvètsiz.

Disorder, *s.* قارشقلق kàrishiklik; پریشانیت pèrīshānìyyèt; اختلال ìkhtilāl; نظامسزلق nìzāmsizlik; —, *v.a.* قارشدرمق kàrishdirmak, نظامنی بوزمق nìzāmini-bòzmak.

Disordered, *a.* قارشق kàrishik; پریشان pèrīshān; مختل mùkhtèll.

Disorganization, *s.* نظامسزلق nìzāmsizlik.

Dispatch, *s.* چابکلك chàbiklik; سرعت sùr"at, عجله "àjélé; تحریرات tàhrirāt, کاغد kyāghid; —, *v.a.* چابك بترمك chābik-bìtirmek, عجله ا "àjélé-et; کوندرمك ghyùndermek, چیقارمق chìkàrmak; اولدرمك ùldurmek, قتل ا kàtl-et. [dèf"-et, ازاله ا ìzālé-et.

Dispel, *v.a.* طاغتمق dàghitmak; دفع ا

Dispense, *v.a.* طاغتمق dàghitmak, توزیع ا tèvzī"-et; —, *v.n.* وازکچمك vāz-ghèchmek. [*v.n.* طاغلمق dàghilmak.

Disperse, *v.a.* طاغتمق dàghitmak; —,

Displace, *v.a.* یرندن چیقارمق yèrindan-chìkàrmak.

Display, *s.* کوسترش ghyùsstérish, سلطنت sàltanàt; —, *v.a.* کوسترمك ghyùss-termek, ابراز ا ìbrāz-et.

Displease, *v.a.* کوجنه کتمك ghyùjuna-ghìtmek, کریه کورنمك kèrīh-ghyùrunmek.

Displeasure, *s.* دارغینلق dàrghinlik, غضب ghàzab.

Dispose, *v.a.* ترتیب ا tèrtīb-et, تنظیم ا tànzīm-et; — of, *v.n.* صاتمق sàtmak; ویرمك vèrmek; قوللانمق kùllànmak; اولدرمك ùldurmek; یاپمق yàpmak; دفع ا dèf"-et, امر ا èmr-et.

Disposed, *a.* میال mèyyāl, کوکلی اولان ghyùngulu-òlan (ghyùnu-òlan); استعدادی اولان ìssti"dādi-òlan; to be well-disposed, سومك sèvmek; to be ill-disposed, سومامك sèvmamek; — of, صاتلمش sàtilmish, ویرلمش vèril-mish, کتمش ghìtmish, دفع اولنمش dèf"-òlunmush, قتل اولنمش kàtl-òlunmush.

Disposition, *s.* ترتیب tèrtīb, نظام nìzām; خوی khùy, طبیعت tàbī"àt, جبلت jìbillèt, خلق khùlk.

Dispossess, *v.a.* محروم ا màhrūm-et.

Disproportion, *s.* عدم تناسب "àdémi-tènāssub.

Dispute, *s.* نزاع nìzā"; غوغا (kàwgha);

—, *v.n.* نزاع ا nìzā''-et, مجادله ا mùjā-délé-et. [-i-èhlìyyèt.

Disqualification, *s.* عدم اهليت ''àdem-

Disregard, *s.* عدم رعايت ''àdémi-rì''āyèt, رعايتسزلك rì''āyetsizlik; —, *v.a.* باقمامق bàkmamak, قولاق اصمامق kùlàk-àssmamak, طنمامق tìnmamak, صايمامق sàymamak, اعتبار ايتمامك i''tibār-ètmamek.

Disreputable, *a.* عيب ''àyb; رذيل rèzīl, ناموسسز nāmūsssiz.

Disrespect, *s.* رعايتسزلك rì''āyetsizlik, عدم احترام ''àdémi-ìhtirām.

Disrespectful, *a.* رعايتسز rì''āyetsiz.

Dissatisfaction, *s.* خشنودسزلق khòshnud-suzluk.

Dissatisfied, *a.* خشنودسز khòshnudsuz; to be —, *v.n.* سويلنمك sùwèylenmek.

Dissect, *v.a.* تشريح ا tèshrīh-et.

Dissemble, *v.n.* مدارا ا mùdārā-et; —, *v.a.* كتم ا kètm-et. [nèshr-et.

Disseminate, *v.a.* يايمق yàymak, نشرا

Dissension, *s.* نفاق nìfāk.

Dissent, *s.* عدم موافقت ''àdémi-mùwā-fakàt, مخالفت mùkhālèfèt.

Dissertation, *s.* بحث bàhss; رساله rìssālé.

Dissimilar, *a.* غير مشابه ghàyri-mùshābih, بكزهمز bèngzémàz.

Dissipate, *v.a.* طاغتمق dàghitmak, محوا màhv-et. [sèfīh.

Dissipated, *a.* چاپقين chàpkin, سفيه

Dissipation, *s.* سفاهت sèfāhàt, چاپقينلق chàpkinlìk.

Dissolute, *a.* فاسق و فاجر چاپقين fāsik-u-fājir-chàpkin.

Dissolution, *s.* اولم ùlum, وفات wèfāt, حل hàll, تفريق اعضا tèfrīki-à''zā.

Dissolve, *v.a.* اريتمك èritmek, حل ا hàll-et; طاغتمق dàghitmak, اعضاسنى تفريق ا à''zāssini-tèfrīk-et; —, *v.n.* اريمك èrimek; طاغلمق dàghilmak, منحل او mùnhàll-òl.

Dissuade, *v.a.* نيتندن چويرمك nìyyè-tindan-chèvirmek, واز كچورمك vāz- [ghèchirmek.

Distaff, *s.* اوركه ùréké.

Distance, *s.* اوزاقلق ùzàklìk, بعد bu''d, مسافه mèssāfé, يول yòl, منزل mènzil; اوزاق ùzàk, اوزاق برير ùzàk-bìr-yèr; اوزاق يرلر ùzàk-yèrler.

Distant, *a.* اوزاق ùzàk, ايراق īràk, بعيد bà''īd; (in manners) صوغوق sòghùk.

Distemper, *s.* مرض màraz, خستهلق khàsstalìk; رنكلى بادانه rènkli-bàdana.

Distend, *v.a.* كرمك ghèrmek, شيشرمك shìshirmek, قبارتمق kàbartmak.

Distension, *s.* شيش shìsh, كركيلك [ghèrghilìk.

Distich, *s.* بيت bèyt.

Distil, *v.a.* انبيقدن چكمك ìnbīkdan-chèkmek, تقطيرا tàktīr-et; —, *v.n.* تقطرا tàkàttur-et. [èden.

Distillation, *s.* تقطير tàktīr.

Distiller, *s.* راقى تقطير ايدن ràki-tàktīr-

Distinct, *a.* بللو bèlli, واضح wāzih, عيان ''àyān; ايرى àyri, بشقه bàshka.

Distinction, *s.* فرق fàrk; تفريق tèfrīk; امتياز ìmtiyāz; رعايت rì''āyèt.

Distinguish, *v.a.* كورمك ghyùrmek, سچمك sèchmek, چيقارمق chìkàr-mak; فرق ا fārk-et, تفريق ا tèfrīk-et;

— one's self, كنديني كوسترمك kèndini-ghyùsstermek, شهرت قزانمق shùhrèt-kàzanmak, تحصيل نام ا tàhsīli-nām-et.

Distinguished, *a.* نامدار nāmdār, مشهور mèshhūr, ممتاز mùmtāz, معتبر mù''tébèr.

Distracted, *a.* چلغين chìlghin.

Distraction, *s.* چلغينلق chìlghinlik, تجنن tèjènnun.

Distress, *s.* صيقندى sìkindi, درد dèrd, كدر kèder; —, *v.a.* صيقمق sìkmak, صيقندى ويرمك sìkindi-vèrmek.

Distressing, *a.* باعث كدر bā''iss-i-kèder.

Distribute, *v.a.* طاغتمق dàghitmak, توزيع ا tèvzī''-et تقسيم ا tàksīm-et.

Distribution, *s.* توزيع tèvzī; تقسيم tàksīm.

District, *s.* ناحيه nāhìyyé.

Distrust, *s.* امنيتسزلك èmnìyyètsizlik, عدم امنيت ''àdémi-èmnìyyèt; —, *v.a.* امنيت ايتمامك èmnìyyèt-ètmamek, امنيت ايده مامك èmnìyyèt-èdamamek.

Disturb, *v.a.* قارشدرمق kàrishdirmak; راحتنى بوزمق rāhatini-bòzmak, راحتسز ا rāhatsiz-et.

Disturbance, *s.* كورلدى ghyùruldu, شماطه shàmata; قارشقلق kàrishiklik, فساد fèssād, اختلال ìkhtilāl.

Ditch, *s.* خندق hèndek.

Dive, *v.n.* دالمق dàlmak.

Diver, *s.* دالغيچ dàlghich.

Diverge, *v.n.* ايرلمق àyrilmak, صاپمق sàpmak.

Divers, *a.* برطاقم bìr-tàkim, بعض bà''zi.

Diversify, *v.a.* چشيد چشيد ا chèshid-chèshid-et.

Diversion, *s.* ايلنجه èylènja; تغليط tàghlīt, شاشرتمه shàshirtma, اشغال ìshghāl, اغفال ìghfāl.

Divert, *v.a.* چويرمك chèvirmek, صاپتمق sàpitmak; ايلندرمك èylèndirmek.

Divest, *v.a.* صويمق sòymak; چيقارمق chìkàrmak; عقلندن چيقارمق ''àklindan-chìkàrmak.

Divide, *v.a.* بولمك bùlmek, ايرمق àyrmak, تقسيم ا tàksīm-et, مقاسمه ا mùkàssémé-et; —, *v.n.* بولنمك bùlunmek, تقسيم قبول ا tàksīm-kàbūl-et.

Divine, *a.* الهى ìlāhī, ربانى ràbbānī; —, *s.* علوم دينيه ده ماهر پاپاس ''ùlūmi-dīnìyyédé-māhir-pàpass.

Divinity, *s.* الله àllāh; الهيت ìlāhìyyèt; معبود باطل mà''būdi-bàtil; علم دين ''ilm-i-dìn.

Division, *s.* تقسيم tàksīm; بولمه bùlmé, بلوك bùluk, قسم kìssm; فرقه fìrka; نفاق nìfāk; اختلاف ìkhtilāf.

Divorce, *s.* طلق tàlak, تطليق tàtlīk; —, *v.a.* بوشامق bòshamak, تطليق ا tàtlīk-et.

Divulge, *v.a.* سويلمك sùwèylémek, فاش ا fàsh-et, افشا ا ìfshā-et.

Dizziness, *s.* باش دونمكلك bàsh-dùnmeklik, كوزلر قرارمق ghyùzlar-kàrarmak.

Do, *v.a.* ايتمك ètmek, ياپمق yàpmak, ايلمك èylémek, قيلمق kìlmak, اجرا ا ìjrā-et, فعله كتورمك fì''lé-ghètirmek; پشورمك pìshirmek; —, *v.n.* حركت ا hàrékèt-et; اولمق òlmak, اويمق

ùymak; يتشمك yètishmek; پشمك pìshmek; — away with, قالدرمق kàldirmak; how do you do? نصل‌سكز nàssl-singiz, نه‌ياپيورسكز nè-yàpiyor-singiz; that will do, الويور èlvérir, يتشر yètishir, أولدى òldu.

Docile, a. مظلوم màzlūm, قوزى‌كبى kùzu-ghìbi, منقاد mùnkād.

Dock, s. حوض hàwz; —, v.a. اوجنى‌كسمك ùjunu-kèssmek; حوضه‌قومق hàwza-kòmak.

Dockyard, s. ترسانه tèrsānè.

Doctor, s. (of medicine) هيكم hèykim, طبيب tàbīb; (of laws and divinity) مدرس mùdèrriss; (of philosophy) علم حكمت مدرسى "ìlm-i-hìkmet-mùdèrrissi; —, v.a. علاجا "ìlāj-et, معالجها mù"ālèjè-et.

Doctrine, s. قول kàvl, قوليات kàv-lìyyāt, علميات "ìlmìyyāt; عقائد "àkā'id.

Document, s. كاغد kyàghid, سند sèned, حجت hùjjèt; documents, اوراق èvrāk.

Doe, s. ديشى‌كيك dìshi-ghèyik, ديشى‌قراجه dìshi-kàraja. [ايت it.

Dog, s. كوپك kyàpèk, كلب kèlb,

Dog-days, s. pl. ايام‌باحور èyyāmi-bāhūr.

Doge, s. ونديك دوغه‌سى Vènèdìk-dòghassi.

Dollar, s. أريال ìriyāl, قره غروش kàra-

Dome, s. قبه kùbbè. [ghùrùsh.

Domestic, a. اوه‌الشمش‌اولان èvè-àlish-mish-òlan; —, s. أوشاق ùshàk, خدمتكار (khìzmètkyār).

Domineer, v.n. باشنه‌ضابط كسلمك bà-shina-zābit-kèssilmek.

Dominion, s. ملكوت mèlèkyūt, حكومت hùkyūmet; dominions, ممالك mèmālik.

Don (the river), s. تن صويى tèn-sùyu.

Donkey, s. اشك èshek, خر khàr, حمار hìmār.

Door, s. قپو kàpi, در dèr, باب bāb.

Door-keeper, s. قپوجى kàpiji, دربان [dèrbān.

Dormitory, s. قوغوش kòghush.

Dose, s. غدا ghìdā.

Dot, s. نقطه nòkta.

Dotage, s. اختيارن بوكالمش حالتى ìkhti-yārin-bùngalmish-hāleti. [ìkhtiyār.

Dotard, s. بونامش اختيار bùnamish-

Double, a. and s. ايكى‌قات ìki-kàt; —, v.a. ايكى‌قاتا ìki-kàt-et.

Doubt, s. شبهه shùbhè, شك shèkk, كمان ghyùmān; —, v.n. شبهها shùbhè-et.

Doubtful, a. شبهه‌لو shùbhèli; مشكوك mèshkyūk. [shùbhèssiz.

Doubtless, ad. البته èlbèttè, شبهه‌سز

Dough, s. خمير (khàmur).

Dove, s. قمرى kùmru. [نكاح nìkyāh.

Dower, s. مهرمؤجل mìhri-mù'èjjèl,

Down, s. توى tùy; پوفله pùfla; —, ad. اشاغى àshàghi, اشاغيده àshàghida; يره yèra, يرده yèrda.

Downcast, a. محزون màhzūn.

Downward, a. Downwards, ad. اشاغى طوغرى àshàghi-dòghru.

Doze, v.n. اويوقلمق ùyuklamak.

Dozen, s. دوزينه dùzina; دسته dèsstè; اون‌ايكى òn-iki.

Drachm, *s.* درهم dìrhèm.

Drag, *v.a.* سوركلمك sùruklémek, چكمك chèkmek.

Dragoman, *s.* ترجمان tèrjumān.

Dragon, *s.* اژدر àzhdèr, اژدها èzhdihā (èjdèrhā).

Dragoon, *s.* قلجلو اتلو عسكرى kilìjli-àtli-"àsskéri.

Drain, *s.* لغم làghim ; لغم سوزگچى làghim-sùzghéchi, لغم دلكى làghim-dèlighi ; —, *v.a.* لغم يا يمق làghim-yàpmak ; رطوبتنى سوزدرمك rùtūbètini-sùzdurmek ; —, *v.n.* سوزمك sùzmek, چكلمك chèkilmek.

Drake, *s.* اركك اوردك èrkek-ùrdek.

Dram, *s.* بر راقى bìr-ràki.

Draper, *s.* چوقه جى (chòhaji); دلبندجى (tùlbentji); بزاز bèzzāz.

Draught, *s.* روزكار rùzghyār; ايچم ìchim, يودم yùdum ; مسوده mùssvèddé ; قبا رسم kāba-rèssim ; كمينك صو چكمسى ghèmining-sù-chèkméssi ; اغ طوليسى àgh-dòlussu ; — board, دامه تختەسى dāma-tàkhtassi ; — horse, عربه باركيرى "àraba-(bèghiri); draughts, دامه dāma.

Draw, *v.a.* چكمك chèkmek ; رسم ا rèssam-et ; —, *v.n.* چكمك chèkmek ; رسم يا يمق rèssim-yàpmak ; — away, چكوب كوترمك chèkup-ghyùturmek ; — back, كيرو چكلمك ghèri-chèkilmek ; كيرو چكمك ghèri-chèkmek ; — breath, نفس المق nèfess-àlmak ; — out, اوزامق ùzamak ; — in, قصالمق kìssàlmak ; — near, — nigh, يقلاشمق yàklashmak ; — on, كچمك ghèchmek ; — up, دورمق dùrmak ; ديزمك dìzmek ; ترتيب ا tèrtīb-et ; قلمه المق kàléma-àlmak, يازمق yàzmak ; يا يمق yàpmak ; يوقارى چكمك yùkàri-chèkmek.

Drawer, *s.* چكمجه chèkméjé ; رسام rèssām ; چكيجى chèkiji.

Drawers, *s. pl.* ايچ طونى ìch-dònu, طون dòn, طوك dòng.

Drawing, *s.* رسم rèssim.

Drawing-room, *s.* مسافر اوطەسى mùssā-fir-òdassi.

Dread, *s.* قورقو kòrku, خوف khàvf ; —, *a.* مهابتلو màhābètlu, مهيب mùhīb ; —, *v.a.* قورقمق kòrkmak.

Dreadful, *a.* قورقولو kòrkulu ; پك فنا pèk-fènā.

Dream, *s.* رؤيا rù'yā, دوش dūsh ; —, *v.n.* رؤيا كورمك rù'yā-ghyùrmek.

Dreamer, *s.* رؤيا كورن كمسه rù'yā-ghyùren-kimsé.

Dreary, *a.* صيقنديلى sìkìntìlì, اسسز èsssiz.

Dredge, **Dredging-machine**, *s.* ايرمق و ليمانك قوم و چاموريني چيقارمق ايچون بر آلت ìrmak-vé-līmànin-kūm-vé-chàmurini-chikàrmak-ìchin-bìr-ālet.

Dredge, *v.a.* مذكور آلت قوللانمق mèzkyūr-ālet-kùllanmak.

Dregs, *s. pl.* تورتى tòrtu, تلوه tèlvé ; — of the people, اياق طاقمى àyak-tàkimi.

Drench, *v.a.* فنا اصلاتمق fènā-ìsslàtmak.

Dress, *s.* روبه rùba (ùruba), اثواب èsswāb (èssbāb), البسه èlbissé ; زى zìy, قلق kìlik, قيافت kìyāfèt, كسوت kìssvèt ; —, *v.a.* كيندرمك ghìyindirmek; (a wound) صارمق sàrmak; (food) پشرمك pìshirmek; (with a dressing) تربيه ا tèrbìyyé-et; (smooth) دوزتمك dùzètmek; —, v.n. كينمك ghìyinmek.

Dresser, s. مطبخ تسخته سى (mùtfak-tèzghyāhi); صاريجى sàriji.

Dressing, s. (surgical) صارغى sàrghi; (for salad, &c.) تربيه tèrbìyyé.

Drift, s. مفهوم mèfhūm, معنا mà''nà, مرام mèrām.

Drill, s. متقب (màtkàb); تعليم tà''līm; —, v.a. دلمك dèlmek; تعليم ايتدرمك tà''līm-ètdirmek.

Drink, s. ايچه جك ìchéjek, ايچقى ìchki; —, v.a. ايچمك ìchmek.

Drip, v.n. طملامق dàmlamak.

Drive, v.a. سورمك sùrmek; — away, — off, — out, قوغمق kòghmak; — back, كيروسورمك ghèri-sùrmek; — on, ايلرو سورمك ìléri-sùrmek.

Driver, s. سوريجى sùruju; عربه جى ''àrabaji; قوچاچ kòchàch.

Drizzling rain, اينجه يغمور ìnjé-yàghmur.

Drogman, Drogoman, s. ترجمان tèrju-mān.

Droll, a. تحاف tùhāf.

Dromedary, s. هجين hèjin.

Drone, s. يبان اريسى yàban-àrissi; تنبل tènbel.

Droop, v.n. صارقمق sàrkmak; اوزلمك ùzulmek.

Drop, s. طمله dàmla; —, v.n. طملامق dàmlamak; دوشمك dùshmek; —, v.a. دوشورمك dùshurmek.

Dropsical, a. سسقه sìsska, مستسقى mùsstàsskī.

Dropsy, s. استسقا ìsstìsskā.

Dross, s. بوق bòk, جروف jùrūf.

Drought, s. قوراقلق kùràklik.

Drove, s. سورى sùru.

Drover, s. صيغرتماج sìghirtmàj, چوبان chòbàn.

Drown, v.a. صويه بوغمق sùya-bòghmak; —, v.n. صويه بوغلمق sùya-bòghulmak; — one's self, v.a. كنديني صويه اتوب بوغلمق kèndini-sùya-àtip-bòghulmak.

Drowsiness, s. اويقوسى كلمكلك ùykussu-ghèlmeklik.

Drowsy, a. اويقوسى كلمش ùykussu-ghèlmish.

Drub, v.a. دوكمك dùghmek.

Drubbing, s. طياق dàyak.

Drudge, s. كوله kyùlé, يسير yèssir; —, v.n. يسيركبى چالشمق yèssir-ghìbi-chàlishmak.

Drug, s. اجزا èjzā, علاج ''ìlāj.

Druggist, s. اجزاجى èjzāji, سپنچيار ìsspènchiyàr.

Drum, s. ترانپته trànpèta; (big) طاول dàwul; (kettle) دنبلك dùnbélèk.

Drum-major, s. طابورماجور tàbur-màjòr.

Drummer, s. ترانپته جى trànpètaji, طاولجى dàwulju, دنبلكجى dùnbélèkji.

Drumstick, s. ترانپته دينكى trànpèta-dèyneghi.

Drunk, a. سرخوش (sàrkhòsh), كيف kèyf.

Drunkard, s. بكرى bèkrī.

Drunkenness, s. سرخوشلق sèr-khòshlik.

Dry, a. قورو or قورى kùru; صوصامش sùssamish; dry land, قره kàra; —, v.n. قورومق kùrumak; —, v.a. قوروتمق kùrutmak; — up, قورومق kùrumak; قوروتمق kùrutmak.

Drynurse, *s.* (woman) دادی dàdi, دادا dàdà; (man) لالا lála.

Dubious, *a.* شبهه‌لو shùbhéli; مشكوك mèshkyūk.

Ducat, *s.* (Dutch) باجاقلی bàjakli, فلمنك التونی fìlémènk-àltini; (Austrian) مجار التونی màjar-àltini; (Venetian) وندك التونی vènédik-àltini, یالدز التونی yàldiz-àltini.

Duck, *s.* اوردك ùrdek; —, *v.a.* صایه دالدرمق sùya-dàldirmak; (one's head) باشنی دالمق bàshini-dàlmak.

Duckling, *s.* اوردك پلازی ùrdek-pàlazi.

Duct, *s.* صو یولی sū-yòlu; طمر dàmar.

Due, *a.* لازم lāzim, واجب wājib; (payable) وعده‌سی كلمش wà''déssi-ghèlmish; —, *s.* رسم rèssim, تكليف tèklīf, ویركو (vèrghi) vìrghyū.

Duel, *s.* غوغا (kàwgha), دوكش dùghush.

Dug, *s.* ممه mèmé.

Duke, *s.* دوقه dùka.

Dukedom, *s.* رتبهٔ ثانیه بكی rùtbé'i-sānìyyé-bèghi, دوقه‌لق حكومت dùkalik-hùkyūmèt; دوقه‌لق پایه‌سی dùkalik-pāyéssi.

Dulcimer, *s.* صنطور sàntur.

Dull, *a.* (boy) استعدادسز ìsstì''dādsiz; (in spirits) كیفی یوق kèyfi-yòk; (place) صیقندیلی sìkintili, ادم بوغلور àdam-bòghulur; (edge) كور kyùr, كسمز kèssmàz; (day) قپانق kàpànik; (pain) اینجه ìnja; (sound) صاغر sàghir, بوغوق bòghuk; (colour) دونك dùnuk; (ear) اغر àghir; (of hearing) صاغر sàghir; (sight) كورمز ghyùrmàz; (trade) دورغون dùrghun, كساد kèssàd.

Dumb, *a.* دلسز dìlsiz; — creature, حیوان hàywān; — show, اشارت ìshārèt.

Dung, *s.* بوق bòk, نجاست nèjāssèt; فشقی fìshki; كوبره ghyùbré.

Dungeon, *s.* حبس (hàpss), محبس màhbèss, زندان zìndàn, بودرم bòdrum.

Dunghill, *s.* مزبله‌لك mèzbélélik.

Dupe, *s.* الدانمش àldànmish; —, *v.a.* الداتمق àldàtmak.

Duplicate, *s.* ایكنجی صورت ìkinji-sūrèt; in —, *ad.* ایكی صورتی اوله‌رق ìki-sūrèti-òlarak.

Duplicity, *s.* یلانجیلق yàlànjìlik, ایكی یوزلولك ìki-yùzluluk, شیطانلق shèytànlik, خیانت khìyānèt, خباثت khàbàssèt.

Durable, *a.* طیانور dàyànir, طیانقلو dàyànikli.

Duration, *s.* مدت mùddèt; سورك sùrèk, امتداد ìmtidād, قرار kàrār, استمرار ìsstimrār.

During, *pr.* اثناسنده èssnāssìnda, ایچنده ìchinda, ده da; بتنجه‌یه قدر bìtinjéyé-kàdar.

Dusk, *s.* اخشام قرارمسی àkhsham-kàràrmassi.

Dust, *s.* توز tòz, غبار ghùbàr; (sweepings) چوپ chùp.

Dustman, *s.* چوپجی chùpju.

Dusty, *a.* (superficially) توز tòz; (mixed with dust) توزلو tòzlu.

Dutch, *a.* فلمنك fìlémènk.

Dutchman, *s.* فلمنك filémènk.

Dutiful, *a.* (person) رضاجو rìzājū; (conduct) رضاجویانه rìzājūyāné.

Duty, *s.* ایش, ìsh, خذمت (khìzmèt); مأموریت mé'mūrìyyèt; واجبهٔ ذمت wājibé'i-zìmmèt; كمرك ghyùmruk, رسم كمرك rèssmi-ghyùmruk; نوبت

nùbèt ; to be on —, نوبتجی nùbètji-òl; to present one's — to a person, اتکنی اللرینی اوپمك ÈllÈrini-ùpmek, اتکنی اوپمك ètéghini-ùpmek.

Dwarf, s. جوجه jùjÉ.

Dwarfish, a. بودور bòdur.

Dwell, v.n. اوطورمق òtùrmak, قالمق kàlmak, ساکن او sākin-òl ; — on, (in thought) دوشونمك dùshunmek, عقلنی ویرمك "àklini-vèrmek, قید ا kàyd-et; (in speech) تکراربتکرارا کدرمق tèkrar-bé-tèkrar-àngdirmak ; پك تفصیلاته کیرشمك pèk-tàfsīlāta-ghìrish-mek ; — (a note) اوزاتمك ùzàtmak.

Dwelling, s. یر yÈr ; او èv, خانه khānÉ, مسکن mèsskèn ; — house, او èv, خانه khānÉ. [مسکن mèsskèn.

Dwelling-place, s. یر yèr, یورد yùrd,

Dye, s. بویا bòya ; —, v.a. بویامق bòyamak ; —, v.n. بویانمق bòyan-mak, بویاالمق bòya-àlmak.

Dyer, s. بویاجی bòyaji.

Dying, s. اولم ùlum ; اولمه ùlmÉ ; —, a. اولیور ùliyor.

Dyke, s. خندق hèndek ; سد sèdd.

Dynasty, s. اوجاق òjak, سلسله silsilÉ.

Dysentery, s. قانلو اسهال kànli-ìsshāl.

Dyspepsia, s. ضعف هضم zà"f-i-hàzm.

E.

Each, pron. s. هربر hÈr-bìr ; —, pron. a. هر hÈr, هربر hÈr-bìr ; each other, بربری bìr-bìri, یکدیکر yèk-dìghÈr.

Eager, a. پك ارزولو pèk-àrzulu, پك استکلو pèk-ìsstèkli.

Eagerness, s. پك استك pèk-isstek, صبرسزلق sàbrsizlik.

Eagle, s. قره قوش kàra-kùsh.

Ear, s. قولاق kùlàk ; (of corn) باشاق bàshak, سنبله sùnbulÉ ; a box on the —, شمار shàmar. [-bèghi.

Earl, s. دردنجی رتبه بکی dùrdinji-rùtbé-

Early, a. ارکن èrken ; طرفانده tùrfàndÉ ; کنجلکده ghènjlikda ; اول ÈvvÈl, اسکی èsski ; ad. ارکن èrken ; پك صباح pèk-sàbah.

Earn, v.a. قزانمق kàzanmak.

Earnest, a. جدی jìddī, حقیقی hàkīkī ; کرمیتلو ghÈrmìyyètli ; —, s. پی pÈy ; نمونه nùmūnÉ. [kùlàk-kàrishdirajak.

Earpick, s. خلال khìlāl, قولاق قارشدره جق

Earring, s. کوپه kyùpÉ.

Earth, s. طپراق tòprak ; یر yÈr, ارض àrz ; the —, یریوزی yÈr-yùzu, دنیا dùnyà, کرهٔ ارض kyùré'i-àrz.

Earthen, a. طپراق tòprak.

Earthenware, s. طپراق ایشی tòprak-ìshi, چناق چوملك chànak-chùmlek, طباق مباق tàbak-màbak.

Earthly, a. دنیوی dùnyÉvì, خاکی khākī.

Earthquake, s. زلزله zèlzÉlÉ (zÈrzÉlÉ).

Earthwork, s. طپراق طابیه tòprak-tàbiya.

Ease, s. راحت rāhat, قولایلق kòlaylik, سهولت sùhūlèt ; رفاه rèfāh, رفاهیت rèfāhìyyèt ; اسایش āsāyish, اسودکی āsūdéghī ; —, v.a. راحت ویرمك rāhat-vèrmek, راحتلندرمق rāhatlan-dirmak ; تسکین ا tèsskīn-et ; کوشتمك ghèvshÈtmek.

Easel, s. رسام صپاسی rèssām sìpassi.

East, *s.* شرق shàrk, مشرق mèshrik, كون طوغيسى ghyùn-dòghussu (dògh-russu).

Easter, *s.* پاسقاليا pàsskàlya.

Eastern, *a.* شرقى sharkī.

Easy, *a.* قولاى kòlay, سهولتلو sùhūlètli, اسان āssān; راحت rāhat; كوشك ghèvshèk; طاتلو tàtli, يواش yàwàsh.

Eat, *v.a.* يمك yèmek, تناول ا tènāvul-et, اكل ا èkl-et.

Eatable, *a.* ينور yènir, ييه جك yèyéjek, ينه جك yènéjek, مأكول mè'kyūl; eatables, *s.pl.* مأكولات mè'kyūlāt, ييه جك شيلر yèyéjek-shèyler, ييه جك yèyéjek.

Eaves, *s. pl.* صاچاق sàchak.

Echo, *s.* يانقو yànko; —, *v.a.* and *n.* عكس ا "àkss-et.

Eclipse, *s.* (sun's) كسوف kyùssūf; (moon's) خسوف khùssūf; —, *v.a.* ايدينلكنى كسمك àydinlighini-kess-mek; (fig.) كيرو براقمق ghèri-bràk-mak, اشمق àshmak; to be eclipsed, طوتلمق tùtulmak.

Economize, *v.a.* ادارة ا idārè-èt.

Economy, *s.* ادارة idārè.

Ecstacy, Ecstasy, *s.* وجد vèjd, وجدان vìjdān.

Eddy, *s.* انافور ànafòr.

Edge, *s.* (margin) كنار kènār; (cutting) اغز àghiz, قلاغى kìlàghi.

Edible, *a.* مأكول mè'kyūl.

Edifice, *s.* ياپى yàpi, بنا binā.

Editor, *s.* غزته مديرى ghàzèta-mùdīri.

Educate, *v.a.* اوقوتمق òkutmak, تعليم ا tà"līm-et, تدريس ا tèdrīss-et, تربية ا tèrbiyyè-et, پرورش ا pèrvèrish-et.

Eel, *s.* يلان بالغى yìlàn-bàlighi.

Efface, *v.a.* بوزمق bòzmak, سلمك sil-mek, چيزمك chìzmek.

Effect, *s.* تأثير tè'ssīr; اثر èsser; —, *v.a.* ياپمق yàpmak, ايتمك ètmek, حاصل ا hàssil-et.

Effective, *a.* صاغ sàgh; يرار yàrar, صالح sālih.

Effectual, *a.* مرامى كلياً منتج اولان mèrāmi-kyùllìyyan-mùntìj-òlan.

Effervesce, *v.a.* قاينامق kàynamàk.

Efficacious, *a.* مؤثر mù'èssir, مرامى منتج اولان mèrāmi-mùntìj-òlan.

Efficiency, *s.* اهليت èhlìyyèt.

Efficient, *a.* مقتدر mùktèdir, اهل èhl, ارباب èrbāb, صالح sālih.

Effluvium, *s.* قوقو kòku, تعفن tà"affun.

Effort, *s.* سعى sà"y, كوشش ghyùshish, ورزش vèrzish; حمله hàmla.

Egg, *s.* يمورطه yìmurta.

Egg-plant, *s.* پاتلجان pàtlijàn.

Egotism, *s.* انانيت ènānìyyèt, خودبينلك khòdbīnlik, خودپسندلك khòdpèssèndlik.

Egotist, *s.* خودبين khòdbīn, خودپسند khòdpèssènd.

Eight, *a.* سكز sèkiz, ثمان sèmān, هشت hèsht.

Eighteen, *a.* اون سكز òn-sèkiz.

Eighth, *a.* سكزنجى sèkizinji, ثامن sāmin; —, *s.* ثمن sùmn.

Eighty, *a.* سكسان sèksen.

Either, *pron.* يااويابو yà-ò-yà-bù; نه اونه بو nè-ò-nè-bù; بر bìr; ايكيسندن بريسى ìkissindan-bìrissi; —, *conj.* يا.

Elaborate, *a.* اينجه ìnja.

Elapse, *v.n.* كچمك ghèchmek, مرور ا mùrūr-et.

Elastic, *a.* اسنر èssnèr ; اوزانور چکلور ùzànir-chèkilir.

Elbow, s. درسك dìrsek.

Elder, *a.* بیوك bìyuk ; —, *s.* قوجه‌باشی kòja-bàshi, اق صقاللی àk-sàkàlli ; — tree, مرور اغاجی mùrver-àghàji.

Eldest, *a.* بیوك bìyuk ; — son, الك اوغل ìlk-òghul ; — brother, اغا àgha ; — sister, ابله àbla.

Elect, *a.* منتخب mùntakhàb ; مجتبی mùjtébà, ناجی nājī ; —, انتخاب ا ìntikhāb-et, بکنمك bèghènmek, سچمك sèchmek, ایرمق àyrmak.

Election, *s.* انتخاب ìntikhāb.

Electricity, *s.* ایلکتریق ilektrik.

Electrify, *v.a.* ایلکتریق چارپدرمق ilek-trik-chàrpdirmak.

Electuary, *s.* معجون mà"jūn, طریاق tìryàk.

Elegance, *s.* کوزللك ghyùzèllik, ظرافت zàrāfèt, لطافت làtāfèt, حسن hūssn.

Elegant, *a.* کوزل ghyùzèl, ظریف zàrīf, لطیف làtīf.

Elegy, *s.* مرثیه mèrsìyyé.

Element, *s.* اساس èssāss ; جزء jùz" ; elements, ارکان èrkyān ; اصول ùssūl ; the four —, عناصر اربع "ànāssiri-èrbà".

Elephant, *s.* فیل fìl.

Elevate, *v.a.* رفع ا rèf"-et, ترفیع ا tèrfī"-et, قالدرمق kàldirmak, یوکسلتمك yùkseltmek.

Elevation, *s.* رفعت rìf"àt ; علو "ùlùvv ; یوکسکلك yùkseklik ; دپه (tèpé).

Eleven, *a.* اون بر òn-bìr.

Elicit, *v.a.* چیقارمق chìkàrmak, استخراج ا isstikhrāj-et.

Eligible, *a.* استنلور ìssténilir, استنله جك ìsstènilèjek, ارانیلور àrànilir.

Elixir, *s.* اکسیر ìksīr.

Ellipse, *s.* بیضی bèyzī, قطع ناقص kàt"i-nākiss.

Elm, *s.* قره اغاج kàra-àghàch.

Elogy, *s.* مدح mèdh, ثنا sènā, ستایش sìtāyish ; مدحیه mèdhìyyé.

Eloquence, *s.* فصاحت fàssāhàt, بلاغت bèlāghàt, جربزه jèrbézé.

Eloquent, *a.* میرکلام mīri-kèlām, جربزه‌لو jèrbézéli.

Else, *pron.* بشقه bàshka, دیکر dìghèr, غیری ghàyri : —, *c.* یوخسه yòkhsa.

Elsewhere, *ad.* بشقه یره bàshka-yèra, بشقه یرده bàshka-yèrda.

Elucidate, *v.a.* ایضاح ا īzāh.

Elucidation, *s.* ایضاح īzāh.

Elude, *v.a.* صنعت ایله صاقنمق sàn"àt-ìla-sàkinmak ; قورتلمق kùrtulmak.

Emanate, *v.n.* صادر او sàdir-òl, صدور ا sùdūr-et.

Emancipate, *v.a.* ازاد ا āzād-et (àzàd).

Embark, *v.n.* کمی یه بنمك ghèmiya-bìnmek ; — *v.a.* کمی یه قومق ghèmiya-kòmak ; کمی یه بندرمق ghèmiya-bìndirmek.

Embarkation, *s.* کمی یه بنمکلك و بندرمکلك ghèmiya-bìnmeklik-vé-bìndirmeklik.

Embarrass, *v.a.* صیقندی ویرمك sìkindi-vèrmek ; to be embarrassed, صیقلمق sìkìlmak ; بوزلمق bòzulmak, دلی طوتلمق dìli-tùtulmak.

Embarrassment, *s.* صیقندی sìkindi ; دلی طوتلمسی dìli-tùtulmassi.

Embassy, *s.* سفارت sèfārèt, سفارتخانه sèfārèt-khanè.

Embellish, *v.a.* تزيين ا tèzyīn-et, زينتلندرمك zīnètlendirmek.

Embellishment, *s.* تزيين tèzyīn.

Embers, *s. pl.* اوطون اتشنك قورلرى òdun-àtèshining-kòrlari, قور اتش kòr-àtèsh.

Embezzle, *v.a.* چالمق chàlmak.

Emblem, *s.* علامت "àlāmèt, اشارت ìshārèt.

Embrace, *v.a.* قوجاقلمق kūjàklamak; صارلمق sàrilmak; اوپشمك ùpush-mek; قوشاتمق kùshàtmak; احاطه ا ìhāta-et, شامل او shāmil-òl, شمولى او shùmūli-òl.

Embrasure, *s.* مزغال màzghal.

Embroidery, *s.* اينه ايشى īné-ìshi, ايشلمه ìshlémé, نقش nàksh (nàghash).

Embryo, *s.* جنين jènin.

Emerald, *s.* زمرد zùmrud.

Emerge, *v.n.* چيقمق chìkmak.

Emergency, *s.* ايجاب ījāb; in case of —, ايجابى تقديرجه ijabi-tàkdīrja.

Emery, *s.* سمپاره sìmpārè (zìmpara).

Emetic, *a.* and *s.* مقيى mùkàyyī.

Emigrant, *s.* مهاجر mùhājir.

Emigrate, *v.n.* ترك وطن ا tèrki-wàtan-et, اختيار غربت ا ìkhtiyāri-ghùrbèt-et, هجرت ا hìjrèt-et.

Emigration, *s.* ترك وطن terki-wàtan.

Eminence, *s.* تفوق tèfèvvuk; طاغ dàgh, ديه (tèpè).

Eminent, *a.* فائق الاقران fā'iku-'l-àkrān; مشهور mèshhūr.

Emissary, *s.* جاسوس jāssūss (shàshid).

Emolument, *s.* معاش mà''āsh; عوائد ''àwā''id.

Empale, *v.a.* قازقلمق kàzìklamak.

Empalement, *s.* قازقلمه سياستى kàzìk-lama-sìyāssèti.

Emperor, *s.* پادشاه pādishāh, حكمدار hùkyumdār, ايمپراطور ìmpèrātòr.

Empire, *s.* دولت dèvlet, حكومت hùkyūmèt; ايمپراطورلق ìmpèrātòrluk; ممالك mèmālik.

Employ, *v.a.* قوللانمق kùllànmak; (persons) استخدام ا ìsstìkhdām-et; (things) استعمال ا ìsstì''māl-et; ايش ويرمك ìsh-vèrmek; —, *s.* ايش ìsh, خدمت (khìzmet).

Employment, *s.* ايش ìsh; خدمت (khìzmet), مأموريت mè'mūrìyyèt; مشغوليت mèshghūlìyyèt.

Empress, *s.* ايمپراطوريچه ìmpèrātòrīcha, (regnant) پادشاه pādishāh.

Empty, *a.* بوش bòsh, خالى khālī, تهى tèhì; —, *v.a.* بوشالتمق bòshaltmak; — itself, *v.n.* بوشالمق bòshalmak, بوشانمق bòshanmak; (by flowing) اقمق àkmak; (by flowing into) منصب او mùnsàbb-òl.

Emulation, *s.* غيرت ghàyrèt.

Enable, *v.a.* اقدار ا ìkdār-et, مقتدر قيلمق mùktèdir-kìlmak.

Enamel, *s.* مينا mīna (mìnè); —, *v.a.* مينا ايشلمك mìnè-ìshlémek.

Enamoured, *a.* عاشق ''āshìk; to be — (delighted) بايلمق bàyìlmak, خوشلانمق kkòshlanmak.

Encamp, *v.n.* اردو قورمق òrdu-kùrmak.

Encampment, *s.* اردو òrdu; اردوگاه òrdughyāh; قورلمش بر قاچ چادرلر kùrulmish-bìr-kàch-chàdirler.

Enchant, *v.a.* سحرا sìhr-et; سوندرمك sèvindirmek; خوشنه گلمك khò-shuna-ghèlmek.

Enchanter, *s.* سحرباز sìhrbāz.

Enchanting, *a.* دلبر dìlber.

Enchantment, *s.* سحر sìhr; سونج sèvinj; خوشلانش khòshlànish.

Enclose, *v.a.* چويرمك chèvirmek, قوشاتمق kùshàtmak; لفا lèff-et, ایچنه قومق ìchina-kòmak.

Enclosure, *s.* حائط hā'it.

Encore, *int.* (French) افرين افرين āfèrim-āfèrim; بر دها bìr-dàha.

Encounter, *s.* راست گلش ràsst-ghèlish, تصادف tèssàduf; دوكش dùghush; —, *v.a.* راست گلمك ràsst-ghèlmek, تصادفا tèssàduf-et; دوكشمك dùghushmek.

Encourage, *v.a.* يوز ويرمك yùz-vèrmek; يوركلندرمك yùreklendirmek, جسارت ويرمك jèssāret-vèrmek; پرورشا pèr-vèrish-et.

Encouragement, *s.* تشويق tèshvīk.

Encumber, *v.a.* بار او bār-òl; صيقندى او sìkindi-òl, صيقندى ويرمك sìkindi--vèrmek.

End, *s.* اوج ùj; صوك sòng; نهايت nìhāyèt, غايت ghāyèt, انجام ènjām; —, *v.n.* بتمك bìtmek, كسلمك kèssilmek, دوكنمك dùkènmek, منقطعا mùnkàti''-òl, منقرضا mùn-kàriz-òl; —, *v.a.* بترمك bìtirmek; كسمك kèssmek; دوكتمك dùkèt-mek; اتماما ìtmām-et; to make an end of . . . . , كسمك kèssmek, بترمك bìtirmek; — — — — of one's self, كندى كنديني اولدرمك kèndi-kèndini-ùldurmek; to put an end to, بترمك bìtirmek, اوكنى المق ùngunu-àlmak, منعا mèn''-et, چاره بولمق chārè-bùlmak; — — — — to life, اولدرمك ùldurmek; — to sufferings, اذيتدن قورتارمق èzìyyètdan-kùrtarmak, قورتلسون ديو اولدرمك kùrtulsun-dèyu-ùldurmek. [-kòmak.

Endanger, *v.a.* تهلكه يه قومق tèhlikèyè-

Endeavour, *v.n.* چالشمق chàlishmak, سعى ا sà''y-et, باقمق bàkmak. [tassi.

Endive, *s.* فرنك صلاطه سى fìrènk-sàla-

Endless, *a.* نهايتسز nìhāyetsiz, دوكنمز dùkènmàz, بى نهايه bì-nìhāyè.

Endow, *v.a.* ايراد باغلامق īrād-bàgh-lamak; متصف قيلمق mùttàssif-kìl-mak.

Endure, *v.n.* طيانمق dàyanmak, سورمك sùrmek, باقى او bāki-òl, پايدار او pàydār-òl.

Enemy, *s.* دشمن dùshmèn, خصم khàssm, عدو ''àdùvv.

Energetic, *a.* ايشكذار ìshghyuzār; چالشقان chàlishkàn. [ilè.

Energetically, *ad.* غيرت ايله ghàyrèt-

Energy, *s.* غيرت ghàyrèt; قوت kùvvèt.

Enfeeble, *v.a.* ضعيفا zà''īf-èt.

Enfilade, *v.a.* ياندن المق yàndan--àlmak, ياندن دوكمك yàndan--dùghmek.

Enforce, *v.a.* اجرا ا ìjrā-et, حكمنى فعله چيقارمق hùkmunu-fì''la-chìkàr-mak.

Engage, *v.a.* طوتمق tòtmak; مشغول ا mèshghūl-et, اشغال ا ìshghāl-et; يازمق yàzmak, تحريرا tàhrīr-et; جنك ا jènk-et; —, *v.n.* سوز ويرمك sùz-vèrmek, تعهد ا tà''àhhud-et; يازلمق yàzilmak; مقاوله ا mùkāvélé-et, قول ا kàvl-et; — one's self, سوزلشمك sùzleshmek, سوز ويرمك sùz-vèrmek.

Engaged, *a.* تعهدايتمش tà'àhhad-ètmish; وعد ويرمش và''d-vèrmish; مشغول اولمش mèshghūl-òlmish.

Engagement, *s.* ايش ìsh, مشغوليت mèshghūlìyyèt; سوز sùz, وعد và''d; جنك jènk, محاربه mùhārébé; مقاوله mùkāvélé, قول kàvl.

Engine, *s.* چرخ chàrkh, الت ālèt.

Engineer, *s.* چرخجى chàrkhji; (civil or military) مهندس mùhèndiss.

England, *s.* انكلتره Inghiltèrra.

English, *a.* انكليز Inghlìz. [hàkk-et.

Engrave, *v.a.* قازمق kAzmak, حك ا

Engraver, *s.* حكاك hèkkyāk.

Engraving, *s.* باصمه رسم bAssma-rèssim.

Enjoy, *v.a.* (possess) مالك او mālik-òl, نائل او nā'il-òl; (derive pleasure) خوشلنمق khòshlanmak, اكلنمك èghlenmek, متلذذ او mùtélèzziz-ol; — one's self, خوشلنمق khòshlanmak, اكلنمك èghlenmek, صفا ا sàfā-et, متلذذ او mùtélèzziz-òl.

Enjoyment, *s.* تلذذ tèlèzzuz.

Enlarge, *v.a.* بيوتمك bìyutmek, كنشلتمك ghènishletmek; —, *v.n.* بيومك bìyumek; — upon, تفصيلاته كيرشمك tAfsīlAta-ghìrishmek.

Enlightenment, *s.* معلومات mà''lūmAt.

Enlist, *v.a.* عسكرلكه يازمق ''Asskerligha-yàzmak, تحريرا tàhrīr-èt; —, *v.n.* عسكرلكه يازلمق ''Asskerligha-yàzilmak.

Enmity, *s.* دشمنلك dùshmenlik, خصومت khùssūmèt, عداوت ''àdāvèt, غرض ghàraz, نفسانيت nèfsānìyyèt.

Ennui, *s.* (French) جان صيقنديسى jàn-sìkindissi.

Enormity, *s.* فضاحت fAzāhat.

Enormous, *a.* پك بيوك pèk-bìyuk, حددن اشورى hàdddan-Ashiri.

Enough, *a.* and *ad.* يتشر yètishir, يتر yèter, يتشه جك قدر yètishéjek-kAdar, كفايت مقدارى kìfāyèt-mìkdāri.

Enquire, *v.n.* صورمق sòrmak; — for, *or* after, صورمق sòrmak.

Enrich, *v.a.* زنكين ا zènghin-et; (embellish) تزيين ا tèzyīn-et; (with jewels) ترصيع ا tèrsī''-et.

Ensign, *s.* سنجاق sAnjak, بيرق bàyrak, باندره bàndara; بيراقدار bàyrakdàr, سنجاقدار sAnjakdàr.

Enslave, *v.a.* اسيرا èssīr-et (yèssir).

Ensue, *v.n.* چيقمق chìkmak, حاصل او hāssil-òl, ترتب ا tèrèttub-et.

Enter, *v.a.* كيرمك ghìrmek, دخول ا dùkhūl-et, داخل او dākhil-ol; (write down) قيد ا kayd-et; — into (commence), كيرشمك ghirishmek, مباشرت ا mùbāshérèt-et.

Enterprise, *s.* ایش ìsh, کار kyār, مباشرت mùbāshérèt.

Entertain, *v.a.* قبول ا kÀbūl-et; اليقومق Àlikòmak; اكلندرمك èghlÈndirmek; يمك ويرمك yèmèk-vÈrmek; بسلمك bèsslémek; اضمار ا ìzmār-et, عقلنه قبول ا "Àklina-kÀbūl-et. [ضيافت zìyāfèt.

Entertainment, *s.* اكلنجه èghlÈnjÉ;

Entice, *v.a.* جزب ا jèzb-et, الداتمق Àl-

Enticing, *a.* دلفريب dìlfirīb. [datmak.

Entire, *a.* يكپاره yèkpārÉ, بتون bìtun, تام tÀmm, تكميل tèkmīl; — horse, ات Àt, ايغر āyghir.

Entrails, *s. pl.* بغرساق bàghirsak.

Entrance, *s.* (act) كيرش ghìrish, دخول dùkhūl; (place) قپو kÀpi, مدخل mèdkhàl.

Entreat, *v.a.* رجا ا rìjā-et, نياز ا nìyāz-et, يالوارمق yÀlvarmak.

Entry, *s.* قپو kÀpi, مدخل mèdkhàl; (registering) قيد kàyd. [tà"dād-et.

Enumerate, *v.a.* صايمق sàymak, تعداد ا

Envelop, *v.a.* صارمق sarmak.

Envelope, *s.* ظرف zàrf. [hàssūd.

Envious, *a.* قزقانج kìzkÀnj, حسود

Environs, *s. pl.* جوار jìwār, اطراف ètrāf, قرب kùrb.

Envoy, *s.* اورطه ايلچى òrta-èlchi, مخصوص ايلچى màkhsūss-èlchi.

Envy, *s.* قزقانمه kìzkÀnma, حسد hàssed; —, *v.a.* قزقانمق kìzkÀnmak, حسد ا

Epilepsy, *s.* صرعه sÀr"à. [hàssed-et.

Equal, *a.* بر bìr, مساوى mùssāvi; (in age) اقران Àkrān; (in rank) كفو kyùfv; —, *v.a.* مساوى او mùssāvi-òl.

Equality, *s.* مساوات mùssāvāt.

Equalize, *v.a.* مساوى ا mùssāvī-et.

Equally, *ad.* مساوات اوزره mùssāvāt-ùzérÉ.

Equalness, *s.* مساوات mùssāvāt.

Equator, *s.* خط استوا khÀtt-i-ìsstiwā.

Equatorial, *a.* خط استوايه منسوب khatt-i-ìsstiwāya-mènsūb.

Equilateral, *a.* متساوى الاضلاع mùtéssā-vìyyu-'l-Àzlā".

Equinoctial, *a.* خط استوايه منسوب khatt-i-ìsstiwāya-mènsūb. [-lèyl-u-nìhār.

Equinox, *s.* تساوىء ليل ونهار tèssāvī'i-

Equip, *v.a.* دوناتمق dònatmak, تجهيز ا tèjhīz-et. [hÀkkÀnìyyèt.

Equity, *s.* عدالت "àdālèt, حقانيت

Equivalent, *a.* مساوى mùssāvi; —, *s.* عوض "ìvèz, قارشيلق kàrshilik.

Era, *s.* مبدأ تاريخ mèbdè'i-tārīkh, حساب تاريخ hìssābi-tārīkh.

Erase, *v.a.* بوزمق bòzmak, ترقين ا tÈrkīn-et, حك ا hàkk-et.

Erect, *a.* ديك dìk, طوغرى dòghru, قائم kā'im, عمود "àmūd; —, *v.a.* دكمك dìkmek, نصب ا nÀssb-et; قالدرمق kÀldirmak; ياپمق yàpmak, بنا ا bìnā-et, انشا ا ìnshā-et.

Erivan (capital of Persian Armenia), *s.* روان شهرى Rèvān-shèhiri.

Ermine, *s.* قاقوم kākūm.

Err, *v.n.* (mistake) ياكلمق yàngilmak, خطا ا khÀtā-et; (wander) طولاشمق dòlashmak. [khÀtā-sàwÀb.

Errata, *s. pl.* erratum, *s.* خطا صواب

Erroneous, *a.* ياكلش yāngilish (yānish).

Error, *s.* یاکلش yàngılish (yānish), یاکلشلق (yānishlik) خطا khàtā, سهو sèhv, ضلالت dàlālèt, ضلال dàlāl; one in error, ضال dāll; one who leads into error, مضل mùdìll. [bàhhir.

Erudite, *a.* عالم "ālim, متبحر mùté-

Erysipelas, *s.* یلانجق yìlànjìk. [-shèhiri.

Erzroum, *s.* ارض‌روم شهری Erzrūm-

Escape, *s.* قورتلش kùrtulush, خلاص khàlāss, سلامت sèlāmèt; قاچش kàchish, فرار firār; —, *v.n.* قورتلمق kùrtulmak, خلاص‌بولمق khàlāss-bùlmak, یقابی‌قورتارمق yàkayi-kùrtarmak; قاچمق kàchmak, فرارا firār-et.

Escort, *s.* یساقجی yàssàkji; احتیاطاً ترفیق‌اولنان‌عسکر ìhtiyàtan-tèrfīk-òlunan-"àsskèr; —, *v.a.* برابرکتمك bèrābèr-ghìtmek. [khàsss.

Especial, *a.* مخصوص màkhsūss, خاص

Especially, *ad.* مخصوصاً màkhsūssan, خصوصا khùssūssā, خاصة khàsssātan.

Espouse, *v.a.* المق àlmak, تزوجا tèzèvvuj-et; (a cause) التزاما ìltizām-et, تصحبا tàssàhhub-et.

Essay, *s.* تجربه tèjribé; رساله rìssālé; —, *v.n.* and *a.* باقمق bàkmak, دنه‌مك dènémek, تجربه‌ا tèjribé-et; امتحانا ìmtihān-et, طارتمق tàrtmak, یوقلامق yòklamak. [روح rūh.

Essence, *s.* اصل àssl, كنه kyunh; (spirit)

Essential, *a.* اصلی àsslī; (volatile) طیار tàyyār; (necessary) لازم lāzim, متحتم mùtahàttim.

Establish, *v.a.* اچمق àchmak, قورمق kùrmak, تأسیسا tè'sīss-et, پایدارا pàydār-et. [dùkkyān.

Establishment, *s.* تأسیس tè'siss; دكان

Estate, *s.* املاك èmlāk, اراضی àrāzī, ملك mùlk; مال‌واشیا māl-u-èshyā; تركه tèréké; حال‌وحیثیت hāl-u-hàysìyyèt; رتبه rùtbé.

Esteem, *s.* اعتبار ì"tibār; نظر nàzar; —, *v.a.* اعتبارا ì"tibār-et, صایمق sàymak, نظرا nàzar-et, عدا "àdd-et.

Estimate, *s.* كشف kèshf, تخمین tàkhmīn; —, *v.a.* تخمینا tàkhmīn-et.

Eternal, *a.* ابدی و ازلی èbédī-vè-èzélī.

Eternity, *s.* (past) ازل èzel; (future) ابد èbed; (state of) ابدیت èbédìyyèt, ازلیت èzélìyyèt.

Ether, *s.* لقمان روحی lòkmān-rùhu; (ethereal matter) اثیر èssīr.

Ethics, *s. pl.* علم‌اخلاق "ìlmi-àkhlāk, ادبیات èdébìyyāt.

Ethiopian, *s.* سیاه‌عرب sìyāh-"àrab.

Etiquette, *s.* عادت "ādèt.

Etymology, *s.* اشتقاق ìshtikāk; علم‌صرف

Eulogy, *s.* ستایش sìtāyish. ["ìlm-i-sàrf.

Eunuch, *s.* خصی khasi; خادم khàdim; طواشی tàwāshī.

Euphrates (the river) *s.* فرات نهری fùrāt-nèhri. [tàkhlìyyé-et.

Evacuate, *v.a.* چیقمق chìkmak; تخلیه‌ا

Evacuation, *s.* تخلیه tàkhlìyyé.

Evaporate, *v.n.* اوچمق ùchmak, قورومق kùrumak; —, *v.a.* قایناتمق kàynatmak, اوچرمق ùchurmak, قوروتمق kùrutmak.

Evaporation, *s.* اوچوب بخار اولمقلق ùchup-bùkhār-òlmaklik.

Eve, *s.* اخشام Akhsham.

Even, *s.* اخشام Akhsham; —, *a.* دوز dùz, هموار hèmvār; طوغری dòghru; برسیاقده bìr-sìyAkda; باشه باش bAsha-bAsh; —, *ad.* بیله bīlé, ده da, دخی dàkhi; even so, *ad.* اویله ùylé.

Evening, *s.* اخشام Akhsham, اخشام وقتی Akhsham-wAkti.

Event, *s.* وقعه wàk''à.

Eventually, *ad.* عاقبت ''ākibet.

Ever, *ad.* دائما dā'imā; بر وقتده bìr-wAkitda; for ever, ابداً èbédEn; for ever and ever, ابد الاباد èbédé-'l-ābād; ever and anon, بردوزیه bìr-dùzìyé; ever since, اول وقتدنبرو òl-wAkitdan-bèri.

Everlasting, *a.* دوکنمز dùkènmaz, بی زوال bī-zèwāl, لم یزل lèm-yèzil.

Evermore, *ad.* فیمابعد fīmābà''d, بوندن بویله bùndan-bùylé, الی الابد ìlé-'l-èbed.

Every, *a.* هر hèr, هربر hèr-bìr; — day, هرکون hèr-ghyùn; — other day, کون اشوری ghyùn-Ashiri, ایکی کونده بر ìki-ghyùnda-bìr; — thing, هرشی hèr-shèy; — one, — body, هرکس hèr-kèss; — where, هریره hèr-yèra, هریرده hèr-yèrda, — whit, — bit, هروجهله hèr-wèjhila; بتون بتون bìtun-bìtun.

Evidence, *s.* شهادت shàhādèt; دلالت dèlālèt.

Evident, *a.* کوز اوکنده ghyùz-ùngunda, میداننده mèydAnda, اشکار Ashikyār, ظاهر zāhir, بدیهی bèdīhī, بدیدار bèdīdār, هویدا hùwèydā.

Evil, *s.* کوتیلك kyùtuluk, فنالق fènalik, سوء sù'; ضرر zàrar, مضرت mAzàrràt; بلا bèlā, مصیبت mùssībèt; فلاکت fèlākèt; علت ''ìllèt, مرض màraz; —, *a.* کوتی kyùtu, فنا fèna, قبیح kAbīh; the evil one, شیطان لعین shèytAni-là''īn; the evil eye, نظر nAzar; evil-doer, *s.* مجرم mùjrìm; evil-speaking, *s.* بهتان bùhtan.

Ewe, *s.* ماریا māriya, دیشی قویون dìshi-kòyun.

Ewer, *s.* ابریق ìbrīk.

Exact, *a.* طوغری dòghru, تمام tAmām, تام tāmm, صحیح sàhīh; —, *v.a.* المق Almak, سوکوب المق sùkyub-Almak, مطلق استیوب المق mùtlAk-ìsstéyub-Almak; تحصیل ا tàhsīl-et; طلب ا tAleb-et.

Exactly, *ad.* تام tāmm, تمام tAmām; صحیحاً sàhīhan.

Exactness, *s.* طوغریلق dòghruluk.

Exaggerate, *v.a.* مبالغه ا mùbAligha-et.

Exaggeration, *s.* مبالغه mùbAligha.

Examination, *s.* یوقلمه yòklama, امتحان ìmtihān.

Examine, *v.a.* یوقلمق yòklamak, باقمق bAkmak, معاینه ا mù''āyéné-et; امتحان ا ìmtihān-et.

Examiner, *s.* ممیز mùmèyyiz.

Exasperate, *v.a.* قیزدرمق kìzdirmak, دارلتمق dArìltmak.

Exasperation, *s.* فنا دارغینلق fèna-dàrghìnlik. [òymak ; حفرا hùfr-et.

Excavate, *v.a.* قازمق kàzmak ; اویمق

Exceed, *v.a.* کچمك ghèchmek, اشمق àshmak, تجاوز ا tèjāvuz-et.

Exceedingly, *ad.* غایت ghāyèt, غایتله ghāyètla, بغایت bèghāyèt.

Excel, *v.n.* and *a.* فائق او fā'ik-òl.

Excellence, *s.* ایولك īyilik, اعلالق à''lālik; تفوق tèfèvvuk, رجحانیت rùjhānìyyèt.

Excellent, *a.* پك ایو pèk-īyi, پك اعلا pèk-à''lā, چوق ایو chòk-īyi.

Except, *ad.* دن بشقه dan-bàshka, دن ماعدا dan-mā''ada, دن فضله dan-fàzla, دن غیری dan-ghàyri; —, *v.a.* استثنا ا ìsstissnā-et, مستثنا طوتمق mùsstèssnā-tùtmak.

Excepting, *ad.* دن بشقه dan-bàshka, دن ماعدا dan-mā''ada, دن فضله dan-fàzla, دن غیری dan-ghàyri.

Exception, *s.* استثنا ìsstissnā.

Excess, *s.* فضله fāzla; افراط ìfrāt; to commit excesses, طاشتمق tàshitmak, اشورمق àshirmak.

Exchange, *s.* دیکش dìghish, ترانپه trànpa, مبادله mùbādélé; bill of —, پولیچه pòlicha; course of —, قانبیو kànbiyo; —, *v.a.* دیکشدرمك dìghishdirmek, تبدیل ا tèbdīl-et; —, *v.n.* دیکش ا dìghish-et, ترانپه ا trànpa-et, مبادله ا mù-bādélé-et.

Exchequer, *s.* خزینه khàzìné.

Excise, *s.* احتساب ìhtissāb.

Exciseman, *s.* احتساب مأموری ìh-tissāb-mè'mūri.

Excite, *v.a.* تحریك ا tàhrīk-et; تأثیرا tè'sīr-et.

Exclaim, *v.n.* چاغرمق chàghirmak, باغرمق bàghirmak, ندا ا nìdā-et.

Exclamation, *s.* ندا nìdā; note of —, حرف ندا hàrf-i-nīda.

Exclude, *v.a.* ایچرو المق ìchèri-àlma-mak, قبول ایتممك kàbūl-et-memek.

Exclusion, *s.* عدم قبول 'àdm-i-kàbūl.

Excusable, *a.* معذور mà''zūr.

Excuse, *s.* عذر ''ùzr; بهانه bàhānė; —, *v.a.* عفو ا ''àfv-et.

Execute, *v.a.* اجرا ا ìjrā-et, فعله کتورمك fì''lé-ghètirmek; قتل ا kàtl-et; اصمق àssmak.

Execution, *s.* اجرا ìjrā; قتل kàtl.

Executioner, *s.* جلاد jèllàd.

Exemplify, *v.a.* مثال کتورمك mìssāl-ghètirmek, تمثیل ا tèmsīl-et.

Exempt, *a.* بری bèrī, معاف mù''àf, ازاد āzād; —, *v.a.* عفو ا ''àfv-et, معاف ا mù''àf-et.

Exemption, *s.* معافیت mù''àfìyyèt.

Exercise, *s.* (bodily) حرکت hàrékèt; (for improvement) تعلیم tà''līm; (military) تعلیم tà''līm; (performance) اجرا ìjrā; (lesson) درس dèrss, تعلیم tà''līm, مطالعه mùtāla''à; —, *v.a.* تعلیم ایتدرمك tà''līm-ètdirmek; (a profession) ایتمك ètmek; (a horse, &c.) کزدرمك ghèzdirmek.

Exert, *v.a.* صرف ا sàrf-et; ابراز ا ìbrāz-et; — one's self, سعی ا sà''y-et, غیرت ا ghàyret-et, چبالمق chàbàla-mak. [چبالمه chàbàlama.

Exertion, *s.* سعی sà''y, غیرت ghàyret,

Exhalation, *s.* بخار bùkhār. [bìtirmek.

Exhaust, *v.a.* دوكتمك dùkètmek, بترمك

Exhaustion, *s.* دوكتمكلك dùkètmeklik; بترمكلك bìtirmeklik.

Exhibit, *v.a.* كوسترمك ghyùsstermek, سير ايتدرمك sèyr-ètdirmek; ابراز ا ìbrāz-et.

Exile, *s.* سوركون sùrghyun, نفى nèfy, منفى mènfī; —, *v.a.* سورمك sùrmek, نفى ا nèfy-et.

Exist, *v.n.* وار او vàr-òl, كائن او kyā'in-òl, موجود او mèvjūd-òl, بولنمق bùlunmak; كچنمك ghèchinmek, تعيش ا tà''àyyush-et.

Existence, *s.* وارلق vàrlik, كون kèvn, كينونت kèynūnèt, موجوديت mèvjūdìyyèt, وجود vùjūd.

Exorbitant, *a.* حددن متجاوز hàdden-mùtéjāviz; پك بهالو pèk-pAhali.

Exotic, *a.* اجنبى èjnébī.

Expand, *v.n.* يايلمق yàyilmak.

Expansion, *s.* يايلمقلق yàyilmaklik.

Expect, *v.a.* باقمق bAkmak, اومق ùmmak, مأمول ا mè'mūl-et.

Expectation, *s.* مأمول mè'mūl, اميد ùmīd (ùmut), ترجى tèrèjjī, ترقب tèràkkùb.

Expectorate, *v.a.* توكورمك tùkyurmek.

Expediency, *s.* مناسبت mùnāssébèt, لزوم lùzūm.

Expedient, *s.* چاره charé, قولاى kòlay, يول yòl; —, *a.* مناسب mùnāssib, لازم lāzim.

Expedite, *v.a.* تعجيل ا tà''jīl-et.

Expedition, *s.* سرعت sùr''àt; عجله ''àjélé; ارسال ìrsāl; سفر sèfer; سفر ارقه داشلرى طاقمى sèfer-àrkadash-lari-tàkimi. [sèrī''.

Expeditious, *a.* چابك chàbik, سريع

Expel, *v.a.* قوغمق kòghmak, دفع ا dèf''-et.

Expend, *v.a.* خرج ا khàrj-et, صرف ا sàrf-et, خرجامق khàrjamak.

Expense, *s.* خرج khàrj, مصرف mAssràf, مصارف mAssārif, مصارفات mAssārifAt.

Expensive, *a.* مصرفلو mAssràfli.

Experience, *s.* كوركى ghyùrghi, معلومات mà''lūmAt, تجربه tèjrubé; —, *v.a.* كورمك ghyùrmek, باشنه كلمك bAshina-ghèlmek, تجربه ا tèjrubé-et, چكمك chèkmek; —, دنه مك dènémek.

Experienced, *a.* معلوماتلو mà''lūmAtli, كارديده kyārdīdé, مجرب mùjèrreb.

Experiment, *s.* تجربه tèjrubé, دنه مه dènémé.

Expert, *a.* استاذ ùsstāz (ùssta).

Expire, *v.n.* اولمك ùlmek; سونمك sùnmek, منطفى او mùntàfi-òl; (a term) كلمك ghèlmek, تمام او tAmAm-òl, منقضى او mùnkAzi-òl.

Explain, *v.a.* تعريف ا tà''rīf-et, اكلاتمق ànglatmak (ànnatmak).

Explanation, *s.* تعريف tà''rìf.

Explicit, *a.* صريح sArīh, اچق àchik.

Explode, *v.n.* پاطلامق pAtlamak; —, *v.a.* اتش ويرمك Atèsh-vèrmek, اتمق Atmak; چوروتمك chùrutmek, ابطال ا ìbtāl-et.

Exploration, *s.* کشف و معاینه kèshf-vé-mù‘‘āyéné.

Explore, *v.a.* یوقلمق yòklamak, معاینه ا mù‘‘āyéné-et, تجسس ا tèjèsssuss-et.

Explosion, *s.* پاطلایش pàtlayish, اتش àtish; سس sèss, صدا sādā.

Export, *s.* اخراجات ìkhrājāt (*pl.*); —, *v.a.* طیشاری کوندرمك dìshàri-ghyùndermek.

Exportation, *s.* اخراج ìkhrāj, طیشاری کوندرمه dìshàri-ghyùnderma, طیشاری کوندریلمه dìshāri-ghyùnderilma.

Exporter, *s.* امتعه طیشاری کوندرر اولان بازرکان èmti‘‘a-dìshàri-ghyùnderer-òlan-bàzirghyān.

Expose, *v.a.* (to view) میدانه قومق mèy-dana-kòmak, میدانه چیقارمق mèy-dana-chìkàrmak; (to shame) رذیل ا rèzīl-et, الەویرمك èla-vèrmek, لسانه کتورمك lìssāna-ghètirmek; (explain) بیان ا bèyān-et, سویلمك sùwèylémek, بسط ا bàsst-et, اچمق àchmak.

Express, *a.* مخصوص màkhsūss; —, *s.* تاتار tàtār, سوریجی sùruju; —, *v.a.* افاده ا ìfādé-et, تعریف ا tà‘‘rīf-et, بیان ا bèyān-et, تعبیر ا tà‘‘bīr-et, سویلمك sùwèylémek, اکلاتمق ànglat-mak; صیقمق sìkmak, صوینی المق sùyunu-àlmak. [تعریف tà‘‘rīf.

Expression, *s.* تعبیر tà‘‘bīr; افاده ìfādé,

Exquisite, *a.* پك نازك pèk-nāzik, پك لطیف pèk-làtīf.

Extempore, *a.* بلا مطالعه و بدیهی bìlā-mūtāla‘‘à-vé-bèdīhī.

Extend, *v.a.* یایمق yàymak; اوزاتمق ùzàtmak; —, *v.n.* یایلمق yàyilmak; وارمق vàrmak.

Extensive, *a.* واسع vàsi‘‘, کنش ghènish, بیوك bìyuk; کلی kyùllī.

Extent, *s.* امتداد ìmtidād; وسعت vùss‘‘àt; مقدار mìkdār; درجه dèréjé; حجم hàjm.

Extenuate, *v.a.* تخفیف ا tàkhfīf-èt.

Extenuation, *s.* تخفیف tàkhfīf.

Exterior, *s.* طیش dìsh, خارج khārij; —, *a.* خارجی khārijī.

Exterminate, *v.a.* بترمك bìtirmek, قیرمق kìrmak, کوکنی قازیمق kyùkunu-kàzimak.

Extermination, *s.* استیصال ìsstīssāl.

External, *a.* خارجی khārijī.

Extinction, *s.* اطفا ìtfā; انقراض ìnkìràz.

Extinguish, *v.a.* سوندرمك sùndurmek, اطفا ا ìtfā-et.

Extirpate, *v.a.* سوکمك sùkmek, چیقارمق chìkàrmak, قلع ا kàl‘‘-et.

Extort, *v.a.* جبراً المق jèbran-àlmak; اجباراً سویلتمك ìjbāran-sùwèyletmek.

Extortion, *s.* جبراً پاره المقلق jèbran-pārè-àlmaklik.

Extra, *a.* زائد zā’id, فضله fàzla, حسابدن خارج hìssābdan-khàrij.

Extract, *v.a.* چیقارمق chìkārmak; المق àlmak; اخراج ا ìkhrāj-et, استخراج ا ìsstikhrāj-et, *s.* نبذه nèbzé; برمقدار bìr-mìkdār; خلاصه khùlāssé.

Extraordinary, *a.* فوق العاده fèvka-’l-‘‘ādé; عجیب (‘‘àjā’ib), غریب ghàrīb.

Extravagance, *s.* أسراف ìssrāf ; صاچمه sAchma, دلیصاچمهسی dèli-sAch-massi.

Extravagant, *a.* مسرف mùssrif ; دلی dèli, مجنون mèjnūn ; مجنونانه mèj-nūnānÉ.

Extreme, *s.* نهایت nìhāyet, غایت ghāyèt, نهایتدرجه nìhāyéti-dèréjÉ ; —, *a.* —ly, *ad.* حددنزیاده hàddddan--ziyādÉ, اشوری Ashiri ; شدید shèdīd.

Extremity, *s.* نهایت nìhāyet, اوج ūj ; شدت shìddèt, فرط fÈrt, افراط ìfrAt.

Extricate, *v.a.* قورتارمق kùrtarmak, خلاص ا khàlāss-et.

Exult, *v.n.* سونملك sÈvinmek, حظ ا hAzz--et, مسرور او mèssrūr-òl, خوشلانمق khòshlanmak.

Exultation, *s.* سونمه sÈvinmÉ.

Eye, *s.* كوز ghyùz, عين ''àyn, چشم chèshm ; (hook and) — قوپچه kòpcha ; —, *v.a.* باقمق bAkmak, كوز دكملك ghyùz-dìkmek.

Eyeball, *s.* كوز ghyùz.

Eyebrow, *s.* قاش kAsh.

Eyelash, *s.* كرپك kìrpik.

Eyesight, *s.* كوز ghyùz, بصر bAssar.

Eye-witness, *s.* كوز شاهدى ghyùz--shāhidi, شاهد shāhid, شاهدالعين shāhidu-'l-''àyn.

F.

Fable, *s.* مثال mìssāl, مصال mAssAl, حكايه hìkyāyÉ.

Fabric, *s.* یاپی yàpi, بنا binā ; هیئت hèy'èt, هیكل hèykÈl ; قماش kùmAsh.

Fabricate, *v.a.* دوزملك dùzmek, یاپمق yàpmak.

Fabulous, *a.* اصلییوق Assli-yòk ; اصلی یوق كبی Assli-yòk-ghìbi, مصال كبی mAssAl-ghìbi.

Face, *s.* یوز yùz, چهره chèhrÉ, صورت sūrÈt (sùrAt) ; —, *v.a.* یوزینهباقمق yùzuna-bAkmak ; قارشیدورمق kàr-shi-dùrmak, طیانمق dàyanmak ; اورتملك ùrtmek, قاپلامق kAplamak.

Facet, *s.* فاچته fàchèta.

Facetious, *a.* لطیفهجی làtīféji.

Facetiousness, *s.* لطیفهجیلك làtīféjilik.

Facilitate, *v.a.* تسهیل ا tèsshīl-et. [lèt.

Facility, *s.* قولایلق kòlaylik, سهولت sùhū-

Facing, *s.* یوز yùz, قاپلامه kAplama ; —, *pr.* قارشیسنه kàrshissina, قارشیسنده kàrshissinda. [-hāl.

Fact, *s.* وقعه vàk''à ; واقعحال vākì''i-

Factor, *s.* صاتیجی sAtiji.

Factory, *s.* فابریقه fàbrika.

Faculty, *s.* خاصه khAsssa, قوت kùvvèt ; اختیار ìkhtiyār, رأی rè'y ; صنف sìnf.

Fade, *v.n.* صولمق sòlmak, اتمق Atmak ; — away, زائلاو zā'il-òl, غائباو ghā'ib-òl. [-ghìbi-chAlishmak.

Fag, *v.n.* حمال كبی چالشمق hAmmāl-

Faggot, *s.* اینجهاوطوندمتی ìnja-òdun--dèméti.

Fail, *v.n.* بوشهچیقمق bòsha-chìkmak, اویمامق ùymamak ; بوزلمق bòzulmak ; اویدرهممق ùyduramamak ; مفلساو mùfliss-òl, طوپ اتمق tòp-Atmak ; قصور ا kùssūr-et ; ایتمامزلك ا ètma-mazlik-et.

Failing, *s.* قصور kùssūr, عيب ''àyb, قباحت kābāhat. [lik.

Failure, *s.* افلاس ìflāss, مفلسلك mùfliss-

Faint, *a.* بايله‌جق bàyilajak; (colour) خفيف khāfīf, اچق àchik; (smell) اغر āghir; (voice) اينجه ìnja, بايغين bàyghin; —, *v.n.* بايلمق bàyilmak.

Fainting-fit, *s.* بايلمه bàyilma.

Fair, *a.* (beautiful) كوزل ghyùzèl, دلبر dìlbēr; (fine) كوزل ghyùzèl, اچق àchik; (favorable) اويغون ùyghun, موافق mùwāfik; (not dark) صارى sāri, بياض bèyaz; (hair) لپشقه lìpìsska; (kind) طاتلو tātli; — play, طوغريلق dòghrùluk, حيله‌سزلك hīléssizlik; to give fair play, حيله ايتمامك hīlé-ètmamek, خارجدن قارشمامق khārijdan-kārishmamak; the fair sex, قاريلر kārilar, طائفهٔ نسا tā'ifè'i-nìssā, قارى قسمى kāri-kìssmi; —, *s.* پناير pānàyir.

Fairy, *s.* پرى pèri.

Faith, *s.* ايمان īmān; دين dīn; اعتقاد ì''tikād; امنيت èmnìyyèt, اعتماد ì''timād; bad faith, يلانجيلق yàlānjilik, خائنلق khā'inlik, خيانت khìyānèt.

Faithful, *a.* صادق sādik; the faithful, *s. pl.* مسلمين mùsslimīn, مؤمنين mù'minīn.

Faithfulness, *s.* صداقت sādākāt.

Falcon, *s.* شاهين shāhin, طوغان dòghan.

Fall, *s.* دوشمه dùshmé; —, *v.a.* دوشمك dùshmek; يقلمق yìkilmak; انمك ènmek; پهاسى انمك pàhassi-ènmek; باشلامق bāshlamak; — asleep, اويقوسى كلوب اويومق ùykussu-ghèlup-ùyumak; اولمك ùlmek, وفات ا vèfāt-et; — away, دونوب براقمق dùnup-bràkmak; دوشمك dùshmek, يقلمق yìkilmak; ضعيفلنمق zà''īflanmak, يالكزكموك قالمق yālingiz-kèmik-kālmak; — back, كيرو چكلمك ghèri-chèkilmek; — down, دوشمك dùshmek, يقلمق yìkilmak; — in with, تصادف ا tèssāduf-et, راست كلمك rāsst-ghèlmek; موافقت ا mùwāfakāt-et; — off, ازالمق āzalmak; براقوب چكلمك bràkip-chèkilmek; — out, تصادف ا tèssāduf-et, واقع او waki''-ol; بوزشمق bòzushmak, غوغا ا (kàwgha)-et; — short, اكسك كلمك èksik-ghèlmek, نصابنى بولمامق nìssābini-bùlmamak; — to, باشلامق bāshlamak; — to leeward, روزكار التنه كتمك rùzghyār-āltina-ghìtmek.

False, *a.* ياكلش yàngilish (yānish), فاسد fāssid; يلان yàlān; يلانجى yàlānji; تقليد tāklīd; يابمه yàpma, دوزمه dùzmé, اويدرمه ùydurma; قالپ kālp; ساخته sākhté; خائن khā'in; بيوفا. bīwèfā, صداقتسز sādākātsiz; مزور mùzèvvir; — witness, يلان شاهدى شاهدزور shāhidi-zūr, yàlān-shāhidi; false-witness, *s.* افترا ìftirā, بهتان bùhtān, يلان yàlān, تزوير tèzvīr.

Falsehood, *s.* يلان yàlān, كذب kìzb; يلانجيلق yàlānjilik; خائنلق khā'inlik; صداقتسزلق sādākātsizlik, عدم وفا ''àdémi-wèfā.

Falseness, *s.* يلان yàlān; ياكلش yàn-gilish (yānish), خطا khAtā, ياكلشلق (yānishlik). [نام nAm.

Fame, *s.* شهرت shùhrèt, اشتهار ìshtihār,

Familiar, *a.* دوست dòsst, صيقى دوست sìki-dòsst; دوستانه dòsstānè; تكليفسز tèklīfsiz; قبا kAba.

Familiarity, *s.* تكليفسزلك tèklīfsizlik.

Familiarize, *v.a.* الشدرمق Alishdirmak; — one's self, الشمق Alishmak.

Family, *s.* چوجق chòjuk, اولاد èvlād; چولق چوجق chòluk-chòjuk, اوبارق èv-bàrk, اهل وعيال èhl-u-"àyāl, او طاقمى èv-tàkimi; اوجاق òjak, سلسله sìlsilè, خانه khānè, خاندان khānédān, دودمان dūdmān, آل āl; نوع nèv", صوى sòy, صوى صوب sòy-sòp, جنس jìnss. [غلا ghìlā.

Famine, *s.* اچلق àchlik; قحط kàht,

Famish, *v.a.* اچ قومق àj-kòmak; —, *v.n.* اچ قالمق àj-kAlmak, اجقمق àjik-mak, اچلق چكمك àchlik-chèk-mek. [pèk-àjikmish.

Famished, *a.* پك اچ pèk-àj, پك اجقمش

Famous, *a.* مشهور mèshhūr; پك ايو pèk-īyi, پك اعلا pèk-à"lā.

Fan, *s.* يلپازه yèlpāzè; قالبور kAlbur; —, *v.a.* يلپازه صاللامق yèlpāzè-sAlla-mak.

Fanatic, *s.* متعصب mùta"Asssib; —al, *a.* متعصبانه mùta"Assibānè.

Fanaticism, *s.* تعصب tà"Assub.

Fancy, *s.* عقل "Akl, ذهن zìhn; قوت متخيله kùvvèti-mùtékhàyyilè; مراق mèrAk; قورونتى kùruntu, صاچمه sAchma; —, *v.a.* قورمق kùrmak, عقلنه كتورمك "Aklina-ghètirmek; ظن ا zànn-et; جانى استمك jAni-ìssté-mek; بكنمك bèghEnmek; to take a fancy to . . . , جانى استمك jāni-ìsstémek; بكنمك bèghEnmek.

Fanfaronade, *s.* لاف lAf.

Far, *a.* اوزاق ùzAk, ايراق īrAk, بعيد bà"īd; — and wide, *ad.* اطرافه ètrāfa, اطرافده ètrāfda; —, *ad.* (much more) دها چوق dàhā-chòk; (very) پك pèk, چوق chòk.

Fare, *s.* (food) ييه جك ايچه جك yèyé-jek-ìchèjek; (reception) معامله mù"-āmélè; (carriage-hire) نوبت پاره سى nùbet-pàrassi; (passenger) مشترى mùshtèri; —, *v.n.* ييوب ايچمك yèyup-ìchmek; كچنمك ghèchinmek; اولمق òlmak; اويمق ùymak.

Farewell, *int.* دعالر dù"ālar, اللهه صمارلدق AllAha-ìssmàrladik; اوغور اوله òghur-òla.

Farm, *s.* چفتلك chìftlik; التزام ìltizām; مقاطعه mùkāta"à; —, *v.a.* كرا ايله طوتمق kirā-ila-tùtmak; كرايه ويرمك kìrāya-vèrmek; التزام ا ìltizām-et; التزامه ويرمك ìltizāma-vèrmek; قوللانمق kùllAnmak, باقمق bAkmak, زراعت ا zìrā"àt-et; — out, كرايه ويرمك kìrāya-vèrmek; التزامه ويرمك ìltizāma-vèrmek.

Farmer, *s.* چفتجى chìftji; اهل زراعت èhli-zìrā"àt; ملتزم mùltèzim.

Farrier, *s.* نعلبند (nAlbAn, nAlbAnt) nā"lbènd.

Farther, *a.* دها اوزاق dàhā-òzàk; —, *ad.* دها اوته یه dàhā-ùtéya, دها اوته ده dàhā-ùtédé; —, *v.a.* یاردم ا yàrdim-et.

Farthermore, *c.* و ینه vè-yìné (vè-ghèné), وهم ده vè-hèm-dé, وهمدخی vè-hèm-dàkhi, وكذا vèkézā.

Farthest, *a.* الڭ اوزاق èng-ùzàk; at farthest, *ad.* اولسه اولسه òlsa-òlsa.

Farthing, *s.* اقچه àkcha.

Fascinate, *v.a.* كوز باغلامق ghyùz-bàghlamak, فریفته ا fèrīfté-et.

Fascine, *s.* چبوق دمتی chìbùk-dèméti.

Fashion, *s.* عادت "ādèt, رسم rèssim, بچم bìchim, مودا mòda, طرز tàrz; —, *v.a.* یاپمق yàpmak; بچم ویرمك bìchim-vèrmek.

Fast, *a.* (tight) صیقی sìki; (firm) محكم mùhkèm; (quick) چابك chàbik; —, *s.* اوروج ùrùj, سیام sìyām; Christian —, پرهیز pèrhīz; —, *v.n.* اج دورمق àj-dùrmak, اج قالمق àj-kàlmak; اوروج طوتمق ùrùj-tùtmak; پرهیز طوتمق pèrhīz-tùtmak.

Fasten, *v.a.* باغلامق bàghlamak; صیقشدرمق sìkishdirmak.

Fastidious, *a.* تتیز tìtiz.

Fasting, *a.* اج àj; اوروجلو ùrùjlu; پرهیزلو pèrhīzli.

Fat, *s.* یاغ yàgh; —, *a.* (meat) یاغلو yàghli; (man) شیشمان shìshmàn; (beast) سمیز sèmiz, تاولو tàwli; —, *v.n.* سمورمك sèmirmek; —, *v.a.* بسلمك bèsslémek, سمورتمك sèmirtmek.

Fatal, *s.* مورث موت mùrissi-mèvt; برایشك بوزلمسنه سبب اولان bìr-ishing-bòzulmassina-sèbeb-òlan; مقدر mù-kàddèr, معین mù"àyyèn; مشئوم mèsh'ūm.

Fatality, *s.* مشئومیت mèsh'ūmìyyèt; شئامت sha'āmèt. [ènjāmi-kyār.

Fate, *s.* قدر kàder; اولم ùlum; انجام كار

Father, *s.* بابا bàba, پدر pèder; wife's —, قاین اتا kàyn-àta; step- —, اویكی بابا ùvèghi-bàba.

Fatherland, *s.* وطن vuàtan.

Fathom, *s.* قولاچ kùlàj; —, *v.a.* اسقاندیل ا ìsskàndil-et; اكلامق ànglamak (ànnamak). [maz.

Fathomless, *a.* دیبی بولنمز dìbi-bùlun-

Fatigue, *s.* یورغونلق yòrghunluk, تعب tà"b; مشقت mèshàkkàt; —, *v.a.* یورمق yòrmak.

Fatigued, *a.* یورغون yòrghun.

Fatiguing, *a.* یورار yòrar.

Fatten, *v.n.* سمورمك sèmirmek; —, *v.a.* بسلمك bèsslémek, سمورتمك sèmirtmek.

Fault, *s.* قباحت kàbāhat, صوچ sùch, قصور kùssūr, جنحه jùnha, جرم jùrm; سقطلق sàkatlik; to find —, *v.n.* قباحت بولمق kàbāhat-bùlmak; بهانه بولمق bàhānè-bùlmak, قصور بولمق kùssūr-bùlmak.

Faultless, *a.* قصورسز kùssūrsiz.

Favour, *s.* كرم kèrem, عنایت "ìnāyet, لطف lùtf; مساعده mùssā"adé; حسن نظر hùssnu-nàzàr; یوز yùz, چهره chèhré, صورت sūrèt; قوردله باغی kòrdèla-bàghi; to curry —, *v.a.*

يلتنمك yeltenmek; مداهنه ا mùdāhéné-èt. [mùssā''id, اويغون ùyghun.
Favourable, *a.* موافق mùwāfik, مساعد
Favourite, *s.* سودك sèvdik.
Fawn, *s.* كيك ياوريسى ghèyik-yàwrissi, قراجه ياوريسى kàraja-yàwrissi; —, *v.n.* يالتاقلنمق yàltaklanmak.
Fear, *s.* قورقو kòrku, خوف khàvf, بيم bīm, دهشت dèhshèt; —, *v.n.* and *a.* قورقمق kòrkmak.
Fearful, *a.* قورقولو kòrkulu, قورقونجلو kòrkunjlu, مخوف màkhūf.
Feasible, *a.* ياقشق الور yàkishìk-àlir, اولور òlur, ممكن mùmkin.
Feast, *s.* ضيافت zìyāfèt; (religious) بيرام bāyram; يورطى yòrti.
Feather, *s.* توى tùy.
Features, *s. pl.* سيما sīmā.
February, *s.* شباط shùbàt.
Fecund, *a.* چوقجه چوجق طوغرر chòkjé-chòjuk-dòghurur; محصولدار màh-sūldār.
Federation, *s.* اتفاق ìttifāk; متفقين mùttèfikīn. [ترى àyak-tèri.
Fee, *s.* رسم rèssim, عوائد ''àwā'id; اياق
Feeble, *a.* ضعيف zà''īf, قوتسز kùvvètsiz.
Feebleness, *s.* ضعف zà''f, قوتسزلك kùvvètsizlik.
Feed, *s.* يمك yèmèk; —, *v.n.* يمك yèmek, يمك يمك yèmèk-yèmek; —, *v.a.* بسلمك bèsslémek; يدرمك yèdirmek.
Feel, *v.a.* دويمق dùymak, حس ا hisss-et; دوقنمق dòkunmak, باقمق bàkmak; يوقلامق yòklamak.
Feeling, *a.* مرحمتلو mèrhàmetli; حساس hàsssāss; —, *s.* حس hìsss; قوت لامسه kùvvèti-lāmissé; حساسلق hàsssāsslìk; مرحمت mèrhàmet, شفقت shèfakàt, رقت قلب rìkkàti--kàlb. [-yàpmak, تقليد ا tàklīd-et.
Feign, *v.a.* يالاندن ياپمق yàlàndan-
Feigned, *a.* يالاندن yàlàndan, ياپمه yàpma, تقليد tàklīd.
Felicitation, *s.* تبريك tèbrīk, تهنيه tèhnìyyé, كوزك ايدين ghyùzung-
Felicity, *s.* سعادت sà''ādèt. [àydin.
Felloe, *s.* اپسد ìpsid.
Fellow, *s.* حريف hèrif, ارقه داش àrka-dash, اياقداش àyakdash, يولداش yòldash; كدكلو ghèdikli; fellows, اخوان ìkhwān.
Fellow-citizen, *s.* همشهرى hèm-shèhri.
Fellowship, *s.* ارقه داشلق àrkadashlìk; اخوانلق ìkhwānlìk; كدك ghèdik.
Felon, *s.* خرسز وقاتل مقوله سى ادم khìr-siz-vè-kātil-màkūléssi-àdam, خبيث khàbīss. [khàbāssètli.
Felonious, *a.* خبيث khàbīss, خباثتلو
Felony, *s.* خرسزلق ياخود قاتللق كبى جنحه khìrsizlìk-yàkhud-kātillik--ghìbi-jùnhà.
Felt, *s.* كچه kèché, كبه kèbé.
Female, *a.* and *s.* ديشى dìshi; قارى kàri; قيز kìz.
Feminine, *a.* (gram.) مؤنث mù'èn-nèss; — (womanlike) قارى يه ياقشور kàrìya-yàkìshir.
Fence, *s.* تخته پرده tàkhta-pèrdé, پرمقلق pàrmaklìk, ديوار dìwar, چيت chìt;

—, *v.a.* چويرمك chèvirmek; —, *v.n.* مچ تعليمى ا mèch-tà''līmi-et.

Fencing, *s.* مچ تعليمى mèch-tà''līmi.

Fennel, *s.* دره اوتى dèré-òtu.

Feoff, *s.* تيمار tīmār, زعامت zi''āmet; يوردلق اوجاقلق yùrdluk-òjaklik.

Ferment, *s.* مايه māyé (màya); قاينامه kàynama; چوريمه chùrumé, قيزمه kìzma; تلاش tèlāsh; —, *v.n.* قبارمق kàbarmak; قايناماق kàynamak; تخمر ا tàkhàmmur-et; —, *v.a.* قبارتمق kàbartmak; قايناتمق kày-natmak; تخمير ا tàkhmīr-et.

Fermentation, *s.* تخمير tàkhmīr, تخمر tàkhàmmur; قبارمه kàbarma, قاينامه kàynama; قيزمه kìzma; چوريمه chùrumé.

Ferret, *s.* صانصار sànsàr (?).

Ferrule, *s.* پرازوانه pràzwàna.

Ferry, *s.* كچيديرى ghèchìd-yèri.

Ferry-boat, *s.* قايق kàyik, تومباز tòm-bàz, كلك kèlek.

Fertile, *a.* منبت mùnbit, بركتلو bèré-kètli, محصولدار màhsūldār.

Fertileness, Fertility, *s.* منبتلك mùn-bitlik, بركتلولك bèrékètlilik.

Fester, *v.n.* جراحت طوپلانمق jèrāhàt-tòplanmak. [يورتى yòrtu.

Festival, *s.* كون ghyùn; بيرام bàyràm;

Fetch, *v.a.* كيدوب كتورمك ghìdup-ghètirmek, كيدوب الوب كلمك ghìdup-àlip-ghèlmek. [àghìr-kòkar.

Fetid, *a.* فنا قوقار fèna-kòkar, اغر قوقار

Fetlock, *s.* طوپوق tòpuk.

Fetters, *s. pl.* تيمور (dèmir), زنجير zìn-jir, بوقاغى bùkàghi.

Feud, *s.* نزاع nìzā''.

Fever, *s.* حما hùmmā; (ague) ايستمه ìssìtma (sìtma); (heat) حرارت

Feverish, *a.* حرارتلو hàrārètli. [hàrārèt.

Feverishness, *s.* حرارت hàrārèt.

Few, *a.* از àz; a few, بر از bìr-àz, برقاچ

Fibre, *s.* تل tèl; ليف līf. [bìr-kàch.

Fibrous, *a.* تل تل tèl-tèl, تللو tèlli, ليف كبى līf-ghìbi.

Fickle, *a.* ثباتسز sèbātsiz, بر دالده دورماز bìr-dàlda-dùrmàz, متلون mùtélèvvin.

Fictitious, *a.* دوزمه dùzma, اويدرمه

Fiddle, *s.* كمان kèmàn. [ùydurma.

Fiddler, *s.* كمانجى kèmànji, كمان چالار kèmàn-chàlar. [kèmàn-òku.

Fiddlestick, *s.* اوق òk, كمان اوقى

Fiddlestring, *s.* كمان تلى kèmàn-tèli.

Fidelity, *s.* صداقت sàdākàt, صادقلق sàdiklik.

Fidget, *s.* مراقلو mèràkli; راحت دورماز rāhat-dùrmaz; —, *v.n.* مراق ا mèràk-et; راحت دورمامق rāhat-dùrma-mak; —, *v.a.* قارشدرمق kàrish-dirmak; راحت براقمامق rāhat-bràkmamak.

Fief, *s.* تيمار tīmār; يوردلق اوجاقلق yùrdluk-òjaklik; مالكانه mālikyāné.

Field, *s.* طرلا tàrla; اووه òwa, چاير chàyir; صحرا sàhrā.

Field-day, *s.* بيوك تعليم كونى bìyuk-tà''līm-ghyùnu.

Field-marshal, *s.* سرعسكر sèr-''àsskèr.

Field-officer, *s.* بيوك ضابط bìyuk-zābit.

Field-piece, *s.* چرخه طوبى chàrkha-tòpu, ابوس (kùbuss).

Fierce, *a.* سرت sèrt, حديد hàdīd, شديد [shèdīd.
Fiery, *a.* آتش‌كبي âtèsh-ghìbi.
Fife, *s.* دودك dùduk.
Fifer, *s.* دودكجي dùdukju.
Fifteen, *a.* اون‌بش òn-bèsh.
Fifty, *a.* اللي èlli.
Fig, *s.* انجير ìnjir.
Fight, *s.* غوغا (kawgha), دوكش dù*g*hush; جنك jènk, محاربه mùhārébé; —, *v.n.* دوكشمك dù*gh*ushmek, غوغا ا (kàwgha)-et, جنك ا jènk-et, محاربه ا mùhārébé-et; — one's way, ايشنى اويدرمق ìshini-òydurm*a*k.
Figure, *s.* شكل (shèkil) shèkl; بچم bìchim, اندام èndām, بوى‌بوص bòy-bòss, هيئت hèy'èt; رقم ràkam; —, *v.n.* كوسترش ا ghy*ù*sstèrish-et; كورنمك ghy*ù*runmek.
Filbert, *s.* تازه‌فندق tāzé-fìnd*i*k.
Filch, *v.a.* چالمق chàlm*a*k.
File, *s.* اكه è*gh*é; (of soldiers) صره sìr*a*; (of papers) طاقم tàk*i*m; —, *v.a.* اكه‌لمك è*gh*élémek, اكه‌ايله‌المق è*gh*é-il*a*-âlm*a*k; (papers) طوپلايوب ترتيب ا tòplayup-tèrtīb-et.
Filial, *a.* بنوى bènévī.
Filings, *s.* اكندى è*gh*enti.
Fill, *v.n.* طولمق dòlm*a*k; —, *v.a.* طولدرمق dòldurm*a*k.
Filly, *s.* قسراق‌طاى kìssrâk-tày.
Film, *s.* زار zār.
Filter, *s.* سوزكچ sùzghèch; —, *v.a.* سوزمك sùzmek; —, *v.n.* سوزلمك sùzulmek.
Filth, *s.* پسلك pìsslik, مردارلق mùrdàr-[lik (mùn-), اوساخ èvsākh.
Filthy, *a.* پس piss, مردار mùrdàr.
Fin, *s.* بالق‌قنادى bàl*i*k-kànad*i*, قناد kànad.
Final, *a.* صوك sòn*g*, آخر ākh*i*r.
Finally, *ad.* عاقبت ʿākìbèt, عاقبتده ʿākìbètd*a*; الحاصل èl-hāss*i*l, حاصل كلام hāss*i*l*i*-kèlām.
Finance, *s.* امور ماليه ùmūru-māliyyé; minister of —, ماليه ناظرى māliyyé-[-nàziri.
Find, *v.a.* بولمق bùlm*a*k.
Fine, *a.* كوزل ghy*ù*zèl; اينجه ìnj*a*; خاص khāss; خالص khāliss; —, *s.* جريمه jèrīmé; —, *v.a.* جريمه‌المق jèrīmé-âlm*a*k, تجريم ا tèjrīm-et; تصفيه ا tàssfiyyé-et.
Finedraw, *v.a.* اورمك *ù*rmek.
Finedrawer, *s.* اوريجى *ù*ruju.
Finger, *s.* پرمق pàrm*a*k; —, *v.a.* دوقنمق dòkunm*a*k, قارشدرمق kàr*i*sh-d*i*rm*a*k.
Finger-post, *s.* يول كوسترن ديرك yòl-ghy*ù*steren-dīrèk.
Finish, *s.* صوك ال sòn*g*-èl; —, *v.n.* بتمك bìtmek; دوكنمك dùkènmek; تمام او tàmàm-òl, تكميل او tèkmīl-òl; —, *v.a.* بترمك bìtirmek; دوكتمك dùkètmek; تكميل ا tèkmīl-et.
Finite, *a.* محدود màhdūd, متناهى mùté-[nāhī.
Fir, *s.* چام chàm.
Fire, *s.* آتش âtèsh; —, *v.a.* آتمق âtm*a*k, انداخت ا èndākht-et; آتش ا âtèsh-et; آتش ويرمك âtèsh-vèrmek; —up, *v.n.* پارلامق pàrlam*a*k, حدتلنمك hìddètlènmek.
Firearms, *s. pl.* تفنك‌طبانجه tùfènk-

-tàbAnja ; اسلحۀ ناریه èsslihé'i-nārìyyÉ.

Firelock, *s.* تفنك tùfènk (tùfèk).

Fireman, *s.* یانغین طلومبه جیسی yànghin-tùlumbajissi. [missi.

Fireship, *s.* آتش كمیسی Atèsh-ghè-

Firewood, *s.* اوطون òdun, حطب hAtAb.

Firework, *s.* فشنك fìshènk (fìshèk).

Firing, *s.* اوطون كمور òdun-kyùmur.

Firm, *a.* محكم mùhkèm, قوی kàwi ; صیقی sìki ; طیانقلو dàyànìkli, متانتلو mètānètli, متین mètīn ; ثابت sābit ; راسخ rāsikh, پایدار pàydār ; —, *s.* امضا ìmzā ; شركت shìrkèt.

Firmament, *s.* كوك یوزی ghyùk-yùzu, سما sèmā, اسمان āssmān ; فلك الافلاك fèleku-'l-èflāk.

Firmness, *s.* ثبات sèbāt, متانت mètā-nèt ; محكملك múhkèmlìk.

First, *a.* برنجی bìrinji, الك ilk, اول Èvvel.

Firstborn, *a.* نخستزاد nùkhùsstzād, نخستزاده nùkhusstzādÉ, بیوك bìyuk, الك ìlk.

Firstfruits, *s. pl.* ترفانده tùrfAndÉ.

Fish, *s.* بالق bAlìk ; —, *v.n.* اولامق Avlamak, بالق اولامق bAlìk-Avlamak ; قاپمغه باقمق kApmagha-bAkmak.

Fishbone, *s.* بالق قیلچغی bAlìk-kìlchighi.

Fisher, Fisherman, *s.* بالقجی bAlìkji, بالق اولاییجی bAlìk-Avlayìji. [dAlyAn.

Fishery, *s.* بالق اوی bAlìk-Avi ; طالیان

Fishmonger, *s.* بالقجی bAlìkji, بالق صاتیجی bAlìk-sAtìji.

Fishpond, *s.* حوض hàwz.

Fissure, *s.* یارق yàrìk, چاتلاق chàtlAk.

Fist, *s.* مشته mùshta, یومرق yùmruk.

Fit, *a.* مناسب mùnāssib, یاقشور yàki-shir, لایق lāyìk, جسبان jùssbān ; اهل èhl, ارباب Èrbāb ; —, *s.* نوبت nùbèt ; صرعه sAr"à; —, *v.a.* ایو كلمك īyi-ghèlmek ; اویمق ùymak ; اویدرمق ùydurmak.

Fitness, *s.* مناسبت mùnāssébèt, یاقشق yàkìshìk ; لیاقت lìyākAt, اهلیت èhlìyyèt.

Fitting, *a.* مناسب mùnāssib ; —, *s.* طاقم tàkìm ; اویدرمقلق ùydurmaklìk.

Five, *a.* بش bèsh, خمس khàmss, پنج pènj.

Fix, *v.a.* ثابت ا sābit-et ; تعیین ا tà"yīn-et ; كسمك kèssmek ; قرار ویرمك kArār-vérmek ; —, one's self, *v.n.* اوطورمق òtùrmak ; اتخاذ مكان ا ìtti-khāzi-mèkyān-et ; —, *s.* كوچلك ghyùchluk, مشكل mùshkil.

Fixed, *a.* ثابت sābit ; معین mù"àyyèn, كسلمش kèssilmish ; دیك dìk.

Flag, *s.* سنجاق sAnjak, بیراق bāyrak, بانده‌ره bAndara ; ساز sAz ; —, *v.n.* قوتی كسلمك kùvvèti-kèssilmek ; یورولمق yòrūlmak ; صارقمق sàrkmak ; كساد او kèssAd-òl.

Flagship, *s.* پاشا كمیسی pàsha-ghèmissi.

Flagstaff, *s.* سنجاق دیركی sAnjak-dìrèghi ; سنجاق كوندری sAnjak-ghyùndéri.

Flake, *s.* (of snow) قوش باشی kùsh-bAshi ; (of pastry) قات kAt.

Flaky, *a.* (pastry) قات قات kAt-kAt.

Flambeau, *s.* مشعله mèsh"ālÉ (mAshAla).

Flame, *s.* علو "àlev, زبانه zàbānᴇ́; شعله shù"lᴇ́; عشق "àshk; معشوقه mà-"shūka; —, *v.a.* علو ويرمك "àlev-vèrmek; to burst into flames, علولنمك "àlevlᴇnmek.

Flaming, *a.* علولو "àlevli, زبانه كش zàbà-nékèsh, شعله ور shù"lévèr.

Flank, *s.* يان yàn; جناح jènāh; —, *v.a.* ياندن المق yàndan-àlmak.

Flannel, *s.* فانله fānèla. [mek.

Flare, *v.n.* پك علولنمك pèk-"àlevlᴇn-

Flash, *s.* علو "àlev; —, *v.n.* علوويرمك "àlev-vèrmek; پارلامق pàrlamak; چاقمق chàkmak; to flash in the pan, الامامق àlmamak. [وزنه vèznᴇ́.

Flask, *s.* شيشه shìshᴇ́; (powder —)

Flat, *a.* دوز dùz; ياصى yàsssi; لذتسز lèzzètsiz, طاتسز طوزسز tàtsiz-tùzsuz;

Flat-iron, *s.* اوتى ùtu. [عقلسز "àklsiz.

Flatten, *v.a.* دوزلتمك dùzletmek, dù-zèltmek; ياصيلتمق yàssilatmak.

Flatter, *v.a.* مداهنه ا mùdāhanᴇ́-et; — one's self, *v.n.* صانمق sānmak; اممق ùmmak, اميد ا ùmīd-et.

Flatterer, *s.* مداهنه جى mùdāhanᴇji.

Flattery, *s.* مداهنه mùdāhanᴇ́.

Flavour, *s.* لذت lèzzèt, چاشنى chāshni (chèshni) طات tàt.

Flaw, *s.* سقط sàkat, عيب "àyb, قصور kùssūr, سقامت sàkāmèt.

Flax, *s.* كتان (kètᴇn).

Flay, *v.a.* يوزمك yùzmek, دريسنى صويمق

Flea, *s.* پيره pīrᴇ́. [dèrissini-sòymak.

Fleabane, *s.* پيره اوتى pīrᴇ́-òtu.

Flee, *v.n.* قاچمق kàchmak, فرار ا fìrār-et.

Fleece, *s.* پوست pòsst; —, *v.a.* صويمق sòymak. [chàbik, سرعتلو sùr"àtli.

Fleet, *s.* دونما dònanma; —, *a.* چابك

Fleeting, *a.* چابك كچر chàbik-ghèchᴇr, سريع الزوال sèrī"u-z-zèwāl, فانى fānī.

Flesh, *s.* ات èt, لحم làhm, كوشت ghyòsht.

Fleshy, *a.* اتلو ètli; ملحم mùlàhhàm.

Flexible, *a.* اكلور èghilir, يموشاق yìmushàk.

Flight, *s.* قاچش kàchish, فرار fìrār; (of birds) سورى sùru; (of arrows) يايلم yàyilim; (of stairs) قات kàt.

Flimsy, *a.* سيرك sèyrèk, قماشى سيرك kùmàshi-sèyrèk.

Fling, *v.a.* اتمق àtmak.

Flint, *s.* چاقمق طاشى chàkmak-tàshi.

Float, *s.* شماندره shàmàndara; —, *v.n.* يوزمك yùzmek; —, *v.a.* يوزدرمك yùzdurmek. [ùshushmek.

Flock, *s.* سورى sùru; —, *v.n.* اوشمك

Flog, *v.a.* دوكمك dùghmek, طياق اتمق dàyak-àtmak.

Flogging, *s.* قامچى kàmchi.

Flood, *s.* سيل sèyl (sèl); طوفان tūfān; مد mèdd; —, *v.a.* صو باصمق sū-bàss-mak; صو باصدرمق sū-bàssdirmak.

Floor, Flooring, *s.* دوشمه dùshémᴇ́, تخته tàkhta; —, *v.a.* دوشه مك

Florid, *a.* قرمزى kìrmizi. [dùshémek.

Florist, *s.* چيچكجى باغچوان chìchekji--bāghchawān.

Flotilla, *s.* اينجه دونما ìnja-dònanma.

Flounder, *s.* پسى بالغى pìssi-bàlighi; —, *v.n.* يوارلنمق yìwarlanmak.

Flour, *s.* اون ūn, دقيق dàkìk.

Flourish, *v.n.* نشو و نما بولمق nèshv-u--nèmā-bŭlmak; برحيات او bèr-hàyāt--ŏl.

Flourishing, *a.* حسن حالده اولان hùssnu-[-hālda-ŏlan.

Flow, *s.* مد mèdd; —, *v.n.* اقمق àkmak, جريان ا jèréyān-et; منصب او mùn-sàbb-ol; مد او mèdd-ŏl.

Flower, *s.* چيچك chìchek; —, *v.n.* چيچك اچمق chìchek-àchmak.

Flowerpot, *s.* صاقسى sàksi.

Fluctuate, *v.n.* بر قرارده دورمامق bìr--kàrārda-dùrmamak.

Flue, *s.* باجه bàja. [vé-sùhūlèt.

Fluency, *s.* مهارت و سهولت màhārèt-

Fluently, *ad.* سهولت ايله sùhūlèt-ìla.

Fluid, *a.* سيال sèyyāl; —, *s.* جسم سيال jìssm-sèyyāl. [kòrkutmak.

Flurry, *s.* تلاش tèlàsh; —, *v.a.* قورقوتمق

Flush, *a.* دوز dùz; —, *v.n.* بردن جولان ا bìrdan-jèvélān-et; — up, قزارمق kìzàrmak.

Flute, *s.* ناى này, نى nèy, فلاوطه flàwta.

Fluting, *s.* ييو yìw, yìv.

Fly, *s.* سينك sìnek; كرا عربه سى kìrā--'àrabassi; —, *v.n.* اوچمق ŭchmak; قاچمق kàchmak; — about, اطرافه فرلامق ètrāfa-fìrlamak; — at, اوزرينه اتلمق ùzériné-àtìlmak; — away, اوچمق ŭchmak; — back, كيرو فرلامق ghèri-fìrlamak; — for refuge, صيغنمق sìghìnmak, التجا iltijā-et; — in pieces, پاره لنمك pārélenmek (pàra-lanmak); — into a passion, پارلامق pàrlamak, حدتلنمك hìddètlenmek; — off, اوچمق ŭchmak; فرلامق fìrla-mak; قاچمق kàchmak; — open, اچليويرمك àchìlivèrmek; — out, اتلمق àtìlmak; صچرامق sìchramak; فرلامق fìrlamak; — up, يوقارى فرلامق yŭkāri-fìrlamak.

Flying-bridge, *s.* عاريتى كوپرى "ārìy-yètī-kyùpru. [dòghurmak.

Foal, *s.* طاى tày; —, *v.n.* طوغرمق

Foam, *s.* كپوك kyùpuk; —, *v.n.* كپورمك kyùpurmek. [مركز mèrkez.

Focus, *s.* نقطهء احتراق nòkta'i-ìhtiràk;

Fodder, *s.* اوت ŏt, ارپه صمان àrpa-sàman.

Foe, *s.* دشمن dùshmèn.

Fœtus, *s.* جنين jìnīn, چوجق chòjuk, ياورى yàwri. [sìss.

Fog, *s.* **Foggy,** *a.* دومان dùmàn, سيس

Foible, *s.* مراق mèrāk.

Fold, *s.* قات kàt; sheep —, اغل àghìl; —, *v.a.* قات قات ا kàt-kàt-et; طوپلامق tòplamak, دوشيرمك dèvshirmek; صارمق sàrmak, بوكمك bùkmek; قيرمق kìrmak; —, *v.n.* قات قات او kàt-kàt-ŏl; طوپلانمق tòplanmak, دوشيرلمك dèvshirilmek, صارلمق sà-rìlmak, بوكلمك bùkyulmek, قيرلمق kìrìlmak. [عالم "ālèm.

Folk, *s.* خلق khàlk, اورطه لق ŏrtalìk,

Follow, *v.a.* ارقه سنه دوشمك àrkassina--dùshmek, اردينه دوشمك àrdina--dùshmek, اردينه كتمك àrdina--ghìtmek, ارقه سى صره كلمك àrkassi--sìra-ghèlmek; تابع او tābi'-ol; —, *v.n.* چيقمق chìkmak, لازم كلمك lāzim-ghèlmek.

Following, *a.* ایرته èrtÉ; اتی ātī; زیرده محرر zīrdÉ-mùhàrrer. [lilik.

Folly, *s.* عقلسزلق ''àklsizlik, دلیلك dè-

Foment, *v.a.* صیجاق صوایله یقامق sìjàk-sù-ila-yìkamak; (troubles) فت ویرمك fit-vèrmek, پرمق ویرمك pàr-mak-vèrmek, تحریك ا tàhrīk-et.

Fond, *a.* پك سور pèk-sèver, چوق سور chòk-sèver; دلیسی dèlissi; بوش bòsh, بیهوده bīhūdÉ.

Fondle, *v.a.* قوجاغنه الوب اوخشامق kùjaghina-àlip-òkhshamak.

Food, *s.* ییه جك yèyéjek, یمك yèmèk, غدا ghìdā. [dìwānÉ.

Fool, *s.* عقلسز ''àklsiz, دلی dèli, دیوانه

Foolery, *s.* مسخره لق màsskharalik.

Foolhardy, *a.* جسور دكل دلی jèssūr-dìghil-dèli.

Foolish, *a.* (person) عقلسز ''àklsiz, دلی dèli, دیوانه dìwānÉ; (thing) عقلسز ''àklsiz.

Foot, *s.* ایاق àyak, قدم kàdem, پا pā, پای pāy, پی pèy; (of hill) اتك ètek.

Footing, *s.* ایاق باصه جق یر àyak-bàssajak-yèr; صفت sìfàt, منزلت mènzélèt.

Footman, *s.* اوشاق ùshàk.

Footpath, *s.* پیاده قالدریمی pìyādÉ-kàl-dirimi; پیاده یولی pìyādÉ-yòlu.

Footstep, *s.* ایاق ایزی àyak-ìzi; اثر èsser; اثر ìssr. [dighi.

Footstool, *s.* ایاق یاصدیغی àyak-yàss-

For, *pr.* ایچون (ichin) ichun; ئه *a*, یه ya; دن dan; دن طولایی dan-dòlayi; —, *c.* زیرا zīrā, چونكه chùnku; for all that, *ad.* ینه yìnÉ (ghèna).

Forage, *s.* اوت òt, ارپه صمان àrpa-sàman; —, *v.n.* ییه جكنی ارامق yèyéjéghini-àramak; — about, *v.n.* اوته بری قارشدره رق ارامق ùtÉ-bèri-kàrishdirarak-àramak.

Forbear, *v.n.* وازكچمك vāz-ghèchmek; كندینی ضبط ا kèndini-zàbt-et, جبر نفس ا jèbri-nèfss-et. [hàmmul.

Forbearance, *s.* صبر sàbr, تحمل tà-

Forbid, *v.a.* ایتمه دیو تنبیه ا ètma-dèyu-tènbīh-et, نهی ا nèhy-et, یساق ا yàssak-et.

Force, *s.* زور zòr, كوچ ghyùch, قوت kùvvèt; جبر jèbr; اجبار ìjbār; —, *v.a.* زورلامق zòrlamak; جبرا jèbr-et, اجبارا ìjbār-et; by —, *ad.* زوراكی zòràki, استمیه رك ìsstéméyérek, جبراً jèbren; to force a sale, طوتدره بلدیكنه صاتمق tùtdura-bìldighina-sàtmak; — back, كیرو ایتمك ghèri-ìtmek, كیرو سورمك ghèri-sùrmek; — down, اشاغی باصمق àshàghi-bàss-mak; — in, ایچرو قاقمق ìchèri-kàk-mak; — out, سوكمك sùkmek.

Forceps, *s.* ماشه màsha, قصاج kìssàj.

Ford, *s.* كچید ghèchid, كچید یری ghè-chid-yèri, معبر mà''ber; —, *v.a.* كچمك ghèchmek; عبور ا ''ùbūr-et.

Fore, *a.* اوكده كی ùngdéki, ایلروكی ìlèriki, ایلروده كی ìlèridéki; — and aft, كمینك بویجه ghèmining-bòyunja.

Forefather, *s.* جد jèdd (pl. اجداد èjdād).

Forefinger, *s.* شهادت پرمغی shàhādet-pàrmaghi.

Forego, *v.a.* وازكچمك vāz-ghèchmek.

Forehead, *s.* الن ʌlin (ànn), جبين jèbīn, جبهه jèbhé.

Foreign, *a.* **Foreigner**, *s.* اجنبى èjnébī.

Foreland, *s.* برون bùrun.

Forelock, *s.* ناصيه nāssìyyé.

Foreman, *s.* استاد (ùssta), قالفه kʌlfa.

Foremast, *s.* پرووه ديركى prùwa-dirèghi, باش ديركى bʌsh-dirèghi.

Foremost, *a.* الك ايلروده كى èng-ìlèridéki.

Foresail, *s.* ترنكت trìnkèt.

Foresee, *v.a.* قبل الوقوع حس ا kʌbla-'l--vùkū"-hìss-et.

Foresight, *s.* بصيرت bʌssīrèt.

Forest, *s.* اورمان òrmʌn.

Foretell, *v.a.* قبل الوقوع خبرويرمك kʌbla-'l-vùkū"-khʌber-vèrmek.

Forge, *s.* تيمورجى دكانى dèmirji-dúk-kyāni; تيمورجى اوجاغى dèmirji--òjaghi; —, *v.a.* ايشلمك ìshlémek, دوكمك dùghmek; (a forgery), *v.a.* تقليد ا tʌklīd-et; —, *v.n.* ساختهكارلق ا sàkhtékyārlik-et.

Forger, *s.* ياپيجى yàpiji; ساختهكار sàkhtékyār.

Forgery, *s.* ساختهكارلق sàkhtékyārlik; ساخته sàkhté.

Forget, *v.a.* اونوتمق ùnùtmak, فراموش ا fèrāmūsh-et, نسيان ا nìssyān-et.

Forgetful, *a.* اونودر ùnùdur.

Forgetfulness, *s.* غفلت ghʌflet.

Forgive, *v.a.* عفو ا "ʌfv-et, بخش ا bàkhsh-et, بخشلامق (bʌghishlamak).

Forgiveness, *s.* عفو "ʌfv; (by God) مغفرت màghférèt, غفران ghùfrān.

Fork, *s.* چتال chàtal; (for digging) بل [bèl.

Forked, *a.* چتال chàtal.

Forlorn, *a.* صاحبسز sāhibsiz.

Form, *s.* شكل shèkil, بچم bìchim, صورت sūrèt, هيئت hèy'èt; رسم (rèssim), عادت "ādèt; صورت sùrèt; صره sìra, پيكه pèykèh; صنف sìnf; —, *v.a.* تشكيل ا tèshkīl-et, ياپمق yàpmak; اولمق òlmak, هيئتنه كيرمك hèy'ètina-ghìrmek.

Formal, *a.* رسمى rèssmī; صورى sūrī.

Formality, *s.* رسم (rèssim), عادت رسميه "ādèti-rèssmìyyé.

Formally, *ad.* رسماً rèssman.

Formation, *s.* ياپش yàpish; ياپلش yà-pilish; تشكيل tèshkīl.

Former, *a.* مقدمكى mùkʌddemki, سابق sābīk; اسبق èssbʌk.

Formerly, *ad.* مقدما mùkʌddémā, سابقا sābikā; بوندن اقدم bùndan-ʌkdem, اوللرده èvvellerdā, كچنلرده ghèchen-lerdé; اسكى زمانلرده èsski-zàmʌn-larda. [màkhūf.

Formidable, *a.* قورقلور kòrkulūr, مخوف

Fornication, *s.* زنا zìnā, زنپارهلك (zàm-paralik). [para).

Fornicator, *s.* زانى zānī, زنپاره (zàm-

Fornicatress, *s.* زانيه zānìyyé, روسپى (òrosspò), فاحشه fāhìshé.

Forsake, *v.a.* براقمق bràkmak, ترك ا tèrk-et, وازكچمك vāz-ghèchmek.

Fort, *s.* قلعه kàl"à (kàylé), پلنقه pʌ-langha.

Forth, *ad.* طشره tʌshra, طيشارى dìshāri; to set —, بيان ا bèyān-et.

Forthwith, *ad.* شمدى shìmdi, درعقب dèr-‘‘àkab, همانندم hèmāndèm, او ساعت ò-sā‘‘at.

Fortification, *s.* استحكامات ìsstìhkyā-[māt.

Fortify, *v.a.* استحكام ويرمك ìsstìhkyām-vèrmek, قلعه يا پمق kàl‘‘a-yàpmak; تقويت ويرمك tàkvìyyèt-vèrmek, قوت ويرمك kùvvèt-vèrmek, متانت ويرمك mètānèt-vèrmek.

Fortitude, *s.* صبر sàbr, تحمل tàhàmmul, ثبات sèbāt, متانت mètānèt.

Fortnight, *s.* ايكى هفته ìki-hàfta.

Fortress, *s.* قلعه kàl‘‘a (kāylé).

Fortuitous, *a.* تصادفى tèssàdufī, اتفاقى ìttifākī, راست كله ràsst-ghèlé.

Fortunate, *a.* بختيار bàkht-yār.

Fortune, *s.* بخت bàkht, طالع tāli‘‘; مال màl, پاره (pàra), زنكينلك zèn-ghinlik; ميراث mīrāss.

Forty, *a.* قرق kìrk, اربعين èrba‘‘īn, چهل chèhil.

Forward, *a.* ايلرو كلمش ìléri-ghèlmish, ايلرولمش ìlèrilémish; اركن يتشور èrken-yètishir; عارسز ‘‘ārsiz, ادبسز èdebsiz; —, *ad.* ايلرو ìléri; ايلرويه طوغرى ìlériyé-dòghru; —, *v.a.* كوندرمك ghyùn-dèrmek; ايلرولتمك ìlréilètmek; ياردم ا yàrdim-et.

Forwards, *ad.* ايلرو ìléri, ايلرويه طوغرى ìlériyé-dòghru.

Fossil, *a.* تحجرايتمش اولان tàhàjjur-ètmish-òlan; —, *s.* تحجرايتمش نسنه tàhàjjur-ètmish-nèssné.

Foster, *v.a.* بسلمك bèsslémek; سود ويرمك sùd-vèrmek.

Foster-brother, Foster-sister, *s.* سود قرنداشى sùd-(kàrdashi).

Foster-daughter, *s.* سود قيزى sùd-kìzi.

Foster-mother, *s.* سودانا sùd-àna.

Foster-son, *s.* سوداوغلى sùd-òghlu.

Foul, *a.* كيرلو kirli, پس pìss, مردار mùrdār (mùndār); چپارز chàpàriz; فنا fèna, بوزق bòzuk; ترس tèrss, مخالف mùkhālif; —, *v.a.* كيرلتمك kìrlètmek; —, *v.n.* كيرلنمك kìrlen-mek; to run foul of, چاتمق chàtmak, اوزرينه دوشمك ùzériné-dùshmek; چپارز او chàpàriz-òl.

Foundation, *s.* تمل tèmel; اساس èssāss, تاسيس tè‘sīss; pious —, وقف wàkf, خيرات khàyrāt, عمارت ‘‘ìmārèt.

Founder, *s.* بانى bānī, واضع الاساس vāzi-‘‘u-'l-èssāss; وقف صاحبى wàkf-sāhibi, صاحب الخيرات sāhibu-'l-khàyrāt; دوكيجى dùkuju; —, *v.n.* باتمق bàtmak, قاينامق kàynamak.

Foundered, *a.* اياقلرى سقط àyaklari-sàkat; dumb —, دلى طوتلمش dìli-tùtulmush.

Foundry, *s.* دوكم خانه dùkyum-khāné.

Fount, Fountain, *s.* چشمه chèshmé; پيكار (pùngàr), ايازمه àyàzma.

Four, *a.* درت dùrt, اربع èrbà‘‘, چهار chihār.

Four-cornered, *a.* درت كوشه dùrt-kyùshé.

Fourfold, *a.* درت قات dùrt-kàt.

Fourfooted, *a.* درت اياق dùrd-àyak.

Fourteen, *a.* اون درت òn-dùrt.

Fowl, *s.* طاوق tàwuk; قوش kùsh; —, *v.n.* قوش اوينه كتمك kùsh-àvìna-ghìtmek.

Fowler, *s.* قوشباز kùshbàz.

Fowlingpiece, *s.* او تفنكى àv-(tùfèghi), فلنته fìlìnta.

Fox, *s.* دلكى or تلكى tìlki; شيطان shèy-tān, ولد vèled.

Foxglove, ارى قوانى àri-kòwāni.

Fraction, *s.* كسر kèssir; پارچه pàrcha, جزء jùz', قسم kìssm.

Fractions, *s.* كسورات kyùsūrāt; vulgar —, كسر kèssr; decimal —, كسراعشارى kèssri-ā''shārī.

Fractious, *a.* ترس tèrrs.

Fracture, *s.* قيرق يرى kìrik-yèri, قيرق kìrik; —, *v.n.* قيرمق kìrmak; —, *v.n.* قيرلمق kìrìlmak.

Fractured, *a.* قيرق kìrik.

Fragile, *a.* قولاى قيريلور kòlay-kìrìlir; اينجه ìnja, يوفقه yūfka; ضعيف zà''īf; متانتسز mètānètsiz.

Fragment, *s.* قيرندى kìrìnti, دوكندى dùkuntu; پارچه pàrcha, قطعه kìt''à, قسم kìssm.

Fragrance, *s.* كوزل قوقو ghyùzèl-kòku, قوقو kòku, رايحه rā'ihà, بوى bùy.

Fragrant, *a.* كوزل قوقولو ghyùzèl-kòkulu, معطر mū''àttàr, خوشبو kòshbū.

Frail, *a.* اينجه ìnja, يوفقه yūfka; ضعيف zà'īf, متانتسز mètānètsiz; نازك nāzik; غير عفيفه ghàyri-''àfīfé.

Frailness, Frailty, *s.* عدم متانت ''àdemi-metānèt; عدم عفت ''àdemi-''iffèt.

Frame, *s.* چرچوه chèrchivé; بنيان bùnyān, بنياد bùnyād; —, *v.a.* ترتيب ا tèrtīb-et.

France, *s.* فرانسه Frànsa.

Franchise, *s.* معافيت mū''āfiyyèt; امتياز ìmtiyāz.

Frank, *a.* كتم ايتميوب طوغرى سويلر kètm-etmeyub-dòghru-sùwèyler.

Frankincense, *s.* كونلك ghyùnluk, بخور bùkhūr.

Fraud, *s.* حيله hīlé.

Fray, *s.* غوغا kàwgha.

Freckle, *s.* سيل sīl.

Free, *a.* سربست sèrbèsst, ازاد àzād; (of a trade) كدكلو ghèdikli; —, *v.a.* ازاد ا àzād-et.

Freebooter, *s.* حيدود hàydūd.

Freedom, *s.* سربستلك sèrbèsstlik, سربستيت sèrbèsstiyyèt, ازاد àzād, ازادلق àzādlìk; (of a trade) كدك ghèdik.

Freehold, *a.* & *s.* ملك mùlk.

Freemason, *s.* فارماصون fàrmàsūn.

Freewill, *s.* ارادهٔ جزئيه irādè'l-jùz'iyyé.

Freeze, *v.n.* طوكمك dòngmak, او منجمد mùnjèmid-òl; —, *v.a.* طوكدرمق dòngdurmak.

Freight, *s.* نول nèvl (nàvlun); يولك yùk, حموله hàmūlé; —, *v.a.* نوله ويرمك nèvla-vèrmek; نولله طوتمق nèvlla-tùtmak; يوكلتمك yùklètmek, طولدرمق dòldurmak.

French, *a.* فرانسز fransiz.

Frenchman, *s.* فرانسز fransiz.

Frenzy, *s.* چلغينلق chìlghìnlìk, جنت jìnnèt, جنون jùnūn.

Frequent, *a.* صيق sìk; —, *v.a.* چوق كتمك chòk-ghìtmek, صيق اوغرامق sìk-òghramak.

Frequently, *ad.* صيق صيق sìk-sìk, چوق chòk.

Fresh, *a.* تازه tàzé; (water) طاتلو tàtli; (new) يكى yèngi; (cool) سرين sèrin; (horse) اويناق òynàk; (wind) صيقيجه sìkija.

Fret, *v.n.* قساوت ا kàssàvèt-et, كدر ا

kèder-et ; —, *v.a.* کوجه کتمك ghyùjé-ghìtmek.

Friable, *a.* قولای ازیلور kòlay-ézilir, قولای اوفانور kòlay-ūfànir.

Friction, *s.* سورنمه sùrunmé, سورشمه sùrushmé.

Friday, *s.* جمعه jùm''à, جمعه کونی jùm''à-ghyùnu.

Friend, *s.* دوست dòsst, محب mùhìbb, مخلص mùkhliss.

Friendly, *a.* (person) دوست dosst ; (thing) دوستانه dòsstānè.

Friendship, *s.* دوستلق dòsstluk, محبت màhàbbèt ; خلوص khùlūss.

Frigate, *s.* فرقتين fìrkatīn.

Fright, *s.* قورقو kòrku, خوف khàvf.

Frighten, *v.a.* قورقوتمق kòrkutmak, تخويف ا tàkhwīf-et, اخافه ا ìkhāfé-et.

Frightful, *a.* قورقولو kòrkulu, قورقونج kòrkunj, مخوف màkhūf.

Fringe, *s.* صاچاق sàchak ; —, *v.a.* اطرافنه پرواز کبی او ètrāfina - pèrwāz-ghìbi-òl.

Fro, *ad.*, to and fro, اوته برو ùté-bèri, اشاغی يوقاری àshaghi-yùkàri, اننه بوينه ènina-bòyuna.

Frock, *s.* فسطان fìsstān.

Frog, *s.* قوربغه kùrbàgha ; (horse's) طبان tàban.

From, *pr.* دن dan.

Front, *s.* اوك ùng, يوز yùz, پيش pīsh.

Frontier, *s.* سنور sìnir, سرحد sèr-hàdd.

Frost, *s.* طوك dòng, قراغی kìràghi.

Frosty, *a.* طوكيور dòngiyor, صوغوق sòghuk.

Froth, *s.* كپوك kyùpuk.

Frown, *s.* قاش چاتمسی kàsh-chàtmassi ; —, *v.n.* قاش چاتمق kàsh-chàtmak.

Frozen, *a.* طوكمش dòngmush, منجمد mùnjèmid.

Fruit, *s.* يمش yèmish, ميوه mèyvé, ثمره sèméré ; محصول màhsūl.

Fruitful, *a.* بركتلو bèrékètli, محصولدار màhsūldār.

Fruitless, *a.* بوش bòsh, بيهوده bīhūdé, نافله nāfilé, فائده سز fā'idéssiz.

Frustrate, *v.a.* بوزمق bòzmak, سكته ويرمك sèkté-vèrmek, مانع او mānì''òl.

Fry, *s.* (of fish) بالق ياورسی bàlìk-yàw-rissi ; (lamb's, &c.) جكر jìgher ; (dish) تاوه tàwa ; —, *v.a.* تاوه ده پشورمك tàwada-pìshirmek, قاورمق kàwurmak ; —, *v.n.* تاوه ده پشمك tàwada-pìshmek, قاورلمق kàwrulmak.

Fryingpan, *s.* تاوه tàwa. کومور kyùmur.

Fuel, *s.* ياقه جق yàkajak, اوطون òdun ;

Fugitive, *s.* and *a.* قاچقين kàchkìn, فراری fìrāri.

Fulcrum, *s.* مسند mèssned.

Fulfil, *v.a.* يرينه كتورمك yèrina-ghè-tirmek, اجرا ا ìjrā-et, ايفا ا īfà-et.

Full, *a.* طولو dòlu, طولغون dòlghūn, مملو mèmlū ; — moon, بدر bèdr, ايك اون بشی àying-òn-bèshi.

Fuller's-earth, *s.* كل kil.

Fumigate, *v.a.* توتسيلتمك tùtsìletmek, توتسيلمك tùtsulémek, توتسی ويرمك tùtsu-vèrmek.

Fumigation, *s.* توتسی tùtsu.

Fun, *s.* شقا shàka, اكلنجه èylènje.

Function, *s.* ايش ìsh, خدمت (khìzmèt).

Fund, *s.* سرمايه sèrmāyé, خزينه (khàzna).

Fundamental, *a.* اصلی àsslī, اساسی èssāssī.

Funeral, *s.* جنازه‌الایی jènāzé-ālayi.
Funk, *s.* قورقو kòrku.
Funnel, *s.* حونی hùni; بوری bòru.
Funny, *a.* تحاف tùhāf. [پوصه pòssa.
Fur, *s.* کورك kyùrk; (dirt) کیر kìr,
Furious, *a.* حدتلو hìddètli, قیزغین kìzghìn; پك سرت pèk-sèrt, حدید hàdīd, شدید shèdīd.
Furnace, *s.* اوجاق òjak.
Furnish, *v.a.* (give) ویرمك vèrmek; (sell) صاتمق sàtmak; (a house) دوشه‌مك dùshémek; (a house by the agency of another person) دوشتمك dùshetmek.
Furniture, *s.* دوشه‌مه dùshémé. [etmek.
Furrier, *s.* کورکجی kyùrkju.
Further, **Furthermore**, **Furthest**, *v.* Farther, &c. [غضب ghàzab.
Fury, *s.* حدت hìddèt; شدت shìddèt;
Fuse, *v.n.* اریمك èrimek; —, *v.a.* ارتمك èritmek; —, *s.* فتیل fītil; طاپه tàpa. [èrimish.
Fusion, *s.* اذابه ìzābé; in —, اریمش
Fuss, *s.* تلاش tèlash; to make a —, *v.n.* تلاش ا tèlash-et.
Fustian, *s.* شیطان‌بزی shèytān-bèzi.
Futile, *a.* بوش bòsh, بیهوده bīhūdé, فائده‌سز fā'idéssiz, نافله nāfilé.
Futility, *s.* بیهوده‌لك bīhūdélik; بیهوده ایش bīhūdé-ìsh.
Future, *a.* کله‌جك ghèlèjek, آتی ātī, اوله‌جق òlajak; —, *s.* کله‌جك‌زمان ghèléjek-zàmān; in —, *ad.* اتیده ātīda, فیمابعد fī-mā-bà''d, بوندن‌بویله bùndan-bùylé, بوندنصکره bùndan-sòngra.
Futurity, *s.* کله‌جك زمان ghèléjek-zàmān.
Fye, *int.* عیب ''àyb, اوطان ùtān.

G.

Gabion, *s.* طابیه سپدی tābiya-sèpedi.
Gad about, *v.n.* حیلازلق‌ایدوب‌کزمك hàylāzlìk-èdup-ghèzmek.
Gadfly, *s.* آت سنکی āt-sìnèghi.
Gaiety, *s.* فراح fèrāh, جنبش jùnbush.
Gain, *s.* کار kyàr, قزانج kàzanj; —, *v.a.* قزانمق kàzanmak, کارا kyār-et; واصل‌او vāssìl-òl, یتشمك yètishmek; ایارتمق àyartmak; — over, ایارتمق àyartmak; — upon, ایلرولیوب طوته‌جق‌او ìlériléyup-tùtajak-òl; — ground, یرقزانمق yèr-kàzanmak, ایلرولمك ìlérilémek; — time, وقت قزانمق wàkìt-kàzanmak. [tèkzīb-et.
Gainsay, *v.a.* انکارا inkyār-et; تکذیب ا
Galata (a quarter of Constantinople), *s.* غلطه Ghàlàta. [bòra, فرطونه fìrtìna.
Gale, *s.* صیقی‌روزکار sìkì-rùzghyār; بوره
Gall, *s.* عود ''ùd, زهره zèhré; مرارت mèrārèt; (rub) یاره yàra; —, *v.a.* اینجتمك ìnjitmek, یاره ا yàra-et; کوجه‌کتمك ghyùjé-ghìtmek; —nut, nutgall, *s.* مازی màzi.
Gallant, *a.* یکیت yìghit, جسور jèssūr, دلاور dìlāvèr, بهادر bàhādir; —, *s.* عاشق ''āshìk; زنپاره (zàmpara).
Gallantry, *s.* یکیتلك yìghitlik, جسارت jèssārèt; زنپاره‌لق (zàmparalìk).
Gallery, *s.* دیوانخانه dīwānkhāné; مناره اوستی شرفه‌سی mìnāré-shùrféssi;

اورتیلو یول àsstu-ùrtulu-yòl, صوقاق sòkAk, کوپری kyùpru.
Galley, s. چکدرمه chèktirma. [prànghα.
Galleys, s. pl. کورك kyùrèk; پرانغه
Galley-slave, s. کورکلو kyùrèklu; پرانغه‌لو prànghali.
Gallipoli (town of), s. کلیبولی Ghélībòli.
Galloon, s. شرید shèrid.
Gallop, s. درت نعل dırt-(nAl); —, v.n. درت نعل کتمك dùrt-(nAl)-ghìtmek.
Gallows, s. داراغاجی dār-Aghaji.
Galvanic, a. غلوانیقی ghalvaniki; — battery, غلوانیق طاقمی ghalvanik-
Galvanism, s. غلوانیق ghalvanik. [tàkimi.
Gamble, v.n. قمارا وینامق kùmàr-òyna-mak. [kùmārbAz.
Gambler, s. قمارجی kùmārji, قمارباز
Gamboge, s. پنطالومبه pàntalòmba.
Game, s. اویون òyun; (chase) او Av, شکار shìkyār, صید sàyd. [kùmārji.
Gamester, s. قمارباز kùmārbAz, قمارجی
Gander, s. ارکك قاز èrkek-kAz. [bùluk.
Gang, s. طاقم tàkim, سوری sùru, بلوك
Gangrene, s. قانغرینه kànghrìna.
Gaol, s. زندان zìndān, حبسخانه hAbss--khānè, محبس māhbèss.
Gaoler, s. زندانجی zìndānji.
Gap, s. ارالق àralik, اچقلق àchiklik, اچق یر àchik-yèr.
Gape, v.n. اسنمك èssnémek; اچلمق àchilmak, اچق قالمق àchik-kAlmak; — after, — at, v.a. باقمق bàkmak.
Garb, s. زی zìy, قیلق kìlik, قیافت kìyāfèt, کسوت kìssvèt. [pp. محرف mùhàrrèf.
Garble, v.a. تحریف ا tàhrìf-et; —ed,

Garden, s. باغچه bàghcha; kitchen —, بوستان bòsstān; سبزوات باغچه‌سی sèbzéwAt-bàghchassi (zèrzawAt).
Gardener, s. باغچوان bàghchawān.
Gargle, s. غرغره ghàrghara; —, v.a. and n. غرغره ا ghàrghara-et.
Garlic, s. صارمصق sàrimsàk.
Garment, s. روبه rùba, ثوب sèvb.
Garnet, s. لعل là''l.
Garret, s. طوان اراسی tàwan-àrassi.
Garrison, s. قلعه‌ده موجود اولان عسکر kAl''àda - mèvjūd - òlAn - ''Assker, مستحفظین عسکری mùsstàhfizīn--''Asskéri, اوطوراق عسکری òturAk--''Asskéri; —, v.a. عسکر قومق ''Assker-kòmak; اوطورمق òturmak; to be in —, v.n. اوطورمق òturmak, اوطوراق او òturAk-òl.
Garter, s. دیز باغی dìz-bàghi.
Gash, s. بچاق یاره‌سی bìchàk-yàrassi.
Gasp, s. نفس nèfess; —, v.n. همان نفس الهمامق (hèmen)-nèfess-Alama-[mak.
Gate, s. قپو kàpi, باب bāb, در dèr.
Gateway, s. قپو التی kàpi-Alti.
Gather, v.a. (pluck) قوپارمق kòparmak; — up, — together, طوپلامق tòplamak, دیوشرمك dèvshirmek, جمع ا jèm''--et; —, v.n. طوپلانمق tòplanmak; (fester) جراحت طوپلانمق jèrāhàt-tòplanmak. [v.a. اولچمك ùlchmek.
Gauge, s. چاپ chàp; اولچی ùlchu; —,
Gauntlet, s. زره الدوانی zìrh-èldivèni.
Gauze, s. بورمجك bùrumjik; wire-gauze, تلدن اورمه tèldan-ùrmè.
Gay, a. جنبشلو jùnbushlu, ایلنجه‌لو

èylènjáli ; كيف kèyf ; أچق àchik, پارلاق pàrlàk ; فراح fèrāh.

Gaze, s. سيرجی كبی باقش sèyrji-ghìbi-bàkish ; —, v.n. سيرجی كبی باقمق sèyrji-ghìbi-bàkmak. [āhū.

Gazelle, s. جيران jèyrān (jèylān), اهو

Gazette, s. غزته ghàzèta, تقويم وقائع tàkwīmī-vàkā'ì''.

Gear, s. طاقم tàkim, ادوات èdāwāt, أوادانلق àwadànlik ; in —, طاقيلو tàkili ; out of —, طاقيلو دكل tàkili-dìghil. [larini-kèssmek.

Geld, v.a. طاشاقلرينی كسمك tàshak-

Gelding, s. اكدش ìghdish, باركير (bèghir.

Gem, s. جوهر jèvhèr (pl. جواهر jèwāhīr).

Genealogy, s. نسب nèsseb.

General, s. پاشا pàsha ; مشير mùshīr ; سرعسكر sèr-''àsskèr, سردار sèrdār, سركرده sèrkèrdé ; lieutenant —, فريق fèrik ; major —, *or* brigadier —, ميرلوا mīri-lìwā ; —, a. عمومی ''ùmūmī ; in —, generally, ad. أكثريا èksériyyā.

Generalissimo, s. سردار اكرم sèrdār-èkrèm.

Generate, v.a. حاصل ا hàssil-et, ايراث ا īrāss-et.

Generation, s. قرن kàrn ; عصر واحد ادملری ''àssri-wāhid-àdamlari ; تكون tèkèvvun ; تناسل tènāssul ; organs of —, الات تناسل ālāti-tènāssul.

Generosity, s. سخاوت sàkhāvèt, جومردلك jùmerdlik ; كرم الشيم kèremu-'sh-shìyèm.

Generous, a. سخاوتلو sàkhāvetli, جومرد jùmerd ; كريم الشيم kèrīmu-'sh- [-shìyèm.

Genesis, s. تورات tèvrāt.

Genie, s. جن jìn, جنی jìnnī.

Genius, s. هنر hùner ; استعداد ìsstì''dād ; هنر صاحبی hùner-sāhibi.

Genoa, s. جنويز jenviz.

Genteel, a. تميز tèmīz ; (person) كشی زاده kìshi-zādé, افندی èfèndi ; (lady) خانم hànim.

Gentle, a. ملايم mùlāyim, يواش yàwàsh ; مظلوم màzlūm ; طاتلو tàtli.

Gentleman, s. كشی زاده kìshi-zādé, بكزاده bèghzādé, افندی èfèndi.

Genuine, a. خالص khāliss, صحيح sàhīh, خاص khàsss.

Geography, s. جغرافيا jàghrāfiya.

Geology, s. علم طبقات ارض ''ìlmi-tàbakāti-àrz.

Geometer, Geometrician, s. مهندس mùhèndiss, اهل هندسه èhli-hèndéssé.

Geometry, s. هندسه hèndéssé.

Georgia, s. كورجستان ghùrjistān. [ghùrji.

Georgian, s. كورجی ghùrji ; —, a. كورجی

Geranium, s. سارد ليه چيچكی sàrdèlya-chìchèghi, ابه كومجی èbé-ghyùmèji.

Germinate, v.n. سورمك sùrmek, كوك صالمق kyùk-sàlmak, فلزلنمك fìliz-lenmek.

Get, v.a. (procure) پيدا ا pèydā-et, تحصيل ا tàhsīl-et ; —, v.n. (go) كتمك ghìtmek ; (become) أولمق òlmak ; — above, دن زياده يوقاری يه چيقمق dan-ziyādé-yùkāriya-chìkmak ; — abroad, نشر اولنمق nèshr-òlunmak ; سويلنلمك sùwèylenilmek, دويولمق dùyulmak ; طيشاری كتمك dìshāri-ghìtmek ; — a fall, دوشمك dùshmek ; — a footing, يرلشمك yèrleshmek; — away, *v.n.* قورتلمق kùrtulmak; ايرلمق āyrɪl-mak; چيقمق chɪ̀kmak; —, *v.a.* چيقارمق chɪ̀kàrmak, ايرمق àyrmak, سوكمك sùkmek; قورتارمق kùrtarmak; — before, اوكنهوارمق ùnguna-vàrmak; — by heart, ازبرلمك èzbèrlémek; — clear, *v.* — away; — down, *v.n.* انمك ènmek; *v.a.* اندرمك èndirmek; — forward, ايلرولمك ilérilémek; — in, كيرمك ghìrmek; — off, *v.* — away; — on, ايلرولمك ìlérilémek; اوستنهچيقمق ùsstuna-chɪ̀kmak; بنمك bìnmek; كيمك ghìymek; — out, *v.* — away; — ready, *v.n.* حاضرلنمق hāzirlanmak, حاضراو hāzir-òl; —, *v.a.* حاضرلمق hāzirlamak, حاضرا hāzir-et; — the better of, حقندنكلمك kàkkindan-ghélmek; ينمك yènmek; غالباو ghālib-òl; صاوشدرمق sàwushdurmak; — through, *v.n.* كچمك ghèchmek; —, *v.a.* كچورمك ghèchirmek; — together, *v.n.* طوپلانمق tòplanmak; —, *v.a.* طوپلامق tòplamak; — up, *v.n.* قالقمق kàlkmak; —, *v.a.* چيقارمق chɪ̀kàrmak; قالدرمق kàldirmak; ديكمك dìkmek; — well, ايواو īyi-òl, افاقتبولمق ìfākàt-bùlmak; — with child, *v.n.* كبهقالمق ghèbé-kàl-mak; —, *v.a.* كبها ghèbé-et; — you gone, *int.* هايدىكيت hàydi-ghìt, ييقلشورادن yìkɪl-shùradan; هايدى سكدر hàydi-sìkdir.

Ghost, *s.* خياله khàyālé; روح rūh, جان jàn; Holy Ghost, روحالقدس rūhu-'l-kùduss; to give up the —, تسليمروحا tèsslīmi-rūh-et; جانى چيقمق jàni-chɪ̀kmak.

Giant, *s.* طاغكبىادم dàgh-ghìbi-àdam.

Gibbet, *s.* داراغاجى dàr-àghaji.

Gibraltar, *s.* جبلالتر Jèbel-tàr.

Giddiness, *s.* سرسملك sèrsèmlik; باش دونمهسى bàsh-dùnméssi, كوزلرقرارمسى ghyùzlar-kàrarmassi; عقلسزلق "àkl-sizlik, خفتمزاج khɪ̀ffèti-mìzāj.

Giddy, *a.* سرسم sèrsèm; عقلسز "àklsiz; to be —, باشىدونمك bàshi-dùnmek, كوزلرى قرارمق ghyùzlari-kàrarmak.

Gift, *s.* هديه hèdìyyé; عطيه "àtìyyé, احسان ìhsān, انعام in"ām; بخشش bàkhshish; موهبهءالاهيه mèvhibé'i-ilàhìyyé. [جسيم jèssīm, مفرط mèfrèt.

Gigantic, *a.* بيوك bìyuk, عظيم "àzīm,

Gild, *v.a.* يالدزلمى yàldizlamak, تذهيبا tèzhīb-et.

Gilding, *s.* يالدز yàldiz. [kùlàklari.

Gills, *s. pl.* بالغكقولاقلرى bàlighing-

Gimlet, *s.* بورغى bùrghu.

Gimp, *s.* قيطان (ghàytān).

Gin, *s.* (spirit) راقى ràki, عرق "àrak; (trap) طوزاق tùzak; (machine) چرخ [charkh.

Ginger, *s.* زنجفيل zènjéfīl.

Gipsy, *s.* چنكانه (chìnghèni) قبطى kìbtī.

Giraffe, *s.* زرافه zùrāfa (zùrāfā).

Gird, *v.a.* قوشاتمق kùshàtmak; — up (a horse) قولاننىچكمك kòlànini--chèkmek, — one's self, قوشانمق kùshànmak.

Girdle, *s.* قوشاق kùshàk, كمر kèmer.

Girl, *s.* قيز kìz.

Girt, *v.a. v.* Gird.

Girth, *s.* محيط mùhīt, چوره chèvré; horse's — bands, قولان kòlān.

Give, *v.a.* ويرمك vèrmek, vìrmek; اعطا ا ì''tā-et; حاصل ا hāssìl-et; —, *v.n.* (stretch) اسنمك èssnémek; (frost) كوشه‌مك ghèvshémek; — a call, چاغريويرمك chàghirivèrmek; اوغرايويرمك òghrayivèrmek; — a guess, بليويرمك bìlivèrmek; برتخمين ا bìr-tàkhmīn-et; — a look, باقيويرمك bàkivèrmek; — a portion, جهاز ويرمك jìhāz-vèrmek (chèhiz); — away, ويريويرمك vèrivèrmek, هبه ا hìbé-et; — back, — back again, كيرو ويرمك ghèri-vèrmek; — battle, جنكه باشلامق jènghé-bàshlamak; — ear, قولاق ويرمك kùlàk-vèrmek; — forth, طيشارى ويرمك dìshàri-vèrmek; اعلان ا ì''lān-et; — ground, كيرو چكلمك ghèri-chèkilmek; سوزندن دونمك sùzundan-dùnmek; — a hand, ياردم ا yàrdim-et; — heed, دقت ا dìkkàt-et; — in charge, تسليم ا tèsslīm-et; — judgment, اعلام ا ì''lām-et; — the lie, تكذيب ا tèkzīb-et; — notice, خبر ويرمك khàber-vèrmek; — one joy, تبريك ا tèbrīk-et; — leave, رخصت ويرمك اذن ìzin-vèrmek; ويرمك rùkhsàt-vèrmek; — one's mind, افكارينى بيان ا èfkyārini-bèyān-et; — one's mind to (a thing), صرف ذهن ا sàrfi-zihn-et, دوشمك dùshmek, توغل ا tèvàghghul-et, مشغول ا mèshghūl-òl; — out, *v.a.* طيشارى ويرمك dìshàri-vèrmek; اعلان ا ì''lān-et; —, *v.n.* يورلمق yòrulmak, اوصانمق ùssànmak; دوكنمك dùkènmek; — over, *v.a.* تسليم ا tèsslīm-et, دور ا dèvr-et; —, *v.n.* وازكچمك wāz-ghèchmek; كسلمك kèssilmek; — place, چكلوب ير ويرمك chèkilup-yèr-vèrmek; — suck, امزرمك èmzirmek, بسلمك bèsslémek; — the slip, صاوشمق sāwushmak; — up, تسليم ا tèsslīm-et; سويلمك sùwèylé-mek; — warning, خبر ويرمك khàber-vèrmek; — way, قيرلمق kìrilmak, قوپمق kòpmak; يقلمق yìkilmak; بوزلمق bòzulmak.

Glad, *a.* ممنون mèmnūn, مسرور mèssrūr; to be —, حظ ا hàzz-et, خوشلنمق, khòshlanmak. [سرور sùrūr.

Gladness, *s.* ممنونيت mèmnūnìyyèt,

Glance, *s.* باقش bàkish; —, *v.n.* سكمك sèkmek; — over, كوز اتمق ghyùz-àtmak.

Gland, *s.* بيض bèyz (bèz).

Glare, *s.* پك پارلايش pèk-pàrlayish — *v.n.* پك پارلامق pèk-pàrlamak; — at, كوزلرى اتش كبى اوله رق باقمق ghyùzléri-àtèsh-ghìbi-òlarak-bàkmak.

Glass, *s.* جام jàm, بللور billūr; (drinking) قدح kàdeh; (looking) آيينه àyina; (eye) كوزلك ghyùzluk; (telescope) دوربين dūrbīn (dùrbun); (hour) قوم ساعت kùm-sā''at.

Glaze, *s.* سر sìrr; —, *v.a.* جام كچورمك jàm-ghèchirmek; جام قاپلامق jàm-kàplamak.

Glazier, *s.* جامجى jamji.

Gleam, *s.* شعاع shù''ā'' ; —, *v.n.* پارلامق pàrlamak. [àkip-ghèchmek.
Glide, *v.n.* قایمق kàymak ; اقوب کچمك
Glitter, *s.* پارلایش pàrlayish ; —, *v.n.* پارلامق parlamak.
Globe, *s.* کوره kyùrÉ.
Globular, *a.* کروی kyùrévī. [hàbāb.
Globule, *s.* حبه hàbbÉ, دانه dānÉ; حباب
Gloom, *s.* قرانلق kàranlìk ; کدر kèder, مغمومیت màghmūmìyyèt.
Gloomy, *a.* قرانلق kàranlìk ; مغموم màghmūm. [tèmjīd-et.
Glorify, *v.a.* حمد ا hàmd-et, تمجید ا
Glorious, *a.* نامدار nāmdār, مشهور mèshhūr ; رونقلو rèvnàklì.
Glory, *s.* حمد hàmd ; مجد mèjd ; شوکت shèvkèt ; رونق rèvnàk, شان shān, شهرت shùhrèt.
Gloss, *s.* جلا jìlā, پارلاقلق pàrlaklìk ; — over, *v.a.* اورتمك ùrtmek.
Glove, *s.* الدوان (èldivèn), الدوانلق (èldivènlik). [àtèsh-késsilmek.
Glow, *v.n.* یانمق yànmak, اتش کسلمك
Glue, *s.* طوتقال tùtkàl ; — *v.a.* طوتقال ایله یاپشدرمق tùtkàl-ila-yà-pishdirmak.
Glutton, *s.* اوبور òbur, اکول èkyūl.
Gluttony, *s.* اوبورلق òburlik.
Gnat, *s.* سوری سنك sìvri-sìnek.
Gnaw, *v.a.* کمرمك ghèmirmek.
Gnomon, *s.* عضاده ''ìzādÉ.
Go, *v.n.* کتمك ghìtmek, یوریمك yùrumek ; — about, دولاشمق dòlashmak ; باشلامق bāshlamak ; — abroad, طیشاری چیقمق dìshāri-chìkmak ; طیشاری کتمك dìshàri-ghìtmek ; طاغلمق dàghìlmak, نشر اولنمق nèshr-òlunmak ; — against, قارشو کتمك kàrshi-ghìtmek ; بد کلمك bèd-ghèlmek ; — along, همان کتمکده او (hèmen)-ghìtmekda-òl ; — ashore, قره یه چیقمق kàraya-chìkmak ; قره یه اوطورمق kàraya-òturmak ; — astray, یولنی شاشرمق yòlunu-shàshirmak ; فنا یوله صاپمق fèna-yòla-sàpmak ; — asunder, قوپمق kòpmak, کسلمك kèssilmek ; — away, کتمك ghìtmek ; — back, کیرو کتمك ghèri-ghìtmek ; — backwards, کیرولمك ghèrilémek ; ترس یوریمك tèrss-yùrumek ; — backwards and forwards, کیدوب کلمك ghìdup-ghèlmek ; — down, انمك ènmek ; باتمق bàtmak ; — for, کیدوب المق ghìdup-àlmak ; — forth, نشر اولنمق nèshr-òlunmak ; چیقمق chìkmak ; — from, دونمك dùnmek, ایرلمق àyrìlmak ; — halves, پایلاشمق pàylashmak ; — in, کیرمك ghìrmek ; ایچرو کتمك ìchèri-ghìtmek ; — off, کیدیویرمك ghìdivèrmek ; بوزلمق bòzulmak, اویمامق ùymamak, اولمامق òlmamak ; کچمك ghèchmek ; کسلمك kèssil-mek ; اتش المق àtèsh-àlmak ; پاطلامق pàtlamak ; اوچمق ùchmak ; — on, ایلرو کتمك ìléri-ghìtmek ; دورمامق dùrmamak, قالمامق kàlmamak, فارغ اولمامق fārigh-òlmamak ; اویمق ùymak, اولمق òlmak, کیلمك

ghìyilmek ; — out, طیشاری چیقمق dìshàri-chìkmak ; سونمك sùnmek, منطفی او mùntàfi-ol ; — over, کچمك ghèchmek ; اوستندن کچمك ùsstun-dan - ghèchmek ; کوزدن کچورمك ghyùzdan - ghèchirmek ; کزمك ghèzmek ; يوقلامق yòklamak ; — through, ایچندن کچمك ìchindan--ghèchmek ; کوزدن کچورمك ghyùz-dan-ghèchirmek ; let go the anchor ! فونده fònda.

Goad, *s.* اوکندره ùghèndérè ; —, *v.a.* دورتمك dùrtmek, دورتشدرمك dùr-tushturmek.

Goal, *s.* سرمنزل sèr-mènzil, محل مقصود [màhàlli-màksūd.

Goat, *s.* کچی kèchi ; he —, ارکچ èrghech.

Goblet, *s.* قدح kàdeh, جام jām, پیاله pìyālé.

God, *s.* الله àllāh, تنکری tànghri, اله [ìlāh.

Godhead, *s.* لاهوت lāhūt.

Godly, *a.* صالح sālih, دیندار dīndār.

Goitre, *s.* اور ùr.

Gold, *s.* التون àltin, زر zèr, ذهب zèheb.

Goldbeater, *s.* ورقجی vàrakji.

Golden, *a.* التون àltin, زرین zèrīn.

Goldfinch, *s.* سقا قوشی sàka-kùshu.

Gold-lace, *s.* سرمه sìrma.

Goldsmith, *s.* قویومجی kùyumju.

Gonorrhœa, *s.* بل صوغوغی bèl-sòghughu.

Good, *s.* خیر khàyr, ایولك īyilik, فلاح fèlāh ; —, *a.* ایو īyi ; یرار yàrar.

Good-humour, *s.* کیف kèyf ; to be in a —, کیفی او kèyfi-òl.

Good-humoured, *a.* کولر یوزلو ghyùler--yùzlu, دارلمز dàrilmàz.

Goodly, *a.* کوزل ghyùzèl ; بیوجك bìyujèk, خیلی khàyli.

Good-nature, *s.* ایو طبیعت īyi-tàbī''àt.

Good-natured, *a.* ایو īyi, طاتلو tàtli, کوزل خویلو ghyùzèl-khùylu.

Goodness, *s.* ایولك īyilik.

Goods, *s. pl.* اشیا èshyā, امتعه èmta''à, اموال èmvāl, مال màl.

Goose, *s.* قاز kàz ; tailor's —, اوتی ùtu.

Gooseberry, *s.* بکطاشی اوزومی bèk-tàshi-ùzumu.

Gorge, *s.* بوغاز bòghàz ; —, *v.a.* دویورمق dòyurmak ; طیقامق tìka-mak ; —ed, *p.p.* دویمش dòymush ; طیقانمش tìkànmish ; to become —, *v.n.* دویمق dòymak ; طیقانمق tìkàn-mak.

Gosling, *s.* قاز پلازی kàz-pàlazi.

Gospel, *s.* انجیل شریف ìnjīli-shèrīf.

Gossamer, *s.* شیطان عربه‌سی shèytān--''àrabassi.

Gossip, *s.* بوشبوغاز bòsh-bòghàz ; انیس [ènīss.

Gourd, *s.* قباق kàbak.

Gourmand, *s.* شکمپرست shikèmpèrèsst.

Gout, *s.* نقریس nìkrīss.

Govern, *v.a.* حکومت ا hùkyūmèt-et, اداره ا idārè-et, ضبط و ربط ا zàbt-u--ràbt-et.

Government, *s.* حکومت hùkyūmèt, اداره idāré, ضبط و ربط zàbt-u-ràbt ; دولت dèvlèt ; وکلای دولت vùkélā'i--dèvlèt, وکلا طاقمی vùkélā-tàkimi.

Governor, *s.* والی vāli, متصرف mútas-sàrrif, متسلم mùtèssèllim ; lieutenant —, قائممقام kā'im-màkàm.

Gown, *s.* (woman's) فسطان fìsstan; (man's outer) جبه jùbbé; بينش bīnish; (inner) انتارى èntāri.

Grace, *s.* كرم kèrem, لطف lùtf, عنايت "ìnāyèt, احسان ìhsān; لطافت làtāfèt, نزاكت nèzākèt, حسن hùssn, ادا èdā; تشكر tèshèkkyur, دعا dù"ā; عفو "àfv; مغفرت màghférèt, غفران ghùfrān; your —, ذات عاليلرى zāti-"ālīléri, ذات دولتلرى zāti-dèv-lètléri; his —, فخامتلو fàkhāmètlù; —, *v.a.* تزيين ا tèzyīn-et, زينت او zīnèt-òl.

Graceful, *a.* حسنلو hùssunlu, نازك nāzik, نزاكتلو nèzākètli.

Gracious, *a.* (person) كريم kèrīm, لطيف làtīf, عنايتكار "ìnāyètkyār, نازك nāzik; (act or word) لطف وعنايت اميز lùtf-vè-"ìnāyet-āmīz, كريمانه kèrīmāné, عنايتكارانه "ìnāyetkyārāné, نازكانه nāzìkyāné.

Gradation, *s.* درجه dèréjé; تدريج tèdrīj.

Gradual, *a.* تدريجى tèdrījī; —ly, *ad.* على التدريج "àlé-'t-tèdrīj.

Graft, *s.* اشى àshi, قلم اشيسى kàlem-àshissi; —, *v.a.* اشلاتمق àshlatmak; اشلامق àshlamak.

Grain, *s.* دانه dāné (tāné), حبه hàbbé; ذخيره zàkhīré; تخم tòkhum; (of wood) طمر dàmar; to go against the grain, ادمك كوجنه كتمك àdaming-ghyùjuna-ghìtmek.

Grammar, *s.* صرف ونحو sàrf-u-nàhv.

Grammar-school, *s.* مكتب عرفان mèk-tеb-i-"ìrfān.

Granary, *s.* انبار ànbār.

Grand, *a.* بيوك bìyuk; عظامتلو "àzā-mètli; طنطنه لو tàntanali.

Grandee, *s.* رجال كباردن برى rìjāli-kìbārdan-bìri, اعاظم رجالدن برى à"āzimi-rìjāldan-bìri.

Grandeur, *s.* عظامت "àzāmèt, طنطنه tàntana, هيبت hèybèt.

Grandfather, *s.* بيوك بابا bìyuk-bàba, دده dèdé, جد jèdd. [turàk-kèlām.

Grandiloquence, *s.* طمطراق كلام tòm-

Grandiloquent, *a.* كلامى طمطراق kèlāmi--tòmturàk. [bìyuk-vālidé.

Grandmother, *s.* بيوك انا bìyuk-àna, بيوك والده

Grandson, *s.* طورون tòrun, حفيد hàfīd, نبيره nèbīré.

Grand-Vizier, *s.* صدر اعظم sàdr-à"zàm.

Grant, *s.* احسان ìhsān; فرمان fèrmān, برات bèrāt; —, *v.a.* ويرمك vèrmek, احسان ا ìhsān-et; تسليم ا tèsslīm-et, اعتراف ا i"tirāf-et; فرض ا fàrz-et.

Grape, *s.* اوزوم ùzum; — shot, مسكت mìsskèt, صالقم sàlkim.

Grapple with, *v.a.* اوغراشمق òghrash-mak, چكشمك chèkishmek.

Grasp, *v.a.* طوتمق tùtmak, قاورامق kàwramak, قبض ا kàbz-et.

Grass, *s.* اوت òt.

Grasshopper, *s.* چكركه chèkirghé.

Grassplot, *s.* چيم chìm.

Grate, *s.* اوجاق òjak; اسقاره ìsskàra; —, *v.a.* رنده لمك rèndélémek; —, *v.n.* سورتمك sùrunmek, غيجردامق ghìjirdamak; — on one's feelings, ادمك بدينه كتمك àdaming-bèdina--ghìtmek.

Grateful, *a.* متشكر mùtéshèkkir, شاكرالنعمه shākiru-'n-nì"mé.

Grater, *s.* رنده rèndé.

Gratification, *s.* ممنونيت mèmnū-niyyèt, صفا sAfā; نعمت nì"mèt; بخشش bàkhshish, احسان ìhsān, انعام ìn"ām; خشنوديت khòsh-nūdìyyèt; حظ hAzz, حظ نفس hAzzi--nèfss.

Gratify, *v.a.* ممنون ا mèmnūn-et, خشنود ا khòshnūd-et; صفا ويرمك sAfā-vèrmek; خوشلاندرمق khòsh-landirmak; حاصل ا hāssil-et; اجرا ا ìjrā-et; اقتضاسنى اجرا ا ìktizāssini--ìjrā-et; تابع او tābi"ol, اويمق ùymak.

Gratis, *ad.* بادهوا bādi-hèwā (bèdāwa), مجانا mèjānan.

Gratitude, *s.* شكر shùkr, تشكر tèshèk-kyur, شكرانيت shùkrānìyyèt.

Gratuitous, *a.* بادهوا bādi-hèwā (bè-dāwa).

Gratuity, *s.* بخشش bàkhshish, احسان ìhsān, انعام ìn"ām.

Grave, *s.* مزار mèzār, قبر kAbr, مقبره mAkbéré; —, *a.* (person) اغر àghir, تمكينلو tèmkīnli; (affair) قورقلور kòrkulur, قورقلهجق kòrkulajak; —, *v.a.* قازمق kAzmak, حك ا hàkk-et.

Gravestone, *s.* مزار طاشى mèzār-tAshi.

Graving-tool, *s.* قلم kàlem.

Gravity, *s.* (personal) اغر àghir, تمكين tèmkīn; (of affairs) قورقلهجق برحال kòrkulajak-bìr-hāl; (of substances) ثقلت sìklèt; specific —, ثقلت ذاتيه sìklèti-zātìyyé.

Gravy, *s.* صو sū. [yàghlamak.

Grease, *s.* ياغ yàgh; —, *v.a.* ياغلامق

Great, *a.* بيوك bìyuk, كبير kèbīr, عظيم "Azīm; چوق chòk; the —, *s. pl.* كبار kìbār, كبارطاقمى kìbār-tàkimi, كبرا kyùbérā; a — many, a — deal, برچوق bìr-chòk; — grandfather, دده نك باباسى dèdéning-bAbAssi; — grandson, طورونك اوغلى tòrunung--òghlu; Alexander the —, اسكندر رومى Isskender-rūmì; Peter the — دلى پترو dèli-Pétro.

Great-coat, *s.* قپود kapòt. ["Azāmèt.

Greatness, *s.* بيوكلك bìyukluk; عظامت

Greece (kingdom of), *s.* يونانستان Yūnānisstān; — (ancient) روم rūm.

Greedy, *a.* اچ كوزلو àch-ghyùzlu; چوق يير chòk-yèr, اوبور òbūr.

Greek (in general), *a.* روم rūm, رومى rūmi; (of the kingdom) يونان yūnān; (language) *s.* رومجه rūmjé.

Green, *a.* يشل yèshil; خام khAm.

Greengrocer, *s.* سبزواتجى sèbzéwātji.

Greenhouse, *s.* ليمونلق lìmònluk.

Greens, *s. pl.* لحنه làhana.

Greet, *v.a.* سلام ويرمك sèlām-vèrmek.

Grey, *a.* قير kìr; بوز bòz; كومشى ghyùmishī; قورشونى kūrshunī; —, *s.* — of the morning, صباح ايدينلغى sàbAh-àydinlighi; — of the evening, اخشام قرانلغى Akhsham-kAranlighi.

Greybeard, *s.* اق صقاللو Ak-sàkAlli.

Greyhound, *s.* تازى tAzi.

Gridiron, *s.* اسقاره ìsskàra.

Grief, *s.* كدر kèder, درد dèrd, قساوت

kassāvèt, الم èlem, غم gham, اندوه èndūh.

Grievance, s. موجب تشکی mùjibi-tèsh-èkki; بلا bèlā, درد dèrd; غدر ghadr; ظلم zùlm.

Grieve, v.a. کدر ویرمك kèder-vèrmek; —, v.n. کدرا kèder-et, قساوت چکمك kassāvèt-chèkmek, غم یمك gham-yèmek, مکدر او mùkèdder-òl.

Grievous, a. عظیم والیم "azīm-vè-èlīm, فنا fèna.

Grill, v.a. قزارتمق kìzàrtmak. اسقاره‌ده ìsskàrada-

Grind, v.a. (flour, &c.) اوکتمك ùghut-mek; چکمك chèkmek; (colours, &c.) ازمك èzmek, سحق‌ا sàhk-et; (iron, &c.) طاشه طوتمق tasha-tùtmak; (the teeth) غجرداتمق ghìjirdatmak.

Grindstone, s. طاش tash, بلکی bilèghi, بلکی طاشی bilèghi-tashi.

Gripe, s. ال èl, پنچه pènché, قبضه kabza; —, v.a. صیقی طوتمق sìki-tùtmak; قارن اغرتمق kàrn-aghritmak; gripes, s.pl. قارن اغریسی kàrn-aghrissi, صانجی sanji.

Gristle, s. قیقرداق kìkirdak.

Groan, s. ایکلدی ìngilti, انین ènīn; —, v.n. ایکلمك ìnglémek.

Grocer, s. بقال bakkāl.

Groin, s. قاصق kassik.

Groom, s. سئیس sè'īss, اسپر ìsspir.

Groove, s. ییو yīv, yīw.

Gross, s. اون ایکی دوزینه òn-ìki-dùzina, یوزقرق درت دانه yùz-kìrk-dùrt-(tānè); —, a. قبا kaba, فنا fèna, دارەسی چیقمامش dàrassi-chìk-mamish.

Grot, Grotto, s. مغاره màghara, این īn.

Ground, s. یر yèr, عرصه "àrsa; زمین zèmīn; اساس èssāss; موجب mùjib, سبب sèbeb, مناسبت mùnāssébèt; —, a. اوکدلمش ùghudulmush; دوکلمش dùghulmush, چکلمش chèkilmish, ازلمش èzilmish; —, v.a. تأسیس‌ا tè'sīss-et; —, v.n. (a ship) اوطورمق òturmak.

Grounded, a. متأسسی mùté'èsssiss, مبتنی mùbténi; اصلی‌وار assli-vàr.

Groundless, a. دیبسز dìbsiz, اصلی‌یوق assli-yòk, بوش bòsh.

Grounds, s. pl. تلوی tèlvi, طورطو tòrtu, پوصه pòssa.

Ground-swell, s. صالنتی salinti.

Ground-work, s. تمل tèmel.

Group, s. کومه kyùmè, بلوك bùluk; —, v.a. طوپ‌ا tòp-et; —, v.n. طوپ‌او tòp-òl.

Grove, s. اورمان òrman.

Grow, v.n. بیومك bìyumek; بویلانمق bòylanmak; سورمك sùrmek; اولمق òlmak, کسلمك kèssilmek.

Growl, v.n. خرلامق khìrlamak.

Gruel, s. یوان‌چوربا yàwan-chòrba.

Gruff, a. بوغوق bòghuk; خویسز khùysuz.

Grumble, v.n. سویلنمك sùwèylenmek.

Guarantee, s. (person) کفیل kèfīl; (thing) کفالت kèfālèt; رهین rèhīn.

Guard, s. (man) یساقجی yàssakji, نوبتجی nùbètji; عسکر "assker, قواص kawass, (soldiers) خاصه عسکری khāsssa-"asskéri, عساکرخاصه "assa-kiri-khāsssa; (time or duty) نوبت nùbèt; (of a sword-handle) چاپراز

chàpràz ; (of a gun-trigger) قورقولق kòrkuluk ; —, *v.a.* صقلامق sàklamak, حفظ ا hìfz-et, محافظه ا mùhāfaza-et ; باقمق bàkmak.

Guard-house, *s.* قوللق kòlluk.

Guardian, *s.* وصی wàssi ; محافظ mùhāfiz.

Guerilla, *s.* باشی بوزق bàshi-bòzuk.

Guess, *s.* ظن zànn, تخمین tàkhmīn ; —, *v.a.* بلمك bìlmek ; تخمین ا tàkh-[mīn-et.

Guest, *s.* مسافر mùssāfir.

Guidance, *s.* هدایت hìdāyet ; دلالت dèlālèt.

Guide, *s.* قلاغوز kìlāghuz, دلیل dèlīl, هادی hādī, رهنما rèhnumā ; —, *v.a.* یول كوسترمك yòl-ghyùsstermek ; قلاغوزلق ا kìlāghuzluk-et.

Guild, *s.* اصناف èssnāf.

Guile, *s.* غل وغش ghìll-u-ghìsh, حیله [hīlé.

Guilt, *s.* قباحت kàbāhàt, جرم jùrm, كناه ghyùnāh.

Guiltless, *a.* قباحتسز kàbāhatsiz, كناهسز ghyùnāhsiz, بیكناه bī-ghyùnāh.

Guilty, *a.* قباحتلو kàbāhatli, جنحه لو [jùnhali.

Guinea-fowl, *s.* بچ طاوغی bèch-tàwughu.

Guitar, *s.* كیتاره ghitāra.

Gulf, *s.* (bay) كورفز kyùrfez ; (abyss) ورطه vàrta, حفره hùfré.

Gull, *s.* (bird) مارطی màrti ; (dupe) شاشقین shàshkin ; —, *v.a.* الداتمق àldatmak.

Gullet, *s.* غرتلاق ghìrtlàk, بوغاز bòghàz.

Gum, *s.* صمغ sàmgh (zàmk) ; (of the eyes) چپاق chàpak ; (of the teeth) دیش اتلری dìsh-ètléri ; —, *v.a.* صمغ ایله یاپشدرمق (zàmk)-ila-yàpishdir-mak.

Gun, *s.* طوپ tòp ; تفنك tùfènk (tùfèk).

Gun-barrel, *s.* تفنك دمیری tùfènk-démiri.

Gun-carriage, *s.* قنداق kùndak.

Gun-cotton, *s.* پاموق باروتی pàmūk-bārūti.

Gunner, *s.* طوپجی tòpji ; طوپجی باشی [tòpji-bàshi.

Gunpowder, *s.* باروت bārùt.

Gunshot, *s.* (distance) طوپ منزلی tòp-mènzili ; قورشون منزلی kùrshun-mèn-zili ; — wound, كله یاره سی ghyùllé-yàrassi ; قورشون یاره سی kùrshun-yàrassi.

Gunsmith, *s.* تفنكجی tùfènkji (tùfèkji), [چقماقجی chàkmakji.

Gunstock, *s.* تفنك قونداغی tùfènk-kùndàghi.

Gush, *v.n.* فشقرمق fìshkirmak.

Gust, *s.* روزكارك براسمه سی rùzghyāring-bìr-èssmassi ; بوره bòra.

Gut, *s.* باغرصق or بغرصاق bàghirsak.

Gutter, *s.* اولق òluk, اولاق àwlàk.

Guzzle, *v.n.* and *a.* ایچمك ìchmek, چاقمق chàkmak.

Gymnasium, *s.* بدن تعلیمی محلی bèden-tà''līmi-màhàli.

H.

Haberdasher, *s.* خرده فروش khùrdé-fùrūsh.

Habit, *s.* عادت ''ādet ; خوی khùy.

Habitable, *a.* اوطوریلور òturulur, قابل سكنی kābili-sùknā.

Habitation, *s.* مسكن mèsskèn, مأوی [mè'và.

Habitual, *a.* عادت حكمنه كيرمش "ādet-hùkmuna-ghìrmish.

Habituate, *v.a.* آلشدرمق alishdirmak; — one's self, آلشمق alishmak.

Hack, *v.a.* چنتمك chèntmek; —, hackney, *s.* باركير bārghīr (bèyghir), كراجى باركيرى kìrāji-(bèyghiri).

Hail, *s.* دولو *or* طولو dòlu; —, *v.n.* دولو ياغمق dòlu-yàghmak; —, *int.* السلام عليك ess-sèlāmu-"àlèyké; —, *v.a.* بيورك بيورك ديو قبول ا bùyurung-bùyurung-dèyu-kabūl-et; چاغرمق chàghirmak.

Hale, *a.* دنج dìnj.

Half, *a.* يارم yàrim; —, *s.* يارى yàri; ... and a half, بچوق ... bùchuk; —, *ad.* يارى يارى يه yàri-yàriya.

Half-moon, *s.* يارم اى yàrim-ày.

Half-pay, *s.* حضر معاشى hàzar-mà"āshi.

Halfpenny, *s.* اون پاره òn-pārė.

Half-seas-over, *a.* سرخوشجه sèrkhòshjė.

Half-witted, *a.* بوداله bùdala.

Hall, *s.* ديوانخانه dīwānkhānė.

Halloo, *int.* اى èy, بكا باق bàna-bāk.

Hallow, *v.a.* تقديس ا tàkdiss-et, مبارك ا mùbārek-et; رعايت ا ri"āyet-et, مبارك عد ا mùbārek-"àdd-et; —ed, *pp.* مبارك mùbārek, مقدس mùkàddèss.

Halt, *s.* ايلنش èylènish; —, *a.* طوپال tòpal; —, *v.n.* ايلنمك èylenmek; طوپاللمق tòpàllamak, اغسيمق aghsimak; —, *int.* حالت hàlt.

Halter, *s.* يولار yùlar; ايپ ìp.

Halve, *v.a.* ايكى يه بولمك ìkiya-bùlmek; پايلاشمق pàylashmak.

Ham, *s.* بوط bùt, قايناق kāynàk; دوكز بوطى پاصدرمسى dònguz-bùtu-pàssdirmassi (dòmuz).

Hamlet, *s.* كويجكز kyùyjèghiz, اوفاق كوى ùfàk-kyùy.

Hammer, *s.* چكيج chèkij; طوقماق tòkmàk; sledge —, واريوس vàriyoss; —, *v.a.* دوكمك dùghmek.

Hammock, *s.* برانده brànda.

Hamper, *s.* قپاقلو سپد kapakli-sèped; —, *v.a.* صيقندى ويرمك sìkinti-vèrmek, النى اياغنى باغلامق èlini-àyaghini-bàghlamak, باغلامق bàghlamak.

Hand, *s.* ال èl, دست dèsst, يد yèd; (man) ادم adam, نفر nèfer, ايشجى ìshji; (signature) امضا ìmzā; hour —, عقرب "àkreb; minute —, يلقوان yèlkowàn; —, *v.a.* ويرمك vèrmek; — over, تسليم ا tèsslīm-et; — in hand, *ad.* ال اله ويره رك èl-èla-vèrèrek; على الاتفاق "àlé-'l-ìttifāk; to live from hand to mouth, اخشام نه ييه جكنى صباحلين بلمامك aksham-nè-yèyé-jéghini-sàbāhléyin-bìlmamek.

Handful, *s.* اوج طوليسى āwuj-dolussu.

Hand-grenade, *s.* ال خمبره سى èl-khùmbarassi.

Handicraft, *s.* صنعت sàn"àt.

Handkerchief, *s.* منديل mèndil, چوره chèvrė, يمنى yèméni, ياغلق yàghlik, مقرمه màkrama-(màh-).

Handle, *s.* صاپ sap, قولپ kùlp, قولاق kùlak, قبضه kabza; —, *v.a.* طوتمق tùtmak, قوللانمق kùllanmak.

Handsome, *a.* كوزل ghyùzèl, كوسترشلو ghyùsstèrishli, ياقشقلو yàkishìkli.

Handspike, *s.* مانوله mànavèla.

Handy, *a.* (man) هزارفن hèzār-fènn (hèzārifènd); (thing) راحت ràhat, قولاى kòlay, ايشه يرار ìsha-yàrar.

Hang, *v.a.* اصمق ássmak; —, *v.n.* اصلمق ássilmak; — about, طولاشمق dòlashmak; — back, ايلرو كلمامك ìléri-ghèlmamek, كيرو طورمق ghèri-dùrmak; — down, صارقمق sàrkmak; — out, *v.a.* اصمق ássmak, سرمك sèrmek; صارقتمق sàrkitmak, قالدرمق kàldirmak, كوسترمك ghyùsstermek; —, *v.n.* صارقمق sàrkmak; اصلمق ássilmak; — over, طاشمق tàshmak; صارقمق sàrkmak; — together, برى برينى براقمامق bìri-bìrini-bràkmamak; — up, اصمق ássmak. [kilij.

Hanger, *s.* قصه جق برقلج kìssajek-bìr-

Hangman, *s.* جلاد jèllād.

Hank, *s.* قنغال kànghal, طره tùrré (tùra).

Hanker after, *v.a.* استمك ìsstémek, ارزولمق àrzulamak, ارامق àramak, اشتياق چكمك ìshtiyāk-chèkmek.

Happen, *v.n.* اولمق òlmak, چيقمق chìkmak, واقع‌او vāki‘‘òl, تصادف‌ا tèssāduf-et, ظهورا zùhūr-et, وقوع بولمق vùkū‘‘-bùlmak.

Happily, *ad.* سعادتله sà‘‘ādètla; بركت ويرسونكه bèrékèt-vèrsin-ki.

Happiness, *s.* سعادت sà‘‘ādèt; ممنونيت mèmnūnìyyèt.

Happy, *a.* ايشى يولنده راحتى يرنده اولان ìshi - yòlunda - rāhati - yèrinda - òlan, سعيد sà‘‘īd, مسعود mèss‘‘ūd; ممنون mèmnūn; مسرور mèssrūr.

Harass, *v.a.* يورمق yòrmak, راحت ويرمامك rāhat-vèrmamek, راحتسزا rāhatsiz-et, تعجيزا tà‘‘jīz-et.

Harbour, *s.* ليمان lìmān, مرسى or مرسا mèrsà; —, *v.a.* طوتمق tùtmak, يتاق‌او yàtak-òl. [dipòrto.

Harbour-master, *s.* قپتان ديپورتو kàptan-

Hard, *a.* قتى kàti, سرت sèrt, پك pèk; صيقى sìki; كوچ ghyùch, چتين chètin, مشكل mùshkil; — of belief, كوچ اينانور ghyùch-ìnànir, اينانمز ìnàn-màz; — to be believed, كوچ اينانلور ghyùch-ìnànilir, اينانلمز ìnànilmàz; — of hearing, صاغر sàghir.

Harden, *v.a.* قتيلاشدرمق kàtilashdirmak, سرتلشدرمك sèrtleshdirmek, پكشدرمك pèkishdirmek; —, *v.n.* قتيلاشمق kàtilashmak, سرتلشمك sèrtleshmek, پكشمك pèkishmek.

Hard-favoured, Hard-featured, *a.* چركين chìrkin.

Hard-hearted, *a.* مرحمتسز mèrhàmetsiz.

Hardihood, *s.* جسارت jèssārèt.

Hardiness, *s.* طيانقلق dàyànìklik.

Hardly, *ad.* همان hèmān (hèmen); كوچ بلا ghyùch-bèlā; هيچ مساعده كوسترميه‌رك hìch-mùssā‘‘adé-ghyùss-terméyérek.

Hardness, *s.* قتيلق kàtilik, سرتلك sèrtlik; صيقيلق sìkilik; كوچلك ghyù-chluk, چتينلك chètinlik, مشكللك mùshkillik, صعوبت sù‘‘ūbèt.

Hardship, *s.* صيقندى sìkindi, مشقت mèshàkkàt.

Hardy, *a.* طيانقلو dàyànikli, دنج dìnj.

Hare, *s.* طاوشان tàwshan. [kulàk-vèr.
Hark, *int.* دكله dìnglé (dīné), قولاق‌ویر
Harlot, *s.* فاحشه fāhishé.
Harm, *s.* ضرر zàrar, زیان zìyān; —, *v.a.* اینجیتمك ìnjitmek, ضررا zàrar-et.
Harmless, *a.* ضررسز zàrarsiz. [mùwāfakàt.
Harmony, *s.* طاتلولق tàtlìlik; موافقت
Harness, *s.* قوشم or قوشوم kòshum; طاقم tàkim; —, *v.a.* قوشمق kòshmak; طاقمنی‌اورمق tàkimini-wùrmak; — maker, سراج sàrrāj.
Harp, *s.* چنك chèngh.
Harpoon, *s.* زبقین zìbkin.
Harpooner, *s.* زبقینجی zìbkinji.
Harpsichord, *s.* كارقدیم پیانو kyàr-kàdīm-piàno.
Harrow, *s.* چفتجی طراغی chìftji-tàraghi; —, *v.a.* طرامق tàramak; — one's feelings, ادمك یوركنی قاناتمق àdam-ing-yùrèghini-kànatmak.
Harsh, *a.* سرت sèrt.
Hartshorn, *s.* نشادر nìshàdir; (spirit of) نشادر روحی nìshādir-rūhu.
Harvest, *s.* حصاد hàssàd, محصول màhsūl; — time, بچم‌وقتی bìchim-wàkti, اوراق‌وقتی òrak-wàkti.
Hash, *s.* یحنی yàhni; —, *v.a.* یحنی‌ا yàhni-et.
Haste, *s.* عجله ''àjélé; چابكلك chà-bìklik, سرعت sùr''àt; —, *v.n.* عجله‌ا ''àjélé-et, چابك‌او chàbik-òl.
Hasten, *v.n.* چابك‌كتمك chàbik-ghìtmek; —, *v.a.* تعجیل‌ا tà''jil-et.
Hastily, *ad.* عجله‌ایله ''àjélè-ila, على العجله ''àlè-'l-''àjélé.
Hasty, *a.* چابك chàbik; صبرسز sàbrsiz, چابك قزار chàbik-kìzar.
Hat, *s.* شاپقه shàpka.
Hatch, *v.a.* یاوری‌چیقارمق yàwri-chì-kàrmak; —, *s.* قپو kàpi; انبارقپاغی ànbar-kàpàghi.
Hatchet, *s.* بالطه bàlta.
Hatchway, *s.* انبار اغزی ànbar-àghizi.
Hate, *s.* بغض bùghz, عداوت ''àdāvèt; نفرت nèfrèt; —, *v.a.* هیچ‌سومامك hìch-sèvmamek; عداوت‌ا ''àdāvèt-et.
Hateful, *a.* منفور mènfūr, مقبوح màkbūh.
Hatred, *s.* بغض bùghz, عداوت ''àdāvèt; نفرت nèfrèt. [(kìbir).
Haughtiness, *s.* تكبر tèkèbbur, كبر kìbr
Haughty, *a.* متكبر mùtékèbbir, كبرلو kìbirli, فرعون fìr''àwn, نوبران nòbràn.
Haul, *v.a.* چكمك chèkmek; هیسه‌ا [hīsa-et.
Haunch, *s.* صغری sàghri.
Haunt, *v.a.* طائف‌او tā'if-ol.
Have, *v.a.* مالك‌او mālik-òl.
Havoc, *s.* زیان zìyān, خسارت khàssārèt.
Hawk, *s.* اتمجه àtmaja; —, *v.a.* كزدروب صاتمق ghèzdirip-sàtmak.
Hawker, *s.* كزدریجی بازركان ghèzdiriji-bàzirghyān.
Hawser, *s.* پلامار pàlamàr.
Hay, *s.* قورو اوت kùru-òt.
Haycock, *s.* اوت یغینی òt-yìghini.
Haymaking, *s.* اوت بچمك òt-bìchmek.
Hayrick, Haystack, *s.* بیوك قورو اوت یغینی bìyuk-kūru-òt-yìghini.
Hazard, *s.* بخت bàkht; تصادف tèssā-duf; —, *v.a.* تهلكه‌یه قومق tèhlikéyé-[kòmak.
Hazardous, *a.* تهلكه‌لو tèhlikéli.
Haze, *s.* سیس sìss, دومان dùmàn.

Hazel, *s.* فندوق fìndìk ; —, *a.* کستانه رنکلو kèsstāné-rènkli.

He, *pr.* او ò, اول òl ; —, *a.* ارکك èrkek.

Head, *s.* باش bāsh ; سر sèr, رأس rè'ss ; (of a ship), باش bāsh ; (of a cask) دیب dìb ; (of an arrow) تمرن tèmrèn ; —, *a.* باش bāsh, برنجی bìrinji ; —, *v.a.* باش او bāsh-ol, سرکرده او sèrkèrdé-òl.

Headache, *s.* باش اغریسی bāsh-āghrissi.

Headland, *s.* بورون bùrun.

Headlong, *ad.* باش اشاغی bāsh-āshàghi, دپه تقلاق (tèpé)-tàklak.

Head-quarters, *s.* مرکز mèrkez.

Headstrong, *a.* سوز دکلهمز sùz-dìnglémàz (dìnémàz).

Headway, *s.* یول yol ; یوریمه yùruma.

Heal, *v.n.* ایواو īyi-òl ; —, *v.a.* ایوا īyi-et.

Health, *s.* صحت sìhhàt, عافیت "āfìyyèt ; کیف kèyf, مزاج mìzāj, طبع tāb" ; your health ! عشقکزه "āshkìngiza.

Healthy, *a.* صاغ sàgh, صاغلام sàghlàm.

Heap, *s.* کومه kyùmé, یغین yìghìn ; —, *v.a.* یغمق yìghmak.

Hear, *v.a.* اشتمك ìshìtmek, استماعا ìsstimā"-et ; دکلهمك dìnglémek (dìnémek), قولاق ویرمك kùlāk-vèrmek ; قبولا kābūl-et, اجابتا ìjābet-et.

Hearing, *s.* قوت سامعه kùvvèti-sāmi"a ; in one's —, اشیتدیکی حالده ìshitdighi-hālda ; to give a —, اذن ویروب سویلتمك ìzin-vèrup-sùwèylètmek, دکلهمك (dìnémek).

Hearken, *v.n.* قولاق ویرمك kùlàkvèrmek.

Hearsay, *s.* مسموعات mèssmū"āt.

Heart, *s.* یورك yùrèk, قلب kālb, دل dìl ; (of a plant) کوبك ghyùbèk ; (middle) اورطه or اورته òrta ; by —, ازبردن èzbèrden ; to learn by —, *v.a.* ازبرلمك èzbèrlémek.

Heart-breaking, Heart-rending, *a.* ادمك یورکی طیانمز ādāmìng-yùrèghi-dàyanmàz.

Heart-broken, *a.* شکسته دل shìkèssté-dìl.

Hearth, *s.* اوجاق òjak.

Heartless, *a.* انسانیتسز ìnsānìyyètsiz, انصافسز ìnsāfsiz.

Heart's-ease, *s.* هرجائی بنفشه hèr-jā'ī-bènèfshé (mènèkshé).

Hearty, *a.* قوی kàwī, صاغلام sàghlàm ; صمیمی sàmīmī, یورکدن yùrèkdan.

Heat, *s.* سیجاق sìjāk, سیجاقلق sìjāklìk, حرارت hàrārèt; اتش ātèsh ; قیزغینلق kìzghìnlìk ; —, *v.a.* استمق ìssìtmak, قیزدرمق kìzdirmak, تسخینا tèsskhīn-et.

Heathen, *s.* and *a.* کاور ghyàwr, کافر kyāfir, کتابسز کافر kìtābsiz-kyāfir.

Heave, *v.a.* اتمق ātmak ; —, *v.n.* باش اورمق bāsh-wūrmak.

Heaven, *s.* جنت jènnèt, فردوس fìrdàvss.

Heavy, *a.* اغر āghir, ثقیل sàkīl.

Hectic, *a.* ورملو vèrèmli ; — fever, کیزلو استمه ghìzli-ìssìtma.

Hedge, *s.* چیت chìt.

Hedgehog, *s.* اوفاق کرپی ùfāk-kìrpi.

Heed, *s.* دقت dìkkāt, تقید tàkàyyud, قید kàyd ; —, *v.a.* and *n.* دقتا dìkkāt-et, قیدا kàyd-et.

Heel, *s.* اوکچه ùkché ; — over, *v.n.* یاتمق yàtmak ; —, *v.a.* یاترمق yàtirmak.

Hegira, *s.* هجرت hìjrèt ; هجرت نبويه hìjréti-nèbévìyyé. [اينك ghènj-ìnek.

Heifer, *s.* ديشى طانه dìshi-dàna, كنج

Height, *s.* بوى bòy ; يوكسكلك yùksèklik, ارتفاع ìrtifā''; طاغ dàgh, دپه (tèpé), باير bàyir, صرت sìrt ; اوج èvj, ذروه zìrvé ; اورته òrta, وسط wàssat.

Heinous, *a.* پك قبيح pèk-kàbīh ; شنيع shènī''; اشنع èshnà''.

Heir, *s.* (after possession) وارث vāriss ; (before possession) ولى عهد vèlī-''àhd.

Heiress, *s. f.* وارثه vārissé ; وليةالعهد vèlìyyétu-'l-''àhd. [-chichèghi.

Heliotrope, *s.* وانليه چيچكى vànìlya-

Hell, *s.* جهنم jìhènnem (jìhànnam), جحيم jàhīm.

Hellenic, *a.* يونانى yūnāni.

Hellespont, *s.* چناق قلعه‌سى بوغازى chànak-kàléssi-bòghàzi. [يكه yèké.

Helm, *s.* دومن يكه‌سى dùmèn-yèkéssi,

Helmet, *s.* تاس tàss, مغفر mìghfèr, تغلغه tùghulgha.

Helmsman, *s.* دومنجى dùmènji.

Helot, *s.* اسير èssir.

Help, *s.* ياردم yàrdim, امداد ìmdād, اعانه ì''āné, معاونت mū''āvénèt, عون ''àvn; ياردمجى yàrdimji, معين mū''īn, معاون mū''āvin ; —, *v.a.* ياردم ا yārdim-et, معاونت ا mū''āvénèt-et ; اعانه ا ì''āné-et ; امداد ا ìmdād-et, امداده يتشمك ìmdāda-yètishmek ; منع ا mèn''-et, چاره بولمق chāré-bùlmak. [Èli-àyaghi-tùtmàz.

Helpless, *a.* بيچاره bīchāré, الى اياغى طوتمز

Helpmate, *s.* ارقه‌داش àrkadàsh.

Hem, *s.* قيورلميس كنار kìvrīlmish--kènar ; —, *v.a.* كنارينى قيورمق kènārini-kìvirmak ; — in, چويرمك chèvirmek, قوشاتمق kùshàtmak, اطرفنى المق ètrāfìni-àlmak.

Hemisphere, *s.* نصف كره nìsfi-kyùré.

Hemistich, *s.* مصراع mìssrā''.

Hemorrhoids, *s.* مايه‌سيل māyéssīl,

Hemp, *s.* كندر kèndir. [باسور bāssūr.

Hen, *s.* طاوق tāwuk.

Hence, *ad.* بوندن bùndan ; بناءً عليه bìnā'an-''àlèyh, بوكا بناءً bùnga-bìnā'an, بوكا مبنى bùnga-mèbni, بناءً على ذلك bìnā'an-''àlà-zālìké.

Henceforth, Henceforward, *ad.* بوندن بويله bùndan-bùylé, بوندنصكره bùndan-sòngra, فيمابعد fī-mā-bà''d, بردها bìr-dàhà, شمديدن كيرو shìmdidan--ghèri.

Her, *pr. s.* انى àni, ònu ; اكا ànga (àna), ònga (òna) ; *pr. a.* ى i, سى si, انك aning, ònung.

Herald, *s.* منادى mùnādi ; —, *v.a.* خبر ويرمك khàber-vèrmek.

Herb, *s.* اوت òt, نبات nèbāt.

Herbalist, *s.* كوكجى kyùkju.

Herd, *s.* سورى sùru ; — together, *v.n.* سورى سورى كزمك sùru-sùru-ghèzmek.

Herdsman, *s.* صغرتماج sìghirtmàj.

Here, *ad.* بورا bùra, بوراسى bùrassi ; بورايى bùrayi, بوراسنى bùrassini ; بورايه bùraya ; بوراده bùrada ; بوراسنه bùrassina ; بوراسنده bùrassinda ; —, *int.* اشته ìshté, نا nà ; — and there,

اوته‌بری ùté-bèri ; تك‌تك tèk-tèk ; here is, اشته ìshté, نا nà. [bùralara.

Hereabouts, *ad.* بورالرده bùralarda, بورالره

Hereafter, *ad.* بوندنصكره bùndan--sòngra ; بعدالموت bà‘‘dé-’l-mèvt ; —, *s.* آخرت ākhirèt.

Hereby, *ad.* بومناسبتله bù-mùnāssé-bètla ; بو واسطه‌ایله bù-wāssità-ila.

Hereditary, *a.* موروث mèvrūss, متوارث mùtévāriss ; وارث vāriss ; ولی عهد vèli-‘‘àhd.

Herein, *ad.* بونده bùnda ; بوندن bùndan ; بوكا bùnga ; بونی bùnu.

Hereof, *ad.* بونك būnūn.

Hereon, *ad.* بونك‌اوزرینه būnūn-ùzeriné.

Heresy, *s.* ضلالت dàlālèt, شیعه shī‘‘à, اعتزال ì‘‘tizāl. [mù‘‘tèzil.

Heretic, *s.* ضال dāll, شیعی shī‘‘ī, معتزل

Heretofore, *ad.* شمدی‌یه‌قدر shìmdiya--kàdar, شمدی‌یه كلنجه shìmdiya--ghèlinja ; از قدیم èz-kādīm (ab antiquo), اوته‌دنبرو ùtédan-bèri.

Herewith, *ad.* (inclosed) لفاً lèffan, ملفوفاً mèlfūfan.

Heritage, *s.* میراث mīrāss.

Hermaphrodite, *s.* خنثی khùnsà.

Hermetically, *ad.* هیچ‌هواالمیه‌جق‌صورتله hìch-hèwā-àlmayajak-sūrètla.

Hermit, *s.* منزوی mùnzévī.

Hermitage, *s.* زاویه zāviyyé, عزلتخانه ‘‘ùzletkhāné. [فتق علتی fètk-‘‘ìllèti.

Hernia, *s.* قاصق‌یاریغی kàssik-yàrighi,

Hero, *s.* یكیت yìghit, بهادر bàhādir ; محكی فیه màhkiyun-fīh.

Heroic, *a.* بهادرانه bàhādirāné.

Heroine, *s.* بهادرقاری bàhādir-kàri ; محكیة‌فیها màhkiyetun-fīhā.

Heroism, *s.* یكیتلك yìghitlik.

Hers, *pr.* انك àning, ònung ; انككی àningki, ònungku.

Herself, *pr.* كندی kèndi, كندیسی kèndissi, كندیسنی kèndissini.

Herzegovina, *s.* هرسك Hèrsèk.

Herzegovinian, هرسكلو Hèrsèklī.

Hesitate, *v.n.* باقنمق bàkinmak ; تردد tèrèddud-et ; تأخر tè‘èkhkhur-et ; استمامك ìsstémamek ; نه‌یاپه‌جغنی بلمامك nè-yàpajaghini-bìlmamek ; سویلیه‌جكنی شاشرمق sùwèyléyé-jéghini-shàshirmak. [shùbhé.

Hesitation, *s.* تردد tèrèddud ; شبهه

Heterodox, *a.* امته مخالف ùmmèta [mòkhālif.

Hetman, *s.* هتمان hètmān.

Hew, *v.a.* یارمق yàrmak ; — down, *v.a.* كسمك kèssmek ; یره یقمق yèra-yìkmak.

Hexagon, *s.* مسدس mùssèddèss.

Hiatus, *s.* ارالق àralik.

Hibernate, *v.n.* قیشلامق kìshlamak.

Hibernation, *s.* قیشلامه kìshlama.

Hiccough, Hiccup, *s.* حنچقرق hìnchki-rik ; —, *v.n.* حنچقرمق hìnchkirmak.

Hide, *s.* دری dèri ; —, *v.n.* صقلانمق sàk-lanmak, كیزلنمك ghìzlenmek ; —, *v.a.* صقلامق sàklamak, كیزلمك ghìzlémek.

Hideous, *a.* پك‌چركین pèk-chìrkin, كریه‌المنظر kèrīhu-’l-mànzàr.

Hieroglyph, Hieroglyphic, *s.* صورتلو یازی اشارتی sūrètlū-yàzi-ìshāreti.

High, *a.* يوكسك yùksèk, مرتفع mùrtèfi", بالا bālā; عالى "ālī, سامى sāmī, رفيع rèfī"; طولغون dòlghun, جوشقون jòshkun, طاشقين tashkin; چوق chòk, پك pèk; the Most High, *s.* حق تعالى hàkk-tà"ālà; — tide, — water, مد كامل mèdd kyāmil.

Highland, *a.* طاغلق يره مخصوص dāghlik-yèra-màkhsūss, طاغى dāghī.

Highlander, *s.* طاغ ادمى dāgh-ādami; — *s. pl.* طاغ اهاليسى dāgh-àhālissi.

Highlands, *s. pl.* طاغلق يرلر dāghlik-yèrler, طاغستان dàghistān.

Highly, *ad.* چوق chòk, خيلى khàyli.

Highness, *s.* يوكسكلك yùkseklik; شوكتمآب shèvket-mà'āb; شوكتلو shèvkètlū.

Highway, *s.* جاده jāddé, يول yòl, طريق عام tàrīki-"āmm, شاهراه shāhrāh.

Highwayman, *s.* يول كسيجى yòl-kèssiji, قاطع الطريق kāti"u-'t-tàrīk.

Hill, *s.* طاغ dàgh, دپه (tèpé).

Hillock, *s.* دپه (tèpé).

Hilly, *a.* طاغلق dāghlik.

Hilt, *s.* قبضه kābza.

Hind, *s.* ديشى كيك dìshi-ghèyik; كويلو kyùylu; —, *a.* ارد àrd, قيچ kìch.

Hinder, *a.* كيروكى ghèriki, كيروده كى ghèridéki; —, *v.a.* مانع او māni"-òl, براقمامق bràkmamak, قومامق kòmamak, سكته ويرمك sèkté-vèrmek.

Hinderance, Hindrance, *s.* مانع māni", سكته sèkté.

Hindermost, Hindmost, *a.* اك كيروده كى èng-ghèridéki.

Hindoo, *s.* هندى hìndī.

Hindoostanee, *s.* هند لسانى Hìnd-lìssāni.

Hinge, *s.* رزه rèzé; منتشه mèntéshé; —, *v.n.* دونمك dùnmek; باقمق bākmak.

Hint, *s.* اورتيلوافاده ùrtulu-ìfādé, ايما īmā; —, *v.a.* اورتيلوافاده ا ùrtulu-ìfādé-et, ايما ا īmā-et.

Hip, *s.* قالچه kālcha.

Hire, *s.* كرا kìrā; —, *v.n.* كرايه ويرلمك kìrāya-vèrilmek; —, *v.a.* كرايه ويرمك kìrāya-vèrmek; كراايله طوتمق kìrā-ila-tùtmak; — out, كرايه ويرمك kìrāya-vèrmek.

His, *pr. a.* انك āning, ònung; انككى āningki, ònungku.

Historian, *s.* مورخ mùvèrrikh.

History, *s.* تاريخ tārīkh, تواريخ tāwārīkh (pl.); حكايه hìkyāyé.

Hit, *v.a.* اورمق wùrmak; دكمك dèghmek, اصابت ا ìssābet-et.

Hither, *ad.* برو bèri, برويه bèriya, بو يانه bù-yàna, بو طرفه bù-tàrafa.

Hitherto, *ad.* شمدى يه قدر shìmdìya-kādar, بو زمانه كلنجه bù-zàmāna-ghèlinja.

Hive, *s.* قوان kòwan, ارى قوانى àri-kòwani.

Hoarfrost, *s.* قراغى kìràghi.

Hoarse, *a.* (person) سسى قصلمش sèssi-kìssilmish; (voice) بوغوق bòghuk.

Hoary, *a.* اق āk, اغارمش āgharmish, قير kìr.

Hobgoblin, *s.* زبانى zèbānī.

Hock, *s.* بر نوع شراب bìr-nèv-"i-shèrāb.

Hocus-pocus, *s.* حيله hīlé.

Hod, *s.* تکنه tèkné.

Hodge-podge, *s.* بر نوع طعام bìr-nèv''i-tà''ām; قارشقلق kàrishìklik.

Hoe, *s.* چاپه chàpa.

Hog, *s.* ایغدش طوکز ìghdish-dònguz (dòmuz).

Hogshead, *s.* بیوك فوچی bìyuk-fìchi, مانجنه mànjana.

Hoist, *v.a.* قالدرمق kàldirmak, چیقارمق chìkàrmak.

Hold, *s.* طوتش tùtush, قبض kàbz, ضبط zàbt; (ship's) انبار ànbār; —, *v.a.* طوتمق tùtmak, قبض ا kàbz-et, ضبط ا zàbt-et; براقمامق bràkmamak, صالیویرمامك sàlivèrmamek; — back, *v.n.* کیرو طورمق ghèri-dùrmak; —, *v.a.* الیقومق àlikòmak; — forth, *v.n.* وعظ ا và''z-et; —, *v.a.* اوزاتمق ùzàtmak; — in, ضبطا zàbt-et; — on, *v.n.* براقمامق bràkmamak, وازکچمامك vāz-ghèchmamek; — one's breath, نفسنی حبس ا nèfessini-hàbss-et; — one's tongue, صوصمق sùssmak; اغزینی قپامق àghzini-kàpamak, دلنی طوتمق dìlini-tùtmak; — out, *v.n.* طیانمق dàyanmak; —, *v.a.* اوزاتمق ùzàtmak; ایراد ا īrād-et; — true, — good, *v.n.* قول صحیح او kàvli-sàhīh-òl; — up, *v.n.* اچلمق àchilmak; —, *v.a.* قالدرمق kàldirmak; طوتمق tùtmak; — with, سوزده برابر او sùzda-bèrābèr-òl.

Hole, *s.* دلیك dèlik, سوراخ sūrākh; قویی kùyu, چقور chùkur.

Holiday, *s.* تعطیل tà''tīl; یورتی yòrtu.

Holland, *s.* فلمنك مملکتی filémènk-mèmlekèti.

Hollander, *s.* فلمنك filémènk.

Hollow, *a.* ایچی بوش ìchi-bòsh, مجوف mùjèvf; چقور chùkur, اویوق òyuk; —, *s.* چقور chùkur; —, *v.a.* قازمق kàzmak, اویمق òymak.

Holy, *a.* شریف shèrīf, مقدس mùkàddèss, مبارك mùbārek; — Ghost, روح القدس rūhu-'l-kùduss, — Land, دارفلسطین dāri-filastīn.

Homage, *s.* عرض عبودیت ''àrzi-''ùbūdìyyèt; عبودیت ''ùbūdìyyèt, بندکی bèndéghī.

Home, *s.* او èv; وطن wàtàn; —, *ad.* یرینه yèrina, یرنده yèrinda; اوه èva.

Homely, *a.* قباجه kàbaja; چرکینجه chìrkinja; فقراجه fùkarāja.

Home-made, *a.* اوده یاپلمش èvda-yàpilmish.

Homeward, *a.* اوه طوغری èva-dòghru; کندی وطننه طوغری kèndi-vwàtanina-dòghru.

Homeward-bound, *a.* کندی وطننه طوغری [kèndi-vwàtanina-dòghru.

Homicide, *s.* قتل kàtl; قاتل kātil.

Homogeneous, *a.* متجانس mùtajāniss.

Homogeneousness, *s.* تجانس téjānus.

Hone, *s.* یاغ بلکیسی yàgh-bilèghissi.

Honest, *a.* (person) اهل عرض èhli-''ìrz, تمیز tèmiz; طوغری dòghru, امین èmīn; (living) حلال hàlāl.

Honesty, *s.* عرض ''ìrz; طوغریلق dòghruluk.

Honey, *s.* بال bàl, انکبین ènghyubīn, عسل ''àssel; — comb, چیك بال chìgh-bàl; — dew, ترنکبین tèrènghyubìn; — suckle, حانم الی hànim-èli.

Honorarium, *s.* عائده à'idé.

Honorary, *a.* اعتباری i''tibārī, باپایه bā-pāyé.

Honour, *s.* استقامت ìsstikāmèt, عرض "ìrz, ناموس nāmūs; نام nām, شان shān; شرف shèref, عزت "ìzzèt; —, *v.a.* احترام ا ìhtirām-et, صايمق sāymak; تشريف ا tèshrīf-et, تبجيل ا tèbjīl-et.

Honourable, *a.* (person) تميز tèmiz, طوغرى dòghru, مستقيم mùsstakīm, صاحب ناموس اهل عرض èhli-"ìrz, sāhib-nāmūss; شريف shèrīf, نجيب nèjīb; (thing) باعث شرف bā"issi-shèref; the Right —, دولتلو dèvlètlū.

Hood, *s.* باشلق bāshlik, قوقولته kùkulèta.

Hoof, *s.* طرنق tìrnak, ظفر zìfr.

Hook, *s.* چنكل chènghel; قانجه kānja; ايلك ìlik; اولطه òlta, زونقه zònka; —, *v.n.* ايلشمك ìlishmek; ايلكلنمك ìliklenmek; —, *v.a.* ايلشدرمك ìlishdirmek; ايلكلمك ìliklémek.

Hoop, *s.* چنبر chènber; حلقه hālka.

Hooping-cough, *s.* بوغمجه اوكسرك bòghmaja-ùksuruk.

Hope, *s.* اميد ùmīd, اوموت ùmut; —, *v.a.* اميد ا ùmīd-et, اوممق ùmmak, مأمول ا mè'mūl-et.

Horizon, *s.* افق ùfuk.

Horizontal, *a.* افقى ùfukī, افقه موازى ùfuka-mùwāzi.

Horn, *s.* بوينوز bòynūz; بورى bòrū.

Horoscope, *s.* زائچه zā'ijé.

Horrible, Horrid, *a.* پك فنا pèk-fèna, پك كريه pèk-kèrīh, پك چركين pèk-chìrkin, پك قورقولو pèk-kòrkulu, پك مخوف pèk-mākhūf, پك مهيب pèk-mùhīb.

Horror, *s.* (active) كراهت kèrāhèt; هيبت hèybèt; (passive) قورقو kòrku, دهشت dèhshèt; نفرت nèfrèt, تنفر tènèffur.

Horse, *s.* ات āt; باركير bàrghīr (bèyghir); اتلو ātli; سوارى sùwāri; clothes —, قفس kāfess; blood —, جنس ات jìnss-āt; led —, يدك yèdek; light —, خفيف اتلو عسكرى khàfīf-àtlu-"asskeri; race —, قوشى اتى kòshu-āti.

Horse-breaker, *s.* ات الشديران جانباز āt-ālishdiran-jānbāz.

Horse-cloth, *s.* جل jùll, چول chūl.

Horse-dealer, *s.* ات جانبازى āt-jānbāzi.

Horse-guards, *s.* سوارى عسكر خاصه سى sùwāri-"assker-khāssassi; سر عسكر قپوسى sèr-"assker-kāpissi.

Horseman, *s.* اتلو ātli; جندى jìndi, بنيجى bìniji. بنيجيلك bìnijilik.

Horsemanship, *s.* جنديلك jìndilik,

Horse-shoe, *s.* نعل nā"l (nāl).

Hose, *s.* چوراب chòrab; خرطوم khòrtum.

Hosier, *s.* چورابجى chòrabji.

Hospitable, *a.* غريب پرور ghàrīb-pèrvèr, مهمان نواز mìhmān-nùwāz.

Hospital, *s.* خسته خانه khāssta-khānè, اسپتاليه ìsspitàlya.

Host, *s.* خانه صاحبى khānè-sāhibi; مسافر mùssāfir; اردو òrdu.

Hostage, *s.* رهين rèhīn, كريو ghìrīv.

Hostile, *a.* دشمن dùshmèn.

Hostility, *s.* دشمنلك dùshmènlik; —ties, *s. pl.* حرب hàrb.

Hot, *a.* سيجاق sìjāk; قيزغين kìzghin; كرم ghèrm, حرارتلو hàrārètli; حار hārr.

Hotel, *s.* لوقانده lòkànda.
Hothouse, *s.* صوبه sòba.
Hough, *s.* حیوانك ارد دیزی hàywāning-àrd-dìzi.
Hound, *s.* زغر zàghar.
Hour, *s.* ساعت sā''at; وقت wàkit, زمان zàmān.
Hourglass, *s.* قوم ساعت kùm-sā''at.
House, *s.* او èv, قوناق kònak, خانه khānè, بیت bèyt, دار dār; —, *v.a.* اورتی التنه قومق ùrtu-àltina-kòmak; ایچرو المق ìchèri-àlmak.
House-breaker, *s.* خرسز khìrsiz.
Household, *s.* او طاقمی èv-tākimi, او اوشاقلری èv-ùshàklari, چولق چوجق chòluk-chòjuk, اهل و عیال èhl-u-''àyāl; — stuff, اشیا èshyā, اثاث èssāss.
Householder, *s.* او صاحبی èv-sāhibi.
Housekeeper, *s.* كتخدا قادین kètkhudā-kàdin.
Housekeeping, *s.* او ادارەسی èv-ìdārèssi.
Housemaid, *s.* بسلمه bèsslémè.
Hovel, *s.* قولبه kùlubè.
Hover, *v.n.* طولاشمق dòlashmak; ایرلمامق àyrilmamak; قناد اوستنده دورمق kànad-ùsstunda-dùrmak.
How? *ad.* نصل nàssl, نیجه nìjè, نه درلو nè-dùrlu (tùrlu), نه صورتله nè-sūrètla, نه وجهله nè-vèjhla; نقدر nàkadar; — much? نقدر nàkadar; — many? قاچ kàch, نقدر nàkadar; — many times? قاچ كره kàch-kèrrè, قاچ دفعه kàch-dèf''à, قاچ نوبت kàch-nùbèt, قاچ سفر kàch-sèfer; — long? نقدر nàkadar, نه مدت nè-mùddèt; — often? — frequently? قاچ وقتده بر kàch-wàkitda-bìr.
However, *c.* ولكن vè-lākin, وینه vè-yìnè, ینه yìnè (ghènè), عما ''àmmā; مع ما فیه mà''a-mā-fīh, بونكله برابر bù-nungla-bèrābèr; —, *ad.* هرنصل hèr-nàssl, نصل nàssl; هرنقدر hèr-nàkadar.
Howitzer, *s.* اوبوس òboss (kùbuz).
Howl, *s.* اولویش ùluyush; —, *v.n.* اولومق ùlumak.
Howsoever, *ad.* هرنصل hèr-nàssl, هرنقدر hèr-nàkadar.
Huckster, *s.* مادراباز màdrabàz, قولتقجی kòltukju, كزدریجی ghèzdiriji.
Hue, *s.* رنك rènk, لون lèvn.
Hug, *s.* صارلش sàrilish; —, *v.a.* صارلمق sàrilmak; یقین صوقلمق yàkin-sòkul-mak.
Huge, *a.* پك بیوك pèk-bìyuk, قوجه مان kòjamān, مفرط mèfrèt, عظیم ''àzīm.
Hulk, *s.* قشلایه چویرلمش كمی kìshlaya-chèvirilmish-ghèmi; — about, *v.n.* سورتنمك sùrtunmek.
Hulks, *s.* پرانغه prànghа.
Hull, *s.* تكنه tèknè.
Hum, *s.* اری سسی àri-sèssi; ترنم tèrèn-num; —, *v.n.* اوتمك ùtmek; ترنم ا tèrènnum-et.
Human, *a.* بشری bèshèrī, ادمی ādémī, انسانی ìnsānī, مردی mèrdī; a — being, انسان ìnsān.
Humane, *a.* انسانیتلو ìnsāniyyètli, مشفق mùshfik, شفقتلو shàfakàtli.
Humanity, *s.* انسانیت ìnsāniyyèt, شفقت shàfakàt; بشریت bèshè-

rìyyèt, انسان‌حالی ìnsān-hāli ; ناسوت nāssūt ; ناس nāss.

Humble, *a.* الچق‌کوکللو àlchàk-ghyùngullu, متواضع mùtéwāzi'', کمتر kèmtèr ; کمترانه kèmtèrānè, فقیر fàkīr, ناچیزانه nāchīzānè ; —, *v.a.* کبرینی قیرمق kìbrini-kìrmak, بورننی‌ازمك bùrnunu-èzmek.

Humbug, *s.* یالانجی yàlànji, یالان yàlan.

Humid, *a.* رطوبتلو rùtūbètli.

Humidity, *s.* نم nèm, رطوبت rùtūbèt.

Humility, *s.* تواضع tèwāzu'', وضوع wùzū'', خشوع khùshū''.

Humour, *s.* خوی khùy, خلق khùlk, طبیعت tàbī''àt ; خلط khìlt (*pl.* اخلاط àkhlāt); صو sù.

Hump, Hunch, *s.* اورکج ùrghyuj ; قانبور kànbur ; — backed, قانبور kànbur.

Hundred, *a.* یوز yùz, مائه or مئه mì'è, صد sàd.

Hunger, *s.* اچلق àchlìk, جوع jū'', کرسنکی ghyùrissnéghī ; —, *v.n.* اچ‌او àj-òl.

Hungered, Hungry, *a.* اچ àj, جائع jā'i'', کرسنه ghyùrissnè.

Hunt, *s.* اوه‌کیدش àva-ghìdish ; ارایش àrayish ; —, اوینه‌کتمك àvina-ghìt-mek ; ارامق àramak.

Hunter, *s.* اوجی àvji ; او اتی àv-àti.

Huntsman, *s.* اوجی‌باشی àvji-bàshi.

Hurricane, *s.* قصرغه kàssirgha (sàkirgha).

Hurry, *s.* عجله ''àjélè ; —, *v.n.* عجله‌ا ''àjélè-et ; —, *v.a.* عجله‌ایتدرمك ''àjélè-ètdirmek, تعجیل‌ا tà''jīl-et.

Hurt, *s.* ضرر zàrar, زیان zìyān ; یاره yàra ; دوکلمش قیرلمش dùkulmush-kìrìlmish ; —, *v.n.* اجیمق àjìmak ; —, *v.a.* اجتمق àjìtmak; اینجتمك ìnjitmek.

Hurtful, *a.* مضر mùzìrr, ضررلو zàrarli.

Husband, *s.* قوجه kòja, زوج zèvj, شوهر shèvhèr ; sister's —, انشته ènishtè ; wife's sister's —, باجناق bàjanàk, باجناخ bàjanàkh, باجناح bā-jènāh ; —, *v.a.* اداره‌ا idārè-et, از قوللانمق àz-kùllanmak.

Husbandman, *s.* چفتجی chìftji, اهل زراعت èhli-zìrā''àt.

Husbandry, *s.* چفتجیلك chìftjilik, زراعت zìrā-''àt, حراست and حراثت hìrāssèt, فلاحت fèlāhàt.

Hush, *int.* صوص sùss ; —, *v.n.* صوصمق sùssmak ; —, *v.a.* صوصدرمق sùssdurmak.

Husk, *s.* قبوق kàbuk.

Hut, *s.* قولبه kùlubè.

Hyacinth, *s.* سنبل sùnbul (zùnbul).

Hybrid, *s.* ملز mèlez ; —, *a.* ملز mèlez.

Hydrogen, *s.* مولدالما mùwèllidu-'l-mā.

Hydrophobia, *s.* قدوز kùduz.

Hyena, *s.* سرتلان sìrtlan.

Hymn, *s.* الاهی ìlāhī.

Hyperbola, *s.* قطع‌زائد kàt''i-zā'id.

Hyperbole, *s.* مبالغه mùbāligha.

Hypocrisy, *s.* ریا rìyā, ایکی‌یوزلولك ìki-yùzluluk.

Hypocrite, *s.* ریاکار rìyākyār, مرایی mùrāyī, ایکی‌یوزلو ìki-yùzlu.

Hypothenuse, *s.* وترقائمه vètèri-kā'imè.

Hypothesis, *s.* فرض fàrz, تقدیر tàkdīr.

I.

I, *pr.* بن bèn.

Ice, *s.* بوز bùz.

Iceberg, *s.* بوز اطه‌سی bùz-àdassi. [durma.

Ice-cream, *s.* سوتلو طوکدرمه sùtlu-dòng-

Idea, *s.* فکر fikr ; تخیل tàkhàyyul ; تصور tàssàvvur, مطالعه mùtāla''à; ظن zànn; I have an idea, عقلمه برشی کلیور ''àklima-bìr-shèy-ghèliyor, برشی تصور ایتدم bìr-shèy-tàssàvvur-ètdim.

Ideal, *a.* ظنی zànnī, تصوری tàssàvvurī, تخیلی tàkhàyyulī.

Identify, *v.a.* بلمك bìlmek, سچمك sèchmek, طانیمق tànimak, تشخیص ا [tèshkhīss-et.

Idiot, *s.* بوداله bùdāla.

Idle, *a.* اشسز ìshsiz, بوش bòsh, بوشده bòshda ; —, *v.n.* اشسز طورمق ìshsiz-dùrmak ; —, *v.a.* بوش کچورمك bòsh-ghèchirmek.

Idleness, *s.* اشسزلك ìshsizlik, بوشلق bòshluk, عطالت ''àtālèt. [sūrèt.

Idol, *s.* بت (pùt), صنم sànem, صورت

Idolater, *s.* بتپرست pùtpérèsst ; —s, *s. pl.* عبدهٔ اصنام ''àbédè'i-àssnām, عبدهٔ اوثان ''àbédè'i-èvsān.

Idolatry, *s.* بتپرستلك pùtpérèsstlik, پرستشِ اصنام pèrèsstishi-àssnām, عبادت اوثان ''ìbādèti-èvsān.

If, *c.* اکر èghèr, èghèr ; (even though) ولو vè-lèv.

Ignite, *v.n.* المق àlmak, طوتشمق tùtush-mak ; —, *v.a.* طوتشدرمق tùtushdur-mak ; الدرمق àldirmak ; اتش ویرمك àtèsh-vèrmek.

Ignominious, *a.* رذیل rèzīl, رسوای rùssvāy.

Ignominy, *s.* رذالت rèzālèt, رسوایلق rùssvāylik.

Ignorance, *s.* جهل jèhl, جهالت jèhālèt, معلوماتسزلق mà''lūmātsizlik.

Ignorant, *a.* جاهل jāhil, معلوماتسز mà''lūmātsiz.

Ill, *s.* فنالق fènalik ; ضرر zàrar ; بلا bèlā, درد dèrd ; —, *a.* فنا fèna ; خسته khàssta, کیفسز kèyfsiz, مزاجسز [mizājsiz.

Ill-bred, *a.* قبا kàba.

Illegal, *a.* یولسز yòlsuz, غیرمشروع ghàyri-mèshrū'', قانونه مغایر kānūna-mù-[ghāyir.

Illegible, *a.* اوقنمز òkunmaz.

Illegitimate, *a.* پیچ pìch ; یولسز yòlsuz ; حرام hàrām.

Illicit, *a.* ممنوع mèmnū'', یساق yàssàk, یولسز yòlsuz ; حرام hàrām.

Illnature, *s.* بدخوی bèd-khùy.

Illness, *s.* خسته‌لق khàsstalik, کیفسزلك kèyfsizlik, مزاجسزلك mìzājsizlik.

Illuminate, *v.a.* قندیل دوناتمق kàndīl-dònatmak ; ایدینلق ا àydinlik-et, تنویر ا tènvīr-et ; (a book) تذهیب وتزیین ا tèzhīb-vè-tèzyīn-et.

Illumination, *s.* قندیل دونانماسی kàndīl-dònanmassi.

Illustrate, *v.a.* مثال کتورمك missāl-ghètirmek, تمثیل ا tèmsīl-et.

Illustration, *s.* رسم rèssm.

Illustrious, *a.* مشهور mèshhūr ; عالی تبار ''ālī-tèbār. [''àdāvèt, غرض ghàraz.

Illwill, *s.* دشمنلك dùshmènlik, عداوت

Image, *s.* صورت sūrèt, تصویر tàssvīr, مجسم mùjèssèm ; عین ''àyn.

Imaginary, *a.* بوش bòsh, دبسز dìbsiz; تخیلی tàkhàyyulī, ظني zànnī.

Imagination, *s.* متخیله mùtakhàyyilé, قوت متخیله kùvvèti-mùtakhàyyilé; عقل ''àkl, فکر fìkir, تفکر tèfèkkyur, تصور tàssàvvur, تخیل tàkhàyyul; ظن zànn, قورنتی kùruntu, مراق mèrāk.

Imagine, *v.a.* تصورا tàssàvvur-et, تخیلا tàkhàyyul-et; قورمق kùrmak, عقلنه کتورمق ''àklina-ghètirmek.

Imbecile, *a.* بوداله bùdala.

Imbecility, *s.* بودالهلق bùdalalik.

Imbibe, *v.a.* ایچمك ìchmek.

Imitate, *v.a.* تقلیدا tàklīd-et, عیننی یاپمق ''àynini-yàpmak.

Imitation, *s.* تقلید tàklīd.

Immaterial, *a.* روحانی rūhānī, غیرهیولانی ghàyri-hèyyulānī; پکده لزومی اولمیان pèkda-lùzūmi-òlmayan; پکده ضرری اولمیان pèkda-zàrari-òlmayan; it is — which, قنغیسی اولورایسه اولسون kànghissi-òlursa-òlsun; — — — how, نصل اولوراسه اولسون nàssl-òlursa-òlsun.

Immature, *a.* خام khām, ناپخته nà-pùkhté.

Immediate, *a.* **Immediately**, *ad.* درعقب dèr-''àkab, اول ساعت òl-sā''at, علی العجله ''àlé-'l-''àjélé; انیده ānida; شمدی shìmdi, چابك chābik, عجله ''àjélé.

Immense, *a.* پك بیوك pèk-bìyuk; پك کلیتلو pèk-kyùllìyyètli.

Immerse, *v.a.* طالدرمق dàldirmak, باترمق bàtirmak. [-yèmūt.

Immortal, *a.* اولمز òlmàz, لایموت lā-

Immunity, *s.* امان èmān; معافیت mù''āfìyyèt, امتیاز ìmtiyāz.

Impair, *v.a.* بوزمق bòzmak, خلل ویرمك khàlel-vèrmek.

Impale, *v.a.* قازقلمق kàziklamak.

Impalement, *s.* قازقلمه kàziklama.

Impart, *v.a.* ویرمك vèrmek; تبلیغا tèblīgh-et, سویلمك sùwèylémek.

Impartial, *a.* منصف mùnsif, منصفانه mùnsifāné. [ghèchid-vèrmàz.

Impassable, *a.* کچلمز ghèchilmàz; کچید ویرمز

Impatience, *s.* صبرسزلق sàbrsizlik.

Impatient, *a.* صبرسز sàbrsiz.

Impeach, *v.a.* ملت مجلسی حضورنده دعوا ا millèt-mèjlissi-hùzūrinda-dà''wà-èt.

Impeachment, *s.* ملت مجلسی حضورنده دعوا ایتمکلك millèt-mèjlissi-hùzurinda-dà''wà-ètmeklik.

Impede, *v.a.* مانع اول māni''-òl, منعا mèn''-et, سکته ویرمك sèkté-vèrmek.

Impediment, *s.* مانع māni'', سکته sèkté; — of speech, پلتکلك pèltèklik.

Impel, *v.a.* سوقا sèvk-et.

Impenitent, *a.* غیر نادم ghàyri-nādim.

Imperative, *a.* آمرانه āmirāné; ضروری zàrūrī; — mood, *s.* صیغهٔ امر sīgha-i-èmr.

Imperceivable, *a.* کورلمز ghyùrulmaz.

Imperfect, *a.* ناقص nākiss, اکسك èksik, نا تمام nā-tàmām, غیرتام ghàyri-tàmm.

Imperfection, نقصان nòksān, اکسکلك èksiklik, قصور kùssūr, عیب ''àyb.

Imperial, *a.* شاهانه shāhāné, پادشاهانه pādishāhāné.

Impertinence, *s.* عارسزلق ‘‘ārs*i*zl*i*k.

Impertinent, *a.* عارسز ‘‘ārs*i*z, ادبسز èdebsiz.

Impervious, *a.* گچلمز ghèchilmàz ; — to rain, يغمورگچمز yàghmūr-ghèchmàz.

Impetuous, *a.* حدتلو hìddètli, شدتلو shìddètli, حزلو hìzli. [kùvvèt, زور zor.

Impetus, *s.* سرعت sùr‘‘àt, حز hiz ; قوت

Impiety, *s.* دينسزلك dīnsizlik, كفر kyùfr.

Impious, *a.* كافر kyāfir, دينسز dīnsiz, اللهدن قورقمز Allàhdan-kòrkmàz ; كافرانه kyāfirānè.

Implement, *s.* الت ālet (*pl.* الات ālāt).

Implicate, *v.a.* قارشدرمق kArishdirmak.

Implicit, *a.* كامل kyāmil, تام tAmm ; ضمنى zìmnī. [nìyāz-et.

Implore, *v.a.* يالوارمق yAlvarmak, نيازا

Imply, *v.a.* متضمن او mùtazàmmin-òl, ضمناً افاده ا zìmnan-ìfādè-et, دلالت ا dè-

Impolite, *a.* تربيه سز tèrbìyyèsiz. [lālet-et.

Impoliteness, *s.* تربيه سزلك tèrbìyyèsizlik.

Import, *s.* معنا mà‘‘nà ; مفهوم mèfhūm ; ادخال ìdkhāl ; —, *v.a.* خارجدن كتورمك khārijdan - ghètirmek ; خارجدن كتورتمك khārijdan-ghètirtmek, ادخال ا ìdkhāl-et ; حكمى او hùkmu-òl, دخلى او dàkhli-òl, مدخلى او mèdkhàli-òl.

Importance, *s.* اهميت èhèmmìyyèt ; نفوذ nūfūz ; of —, خاطرى صايلور khātiri-sàyilir ; مهم mùhìmm.

Important, *a.* مهم mùhìmm ; خاطرى صايلور khātiri-sàyilir, معتبر mù‘‘tébèr.

Importer, *s.* طشره دن امتعه جلب ايدن بازركان dìshāridan-èmti‘‘à-jèlb--èden-bAzirghyān.

Imports, *s. pl.* ادخالات ìdkhālāt.

Importunate, *a.* معجز mù‘‘jiz, تعجيزايدر tà‘‘jīz-èder.

Importune, *v.a.* صيقشدرمق sìkishdirmak, تعجيزا tà‘‘jīz-et, ابرام ا ìbrām-et.

Impose, *v.a.* قومق kòmak, باغلامق bAghlamak, وضع ا wAz‘‘-et ; — upon, اويون ا òyun-et, الداتمق Aldàtmak.

Imposing, *a.* هيبتلو hèybètli. [mak.

Imposition, *s.* وضع wAz‘‘ ; اويون òyun, دك dèk, حيله hīlè. [imkyān.

Impossibility, *s.* عدم امكان ‘‘àdem-i-

Impossible, *a.* محال mùhāl, غيرممكن ghàyri-mùmkin, عديم الامكان ‘‘àdīmu-'l-ìmkyān. [kyāzib, حيله كار hīlèkyār.

Impostor, *s.* يلانجى yàlAnji, كاذب

Imposture, *s.* حيله hīlè, اويون òyun, دك dèk, دولاب *or* طولاب dòlAb.

Impotence, Impotency, *s.* عنينلك ‘‘ìnnīnlik. [ghāyri-mùktèdir.

Impotent, *a.* عنين ‘‘ìnnīn ; غير مقتدر

Impracticable, *a.* ياپله مز yApilamaz.

Impregnable, *a.* النه مز Alinamàz, تسخيرى غيرممكن tèsskhìri - ghàyri - -mùmkin.

Impregnate, *v.a.* تأثيرا tè‘sīr-et ; تأثير ايتدرمك tè‘sīr-ètdirmek, مساماتنه كچورمك mèssāmmātina-ghèchirmek ; كبه ا ghèbè-et.

Impression, *s.* تأثير tè‘sīr ; اثر èsser ; ظن zànn, قياس kìyāss.

Imprison, *v.a.* حبس ا hAbss-et, تسجين ا tèssjīn-et, قپامق kApAmak.

Imprisonment, *s.* حبس hAbss. [māl.

Improbability, *s.* عدم احتمال ‘‘àdmiìhti-

Improbable, *a.* غیرمحتمل ghàyri-mùhtèmil, غیرمأمول ghàyri-mè'mūl.

Improper, *a.* لایقسز làyiksiz, یاقشمز yàkishmàz, مناسبتسز mùnāssébètsiz.

Impropriety, *s.* مناسبتسزلك mùnāssébètsizlik.

Improve, *v.n.* ایلرولمك ìlèrilémek; ایولشمك īyileshmek; كوزللشمك ghyùzèlleshmek; یولنه كیرمك yòluna-ghìrmek; —, *v.a.* ایلرولتمك ìlèriletmek; ایولشدرمك īyileshdirmek, كوزللشدرمك ghyùzèlleshdirmek, اصلاح ا ìsslāh-et, دها بر یولنه قومق dàhà-bìr-yòluna-kòmak.

Improvement, *s.* اصلاح ìsslāh. [ìktiyyAt.

Improvidence, *s.* عدم احتیاط "àdm-i-

Imprudent, *a.* عقلسز "àklsiz, دلی dèli.

Impudent, *a.* عارسز "ārsiz, ادبسز èdebsiz, حیاسز hàyāssiz.

Impulse, *s.* وهله vèhlé; on the first —, وهله اولاده vèhlé'i-ūlāda.

Impunity, *s.* مجازاتدن بری اولمقلق mùjāzātdan-bèrī-òlmaklik; with —, بلا مقابله bìlā-mùkābèlé, بلا مجازاة bìlā-mùjāzātin.

Impure, *a.* پس piss, مردار mùrdār, نجس nèjiss, ناپاك nā-pāk.

Impurity, *s.* پیسلك pìsslik; نا پاكلك nā-pāklik.

Imputation, *s.* اسناد ìssnād; عزو "azv.

Impute, *v.a.* ویرمك vèrmek, اسناد ا ìssnād-et, عزو ا "àzv-et.

In, *pr.* ه é, a, ده dé, da; ایچنه ìchina, ایچنده ìchinda, درونه dèrūnina, درونده dèrūninda; ظرفنه zàrfina, ظرفنده zàrfinda; مرورنده mùrūrinda; ایله ìla; ایكن ìken.

Inability, *s.* قابلیتسزلك kābiliyyétsizlik; عدم اقتدار "àdémi-ìktidār, عجز "àjz.

Inaccuracy, *s.* یاكلش yàngilish, سهو sèhv.

Inaccurate, *a.* یاكلش yàngilish (yànish), غیر صحیح ghàyri-sàhīh. [-hàrékèt.

Inaction, *s.* عدم حركت "àdm-i-

Inactive, *a.* تنبل tènbel. [-kifāyet.

Inadequacy, *s.* عدم كفایت "àdm-i-

Inadequate, *a.* الویرمز èlvermàz, یتشمز yètishmàz, غیركافی ghàyri-kyāfī.

Inattention, *s.* دقتسزلق dìkkAtsizlik.

Inattentive, *a.* دقتسز dìkkAtsiz.

Inaudible, *a.* ایشیدلمز ìshìdilmàz.

Inaugurate, *v.a.* كشاد ا kyùshād-èt.

Inauguration, *s.* رسمی كشاد rèssmi-kyùshad.

Inauspicious, *a.* منحوس mènhūs.

Inborn, Inbred, *a.* خلقی khàlkī, جبلی jìbìllī, طبیعی tAbī"ī.

Incapable, *a.* الندن كلمز èlindan-ghèlmàz, غیرمقتدر ghàyri-mùktèdīr, نااهل nā-èhl, عاجز "ājiz.

Incapacitate, *v.a.* صلاحیتنی بوزمق sAlā-hìyyètini-bòzmak.

Incapacity, *s.* عدم صلاحیت "àdémi-sAlāhìyyèt, عدم اهلیت "àdémi-èhlìyyèt.

Incendiary, *s.* قونداقجی kùndAkji; مفسد mùfsid, محرك mùhàrrik.

Incense, *s.* كونلك ghyùnluk, بخور bùkhūr; عبودیت "ùbūdiyyèt; —, *v.a.* قیزدرمق kìzdirmak, دارلتمق

dàriltmak, كوجندرمك ghyùjèndirmek. [ساٸق sā''ik, تازيانه tāziyānè.

Incentive, s. سبب sèbeb, موجب mūjib,

Incertitude, s. شبهه shùbhè, شك shèkk, مشكوكيت mèshkyūkiyyèt.

Incessant, a. لاينقطع lā-yànkàti'', اردى اراسى اولميان àrdi-àrassi-òl-mayan.

Inch, s. پرمق pàrmak, اصبع ùssbu''.

Incident, s. ماده māddè, فقره fìkra, منقبه mànkabè; —, a. عارض ''āriz, لازم lāzim. [ìttifākī.

Incidental, a. عرضى ''àrazī, اتفاقى

Incite, v.a. تحريك ا tàhrīk-et, تحريض ا tàhrīz-et, ترغيب ا tèrghīb-et.

Inclement, a. فرطونه لو fìrtinali; صوغوق sòghuk, يغمورلو yāghmùrlu.

Inclination, s. ميل mèyl; رغبت ràghbet, استك ìsstèk, خواهش khāhish.

Incline, v.n. ميل ا mèyl-et, ياتمق yàtmak; مائل او mā'il-òl, استعداد كوسترمك ìssti''dād-ghyùsstermek; رغبت ا ràghbet-et, جانى استمك jāni-ìsstèmek; —, v.a. ياترمق yàtirmak, اماله ا ìmālè-et, ميل ويرمك mèyl-vèrmek.

Inclined, a. مائل mā'il; مستعد mùsstà''idd; استكلو ìsstèkli, استكى اولان ìsstèghi-òlan, رغبتى اولان ràghbeti-òlan. [lèf-et.

Inclose, v.a. احاطه ا ìhātè-et; لف ا

Include, v.a. داخل ا dākhil-et; شامل او shāmil-òl, شمولى او shùmūli-òl, المق àlmak, احاطه ا ìhāta-et, مشتمل او mùshtèmil-òl.

Incog, Incognito, a. تبديل tèbdīl.

Incoherent, a. ربطسز ràbtsiz.

Incombustible, a. يانمز yànmàz.

Income, s. ايراد īrād; واريت vārìyyèt, كلور ghèlir. [-vèrghissi.

Income-tax, s. ايراد ويركوسى īrād-

Incompetence, Incompetency, s. عدم صلاحيت ''àdm-i-sàlāhìyyèt.

Incompetent, a. نااهل nā-èhl, اربابى دكل èrbābi-dìghil, صلاحيتسز sàlāhìyyètsiz.

Incomplete, a. اكسك èksik, ناقص nākiss, ناتمام nā-tàmām, غيرتام ghàyri-tàmm.

Incomprehensible, a. اكلاشلمز ànglàshìlmàz (ànnàshìlmàz).

Inconsiderable, a. از àz, قليل kàlīl; كچوك kùchuk, صغير sàghīr; جزئى jùz'ī.

Inconsistent, a. غيرمتطابق ghàyri-mùtatābìk, بروقتى بروقتنه اويمز bìr-wàkti-bìr-wàktina-ùymàz, برسوزى برسوزينه اويمز bìr-sùzu-bìr-sùzuna-ùymàz, سوزى فعلنه اويمز sùzu-fì''lina-ùymàz.

Inconstancy, s. عدم قرار ''àdm-i-kàrār.

Inconstant, a. قرارسز kàrarsiz, ثباتسز sèbātsiz; بيوفا bī-wèfā.

Inconvenience, s. زحمت zàhmet.

Inconvenient, a. راحتسز rāhatsiz, صيقندى sìkindi, صيقنديلو sìkindili.

Incorporate, v.a. قارشدرمق kàrishdirmak, مزج ا mèzj-et; قاتمق kàtmak.

Incorrect, a. ياكلش yàngilish (yānish), غيرصحيح ghàyri-sàhīh.

Increase, s. زياده zìyādè, ازدياد ìzdiyād, ترقى tàràkki; —, v.n. بيومك biyumek ; ارتمق àrtmak, چوغالمق chò-ghAlmak, زیادەلنمك zìyādÉlEnmek, زیادەلشمك zìyādÉlEshmek, ازدیاد izdiyād-bùlmak, ترقی بولمق tàràkki-būlmak, مزداداو mùzdād-òl, مترقی‌او mùtaràkki-òl ; —, v.a. بیوتمك bìyutmek ; ارترمق àrtirmak, چوغالتمق chòghAltmak.

Incredible, a. اینانلمز inànilmàz, کوچ ایناتلور ghyùj-inànilir.

Incredulous, a. اینانمز inànmàz, کوچ اینانور ghyùj-inànir.

Incubation, s. حضون hùzūn.

Inculcate, v.a. تعلیم‌ا tà''līm-et, اوکرتمك ùghrÉtmek. [اغرلق Aghirlik.

Incumbrance, s. بار bār, یوك yùk,

Incur, v.a. ارایوب بولمق Arayub-būlmak, کیرمك ghìrmek, اوغرامق òghramak.

Incurable, a. شفاقبول ایتمز shìfā-kAbūl-

Incursion, s. اقین Akin. [-ètmàz.

Indebted, a. بورجلو bòrjlu, مدیون mèdyūn ; مجبور mèjbūr.

Indecent, a. عیب ''àyb, مغایر ادب mūghāyiri-èdeb.

Indeed, ad. حقیقت hAkīkAt, حقیقةً hAkīkAtan, فی‌الحقیقه fī-'l-hAkīka ; —, c. بیله bīlÉ ; —? کرچکمی ghÈrchèkmi, اویله‌می ùylÈmi.

Indefatigable, a. یورلمز yòrulmàz, یورلمق بلمز yòrulmak-bilmàz.

Indefinite, a. نا محدود nā-màhdūd, غیرمحدود ghàyri-màhdūd, غیرمعین ghàyri-mù''àyyen ; — article, s. حرف تنکیر hàrf-i-tènkīr.

Indemnify, v.a. تضمین‌ا tAzmīn-et.

Indemnity, s. تضمین tAzmīn, تضمینات tAzmīnAt ; معافیت mù''āfiyyèt, براثةالذمه bèrā'atu-'z-zimmÉ.

Independence, Independency, s. استقلال isstiklāl.

Independent, a. باشلی باشنه bAshli-bAshina, خودبخود khòd-bé-khòd, کندی کندینه kendi-kèndina; سربست sÈr-bèsst, مطلق mùtlAk, مستقل mùsstAkill ; کمسه‌یه محتاج دکل kìm-sÉyÉ-mùhtāj-dìghil ; زنکین zÈnghin.

Index, s. شهادت پرمغی shàhādet-pàrmaghi ; فهرس fihriss, فهرست fihrisst. [tān.

India, s. هند hìnd, هندستان hìndiss-

Indiaman, s. هنده سفر ایدن کمی hìnda-sèfer-èden-ghèmi.

Indian, a. هندی hìndi. [-bòghdayi.

Indian-corn, s. مصر بوغدایی mìssir-

Indian-ink, s. چینی مرکب chīnī-mùrèkkÉb.

India-rubber, s. قومناستق kòmnāstik.

Indicate, v.a. دلالت‌ا dèlàlet-et, اشارت‌او ishārèt-òl.

Indifference, s. قیدسزلق kàydsizlik, عدم تمیل ''àdÉmi-tèmèyyul, عدم رغبت ''àdÉmi-ràghbet.

Indifferent, a. قیدسز kàydsiz, لاقید lā-kàyd, وظیفه‌سنده‌دکل wAzīfÉssindÉ-dìghil ; همپ بر hèp-bìr, برابر bÈrābÈr, لافرق lā-fārk ; بیاغی bàyaghi, عادی ''ādī, اشاغی Ashàghi, فنا fÈna, قبا [kAba.

Indigenous, a. یرلو yÈrli.

Indigestible, a. اغر Aghir, هضمی کوچ hAzmi-ghyùch.

Indigestion, *s.* معده‌فسادی mì''dé-fès-sādi, امتلا ìmtilā.

Indignant, *a.* کوجنمش ghyùjènmish, دارلمش dārilmish. [dārghinlik.

Indignation, *s.* غضب ghāzab, دارغینلق

Indignity, *s.* بدمعامله bèd-mū''āmélé, حقارت-hàkārèt.

Indigo, *s.* چوید chìvid.

Indispensable, *a.* اهم èhèmm, متحتم mùtahàttem, مطلقا لازم mūtlaka-lāzim.

Indisposition, *s.* کیفسزلك kèyfsizlik, انحراف مزاج ìnhirāfi - mìzāj; عدم استمامکلك ìsstémameklik, رغبت ''àdémi-ràghbet.

Indisputable, *a.* مسلم mùsèllèm.

Indistinct, *a.* بللوسز bèllisiz.

Indistinctness, *s.* بللوسزلك bèllisizlik.

Individual, *s.* فرد fèrd, نفر nèfer, کشی kìshi; —, *a.* ایری àyri, منفرد mùn-fèrid.

Indolent, *a.* تنبل tènbèl.

Indorse, *v.a.* قبول و تصدیق ا kābūl-vé-tāssdīk-et.

Induce, *v.a.* سوق ا sèvk-et, تحریك ا tàhrīk-et, سبب او sèbeb-òl.

Indulge, *v.n.* مبتلا او mùbtélā-òl, کندینی ویرمك kèndini-vèrmek; —, *v.a.* مساعده ا mùssā''adé-et. [ابتلا ìbtilā.

Indulgence, *s.* مساعده mùssā''adé;

Industrious, *a.* چالشقان chālishkān, ایشکذار ìshghyuzār, مقدم mūkdim.

Industry, *s.* چالشقانلق chālishkānlik, ایشکذارلك ìshghyuzārlik, اقدام ìk-dām; حرفت hìrfèt, صناعت sànā-''at.

Inebriated, *a.* سرخوش sèr-khòsh.

Inefficient, *a.* نا اهل nā-èhl.

Inert, *a.* تنبل tènbel.

Inertia, *s.* عطالت ''ātālèt.

Inestimable, *a.* قیمتی تقدیراولنه‌مز kīmé-ti-tākdīr-òlunamàz.

Inevitable, *a.* قورتلنه‌مز kùrtulunamàz, چاره‌سز chārèssiz.

Inexact, *a.* یاکلش yàngilīsh.

Inexcusable, *a.* معذور طوتله‌مز mà''zur-tùtulamàz.

Inexperienced, *a.* عجمی ''ājémī, مبتدی mùbtédi, غیر مجرب ghàyri-mùjèrreb.

Infamous, *a.* عیب ''àyb, رذیل rèzīl, رسوای rùssvāy, ناموسسز nāmūssuz.

Infamy, *s.* رذالت rèzālèt, رسوایلق rùssvāylik, ناموسسزلق nāmūsssuzluk.

Infancy, *s.* چوجقلق chòjukluk, صباوت sābāvèt, طفولیت tùfūlìyyèt.

Infant, *s.* چوجق chòjuk, اوفاق چوجق ùfāk-chòjūk, ببك bèbek. [kéri.

Infantry, *s.* پیاده‌عسکری piyādé-''āss-

Infatuation, *s.* دلیلك dèlilik.

Infection, *s.* علت‌ساریه ''ìllèti-sārìyyé; بولاشقلق bùlàshiklik; سرایت sìrāyet.

Infectious, *a.* ساری sārī, کچر ghèchèr, بولاشور bùlàshir.

Infer, *v.a.* اکلامق ànglamak (ànnamak), چیقارمق chìkàrmak, استدلال ا ìsstid-lāl-et. [ìsstidlāl.

Inference, *s.* معنا mà''nà; استدلال

Inferior, *a.* اشاغی āshàghi, دون dūn; بیاغی bàyaghi, فنا fèna; —, *s.* کچوك kùchuk, مادونده اولان کمسنه mā-dūnda-òlan-kìmèssné.

Infernal, *a.* جهنمی jihènnémī, شیطانی shèytānī; پك فنا pèk-fèna.

Infidel, *s.* كافر kyāfir, منكربالله mùnkir-bì-'llāh.

Infidelity, *s.* كفر kyùfr, عدم صداقت "àdémi-"sàdakāt; عدم وفا "àdémi-wèfā; عدم عصمت àdémi-"ìssmèt; عدم عفت "àdémi-"ìffèt.

Infinite, *a.* نامتناهى nā-mùténāhī, بينهايه bī-nìhāyé, بيغايه bī-ghāyé.

Infirm, *a.* سقط sàkat, الى اياغى طوتمز èli-àyaghi-tùtmàz.

Infirmary, *s.* خسته خانه khàssta-khāné.

Infirmity, *s.* علت "ìllèt, درد dèrd; نقيصه nàkīssa, قصور kùssūr.

Inflame, *v.a.* علولندرمك "àlevlendir-mek; التهاب كتورمك ìltihāb-ghètir-mek. [nar, طوتشور tùtushur.

Inflammable, *a.* علوايله ينار "àlèv-ila-yà-

Inflammation, *s.* التهاب ìltihāb, حمرت hàmrèt.

Inflate, *v.a.* هوا طولدروب شيشرمك hà-wā-dòldurup-shìshirmek.

Inflexible, *a.* اكلمز èghilmàz; قصدندن دونمز kàssdindan-dùnmàz.

Inflict, *v.a.* ترتيب واجرا ا tèrtīb-vè-ìjrā-et, عارض ا "āriz-et.

Influence, *s.* نفوذ nùfūz; تأثير tè'sīr; حكم hùkm; —, *v.a.* سوز كچورمك sùz-ghèchirmek, دكلتمك dìngletmek (dīnetmek); تأثيرا tè'sīr-et.

Influential, *a.* نفوذ صاحبى nùfūz-sāhibi, سوزى كچر sùzu-ghècher.

Influenza, *s.* زكام zùkkyām, نزله nèzlé, نوازل nèwāzil.

Inform, *v.a.* خبر ويرمك khàber-vèr-mek, سويلمك sùwèylémek.

Informant, *s.* خبر ويرن khàber-vèren, سويلين sùwèyléyen, مخبر mùkhbir.

Information, *s.* خبر khàber, معلومات mà"lūmàt, علم "ìlm. [-hàrékèt.

Infraction, *s.* مغاير حركت mùghāyir-

Infringe, *v.a.* بوزمق bòzmak, اخلال ا ìkhlāl-et, مغاير حركت ا mùghāyir-hàrékèt-et.

Infringement, *s.* نقض nàkz.

Ingenious, *a.* (person) هنرلو hùnerli, هزارفن hèzār-fènn (hèzārifènd); (thing) هنرلو hùnerli, معرفتلو mà"-rifètli.

Ingenuity, *s.* هنر hùner, معرفت mà"rifèt, صنعت sàn"àt, عقل "àkl.

Ingenuous, *a.* ساده دل sādé-dìl, صاف درون sāf-dèrūn, طوغرى سويلر dòghru-sùwèyler.

Ingot, *s.* كولچه kyùlché, سبيكه sèbīké.

Ingraft, *v.a.* اشلامق àshlamak.

Ingratitude, *s.* نانكورلك nān-kyùrluk (nàmkyùrluk), كفران نعمت kyùfrāni-nì"mèt.

Ingredient, *s.* جزء مركب jùz'u-mùrèkkib (*pl.* اجزاى مركبه èjzā'i-mùrèkkibé).

Ingress, *s.* كيرش ghìrish; كيره جك ير ghìréjek-yèr; دخول dùkhūl; مدخل mèdkhàl.

Inhabit, *v.a.* اوطورمق òturmak, ساكن او sākin-òl, متمكن او mùtémèkkin-òl.

Inhabitant, *s.* يرلو yèrli, ساكن sākin (*pl.* سكنه sèkéné), (*pl.*) اهالى àhālī.

Inhale, *v.a.* نفسله ايچرو چكمك nèfèssla-ìchèri-chèkmek. [mīrāss-yèmek.

Inherit, *v.a.* وارث او vāriss-òl, ميراث يمك

Inheritance, *s.* میراث mīrāss, وراثت vèrāssèt; ارث ìrss, توارث tèvāruss.

Inheritor, *s.* وارث vāriss, میراثخور mīrāsskhòr.

Inhuman, *a.* انسانیتسز ìnsānìyyètsiz.

Inimical, *a.* دشمن dùshmèn, خصم khàssm, خصومتلو khùssūmètli.

Inimitable, *a.* تقلید اولنه‌مز tàklīd-òluna-màz, بشقه کمسه‌نك یاپه‌میه‌جغی bàshka-kìmsèning-yàpamayajaghi.

Iniquitous, *a.* فاسد fāssid.

Iniquity, *s.* گناه ghyùnāh, فسق وفجور fìssk-u-fùjūr, معصیت mà''sìyyèt.

Initiate, *v.a.* اوگرتمك ùghrètmek, یولنی گوسترمك yòlunu-ghyùsstermek, تعلیم ا tà''līm-et.

Injudicious, *a.* عقلسز 'àklsiz, اویغونسز ùyghunsuz, مناسبتسز mùnāssébètsiz.

Injunction, *s.* أمر èmr (èmir), تنبیه tènbīh, سپارش sìpàrish.

Injure, *v.a.* ضرر ا zàrar-et, سقط ا sàkat-et, بوزمق bòzmak, خلل ویرمك khàlel-vèrmek, اخلال ا ìkhlāl-et.

Injurious, *a.* ضررلو zàrarli, مضر mùzìrr.

Injury, *s.* ضرر zàrar, خلل khàlel, سقامت sàkāmèt, سقطلق sàkatlìk. [hàkksizlìk.

Injustice, *s.* غدر ghàdr, ظلم zùlm, حقسزلق

Ink, *s.* مرکب mùrèkkèb; —, *v.a.* مرکب سورمك mùrèkkèb-sùrmek; red —, *s.* سرخ sùrkh.

Inkstand, *s.* مرکب حقه‌سی mùrèkkèb-hòkkassi, حقه hòkka. [kyùrfez.

Inlet, *s.* اغز àghiz, بوغاز bòghàz, کورفز

Inn, *s.* خان khān, لوقانده lòkànda, مسافرقوناغی mùssāfir-kònaghi.

Inner, *a.* ایچروکی ìchèriki, داخلی dākhilī.

Innermost, *a.* الْ ایچروده‌کی èng-ìchè-rìdéki.

Innkeeper, *s.* لوقانده‌جی lòkàndaji.

Innocence, *s.* قباحتسزلق kàbāhatsizlìk, معصومیت mà''sūmìyyèt, براءت ذمت bèrā'àti-zìmmèt.

Innocent, *a.* قباحتسز kàbāhatsiz, بری الذمه bèrìyyu-'z-zìmmé, معصوم mà''sūm.

Innocuous, *a.* ضررسز zàrarsiz.

Innovation, *s.* بدعت bìd''àt, یکی اصول yèngi-ùssūl.

Innumerable, *a.* صایلمز sàyìlmàz, لایعد lā-yù''àdd, لایحصا lā-yùhsā.

Inoculate, *v.a.* اشلامق àshlamak; چیچك اشلامق chìchek-àshlamak.

Inoculation, *s.* اشلامقلق àshlamaklìk.

Inoffensive, *a.* ضررسز zàrarsiz.

Inquest, *s.* تفتیش رسمی tèftīsh-rèssmī.

Inquire, *v.a.* صورمق sòrmak, سؤال ا sù'āl-et; استفسار ا ìsstifsār-et; استعلام ا ìssti''lām-et; استفتا ا ìsstiftā-et; تجسس ا tèjèsssuss-et, تحری ا tàhàrrī-et.

Inquiry, *s.* صورش sòrush, سؤال sù'āl; استفسار ìsstifsār; استعلام ìssti''lām; استفتا ìsstiftā, تجسس tèjèsssuss, تحری tàhàrrī; پرسش pùrsish.

Inquisitive, *a.* مراقلو mèràkli, چوق شی صورار chòk-shèy-sòrar.

Inroad, *s.* اقین àkìn.

Insane, *a.* دلی dèli, چلغین chìlghìn, قاچیق kàchìk, مجنون mèjnūn.

Insanity, *s.* دلیلك dèlilik, چلغینلق chìlghìnlìk, قاچقلق kàchìklìk, جنت jìnnèt, جنون jùnūn.

Insatiable, *a.* دويمق بلمز dòymak-bilmàz, دائما اج dā'imā-àj.

Inscribe, *v.a.* يازمق yàzmak, قيد ا kàyd-et, تحرير ا tàhrīr-et.

Inscription, *s.* يازى yàzi; كتابه kìtābé.

Insect, *s.* بوجك bùjek, (*pl.*) حشرات hAsharĀt.

Insecure, *a.* قورقلور kòrkulur, امين دكل [èmīn-dìghil.

Insecurity, *s.* امنيتسزلك èmnìyyètsizlik; مخاطره mùkhĀtara.

Insensible, *a.* حس ايتمز hìsss-etmàz; بلمز bìlmàz; بايلمش bàyilmish, بيخود bīkhòd.

Insert, *v.a.* صوقمق sòkmak, صوقشدرمق sòkushdurmak; درج ا dèrj-et, ادخال ا [ìdkhāl-et.

Insertion, *s.* درج dèrj.

Inside, *s.* ايچ ìch, ايچرو ìchèri, درون dèrūn, داخل dākhil; —, *a.* داخلى dākhilī.

Insinuate, *v.a.* بريول ايله اكلاتمق bìr-yòl-ila-ànglàtmak (ànnàtmak), ايما ا īmā-et; — one's self, صوقلمق sòkulmak.

Insipid, *a.* طاتسز tàtsiz.

Insipidity, *s.* طاتسزلك tàtsizlik, لذتسزلك [lèzzètsizlik.

Insist, *v.n.* وازكچمامك vāz-ghèchma-mek, مطلق استمك mùtlAk-ìsstémek.

Insobriety, *s.* سرخوشلق sErkhòshlik.

Insolence, *s.* ادبسزلك èdebsizlik, عارسزلق ''ārsizlik.

Insolent, *a.* ادبسز èdebsiz, عارسز ''ārsiz, كستاخ kyùsstākh; كستاخانه kyùsstā-khānÉ.

Insolvent, *a.* مفلس mùfliss; —, *s.* مفلس [mùfliss.

Inspect, *v.a.* يوقلامق yòklamak; نظارت ا nAzārèt-et, معاينه ا mù''āyénÉ-et.

Inspection, *s.* يوقلمه yòklama, نظارت nAzārèt; معاينه mù''āyénÉ.

Inspector, *s.* يوقلمه جى yòklamaji; — of schools, مميز mùmèyyiz.

Inspiration, *s.* وحى vàhy, الهام ìlhām; نفس چكشى nèfess-chèkishi; تعليم tà''līm, تشويق tèshvīk.

Inspire, *v.a.* الهام ا ìlhām-et, وحى طريقيله بلدرمك vàhy-tàrīkila-bìldirmek; يوركنه قومق yùrèghina-kòmak; تعليم ا tà''līm-et, تشويق ا tèshvīk-et, عقلنه قومق ''Aklina-kòmak; —, *v.n.* نفس چكمك nèfess-chèkmek, صولق المق sòluk-Almak.

Instalment, *s.* تقسيط tAksīt, قسط kìsst.

Instance, *s.* رجا rìjā, نياز nìyāz; تكليف tèklīf; دعوت dà''vèt; مثال missāl, نمونه nùmūné; دفعه dèf''à, كره kèrrÉ; —, *v.a.* مثال ايراد ا mìssāl-īrād-et.

Instant, *s.* آن ān, دقيقه dAkīka, دم dèm; —, *a.* صيقى sìki, مبرم mùbrèm.

Instantly, *ad.* درحال dèr-hāl, درعقب dèr-''àkab, انيده ānīda.

Instead, *ad.* يرينه yèrina, بدل اولهرق bèdel-òlarak, بدل bèdel, بدلاً bèdelan.

Instep, *s.* اياغك اوستى àyaghing-ùsstu, اينجك ìnjik.

Instigate, *v.a.* قيندرمق kìndirmak, ايارتمق àyartmak, پرمقلمق pàrmak-lamak, تحريك ا tàhrīk-et, تحريض ا tàhrīz-et, تشويق ا tèshvīk-et.

Instigation, *s.* تحريك tàhrīk, تحريض tàhrīz, تشويق tèshvīk.

Instinct, *s.* حس hìsss, حس حيوانى hìsssi-hàywAnī.

Institute, *s.* مكتب mèktɐb ; قاعده kā-"idé, موضوع mèvzū" ; —, *v.a.* چيقارمق chɪkàrmak, باشلامق bàsh-lamak, ابداع ا ìbdā"-et, اختراع ا ìkhtirā"-et ; وضع ا wàz"-et, ترتيب ا tɐrtīb-et, تاسيس ا tè'sīss-et.

Instruct, *v.a.* اوكرتمك ùghrètmek, تعليم ا tà"līm-et, تدريس ا tèdrīss-et.

Instruction, *s.* علم "ìlm, معلومات mà"lū-māt ; تعليم tà"līm, تدريس tèdrīss ; تحصيل tàhsīl ; —s, *s. pl.* تعليمات tà"līmāt.

Instructor, *s.* خواجه khòja ; معلم mù"àllim, تعليمجى tà"līmji.

Instrument, *s.* الت ālèt (*pl.* آلات ālāt).

Insubordinate, *a.* اطاعتسز ìtā"atsiz.

Insubordination, *s.* اطاعتسزلق ìtā"atsizlik.

Insufferable, *a.* تحمل اولنه مز tàhàmmul-òlunamàz.

Insufficient, *a.* الويرمز èlvɐrmàz, يتشمز yètishmàz, كفايت ايتمز kìfāyet-ètmàz, غير كافى ghàyri-kyāfī.

Insult, *s.* حقارت hàkārèt ; —, *v.a.* حقارت ا hàkārèt-et ; ناموسه دوقنمق nāmūssa-dòkūnmak.

Insupportable, *a.* چكلمز chèkilmàz, تحمل اولنه مز tàhàmmul-òlunamàz.

Insurance, *s.* سيغورته sìghūrta ; — company, *s.* سيغورته قومپانيه سى sìghūrta-còmpànyassi.

Insurgent, *s.* عاصى "āssi.

Insurrection, *s.* اياقلانش àyaklànish, عصيان "ìssyān, طغيان tùghyān.

Integer, *s.* عدد صحيح "àdédi-sàhīh.

Integrity, *s.* تماميت tàmāmìyyèt ; طوغريلق dòghrulɐk, استقامت ìssti-kāmet.

Intellect, *s.* عقل "àkl, ذهن zìhn.

Intellectual, *a.* عقلى "àkli, عاقل "ākɪl.

Intelligence, *s.* عقل "àkl, قوت عقليه kùvvèti-"àklìyyé, فهم fèhm, ادراك ìdrāk, ذكا zèkyā, ذكاوت zèkyāvèt, خبر درايت dìrāyèt, فطانت fàtānèt ; خبر khàbɐr, معلومات mà"lūmāt.

Intelligent, *a.* عقللو "àklli, عاقل "ākɪl, ذكى zèkī, درايتلو dìrāyètli, فطين fàtīn.

Intemperance, *s.* بكريلك bèkrīlik.

Intemperate, *a.* سرت sɐrt, شديد shèdīd, حديد hàdīd ; بكرى bèkrī ; ناپرهيزكار nā-pɐrhīzkyār.

Intend, *v.a.* نيت ا nìyyèt-et, نيتنده او nìyyètinda-òl, تصميم ا tàssmīm-et, قورمق kūrmak. [صيقى sɪki.

Intense, *a.* سرت sɐrt, شديد shèdīd ;

Intent, Intention, *s.* نيت nìyyèt, تصميم tàssmīm, مراد mùrād, قصد kàssd.

Intentional, *a.* قصدى kàssdī, مخصوص màkhsūss ; —ly, *ad.* بلهرك bilérek, عمداً "amdan, قصداً kàssdan.

Inter, *v.a.* كومك ghyùmmek, دفن ا dèfn-et.

Intercede, *v.n.* شفاعت ا shìfā"at-et, ارايه كيرمك àraya-ghìrmek, رجا ا rìjā-et.

Intercept, *v.a.* طوتمق tùtmak, يولنى كسمك yòlunu-kèssmek ; حائل او hā'il-òl. [rìjā.

Intercession, *s.* شفاعت shìfā"at, رجا

Intercessor, *s.* شفيع shèfī", رجاجى rìjaji.

Intercourse, *s.* اختلاط ìkhtilāt, الفت ùlfet, مؤانست mū'ānéssèt.

Interdict, *s.* افروز àforòz, لعنت là''nèt; —, *v.a.* یساق ا yàssāk-et, نهی ا nèhy-et, ممنوع ا mèmnū''-et.

Interest, *s.* فائض fā'iz, کذشته ghyù-zèshtē, نما nèmā (nàmā), ربو rìbv, ربا rìbā, معامله mū''āmélē; نفوذ nūfūz, خاطر khātir, اعتبار ì''tibār; تعصب tàssàhhub, التزام ìltizām, ارقه àrka; محبت màhàbbèt; رغبت ràghbèt, مراق mèrāk; تلذذ tèlèzzuz, ایلنجه èylènjē; الوب ویره جك ālip-vèrējek, اوکرنه جك ùghrènējek, بله جك bìlējek, کوره جك ghyùrējek, وظیفه wāzīfē, حصه hìsssē; غرض ghàraz, منفعت mènfà''àt, فائده fā'idē; —, *v.a.* تعصب ایتدرمك tàssàhhub-ètdirmek, التزام ایتدرمك ìltizām-ètdirmek; ایلنجه ویرمك èylènjē-vèrmek, یورکنی جزب ا yù-règhini-jèzb-et, قلبه تأثیرا kālba-tè'sīr-et, قلبه رقت کتورمك kālba-rìkkāt-ghètirmek; to take an —, سومك sèvmek, التزام ا ìltizām-et, تعصب ا tàssàhhub-et; to have an —, الوب ویره جکی او ālip-vèréjéghi-òl, وظیفه سی او wāzīféssi-òl; حصه دار او hìsssédār-òl; compound —, فائض ایله فائضك فائضی fā'iz-ìla-fā'izin-fā'izi.

Interesting, *a.* کوزل ghyùzèl; دلبر dìlber; ایلنجه لو èylènjéli.

Interfere, *v.n.* قارشمق kārishmak, مداخله ا mùdākhala-et; سکته ویرمك sèktē-vèrmek, مانع او māni''-òl.

Interference, *s.* قارشمه kārishma; مداخله mùdākhala.

Interim, *s.* ارالق àralik, مدت mùddèt; in the —, دیرایکن dèr-iken (dèr-'ken), اول ارالق ò'-àralik, اول اثناده òl-èss-nāda; ad —, موقت mùwākkàt; موقتاً mùwākkatan.

Interior, *s.* ایچ ìch, درون dèrūn, داخل dākhil; باطن bātin; —, *a.* درونی dèrūnī, داخلی dākhilī, باطنی bātini; Minister of the —, داخلیه ناظری dākhilìyyē-nāziri.

Interment, *s.* دفن dèfn, جنازه دفنی [jènāzē-dèfni.

Internal, *a.* داخلی dākhilī, باطنی bātinī.

Interpose, *v.a.* ارایه قومق àraya-kòmak, ارایه صوقمق àraya-sòkmak; —, *v.n.* ارایه کیرمك àraya-ghìrmek, توسط ا tàwāsssut-et.

Interpret, *v.a.* ترجمه ا tèrjumē-et; —, *v.n.* ترجمانلق ا tèrjumānlik-et.

Interpretation, *s.* ترجمه tèrjumē; معنی mà''nà.

Interpreter, *s.* ترجمان tèrjumān.

Interrogate, *v.a.* استنطاق ا ìsstintāk-et.

Interrogation, *s.* استنطاق ìsstintāk; note of —, علامت استفهام ''àlāmèt-i-ìsstifhām.

Interrupt, *v.a.* کسمك kèssmek; منع ا mèn''-et, مانع او māni''-òl.

Intersect, *v.a.* قطع ا kāt''-et; — one another, تقاطع ا tàkātu''-et.

Interstice, *s.* ارالق àralik; یارق yàrik, چتلاق chàtlāk.

Interval, *s.* ارالق àralik, مابین mā-bèyn.

Intervene, *v.n.* كچمك ghèchmek; ارایه كیرمك àraya-ghìrmek; ارادهبولنمق àrada-bùlunmak, حائل او hā'il-òl.

Intervention, *s.* توسط tàvàsssut; ارایه كیرمكلك àraya-ghìrmeklik.

Interview, *s.* ملاقات mùlākāt, كورشمه ghyùrushma.

Intestines, *s. pl.* بغرصاق bàghirsàk.

Intimacy, *s.* صیقی دوستلق sìki-dòsstluk.

Intimate, *a.* محرمانه màhrémānÉ; —, *s.* محرم màhrèm; —, *v.a.* بلدرمك bìldirmek, اكلاتمق ànglatmak (ànnatmak), خبر ویرمك khàber-vèrmek, سویلمك sùwèylémek.

Intimation, *s.* خبر khàber, افاده ìfadé, تبلیغ tèblīgh.

Intimidate, *v.a.* قورقوتمق kòrkùtmak, تخویف ا tàkhwīf-et, اخافه ا ìkhāfé-et.

Intimidation, *s.* اخافه ìkhāfé. [dèrūnina.

Into, *prep.* ه É, a, ایچنه ìchina, درونته

Intolerable, *a.* چكلمز chèkilmàz, تحمل اولنمز tàhàmmul-òlunmàz.

Intoxicate, *v.a.* سرخوش ا sèrkhòsh-et, كیف ا kèyf-et; —ed, *a.* كیف kèyf, سرخوش sèrkhòsh (sàr-).

Intoxication, *s.* كیف kèyf, سرخوشلق sèrkhòshluk (sàr-), سكر sèkir.

Intrench, *v.n.* مترس یاپمق mètériss-yàpmak, تحصن ا tàhàsssun-et; —, *v.a.* مترس ایله استحكام ویرمك mèté-riss-ila-ìsstìhkyām-vèrmek.

Intrenchment, *s.* مترس mètériss.

Intrepid, *a.* یكیت yìghit, جسور jèssūr, بیباك bībāk, بیپروا bīpèrwā.

Intricacy, *s.* قارشقلق kàrishìklìk.

Intricate, *a.* قارشق kàrishìk, طولاشق dòlàshìk, مشتبك mùshtébèk.

Intrigue, *s.* فتنه fìtnÉ, فساد fèssād, اویون òyun; —, *v.n.* فتنهچیقارمق fìtnÉ--chìkàrmak, فسادچیقارمق fèssād--chìkàrmak, اویون چیقارمق òyun--chìkàrmak.

Introduce, *v.a.* ایچرو صوقمق ìchèri-sòk-mak; ایچرو كتورمك ìchèri-ghètir-mek, ادخال ا ìdkhāl-et; كورشدرمك ghyùrushdurmek, قوكشدرمق kòngushdurmak, طانشدرمق tànish-dirmak; چیقارمق chìkàrmak, ابداع ا ìbdā''-et, اختراع ا ìkhtirā''-et, ایجاد ا ījād-et; اچمق àchmak, لقردیسنی اچمق làkirdissini-àchmak; درج ا dèrj-et; تقدیم ا tàkdīm-et, ابراز ا ìbrāz-et.

Introduction, *s.* مقدمه mùkàddimé; توصیه tàvsìyyé.

Intrude, *v.n.* تعجیز ا tà''jīz-et, اشغال ا ìshghāl-et, مانع او māni''-òl.

Intrust, *v.a.* امانة تسلیم ا èmānéten-tèss-līm-et.

Inundation, *s.* سیل sèyl (sèl), صوباصمسی sù-bàssmassi; طغیان tùghiyyān.

Inure, *v.a.* الشدرمق àlishdirmak.

Invade, *v.a.* باصمق bàssmak, تجاوز و تخطی ا tèjāvuz-vè-tàkhàttī-et.

Invalid, *a.* غیر صالح ghàyri-sālih, بوش bòsh; —, *s.* چوروك chùruk; —, *v.n.* چوروكه چیقمق chùrughÉ-chìk-mak; —, *v.a.* چوروكهچیقارمق chù-rughÉ-chìkàrmak.

Invalidate, *v.a.* بوزمق bòzmak, حكمنی بوزمق hùkmunu-bòzmak.

Invaluable, *a.* پك قيمتلو pèk-kīmètli, قيمتى بلنه‌مز kīmèti-bìlin*a*m*à*z.

Invasion, *s.* تجاوز tèjāvuz, تخطى tà-khàttī, استيلا isstīlā. [tirā''-et.

Invent, *v.a.* ايجاد ا ījād-et, اختراع ا ìkh-

Invention, *s.* ايجاد ījād, اختراع ìkh-tirā''. [téri''.

Inventor, *s.* موجد mūjid, مخترع mùkh-

Inventory, *s.* دفتر dèftᴇʀ.

Inverse, *a.* عكسى ''àksī, ترش tèrss; —, *s.* عكس ''àks, ترس tèrss.

Invest, *v.a.* اكسا ا ìksā-et, متصف ا mùt-tᴀssif-et; قوشاتمق kùshᴀtm*a*k, چويرمك chèvirmek, محاصره ا mù-hᴀss*a*r*a*-et; ياترمق yàt*i*rm*a*k, ويرمك vèrmek.

Investigate, *v.a.* تفتيش ا tèftīsh-et; تحرى ا tàhàrri-et, تجسس ا tèjèsssuss-et. [-dā'imā.

Invincible, *a.* المظفر دائما èl-mùzᴀffᴇʀ-

Invisible, *a.* كورنمز ghy*ù*runm*à*z, كوزكمز ghy*ù*zikm*à*z.

Invitation, *s.* دعوت dà''vèt.

Invite, *v.a.* دعوت ا dà''vèt-et.

Invoice, *s.* علم و خبر ''ìlm-u-khᴀbᴇʀ, پوصله pùssl*a*, دفتر dèftᴇʀ.

Involuntary, *a.* غير اختيارى ghàyri-ìkh-tiyārī, الده‌دكل ᴇldé-dì*gh*il.

Involve, *v.a.* قارشدرمق kᴀr*i*shd*i*rm*a*k, داخل ا dākhil-et; ايجاب ايتدرمك ījāb-ètdirmek.

Inward, *a.* داخلى dākhilī.

Inwards, *ad.* ايچرويه طوغرى ìchèriy*a*-

Ireland, *s.* ايرلانده Irlànd*a*. [dò*gh*ru.

Iris, *s.* زنبق zànbᴀk.

Irish, *a.* ايرلانده‌لو Irlànd*a*li.

Iron, *s.* تيمور tīmūr (dèmir), حديد hàdīd,

Iron-clad, *a.* زره‌لو zìrhli. [آهن āhèn.

Iron-monger, *s.* تيمورجى dèmirji.

Irony, *s.* استهزا ìsstihzā.

Irregular, *a.* اطرادسز ìttirādsiz; نظامسز nìzᴀmsiz, انتظامسز ìntizāmsiz; قاعده‌سز kā'idéssiz; يولسز yòlsuz; شاذ shᴀzz; باشى بوزق bᴀsh*i*-bòzuk.

Irreparable, *a.* تعميرقبول ايتمز tà''mīr-kᴀbūl-ètm*à*z; چاره‌سز chāréssiz.

Irresistible, *a.* قارشى قونلمز kàrsh*i*-kò-nulm*à*z.

Irresolute, *a.* كندى عقلنى بلمز kèndi-''ᴀkl*i*n*i*-bìlm*à*z, مترددد mùtérèddid.

Irritable, *a.* تيزقيزار tèz-kìzar, چابك دارلور chàb*i*k-dᴀr*i*l*i*r.

Irritate, *v.a.* قيزدرمق kìzd*i*rm*a*k, دارلتمق dᴀr*i*ltm*a*k. [k*i*n.

Irruption, *s.* هجوم hùjūm, باصقين bᴀss-

Isinglass, *s.* بالق طوتقالى bᴀl*i*k-tùtkᴀl*i*.

Island, Isle, Islet, *s.* اطه ᴀd*a*, جزيره jèzīré.

Ispahan (town of), *s.* اصفهان ìssfâhān.

Israelite, *s.* يهودى yàhūdī.

Issue, *s.* چيقه‌جق‌ير chìkajak-yèr, مخرج màkhrèj, قپو kᴀp*i*; نخودياقيسى nòkhud-yàkissi; چوجق chòjuk, اولاد èvlād, ذريت zùrrìyyèt; دعوى dà''wà, اختلاف ìkhtilāf, معارضه mù''āraza; —, *v.n.* چيقمق chìkmak; نشئت ا nèsh'èt-et.

Isthmus, *s.* بوغاز bò*gh*ᴀz, دل dìl.

It, *pr.* اول òl (ò); انى ᴀn*i*, ònu; اكا ᴀng*a* (òng*a*).

Italian, *a.* ايتاليا Itàli*a*.

Italy, *s.* ايتاليا Itàli*a*.

Itch, *s.* اويوز ŭyʊz ; —, *v.n.* كيدشمك ghìdishmek, قاشنمق kʌshɪnmak.

Item, *s.* قلم kàlɪm. [ʌn*ingki*, ònʊn*g*kʊ.

Its, *pr. a.* انك ʌn*ing*, ònʊn*g* ; انككى

Itself, *pr.* كندى kèndi, كنديسى kèndissi ; كنديسنى kèndissini ; كنديسنه kèndissinɛ.

Ivory, *s.* فيل‌ديشى fīl-dìshi.

Ivy, *s.* صارماشق sàrmʌshɪk.

J.

Jackal, *s.* چقال chàkāl. [hìmār.

Jackass, *s.* اشك èshek, خر khàr, حمار

Jackdaw, *s.* الا قارغه ʌl*a*-kàrgh*a*(?).

Jacket, *s.* منطان mìntʌn.

Jack-ketch, *s.* جلاد jèllād.

Jail, *s.* زندان zìndān, حبسخانه hʌbss-

Jailer, *s.* زندانجى zìndānji. [khānɛ.

Jalap, *s.* جلاپه jʌlap*a*.

Jam, *s.* رچل rèchel, طاتلو tʌtl*i*.

Janissary, *s.* يكيچرى yèn*g*ichéri.

January, *s.* كانون‌ثانى kyānūni-sānī.

Japan, *s.* ياپونيا yàpòni*a* ; روغن rūghʌn ; —, *v.a.* روغن‌اورمق rùghʌn-wūrm*a*k.

Japanese, *a.* ياپونيالو yàpòni*a*li.

Japhet, *s.* يافث yàfeth.

Jar, *s.* قوانوس kàwanòss ; on the —, *ad.* اچق àch*ɪ*k ; —, *v.n.* قارشمق

Jasper, *s.* يشم yèshem. [kʌr*ɪ*shm*a*k.

Jaundice, *s.* صاريلق s*à*r*ɪ*l*ɪ*k.

Jaw, *s.* چكه chèn*g*ɛ.

Jealous, *a.* قزقانج kɪzkʌnj ; غيور ghàyūr ; حسود hʌssūd, حسدلو hʌssedli.

Jealousy, *s.* قزقانجلق kɪzkʌnjl*ɪ*k, غيرت ghàyrèt ; حسد hʌssed.

Jeer, *v.n.* and *a.* زوقلنمق zèvklɪnmek.

Jehovah, *s.* الحى القيوم el-Hàyyu-'l--Kàyyūm. [lù''āb.

Jelly, *s.* الماسيه èlmʌssiyyɛ ; لعاب

Jeopardy, *s.* تهلكه tèhlikɛ. [shèrīf.

Jerusalem, *s.* قدس شريف kūdssi-

Jessamine, *s.* ياسمين yāssémīn.

Jest, *s.* شقا sh*à*ka, لطيفه lȧtīfɛ.

Jesus-Christ, *s.* عيسى المسيح ''Īssà-'l--Messīh, حضرت‌عيسى hàzrèti-''Īssà.

Jet, *s.* فسقيه fɪsskɪyyɛ.

Jetty, *s.* اسكله ìsskèlɛ.

Jew, *s.* يهودى yàhūdī ; Jewess, يهودى قاريسى yàhūdī-kʌrissi.

Jewel, *s.* Jewels, *s. pl.* مجوهرات mù-jèvhérāt. [jèwāhirji.

Jeweller, *s.* قيومجى kùyumju, جواهرجى

Jib, *s.* فلوق flòk.

Jibboom, *s.* باستون bāsstūn. [ايش ìsh.

Job, *s.* حضرت ايوب hàzrèti-èyyūt ;

Jobber, *s.* سمسار sìmsār.

Jockey, *s.* بنيجى bɪn*i*j*i*. [lȧtīféj*i*.

Jocular, *a.* تحاف tùhāf, لطيفه‌جى

Jog, Joggle, *v.a.* صارصمق sàrssm*a*k.

John Bull, *s.* انكلتره ملتى ìnghiltèrra-millèti.

Join, *v.n.* بتشمك bìtishmek, التحاق‌ا ìltihʌk-et, ملاصق‌او mùlässɪk-ol ; واصل‌او vʌssɪl-ol ; — *v.a.* بتشدرمك bìtishdirmek ; الحاق‌ا ìlhʌk-et ; وصل‌ا vʌssl-et.

Joiner, *s.* دوغرامه‌جى dòghram*a*j*i*.

Joint, *s.* اك‌يرى èk-yèri ; اويناق‌يرى

òynak-yèri, مفصل mAfsAl; out of —, چیقق chìkìk; get out of —; be put out of —, چیقمق chìkmak; put out of —, چیقارمق chìkàrmak.

Jointly, *ad.* مشترکاً mùshtèrékEn, اشتراکاً ìshtirākEn.

Joint-stock Company, شرکت shìrkèt.

Jointure, *s.* زوجه یه باغلنان ایراد zèvjéya-bAghlanAn-īrād.

Joke, *s.* شقا shàka, لطیفه làtīfé; —, *v.n.* شقا ا shàka-et, لطیفه ا làtīfé-et.

Jolly, *a.* کولر یوزلو ghyùlEr-yùzlu; کیف kèyf; ذوقلو zèvkli; — boat,

Jolt, *v.a.* صارصمق sàrssmak. [فلوقه fìlìka.

Jonquil, *s.* فولیه fùlya.

Journal, *s.* روزنامه rūznāmé; تقویم وقائع tAkwīmi-vàkā'i''; ژورنال zhùrnAl.

Journalist, *s.* غزته جی ghàzètaji, جریده جی jèrīdéji.

Journey, *s.* یول yòl, یولجیلق yòljuluk, سفر sèfEr; —, *v.n.* کزمك ghèzmek, یولجیلق ا yòljuluk-et, سفر ا sèfEr-et.

Journeyman, *s.* کوندهلکجی ghyùndélikji.

Joy, *s.* سونج sEvinj, ممنونیت mèmnūnìyyèt, سرور sùrūr, حبور hùbūr, شادمانی shādumānī.

Joyful, *a.* ممنون mèmnūn, مسرور mèssrūr, شاد shAd (shAz), شادمان shAdumAn.

Judge, *s.* حاکم hākim, قاضی kAzī (kAdi), مولا mèvlà (mòlla); deputy —, نائب nā'ib; —, *v.n.* قیاس ا kìyāss-et; ظن ا zànn-et, عد ا ''àdd-et; —, *v.a.* محاکمه ا mù-hākémé-et; حکومت ا hùkyūmet-et.

Judgment, *s.* ظن zànn, قیاس kìyāss; عقل ''Akl, تدبیر tèdbīr; حکومت hùkyūmèt; جزا jèzā, بلا bèlā; day of —, قیامت کونی kìyāmèt-ghyùnu; — seat, مسند حکومت mèssnèdi-hùkyūmèt.

Judicious, *a.* عقللو ''Aklli.

Jug, *s.* دستی dèssti, تستی tèssti.

Juggler, *s.* حقه باز hòkka-bāz. [bāzlik.

Jugglery, Juggling, *s.* حقه بازلق hòkka-

Jugular-vein, *s.* حبل الورید hablu-'l-

Juice, *s.* صو sū; شیره shìra. [-vèrīd.

Juicy, *a.* صولو sùlu.

Jujube, *s.* عناب ''ùnnāb.

July, *s.* تموز tèmmūz.

Jumble, *v.a.* قارشدرمق kArishdirmak; —, *s.* قارمه قارشق شی kàrma-karishik-shèy.

Jump, *s.* صچرایش sìchrayish, اتلایش Atlayish; —, *v.n.* صچرامق sìchramak, اتلامق Atlamak. [موصل mèvsàl.

Junction, *s.* اتصال ìttissAl; تلاقی tèlākī;

Juncture, *s.* ارالق àralìk, اثنا èssnā, وقت wAkit, زمان zàmAn; حال hāl.

June, *s.* حزیرن hàzīrān.

Jungle, *s.* اورمان òrmAn; اورمانلق یر òrmAnlìk-yEr, چنکلستان chènghè-lisstān. [اوغلی òghlu, زاده zādé.

Junior, *a.* سنجه کچوك sìnnja-kùchuk;

Juniper, *s.* اردج اغاجی àrdij-Aghaji; — berries, اردج تخمی àrdij-tòkhmi.

Junk, *s.* چین کمیسی chìn-ghèmissi.

Jurisconsult, *s.* مفتی mùftī; فقیه fàkīh.

Jurisdiction, *s.* حكومت hùkyūmèt.
Jurisprudence, *s.* علم فقه "ìlmi-fìkh.
Jurist, *s.* فقيه fàkīh.
Jury, *s.* اون ايكى يمينلو كمسنه مجلسى òn-ìki-yèmīnlī-kìmèssné-mèjlissi.
Juryman, *s.* مذكور يمينلولرك برى mèzkyūr-yèmīnlīlerīn-bìri. [dīrèk.
Jury-mast, *s.* عاريتى ديرك āriyyèti-
Just, *a.* عادل "ādil, حق شناس hàkk-shìnāss, منصف mùnsif, حقانيتلو hàkkānìyyètli; —, *ad.* تمام tàmām, تام tāmm, تماماً tàmāman; — as, همان . . . ايكن hèmān . . . iken; — now, همان شمدى hèmān-shìmdi; — so, تمام بويله tàmām-bùylé, تمام اويله tàmām-ùylé, همان بويله hèmān-bùylé, همان شويله hèmān-shùylé, همان اويله hèmān-ùylé.
Justice, *s.* عدالت "àdālèt, حقانيت hàkkānìyyèt, انصاف ìnsāf, حق hàkk; حاكم hākim.
Justifiable, *a.* جائز jā'iz. [-zìmmèt.
Justification, *s.* تبرئهٔ ذمت tèbrìyyè'i-
Justify, *v.a.* تبرئهٔ ذمت ا tèbrìyyè'i-zìmmèt-et; حق ويرمك hàkk-vèrmek; جائز قيلمق jā'iz-kìlmak, تجويز ا tèjvīz-
Juvenile, *a.* كنج ghènj, جوان jìwān. [-et.
Juxtaposition, *s.* اتصال ìttissāl.

K.

Kalendar, *s.* تقويم tàkvīm.
Keel, *s.* اوكرغه òngurgha (òmurgha).
Keen, *a.* كسكين kèsskin, قلاغيلو kìlāghìli, بران bùrrān, حديد hàdīd.
Keep, *s.* بوغاز bòghāz, ييه جك yèyéjek, تغديه tàghdìyyé; *v.a.* صاقلامق sàklamak, حفظ ا hìfz-et; طوتمق tùtmak, اليقومق àlìkòmak, براقمامق bràkmamak, صاليويرمامك sàlìvèrmamek; بسلمك bèsslémek; —, *v.n.* طيانمق dàyanmak, بوزلمامق bòzulmamak; دورمق dùrmak, قالمق kàlmak.
Keeper, *s.* حافظ hāfiz, محافظ mùhāfiz, بكجى bèkji.
Keep-sake, *s.* يادگار yādighyār.
Keg, *s.* اوفاجق فوچى ùfàjèk-fichi.
Kennel, *s.* اولوق òluk.
Kernel, *s.* ايچ ìch, مغز màghz, لب lùbb; بيض bèyz (bèz).
Kerseymere, *s.* قازمير kàzmīr.
Kettle, *s.* قزغان kàzghān (kàzan); كوكم ghyùghum. [دمبلك dùmbélèk.
Kettledrum, *s.* نقاره nàkkāré (nàghara);
Key, *s.* اناختار ànakhtār, مفتاح mìftāh.
Khan, *s.* خان khān.
Kick, *s.* تكمه tèkmé; چفته chìfté; —, *v.n.* تكمه اتمق tèkmé-àtmak; چفته اتمق chìfté-àtmak; —, *v.a.* تپمك or دپمك tèpmek; — out, *v.a.* قوغمق kòghmak, سكدر ا sìkdir-et.
Kid, *s.* اوغلاق òghlàk.
Kidney, *s.* بوكرك bùghrek (bùbrek); — beans, فصوليه fàssòlya.
Kill, *v.a.* اولدرمك ùldurmek, قتل ا kàtl-et, تلف ا tèlef-et, هلاك ا hèlāk-
Kiln, *s.* اوجاق òjak. [-et.
Kind, *s.* درلو dùrlu, صوى sòy, جنس jìnss, نوع nèv"; —, *a.* ايو ìyi, طاتلو tàtli.

Kindle, *v.n.* طوتشمق tùtushm*a*k ; —, *v.a.* ياقمق yàkm*a*k ; طوتشدرمق tù-tushdurm*a*k, ايقاد ا īkĀd-et.

Kindness, *s.* ايولك īyilik, كرم kèrem, عنايت ‘‘ìnāyet, لطف lùtf ; افنديلك éfèndilik.

Kindred, *s.* اقربا Akrabā, خصماقربا khìss*i*m-Akr*a*bā ; قرابت kArābèt, خصملق khìss*i*ml*i*k.

King, *s.* قرال k*i*rAl, حكمدار hùkmdār, پادشاه pādishāh, شاه shāh, ملك mèlik, مالك mālik.

Kingdom, *s.* قراللق k*i*rAll*i*k, پادشاهلق pādishāhl*i*k, حكومت hùk*y*ūmèt, دولت dèvlèt, ملك milk *or* mùlk, مملكت mèmlékèt, ملكوت mèlé-k*y*ūt.

[-‘‘illèti.

King's-evil, *s.* صراجه علتى sàr*a*j*a*-

Kinsman, Kinswoman, *s.* خصم khìssm, اقربادن Akr*a*bād*a*n.

Kiss, *s.* اوپش ùpush, شفتالو shèftāl*i*, بوسه būssé ; —, *v.a.* اوپمك ùpmek, بوس ا būss-et.

Kitchen, *s.* مطبخ mAtbAkh (mūtfAk).

Kite, *s.* (bird) چايلاق chàylāk ; (toy) اوچرتمه ùchurtm*a*.

Kitten, *s.* كدى ياوريسى kèdi-yàwrussu.

Knapsack, *s.* چانطه chAnt*a*.

Knave, *s.* حيله‌كار hīlékyār, چاپقين chApk*i*n, پزونك pèzéwènk.

Knead, *v.a.* يوغورمق yòg*h*urm*a*k.

Knee, *s.* ديز dìz, زانو zānū ; (of timber) ديرسك dìrsèk.

Kneel, *v.n.* ديز چوكمك dìz-chùkmek.

Knife, *s.* بچاق bìchAk ; (pocket —) چاقى chàk*i* ; (turkish pen—) قلمتراش kàlem-trāsh ; (carver) ساطور sAt*i*r ; (long weapon) يتاغان yàtag*h*An.

Knight, *s.* بك bèg*h*, قواليرِ kàwalīr ; (chess) ات At.

Knit, *v.a.* اورمك ùrmek ; —, *a.* اوريلو ùrulu, اورلمش ùrulmush.

[bAbA.

Knob, *s.* طوپ tòp, طوپوز tòpuz ; بابا

Knock, *s.* اورش wūrush ; قپوچالنمسى kApi-chAl*i*nm*a*ss*i* ; —, *v.a.* اورمق wūrm*a*k ; چالمق chAlm*a*k ; — against, چاتمق chàtm*a*k ; — down, يقمق y*i*km*a*k ; — in, ايچرو قاقمق ìchèri-kAkm*a*k ; — off, اندرمك èndirmek, دوشرمك dùshurmek ; كسمك kèssmek ; بترمك bìtirmek ; — out, چيقارمق ch*i*kàrm*a*k, دوشرمك dùshurmek ; — under, *v.n.* تسليم او tèsslīm-òl.

Knocker, *s.* قپو طوقماغى kApi-tòkm*a*g*h*i.

Knot, *s.* دوكم dùg*h*um ; —, *v.a.* باغلامق bAg*h*lamak, دوكملمك dùg*h*umlémek ; —, *v.n.* دوكملنمك dùg*h*umlenmek.

Know, *v.a.* بلمك bìlmek ; خبرى او khAbéri-òl, خبردار او khAberdār-òl, واقف او wāk*i*f-òl ; طانيمق tAn*i*m*a*k ; معلوماتى او mà‘‘lūmAt*i*-òl ; — one another, بربرينى طانيمق bìr-bìrini-tAn*i*m*a*k, معارفه‌لرى او mū‘‘āréféléri-òl ; — again, طانيمق tAn*i*m*a*k ; — carnally, سكمك sìkmek, جماع ا jìmā‘‘-et, وطى ا wAty-et.

Knowledge, *s.* علم ‘‘ìlm, خبر khAber,

معلومات mà"lūmāt, عرفان "ìrfān, دانش dānish.

Knuckle-bone, *s.* اشق ȧshik.

Kufic, *a.* كوفى kyūfī.

L.

Label, *s.* يافته yȧfta; —, *v.a.* يافته طاقمق yȧfta-tàkmak, يافته يا پشدرمق yȧfta-yàpishdirmak.

Laborious, *a.* اغر ȧghir, كوچ ghyùch.

Labour, *s.* امك èmek, ايش ìsh, ايشجيلك ìshjilik; —, *v.n.* ايشلمك ìshlémek.

Labourer, *s.* رنجبر rènjbėr (rènchpėr), ايشجى ìshji, ارغاد ȧrghād, يناشمه yànashma.

Lace, *s.* قيطان (ghàytān); شريد shèrid; دانتله dȧntèla; (gold) سرمه sìrma; قلاپطان kìlȧptȧn *or* قلابدان kìlȧbdȧn; —, *v.a.* قيطاننى كچورمك ghàytānini-ghèchirmek.

Lack, *s.* نقصان nòksān, اكسكلك èksiklik; —, *v.a.* اكسك او èksik-ȯl; اكسكى او èksighi-ȯl.

Lacker, *s.* روغن rūghȧn; —, *v.a.* روغن اورمق rūghȧn-wùrmak.

Lackey, *s.* اوشاق ùshȧk.

Laconic, *a.* قصه kìssa. [جوان jùwȧn.

Lad, *s.* اوغلان ȯghlȧn, دليقانلو dèlikȧnli,

Ladder, *s.* نردبان nėrdibān (mėrdivėn); اسكله ìsskèlé.

Lade, *v.a.* يوكلتمك yùklėtmek, تحميل ا tàhmīl-et; —, *v.n.* يوك المق yùk-ȧlmak.

Lading, *s.* يوكلنمكلك yùklėnmeklik; يوكلتمكلك yùklėtmeklik; يوك yùk, حموله hàmūlé; bill of —, يوك سندى yùk-sènedi; پوليچه دى قاريقو pòlicha-dì-kàriko.

Ladle, *s.* كفچه kèfché, كپچه kèpché.

Lady, *s.* خانم hànim; قوقونه kòkona; دودو dūdu; مادامه màdama.

Lake, *s.* كول ghyùl. [dòghurmak.

Lamb, *s.* قوزى kùzu; —, *v.n.* طوغرمق

Lame, *a.* طوپال tòpȧl; — of one hand, چولاق chòlȧk; —, *v.a.* اياغنى سقطا àyaghini-sȧkȧt-et.

Lameness, *s.* طوپاللق tòpȧllik.

Lament, *v.a.* and *n.* اغلامق ȧghlamak.

Lamentation, *s.* اغلامه ȧghlama, فغان fìghān, نالش nālish.

Lamp, *s.* قنديل kȧndīl. [hìjv-èt.

Lampoon, *s.* هجو hìjv; —, *v.a.* هجو ا

Lance, *s.* مزراق mèzrȧk; —, *v.a.* دشمك dèshmek, اچمق ȧchmak.

Lancet, *s.* نيشتر nīshtėr (nèshtėr).

Land, *s.* قره kȧra, بر bèrr; ارض àrz (pl. اراضى àrāzī), الكا (ùlké), ملك mìlk, مملكت mèmlékèt, طپراق tòprȧk; plot of —, عرصه "àrsa; —, *v.n.* قره يه چيقمق kȧraya-chìkmak; —, *v.a.* قره يه چيقارمق kȧraya-chìkàr-mak. [ùsstu-ȧchilir-bìr-nèv-"i-hìnto.

Landau, *s.* اوستى اچلور بر نوع هنطو

Landholder, *s.* املاك صاحبى èmlāk-sāhibi. [ìsskèlé.

Landing, Landing-place, *s.* اسكله

Landlady, *s.* او صاحبى قادين èv-sāhibi-kȧdin.

Landlord, *s.* ملك صاحبی mùlk-sāhibi; خانه صاحبی او صاحبی èv-sāhibi, khānè-sāhibi. [اشارت ìshāret.

Landmark, *s.* سنور طاشی sìnir-tàshi;

Landowner, *s.* املاك صاحبی èmlāk-[-sāhibi.

Landscape, *s.* نظارت nàzārèt.

Lane, *s.* دار یول dàr-yòl; دار صوقاق dàr-sòkak; چیقمز صوقاق chìkmàz-sòkak. [زبان zàbān.

Language, *s.* دل dìl, لسان lìssān,

Languid, *a.* بایغین bàyghin, جانسز jānsiz. [-ghìbi-òl.

Languish, *v.n.* بایغین کبی او bàyghin-

Lantern, *s.* فنار (fèner); magic —, *s.* خیالجی فنری khàyālji-fèneri.

Lap, *s.* قوجاق kùjak; —, *v.a.* یالایه یالایه ایچمك yālaya-yālaya-ìchmek.

Lapidate, *v.a.* رجم ا rèjm-et, طاشلامق tāshlamak.

Lapse, *s.* مرور mùrūr; —, *v.a.* قالمق kālmak, عائد او "ā'id-òl.

Larboard, *s.* اسکله ìsskèlé.

Larceny, *s.* خرسزلك khìrsizlik.

Larder, *s.* کیلار kìlar (kìler).

Large, *a.* بیوك bìyuk, کبیر kèbīr, عظیم "āzīm; کلی kyùllī, کلیتلو kyùllìyyètli.

Larkspur, *s.* هزاررنك چیچکی hèzār-rènk-chìchèghi (هزارن hèzārèn).

Lash, *s.* قامچی kàmchi; —, *v.a.* قامچیلمق kàmchilamak; باغلامق [bàghlamak.

Lass, *s.* کیز kìz.

Last, *s.* قالب kālip; صوك sòng; —, *a.* الك صکره کی èng-sòngraki, اخر ākhir, پسین pèssīn; —, *v.n.* سورمك sùrmek; طیانمق dàyanmak; باقی قالمق bākī-kālmak, پایدار او pàydār-òl, مستمر او mùsstémèrr-òl; at —, *ad.* عاقبت "ākibèt, صوك صوکنده sòng-sòngunda, انجام کار ènjāmi-kyār.

Lasting, *a.* طیانقلو dàyànikli; چوق سورر chòk-sùrer, پایدار pàydār, مستمر mùsstémèrr.

Lastly, *ad.* خلاصهٔ کلام khùlāssa'i-kèlām, الحاصل èl-hāssil.

Latch, *s.* سندال màndāl, دل dìl.

Late, *a.* کج ghèj, کیچ ghèch; سابق sābik; مرحوم mèrhūm, متوفا mùtéwèffà; —, *ad.* سابقا sābika.

Lately, *ad.* بر از اول bìr-āz-èvvel; یقینلرده yàkinlarda, مؤخرا mù'àkh-kharan. [-tàkhta, پداوره pàdàwra.

Lath, *s.* شیشه shìshé; چام تخته chàm-

Lathe, *s.* چرخ chàrkh.

Lather, *s.* صابون کپوکی sàbun-kyùpughu; —, *v.a.* صابونلمق sàbūnlamak.

Latin, *a.* لاطین Lātīn; —, *s.* لاطینجه Lātīnjé.

Latitude, *s.* عرض "àrz, عرض بلد 'àrzi-bèled; وسعت vùss"àt; مساعده mùssā"adé.

Latter, *a.* صکره کی sòngraki, اخر ākhir.

Latterly, *ad.* یقینده yàkinda, بو یقینلرده bù-yàkinlarda, مؤخرا mù'àkhkharan.

Lattice, *s.* قفس kāfess, شبیکه shèbīké.

Laud, *v.a.* مدح ا mèdh-èt.

Laudable, *a.* مستحسن mùsstàhsèn.

Laudanum, *s.* افیون روحی āfyòn-rūhu.

Laudation, *s.* مبالغه ایله مدح mùbālagha-ìla-mèdh.

Laudatory, *a.* مدح متضمن mèdh-mùta-zàmmin.

Laugh, *s.* كولش ghyùlush, خنده khàndé; —, *v.n.* كولمك ghyùlmek, خنده ا khàndé-et; — at one, برينه كولمك bìrina-ghyùlmek; — in one's sleeve, ايچرودن كولمك ìchèriden-gyùlmek; — out loud, قهقهه كولمك kàhkaha-gyùlmek.

Laughable, *a.* كولنه جك ghyùlenejek.

Launch, *s.* صندال sàndàl; —, *v.a.* دكزه اندرمك dèngizé-èndirmek; — out, *v.n.* پاره خرج ا pàra-khàrj-et; تفصيله باشلامق tàfsīla-bàshlamak.

Laundress, *s.* چماشيرجي قارى chàmà-shirji-kàri.

Laureate, *s.* باش شاعر bàsh-shā"àr.

Laurel, *s.* يبان دفنه سى yàban-dèfnéssi.

Lavender, *s.* لوانده làvànda.

Lavish, *a.* مسرف mùssrif; بذول bèzūl; —, *v.a.* بذل ا bèzl-et, اتمق àtmak.

Law, *s.* شرع shèr", شريعت shèrī"àt, قانون kānūn, نظام nìzām.

Lawful, *a.* مشروع mèshrū"; جائز jā'iz; حلال hàlāl; مأذون mè'zūn.

Lawgiver, *s.* قانونجى kānūnji.

Lawless, *a.* نظامسز nìzāmsiz.

Lawlessness, *s.* نظامسزلك nizamsizlik.

Lawmaker, *s.* قانونجى kānūnji.

Lawsuit, *s.* دعوى dà"wà.

Lawyer, *s.* مفتى mùftī, فقيه fàkīh; دعوى وكيلى dà"wà-vèkīli; اووقات àvokàt.

Lax, *a.* كوشك ghèvshèk; مساعده جى mùssā"adéji, مسامحه جى mùssāma-haji; لينتلوجه līnètlija.

Laxative, *a.* ملين mùlèyyin.

Laxity, Laxness, *s.* كوشكلك ghèvsheklik.

Lay, *v.n.* يمورطلمق yìmurtlamak; —, *v.a.* قومق kòmak, ياترمق yàtirmak, وضع ا wàz"-et; قورمق kùrmak, طرح ا tàrh-et; — aside, براقمق bràkmak, ترك ا tèrk-et; — before, عرض ا "àrz-et; — by, *v.a.* صاقلامق sàklamak; —, *v.n.* دينلمك dìnènmek, راحت ا rāhat-et; — down, يره قومق yèra-kòmak, براقمق bràkmak, ترك ا tèrk-et; — hold of, طوتمق tùtmak, ياپشمق yàpishmak, يقالمق yàkalamak; — in, طوپلامق tòplamak, تدارك ا tèdāruk-et (tèdārik); — on, سورمك sùrmek; صالدرمق sàldirmak, وضع ا wàz"-et, طرح ا tàrh-et; — open, آچمق àchmak; — out, خرج ا khàrj-et, صرف ا sàrf-et, خرجامق khàrjamak; — over, قاپلامق kàplamak; — up, *v.a.* صاقلامق sàkla-mak, خسته ا khàssta-et; —, *v.n.* خسته او khàssta-òl; — waste, *v.a.* خراب ا khàrāb-et; —, *v.n.* ويران قالمق vīrān-kālmak; خالى قالمق khālī-kālmak.

Layer, *s.* قات kàt, طبقه tàbàka.

Lazaretto, *s.* تحفظ خانه tàhàffuz-khāné, قارنتينه kàrantīna.

Laziness, *s.* تنبللك tènbèllik.

Lazy, *a.* تنبل tènbèl.

Lead, *s.* قورشون kùrshun, اسرب ùssrub; اسقنديل ìsskàndil; قلاغوزلق kìlàghuz-luk, ارباشيلق èr-bàshìlìk, سوزباشيلق sùz-bàshìlìk; —, *v.a.* كوترمك ghyù-turmek, يدمك yèdmek; —, *v.n.* باشه كچمك bàsha-ghèchmek, ايلرو دوشمك

ìléri-dùshmek, اوكه دوشمك ùngé-dùshmek, قلاغوزلق اولمق kìlàghuzluk-et, هادی او hādī-òl; — away, الوب كوترمك Alip-ghyùturmek; الداتمق Aldatmak, ازدرمق Azdirmak, اضلال ا ìdlāl-et, افساد ا ìfsād-et; — astray, يولدن چيقارمق yòldan-chìkàrmak; الداتمق Aldatmak, ازدرمق Azdirmak, اضلال ا ìdlāl-et, افساد ا ìfsād-et; to cast the —, اسقندل اتمق ìsskAndil-Atmak.

Leader, *s.* باش bAsh, رئيس rè'īss, سر sèr; اوك اتی ùng-Ati, اوك حيوانی ùng-hàywAni, غزته نك باشلوجه بندی ghàzètaning-bAshlija-bèndi.

Leaf, *s.* ييراق yàprAk, ورق vàrak, ورقه vàraka; — gold, التون ورقی Altin-vàraki; — silver, كومش ورقی ghyù-mush-vàraki; — copper or brass, ورق vàrak.

League, *s.* ساعت sā"at, ساعتلق يول sā"atlik-yòl; اتفاق ìttifāk; — together, *v.n.* اتفاق ا ìttifāk-et.

Leak, *s.* دليك dèlik, اچقلق àchiklik, يارق yàrik; —, *v.n.* اقمق Akmak; صزمق sìzmak; صوا sù-et.

Lean, *a.* ضعيف zà"īf, زبون zàbun, اريق Arīk; —, *s.* ياغسز ات yàghsiz-èt; —, *v.n.* اكری دورمق èghri-dùrmak, اكلمك èghilmek, ياتمق yàtmak; — against, *v.n.* طيانمق dàyanmak, يصدانمق yàssdanmak; —, *v.a.* طيامق dàyamak.

Leap, *s.* اتلايش Atlayish, صچرايش sìch-rayish; —, *v.n.* اتلامق Atlamak, صچرامق sìchramak.

Leapyear, *s.* كبيسه kèbīssé.

Learn, *v.a.* اوكرنمك ùghrènmek, تحصيل ا tàhsīl-et, استفاده ا ìsstifādé-et, تعلم ا tà"àllum-et. [دانشمند dānishmènd.

Learned, *a.* عالم "ālim, اوقومش òkumush,

Learner, *s.* شاكرد shāghird.

Learning, *s.* علم "ìlm, عرفان "ìrfān, دانش dānish. [-vé-ìsstījārin-hùjjeti.

Lease, *s.* ايجار واستيجارك حجتی ījār-

Least, *a.* الك اوفاق èng-ùfAk, الك كچوك èng-kùchuk; الك از èng-Az; ادنا èdnā, يك جزئی pèk-jùz'ī; at —, *ad.* هيچ اولمزايسه hìch-òlmàz-ìssa; —, *c.* ياخود yākhūd; not in the —, *ad.* هيچ hìch, اصلا àsslā, قطعا kAt"ā, قطعاً وقاطبة kAt"àn-vè-kAtibétan.

Leather, *s.* مشين mèshīn, سختيان sàkhtiyān, بولغاری bùlghārī; (sole) كوسله kyùssélé, كون ghyùn.

Leave, *s.* اذن ìzn, ìzin, رخصت rùkhsAt; —, *v.a.* براقمق bràkmak, ترك ا tèrk-et; — off, براقمق bràkmak, واز كچمك vāz-ghèchmek; كسلمك kèssilmek, ديكمك dìngmek, منقطع او mùnkAti"-òl; — out, كچمك ghèchmek, اتلامق Atlamak, يازمامق yàzmamak.

Leaven, *s.* مايه māyé; —, *v.a.* مايه لتمك māyéletmek.

Lecture, *s.* درس dèrss; درس عام dèrssi-"āmm; وعظ và"z; —, *v.n.* درس ويرمك dèrss-vèrmek; وعظ ا và"z-et; —, *v.a.* ازارلمق Azarlamak, نصيحت ويرمك nAssīhat-vèrmek. [-"āmm-khòjassi.

Lecturer, *s.* درس عام خواجه سی dèrssi-

Led-horse, *s.* يدك yèdek.

Lee, *s.* روزكار التى rùzghyār-ʌltì.

Leech, *s.* سولوك sùluk; هكيم hèkim, طبيب tàbīb; —, *v.a.* سولوك ياپشدرمق sùluk-yàpìshdìrmak.

Leek, *s.* پراصه prāssa.

Left, *s.* صول sòl, صول طرفى sòl-tàrafi, يسار yèssār, چپ chèp; — handed, صولاق sòlʌk.

Leg, *s.* اياق àyak, باجاق bʌjak; بوط bùt.

Legacy, *s.* وصيت wʌssìyyèt.

Legal, *a.* شرعى shèr''ī, مشروع mèshrū'', جائز jā'iz, مأذون mè'zūn, حلال hàlāl.

Legation, *s.* سفارت sèfārèt; — house, سفارتخانه sèfārèt-khānè.

Legible, *a.* اوقونور òkunur, اوقوناقلو òkunʌkli, عيان ''àyān, جلى jèlī.

Legibility, *s.* اوقوناقلق òkunʌklik.

Legion, *s.* الاى ʌlay, لوا lìvā.

Legislate, *v.n.* قانون وضع ا kānūn-wʌz''et.

Legislation, *s.* وضع قانون wʌz''-i-kānūn.

Legislator, *s.* واضع قوانين دولت vwʌzi''-kàwānīn-i-dèvlet.

Legislature, *s.* وضع قوانين دولت ايچون مجلس waz''-i-kawanin-i-dèvlet-ìchin-mèjliss.

Legitimate, *a.* يوللو yòllu, يولنده yòlunda; شرعى shèr''ī, مشروع mèshrū'', حلال hàlāl.

Leisure, *s.* بوش وقت bòsh-wʌkit, خالى وقت khālī-wʌkit.

Lemon, *s.* ليمون līmòn.

Lemonade, *s.* ليموناطه līmonāta.

Lend, *v.a.* ويرمك vèrmek, عارية ويرمق ''āriyyètʌn - vèrmek; اودنج ويرمك ùdunj-vèrmek, قرض ا kàrz-et.

Length, *s.* بوى bòy, طول tūl, اوزونلق ùzūnluk; at —, *ad.* عاقبت ''ākibet, نهايت nìhāyet.

Lengthen, *v.n.* اوزامق ùzamak, بويلانمق bòylanmak; —, *v.a.* بوى ويرمك bòy-vèrmek, اوزاتمق ùzʌtmak.

Lengthy, *a.* اوزون ùzun.

Lenient, *a.* شفقتلو shàfakʌtli.

Lenity, *s.* سفقت shàfakʌt.

Lens, *s.* جام jàm.

Lentile, *s.* مرجمك mèrjumèk.

Leopard, *s.* قپلان kàplàn. [ابرص ʌbràss.

Leper, *s.* مسكين mìsskin, الا تنلو ʌla-tènli,

Leprosy, *s.* مسكينلك علتى mìsskinlik-''illèti; الا تنلولك ʌla-tènlilik.

Leprous, *a.* مسكين mìsskin.

Less, *a.* كچوك kùchuk, دها كچوك dàhà-kùchuk; از ʌz, دها از dàhà-ʌz, اكسك èksik.

Lessen, *v.n.* كچولمك kùchulmek, اوفالمق ùfʌlmak; ازالمق ʌzʌlmak; —, *v.a.* كچولتمك kùchultmek, اوفالتمق ùfʌltmak, ازالتمق ʌzʌltmak, كسمك kèssmek.

Lesson, *s.* درس dèrss; عبرت ''ìbrèt.

Lest, *c.* شايدكه shāyed-ki, مباداكه mèbādā-ki, قورقوسندن kòrkussundan, مطالعهسندن mùtāla''àssindan.

Let, *s.* مانع māni''; —, *v.a.* براقمق bràkmak, قومق kòmak; كرايه ويرمك kìrāya-vèrmek; —, *v.n.* كرايه ويرلمك kìrāya-vèrilmek; — down, اندرمك èndirmek; — loose, صاليويرمك sʌlivèrmek; براقمق bràkmak; — off, صاليويرمك sʌlivèrmek; اتمق ʌtmak; عفو ا ''ʌfv-et; — fly, اتمق ʌtmak;

— out, طیشاری براقمق dìshàri-bràkmak ; کرایه‌ویرمك kìràya-vèrmek ; — in, ایچروالمق ìchèri-àlmak ; ایچرو قومق ìchèri-kòmak ; پارچه‌قومق pàrcha-kòmak ; — blood, قان‌المق kàn-àlmak ; —, pp. کراده kìrāda.

Letter, s. حرف hàrf (pl. حروف hùrūf, حروفات hùrūfāt) ; مکتوب mèktūb (mèktup), نامه nāmé.

Lettuce, s. ماروال mārul, صلاطه sàlata.

Levant, s. ممالك عثمانیه mèmāliki-"òssmānìyyé.

Levantine, s. ممالك عثمانیه‌ده طوغمش فرنك mèmāliki-"ossmānìyyéda-dòghmish-firènk.

Levee, s. بینش bīnish ; رکاب rìkyab.

Level, s. افق ùfuk ; دوز dùz ; —, a. افقی ùfukī, دوز dùz, طوغری dòghru ; —, v.a. دوزلتمك dùzlètmek ; — at, نشان‌المق nìshān-àlmak.

Lever, s. قول kòl, مانوله mànavèla.

Levity, s. خفت khìffèt ; خفت‌مزاج khìffèti-mìzāj.

Levy, s. عسکرتحریری "àsskèr-tàhrīri ; یکی یازلمش عسکر yèngi-yàzìlmish-"àsskèr ; صالغین sàlghin ; تحصیل tàhsīl ; —, v.a. تحریرا tàhrīr-et, جمعا jèm"-et, طوپلامق tòplamak ; تحصیلا tàhsīl-et, طوپلامق تحصیلا tòplamak, المق àlmak.

Lewd, a. شهوتی غالب shehvèti-ghālib.

Lexicographer, s. لغت مؤلفی lughàt-mù'èllifi.

Lexicon, s. لغت lughàt.

Liability, s. مسئولیت mèss'ūliyyèt.

Liable, a. قابل kābil, مستعد mùsstà"ìdd ; [مسئول mèss'ūl.

Liar, s. یلانجی yàlànji.

Libel, s. افترا ìftirā ; —, v.a. افترا ا ìftirā-et. ["inden.

Libellous, a. افترا نوعندن ìftirā-nèv-

Liberal, a. الی‌اچیق èli-àchik, جومرد jùmèrd, سخاوتلو sàkhāvètli, سخی sàkhī ; مکمل mùkèmmèl.

Liberate, v.a. آزاد ا āzād-et.

Liberation, s. ازاد āzād.

Liberator, s. ازاد ایدن āzād-èden.

Libertine, s. چاپقین chàpkin, زنپاره zèn-pāré (zàmpara). [زنپاره‌لق zàmparalik.

Libertinism, s. چاپقینلق chàpkinlik ;

Liberty, s. سربستلك sèrbèsstlik (sèrbèsslik), سربستیت sèrbèsstìyyèt, سربستی sèrbèsstī ; حریت hùrrìyyèt, ازاد āzād, ازادکی āzādéghī ; اذن ìzn, مأذونیت mè'zūnìyyèt, رخصت rùkhsàt ; ترك ادب tèrki-èdèb, عارسزلق "ārsizlik, جسارت jèssārèt ; امتیاز ìmtiyāz, معافیت mù"āfiyyèt ; حدود hùdūd ; to be at —, کزمك ghèzmek, محبوس‌اولمامق màhbūss-òlmamak ; بوشده‌او bòshda-òl, خالی وقتی‌او khālī-wàkti-òl ; مأذون‌او mè'zūn-ol, اذنی‌او ìzni-òl ; to take the —, اجتسارا ìjtissār-et, جسارت ا jèssāret-et, اجترا ا ìjtirā-et, جرئت ا jùr'èt-et ; to take liberties, عارسزلنمق "ārsizlanmak, عاسزلق ا "ārsizlik-et.

Libidinous, a. شهوانی shèhwānī.

Libidinousness, s. شهوت shèhvèt.

Librarian, s. حافظ کتب hāfiz-kyùtub.

Library, s. کتبخانه kyùtub-khāné.

Lice, *s.* بتلر bìtler.

License, *s.* تذكره tèzkéré.

Licentious, *a.* چاپقين chàpkin; فاسق fāssik.

Lick, *v.a.* يالامق yàlamak; دوكمك dùghmek; الت ا ālt-et, مغلوب ا màghlūb-et, ينمك yènmek.

Lid, *s.* قپاق kàpak, اورتى ùrtu.

Lie, *s.* يلان yàlān, كذب kìzb, دروغ dùrūgh; كول صويى kyùl-sùyu, بوغاده bùghāda; —, *v.n.* ياتمق yàtmak; اولمق òlmak, بولنمق bùlunmak, واقع او vāki"-òl; موضوع او mèvzū"-ol; يلان سويلمك yàlān-sùwèylémek; — down, ياتمق yàtmak, اشاغى ياتمق àshàghi-yàtmak, اوزانمق ùzānmak; — with, مجامعه ا mùjāma"à-et; محول او mùhàvvel-ol, رأينه منوط او rè'yina-mènūt-òl, حواله اولنمق hàwālé-òlunmak; — at stake, اراده او àrada-òl.

Lieutenant, *s.* (navy) يوزباشى yùz-bāshi; (army) ملازم mùlāzim; — colonel, — governor, &c., — of grand-vizier, قائممقام kā'im-màkām (kàymakām); — of a judge, نائب nā'ib; — general, فريق fèrīk; — of a civil functionary, or individual, وكيل vèkīl.

Life, *s.* جان jān, حيات hàyāt; — time, عمر "ùmr, مدت عمر mùddèti-"ùmr; this —, دنيا dùnyā, عالم دنيا "ālémi-dùnyā, عالم فنا "ālémi-fènā, عالم كون وفساد "ālémi-kèvn-u-fèssād; the — to come, اخرت ākhirèt, دار بقا dāri-bākā.

Life-assurance, *s.* عمر سيغورته سى "ùmr-sìghūrtassi.

Life-boat, *s.* قضازده لرى قورتارمق ايچون بيوك صندال kàzāzèdéleri-kùrtarmak-ìchin-bìyuk-sàndal.

Lifeless, *a.* جانسز jānsiz.

Lifelessness, *s.* جانسزلق jānsizlik.

Life-preserver, *s.* بر نوع ال دينكى bìr-nèv-"èl-dèyneghi.

Lift, *v.a.* قالدرمق kàldirmak.

Light, *s.* اشيق ìshik, ايدينلق àydinlik, ضيا zìyā, نور nūr; اتش ātèsh; موم mùm; —, *a.* خفيف khàfīf; —, *v.n.* طوتشمق tùtushmak, يانمق yànmak; ايدينلنمق àydinlanmak; انمك èn-mek, قونمق kònmak; —, *v.a.* ياقمق yàkmak, طوتشدرمق tùtushdurmak, ايقاد ا īkād-et; — up, *v.n.* ايدينلنمق àydinlanmak; —, *v.a.* ياقمق yàkmak; ايدينلندرمق àydinlandirmak; — upon, راست كلمك rāsst-ghèlmek, تصادف ا tèssāduf-et, اوزرينه قونمق ùzèrina-kònmak.

Lighten, *v.n.* شمشك چاقمق shìmshek-chàkmak; —, *v.a.* خفيفلتمك khàfīfletmek, تخفيف ا tàkhfīf-et; ايدينلندرمق àydinlandirmak, تنوير ا tènvīr-et, اضائه ا ìzā'a-et; فراحلندرمق fèrāhlandirmak, تفريح ا tèfrīh-et.

Lighter, *s.* مغونه màghūna, صلاپوريه sàlapùriya, طومباز tòmbāz.

Lighthouse, *s.* فنار fèner.

Lightning, *s.* شمشك shìmshek, برق bèrk.

Lignum-vitæ, *s.* پلسنك اغاجى pèlé-ssènk-àghaji.

Like, *s.* اش èsh, شبه shìbh; —, *a.* بكزر bèngzer, مشابه mùshābih, شبيه shèbīh; —, *v.a.* سومك sèvmek, حظا

hAzz-et, تلذذ ا tèlèzzuz-et, خوشلنمق khòshlanmak ; —, *ad.* كبی ghìbi, وش vèsh.

Likelihood, *s.* احتمال ìhtimāl.

Likely, *a.* احتمال ìhtimāl, محتمل mùhtèmil, مأمول mèʿmūl, ملحوظ mèlhūz ; كوزل ghyùzèl, یاقشقلو yàkishìkli, كوسترشلو ghyùsstèrishli, دلبر dìlbèr. [تشبیه ا tèshbīh-et.

Liken, *v.a.* بكزتمك bèngzètmek,

Likeness, *s.* مشابهت mùshābéhèt ; رسم rèssm, تصویر tAssvīr.

Likewise, *ad.* هكذا hākézā, وكذا vèkézā, كذلك kèzālik.

Lilac, *s.* لیلاك lèylāk ; —, *a.* مور mòr.

Liliputian, *a.* اوفاق ùfAk.

Lily, *s.* زنبق zànbAk ; — of the valley, اینجوچیچكی ìnji-chìchèghi.

Limb, *s.* عضو ʿʿùzv (pl. أعضا àʿʿzā) ; كنار kènār, محیط mùhīt.

Lime, *s.* كرج or كیرج kìrèj ; لیمون līmòn ; — tree, فلامور filāmūr (ìkhlāmūr) ; bird —, — twig, اوكسه ùksé.

Limit, *s.* حد hàdd, پایان pàyān, اوج ùj, غایت ghāyet, نهایت nihāyet ; حدود hùdūd, سرحد sèr-hàdd, سنور sìnir ; —, *v.a.* حدتعیین ا hàdd-tàʿʿyīn-et ; حصرا hAssr-et, باغلامق bAghlamak.

Limited, *a.* محدود màhdūd.

Limp, *a.* كوسك ghèvshèk, یمشاق yìmushAk ; —, *v.n.* طوپاللمق tòpAllamak, اقصیمق Aksìmak.

Limpid, *a.* براق bèrrāk.

Limpidity, Limpidness, براقلق bèrrāklik.

Linden-tree, *s.* فلامور filāmūr (ikhlāmūr).

Line, *s.* چیزی chìzi, خط khAtt ; سطر sAtr ; ایپ ìp, حلاط hAlAt ; —, *v.a.* استار چكمك Asstar - chèkmek ; قاپلامق kAplamak ; branch —, شعبه یول shùʿʿbé-yòl ; main —, انا یول àna-yòl ; ship of the —, قالیون kàlyòn.

Lineage, *s.* نسل nèssl.

Linen, *a.* كتان kèten ; —, *s.* كتان بزی kèten-bèzi ; بز bèz ; چماشیر chàmAshir ; body —, چماشیر chàmAshir ; table —, سفره بزلری sòfra - bèzléri, پیشكیر میشكیر (pèshghir - mèshghir) ; bed —, چارشب مارشب (chàrshaf-màrshaf) ; — draper, بزجی bèzji.

Linger, *v.n.* كتمیوب وقت كچورمك ghìtméyup - wAkit - ghèchirmek ; أولوم درجه‌لرنده چوق وقت یاتمق ùlum-dèréjélerinda-chòk-wAkit-yàtmak.

Linguist, *s.* چوق لسان بلور اولان كمسنه chòk-lìssān-bìlir-òlan-kìmèssné.

Liniment, *s.* یاغ yàgh.

Lining, *s.* استار Asstar ; قاپلامه kAplama.

Link, *s.* زنجیرحلقه‌سی zìnjir-hAlkassi ; مشعله mèshʿʿàlé (mAshala).

Linseed, *s.* كتان تخمی kèten-tòkhumu, بذرتخمی bèzir-tòkhumu ; — oil, بذر یاغی bèzir-yàghi.

Lint, *s.* یاره بزی yàra-bèzi, مرهم بزی mèrhèm - bèzi ; دیتلمش كتان dìtilmish-kèten.

Lintel, *s.* اوست اشیكی ùsst-èshighi.

Lion, *s.* ارسلان àrsslan (Asslan), شیر shīr, اسد èssed, غضنفر ghAzanfèr ; —ess, دیشی ارسلان dìshi-(Asslan).

Lip, *s.* دوداق dùdàk, شفه shèfé, لب lèb; كنار kènar.

Liqueur, *s.* عنبريه ʻʻànbèrìyyé.

Liquid, *a.* سيال sèyyāl, مائع mā'iʻʻ; —, *s.* سياله sèyyālé, اقيجى نسنه àkiji-nèssné.

Liquidate, *v.a.* اودهمك ùdémek, قپاتمق kàpatmak, ايفا īfā-et, استيفا isstīfā-et.

Liquor, *s.* صو sù; ايچقى ìchki; in —, كيف kèyf, سرخوش sèrkhòsh.

Liquorice, *s.* ميان بالى mìyān-bàli; — root, ميان كوكى mìyān-kyukyu.

List, *s.* دفتر dèfter, پوصله pùssla; چوقه كنارى (chòha)-kènàri; ياتمه yàtma, اكريلك èghrilik; lists, *s. pl.* ميدان mèydān; —, *v.n.* استمك isstémek, جانى استمك jāni-isstémek; قولاق ويرمك kùlàk-vèrmek, دكلهمك dìnglémek (dīnémek); ياتمق yàtmak, اكلمك èghilmek; civil —, *s.* جيب همايون jèyb-hùmāyūn.

Listen, *v.n.* قولاق ويرمك kùlàk-vèrmek, دكلهمك dìnglémek (dīnémek).

Literal, *a.* لغوى lùghavī.

Literally, *ad.* حرف بحرف hàrf-bé-hàrf.

Literary, *a.* كتابه متعلق kìtābé-mù-taʻʻàllik.

Literati, *s. pl.* اصحاب دانش àsshābi-dānish.

Literature, *s.* مؤلفات mùʻèlléfāt; تأليف tèʻlīf.

Lithography, *s.* ليتوغرافيا lìtografía.

Litigation, *s.* احتجاج ìhtijāj, دعوى dàʻʻwà.

Litter, *s.* پسلك pìsslik; دسكره dèss-kéré, تختروان tàkhti-ràwān; كوبره ghyùbré, صاپ sàp; — down, *v.a.* التنه كوبره سرمك àltina-ghyùbré-sèr-mek (*or* صاپ sàp); — about, *v.a.* اتمق àtmak, دوكمك dùkmek.

Little, *a.* كچوك kùchuk, اوفاق ùfàk, صغير sàghīr; —, *ad.* از àz, ازبرشى àz-bìr-shèy, جزئيجه jùzʻījа; a —, *s.* جزئى براز bìr-àz, ازبرشى àz-bìr-shèy, جزئى برشى jùzʻī-bìr-shèy, ازبچوق برشى àz-bùchuk-bìr-shèy; — one, ياورى yàvri; چوجق chòjuk; — by —, ازرازر àzer-àzer, يواش يواش yāwàsh-yāwàsh, تدريجله tèdrījla, على التدريج ʻʻàlè-'t-tèdrīj, جسته جسته jèssté-jèssté.

Live, *v.n.* يشامق yàshamak, معمراو mùʻʻàmmer-òl; كچنمك ghèchinmek, تعيش ا tàʻʻàyyush-et, كفاف نفس ا kèfāfi-nèfss-et; بسلنمك bèsslènmek, تغدى ا tàghàddī-et; — upon, يمك yèmek, بسلنمك bèsslènmek; كچنمك ghèchinmek.

Livelihood, *s.* كچنهجك ghèchinéjek, كفاف نفس kèfāfi-nèfss.

Liveliness, *s.* جانلولق jānlulik; اويناقلق òynaklik; فرح fìrah; the livelong day, بتون كون bìtun-ghyùn.

Lively, *a.* اوينيور òyniyor, اويناق òynàk; شن شوخ shèn-shūkh; مفرح mùfèrrih, طرب انكيز tàrab-ènghīz.

Liver, *s.* قره جكر kàra-jìgher, جكر jìgher.

Livery, *s.* خدمتكارك رسمى البسهسى hìzmetkyārin-rèssmī-èlbisséssi.

Live-stock, *s.* حيوانات hàywānàt.

Livid, *a.* مور mòr; الق بولاق àlak-bùlak.

Living, *s.* کچنه‌جك ghèchinéjek, کفاف نفس kèfāfi-nèfss; صورت تعیش sūrèti-tà''àyyush; یمك yèmèk, طعام tà''ām; امامت imāmèt; —, *a.* دیری diri, صاغ sàgh, حیاتده hàyātda, برحیات bèr-hàyāt, حی hàyy, جانوار jānvār.

Lizard, *s.* کرتنکلر kèrtènkèlèr (kèrtènkèlé).

Load, *s.* یوك yùk, بار bār, حموله hà-mūlé; —, *v.a.* یوکلتمك yùklètmek; طولدرمق dòldurmak.

Loadstone, *s.* مقناطیس miknātiss (mìkhlàdiz-tāshi).

Loaf, *s.* صومون sòmun; کله kèllé.

Loan, *s.* اودنج ùdunj, قرض kàrz, استقراض isstikrāz.

Loathe, *v.a.* ایکرنمك ighrènmek, تکسنمك tiksinmek, استکراه ا isstik-rāh-et, اکراه ا ikrāh-et.

Lobster, *s.* استاقوز isstàkoz.

Local, *a.* یرلو yèrli, موقعی mèvki''ī; جزئی jùz'ī, منحصر mùnhàssir.

Locality, *s.* یر yèr, محل màhàll, موقع mèvki'', موضع mèvzi''.

Lock, *s.* کلید kìlid; چقماق chàkmak; حوض hàwuz; دمت dèmet; —, *v.n.* کلیدلنمك kilidlènmek, کتلنمك kìtlènmek; —, *v.a.* کلیدلمك kìlidlémek, کتلمك kìtlémek; — in, ایچروکتلمك ìchèri-kìtlémek; — out, طیشاری کتلمك dìshāri-kìtlémek; — up, کتلمك kìtlémek, کتلیویرمك kìtléyivèrmek.

Locksmith, *s.* چلنکیر chìlinghir.

Locust, *s.* چکرکه chèkirghé; کچی بوینوزی kèchi-bòynuzu.

Lodge, *s.* قپوجی اوطه‌سی kāpiji-òdassi, قپوجی اوی kāpiji-èvi; باغ اوی bāgh-èvi; —, *v.n.* اوطورمق òturmak, مسافراو mùssāfir-òl, مسافرة اوطورمق mùssāférétèn-òturmak; قالمق kàl-mak; —, *v.a.* اوطورتمق òturtmak; اتمق ātmak; عرض ا ''àrz-et.

Lodger, *s.* کراجی kìrāji, مسافر mùssāfir.

Lodging, Lodgings, *s.* اوطه òda, قوناق kònak.

Loft, *s.* طوان اراسی tāwan-àrassi. [tèfi''.

Lofty, *a.* یوکسك yùksèk, مرتفع mùr-

Log, *s.* اوطون òdun; کتوك kyùtuk; پراکته pàrakèta; انساب ènsāb; log. sine, نسبت جیبیه nìssbèti-jèy-bìyyé; log. cosine, تمام نسبت جیبیه tāmāmi-nìssbèti-jèybìyyé; log. tan-gent, نسبت ظلیه nìssbèti-zìllìyyé; to heave the —, پراکته اتمق pàrakèta-ātmak. [انساب ènsāb.

Logarithm, *s.* لغارتمه lùghārìtma;

Log-book, *s.* گمی ژورنالی ghèmi-zhūrnāli.

Loggerhead, *s.* احمق àhmàk; to fall, go to loggerheads, بوزشمق bòzush-

Logic, *s.* منطق māntik. [mak.

Log-line, *s.* پراکته سجیمی pàrakèta-

Logwood, *s.* بقام bākkàm. [sìjimi.

Loins, *s.* بل bèl, صلب sùlb.

Loiter, *v.n.* کزنمك ghèzinmek, طولاشمق dòlashmak, وقت کچورمك wākit-ghèchirmek, وقت غائب ا wākit-(kā'ib)-et.

Lombard, *s.* لومبارد یالو lòmbardìali.

Lombardy, *s.* لومباردیا lòmbardìa.

London (town of), *s.* لوندره شهری Lòndra-shèhiri.

Londoner, *s.* لوندره‌لو lòndrali. [ìsssiz.

Lonely, *a.* تنها tènhā; یالکز yàlingiz; اعسز

Long, *a.* اوزون ùzun, طویل tàwīl; as — as, قدر kàdar; —, *v.n.* اش یرمك àsh-yèrmek; — for, استمك ìsstémek, جانی استمك jāni-ìsstémek; ارامق àramak; — after, ارامق àramak, مشتاق او mùshtāk-òl, اشتیاق ا ìshtìyāk-et.

Longer, *a.* دها اوزون dàhà-ùzun; —, *ad.* any —, no —, ارتق àrtik, زیاده zìyādé; a little —, بر از دها bìr-àz-dàhà.

Longevity, *s.* طول عمر tùl-i-''ùmr.

Longitude, *s.* طول tūl, طول بلد tūlibèled.

Look, *s.* باقش bàkish, نظر nàzar, لحظه làhza; بکز bèngz, چهره chèhré, سیما sīmā; قیافت kìyāfèt, صورت sūrèt, هیئت hèy'èt, قیلق kìlik; —, *v.n.* باقمق bàkmak, نظرا nàzar-et; سیرا sèyr-et, تماشا ا tàmāshā-et; کلمك ghèlmek, کوزه کورنمك ghyùzé-ghyùrunmek; — like, بکزمك bèngzémek; — about, باقنمق bàkinmak; ارامق àramak; — after, باقمق bàkmak, کوزتمك ghyùzetmek; ارامق àramak; — big, قورلمق kùrulmak, قبادایلق ا kàba-dàylik-et; — down upon, یوقاریدن اشاغی باقمق yùkàri-dan-àshaghi-bàkmak; استحقارا ìss-tìhkār-et, خوارباقمق khòr-bàkmak; — for, ارامق àramak; بکلمك bèklé-mek, منتظراو mùntàzir-òl, مأمول ا me'mūl-et; — into, تفتیش ا tèftīsh-et; تجسس ا tèjèsssuss-et; — on, باقمق bàkmak, سیرا sèyr-et; — out, ایوجه باقمق īyija-bàkmak, دقت ا dikkàt-et; — well, کوزل او ghyùzèl-òl, یاقشمق yàkishmak, یراشمق yàrashmak; چهره‌سی ایواو chèhréssi-īyi-òl. [mìr'àt.

Looking-glass, *s.* ایینه āyiné, مرآت

Loom, *s.* بزدستکاهی bèz-dèsstghyāhi, دستکاه dèsstghyāh (tèzghyāh); —, *v.n.* خیال میال کوزکمك khàyāl-màyāl-ghyùzukmek.

Loop, *s.* الملك ìlmik; الیك ìlik.

Loophole, *s.* باجه bàja, ایدینلق باجه‌سی àydinlik-bàjassi; قاچامق kàchamak.

Loose, *s.* اطلاق عنان ìtlàki-''ìnān; —, *a.* کوشك ghèvshèk; چوزیلو chùzulu; صاللانیور sàllàniyor; مبهم mùbhèm; ربطسز ràbtsiz; رابطه‌سز ràbitassiz, یرامز yàramàz, چاپقین chàpkin; —, *v.a.* اچمق àchmak, چوزمك chùzmek; براقمق bràkmak; صالیویرمك sàli-vèrmek. [لینت ویرمك līnèt-vèrmek.

Loosen, *v.a.* کوشتمك ghèvshètmek;

Looseness, *s.* کوشکلك ghèvsheklik; (of bowels) لینت līnèt; اسهال ìsshāl; (of morals) چاپقینلق chàpkinlik.

Loquacious, *a.* کوزه ghèvézé; لافزن lāfzèn.

Loquacity, *s.* کوزه‌لك ghèvézèlik.

Lord, *s.* افندی èfèndi, بك bègh; the Lord God, رب العالمین ràbbu-'l-''ālémīn; the Lord of glory, رب العزت ràbbu-'l-''ìzzèt; our Lord, افندیمز èfèndimiz; ربمز تعالی ràbbimiz-tà''ālà;

our Lord Jesus Christ, عیسی المسیح افندیمز حضرتلری "Īssà - 'l - Mèssīh- -èfèndimiz - hÀzrètléri, *or* ربمز تعالی عیسی المسیح حضرتلری rÀbbimiz-tà- "ālà-"īssà-'l-mèssīh-hÀzrètléri; our Lord and Saviour, ربمز وخلاصمز rÀbbi-miz-vÈ-khàllāssimiz; our sovereign Lord, پادشاهمز افندیمز pādishāhimiz- -èfèndimiz; our Lord and Master, ولی نعمتمز افندیمز vèlī-nì"mètimiz- -èfèndimiz.

Lose, *v.a.* غائب ا ghā'ib-et (kàybet), ضائع ا zā'i"-et, الدن قاچرمق Èldan- -kÀchirmak, دن او dan-òl; — ground, یر غائب ا yÈr-ghā'ib-et, کیرولمك ghè-rilémek; — one's way, یول غائب ا yòl-ghā'ib-et, یول شاشرمق yòl-shà-shirmak, [tèlef; تلفیات tèlefìyyāt.

Loss, *s.* ضرر zàrar, زیان zìyān; تلف

Lot, *s.* قسمت kìssmèt; lots, قرعه kùr"à; to draw lots, قرعه چکمك [kùr"à-chèkmek.

Lotion, *s.* صو sù.

Lottery, *s.* پیانقو pìyànko. [بلند bùlènd.

Loud, *a.* پك pèk, پك سسلو pèk-sèssli,

Louse, *s.* بت bìt, کهله kèhlÉ; —, *v.n.* بتلنمك bìtlÈnmek; —, *v.a.* کهله لرینی قیرمق kèhlÈlérini-kìrmak.

Lout, *s.* اشك èshek.

Love, *s.* عشق "Àshk, سوکی sÈvghi; محبت màhàbbet; —, *v.a.* سومك sÈvmek; عاشق او "àshik-òl.

Love-apple, *s.* فرنك پاطلیجانی firÈnk- -pÀtlìjāni; (green) قواته kÀwAtà.

Lovely, *a.* سوکیلو sÈvghili, کوزل ghyùzèl, دلبر dìlbÈr.

Lover, *s.* عاشق "Āshik; زنپاره (zàm-para); هوسلو hàvèssli; مراقلو mèrĀkli.

Low, *a.* اشاغی Àshāghi; الچق Àlchàk; باصق bÀssik; حقیر hàkīr; دنی dènī; چاپقین chÀpkin, نامرد nā-mèrd; یواش yāwÀsh; پس pèss; —, *v.n.* اینك کبی سس ویرمك īnèk-ghìbi-sèss-vÈrmek. [-dìyāri.

Low Countries, فلمنك دیاری fìlÉmÈnk-

Lower, *a.* دها الچق dàhà-Àlchàk; دها اشاغی dàhà-Àshàghi; —, *v.a.* اندرمك èndirmek; اشاغیلتمق Àshäghìlatmak; صارقتمق sàrkitmak; ماینه ا màyna-et; ترذیل ا tèrzīl-et, محقرا mÙhÀkkàr-et; ضعیفلتمق zà"īflatmak; —, *v.n.* قرارمق kÀrarmak. [منقاد mùnkĀd.

Loyal, *a.* صادق sĀdik, مطیع mùtī",

Lucid, *a.* واضح vwāzih.

Lucidity, *s.* وضوح vwÙzÙh.

Lucifer, *s.* کبریت kìbrīt; زهره zùhrÉ; شیطان shèytān.

Luck, *s.* بخت bàkht, طالع tāli".

Lucky, *a.* بختلو bàkhtli.

Lucrative, *a.* کارلو kyārli.

Lucre, *s.* کار kyār; پاره pārÉ.

Ludicrous, *a.* کولنه جك ghyùlenejek.

Luff, *v.n.* اورصه ا òrsa-èt.

Luggage, *s.* اشیا èshyā, پرتی pàrti, اثقال èsskĀl, یوك yùk, صندق ماندق sÀndik-mÀndik.

Lugger, *s.* بیوك صندال bìyuk-sÀndAl.

Lukewarm, *a.* ایلیجق ìlijàk; اغر Àghir, کوشك ghèvshèk, غیرتسز ghàyretsiz.

Lull, *v.n.* یاتشمق yàtishmak; —, *s.* تسکین tèsskīn.

Luminary, *s.* جسم منیر jìssm-mùnīr.

Luminous, *a.* منیر mùnīr.

Lump, *s.* پارچه pàrcha, طوپ tòp ; —, *v.a.* کوتری المق ghyùturu - àlmak ; کوتری ویرمك ghyùturu - vèrmek ; کوتری یاپمق ghyùturu - yàpmak ; کوتری یاپدرمق ghyùturu-yàpdirmak.

Lunacy, *s.* دلیلك dèlilik, جنت jìnnèt, [جنون jùnūn.

Lunar, *a.* قمری kàmérī.

Lunatic, *a.* and *s.* دلی dèli, مجنون mèjnūn. [altissi.

Lunch, *s.* اویله قهوالتیسی ùylé-kàhwé-

Lungs, *s. pl.* جگر jìghèr, اق جگر àk-[jìghèr.

Luscious, *a.* پك طاتلو pèk-tàtli.

Luserne, Lucerne, *s.* یونجه yònja.

Lust, *s.* شهوت shèhvèt ; — after, *v.n.* شهوتلنمك shèhvètlenmek.

Lustre, *s.* پارلاقلق pàrlalik, رونق rèvnàk ; اویزه àvīzé.

Lusty, *a.* دنج dìnj, قوتلو kùvvètli.

Lute, *s.* ساز sāz ; لاوطه làwuta ; عود ūd.

Luxuriant, *a.* قوتلو kùvvètli, برکتلو bèré-kètli, چوق chòk, مبذول mèbzūl.

Luxurious, *a.* سلطنتلو sàltanàtli, طنطنه‌لو tàntanali ; اعلی à''là, نفیس nèfiss.

Luxury, *s.* سلطنت sàltanàt, طنطنه tàntana ; سفاهت sèfāhàt ; نفیس شی nèfīss-shèy.

Lying-in, *s.* چوجق طوغره جق وقت chò-juk-dòghurajak-wàkit ; لوغوسه لق وقتی lòghussalik-wàkti.

Lymphatic, *a.* بلغمی bàlghàmī. [làk.

Lynx, *s.* وشق vàshak, قره قولاق kàra-kù-

Lyre, *s.* بربط bèrbèt.

Lyric, *s.* غزل ghàzèl.

M.

Macaroni, *s.* مقارنه màkàrna.

Mace, *s.* طوپوز tòpuz, بوزطغان bòzdaghàn ; هندوستان جوزی قبوغی hìndusstān-jèvizi-kàbughu. [lìwā-i-sélanīk.

Macedonia, *s.* فلبه filibé ; لواء سلانیك

Machine, Machinery, *s.* چرخ chàrkh, ماکینه màkina, الت ālet, الات ālāt.

Machinist, *s.* چرخجی chàrkhji.

Mackerel, *s.* اسقومری ùsskùmru.

Mad, *a.* دلی dèli, دیوانه dīwāné ; مجنون mèjnūn, قاچق kàchik, چلدرمش chìldirmish ; to go —, *v.n.* چلدرمك chìldirmek, دلی او dèli-òl, تجنن ا tè-jènnun-et, جنت کتورمك jìnnèt-ghè-tirmek. [قوقونا kòkona.

Madam, *s.* حانم افندی khànim-èfèndi ;

Madder, *s.* کوك بویا kyùk-bòya.

Mad-house, *s.* تیمارخانه tīmar-khāné, بیمارخانه bīmar-khāné.

Madman, *s.* دلی dèli.

Madness, *s.* دلیلك dèlilik, جنت jìnnèt, جنون jùnūn. [yém.

Madona, *s.* حضرت مریم hàzrèti-mèr-

Magazine, *s.* مغازه màghaza ; انبار ànbār ; مخزن màkhzèn ; غزته ghàzèta ; powder —, جبخانه jèb-khāné.

Maggot, *s.* قورت kùrt.

Magic, *s.* سحر sìhr ; — lantern, خیالجی فناری khàyālji-fènéri.

Magician, *s.* سحرباز sìhrbāz, سحار sàhhār.

Magistracy, *s.* حاکملك hākimlik ; حکام hùkkyām. [مأمور mè'mūr.

Magistrate, *s.* حاکم hākim, ضابط zābit,

Magnanimity, *s.* علوجناب "ùlùvvi-jènāb, علوفطرت "ùlùvvi-fitrèt.

Magnanimous, *a.* على جناب "āli-jènāb.

Magnesia, *s.* كهرچاله‌قايمغى ghyùhèr-chilé - kàymaghi; مغنيسا قصبه‌سى màghnìsia-kàssabassi. [lādiz).

Magnet, *s.* مقناطيس mìknātiss (mìkh-

Magnificence, *s.* سلطنت sàltanàt, طنطنه tàntana, دبدبه dèbdébé; فخامت fàkhāmèt.

Magnificent, *a.* پك‌كوزل pèk-ghyùzèl; سلطنتلو sàltanàtli; فخيم fàkhīm, فخامتلو fàkhāmètlū.

Magnify, *v.a.* بيوتمك bìyutmek; تحميد وتمجيدا tàhmīd-u-tèmjīd-et.

Magnifying-glass, *s.* پرتوسوز pèrtevsūz (pèrtevsiz).

Magnitude, *s.* بيوكلك bìyuklik, حجم hàjm; اهميت èhèmmìyyèt.

Magpie, *s.* صقصغان sàksaghàn. [-àghaji.

Mahogany, *s.* ماغون‌اغاجى màghon-

Mahometan, *a.* محمدى mùhàmmédī, اسلامى ìsslāmī; —, *s.* مسلم mùsslim, اهل‌اسلام èhli-ìsslām, مسلمان mùss-limān. [اسلام dīni-ìsslām.

Mahometanism, *s.* اسلام ìsslām, دين

Maid, Maiden, *s.* قيز kìz, قيزاوغلان‌قيز kìz-òghlan-kìz, باكره bākiré.

Maidenhead, *s.* قيزلق kìzlìk, بكر bìkr.

Maidservant, *s.* (free) بسلمه bèssléмé; (slave) خلايق khàlāyìk, جاريه jārìyyé.

Mail, *s.* پوسته pòssta; زره zìrh.

Maim, *v.a.* الني‌سقطا èlini-sàkat-et, قولني‌سقطا kòlunu-sàkat-et.

Main, *a.* بيوك bìyuk, انا àna, اصل àssl; —, *s.* دكز dèngiz; قوت kùvvèt; with all his might and main, وارقوتيله vār-kùvvètīla; — land, اصل‌قره àssl-kàra; — mast, اورطه‌ديرك òrta-dìrèk, غراندى ديركى ghràndi-dìrèghī; — sail, غراندى ghràndi; — topsail, غابيه‌غراندى ghàbiya-ghràndi.

Maintain, *v.a.* بسلمك bèsslémek; ارقه او àrka-òl, طوتمق tùtmak; ادعاا ìddi"ā-et; ابقاا ìbkā-et; صيانتا sìyānèt-et, وقايها vìkāyé-et.

Maintenance, *s.* كچنه‌جك ghèchinéjek, تعيش tà"àyyush, نفقه nàfaka, كفاف نفس kèfāfi-nèfss; ابقا ìbkā; صيانت sìyānèt, وقايه vìkāyé.

Maize, *s.* مصر بغدايى mìssir-bòghdayi.

Majestic, *a.* كوسترشلو ghyùssterishli; هيبتلو hèybetli.

Majesty, *s.* شوكت shèvkèt, مهابت màhābèt; His Majesty (the Sultan), سوكتلو افنديمز shèvkètli - èfèndimiz; His (or Her) Majesty the King, حشمتلوقرال‌جنابلرى hàshmètli-kìràl-jènàbléri, (or قراليچه kìrālìcha, the Queen, *or* ايمپراطور ìmpérātòr, the Emperor, &c.)

Major, *a.* اكثرى èksérī; اعظم à"zàm, اكبر èkbèr; كلى kyùllī; بالغ bāligh; —, *s.* بيكباشى bìng-bàshi; drum —, طامبورماژور tàmbur-màzhòr; — domo, كتخدا kyāya; وكيلخرج vèkīl-khàrj; — general, لواپاشا lìwā-pàsha.

Majority, *s.* اكثريت èksèrìyyèt; بلوغ bùlūgh, سن‌بلوغ sìnni - bùlūgh; بيكباشيلك bìng-bàshìlìk.

Make, *s.* بچم bìchim, صورت sūrèt, هيئت hèy'èt, ياپلش yàpılish; اعماليه ì''mālìyyé; —, *v.a.* ياپمق yàpmak, اعمال ا ì''māl-et; وجوده كتورمك vùjūda-ghètirmek; يراتمق yèratmak, خلق ا khàlk-et; ايتمك ètmek, ايلمك èylémek, قيلمق kılmak; — a fool of, الداتمق aldatmak, كپازه ا képāzé-et, مسخره يه چويرمك massharaya-chèvirmek; — a mistake, ياكلمق yàngılmak, سهوا sèhv-et, خطاا khata-et, ياكلشلق ا yàngılishlık-et; — angry, دارلتمق darıltmak, قيزدرمق kızdırmak, كوجندرمك ghyùjèndirmek; — a pen, قلم يونتمق kàlem-yòntmak, (a new pen) قلم اچمق kàlem-àchmak; — at, صالدرمق saldırmak, هجوم ا hùjūm-et; — away with, اوچرمق ùchurmak, تلف ا tèlef-et; — for, يول طوتمق yòl-tùtmak; — good, يرينه كتورمك yèrina-ghètirmek; — haste, چابك او chàbık-òl, عجله ا ''ajélé-et; — land, دكزده قره كورنمك dèngizda-kàra-ghyùrunmek; — many words, اوزاتمق ùzatmak, چوق سويلمك chòk-sùwèylémek; — off, كتمك ghitmek, صاوشمق sàwushmak; — off with, المق almak; چالمق chalmak; — one of a company, رفاقت ا rèfākàt-et, داخل ا dākhil-òl; — one's escape, قاچمق kachmak; قورتلمق kùrtūlmak; — out, چيقارمق chìkàrmak, اوقومق òkumak; اثبات ا ìssbāt-et; حساب ا hissāb-et; — over, دورا dèvr-et; حواله ا hàwālé-et; — towards, يول طوتمق yòl-tùtmak; — up, طوپلامق tòplamak; تكميل ا tèkmīl-et, تمام ا tamam-et; — up to, يانينه وارمق yànina-vàrmak; — it up, بارشمق barishmak; — it up to, تضمين ا tazmīn-et, تماملمق tamamlamak; — use of, قوللانمق kùllanmak, استعمال ا ìsstì''māl-et.

Maladministration, *s.* سؤ اداره sù'i-ìdāré.

Malady, *s.* درد dèrd, علت ''ìllèt.

Malaria, *s.* هواى وخيم hàwa-i-vwàkhīm.

Male, *a.* and *s.* اركك èrkek, نر nèr, ذكر zèker (pl. ذكور zùkyūr).

Malediction, *s.* بد دعا bèd-dù''ā.

Malefactor, *s.* صاحب جنحه sāhib-jùnhà, مجرم mùjrim.

Malevolence, *s.* عداوت ''àdāvèt, عدوان ''ùdvan, حقد hìkd, بغض bùghz.

Malevolent, *a.* كوتى kyùtu.

Malice, *s.* سوء قصد sù'i-kassd, سوء نيت sù'i-nìyyèt, كوتيلك kyùtulik.

Malicious, *a.* كوتى kyùtu.

Maliciousness, *s.* كوتيلك kyùtuluk.

Malign, *v.a.* افترا ا ìftirā-et.

Malignant, *a.* كوتى kyùtu.

Malignity, *s.* كوتيلك kyùtuluk.

Mallet, *s.* طوقمق tòkmak.

Mallows, *s.* ابه كومجى èbé-ghyùmèji.

Malt, *s.* بيرالق ارپه bìralik-àrpa.

Malta, *s.* مالطه Màlta.

Malt-liquor, *s.* بيرا bìra.

Maltreatment, *s.* اذيت èzìyyèt.

Mamma, *s.* انا àna, نينه nìné, والده vālìdé.

Man, *s.* ادم ādem (adam), انسان ìnsān,

مرد mèrd, مردم mèrdum; — of war, جنك كميسى jènk-ghèmissi, قاليون kàlyòn, — of war's man, قاليونجى نفرى kàlyònji-nèféri; —, v.a. ادم ايله دوناتمق Adam-ila-dònatmak, ادم قومق Adam-kòmak; دوناتمق dònat-mak, باشنه وارمق bAshina-vàrmak.

Manage, v.n. اويدرمق ùydurmak; ايدنمك èdinmek; كچنمك ghèchin-mek; —, v.a. قوللانمق kùllAnmak; ضبط ا zAbt-et; اداره ا idārÉ-et; اويدرمق ùydurmak, ياپمق yàpmak, كورمك [ghyùrmek.

Management, s. اداره idārÉ.

Manager, s. مدير mûdīr.

Mandate, s. اراده iradÉ, فرمان fèrmān, حكم hùkm, امر èmr.

Mane, s. يله yèlÉ.

Mange, s. اويوز ùyuz.

Manger, s. يملك yèmlik.

Mangle, s. جندره jèndérÉ; —, v.a. يرتمق yìrtmak, پاره لمك pārÉlémek; جندره دن كچورمك jèndérÉdan-ghè-[chirmek.

Manhood, s. ادملق Adamlik.

Mania, s. دليلك dèlilik.

Maniac, s. دلى dèli, چلغين chìlghin, ديوانه dīwānÉ, مجنون mèjnūn.

Manifest, s. كمينك حجتى ghèmining-hùjjèti; —, a. اشكار Ashikyār, بديهى bèdihī, ظاهر zāhir, بديدار bèdīdār, هويدا hùwèydā; —, v.a. كوسترمك ghyùsstermek, اظهارا izhār-et.

Manifesto, s. بياننامه bèyān-nāmÉ, اعلاننامه ì''lān-nāmÉ.

Mankind, s. بنى ادم bèni-ādem, نوع بنى بشر nèv''i-bèni-bèsher, ناس nāss.

Manly, a. مرد mèrd, مردانه mèrdānÉ, ادم Adam.

Manna, s. قدرت حلواسى kùdrèt-[hèlwāssi.

Manner, s. طرز tàrz, درلو dùrlu (tùrlu), وجه vèjh; manners, s. pl. اطوار Atwār; اخلاق àkhlāk; اداب ādāb.

Manœuvre, s. طولاب dòlAb, اويون òyun; مانوره mànèvra; —, v.n. طولاب چويرمك dòlAb-chèvirmek, اويون چيقارمق òyun-chìkàrmak; مانوره چويرمك mànèvra-chèvirmek.

Mansion, s. قوناق kònak.

Mantel-piece, Mantel-shelf, s. اوجاق اوستنده اولان راف òjak-ùsstindÉ-òlan-rAf.

Mantua (town of), s. مانتوا شهرى [màntua-shèhiri.

Manual, s. رساله rìssālÉ; —, a. ال ايله اجرا اولنان Èl-ila-ijrā-òlunan; — exer-cise, عجمى تفنك تعليمى ''Ajémi-tùfèk-tà''līmī; sign —, امضا imzā.

Manufactory, s. فابريقه fàbrika.

Manufacture, s. فابريقه fàbrika, كارخانه kyār-khānÉ; مال māl, (pl.) اعمالات i''mālāt, مصنوعات mAssnū''āt; اعمال ì''māl; —, v.a. ياپمق yàp-mak, اعمال ا ì''māl-et.

Manufacturer, s. فابريقه جى fàbrikaji.

Manumission, s. ازاد āzād.

Manumit, v.a. ازاد ا āzād-et.

Manure, s. كوبره ghyùbrÉ; —, v.a. كوبره ويرمك ghyùbrÉ-vèrmek.

Manuscript, a. ال يازيسى Èl-yàzissi; —, s. ال يازيسى كتاب Èl-yàzissi-kìtAb.

Many, *a.* چوق chòk, وافر wāfir; a great —, چوق chòk, برچوق bìrchòk; — a, [نیجه nījé.

Map, *s.* جریطه khàrīta.

Maple, *s.* بر جنس أغاج bīr-jìnss-àghaj.

Marauder, *s.* یغماجی yàghmaji.

Marble, *s.* مرمر mèrmer.

March, *s.* مارت màrt; مارش màrsh; عسکریورومسی ʿàsskèr-yùruméssi; یول yòl; —, *v.n.* یورومك *or* یوریمك yùrumek; —, *v.a.* یوروتمك yùrutmek; سوق ا sèvk-et, کوترمك ghyùturmek; —, *int.* ارش àrsh; — in, کیرمك ghìrmek; — off, کتمك ghìtmek; کوترمك ghyùturmek; — on, ایلرو کتمك ìléri-ghìt-mek; — out, چیقمق chìkmak.

Mare, *s.* قسراق kìssràk.

Margin, *s.* کنار kènār; فضله fàzla; marginal note, کنار kènār; حاشیه [hāshìyyé.

Marigold, *s.* نرکس nèrghiss.

Marine, *a.* بحری bàhrī, بحریه bàhrìyyé; —, *s.* کافهٔ تجملات بحریه kyāffé'i-tèjèmmulāti-bàhrìyyé; بحریه تفنکجیسی bàhrìyyé-tùfènkjissi; نوش پوتقال bòsh-pùtkal.

Mariner, *s.* کمیجی ghèmiji.

Maritime, *a.* بحری bàhrī; ساحلی sāhilī.

Mark, *s.* چیزی chìzi, اشارت ìshāret, نشان nìshān; اثر èsser; تمغا (dàmgha); شخص shàkhss; نشان nìshān, هدف hèdef; —, *v.n.* یازمق yàzmak, چیزمك chìzmek; دقت ا dìkkàt-et; —, *v.a.* اشارت قومق ìshāret-komak, نشان قومق nìshān-kòmak; تمغا اورمق dàmgha-wùr-mak; داغلامق dàghlamak; اثربراقمق èsser-bràkmak; دقت ا dìkkàt-et; of —, معتبر mù''tébèr, بلاوباشلو bèlli-bàshli, متعارف mùtaʿ'ārif, معلوم mà''lūm. [چارشی chàrshi.

Market, *s.* پازار pàzàr; چارسو chàrsū,

Marking-iron, *s.* داغ dàgh.

Marmalade, *s.* رچل rèchel.

Marque (letters of), *s.* قورصانلق فرمانی kùrsānlik-fèrmāni.

Marquee, *s.* ایکی دیرکلوچادر ìki-dìrèkli-chàdir; بیوك چادر bìyuk-chàdir.

Marquess, Marquis, *s.* رتبهٔ ثالثه بکی rùtbé'i-sālissé-bèghi.

Marriage, *s.* نکاح nìkyāh, اولنش èvlènish, تزوج tèzèvvuj, ازدواج ìzdiwāj.

Marriageable, *a.* اوره جك èvéréjek; کلینلك ghèlinlik.

Married, *a.* اولو èvli, متأهل mùtéʿèhhil; قوجه‌ده kòjada, منکوحه mènkyūha.

Marrow, *s.* الك ìlik, مغز màghz.

Marry, *v.n.* اولنمك èvlenmek, قاری المق kàri-àlmak, تأهل ا tèʿèhhul-et; قوجه‌یه وارمق kòjaya-vàrmak; —, *v.a.* المق àlmak, تزوج ا tèzèvvuj-et; اولندرمك èvlèndirmek, تزویج ا tèzvīj-et; قوجه‌یه ویرمك kòjaya-vèrmek; عقدا ''àkd-et, نکاح ا nikyāh-et.

Mars, *s.* مریخ یلدیزی mèrrīkh-yìldìzi; جنك معبودك اسمی jènk-mà''būdūn-ìssmi.

Marsh, *s.* بطاق bàtàk, بطاقلق bàtaklìk.

Marshal, *s.* چاوش chàwush; earl —, lord —, جاوش باشی chàwush-bàshi;

field —, سردارپایه‌لوسی sèrdār-pàyé-lissi; —, *v.a.* ترتیب‌ا tèrtīb-et.

Mart, *s.* بدستان bèdisstèn, بزستان bèzisstèn, بزازاستان bèzzāzisstān; قپان kàpan; چارشی chàrshi.

Marten-sable, *s.* سمور (sàmūr).

Martial, *a.* حربی hàrbī; عسکری "àsskérī; court —, دیوان حرب dīwāni-hàrb.

Martyr, *s.* شهید shèhīd.

Martyrdom, *s.* شهادت shàhādèt, شهیدلك shèhīdlik. [غریب ghàrīb.

Marvellous, *a.* عجیب "àjīb ("àjā'ib),

Masculine, *a.* مذكر mùzèkker.

Mason, *s.* طاشجی tàshji; دیوارجی dìwàrji.

Masonry, *s.* طاش دیوار tàsh-dìwàr; طاشجیلق tàshjilik; دیوارجیلق dìwàrjilik.

Mass, *s.* حجم hàjm, جرم jùrm; یغین yìghin; طوپ tòp, كومه kyùmé; طابور tàbur, فوج fèvj; قتولیكلرك بادراقی kàtoliklèring-bàdaràki; —, *v.a.* طوپ‌ا tòp-et; یغمق yìghmak.

Massacre, *s.* قتل عام kàtli-"āmm; —, *v.a.* قیرمق kìrmak, قتل‌ا kàtl-et, اولدرمك ùldurmek, پاره‌لمك (pàralamak). [اغر àghir, قالین kàlin.

Massive, *a.* متین mètīn, قونت kùnt,

Mast, *s.* دیرك dìrèk, ستون sùtūn, عمود "àmūd; كولكن اغاجنك یمشی ghyùlghèn-àghajining-yèmishi; top —, غابیه‌چبوغی ghàbiya-chìbùghu; top-gallant —, بابافنغوچبوغی bàba-fingo-chìbùghu.

Master, *s.* افندی èfèndi; اغا àgha; استاد ùsstād (ùssta); خوجه khòja; معلم mù"àllim; ضابط zābit; غالب ghālib; كمی رئیسی ghèmi-rè'īssi, قپودان kàpudān (kàptan); —, *v.a.* حقندن كلمك hàkkindan-ghèlmek, غالب‌او ghālib-òl; — hand, استادالی ùsstād-èli; — key, تام‌اناختار tàmm-ànakhtàr; — of the Horse, میراخور mīrì-àkhòr (èmrakhòr).

Masterpiece, *s.* استادایشی ùsstād-ìshi.

Mastic, *s.* مصطقی màsstaki, ساقز sàkiz; معجون mà"jūn.

Mat, *s.* حصیر hàssir; —, *v.n.* بربرینه یاپشمق bìr-bìrina-yàpishmak, كچه‌لنمك kèchélènmek.

Match, *s.* كبریت kìbrit; اش èsh, عین "àyn, مثل missl; كفو kyùfv, اقران àkrān, ارقه‌داش àrkadash, باش bàsh, بر bìr, برابر bèrābèr, مساوی mùssāvi; چیقشیر chìkishir, چیقشه‌جق chìkishajak, حقندن كلور hàkkindan-ghèlir; التده قالمز àltda-kàlmàz, اشاغی قالمز àshàghi-kàlmàz; تزوج tèzèvvuj; —, *v.n.* براو bìr-òl; برابر كتمك bèrābèr-ghìtmek, اش‌او èsh-òl; —, *v.a.* اش بولمق èsh-bùlmak; اش‌ارامق èsh-àramak; اشی یوق دیو ادعاا èshi-yòk-dèyu-ìddi"ā-et, اشی یوق دیومیدانه قومق èshi-yòk-dèyu-mèydāna-kòmak.

Matchless, *a.* بینظیر bī-nàzīr.

Mate, *s.* ارقه‌داش àrkadash; اش èsh; یماق yàmak; ملازم mùlāzim; یازیجی yàziji; مات màt; شاهمات shāhmāt.

Material, *a.* جسمانی jìssmānī, هیولانی hèyyūlānī ; خیلی khàyli, کلی kyùllī, عظیم ''àzīm, چوق chòk ; —, *s.* قماش kùmàsh ; كرستة kèresstÉ, خرج khàrj ; —s, *s. pl.* لوازمات lèwāzimāt; (old) انقاض ènkāz.

Maternal, *a.* مادرانه mādérānÉ ; انا طرفندن àna-tàrafīndan.

Mathematical, *a.* هندسی hèndéssi.

Mathematician, *s.* مهندس mùhèndiss, أهل هندسه èhli-hèndéssÉ.

Mathematics, *s. pl.* هندسه hèndéssÉ ; علوم رياضيه ''ùlūmi-rìyāzìyyÉ.

Matrimony, *s.* ازدواج ìzdivāj, تزوج tèzèvvuj ; نكاح nìkyāh.

Matron, *s.* ثيبه sèyyibÉ, ثيب sèyyib, قاری kàri ; كتخدا قدين (kyāya)-kàdin.

Matter, *s.* هيولا hèyyùlā ; جسم jìssm ; مادة māddÉ (màddÉ); خصوص khùssūss, كيفيت kèyfìyyèt, امر èmr (pl. امور ùmūr), ايش ìsh, مصلحت màsslāhat ; جراحت jèrāhàt, ايرك ìring ; چپاق chàpak ; ضرر zàrar, بأس bè'ss ; —, *v.n.* ضرری او zàrari-òl ; no — ! ضرريوق zàrar-yòk, بأس يوق bè'ss-yòk; that does not —, ضرری يوق zàrari-yòk ; what is the — ? نه وار nè-vàr, مصلحت نه ايمش màsslahat-nè-imish (*or* در dir).

Mattock, *s.* قازمه kàzma.

Mattress, *s.* مندر mìnder ; شلته shìltÉ.

Mature, *a.* اولمش òlmush, يتمش yètmish, يتشمش yètishmish, يرشمش yèrishmish, كماله وارمش kèmāla-vàrmish, كمال بولمش kèmāl-bùlmush, قوام بولمش kìwām-bùlmush, قرارينی بولمش kàrārini-bùlmush ; پشمش pìshmish ; —, *v.n.* اولمق òlmak, كماله وارمق kèmāla-vàrmak ; —, *v.a.* قرارلاشدرمق kàrārlashdirmak, تكميل ا tèkmīl-et, قوامه كتورمك kìwāma-ghètirmek.

Maturity, *s.* قوام kìwām, قرار kàrār ; بلوغ bùlūgh ; كمال kèmāl ; انقضا ìnkizā.

Maxim, *s.* قاعده kā''idÉ, قانون kānūn ; ضرب مثل zàrbi-mèssèl, موضوع mèvzū''. [Grammar.

May, *s.* مايس māyiss ; —, *v. aux.* See

Mayor, *s.* عيان باشی ''àyān-bàshi.

Me, *p.* بنی bèni ; بكا bànga.

Meadow, *s.* چاير chàyr.

Meal, *s.* اون ūn, دقيق dàkīk ; يمك yèmèk, طعام tà''ām, اوين *or* اويون ùyun, *or* اوكون ùghun.

Mean, *a.* وسطی vàssàtī, اورته òrta ; الچق àlchàk, دنی dènī ; خسيس khàssīss, طمعكار tàmà''kyār ; لايقسز lāyìksiz, فنا fènā ; —, *s.* وسط vàssàt, اورته òrta ; —, *v.a.* ديمك استمك dèmek-isstémek ; ديمك dèmek, معناسی ma''nàssi-òl ; مراد ايتمك mùrād-et, تصميم ا tàssmīm-et, قورمق kùrmak, نيت ا nìyyèt-et.

Meaning, *s.* معنا mà''nà ; مراد mùrād.

Meanness, *s.* دونلق dūnluk ; طمعكارلك tàmà''kyārlik ; فقيرلق fàkīrlik.

Means, *s.* واسطه vāssita, وساطت vàssātàt ; اقتدار ìktidār, قدرت kùdrèt ; پاره (pàra), اقچه àkcha.

Meantime, Meanwhile, *ad.* اول ارالق (ه)-àralik; دیرایکن dèr-ikèn.

Measles, *s. pl.* قزاموق *or* قزامق kìzāmuk.

Measure, *s.* اولچی ùlchu; اولچك ùlchek; ارشون àrshin, اندازه ÈndāzÉ, ذراع zìrā''; تدبیر tèdbīr; (of poetry) وزن vèzn; —, *v.n.* کلمك ghÈlmek, ایتمك ètmek; —, *v.a.* اولچمك ùlchmek, اولچیسنی المق ùlchussunu-Almak.

Meat, *s.* ات èt, لحم làhm, کوشت ghyòsht; یمك yèmèk, طعام tà''ām.

Mechanic, *s.* اهل حرفت èhli-hìrfèt, اهل صنعت èhli-sàn''àt. [èsskāl.

Mechanics, *s. pl.* علم جراثقال ''ìlmi-jèrri-

Mechanism, *s.* چرخ chàrkh, چرخلر chàkhlar, الات ālāt, معرفت mà''-rifèt.

Medal, *s.* نشان nìshĀn; سکه sìkkÉ.

Meddle, *v.n.* قارشمق kĀrishmak, مداخله ا mùdākhala-et.

Mediate, *v.n.* قارشمق kĀrishmak, ارایه کیرمك àraya-ghìrmek, توسطا tàwĀss-

Mediation, *s.* توسط tàwĀsssut. [sut-et.

Mediator, *s.* متوسط mùtawĀsssit, واسطه wāssita.

Medical, *a.* طبی tìbbī; — attendant, حکیم hèkim, طبیب tĀbīb; — attendance, حکیملك خدمتی hèkimlik-khìdméti, حکیملك باقمسی hèkiming-bĀkmassi.

Medicine, *s.* علاج ''ìlāj, دوا dèwā.

Meditate, *v.n.* دوشنمك dùshunmek, طاشنمق tĀshinmak, مطالعه ا mùtāla''à-et; مراقبه ا mùrākaba-et.

Mediterranean, Mediterranean Sea, *s.* اق دکز Ak-dèngiz.

Medium, *s.* واسطه wāssita.

Medlar, *s.* موشمله mùshmula.

Meed, *s.* مستحق mùsstahAkk, مکافات mùkyāfat; مجازات mùjāzāt.

Meek, *a.* مظلوم màzlūm, حلیم hàlīm.

Meet, *a.* مناسب mùnāssib, لایق lāyik, جسبان jùssbān; —, *v.n.* قاوشمق kàwushmak, تلاقی ا tèlāki-et; طوپلانمق tòplanmak, جمع او jèm''-òl, برارایه کلمك bìr-àraya-ghÈlmek; —, *v.a.* راست کلمك rAsst-ghÈlmek, ملاقات ا mùlākAt-et; — one another, بولشمق bùlushmak.

Meeting, *s.* ملاقات mùlākAt; مجلس mèjliss, جمعیت jèm''ìyyèt; جماعت jèmā''àt; ملتقی mùltakà; — house, مسجد mèssjid, جامع jāmi'', معبد mà''bèd.

Melancholy, *s.* غم ghAmm, کدر kÈdEr; قره سودا kĀra-sÉvdā; —, *a.* مغموم màghmūm, مکدر mùkèddEr; صیقندیلو sìkindili; فنا fÈna.

Mellow, *a.* اولمش òlmush.

Melodious, *a.* طاتلو tAtli.

Melody, *s.* ترانه tèrānÉ; نغمه nàghma.

Melon, *s.* (water) قارپوز kàrpuz; (musk) قاون kàwun.

Melt, *v.n.* اریمك èrimek; —, *v.a.* ارتمك èritmek, اذابه ا ìzābÉ-et.

Member, *s.* عضو ''ùzv (pl. اعضا à''zā).

Membership, *s.* اعضالق à''zālik.

Membrane, *s.* زار zār, دریجك dèrijik.

Memoir, *s.* تذکره tèzkérÉ; لائحه lā'iha.

Memorable, *a.* مشهور mèshhūr.

Memorandum-book, *s.* مجمعه mèjma"a, احمق دفتری àhmàk-dèftéri.

Memorial, *s.* عرضحال "àrzihāl, عریضه "àrīza; برکذار bèrghyùzār; اثر èsser.

Memory, *s.* قوت حافظه kùvvèti-hāfiza; ذهن zìhn, عقل "àkl, خاطر khātir; in — of, نامنه nāmina, نامنی ابقانیتیله nāmini-ìbkā-nìyyètīla; within the — of, عقلنه کلمك اوزره "àklina-ghèlmek-ùzéré, وقتنده wàktinda.

Menace, *s.* قورقو kòrku, قولاً اخافه kàvlan-ìkhāfé, فعلاً اخافه fi"lan-ìkhāfé; —, *v.a.* قورقتمق kòrkutmak; اخافه ا ìkhāfé-et; لسان حال ایله اخافه ا lìssāni-hāl-ìla-ìkhāfé-et.

Menagerie, *s.* ارسلانخانه àrsslankhāné.

Mend, *v.n.* ایواو īyi-òl, ایولشمك īyi-lèshmek, ایولکه یوزطوتمق īyiligha-yùz-tùtmak; اصلاح اولنمق ìsslāh-òlunmak; —, *v.a.* اصلاح ا ìsslāh-et; تعمیرا tà"-mīr-et, ترمیم ا tèrmīm-et.

Mendacious, *a.* یالانجی yàlànji.

Mendacity, *s.* یالانجیلق yàlànjilik.

Mendicant, *s.* دیلنجی dìlènji.

Mendicity, *s.* دیلنجیلك dìlènjilik.

Menses, *s. pl.* عادت "ādet, ای باشی ày-bàshi, حیض hàyz.

Mensuration, *s.* علم مساحه "ìlmi-mèssāha.

Mental, *a.* ذهنی zìhnī, عقلی "àklī.

Mention, *s.* ذکر zìkr, لقردی làkirdi; —, make — of, *v.a.* اکمق àngmak, اغزه المق àghza-àlmak, ذکرا zìkr-et, قاله المق kāla-àlmak, لقردیسنی ا làkir-dissini-et.

Mentor, *s.* خواجه khòja; نصیحتجی nàssīhàtji.

Mercantile, *a.* تجاری tùjjārī, تجاره متعلق tùjjāra-mùta"àllik, تجارته متعلق tìjārèta-mùta"àllik.

Mercenary, *a.* اجرت وبخشش املنده اولان ùjrèt-vè-bàkhshish-èmelindé-òlan; —, *s.* اجرتلو خدمتکار ùjrètlu-hìzmet-kyār; یالکز اجرت ایچون خدمت ایدن yàlingiz-ùjrèt-ìchin-hìzmet-èden.

Merchandise, *s.* مال māl (pl. اموال èmwāl), متعه mat"à (pl. امتعه èmta"à).

Merchant, *s.* بازرکان bàzirghyān (bèzir-ghèn), تاجر tājir (pl. تجار tùjjār, generally used as a singular).

Merchantman, *s.* تجار کمیسی tùjjār-ghèmissi, بازرکان تکنه سی bàzir-ghyān-tèknéssi.

Merciful, *a.* مرحمتلو mèrhàmetli, رأفتلو rè'fètli, شفقتلو shèfakàtli; the Merciful (God) رحمن Ràhmān; the Most Merciful (God) رحیم Rahīm.

Mercury, *s.* (metal) جیوه jìwa, زیبق zībàk; (planet) عطارد "ùtārid.

Mercy, *s.* مرحمت mèrhàmet, شفقت shèfakàt, رأفت rè'fèt; (of God to the blessed) رحمت ràhmèt.

Mere, *a.* قورو kùru, ساده sādé, صالت sàlt, یالکز yàlngiz.

Meridian, *s.* دائرهٔ نصف نهار dā'iré'i-nìssfi-nìhār; — altitude, غایت ارتفاع ghāyéti-ìrtifā".

Meridional, *a.* جنوبی jènūbī.

Merit, *s.* استحقاق ìsstihkāk, لیاقت

lìyàkAt, اهليت èhlìyyèt; هنر hùner, كمال kèmāl, فضيلت fAzīlèt; —, *v.a.* مستحق او mùsstahAkk-òl, سزا او sèzā-òl, شايسته او shāyèsstè-òl, شايان او shāyAn-òl, جسبان او jùssbAn-òl; قزانمق kAzAnmak, تحصيل ا tàhsīl-et.

Meritorious, *a.* ثواب sèwāb; مستحسن mùsstàhsèn. [kèyf, كيفلو kèyfli.

Merry, *a.* شن shèn, فراح fèrāh, كيف

Mesh, *s.* كوز ghyùz.

Mess, *s.* مردارلق mùrdārlik, برابر يمك يبان طاقم bèrābèr-yèmèk-yèyan-tàkim; —, *v.n.* برابر يمك bèrābèr-yèmek.

Message, *s.* خبر khAber, پيام pèyām; سپارش sìpārish, امر èmr.

Messenger, *s.* ادم Adam; پيامبر pèyām-bèr, پيامرس pēyāmrèss; تاتار tātār, اولاق ùlAk; قاصد kāssid, ساعى sā"ī.

Messiah, *s.* حضرت مسيح Hàzrèti-Mèssīh.

Metal, *s.* معدن mà"dèn.

Metaphysics, *s.* علم حكمت "ìlmi-hìkmèt.

Method, *s.* يول yòl, اصول ùssūl, ترتيب tèrtīb, تقريب tAkrīb.

Methodical, *a.* منتظم mùntazàm; نظاملو nìzāmli.

Methodically, *ad.* اصول ايله ùssūl-ìla.

Metre, *s.* وزن vwèzn.

Metropolis, *s.* پايتخت pāyi-tàkht, مركز حكومت mèrkèzi-hùkyūmèt.

Mettlesome, *a.* اويناق òynàk; يكيت yìghit, جسور jèssūr.

Mews, *s.* صره اخورلر sìrà-akhorler.

Miasma, *s.* وخيم بخار vwàkhīm-bùkhār.

Microscope, *s.* خردهبين khùrdabīn.

Mid, *a.* يارى yāri, اورته òrta.

Midday, *s.* كوندز اورتهسى ghyùnduz-òrtassi, نصف نهار nìssfi-nìhār.

Middle, *s.* اورته òrta, اورتهيرى òrta-yèri, وسط vAssAt; بل bèl, ميان mèyān; — ages, قرون متوسطه kūrūn-mùtéwàssìtè; — aged, اورتا يشلو òrta-yashli.

Middling, *a.* اورته òrta; شويله بويله shùylè-bùylè, نهپك ايو نهپك فنا nè-pèk-īyi-nè-pèk-fèna.

Midshipman, *s.* بحريه ملازم ثانيسى bàhrìyyè-mùlāzim-sānissi.

Midst, *s.* اورته òrta, وسط vAssAt; ارا àra, ميانه mèyānè, مابين mābèyn.

Midsummer, *s.* ياز اورتاسى yàz-òrtassi.

Midwife, *s.* ابه èbè.

Midwifery, *s.* ابهلك èbèlik.

Mien, *s.* چهره chèhrè, قيافت kìyāfèt, سيما sīmā.

Might, *s.* قوت kùvvèt, قدرت kùdrèt, اقتدار ìktidār, مكنت mìknèt, زور zòr; —, *v. aux.* See Grammar.

Mighty, *a.* قدرتلو kùdrètli, مكنتلو mìknètli, صاحب اقتدار sāhib-ìktidār; بيوك bùyuk, كليتلو kyùllìyyètli, كلى kyùllī.

Mignonette, *s.* محبت چيچكى màhà-bbèt-chìchèghi.

Migrate, *v.n.* كوچمك ghyùchmek.

Migration, *s.* كوچ ghyùch.

Migratory, *a.* كوچبه ghyùchébè.

Mild, *a.* يواش yàwAsh, ملايم mùlàyim, طاتلو tàtli.

Mildew, *s.* كف *or* كوف kyùf.

Mildness, *s.* يواشلق yàwÀshlik; ملايمت mùlāyémèt.

Mile, *s.* ميل mìl.

Military, *a.* حربيه hàrbī, عسكرى "Àsskérī.

Militia, *s.* رديف عسكرى rèdīf-"Àsskéri.

Milk, *s.* سوت sùt.

Milkman, *s.* سوتجى sùtji.

Milkwoman, *s.* سوتجى قارى sùtji-kÀri.

Mill, *s.* دكرمن dèghirmÈn; rolling —, حادّه hāddÉ; hand —, ال دكرمنى Èl-dèghirméni.

Miller, *s.* دكرمنجى dèghirmÈnji.

Millet, *s.* دارى dàri.

Milliner, *s.* قارى شاپقه جيسى kÀri-shÀpkajìssi.

Million, *s.* ميليون mìliòn.

Millionaire, *s.* پك زنكين ادم pèk-zÈnghin-ÀdAm.

Mimick, *s.* مقلد mÙkÀllid; —, *a.* تقليد tÀklīd, بكزتمه bèngzÈtma, ياپمه yàpma; —, *v.a.* تقليد ا tÀklīd-et.

Mimicry, *s.* تقليد tÀklīd.

Mince, *s.* قيمه kÌyma; —, *v.a.* قيمق kìymak; — meat, قيمه kÌyma; it won't do to mince matters, نزاكت وقتى دكل nèzākÈt-wÀkti-dìghil.

Mind, *s.* عقل "Àkl, ذهن zihn; افكار èfkyār; رغبت ràghbèt, هوس hàvess, استك ìsstek; —, *v.n.* قيدا kàyd-et, وظيفه ايدنمك wÀzifÉ-èdinmek; —, *v.a.* باقمق bÀkmak, كوزتمك ghyùz-ètmek, دقت ا dìkkAt-èt; دكله مك dìnglÉmek (dīnÉmek); I have a — to . . . . , عقلمه كليور "Àklima-ghè-liyor, همان ايده جكم كليور hÈmEn-èdéjéghim-ghèliyor; I don't — that, اوراسى وظيفه مده دكل òrassi-wÀzīf-Èmda-dìghil; all of one —, هپ بر افكارده hèp-bìr-èfkyārda; to bear in —, عقلده طوتمق "Àklda-tÙtmak, عقلده صقلامق "Àklda-sàklamak, اونوتمامق Ùnùtmamak.

Mindful, *a.* اكاه āghyāh, خبردار khÀbEr-dār, انتباه اوزره ìntibāh-ùzérÉ; to be —, باقمق bÀkmak, دقت ا dìkkAt-et; اونوتمامق Ùnùtmamak; غافل اولمامق ghāfil-òlmamak.

Mine, *p.* بنم bènim; بنمكى bènimki, بنمكيلر bènimkilar; —, *s.* معدن mà"dEn; لغم làghim; —, *v.a.* لغملمق làghimlamak. [làghimji.

Miner, *s.* معدنجى mà"dEnji; لغمجى

Mineral, *a.* معدنى mà"dEnī; —, *s.* معدن mà"dEn, طاش tàsh, فلز fìlìzz; — water, معدن صويى mà"dÈn-sùyu.

Mingle, *v.n.* قارشمق kÀrishmak; اختلاطا ìkhtilÀt-et; —, *v.a.* قاتمق kÀtmak, قارشدرمق kÀrishdirmak, خلط ا khÀlt-et, مزج ا mèzj-et.

Minister, *s.* خدمتكار khÌdmetkyār (hìz-), خادم khādim, عبد "àbd, نوكر nùkEr; (of state) وكلادن برى vùké-lādan-bìri, ناظر nāzir, وكيل vèkīl; (foreign —) ايلچى Èlchi, سفير sèfīr; (of religion) پاپاس pÀpAss, امام ìmAm, خخام khÀkhAm; —, *v.n.* خدمت ا khÌdmet-et; باقمق bÀk-mak; حوائجنى ويرمك hàwā'ijini-vÈrmek.

Ministry, *s.* خدمت khÌdmet, عبوديت

"ùbūdìyyèt; وكالت vèkyālèt, نظارت nAzārèt; وكلا طاقمى vùkélā-tàkimi; پاپاسلق pApAsslik, امامت ìmāmèt, خخاملق khAkhAmlik.

Minor, *s.* جوجق chòjuk, صبى sAbī, طفل tìfl; —, *a.* جزئى jùz'ī, ادنى èdnà; Asia —, اناطولى ànàdolī.

Minority, *s.* چوجقلق chòjukluk, صباوت sAbāvèt, طفوليت tùfūlìyyèt; ازلق Azlik. [shā"ir.

Minstrel, *s.* مطرب mùtrib; شاعر

Minstrelsy, *s.* مطربلك mùtriblik; شعر shì"r.

Mint, *s.* (herb), and peppermint, نعنه *or* نعنا *or* نعنع *or* نعناع (nānÉ); (for coining) ضربخانه zàrb-khānÉ.

Minute, *s.* دقيقه dAkīka; (paper) مضبطه mAzbAta; —, *a.* دقيق dAkīk, اوفاق ùfAk, اينجه ìnja; — down, *v.a.* ضبطا zAbt-et, يازمق yàzmak.

Minutiæ, *s.* تفصيلات tAfsīlAt.

Miracle, *s.* معجزه mù"jizÉ; كرامت kèrāmèt; خارق العاده khārikv-'l-"ādÉ.

Miraculous, *a.* غريب ghàrīb. [-"ādÉ.

Mire, *s.* چامور chàmur; mired, *a.* چاموره باتمش chàmura-bAtmish.

Mirror, *s.* ايينه āyinÉ, جام jām.

Mirth, *s.* كيف kèyf, فراح fèrāh, حبور hùbūr, انبساط ìnbissAt, شادمانى shAdmānī.

Misanthrope, *s.* ادملردن تنفر ايدن AdAmlerden-tènèffur-èden.

Misapprehend, *v.a.* ياكلش اكلامق yānish-ànnamak. [yānish-ànnamaklik.

Misapprehension, *s.* ياكلش اكلامقلق

Misbehave, *v.n.* يرامزلق ا yàramàzlik-et.

Misbehaviour, *s.* يرامزلق yàramàzlik.

Misbeliever, *s.* كافر kyāfir, ايمانسز īmAnsiz, كاور ghyāwur.

Miscalculate, *v.a.* and *n.* ياكلش حساب ا yānish-hìssāb-et. [hìssāb.

Miscalculation, *s.* ياكلش حساب yānish-

Miscarriage, *s.* چوجق دوشرمسى chòjuk-dùshurméssi, اسقاط جنين ìsskAti-jìnīn.

Miscarry, *v.n.* چوجق دوشرملك chòjuk-dùshurmek; ياكلش كتملك yàngilish-ghìtmek (yānish), غائب او ghā'ib-òl; بوشه چيقمق bòsha-chikmak.

Miscellaneous, *a.* متنوع mùténèvvi.

Mischief, *s.* يرامزلق yàramàzlik; زيانكارلق zìyānkyārlik, خسارت khAssārèt.

Mischievous, *a.* يرامز yàramàz.

Mischievousness, *s.* يرامزلق yàramàzlik.

Misconception, *s.* ياكلش yānish.

Misconduct, *s.* سو حركت sù'hàrÉkÈt.

Misdeed, *s.* جنحه jùnha.

Misdirect, *v.a.* ياكلش صاغلق ويرملك yānish-sàghlik-vÈrmek.

Miser, *s.* خسيس khàssīss, جمرى jìmri, پنتى pìnti, طمعكار tAma"kyār.

Miserable, *a.* دوشكون dùshkyun, پريشان pèrishAn, فقير fàkīr, محنتكش mìhnet-kèsh, دردمند dèrdmènd; خبيث khàbīss; بوق bòk, پك فنا pèk-fēna, مسكين mìsskin.

Misery, *s.* درد dÈrd, محنت mìhnèt, جفا jèfā, صيقندى sikindi, بلا bèlā; ازيت èzìyyèt.

Misfortune, *s.* قضا kàzā, بلا bèlā, فلاكت fèlākèt, داهيه dāhìyyé; —s, *s. pl.* دوشكونلك dùshyunluk, نكبت nìkbèt.

Misgovern, *v.a.* يولسز حكومت ا yòlsiz-hùkyūmèt-èt.

Misgovernment, *s.* يولسز حكومت yòl-siz-hùkyūmèt.

Mishap, *s.* قضا kàzā.

Misinform, *v.a.* ياكلش خبر ويرمك yānish-khaber-vèrmek.

Mislead, *v.a.* الداتمق àldatmak; ياكلتمق yàngıltmak, اغفال ا ìghfāl-et.

Misrepresent, *v.a.* ياكلش اكلاتمق yānish-ànnatmak.

Miss, *s.* خانم قيز hànim-kìz, قيز kìz, خانم hànim; —, *v.a.* اورمامق wùr-mamak, اصابت ايتمامك ìssābet-ètmamek; اتلامق àtlamak; قصورا kùssūr-et; ارامق àramak; —fire, الماما الماماق àlmamak, اتش الماماق àtèsh-àlmamak; do not — coming, صاقن كلما مزلك ايتمه sàkin-ghèlma-màzlik-ètma; I must not — seeing, البته كوره جكم èlbètta-ghyùréjéghim (*or* كورمليوم ghyùrmàliyim).

Missile, *s.* جسم مرمى jìssmi-mèrmī.

Missing, *a.* غائب ghā'ib.

Mission, *s.* مأموريت mè'mūrìyyèt, خدمت khìdmèt (hìz-); ايلچيلك èlchilik, سفارت sèfārèt; سفارت طاقمى sèfāret-tàkimi; ناسى دينه دعوت ضمننده اختيار اولنان پاپاس ايلچيلكى nāssi-dīna-dà''vet-zìmnin-da-ìkhtiyār-òlunan-pāpass-èlchilighi; پاپاسلر سفارتى pāpasslar-sèfārèti.

Missionary, *s.* ناسى دينه دعوت ايچون كوندريلن پاپاس nāssi-dīna-dà''vet-ichin-ghyùndérilen-pàpass.

Missive, *s.* مكتوب mèktūb, تذكره tèzkéré, پوصله pūssla, نامه nāmé.

Misspell, *v.a.* ياكلش املا ايله يازمق yānish-ìmlā-ìla-yàzmak.

Misspelt, *a.* ياكلش املا ايله يازلمش yanish-ìmlā-ìla-yàzilmish.

Misstatement, *s.* ياكلش افاده yānish-ìfādé; يالان yàlan.

Mist, *s.* سيس sìss, دومان dùmàn.

Mistake, *s.* ياكلش yàngilish (yānish), سهو sèhv, خطا khàtā; —, to be mistaken, *v.n.* ياكلمق yàngılmak, سهوا sèhv-et, خطا ا khàtā-et; —, *v.a.* بشقه سنه بكزتمك bàshkassina-bèng-zetmek.

Mistaken, *a.* ياكلش yānish.

Mister, *s.* اغا àgha; افندى èfèndi.

Mistranslation, *s.* ياكلش ترجمه yānish-tèrjumé.

Mistress, *s.* خانم hànim, افندى èfèndi, قوقونه kòkòna, مادامه màdama; معشوقه mà''shūka; اوطه لق òdalik; مخصوص روسپى màkhsūss- (òrosspo), زانيه zānìyyé; استاد قارى (ūssta)-kàri, اوسته ùssta; قالفه kàlfa.

Mistrust, *s.* عدم امنيت ''àdémi-èmnìy-yèt, شبهه shùbhé; —, *v.a.* شبهه ا shùbhé-et. [(yānish)-(ànnamak).

Misunderstand, *v.a.* ياكلش اكلامق

Misunderstanding, *s.* ياكلش اكلاملق yanish-ànnamaklik; بوزشلق bòzush-luk. [تخفيف ا tàkhfīf-et.

Mitigate, *v.a.* خفيفلتمك khàfifletmek,

Mitigation, *s.* تخفيف tàkhfīf.

Mix, *v.n.* قارشمق kArishmak ; اختلاط ا ìkhtilĀt-et ; —, *v.a.* قارشدرمق kArish-dirmak.

Mixture, *s.* قارشق شی kàrishik-shèy, ترکیب tErkīb ; شربت shErbèt.

Mizen, *s.* قونطره مجانه kòntra-màjāna.

Moan, *s.* ایکلتی ìngilti, اه āh, انین ènīn, فغان fìghān ; —, *v.n.* اه چکمك āh-chèkmek, ایکلهمك ìnglémek.

Moat, *s.* خندق (hèndek).

Mob, *s.* ایاقلنمش خلق غلبهلغی àyak-lanmish - khAlk - (kAlabAlighi) ; *v.a.* خلق چویروب بد معامله ا khAlk-chèvirup-bèd-mū"āmélé-et.

Mock, *a.* تقلید tàklīd, یاپمه yàpma, یلانجی yàlAnji ; *v.a.* ذوقلنمك zèvk-lEnmek, استهزا ا ìsstìhzā-et, مسخره یه مسخرهیه چویرمك mAsskharaya-chèvirmek ; تقلید ا tàklīd-et.

Mockery, *s.* مسخرهلق mAsskharalik.

Model, *s.* مودل mòdèl, اورنك ùrnek, رسم rèssm, قالب kĀlib ; نمونه nù-mūné, مثال mìssāl.

Moderate, *a.* معتدل mù"tèdil ; خفیف khAfīf ; یواش yàwAsh, ملایم mùlāyim ; انصافلو ìnsĀfli, یولنده yòlunda, قرارنده kArārinda ; قراردن زیادهیهمازایچمز kArārdan-zìyādé-yèmàz-ìchmàz ; —, *v.n.* انمك ènmek, ازالمق AzAlmak, کسلمك kèssilmek, قالمق kAlmak ; خفیفلشمك khAfīflEshmek ; —, *v.a.* تعدیل ا tà"dīl-et, تسکین ا tèsskīn-et, تخفیف ا tàkhfīf-et.

Moderately, *ad.* اولدقجه òldùkjé. [sAbr.

Moderation, *s.* اعتدال ì"tidāl ; صبر

Modern, *a.* یکی yèngi, یکی اصول yèngi-ùssūl ; دها صکره dàhà-sòngra, متأخر mùta'àkhkhir ; moderns, *s. pl.* متأخرین mùta'àkhkhirīn, یکی زمان ادملری yèngi-zùmĀn-AdAmlari.

Modest, *a.* محجوب màhjūb ; أدیب èdīb ; اهل پرده èhli-pErdé, عفیفه "àfīfé.

Modesty, *s.* حجاب hìjĀb, ادب èdeb ; عفت "ìffèt, عصمت "ìssmèt.

Modification, *s.* تبدیل جزئی tèbdìl-jùz'ī.

Modify, *v.a.* براز تبدیل ا bìr-Az-tèbdìl-èt.

Mogul, *s.* مغل mùghùl. [اسلام ìsslām.

Mohammedan, *a.* اسلامی ìsslāmī ; —, *s.*

Moist, *a.* نملو nèmli, رطوبتلو rùtūbètli ; — sugar, خام شکر khĀm-shèkEr.

Moisture, *s.* رطوبت rùtūbèt.

Mole, *s.* کوستبك kyùsstébèk ; (pier) اسکله ìsskèlé, ریختم rìkhtim ; (on the skin) بن bèn *or* بك bèng.

Molest, *v.a.* اذیت ا èzìyyèt-et, صاتاشمق sAtashmak, ایلشمك ìlishmek, قارشمق kArishmak, رنجش ا rènjish-et, رنجیده ا rènjīdé-et.

Molestation, *s.* رنجش rènjish.

Moment, *s.* ان ān, لحظه làhza ; اهمیت èhèmmìyyèt.

Momentaneous, *a.* ان واحد سوررسورمز āni-wāhid-sùrEr-sùrmàz.

Momentous, *a.* مهم mùhìmm.

Monarch, *s.* پادشاه pādishāh.

Monarchy, *s.* پادشاهلق pādishāhlik.

Monastery, *s.* مناسطیر (*or* مناستر) mAnasstir, دیر dèyr.

Monday, *s.* پازارارتسی pàzàr-èrtéssi, یکشنبه yèkshènbih, یوم‌أحد yùvmi-àhàd.

Money, *s.* اقچه Akcha, پاره (pàra); نقد nAkd; ready —, پیشین‌پاره (pèshin-pàra); — changer, صراف sàrrāf (sàraf).

Monk, *s.* راهب rāhib, رهبان rùhbān.

Monkey, *s.* میمون màymūn.

Monopoly, *s.* انحصار ìnhissār, یدواحداصولی yèdi-wāhid-ùssūlu.

Monosyllable, *s.* برهجالو کلمه bìr-hèjāli-kèlimé.

Monotonous, *a.* ادمك جاننی صیقار اولان Adamin-jānini-sìkar-òlan.

Monsoon, *s.* موسم نام روزکارلر mòssim-nām-rūzghyārler.

Monster, *s.* خبیث کمسنه khàbīss-kìmèssné; پك بیوك نسنه pèk-bìyuk-nèssné.

Monstrous, *a.* خبیث khàbīss.

Month, *s.* ای ày, ماه māh, شهر shèhr; calendar —, الافرانقه آیی àllafrànka-àyi; lunar —, عربی آیی àrábi-àyi.

Monthly, *a.* ایده برکره àyda-bìr-kèrré.

Monument, *s.* اثر èsser, برکذار bèr-ghyùzār; طاش tAsh; بنا bìnā.

Moon, *s.* ای ay, ماه māh, قمر kAmer; new —, ای‌باشی ày-bAshi; هلال hilāl; full —, بدر bèdr.

Moonlight, Moonshine, *s.* ای‌ایدینلغی ày-àydinlighi, ساهتاب māhitāb, مهتاب mèhtāb.

Moor, *s.* قیر kìr, صحرا sàhrā; (man) مغربی màghribī; عرب ''àrab.

Mop, *s.* پاپاس pàpass; —, *v.a.* پاپاس ایله صلمك papass-ìla-silmek.

Moral, *a.* صالح sālih, مستقیم mùsstakīm; معنوی mà''névī; morals, *s. pl.* اخلاق àkhlāk, اداب ādāb, ادبیات èdebìyyāt.

Morass, *s.* بتاق bAtak.

More, *a.* دها dàhà, زیاده zìyādé, دهاز یاده dàhà-zìyādé; no —, not any —, ارتق àrtik, بردها bìr-dàhà; — and —, کتدکجه‌زیاده ghìtdikja-zìyādé.

Moreover, *c.* وبرده vè-bìrdé, ودخی vè-dàkhi.

Morn, Morning, *s.* صبح sàbāh, قوشلق‌وقتی kùshluk-wAkti.

Morocco, *s.* سختیان sàkhtiyān; مغرب màghrib; مراکش شهری mèrākèsh-shèhiri.

[Morose, *a.* ترس tèrss; خویسز khùysuz, اکشی صورتلو èkshi-sūrètli.] اکشی صورتلو èkshi-sūrètli.

Morrow, *s.* ایرته *or* ارته èrté, فردا fèrdā, صباح sàbāh; to-morrow, یارین yārin.

Morsel, *s.* لقمه lòkma.

Mortal, *a.* یموت yèmūt, اوله‌جك ùléjek; مهلك mùhlik, باعث‌موت bā''issi-mèvt; —, *s.* انسان ìnsān, بنی‌ادم bèni-ādem, بشر bèsher.

Mortality, *s.* یموتیت yèmūtìyyèt, فنا fènā; بشریت bèshèrìyyèt, ناسوت nāssūt; جسدفانی jèssedi-fānī; قیرم kìrim, تلف tèlef, وفات wèfāt.

Mortar, *s.* خرج khàrj; صیوه sìwa; (artillery) هاون (hAwan).

Mortgage, *s.* استغلال ìsstighlāl; —, *v.a.* استغلال‌ا ìsstighlāl-et.

Mortgagee, *s.* مستغل له mùsstàghèl-lahū.

Mortmain, *s.* وقف wʌkf (*pl.* اوقاف èvkāf); in —, موقوف mèvkūf.

Mosaic, *s.* صدفجی کاری و قاقمه‌جی ایشی sʌdefji-kyāri-vé-kʌkméji-ìshi.

Moscow, مسقو شهری mòsskof-shèhiri.

Moslem, *s.* اهل‌اسلام èhli-ìsslām, مسلم mùsslim, مؤمن mù'min.

Mosque, *s.* (large) جامع jāmi'', (small) مسجد mèssjid.

Moss, *s.* یوصون yòssun; — rose, یوصونلوکل yòssunlu-ghyùl.

Most, *a.* and *ad.* پك pèk, چوق chòk, غایت ghāyet, غایتله ghāyètla, بغایت bìghāyèt; the —, الك èng, الك زیاده èng-zìyādé; for the — part, mostly, اکثریا èksèrìyyā.

Mosul, (town of) *s.* موصل mòssul.

Moth, *s.* پروانه pèrwāné; کوه ghyùwé; — eaten, کوه‌یمش ghyùwé-yèmish.

Mother, *s.* انا àna, نینه niné, والده vālidé, مادر mādər; پوصی pòssu, طورطی tòrtu; wife's —, قاین‌انا kàyn-àna; —, *a.* انا àna, اصل ʌssl; — country, اصل‌وطن ʌssl-wʌtan, — of pearl, صدف sʌdef (sèdef).

Motion, *s.* حرکت hàrékèt, قیملدانش kìmìldʌnish; عمل ''ʌmel; تکلیف tèklīf, اخطار ìkhtār; اشارت ìshāret; — *v.a.* اشارت‌ا ìshāret-et.

Motionless, *a.* حرکتسز hàrékètsiz.

Motive, *a.* محرك mùhàrrik; —, *s.* سبب sèbeb, علت ''ìllèt, باعث bā''iss, ذریعه zèrī''à, موجب mūjib, مورث mūriss.

Motley, *a.* رنکارنك rènghyārèngh.

Mottled, *a.* بنکلو bènekli.

Mould, *s.* طپراق tòprʌk; کف or کوف kyùf; قالب kʌlib; —, *v.a.* قالب‌یاپمق kʌlib-yàpmak; پرواز چکمك pèrwāz-chèkmek; اویمق òymak. [دوکلمك dùkyulmek.

Moulder, *v.n.* چوروملك chùrumek,

Mouldiness, *s.* کف or کوف kyùf.

Mouldy, *a.* کوفلو kyùflu.

Mound, *s.* دپه (tèpé); یغین yìghin, یغینتی yìghinti.

Mount, *s.* دپه (tèpé); —, *v.n.* چیقمق chìkmak, یوکسلمك yùkselmek; —, *v.a.* بنمك binmek, اوستنه‌چیقمق ùsstuna-chìkmak; طاقم‌یاپمق tàkim-yàpmak, دوناتمق dònatmak; — Ararat, اغری طاغی ʌghri-dʌghi; — Carmel, کرمل طاغی kìrmìl-dʌghi; — Hermon, جبل الشیخ jèbel-u-shèykh; — Hor, جبل هارون jèbeli-hārūn; — Lebanon, جبل لبنان jèbeli-lìbnān; درزی طاغی dùrzī-dàghi; — Olympus (Bithynian), کشیش طاغی keshīsh-dʌghi; — Sinai, جبل موسی jèbeli-mūssà. [jèbel.

Mountain, *s.* طاغ dàgh, کوه kyūh, جبل

Mountaineer, *s.* طاغ اهلی ادم dʌgh-èhli-ʌdam.

Mounted, *a.* بنمش bìnmish, بنیلو bìnili; اتلو ʌtli, سوار sùwār; طاقملو tàkimli, دونالو dònʌli.

Mourn, *v.n.* اغلامق ʌghlamak, اجیمق ʌjimak; یاس‌ا yàss-et, ماتم‌ا mātèm-et.

Mourning, *s.* یاس yass, ماتم mātèm; کدورت kèdūrèt.

Mouse, *s.* فاره fāré, فندق صیچانی fìndik-sìchāni ; — trap, قپان kàpan.

Moustache, *s.* بیق bìyik.

Mouth, *s.* اغز àghiz, دهان dìhān, فم fèm ; بوغاز bòghāz.

Mouthful, *s.* لقمه lòkma.

Mouthpiece, *s.* اغزلق àghizlik.

Move, *v.n.* قیملدانمق kìmildanmak, حرکت ا hàrékèt-et ; طاشنمق tàshinmak, کوچ ا ghyùch-et, نقل ا nàkl-et ; اودیکشمك èv-dìghishmek ; —, *v.a.* قیملداتمق kìmildatmak, دورتمك dùrtmek, تحریك ا tàhrīk-et ; یموشاتمق yìmushàtmak, ترحم ایتدرمك tèràhhum-ètdirmek, رقت کتورمك rìkkāt-ghètirmek ; begin to —, حرکته کلمك hàrékèta-ghèlmek.

Movement, *s.* قیملدانش kìmildanish, حرکت hàrékèt.

Mow, *v.a.* بچمك bìchmek, طرپان ایله بچمك tìrpān-ila-bìchmek.

Mower, *s.* طرپانجی tìrpānji.

Much, *a.* چوق chòk ; کلی مقدار kyùllī-mìkdār ; —, *ad.* چوق chòk, کلیاً kyùllìyyān.

Muck, *s.* کوبره ghyùbré, پیسلك pìsslik.

Mucus, *s.* سموك sùmuk.

Mud, *s.* چامور chàmur.

Muddle, *v.a.* قارشدرمق kàrishdirmak ; —, *s.* قارشقلق kàrishiklik.

Muddy, *a.* چامورلو chàmurlu ; بولانق bùlànik.

Muff, *s.* ال کورکی èl-kyùrghi.

Mufti, *s.* مفتی mùftī.

Mug, *s.* برداق *or* بارداق bàrdak, مشربه (màshraba) ; یوز yuz, چهره chèhré, صورت (sūrat).

Mulatto, *s.* ملز mèlez.

Mulberry, *s.* دوت dùt.

Mulct, *v.a.* تجریم ا tèjrīm-et.

Mule, *s.* قاطر kàtir, بغل bàghl, أستر èsstèr.

Muleteer, *s.* قاطرجی kàtirji.

Mullet, *s.* (grey) لوفر lùfer ; (red) تکیر بالغی *or* تکفور بالغی tèkir-bàlighi, مرجان بالغی mèrjān-bàlighi, باربونیه bàrbūnya.

Multifarious, *a.* کوناکون ghyūn-ā-ghyūn.

Multiplication, *s.* تورهیش türéyish, چوغالش chòghalish, تکثر tèkèssur ; توردش türédish, چوغالدش chòghal-dish, تکثیر tèksīr ; (arith.) ضرب zàrb.

Multiplicity, *s.* کثرت kèssret.

Multiply, *v.n.* تورهمك türémek, چوغالمق chòghalmak, تکثر ا tèkèsssur-et ; —, *v.a.* تورتمك türetmek, چوغالتمق chòghaltmak, تکثیر ا tèksīr-et ; ضرب ا zàrb-et.

Multitude, *s.* وفرت wèfrèt, کثرت kèssrèt ; غلبه لق (kàlabàlik), ازدحام ìzdìhām, جمعیت jèm''iyyèt ; great —, جم غفیر jèmmi-ghàfīr.

Mummy, *s.* موصیا mūmiyā.

Mumps, *s.* بوغاز بیضارینك شیشمسی bòghāz-bèyzlérining-shìshmessi.

Munch, *v.a.* چینهمك chīnémek.

Mundane, *a.* دنیوی dùnyévī.

Municipality, *s.* شهر shèhir, قصبه kàssaba ; اهالی àhālī.

Munificence, *s.* سخاوت کلیه sàkhāvèti-kyùllìyyé, دریای سخاوت déryā'i-sàkhāvèt.

Munificent, *a.* سخی sàkhī, سخاوتلو sàkhāvetli, بذول bèzùl, جومرد; jùmèrd; (gift) کلی kyùllī.

Munitions, *s. pl.* لوازمات lèwāzimAt.

Murder, *s.* قتل نفس بغیر حق kAtlī-nèfss--bi-ghàyri-hAkk; —, *v.a.* اولدرمق ùldurmek, تلف ا tèlef-et, قتل ا kAtl-et, تپه لمك tèpélémek, قا نه کیرمك kAnina-ghìrmek.

Murderer, *s.* قاتل kAtil, قانلوقاتل kAnli-[-kAtil.

Murmur, *s.* مرلدامه mìrìldama; سویلنمه sùwèylenma; —, *v.n.* سویلنمك sùwèylenmek, مرلدانمق mìrìldAnmak.

Muscle, *s.* بالق اتی bAlik-èti, قباات kAba-et; عصبه ''Assaba; (fish) میدیه mìdiyé.

Muscovy, *s.* مسقو مملکتی mòsskof--mèmlékèti.

Muscular, *a.* عضله ناك àzàlénāk; قوتلو kùvvetlu. [kùvvetlu.

Mushroom, *s.* ینور اولان منتار yènir-òlan--mAntar.

Music, *s.* چالغی chAlghi; موسیقی mūsīkī. [mūssīkī.

Musical, *a.* موسیقی یه منسوب mūsīkīyyé--mènsūb.

Musician, *s.* اهل موسیقی èhli-mūsīkī; چالغیجی chAlghiji; سازنده sāzèndé.

Music-master, *s.* چالغی خواجه سی chAlghi-khòjassi.

Musk, *s.* مشك mìshk (mìsk); — melon, قاون kàwun.

Musket, *s.* تفنك tùfènk (tùfèk); — proof, *a.* قورشون کچمز kūrshūn-gèch-màz.

Musketry, *s.* تفنك اتمقلق صنعتی tùfek-[Atmaklik-sàn''ati.

Muslin, *s.* دلبند dùlbènd (tùlbent).

Musquito, *s.* سیوری سینك sìvri-sìnek.

Mussel, *s.* میدیه mìdiyé.

Mussulman, *s.* اهل اسلام èhli-ìsslām, مسلم musslim, مسلمان mùsslimān.

Must, *v. aux.* see Grammar; —, *s.* کوف kyùf; شیره shìra.

Mustaches, Mustachio, *s.* بیق bìyik.

Mustard, *s.* خردل khàrdAl.

Muster, *s.* یوقلمه yòklama; —, *v.a.* یوقلمق yòklamak, یوقلمه ا yòklama-et; طوپلامق toplamak; — roll, یوقلمه دفتری yòklama-dèfteri.

Musty, *a.* کوفلو kyùflu, اکشی èkshi, چوروك chùruk.

Mute, *a.* and *s.* دلسز dìlsiz, اخرس àkhrèss; —, *v.n.* صیچماق sìchmak.

Mutilate, *v.a.* بعض یرلرینی کسمك bA''zi--yèrlerini-kèssmek.

Mutilation, *s.* کسوب سقط ایتمکلك kès-sub-sàkAt-ètmeklik.

Mutineer, *s.* عاصی ''Assī, زوربا zòrbā.

Mutiny, *s.* عصیان ''ìssyān, طغیان tùghyān, زوربالق zòrbalik; —, *v.n.* اياقلنمق àyaklanmak, اياغه قالقمق àyagha-kAlkmak, عصیان ا ''ìssyān-et, طغیان ا tùghyān-et.

Mutter, *v.n.* and *a.* دیش اراسنده سویلنمك dìsh-àrassinda-sùwèylenmek.

Mutton, *s.* قویون اتی kòyun-èti; — chop, *s.* بریزوله brìzòla.

Mutual, *a.* مشترك mùshtérèk, ایکی طرفدن اولان ìki-tàrafdan-òlAn.

Muzzle, *s.* اغز àghz, بورون bùrun; —, *v.a.* اغزینی باغلامق Aghzini-bAghlamak.

My, *p.* م im, ìm, بنم bènim.

Myriad, *s.* اون بيك òn-bìn ; بيكلر bìnler.

Myrrh, *s.* مر صافي mùrri-sāfī.

Myrtle, *s.* مرسين اغاجي mèrsin-àghaji.

Mysterious, *a.* اكلاشلمز ànglashilmàz (ànnashilmaz), مراق ويرر mèrak-vèrir ; كيزلو ghìzli, صاقلو sàkli, خفى khàfı, مخفى màkhfī.

Mystery, *s.* اكلاشلمز برماده (ànnashil-màz)-bìr-māddé, معما mù"àmmā, سر sìrr, (pl. اسرار èssrār), رمز rèmz (pl. رموز rūmūz).

Mystic, Mystical, *a.* باطنى bātinī, مخفى màkhfī, معنوى mà"névī, تصوفى tàssàvvufī ; mystic, *s.* اهل تصوف èhli-tàssàvvuf, صوفى sūfī (pl. صوفيون sūfiyyūn).

Mysticism, *s.* تصوف tàssàvvuf.

Myth, *s.* مصال màssal ; اساطير الاولين مقوله سى èssātiru-'l-èvvélīn-màkūléssi.

Mythology, *s.* اساطير الاولين èssātīru-'l-èvvélīn, اسكى زمان حكايه لرى èsski-zàmān-hìkyāyéléri.

N.

Nadir, *s.* حضيض hàdīd ; سمت قدم sèmti-kàdem.

Nag, *s.* آت àt, باركير (bèghir).

Nail, *s.* (natural) طرناق tìrnak ; (metal) چيوى chìvi, انكسر ènkser, ميخ mìkh ; —, *v.a.* ميخلامق mìkhlamak, چيويلمك chivilémek.

Naked, *a.* چيپلاق chìplak, عارى "ārī, برهنه bèrèhné.

Nakedness, *s.* چيپلاقلق chìplaklik.

Namby-pamby, *a.* حوپا مزاج hòppa-mìzāj.

Name, *s.* اد àd, اسم issm, نام nām ; —, *v.a.* ديمك dèmek, تسميه ا tèssmiyyé-et ; ادقومق àd-kòmak, اد ويرمك àd-vèrmek, اد طاقمق àd-tàkmak ; to call names, سوكوب صايمق sùghup-sàymak, بدنام ا bèd-nām-et.

Namely, *ad.* يعنى yà"nī ; مثلا mèssélā.

Namesake, *s.* ادداش àddàsh, همنام hèmnām.

Nap, *s.* اويقو ùyku ; (of cloth) حاو hàw.

Nape of the neck, اكسه èngsé, عنق "ùnuk.

Naphtha, *s.* نفت nèft.

Napkin, *s.* پيشكير (pèshkir).

Naples, *s.* ناپولى nàpoli.

Narcissus, *s.* زرين قدح zèrīn-kàdeh, زرن zèren ; trumpet —, بورو چيچكى bòru-chìchéghi ; globe —, *or* daffodil, التون طوپ àltin-tòp.

Narcotic, *s.* مخدر mùkhèddīr.

Narrate, *v.a.* نقل ا nàkl-et, حكايه ا hìk-yāyé-et.

Narration, Narrative, *s.* حكايه hìkyāyé.

Narrator, *s.* راوى rāvī.

Narrow, *a.* دار dàr, انسز ènsiz.

Nasal, *a.* بورونه ياخود ككزه منسوب bùruné-yākhod-ghèngzé-mènsūb.

Nasty, *a.* فنا fèna, پس pìss, مردار mùrdār (mùn-).

Nation, *s.* قوم kàvm, قبيله kàbīlé, ملت millèt, جنس jìnss.

National, *a.* ملته منسوب millèté-mèn-sūb.

Native, *a.* يرلو yèrli ; طوغمه dòghma, خلقى khìlkī, طبيعى tàbī"ī ; — country, وطن vwàtan.

Nativity, *s.* ولادت vèlādèt, مولد mèvlèd, مولود mèvlūd, میلاد mīlād; the — میلاد milad; میلاد عیسی mīlādi-"īssà; to cast a —, زائچه استخراج ا zāi'ché-isstikhrāj-èt.

Natural, *a.* طبیعی tābī"ī; خلقی khilkī, جبلی jìbillī; — history, علم حیوانات "ilmi-hàywānāt; — philosophy, حکمت طبیعه hikméti-tābi"iyyé; — child, پیچ pìch.

Naturalization, *s.* اجنبیی تبعیته قبول ا èjnébīyyi-tèbà"ìyyèta-kābūl-èt; letters of —, تبعیتنامه tebà"ìyyètnāmé; پاتنته pàtènta.

Naturalize, *v.a.* اجنبیی تبعیته قبول ا èjnébīyi-tèbà"ìyyèta-kābūl-èt.

Naturalized, *a.* یرلو کبی اولمش yèrli-ghìbi-òlmush; یرلشمش yèrleshmish.

Nature, *s.* طبیعت tābī"àt; خالق khālik, الله Allāh.

Naught, *s.* هیچ hìch.

Naughtiness, *s.* یرامزلق yàramàzlik.

Naughty, *a.* یرامز yàramàz.

Nausea, *s.* یورك بولانمسی yùrèk-būlàn-massi.

Nautical, *a.* بحری bàhrī.

Naval, *a.* بحری bàhrī, دونتمایه متعلق dònanmaya-mùta"àllik.

Nave, *s.* (church) صحن sàhn; (wheel) مویلو mòylu, باشلق bāshlik.

Navel, *s.* کوبك ghyùbèk.

Navigability, *s.* کمی و قایق ایله کشت و کذارینك امکانی ghèmi-vé-kàyik-ìla-ghèsht-u-ghyùzārinin-imkyāni.

Navigable, *a.* کشت و کذاری ممکن ghèsht-u-ghyùzāri-mùmkin.

Navigate, *v.a.* کمی ایله کزمك ghèmi-ìla-gèzmek.

Navigation, *s.* علم سیر سفائن "ìlmi-seyri-sèfā'in.

Navigator, *s.* کمی ایله کزك کمسنه ghèmi-ìla-gèzen-kimèssné.

Navy, *s.* دونتما dònanma.

Nay, *ad.* یوق yòk.

Naze, *s.* بورون bùrun.

Neapolitan, *a.* ناپولیلو nàpolili.

Near, *a.* یقین yàkin, قریب kārīb, نزدیك nèzdīk; خسیس khāssīss, طمعکار tāmà"kyār; صول sòl, صول طرفده کی sòl-tàrafdaki; —, *ad.* همان (hèmen), تقریبا tākrībā; —, *pr.* یاننه yànina, یاننده yàninda; قربنه kùrbina, قربنده kùrbinda; نزدینه nèzdina, نزدنده nèzdinda; جوارینه jìwārina, جوارنده jìwārinda, حوالیسنه hàwālīssina, حوالیسنده hàwālīssinda; (in time) صولرنده sūlarinda, قرارلرنده kārārlarinda.

Nearsighted, *a.* کوتاهبین kyùtāhbīn.

Nearsightedness, *s.* کوتاهبینلك kyù-tāhbīnlik.

Neat, *a.* تمیز tèmiz; کوزل ghyùzèl, ساده کوزل sādé-ghyùzèl; — cattle, صیغر مقوله سی حیوانات sighir-màkūléssi-hàywānāt.

Nebula, *s.* خفیف بلوط khàfif-būlut.

Nebular, *a.* بلوط کبی būlut-ghìbi.

Nebulosity, *s.* بلوطلولق būlutluluk.

Necessaries, *s.pl.* حوائج ضروریه hàwā'iji-zàrūrìyyé, لوازمات làwāzimāt.

Necessarily, *ad.* البته elbètta, بالضرور bì-'z-zàrūr, بالضروره bì-'z-zàrūré.

Necessary, *a.* لازم lāzim ; (very) الزم èlzèm ; —, *s.* لازمه lāzimé ; كنف kènef, ممشا mèmshā, ابدستخانه àb-dest-khānè. [ètdirmek.

Necessitate, *v.a.* ايجاب ايتدرمك ījāb-

Necessitous, *a.* محتاج mùhtāj, فقير fàkīr, حاجتمند hājetmènd.

Necessity, *s.* احتياج ìhtiyāj, ضرورت zàrūrèt ; حاجت hājet.

Neck, *s.* بويون bòyun, كردن ghèrdèn, عنق "ùnuk.

Neckcloth, *s.* بويون باغى bòyun-bàghi.

Necklace, *s.* كردنلك ghèrdenlik, قلاده kìlàdé.

Necktie, *s.* بويون باغى bòyun-bàghi.

Nectarine, *s.* دراقى dùrrākī, تويسزشفتالو tùysuz-shèftāli.

Need, *s.* احتياج ìhtiyāj, ضرورت zàrūrèt, حاجت hājet ; —, *v.a.* محتاج او mùhtāj-òl.

Needful, *a.* لازم lāzim ; the —, ايجاب مصلحت ījābi-màsslāhat ; اقچه àkcha, پاره (pàra).

Needle, *s.* ايكنه ìghné, سوزن sūzèn.

Needlework, *s.* دكش dìkish ; ايكنه ايشى ìghné-ìshi.

Needy, *a.* محتاج mùhtāj, فقير fàkīr, حاجتمند hājetmènd.

Negation, *s.* انكار ìnkyār ; نفى nèfy.

Negative, *a.* نفى ايدن nèfy-èden ; رد ايدن rèdd-èden ; —, *s.* حرف نفى hàrfi-nèfy ; —, *v.a.* رد ا rèdd-èt.

Neglect, *s.* دقتسزلق dìkkàtsizlik, اهمال ìhmāl ; —, *v.a.* اهمال ا ìhmāl-et, باقمامق bàkmamak.

Neglectful, *a.* اهمالجى ìhmālji.

Negligence, *s.* اهمال ìhmāl.

Negligent, *a.* اهمالجى ìhmālji.

Negociate, *v.a.* مكالمه ا mùkyālémé-et, سويلشمك sùwèyleshmek ; صاتمق sàtmak, سورمك sùrmek.

Negociation, *s.* مكالمه mùkyālémé, مذاكره mùzākéré, مباحثه mùbāhassé.

Negro, *s.* عرب "àrab, سياه عرب sìyāh-"àrab.

Neigh, *v.n.* كشنمك kìshnémek.

Neighbour, *s.* قوكشى kòngshu (kòm-shu), جار jār ; مجاور mùjāvir.

Neighbourhood, *s.* قوكشيلق kòngshu-luk ; جوار jìwār ; مجاورت mùjāvérèt.

Neighbouring, *a.* يقين yàkin, يقينده اولان yàkinda-òlan, جوارده اولان jìwārda-òlan.

Neither, *p.* هيچ بريسى hìch-bìrissi, نه او نه او nè-ò-nè-ò ; —, *ad.* ونده vè-nèdé, نه nè.

Nephew, *s.* يكن yèghen, برادرزاده bìrāder-zādé, همشيره زاده hèmshīré--zādé, قاينزاده kàyn-zādé, انشته زاده ènishté-zādé, باجناخزاده bàjénàkh--zādé, &c. &c.

Neptune, *s.* نپطون يلديزى nèptūn-yìldizi.

Nerve, *s.* سگير sìngir, عصبه "àssaba ; اق طمر àk-dàmar ; متانت mètānèt, جسارت jèssārèt.

Nervous, *a.* قورقاق kòrkàk ; متانتلو mètānètli ; اق طمردن عبارت اولان àk-dàmardan-"ìbāret-òlan ; اق طمرلره متعلق اولان àk-dàmarlara-mùta"àllik-òlan.

Nest, *s.* يوه yìwa, لانه lānè.

Net, *s.* اغ àgh; (cast) صاچمه sAchma; —, *a.* دارهسی چیقمش dàrassi-chìk-mish; مصرفی چیقمش mAssrafi-chìk-mish; —, *v.a.* قزانمق kAzanmak.

Nettle, *s.* اصرغان اوتی ìssirghAn-òtu; —, *v.a.* اغرینهدوقنمق Aghirina-dò-kunmak, کوجنه کتمك ghyùjuna-ghìtmek.

Neuralgia, *s.* سکیر اغریسی singir-Aghrissi.

Neuter, *a.* قارشمیان kArishmayan, نه ارکك نه دیشی اولان nè-èrkek-nè-dìshi-òlan.

Neutral, *a.* قارشمیان kArishmayan.

Neutrality, *s.* بیطرفلق bītàraflik.

Neutralize, *v.a.* محو ا màhv-èt.

Never, *ad.* هیچ hìch, اصلا Assla, ابداً èbédEn.

Nevertheless, *c.* ینه yìnÉ (ghènÉ), مع ما فیه mà"a-mā-fīh.

New, *a.* یکی yèngi, جدید jèdīd, نو nèv; مجدد mùjèdded; تازه tāzÉ.

News, *s. pl.* خبر khAber, حوادث hàwādiss.

Newspaper, *s.* غزته ghàzèta, تقویم tAkwīm, جریده jèrīdÉ.

Newsvender, *s.* غزته صاتان ghàzèta-sAtan.

Next, *a.* یاندهکی yàndaki; الت یاندهکی Alt-yàndaki, صکرهکی sòngraki; —, *ad.* صکره sòngra, بعده bà"dahu, پس pèss; — day, ایرتهسی کون èrtéssi-ghyùn, فرداسی کون fèrdassi-ghyùn, برکون صکره bìr-ghyùn-sòngra; اوبرکون ò-bìr-ghyùn.

Nib, *s.* بورون bùrun; —, *v.a.* قطع ا kAt"-et.

Nibble, *v.a.* اوك دیشلر یله یواش یواش اصرمق ùn-dìshlarīla-yàwAsh-yàwAsh-ìssirmak.

Nice, *a.* ایو īyi, کوزل ghyùzèl, طاتلو tAtli; مراقلو mèrAkli, پك دقت ایدیجی pèk-dìkkAt-èdiji.

Niche, *s.* هجره hūjrÉ.

Nick, *s.* چنتك chèntik, کدك ghèdik; in the very — of time, تمام وقتنده tAmAm-wAktinda.

Niece, *s.* برادرزاده قیز bìrādèr-zādÉ-kìz, &c. See Nephew.

Niggard, *s.* خسیس khAssīss, طمعکار tàmà"kyār, جمری jìmri.

Nigh, *a.* یقین yàkin, قریب kArīb, نزدیك nèzdīk; well —, *ad.* ازقالدی Az-kàldi.

Night, *s.* کیجه ghèyja, لیل lèyl, شب shèb.

Nightgown, *s.* کیجهلك ghèyjalik.

Nightingale, *s.* بلبل bùlbul, عندلیب "àndélīb (pl. عنادل "ànādil).

Nightman, *s.* لغمجی làghimji.

Nightmare, *s.* کابوس kyābūs.

Nightshirt, *s.* کیجهلك ghèyjalik.

Nile (river), *s.* نیل نهری nīl-nèhri.

Nimble, *a.* چابك chàbik, تتك tètik.

Nine, *a.* طقوز dòkuz, تسع tìss", تسعه tìss"à, نه nùh.

Nineteen, *a.* اون طقوز òn-dòkuz.

Ninety, *a.* طقسان dòksan, تسعین tìss"īn.

Nip, *v.a.* قسمق kìssmak.

Nippers, *s. pl.* قساج kìssAj.

Nipple, *s.* ممه mèmÉ, ممه باشی mèmÉ-bAshi.

Nitre, *s.* کهرچله ghyùhèrchilÉ.

Nitrogen, *s.* مولد الکهرچله mùwèllidu-'l-ghyùhèrchilÉ.

No, *ad.* يوق yòk, خير khàyr, لا lā; —, *p.* هيچ hìch, هيچ بر hìch-bìr; — matter, ضرريوق zàrar-yòk; — more, *ad.* ارتق àrtik; فيمابعد fī-mā-bà''d.

Nobility, *s.* شرفا shùréfā; اصالت àssālèt; اصلزادكان àsslzādé-ghian.

Noble, *a.* نجيب nèjīb, شريف shèrīf, كريم kèrīm; اصيل àssīl, اصالتلو àssālètlū.

Nobleman, *s.* بكزاده بك bè*gh*-zādé-bè*gh*, اصلزاده àsslzādé.

Nobody, *p.* كمسه kìmsé, هيچ كمسه hìch-kìmsé.

Nocturnal, *a.* كيجه وقتنده اولان ghèyj*a*-wàkt*i*nd*a*-òlan, ليلى lèylī.

Nod, *s.* باش ايله ايديلن اشارت bàsh-il*a*-èdilen-ìshāret; —, *v.a.* and *n.* باش ايله اشارت ا bàsh - il*a* - ìshāret - et; اويقوده باشى كوكسنه دوشمك ùyku-d*a*-bàsh*i*-gh*yù*kssun*a*-dùshmek.

Noise, *s.* سس sèss, صدا sàdā; كورلدى ghyùruldu, شماته shàmat*a*.

Noisy, *a.* شماته shàmat*a*; شماته لو shàmat*ali*; شماته جى shàmat*aji*.

Nomad, Nomade, *a.* كوچبه ghyùchébé, بدوى bèdévī.

Nominal, *a.* لفظى làfzī; اسمى ìssmī; اعتبارى ì''tībārī. [nàssb-et.

Nominate, *v.a.* تعيين ا tà''yīn-et, نصب ا

Nominative, *s.* مبتدا mùbtédà.

Nonchalance, *s.* قيدسزلق kàydsizlik.

None, *p.* هيچ hìch, هيچ بر hìch-bìr; كمسه kìmsé, هيچ كمسه hìch-kìmsé, هيچ بركمسه hìch-bìr-kìmsé (*or* كمسنه kìmèssné).

Nonsense, *s.* صاچمه sàchm*a*, بوش لقردى bòsh-làk*i*rd*i*, معناسزشى mà''nàssiz-shèy. [-bìr-yèr.

Nook, *s.* كوشه ky*ù*shé, قويتى برير kòytu-

Noon, Noonday, Noontide, *s.* اويله وقتى *ù*ylé-wàkt*i*, ظهر zùhr, زوال وقتى zèwāl-wàkt*i*.

Noose, *s.* ايلمك ìlmik.

Nor, *c.* ونه ده vè-nè-d*a*, نه nè.

North, *s.* شمال shìmāl, يلدز y*ì*ldiz; —, *a.* شمالى shìmālī; — east, پويراز pòyraz; — west, قره يل kàr*a*-yèl.

Northerly, *a.* Northward, *ad.* يلدزه طوغرى y*ì*ldiz*a*-dòghru.

Northern, *a.* شمالى shìmālī.

Norway, *s.* نوروجيا nòrvéji*a*.

Norwegian, *a.* نوروجيالو nòrvéjiali.

Nose, *s.* بورون bùrun, انف ènf.

Nosegay, *s.* چيچك دمتى chìchek-dèmeti, كلدسته gh*yù*ldessté.

Nostril, *s.* بورون دليكى bùrun-dèli*ghi*.

Not, *ad.* See Grammar.

Notch, *s.* كدك ghèdik, چنتك chèntik, ديش dìsh; —, *v.a.* چنتمك chèntmek.

Note, *s.* تذكره tèzkéré, پوصله pùssl*a*; نوطه nòt*a*; تعين tà''àyyun, اعتبار ì''tibār; —, *v.a.* دقت ا dìkkat-et; — down, ضبط ا zàbt-et, يازيويرمك yàz*i*vèrmek; of —, متعين mùt*a*-''àyyin, معتبر mù''tébèr, بللوباشلو bèlli-bàshli; — of hand, تحويل tàhvīl; bank —, قائمه kā'imé.

Note-book, *s.* مجمعه mèjm*a*''à.

Noted, *a.* مشهور mèshhūr.

Nothing, *s.* هيچ hìch, هيچ برشى hìch-bìr-shèy; عدم ''àdem, نيستى nīsstī.

Notice, *s.* خبر khÀbᴇr; اعلان ì''lān; دقت dìkkÀt; to give —, خبر ويرمك khÀbᴇr-vÈrmek; — — public —, اعلان ا ì''lān-et; to take —, دقت ا [dìkkÀt-et.
Notification, *s.* خبر khÀber.
Notify, *v.a.* خبريني ويرمك khÀberini-vÈrmek. [èfkyār),
Notion, *s.* عقل ''àkl, فكر fìkr (pl. افكار
Notoriety, *s.* شهرت رديه shùhrèt-rèdiyyé.
Notorious, *a.* متواتر mùtéwātir, عالمك معلومى ''ālᴇming-mà''lūmi.
Notwithstanding, *c.* ينه yìné (ghèné), مع مافيه mà''a-mā-fīh.
Nought, *s.* صفر sìfr; هيچ برشى hìch-bìr-shèy; to come to —, بوشه چيقمق bòsha-chìkmak, ارقه سى ايشلمامك ărkassi-ìshlémamek.
Nourish, *v.a.* بسلمك bèsslémek.
Nourishment, *s.* يمك yèmèk, ييه جك yèyéjek; بسلمك خاصه سى bèsslémek-khĀsssassi. [hìkyāyé.
Novel, *a.* يكى yèngi; —, *s.* حكايه
Novelist, *s.* حكايه طراز hìkyāyé-tìrāz.
Novelty, *s.* يكيلك yèngilik; تحاف شى tùhāf-shèy.
November, *s.* تشرين ثانى tèshrīnī-sānī.
Novice, *s.* عجمى ''Àjémi.
Now, *ad.* شمدى shìmdi, حالا hālā, الان èl-ān, اليوم el-yèvm, الحالة هذه èl-hālétu-hāzihi; —, *c.* امدى ìmdi; — and then, بعضاً bÀ''zan, بعض كره bÀ''zi-kèrré, اراصره àra-sàra, اراده صره ده àrada-sàrada, احياناً ìhyānan.
Now-a-days, *ad.* شمدى shìndi.

Nowhere, *ad.* هيچ بريرده hìch-bìr-yèrda.
Noxious, *a.* مضر mùzìrr, مضرتلو mÀzàr-rÀtli. [burun.
Nozzle, *s.* امزك èmzik, غاغا ghàgha, بورون bùrun.
Nucleus, *s.* مركز mèrkèz.
Nude, *a.* چپلاق chìplAk.
Nuisance, *s.* بلا bèlā. [bātil.
Null, *a.* بوش bòsh, حكمسز hùkmsuz, باطل
Numb, Numbed, *a.* اويوشق ùyushuk, اويوشمش ùyushmush.
Number, *s.* صايى sàyi, عدد ''àded; —, *v.n.* اولمق òlmak, بالغ او bÀligh-òl; —, *v.a.* صايمق sàymak, تعداد ا tà''dād-et; a great —, چوق chòk, كثير kèssīr, وافر wāfir. [kèssrèt-ùzéré.
Numerous, *a.* چوق chòk, كثرت اوزره
Nuptial, *a.* اولنمه دوكوننه متعلق èvlᴇnma-dùghununa-mùta''àllik; nuptials, *s. pl.* اولنمه دوكونى èvlènma-dùghunu, وليمه vèlīmé, سور sūr.
Nurse, *s.* خسته يه باقيجى khĀsstaya-bĀkiji; چوجغه باقيجى chòjugha-bĀkiji, دادى dàdi; wet —, دايه dāyé, سوت انا sùt-àna; —, *v.a.* باقمق bĀkmak, خدمت ا khìdmet-et(hìz-); سوت ويرمك sùt-vèrmek, امزرمك èmzirmek; صاقلمق sàklamak.
Nursery, *s.* چوجقلره مخصوص اوطه chò-juklera-màkhsūss-òda; فدان بغچه سى fìdAn-bĀghchassi.
Nurserymaid, *s.* دادى dàdi.
Nut, *s.* فندق fìndik; (of a screw) صمون [sòmun.
Nutgall, *s.* مازى mĀzi.
Nutmeg, *s.* هندوستان جوزى hìndisstān-jèvizi, جوزبوا jèvzi-bèwwā.

Nutriment, *s.* يمك yèmèk, ييه‌جك yèyéjek; بسلمك خاصه‌سى bèsslémek-khāssassi. [-vèrir-òlan.

Nutritious, *a.* قوت ويرر اولان kùvvet-

O.

O, *int.* اى èy, يا yā. [mèyshé-aghaji.

Oak, *s.* ميشه mèyshé, ميشه اغاجى

Oakum, *s.* استوپى ùsstùpu.

Oar, *s.* كورك kyùrèk.

Oath, *s.* أند and, يمين yèmīn; to take an —, اندا يچمك and-ichmek, يمين ا

Oats, *s. pl.* يولاف yùlaf. [yèmīn-et.

Obdurate, *a.* عنادجى ʿìnādji.

Obdurateness, *s.* عناد ʿìnād.

Obedience, *s.* اطاعت ìtāʿʿat, انقياد inkiyād, امتثال imtissāl, مماثلت mùmāssélèt. [mùnkād, رام rām.

Obedient, *a.* مطيع mùtīʿ, منقاد

Obese, *a.* شيشمان shìshmān.

Obey, *v.a.* دكله‌مك dìnglémek (dīné-mek), اطاعت ا ìtāʿʿat-et, منقاد او mùnkād-òl.

Object, *s.* جسم jìssm, مرئى mèrʾī; مرام mèrām, مراد mùrād, مقصود maksūd; مفعول به mèfʿʿūlun-bìh; —, *v.n.* اعتراض ا ìʿʿtirāz-et.

Objection, *s.* اعتراض ìʿʿtirāz.

Obligation, *s.* مجبوريت mèjbūrìyyèt; بورج bòrj; تحويل tàhvīl, تمسك tèmèssuk.

Oblige, *v.a.* جبر ا jèbr-et, اجبار ا ìjbār-et; مجبور ا mèjbūr-et; كرم ا kèrem-et, عنايت ا ʿìnāyet-et, لطف ا lùtf-et.

Obliging, *a.* عنايتكار ʿìnāyetkyār.

Oblique, *a.* مائل māʾil, منحرف mùn-hàrif, أكرى èghri. [lik.

Obliqueness, Obliquity, *s.* اكريلك èghri-

Obliterate, *v.a.* بوزمق bòzmak, سلمك silmek, چيزمك chìzmek.

Oblivion, *s.* نسيان nìssyān, فراموشى fèrāmūshī. [mūsstatīl.

Oblong, *a.* اوزون ùzun; —, *s.* مستطيل

Obscene, *a.* پش piss, فاحش fāhish, ادبه‌مغاير èdeba-mùghāyir. [shèt.

Obsceneness, Obscenity, *s.* فحاشت fèhā-

Obscure, *a.* قرانلق kāranlik, مظلم mùzlim; مغلق mùghlàk, مبهم mùbhèm.

Obscurity, *s.* قرانلق kāranlik.

Obsequious, *a.* متواضع mùtéwāzi.

Observation, *s.* نظر nazar; نظرايتمكلك nāzar-ètmeklik; رصد rassad; ملاحظه mùlāhaza.

Observatory, *s.* رصدخانه rassad-khāné.

Observe, *v.a.* باقمق bakmak, كوزتمك ghyùzètmek, دقت ا dìkkat-et; طوتمق tùtmak, رعايت ا riʿʿāyet-et, اتباع ا ittibāʿʿ-et, امتثال ا imtissāl-et; سويلمك sùwèylémek, بيورمق bùyurmak.

Obstacle, *s.* مانع māniʿʿ, سكته sèkté.

Obstinacy, *s.* عناد ʿìnād, معاندت mùʿʿānédèt, تمرد tèmèrrud.

Obstinate, *a.* عنادجى ʿìnādji, معند mùʿʿànnid, متمرد mùtémèrrid.

Obstruct, *v.a.* كسمك kèssmek, قپامق kapamak, طيقامق tikamak, سد ا sèdd-et.

Obstruction, *s.* مانع mānì'', سده sùddé.

Obtain, *v.a.* تحصيل ا tàhsīl-et, استحصال ا ìsstihsāl-et, نائل او nā'il-òl, مظفراو mùzAffer-òl, بولمق bùlmak, المق Almak, قوپارمق kòparmak.

Obtuse, *a.* كور kyùr, كسمز kèssmàz; درايتسز dìrāyetsiz, احمق àhmàk; منفرج mùnfèrij (fem. منفرجه mùnfèrijé).

Obviate, *v.a.* چارەسنى بولمق chāréssini-bùlmak, علاجنى بولمق ''ìlājini-bùlmak.

Obvious, *a.* اچيق àchìk, اشكار āshikyār, ميداندە mèydānda, واضح wāzih, عيان ''àyān.

Occasion, *s.* كره kèrré, دفعه dèf''à; مناسبت mùnāssébèt, اقتضا ìktizā, حاجت hājet; سبب sèbeb, علت ''ìllèt, ذريعه zèrī''à, وسيله vèssīlé; فرصت fìrsAt, ايپ اوجى ìp-ùju, سررشته sèr-rìshté; —, *v.a.* ايراث ا īrāss-et, انتاج ا ìntāj-et, جلب ا jèlb-et, دعوت ا dà''vèt-et, بادى او bādī-òl, باعث او bā''iss-òl, مورث او mūriss-òl, منتج او mùntij-òl, وسيله او vèssīlé-òl.

Occasional, *a.* ظهورى zùhūrī, اراصره واقع اولان àra-sìra-wākì''-òlAn; —ly, *ad.* بعضاً bà''zan, اراصره àra-sìra, احياناً ìhyānan, ايكيدەبر ìkida-bìr.

Occupation, *s.* مشغوليت mèshghūlìyyèt, ايش ìsh, شغل shùghl (*pl.* اشغال èshghāl), كار kyār, پيشه pīshé; استيعاب ìsstī''Ab; ضبط ومحافظه zAbt-u-mùhAfaza.

Occupy, *v.a.* ايش ويرمك ìsh-vèrmek, ايش بولمق ìsh-bùlmak, اشغال ا ìshghāl-et; مشغول ا mèshghūl-et; طوتمق tùtmak, وقتنى طوتمق wAktìni-tùtmak, ايشندن اليقومق ìshindan-Alìkòmak, مانع او mānì''òl; استيعاب ا ìsstī''Ab-et, طوتمق tùtmak, طولدرمق dòldurmak; ضبط ومحافظه ا zAbt-u-mùhAfaza-et, وجودى ايلەغيرك دخولنى منع ا vùjūdi-ìla-ghāyrìng-dùkhūlini-mèn''-et; استمك ìsstémek.

Occur, *v.n.* اولمق òlmak, واقع او wAkì''òl, ظهورا zùhūr-et, فعلەكلمك fì''la-ghèlmek.

Occurrence, *s.* ايش ìsh, شى shèy, وقعه wàk''à (*pl.* وقائع wàkā'ì''); —s, *s. pl.* وقوعات wùkū''At, ظهورات zùhūrAt, حوادثات hàwAdissAt.

Ocean, *s.* طيش دكزى dìsh-dèngizi, بحر محيط bàhri-mùhìt, عمان ''ùmmAn, قاموس kAmūss, اقيانوس ìkyānūss, دريا dèryā.

Ochre, *s.* (red) اشى بوياسى Ashi-bòyassi.

Octagon, *s.* **Octagonal,** *a.* مثمن mùssèmmen, سكزكوشەلو sèkiz-kyùshéli.

October, *s.* تشرين اول tèshrīni-èvvel.

Ocular, *a.* كوزايله كوريلان ghyùz-ìla-ghyùrulen; to give — proof, — demonstration, كوزايله كوسترمك ghyùz-ìla-ghyùsstermek; to have — —, — —, كوزايله كورمك ghyùz-ìla-ghyùrmek, رأى العين مشاهده ا rè'ya-'l-''àyn-mùshāhédé-et; — witness, كوزيله كورن ghyùzila-ghyùren,

شاهدا لعين shāhidu-'l-"àyn, شاهد shāhid.

Oculist, *s.* كوزجى هكيم ghyùzju-hèkim.

Odd, *a.* تك tèk; عجيب "ȃjīb (ȃjā'ib), غريب ghȃrīb, تحاف tùhȃf.

Ode, *s.* (long) قصيده kȂssīdé, (short) غزل ghàzèl.

Odious, *a.* منفور mènfūr, مكروه mèkrūh, كريه kèrīh, مستكره mùsstèkrēh.

Odorous, *a.* قوقولو kòkulu, رائحه لو rā'ihàli.

Odour, *s.* قوقو kòku, رائحه rā'ihà, بو bū, بوى bùy; sweet —, كوزل قوقو ghyùzèl-kòkū, رائحه طيبه rā'ihà'i-tàyyibé, بوى شيرين bùyi-shīrīn; bad —, فنا قوقو fèna-kòku, اغر قوقو ȃghir-kòku, رائحه كريهه rā'ihà'i-kèrīhé; in bad —, منكوب mènkyūb, اعتباردن دوشمش ì"tibārdan-dùshmush.

Of, *pr.* ك ing, نك ning; دن dan; لو li, lū, ايله ìla; دن اوتورى dan-ȗturu, دن طولايى dan-dòlayi; از èz; من mìn; عن "àn.

Off, *ad.* اوستندن ùsstundan, اوزرندن ùzerindan; اوزاق ùzȂk; اوزاقده ùzȂkda, اوزاغه ùzȂgha; to be —, كتمك ghìtmek; يقلمق yìkilmak, سكدرمك sìkdirmek, جهنم او jìhànnam-òl; to be well —, حسن حالده او hùssnu-hālda-òl, حالى اويغون او hāli-ùyghun-òl, رفاه حالى او rèfāhi-hāli-òl, مرفه الحال او mùrèffahu-'l-hāl-òl; to come —, چيقمق chìkmak, قوپمق kòpmak; اولمق òlmak, واقع او wāki"-òl, وقوع بولمق wùkū"-bùlmak; to go —, كتمك ghìtmek; اتش المق Ȃtèsh-Ȃlmak; اولمق òlmak, اويمق ùymak; to take —, چيقارمق chìkàr-mak, قالدرمق kȂldirmak; كسمك kèssmek, قطع ا kȂt"-et; تقليد ا tȂklīd-et; to pull —, قوپارمق kòpàrmak; اوستندن المق ùsstundan-Ȃlmak; —, *a.* صاغ sàgh, صاغ طرفده كى sàgh-tàrafdaki.

Offal, *s.* حيوانك ات صايلميان طرفلرى hàywȂning-èt-sàyilmayȂn-tàraflari.

Offence, *s.* قباحت kȂbāhat, جنحه jùnhà, جرم jùrm, صوچ sùch; تجاوز tèjāvuz; to give —, كوجندرمك ghyùjèndirmek; to take —, كوجنمك ghyùjènmek.

Offend, *v.a.* كوجندرمك ghyùjèndirmek; —, *v.n.* قباحت ا kȂbāhat-et; صوچ ا sùch-et; كناه ا ghyùnāh-et; — against, مغاير حركت ا mùghāyir-hàrékèt-et.

Offender, *s.* صوچلو sùchlù, قباحتلو kȂbāhatli, مجرم mùjrim, جنحه صاحبى jùnhà-sāhibi; old —, سابقه لو sābikali, اسكى قورت èsski-kùrt.

Offensive, *a.* كريه kèrīh, بد bèd; تجاوزى tèjāvuzī; — and defensive, تجاوزى وتدافعى tèjāvuzī-vè-tèdāfu"ī.

Offer, *s.* تكليف tèklīf; ويرش vèrish; —, *v.n.* كورنمك ghyùrunmek, ظهور ا zùhūr-et; —, *v.a.* ويرمك vèrmek; تكليف ا tèklīf-et; عرض ا "àrz-et; — violence, زورلامق zòrlamak; — — to one's feelings,

صوغوق برشی تکلیف ا sòghuk-bìr-shèy-tèklīf-et.

Off-hand, *a.* پك تكليفسز pèk-tèklifsiz; عارسز "ārsiz; چابك chàbik; —, *s.* صاغ طرفی sàgh-tàrafi.

Office, *s.* قلم kàlem; اوطه òda; مغازه màghaza; خدمت khìdmet (hìz-), مأموريت mè'mūrìyyèt, ایش ìsh.

Officer, *s.* ضابط zābit; مأمور mè'mūr.

Official, *a.* رسمی rèssmī; —ly, *ad.* رسماً [rèssman.

Offing, *s.* انكين ènghin.

Oft, Often, Oftentimes, Ofttimes, *ad.* چوق chòk, چوق كره chòk-kèrré, چوق دفعه chòk-dèf"à, نيجه كره nìjé-kèrré, قاچ كره kàch-kèrré; صيق sìk, صيق صيق sìk-sìk, كراراً kèrāran, مراراً mèrāran.

Ogle, *v.a.* عشوه كارانه يان باقمق "ìshvé-kyārané-yàn-bàkmak.

Ogre, *s.* مردمخوار mèrdumkhār.

Oh! *int.* آه àh, وای vày, واه wàh.

Oil, *s.* ياغ yàgh, روغن rūghàn; —, *v.a.* ياغلامق yàghlamak, تدهين ا tèdhīn-et.

Ointment, *s.* ياغ yàgh, مرهم mèrhèm.

Old, *a.* اسكی èsski, قديم kàdīm; اسكيمش èsskimish, كهنه kyùhné; (person) قوجه kòja, اختيار ìkhtiyār, مسن mùssinn, سالديده sāl-dīdé, سالخورده sāl-khūrdé; — man, پير pīr, شيخ shèykh, اختيار ìkhtiyār; — woman, قوجه قاری kòja-kàri, پيره زن pìré-zèn, عجوز "àjūz; — Testament, تورات tèvrāt, كتب عهد عتيق kyùtubu-"àhdi-"àtik; of —, اسكيدن èsskidan, ازقديم èz-kàdīm, من القديم mìn-el-kàdīm, عن اصل "àn-àsslin, فی الاصل fī-'l-àssl, اوتەدنبرو ùtédan-bèri, اسكيدنبرو èsskidan-bèri.

Oldfashioned, *a.* اسكی زمان طرزی èsski-zèmān-tàrzi.

Oleander, *s.* زقوم zàkkūm.

Olive, *s.* زيتون zèytūn (zèytin); — tree, زيتون اغاجی zèytun-àghàji; — oil, زيتون ياغی zèytun-yàghi.

Omelet, *s.* قيغنه kàyghana.

Omen, *s.* فال fàl.

Ominous, *a.* فال نوعندن fàl-nèv"inden; منحوس mènhūss.

Omission, *s.* قصور kùssūr; تقصير tàksīr; اتلايش àtlayish; ترك tèrk.

Omit, *v.a.* اتلامق àtlamak, براقمق bràkmak, ترك ا tèrk-et, صرف نظر ا sàrfi-nàzar-et; — an opportunity, قصور ا kùssūr-et, فرصت قاچرمق fìrsat-kàchirmak.

Omnibus, *s.* چارشی عربه سی chàrshi-"arabassi.

Omnipotence, Omnipotency, *s.* قدرت علی الاطلاق kùdret-"alé-'l-ìtlàk.

Omnipotent, *a.* قدير kàdīr.

Omnipresent, *a.* مكاندن منزه. mèkyān-dan-mùnèzzèh.

Omniscience, *s.* علم مطلق "ìlmi-mùtlàk.

Omniscient, *a.* اعلم à"lèm, عليم "àlīm, علام "àllām.

On, *pr.* ده é, a; ده dé, da; اوستنه ùsstuna, اوستنده ùsstunda; اوزرينه ùzerina, اوزرنده ùzerindā; بر bèr; علی "àla; —, *ad.* ايلرو ìléri; اوسته ùssté, اوستده ùsstdé; ينه yìné (ghènÉ); بردوزی یه bìr - dùziyÉ, متمادیاً mùtémādiyan; — foot, *ad.* یایان yàyan, ماشیاً māshiyan; —, *a.* پیاده pìyādÉ; — high, یوکسکه yùksegha, یوکسکده yùksekda; کوکه ghyùghÉ, کوکده ghyùkdÉ, فی السموات fì-'ss-sèmāvāti; — horseback, اتایله Àt-ila; اتلو Àtli, سوار sùwār, سواری sùwāri; — purpose, مخصوص màkhsūss, قصداً kÀssdan, عمداً "àmdan; — that day, اول کون òl-ghyùn, یوم مذکور yèvmi-mèzkyūr; to put —, کیمک ghīmek; کیدرمک ghìdirmek; to go —, ایلروکتمک ìléri-ghìtmek; اولمق òlmak, کچمک ghèchmek; کیلمك ghìyilmek; to come —, کلمك ghèlmek, کلیویرمك ghèlivèrmek, ایلرو کلمك ìléri-ghèlmek.

Once, *ad.* برکره bìr-kÈrrÉ, بردفعه bìr-dèf"à, برسفر bìr-sèfer; بروقت bìr--wÀkit, برزمان bìr-zàmÀn, وقتامن الاوقات wÀktan-mìn-el-èvkÀt; — more, بردها bìr-dàhà.

One, *a.* بر bìr; یك yèk; احد àhàd, واحد wàhid (fem. احدی ìhdà); —, *pr.* ادم ÀdAm, کشی kìshi; some —, بری bìri, بریسی bìrissi, ادم ÀdAm; no —, کمسه kìmsÉ; every —, هرکس hèr-kèss; any —, بری bìri, بریسی bìrissi, ادم ÀdAm; کمسه kìmsÉ; —'s-self, کندی kèndi.

One-eyed, *a.* یکچشم yèkchèshm. [ìnsÀf.

Onesidedness, *s.* عدم انصاف "àdemi-

Onion, *s.* صوغان sòghAn, بصل bÀssl.

Only, *ad.* یالکز yÀlingiz, فقط fàkAt, صالط sÀlt, ساده sādÉ, صافی sāfi, مجرد mùjèrred. [kìtAbi.

Onomasticon, *s.* لغات کتابی lùghAt-

Onset, *s.* هجوم hùjūm.

Onslaught, *s.* هجوم hùjūm.

Onward, *ad.* ایلرو ìléri. [-tÀshi.

Onyx, *s.* سلیمانی طاشی sùlèymĀnī-

Ooze, *v.n.* صزمق sìzmak, نشوا nèshv-et (or نشفا nèshf-et), تقاطرا tàkĀtur-et.

Opal, *s.* عین الشمس "àynu-'sh-shèmss.

Opaque, *a.* دونق dùnuk, کثیف kèssīf.

Open, *a.* اچق àchik, باز bĀz, کشاده kyùshādé, مفتوح mèftūh; —, *v.a.* اچمق àchmak, فتحا fèth-et (fèt-h); —, *v.n.* اچلمق àchilmak.

Opening, *a.* مسهل mùsshìl; —, *s.* اچقلق àchiklik, ارالق àralik, قپو kÀpi; فرصت fìrsAt; اچمه àchma; اچلمه àchilma; فتح fèth (t-h), کشاد kyùshād.

Openly, *ad.* اچق àchik, اچقدن اچغه àchikdan-àchigha, جهراً jèhran, عیاناً "àyānan, اشکار Āshikyār.

Opera, *s.* اوپرا òpÉra. [dūrbīnī.

Opera-glass, *s.* اوپرا دوربینی òpÉra-

Operate, *v.n.* ایشلمك ìshlémek, ایش کورمك ìsh-ghyùrmek; تأثیرا tè'sīr-et; عمل ویرمك "ÀmEl-vÈrmek; اجرای صنعتا ìjrāyi-sàn"àt-et.

Ophthalmia, *s.* رمد rèmed.

Opiate, *s.* اویومق ایچون بر علاج ÙyÙmak-ìchin-bìr-"ìlÀj.

Opine, *v.n.* ظن ا zànn-et.

Opinion, *s.* رأى rèʿy, ظن zànn, قياس kìyāss, قول kȦvl, سوز sùz; (legal) فتوا fètwà.

Opinionated, *a.* عنادجى ʿʿìnādji.

Opium, *s.* افيون Ȧfyūn.

Opponent, *s.* خصم khȦssm, مخالف mùkhālif.

Opportune, *a.* تمام وقتندە اولان tȦmĀm-wȦktinda-òlan, مناسبتلو mùnāssébètli.

Opportuneness, *s.* تمام وقتندە اولمقلق tàmĀm-wȦktinda-òlmaklik.

Opportunity, *s.* فرصت fìrsȦt, وقت wȦkt, مناسبت mùnāssébèt.

Oppose, *v.a.* قارشى دورمق kàrshi-dūrmak, مخالفت ا mùkhāléfèt-et, ممانعت ا mùmānaʿʿàt-et; قارشى كوندرمك kàrshi-ghyùndərmek, قارشى تعيين ا kàrshi-tàʿʿyīn-et.

Opposite, *a.* قارشى kàrshi, مقابل mùkābil, مواجه mùwājih.

Opposition, *s.* مخالفت mùkhāléfèt, ممانعت mùmānaʿʿàt.

Oppress, *v.a.* صيقندى ويرمك sìkindi-vèrmek; صيقمق sìkmak, ظلم ا zùlm-et, تعدى ا taʿʿàddi-et.

Oppressor, *s.* ظالم zālim.

Opprobrium, *s.* عيب ʿʿayp.

Optician, *s.* كوزلكجى ghyuzlukji.

Option, *s.* اختيار ìkhtiyār.

Opulence, *s.* ثروت sèrvèt, سامان sāmān, زنكينلك zènghinlik.

Opulent, *a.* زنكين zènghin, متمول mùtémèvvil.

Oracle, *s.* مكهن mèkhèn (k-h) كاهن جوابى kyāhin-jéwȦbi.

Oral, *a.* اغزدن Ȧghzdan, شفاهى shìfāhī; —ly, *ad.* شفاهاً shìfāhan.

Orange, *s.* پورتقال pòrtakȦl; (Seville) ترنج tùrunj.

Orangoutang, *s.* ميمون màymūn.

Oration, *s.* نطق nùtk.

Orator, *s.* مير كلام mīri-kèlām.

Orbit, *s.* فلك fèlek; دائرە dāʿirè; يول yòl.

Orchard, *s.* ميوە باغى mèyvé-bȦghi.

Orchestra, *s.* چالغيجيلر chȦlghijiler.

Ordain, *v.a.* ترتيب ا tèrtīb-et, تنظيم ا tànzīm-et; امر ا èmr-et; نصب ا nȦssb-et.

Order, *s.* نظام nìzȦm, انتظام ìntizȦm; ترتيب tèrtīb, صرە sìra; امر èmr, ارادە ìrādé, تنبيه tènbīh, سپارش sìpārish; صنف sìnf, جنس jìnss; طريقت tàrīkȦt; نشان nìshȦn; —, *v.a.* ترتيب ا tèrtīb-et, تنظيم ا tànzīm-et; امر ا èmr-et, ارادە ا ìrādé-et, تنبيه ا tènbīh-et; سپارش ا sìpārish-et, اصمارلمق ìssmàrlamak; to —, *a.* اصمارلمە ìssmàrlama.

Ordinary, *a.* بياغى bàyàghi, عادى ʿʿādī.

Ordnance, *s.* طوپ tòp, هاون (hȦvan).

Ore, *s.* معدن màʿʿdèn, فلز filìzz, جوهر jèvhèr.

Organ, *s.* آلت ālet; ارغانون èrghanòn.

Organization, *s.* ترتيب tèrtīb, تنظيم tànzīm.

Organize, *v.a.* ترتيب ا tèrtīb-et, تنظيم ا tànzīm-et, تنسيق ا tènsīk-et, صرەسنە قومق sìrassina-kòmak.

Orgie, *s.* عيش و عشرت ʿʿīsh-u-ʿʿìshrèt.

Oriental, *a.* شرقى shàrkī.

Orientalist, *s.* السنه شرقيه اشنا èlsinÉ-shàrkìyyÉ-āshinā.

Orifice, *s.* دليك dèlik, اغز Aghz, كوز ghyùz, فم fèm, دهان dìhān, سوراخ sūrākh.

Origin, *s.* اصل àssl, مبدأ mèbdè', منشأ mènshè', باش bAsh, باشلانغيج bAsh-langhij, تمل tèmel, اول Èvvèl, ابتدا ibtidā, بدء bèd'.

Original, *a.* أصلى Asslī ; تحاف tùhāf, عجيب "àjīb ("àjā'ib), غريب gharīb ; دلى dèli ; —, *s.* اصل Assl ; تحاف ادم tùhāf-AdAm, دلى dèli.

Originate, *v.a.* چيقمق chìkmak, ظهورا zùhūr-et; نشئت ا nèsh'èt-et ; —, *v.a.* چيقارمق chìkàrmak, دوشنمك dùshunmek, ابداع ا ìbdā"-et.

Ornament, *s.* زينت zīnèt, زيب zīb, زيبا zībā, زيبايش zībāyish ; —, *v.a.* تزيين ا tèzyìn-et, زينتلندرمك zīnet-lendirmek, دوناتمق dònatmak ; — one's self, بزنمك bèzenmek.

Orphan, *s.* يتيم yètīm, اوكسز ùksuz.

Orthography, *s.* املا ìmlā.

Oscillate, *v.a.* صلانمق sAllànmak.

Oscillation, *s.* صلانمه sAllànma.

Ostensible, *a.* ظاهرى zāhirī, علنى "àlénī.

Ostentation, *s.* كوسترش ghyùsstèrish.

Ostler, *s.* سئيس sè'īss.

Ostrich, *s.* دوه قوشى dèvÉ-kùshu, شتر مرغ shùtur-mùrgh. [àkhàr, سائر sā'ir.

Other, *a.* بشقه bAshka, ديكر dìgher, اخر

Otherwise, *ad.* بشقه درلو bAshka-(tùrlu) ; —, *c.* ياخود yākhud ; نام ديكر nāmi-dìgher.

Otter, *s.* صوسمورى sù-sàmūru.

Otto of roses, *s.* كل ياغى ghyùl-yāghi.

Ottoman, *a.* عثمانلو "òssmānlí. ["āliyyÉ.

Ottoman Empire, *s.* دولت عليه dèvleti-

Ought, *v. aux.* See Grammar.

Ounce, *s.* (troy) اون درهملك طارتى òn-dìrhèmlik-tàrti ; (avoirdupois) سكز بچوق درهملك طارتى sèkiz-bùchuk-dìrhèmlik-tàrti ; (animal) برنوع قاپلان bìr-nèv"-kAplAn.

Our, *a. pro.* مز miz, يمز imiz ; بزم bìzim.

Ours, *pro.* بزم bìzim ; بزمكى bìzimki, بزمكيلر bìzimkilar.

Ourself, *s.* كنديمز kèndimiz.

Ourselves, *s. pl.* كنديمز kèndimiz.

Oust, *v.a.* چيقارمق chìkàrmak.

Out, *ad.* خارج khārij, طشره tAshra, طيشارى dìshāri ; طيشارى يه dìshāriya; طيشارده dìshàrda ; —, *a.* طيشارى چيقمش dìshāri-chìkmish ; سونمش sùnmush, منطفى mùntàfi ; بتمش bìtmish, دوكنمش dùkènmish, منقضى mùnkAzi ; منقرض mùnkàriz, منقطع mònkAti" ; — of, *pr.* دن dan ; دن خارج dan-khārij ; — —, *a.* سز siz, بلا bìlā, بى bī, نا nā ; — of hand, الدن چيقمش Èldan-chìkmish ; to put — — —, الدن چيقارمق Èldan-chìkàr-mak ; — — humour, دارغين dàrghin ; — — place, وقتسز wAkitsiz, مناسبتسز mùnāssébètsiz, نابمحل nā-bè-màhàll ; بوشده bòshda ; معزول mà"zūl ; — — pocket, ضررلو zàrarli, ضررايتمش zàrar-ètmish, پاره غائب ايتمش (pàra)-(kayb)-ètmish ; — — sight, غائب

ghā'ib, مفقود mèfkūd, کورنمیور ghyùrunmiyor, کوزکمیور ghyùzik-miyor; — — tune, اهنکی بوزلمش āhÈnghi-bòzulmush.

Outbreak, *s.* عصیان "ìssyān; ظهور zùhur.

Outcast, *s.* مطرود کمسنه mÀtrūd-kìmèssnÉ.

Outcry, *s.* ولوله vèlvélÉ, فریاد fÈryād.

Outdo, *v.a.* یاپمقده کچمك yÀpmakda-gèchmek.

Outer, *a.* طیش dìsh, خارجی khāriji.

Outfit, *s.* خرجراه khàrji-rāh; طاقم tàkim.

Outflank, *v.a.* کندی جنابی دشمنك جنابندن کچمك kèndi-jènÀbi-dùsh-mÈnin-jènÀbinden-gèchmek.

Outgoing, *s.* خرج khàrj, مصرف mÀss-raf; خروج khùrūj, چیقش chìkish.

Outguard, *s.* ایلروکی قره قول ìlériki-kÀra-kol, نوبتجی nùbètji.

Outhouse, *s.* صوندرمه sùndurma.

Outlandish, *a.* یاقشقسز yàkishiksiz.

Outlaw, *s.* فرمانلو fÈrmÀnli, عاصی "Àssi, قتلی حلال اولان kÀtli-hàlāl-òlAn.

Outlay, *s.* مصرف mÀssraf; —, *v.a.* صرف ا sàrf-et.

Outlet, *s.* مخرج màkhrèj, چیقه جق یر chìkajak-yÈr, قپو kÀpi; نفسلك nèfesslik.

Outline, *s.* قورو چیزلمش رسم kùru-chìzilmish-rèssim, تصلاق tÀsslAk; شکل shèkil, بچم bìchim.

Outlive, *v.a.* بشقه سی اولدکدنصکره بیله یاشامق bÀshkassi-ùldukdan-sòngra-bìlÉ-yàshamak, بشقه بر شیئك اثری بیله قالمدقدنصکره یاشامق bÀshka-bir-shèy'ing-ÈssEri-bìlÉ-kÀlmadikdan-sòngra-yàshamak.

Outlook, *s.* نظارت nÀzarèt; تیقظ tèy-àkkuz; on the —, مقید mùkàyyed.

Outlying, *a.* خارجده اولان khārijda-òlAn, اوزاق دوشن ùzÀk-dùshEn.

Out-manœuvre, *v.a.* حیله و دسیسه ده فائق کلمك hìlÉ-vÉ-dèssīssÉdÉ-fā'ik-gèlmek.

Outnumber, *v.a.* عددی زیاده او "àdédi-zìyādÉ-òl, متجاوز او mùtéjāviz-òl, کچمك ghèchmek. [léssi.

Outport, *s.* طشره اسکله سی tÀshra-isskè-

Outpost, *s.* ایلروکی قره قول ìlèriki-kÀrakol.

Outrageous, *a.* طاشقین tÀshkin, فاحش fāhish; قیزغین kìzghin, دارغین dàrghin.

Outreach, *v.a.* الداتمق Àldatmak.

Outright, *ad.* بتون بتون bìtun-bìtun, کلیاً [kyùllìyyan.

Outset, *s.* ابتدا ìbtidā.

Outside, *s.* طیش dìsh, طیشاری dìshàri, طشره tÀshra, خارج khārij, بیرون bīrūn; —, *a.* خارجی khāriji; at the —, اولسه اولسه òlsa-òlsa, نهایت nìhāyet; — price, نهایت پهاسی nìhāyet-pÀhÀssi.

Outskirt, *s.* طیشاری یری dìshàri-yÈri.

Outspoken, *a.* طوغری سویلر dòghru-sùwèyler. ["ìnād-et.

Outstand, *v.a.* انکار ا ìnkyār-et, عناد ا

Outstanding, *a.* هنوز تسویه اولنمیوب مطلوب بولنان hènuz-tèssvìyyÉ-òlun-mayub-mÀtlūb-bùlunan.

Outward, *a.* خارجی khāriji.

Outwards, *ad.* طیشاری یه طوغری dìshàriya-dòghru.

Outweigh, *v.a.* باصقین کلمك bàsskin-ghèlmek ; غالب او ghālib-òl.

Outwit, *v.a.* دسیسه ایله آلداتمق dèssīssé-ìlla-àldatmak.

Outwork, *s.* قلعه خارجنده اولان استحکامات kàlé-khàrijinda-òlan-ìsstìhkyāmāt.

Oval, *a.* بیضی bèyzī ; —, *s.* قطع ناقص kàt''i-nākiss.

Oven, *s.* فرون fìrìn.

Over, *a.* کچمش ghèchmish, بتمش bìtmish, تمام اولمش tàmām-òlmùsh ; فضله fàzla, الده èlda ; —, *ad.* اوستنه ùsstuna, اوستنده ùsstunda, مافوقنه mā-fèvkina, مافوقنده mā-fèvkinda ; بالاسنه bālāssina, بالاسنده bālāssinda ; دن زیاده dan-zìyādé, متجاوز mùté-jāviz ; دوریله‌رك dèvrilérek ; طاشه‌رق tàsharak ; —, *pr.* دن dan, اوستندن ùsstundan, اوزرندن ùzérindan ; — and above, دن فضله dan-fàzla, دن ماعدا dan-mā''ada, دن بشقه dan-bàshka ; — against, ئه قارشی a-kàrshi, قارشیسنه kàrshissina, قارشیسنده kàrshissinda ; to run —, *v.n.* طاشمق tàshmak ; *v.a.* اوستندن کچوب چینه‌مك ùsstun-dan-ghèchup-chìnémek ; to fall —, دوریلوب دوشمك dèvrilup-dùshmek ; to go —, to pass —, کچمك ghèch-mek ; to give —, وازکچمك wāz-ghèchmek, براقمق bràkmak ; کسلمك kèssilmek ; دورا dèvr-et, تسلیم ا tèsslīm-et ; all —, هپ hèp, بتون bìtun, تکمیل tèkmīl, باشدن باشه bàshdan-bàsha ; — again, یکیدن yèngidan, تکرار tèkrār, یکی باشدن yèngi-bàshdan ; all is —, بتمش bìtmish, بتدی bìtdi ; ایشی بتمش ìshi-bìtmish ; ایش ایشدن کچمش ìsh-ìshdan-ghèchmish.

Overbear, *v.a.* غالب او ghālib-òl ; —ing, *a.* ظالم zālim, متحکم mùtahàkkim.

Overboard, *ad.* دکزه dèngiza, دکزده dèngizda.

Overburden, *v.a.* تحملندن زیاده یوك یوکلتمك tàhàmmulinden-zìyadé-yùk-yùklətmek.

[nìk, سنبلی sùnbulī.

Overcast, *a.* بلوطلو bùlutlu, قپانق kàpà-

Overcharge, *v.a.* زیاده بها سویله‌مك والمق zìyadé-bàha-sùwèylémek-vé-àlmak.

Overcome, *v.a.* غالب او ghālib-òl, ینمك yènmek, الت ا àlt-et, بوزمق bòzmak.

Overdue, *a.* وعده‌سی کچمش vwà''déssi-gèchmish.

Overflow, *s.* سیل sèyl (sèl), طغیان tùghyān ; —, *v.n.* طاشمق tashmak ; —, *v.a.* باصمق bàssmak.

Overgrown, *s.* پك بیومش pèk-bìyu-mish, پك بویلنمش pèk-bòylanmish ; قاپلنمش kàplanmish, اورتلمش ùrtul-mush.

Overhang, *v.n.* صارقمق sàrkmak, اصلمق àssìlmak ; حواله لو او hàwāléli-òl.

Overhaul, *v.a.* یوقلامق yòklamak ; یتشمك yètishmek, طوتمق tùtmak.

Overhear, *v.a.* اشیتمك ìshìtmek, استماع ا ìsstimā''-et.

Overjoyed, *a.* پك سونمش pèk-sèvin-mish.

Overlook, *v.a.* باقمق bàkmak, ناظر او

nāzir-ôl, نظارت ا nAzārèt-et; عفوا ''Afv-et.

Overlooker, *s.* ناظر nāzir, باقيجى bAkiji.

Overpower, *v.a.* غالب او ghālib-ôl, ينمك yènmek; بوغمق bògh*mak*, مستغرق ا mùsst*a*ghr*à*k-et.

Overreach, *v.a.* الداتمق Aldatmak.

Overrule, *v.a.* اسكات ا ìssk*y*āt-et, جرح ا jèrh-et.

Overseer, *s.* ناظر nāzir, مدير mùdīr.

Oversight, *s.* ياكلش y*à*ngilish (yānish), سهو sèhv.

Overspread, *v.a.* اورتمك *ù*rtmek, [قاپلامق kAplam*a*k.

Overtake, *v.a.* يتشمك yètishmek, اولاشمق ùlàshm*a*k, طوتمق tùtm*a*k.

Overthrow, *s.* انهزام ìnhizām; خراب khàrāb, انهدام ìnhidām; —, *v.a.* بوزمق bòzm*a*k, منهزم قيلمق mùnhè-zim-kìlm*a*k; يقمق yìkm*a*k, هدم ا hèdm-et.

Overture, *s.* تكليف tèklīf; تياتروكشادى چالغيسى tèyātro-kyùshAd*i*-chAlghiss*i*.

Overturn, *v.a.* دويرمك dèvirmek; —, *v.n.* دوريلمك dèvrilmek.

Overwhelm, *v.a.* مستغرق ا mùsst*a*ghr*à*k-et, بوغمق bògh*mak*.

Overwork, *v.a.* تحملندن زياده چالشدرمق tàh*à*mmulinden-zìyadÉ-chAlishd*i*rm*a*k.

Owe, *v.a.* بورجلو او bòrjlu-ôl, بورجى او bòrju-ôl, دينى او dèyni-ôl, مديون او mèdyūn-ôl.

Owing, *ad.* مبنى mèbni, مناسبتيله mùnāssébètīl*a*, سببيله sèbébīl*a*, سببندن sèbébind*a*n.

Owl, *s.* بايقوش bàykush, بوغوقوشى [bùgh*u*-kùshu.

Own, *pro. a.* كندى kèndi; —, *pro. s.* my —, كنديمككى kèndiming*k*i, thy —, كندوككى kèndingingki, his, her, its —, كندونككى kèndiningki, &c.: see Grammar; —, *v.a.* مالك او mālik-ôl, صاحب او sāhib-ôl; اقرارا ìkrār-et, اعتراف ا ì''tirAf-et.

Owner, *s.* صاحب sāhib, مالك mālik.

Ownership, *s.* صاحبلك sāhiblik.

Ox, *s.* صيغر sìghir, اوكوز *ù*kyuz.

Oyster, *s.* استريديه ìsstrìdiyÉ.

P.

Pace, *s.* كيدش ghìdish, يورويش yùru-yush; يوريمه yùrumÉ, اديم Ad*i*m, خطوه khAtvÉ.

Pacific, *a.* صلح سور اولان sùlh-sÈver-ôlan; — (Ocean), *s.* بحر محيط غربى bàhri--mùhīt-ghàrbī.

Pacification, *s.* صلح sùlh, مصالحه mùssā-l*a*h*a*, بارش كورش bArish-ghyùrush, بارشق bAr*i*sh*i*k; تسكين tèsskīn.

Pacify, *v.a.* تسكين ا tèsskīn - et, يموشاتمق yìmushAtm*a*k.

Pack, *s.* دنك dènk; بوغچه bògh*c*ha; دسته dèsstÉ; طاقم tàkim; —, *v.a.* استيف او ìsstif-et; —, *v.n.* استيف ا ìsstif-ol; — away, قالدروب استيف ا kAld*i*r*i*p-ìsstif-et; — off, كتمك ghìtmek; — up, ديوشروب صندوقه قومق dèvshirup - sAnd*i*gh*a* - kòm*a*k, بوغچه ا bògh*c*ha-et.

Package, *s.* بوغچه bògh*c*ha, صندوق sAnd*i*k, كاغد kyàg*h*id.

Packet, *s.* اوفاق بوغچه ūfAk-bòghcha, كاغد kyàghid, طوپ tòp ; —, packet-boat, يولجى كميسى yòljυ-ghèmissi ; تحريرات كميسى tàhrīrāt-ghèmissi.

Packhorse, *s.* سمر باركيرى sèmer-(bèghiri), يوك حيوانى yùk-hàywAni.

Packneedle, Packing-needle, *s.* چوالدوز [chùwAldiz.

Packsaddle, *s.* سمر sèmer.

Packthread, *s.* سجيم sìjim.

Pad, *s.* كچوك يصدق kùchuk-yàssdik, پاموق pAmυk (pàmbυk) ; باركير (bèghir) ; —, *v.a.* طولدرمق dòldυr-mak ; foot —, خرسز khìrsiz.

Paddle, *s.* كورك kyùrèk ; واپور چرخنك تختەسى vàpòr-chàrkhining-tàkhtassi ; —, *v.n.* كورك چكمك kyùrèk-chèk-mek ; — box, داولمباز dàwlυmbAz.

Padlock, *s.* اصمه كليدى Assma-kìlidi.

Pagan, *s.* پتپرست pùt-pèrèsst.

Page, *s.* صحيفه sàhīfé, يوز yùz ; ايچ اوغلانى ìch - òghlAni, ايچ اغاسى [ìch-AghAssi.

Pail, *s.* قوغه kògha.

Pain, *s.* اجى Aji, اغرى Aghri, وجع vèjà'', الم èlem, رنج rènj, رنجش rènjish ; *v.n.* اجيمق àjimak, اغريمق Aghrimak ; *v.a.* اجتمق Ajitmak ; كدر ويرمك kèder-vèrmek.

Painful, *a.* اجيور Ajiyor, اجر Ajir, اليم èlīm ; مورث كدر mūrissi-kèder.

Pains, *s.* سعى sà''i ; اوزنمه ùzènmé ; to take —, اوزنمك ùzènmek.

Paint, *s.* بويا bòya ; (for the face) دوزكون dùzghyun ; (for the eyebrows) راستق rAsstik ; —, *v.a.* بويامق bòyamak ; —, *v.n.* (as artists) رسم ياپمق rèssim-yàpmak ; (as ladies) دوزكون قوللانمق dùzghyun-kùllAnmak.

Painter, *s.* (house) نقاش nAkkAsh ; (artist) رسام rèsssām.

Painting, *s.* بويالو رسم bòyali-rèssim.

Pair, *s.* چفت chìft ; —, *v.n.* چفت او chìft-òl ; —, *v.a.* اشنى بولمق èshini-bùlmak ; چفت چفت قومق chìft-[-chìft-kòmak.

Palace, *s.* سراى sàrāy.

Palate, *s.* دماغ dìmāgh.

Pale, *a.* (colour) اچق àchik ; (face) صارى sàri ; —, *s.* حولى hàvli, دائره dā'iré ; پرمق pàrmak, تخته tàkhta ; to turn —, بكزى بم بياض كسلمك bèngzi-bèm-bèyAz-kèssilmek, بكزى قالمامق bèngzi-kAlmemak.

Paling, Palings, *s.* تخته پرده tàkhta-pèrdé. [pàrmaklik.

Palissade, *s.* شرامپو shàrampò ; پرمقلق

Palliate, *v.a.* تخفيف ا tàkhfīf - et ; رنك ويرمك rènk-vèrmek. [lighi.

Pallor, *s.* بكزك صاريلغى bèngzin-sAri-

Palm, *s.* (tree) خرما اغاجى khùrma-Aghaji ; (of the hand) ال ايەسى èl-àyassi ; (measure) سره sèré ; to palm off, سورمك sùrmek, صاتمق sAtmak.

Palpable, *a.* ظاهر zāhir, اشكار āshikyār.

Palpitate, *v.n.* نبض كبى اورمق nAbz-ghìbi-wùrmak, چالقانمق chAlkAn-mak, اوينامق òynamak. [khAfakān.

Palpitation of the heart, *s.* خفقان

Palsy (paralysis), *s.* فلج علتى fèlij-''illèti, بريانى طوتلمسى bìr-yàni-tùtυlmassi, اجنى چارپمسى ìjìnni-

-chàrpmassi; palsied, *a.* مفلوج mèflūj; طوتلمش tòtulmush, چارپلمش chàrpilmish. [sAchma, بوش bòsh.

Paltry, *a.* مسكين misskin; صاچمه

Pampas, *s. pl.* امريقا جنوبی قيرلری amèrica-jènūbī-kirleri.

Pamper, *v.a.* نازونعيمه مستغرق ايدوب فنا الشدرمق nāz-vè-nà''īmé-mùss-tàghràk-èdup-fèna-Alishdirmak.

Pamphlet, *s.* رساله rissālé, جزء jùz'.

Pan, *s.* چناق chànak, طباق tAbAk; كوكچ ghyùghèch; — of a gunlock, چقماق تابه‌سی chàkmak-(tAwassi); knee —, ديزقپاغی dìz-kApAghi.

Panacea, *s.* علاج مطلق ''ilāj-mùtlàk.

Pancake, *s.* كوزلمه ghyùzlémé.

Pandemonium, *s.* مجمع شياطين mèjmà-i-shèyàtīn.

Pander, *s.* پزونك pèzéwènk; —, *v.n.* پزونكلك ا pèzéwènklik-èt.

Pane of glass, *s.* جام jàm.

Panegyric, *s.* مديحه mèdīha.

Panegyrize, *v.a.* مدح ا mèdh-èt.

Pang, *s.* وجع vèjà'', درد dèrd.

Panic, *s.* انسزين مستولی اولان خوف عمومی ānsizin-mùsstèvli-òlan-khàvf-ùmūmī.

Pannier, *s.* كوفه kyùfé. [rèssm.

Panorama, *s.* وسعتلو رسم vwùss''àtli-

Pant, *v.n.* پك صولومق pèk-sòlumak.

Pantaloons, *s.* پانطاون pàntalòn.

Panther, *s.* پارس pārss.

Pantile, *s.* كراميد kìrémid.

Pantomime, *s.* برنوع مسخره‌لق تياترو اويونی bìr-nèv''i-mAsskharalik-teàtro-

Pantry, *s.* كيلار (kilEr). [òyunu.

Pap, *s.* لاپه lApa; مه‌مه mèmé.

Papa, *s.* بابا bAbA, پدر pèdEr.

Papacy, *s.* روما پاپالغی ròma-pàpàlighi.

Papal, *a.* روما پاپاسنه متعلق ròma-pàpàssina-muta''allik.

Paper, *s.* كاغد kyāghid, قرطاس kirtAss; غزته ghàzèta; papers, *s. pl.* اوراق èvrAk.

Paper-mill, *s.* كاغد فابريقه سی kyaghid-

Papist, *s.* قتولك kàtolik. [fàbrikassi.

Parable, *s.* مثال missāl, تمثيل tèmsīl.

Parabola, *s.* قطع مكافی kAt''i-mùkyāfi.

Paradise, *s.* فردوس fìrdèvss, جنت jènnEt. [فقره fikra.

Paragraph, *s.* بند bènd, جمله jùmlé,

Parallax, *s.* اختلاف منظر ikhtilAfi--mAnzàr.

Parallel, *a.* موازی mùwāzi; (similar) نظير nAzīr; — to each other, متوازی mùtéwāzi; —, *s.* خطموازی khAtti-mùwāzi; (similar thing) نظيره nAzīré. [wāziyu-'l-AdlA''.

Parallelogram, *s.* متوازی الاضلاع mùté-

Paralysis, *s.* فلج علتی fèlij-''illèti, برطرفلك طوتلمسی bir-tàrafing-tòtul-massi, اجنی چارپمسی ìjinni--chàrpmassi. [فلج علتی fèlij-''illèti.

Paralytic, *a.* مفاوج mèflūj; — stroke,

Paralyze, *v.a.* حركتدن محروم ا hàrékEt-den-màhrūm-èt. [para).

Paramour, *s.* زانی zānī, زنپازه (zàm-

Parapet, *s.* سپر sipEr.

Paraphernalia, *s. pl.* اغرلق Aghirlik; طاقم tàkim, الات ادوات ālāt-èdāwāt.

Paraphrase, *s.* شرح shErh.

Parasite, *s.* کاسه‌لیس kyāssé-līss.

Parasol, *s.* شمسیه shèmsiyyé.

Parboil, *v.a.* یاری بچق حاشلامق yàri--bàchuk-hàshlamak.

Parcel, *s.* بوغچه bòghcha, کاغد kyāghid; طاقم tàkim; سورو sùru.

Parch, *v.a.* قاورمق kàwurmak; صوصاتمق sùssatmak; قوروتمق kùrutmak; —, *v.n.* قاورلمق kàwrulmak; صوصامق sùssamak; قورومق kùrumak.

Parchment, *s.* ترشه tìrshé.

Pard, *s.* قپلان kàplan.

Pardon, *s.* عفو ‘‘àfv; —, *v.a.* عفو ا ‘‘àfv-et, بخش ا bàkhsh-et, باغشلامق bàghishlamak.

Pare, *v.a.* صویمق sòymak, قبوغنی صویمق kàbughunu-sòymak; کسمك kèss-mek, قرقمق kìrkmak, یونتمق yònt-mak; قازیمق kàzimak.

Parent, *s.* بابا bàba, پدر pèder; انا àna, ننه ninė, والده vālidé; both parents, والدین vālidèyn. [mādérāné.

Parental, *a.* پدرانه pèdérāné; مادرانه

Parenthesis, *s.* معترضه mù‘‘tériza.

Pariah, *s.* هند مسکین مطرودی hìnd--mèsskin-màtrūdi.

Paring, *s.* قبوق kàbuk; کسندی kès-sinti; قرقندی kìrkinti.

Paris (town of), *s.* پارس شهری pàris-

Parish, *s.* محله màhàllé. [-shèhiri.

Parity, *s.* مشابهت mùshābéhèt. [cha.

Park, *s.* اورمانلق باغچه òrmànlik-bàgh-

Parley, *s.* مکالمه mùkyālémé.

Parliament, *s.* مبعوثان ملت مجلسی mèb‘‘ūssāni-millèt-mèjlissi.

Parliamentary, *a.* ملت مجلسنه متعلق millèt-mèjlissina-mùta‘‘àlik.

Parlour, *s.* سلاملق اوطه‌سی sèlāmlik-

Parole, *s.* پاروله pàròla. [-òdassi.

Parricide, *s.* کندی باباسنی قتل ایتمش خبیث kèndi-bàbassini-kàtl-ètmish--khàbīss; کندی باباسنی قتل ایتمك جنحه‌سی kèndi-bàbassini-kàtl-èt-mek-jùnhassi.

Parrot, *s.* پپغان pàpaghān, ببغا bèbghā, *or* bèbéghā, طوطی tūtī.

Parry, *v.a.* دفع ا def‘‘-èt.

Parsee, *s.* کبر ghèbr.

Parsimonious, *a.* خسیس khàssīss, طمعکار tàma‘‘kyār, مسکین misskīn.

Parsimoniousness, Parsimony, *s.* طمعکارلق tàma‘‘kyārlik.

Parsley, *s.* مایدنوس màydanòss.

Parsnip, *s.* یبان هاوجی yàban-hàwuju.

Parson, *s.* پاپاس pàpass.

Part, *s.* پارچه pàrcha, یان yàn, قسم kìssm, جزء jùz‘, حصه hìssé, قسط kìsst, پای pày; تعصب tàssàhhub; طرف tàraf, جانب jānib; حوالی hàwālī, جوار jìwār; خدمت khìdmet, واجبه ذمت wājibè‘i-zìmmèt; parts, *s. pl.* ذکا zèkyā, استعداد issti‘‘dād; طرفلر tàraflar, جوانب jèwānib, حوالی hàwāli, جوارلر jìwārlar; privy —, عورت یرلری ‘‘àvret-yèrléri; —, *v.n.* ایرلمق àyrilmak, مفارقت ا mùfāra-kàt-et; قوپمق kòpmak, کسلمك kèssilmek; — with, ایرلمق àyrilmak; ویرمك vèrmek; صاتمق sàtmak; قوغمق kòghmak.

Partake, *v.n.* حصه‌منداو hìsssémènd-òl; يمك yèmek.

Partial, *a.* جزئی jùz'ī, غيرعمومی ghày-ri-"ùmūmī, غيرتام ghàyri-tàmm; ميال mèyyāl, محب mùhìbb; غرضكار ghàrazkyār, نفسانيتلو nèf-sānìyyètli; to be — to, سومك sèv-mek. [حصه‌سی‌او hìsssèssi-òl.

Participate, *v.n.* شريك‌او shèrik-òl,

Participation, *s.* حصه‌ياب اولمقلق hissa-yāb-òlmaklik.

Participle, *s.* (active) اسم‌فاعل ìssmi-fā"il; (passive) اسم‌مفعول ìssmi-mèf"ūl.

Particle, *s.* ذره zèrré; ادات èdāt.

Particular, *a.* مخصوص màkhsūss, خاص khāsss, مختص mùkhtàsss, مخصص mùkhàsssàss; ايری àyri, بشقه bàshka; اينجه‌بقار ìnja-bàkar, پك دقت‌ايدر pèk-dìkkàt-èder, مراقلو mèrākli; —s, *s. pl.* تفصيلات tàf-sīlàt.

Particularly, *ad.* خصوصا khùssūssā.

Parting, *s.* ايريلش àyrìlish, مفارقت mùfārakàt. [ghàyretkèsh.

Partisan, *s.* طرفدار tàrafdār, غيرتكش

Partisanship, *s.* طرفدارلق tàrafdārlik.

Partition, *s.* بولمه bùlmé; — off, *v.a.* بولمك bùlmek.

Partly, *ad.* بعض‌مرتبه bà"zi-mèrtébé, بيردرجه‌يه‌قدر bìr-dèréjéyé-kàdar.

Partner, *s.* اورتاق òrtàk, شريك shèrīk.

Partnership, *s.* شركت shìrkèt.

Partridge, *s.* ككلك kèklik,

Parturition, *s.* وضع حمل wàz"i-hàml.

Party, *s.* طاقم tàkim, بلوك bùluk, فرقه fìrka; جمعيت jèm"ìyyèt.

Pasha, *s.* پاشا pàsha.

Pass, *s.* كچيد ghèchid, دربند dèrbènd (dèvrènd), بوغاز bòghāz, دره dèré; تذكره tèzkéré, يول‌امری yòl-èmri, بيورلدی bùyuruldu; حال hāl, هيئت hèy'èt; —, *v.n.* كچمك ghèchmek; (through) مرورا mūrūr-et; (over) عبورا "ùbūr-et; (current) تداولا tèdāvul-et; —, *v.a.* كچورمك ghè-chirmek; امرارا ìmrār-et; — along, يولنجه كچمك yòlunja-ghèchmek, كچمك ghèchmek; — away, كچوب كتمك ghèchup-ghìtmek; بتمك bìtmek, دوكنمك dùkènmek; فنا بولمق fènā-bùlmak; — by, *v.n.* اوكدن‌كچمك ùngdan-ghèchmek, ياندن‌كچمك yàndan-ghèchmek; اورادن‌كچمك òradan-ghèchmek, كچمك ghèchmek; —, *v.a.* كچورمك ghèchirmek, عفوا "àfv-et; — for, *v.n.* ظن‌اولنمق zànn-òlun-mak; —, *v.a.* ديوويرمك dèyu-vèrmek, ديوصاتمق dèyu-sàtmak; — one's word, سوز ويرمك sùz-vèrmek, كفيل‌او kèfīl-òl, — over, *v.a.* عفوا "àfv-et; — sentence, اعلاما ì"lām-et; to come to —, اولمق òlmak, واقع‌او wākì"-òl, وقوع بولمق wùkū"-bùlmak, ظهورا zùhūr-et, جايكيراو jāyghīr-òl.

Passable, *a.* كچيلور ghèchilir, قابل‌مرور kābili-mùrūr; اپ‌ايوجه èp-īyija, كچر ghècher.

Passably, *ad.* اپ أيوجه èp-īyija.

Passage, *s.* مرور mūrūr, عبور ‟ūbūr, كچش ghèchish ; ممر mèmèrr, معبر mà‟bèr, كچه جلك يير ghèchéjek-yēr, يول yòl ; اثناى راه èssnāyi-rāh ; صوقاق sòkak, قپو دهليزى kāpi-dèhlīzi ; عباره ‟ìbārē, بند bènd.

Passenger, *s.* يولجى yòlju.

Passer-by, *s.* كچك gèchen.

Passion, *s.* دارغينلق dàrghinlik, اويكه (ùfké), غضب ghāzab ; هوس hàwèss, مراق mèrāk ; عشق ‟āshk ; ابتلا ìbtilā, انفعال ìnfi‟āl ; — flower, چرخ فلك چيچكى chàrkhi-fèlèk-chìchéghi.

Passionate, *a.* دارغين dàrghin, غضوب ghāzūb ; —ly, *ad.* پك pèk, اشورى āshiri.

Passive, *a.* الى قولى باغلو كبى Èli-kòlu-bāghli-ghìbi ; verb —, فعل مجهول fì‟li-mèjhūl ; — participle, اسم مفعول ìssmi-mèf‟ūl.

Passport, *s.* يول أمرى yòl-èmri, يول تذكره سى yòl-tèzkèrēssi, بيورلدى bùyuruldu, پاسه پورطه pàssapòrta.

Pass-word, *s.* پاروله pàròla ; شعار shì‟ār.

Past, *a.* كچمش ghèchmish ; ماضى māzi ; the —, كچمش زمان ghèch-mish-zàmān, ايام سابقه èyyāmi-sābika ; —, *pr.* دن اوته يه dan-ùtéyē ; دن خارج dan-khārij ; — cure, — recovery, چاره سز chārēssiz, علاج قبول ايتمز ‟ìlāj-kābūl-ètmàz, بتمش bìtmish.

Paste, *s.* خمير (khāmur) ; چريش chìrish ; —, *v.a.* چريش ايله ياپشدرمق chìrish-ila-yàpishdirmak.

Pasteboard, *s.* مقوا mùkàwwà.

Pastil, Pastille, قرص kùrss.

Pastime, *s.* ايلنجه èylènja. [pass.

Pastor, *s.* چوبان chòbān ; پاپاس pà-

Pastry, *s.* خميرايشى (khāmur)-ìshi ; — cook, بوركجى bùrèkji.

Pasture, Pasturage, *s.* اوتلاق òtlak ; چاير chàyr ; اوت òt ; —, *v.n.* اوتلامق òtlamak ; —, *v.a.* اوتارمق òtarmak, اوتلاتمق òtlātmak.

Pasty, *s.* بورك bùrèk.

Patch, *s.* يامه yàma ; پارچه pàrcha ; —, *v.a.* يامه اورمق yàma-wùrmak, پارچه قومق pàrcha-kòmak ; — up, قباجه تعميرا kābaja-tà‟mīr-et ; اويدريويرمك ùydurivèrmek.

Patent, *s.* برات bèrāt, فرمان fèrmān ; پاتنته pàtènta, امتيازبراتى ìmtiyāz-bèrāti ; —, *a.* پاتنته لو pàtèntali, امتيازلو ìmtiyāzli.

Patented, *a.* پاتنته لو pàtèntali.

Patentee, *s.* نوايجاد نسنه نك پاتنته سى صاحبى nèv-ijād-nèssnénin-pàtèn-tassi-sāhibi. [rānē.

Paternal, *a.* ابوى èbévī, پدرانه pèdē-

Path, Pathway, *s.* يول yòl, طريق tàrīk, راه rāh.

Pathetic, *a.* جكرسوز jīgher-sūz.

Patience, *s.* صبر sābr, تحمل tàhàmmul, شكيبائى shèkībā'ī.

Patient, *a.* صبرلو sābrli, صبور sābūr, متحمل mùtàhàmmil, شكيب shèkīb ; —, *s.* خسته khāssta.

Patriarch, *s.* پطريق pātrīk; —s, *s. pl.* اجدادبنی اسرائيل èjdādi-bèni-ìssrā'īl.

Patriarchate, *s.* پطريقلق صفتی pātrīk-lik-sìfāti; پطريق قوناغی pātrīk-kònaghi.

Patrician, *s.* اصلزاده āsslzādé.

Patrimony, *s.* ميراث mirāss, ملك موروث mìlki-mèvrūss.

Patriot, *s.* وطن غيرتنده اولان كمسنه wātan-ghàyrètinda-òlan-kìmèssné.

Patriotic, *a.* وطننی سور اولان wātanini-sèver-òlan.

Patrol, *s.* قول kòl; —, *v.n.* قول كزمك kòl-ghèzmek; —, *v.a.* كزمك ghèzmek, طولاشمق dòlashmak.

Patron, *s.* ولی نعمت vèlī-ni''mèt, افندی èfèndi; راغب rāghib. [zām.

Patronage, *s.* حمايه hìmāyé; التزام ìlti-

Patronize, *v.a.* التزام ا ìltizām-et; مشتريسی او [mùshtérìssī-ol. افنديلك ا èfèndilik-et;

Patten, *s.* نعلين (nālin).

Pattern, *s.* اورنك ùrnek; رسم rèssim; قالب kālib; نمونه nùmūné.

Paunch, *s.* قارن kàrn; اشكنبه ìshkènbé.

Pauper, *s.* فقير fàkir.

Pause, *s.* قالش kālish; سكوت sùkyūt, سكون sùkyūn; دوراق يری dùrak-yèri; —, *v.a.* قالمق kālmak, دورمق dùrmak; باقمق bākmak, باقنمق bākinmak, دوشنمك dùsh-unmek, تأنی ا tè'ènni-et, تأمل ا tè'èm-mul-et. [-dùshémek.

Pave, *v.a.* طاش ايله دوشه‌مك tàsh-ila-

Pavement, *s.* قالدريم kàldirim; foot —, پياده قالدريمی pìyādé-kāldirimi.

Pavilion, *s.* كوشك kyùshk, قصر kāssr; مهتابيه mèhtābìyyé; چادر chādir.

Paving, *s.* دوشه‌مه dùshemé.

Pavior, *s.* قالديرمجی kàldirimji.

Paw, *s.* اياق àyak, پنچه pènché, پا pā, پای pāy.

Pawn, *s.* رهن rèhn; رهين rèhīn; (at chess) پيداق pàydàk; —, *v.a.* رهينه ويرمك rèhīna-vèrmek, رهينه قومق rèhīna-kòmak.

Pay, *s.* كونده‌لك ghyùndélik; هفته‌لق hāftalik; ايلق àylik, ماهيه māhìyyé, شهريه shèhrìyyé; يللق yìllik; معاش mà''āsh; —, *v.a.* اوده‌مك ùdémek, ويرمك vèrmek, ادا ا èdā-et, ايفا ا īfā-et, استيفا ا ìsstīfā-et; — a visit, اوغرامق òghramak, زيارت ا zìyārèt-et; — away, ويرمك vèrmek, خرج ا khàrj-et; — —, — out (a rope), موله ا mòla-et; — down, پيشين ويرمك pèshin-vèrmek; — off, قارشيلغنی ا kàrshilighini-et, اجيسنی چيقارمق ājissini-chìkàrmak; اذن ويرمك ìzin-vèrmek, ادملرينه اذن ويرمك ādamlarina-ìzin-vèrmek.

Payable, *a.* وعده‌سی كلمش wà''déssi-ghèlmish, واجب الادا wājibu-'l-èdā.

Paymaster-General, *s.* عسكرك عمومی معاش ناظری ''āsskerin-ùmūmī-mà''āsh-nāziri.

Payment, *s.* تأديه tè'dìyyé.

Paynim, *s.* كافر kyāfir.

Pay-office, *s.* سركی sèrghi.

Pea, *s.* نخود nòkhud, بزليه bèzèlya; sweet —, عطرشاهی ''ìtri-shāhī.

Peace, *s.* بارشق bârishik, بارش‌کورش bârish-ghyùrush, صلح sùlh, مصالحه mùssâlahà; go in —! سلامتله sèlâmètla, بالامن والامان bì-'l-ùmni-vè-'l-èmân; —! *int.* صوص sùss; to be at —, بارشق او bârishik-òl; to hold one's —, صوصمق sùssmak.

Peaceable, *a.* اسایشلو âssâyishli.

Peacemaker, *s.* بارشدریجی bârishdiriji.

Peach, *s.* شفتالو shèftâli; melting —, یارمه‌شفتالو yàrma-shèftâli; cling stone —, کباد kèbâd, صاری‌کباد sâri-kèbâd, ات‌شفتالوسی èt-shèftâlissi.

Peacock, *s.* طاوس tàwuss, طاوس‌قوشی tàwuss-kùshu. [tàwuss-kùshu.

Peahen, *s.* دیشی طاوس قوشی dìshi-

Peak, *s.* دپه (tèpé), ذروه zìrvé, کنکره kyùnghyuré.

Peal, *s.* مکرر سس mùkèrrèr-sèss; —, *v.n.* مکرر سس ا mùkèrrèr-sèss-et.

Pear, *s.* ارمود àrmud, امرود èmrûd.

Pearl, *s.* اینجو ìnji, در dùrr, لؤلؤ lù'lù', مروارید mèrvârîd.

Peasant, *s.* کویلو kyùylu. [chàkil-tâshi.

Pebble, *s.* چاقل chàkil, چاقل‌طاشی

Peculation, *s.* خرسزلق khèrsizlik, مأمور سرقتی mè'mûr-sirkàti.

Peculiar, *a.* مخصوص màkhsûss; عجیب "âjîb (àjâ'ib), غریب ghàrîb, تحاف tùhâf.

Peculiarity, *s.* کیفیت مخصوصه kèyfiyyèti-màkhsûssa, خاصه khâsssa.

Pecuniary, *a.* اقچه‌یه متعلق âkchaya-mùta"àllik, اقچه‌جه âkchaja.

Pedestal, *s.* کرسی kyùrsî.

Pedigree, *s.* شجره shèjéré, نسب nèsseb.

Pedlar, *s.* قولتقجی kòltukju, کزدریجی ghèzdiriji, مادراباز mâdrabâz.

Peel, *s.* قبوق kâbuk; —, *v.a.* صویمق sòymak, قبوغنی صویمق kâbughunu-sòymak; —, — off, *v.n.* صویلمق sòyulmak. [mak.

Peep, *v.n.* ارالقدن باقمق àralikdan-bâk-

Peer, *s.* زادکاندن اولان zâdéghyândan-òlan; کفو kyùfv, همپایه hèm-pâyé.

Peerage, *s.* اصلزادکان âsslzâdéghyân.

Peeress, *s.* اصلزاده قاریسی âsslzâdé-

Peerless, *a.* بی نظیر bî-nâzîr. [kârissi.

Peevish, *a.* ترس tèrss, خویسز khùysuz.

Peevishness, *s.* ترسلك tèrsslik.

Peg, *s.* چیوی chìvi.

Pelican, *s.* سقاقوشی (sàka)-kùshu.

Pell-mell, *ad.* قارمه‌قارش kàrma-kârish.

Pelt, *v.a.* طاشلامق tâshlamak; —, *v.n.* شدت ایله یاغمق shiddèt-ìla-yàghmak.

Pen, *s.* قلم kàlem; اغل âghil; —, *v.a.* یازمق yàzmak; اغله‌قپامق âghìla-kâpamak; — down, یازمق yàzmak; — up, اغله‌قپامق âghìla-kâpamak; — in, چینیلمك chìnilémek, مرکبلمك mùrèkkèblémek; اغله قپامق âghìla-kâpamak. [nèv"inden.

Penal, *a.* مجازات نوعندن mùjâzât-

Penalty, *s.* جریمه jèrîmé; مجازات mùjâzât, جزا jèzâ; under —, مجازات اولنمق شرطیله mùjâzât-òlunmak-shàrtìla, جریمه النمق شرطیله jèrîmé-âlinmak-shârtìla.

Penance, *s.* اختیاری جزا ìkhtiyâri-jèzâ.

Pencase, *s.* قبور kùbur, قلمدان kàlem-dān.

Pence, *s. pl.* باقرلر bàkirlar, منغرلر màn-ghirlar.

Pencil, *s.* قلم kàlem ; lead —, قورشون قلم kùrshun-kàlem ; hair —, توى قلم tùy-kàlem, فرچه fìrcha ; slate —, طاش قلم tàsh-kàlem ; — of light, شعاع shù''ā''.

Pendulum, *s.* رقاص ràkkāss.

Penetrate, *v.a.* كيرمك ghìrmek, ايشلمك ìshlémek.

Peninsula, *s.* اطه àda, جزيره jèzīré, نيم جزيره nìm-jèzīré, شبه جزيره shì-bhi-jèzīré.

Penitence, *s.* پشيمانلق pèshīmānlik (pìshmanlik), ندامت nèdāmèt ; چله chìllé. [نادم nādim.

Penitent, *a.* پشيمان pèshīmān (pìshman),

Penknife, *s.* قلمتراش kàlemtràsh, (pocket —) چاقى chàki.

Penman, *s.* خطاط khàttāt ; —ship, خط khàtt. [bàyrak.

Pennant, *s.* فلاندره filàndara ; بيراق

Penniless, *a.* پارەسز pārèssiz.

Pennon, *s.* بيراق bàyrak.

Penny, *s.* باقر bàkir, منغر mànghir.

Pension, *s.* تقاعد معاشى tàkā''ud-mà''āshi, معاش mà''āsh, ايلق àylik ; —, — off, *v.a.* معاشله تقاعد ا mà''āshla-tàkā''ud-et, ايلق باغلامق àylik-bàghlamak.

Pensioner, *s.* معاش ايله متقاعد اولان كمسنه mà''āsh-ìla-mùtakā''id-òlan-kìmèssné ; Greenwich —, بحريه متقاعدى bàhriyyé-mùtakā''idi ; Chelsea —, بريه متقاعدى bèrrìyyé-mùtakā''idi.

Pentagon, *s.* مخمس mùkhàmmess.

Penthouse, *s.* صوندرمه sùndurma.

Penurious, *a.* طمعكار tàma''kyār.

Penuriousness, *s.* طمعكارلق tàma''kyārlik.

Penury, *s.* فقيرلق fàkīrlik.

Peony, *s.* شقائق shàkā'ik.

People, *s.* ملت millèt, قوم kàvm, قبيله kàbīlé, طائفه tā'ifé, جنس jìnss ; خلق khàlk, اورتەلق òrtalik, عامه ''āmmé ; عوام ناس ''àwàmmi-nāss, اياق طاقمى àyak-tàkimi, قباخلق kāba-khàlk ; great —, كبار طاقمى kìbār-tàkimi, اكابر ناس èkyābiri-nāss ; —, *v.a.* معمورا mà''mūr-et, ابادان ا àbādān-et, شنلندرمك shènlèndirmek ; —d, *p.p.* معمور mà''mūr, ابادان àbādān, شن shèn.

Pepper, *s.* ببر bìber ; —, *v.a.* ببر قاتمق bìber-kàtmak ; — corn, ببر دانەسى bìber-(tànèssi) ; — box, ببر قوتيسى bìber-kùtussu ; — mint, نعنه nà''né.

Peradventure, *ad.* بلكه bèlki.

Perambulate, *v.n.* طولاشمق dòlashmak.

Perambulator, *s.* چوجق ايچون ال عربەسى chòjuk-ichin-èl-''àrabassi.

Per annum, *ad.* ييلده yìlda, سنوى sènèvī

Perceive, *v.a.* كورمك ghyùrmek, تشخيص ا tèshkhīss-et ; اكلامق àngla-mak (ànnamak), درك ا dèrk-et, ادراك ا ìdrāk-et, فهم ا fèhm-et.

Per cent., *ad.* يوزده yùzda.

Per-centage, *s.* يوزدەلك yùzdalik.

Perceptible, *a.* محسوس màhsūss.

Perch, *s.* طاوق قونه جق صيرق tàwuk-kònajak-sìrìk, صيرق sìrìk, اغاج àghàj; تربيعى اللى ارشينلق مسافه tèrbī''ī-èlli-àrshinlìk-mèssāfé; —, *v.n.* قونمق kònmak; —, *v.a.* دكمك dìkmek.

Perchance, *ad.* بلكه bèlki.

Percussion, *s.* اورش wùrush.

Percussion-cap, *s.* قاپسول kàpsūl.

Perdition, *s.* خراب khàrāb.

Peregrinate, *v.n.* اوته برو كزمك uté-bèri-ghèzmek. [brìm.

Peremptory, *a.* قطعى kàt''ī, مبرم mù-

Perfect, *a.* تام tāmm, كامل kyāmil, عيب ونقصاندن خالى ''àyb-ū-nòksān-dan-khāli; —, *v.a.* اتمام ا ìtmām-et, تتميم ا tètmīm-et, اكمال ا ìkmāl-et, تكميل ا tèkmīl-et.

Perfection, *s.* كمال kèmāl.

Perfidious, *a.* خائن khā'in.

Perfidy, *s.* خائنلق khā'inlik.

Perforate, *v.a.* دلمك dèlmek, اچمق àchmak, ثقب ا sàkb-et.

Perforce, *ad.* ناچار nā-chār.

Perform, *v.a.* ياپمق yàpmak, ايتمك ètmek, اجرا ا ìjrā-et, فعله كتورمك fi''la-ghètirmek, فعله اخراج ا fi''la-ìkhrāj-et, قوه دن فعله اخراج ا kùvvé-dan-fi''la-ìkhrāj-et; (as a machine) ايشلمك ìshlémek, كتمك ghìtmek.

Performance, *s.* اجرا ìjrā; ايش ìsh; اويون òyun. [mùkallid.

Performer, *s.* اجرا ايدن ìjrā-èden; مقلد

Perfume, *s.* قوقو kòku, عطر ''ìtr, طيب tīb; بخور bùkhūr, توتسى tùtsu; —, *v.a.* معطر ا mù''àttar-et, مطيب ا mù-tàyyeb-et; —ed, *a.* معطر mù''àttar, مطيب mùtàyyeb; —ing-pan, بخوردان bùkhūrdān (bùkhurdanlik).

Perfumer, *s.* عطرجى ''itrji; ياغى yàghji.

Perfumery, *s.* عطرجينك صاتديغى اشيا ''itrjinin-sàtdighi-èshyā.

Perhaps, *ad.* بلكى bèlki.

Perihelium, *s.* اوج èvj.

Peril, *s.* قورقو kòrku, تهلكه tèhliké, مخاطره mùkhātara, خطر khàtar; —, *v.a.* تهلكه يه قومق tèhlikéyé-kòmak; at your —! ايتده باق èt-da-bàk, ايتده كوررسن èt-da-ghyùrursun, سن sèn-bìlirsin, بلورسن كناهى بويونكده ghyùnāhi-bòyunungda. [mùkhātarali.

Perilous, *a.* تهلكه لو tèhlikéli; مخاطره لو

Perilousness, *s.* تهلكه ليلك tèhlikélilik.

Period, *s.* مدت mùddèt.

Periodical, *a.* اوقات معينه ده واقع اولان èvkāt-mù''ayyènéda-vwākì''-olan; —, *s.* اوقات معينه ده نشر اولنان غزته و امثالى èvkāt-mù''ayyenéda-nèshr-òlunan-ghàzèta-vé-èmsāli.

Perish, *v.n.* هلاك او hèlāk-òl, تلف او tèlef-òl, بتمك bìtmek; اولمك ùl-mek; قورومق kùrumak; چورومك chùrumek; —, *v.a.* چوروتمك [chùrutmek.

Periwig, *s.* پروقه pèrūka.

Perjure one's self, *v.a.* حنث ا hìnss-et, يلان يره يمين ا yàlan-yèra-yèmīn-et; خلف يمين ا khùlfi-yèmīn-et.

Permanence, *s.* دوام dèwām, بقا bàkā, استمرار ìsstimrār.

Permanent, *a.* دائم dā'im, باقى bākī, مستمر mùsstémèrr; تمللو tèmèlli;

چيقمز chikmàz, بوزلمز bòzulmàz; چيقميه‌جق chìkmayajak, بوزلميه‌جق bòzulmayajak.

Permission, s. اذن ìzn (ìzin), رخصت rùkhsAt, اجازت ìjāzet, جواز jèwāz.

Permit, s. تذكره tèzkÉRÉ; —, v.a. اذن ويرمك ìzin-vÈrmek, رخصت ويرمك rùkhsAt-vÈrmek, تجويزا tèjvīz-et, ترخيصا tÈrkhīss-et.

Pernicious, a. مضر mùzìrr, ضررلو zàrārli.

Perpendicular, s. عمود "àmūd; —, a. قائم kā'im, عمودى "àmūdī, طوغرى dòghru, دك dìk.

Perpetrate, v.a. ياپمق yàpmak, ايتمك ètmek, ارتكابا ìrtikyāb-et.

Perpetual, a. دائم dā'im; —ly, ad. دائما dā'imā.

Perplex, v.a. باش اغرتمق bAsh-Aghrit-mak, صيقندى ويرمك sìkìndi-vèrmek.

Perplexity, s. اضطراب ìztirāb.

Perquisites, s. pl. عوائد "àwā'id, عائدات "ā'idāt.

Persecute, v.a. قوغالمق kòghalamak, دالنه بنمك dAlina-bìnmek, راحت ويرمامك rāhat-vÈrmamek, رنجيده‌ا rènjīdÉ-et, دشمنلكا dùshmÈnlik-et, خصومتا khùssūmèt-et, عداوتا "àdāvèt-et.

Perseverance, s. اقدام ìkdĀm, دوام dèwām; —re, v.n. اقداما ìkdĀm-et, دواما dèwĀm-et; —ing, a. مقدم mùkdim.

Persia, s. ايران ìrān.

Persian, a. ايرانى ìrānī; —, s. عجم "Ajem; ايرانى ìrānī; عجم لسانى "Ajem-lìssAni.

Persian Gulf, بصره كورفزى bàssra-kyùr-fezi.

Persist, v.n. عنادا "ìnād-et, وازكچمامك vāz-ghèchmamek.

Persistence, Persistency, s. اصرار ìssrār.

Persistent, Persisting, a. مصر mùssìrr.

Person, s. كشى kìshi, كمسنه kìmèssnÉ, شخص shàkhss, ادم AdAm, نفر nèfEr; (hypostasis) اقنوم ùknūm (pl. اقانيم àkānīm); the three —s of the Trinity, اقانيم ثلثه àkānīmi-sèlāssÉ; (gram.) first —, نفس متكلم nèfssi-mùtékèllim; second —, مخاطب mùkhĀtAb; third —, غائب ghā'ib.

Personage, s. ذات عالى zāt-"ālī.

Personal, a. ذاتى zāti; — pronoun, ضمير zamīr.

Perspective, s. علم مناظر "ìlmi-mènāzir.

Perspicacious, a. فطانتلو fAtānètli.

Perspicaciousness, Perspicacity, s. فطانت fAtānèt.

Perspicuity, s. اچقلق àchìklìk.

Perspicuous, a. اچق àchìk.

Perspiration, s. تر or در tÈr.

Perspire, v.n. ترلمك tÈrlÉmek.

Persuade, v.a. ايناندرمق inàndìrmak, قاندرمق kAndìrmak, اسكاتا isskyāt-et; عقلنى چلمك "Aklìni-chèlmek; عقلنه قومق "Aklina-kòmak.

Persuasion, s. عقلنى چلمكلك àklìni-chèlmeklik.

Pert, a. عارسز "ārsiz.

Pertain, v.n. متعلق او mùta"àllik-òl, راجع او rāji"-òl, منوط او mènūt-òl, مربوط او mÈrbūt-òl, محول او mùhàvvel-òl, مخصوص او màkhsūss-òl, منسوب او mènsūb-òl, باقمق bAkmak, دوقنمق dòkunmak.

Pertinacious, *a.* مصر mùssìrr.

Pertinacity, *s.* عناد "ìnād ; ثبات sèbāt, اقدام ìkdām. [mùnāssébèt.

Pertinence, Pertinency, *s.* مناسبت

Pertinent, *a.* مناسبتلو mùnāssébètli.

Pertly, *ad.* عارسز "ārsiz ; —, *s.* عارسزلق [ārsizlik.

Perusal, *s.* اوقومه òkuma.

Peruse, *v.a.* اوقومق òkumak.

Pervade, *v.a.* تأثيرى او tè'sīri-òl; ايشلمك ìshlémek, كچمك ghèchmek, نافذ او nāfiz-òl.

Perverse, *a.* ترس tèrss ; خيرسز khàyrsiz.

Pervert, *v.a.* ايارتمق àyartmak, افساد ا ìfsād-et, اضلال ا ìdlāl-et ; —, *s.* مرتد mùrtèdd (mùrtàd).

Pest, Pestilence, *s.* وبا vèbā, طاعون tā"ūn, خسته لق khàsstalìk, يمورجق yìmurjàk.

Pestle, *s.* هاون الى (hàwan)-èli.

Pet, *s.* سودك sèvdik, جان jān, قوزى kùzu, جكركوشه jìgher-kyùshé, ايكى كوز ìki-ghyùz ; دارغينلق حالى dàrghinlìk-hāli ; —, *v.a.* سومك sèvmek ; اوخشامق òkhshamak ; يك يوز ويرمك pèk-yùz-vèrmek.

Petition, *s.* عرضحال "àrzi-hāl, عريضه "àrīza ; رجا rìjā, نياز nìyāz, در خواست dèr-khāsst ; —, *v.a.* عرضحال ويرمك "àrzi-hāl-vèrmek. [àrzuhāl.

Petitioner, *s.* صاحب عرضحال sāhibi-

Petrel, *s.* فرطونه مارطيسى fìrtina-màrtissi.

Petrifaction, Petrification, *s.* تحجر tàhàjjur.

Petrify, *v.a.* طاش ا tàsh-et ; —, *v.n.* طاش كسلمك tàsh-kèssilmek, تحجر ا tàhàjjur-et.

Petroleum, *s.* معدن نفتى mà"dan-nèfti ; غاز ghàz.

Petticoat, *s.* ايچ فسطانى ìch-fìsstāni.

Petty, *a.* اوفاق تفك ùfàk-tèfèk, جزئى jùz'ī, صاچمه sàchma.

Pewter, *s.* بياض معدن bèyàz-mà"dan.

Pharmacy, *s.* اجزاجى دكانى èjzāji-dùkkyāni (dùkkèni).

Pheasant, *s.* سوكلون sùghlun (sùlun *or* sùylun), تذرو tèzrèv.

Phenix, *s.* عنقا "ànkā, ققنوس kàknūss *or* ققنس kàknuss.

Phenomenon, *pl.* **Phenomena,** *s.* علامت "àlāmèt, غريبه ghàrībé ; *pl.* علائم "àlā'im, غرائب ghàrā'ib.

Phial, *s.* اوفاق شيشه ùfàk-shīshé.

Philanthropic, Philanthropical, *a.* اهل شفقت èhli-shàfakat. [kat.

Philanthropist, *s.* اهل شفقت èhli-shàfa-

Philanthropy, *s.* شفقت shàfakat.

Philology, *s.* علم تدقيق غور لسان "ìlmi-tèdkiki-ghàvri-lissan.

Philomel, *s.* بلبل bùlbul.

Philosopher, *s.* حكيم hàkīm (*pl.* حكما hùkémā) فيلسوف fèylasòf (*pl.* فلاسفه fèlāséfé) ; —'s stone, كيميا kìmiyā, اكسير ìksīr, التون اوتى àltin-òtu.

Philosophy, *s.* علم حكمت "ìlmi-hìkmèt.

Phlebotomy, *s.* قان المقلق kàn-àlmaklik.

Phlegm, *s.* بلغم bàlgham.

Phlegmatic, *a.* بلغمى bàlghami ; صوغق طبيعتلو sòghuk-tàbi"atli.

Phosphorus, *s.* فوسفوره fòssfora.

Photograph, *s.* رسم rèssm. [fìaji.

Photographer, *s.* فوتوغرافيه جى fòtogra-

Photography, *s.* فوتوغرافيه fòtografìa.
Phrase, *s.* عبارة ''ìbārɛ́; تعبير tà''bīr.
Phraseology, *s.* تعبيرات tà''birāt.
Phrenology, *s.* علم قيافت دماغ ''ìlmi-kìyāfèti-dìmāgh.
Phrensy, *s.* جنون موقت jùnūn-mùwʌkkàt.
Phthisis, *s.* ورم علتى vèrem-''ìllèti.
Physic, *s.* علاج ''ìlāj; —s, *s. pl.* حكمت طبيعيه hìkmèti-tàbī''ìyyɛ́.
Physical, *a.* طبيعى tàbī''ī; جسمانى jìssmʌnī; —ly, *ad.* طبعاً tʌb''an.
Physician, *s.* هكيم hèkīm.
Physiognomist, *s.* اهل علم قيافت èhli-''ìlmi-kìyāfèt.
Physiognomy, *s.* قيافت kìyāfèt, چهره chèhrɛ́, سيما sīmā; علم قيافت ''ìlmi-kìyāfèt.
Physiology, *s.* علم بحث حيات بدنيه ''ìlmi-bàhssi-hàyāt-bèdɛnìyyɛ́.
Pianist, *s.* پيانو چالان استاد piàno-chʌlan-ùstād.
Piano, Pianoforte, *s.* پيانو piàno.
Piastre, *s.* غروش ghùrùsh.
Pick, (pickaxe), *s.* قازمه kʌzma; tooth —, ear —, خلال khìlāl; —, *v.a.* (pull off) قوپارمق kòparmak; (a lock), آچمق àchmak; (teeth, &c.) قارشدرمق kʌrìshdirmak, ارقلامق ʌrìklamak (àytlamak); (a bone) تميزلمك tèmiz-lɛ́mek; (a quarrel) آرامق ʌramak; — pockets, يان كسيجيلك ا yàn-kèssiji-lik-et; — out, آيرمق àyrmak, سچمك sèchmek, انتخاب ا ìntìkhāb-et; — up, *v.a.* قالدرمق kʌldirmak; طوپلامق tòplamak, دوشيرمك dèvshirmek, جمع ا jèm''-et; تحصيل ا tàhsīl-et; —, —, *v.n.* ايولشمك īyilɛshmek, قوتى يرينه كلمك kùvvèti-yɛ̄rina-ghɛ̀lmek; سمورمك sèmirmek; — to pieces, سوكمك sùkmek; دالدرمق dʌldirmak.
Picket, *s.* ايلروقراغولى ìléri-kʌragholi.
Pickle, (brine) صلاموره sʌlamūra; (of vegetables) ترشى tùrshu; —, *v.a.* ترشى باصمق tùrshū-bʌssmak.
Pickpocket, *s.* يان كسيجى yàn-kèssiji, خرسز khìrsiz.
Picnic, *s.* قير يمكى kir-yèmèghi.
Picture, *s.* رسم rèssim.
Picturesque, *a.* رسم كبى rèssim-ghìbi; كوزل ghyùzèl.
Piddle, *s.* چيش chìsh, كچوك چيش kùchuk-chish; سيدك sìdik, بول bèvl; —, *v.n.* ايشه مك ìshémek, صو دوكمك sù-dùkmek, تبول ا tèbèvvul-et.
Pie, *s.* بورك bùrèk.
Piebald, *a.* الا ʌla, الاجه ʌlaja.
Piece, *s.* پارچه pàrcha, قطعه kìt''à, جزء jùz', قسم kìssm; —, *v.a.* اكله مك èklémek.
Piecemeal, *ad.* پارچه پارچه pàrcha-pàrcha.
Pier, *s.* اسكله ìsskèlɛ́; ريختم rìkhtim.
Pierce, *v.a.* دلمك dèlmek, ثقب ا sàkb-et; ايشلمك ìshlémek.
Piety, *s.* ديانت dìyānèt, ديندارلق dīndārlik, تقوى tʌkwà, صلاح sʌlāh.
Pig, *s.* طوكز dònguz (dòmuz), خنزير khìnzīr, خوك khūk; — of lead, صمون sòmūn, كولچه kyùlchɛ́.
Pigeon, *s.* كوكرجين ghyùghɛ̀rjin, كبوتر kèbutɛ̀r, حمامه hʌmʌmɛ́.
Pigeon-hearted, *a.* قورقاق kòrkak.

Pig-headed, *a.* عنادجی ''ìnādji.

Pig-headedness, *s.* عناد ''ìnād.

Pigmy, *s.* جوجه jùjé. [nèvi''-bālìk.

Pike, *s.* حربه hàrba; برنوع بالق bìr-

Pile, *s.* یغین yìghin; بنا bìnā; قازق kāzìk; (of velvet) حاو hàw; —s, *s. pl.* باسور bāssūr, مایەسیل māyassīl; —, *v.a.* یغمق yìghmak, یغین‌ا yìghin-et.

Pilfer, *v.a.* چالمق chālmak; —, *v.n.* خرسزلق‌ا khèrsìzlìk-et, سرقت‌ا sìrkāt-et.

Pilgrim, *s.* حاج hājj, حجی hājjī (hāji); زائر zā'ir (*pl.* زوار zùwwār).

Pilgrimage, *s.* حج hājj; زیارت zìyārèt.

Pill, *s.* حب hàbb (hāp).

Pillage, *s.* یغما yàghma, غارت ghāret, صویغون sòyghun; اموال‌منهوبه èmwāli-mènhūbé; *v.a.* صویمق sòymak, یغماا yàghma-et, غارت‌ا ghāret-et, نهب‌ا nèhb-et.

Pillar, *s.* دیرك dìrèk, ستون sòtūn, عمود ''àmūd.

Pillion, *s.* پلان pālān.

Pillow, *s.* یوزیصدیغی yùz-yàssdighi, بالین bālīn; — case, یصدق یوزی yàssdìk-yùzu.

Pilot, *s.* قلاغوز kìlàghuz; —, *v.a.* قلاغوزلق‌ا kìlàghuzluk-èt.

Pimento, *s.* یکی‌بهار yèngi-bàhār.

Pimple, *s.* سویلجه sìvilja; (on the lip) اوچق ùchuk.

Pin, *s.* طوپلو tòplu, طوپلوایکنه tòplu-ìghné; چیوی chìvi; جیواطه jìwāta; —, *v.a.* طوپلوایله ایلشدرمك tòplu-ila-ìlishdirmek; چیویلمك chìvilé-mek, میخلامق mìkhlamak.

Pincers, *s. pl.* قصاج kìssāj.

Pinch, *s.* چمدك chìmdik; قصدرش kìssdirish; (of snuff) طوتم tùtum; (necessity) صیقی sìki, ضرورت zàrū-rèt; —, *v.a.* چمدكلمك chìmdiklé-mek; قصمق kìssmak; قصدرمق kìss-dirmak; صیقمق sìkmak.

Pinchbeck, *s.* تومبق tòmbàk.

Pine, *s.* چام chàm; چام اغاجی chàm-àghaji; —, *v.n.* اوزلمك ùzulmek; دردچكمك dèrd-chèkmek; اشتیاق چكمك ìshtiyāk-chèkmek.

Pineapple, *s.* اناناس ànanàss.

Pinion, *s.* (feather) شهپر shèh-pèr; (wheel) فنر fèner; —, *v.a.* قوللرینی باغلامق kòllarini-bāghlamak.

Pink, *s.* قرنفل چیچكی kàrenfìl-chì-chéghi; —, *a.* پنبه pènbé; —, *v.a.* اویمه‌اچمق òyma-àchmak.

Pinnace, *s.* فلوقه fìlìka.

Pint, *s.* یوز قرق درهملك اولچی yùz-kìrk-dìrhèmlik-ùlchu.

Pintle, *s.* ایكنه‌جك ìghnéjik.

Pioneer, *s.* بالطه‌جی bāltaji.

Pious, *a.* دیندار dīndār, اهل‌تقوی èhli-tàkwà, متقی mùttàki, صوفی sòfu.

Pip, *s.* چكردك chèkirdek.

Pipe, *s.* بوری *or* بورو bòru; چبوق chìbùk; دودوك dùduk; بیوك فوچی bìyuk-fìchi, مانجنه mànjana.

Pipkin, *s.* طوپراق تنجره tòprak-tènjéré.

Pirate, *s.* دكزخرسزی dèngiz-khìrsizi, خرسز khìrsiz; خرسزتكنەسی khìrsiz-tèknéssi; —, *v.a.* چالمق chālmak, سرقت‌ا sìrkāt-et.

Piss, *s.* چیش chîsh, کچوك چیش kùchuk-chìsh, بول bèvl; —, *v.n.* چیش ا chish-et, صو دوكمك sū-dùk-mek, کچوك صودوكمك kùchuk-sū-dùkmek, تبول ا tèbèvvul-et.

Pistachio, *s.* فستق fìsstìk.

Pistol, *s.* طبانجه tàbànja, پشطو pìshtow.

Piston, *s.* بقراج bàkraj.

Pit, *s.* قویو kūyu, چقور chùkur, حفره [hùfra.

Pitch, *s.* زفت zìft; درجه dèréjé, كرته kèrté, راده rāddé, مرتبه mèrtébé, منزله mènzilé; نهایت درجه سی nìhā-yet-dèréjéssi; —, *v.a.* اتمق àtmak; زفتلمك zìftlémek; قورمق kùrmak; — upon, ایرمق àyrmak, سچمك sèchmek; — — one's head, باش اشاغی یره دوشمك bàsh-àshàghi-yèra--dùshmek.

Pitcher, *s.* دستی dèssti (tèssti).

Piteous, اجی àjì; اجنه جق àjìnajak.

Pith, *s.* اوز ùz, مغز màghz.

Pittance, *s.* قوت لا یموت kūti-lā-yèmūt.

Pitted with the small-pox, *a.* چیچك بوزوغی chìchèk-bòzughu.

Pity, *s.* ترحم tèràhhum, مرحمت mèr-hàmet; —, *v.a.* اجیمق àjìmak, مرحمت ا mèrhàmet-et; what a —! یازق yàzìk.

Pivot, *s.* میل mìl, محور mìhvèr.

Placard, *s.* یافته yàfta; —, *v.a.* یافته یاپشدرمق yāfta-yàpìshdìrmak.

Place, *s.* یر yèr, محل màhàll, موقع mèvkì'', موضع mèvzì'', مکان mèkyān; یر yèr, خدمت khìdmèt (hìzmet), مأموریت mè'mūrìyyèt; *v.a.* قومق kòmak, وضع ا wàz''-et; اوطورتمق òturtmak; دکمك dìkmek, رکز ا rèkz-et, نصب ا nàssb-et, تعیین ا [tà''yīn-et.

Placid, *a.* یواش yàwàsh.

Plague, *s.* وبا vèbā, طاعون tā''ūn, یمورجق yìmurjàk, خسته لق khàss-talìk; بلا bèlā, مصیبت mùssìbèt, درد dèrd; —, *v.a.* درد او dèrd-òl, بلا او bèlā-òl.

Plain, *s.* دوزلك dùzluk, اووه òwa, قیر kìr, صحرا sàhrā; —, *a.* دوز dùz; ساده sādé; ساده کوزل sādé-ghyùzèl; چرکین chìrkin; اچق àchìk, بللو bèlli, عیان ''àyān, مستبان mùsstébān; عادی ''ādī, بیاغی bàyàghi; — spoken, طوغری سویلر dòghrū-sù-wèylər, لقردیسنی اسرکماز làkìrdìssìni-èssirghémàz.

Plaintiff, *s.* دعواجی dà''wàjì.

Plait, *s.* قیرمه kìrma; اورمه ùrmé; —, *v.a.* قیرمق kìrmak, قیرمه قیرمه ا kìrma-kìrma-et; اورمك ùrmek.

Plan, *s.* رسم rèssim, خریطه khàrīta; ترتیب tèrtīb, تدبیر tèdbīr; اصول ùssūl, یول yòl; —, *v.a.* ترتیب ا tèrtīb-et, تدبیر ا tèdbīr-et, دوشونمك dùshunmek, عقل ا ''àkl-et.

Plane, *s.* سطح مستوی sàthì-mùsstèvī; رنده rèndé; —, *a.* مستوی mùsstèvī; —, *v.a.* رنده لمك rèndélémek; — tree, چنار chìnar.

Planet, *s.* سیاره sèyyāré.

Plank, *s.* تخته tàkhta; —, *v.a.* تخته قاپلامق tàkhta-kàplamak; تخته دوشه مك tàkhta-dùshémek.

Plant, *s.* اوت òt ; اغاج àghàj ; فدان fidàn ; نبات nèbāt ; —, *v.a.* دكمك dìkmek, غرس ا gharss-et ; نصب ا nàssb-et, ركزا rèkz-et.

Planter, *s.* غرس ايدر اولان ادم gharss-èder-òlan-àdam.

Plaster, *s.* صيوه siwa *or* صيغه sìgha ; (of Paris) الجى àlchi ; (for wounds) ياقى yàki ; —, *v.a.* صيوامق siwamak, صيغامق sìghamak.

Plate, *s.* طباق tàbāk ; تخته tàkhta ; كموش طاقم ghyùmush - tàkim ; باصمه رسم bàssma - rèssim ; شكل shèkil ; —, *v.a.* كموش قاپلامق ghyùmush - kàplamak ; — glass, آيينه جامى àyina-jàmi.

Plater, *a.* كومش قاپلمه ghyùmish-kàp-[lama.

Platinum, *s.* پلاتينه plàtina.

Plato, *s.* افلاطون ìflàtūn.

Play, *s.* اويون òyun ; شقا shàka ; قمار kùmār ; —, *v.n.* اوينامق òynamak ; قمار اوينامق kùmār-òynamak ; —, *v.a.* چالمق chàlmak ; قومق kòmak, باصمق bàssmak ; — high, چوق پاره قومق chòk-pàra-kòmak ; — a high game, كوزى پك ايلروده او ghyùzu-pèk-ilèrida-ol ; — the fool, *v.n.* اشكلك ا èsheklik-et ; دالقاوقلق ا dàlkàwuklùk - et ; مسخره لق ا màsskharalik-et ; — — with, *v.a.* اشك يرينه قومق èshek-yèrina-kòmak, الداتمق àldatmak ; — the truant, مكتبه كتمامك mèk-tèbé - ghitmamek, مكتبدن قاچمق mèktèbdan - kàchmak ; — upon, چالمق chàlmak ; — — a word, مضمون سويلمك màzmūn-sùwèylé-mek. [òyunju.

Player, *s.* مقلد mùkàllid ; اويونجى

Plaything, *s.* اويونجق òyunjak ; ايلنجه èylènja. [bàhānè.

Plea, *s.* لقردى làkirdi ; عذر "ùzr ; بهانه

Pleasant, *a.* كوزل ghyùzèl, خوش khòsh, طاتلو tàtli ; صفالو sàfāli ; لذيذ lèzīz.

Pleasantry, *s.* شقا shàka, لطيفه làtīfè.

Please, *v.n.* تنسيب ا tènsīb - et, مناسب كورمك mùnāssib-ghyùr-mek ; استمك ìsstémek, ديلهمك dìlémek ; —, *v.a.* خوش كورنمك khòsh - ghyùrunmek, خوشه كچمك khòsha - ghèchmek, مقبوله كچمك màkbūla-ghèchmek, بكنلمك bèghén-ilmek ; — one's self, استديكى كبى ا ìsstédighi - ghibi-et, كيفنجه حركت ا kèyfinja-hàrèkèt-et.

Pleasure, *s.* كيف kèyf, جنبش jùn-bush, صفا sāfā, ايلنجه èylènja, حظ نفس hàzzi-nèfss, تلذذ tèlèzzuz.

Plebeian, *a.* قبا kàba ; —, *s.* قبا ادم kàba-àdam.

Pledge, *s.* رهين rèhīn ; —, *v.a.* رهينه قومق rèhīna - kòmak ; عشقنه ايچمك "àshkina-ichmek.

Pleiades, *s.pl.* ثريا sùrèyyā, يدى قرنداش yèdi-(kàrdash).

Plenipotentiary, *s.* مرخص mùràkh-khàss.

Plenteous, Plentiful, *a.* بول bòl, چوق chòk, بركتلو bèrékètli, غنى ghànī.

Plenty, *s.* بوللق bòllʊk, چوقلق chòklʊk, برکت bèrékèt, غنیمت ghànīmèt.

Pleurisy, *s.* ذات الجنب zātu-'l-jènb (sAtlijAn). [قولای اکلور kòlay-èghilir.

Pliable, Pliant, *a.* يموشاق yìmʊshAk,

Plight, *s.* حال hāl ; —, *v.a.* ويرمك vèrmek ; وعد ا wà''d-et.

Plot, *s.* فتنه fìtné, فساد fèssād ; — of ground, عرصه ''àrsa ; — of a tale, خلاصه khʊ̀lāssa ; grass —, چيم chìm ; —, *v.n.* فتنه قورمق fìtné-kʊ̀rmak, فساد قايناتمق fèssād-kày-natmak.

Plough, *s.* صبان sàbAn ; —, *v.a.* صورمك sùrmek ; —, *v.n.* صبان سورمك sàbAn-sùrmek.

Pluck, *s.* ايچ ìch, جكرمكر jìgher--mìgher ; مردلك mèrdlik, يكيتلك yìghitlik ; —, *v.a.* قوپارمق kòpàrmak ; المق Almak ; صويمق sòymak ; يولمق yòlmak.

Plug, *s.* طيقاج tìkAj ; (for a wound), فتيل fìtil ; —, *v.a.* طيقامق tìkamak, قپامق kApamak ; فتيل صوقمق fìtil--sòkmak.

Plum, *s.* اريك èrik ; قوری اوزوم kʊ̀rʊ--ùzum ; يوزبيك ليره مبلغی yùz-bìng--lìra-mèblàghi.

Plumb, *v.a.* لهيملمك lèhīmlémek ; اسقانديل ا isskAndīl-et ; — line, *s.* شاقول shākʊ̄l (shàghʊl). [èkmek.

Plum-cake, *s.* اوزوملو اكمك ùzumlu-

Plume, *s.* صورغوچ sòrghʊch ; توی tùy ; — one's self, *v.n.* افتخار ا ìftikhār-et.

Plummet, *s.* قورشون قلم kʊ̀rshʊn--kàlem ; اسقانديل isskAndīl.

Plump, *a.* سميز *or* سموز sèmiz ; — up, *v.n.* طولمق dòlmak, شيشمك shìsh-mek ; — (into), *v.n.* دوشمك dùsh-mek, اتلمق Atìlmak, پاطه‌دق دوشمك pAtadak-dùshmek ; —, *ad.* پاطه‌دق pAtadak, لاپه‌دق lApadak.

Plunder, *s.* يغما yàghma, غارت ghāret, غنيمت ghànīmèt (*pl.* غنائم ghànā'im) ; —, *v.a.* يغما ا yàghma-et, غارت ا ghāret-et, نهب ا nèhb-et ; صويمق sòymak.

Plunderer, *s.* يغماجی yàghmaji.

Plunge, *s.* دالش dAlish ; —, *v.n.* دالمق dAlmak, غطس ا ghàtss-et ; —, *v.a.* دالدرمق dAldirmak, صوقمق sòkmak, غطس ا ghàtss-et.

Plural, *s.* جمع jèm''.

Plurality, *s.* كثرت kèssret.

Plus, *ad.* زائد zā'id.

Plush, *s.* قبا قطيفه kAba-kAdīfé.

Ply, *v.n.* ايشلمك ìshlémek ; —, *v.a.* ايشلمك ìshlémek, ايتمك ètmek ; صيقشدرمق sìkishdirmak.

P.M. (post meridiem), *ad.* بعد الزوال bà''d-ez-zèwāl. [yèrda-Avlamak.

Poach, *v.n.* يساق يرده آولامق yassAk-

Poacher, *s.* يساق يرده آولايان خرسز yassAk-yèrda-Avlayan-khàrsiz.

Pock, *s.* چبان chìbAn.

Pocket, *s.* جيب (jèb) ; —, *v.a.* جيبنه قومق jèbina-kòmak ; — book, جزدان jùzdān ; — money, جيب خرجلغی jèb-khàrjlighi.

Pock-marked, *a.* چیچك بوزق chìchek--bòzuk.

Pod, *s.* قبوق kàbuk ; —, *v.n.* باغلمق bāghlamak ; —, *v.a.* قبوغنی صویمق kàbughunu-sòymak, قبوقدن چیقارمق kàbukdan-chìkàrmak.

Poem, *s.* (short) غزل ghàzèl, (long) [قصیده kàssīdé.

Poesy, *s.* شعر shì"r.

Poet, *s.* شاعر shā"ir (*pl.* شعرا shù"arā).

Poetry, *s.* شعر shì"r.

Poignant, *a.* فنا fèna, اجی àji, کسکین kèsskin, الیم èlīm, وجیع vèjī", جکرسوز jìgher-sūz.

Point, *s.* نقطه nòkta ; اوج ūj ; بورون bùrun ; خصوص khùssūss, ماده māddé, باب bāb, امر èmir, کیفیت kèyfiyyèt, نکته nùkté, دقیقه dàkīka, بحث bàhss, مبحث mèbhàss مطلب màtlàb ; درجه dèréjé, مرتبه mèrtébé, راده rāddé, منزله mènzilé, کرته kèrté, پرسه pèréssé ; (of the compass) کرته kèrté, روزکار rùzghyār ; —, *v.n.* باقمق bàkmak, دونمك dùnmek ; پرمق ایله اشارت ا pàrmakla-ishāret-et; —, *v.a.* طوغرلتمق dòghrultmak ; make a —, مخصوص یاپمق màkhsūss--yàpmak.

Point blank, *ad.* طوغری dòghru ; — range, تام منزل tāmm-mènzil.

Pointed, *a.* سیوری اوجلو sìvri-ūjlu, سیوری sìvri ; طوغرلمش dòghrulmush ; باقیور bàkiyor ; مخصوص màkhsūss, اشکار àshikyār.

Poison, *s.* زهر zèhir, سم sèmm, اود òd (òt), اغو àghu ; —, *v.a.* زهرلمك zèhirlémek, تسمیم ا tèssmīm-et ; بوزمق bòzmak, افساد ا ìfsād-et.

Poke, *v.a.* صوقمق sòkmak, صوقوب قارشدرمق sòkup - kàrishdìrmak ; دورتمك dùrtmek.

Poland, *s.* لهستان lèhisstān.

Pole, *s.* صیرق sìrìk ; دیرك dìrèk ; سرن sèren ; لهلو lèhli ; قطب kùtb (kùtub) ; التی بچوق ارشون àlti-bù-chuk-àrshin ; — star, قطب یلدزی kùtub - yìldizi, تیمور قازق (dèmir)--kàzìk, جدی jùdèyy.

Police, *s.* (matters of) امور ضبطیه ùmūri--zàbtìyyé ; —man, ضبطیه قواصی zàb-tìyyé-kàwwàssi ; — agent, ضبطیه مأموری zàbtìyyé-mè'mūru.

Policy, *s.* تدبیر tèdbīr, اصول ùssūl, روش rèvish ; سند sèned.

Polish, *a.* لهلو lèhli ; —, *s.* لهجه lèhjé ; جلا jìlā ; تربیه tèrbìyyé ; —, *v.a.* جلا ا jìlā-et, جلاویرمك jìlā-vèrmek ; تربیه ا tèrbìyyé-et.

Polite, *a.* چلبی chèlébi, افندی èfèndi, تربیه لو tèrbìyyéli, مکرم mùkrim, نوازشلو nùwāzishli.

Political, *a.* امور ملکیه یه متعلق ùmūr-i--mìlkīyyéya-mùta"allik ; — economy, علم ادارهٔ ملکیه "ìlmi-ìdāréi-mìlkīyyé.

Politically, *ad.* دولتجه dèvletjé.

Politician, *s.* امور ملکیه اشنا ùmūri--mìlkīyyé-āshinā. [-dèvlet.

Politics, *s.* علم تدبیر دولت "ìlmi-tèdbīrī-

Pollard, *s.* اینجه کپك ìnja-kèpek ; داللری هپ بودنمش اغاج dàllari-hèp--bùdànmish-àghàj.

Pollute, *v.a.* تنجيس ا tènjīss-et, مردار ا mùrdàr-et, پس ا pìss-et.

Poltroon, *s.* قورقاق kòrkak.

Poltroonery, *s.* قورقاقلق kòrkaklik.

Polyanthus, *s.* چوقه‌چیچکی (chòha)-chìchèghi.

Pomegranate, *s.* نار nàr, انار ènār.

Pommel, *s.* ایرقاشی èyer-kàshi; —, *v.a.* دوکمك dùghmek, اورمق wùrmak.

Pomp, *s.* طنطنه tàntana, دبدبه dèbdébé, سلطنت sàltanàt.

Pond, *s.* کول ghyùl, حوض hàwuz.

Ponderous, *a.* اغر àghir, ثقیل sàkīl, کران ghìrān.

Pontiff, *s.* امام ìmām, همام hùmām.

Pontoon, *s.* طومباز tòmbàz.

Pony, *s.* مدللی midìlli.

Pool, *s.* کول ghyùl, حوض hàwuz.

Poop, *s.* اوصورق òssuruk, ضرطه zàrta; (of a ship) قامره‌اوستی kàmara-ùsstu.

Poor, *a.* فقیر fàkīr (*pl.* فقرا fukarā), غریب‌یکیت (kàripīt); ضعیف zà"īf (*pl.* ضعفا zù"afā, the origin of the French denomination of "Zouave," the *infantry* in Africa being called "the poor," or "the weak," because not able to afford themselves horses to ride against the enemy); فنا fèna, ایش‌یوق ìsh-yòk.

Poorly, *a.* کیفسز kèyfsiz, مزجسز mìzājsiz, خسته khàssta; —, *ad.* فقیرجه fàkīrja; فنا fèna.

Pop, *v.n.* پاطلامق pàtlamak; اتلمق àtilmak, فرلامق fìrlamak; —, *v.a.* اتیویرمك àtivèrmek; — in, *v.n.* لاپ‌ایچروکیرمك اوغرامق òghramak; làp-ìchèri-ghìrmek; — —, *v.a.* ایچرو اتیویرمك ìchèri-àtivèrmek; — out, *v.n.* طیشاری‌اوغرامق dìshāri-òghramak; — —, *v.a.* سوندربویرمك sùndurivèrmek; طیشاری قویویرمك dìshàri-kòyuvèrmek; — on, *v.a.* کیویرمك ghìyivèrmek; — off, *v.n.* صاوشیویرمك sàwushuvèrmek; اولیویرمك ùluvèrmek; — —, *v.a.* چیقاریویرمك chìkàrivèrmek.

Poplar, *s.* قواق اغاجی kàwak-àghaji, قواق kàwak.

Poppy, *s.* حشحاش hàshhāsh; (wild) کلینجك‌چیچکی ghèlinjik-chìchèghi.

Populace, *s.* عوام‌ناس "àwāmmi-nāss, اسافل‌ناس èssāfili-nāss, ایاق طاقمی àyak-tàkimi.

Popular, *a.* مقبول‌عام màkbūlu-"āmm, عوام‌پسند "àwāmm-pèssènd.

Populate, *v.a.* معمورا mà"mūr-et.

Population, *s.* اهالی àhālī, نفوس nùfūss.

Populous, *a.* معمور mà"mūr.

Porcelain, *s.* فغفور fàghfūr.

Porch, *s.* دهلیز dèhlīz.

Porcupine, *s.* اوقلوکرپی òklu-kìrpi.

Pore, *s.* (*pl.* مسامات mèssāmmāt); — over, *v.a.* دالمق dàlmak, پك‌باقمق pèk-bàkmak.

Pork, *s.* طوکز اتی dònguz-èti (dòmuz), لحم‌الخنزیر làhmu-'l-khènzīr.

Porous, *a.* مساماتلو mèssāmātli.

Porphyry, *s.* سماقی sòmmākī.

Porpoise, *s.* یونس‌بالغی yònuss-bàlighi.

Porringer, *s.* طوپراق‌تنجر tòprak-tènjéré.

Port, *s.* ليمان lìmān; اسكله ìsskèlé; لومبار قپاغى lùmbar-kàpaghi; لومبار lùmbar; پورت شرابى pòrt-shèrābi.

Portable, *a.* خفيف khàfīf, طاشيمسى قولاى tàshimassi-kòlay.

Porte, *s.* باب عالى bābi-"ālī, پاشاقپوسى pàsha-kàpissi; دولت عليه dèvlèti-"àlìyyé.

Porter, *s.* حمال hàmmāl (hàmal); قپوجى kàpiji; سياه ارپه صويى sìyāh-àrpa-sùyu.

Porterage, *s.* حماللق hàmmāllik.

Port-hole, *s.* لومبار دليكى lùmbar-dèlighi.

Portico, *s.* قپو دهليزى kàpi-dèhlīzi.

Portion, *s.* پارچه pàrcha, بلوك bùluk, جزء jùz', قسم kìssm, قطعه kìt"à; حصه hìsssé, پاى pày; سهم sèhm, سهيم sèhīm; قسمت kìssmèt; —, — out, *v.a.* تقسيم ا tàksīm-et, بولمك bùlmek; — off, *v.a.* حصه سنى ويروب دفع ا hìsssésini-vèrup-dèf"-et; marriage —, جهاز jìhāz (chèhiz), اغرلق àghirlik.

Portmanteau, *s.* صندق sàndik, چانطه chànta.

Portrait, *s.* رسم rèssim, تصوير tàssvīr, [صورت sūrèt.

Portrait-painter, *s.* تصوير رسامى tàssvīr-rèssāmi.

Portray, *v.a.* رسم ا rèssm-et, توصيف ا [tàvsīf-et.

Position, *s.* موقع mèvki"; حال hāl.

Positive, *a.* صحيح sàhīh, صحيحاً معلوم sàhīhan-mà"lūm, محقق mùhàkkàk; ايو بلور īyi-bilir; پك قوى سويلر pèk-kàvi-sùwèyler; عنادجى "ìnādji; مطلق mùtlàk.

Possess, *v.a.* مالك او mālik-òl, متملك او mùtémèllik-òl; — one's self of, ضبط ا zàbt-et, اله كتورمك èlé-ghètirmek, استحصال ا ìsstihsāl-et; whatever possessed you? قنغى شيطانه اويدك (hànghi)-shèytāna-ùydung, نه درلو عقله خدمت ايتدك nè-dùrlu-"àkla-(hìzmet)-ètding; —ed, *p.p.* دلى dèli, مجنون mèjnūn, ديوانه dīwāné.

Possessed, *a.* دلى dèli; تصرفنده اولان tàssàrrufinda-òlan.

Possession, *s.* تصرف tàssàrruf. [-ilèyh.

Possessive case, مضاف اليه mūzàfun-

Possessor, *s.* صاحب sāhib; متصرف mùtéssàrrif.

Possibility, *s.* امكان ìmkyān. [بلكه bèlki.

Possible, *a.* ممكن mùmkin; —bly, *ad.*

Post, *s.* (wooden) قازق kàzik, ديرك dìrèk; (for letters) پوسته pòssta; (for horses) منزل mènzil; (office) پوست pòsst, مأموريت mè'mūrìyyet, مسند mèssnèd, صدر sàdr; (sentry) قول kòl, قره قول kàra-kòl, قره غول kàraghol, نوبتجى nùbètji; (place) ير yèr, موقع mèvki", —, *v.a.* پوسته يه ويرمك pòsstaya-vèrmek; قومق kòmak, براقمق bràkmak, تعيين ا tà"yīn-et; —, — up, *v.a.* (accounts) يازمق yàzmak, قيد ا kàyd-et, دفتره كچورمك dèftera-ghèchirmek; (persons) يافته يه يازمق yàftaya-yàzmak; —, *v.n.* منزل سورمك mènzil-sùrmek, منزل كتمك mènzil-ghìtmek; — office, پوسته خانه pòssta-khāné; — house, منزلخانه mènzil-khāné; — master,

پوسته مأموری pòssta - mè'mūrū ; منزلجی mènzilji ; — — general, پوسته ناظری pòssta-nāziri, — horse, منزل بارکیری mènzil-(bèghiri).

Postage, *s.* پوسته اجرتی pòssta-ùjrèti.

Post-boy, *s.* سوریجی sùruju.

Post-chaise, *s.* منزل عربه‌سی mènzil-"àrabassi.

Posterity, *s.* ذریت zùrrìyyèt, اولاد احفاد èvlād-u-àhfād.

Postilion, *s.* سوریجی sùruju.

Postpone, *v.a.* تأخیرا tè'khīr-et, صکره‌یه براقمق sòngraya-bràkmak.

Postscript, *s.* کنار kènar, حاشیه hāshìyyé.

Pot, *s.* قاب kāb, قوانوس kàwanoss, برداق bàrdak ; حقه hòkka ; تستی tèssti ; کوپ kyùp ; تنجره tènjéré, قزغان (kāzan) ; flower —, صقسی sāksi ; —, *v.a.* قوانوسه‌باصمق kàwanossa - bāssmak ; صقسی‌یه دکمك sāksiya-dìkmek.

Potash, *s.* پوتاس pòtāss.

Potassa, *s.* پوتاس pòtāss.

Potassium, *s.* پوتاسیوم pòtāssium.

Potato, *s.* یرالماسی yèr-èlmassi.

Pot-bellied, *a.* قارنلو kàrnli.

Potency, *s.* قوت kùvvet.

Potent, *a.* قوتلو kùvvetli.

Potentate, *s.* حکمدار hùkmdār.

Potential mood, *s.* صیغهٔ اقتداریه sīgha'i-ìktidāriyyé.

Potion, *s.* علاج "ìlāj.

Pottage, *s.* چوربا chòrba ; لاپه lāpa.

Potter, *s.* چوملکجی chùmlekji ; — about, — over, بوش شیلرایله ایلنوب وقت کچورمك bòsh - shèylèr - ila - -èylènup-wākit-ghèchirmek.

Poulterer, *s.* طاوقجی tàwukju.

Poultice, *s.* لاپه lāpa ; —, *v.a.* لاپه‌اورمق lāpa-wùrmak.

Poultry, *s.* طاوق tàwuk, طاوق ماوق tàwuk-màwuk.

Pound, *s.* (weight) لیبره lìbra ; (Turkish = $2\frac{3}{4}$ avoirdupois) قیه kìyyé (òkka) ; (sterling) لیره lìra ; (for cattle) اغل āghil ; —, *v.a.* دوکمك dùghmek, ازمك èzmek, دق ا dàkk-et.

Pour, *v.a.* دوکمك dùkmek, اقتمق ākitmak ; —, *v.n.* سیل کبی یاغمق (sèl)-ghìbi-yàghmak ; سیل کبی اقمق (sèl)-ghìbi-ākmak.

Pout, *v.n.* صوموتمق sòmutmak.

Poverty, *s.* فقر fàkr, فاقه fāka, فقیرلق fàkīrlik, فقرالق fàkarālik, ضرورت zàrūrèt.

Powder, *s.* توز tòz, غبار ghùbār ; (medicine) سفوف sùfūf ; gun —, باروت bàrut ; —, *v.a.* اوستنه توز سلکمك ùsstuna - tòz - silkmek ; توز ا tòz-et, ازمك èzmek ; — horn, — flask, وزنه vèzné, باروت وزنه‌سی bàrut-vèznéssi ; — mill, باروتخانه bārut-khāné ; — room, — magazine, جبخانه jèb-khāné.

Power, *s.* زور zòr, قوت kùvvèt, قدرت kùdrèt, مکنت mìknèt, اقتدار ìktidār ; دولت dèvlèt, حکومت hùkyūmèt ; نفوذ nùfūz ; تأثیر tè'sīr ; حاسه hāsssa (*pl.* حواس hàwāss).

Powerful, *a.* زورلو zòrlu, قوتلو kùvvètli, قوی kàvī, قدرتلو kùdrètli, مکین mèkīn, مقتدر mùktèdir ; نفوذلو nūfūzlu, نافذالكلمتين nāfizu-'l-kèlimé-tèyn; مؤثر mù'èssir; سرت sèrt; all —, قدير kādīr. [-kùvveti-yòk.

Powerless, a. هيچ برقوتى يوق hìch-bìr-

Powerlessness, s. هيچ برقوتى اولمامقلق hìch-bìr-kùvveti-òlmamaklik.

Pox, s. فرنكى fìrènghi.

Practicable, a. ممكن mùmkin, ياپلور yàpılır; قوللانلور kùllānılır.

Practice, s. تعليم tà''līm, دوام dèwām, مداومت mùdāvémèt; عمل ''āmel; عمليات ''āmélìyyāt; عادت ''ādèt; طبيبك مشتريلرى tābībing-mùshtèr-iléri; —, v.a. ايتمك ètmek, ياپمق yàpmak; تعليم ا tà''līm-et, دوام ا dèwām-et; هكيملك ا hèkimlik-et.

Praise, s. مدح mèdh, ثنا sènā, ستايش sitāyish; (to God) حمد hàmd, شكر shùkr; —, v.a. مدح ا mèdh-et, ثنا ا sènā-et, ستايش ا sìtāyish-et; حمد ا hàmd-et, شكر ا shùkr-et. [mèbrūr.

Praiseworthy, a. مرضى mèrzī; مبرور

Prance, v.n. اوينامق òynamak, صچرامق [sìchramak.

Prawn, s. تكه tèké.

Praxis, s. تعليم tà''līm.

Pray, v.n. يالوارمق yālvarmak, رجا ا rìjā-et, نياز ا nìyāz-et; دعا ا dù''ā-et; نمازقيلمق nāmaz-kìlmak.

Prayer, s. رجا rìjā, نياز nìyāz; دعا dù''ā; (stated) نماز namāz, صلات or صلوت sālāt.

Prayer-book, s. دعا كتابى dù''ā-kìtābi.

Preach, v.n. وعظ ا wà''z-et.

Preacher, واعظ vwā''iz. [meklik.

Preaching, s. وعظ ايتمكلك wà'z-èt-

Preamble, s. مقدمه mùkāddimé, ديباجه dībājé. [rèr.

Precarious, a. غير مقرر ghàyri-mùkàr-

Precaution, s. حذر hāzar, احتذار ìhti-zār, احتياط ìhtiyāt, انتباه ìntibāh; to take —, صاقنمق sàkinmak, كوز اچمق ghyùz-àchmak, حذر ا hāzar-et, احتياطلو بولنمق ìhtiyātli-bùlun-mak, انتباه اوزره او ìntibāh-ùzéré-òl.

Precede, v.a. and n. سبقت ا sàbkāt-et; مسابقت ا mùssābakāt-et; —ding, سابق sābık.

Precedence, s. مسابقت mùssābakāt.

Precedent, s. امثال èmsāl (pl.)

Precept, s. قاعده kā'idé; نصيحت nāssihàt; ضرب مثل zārbi-mèssel.

Preceptor, s. نصيحتجى nāssihàtji, خواجه khoja.

Precious, a. قيمتلو kīmètli, ذى قيمت zī-kīmèt; عزيز ''āzīz; — stone, جوهر jèvhèr (pl. جواهر jèwāhir); — rogue, كدكلو چاپقين ghèdikli-chāpkin. [ورطه vàrta.

Precipice, s. يار yàr, اوچروم ūchurum,

Precipitate, a. —ly, ad. عجله ايله ''ājélè-ila, على العجله ''àlā-'l-''ājélé; — retreat, رجعت قهقرى rìj''àti-kàhkarà; —, s. توز toz, چوكندى chùkundu; —, v.a. اشاغى اتمق āshàghi-àtmak; تعجيل ا tà''jīl-et; —, v.n. ديبه چوكمك dìbé-chùkmek; — things, — matters, عجله ا ''ājélé-et.

Precipitation, s. عجله ''ājélé. [-et.

Precise, a. (person) مراقلو mèrākli, اهل دقت èhli-dìkkāt; (time, &c.)

تام tāmm, تمام tàmām; —, *v.a.* تعيين ا tà''yīn-et, تفريق ا tèfrīk-et, مخصوص بريني كوسترمك màkhsūss--bìrini-ghyùsstermek.

Precision, *s.* مراق mèrāk; دقت dìk-kāt; صحت sìhhàt.

Preclude, *v.a.* مانع او mānì''-òl.

Precocious, *a.* وقتندن اول يتشمش vwāktinden-èvvel-yètishmish.

Predecessor, *s.* سلف sèlef (*pl.* اسلاف èsslāf).

Predestination, *s.* قدر kāder.

Predicament, *s.* فنا حال fēnahāl.

Predicate, *s.* خبر khāber.

Predict, *v.a.* وقوعندن اول خبر ويرمك wùkū''undan-èvvel-khāber-vèrmek, استخراج ا ìsstikhrāj-et.

Prediction, *s.* وقوعندن اول خبر ويرمكلك wùkū''undan-èvvel-khāber-vèrmek-lik.

Predilection, *s.* ميل mèyl.

Predispose, *v.a.* استعداد ويرمك ìsstì''-dād-vèrmek.

Predisposition, *s.* استعداد ìsstì''dād.

Predominant, *a.* غالب ghālib.

Predominate, *v.n.* غالب او ghālib-òl, چوق او chòk-òl, زياده او zìyādé-òl.

Preface, *s.* مقدمه mùkāddimé, ديباجه dībājé; —, *v.n.* بسط مقدمه ا bāssti--mùkāddimé-et.

Prefer, *v.a.* ترجيح ا tèrjīh-et; ترفيع رتبه ا tèrfī''i-rùtbé-et.

Preferable, *a.* مرجح mùrèjjàh.

Preference, *s.* ترجيح tèrjīh.

Pregnancy, *s.* كبه لك ghèbélik.

Pregnant, *a.* كبه ghèbé, حامله hāmilé.

Prejudice, *s.* ضرر zàrar, فنالك fènalik; — against, سوءظن sù'īzànn; — in favour, حسن ظن hùssni-zànn; vulgar —, ظن باطل zànni-bātil; —, *v.a.* ضررا zàrar-et; —, ذهننه شي قومق zìhnina-shèy-kòmak.

Prelate, *s.* پسقپوس pìsskoposs.

Premature, *a.* —ly, *ad.* وقتندن اول wāktindàn-èvvel, وقتي كلمدن wākti-ghèlmadan.

Premeditate, *v.a.* دوشونوب قورمق dùshunup-kùrmak, قصدا kāssd-et; —d, *p.p.* قصدى kāssdī; —dly, *ad.* قصداً kāssdan, عمداً ''àmdan.

Premier, *s.* صدراعظم sādri-à''zàm (sàd-razàm), باش وكيل bāsh-vèkīl.

Premises, *s. pl.* او èv, دكان dùkkyān (dùkkèn), اوطه òda, باغچه bāghcha, عرصه ''àrsa, ير yèr, حدود hùdūd; (logic) مقدمه mùkāddimé (single), مقدمتين mùkāddimétèyn (double), مقدمات mùkāddimāt (several).

Premium, *s.* باش bāsh, كار kyār; اجرت ùjrèt; مكافات mùkyāfāt; شاكرديه اقچه سى shāghirdìyyé-āk-chassi.

Preoccupy, *v.a.* ذهنني مشغول ا zìhnini--mèshghūl-et; —ied, *a.* ذهنى مشغول zìhni-mèshghūl.

Preparation, *s.* تدارك tèdāruk (tèdārik, *pl.* تداركات tèdārikyāt); (compound) تركيب tèrkīb.

Prepare, *v.n.* حاضرلنمق hāzirlanmak, حاضراو hāzir-òl; —, *v.a.* حاضرا hāzir-et; — a table, صفره قورمق sòfra--kùrmak; (cook) ياپمق yàpmak, پشورمك pìshirmek; (compound)

ترکیب ا tèrkīb-et; (arrange) ترتیب ا tèrtīb-et.

Preponderance, *s.* غلبه ghàlébé.

Preponderate, *v.n.* غالب او ghālib-òl, باصقین کلمك bàsskin-ghèlmek.

Preposition, *s.* حرف جر hàrfi-jèrr, جار jārr.

Prepossess, *v.a.* کوکل ضبط ا ghyùngul-[zàbt-et.

Prepossession, *s.* میل mèyl; عداوت "àdāvèt.

Preposterous, *a.* عقله مغایر "àkla-[-mùghāyir.

Prerogative, *s.* خاصه khàsssa.

Presage, *s.* علامت "àlāmèt, دلیل dèlīl; فال fàl; —, *v.a.* علامت او "àlāmèt-ol, دلالت ا dèlālèt-et; اکلامق ànglamak (ànnamak), استخراج ا ìss-tikhrāj-et. [bīh-et; ترتیب ا tèrtīb-et.

Prescribe, *v.a.* امر ا èmr-et, تنبیه ا tèn-

Prescription, *s.* حکیم ترتیبی hèkim-tèr-tībi, رچته rèchèta.

Presence, *s.* حضور hùzūr; وارلق vàrlìk, موجودیت mèvjūdìyyèt, وجود vùjūd; — of mind, عقلی باشنده اولمقلق "àkli - bàshinda - òlmaklìk; فتور کتورمامکلك fùtūr-ghètirmameklik; to have, to be in possession of — of mind, هیچ بوزلمامق hìch - bòzulmamak, عقلی باشنده او "àkli-bàshinda-òl, هیچ فتور کتورمامك hìch-fùtūr-ghètir-mamek.

Present, *a.* حاضر hàzir, وار vàr, موجود mèvjūd, بولنور bùlunur, بولنمش bùlunmush; شمدیکی shìmdiki, حالی hālī; —, *s.* هدیه hèdìyyé; پیشکش pīshkèsh; عطیه "àtìyyé; بخشش bàkhshish; شمدیکی حال shìmdiki-hāl, شمدیکی وقت shìm-diki-wàkit, شمدی shìmdi, حال hāl; at —, شمدی shìmdi, شمدیلك shìmdilik, الحال èl-hāl, الان èl-ān, حالا hālā; —, *v.a.* عرض ا "àrz-et, تقدیم ا tàkdīm-et; ابراز ا ìbrāz-et, کوسترمك ghyùsstermek; طوغرلتمق dòghrultmak; — arms! سلام طور sèlām-dùr; present! نشان ال nì-shān-àl. [dīm, ابراز ìbrāz.

Presentation, *s.* عرض "àrz, تقدیم tàk-

Presently, *ad.* شمدی shìmdi, همان (hèmen)-shìmdi, برازدن bìr-àzdan. [mùhāfaza.

Preservation, *s.* حفظ hìfz; محافظه

Preserve, *s.* طاتلو tàtli, رچل rèchel, شکرلمه shèkerlémé; ترشی tùrshu; قورو kòru, قورولق kòruluk; —, *v.a.* قورومق kòrumak, صقلامق sàklamak, حفظ hìfz-et, وقایه ا vìkāyé-et, صیانت ا sìyānèt-et, محافظه ا mùhāfaza-et; رچلنی یاپمق rèchelini-yàpmak; ترشیسنی یاپمق tùrshusunu-yàpmak; —, *v.n.* رچل او rèchel-òl; ترشی او tùrshu-òl. [-èden-kìmèssné.

Preserver, *s.* حفظ ایدن کمسنه hìfz-

Preside, *v.n.* ریاست ا rìyāssèt-et; باشده او bàshda-òl. [سر sèr.

President, *s.* رئیس rèʾīss; باش bàsh,

Presidentship, *s.* ریاست rìyāssèt.

Press, *s.* باصمه دستکاهی bàssma-dèsst-ghyāhi; منکنه mènghéné; جندره jèndéré, باصقی bàsski; طولاب dòlap, یوك yùk; باصمه جیلر اصنافی bàssmajilar-èssnāfi ; غزته‌لر ghàzètalar ; زوراکی عسکرطوپلایان قول zòràki-‘‘ASS-KER-tòplayAn-kòl ; —, v.a. صیقمق sìkmak; باصمق bAssmak ; صیقشدرمق sìkishdirmak ; تضییق ا tAzyīk-et, جبرا jèbr-et, اجبارا ìjbār-et ; زوراکی عسکریازمق zòràki-‘‘Assker-yàzmak.

Pressure, s. صیقش sìkish, باصش bAss-ish ; صیقی sìki, باصقی bAsski ; زور zòr, تضییق tAzyīk.

Pretence, s. بهانه bàhānÉ ; کوسترش ghyüsstERish, تقلید tAklīd, یلان yàlAn.

Preterite, s. فعل ماضی fìli-māzi.

Pretext, s. بهانه bàhānÉ ; وسیله vèssīlÉ.

Pretty, a. کوزل ghyùzèl, دلبر dìlbÈr, حسنلو hùssnlu ; —, ad. اپ ایوجه èp-īyija, اولدقجه òldυkja, چوقجه chòkja, کرکی کبی ghèrèghi-ghìbi ; — well, ایوجه īyija, اولدقجه ایو òldυkja-īyi.

Prevail, v.n. غالب او ghālib-òl ; — with, — upon, راضی ا rāzi-et, کوکلنی ا ghyùngulunu-et (ghyùnunu-et).

Prevalent, a. جاری jārī.

Prevent, v.a. منع ا mèn‘‘-et.

Preventable, a. منعی ممکن mèn‘‘i-mùmkin.

Prevention, s. منع mèn‘‘.

Preventive, s. مانع māni‘‘.

Previous, a. اولکی ÈvvElki, مقدمکی mùkAddEmki, اسکی èsski.

Previously, ad. اسکیدن èsskidan, اول ÈvvEl, مقدم mùkAddEm, مقدما mùkAddEma, اول امرده Èvvéli-èmirdÉ, اولا ÈvvÉla.

Prey, s. او Av, شکار shìkyār, صید sàyd ; طعمه tà‘‘ma ; — upon, v.a. یملک yèmek ; اولامق Avlamak, طوتمق tùtmAk, صید ا sàyd-et, شکارا shìkyār-et ; beast of —, یرتیجی حیوان yìrtiji-hàywAn.

Price, s. بها bàhā, فیأت fì‘àt ; high —, اغر فیأت Aghir-fì‘àt, طولغون فیأت dòlghυn-fì‘àt ; low —, دون بها dūn-bàhā, اهون بها Èhvèn-bàhā ; fixed —, کسلمش بها kèssilmish-bàhā, مقطوع فیأت mAktū‘‘-fì‘àt ; assize —, نرخ nàrkh, میری فیأتی mīrī-fì‘àti ; — of blood, دیت dìyyèt, خونبها khūn-bàhā.

Prick, s. دیکن dìkÈn, خار khār ; سك sìk, ذکر zèkEr, الت تناسل āleti-tènāssul ; ایکنه یاره‌سی ìghnÉ-yàrassi ; —, v.a. سیوری شی ایله یاره ا sìvri-shèy-ila-yàra-et ; —, v.n. باتمق bAtmak ; — up one's ears, قولاق دیکمك kùlAk-dìkmek.

Prickle, s. دیکن dìkÈn, خار khār.

Pride, s. کبر kìbr (kibir), نخوت nàkhvèt, تکبر tèkèbbur, تعظم tà‘‘àzzum ; فخر fàkhr ; افتخار ìfti-khār ; — one's self in, v.n. افتخارا ìftikhār-et, مراق ایدنمك mèrāk-èdinmek.

Priest, s. امام ìmām ; پاپاس pApAss, رهبان rùhbān, کشیش kèshīsh ; خخام khàkhām.

Prime, a. اعلا à‘‘là, علی الاعلا ‘‘àliyyu-'l-à‘‘là, باشدن باش bAshdan-bAsh ; اعظم à‘‘zàm, باش bAsh, اول ÈvvEl ; اصلی Asslī ; —, s. الك علاسی èng-

-à"làssi ; — of youth, عنفوان شبابت "ùnfuvāni-shèbābèt ; —, *v.a.* اغزلامق àghzlamak, يملمك yèmlémek ; لقردی قفا اوکرتمك làkirdi-ùghretmek ; kàfā-kurdurmak. ; بويانك قوردرمق boyaning-àsstarini-wùrmak ; — one's-self, قفاقورمق kàfā-kùrmak.

Primer, *s.* الفباجزئی èlif-bé-jùz'u.

Priming, *s.* اغزاوتی àghz-òtu ; يملمه yèmlémé ; بويا استاری bòya-àsstari ; — horn, وزنه vèzné.

Prince, *s.* شهزاده shèhzādé ; برنجی رتبه بكی bìrinji-rùtbé-bèghi.

Principal, *a.* باش bàsh, بيوك bìyuk, انا àna, اصل àssl ; —, *s.* سرمايه sèrmāyé, رأس المال rè'ssu-'l-māl ; سركرده sèrkèrdé ; اصل مال صاحبی àssl-māl-sāhibi ; اصل مصلحت صاحبی àssl-màsslāhat-sāhibi. [-mèmlékèt.

Principality, *s.* بكلك مملكت bèghlik-

Principle, *s.* اساس èssāss, تمل tèmel ; موضوع mèvzu", ركن rùkn, مادهٔ اصليه māddè'i-àsslìyyé ; عقيده "àkìdé ; قاعده kā"idé ; —s, *s.pl.* اصول ùssūl ; اوليات èvvelìyyāt ; اركان èrkyān ; عقائد "àkā'id ; انصاف ìnsāf, استقامت ìsstikāmet ; good —, استقامت ìss-tikāmet ; bad —, شقاوت shàkāvèt.

Print, *s.* باصمه bàssma ; —, *v.a.* باصمق bàssmak, طبع tàb"-et ; —ing-office, باصمه خانه bàssma-khāné, مطبعه màtba"à, مطبع màtbà".

Printer, *s.* باصمه جی bàssmaji.

Prison, *s.* زندان zìndān, حبس hàbss, حبسخانه hàbss-khāné, محبس màh-bèss.

Prisoner, *s.* حبس (hàpiss), محبوس màhbūss ; — of war, اسير èssīr (yèssir). [ghìzlilik.

Privacy, *s.* خلوت khàlvet ; كيزلولك

Private, *a.* بياغی bàyaghi, عادی "ādī ; خاص khàsss ; كيزلو ghìzli, صاقلو sàkli, خفی khàfī, مخفی màkhfi ; — person, عوام ناسدن بری "àwāmmi-nāssdan-bìri ; —, *s.* عسكرنفری "àsker-nèféri ; ادب يری èdeb-yèri, عورت يری "àv-ret-yèri.

Privateer, *s.* جنكه مأذون بازركان كميسی jènghé-mè'zūn-bàzirghyān-ghèmissi.

Privately, *ad.* كيزلو ghìzli.

Privilege, *s.* امتياز ìmtiyāz, مأذونيت mè'zūnìyyèt.

Privy, *a.* خاص khàsss ; محرم màhrèm, خبردار khàberdār ; —, *s.* كنف kènef, ممشا mèmshā, ابدستخانه àb-desst-khàné.

Prize, *s.* قزانلهجق شی kàzànìlajak-shèy, قزانلان شی kàzànìlan-shèy ; مكافات mùkyāfāt ; —, *v.a.* عزيز طوتمق "àzīz-tòtmak ; — open, اوجی سيوری برشی صوقوب اچمق ūju-sìvri-bìr-shèy-sòkup-àchmak.

Prize-fighter, *s.* پهلوان pèhluwān.

Probable, *a.* محتمل mùhtèmil, احتمال ìhtimāl ; —bly, *ad.* احتمال ìhtimāl, احتمالاً ìhtimālan ; —bility, *s.* احتمال ìhtimāl.

Probably, *ad.* غالبا ghālbā. [ìhtimāl.

Probe, *s.* ميل mīl, اسقنديل ìsskàndīl ;

—, *v.a.* يوقلامق yòklamak, اسقنديل ا ìsskāndūl-et, ميل صوقمق mīl-sòkmak.

Probity, *s.* أستقامت ìsstikāmet, طوغريلق dòghruluk, راستى ràsstī.

Problem, *s.* دعواى عملى dà"wàyi-"āmélī.

Problematic, *a.* شبهه لو shùphéli.

Proboscis, *s.* خرطوم khòrtūm.

Proceed, *v.n.* چيقمق chìkmak, حاصل او hāssil-òl, نشئت ا nèsh'èt-et, ترتب ا tèrèttub-et, لازم كلمك lāzim-ghèlmek; الت طرفنى سويلمك àlt-tàrafini-sù-wèylémek; كچمك ghèchmek; ايلرو كتمك ìléri-ghìtmek. [*pl.* دعوا dà"wà.

Proceeding, *s.* معامله mù"āmélé; —s, *s.*

Proceeds, *s. pl.* حاصلات hāssilāt.

Process, *s.* أصول ùssūl; اعمال ì"māl; دعوا dà"wà. [نشئت nèsh'èt.

Procession, *s.* الاى àlay; حصول hùssūl,

Proclaim, *v.n.* ندا ا nìdā-et, اعلان ا ì"lān-

Proclamation, *s.* اعلان ì"lān. [-et.

Procrastinate, *v.n.* ايشنى صكره يه براقمق ìshini-sòngraya-bràkmak.

Procrastination, *s.* تأخر tà'àkhkhur.

Procreator, *s.* مولد mùwèllid.

Procure, *v.a.* بولمق bùlmak, المق àlmak, اله كتورمك èla-ghètirmek, حاصل ا hāssil-et, تحصيل ا tàhsīl-et, استحصال ا ìsstihsāl-et.

Prodigal, *a.* مسرف mùssrif; بذول bèzūl; —ity, *s.* اسراف ìssrāf; مبذوليت mèbzūlìyyèt. [bìyuk; چوق chòk.

Prodigious, *a.* عجيب "àjīb; بيوك

Prodigy, *s.* معجزه mù"jizé.

Produce, *v.a.* حاصل ا hāssil-et, ويرمك vèrmek; احضار ا ìhzār-et, چيقارمق chìkàrmak, كوسترمك ghyùsstermek, ميدانه قومق mèydāna-kòmak, ابراز ا ìbrāz-et; اشهاد ا ìshhād-et; —, *s.* حاصلات hāssilāt (*pl.*); ثمره sèméré; ايراد īrād; محصول màhsūl.

Product, *s.* محصول màhsūl.

Production, *s.* حصول hùssūl; اثر èsser.

Profane, *a.* عادى "ādī; دينه غير متعلق dīné-ghàyri-mùta"àllik; مقتضاى ديانته مغاير اولان mùktāzāyi-dìyānèta-mùghāyir-òlan; —, *v.a.* مبارك نسنه حقنده مغاير احترام اوضاعه مباشرت ا mùbārek-nèssné-hàkkinda-mùghāyiri-ìhtirām-èvzā"a-mùbāshéret-et.

Profess, *v.a.* علناً اقرار ا "àlénen-ìkrār-et, دعواسنده او dà"wàssinda-òl, صاتمق sātmak; مدرسلك ا mùdèrrisslik-et, تدريسيله مشغول او tèdrīssīla-mèsh-ghūl-òl.

Profession, *s.* اقرار علنى ìkrār-"àlénī; دعوى dà"wà, ادعا ìddi"ā; مشغوليت mèshghūlìyyèt, حرفت hìrfèt, صنعت sàn"àt. [khòja, معلم mù"àllim.

Professor, *s.* مدرس mùdèrriss; خواجه

Proficiency, *s.* مهارت màhārèt.

Proficient, *a.* ماهر māhir.

Profile, *s.* رسم مسنم rèssmi-mùssènnem; يان باقشى رسمى yàn-bākishi-rèssmi.

Profit, *s.* كار kyār, قزانج kāzànj; فائده fā'idé, نفع nèf", منفعت mènfa"àt; —, *v.n.* كار ا kyār-et, قزانمق kāzan-mak, انتفاع ا ìntifā"-et, فائده كورمك fā'idé-ghyùrmek, فائده مند او fā'idé-mènd-òl; —, *v.a.* كار ويرمك kyār-vèrmek, فائده ويرمك fā'idé-vèrmek,

فائده ا fā'idé-et, فائده او fā'idé-ȯl, فائدەسی او fā'idéssi-ȯl, فائده لو او fā'i-déli-ȯl.

Profligacy, *s.* چاپقینلق chȧpkinlik, فسق وفجور fisk-u-fùjūr, سفاهت sèfāhȧt.

Profligate, *a.* چاپقین chȧpkin, سفیه sèfīh, فاسق fāssik, فاجر fājir.

Profound, *a.* درین dèrīn, عمیق ‘‘ȧmīk; —ly learned, متبحر mùtébȧhhir.

Profoundness, Profundity, *s.* درینلك dèrīnlik.

Profuse, *a.* بول bȯl, غنی ghȧnī; مسرف mùssrif; بذول bèzūl.

Profusion, *s.* چوقلق chȯkluk.

Progenitor, *s.* جد jèdd.

Progeny, *s.* ذریت zùrriyyèt.

Prognostic, *s.* علامت ‘‘ȧlāmèt.

Programme, *s.* لائحه lā'iha.

Progress, *s.* ایلرولیش ìlériléyish; ترقی tèrȧkki; —, *v.n.* ایلرولمك ìlerilé-mek, کتمك ghìtmek.

Prohibit, *v.a.* یساق ا yȧssȧk-et, ممنوع ا mèmnū‘‘-et, نهی ا nèhy-et.

Prohibition, *s.* یساق yȧssȧk; نهی nèhy.

Project, *s.* تصور tȧssȧvvur, مطالعه mù-tāla‘‘à; —, *v.a.* تصور ا tȧssȧvvur-et, مطالعه ا mùtāla‘‘à-et; آتمق ȧtmak, انداخت ا ȅndākht-et, رمی ا rèmy-et; ایتمك ètmek; —, *v.n.* چیقمق chìkmak, ایلرو کلمك ìléri-ghèlmek, اوزامق ȕzamak.

Projectile, *s.* جسم مرمی jìssmi-mèrmī.

Prolific, *a.* برکتلو bèrékȅtli; یدی ویرن yèdi-vȅren; مثمر mùssmir, محصولدار màhsūldār.

Prolix, *a.* اوزون ȕzun, مفصل mùfȧssȧl.

Prologue, *s.* مقدمه mùkkȧddimé.

Prolong, *v.a.* اوزاتمق uzȧtmak, مد ا mèdd-et, استقامتی اوزره اخراج ا ìssti-kāméti-ùzéré-ikhrāj-et.

Promenade, *s.* سیر sèyr, سیر و تماشا sèyr--u-tȧmāshā; سیریری sèyr-yȅri, مسیره mèssiré, مسیره کاه mèssīréghyāh, مسیر mèssīr; —, *v.n.* کزمك ghèzmek, طولاشمق dȯlashmak; —, *v.a.* کزدرمك ghèzdirmek, طولاشدرمق dȯlȧshdirmak.

Promiscuous, *a.* قارشق kȧrishik.

Promise, *s.* سوز sùz, وعد vȧ‘‘d; —, *v.a.* سوز ویرمك sùz-vèrmek, وعد ا vȧ‘‘d-et; —, *v.n.* کورنمك ghyùrunmek, امید ویرمك ùmīd-vȅrmek.

Promontory, *s.* بورون bùrun.

Promote, *v.a.* رتبه ویرمك rùtbé-vèrmek, ترفیع رتبه ا tȅrfī‘‘i-rùtbé-et; یاردم ا yȧrdim-et, معاونت ا mù‘‘āvénèt-et, ایلرولتمك ìlérilȅtmek.

Promotion, *s.* ترفیع رتبه tȅrfī‘‘i-rùtbé.

Prompt, *a.* چابك chȧbik, تیز tīz (tèz), سرعتلو sùr‘‘ȧtli, سریع sèrī‘‘; —, *v.a.* عقلنه‌ش قومق ‘‘ȧklina-shèy--kȯmak; لقردی اوکرتمك lȧkirdi-ùghrȅtmek, تعلیم ا tȧ‘‘līm-et.

Promptitude, *s.* چابکلك chȧbiklik.

Promulgate, *v.a.* اعلان ا ì‘‘lān-et, نشر ا nèshr-et, یایمق yȧymak.

Prone, *a.* میال mèyyāl, مستعد mùss-tȧ‘‘ìdd; یوزی قوین yùzu-kȯyun.

Pronoun, *s.* ضمیر zȧmīr.

Pronounce, *v.a.* تلفظ ا tèlȧffuz-et;

اغزه‌المق Aghza-Almak, قاله‌المق kāla--Almak, تفوه‌ا tèfèvvuh-et.

Pronunciation, *s.* تلفظ tèlAffuz.

Proof, *s.* اثبات ìssbāt, سند sèned, حجت hùjjèt, برهان bùrhān, فرقان fìrkān, سلطان sùltAn, دليل dèlīl; شاهد shāhid; امتحان ìmtihān, تجربه tèjrubÉ; قرار kArār, قوام kìwām; تصحيح ايچون باصلان صحيفه tAsshīh - ìchin - bAssilAn - sàhīfÉ; رسملك الك باصلان نسخه‌لرى rèssming--ìlk-bAssilAn-nùsskhalari; —, *a.* تام قرار tāmm-kArār; قبول ايتمز kAbūl-ètmàz, قورقمز kòrkmàz, طيانور dàyànir.

Prop, *s.* دستك dèsstek, طياق dàyak, پاينده pàyèndÉ; —, *v.a.* دستك اورمق dèsstek-wùrmak, طوتدرمق tùtdurmak; طوتمق tùtmak.

Propagate, *v.a.* اولاد يتشدرمك èvlād--yètishdirmek, چوجق ياپمق chòjuk--yàpmak; ياورى ياپمق yàvri-yàpmak; تورتمك tùrEtmek; نشرا nèshr-et, يايمق yàymak. [نشر nèshr.

Propagation, *s.* ايلاد īlād; تولد tèvèllud;

Propel, *v.a.* يوروتمك yùrutmek, سوق‌ا sèvk-et, تحريك‌ا tàhrīk-et, سورمك [sùrmek.

Propensity, *s.* ميل mèyl.

Proper, *a.* مناسب mùnāssib, لايق lāyik, سزا sèzā, شايان shāyān; شايسته shāyèsstÉ, جسبان jùssbān; اهل èhl, ارباب èrbāb; كندو *or* كندى kèndi, اصل Assl, اصل كندى Assl--kèndi, ذاتى zātī; خاص khAsss.

Property, *s.* مال māl, منال mènāl, واريت vàrìyyèt; خاصه khāsssa.

Prophecy, *s.* پيغمبر طرفندن ويريلان خبر pèy-ghAmbèr-tàrafindan-vèrilen-khAber.

Prophesy, *v.n.* خبر ملهمى اخبار ا khAberi - mùlhèmi - ìkhbār - et, الهام طريقيله ناسه غائبدن خبر ويرمك ìlhām - tàrīkila-nāssa - ghā'ibdan - - khAber - vErmek, پيغمبرلك‌ا pèy-ghAmbèrlik-et; مستقبلدن بحثله قطعيا حكم‌ا mùsstAkbeldan-bàhssla-kA-t''ìyyan-hùkm-et.

Prophet, *s.* پيغمبر pèyghAmbèr, رسول rèssūl, نبى nèbī. [fakAtini-tàhsīl-et.

Propitiate, *v.a.* شفقتنى تحصيل ا shè-

Propitious, *a.* مساعد mùssā''id.

Proportion, *s.* نسبت nìssbèt; تناسب tènāssub; rule of —, اربع متناسبه èrbà''i - mùténāssébÉ; —, *v.a.* تناسب اوزره تقسيم ا tènāssub-ùzÉrÉ--tàksīm-et; نسبتنده ياپمق nìssbètinda-yàpmak.

Proportionate, *a.* متناسب mùténāssib.

Proposal, *s.* تكليف tèklīf.

Propose, *v.a.* تكليف‌ا tèklīf-et; —, *v.n.* نيت‌ا nìyyèt-et, قورمق kùrmak; ديمك dèmek, سويلمك sùwèylémek; كنديني عرض‌ا kèndini-''àrz-et, طالب او tālib-òl.

Proposition, *s.* قول kAvl, دعوى dà''wà, سوز sùz, لقردى làkirdi; قضيه kAzìyyÉ.

Propound, *v.a.* درميان‌ا dèr-mèyān-et, بسط ا bAsst-et, بيان‌ا bèyān-et.

Proprietor, *m.* **Proprietress,** *f. s.* مال صاحبى māl-sāhibi; ملك صاحبى mùlk-sāhibi; صاحب sāhib.

Propriety, *s.* مناسبت mùnāssébèt.

Prorogation, *s.* تعطيل tà''tīl.

Prorogue, *v.a.* تعطيل ا tà''til-et.

Prosaic, *a.* منشور mènsūr ; ثقلت ويرر sìklet-vèrir.

Prose, نثر nèssr (nèssir).

Prosecute, *v.a.* مجرمه دعوى اچمق mùjrima - dà''wà - àchmak, دعواجى او dà''wàji-òl ; دوام ا dèwām-et.

Prosecution, *v.a.* دعوا اچمقلق dà''wa-àchmaklìk.

Prosecutor, *s.* جنحه دعواسنده مدعى اولان ادم jùnha - dà''wassinda - mùddà''i - òlan-ÀDAM.

Proselyte, *s.* مهتدى mùhtédī, دونمه dùnmé.

Prosody, *s.* عروض ''àrūz.

Prospect, *s.* نظارت nÀzārèt ; اميد ùmìd, مأمول mè'mūl.

Prospectus, *s.* اعلاننامه i''làn-nāmé.

Prosper, *v.n.* فلاح بولمق fèlāh-bùlmak, ايشى طوغرى كتمك ìshi-dòghru-ghìtmek, ايشى يولنده او ìshi-yòlunda-òl.

Prosperity, *s.* دولت dèvlèt, اقبال ìkbāl.

Prosperous, *a.* صاحب دولت و اقبال sāhibi - dèvlet - vé-ìkbĀl ; مساعد mùssā''id.

Prostitute, *s.* فاحشه fāhishé, صوقاق روسپيسى sòkAk-(òrosspossu) ; —, *v.a.* فاحشه كبى راست كلنه رام ا fāhishé-ghìbi-rÀsst-ghÈlÉna-rām-et ; — one's self, فاحشه او fāhishé-òl, فاحشه لك ا fāhishÉlik-et.

Prostitution, *s.* فاحشه لك fāhishÉlik.

Prostrate, *a.* يوزى قوين yùzu-kòyun ; —, *v.a.* يقمق yèkmak, يره چاريمق yèra - chàrpmak ; قوتنى كسمك kùvvètini - kèssmek ; كدره بوغمق kÈdÉra-bòghmak.

Prostration, *s.* يره اتمقلق yÈra-Àtmaklik; مجالسزلك mèjālsizlik.

Protect, *v.a.* حفظ ا hìfz-et, محافظه ا mūhĀfaza-et, حمايه ا hìmāyÉ-et, صيانت ا sìyānèt-et ; ارقه او àrka-òl, تصحب ا tÀssàbhub-et.

Protection, *s.* محافظه mùhĀfaza; حمايه hìmāyÉ.

Protector, *s.* حافظ hĀfiz, محافظ mūhĀfiz ; حامى hāmī ; ارقه àrka ; محفظه màhfaza.

Pro tem., *ad.* موقتاً mùwÀkkatan.

Protest, *s.* پروتسطو pròtèssto ; —, *v.n.* پروتسطو ويرمك pròtèssto - vÈrmek ; يمين ا yèmīn-et; —, *v.a.* ادعا ا iddi''ā-et, قوياً بيان ا kàviyyan - bèyān-et ; پروتسطو ا pròtèssto-et.

Protestant, *a.* پروتستانت pròtesstānt ; —, *s.* پروتستانت pròtesstānt.

Protestantism, *s.* پروتستانتلق pròtesstāntlik.

Protocol, *s.* مضبطه mÀzbAta.

Protract, *v.a.* اوزاتمق ùzÀtmak, تمديد ا tèmdīd-et ; رسم ا rèssm-et.

Proud, *s.* كبرلو kìbirli, متكبر mùtékèbbir, فضول fàdūl (fòdul), فرعون fìr''àvn ; مفتخر mùftàkhir.

Prove, *v.a.* اثبات ا ìssbĀt-et ; —, *v.n.* چيقمق chìkmak.

Provender, *v.a.* اوت ارپه صمان òt-àrpa-sàmAn.

Proverb, *s.* ضرب مثل zàrbi-mèssel, لقردى làkirdi.

Proverbial, *a.* ضرب مثل حكمنه كيرمش zàrbi-mèssel-hùkmuna-ghirmish.

Provide, *v.a.* تدارك ا tèdāruk-et(-rik) ; ترتيب ا tÈrtīb-et ; ويرمك vÈrmek ;

— for, *v.n.* تعیشنی ویرمك tà''àyyu-shunu - vèrmek, حوائجنی ویرمك hāwā'ijini-vèrmek, باقمق bàkmak, بسلمك bèssléмek; خدمت بولمق khìdmet - bùlmak, خدمته صوقمق khìdméta-sòkmak; —ded that, شو بشرطانكه شرطلهكه shù - shàrtla - ki, bì-shàrti-ān-ki.

Providence, *s.* عاقبت اندیشلك ''āki-bet-èndīshlik, عقل ''àkl, بصیرت bàssīret; الله Allāh, حق تعالی hàkk-tà''ālà; رزاق rèzzāk, حافظ hāfiz, پروردگار pèrvèrdighyār; عنایت ''ìnāyet, احسان ìhsān, مرحمت mèrhàmet. [ایش ìsh.

Province, *s.* ایالت èyālèt; وظیفه wàzīfé,

Provision, *s.* تدارك tèdāruk (-ik); اكمك èkmek, نانپاره nān-pārÉ; شرط shàrt; —s, *s. pl.* ذخیره zàkhīrÉ (*pl.* ذخائر zàkhā'ir).

Proviso, *s.* شرط shàrt. [īrāss.

Provocation, *s.* اغضاب ìghzāb; ایراث

Provoke, *v.a.* قزدرمق kìzdìrmak, دارلتمق dàrìltmak; ایراث ا īrāss-et, سبب او sèbeb-òl.

Proximity, *s.* قرب kùrb, جوار jìwār.

Proxy, *s.* وكیل vèkīl; وكالتنامه vèkyālet-nāmÉ. [بصیرتلو bàssīrètli.

Prudent, *a.* عقللو ''àkllì, عاقل ''ākìl,

Prune, *s.* قورو اریك kùru-èrik; —, *v.a.* بودامق bùdamak.

Prussia, *s.* پروسیا دولتی Prūssia-dèvleti.

Prussian, *s.* and *a.* پروسیالو Prūssiali.

Puberty, *s.* بلوغ bùlūgh.

Public, *a.* علنی ''àlÉnī; رسمی rèssmī; عمومی ''ùmūmī; میری mīrī, بكلك bèghlik; عامره ''āmirÉ; معموره mà''mūrÉ; خاص khāsss; — paper, غزته ghàzèta; — house, میخانه mèy-khānÉ, لوقانده lòkànda; — service, دولت خدمتی dèvlet-khìdméti (hìz-); —, *s.* عالم ''ālem, ناس nāss, خلق khàlk, اورتهلق òrtalìk; جمهور jùmhūr.

Publican, *s.* میخانهجی mèy-khānÉji.

Publication, *s.* نشر nèshr.

Public-house, *s.* میخانه mey-khānÉ.

Publish, *v.a.* اعلان ا ì''lān-et, نشر ا nèshr-et; باصمق bàssmak, طبع ا tàb''-et, طبع وتمثیل ا tàb''-u-tèmsīl-et.

Publisher, *s.* كتابجی kìtābji.

Puddle, *s.* كول ghyùl; — about, *v.n.* چامورلرده گزنمك chàmūrlarda-ghè-zinmek. [''àbess, صاچمه sàchma.

Puerile, *a.* چوجقلق chòjukluk, عبث

Pugilism, *s.* مشته غوغاسی تعلیمی صنعتی mùshta-kàwghassi-tà''limi-sàn''àti.

Pugilist, *s.* مشته غوغاسیجی mùshtÉ-kàwghassiji.

Puke, *v.n.* قوسمق kùssmak, قی كتورمك kày-ghètirmek, استفراغ ا ìsstifrāgh-et.

Pull, *s.* چكش chèkish; —, *v.a.* چكمك chèkmek; — back, *v.a.* كیرو چكمك ghèri-chèkmek; —, *v.n.* كیرو چكلمك ghèri-chèkilmek; — down, یقمق yìkmak, هدم ا hèdm-et; دوشرمك dùshurmek; — in, ایچرو چكمك ìchèri-chèkmek; — off, چیقارمق chìkàrmak, اندرمك èndirmek; قوپارمق kòpàrmak; — out, طیشاری چكمك dìshàri-chèkmek; سوكمك

sùkmek, چیقارمق chìkàrmak; — up, v.a. سوکمك sùkmek, چیقارمق chìkàrmak; ضابطه کوترمك zābita-ghyùturmek; — —, v.n. دورمق dùrmak. [بیومش پلیج bìyumush-pìlij.

Pullet, s. کنج طاوق ghènj-tàwuk,

Pulley, s. مقره màkara. [ghera-mènsūb.

Pulmonary, a. اق جکره منسوب Àk-jì-

Pulp, s. میوه نك اتی mèyvéning-èti; لاپه کبی هیئت làpa-ghìbi-hèy'èt.

Pulpit, s. کرسی kyùrsi, منبر mìnber.

Pulsate, v.n. نبض کبی اورمق nàbz-ghìbi-wùrmak. [-hàrékèti.

Pulsation, s. نبضك حرکتی nàbzin-

Pulse, s. نبض nàbz; حبوبات hùbūbàt.

Pulverize, v.a. توز ا tòz-et, سحق ا sàhk-et, ازمك èzmek. [-tàshi.

Pumice-stone, s. سونکر طاشی sùngher-

Pump, s. طلومبه tùlumba; اینجه قوندره ìnja-kùndura; —, v.a. طلومبه ایشلتمك tùlumba-ìshletmek; طلومبه ایله چکمك tùlumba-ila-chekmek (or المق àlmak), اغزندن لقردی قاپمق àghzindan-làkirdi-kàpmak.

Pumpkin, s. قباق kàbak.

Pun, s. مضمون mazmūn; —, v.n. مضمون سویلمك màzmūn-sùwèylé-mek.

Punctual, a. وقتیله کلان wàktīla-ghèlan.

Punctuality, s. وقتیله کلمکلك wàktīla-gèlmeklik. [-wàktinda.

Punctually, ad. وقتلو وقتنده wàkitli-

Punctuate, v.a. طوراق یرلرینی اشارت ا dùrak-yèrlerini-ìshāret-et.

Punctuation, s. طوراق یرلرینی اشارت ایتمکلك dùrak-yerlerini-ìshāret-ètmeklik.

Pungent, a. سرت sèrt, کسکین kèsskin.

Punish, v.a. تأدیب ا tè'dīb-et, تکدیر ا tèkdīr-et, مجازات ا mùjāzāt-et, جزاسنی ویرمك jèzāssini-vèrmek; اینجتمك ìnjitmek.

Punishment, s. تأدیب tè'dīb, مجازات mùjāzāt, جزا jèzā, عقوبت ''ùkūbèt.

Punning, s. مضمون سویلمکلك màzmūn-sùwèylémeklik.

Punster, s. مضمونجی màzmūnju.

Puny, a. علیل ''àlīl.

Pup, s. کوپك یاوریسی kyùpek-yàvrissi.

Pupil, s. شاکرد shàghird, تلمیذ tèlmīz; وصی یه سپارش اولنمش یتیم wàssīya-sìpārish-òlunmush-yètīm; — of the eye, کوز ببکی ghyùz-bèbèghi, مردمك چشم mèrdumèki-chèshim, انسان العین ìnsānu-'l-''àyn.

Puppy, s. کوپك یاوریسی kyùpek-yàwrussu; impertinent —, ادبسز قاطر èdebsiz-kàtir.

Purchase, s. صاتون النان شی sàtīn-àlinan-shèy; الش àlish, الم àlim, شرا shìrā, اشترا ìshtirā, ستد sìtèd; جراثقال قوتی jèrri-èsskāl-kùvvèti; مسند قوت mèssnedi-kùvvèt; واسطهٔ قوت wàssita'i-kùvvèt; —, v.a. المق àlmak, صاتون المق sàtin-àlmak, اشترا ا ìshtirā-et.

Purchaser, s. مشتری mùshtérī.

Pure, a. خالص khāliss, صافی sàfī, صاف sàf; تمیز tèmīz, پاك pāk, طاهر tāhir.

Purgative, a. and s. مسهل mùsshil.

Purgatory, s. اعراف à''rāf, برزخ bèrzàkh.

Purge, *s.* مسهل mùsshìl; —, *v.a.* عمل ويرمك ''àmel-vèrmek; تميزلمك tèmizlémek.

Purify, *v.a.* تميزلمك tèmizlémek, تطهيرا tàthīr-et, تصفيه ا tàssfìyyé-et.

Purity, *s.* تميزلك tèmizlik, خالصلق khālisslik, صفوت sàfvèt; عفت ''ìffèt, عصمت ''ìssmet, پاكدامنلك pākdāmenlik; طهارت tàhārèt.

Purloin, *v.a.* چالمق chàlmak, سرقت ا sìrkàt-et.

Purple, *a.* مور mòr; —, *s.* كسوت پادشاهى kìssvèti-pādishāhī.

Purport, *s.* مآل mà'āl, معنا mà''nà, فحوى fàhwà, مفهوم mèfhūm; —, *v.n.* مآلنده او mà'ālinda-òl.

Purpose, *s.* نيت nìyyèt, مرام mèrām; —, *v.a.* قورمق kùrmak, نيت ا nìyyèt-et; on —, مخصوص màkhsūss; قصداً kàssdan, عمداً ''àmdan.

Purse, *s.* كيسه kèyssé, هميان hìmyān; (sum of 500 piastres) كيسه اقچه kèyssé-àkcha. [jassi.

Purser, *s.* كمى خواجه سى ghèmi-khò-

Purslain, *s.* سميزاوت sèmiz-òt.

Pursue, *v.a.* قوغالمق kòghalamak, تعقيب ا tà''kīb-et; پيشنه دوشمك pèsbina-dùshmek; دوام ا dèwām-et, مشغول او mèshghūl-òl.

Pursuit, *s.* تعقيب tà''kib. [-mè'mūru.

Purveyor, *s.* ذخيره مأمورى zàkhiré-

Pus, *s.* ارنك ìring, جراحت jèrāhàt.

Push, *v.a.* ايتمك ìtmek, سورمك sùrmek, قاقمق kàkmak; — back, *v.a.* كيرو سورمك ghèri-sùrmek; — —, *v.n.* كيرولمك ghèrilémek; — in, *v.a.* صوقمق sòkmak; — —, *v.n.* صوقلمق sòkulmak; — on, *v.n.* ايلرو سورمك ìléri-sùrmek; — out, *v.a.* طيشارى سورمك dìshàri-sùrmek; — —, *v.n.* طيشارى چيقمق dìshàri-chìkmak.

Pusillanimity, *s.* قورقاقلق kòrkaklik, جبن jùbn. [اوچق ùchuk.

Pustule, *s.* سويلجه sìvilja, چبان chìbàn,

Put, *v.a.* قومق kòmak, وضع ا wàz''-et; — about, *v.a.* راحت براقمامق rāhat-bràkmamak; — —, *v.n.* كمى يى چويرمك ghèmiyi-chèvirmek; — a stop to, منع ا mèn''-et; — away, صاقلامق sàklamak; يرينه قومق yèrina-kòmak; دفع ا dèf''-et; بوشامق bòshamak; — back, *v.n.* كيرو دونمك ghèri-dùnmek; — —, *v.a.* كيرو قومق ghèri-kòmak; — by, صاقلامق sàklamak; اداره ا ìdāré-et; — down, باصدرمق bàssdirmak, منع ا mèn''-et; باصمق bàssmak; ياترمق yàtirmak; — forth, چيقارمق chìkàrmak; اوزاتمق ùzàtmak; اچمق àchmak; طيشارى ا dìshàri-et; — forward, درپيش ا dèr-pīsh-et; — in fear, قورقتمق kòrkutmak; — in for, طالب او tālib-òl; — in print, غزته يه باصمق ghàzètaya-bàssmak; — off, چيقارمق chìkàrmak; دفع ا dèf''-et; صكره يه براقمق sòngraya-bràkmak, تأخيرا tà'khīr-et; — — one's clothes, صويينمق sòyunmak; — on, *v.a.* كيمك ghìymek; طاقنمق

tàkinmak ; — out, سوندرمك sùn-durmek, اطفا ا ìtfā-et ; چيقارمق chìkàrmak ; اچمق àchmak ; اوزاتمق ùzAtmak ; — — at interest, فائضه ويرمك fā'iza-vèrmek, فائضه ياترمق fā'iza-yàtirmak ; — out of conceit, قيرمق kìrmak, بورننى قيرمق bùrnunu--kìrmak ; — — — — with, بزدرمك bèzdirmek ; — up, *v.n.* قونمق kòn-mak, قوناق ا kònak-et, انمك ènmek ; — —, *v.a.* يرينه قومق yèrina-kòmak ; — — for sale, صاتيلق ا sAtilik-et ; — — to auction, مزاده ويرمك mè-zāda-vèrmek ; — up with, صبر ا sAbr--et, چكمك chèkmek, تحمل ا tà-hàmmul-et ; اوينه انمك èvina-ènmek, اونده مسافر او èvinda - mùssāfir - òl ; — upon, الداتمق Aldatmak ; ازيت ا èzìyyèt-et, راحتسز ا rāhatsiz-et.

Putrefy, *v.n.* چورومك chùrumek, قوقمق kòkmak. [mùta''Affin.

Putrid, *a.* قوقمش kòkmush, متعفن

Putty, *s.* جامجى معجونى jàmji-mà''jūnu ; —, *v.a.* معجونلمق mà''jūnlamak.

Puzzle, *s.* ياكلتماج yàngiltmàj (yànilt-), اويونجق òyunjak ; —, *v.a.* ياكلتمق yàngiltmak (yànilt-), شاشرتمق shà-shirtmak.

Pyramid, *s.* اهرام èhrām ; the pyramids of Egypt, فرعون ده پەلرى fìr'àvn-tèpé-léri.

Pyramidal, *a.* اهرامى الشكل èhrāmiyyu-'sh-shèkil.

Pyrotechnics, *s. pl.* فشنكجيلك صنعتى fishènkjilik-sàn''àti (fishèk-).

Q.

Quack, *s.* يالاندن حكيم yàlàndan-hèy-kim, بوقدن حكيم bòkdan-hèykim, حقه باز hòkkabAz ; اوردك سسى ùr-dek-sèssi ; —, *v.a.* لاعن علم معالجه ا lā-''àn-''ìlmin-mù''āléjé-et ; —, *v.n.* اوردك سس ا ùrdek-sèss-et ; اوردك كبى سس ا ùrdek-ghìbi-sèss-et.

Quadrangle, *s.* اورته سى حولى درت يانى بنا اولان هيئت òrtassi-hàvli-dùrt-yàni--bìnā-òlAn-hèy'et.

Quadrant, *s.* ربع دائره rùb''i - dā'irÉ ; اوقتانت òktànt.

Quadrilateral, *a.* and *s.* ذو اربعة الاضلاع zū - èrbà''atu -'l-Adlā'', درت كوشه dùrt-kyùshÉ.

Quadrille, *s.* بر نوع رقص bìr-nev''i-ràkss.

Quadruped, *s.* درت اياقلو حيوان dùrt--àyakli-hàywān, چارپا chàrpā.

Quadruple, *s.* درت قات dùrt-kAt, درت مثلى dùrt-mìssli ; —, *v.a.* درت قات ا dùrt-kAt-et ; —, *v.n.* درت قات او dùrt-kAt-òl.

Quaff, *v.a.* ايچمك ìchmek, اتمق Atmak, چاقمق chàkmak. [lìk.

Quagmire, *s.* بتاق bAtak, بتاقلق bAtak-

Quail, *s.* بلدرجين bùldurjin ; —, *v.n.* قورقمق kòrkmak, يلمق yèlmak.

Quaint, *a.* تحاف tùhāf, عجيب ''Ajīb (Ajā'ib).

Quake, *v.n.* تترەمك tìtrémek, دترەمك dìtrémek, لرزان او lèrzān-òl.

Qualification, *s.* استحقاق ìsstihkAk ; صورت استحقاق sūrèti - ìsstihkAk ;

استثنا ìsstissnā, اعتراض i''tirāz, تعديل tà''dīl, تنبيه tènbīh, شرط shàrt.

Qualify, *v.a.* تعديل ا tà''dīl-et; استحقاق ويرمك ìsstihkāk-vèrmek, وسيلهٔ استحقاق او vèssīlé'i-ìsstihkāk-òl; —, *v.n.* استحقاق كسب ا ìsstihkāk-kèssb-et.

Quality, *s.* كيفيت kèyfìyyèt, خاصه khāsssa; رتبه rùtbé; صوى sòy, جنس jìnss.

Qualm, *s.* كوكل بولانمسى ghyùngul-bù-lànmassi, يورك بولانديسى yùrèk-bù-làndissi; — of conscience, شبهه shùbhé; ندامت nèdāmèt.

Quantity, *s.* كميت kèmìyyèt, مقدار mìkdār, قدر kādr (kādar).

Quarantine, *s.* قرانتينه kārantìna; تحفظ خانه tàhàffuz-khāné.

Quarrel, *s.* غوغا (kàwgha), نزاع nìzā'', منازعه mùnāza''à; —, *v.n.* بوزشمق bòzushmak; غوغا ا (kàwgha)-et, نزاع ا nìzā''-et.

Quarry, *s.* طاش اوجاغى tāsh-òjaghi; آو āv, صيد sàyd, شكار shikyār; بيوك اوق bìyuk-òk; —, *v.a.* چيقارمق chìkàrmak; ايشلتمك ìshlètmek.

Quart, *s.* ايكيوزسكسان درهملك اولچى ikiyuz-sèksen-dìrhèmlik-ùlchu.

Quarter, *s.* دردده بر dùrtda-bìr, ربع rùb'', چاريك chàr-yèk (chèyrek); ديلم dìlim; طرف tàraf, يان yàn, جانب jānib, سو sū; حوالى hàwāli; جهت jìhèt; سكز كيله لك ذخيره اولچيسى sèkiz-kìlélik-zàkhīré-ùl-chussu; —s, *s. pl.* قوناق kònak; دائره dā'iré; اوطه òda; —, *v.a.* دردده بولمك dùrda-bùlmek; اوطورتمق òturtmak, قوناق ا kònak-et; winter-quarters, قشلا kìshla, قشلاق kìshlāk, قشلاغ kìshlāgh.

Quarterdeck, *s.* كوكرته نك قيچ طرفى ghyùghèrtaning-kìch-tàrafi.

Quatrain, *s.* رباعى rùbā''ī.

Quay, *s.* اسكله ìsskèlé, ريختم rìkhtim.

Queen, *s.* قراليچه kìrālicha.

Queer, *a.* عجيب ''ājīb (''àjā'ib).

Quell, *v.a.* باصدرمق bāssdirmak, حقندن كلمك hàkkìndan-ghèlmek, زجر ا zèjr-et.

Quench, *v.a.* سوندرمك sùndurmek, اطفا ا ìtfā-et; صوسزلق دفع ا sùssuzluk-dèf''-et.

Query, *s.* سؤال sù'āl; جاى سؤال jāyi-sù'āl; —, *v.n.* شبهه ا shùbhé-et.

Quest, *s.* ارامقلق āramaklik; to go in — of, كيدوب ارامق ghìdup-āramak.

Question, *s.* سؤال sù'āl; اذيت èzìyyèt, شكنجه shikènjé; —, *v.a.* سؤال صورمق sù'āl-sòrmak, سؤال ا sù'āl-et; استنطاق ا ìsstintāk-et; شبهه ا shùbhé-et; to put to the —, اذيت ا èzìyyèt-et.

Quick, *a.* چابك chàbik, تيز tīz (tèz), سريع sèri'', سرعتلو sùr''àtli; جانلو jānli, ديرى dìri, حى hàyy; حيوانك ديرى اتى hàywāning-dìri-èti, ات èt.

Quicken, *v.a.* تعجيل ا tà''jīl-et, تسريع ا tèssri''-et; جان ويرمك jān-vèrmek, جانلندرمق jānlandirmak, ديرلتمك dìriltmek, احيا ا ìhyā-et; ديرلمك

dìrilmek ; چوجغى ديرلمك chòjughu-dìrilmek. [mish-kìrèch.

Quicklime, s. سونمامش كيرچ sùnma-

Quickly, ad. چابك chàbik.

Quickmatch, s. فتيل fìtil.

Quickness, s. چابكلك chàbiklik.

Quicksilver, s. جيوه jìwa, زيبق zìbàk.

Quiet, a. صوص sùss ; اوصلو ùsslu, تمكينلو tèmkīnli, سكونتلو sùkyūnètli ; أسوده āssūdé ; —, a. and s. راحت rāhat, اسايش āssāyish ; —, s. سكونت sùkyūnèt ; —, v.a. تسكين ا tèsskīn-et ; سسنى كسمك sèssini-kèssmek, صوصدرمق sùssdurmak ; — ! int. صوص sùss ; to be —, تك دورمق tèk-dùr-mak ; in a — way, اصوللە ùssūlla.

Quietly, ad. يواش يواش yàwāsh-yàwāsh.

Quietness, s. سسسزلك sèsssizlik, تلاشسزلك tèlashsizlik.

Quill, s. قوش تويى kùsh-tùyu ; اچلمامش توى قلم àchilmamish-tùy-kàlem ; —, v.a. اينجه اينجه قيرمق ìnja-ìnja-kìr-mak, قيرمه قيرمه ا kìrma-kìrma-et.

Quilt, s. يورغان yùrghan ; —, v.a. پاموقلو خرقه كبى ديكمك pàmukli-khìrka-ghìbi-dìkmek.

Quince, s. ايوه àywa. [sùlfātò.

Quinine, Sulphate of Quinine, s. صولفاتو

Quinsy, s. خناق khùnnāk. [-'l-khùlāssa.

Quintessence, s. خلاصة الخلاصه khùlāssatu-

Quire, s. كاغد دسته سى kyāghid-dèsstéssi, دسته dèssté ; خواندكان كروهى khā-nèndéghyān-ghyùrūhu.

Quit, v.a. براقمق bràkmak, ترك ا tèrk-et ; —, v.n. چيقمق chìkmak.

Quite, ad. بتون بتون bìtun-bìtun, كلياً kyùllìyyan ; كاملاً kyāmilan, هر وجهله [hèr-wèjhla.

Quitrent, s. اجاره ìjāré.

Quits, ad. باش bàsh, بر bìr, برابر bèrābèr, نه الەجق نه ويره جك nè-àlajak-nè-vèréjek.

Quiver, s. اوقدان òkdān, اوقدانلق òk-danlik, تيركش tīrkèsh ; —, v.n. اوينامق òynamak, تترەمك tìtrémek.

Quiz, v.a. ذوقلنمك zèvklenmek.

Quondam, a. سابق sābik ; —, ad. سابقا sābikā.

Quota, s. پاى pày, حصه hìsssé.

Quotation, s. اقتباس ايله ايراد ايتمكلك ìktibāss-ila-īrād-ètmeklik.

Quote, v.a. بشقەنك الفاظنى ايراد ا bàsh-kaning-èlfāzini-īrād-et. [met.

Quotient, s. خارج قسمت khāriji-kìss-

R.

Rabbi, Rabbin, s. خخام khàkhām.

Rabbit, s. اطه طوشانى àda-tàwshani.

Rabble, s. اياق طاقمى àyak - tàkimi, اسافل ناس èssāfili-nāss. [mush.

Rabid, a. قدوز kùduz, قدورمش kùdur-

Race, s. قوشى kòshu ; جنس jìnss, صوى sòy, صوى صوب sòy-sòp, سلسله silsilé ; —, v.n. قوشمق kòshmak.

Racecourse, s. قوشى ميدانى kòshu-mèydāni.

Racehorse, s. يارش ايچون بسلنان آت yàrish-ìchin-bèsslénan-àt.

Racer, s. يارش ايدن ات yàrish-èden-àt.

Rack, s. شكنجه shìkènjé.

Radiance, Radiancy, *s.* لمعان lèm‘‘ān ; نور nūr.

Radiant, *a.* پارلاق pārlàk, منير mùnīr.

Radiate, *a.* مركزدن اطرافه داغتمق mèrkezdan-ètrāfa-dàghitmak ; —, *v.n.* مركزدن اطرافه داغلمق mèrkezdan-ètrāfa-dàghilmak.

Radical, *a.* كلى kyùllī, اساسدن èssāssdan, كوكدن kyùkdan ; —, *s.* جمهورجى [jùmhūrju.

Radish, *s.* طورپ tùrp.

Radius, *s.* نصف قطر nìssfi-kùtr ; تكرلك پرمغى tèkerlek-pàrmaghi.

Raffle, *s.* پيانقو pìyànko ; —, *v.a.* پيانقويه قومق pìyànkoya-kòmak.

Raft, *s.* صال sàl, كلك kèlek.

Rafter, *s.* كريش kìrish.

Raftsman, *s.* صالجى sàlji.

Rag, *s.* پچاوره pàchàvra, بزپارچه‌سى bèz-pàrchassi ; rags and tatters, اسكى پوسكى èsski-pùssku. [chàpkìni.

Ragamuffin, *s.* صوقاق چاپقينى sòkak-

Rage, *s.* اويكه (ùfké), حدت hìddèt, غضب ghàzab, خشم khìshm ; —, *v.n.* حدتلنمك hìddetlenmek ; (wind or sea) پك فرطونه اولmak pèk-fìrtina-òl.

Ragged, *a.* يرتق yìrtik ; پروزلو pùruzlu ; اسكيلركييلو èsskilar-ghìyili.

Raid, *s.* اقين àkin.

Rail, *s.* پرمق pàrmak ; —s, *s. pl.* پرمقلق pàrmaklik ; —, *v.n.* تزييف ا tèzyīf-et, اغزينى اچمق àghzini-àchmak, اطاله لسان ا ìtālé‘i-lìssān-et.

Railing, *s.* Railings, *s. pl.* پرمقلق pàrmaklik. [-yòl.

Railroad, Railway, *s.* تيمور يول (dèmir)

Raiment, *s.* روبه (ùruba), اثواب èsswāb (èssbāb), لباس lìbāss (*pl.* البسه èlbissé).

Rain, *s.* يغمور yàghmur, باران bārān, رحمت ràhmèt, مطر màtar ; —, *v.a.* ياغمق yàghmak ; —, *v.n.* يغمور ياغمق yàghmur-yàghmak.

Rainbow, *s.* علائم السما ‘‘àlā‘imu-’ss-sèmā (èléghim-sāmā), قوس قزح kàvssi-kùzāh.

Raise, *v.a.* قالدرمق kàldirmak ; يوكسلتمك yùkseltmek, ترفيع ا tèrfī‘‘-et ; نصب ا nàssb-et, دكمك dìkmek ; (the dead) ديرلتمك dìriltmek, احيا ا ìhyā-et ; (the dead at the resurrection) حشر ا hàshr-et, نشر ا nèshr-et ; (plants) اكوب فلزلندرمك èkip-fìlizlendirmek ; — a siege, محاصره‌دن چكلمك mùhāssaradan-chèkilmek ; — the voice, پك سويلمك pèk-sùwèylémek, پك اوقومق pèk-òkumak, پك چاغرمق pèk-chàghirmak ; — the price, بها ارترمق bàhā-àrtirmak ; — an outcry, ييغره چيقارمق yàyghara-chìkàrmak ; — seed, چوجق يتشدرمك chòjuk-yètishdirmek ; — one's spirits, كيف يتشدرمك kèyf-yètishdirmek, شنلندرمك shènlendirmek, فراحلندرمق fèrāhlandirmak ; — the wind, پاره بولمق (pàra)-bùlmak.

Raisin, *s.* قورو اوزوم kùru-ùzum.

Rake, *s.* طراق tàrak, باغچه طراغى bàghcha-tàraghi ; زندوست zèndòsst, زنپاره (zàmpàra) ; —, *v.a.* طرامق tàramak.

Rally, *v.n.* عقلى باشنه كلمك ''ăkli-băshina-ghèlmek, ايلمق àyilmak, داورانمق dàvranmak; طوپلانمق tòplanmak, يكيدن نظامه كيرمك yèngidan-nizāma-ghirmek; —, *v.a.* يكيدن نظامه قومق طوپلامق tòplamak, yèngidan-nizāma-kòmak; اولاشمق ùlashmak, ملاقى او mùlāki-òl; طاقلمق tàkilmak, صاتاشمق sătashmak, ذوقلنمك zèvklenmek.

Ram, *s.* قوچ kòch; شاهمردان shāh-mèrdān; —, *v.a.* صيقشدرمق sikish-dirmak; — in, صوقمق sòkmak, سورمك sùrmek; — home, يرينه سورمك yèrina-sùrmek.

Ramble, *s.* كزمه ghèzmè, تفرج tèfèr-ruj; —, *v.n.* كزمك ghèzmek, طولاشمق dòlashmak.

Ramification, *s.* قول kòl, چتال chàtal, فرع fèr'', شعبه shù''bé; —s, *pl.* متفرعات mùtéfèrri''āt.

Rammer, *s.* طوقماق tòkmak.

Rampart, *s.* قلعه ديوارى kàl''à-dìwāri, قلعه بدنى kàl''à-bèdéni.

Ramrod, *s.* تفنك چبوغى tùfènk-chi-bùghu, چبوق chìbùk. [bòzuk.

Rancid, *a.* اكشيمش èkshimish, بوزق

Rancour, *s.* كين kìn, بغض bùghz.

Random, *a.* at —, *ad.* راست كلشنه răsst-ghèlishina, راست كلهسى يه răsst-ghèléssiya.

Range, *s.* صره sìra; منزل mènzil; بوى bòy; طولاشش dòlàshish, كزمه ghèzmé; مطبخ اوجاغى mătbăkh-òjàghi; —, —, *v.n.* طولاشمق dòlashmak, كزمك ghèzmek; سورمك sùrmek, كتمك ghìtmek; —, *v.a.* ديزمك dìzmek, ترتيب ا tèrtīb-et.

Rank, *s.* رتبه rùtbé; صف săff, صره sìra; — and file, نفرات nèfĕrāt; —, *a.* اجى ăji, اكشى èkshi, قوقار kòkar; قوتلو kùvvètli, صيق sìk, بويلو bòylu; —, *v.n.* كلمك ghèlmek; —, *v.a.* صايمق sàymak, عدا ''àdd-et.

Rankle, *v.n.* يارهيه صاپلنوب قالمق yà-raya-sàplanip-kălmak.

Ransom, *s.* فديه fìdyé; —, *v.a.* فديه ويرب قورتارمق fìdyé-vèrup-kùrtàrmak, تخليص ا tàkhlīss-et.

Ranunculus, *s.* كريد لالهسى ghìrid-lālēssi.

Rap, *s.* چالش chălish, اورش wùrush; —, *v.n.* چالمق chălmak, اورمق wùrmak.

Rape, *s.* غصباً قارىيهواقع اولان تصرف ghàssban-kăriyyé-vwăki''-òlan-tàs-sàrruf; —, *v.a.* غصباً تصرف ايتمك ghàssban-tàssàrruf-ètmek.

Rapid, *a.* چابك chăbik, تيز tīz (tèz), حيزلو سرعتلو sùr''àtli, سريع sèri'', hìzli; rapid, rapids, *s.* اقندىيرى ăkìndi-yèri. [sùr''àt, حيز hìz.

Rapidity, *s.* چابكلك chàbiklik, سرعت

Rapine, *s.* يغما yàghma, غارت ghāret.

Rapture, *s.* سونج sèvinj, سرور sùrūr, ممنونيت mèmnūniyyèt; حال hāl, وجدان vìjdān.

Rare, *a.* نادر nādir, از بولنور ăz-bùlunur, ناديده nā-dìdé.

Rarefy, *v.a.* خفيفلتمك khàfīflɛtmek; قبارتمق kÀbartm*a*k, تخلخل ايتدرمك tàkh*à*lkhŭl-ètdirmek.

Rarely, *ad.* از Àz, نادراً nādir*a*n.

Rascal, *s.* چاپقين پزونك chÀpk*i*n-pèzé-wɛnk, خبيث khàbīss.

Rascality, *s.* خباثت khàbàssèt; مزوّرلك mùzèvvirlik.

Rash, *s.* قرمزيلق kìrm*i*z*i*l*i*k, حمرت h*à*mrèt, كيدشمه ghìdishm*a*; —, *a.* دلى dèli, عقلسز "Àklsiz, بصيرتسز bÀssīrètsiz. [-dilimi.

Rasher, *s.* پصدرمه دليمى pÀssd*i*rm*a*-

Rasp, *s.* تورپى tùrpu; —, *v.a.* تورپيلمك tùrpulɛ́mek.

Raspberry, *s.* اغاچ چيلكى Àgh*à*j-chì-lèghi, ايزماوله ìzmàwl*a*. [-sìchÀni.

Rat, *s.* صچان sìchÀn, كمرصچانى ghèmɛr-

Rate, *s.* فيأت fī'àt; حساب hìssāb; رتبه rùtbɛ́; مرتبه mɛ̀rtébɛ́; جنس jìnss, صوى sòy; كيدش ghìdish; —, *v.a.* حساب ا hìssāb-et; صايمق sày-m*a*k; first-rate, *a.* اعلى à"là; second-rate, اوسط èvsÀt; third-rate, &c. ادنى èdnā, بياغى bàyāghi, اشاغى Àshàghi, فنا fɛ̀na.

Rather, *ad.* براز bìr-Àz; جق jak *or* jìk, جك jek *or* jik, جه j*a*; I would —, ترجيح ايدرم tɛ̀rjīh-èdèrim; which would you —, قنغيسنى ترجيح ايدرسن kànghìssini-tèrjīh-èdèrsin; death — than slavery, اسيراوله جغمزه اوله لم èssīr--òlajàghimiza-ùlèlim.

Ratification, *s.* تصديق tÀssdìk.

Ratify, *v.a.* تصديق ا tÀssdīk-et.

Ratio, *s.* نسبت nìssbèt. [lānɛ́.

Rational, *a.* عاقل "Àkìl; عاقلانه "Àkì-

Rations, *s. pl.* تعيينات tà"yināt.

Ratsbane, *s.* صچان اوتى sìchAn-òtu.

Rattle, *s.* زريلتى zìrìlti; سس sèss; —, *v.n.* سس ا sèss-et; —, *v.a.* سسلندرمك sèsslɛndirmek.

Ravage, *s.* ضرر zàrar, زيان ziyān, خسارت khÀssārèt; —, *v.a.* خراب ا khàrāb-et, تخريب ا tàkhrīb-et, ويران ا vīrān-et.

Rave, *v.n.* دلى كبى سويلنمك dèli-ghìbi--sùwèylɛnmek, چلدرمق chìld*i*rm*a*k, قاچرمق kÀch*i*rm*a*k.

Raven, *s.* قوزغون kŭz*gh*ūn. [jìk-dɛ̀rɛ́.

Ravine, *s.* صرپ داره جق دره sàrp-dār*a*-

Ravish, *v.a.* يغما ا yàghma-et, زورايله المق zòr-il*a*-Àlm*a*k; زورلامق zòrlam*a*k, زورايله سكمك zòr-il*a*-sìkmek; سونج ايله دلى كبى ا sɛ̀vinj-il*a*-dèli-ghìbi-et, چلدرتمق chìld*i*rtm*a*k.

Raw, *s.* چيك chìgh, چى chī, پشمامش pìshm*a*mish, ناپخته nā-pùkhtɛ́, خام khām; صوغوق sò*gh*uk.

Ray, *s.* شعاع shù"Ā", پرتو pèrtev.

Raze, *v.a.* يقمق yìkm*a*k, هدم ا hèdm--et, يرايله يكسان ا yɛ̀r-il*a*-yèksān-et; كسمك kèssmek, برقاتنى اندرمك bìr-kÀt*i*ni-èndirmek.

Razor, *s.* اوستره *or* استوره *or* استره ùsstur*a*, موسى mūssà.

Reach, *s.* منزل mènzil; نهرك ايكى ديرسكى اراسنده اولان طوغريجه يرى nèhring-ìki-dìrsèghi-àrass*i*nd*a*-òlAn--dòghruj*a*-yɛ̀ri; within —, يتشلور

yètishilir; out of —, ال يتشمز èl-yètishmàz; —, *v.a.* يتشمك yètishmek, اولاشمق òlashmak, وارمق vàrmak; اليويرمك àlivèrmek.

Reaction, *s.* مقابله mùkàbélé; قارشيلق kàrshilik.

Read, *v.a.* اوقومق òkumak, قرائت ا kìrā'at-et; تلاوت ا tilāvet-et; چيقارمق chìkàrmak; —, *v.n.* اوقونمق òkunmak; — well, كاغد اوزرندهكوزل اوقونمق kyāghid-ùzér-inda-ghyùzèl-òkunmak; — out, — aloud, — out loud, *v.a.* پك اوقومق pèk-òkumak; — on, قالميوب همان اوقومق kàlmayup-hèmen-òkumak, دها اوقومق dàhā-òkumak; — over, هپسنى اوقومق hèpsini-òkumak; — again, — over again, بر دها اوقومق bir-dàhā-òkumak; —, *p.p.* اوقومش òkumush, عالم ''ālim; اوقنمش òkun-mush.

Reader, *s.* اوقويجى òkuyuju.

Reading, *s.* اوقومقلق òkumaklik.

Ready, *a.* حاضر hāzir; مهيا mùhèyyā, آماده āmādé, السته àlèssta; to make —, *v.a.* حاضرلمق hāzirlamak, حاضرا hāzir-et; — —, *v.n.* حاضرلنمق hāzirlanmak, حاضر او hāzir-òl.

Real, *a.* كرچك ghèrchèk, حقيقى hàkīkī, صحيح sàhīh; — estate, املاك èmlāk.

Reality, *s.* حقيقت hàkīkàt, كنه kyùnh.

Realize, *v.a.* اينانمق inanmak, حقيقتنه اينانمق hàkīkàtina-inanmak; صاتوب پارهسنى المق sàtip-(pàrassini)-àlmak.

Really, *ad.* كرچكدن ghèrchèkdan, حقيقة hàkīkatan, صحيحاً sàhīhan.

Realm, *s.* ممالك mèmālik.

Ream, *s.* طوپ tòp. [hàssād-et.

Reap, *s.* بچمك bìchmek, حصاد ا

Reaper, *s.* اوراقجى òrakji.

Reaping-hook, *s.* اوراق òrak.

Rear, *s.* كيرو يانى ghèri-yàni, ارد àrd, ورا vèrā; —, *v.a.* بسلمك bèsslémek; يتشدرمك yètishdirmek; بيوتمك bìyutmek; بنا ا binā-et; تحصيل ا tàhsīl-et; —, *v.n.* شاخ قالقمق shākh-kàlkmak (*or* شاه shāh); — admiral, اريالهپاشا iriyàla-pàsha.

Reason, *s.* عقل ''àkl; سبب sèbeb, علت ''illèt, موجب mūjib, ذريعه zèrī''à; —, *v.n.* دوشنمك dùshun-mek; سويلمك sùwèylémek; — with, لقردى اكلاتمق làkirdi-ànglat-mak (ànnat-).

Reasonable, *a.* عاقل ''ākil; معقول mà''kūl. [ghìrmek.

Reassume, *v.a.* تكرار كيرمك tèkrār-

Reassure, *v.a.* يكيدن تأمين ا yèngidan-tè'mīn-et.

Rebel, *s.* عاصى ''āssi, زوربا zòrba; —, *v.n.* عصيان ا ''issyān-et, طغيان ا tùgh-yān-et, زوربالق ا zòrbalik-et, اياقلنمق àyaklanmak, اياغه قالقمق āyagha-kàlkmak.

Rebellion, *s.* زوربالق zòrbalik, عصيان ''issyān, طغيان tùghyān.

Rebellious, *a.* عاصى ''āssi; عصيان معناسنده اولان ''issyān-mà''nàssinda-òlan.

Rebound, *v.n.* سكمك sèkmek ; كيرو تپمك ghèri-tèpmek. [-et.

Rebuild, *v.a.* يكيدن بنا ا yèn*g*id*a*n-bìnā-

Rebuke, *s.* ازار āzār (ᴀzār), ازارش āzā-rish ; —, *v.a.* ازارلمق ᴀzarl*a*m*a*k.

Rebut, *v.a.* تكذيب ا tèkzīb-et ; انكارا ìnk*y*ār-et ; جرح ا jèrh-et.

Recall, *s.* عزل ''ᴀzl ; عودت بوروسى ''àvdèt-bòrussu ; —, *v.a.* عزل ا ''ᴀzl--et ; كيرو چاغرمق ghèri-chà*ghi*rm*a*k ; كيرو المق ghèri-ᴀlm*a*k.

Recapitulate, *v.a.* and *n.* اجمالاً خلاصه ا ìjmāl*a*n-khūlāss*a*-et.

Recapitulation, *s.* خلاصه khūlāss*a*.

Recapture, *v.a.* كيرو ضبط ا ghèri-zᴀbt-et.

Recede, *v.n.* كيرو چكلمك ghèri-chè-kilmek, چكلمك chèkilmek ; دونمك dùnmek.

Receipt, *s.* اخذ àkhz, قبض kᴀbz, الش ᴀl*i*sh ; مقبوض سندى mᴀkbūz-sènédi ; رچته rèchèt*a*, ترتيب tᴇrtīb.

Receive, *v.a.* المق ᴀlm*a*k, اخذ ا àkhz-et, قبض ا kᴀbz-et ; نائل او nā'il-òl, مظهر او mᴀzhàr-òl ; قبول ا kᴀbūl-et ; يمك yèmek ; كرفتار او ghìriftār-òl, دوچار او dūchār-òl, مبتلا او mùbtélā-òl.

Receiver, *s.* اخذ ايدن àkhz-èden.

Recent, *a.* يكى yèn*g*i, مجدد mùjèdded, تازه tāzᴇ.

Recently, *ad.* كچنلرده ghèchᴇnlᴇrd*a*.

Receptacle, *s.* قاب kᴀb.

Reception, *s.* قبول kābūl.

Recess, *s.* حجره hùjrᴇ, طولاب يرى dòlāb-yèri ; تعطيل وقتى tà''tīl-wᴀkt*i*.

Recipe, *s.* رچته rèchèt*a*, ترتيب tᴇrtīb.

Reciprocal, *a.* طرفيندن اولان tàrafèynd*a*n-òlᴀn. [òkυm*a*klik.

Recitation, *s.* ازبردن اوقومقلق èzbᴇrd*a*n-

Recite, *v.a.* ذكرا zìkr-et ; اوقومق òkυ-

Reckless, *a.* قيدسز kàyds*i*z. [m*a*k.

Reckon, *v.a.* حساب ا hìssāb-et, صايمق sàym*a*k ; داخل ا dākhil - et ; عد ا ''àdd-et ; تعداد ا tà''dād-et ; — up, حساب ا hìssᴀb-et, صايمق sàym*a*k ; — upon, اعتماد ا ì''timᴀd-et, امنيت ا èmnìyyèt-et.

Reclaim, *v.a.* اصلاح ا ìsslāh-et ; (land) معمور ا mà''mūr-et, احياى موات ا ìhyāy*i*-mèwāt-et ; كيرو استمك ghèri-ìsstᴇmek. [ùzᴀnm*a*k.

Recline, *v.n.* ياتمق yàtm*a*k, اوزانمق

Recluse, *s.* منزوى mùnzèvi, عزلت كزين ''ùzlet-gh*y*ùzīn, دنيادن چكلمش dùn-*y*ad*a*n-chèkilmish.

Recognition, *s.* طانيمه tᴀn*i*m*a* ; اعتراف ì''t*i*rᴀf. [bìlmek.

Recognize, *v.a.* طانيمق tᴀn*i*m*a*k, بلمك

Recoil, *s.* كيرو تپش ghèri-tèpish ; —, *v.n.* كيرو تپمك ghèri-tèpmek.

Recollect, *v.a.* خاطرلمق khᴀt*i*rlam*a*k, درخاطر ا dᴇr-khᴀt*i*r-et ; خاطرده طوتمق khᴀt*i*rd*a*-tùtm*a*k, اونوتمامق ùnùtma-m*a*k.

Recollection, *s.* خاطرلمه khāt*i*rlam*a*.

Recommend, *v.a.* اصمارلمق ìssmàrlam*a*k, نصيحت ا nᴀssīhàt-et ; توصيه ا tᴀv-sìyy*a*-et ; مدح ا mèdh-et.

Recommendation, *s.* توصيه tàvs*i*yy*a*.

Recompense, *s.* مكافات mùk*y*āfāt, اجر èjr ; بخشش bàkhshish ; —, *v.a.*

مكافاتنى ويرمك mùkyāfātini-vèrmek, اجرينى ويرمك èjrini - vèrmek, بخششنى ويرمك bàkhshishini--vèrmek.

Reconcile, *v.a.* بارشدرمق bàrishdirmak, اوزلاشدرمق ūzlashdirmak, بينلرينى اصلاح ا bèynlérini - ìsslāh - et, ذات البينلرينى اصلاح ا zātu -'l - bèynlérini-ìsslāh-et; خشنود ا khòshnūd-et, ارضا ا ìrzā-et, تسلى ويرمك tèssèlli-vèrmek.

Reconnoissance, *s.* دشمن حواليلرينى يوقلايوب كشف و معاينه ايتمكلك dùshmen-hàwālilérini-yòklayup-kèshf--u-mū''ayéné-ètmeklik.

Reconnoitre, *v.a.* دشمن حواليلرينى يوقلايوب كشف و معاينه ا dùshmen--hàwālilérini - yòklayup - kèshf - u--mū''āyéné-et.

Reconquer, *v.a.* يكيدن فتح ا yèngidan-fèth-et.

Reconsider, *v.a.* بر دها دوشنمك bìr-[dàha-dùshènmek.

Reconstruct, *v.a.* يكيدن ياپمق yèngidan--yàpmak.

Record, *s.* قيد kàyd, سجل sìjìll; *pl.* قيود kùyūd, قيودات kùyūdāt, سجلات sìjillāt; —, *v.a.* يازمق yàzmak, قيد ا kàyd-et, تسجيل ا tèssjīl-et; ضبط ا zàbt-et, تحرير ا tàhrīr-et.

Recount, *v.a.* نقل ا nàkl-et, حكايه ا hìkyāyé-et, ذكر ا zìkr-et.

Recourse, *s.* مراجعت mùrāja''àt, تشبث tèshèbbuss; to have —, دوشمك dùshmek, مراجعت ا mùrā-ja''àt-et, تشبث ا tèshèbbuss-et.

Recover, *v.a.* كيرو المق ghèri-àlmak; ينه بولمق (ghèna)-bùlmak; —, — one's health, ايو او īyi-òl, افاقت بولمق ìfākàt-bùlmak; — one's self, كنديني طوتمق kèndini-tùtmak.

Recovery, *s.* كيرو المه ghèri-àlma; شفا بولمه shifā-bùlma.

Recreant, *a.* قورقاق kòrkàk; مرتد mùr-[tèdd (mùrtàd).

Recreation, *s.* اكلنجه èylènja.

Recriminate, *v.a.* قارشيلقلو اوله رق تهمت اسناد ا kàrshilikli - òlarak - tùhmèt--ìssnād-et.

Recruit, *s.* عسكر عجميسى ''àsskèr--''àjemissi; يكى يازلمش عسكر نفرى yèngi-yàzilmish-''àsskèr-nèféri; —, *v.n.* يكى عسكر طوپلامق yèngi-''àsskèr--tòplamak; استراحت ا ìsstirāhat-et; بدنه خدمت ا bèdéna-khìdmet-et; —, *v.a.* يكيدن تقويت ويرمك yèngidan-tàkvìyyèt-vèrmek.

Rectangle, *s.* مستطيل mùsstatīl.

Rectification, *s.* تصحيح tàsshīh.

Rectify, *v.a.* تصحيح ا tàsshīh-et, طوغرلتمق dòghrultmak; مكرراً انبيقدن چكمك mùkèrréran-ìnbikdan-chèkmek.

Rectitude, *s.* طوغريلق dòghruluk, استقامت ìsstikàmet, راستى ràsstī.

Recur, *v.n.* تكرار وقوع بولمق tèkrār--wùkū''-bùlmak; دونمك dùnmek, تكرار اكمق tèkrār-àngmak.

Recurrence, *s.* تكرار وقوع بولمقلق tèkrār--wùkū-bùlmaklik.

Red, *a.* قرمزى kìrmizi, قزل kìzil, احمر àhmèr, سرخ sùrkh; (hair) صارى sàri.

Redden, *v.n.* قزارمق kìzàrmak; —, *v.a.* قرمزيلق ويرمك kìrmizilik-vèrmek.

Redeem, *v.a.* قورتارمق kùrtarmak, تخليص ا tàkhlīss-et.

Redeemer, *s.* قورتاران kùrtàran, قورتاريجى kùrtàriji, خلاص khàllāss.

Redemption, *s.* قورتارش kùrtàrish, تخليص tàkhlīss; قورتلش kùrtulush, خلاص khàlāss.

Redhot, *a.* قيزغين kìzghin.

Redistribute, *v.a.* يكيدن توزيع ا yèngidan-tèvzi"-et. [-tèvzi".

Redistribution, *s.* يكيدن توزيع yèngidan-

Redoubt, *s.* طابيه tàbiya, پلانقه pàlangha.

Redoubtable, *a.* قورقولو kòrkulu, مهيب mùhīb; كوچ ghyùch, زور zòr.

Redress, *s.* احقاق حق ìhkāki-hàkk; —, *v.a.* احقاق ا ìhkāk-et.

Reduce, *v.a.* ازالتمق àzaltmak, تنزيل ا tènzīl-et, تقليل ا tàklīl-et; كچولتمك kùchultmek; تحويل ا tàhvīl-et, چويرمك chèvirmek, ايتمك ètmek; قومق kòmak, صوقمق sòkmak, كتورمك ghètirmek; جبر ا jèbr-et, يرينه قومق yèrina-kòmak, صارمق sàrmak; تنزيل رتبه ا tènzīli-rùtbé-et; فتح ا fèth-et (t-h), ضبط ا zàbt-et, تسخير ا tèsskhīr-et.

Reduction, *s.* تنزيل tènzīl, تقليل tàklīl; تحويل tàhvīl; جبر jèbr; فتح fèth, تسخير tèsskhīr.

Redundance, Redundancy, *s.* فضله وزائد اولان مقدار fàzla-vé-zā'id-òlan-mìkdār.

Redundant, *a.* زائد zā'id, فضله fàzla.

Reed, *s.* قامش kàmish; قلم kàlem.

Reef, *s.* (rocks) دوكنتى dùkuntu, قيالر kàyalar; يلكنك بر قات جامه دانى yèlkenin-bìr-kàt-jāmédānī; —, *v.a.* جامه دانني باغلامق jāmédānini-bàghla-[mak.

Reef-point, *s.* جامه دان jāmédān.

Reek, *s.* دومان dùmàn, بوغو bùghu; —, *v.n.* دومانى چيقمق dùmàni-chìkmak, بوغوسى چيقمق bùghussu-chìkmak.

Reel, *s.* مقره màkara, طولاب dòlap; —, *v.n.* سندله مك sèndélémek, يقله جق او yìkìlajak-òl, سرسم اولوب اياقلرى طوتمامق sèrsem-òlup-àyak-lari-tùtmamak; —, *v.n.* صارمق sàrmak.

Re-elect, *v.a.* يكيدن انتخاب ا yèngidan-[ìntìkhāb-et.

Re-embark, *v.n.* يكيدن كمى يه بنمك yèngidan-ghèmiyyé-bìnmek.

Re-establish, *v.a.* تجديد ا tèjdīd-et.

Re-establishment, *s.* تجديد tèjdīd.

Refer, *v.a.* كوندرمك ghyùndermek, حواله ا hàwālé-et; —, *v.n.* باقمق bàkmak; مراجعت ا mùrāja"àt-et; كتمك ghìtmek; كلمك ghèlmek; كنايه او kìnāyé-ol, طولابى او dòlayi-òl.

Referee, *s.* حكم hàkem.

Reference, *s.* حواله hàwālé; مراجعت mùrāja"àt; كنايه kìnāyé; كفيل kèfīl; to give a —, كفيل كوسترمك kèfīl-ghyùsstermek; to ask for a —, كفيل استمك kèfīl-ìsstémek.

Refine, *v.a.* تصفيه ا tàssfìyyé-et; —, *v.n.* اينجلتمك ìnjeltmek.

Refined, *a.* پك نازك pèk-nāzik.

Refinement, *s.* نزاكت nèzākèt.

Reflect, *v.a.* عكس ا "àkss-et, كيرو

اورمق ghèri-wòrmak; —, *v.n.* دوشنمك dùshunmek, طاشنمق tàshinmak, مطالعه ا mùtāla''à-et; — upon, توبيخ ا tèvbīkh-et; عيب او ''àyb-òl.

Reflection, *s.* عكس ''àkss, انعكاس ìn''ikyāss; مطالعه mùtāla''à; توبيخ tèvbīkh, تعييب tà''yìb.

Reflector, *s.* ايينه àyina.

Reform, *s.* اصلاح ìsslāh; اصلاحات ìsslāhāt, تنظيمات tànzīmāt, تنسيقات tènsīkāt; —, *v.a.* يولنه قومق yòluna-kòmak, اصلاح ا ìsslāh-et, نظامنه قومق nìzāmina-kòmak.

Reformation, *s.* تهذيب اخلاق tèhzībi-àkhlāk; اصلاح ìsslāh.

Reformer, *s.* مصلح mùsslih.

Refraction, *s.* انكسار شعاعات ìnkissāri-shù''ā''āt.

Refractory, *a.* عاصى ''āssī, عنادجى ''ìnàdji, معند mù''ànnid, متمرد mùtémèrrid.

Refrain, *v.n.* واز كچمك wāz-ghèchmek, صاقنمق sàkinmak, چكنمك chèkinmek, كنديني طوتمق kèndini-tùt-mak, طيانمق dàyanmak.

Refresh, *v.a.* تازه لندرمك tāzélendir-mek; تازه لتمك tāzéletmek; — one's self, دينلنمك dīnenmek, يورغونلغنى المق yòrghunlughunu-àlmak; تفريح بدن ا tèfrīhi-bèden-et; to feel refreshed, اچلمق àchilmak.

Refreshment, *s.* يمك yèmèk, ييه جك ايچه جك yèyéjek-ìchéjek.

Refuge, *s.* صيغنه جق ير sìghinajak-yèr, بارينه جق ير bàrinajak-yèr, ملجا mèljà; to take —, صيغنمق sìghinmak, بارنمق bàrinmak, التجا ìltijā-et.

Refugee, *s.* ملتجى mùltèji.

Refulgence, Refulgency, *s.* پارلاقلق pàrlaklik.

Refulgent, *a.* پارلاق pàrlàk.

Refund, *v.a.* كيرو ويرمك ghèri-vèrmek, رد ا rèdd-et, استرداد ا ìsstirdād-et.

Refusal, *s.* رد rèdd.

Refuse, *v.a.* قبول ايتمامك kàbūl-ètmamek, رد ا rèdd-et; ويرمامك vèrmamek; راضى اولمامق rāzi-òlmo-mak.

Refutation, *s.* جرح jèrh.

Refute, *v.a.* جرح ا jèrh-et, هبت ا *or* هبط ا hàbt-et, چوروتمك chùrutmek.

Regain, *v.a.* تكرار بولمق tèkrār-bùlmak; تكرار واصل او tèkrār-wāssil-òl; تكرار قزانمق tèkrār-kàzanmak.

Regal, *a.* قراله مخصوص kìrāla-màkhsūss, قرالانه kìrālāné, حكمدارانه hùkmdārāné, تاجدارانه tājdārāné.

Regale, *v.a.* ضيافت ا ziyāfèt-et (*or* ايوجه يمك يدرمك ويرمك vèrmek); īyija-yèmèk-yèdirmek, قارننى دويورمق kàrnini-dòyurmak; فرحلندرمق fèrāhlandirmak, خوشلندرمق khòshlandirmak; —, *v.n.* يمك ايچمك yèmek-ìchmek, قارننى دويورمق kàrnini-dòyurmak.

Regalia, *s. pl.* پادشاهك تزيينات رسميه سى pādishāhin-tezyinat-rèssmīyyéssi.

Regard, *s.* باقش bàkish; نظر nàzar, حسن نظر hùssnu-nàzar, اعتبار ì''tibār, احترام ìhtirām, التفات ìltifāt, محبت

màhàbbet; —, *v.a.* باقمق bàkmak; with — to, نظراً nàzaran; بحثنه كلنجه bàhssina-ghèlinja; to have a — for, صايمق sàymak.

Regarding, *ad.* or *pr.* بابنده bābinda.

Regardless, *ad.* باقميه‌رق bàkmayyérek.

Regatta, *s.* قايق و صندالّلر يارشى kàyik-vé-sàndaller-yàrishi. [-sàltanàt.

Regency, *s.* نيابت سلطنت nìyābèti-

Regenerate, *a.* معناً يكيدن احيا اولنمش mà''nan - yèngidan - ìhyā - òlunmush; —, *v.a.* معناً يكيدن احيا ا mà''nan-yèngidan - ìhyā - et, تجديد قلب ا tèjdīdi-kàlb-et.

Regent, *s.* نائب سلطنت nā'ibi-sàltanàt.

Regimen, *s.* پرهيز pèrhīz, حميه hìmyé.

Regiment, *s.* آلاى àlay, عسكرآلايى ''àsskèr-àlayi.

Regimentals, *s.* فورمه fòrma.

Region, *s.* ارض àrz, مملكت mèmlékèt, ديار dìyār.

Register, *s.* دفتر dèfter; —, *v.a.* قيد ا kàyd-et, دفتره كچورمك dèftera-ghè-chirmek, يازمق yazmak.

Registrar, *s.* دفتر امينى dèfter-èmīnī; سجلات كاتبى sìjillat-kyàtibi.

Registry, *s.* تسجيل tèssjīl; دفترخانه dèfter-khāné.

Regret, *s.* اسف èssef, تأسف tè'èsssuf, كدر kèder, غم ghàm; —, *v.a.* اسف ا èssef-et, تأسف ا tè'èssuf-et, كدر ا kèder-et.

Regular, *a.* يولنده اولان yòlunda-òlan; منتظم mùntazàm; مطرد mùttàrid, قياسى kìyāssī; اصل àssl; سالت sàlt; — troops, نظام عسكرى nìzām-''àsskéri, عساكر منتظمه ''àssākiri-mùntàzama.

Regularity, *s.* نظام nìzām.

Regularly, *ad.* نظام اوزره nìzām-ùzèré.

Regulate, *v.a.* نظام ويرمك nìzām-vèr-mek, تنظيم ا tànzīm-et; (a watch) عيار ا ''àyār-et.

Regulation, *s.* نظام nìzām.

Reign, *s.* سلطنت sàltanàt; ايام سلطنت èyyāmi-sàltanàt; —, *v.n.* سلطنت ا sàltanàt-et, حكومت ا hùkyūmet-et, پادشاهلق ا pādishāhlik-et.

Reimburse, *v.a.* ويرمك vèrmek, ينه ويرمك (ghèné) - vèrmek, اوده‌مك ùdémek.

Rein, *s.* ديزكين dìzghin, عنان ''ìnān, زمام zìmām; to give —, اطلاق عنان ا ìtlāki-''ìnān-et.

Reinforce, *v.a.* امداد ويرمك ìmdād-vèrmek, موجوده دها عسكر قاتمق mèvjūda-dàhā-''àsskèr-kàtmak.

Reiterate, *v.a.* تأكيد ا tè'kīd-et, تكرار سويلمك tèkrār-sùwèylémek.

Reiteration, *s.* تكرر tèkèrrùr; تكرير tékrīr.

Reject, *v.a.* رد ا rèdd-et, طرد ا tàrd-et, دفع ا dèf''-et. [tàrd.

Rejection, *s.* دفع def''; رد rèdd; طرد

Rejoice, *v.n.* سونمك sèvinmek, حظ ا hàzz-et, محظوظ او màhzūz-òl, مسرور او mèssrūr - òl; —, *v.a.* سوندرمك sèvindirmek, محظوظ ا màhzūz - et, مسرور ا mèssrūr-et. [màhzūzìyyèt.

Rejoicing, *s.* شنلك shènlik; محظوظيت

Rejoin, *v.a.* جواب ويرمك jèwāb-vèrmek.

Rejoinder, *s.* جواب jèwāb.

Relapse, *s.* نكس nùkss; أرتداد ìrtidād; —, *v.n.* يكيدن فنالشمق yèngidan-fènālashmak, علتى نكس ا "ìllèti-nùkss-et; مرتد او mùrtèdd-òl (mùrtàd); يكيدن فنالغه صاپمق yèngidan-fènaligha-sàpmak.

Relate, *v.a.* نقل ا nàkl-et, حكايه ا hikyāyé-et, بيان ا bèyān-et, تقرير ا tàkrīr-et; —, *v.n.* منسوب او mènsūb-òl; متعلق او mùta"àllik-ol; —ted, *p.p.* منسوب mènsūb, متعلق mùta"-àllik, خصم khìssm; اقربا àkrabā (*pl.*).

Relation, *s.* حكايه hìkyāyé, تقرير tàkrīr; مناسبت mùnāssébèt, تعلق tà"àlluk, منسوبيت mènsūbìyyèt; خصملق khìssmlìk, اقربالق àkrabālìk, قربت kùrbèt; انتساب ìntissāb; نسبت nìssbèt; خصم khìssm, اقربا àkrabā (*pl.*)

Relative, *s.* خصم khìssm, اقربا àkrabā (*pl.*); —, *a.* نسبتله واقع اولان nìssbètla-wākì"-òlan; — pronoun, موصول mèvsūl; —ly, *ad.* نسبتله nìssbètla, نسبةً nìssbéten, قياسله kìyāssla, نظراً nāzaran, كوره ghyùré.

Relax, *v.a.* كوشتمك ghèvshètmek; كوشكلك كتورمك ghèvsheklik-ghètirmek; لينت ويرمك līnet-vèrmek; —, *v.n.* يموشانمق yìmushànmak; يموشامق yìmushamak; كوشه‌مك ghèvshémek.

Relaxation, *s.* اكلنجه èylenja; تنفس tènèffuss.

Release, *s.* قورتلش kùrtulush, خلاص khàlāss; —, *v.a.* صاليويرمك sàli-vèrmek, خلاص ا khàlāss-et; قورتارمق kùrtarmak, تخليص ا tàkhlīss-et, ازاد ا āzād-et.

Relent, *v.n.* يموشامق yìmushamak, رقت كتورمك rìkkàt-ghètirmek.

Reliance, *s.* اعتماد ì"timād, امنيت èmnìyyèt.

Relief, *s.* راحت rāhat; امداد ìmdād; اعانه ì"āné; قورتلش kùrtulush, خلاص khàlāss; in —, قاقمه kàkma, قبارتمه kàbàrtma.

Relieve, *v.a.* راحت ويرمك rāhat-vèrmek, راحت ايتدرمك rāhat-ètdirmek; امداد يتشدرمك ìmdād-yètishdirmek; قورتارمق kùrtarmak, اعانه ا ì"āné-et, دفع ا dèf"-et, تسكين ا tèsskīn-et; — the guard, نوبتجى ديكشمك nùbètji-dìghishmek.

Religion, *s.* دين dīn.

Religious, *a.* ديندار dīndār, متدين mùtédèyyin, صوفى sòfu.

Relinquish, *v.a.* وازكچمك wāz-ghèchmek, براقمق bràkmak, ال چكمك èl-chèkmek, ترك ا tèrk-et, قصر يد ا kàssri-yèd-et, كف يد ا kèffi-yèd-et.

Relinquishment, *s.* ترك tèrk.

Relish, *s.* مزه mèzé, قاتق kàtìk; لذت lèzzèt; —, *v.a.* لذيذ بولمق lèzīz-bùlmak, تلذذ ا tèlèzzuz-et, خوشلانمق khòshlanmak.

Reluctance, *s.* كوكلسزلك ghyùngul-suzluk; with —, reluctantly, استميه‌رك ìsstéméyérek, مع كراهة mā"a-kèrāhétin, مع الكراهة mà"a-'l-kèrāhé.

Reluctant, *a.* كوكلسز ghyùngulsuz.

Rely, *v.n.* كوكنمك ghyùghenmek, اعتماد ا ì''timād-et, استناد ا ìsstinād-et; — upon God, توكل ا tèvèkkyul-et, متوكل او mùtévèkkil-òl.

Remain, *v.n.* قالمق kàlmak, اوطورمق òturmak, ساكن ا sākin-òl; باقى قالمق bākì-kàlmak, فضله قالمق fàzla-kàlmak, ارتمق àrtmak.

Remainder, *s.* قالان kàlan.

Remains, *s.* بقايا bàkāyā, —, *s. pl.* فضله fàzla; mortal —, جنازه jènāzé.

Remark, *s.* لقردى làkirdi; تنبيه tènbīh; اعتراض ì''tirāz; —, *v.n.* كورمك ghyùrmek; دقت ا dìkkàt-et; —, *v.a.* سويلمك sùwèylémek; اشعار ا ìsh''ār-et.

Remarkable, *a.* دقته شايان dìkkàta-shāyān.

Remedy, *s.* چاره chāré; —, *v.a.* چاره بولمق chāré-bùlmak.

Remember, *v.n.* and *a.* خاطرلمق khātirlamak, ياد ا yād-et.

Remind, *v.a.* اخطار ا ìkhtār-et, خاطرينه كتورمك khātirina-ghètirmek.

Remiss, *a.* تنبل tènbèl, اهمالجى ìhmālji; to be —, اهمال ا ìhmāl-et, قصور ا kùssūr-et; —ness, *s.* اهمال ìhmāl, قصور kùssūr.

Remission, *s.* عفو ''àfv, صفح sàfh.

Remit, *v.a.* عفو ا ''àfv-et, صفح ا sàfh-et, بخش ا bàksh-et, بخشلمق (bàghishlamak); كوندرمك ghyùndermek; —, *v.n.* كوشهمك ghèvshémek, كسلمك kèssilmek, ازالمق àzalmak, خفيفلشمك khàfīfleshmek.

Remittance, *s.* مكتوب ايله كوندريلان پاره mèktūp-ìla-ghyùnderīlan-pāré; پاره كوندرلمسى pāré-ghyùnderilmassi.

Remnant, *s.* فضله fàzla, بقيه bàkìyyé; ارتمش àrtmish; ارتمش پارچه àrtmish-pàrcha.

Remonstrate, *v.n.* اعتراض كونا بعض افاداتى واقع او ì''tirāz-ghyūnā-bà''zi-ìfādāti-wākì''òl.

Remorse, *s.* ندامت كليه nèdāmèti-kyùllìyyé, ندامت مع يأس nèdāmèt-mà''à-yè'ss.

Remote, *a.* اوزاق ùzàk, بعيد bà''īd.

Removal, *s.* نقل nàkl, كوچ ghyùch; عزل ''àzl; دفع dèf'', اخراج ìkhrāj.

Remove, *v.a.* قالديرمق kàldirmak, نقل ا nàkl-et; عزل ا ''àzl-et; دفع ا dèf''-et; چيقارمق chìkàrmak, اخراج ا ìkhrāj-et; —, *v.n.* او ديكشمك èv-dìghishmek.

Remunerate, *v.a.* حقنى ويرمك hàkkinì-vèrmek, مكافاتنى ويرمك mùkyāfātini-vèrmek. [اجر èjr; پاره pāré.

Remuneration, *s.* مكافات mùkyafāt;

Rend, *v.a.* يارمق yàrmak, يرتمق yìrtmak, چاك ا chāk-et.

Render, *v.a.* ايتمك ètmek, قيلمق kìlmak; ويرمك vèrmek; تسليم ا tèsslīm-et; كيرو ويرمك ghèri-vèrmek.

Renegade, Renegado, *s.* مهتدى mùhtédī, دونمه dùnma.

Renew, *v.a.* يكيلتمك yèngiletmek, تجديد ا tèjdīd-et.

Renewal, *s.* تجديد tèjdīd.

Renounce, *v.a.* قطع علاقه ا kàt''ì-''àlāka-[-et.

Renovate, *v.a.* تازه‌لتمك tāzéletmek, تجديد ا tèjdīd-et.

Renown, *s.* صيت sīt, شهرت shùhrèt, نام nām, نيكنام nīk-nām, شان shān, اشتهار ìshtihār.

Renowned, *a.* مشهور mèshhūr.

Rent, *s.* كرا kìrā; quit —, اجاره ìjāré; يرتق yìrtìk; يارق yàrìk; —, *v.a.* كرا ايله طوتمق kìrā-ila-tùtmak; — out, كرايه ويرمك kìrāya-vèrmek.

Repair, *s.* تعمير tà''mīr; ترميم tèrmīm; يتاق yàtak, ير yèr, ملجا mèljā; —, —, *v.a.* تعميرا tà''mīr-et, ترميما tèrmīm-et; تسويه‌ا tèssvìyyé-et; اصلاحا ìsslāh-et; چاره‌سنى بولمق chāréssini-bùlmak; —, *v.n.* كتمك ghìtmek, صيغنمق sìghìnmak; in —, in good —, تعميره‌غير محتاج tà''mīra-ghàyri-mùhtāj; out of —, in bad —, تعميره محتاج tà''mīra-mùhtāj.

Reparation, *s.* تعمير tà''mīr, ترميم tèrmīm; تضمين tāzmīn, ترضيه tàrzìyyé.

Repartee, *s.* جواب jèwāb; quick at —, حاضرجواب hāzìr-jèwāb.

Repeal, *s.* فسخ fèsskh, لغو làghv; —, *v.a.* فسخا fèsskh-et, لغوا làghv-et.

Repeat, *v.a.* تكراريا پمق tèkrār-yàpmak, تكرار سويلمك tèkrār-sùwèylémek.

Repeatedly, *ad.* مكرراً mùkèrréran.

Repeater, *s.* باصمغله چالار اولان قوين ساعتى bāssmaghila-chālar-òlan-kòyn-sā''ati.

Repel, *v.a.* دفعا dèf''-et; — an attack, مدافعه‌ا mùdāfa''a-et.

Repent, *v.n.* پشيمان‌او pèshīmān-òl (pìshmān), نادم‌او nādim-òl; توبه‌ا tùbé-et.

Repentance, *s.* ندامت nèdāmèt, پشيمانلق (pìshmanlìk); vow of —, [توبه tùbé.

Repetition, *s.* تكرر tèkèrrur.

Repine, *v.n.* تشكى‌ا tèshèkki-et, متشكى‌او mùtéshèkki-òl.

Reply, *s.* جواب jèwāb; —, *v.n.* جواب ويرمك jèwāb-vèrmek, جوابا jèwāb-et.

Report, *s.* سس sèss, صدا sādā, آواز āwāz, آوازه āwāzé; تواتر tèwātur, خبر khāber, حوادث hàwādiss; تقرير tākrīr, افاده ìfādé, بيان bèyān; —, *v.a.* افاده‌ا ifādé-et, بيانا bèyān-et, تقريرا tàkrīr-et, خبر ويرمك khāber-vèrmek; تواترا tèwàtur-et.

Reporter, *s.* ضبط كاتبى zābt-kyātibi.

Repose, *s.* راحت rāhat, استراحت ìsstirāhat, آسايش āssāyish, آسودكى āssūdéghī, سكون sùkyūn, سكونت sùkyūnèt; —, *v.n.* راحتا rāhat-et, استراحتا ìsstirāhat-et, آسوده‌او āssūdé-òl, آسايشده‌او āssāyishda-òl; — confidence, اعتمادا ì''timād-et.

Repository, *s.* مخزن màkhzen.

Reprehend, *v.a.* آزارلمق āzàrlamak, توبيخا tèvbīkh-et, تقبيحا tākbīh-et, تعييبا tà''yīb-et.

Represent, *v.a.* كوسترمك ghyùsstermek, رسمى‌او rèssmi-ol; افاده‌ا ìfādé-et, بيانا bèyān-et; وكيلى‌او vèkīli-ol, يرينه قائم‌او yèrina-kā'im-òl.

Representation, *s.* ترسيم tèrsīm; افاده [ìfādé.

Representative, *s.* وكيل vèkīl.

Repress, *v.a.* منعا mèn''-et, زجرا zèjr--et, حقندن كلمك hȧkkindan-ghèl-mek ; باصدرمق bȧssdirmak.

Reprieve, *v.a.* قتلنى امهال ا kȧtlini-ìmhāl-et.

Reprimand, *s.* ازار āzār (ȧzàr), تكدير tèkdìr ; —, *v.a.* ازارلمق ȧzàrlamak, تكديرا tèkdīr-et. [mak.

Reprint, *v.a.* تكرار باصمق tèkrār-bȧss-

Reprisal, Reprisals, *s.* مقابله بالمثل mùkȧbélé-bì-'l-mìssl.

Reproach, *s.* عيب ''àyb, عار ''ār, رسوايى rùssvāyī ; تعييب tà''yīb, قدح kȧdh, توبيخ tèvbīkh, تقبيح tȧk-bīh ; —, *v.a.* تعييبا tà''yīb-et, قدحا kȧdh-et, توبيخا tèvbīkh-et ; — with, يوزينه اورمق yùzuna-wūrmak.

Reprobate, *s.* فاسق fāssik.

Reproduce, *v.a.* يكيدن حاصلا yèngi-dan-hȧssil-et. [āzārish, تكدير tèkdīr.

Reproof, *s.* ازار āzār (ȧzar), ازارش

Reprove, *v.a.* ازارلمق ȧzarlamak, تكديرا tèkdīr-et.

Reptile, *s.* قارنى اوستنده سورنان حيوان kàrni-ùsstunda-sùrunen-hàywān.

Republic, *s.* جمهور jùmhūr.

Republican, *a.* جمهورى jùmhūrī ; —, *s.* اهل جمهور èhli-jùmhūr.

Republication, *s.* يكيدن نشر ايتمكلك yèngidan-nèshr-ètmeklik. [-nèshr-et.

Republish, *v.a.* يكيدن نشر ا yèngidan-

Repudiate, *v.a.* بوشامق bòshamak, تطليقا tȧtlīk-et ; قبول ايتمامك kȧbūl--ètmamek, انكارا inkyār-et. [ìnkyār.

Repudiation, *s.* تطليق tȧtlīk ; انكار

Repugnance, *s.* كراهت kèrāhèt, استكراه ìsstikrāh. [fūr.

Repugnant, *a.* كريه kèrīh ; منفور mèn-

Repulse, *s.* مغلوبيت màghlūbìyyèt, بوزغونلق bòzghunluk ; —, *v.a.* هجومنى دفعا hùjūmunu-dèf''-et ; رجاسنى قبول ايتمامك rìjāssini-kȧ-būl-ètmamek.

Reputation, *s.* شهرت shùhrèt, نام nām.

Repute, *v.a.* صايمق sàymak, عدا ''àdd--et, اعتبارا ì''tibār-et.

Request, *s.* رجا rìjā, نياز nìyāz ; —, *v.a.* رجاا rìjā-et, نيازا nìyāz-et.

Require, *v.a.* استمك ìsstémek, محتاج او mùhtāj-òl, احتياجى او ìhtiyāji-òl.

Requisite, *a.* لازم lāzim ; —, *s.* لازمه lāzimé (*pl.* لوازمات làwàzimāt).

Requisition, *s.* استدعا ìsstid''ā, مطالبه mùtālébé.

Rescript, *s.* اراده ìrādé, خط khȧtt.

Rescue, *s.* امداد ìmdād ; —, *v.a.* قورتارمق kùrtarmak, تخليصا tàkh-līss-et. [tàhàrri.

Research, *s.* تجسس tèjèsssus, تحرى

Resemble, *v.a.* بكزهمك bèngzémek, مشابه او mùshābih-òl, مشابهتى او mùshābéhèti-òl.

Resent, *v.a.* داريلوب قارشيلغنى ا dȧrilip--kàrshilighini-et. [غضب ghȧzab.

Resentment, *s.* دارغينلق dàrghinlik,

Reserve, *s.* كتم kètm, كتوملك kètūm-lik, احتراز ìhtirāz ; احتياط ìhtiyȧt ; —, *v.a.* صاقلامق sàklamak, احتياطاً صاقلامق ìhtiyȧtan-sàklamak.

Reservoir, *s.* حوض hàwz, خزينه khà-zīné (hàzna).

Reside, *v.n.* اوطورمق òturmak, ساکن او sākin-òl, متمکن او mùtémèkkin-òl, اقامت ا ikāmet-et, مقيم او mùkīm-òl.

Resident, *a.* ساکن sākin, متمکن mùtémèkkin, مقيم mùkīm; —s, *s. pl.* اهالی àhālī, سکنه sèkéné; minister —, کچوك ايلچی kùchuk - èlchi, اقامتهمأمور ايلچی ìkāméta-mè'mūr-èlchi.

Residue, *s.* باقی bākī, فضله fàzla, قالان kàlan, ارتان àrtan, بقيه bàkìyyé.

Resign, *v.n.* استعفا ا ìssti''fā-et; —, *v.a.* براقمق bràkmak, ترك ا tèrk-et.

Resignation, *s.* استعفا ìssti''fā; تسليم tèsslīm. [chàm-sàkizi; ساقز sàkiz.

Resin, *s.* رچينه rèchina, چام ساقزی

Resist, *v.a.* and *n.* طيانمق dàyanmak, تحمل ا tàhàmmul-et; قارشی قومق kàrshi-kòmak.

Resistance, *s.* مقاومت mùkāvémèt.

Resolute, *a.* يوركی پك yùrèghi-pèk, كوزی پك ghyùzu-pèk, ثابتقدم sābit-kàdem; جسور jèssūr.

Resolution, *s.* ثبات sèbāt, متانت mètānèt; نيت nìyyèt; قرار kàrār; حل hàll, كشف kèshf.

Resolve, *v.n.* نيت ا nìyyèt-et; قرار ويرمك kàrār-vèrmek; —, *v.a.* حل ا hàll-et, كشف ا kèshf-et; — itself into, دونمك dùnmek, اولمق òlmak, اوليويرمك òluvèrmek, كسلمك kèssilmek.

Resort, *s.* يتاق yàtak, مرجع mèrjà'', —, *v.n.* كثرت اوزره كتمك kèssret-ùzéré-ghìtmek; تشبث ا tèshèbbuss-et, دوشمك dùshmek.

Resound, *v.n.* اوتمك ùtmek, سس ويرمك sèss-vèrmek; طنين انداز او tìnīn-èndāz-òl.

Resource, *s.* چاره chāré; منبع ثروت mènbà''i-sèrvèt; اسباب قوت èss-bābi-kùvvèt, وسيلهٔ خلاص vèssīlé'i-khàlāss.

Respect, *s.* حرمت hùrmèt, رعايت rì''āyet, احترام ìhtirām, اعتبار ì''tibār; ماده māddé, خصوص khūs-sūss, باب bāb, امر èmir; نظر nàzar, نسبت nìssbèt, مناسبت mùnās-sébèt; —, *v.a.* حرمت ا hùrmèt-et, رعايت ا rì''āyet-et; in —, with —, نظراً nàzaran, نسبتله nìssbètla; بحثنه كلنجه bàhssina-ghèlinja.

Respective, *a.* بشقه بشقه bàshka-bàshka, ايری ايری àyri-àyri.

Respite, *s.* مهلت mùhlèt, مهل mèhl; —, *v.a.* امهال ا ìmhāl-et, مهلت ويرمك mùhlèt-vèrmek.

Resplendent, *a.* پارلاق pàrlàk, تابناك tābnāk, پرتوانداز pèrtev-èndāz.

Respond, *v.n.* جواب ويرمك jèwāb-vèrmek; مقابله ا mùkābélé-et.

Responsibility, *s.* مسئوليت mèss'ūliyyèt.

Responsible, *a.* مسئول mèss'ūl.

Rest, *s.* راحت rāhat, استراحت ìsstirāhat; باقی bākī, فضله fàzla, قصور kùssūr; طيانهجق نسنه dàyanajak - nèssné; —, — one's self, *v.n.* قالمق kàlmak, استراحت ا

ìsstirāhat-et, دينمك dìnenmek; —, v.a. ديندرمك dìnèndirmek; — on, — upon, v.n. طيانمق dàyanmak, ياتمق yàtmak; — —, — —, v.a. طيامق dàyamak, طياندرمق dàyandirmak, ياترمق yàtirmak.

Restaurant, s. لوقانده lòkànda.

Restitution, s. كيرو ويرش ghèri-vèrish, استرداد ìsstirdād; to make —, كيرو ويرمك ghèri-vèrmek, يرينه قومق yèrina-kòmak, ردا rèdd-et.

Restless, a. هيچ طورمز hìch-dùrmàz.

Restlessness, s. راحتسزلق rāhatsizlik.

Restoration, s. رد rèdd; اعاده ì''ādé; تعمير tà''mīr; تصحيح مزاج tàsshīhī-mìzāj.

Restore, v.a. كيروويرمك ghèri-vèrmek, ردا rèdd-et, اعادها ì''ādé-et; تعميرا tà''mīr-et; صاغالتمق sàghaltmak, شفاويرمك shìfa-vèrmek.

Restrain, v.a. ضبطا zàbt-et, طوتمق tùtmak, جبرا jèbr-et, زجرا zèjr-et, منعا mèn''-et.

Restraint, s. ضبط zàbt; زجر zehjr.

Restrict, v.a. حصرا hàssr-et.

Restriction, s. حصر hàssr.

Result, s. حاصل hāssil, ثمره sèmèré, نتيجه nètījé, فائده fā'idé; —, v.n. حاصل او hāssil-òl, چيقمق chìkmak, ترتبا tèrèttub-et.

Resume, v.a. تكرار باشلامق tèkrār-bàshlamak, تكراراله المق tèkrār-èla-àlmak; خلاصها khùlàssa-et.

Resurrection, s. قيامت kìyāmèt, قيام kìyām, بعث bà''ss.

Retail, s. قيه اندازهايله صاتش (òkka-)-èndāzé-ìla-sàtish; —, a. قيه اندازهايله اولان (òkka)-èndāzé-ìla-òlan; —, v.a. قيه اندازه ايله صاتمق (òkka)-èndāzé-ìla-sàtmak.

Retain, v.a. اليقومق àlìkòmak, طوتمق tùtmak; صاليويرمامك sàlivèrmamek, براقمامق bràkmamak; غائب ايتمامك ghā'ib-ètmamek.

Retainer, s. اوشاق ùshàk.

Retaliate, v.n. مقابله بالمثلا mùkàbélé-bì-'l-mìssl-et, قارشيلغنىا kàrshìlighini-et.

Retaliation, s. مقابله بالمثل mūkābélé-bì-'l-missl.

Retard, v.a. كجكدرمك ghèjikdirmek; اليقومق àlìkòmak, مانعاو māni''-òl.

Retentive, a. اونوتماز اولان ùnùtmàz-òlan.

Retinue, s. اتباع طاقمى ètbā''-tàkimi, خدم وحشم khàdem-u-hàshem.

Retire, v.n. چكلمك chèkilmek; — from the world, عزلتا ''ùzlèt-et.

Retirement, s. عزلت ''ùzlet.

Retiring, a. محجوب màhjūb.

Retract, v.a. كيرو چكمك ghèri-chèkmek.

Retreat, s. كيرو چكلش ghèri-chèkilish, رجعت rìj''àt, رجوع rùjū''; دليك dèlik, سوراخ sūrākh; كوشه kyùshé, زاويه zāvìyyé, عزلتخانه ''ùzlet-khāné; —, v.n. كيرو چكلمك ghèri-chèkilmek; چكلمك chèkilmek.

Retrench, v.n. مصارفنى ازالتمق màssārifini-àzaltmak.

Retrenchment, s. مترس mètériss; تقليل مصارف tàklili-màssārif.

Retribution, *s.* مكافات mùkyāfāt; مجازات mùjāzāt, جزا jèzā, لايق lāyik.

Retrieve, *v.a.* الدن كتمش شى يى تكرار اله كتورمك èldan - ghìtmish - shèy'yi - -tèkrār-èla-ghètirmek.

Retrograde, *a.* كيرويه طوغرى ghèriya- -dòghru, قيچين قيچين kìchin-kìchin, —, *v.n.* كيروكتمك ghèri-ghìtmek, قيچين قيچين كتمك kìchin-kìchin- -ghìtmek, رجعت ا rìj''āt-et.

Return, *s.* عودت ''àvdet, دونش dùnush; معاودت mù''āvèdet, رجعت rìj''āt, رجوع rùjū''; مقابله mùkābélé; (of a disease) نكس nùkss; —, *v.n.* دونمك dùnmek, عودت ا ''àvdet - et; كيرو دونمك ghèri - dùnmek, رجوع ا rùjū'' - et; نكس ا nùkss-et, كيرو دپمك ghèri- -tèpmek; —, *v.a.* كيرو ويرمك ghèri-vèrmek, رد ا rèdd-et; مقابله ا mùkābélé-et.

Reveal, *v.a.* فاش ا fāsh - et, افشا ا ìfshā-et, اچمق àchmak, كشف ا kèshf-et; الهام ا ìlhām-et, وحى ايله بلدرمك vàhy-ila-bìldirmek.

Revealed, *a.* ملهم mùlhèm.

Revelation, *s.* كشف اسرار kèshfi-èssrār; الهام ìlhām, وحى vàhy.

Revenge, *s.* اوج ùj, انتقام ìntikām; —, *v.a.* انتقامنى المق ìntikāmini-àlmak.

Revengeful, *a.* كينه خواه kīné-khāh.

Revengefulness, *s.* كينه خواهى kīné-khāhī. [واردات vāridāt.

Revenue, *s.* ايراد īrād, كلور ghèlir,

Revere, *v.a.* احترام ا ìhtirām-et, عزيز طوتمق ''àzīz - tùtmak, حرمت ا hùrmet - et; مبارك عد ا mùbārek - ''àdd-et.

Reverence, *s.* حرمت hùrmet, احترام ìhtirām, رعايت rì''āyet; دامنبوسى dāmen-būsī; his —, ذات فضيلتمأبلرى zāti-fàzīlèt-mà'àbléri, ذات عاليلرى zāti - ''ālīléri; —, *v.a.* حرمت ا hùrmet-et; رعايتى او rì''āyèti-òl.

Reverse, *a.* and *s.* ترس tèrss, أرقه àrka; فلاكت fèlākèt, بلا bèlā; —, *v.a.* ترس چويرمك tèrss-chèvirmek, ترسنه چويرمك tèrssina-chèvirmek; قلب ا kàlb-et, تعكيس ا tà''kīss-et.

Revert, *v.n.* دونمك dùnmek, كيرو دونمك ghèri-dùnmek; تكرار عطف افكار ا tèkrār - ''àtfi - èfkyār - et, تكرار اكمق tèkrār-àngmak.

Review, *s.* بيوك تعليم bìyuk-tà''līm; معاينه mù''āyéné; غزته ghàzèta; —, *v.a.* معاينه ا mù''āyéné - et, مكرراً كوزدن كچورمك mùkèrrérèn-ghyùz- dan-ghèchirmek.

Revile, *v.a.* سب ا sèbb-et, دشنام ا dùshnām-et, شتم ا shètm-et.

Revise, *v.a.* تنقيح ا tènkīh-et, تصحيح ا

Revision, *s.* تصحيح tàsshīh. [tàsshīh-et.

Revive, *v.n.* ايلمق àyilmak, ديرلمك dìrilmek, جانلنمق jānlanmak, عقلى باشنه كلمك ''àkli-bàshina-ghèlmek, اچلمق àchilmak; ينه پارلامق (ghèné)- -pàrlamak; —, *v.a.* ديرلتمك dìrilt- mek, عقلنى باشنه كتورمك ''àklini- -bàshina-ghètirmek; اچمق àchmak; تكرار پارلاتمق tèkrār-pàrlatmak.

Revocation, *s.* فسخ fèsskh.

Revoke, *v.a.* فسخ ا fèsskh-et ; كيرو المق ghèri-Almak.

Revolt, *s.* عصيان "ìssyān, طغيان tùghyān, اياقلنش àyaklanish ; —, *v.n.* عصيان ا "ìssyān-et, اياقلنمق àyaklanmak ; —, *v.a.* اكراه ايتدرمك ìkrāh-ètdirmek.

Revolution, *s.* دور dèvr, دوران dèvérān, كردش ghìrdish ; تبدل tèbèddul, انقلاب ìnkilāb, تحول tàhàvvul ; تبدل كلى tèbèddulu-kyùllī ; اختلال ìkhtilāl.

Revolve, *v.n.* دونمك dùnmek, دور ا dèvr-et, دوران ا dèvérān-et ; —, *v.a.* چويرمك chèvirmek.

Reward, *s.* مكافات mùkyāfāt ; بخشش bàkhshish ; —, *v.a.* مكافاتنى ويرمك mùkyāfātini-vèrmek.

Rhetoric, *s.* علم تزيينات كلام "ìlmi-tèzyīnāti-kèlām.

Rheumatism, *s.* يل yel, ريح طيار rīhi-tàyyār, وجع المفاصل vèjà"u-'l-mèfāssil.

Rhinoceros, *s.* كركدان ghèrghédān.

Rhodes, *s.* رودوس ròdòs.

Rhomb, Rhombus, *s.* معين mà"īn.

Rhomboid, *s.* شبه معين shìbhi-mà"īn.

Rhubarb, *s.* (drug) راوند rāvènd ; (garden) رباس rùbāss.

Rhyme, *s.* قافيه kāfìyyé ; سجع sèj" ; شعر shì"r, —d, *a.* مقفا mùkAffà,

Rhythm, *s.* وزن vèzn. [مسجع mùsèjjà".

Rib, *s.* قبورغه kAburgha ; اهل بيت èhli-bèyt, قارى kAri, زوجه zèvjé.

Ribald, *a.* اغزى پيس Aghzi-pìss.

Ribaldry, *s.* هزليات hèzlìyyāt.

Riband, Ribbon, *s.* قورده له kòrdèla.

Rice, *s.* پرنج pìrinj, ارز ùrùzz.

Rice-pudding, *s.* سوتلاج sùtlāj.

Rich, *a.* زنكين zènghin, غنى ghànī (*pl.* اغنيا àghniyā), متمول mùtémévvil, مالدار māldār, صاحب ثروت sāhib-sèrvèt ; اغر Aghir, طاتلو tAtli, ياغلو yàghli.

Riches, *s. pl.* مال māl, ثروت sèrvèt, زنكينلك zènghinlik, پاره (pàra).

Rickety, *a.* محكم اولميان mùhkèm-òlmayan. [قورتارمق kùrtarmak.

Rid, *a.* قورتلمش kùrtulmush ; —, *v.a.*

Riddance, *s.* قورتلش kùrtulush ; دفع dèf". [معما mù"àmmà.

Riddle, *s.* قالبور kAlbur ; بلمجه bìlméjé,

Ride, *v.n.* and *a.* بنمك bìnmek, سوار او sùwār-òl, راكب او rākib-òl ; آت ايله كزمك At-ila-ghèzmek, عربه ايله كزمك "àrabà-ila-ghèzmek ; — at anchor, دميرده ياتمق dèmirda-yàtmak ; — out a gale, فرطونه بتنجه يه قدر دميرلو دورمق fìrtina-bìtinjaya-kAdar-dèmirli-dùrmak.

Ridge, *s.* صرت sirt ; بل bèl, بويون bòyun ; صره sira.

Ridicule, *s.* استهزا ìsstìhzā ; هجو hìjv ; مسخره لق mAsskharalik ; —, *v.a.* استهزا ا ìsstìhzā-et ; هجو ا hìjv-et ; كولمك ghyùlmek.

Ridiculous, *a.* كولنه جك ghyùlenéjèk.

Rifle, *s.* ششخانه shèsh-khāné (shìshāné) ; —, *v.a.* صويمق sòymak.

Rig, *s.* زى zìy, قيلق kìlìk, قيافت kìyāfèt ; ارمه àrma ; —, *v.a.* دوناتمق dònatmak ; اورويه ويرمك ùrùba-vèr-mek ; طاقلمق tàkìlmak, ذوقلنمك zèvklènmek.

Rigging, *s.* ارمه àrma ; اورويه ùrùba, اثواب èsswāb (èssbab).

Right, *a.* طوغرى dòghru ; صحيح sàhīh ; تام tāmm, تمام tàmām ; مستقيم mùsstakīm ; قائم kā'im (fem. قائمه kā'imé) ; صاغ sàgh, يمين yèmīn, راست rāsst ; حقلو hàkkli ; —, *s.* حق hàkk ; صاغ طرفى sàgh-tàrafi ; —, *ad.* پك pèk, چوق chòk, كركى كبى ghèrèghi-ghibi ; —, *v.n.* طوغرولمق dòghrulmak ; —, *v.a.* طوغرولتمق dòghrultmak ; حقنى اليويرمك hàk-kini-àlìvèrmek.

Righteous, *a.* اهل صلاح èhli-sàlāh, صالح sālih (*pl.* صلحا sùlahā).

Righteousness, *s.* صلاح sàlāh. [èghilmàz.

Rigid, *a.* قتى kàti, سرت sèrt, اكلمز

Rigorous, *a.* سرت sèrt, شديد shèdīd ; صيقى sìki ; دقتلو dikkàtli ; مدققانه mùdàkkìkàné. [شدت shìddèt.

Rigorousness, Rigour, *s.* سرتلك sèrtlik ;

Rill, *s.* صوجغز sùjàghiz.

Rim, *s.* كنار kènar, لب lèb.

Rime, *s.* قراغى kìràghi.

Rind, *s.* قبوق kàbuk, قشر kàshr.

Ring, *s.* حلقه hàlka ; يوزك yùzuk ; چالش chàlish ; سس sèss, سدا sàdā ; —, *v.a.* چالمق chàlmak ; —, *v.n.* چالنمق chàlinmak ; اوتمك ùtmek ; سس ويرمك sèss-vèrmek.

Ringleader, *s.* ارباشى èr-bàshi, باش bàsh, سركردۀ فساد sèrkèrdé'i-fèssād.

Ringlet, *s.* كاكل kyākyùl, زلف zùlf.

Rinse, *v.a.* چالقامق chàlkamak ; خفيفجه يقامق khàfīfja-yìkamak.

Riot, *s.* قارشقلق kàrishiklik, غوغا (kàwgha) ; چاپقينلق chàpkinlik, سفاهت sèfāhàt ; —, *v.n.* قارشقلق چيقارمق kàrishiklik-chìkàrmak ; باشدن چيقمق bàshdan-chìkmak, طاشرمق tàshirmak.

Rip, *v.a.* سوكمك sùkmek ; يارمق yàrmak.

Ripe, *a.* اولمش òlmush, كمالهيتشمش kèmālé-yètishmish.

Ripen, *v.n.* اولمق òlmak, كماله يتشمك kèmālé-yètishmek ; —, *v.a.* اولدرمق òldurmak, يتشدرمك yètishdirmek.

Ripple, *s.* بوروشق bùrushuk ; —, *v.a.* بورشدرمق bùrushdurmak ; —, *v.n.* بورشمق bùrushmak.

Rise, *s.* منبع mènbà'', باش bàsh, باشلانغج bàshlanghij, منشأ mènshè', مبدأ mèbdè' ; نشئت nèsh'èt, ابتدا ìbtidā ; طلوع tùlū'', طوغش dòghush ; —, *v.n.* قالقمق kàlkmak ; اياغه قالقمق àyàgha-kàlkmak, قيام ا kìyām-et ; چيقمق chìkmak ; يوكسلمك yùk-selmek ; ايلرولمك ìlèrilémek, طى مراتب ا tàyi-mèràtib-et ; طوغمق dòghmak, طلوع ا tùlū''-et ; چيقمق chìkmak, نبع ا nèb''-et ; بدء ا bèd''-et, نشئت ا nèsh'èt-et ; ديرلمك dìrilmek, بعث اولنمق bà''ss-òlun-mak ; طولمق kàbàrmak ; قبارمق

dòlmak ; بهايه چيقمق bàhāya-chìk-mak ; اياقلنمق àyaklanmak.

Risk, s. قورقو kòrku, تهلكه tèhlikÉ, مخاطره mùkhātara ; —, v.a. قومق kòmak, بخته حواله ا bàkhta-hàwālÉ-et, تهلكه يه قومق tèhlikéyÉ-kòmak.

Rite, s. ايين āyīn, رسم عبادت rèssmi-'ibādèt.

Rival, s. انكل ènghel, رقيب ràkīb ; —, v.a. باش او bàsh-òl ; رقابت ا ràkābèt-et.

Rivalry, Rivalship, s. رقابت rakābèt.

River, s. صو sù, چاى chày, ايرمق ìrmak, دره dèrÉ, نهر nèhr (nèhir).

Rivet, s. ميخ mìkh ; —, v.a. ميخلامق mìkhlamak.

Rivulet, s. صو sù, چاى chày, دره dèrÉ.

Road, s. يول yòl, طريق tàrīk, جاده jāddÉ, راه rāh ; ليمان lìmàn ; اچيق àchìk.

Roadstead, s. ليمان līmàn ; مرسا mèrsà.

Roam, v.n. كزمك ghèzmek, طولاشمق dòlashmak.

Roar, s. صيحه sàyhà, پك سس pèk-sèss, كورليش ghyùrléyish ; —, v.n. پك سس ويرمك pèk-sèss-vèrmek, حيقرمق hàykirmak, باغرمق bàghir-mak ; كورلمك ghyùrlÉmek.

Roast, s. شيش كبابى shìsh-kèbābi, اورمان كبابى òrmàn-kèbàbi ; —, v.a. كباب ا kèbāb-et.

Robber, s. خرسز khìrsiz, حرامى hàrāmī, دزد dùzd.

Robbery, s. خرسزلق khìrsizlìk.

Robe, s. اوزون البسه ùzun-èlbissÉ ; —, v.n. اوزون البسه سنى كيمك ùzun-èlbissÉssini-ghìmek. [kùvvètli.

Robust, a. دنج dìnj, قوى kàwī, قوتلو

Rock, s. قيا kàya ; قياپارچه سى kàya-pàrchAssi ; صاللانش sAllanish ; —, v.n. صاللانمق sAllanmak ; —, v.a. صاللامق sAllamak, صاللاندرمق sAllàn-dirmak. [هوائى hàwā'ī.

Rocket, s. هوائى فشنك hàwā'ī-fìshènk,

Rocky, a. قيالق kàyalìk.

Rod, s. چبوق chìbùk, دينك dèynek ; اينجه داللردمتى ìnja-dAllar-dèméti ; التى بچوق ارشونلق اولچى Altì-bùchuk-àrshìnlìk-ùlchu.

Rodomontade, s. قورولاف واوكنمه لاقيرديسى kùru-lāf-vÉ-ùghunmÉ-làkirdissi.

Roe, s. ديشى قراجه dìshi-kAraja ; بالق يمورطه سى bAlìk-yìmurtassi ; — buck, قراجه kAraja.

Rogue, s. چاپقين chApkin, كولخانى kyùlkhānī, طولاندريجى dòlandiriji, مزور mùzèvvir. [مزورلك mùzèvvirlik.

Roguery, s. طولاندريجيلق dòlandirijilik;

Roguish, a. چاپقينجه chApkinjÉ.

Roguishness, s. چاپقينلق chApkinlìk.

Roll, s. تومار tòmar ; طوپ tòp ; يوارلنش yìwarlanish ; تكرلنش tèkerlenish ; —, v.n. يوارلنمق yìwarlanmak ; — over, تكرلنمك tèkerlenmek, دوريلمك dèvrilmek ; —, v.a. يوارلمق yìwarla-mak ; — up, طوپلامق tòplamak, ديوشرمك dèvshirmek, صارمق sàrmak.

Roller, s. يوالق yìwalàk ; صالنتى طالغه سى sAlinti-dAlghassi ; طوپ tòp, پصطال pAsstAl.

Rolling-pin, *s.* اقلاغی òkla*ghi*.

Roman, *a.* رومی rūmī ; رومالو ròmali ; —, *s.* روم rūm ; اسکی روما آدمی èsski-ròmà-ĀdAmi.

Romance, *s.* مصال mÀssAl ; —, *v.n.* مصال سویلمك mÀssAl-sùwèylémek.

Rome, *s.* روما شهری ròm*a*-shèhiri.

Romp, *s.* چوجق اویونی chòjuk-òyunu ; پك اویناماق سون چوجق pèk-òynam*a*k--sèven-chòjuk ; —, *v.a.* اویناماق òynam*a*k.

Roof, *s.* دام dàm ; flat —, باجه bÀj*a*, سطح sÀth (t-h) *pl.* سطوح sùtūh ; —, *v.a.* اورتمق ùrtmek.

Rook, *s.* قارغه kàrgh*a* ; (chess) رخ rùkh.

Room, *s.* اوطه òd*a* ; یر yèr ; لزوم lùzūm, سبب sèbeb, مناسبت mùnāssébèt.

Roomy, *a.* کنش ghènish, وسعتلو vùss''àtl*i*.

Roost, *s.* کومس kyùmèss ; —, *v.n.* قونوب اویومق kònup-ùyum*a*k.

Root, *s.* کوك kyùk, اصل Àssl ; —, *v.n.* طوتمق tùtm*a*k, کوك صالمق kyùk--sÀlm*a*k ; — up, سوکمك sùkmek, چیقارمق chìkàrm*a*k, استئصال ا ìss-tì'sāl-et, قلع ا kÀl''-et.

Rope, *s.* ایپ ìp, حلاط hÀlAt.

Rope-dancer, *s.* جانباز jānbāz (jàmbÀz).

Rope-maker, *s.* ایپجی ìpji.

Ropery, Rope-walk, *s.* ایپجی کارخانه سی [ìpji-kyār-khānéssi.

Ropeyarn, *s.* تل tèl.

Rosary, *s.* تسبیح tèssbīh.

Rose, *s.* کل ghyùl, ورد vèrd ; — bud, غنچه ghònch*a* ; — bush, کل اغاجی ghyùl-À*gh*Aj*i* ; — water, کل صویی ghyùl-sùyu ; — wood, کل اغاجی ghyùl-À*gh*Aj*i* ; otto of —, عطر ''ìtr, عطر یاغی ''ìtr-yà*ghi*.

Roseate, *a.* قرمزی k*i*rmiz*i*.

Rosin, *s.* چام ساقزی chàm-sàkiz*i*.

Rosy, *s.* (cheeks) قرمزی kìrmiz*i*, کلکون ghy*ù*lghy*ū*n, کلفام ghyùlfām ; (lips) ال Àl. [چوروتمك chùrutmek.

Rot, *v.n.* چورومك chùrumek ; —, *v.a.*

Rotary, Rotatory, *a.* دوری dèvrī ; دوار dèvvār ; دونیجی dùnuju.

Rotation, *s.* دور dèvr, دوران dèvérān, تدور tèdèvvur ; in —, نوبتله nùbètl*a*, صره ایله s*ì*rà-il*a*.

Rote, *s.* ازبر èzbèr ; to know by —, ازبردن بلمك èzbèrd*a*n-bìlmek ; to do by —, دوشونمیه رك الت کبی یاپمق dùshunméyérek-ālet-ghìbi-[-yàpm*a*k.

Rotten, *a.* چوروك chùruk.

Rouge, *s.* دوزکون dùzghyun, قزلجه k*ì*z*i*lj*a*.

Rough, *a.* پوروزلو pùruzlu ; قبا kÀba ; طاصلاق tÀsslÀk ; — draft, تسوید tèssvīd, مسوده mùssvèddé ; طاصلاق tÀsslÀk.

Roughness, *s.* پوروزلولك pùruzluluk ; قبالق kàbalik ; سرتلك sèrtlik.

Round, *s.* قول kòl ; دور dèvr ; —, *a.* (circular) دکرمی dè*gh*irmi, مدور mùdèvvèr ; (globular) طوپ tòp, کروی kyùrévi ; *ad.* and *pr.* اطرافنه ètrāf*i*n*a* ; اطرافنده ètrāf*i*nd*a* ; هرطرفنه hèr-tàrafin*a* ; هرطرفنده hèr--tàrafìnd*a* ; all —, *ad.* هرطرفه hèr-tàraf*a*, هرطرفده hèr-tàrafd*a* ; to go —, to come —, طولاشمق dòlashmak; to come — again, طولاشوب ينه كلمك dòlaship-(ghèné)-ghèlmek; — about, اطرافده ètrāfda, جوارده jìwārda.

Roundabout, *a.* طولاشق dòlàshìk; صاپه sàpa.

Roundness, *s.* دكرميلك dèghirmilik.

Rouse, — up, *v.a.* اوياندرمق ùyàndirmak, قالدرمق kàldirmak; — —, *v.n.* اويانمق ùyanmak, كوزينى اچمق ghyùzunu-àchmak, قالقمق kàlkmak.

Rout, *s.* بوزغونلق bòzghunluk, انهزام ìnhizām; اخشام جمعيتى àkhsham-jèm"ìyyèti; —, *v.a.* بوزمق bòzmak, طاغتمق dàghitmak; — out, كركى كبى سلوب سپورمك ghèrèghi-ghìbi-sìlip-sùpurmek; چيقاروب دفع ا chìkàrip-dèf"et.

Route, *s.* يول yòl; عسكرك يول تذكرهسى "àsskéring-yòl-tèzkèréssi.

Rove, *v.n.* كزمك ghèzmek, طولاشمق dòlashmak.

Rover, *s.* اواره اولهرق چوق يرلر كزر اولان آدم āwārè-òlarek-chòk-yèrler-ghèzer-òlan-àdam; قورصان kùrsān.

Row, *s.* صره sìra, ديزى dìzi, صف sàff; غوغا (kàwgha); كورلدى ghyùrultu, شماطه shàmàta, —, *v.n.* كورك چكمك kyùrèk-chèkmek.

Rower, *s.* كوركجى kyùrèkji.

Rowing, *s.* كورك چكمه kyùrèk-chèkma.

Rowlock, *s.* اسقارموز ìsskàrmuz.

Royal, *a.* قرالانه kìrālānè, حكمدارانه hùkmdārānè, شاهانه shāhānè; —, *s.* قونطره باباقنغو kòntra-bàbàfingho.

Royalty, *s.* قراللق kìràllìk.

Rub, *s.* اوغالايش òghalayish; سورتش sùrtush; سوورنش sùrunush; شمار shàmar, توقات tòkàt; مشكل mūshkil, كوچلك ghyùchluk, درد dèrd; —, *v.a.* اوغالمق òghalamak; — on, — in, سورمك sùrmek; — against, سوورونمك sùrunmek.

Rubber, *s.* سله جك sìléjek, بز bèz, پچاوره pàchàvra; India —, قومالاستق kòmalàsstìk (*or* kòmanàsstìk).

Rubbish, *s.* سپورندى sùpuruntu; heap of —, سپورنديلك sùpuruntuluk, مزبله mèzbélè.

Ruby, *s.* ياقوت yākūt; —, *a.* ال àl, قرمزى kìrmizi.

Rudder, *s.* دومن dùmèn.

Ruddiness, *s.* قرمزيلق kìrmizilìk.

Ruddle, *s.* اشى بوياسى àshi-bòyassi.

Ruddy, *a.* قرمزى kìrmizi, قزل kìzil.

Rude, *a.* قبا kàba, حنطال hàntàl; ادبسز èdebsiz, عارسز "ārsiz, خويرات khòyràt. وحشيلك [vwàhshīlīk.

Rudeness, *s.* قبالق kàbalik, وحشيلك

Rudiment, *s.* باشلانغج bàshlanghìj, ابتدا ìbtidā, مبدأ mèbdè'; (*pl.*) اصول ùssūl, مبادى mèbādi, اوليات èvvéliyyàt.

Rue, *s.* صدف اوتى *or* سدف sèdef-òtu; —, *v.a.* پشيمان او (pìshmàn)-òl.

Ruffian, *s.* خنزير khìnzir, خبيث khàbīss.

Ruffle, *s.* قيرمەلو ينلك kìrmali-yènlik; بوروشق bùrushuk; —, *v.a.* بوروشدرمق bùrushdurmak; دارلتمق dàrìltmak.

Rug, *s.* سجاده sèjjādè, كبه kèbè, كچه kèchè, پوست pòsst.

Rugged, *a.* پوروزلو pùruzlu, سیوری‌سیوری sìvri-sìvri, دیش‌دیش dìsh-dìsh.

Ruin, *s.* خراب khàrāb, خرابیت khàrābìyyèt, پریشانی pèrīshānī, پریشانلق pèrīshānlik; خرابه khàrābé, ویرانه vīrāné; آثار قدیمه āssāri-kādīmé; —, *v.a.* خراب‌ا khàrāb-et, پریشان‌ا pèrīshān-et, کول‌ا kyùl-et; —ed, *a.* ویران vīrān, خراب khàrāb, پریشان pèrīshān.

Ruinous, *a.* ویران vīrān, خراب khàrāb, پریشان pèrīshān; مخرب mùkhrib, خراب‌ایدر khàrāb-èder, باعث‌خراب bā''issi-khàrāb.

Rule, *s.* قاعده kā''idé; نظام nìzām; دستورالعمل dèsstūru-'l-''āmel; اصول ùssūl; حکومت hùkyūmèt; حکم hùkm; جدول تخته‌سی jèdvel-tàkhtassi; جدول jèdvel; ارشون àrshin; foot —, قدم kādem; —, *v.a.* حکومت‌ا hùkyūmèt-et; چیزمك chìzmek.

Ruler, *s.* حاکم hākim, حکمدار hùkmdār; جدول تخته‌سی jèdvel-tàkhtassi.

Rum, *s.* روم rūm; —, *a.* عجیب ''ājīb (''ājā'ib).

Rumour, *s.* تواتر tèwātur; false —, (*pl.*) اراجیف èrājīf; —, *v.a.* تواترا tèwātur-et.

Rump, *s.* صغری sàghri, قیچ kìch, کوت ghyùt, قایناق kàynak.

Rumple, *s.* بوروشق bùrushuk; —, *v.n.* بوروشمق bùrushmak; —, *v.a.* بوروشدرمق bùrushdurmak.

Run, *s.* قوشش kòshush; سورك sùrèk, دوام dèwām; بچم bìchim; —, *v.a.* یوروتمك yùrutmek, اوغراتمق òghratmak; —, *v.n.* قوشمق kòshmak, سکرتمك sèghirtmek, چاپمق chàpmak, اشمك èshmek; اقمق ākmak; کسمك kèssmek, قطعا ایتمك kāt''-et, ètmek, کتمك ghìtmek, یورومك yùrumek; — against, چاتمق chàtmak; — aground, *v.n.* دیبه‌دوقنمق dìba-dòkunmak, اوطورمق òturmak; — —, *v.a.* اوطورتمق òturtmak; — a race, قوشی‌ا kòshu-et; — ashore, *v.n.* قره‌یه اوطورمق kàraya-òturmak, قره‌یه اوغرامق kàraya-òghramak; — —, *v.a.* قره‌یه‌اوطورتمق kàraya-òturtmak, قره‌یه‌اوغراتمق kàraya-òghratmak; — away, قاچمق kāchmak, صاوشمق sàwushmak, فرارا fìrār-et; — — with, الوب قاچمق ālip-kāchmak, برابر قاچمق bèrābèr-kāchmak; — — — the idea, ظن‌ا zànn-et; — smoothly, اقمق ākmak, قایمق kàymak, کوزل کتمك ghyùzèl-ghìtmek, یولنجه کتمك yòlunja-ghìtmek; — the gauntlet, صره ایله جمله‌نك شماریـنی ییوب تحمل‌ا sìrà-ila-jùmléning-shàmarini-yèyup-tàhàmmul-et; — through, *v.n.* ایچندن کچمك ìchindan-ghèchmek, ایچندن اقمق ìchindan-ākmak; — —, *v.a.* ییوب بترمك yèyup-bìtirmek; — over, *v.n.* طاشمق tāshmak, دوکلمك dùkyulmek; —, *v.a.* اوستندن کچمك ùsstundan-ghèchmek, چینهمك chīné-mek.

Runaway, *s.* قاچقين kàchkin, فرارى fìrārī.

Runner, *s.* قوشيجى kòshujū; اشكين آت èshkin-àt; قاصد kāssid.

Running, *a.* اقار àkar, جارى jārī.

Rupee, *s.* هندستانك بر سكه‌سى hìn-disstānin-bìr-sìkkéssi.

Rupture, *s.* قاصق ياريغى kàssik-yàrighi; بوزشقلق bòzushukluk.

Rural, *a.* كويلو kyùylu, طشره‌لو tàshrali, طيشاريلو dìshàrili, صحراوى sàhrāvī.

Ruse, *s.* خدعه khùd''à, حيله hīlé, دسيسه dèssīssé.

Rush, *s.* ساز sāz; حيزلواقش hìzli-àkish; حيزلوقوشش hìzli-kòshush; —, *v.n.* حيزلواقمق hìzli-àkmak; حيزلوقوشمق hìzli-kòshmak.

Rusk, *s.* كورك ghèvrèk.

Russia, *s.* روسيه rūssia. [kov.

Russian, *a.* روسيه‌لو rūssiali; مسقو mòss-

Rust, *s.* پاس pàss; —, *v.n.* پاسلانمق pàsslanmak; —, *v.a.* پاشلاندرمق pàsslandirmak.

Rustic, *a.* كويلو kyùylu.

Rusticate, *v.n.* بر مدت كويده اوطورمق bìr-mùddèt-kyùyda-òturmak.

Rusty, *a.* پاسلو pàssli, پاسلانمش pàss-lanmish.

Rut, *s.* تكرلك ايزى tèkerlèk-ìzi; —, rutting-time, قزغينلق وقتى kìzghinlik-wàkti.

Ruthless, *a.* مرحمتسز mèrhàmetsiz, بى امان bī-āmān.

Rye, *s.* چاودار chàvdàr, قره‌باش kàra-bàsh.

S.

Sabbath, *s.* پازار كونى pàzar-ghyùnu; جمعه ايرتسى jùm''à-èrtéssi; يوم السبت yùvmu-'ss-sèbt, تعطيل كونى tà''tīl-ghyùnu.

Sable, *s.* سمور sèmmūr (sàmur); —, *a.* قره kàra, سياه siyāh, اسود èsswèd.

Sabre, *s.* قلج kìlij, سيف sèyf, تيغ tīgh; —, *v.a.* چال قلج ا chàl-kìlij-et.

Sack, *s.* چوال chòwàl; يغما yàghma, غارت ghāret; —, *v.a.* يغما ا yàghma-et; —cloth, غرر (hàrer); large sack of —, غراره (hàrer).

Sacred, *a.* حرام hàrām, مبارك mù-bārek, مقدس mùkàddess, عزيز ''àzīz; مخصوص màkhsūss, مختص mùkhtàss, مخصص mùkhàsssess.

Sacrifice, *s.* قربان kùrbān; فداكارلق fèdākyārlik; ضرر zàrar; —, *v.a.* قيمق kìymak; قربان ا kùrbān-et; فدا ا fèdā-et; قيرمق kìrmak.

Sad, *a.* مكدر mùkèdder, كدرلو kèderli, غمناك ghàmnāk; فنا fèna, پريشان pèrīshān; باعث كدر bā''issi-kèder, فنا fèna.

Saddle, *s.* اير èyer; (pillioned) پلان pàlan; (pack) سمر sèmer; —, *v.a.* ايرلمك èyerlémek, ايريشى اورمق èyérini-wùrmak, ياپمق yàpmak.

Saddle-bow, *s.* اير قاشى èyer-kàshi.

Saddler, *s.* سراج sèrrāj (sàraj).

Safe, *a.* امين èmīn, صاغلم sàghlàm, قورقوسز kòrkussuz; صاغ sàgh, سليم

sèlīm ; قورتلمش kùrtulmush ; —, *s.* صندق sàndìk, طولاب dòlap.

Safe-conduct, *s.* يول تذكرەسى yòl-tèz-kéréssi.

Safeguard, *s.* حفظ hifz ; صيانت sìyā-nèt.

Safety, *s.* امنيت èmnìyyèt, سلامت sèlāmèt, سلم sèlm, امن ùmn, امان èmān.

Saffron, *s.* زعفران zà''férān (sàfràn).

Sag, *v.n.* بل ويرمك bèl-vèrmek, اكلمك èghilmek.

Sagacious, *a.* عقللو ''àklli, درايتلو dìrā-yètli, فطين fàtīn ; حساس hàsssāss.

Sagacity, *s.* عقل ''àkl, درايت dìrāyèt, فطانت fàtānèt ; حس hìsss.

Sage, *a.* عقللو ''àklli ; تمكينلو tèm-kīnli, اوصلو ùsslu ; —, *s.* حكيم hàkīm ; اطه چايى àda-chàyi.

Sagittarius, *s.* قوس برجى kàvss-bùrju.

Sail, *s.* يلكن yèlken, بادبان bādibān, شراع shìrā'' ; تكنه tèkné, كمى ghèmi, سفينه sèfīné ; پاره pāré (pàra), قطعه kìt''à ; —, *v.n.* كتمك ghìtmek, يورومك yùrumek ; قالقمق kàlkmak, يالكن اچمق yèlken - àchmak, قيام ا kìyām - et, عزيمت ا ''àzīmèt-et, بادبانكشا او bādibān-kyùshā-òl.

Sailcloth, *s.* كرباس kirbāss ; يلكن بزى yèlken-bèzi.

Sailing-master, *s.* قلاغوز kìlaghuz.

Sailmaker, *s.* يلكنجى yèlkenji.

Sailor, *s.* كميجى ghèmiji, ملاح mèllāh, كشتيبان kèshtībān.

Sainfoin, *s.* يونجه yònja. [عزيز ''àzīz.

Saint, *s.* ولى vèlī, ولى الله vèlìyyu-'llāh,

Sake, *s.* خاطر khātir, محبت màhàbbet ; for the sake, حبة hìbbétan ; — — — of God, حبةلله hìbbétan-lì-'llāh ; for God's sake ! اللهى سورسه كز àllāhi-sèversén*g*iz.

Salad, *s.* سلاطه sàlata.

Salary, *s.* معاش mà''āsh, أيلق àylìk, ماهيه māhìyyé.

Sale, *s.* صاتم sàtim, صاتش sàtish ; for —, on —, صاتيلق sàtilik ; — by auction, مزاد mèzād, مزايده mùzāyédé.

Saleable, *a.* صاتلور sàtilir.

Saliva, *s.* توكرك tùkruk, اغزك صويى àghzing-sùyu, صليار sàlyār.

Sallow, *a.* بكزى صرارمش bèngzi-sàràr-mish ; صارى sàri.

Sally, *s.* هجوم hùjūm, يورويش yùruyush ; — out, *v.n.* يورويش ا yùruyush-et.

Salmon, *s.* صومون بالغى sòmòn-bālighi.

Salonica, *s.* سلانيك شهرى sèlānik-shè-hiri.

Saloon, *s.* بيوك اوطه bìyuk-òda.

Salt, *s.* طوز tùz, نمك nèmek, ملح mìlh ; —, *a.* طوزلو tùzlu ; —, *v.a.* طوزلمق tùzlamak ; —, *v.n.* طوزلنمق tùzlan-mak.

Saltcellar, *s.* طوزلق tùzluk.

Saltpetre, *s.* كهرچله ghyùhèrchilé.

Salts, *s. pl.* انكليز طوزى ìnglīz-tuzu.

Saltworks, *s. pl.* طوزله tùzla.

Salubrious, *a.* ايو īyi, صاغ sàgh, صاغلم sàghlàm.

Salutary, *a.* شفالو shìfāli ; فائدهلو fā'idéli.

Salutation, *s.* سلام sèlām ; اشنالق àshnalìk.

Salute, *v.a.* سلام ويرمك sèlām-vèrmek ; سلام كوندرمك sèlām-ghyùndermek ; اشنالق ا àshnalìk-et ; سلاملمق sèlām-lamak ; سلام دورمق sèlām-dùrmak ; اوپمك ùpmek, بوس ا būss-et, تقبيل ا

tàkbīl-et; — in return, سلام المق sèlām-àlmak; —, v.n. طوپ اتمق tòp-àtmak; —, s. سلام sèlām; اوپش ùpush, بوسه būssé; طوپ اتشی tòp-àtishi.

Salvation, s. قورتلش kùrtulush, نجات nèjāt, خلاص khàlāss, سلامت sèlāmèt.

Salve, s. یاغ yàgh, مرهم mèrhèm; —, v.a. یاغ سورمك yàgh-sùrmek, مرهم سورمك mèrhèm-sùrmek.

Salver, s. تپسی tèpsi, سینی sìni.

Salvo, s. شرط shàrt; استثنا isstissnā; طوپ یایلمی tòp-yàyilimi, الاباندە àlabànda.

Sal-volatile, s. نشادر روحی nèshādir-rūhu.

Samaria, s. نابلس nābulus.

Same, a. ینه او yīné (ghèné)-ò; او ò; کندی kèndi; بر bìr; عین "àyn, اش èsh; —, a. شیء واحد shèyi-wāhid, هپ بر hèp-bìr, فرقی یوق fàrki-yòk.

Sample, s. اورنك ùrnek, موسطره mòss-tra, نمونه nùmūné.

Sanctify, v.a. تقدیس ا tàkdīss-et.

Sanction, s. اذن ìzin, رخصت rùkhsàt, جواز jèwāz, تجویز tèjvīz, تصویب tàsswīb, استصواب isstisswāb, رضا rìzā; —, v.a. تجویز ا tèjvīz-et, تصویب ا tàsswīb-et.

Sanctity, s. حرمت hùrmèt, قدسیت kùdsìyyèt, مبارکلك mùbāreklik.

Sanctuary, s. حرم hàrem; ملجا mèljā; معبد mà"bèd; to take —, مبارك بر محله التجا ا mùbārek-bìr-màhàlla-iltijā-et.

Sand, s. قوم kùm, ریك rīgh, رمل rèml; — bank, قومصال kùmsàl.

Sandal, s. چاریق chàrìk.

Sand-fly, s. تاتارجق tàtarjìk.

Sandy, a. قومصال kùmsàl, قوم kùm; (hair) صاری sàri, لیپسقه lìpìsska.

Sane, a. عاقل "ākil, عقلی باشنده "àkli-bàshinda.

Sanguinary, a. قانلو kànli, سفاك sèffāk, خونریز khūnrīz; خونریزانه khūnrīzāné.

Sanguine, a. دموی dèmévī, خونین khūnīn; پك امیدجی pèk-ùmīdji.

Sanguineness, s. پك امیدجیلك pèk-ùmīdjilik; دمویت dèmévīyyèt.

Sanity, s. صحت عقل sìhhati-"akl.

Sap, s. نباتلرك صویی nèbātlèring-sòyu; صو sù; خام اغاج khām-àghaj; صیچان یولی sìchan-yòlu; —, v.a. التنی قازمق àltini-kàzmak, اشمك èshmek.

Sapper, s. لغمجی làghimji.

Sapphire, s. كوك یاقوت ghyùk-yākūt, صفیر sàfīr.

Saracen, s. عرب "àrab.

Sarcasm, s. استهزا isstihzā.

Sarcastic, a. استهزا ایدر اولان isstihzā-èder-òlan.

Sardine, s. سارده له بالغی sàrdèlé-bàlighi.

Sarmatia, s. اسكی لهستان èsski-lèhisstān.

Sarmatian, a. اسكی له ولایتنه منسوب èsski-lèh-vìlāyètina-mènsūb.

Sarsaparilla, s. سپارینه sèpāriné.

Sash, s. كمر kèmer, قوشاق kùshàk; (window) چرچوه chèrchivé, قناد kànad.

Satan, s. شیطان shèytān, ابلیس iblīss.

Satchel, s. كتاب توربه سی kìtāb-tòrbéssi.

Satellite, *s.* پیك pèyk; ملازم mùlāzim, ایرلمزكولكه‌سی àyrilmàz-ghyùlghéssi.

Satiate, *v.a.* طویورمق dòyurmak, اقناع‌ا ìknā"-et.

Satin, *s.* اطلس Atlàss.

Satire, *s.* هجو hìjv; **—rize**, *v.a.* هجوا hìjv-et.

Satisfaction, *s.* رضا rìzā, خشنودی khòshnūdī; ترضیه tàrzìyyé; to give —, خشنودا khòshnūd-et; ترضیه ویرملك tàrzìyyé-vèrmek.

Satisfactory, *a.* خشنود اولنور khòshnūd-òlunur.

Satisfied, *a.* قانمش kAnmish; خشنود khòshnūd.

Satisfy, *v.a.* طویورمق dòyurmak; قاندرمق kAndirmak.

Saturday, *s.* جمعه‌ایرتسی jùm"à-èrtéssi, سبت sèbt.

Saturn, *s.* زحل‌یلدزی zùhàl-yildizi.

Sauce, *s.* تربیه tèrbìyyé; صو sù; ادبسزلك èdebsizlik.

Saucepan, *s.* تنجره tènjéré.

Saucer, *s.* ظرف zàrf, فنجان طباغی fìnjān (fìl-)-tàbAghi.

Saucy, *a.* عارسز "ārsiz, ادبسز èdebsiz.

Saunter, *s.* كزنش ghèzinish; —, *v.n.* كزنملك ghèzinmek.

Sausage, *s.* سوجق *or* سجوق sùjuk, مومبار mùmbār (bùmbar); — meat, قیمه kìyma, — — balls, كوفته kyūfté.

Savage, *a.* صالدرر sAldirir, اصرر ìssirir; قزغین kìzghin, دارغین dàrghin; وحشی wàhshī, یبانی yàbānī; —, *s.* یبان‌ادمی yàbān-Adami, وحشی wàhshī.

Savanna, *s.* قیر kir.

Savant, *s.* عالم "ālim.

Save, *v.a.* قورتارمق kùrtarmak, خلاص‌ا khàlāss-et, تخلیص‌ا tàkhlīss-et; صقلامق sàklamak, حفظ‌ا hìfz-et; محافظه‌ا mùhāfaza-et, قورومق kòrumak; اداره‌ا ìdāré-et, ارترمق àrtirmak; —, *pr.* نقصان‌اوله‌رق nòksān-òlarak, مستثنا اوله‌رق mùsstessnā-òlarak.

Saving, *a.* قورتاریجی kùrtàriji; اداره‌جی ìdāréji; —, *s.* اداره ìdāré; قورتارش kùrtàrish, خلاص khàlāss; —, *pr.* نقصان اوله‌رق nòksān-òlarak, مستثنا اوله‌رق mùsstessnā-òlarak.

Saviour, *s.* قورتاران kùrtaran, قورتاریجی kùrtariji, خلاص khàllāss; our —, خلاصمز khàllāssimiz; our Lord and —, ربمزوخلاصمز rAbbimiz-vé-khàllāssimiz.

Savour, *s.* لذت lèzzèt, چاشنی chāshni (chèshni), داد dAd (tAd); —, *v.a.* دادمق dAdmak; —, *v.n.* لذتی‌او lèzzèti-òl.

Saw, *s.* دستره dèsstéré (tèsstéré), اره èrré; (large) بچقی bìchki; ضرب‌مثل zàrbi-mèssel.

Sawdust, *s.* دستره توزی dèsstéré-tùzu.

Sawmill, *s.* اره‌خانه èrrékhāné.

Sawyer, *s.* بچقیجی bichkiji.

Saxon, *s.* ساقسون قبائلی ادمی sàksòn-kàbā'ili-Adami; —, *a.* مذكور قبائله منسوب mèzkyūr-kàbā'ila-mènsūb.

Say, *v.a.* سویلملك sùwèylémek, دیمك dèmek; —, *s.* لقردی làkirdi, سویلیه‌جك sùwèyléyéjek.

Saying, *s.* لقردی làkirdi, قبا لقردی kàba-làkirdi, ضرب‌مثل zàrbi-mèssel.

Scab, *s.* یاره‌قبوغی yàra-kAbughu, قبوق kAbuk; كل kĕl, اویوز ùyuz; —, *v.n.* قبوقلنمق kAbuklanmak.

Scabbard, *s.* قین kìn, نیام nìyām, غلاف ghìlāf (kìlif).

Scaffold, Scaffolding, *s.* اسكله ìsskèlĕ.

Scald, *s.* قاینارصویاره‌سی kàynar-sù-yārassi; —, *v.a.* حاشلامق hAsh-lamak.

Scale, *s.* مقیاس mìkyāss, جدول jèdvel; بالق‌پولی bAlìk-pùlu, پول pùl; (of a balance) كوز ghyùz; pair of —s, ترازو tèrāzi, میزان mīzān; —, *v.a.* دیواردن یوقاری چیقمق dìwārdan-yùkàri-chìk-mak, اتلامق Atlamak; (a gun) یاقمق yàkmak.

Scalene, *a.* مختلف‌الاضلاع mùkhtèlifu-l-Azlā".

Scamp, *s.* یرامز yàramàz.

Scamper, *v.n.* قوشمق kòshmak.

Scan, *v.a.* (poetry) تقطیع‌ا tAktī"-et; باقمق bAkmak, نظرا nAzar-et, كوز كزدرمك ghyùz-ghèzdirmek.

Scandal, *s.* افترا ìftirā, بهتان bùhtān; اراجیف èrājīf; رذالت rèzālèt, عیب "àyb.

Scandalous, *a.* عیب "ayb.

Scant, Scanty, *a.* از Az, قیت kìt; دار dàr; قصه kìssa.

Scapegrace, *s.* یرامز yàramàz.

Scar, *s.* یاره‌نشانی yàra-nìshAni; —, *v.a.* نشان‌براقمق nìshAn-bràkmak.

Scarce, *a.* از Az, قیت kìt, بولنمزكبی bùlunmàz-ghibi, نادربولنور nādir-bùlunur; —ly, *ad.* كوچ‌بلا ghyùch-bèlā, همان hèmān (hèmen).

Scarcity, *s.* قیتلق kìtlìk, ندرت nèdrèt, قحط kàht, غلا ghìlā.

Scare, *v.a.* اوركتمك ùrkyutmek, قورقوتمق kòrkutmak.

Scarf, *s.* شال shAl, اوزون‌شال ùzun-shAl.

Scarlatina, *s.* خفیف قزل حما khàfīf-kìzìl-hùmmà.

Scarlet, *a.* ال Al; — fever, قزل‌حما kìzìl-hùmmà; — runner, چیچك فصولیه‌سی chìchek-fAssūlyassi.

Scarp, *s.* خندقك‌شیوداخلیسی (hèn-dèghing)-shèvi-dākhilīssi.

Scatter, *v.a.* داغتمق dAghìtmak, تارومارا tAr-u-mār-et, پریشان‌ا pèrīshAn-et; —, *v.n.* داغلمق dAghìlmak, تاروماراو tār-u-mār-òl, پریشان‌او pèrīshAn-òl.

Scavenger, *s.* چوپجی chàpju.

Scene, *s.* نظراولنان‌هیئت nAzar-òlunAn-hèy'èt; نظارت nAzārèt; وقعه wàk"à; (of a play, or as a picture of life) مجلس mèjliss; (place) موقع mèvki".

Scent, *s.* قوقو kòku, رائحه rā'iha, بوی bùy; —, *v.a.* قوقتمق kòkutmak; قوقو سورمك kòku-sùrmek; قوقوسنی المق kòkussunu-Almak, حس‌ا hìsss-et.

Sceptic, *s.* لاادری lā-ìdrī.

Sceptre, *s.* عصای‌حكومت "àssāyi-hùkyūmèt.

Scheme, *s.* ترتیب tèrtīb; تصور tàssAv-vur; حیله hīlĕ; —, *v.n.* شی‌قورمق shèy-kùrmak.

Schism, *s.* نفاق nìfAk; اعتزال ì"tizāl, شیعه shī"à; تفرق tèfèrruk.

Schismatic, *s.* اهل‌اعتزال èhli-ì"tizāl,

معتزل mù''tèzil, شیعی shī''ī, متفرق mùtéfèrrik.

Scholar, *s.* عالم ''ālim, فاضل fĀzil; شاگرد shāghird, طالب علم tālibi-''ìlm.

Scholarship, *s.* علم ''ìlm.

School, *s.* مکتب mèktɛb; —, *v.a.* معلومات ویرمك mà''lūmāt-vèrmek, تعلیمات ویرمك tà''līmāt-vèrmek, — master, خواجه khòja, مکتب خواجه‌سی mèktɛb-khòjassi.

Schooner, *s.* اسقونه ùsskūna; brig —, غولت ghùlèt.

Sciatica, *s.* عرق النسا ''ìrku-nìssā.

Science, *s.* علم ''ìlm.

Scimitar, *s.* پاله pĀla.

Scirocco or Sirocco, *s.* لدوس کبی اق دکزده اسر بر روزکار lòdos-ghìbi-Āk--dèngizda-èssɛr-bìr-rūzghyār.

Scissors, *s. pl.* مقاص màkass, مقراض mìkrĀz. [zèvklɛnmek.

Scoff, *v.n.* استهزا ا ìsstihzā-et, ذوقلنمك

Scoffer, *s.* حرمتسز مستهزی hùrmetsiz-mùsstèhzī.

Scold, *s.* دارغین قاری dàrghin-kĀri; —, *v.a.* دارلمق dĀrilmak; ازارلمق Āzàrlamak.

Scollop, *v.a.* اویمق òymak, اویه ا òya-et.

Scoop, *s.* خلال khìlāl; —, *v.a.* اویمق òymak; — out, ایچنی اویمق ìchini--òymak, بوشالتمق bòshĀltmak.

Scope, *s.* مطمح نظر mĀtmàhi-nĀzar; اریم èrim; بوی bòy; منزل mènzil; to give —, میدان ویرمك mèydĀn-vèrmek.

Scorch, *v.a.* یاقمق yàkmak.

Score, *s.* یکرمی yìghirmi; حساب hìssĀb; خصوص khùssūss; باب bĀb; خاطر khĀtir, سبب sèbeb, وسیله vèssīlé; —, *v.a.* چیزمك chìzmek, اشارت ا ìshāret-et.

Scorn, *s.* استحقار ìsstihkār, استخفاف ìsstìkhfāf; —, *v.a.* تنزل یتمامك tènèzzul-ètmamek.

Scornful, *a.* اهانت و استحقار ایدر ìhānet-vé-ìsstìhkār-èdɛr.

Scornfully, *ad.* اهانت و استحقار صورتی ایله ìhānet-vè-ìsstìhkār-sūrèti-ìla.

Scorpio, *s.* (Latin) عقرب ''àkreb.

Scorpion, *s.* عقرب ''àkreb.

Scotch, *a.* اسقوچیالو ìsskòchiali.

Scotland, *s.* اسقوچیا ìsskòchia.

Scoundrel, *s.* کولخانی kyùlkhānī, چاپقین chĀpkin, اوغورسز ùghursuz, خبیث khĀbīss.

Scour, *v.a.* سلمك sìlmek, یقامق yìka-mak; یاغنی لکه‌سنی چیقارمق yà-ghini-lèkéssini-chìkarmak; اسهال ویرمك ìsshāl-vèrmek; — over, — about, *v.n.* قوشمق kòshmak, قوششمق kòshushmak.

Scourer, *s.* لکه‌جی lèkéji.

Scourge, *s.* قامچی kĀmchi, قرباچ kìr-bĀch, تازیانه tāziyāné; افت āfet, بلا bèlā, داهیه dāhìyyé; —, *v.a.* دوکمك dùghmek, ضرب ا dàrb-et.

Scout, *s.* اوزاقده طولاشان قره‌قول ùzĀkda--dòlashĀn-kĀrakol.

Scowl, *v.n.* قاش چاتمق kĀsh-chàtmak, یوز بورشدرمق yùz-bùrushdurmak.

Scramble, *v.n.* قاپشمق kĀpishmak, طرماشمق tìrmĀshmak; —, *s.* قاپش

kàpish ; طرماشه‌رق کیدش tìrmasha-rek-ghìdish.

Scrap, *s.* اوفاق پارچه ùfàk-pàrcha.

Scrape, *s.* بلا bèlā, قضا kàzā, درد dèrd ; —, *v.a.* قازیمق kàzimak ; — together, چالشه‌چالشه‌طوپلامق chàlisha-chàlisha-tòplamak, هزارکلفت ایله‌الاکتورمك hèzār-kyùlfèt-ila-èla-ghètirmek.

Scratch, *s.* طرناق یاره‌سی tìrnak-yàrassi ; —, *v.a.* قاشیمق kàshimak ; طرمه‌لمق tìrmalamak, جزئی یاره‌ا juz'ī-yàra-et ; —, *v.n.* قاشنمق kàshinmak ; — out, *v.a.* چیزمك chìzmek, ترقین ا tèrkīn-et. [فنایازمق fèna-yàzmak.

Scrawl, *s.* فنایازی fèna-yàzi ; —, *v.n.*

Scream, *s.* فریاد fèryād, صیحه sàyha ; —, *v.n.* باغرمق bàghirmak ; فریاد ا fèryād-et.

Screen, *s.* پرده pèrdé, سپر sìpèr, حائل hā'il ; قالبور kàlbur ; —, *v.a.* حائل او hā'il-òl ; اورتمك ùrtmek, محافظه‌ا mùhāfaza-et ; قالبورلمق kàlburlamak.

Screw, *s.* ویده vīde, بورغی bùrghu ; بورمه bùrma ; خسیس khàssīss, طمعکار tàma''kyār, جمری jìmri ; —, *v.n.* ویده‌لنمك vīdélenmek ; —, *v.a.* چویرمك chèvirmek ; ویده‌لمك vīdélémek ; — in, بریول ایله صوقمق bìr-yòl-ila-sòkmak ; — up, کیف ا kèyf-et ; — — courage, جسارت ا jèssāret-et ; — down, تابوته قپایوب ویده‌لمك tàbuta - kàpayup - vīdé-lémek.

Scribble, *v.a.* قره‌لمق kàralamak ; چابك یازمق chàbik-yàzmak ; فنایازمق fèna-yàzmak ; دقتسزیازمق dìkkàtsiz--yàzmak. [-yàzan-mù'èllif.

Scribbler, *s.* فنا یازان مؤلف fèna-

Scribe, *s.* کاتب kyātib ; خطاط khàttāt.

Scripture, *s.* ایت کریمه āyéti-kèrīmé ; —s, *s. pl.* کتب سماویه kyùtubi--sèmāvìyyé.

Scrofula, *s.* صراجه علتی sàraja-''ìllèti.

Scrofulous, *a.* صراجه‌لو sàrajali.

Scroll, *s.* تومار tòmār. [khayé-tòrbassi.

Scrotum, *s.* (Latin) خایه توربه‌سی

Scrub, *v.a.* سرت برشی ایله یقامق sèrt--bìr-shèy-ila-yìkamak ; باتمق bàt-mak ; —, *s.* اوفاق چالیلق ùfàk-chà-lìlik. [-fìrcha.

Scrubbing-brush, سرت فرچه sèrt-

Scruple, *s.* اجزاجی درهمنك اوچده بری èjzāji-dìrhèmining-ùchda-bìri, ثلث درهم sùlssu-dìrhèm ; چکندك chèkindik, اعتراض ì''tiràz, قورقو kòrku ; —, *v.n.* چکنمك chèkinmek.

Scrupulous, *a.* پك چکنور pèk-chèkinir.

Scrutiny, *s.* یوقلایش yòklayish, یوقلمه yòklama ; امتحان ìmtihān, تحری [tàhàrri.

Scuffle, *s.* غوغا kàwgha.

Scull, *s.* خفیف کورك khàfīf-kyùrèk.

Scullion, *s.* اشجی یماغی àshji-yàmaghi.

Sculptor, *s.* اویمه‌جی òymaji ; مجسمجی mùjèsssemji, تصویرجی tàssvīrji, مصور mùssàvvir. [اویمق òymak.

Sculpture, *s.* اویمه òyma ; —, *v.a.*

Scum, *s.* کپوك kyùpuk ; — of the people, اسافل ناس èssāfili-nāss, ایاق طاقمی àyak-tàkimi.

Scurf, *s.* كپك kèpek, توز tòz.

Scurrility, *s.* شتم shètm. [shètm-āmīz.

Scurrilous, *a.* شتام shètām, شتم آميز

Scurvy, *a.* مروتسز mùrùvètsiz, طمعكار tàma"kyār; —, *s.* اسقورپيت علتى ìsskòrpìt-"ìllèti.

Scutcheon, *s.* ارما àrma.

Scythe, *s.* طرپان tàrpàn.

Sea, *s.* دكز dèngiz, دريا dèryā, بحر bàhr; طالغه dàlgha, موج mèvj.

Seafaring, *a.* كميجى اولان ghèmiji-[-òlan.

Sea-gull, *s.* مارطى màrti.

Sea-kale, *s.* دكز لخنه سى dèngiz-làhanéssi.

Seal, *s.* مهر mùhr, خاتم khātèm; (animal) كوپك بالغى kyùpèk-bàlighi (?); —, *v.a.* مهرلمك mùhurlémek; —ing wax, مهربالمومى mùhr-bàl-mùmu.

Seam, *s.* دكش dìkish, دكش يرى dìkish-yèri; الك يرى èk-yèri; يارة نشانى yàra-nishāni; (of ship's planks) اسقارموز ìsskàrmoz (?).

Seaman, *s.* كميجى ghèmiji, ملاح mèllāh, كشتيبان kèshtībān.

Seamanship, *s.* كميجيلك ghèmijilik.

Seaport, *s.* اسكله ìsskèlé.

Sear, *v.a.* ياقمق yàkmak, داغلامق dàgh-[lamak.

Search, *s.* ارايش àrayish, ارامه àrama, يوقلمه yòklama, تحرى tàhàrri; —, *v.a.* ارامق àramak, يوقلامق yòklamak, تحرى ا tàhàrri-et; — for, ارامق àramak; — into, حقيقتنى تجسس ا hàkīkàtini - tèjèsssuss - et; — out, ارايوب بولمق àrayup-bùlmak.

Seashore, Seaside, *s.* دكزكنارى dèngiz-kènāri, يالى كنارى yàli - kènāri, ساحل sāhil, دكز قييسى dèngiz-kìyissi.

Seasick, *a.* دكزطوتمش dèngiz-tùtmush; —ness, *s.* دكزطوتمسى dèngiz-tùtmassi.

Season, *s.* موسم mèvsim, فصل fàssl; وقت wàkit; —, *v.a.* طوز ببر قاتمق tùz - bìber - kàtmak; خاملغنى المق khàmlighini - àlmak; the four —s, فصول اربع fùssūli-èrbà".

Seat, *s.* اوطوره جق ير òturajak-yèr, ير yèr, جاى jày, محل màhàll; مسند mèssned; مركز mèrkez, كرسى kyùrsī; مقعد màk"àd, كوت ghyùt, قايناق kàynak, دبر dùbr, ورا vèrā, قيچ kìch; —, *v.a.* اوطورتمق òturt-mak, اقعادا ìk"ād-et; — one's self, be seated, اوطورمق òturmak, قعود ا kù"ūd-et; — — on the throne, تخته جلوس ا tàkhta-jùlūss-et, جلوس ا jùlūss-et; *v.a.* اجلاس ا ìjlāss-et.

Secant, *s.* قاطع kàti".

Secede, *v.n.* ايرلمق àyrìlmak, اعتزال ا ì"tizāl-et.

Secession, *s.* افتراق و اعتزال ìftirāk-vé-ì"tīzāl.

Seclude, *v.a.* ايرمق àyrmak, ايرى قپامق àyri-kàpamak; — one's self, قپانمق kàpanmak, چكلمك chèkilmek, عزلت ا "ùzlet-et. [ìkhtilātsiz.

Secluded, *a.* تنها tènha; اختلاطسز

Seclusion, *s.* عزلت ùzlet; تنهالك tènhalik.

Second, *a.* ايكنجى ìkinji, ثانى sānī,

دوم dùwum ; —, *s.* ثانيه sānìyyé ; معاون mŭ''āvin ; يماق yàmak ; —, *v.a.* ياردم ا yàrdim-et, معاونت ا mŭ''āvénèt-et ; — hand, *a.* قوللانلمش kŭllànilmish, مستعمل mùsstà''mel ; —ly, *ad.* ثانيا sānìyyā.

Secrecy, *s.* كيزلولك ghìzlilik, مكتوميت mèktūmìyyèt ; كتم kètm, اخفا ìkhfā.

Secret, *s.* سر sìrr (*pl.* اسرار èssrār) ; —, *a.* كيزلو ghìzli, صاقلو sàkli, مخفى màkhfī, خفى khàfī, مكتوم mèktūm.

Secretary, *s.* كاتب kyātib, سركاتبى sìrr-kyātibi, كاتب اسرار kyātibi-èssrār.

Secrete, *v.a.* كيزلمك ghìzlémek, صاقلمق sàklamak, اخفا ا ìkhfā-et ; كتم ا kètm-et ; (organs) اعمال ا i''māl-et, اخراج ا ìkhrāj-et, ويرمك vèrmek.

Secretly, *ad.* سراً sìrran.

Sect, *s.* فرقه fìrka, مذهب mèzhèb.

Section, *s.* قسم kìssm, بلوك bùluk ; قطع kàt'', تقسيم tàksīm ; طاقم tàkim ; رسم مسنم rèssmi-mùssènnèm.

Secular, *a.* عصرى ''àssrī, دهرى dèhrī ; اسكى èsski, قديم kàdīm ; دنيوى dùnyévī ; عادى ''ādī.

Secundine, *s.* صوك sòng.

Secure, *a.* امين èmīn ; صاغ sàgh ; صاغلم sàghlàm ; قوى kāvī, محكم mùhkèm ; شبهه سز shùbhéssiz ; —, *v.a.* صاغلاتمق sàghlatmak ; قويلشدرمك kàvileshdirmek, محكم ا mùhkèm-et ; يقالمق yàkalamak, طوتمق tùtmak ; قزانمق kàzanmak, جلب ا jèlb-et ; امين يره قومق èmīn-yèra-kòmak ; محكم باغلامق mùhkèm-bàghlamak ; وقايه ا vìkāyé-et, صيانت ا sìyānèt-et, قورومق kòrumak.

Security, *s.* امنيت èmnìyyèt ; امن ùmn, امان èmān, امينلك èmīnlik ; صاغلملق sàghlamlik, قويلك kàvilik ; كفيل kèfīl ; كفالت kèfālèt ; رهن rèhn, رهين rèhīn.

Sedan-chair, *s.* سديه sédia.

Sedate, *a.* اغر àghir, تمكينلو tèmkīnli.

Sedateness, *s.* اوصلولق ùsslulùk.

Sedative, *s.* تسكين اضطراب ايدن علاج tèsskīnī-ìztirāb-èden-''ìlāj.

Sedentary, *a.* طيشارى چيقمز حركت ايتمز dìshari-chìkmaz-hàrékèt-ètmàz.

Sediment, *s.* طورطى tòrtu, پوصه pòssa.

Sedition, *s.* فساد fèssād, نفاق nìfāk, فتنه fìtné.

Seditious, *a.* فتنه كار fitnékyār, عاصى ''āssi.

Seduce, *v.a.* ايارتمق àyartmak, الداتمق àldatmak, افساد ا ìfsād-et, اغفال ا ìghfāl-et, اضلال ا ìzlāl-et ; قائل ايدوب جماع ا kā'il-èdup-jìmā''-et.

Seduction, *s.* اضلال ìzlāl ; قائل ايدوب جماع ايتمه kā'il-èdup-jìma''-ètma.

Sedulous, *a.* مقدم mùkdim, ملازم mùlāzim.

Sedulousness, *s.* مداومت mùdāvémèt.

See, *s.* پسقپوسلق pìsskapòsslùk ; —, *v.a.* كورمك ghyùrmek, مشاهده ا mùshāhédé-et ; اكلامق ànglamak (ànnamak), سزمك sèzmek ; صاقنمق sàkinmak, باقمق bàkmak ; — into, حقيقتنى اكلامق hàkīkàtīni-àngla-mak ; — to, باقمق bàkmak, اقتضاسنه باقمق ìktizāssina-bàkmak.

Seed, *s.* تخم tòkhum, بذر *and* بزر bèzr ; —, *v.n.* تخمه‌وارمق tòkhuma-varmak ; — time, اكين‌وقتى èkin-wakti.

Seek, *v.a.* ارامق aramak ; — for, — after, ارامق aramak, تفقد ا tàfàkkud-et ; — out, ارايوب‌بولمق arayip-bùlmak.

Seem, *v.n.* كلمك ghèlmek, كورنمك ghyùrunmek, كوزكمك ghyùzuk-mek, كوسترمك ghyùsstermek, بكزه‌مك bèngzémek.

Seemly, *a.* ياقشور yàkishir, مناسب mùnāssib.

Seer, *s.* پيغمبر pèyghàmbèr, نبى nèbī.

Seesaw, *s.* صالنجق sàlïnjàk ; —, *v.n.* صاللانمق sàllànmak.

Segment, *s.* قطعه kìt"à.

Seize, *v.a.* قاپمق kapmak, يقالمق yàka-lamak, ضبط ا zabt-et ; طوتمق tùtmak, اخذ و كرفت ا àkhz-u-ghìrift-et.

Seldom, *ad.* نادر nādir, نادراً nādiran.

Select, *a.* سچمه sèchma, كزيده ghyù-zīdé, منتخب mùntakhàb ; —, *v.a.* سچمك sèchmek, ايرمق àyrmak, انتخاب ا ìntikhāb-et.

Selection, *s.* انتخاب ìntikhāb, ايرمه àyrma.

Self, *s.* كندى kèndi, ذات zāt, اوز ùz, خود khòd.

Self-conceit, *s.* خودپسندلك khòd-pèssèndlik.

Self-denial, *s.* جبر نفس jèbri-nèfss.

Self-destruction, *s.* كندى كنديني تلف ايتمكلك kèndi-kèndini-tèlef-ètmek-lik.

Self-esteem, *s.* خودپسندلك khòd-pèssèndlik.

Selfish, *a.* خودبين khòdbīn.

Selfishness, *s.* خودبينلك khòdbīnlik.

Self-will, *s.* عناد "ìnād.

Self-willed, *a.* عنادجى "ìnādji.

Sell, *v.a.* صاتمق sàtmak, ويرمك vèrmek, فروخت ا fùrūkht-et, بيع ا bèy"-et ; — off, جملةً صاتوب دفع ا jùmlétèn-sàtip-dèf"-et ; — by auction, مزاد ا mèzād-et ; مزاده ويرمك mèzāda-vèrmek.

Seller, *s.* صاتيجى sàtiji.

Selvage, *s.* كنار kènār.

Semblance, *s.* بكزه يش bèngzéyish, مشابهت mùshābéhèt.

Semi, *a.* يارم yàrim, نصف nìssf ; —circle, نصف دائره nìssfi-dā'iré ; —diameter, نصف قطر nìssfi-kùtr.

Seminary, *s.* مكتب mèkteb.

Sempiternal, *a.* ازلى وابدى èzelī-vé-èbédī, جاودانى jāvidānī.

Senate, *s.* مجلس والا mèjlissi-vālā.

Send, *v.a.* كوندرمك ghyùndermek, ارسال ا ìrsāl-et, اسبال ا ìssbāl-et, تسيار ا tèssyār-et ; — for, استتمك ìsstetmek ; كتورتمك ghètirtmek ; اراتمق aratmak ; — word, خبر كوندرمك khàber-ghyùndermek.

Senior, *a.* سنجه بيوك sìnnja-bìyuk, ياشجه بيوك yàshja-bìyuk ; اسكى èsski ; بابا baba, پدر pèder.

Senna, *s.* سنا sènā, سنامكى sènā'i-mèkkī (sènaméki).

Sensation, *s.* حس hìsss (*pl.* احساس àhsāss) ; تعجب tà"àjjub ; سونج sèvinj ; كدر kèder.

Sense, *s.* حس hìsss, حاسه hāsssa (*pl.* حواس hàwasss) ; معنى mà"nà,

مفهوم mèfhūm ; عقل "ʌkl, ذكا zèkyā, درايت dìrāyet ; the five senses, حواس خمسهٔ ظاهره hàwāsssi-khàm-sa'i-zāhirᴇ.

Sensible, *a.* حساس hàsssāss ; دويلور dùyulur, محسوس māhsūss ; عقللو "ʌklli, درايتلو dìrāyetli ; عاقلانه "āki-lānᴇ, درايتكارانه dìrāyetkyārānᴇ ; متشكر mùtéshèkkir ; خبردار khʌ-berdār.

Sensitive, *a.* حساس hàsssāss ; چكنيجى chèkiniji ; — plant, كوسكون kyùsskyun.

Sensual, *a.* حسى hìsssī ; نفسانى nèfsānī ; شهوانى shèhwānī.

Sensualist, *s.* هوا پرست hèwā-pèrèsst.

Sensuality, *s.* هوا پرستلك hèwā-peresstlik.

Sentence, *s.* عباره "ìbārᴇ, قضيه kʌzìyyᴇ ; اعلام ì"lām, فتوى fètwā, حكم hùkm ; —, *v.a.* حقنده اعلام ويرمك hàkkinda-ì"lām-vèrmek.

Sentiment, *s.* حس hìsss ; فكر fikr (*pl.* افكار èfkyār).

Sentinel, Sentry, *s.* نوبتجى nùbètji.

Separate, *a.* ايرى àyri, بشقه بشقه bʌshka-bʌshka, منفصل mùnfʌssil, منفرد mùnfèrid ; —, *v.a.* أيرمق àyrmak, ايرى ايرى قومق àyri - àyri - kòmak, تفريق ا tèfrīk-et ; —, *v.n.* ايرلمق àyrilmak.

Separation, *s.* تفريق tèfrīk ; مفارقت mùfārakʌt.

September, *s.* ايلول èylūl.

Sepulchre, *s.* مزار mèzār, قبر kʌbr, لحد làhd.

Sepulture, *s.* دفن dèfn, تدفين tèdfīn.

Sequel, *s.* صوك sòng, الت يانى ʌlt-yàni ; نتيجه nètījᴇ.

Sequester, *v.a.* مصادره ا mùssʌdara-et ; توقيف ا tèvkīf-et.

Seraglio, *s.* سراى sàrāy ; public apartments of the —, مابين mābèyn ; private — —, حرم hàrem.

Serene, *a.* اچيق àchik, كوزل ghyùzèl, لطيف làtīf, ساكن sākin, سكونتلو sùkyūnetli.

Serf, *s.* روسيه ده يرلو كوله rūssiada-yèrli-kyùlᴇ.

Serfdom, *s.* كوله لك kyùlᴇlik.

Sergeant, *s.* چاوش chàwush.

Series, *s.* صره sèra.

Serious, *a.* اغر ʌghir, تمكينلو tèmkīnli ; صوفى sòfu, متدين mùtédèyyin ; كلى kyùllī, خيلى khàyli, عظيم "ʌzīm.

Sermon, *s.* وعظ wà"z.

Serpent, *s.* يلان yìlʌn, حيه hàyyᴇ, مار mār.

Servant, *s.* (male) خدمتكار khìdmet-kyār (hìz-), اوشاق ùshʌk, اغا ʌghʌ ; (waiter) خدمتجى khìdmètji (hìz-) ; (maid) بسلمه bèsslémᴇ ; (male-slave) كوله kyùlᴇ, (female - slave) جاريه jārìyyᴇ, خلائق khʌlā'ik.

Serve, *v.a.* خدمت ا khìdmet-et (hìz-) ; ايشنى كورمك ìshini - ghyùrmek ; —, *v.n.* يرامق yàramak, فائده سى او fā'idéssi-òl ; عسكرلك ا "ʌsskerlik-et ; استخدام او mùsstàkhdem-òl, مستخدم اولنمق isstikhdām-òlunmak ; — as, — for, —لك ا, —lik-et ; ايشنى كورمك ìshini-ghyùrmek ; — one a trick, اويون ا òyun-et ; — out, (distribute) داغتمق dʌghìtmak, ويرمك vèrmek ; (punish) ياپمق yàpmak ;

— one's turn, أيشنى كورمك ìshini-ghyùrmek, الويرمك èlvermek, اولمق òlmak.

Servia, *s.* سربستان sèrpisstān.

Servian, *a.* سرب sèrp; سربلو sèrpli; —, *s.* سربلو serpli.

Service, *s.* خدمت khèdmet (hìz-); مأموريت mèʻmūrìyyèt; ايش ìsh; منفعت mènfàʻʻat, فائده fāʻidé; كرم kèrem, عنايت ʻʻìnāyet, افنديلك èfèndilik; to render a —, ايشنى كورمك ìshini-ghyùrmek; ايولك‌ا ìyilik-et, افنديلك‌ا èfèndilik-et; to be of —, فائده‌سى‌او fāʻidéssi-òl, ايشه يرامق ìsha-yàramak, ايش‌كورمك ìsh-ghyùrmek.

Serviceable, *a.* ايشه يرار ìsha-yàrar.

Serviceableness, *s.* ايشه يرارلق ìsha-yàrarlik.

Servile, *a.* حقير hàkīr; ذليل zèlīl.

Servility, *s.* رقيت rìkkìyyèt; عبوديت ʻʻùbūdìyyèt.

Servitor, *s.* خدمتكار hìzmetkyār.

Servitude, *s.* رقيت rìkkìyyèt.

Sesame, *s.* سيسام sīssām (sùssàm); oil of —, شيرلغان‌ياغى shìrlaghàn-yàghi.

Session, *s.* جلسه jìlsé.

Set, *s.* طاقم tàkim; —, *a.* رسمى rèssmī; معين mùʻʻàyyen, كسلمش kèssilmish; —, *v.a.* قومق kòmak, وضع‌ا wàzʻʻ-et; دكمك dìkmek, نصب‌ا nàssb-et; ركز‌ا rèkz-et; قورمق kùrmak; باشلاتمق bàshlatmak, ايتدرمك ètdirmek; (bones) صارمق sàrmak, جبرا jèbr-et; (razors, &c.) بلهمك bìlémek; (a diamond, &c.) اوطورتمق òturtmak, ميخلامق mìkhlamak; (seed) اكمك èkmek; (plants) دكمك dìkmek, غرس‌ا ghàrss-et; —, *v.n.* (stars, &c.) باتمق bàtmak, غروب‌ا ghùrūb-et; (clothes, &c.) اولمق òlmak; (jelly, &c.) طوكمق dòngmak; — in, (commence) باشلامق bàshlamak; — about, باشلامق bàshlamak, الهالمق èla-àlmak, مباشرت‌ا mùbāshérèt-et, مبادرت‌ا mùbādérèt-et, ابتدار ا ìbtidār-et, مسابرت‌ا mùssābérèt-et; — against, (indispose) كوجندرمك ghyùjèndirmek, خصومت ايتدرمك khùssūmèt-ètdirmek, خصم‌ا khàssim-et; (as a counterbalance) قارشيلق‌طوتمق kàrshilik-tùtmak, قارشيلق‌صايمق kàrshilik-sàymak; — aside, برطرفه‌قومق bìr-tàrafa-kòmak; برطرف ا bèr-tàraf-et, دفع‌ا dèfʻʻ-et, طرد ا tàrd-et, صاومق sàwmak; — at, *v.a.* هجوم‌ا hùjūm-et; هجوم ايتدرمك hùjūm-ètdirmek; — at defiance, — at nought, قارشى‌قومق kàrshi-kòmak; هيچ صايمامق hìch-sàymamak, هيچ يرينه قومق hìch-yèrina-kòmak; — by, برطرفه‌قومق bìr-tàrafa-kòmak; — great store by, عزيزطوتمق ʻʻàzīz-tùtmak; — down, يره‌قومق yèra-kòmak; قيد ا kàyd-et, يازمق yàzmak; صانمق sànmak, ظن‌ا zànn-et; — forth, *v.n.* يوله‌چيقمق yòla-chìkmak, قيام‌ا kìyām-et, عزيمت‌ا ʻʻàzìmèt-et; — —, *v.a.* بيان‌ا bèyān-et; — free, ازاد ا āzād-et (àzad); — off, *v.n.* كتمك ghìtmek,

قالقمق kàlkmak, چیقمق chìkmak; — —, *v.a.* صالیویرمك sÀlivÈrmek; باشلاتمق bÀshlatmak; ایشلتمك ìshlEtmek; كوسترمك ghyùsstErmek, حسن ویرمك hùssn-vÈrmek, زیبایش ویرمك zībāyish-vÈrmek, یاقشمق yàkishmak; — on edge, قماشدرمق kàmÀshdirmak; — on, تشویق‌ا tèsh-vīk-et; — one's hand to, امضاا ìmzā-et; — out, *v.n.* یوله چیقمق yòla-chìkmak, قیام‌ا kìyĀm-et, عزیمت‌ا "àzīmèt-et; — —, *v.a.* سرمك sÈrmek, دیزمك dìzmek, ترتیب‌ا tÈrtīb-et; — sail, یللكن اچمق yèlken-àchmak, قالقمق kÀlk-mak, بادبان كشای عزیمت او bādi-bĀn-kyùshāyi-"Àzīmèt-òl; — to, باشلامق bÀshlamak, اغازا àghāz-et, مبادرت‌ا mùbādérèt-et; — up, *v.n.* دكان اچمق dùkkyān-àchmak, تجارته باشلامق tìjārèta-bÀshlamak; باشلامق bÀshlamak; — —, *v.a.* دكمك dìkmek, قالدرمق kÀldirmak, نصب‌ا nÀssb-et, ركزا rèkz-et; كرمك ghÈrmek; مالزمه‌سنی ویرمك mā-lèzéméssini-vÈrmek; — up for, كندینی صاتمق kèndini-sÀtmak, دعوی‌ا dà"wà-et, ادعاا ìddi"ā-et.

Settle, *s.* صندق sÀndik; پیكه pèyghèh (pèykÉ), صره sìra; —, *v.a.* اوطورتمق òturtmak, اسكان‌ا ìsskyān-et; ویرمك vÈrmek, اوده‌مك ùdÉmek, اداا èdā-et, ایفاا īfā-et; قرارلاشدرمق kÀrār-lashdirmak, قرار ویرمك kÀrār-vÈrmek; ارضاا ìrzā-et, اغزینی قپاتمق Àghzini-kÀpAtmak, صوصدرمق sùssdurmak اولدرمك ùldurmek; (money upon) باغلامق bÀghlamak; (accounts) حسابلشمك hìssāblEshmek; —, *v.n.* اوطورمق òturmak; توطن‌ا tàwÀttun-et, اتخاذ مكان‌ا ìttikhāzi-mèkyān-et; تمللو اوطورمق tèmèlli-òturmak, تمللو كیرشمك tèmèlli-ghìrishmek; (weather) قرارلشمق kÀrārlashmak; (liquors) دورلمق dùrulmak, طورطیسی چوكمك tòrtussu-chùkmek; (walls, &c.) چوكمك chùkmek; اوطورمق òturmak, یرلشمك yÈrlEshmek.

Settlement, *s.* فصل fÀssl; تأدیه tè'dìyyÉ; مهر مؤجل mèhri-mù'èjjèl; اوجاق òjak.

Settler, *s.* خالی مملكتده توطن ایدن ادم khāli-mèmlékÈtda-tèwÀttun-èden-Àdam.

Settling, *s.* خالی مملكتده اسكان khāli-mèmlÉkètda-ìsskyān; محاسبه mùhāssébÉ.

Seven, *a.* یدی yèdi, سبع sèb", سبعه sèb"à, هفت hèft; the — planets, سبعهٔ سیاره sèb"à'i-sèyyārÉ.

Seventeen, *a.* اون یدی òn-yèdi.

Seventh, *a.* یدنجی yèdinji, سابع sābi", هفتم hèftum, هفتمین hèftumīn; —, *s.* سبع sùb".

Seventy, *a.* یتمش yètmish, سبعون sèb"ūn, سبعین sèb"īn, هفتاد hèftād.

Sever, *v.a.* ایرمق àyrmak, فصل‌ا fÀssl-et; —, *v.n.* ایرلمق àyrilmak; مفارقت‌ا mùfārakÀt-et.

Several, *a.* برقاچ bìr-kÀch, چند chènd;

أيرى أيرى àyri-àyri; بشقه بشقه bàshka-bàshka.

Severally, *ad.* برر برر bìrer-bìrer, أيرى أيرى àyri-àyri, بشقه بشقه bàshka-bàshka, منفرداً mùnfèridan, يكان يكان yèghyān-yèghyān.

Severe, *a.* سرت sèrt, شديد shèdīd; صيقى sìki; فنا fènā, اغر àghir, كلى kyùllī; اليم èlīm.

Severity, *s.* سرتلك sèrtlik, شدت shìd-dèt; افراط دقت ìfrāti-dìkkàt; (of life) رياضت rìyāzèt, فرط عفت fèrti-"ìffèt, افراط پرهيزكارى ìfrāti-pèrhīz-kyārī. [dìkish-dìkmek.

Sew, *v.a.* دكمك dìkmek, دكش دكمك

Sewer, *s.* لغم làghim, كاريز kyāriz (ghìriz). [fàzlāt.

Sewerage, *s.* لغملر làghimler; فضلات

Sex, *s.* ارككلك ديشيلك عرضى èrkek-lik-dìshilik-"àrazi.

Sextant, *s.* سكستانت sèkisstānt.

Sexton, *s.* مزارجى mèzārji.

Shabby, *a.* اسكيمش èsskimish, اسكى èsski, فرسوده fèrsūdé; عيب "àyb, رذالت rèzālèt; خسيس khàssìss, طمعكار tàma"kyār, چنكانه chìn-ghyāné (chìnghèni).

Shade, *s.* كولكه ghyùlghé, سايه sāyé, ظل zìll; كولكه لك ghyùlghélik; (in drawing) سوس sùss; —, *v.a.* كولكه ا ghyùlghé-et, سايه انداز او sāyé-èndāz-ól; اورتمك ùrtmek; (drawings) سوسنى ياپمق sùssunu-yàpmak.

Shadow, *s.* كولكه ghyùlghé, سايه sāyé, ظل zìll; — forth, دومان ايچنده سويلمك dùmàn-ìchinda-sùwèylémek, اوزاقدن ايما ا ùzàkdan-īmā-et.

Shady, *a.* كولكه ghyùlghé, سايه انداز sāyé-èndāz.

Shaft, *s.* (arrow) اوق òk, تير tīr, سهم sèhm; (well) قويى kùyu, چاه chāh; (column) ديرك dìrèk, ميل mìl; (cart, &c.) اوق òk, قول kòl.

Shagreen, *s.* كلر kèler.

Shake, *s.* صاللانش sàllànish; صالليش sàllayish; —, *v.a.* صاللامق sàllamak; صارصمق sàrssmak; —, *v.n.* صاللانمق sàllanmak; صارصلمق sàrsilmak; — off, سلكمك sìlkmek; دفع ا dèf"-et; — one's self, سلكنمك sìlkinmek.

Shako, *s.* عسكر شاپقه سى "àssker-shàpkassi. [kèyfsiz.

Shaky, *a.* يارق يارق yàrik-yàrik; كيفسز

Shall, *v. aux.* See Grammar.

Shallot, *s.* يبانى صارمساق yàbānī-sārimsàk.

Shallow, *a.* صيغ sìgh; احمق àhmak, درايتسز dìrāyetsiz; قبا kàba, صاچمه sàchma.

Sham, *s.* and *a.* تقليد tàklīd, يلان yàlàn; —, *v.n.* تقليد ا tàklīd-et.

Shambles, *s. pl.* سلخ خانه sèlkh-khāné (sàl-khāné).

Shame, *s.* عار "ār, حيا hàyā, شرم shèrm, حجاب hìjāb; عيب "àyb, رذالت rèzālèt; —, *v.a.* اوطاندرمق ùtàndirmak, محجوب ا màhjūb-et; —, *int.* عيب "àyb!

Shameful, *a.* عيب "àyb.

Shameless, *a.* اوتانمز ùtànmàz.

Sham-fight, *s.* جنك تقليدى jènk-tÀklīdī.

Shampoo, *v.a.* عثمانلو دلاك كبى آدمى اوغالمق òssmĀnli-tèllāk-ghibi-ÀdAmi-òghalamak.

Shampooer, *s.* دلاك tèllāk.

Shank, *s.* قويروق *or* قويرق kùyruk, حلقه hÀlka; (anchor) انا àna.

Shape, *s.* بچم bìchim, شكل shèkil, رسم rèssim, هيئت hèy'èt; —, *v.a.* بچم ويرمك bìchim-vèrmek, بچمه صوقمق bìchima-sòkmak; (a course) طوتمق tùtmak.

Share, *s.* پاى pày, حصه hìsssé, بهره bèhré; —, *v.a.* تقسيم ا tàksīm-et; حصه مند او hìsssémènd-òl; —, *v.n.* حصه مند او hìsssémènd-òl, شريك او shèrīk-òl, مشترك او mùshtérèk-òl.

Shareholder, *s.* حصه دار hissé-dār.

Shark, *s.* كوپك بالغى kyùpek-bàlighi (?), ايو بالغى àyi-bàlighi (?); طولاندريجى dòlandiriji.

Sharp, *a.* (cutting) كسكين kèsskin, حديد hàdīd, بران bùrrān; (pointed) تيز tīz (tèz), سيورى sìvri; (violent) سرت sèrt, شديد shèdīd; (pain) اجى Àji, اليم èlīm; (intellect) مستعد mùsstà''idd, جن عقللو jìnn-''Àklli; (sound) ديك dìk; (taste) اكشى èkshi, ترش tùrsh, مايخوش màykhòsh.

Sharpen, *v.a.* بلهمك bìlémek, طاشه طوتمق tÀsha-tùtmak, مصاده سورمك mÀssĀda-sùrmek; (the wits) اچمق àchmak.

Sharper, *s.* طولاندريجى dòlàndiriji.

Sharpness, *s.* كسكينلك kèsskinlik; سرتلك sèrtlik; اكشيلك èkshilik.

Shatter, *v.a.* پاره لمك pārélémek (pàralamak), پارچه پارچه ا pàrcha-pàrcha-et.

Shave, *v.a.* تراش ا tràsh-et; —, *v.n.* تراش او tràsh-òl; — off, تراش ا tràsh-et, اوستره ايله المق òsstura-ila-Àlmak; رنده ايله المق rendé-ila-Àlmak. [رنده طلاشى rènda-tÀlàshi.

Shavings, *s. pl.* تلاش *or* طلاش tÀlash,

Shawl, *s.* شال shÀl.

She, *pr.* او ò, اول òl; —, *a.* ديشى dìshi, قارى kÀri; قيز kìz.

Sheaf, *s.* دمت dèmet, باغ bÀgh.

Shear, *v.a.* قرقمق kìrkmak.

Shears, *s. pl.* مقاص màkass, مقراض mìkrĀz; (for masts) مقاص màkass, داراغاجى dàr-AghAji.

Sheath, *s.* قين kìn, نيام nìyām, غلاف ghìlāf (kìlif); — (sheathe), *v.a.* قپامق kÀpAmak, قيننه قومق kìnina-kòmak, در نيام ا dèr-nìyām-et; with sheathing, قاپلامق kÀplamak.

Sheave, *s.* دل dìl, مقره دلى màkara-dìli.

Shed, *s.* سوندرمه sùndurma *or* صوندرمه sùndurma, اورتى ùrtu; —, *v.a.* دوكمك dùkmek, اراقه ا ìrāka-et, سفك ا sèfk-et; —, *v.n.* دوكلمك dùkyulmek, اقمق Àkmak; دوشمك dùshmek.

Sheep, *s.* قويون kòyun, طوار dÀwar, مال māl; (small-tailed) قويرجق kìvirjik; (large-tailed) قرمان kÀraman; —fold, اغل Aghil.

Sheep-walk, *s.* مرعا mèr‘‘a.

Sheer, *a.* صافی sāfī, ساده sādé, خالص khāliss, محض màhz, صالت sàlt, قورو kùrū; (steep) دیك dìk; — hulk, قورو تکنه kùru-tèkné; —, — off, *v.n.* ایرلمق àyrīlmak; کتمك ghìtmek; صوقلمامق sòkulmamak.

Sheet, *s.* (bed) جارشب jārshèb, چارشاف chàrshaf; (of paper) طبقه tàbaka; (of a sail) اسقوط ìsskòt (shkòt); winding—, کفن kèfen (kèfin); — anchor, اوجاقلق تیموری òjaklik-dèmiri; — iron, *s.* تیمور تختەسی dèmir-tàkhtassi; — lead, *s.* قورشون تختەسی kùrshun-tàkhtassi.

Shelf, *s.* راف rāf; (of rocks) قیا kàya.

Shell, *s.* قبوق kàbuk; bomb —, خمبره (kòmbara); —, *v.a.* قبوغندن چیقارمق kàbughundan-chìkàrmak, قبوغنی صویمق kàbughunu-sòymak; (with shells) خمبره اتمق kùmbara-àtmak; —fish, بوجك bùjek.

Shelter, *s.* اورتی ùrtu, ملجا mèljā, مأوی mè'và, صیغنەجق یر sìghinajak-yèr, بارینەجق یر bàrinajak-yèr, سایه sāyé, معاذ mà‘‘āz; —, *v.a.* قورومق kòrumak, حفظ ا hìfz-et; ایچرو المق ìchèri-àlmak.

Sheltered, *a.* قویتی kùytu.

Shelving, *a.* دیك dìk, چقور chùkur, باش اشاغی bàsh-àshàghi.

Shepherd, *a.* چوبان chòbàn, راعی rā‘‘ī.

Sherbet, *s.* شربت shèrbèt.

Sherry, *s.* بیاض بر شراب bèyàz-bìr-shèrāb.

Shield, *s.* قلقان kàlkan, سپر sìper, ترس tùrss; —, *v.a.* قورومق kòrumak, حفظ ا hìfz-et, وقایه ا vìkāyé-et, صیانت ا sìyānèt-et, محافظه ا mùhā-faza-et.

Shift, *s.* (chemise) کوملك ghyùmlek, قمیص kàmīss, پیراهن pìrāhèn; (of linen) قات kàt; (distress) صیقندی sìkindi, ضرورت zàrūrèt; (substitute) قولای kòlay, چاره chāré; —, *v.a.* یرینی دیکشدرمك yèrini-dìghishdir-mek; دیکشدرمك dìghishdirmek; — one's self, چماشیر دیکشدرمك chàmàshir-dìghishdirmek; —, *v.n.* (in place) یرندن اوینامق yèrindan-òynamak; (manage) اویدرمق ùydurmak; کچنمك ghèchinmek; ایشنی کورمك ìshini-ghyùrmek; قولاینی بولمق kòlayini-bùlmak.

Shin, *s.* اینجك ìnjik.

Shine, *v.n.* پارلامق pàrlamak, ضیا ویرمك zìyā-vèrmek, ایدینلق ویرمك àydin-lìk-vèrmek, اشیق ویرمك ìshik-vèr-mek, منیر او mùnīr-òl, (with borrowed light) مستنار او mùsstènār-òl, منور او mùnèvver-òl.

Shingle, *s.* (sea) یالی چاقللری yàli-chàkillari, قبا قوملق kàba-kùmluk; (roofing) پداوره pàdàvra, یارمه چام تختەسی yàrma-chàm-tàkhtassi.

Shining, *a.* پارلاق pàrlàk, منیر mùnīr, منور mùnèvver, مستنار mùsstènār.

Ship, *s.* کمی ghèmi, تکنه tèkné, سفینه sèfīné, کشتی kèshtī; —, *v.a.* کمی‌یه قومق ghèmiya-kòmak; کمی‌یه المق ghèmiya-àlmak; (in its place) طاقمق tàkmak, كچورمك ghèchirmek; (a sea) يمك yèmek, ایچرو المق ìchèri - àlmak; (men) یازمق yàzmak; —, v.n. کمی یه یازلمق ghèmiya - yàzìlmak; (in its place) طاقلمق tàkìlmak, كچمك ghèchmek.

Ship-broker, s. کمی سمساری ghèmi-sìmsāri.

Ship-builder, s. کمی معماری ghèmi-mì''māri.

Shipbuilding, s. فن انشای سفائن fènni-ìnshāy-sèfā'in. [sāhibi.

Shipowner, s. کمی صاحبی ghèmi-

Shipper, s. کمی یه مال یوکلدان کمسنه ghèmiyyé-māl-yùklédan-kìmèssné.

Shipping, s. کمیلر ghèmiler, سفائن sèfā'in.

Shipwreck, s. قضا kàzā; to be shipwrecked, کضایه اوغرامق kàzāya-òghramak, قضازده او kàzāzèdé-òl.

Shipwright, s. مرانقوز (màranghòss), دولکر dùlghèr.

Shire, s. سنجاق sànjak, لوا lìwā; قضا kàzā; ایالت èyālèt.

Shirt, s. کوملك ghyùmlek, قمیص kàmìss, پیراهن pīrāhèn.

Shiver, s. اوشومه ùshumé; دترەیش (tìtréyish), لرزه lèrzé, رعشه rà''shé; پارچه pàrcha, قیرندی kìrindi; —, v.n. اوشومك ùshumek, دترەمك (tìtrémek), لرزان او lèrzān -òl, لرزەناك او lèrzénāk-òl; —, v.a. قیرمق kìrmak, پارەلمك (pàralamak).

Shoal, s. صیغ یر sìgh - yèr, قومصال kùmsàl; بالق سوروسی bàlìk-sùrussu, سوری sùru; —, a. صیغ sìgh; —, v.n. صیغلشمق sìghlashmak.

Shock, s. چاتش chàtish, تصادم tàssādum; صارصش sàrsish; خلل khàlel, ضرر zàrar; (of sheaves) اون دمت طاقمی òn-dèmet-tàkimi; —, v.a. صارصمق sàrssmak; پك فنا كلمك pèk - fèna - ghèlmek, کریه کورنمك kèrīh-ghyùrunmek.

Shoe, s. ایاق قابی àyak-kàbi, قوندره kùndura, لاپچین làpchin, پاپوش pāpūsh (pàbuch); (horse) نعل nà''l (nàl); —, v.a. نعللمق (nàllamak).

Shoeblack, s. پابوچ بویایان چوجق pàbuch-bòyayan-chòjuk.

Shoemaker, s. پاپوچجی pàpuchji.

Shoot, s. دال dàl; پیچ pìch; اتش àtish, اتم àtim; فرلایش fìrlayish; —, v.n. (plant) دال سورمك dàl--sùrmek; پیچ ویرمك pìch-vèrmek; (pain) زونقلامق zònklamak, صیزلامق sìzlamak; (in motion) فرلامق fìrlamak, اتلمق àtìlmak; (with a gun) تفنك اتمق tùfènk - àtmak; (with a bow) اوق اتمق òk - àtmak; —, v.a. اولدرمك ùldurmek; یارەلمق yàralamak; اورمق wùrmak; (as a punishment) قورشونه دیزمك kùrshuna - dìzmek; (branches, &c.) سورمك sùrmek; — out, — forth, سورمك sùrmek; — down, v.a. (coals, &c.) دوكمك dùkmek, بوشالتمق bòshaltmak; (a man, ox) اولدرمك ùldurmek, اوروب دوشرمك wùrup-dùshurmek.

Shop, *s.* دكان dùkkyān (dùkkèn), مغازه màghaza ; —, *v.n.* چارشی‌یه كتمك chàrshiya-ghìtmek.

Shopkeeper, *s.* دكانجی dùkkyānji.

Shoplifter, *s.* دكان خرسزی dùkkyān-khìrsizi. [-khìrsizlighi.

Shoplifting, *s.* دكان خرسزلكی dùkkyān-

Shopman, *s.* دكانجی قالفه‌سی dùkkyānji-kàlfassi. [dùkkyānji-kàlfassi-kàri.

Shopwoman, *s.* دكانجی قالفه‌سی قاری

Shore, *s.* ساحل sāhil, دكز كناری dèngiz-kènari, قیی kìyi, یالی yàli ; (prop) پاینده pāyèndé, دستك dèsstek ; —, — up, پاینده اورمق pāyèndé-wùrmak, دستك اورمق dèsstek-wùrmak.

Short, *a.* قصه kìssa, بویسز bòysuz ; (abridged) مختصر mùkhtàssàr, مجمل mùjmèl ; (wanting) اكسك èksik, ناقص nākiss, نقصان nòksān ; to be taken —, چیشی كلمك chìshi-ghèlmek ; to be — of breath, نفس الهمامق nèfess-àlamamak, ضیق النفس او zīku-'n-nèfess-òl (tìk-nèfess-òl) ; in —, *ad.* الحاصل èl-hāssil, القصه èl-kìsssa.

Shortcoming, *s.* قصور kùssūr.

Shorten, *v.a.* قصالتمق kìssàltmak ; —, *v.n.* قصالمق kìssàlmak.

Shorthand, *s.* پك چابك یازیلور برنوع اشارت یازیسی pèk-chàbik-yàzilir-bìr-nèv"i-ìshāret-yàzissi.

Shortly, *ad.* قصه kìssa ; مختصراً mùkhtàssaran ; — after, برازصكره bìr-àz-sòngra, از صكره àz-sòngra, متعقبا mùta-"àkkìban.

Short-sighted, *a.* كوركبی kyùr-ghìbi, كوزی كورمز ghyùzu-ghyùrmàz, قصیرالبصر kàssīru-'l-bàssar ; (morally) قصه دوشنور kìssa-dùshunur, بصیرتسز bàssīrètsiz, فراستسز fèrāssètsiz.

Shot, *s.* صاچمه sàchma ; كله ghyullé ; قورشون kùrshun ; آتش àtish, اتم àtim ; اتلش àtìlish, اتلمه àtìlma ; اتار àtar, اتیجی àtiji, نشانجی nìshànji ; حساب hìssāb ; small —, صاچمه sàchma ; gun— wound, قورشون یاره‌سی kùrshun-yārassi.

Should, *v. aux.* See Grammar.

Shoulder, *s.* اوموز òmuz (òmz) ; —, *v.a.* اوموزلمق òmuzlamak, اوموزینه اورمق òmuzina-wùrmak, اوموزینه المق òmuzina-àlmak ; — blade, — bone, كورك kyùrek, كتف kètf (*pl.* اكتاف èktāf) ; — arms ! دیوان دور dīwàn-dùr.

Shout, *s.* صیحه sàyha, فریاد fèryād, ولوله vèvélé, باغرش bàghirish, جاغرش chàghirish ; باغرشمه bàghirishma, چاغرشمه chàghirishma ; —, — out, باغرمق bàghirmak, چاغرمق chàghirmak ; (together or repeatedly) باغرشمق bàghirishmak, چاغرشمق chàghirishmak.

Shove, *s.* قاقش kàkish, ایتش ìtish ; —, *v.a.* (move) قاقمق kàkmak, ایتمك ìtmek, سورمك sùrmek ; (without moving) دورتمك dùrtmek.

Shovel, *s.* كورك kyùrèk ; —, *v.a.* كوركله‌اتمق kyùrèkla-àtmak.

Show, *s.* كوسترش ghyùsstèrish ; كورنش

ghyùrunush; سیر sèyr; —, *v.a.* کوسترمك ghyùsstɛrmek; اراءه ا ìrā'ɛ-et, ابرازا ìbrāz-et.

Shower, *s.* خفیف یاغمور khāfīf-yàgh-mūr; heavy —, سرت یاغمور sèrt-yàghmur; صاغناق sàghanak; —, *v.a.* یاغمق yàghmak; یاغدرمق yàghdirmak. [پارلاق pàrlàk.

Showy, *a.* کوسترشلو ghyùsstérishli;

Shrapnell shell, *s.* بر نوع خمبره bìr-nev''i-khùmbara.

Shred, *s.* دیلم dìlim, کسندی kèssindi, پارچه pàrcha; —, *v.a.* دتمك dìtmek.

Shrewd, *a.* شیطان shèytān, جن عقللو jìnn-''akkli, درایتلو dìrāyetli, فراستلو fèrāssètli.

Shriek, *s.* صیحه sàyha, فریاد fèryād; —, *v.n.* باغرمق bàghirmak, فریاد ا fèryād-et.

Shrill, *a.* دیك dìk, اینجه ìnja.

Shrimp, *s.* تكه tèkɛ.

Shrink, *v.n.* چكلمك chèkilmek, قصالمق kìssAlmak; بوزلمك bùzulmek; —, *v.a.* اصلادوب چكدرمك ìsslAdip-chèkdirmek; — from, چكنمك chèkinmek, قورقمق kòrkmak.

Shrivel, *v.n.* بوزلمك bùzulmek.

Shroud, *s.* كفن kèfen (kèfin); (of a mast) چارمیخ chàrmīkh; —, *v.a.* صارمق sàrmak, اورتمك ùrtmek, تكفین ا tèkfīn-et.

Shrub, *s.* اغاج Aghaj, چالی chAli.

Shrug, *s.* قالدرش kAldirish; —, — up, *v.a.* قالدرمق kAldirmak.

Shudder, *v.n.* تویلری اورپرمك tùyléri-ùrpɛrmek; قانی صوغومق kAni-sòghumak.

Shuffle, *v.a.* (mix) قارشدرمق kArishdirmak; —, *v.n.* حیله ا hīlɛ-et; یلان سویلمك yàlAn-sùwèylɛmek.

Shun, *v.a.* قاچنمق kAchinmak.

Shut, *a.* قپالو kApAli; —, *v.a.* قپامق kApamak, سد ا sèdd-et; —, *v.n.* قپانمق kApAnmak; — in, ایچرو قپامق ìchèri-kApAmak; — out, طیشاری براقمق dìshàri-brAkmak; — up, قپامق kApAmak.

Shutter, *s.* قناد kAnAd, كپنك kèpenk.

Shy, *s.* اوطانور ùtAnir, اوطانغاج ùtAnghàj; (horse) اوركك ùrkèk; —, *v.n.* اوركمك ùrkmek.

Sicily, *s.* سیجیلیه اطهسی sìcilia-Adassi.

Sick, *a.* خسته khAssta, كیفسز kèyfsiz, مریض màrīz; to be —, قوصمق kùssmak, استفراغ ا ìsstifrāgh-et, قی كتورمك kàyy-ghètirmek, قی ا kàyy-et.

Sicken, *v.n.* خسته لنمق khAsstalanmak, كیفسز او kèyfsiz-òl; —, *v.a.* بزدرمك bèzdirmek. [محصد mìhsAd.

Sickle, *s.* اوراق òrAk, داس dāss,

Sickness, *s.* كیفسزلك kèyfsizlik, خسته لق khàsstalik, علت ''ìllèt, مرض màraz, درد dèrd; قی kàyy, استفراغ ìsstifrāgh, قوصمه kùsssma; sea —, دكز طوتمسی dèngiz-tùtmassi.

Side, *s.* یان yàn, طرف tàraf, جانب jānib, سو sū; (of the body) جنب jènb; —, *v.n.* دن یانه او dan-yàna-òl,

طرفنی طوتمق tàrafini-tŭtmak, طرفدار او tàrafdār-ŏl.

Side-saddle, *s.* قاری ایری kàri-èyeri.

Siege, *s.* محاصره mŭhāssara.

Sieve, *s.* الك èlek, قالبور kālbur.

Sift, *v.a.* الهمك èlémek, قالبوردن کچورمك kālburdan-ghèchirmek; (any one) اغزندن لاقردی المغه باقمق āghzindan-làkirdi-ālmagha-bākmak; — out, ارایوب بولمق ārayip-bŭlmak, اکلامق ànglamak (ànnamak).

Sigh, *s.* آه àh; —, *v.n.* آه چکمك àh-chèkmek; — for, پك استمك pèk-ìsstémek; ارامق āramak, حسرت چکمك hàssret-chèkmek, تحسر ا tàhàsssur-et; — to, قولاغنه آه دیمك kŭlāghina-àh-dèmek, عاشق او "āshik-ŏl.

Sight, *s.* بصر bāssar, قوت بصر kŭvvèti-bāssar; نظر nāzar, مشاهده mùshāhédé; سیر sèyr, کورینه جك شی ghyùrunéjek-shèy; کورینان شی ghyùrunen-shèy; in —, کورنیور ghyùruniyor, کوزکیور ghyùzukiyor, میدانده mèydānda; in one's —, کوزی اوکنده ghyùzu-ùngunda; — of a gun, نشانکاه nìshānghyāh.

Sign, *s.* اشارت ìshāret; علامت "àlāmèt; (of zodiac) برج bŭrj; —, *v.a.* امضا ا ìmzā-et; —, *v.n.* اشارت ا ìshāret-et; — manual, امضا ìmzā.

Signal, *s.* اشارت ìshāret; —, *a.* باهر bāhir, ظاهر zāhir; —, *v.n.* اشارت ا ìshāret-et.

Signature, *s.* امضا ìmzā.

Signet, *s.* مهر mùhr.

Significance, *s.* معنادارلق mà"nadārlik.

Significant, *a.* معنادار mà"nadār.

Signification, *s.* معنی mà"nà.

Signify, *v.a.* دیمك dèmek, دلالت ا dèlālet-et, معناسی او mà"nàssi-ŏl; —, *v.n.* ضرری او zàrari"-ŏl.

Sign-post, *s.* یول کوسترمك ایچون دیکلمش دیرك yòl-ghyùsstermek-ìchin-dìkilmish-dīrèk.

Silence, *s.* سکوت sùkyūt; —, *v.a.* صوصدرمق sŭssdurmak, اسکات ا ìsskyāt-et; —! *int.* صوص sŭss.

Silent, *a.* صوص sŭss, ساکت sākit; سسسز sèsssiz, صداسز sādāsiz.

Silk, *s.* ایپك ìpèk, حریر hàrīr; (sowing) ابریشیم ìbrishim; (stuff) جانفس jān-fèss (jàmfèss).

Silkworm, *s.* ایپك بوجکی ìpèk-bùjeghi.

Silky, *a.* ایپك کبی ìpèk-ghìbi.

Sill, *s.* اشك èshik, الت اشیکی āltèshighi.

Silly, *a.* عقلسز "āklsiz, بوداله bŭdāla; چوجقلق chòjukluk; معناسز mà"nàssiz.

Silver, *s.* کموش *or* کومش ghyùmush, سیم sīm, فضه fìdda, نقره nŭkra; (of looking-glasses) سر sìrr; —, *v.a.* کومش ایله یالدزلمق ghyùmush-ìla-yāldizlamak; (looking-glasses) سر چکمك sìrr-chèkmek, سرلمق sìrr-lamak; —smith, قویومجی kùyumju.

Similar, *a.* بکزر bèngzer, مشابه mùshābih, شبیه shèbīh, مماثل mùmāssil.

Similarity, *s.* مشابهت mùshābéhèt.

Simile, *s.* تجنيس tèjnīss, مثال mìssāl, تشبيه tèshbīh, تمثيل tèmsīl.

Similitude, *s.* مشابهت mùshābéhèt; صورت sūrèt, هيئت hèy'èt.

Simple, *a.* ساده sādé; عادى "ādī, بياغى bàyaghi; (in mind) سادهدل sādé-dìl; —, *s.* قوجه قارى علاجى kòja-kàri-"ìlāji.

Simplicity, *s.* سادهلك sādélik; قولايلق kòlaylik.

Sin, *s.* كناه ghyùnāh, معصيت mà"sìyyèt, اثم ìssm (*pl.* اثام āssām), سوء عمل sù'i-"àmel; —, *v.n.* كناه ا ghyùnāh-et, كناه ايشلمك ghyùnāh-ìshlémek.

Since, *pr.* دنبرو dan-bèri; —, *c.* چونكه chùnki, مادامكه mādāmki.

Sincere, *a.* صميمى sàmīmī, حقيقى hàkīkī, حقيقتلو hàkīkàtli, خالص khāliss, بيريا bī-rìyā.

Sine, *s.* جيب jèyb; log. —, نسبت جيبيه nìssbèti-jèybìyyé.

Sinew, *s.* سكير sìngir, عصبه "àssaba.

Sinful, *a.* (person) كناهكار ghyùnāhkyār, آثم āssim; (thing) كناه ghyùnāh.

Sing, *v.n.* تركى چاغرمق tùrku-chà-ghirmak; (birds) اوتمك ùtmek; —, *v.a.* مقاملهسويلمك màkāmla-sùwèy-[lémek.

Singer, *s.* خواننده khānèndé.

Single, *a.* (alone) يالكز yàlingiz; تك tèk, تاك tāk; (not double) يالينقات yàlinkat *or* يالڭقات yàlingkat; (unmarried) بيكار bīkyār (bèykyār), مجرد mùjèrred; — out, *v.a.* ايرمق àyrmak, سچمك sèchmek; — life, بيكارلق (bèykyārlik), تجريد tèjrīd, تجرد tèjèrrud.

Singly, *ad.* يالكز yàlingiz, منفرداً mùn-fèridan, تك تك tèk-tèk, برو برو bìrer--bìrer, يكان يكان yèghyān-yèghyān.

Singular, *a.* مفرد mùfrèd; يالكز yàlingiz; غريب ghàrīb, تحاف tùhāf, عجيب ("àjā'ib). [تحافلق tùhāflik.

Singularity, *s.* مفردلك mùfrèdlik,

Sinister, *a.* اوغورسز òghursiz.

Sink, *s.* قرنه kùrna; —, *v.n.* باتمق bàtmak, قينامق kàynamak; —, *v.a.* باترمق bàtirmak; (a well) قازمق kàzmak; (a die) قازمق kàzmak, حك ا hàkk-et. [āssim, عاصى "àssi.

Sinner, *s.* كناهكار ghyùnāhkyār, آثم

Sir, *s.* افندم èfèndim; بك bègh.

Sire, *s.* بابا bàba.

Siren, *s.* جاذبهلو قارى jāzibéli-kàri.

Sirname, *s.* فامليا آدى fāmīlia-àdi.

Sister, *s.* قيزقرنداش kìz-kàrindash (kārdash), همشيره hèmshīré, باجى bàji; eldest —, ابله àbla; wife's —, بالدز bàldiz; husband's —, كورمجه ghyùrumjé.

Sit, *v.n.* اوطورمق òturmak, قعود ا kù"ūd--et; (in council) مجلس عقد ا mèjlīss-"àkd-et; (fowls) قولوچقه يه اوطورمق kùlùchkaya-òturmak; — up; طوغرى اوطورمق dòghru-òturmak; — — late, كيچ اوطورمق ghèch-òturmak; — — all night, بتون كيجه ياتمامق bìtun--ghèyjé-yàtmamak; — in judgment, حاكم او hākim-òl.

Site, *s.* یر yĕr, موقع mèvki'', محل màhàll, موضع mèvzi''.

Situate, Situated, *a.* (place) واقع vāki'', کائن kyā'in, موضوع mèvzū''; (person) حالده hālda; situated as I am, بنم حالمده bènim-hālimda, بنم بولندیغم حالده bènim-bŭlundughum-hālda.

Situation, *s.* (place) موقع mèvki'', موضع mèvzi'', محل màhàll; (moral) حال hāl; هیئت hèy'èt; (employ) یر yĕr, خدمت khìdmet (hìzmet), مأموریت mè'mūrìyyèt.

Six, *a.* التی àlti, ست sìtt, ستة sìtta, شش shèsh.

Sixteen, *a.* اون التی òn-àlti.

Sixth, *a.* التنجی àltinji, سادس sādiss, ششم shèshum; —, *s.* التیده بر àltida-bìr, سدس sŭdss.

Sixty, *a.* التمش àltmish, ستون sìttūn, ستین sìttīn, شصت shàsst.

Size, *s.* بیوکلك bìyukluk, قطعه kàt''à, حجم hàjm; (height) بوی bòy, قامت kāmet, اندام èndām, قد kàdd, بالا bālā; (glue) طوتقال tŭtkal.

Skein, *s.* دمت dèmet.

Skeleton, *s.* قورو kŭru, تشریح tèshrīh; — key, میمونجق màymūnjuk.

Sketch, *s.* طاصلاق رسم tàsslak-rèssim; (in words) قباجه تعریف kàbaja-tà''rīf; —, *v.a.* قباجه رسم ا kàbaja-rèssm-et; قباجه تعریف ا kàbaja-tà''rīf-et.

Skewer, *s.* کباب شیشی kèbāb-shìshi, سیخ sīkh.

Skiff, *s.* خفیف یلکنلو فلوقه khàfīf-yèlkènli-fèlika.

Skilful, *a.* هنرلو hùnerli, معرفتلو mà''ri-fètli, استاد ùsstād (ŭssta), ماهر māhir; (physician) حاذق hāzik.

Skill, *s.* هنر hùner, معرفت mà''rifèt, استادلق (ŭsstalik), مهارت màhāret; (medical) حذاقت hàzākàt.

Skim, *v.a.* یوزندن المق yùzundan-àlmak; یاغنی المق yàghini-àlmak; قایمغنی المق kàymaghini-àlmak; (a book) کوزکزدرمك ghyùz-ghèzdirmek; —, *v.n.* (as a bird) یره همان دوقنه رق اوچمق yĕra (*or* صویه sūya)-hèmen-dòkunarak-ŭchmak; (as a boat) اوچمق ŭchmak.

Skin, *s.* دری dèri, جلد jìld; (animal's) پوست pòsst; sheep —, پوستکی pòsstéki; whole sheep or goat —, طلوم tŭlum; whole ox —, یدك yèdek; —, *v.a.* یوزمك yùzmek, صویمق sòymak, سلخ ا sèlkh-et.

Skip, *v.a.* اتلامق àtlamak; —, *v.n.* صیچرامق sìchramak.

Skirmish, *s.* چرخه جیلرك چاتشمسی chàrkhajìlaring-chàtishmassi; —, *v.n.* چاتشمق chàtishmak.

Skirmisher, *s.* چرخه جیلر chàrkhajiler.

Skirmishing, *s.* چرخه جیلق chàrkha-jilik.

Skirt, *s.* اتك ètek, ذیل zèyl, دامن dāmen; —, *v.a.* جوارنده او jìwārinda-òl, قربنده او kùrbunda-òl.

Skittish, *a.* اورکك ùrkek, اویناق òynàk.

Skulk, *v.n.* ایشدن قاچمق ìshdan-kàch-mak, حیلازلق ا hàylazlìk-et; کزلنمك ghìzlenmek.

Skull, *s.* قفا kàfa.

Sky, *s.* کوك ghyùk, کوك یوزی ghyùk-

-yùzu, سما sèmā (*pl.* سموات sèmā-wāt), اسمان āssmān ; — light, دپه (tèpé)-jàmi ; — rocket, هوائی فشنك hàwā'ī-fishènk (fishèk).

Slab, *s.* پارچه pàrcha, لوحه lèvha, تخته tàkhta.

Slack, *a.* كوشك ghèvshek ; — lime, سونمش كيرج sùnmush-kìrèch ; —, *v.a.* كوشتمك ghèvshetmek ; سوندرمك sùndurmek.

Slacken, *v.n.* كوشمك ghèvshémek ; —, *v.a.* كوشتمك ghèvshetmek.

Slag, *s.* معدن بوقی mà''den-bòku.

Slain, *a.* مقتول maktūl.

Slake, *v.a.* اطفا ا itfā-et.

Slander, *s.* افترا ìftirā, بهتان bùhtān, قذف kazf ; —, *v.a.* افترا ا ìftirā-et.

Slanderer, *s.* افتراجی ìftirāji.

Slanderous, *a.* افترا نشر ايدر اولان ìftirā-nèshr-èder-òlan.

Slang, *s.* چاپقين لسانی chapkin-lìssāni.

Slanting, *a.* اكری èghri, يان yàn, ياتق yàtik, ارقوری àrkuri (àykiri) مائل mā'il.

Slap, *s.* سيلی sīlī (silé), شمار shàmar ; —, *v.a.* شمار اتمق shàmar-atmak ; —, *ad.* تمام tamām.

Slash, *v.a.* كسمك kèssmek.

Slate, *s.* يازی طاشی yàzi-tashi ; سياه مرمر sìyāh-mèrmer.

Slattern, *a.* پك صاپسال قاری pèk-sàpsàl-kari.

Slaughter, *s.* قيرم kìrim, قتل عام katli-''amm ; —, *v.a.* كسمك kèssmek, ذبح ا zìbh-et ; اولدرمك ùldurmek, قتل ا katl-et ; قيرمق kìrmak, هلاك ا hèlāk-et ; —house, سلخخانه sèlkh-khāné (sal-khāné).

Slave, *s.* (male) كوله kyùlé, بنده bèndé, عبد ''àbd ; (female) جاريه jāriyyé, خلائق khalā'ik ; (concubine) اوطه لق òdalik ; — (while on sale) اسير èssīr (yèssir) ; — market, اسير پازاری èssīr-pàzāri (yèssir) ; — dealer, اسيرجی èssīrji (yèssirji) ; —, *v.n.* اسير كبی چالشمق (yèssir)-ghibi-chalishmak.

Slavery, *s.* اسيرلك èssīrlik (yès-), كوله لك kyùlélik, رقيت rìkkìyyèt.

Slay, *v.a.* اولدرمك ùldurmek, قتل ا katl-et, هلاك ا hèlāk-et.

Slayer, *s.* قاتل kātil.

Sledge, *s.* قزاق kìzak ; — hammer, واريوس vàriyoss.

Sleek, *a.* سميز sèmiz, تاولو tàvli.

Sleep, *s.* اويقو ùyku, نوم nèvm, خواب khāb ; —, *v.n.* اويومق ùyumak ; —ing, asleep, اويويور ùyuyor, اويقوده ùykuda, نائم nā'im, خوابيده khābīdé ; —less, اويقوسز ùykussuz.

Sleepy, *a.* اويقوسی كلمش ùykussu-ghèlmish, خواب آلود khāb-ālūd ; (pear) چوروك chùruk.

Sleet, *s.* صولو سپكن sùlu-sèpken ; —, *v.n.* صولو سپكن ياغمق sùlu-sèpken-yàgh-mak ; سپمك sèpmek.

Sleeve, *s.* قول kòl, ين yèn, *or* يك yèng, استين āssitīn, كم kyùmm.

Sleigh, *s.* قزاق kìzak.

Slender, *a.* اينجه ìnja, نارين nàrin, يوفقه yūfka, رقيق ràkīk.

Slice, *s.* دليم dìlim ; —, *v.a.* كسمك kèssmek, دليم دليم كسمك dìlim--dìlim-kèssmek.

Slide, *v.n.* قايمق kàymak ; —, *v.a.* قايدرمق kàydirmak ; —, *s.* كچمه‌قپاق ghèchma-kàpak ; قايله‌جق ير kàyila-jak-yèr.

Slight, *s.* حقارت hàkārèt ; —, *a.* خفيف khāfīf, اينجه ìnja, نارين nàrin ; —, *v.a.* باقمامق bàkmamak, صايمامق sàymamak, حقارت‌ا hàkārèt-et.

Slim, *a.* اينجه ìnja, نارين nàrin.

Slime, *s.* سموك sùmuk ; چامور chàmur.

Sling, *s.* صپان sàpan ; اصقى āsski ; —, *v.a.* صپان ايله اتمق sàpan-ila-àtmak ; اصمق àssmak.

Slip, *s.* قايش kàyish, قايمه kàyma, صورچش sùrchush, زله zèllé ; (of paper) شقه shùkka ; (mistake) ياكلش yàngilish (yànish), سهو sèhv, خطا khàtā ; (for ships) اسكله ìsskèlé ; — of the tongue, اغز ياكلشلغى àghz--yàngilishlighi (yànishlighi) ; —, *v.a.* قايمق kàymak, سورچمك sùrchmek ; —, *v.a.* قايدرمق kàydirmak ; — in, *v.n.* كيريويرمك ghìrivèrmek ; كليويرمك ghèlivèrmek, اوغرايويرمك òghrayivèrmek ; — —, *v.a.* صوقيويرمك sòkuvèrmek ; — out, *v.n.* چيقيويرمك chìkivèrmek ; صاوشيويرمك sàwushuvèrmek ; قاچمق kàchmak ; — —, *v.a.* قاچرمق kàchirmak ; — on, *v.a.* كييويرمك ghìyivèrmek ; — off, *v.a.* چيقاريويرمك chìkàrivèrmek ; — —, *v.n.* چيقيويرمك chìkivèrmek ; صاوشيويرمك sàwushuvèrmek ; — knot, الملك ìlmik. [ترلك tèrlik.

Slipper, *s.* پاپوش pāpūsh (pàbuch) ;

Slippery, *a.* قيار kàyar, قيپاخ kàypàkh.

Slit, *s.* يارق yàrik, يارمه yàrma ; دليك dèlik ; يرتق yìrtik ; يرتماج yìrtmàj ; —, *v.a.* يارمق yàrmak ; يرتمق yìrt-mak ; اچمق àchmak ; شق‌ا shàkk--et ; —, *v.n.* يارلمق yàrilmak ; يرتلمق yìrtilmak. [قوتره kòtra.

Sloop, *s.* قوروت kùrvèt ; ابريق ìbrik ;

Slop, *s.* دوكلن صو dùkyulen-sù ; —, — over, — about, *v.a.* دوكمك dùkmek ; —s, *s. pl.* خسته‌يه يدريلان چوربا موربا khàsstaya - yèdirilen--chòrba - mòrba ; حاضر صاتلان اثواب hāzir-sàtilan-èsswāb (èssbab).

Slope, *s.* شيو shèv ; باير bàyir ; —, — off, *v.a.* المق àlmak, شيو ياپمق shèv--yàpmak. [mā'il.

Sloping, *a.* شيو shèv ; باير bàyir, مائل

Sloth, *s.* تنبللك tènbellik.

Slothful, *a.* تنبل tènbel.

Slothfulness, *s.* تنبللك tènbellik.

Slough, *s.* چامور chàmur ; بتاق bàtak, بتاقلق bàtaklik ; (of a sore) جراحت jèrāhàt ; —, *v.n.* چورويوب جراحت او chùruyup-jèrāhàt-òl.

Sloven, *s.* پس كزن ادم pìss-ghèzen-àdam.

Slow, *a.* اغر àghir, يواش yāwàsh, بطى bàtī ; (watch) كيرو ghèri ; — match, ماهتاب māhitāb, فتيل fitil.

Slug, *s.* قبوقسز سموكلو بوجك kàbuksuz--sùmuklu - bùjek ; قورشون كسنديسى kùrshun-kèssindissi.

Sluggard, *s.* دائما اویور اولان تنبل dā'imā-ùyur-òlan-tènbel. [ùyumak.

Slumber, *s.* اویقو ùyku ; —, *v.n.* اویومق

Sly, *a.* شیطان shèytān, حیله کار hīlé-kyār ; on the —, کیزلو کیزلو ghizli-ghizli, مخفیاً màkhfiyyan.

Smack, *s.* شمار shàmar, سیلی sīlī (silé); لذت lèzzèt ; قوقو kòku ; قایق kàyik ; —, *v.a.* شمار اتمق shàmar-àtmak ; (one's lips) سس ایله اغزینی یالامق sèss-ila-àghzini-yàlamak. [صغیر sàghīr.

Small, *a.* اوفاق ùfāk, کچوك kùchuk,

Smallpox, *s.* چیچك علتی chìchek-'illeti, جدری jùdérī.

Smart, *a.* پارلاقجه کینمش pàrlàkja-ghìyinmish ; پارلاقجه pàrlàkja, جیجیلو jìjili ; تتك tètik, مستعد mùsstà''idd ; سرت sèrt, صیقی sìki ; —, *s.* اجی àji, وجع vèjà'' ; —, *v.n.* اجیمق àjimak.

Smash, *s.* قیرلش kìrilish, پاره لنش pàra-lanish ; (bankruptcy) طوپ اتش tòp-àtish ; —, *v.a.* قیرمق kìrmak, پارچه پارچه ا pàrcha-pàrcha-et.

Smattering, *s.* پك جزئی اولان معلومات pèk-jùz'i-òlan-ma''lūmāt.

Smear, *v.a.* سورمك sùrmek, بولاشدرمق bùlàshdirmak.

Smell, *s.* قوقو kòku, رائحه rā'ihà, بوی būy ; (sense of) قوت شامه kùvvèti-shāmmé ; —, *v.n.* قوقمق kòkmak ; —, *v.a.* قوقلامق kòklamak ; قوقوسنی المق kòkussunu-àlmak ; استشمام ا ìsstishmām-et ; — a rat, حیله سزمك hīlé-sèzmek.

Smelt, *v.a.* معدن قال ا mà''dèn-kàl-et.

Smelter, *s.* قالجی kàlji.

Smelting, *s.* قال kàl.

Smelting-furnace, *s.* قال اوجاغی kàl-òjaghi.

Smelting-works, *s.* قالخانه kàlkhāné.

Smile, *s.* خفیف کولمه khàfīf-ghyùlmé, تبسم tèbèssum ; —, *v.n.* خفیف کولمك khàfīf-ghyùlmek, تبسم ا tèbès-sum-et. [dàrb-et.

Smite, *v.a.* اورمق wùrmak, ضرب ا

Smith, *s.* تیمورجی tīmūrji (dèymirji), حداد hàddād, اهنکر āhenghèr.

Smithy, *s.* تیمورجی دکانی dèymirji-dùkkyāni. [chārpilmish.

Smitten, *a.* افتاده ùftādé ; چارپلمش

Smoke, *s.* تتون tùtun, دومان dùmàn, دخان dùkhān ; —, *v.n.* توتمك tùtmek, دومان ویرمك dùmàn-vèr-mek, دومانی چیقمق dùmàni-chìk-mak ; (tobacco) تتون ایچمك tùtun-ìchmek, چبوق ایچمك chìbùk-ìch-mek ; —, *v.a.* توتسی ویرمك tùtsu-vèrmek, توتسیلمك tùtsulémek, تدخین ا tèdkhīn-et ; دومانه اصمق dùmàna-àssmak.

Smoking, *a.* دومانی چیقان dùmāni-chìkan ; —, *s.* توتون ایچمکلك tùtun-ìchmeklik. [dùmànli.

Smoky, *a.* توتونلو tùtunlu ; دومانلو

Smooth, *a.* دوز dùz, هموار hèmvār.

Smother, *s.* قویو دومان kòyu-dùmàn ; پك صیقلق غلبه لق pèk-sìklik-(kàlabà-lik) ; —, *v.a.* بوغمق bòghmak ; اورتوب باصدرمق ùrtup-bàssdirmak.

Smuggle, *v.a.* کمرکدن قاچرمق

ghyùmrukdan - kAchirmak; کیزلـو کتورمك ghìzli-ghètirmek.

Smuggler, *s.* کمرکدن مال قاچران آدم ghyùmrukdan-māl-kAchiran-AdAm.

Smuggling, *s.* کمرکدن مال قاچرمقلق ghyùmrukdan-māl-kAchirmaklik.

Smut, *s.* قوروم دانه‌سی kùrum-tānéssi.

Smutty, *a.* قوروملو kùrumlu.

Smyrna (town of), *s.* اسمیرشهری èssmir-shèhiri.

Snail, *s.* قبوقلوسموکلوبوجك kAbuklu--sùmuklu-bùjek, صلیانقوس sAlyankòss.

Snake, *s.* یلان yìlAn, حیه hàyyé, مار mār; (of waterpipe) مارپیچ mārpīch (màrpuch).

Snap, *s.* قیرش kìrish; چاقش chàkish; (of necklace, &c.) قوپچه kòpcha; —, *v.n.* قیرلمق kìrìlmak, قوپمق kòpmak; —, *v.a.* قیرمق kìrmak, قوپارمق kòparmak; (a pistol, &c.) چکمك chèkmek, چاقمق chàkmak, صیقمق sìkmak; (one's fingers) پرمق چاتردادمق pàrmak - chàtirdAtmak; (one's fingers in one's face) صقالنه ذوقلنمك کولمك sàkAlìna-ghyùlmek, zèvklEnmek; — up, قاپمق kApmak; — at, اصرمق ìssirmak, اصرمغه چبالمق ìssirmagha-chàbAlamak.

Snare, *s.* توزاق *or* طوزاق tùzAk, دام dām, حباله hìbālé (*pl.* حبائل hàbā'il); حیله hīlé, دسیسه dèssīssé; —, *v.a.* توزاغه طوتمق tùzAgha-tùtmak.

Snarl, *v.n.* خرلامق khìrlamak.

Snatch, *v.a.* قاپمق kApmak.

Sneak, *s.* سینسی sìnsi.

Sneaking, *a.* سنسی کبی sinsi-ghìbi.

Sneer, *s.* استهزا ìsstìhzā, هجو hìjv; —, *v.n.* استهزا ا ìsstìhzā-et, هجو ا hìjv-et.

Sneeze, *s.* اقسرق Aksirik, اقسرش Aksirish, عطسه "Atsa; —, *v.n.* اقسرمق Aksirmak, عطسان ا "AtsAn-et.

Sniff, *s.* قوقلایش kòklayish, شمه shèmmé; —, *v.a.* قوقلامق kòklamak.

Snip, *s.* قرقندی kìrkindi; (tailor) ترزی *or* درزی tèrzi; —, *v.a.* قرقمق kìrkmak, کسمك kèssmek.

Snipe, *s.* یلوه قوشی yèlvé-kùshu, یلوه yèlvé.

Snob, *s.* قوندره‌جی یماغی kùnduraji-yàmaghi; الچق Alchàk.

Snobbish, *a.* الچق Alchàk.

Snot, *s.* سموك sùmuk.

Snout, *s.* بوروون bùrun, انف ènf, بینی bīnī.

Snow, *s.* قار kAr, برف bèrf, ثلج sèlj; —, *v.n.* قار یاغمق kAr-yàghmak; — ball, قار طوپی kAr-tòpu.

Snuff, *s.* انفیه ènfìyyé, سعوط sù"ūt; (of a candle) مومك بورنی mùmung-bùrnu; —, *v.a.* بورننی المق bùrnunu--Almak; — box, انفیه قوطیسی ènfìyyé-kùtussu.

Snuffers, *s. pl.* موم مقاصی mùm-màkassi.

Snug, *a.* راحت rāhat.

So, *ad.* (absolutely) بویله bùylé; شویله shùylé; اویله ùylé, بو وجهله bù-wèjhla; (in comparison) قدر kAdar; —, *c.* بناءعلیه bìnā'an-"àlèyh, بنابرین bìnābèrīn, بو سببدن bù-sèbebdan; so much, بوقدر bù-kAdar, شوقدر shù-kAdar, اولقدر òl(ò)-kAdar; — that, شویله که shùylé-ki.

Soak, *v.a.* صویه قویوب براقمق sùya-

-kòyup-bràkmak, كركى كبى اصلاتمق ghèrèghi - ghìbi - ìsslAtmak ; —, v.n. صودە دوروب كركى كبى اصلانمق sùda-dùrup-ghèrèghi-ghìbi-ìsslAnmak ; — into, ايچنه كچمك ìchina-ghèchmek ; — through, كچمك ghèchmek.

Soap, s. صابون sàbun ; —, v.a. صابونلمق sàbunlamak ; —wort, چوكن chùghen.

Soap-boiler, s. صابون ياپان صابونجى sàbun-yàpan-sàbunji. [-kyùpughu.

Soap-suds, s. صابون كوپوكى sàbun-

Soar, v.n. اوچوپ يوكسكدە دورمق ùchup-yùksekda-dùrmak.

Sob, s. اغلامقدە نفسك شدتله ايچرو چكلمسى Aghlamakda-nèfessing-shìd-dètla - ìchèri - chèkilméssi ; —, v.n. اغلامقدە نفسى ايچرو چكمك Aghla-makda-nèfessi-ìchèri-chèkmek.

Sober, a. (person) ايق àyik ; عقللو "Aklli, عاقل "Akil ; قناعتجى kAnā-"atji ; (thing) قناعتكارانه kAnā"atkyā-ràné ; (colour) دونق dùnuk ; —, v.a. عقلنى باشنه كتورتمك ايلتمق àyiltmak, "Aklini-bAshina-ghètirtmek.

Soberness, Sobriety, s. ايقلق àyiklik.

Sociable, a. انيس ènīss, الوف èlūf, طاتلو tAtli ; —ness, s. انسيت ùnsìyyèt.

Socialism, s. كافهٔ اموالك مشتركاً تصرف اولنمسى اوصولى kyāffé - èmwālin - - mùshtérèkan - tàssàruf - òlunmassi - -ūsūlu.

Socialist, s. اشتراكى اموالك اصولى طرافدارى ìshtirāki - èmwālin - ūsūlu- -tàrafdāri.

Society, s. الفت ùlfèt ; اختلاط ìktilAt ; جمعيت احباب طاقمى àhbāb-tàkimi ; jèm"ìyyèt ; مجلس mèjliss ; (at large) مجالس و محافل mèjāliss-vé-màhāfil.

Sock, s. قصه چوراب kìssa-chòrab.

Socket, s. كچمه دليكى ghèchma-dèlighi, دليك dèlik, ير yer.

Sod, s. چيم chìm.

Soda, s. صودا sòda.

Soda-water, s. صودا واطر sòda-vàter.

Sodom (town of), s. شهر لوط shèhiri-lūt.

Sodomite, s. لوطى lūtī ; غلامپاره [kùlAmbara.

Sodomy, s. لواطه lìwāté.

Soever, pro. هر hèr ; whosoever, هركيم hèr-kìm ; whatsoever, هرنه hèr-nè.

Sofa, s. مندر mìnder ; (European) قناپه kànapé ; raised platform for a —, صدر sAdr (sèdir).

Soft, a. يموشاق yìmùshAk, نرم nèrm ; (water) طاتلو tAtli.

Soften, v.n. يموشامق yìmushamak ; —, v.a. يموشاتمق yìmushAtmak.

Soil, s. (earth) طوپراق or طپراق tòprAk, تراب tùrAb ; (dirt) لكه lèké ; night —, ممشا مزخرفاتى mèmshā-mùzà-khréfAti, —, v.a. كيرلتمك kìrletmek ; —, v.n. كيرلنمك kìrlenmek ; —ed, a. كيرلو kìrli, لكه لو lèkéli.

Sojourn, s. اقامت ìkAmet ; —, v.n. مسافرة قالمق mùssāfiréten - kàlmak, قالمق kAlmak, اوطورمق òturmak, اقامت ا ìkAmet-et, ساكن او sākin-òl, مقيم او mùkīm-òl.

Solace, s. تسلى tèssèlli ; صفا sAfā ; —, v.a. تسلى ويرمك tèssèlli-vèrmek, صفا ويرمك sAfā-vèrmek.

Solar, *a.* شمسی shèmsī ; — system, منظومهٔ شمسیه mAnzūmEi-shèmsìyyÉ.

Solder, *s.* لهیم lèhīm ; —, *v.a.* لهیملمك lèhīmlémek ; —, *v.n.* لهیملنمك lèhīmlEnmek. [نفر nèfEr.

Soldier, *s.* عسكر ‘‘Asskèr ; (private)

Sole, *s.* (foot) طبان tàbAn ; (shoe) كوسله kyùssélÉ ; (fish) دل بالغی dìl-bA-*lighi* (?), پسی بالغی pìssi, pìssi-*-bAlighi* (?) ; — *a.* یالكز yAl*in*g*iz*, باشلو باشنه bAshl*i* - bAsh*in*a, واحد wāhid, احد àhàd ; —, *v.a.* كوسلهسنی اورمق kyùsséléssini-wùrmak.

Solemn, *a.* اغر Aghir ; مكلف mùkèllèf, مطنطن mùtAntàn ; رسمی rèssmī.

Solemnize, *v.a.* رسماً اجرا ا rèssmEn-ìjrā--et ; رسمیاتنی اجرا ا rèssmìyyAtini--ìjrā-et. [mak, نیازا nìyāz-et.

Solicit, *v.a.* رجا ا rìjā-et, یلوارمق yAlvar-

Solicitor, *s.* دعوا وكیلی dà‘‘wa-vèkīlī.

Solicitous, *a.* ارزومند àrzumènd.

Solicitude, *s.* مراق mèrāk ; اشتیاق ìshtiyAk ; خیر خواهانه آرزو khàyr--khāhānÉ-àrzu.

Solid, *a.* یكپاره yèkpārÉ ; مجسم mùjès-sem ; قونت kùnt, قالین kAl*in*, اغر Agh*ir* ; محكم mùhkèm, متین mètīn, قوی kàwī, مستحكم mùsstàhkEm ; —, *s.* جسم jìssm.

Soliloquize, *v.n.* كندی كندینه سویلنمك kèndi-kèndinÉ-s*ù*wèylEnmek.

Soliloquy, *s.* كندی كندینه سویلنلان كلام kèndi-kèndinÉ-suweylenilan-kèlām.

Solitary, *a.* تنها tènhā, یالكز yAl*in*g*iz*, یاپه یالكز yàp*a*-yAl*in*g*iz* ; اسسز ìsss*iz*.

Solitude, *s.* تنهالق tènhāl*ik*, یالكزلق yAl*in*g*iz*l*ik* ; بیابان bèyābAn, اسسزیر ìsssiz-yèr.

Solomon, *s.* سلیمان sùlèymAn.

Solstice, *s.* انقلاب ìnk*i*lAb ; summer —, انقلاب سرطان ìnk*i*lAb*i*-sèratAn ; winter —, انقلاب جدی ìnk*i*lAb*i*-jèdī.

Solution, *s.* حل hàll.

Solve, *v.a.* حل ا hàll-et.

Solvency, *s.* بالجمله بورجلرینی ادایه اقتدار bì'l - jùmlÉ - bòrjlerini - èdāy*a*--ìkt*i*dār.

Solvent, *a.* بالجمله بورجلرینی ادایه مقتدر bì'l-jùmlÉ-bòrjlerini-èdāy*a*-mùktèdir.

Sombre, *a.* قویو kòyu ; قرانلق kAranl*i*k.

Some, *a.* (one) بر bìr ; (few) بعض bA‘‘*zi* ; (quantity) براز bìr-Az, برمقدار bìr-mìkdàr; (number) برقاچ bìr-kAch ; —body, — one, — person, بری bìri, بریسی bìrissi, برادم bìr-Adam, بر كمسنه bìr-kìmèssnÉ ; — how, بردرلو bìr-(tùrlu) ; — thing, برشی bìr-shèy ; — time, مقدما mùkàddémā, سابقا sāb*i*kā ; — times, بعضاً bA‘‘zan, بعض كره bA‘‘*zi* - kèrrÉ, — what, بعض مرتبه bA‘‘*zi*-mèrtébÉ ; — where, بر یره bìr-yèr*a* ; بر یرده bìr-yèrd*a*.

Son, *s.* اوغل òghul ; مخدوم màkhdūm ; — of, اوغلی òghlu, ابن ìbni, زاده zādÉ ; — in-law, داماد dāmād ; step —, اویكی اوغل ùwèghi-òghul.

Song, *s.* تركی tùrku, شرقی shàrk*i*, مانی mān*i*.

Soon, *ad.* چابك chàb*i*k, تیز tīz (tèz) ; I would *as soon* stay *as* go,

كتمك ايله قالمق بكا بردر ghìtmek--ila-kÀlmak-bÀnga-bìr-dir; I would *sooner* stay than go, كتمكدن ايسه قالمق بكا يكدر ghìtmekdan-issa-kÀlmak-[bÀnga-yègh-dir.

Soot, *s.* ايس ìss.

Sooth, *s.* حقيقت hÀkīkÀt; in —, in good —, حقيقت hÀkīkÀt, فى الحقيقه fī'l-hÀkīka.

Soothe, *v.a.* تسكين ا tèsskīn-et.

Sophism, *s.* سفسطه sÀfsÀta.

Sophist, *s.* سفسطه جى sÀfsÀtaji.

Sophistry, *s.* سفسطه sÀfsÀta.

Sorcerer, *m.* **Sorceress**, *f. s.* جادى jÀdi, سحرباز sìhrbāz, بوكوجى bùghuju *or* بويوجى bùyuju. [bùyu.

Sorcery, *s.* سحر sìhr, بوكو bùghu *or* بويو

Sordid, *a.* چنكانه (chìnghèni), دنى dènī.

Sore, *a.* اجر Àjir, وجيع vèjī'; دارغين dàrghin, جانى صيقلمش jāni-sìkil-mish; —, *s.* ياره yàra, زخم zàkhm, جرح jùrh; — throat, بوغاز bòghāz, خناق khùnnāk.

Sorrel, *s.* قوزى قولاغى kùzu-kùlÀghi.

Sorrow, *s.* كدر kèder, الم èlem, درد dèrd, قساوت kÀssāvèt, تأسف tè'èsssuf, غم ghÀm, اندوه èndūh.

Sorrowful, *a.* مكدر mùkèddèr, غمناك ghÀmmnāk.

Sorry, *a.* مكدر mùkèdder, متأسف mùté'èsssif; فنا fèna, مسكين miss-kīn.

Sort, *s.* درلو dùrlu (tùrlu), صوى sòy, جنس jìnss, نوع nèv'; —, *v.a.* ايرمق àyrmak, جنس جنس ايرمق jìnss-jìnss-àyrmak; —, *v.n.* اويمق ùymak, يراشمق yàrashmak.

Sortie, *s.* محاصره اولنان عسكرك طيشارى يه بر هجومى mùhÀssara-òlunan-'Asskerin-dìshàriyyé-bìr-hùjūmi.

Sot, *s.* بكرى bèkrī; —, *v.n.* ايچوب ايچوب سرخوش اولمق ìchub-ìchub--sèrkhòsh-òlmak.

Soul, *s.* جان jÀn, روح rūh, جنان jènān.

Sound, *s.* سس sèss, صدا sÀdā, آواز āwāz; (gulf) كورفز kyùrfez, خليج khàlīj; —, *a.* صاغ sàgh, صاغلم sàghlàm; ايو īyi; قوى kàwī; دنج dìnj; محكم mùhkèm; (sleep) اغر Àghir, درين dèrin; —, *v.a.* چالمق chÀlmak, ضرب ا dàrb-et, اوتدرمك ùtdurmek; (depth, &c.) اسقنديل ا ìsskÀndīl-et; (persons) اغزينى يوقلمق Àghzini-yòklamak; —, *v.n.* اوتمك ùtmek, سس ويرمك sèss-vèrmek.

Soundings, *s. pl.* اسقانديل ايله تحقيق اولنان صو درينلكى ìsskÀndīl-ìla-tàhkīk--òlunan-sū-dèrinlighi; to take —, اسقانديل اتمق ìsskàndīl-Àtmak.

Soup, *s.* چوربا chòrba.

Sour, *a.* اكشى èkshi, ترش tùrsh; —ish, *a.* مايخوش màykhòsh.

Source, *s.* پيكار pùnàr, پيكار باشى pùnàr-bÀshi, منبع mènbā'.

South, *s.* جنوب jènūb, قبله kìbla; —, *a.* جنوبى jènūbī; — east, كششلمه kèshishlémé.

Southerly, *a.* and *ad.* قبله كبى kìbla-ghìbi.

Southern, *a.* جنوبى jènūbī.

Southernwood, *s.* كافوريه kyāfūriyyé.

Southward, *a.* and *ad.* قبله‌يه طوغری kìblaya-dòghrʊ.

South-west, *s.* لدوس lòdoss.

South-wester, *s.* لدوس lòdoss; لدوس روزكاری lòdoss-rūzghyāri. [ghìbi.

South-westerly, *a.* لدوس كبی lòdoss-

South-western, *a.* لدوس . طرفنده واقع lòdoss-tàrafinda-vwāki.

Sovereign, *s.* پادشاه pādishāh, حكمدار hùkmdār; (coin) ليره lìra; —, *a.* مستقل mùsstàkill.

Sovereignty, *s.* حكومت hùkyūmèt; ملكيت mìlkìyyèt; استقلال ìsstiklāl, استبداد ìsstibdād; دولت dèvlet.

Sow, *s.* ديشی طوكز dìshi-dònguz (dòmuz); —, *v.a.* اكمك èkmek, زرع ا zèr''-et.

Space, *s.* ير yèr; محل màhàll, مكان mèkyān; ميدان mèydān; open —, اچق‌ير àchik-yèr, اچق ميدان àchik-mèydān; ارالق àralik; absolute —, خلا وملا khàlā-u-mèlā; absolute vacant —, خلا khàlā; — of time, مدت mùddèt, ارالق àralik.

Spacious, *a.* كنش ghènish, واسع wāssi'', وسعتلو vùss''àtli, اچق àchik.

Spade, *s.* بل bèl, كورك kyùrèk.

Spain, *s.* اسپانيا ìsspānia.

Span, *s.* قارش kàrish; (of thumb and fore-finger) سره sèrè; (of an arch) كمر kèmer, اچقلق àchiklik, وتر wèter; (of life) مدت mùddèt; —, *v.a.* قارشلامق kàrishlamak; اوستنده كمركنی دورمق ùsstunda-kèmer-ghibi-dùrmak; احاطه ا ìhāta-et, المق àlmak; — new, spick and — new, يپ‌يكی yèp-yèngi, جديد و مجدد jèdīd-u-mùjèdded.

Spangle, *s.* پول pūl.

Spaniard, *s.* اسپانيالو ìsspānìali.

Spanish, *a.* اسپانيالو ìsspānìali; —, *s.* اسپانيولجه ìsspānìoljé.

Spanish fly, *s.* قندوز بوجكی kùnduz-bùjèghi; — liquorice, ميان بالی mìyān-bàli.

Spanker, *s.* (sail) رانده rànda.

Spar, *s.* (timber) سرن sèren; چبوق chìbùk; (mineral) معدن طاشی mà''den-tàshi; —, *v.a.* مشته تعليمنی ا mùshta-tà''līmini-et.

Spare, *a.* (extra) يدك yèdek, يدكلك yèdeklik; (superabundant) فضله fàzla; بوش bòsh, بوشده bòshda; (lean) ضعيف zà''īf, زبون zàbun, (diet) يوان yàwan, ياغسز yàghsiz; —, *v.a.* عفو ا ''àfv-et, بخش ا bàksh-et, باغشلمق bàghishlamak; اداره‌لو قوللانمق ìdàréli-kùllànmak; اسركمك èssirghémek; ويرمك vèrmek, ويره‌بلمك vèré-bilmek.

Spark, *s.* قغلجيم kìghìljim, شراره shèrāré; (beau) حوپه hòppa.

Sparkle, *v.n.* پارلامق pàrlamak, پرلدامق pìrildamak.

Sparrow, *s.* سرچه sèrché, سرچه قوشی sèrche-kùshu, عصفور ''àssfūr, كنجشك kyùnjìshk; — hawk, اتمجه [àtmaja.

Sparse, *a.* سيرك sèyrèk.

Sparseness, *s.* سيركلك sèyrèklik.

Spasm, *s.* اسپازموس ìsspāzmūss.

Spatula, *s.* مبلق mȁblȁk.

Spavin, *s.* شیش shìsh.

Spawn, *s.* بالق یمورطه سی bȁlik-yìmur-tassi; —, *v.n.* and *a.* یمورطلمق yìmurtlamak.

Speak, *v.n.* لقردی ا làkirdi-et, تکلم ا tèkèllum-et; —, *v.a.* سویلمك sùwèylémek, دیمك dèmek.

Speaker, *s.* سویلیان ادم sùwèyléyan-ȁdam; نطق ایدر اولان ادم nùtk-èder-òlan-ȁdam; رئیس rè'īss.

Speaking-trumpet, *s.* اغز بوریسی ȁghz-bòrussu.

Spear, *s.* مزراق mìzrȁk, غرغی ghàrghi, نیزه nīzé; —, *v.a.* مزراقله اورمق mìzrȁkla-wùrmak.

Special, *a.* خاص khāsss, مخصوص màkh-sūss, مختص mùkhtȁsss; خصوصی khùssūssī.

Speciality, *s.* خصوصیت khùssūssìyyèt; علم مخصوص "ìlmi-màkhsūss, فن مخصوص fènni-màkhsūss, صنعت مخصوصه sàn"àti-màkhsūssa.

Specially, *ad.* خصوصا khùssūssā, علی الخصوص "àlé-'l-khùssūss.

Specie, *s.* نقد nȁkd.

Species, *s.* نوع nèv".

Specify, *v.a.* تخصیص ا tàkhsīss-et, تعیین ا tà"yīn-et.

Specimen, *s.* نمونه nùmūné. [zèrré.

Speck, *s.* لکه lèké; نقطه nòkta; ذره

Spectacle, *s.* سیر sèyr; سیره شایان نسنه sèyra-shāyān-nèssné; —s, *s. pl.* کوزلك ghyùzluk. [شاهد shāhid.

Spectator, *s.* سیرجی sèyrji; ناظر nāzir,

Spectre, *s.* خیاله khàyālé.

Speech, *s.* نطق nùtk; قوت ناطقه kùvvèti-nȁtika; تکلم tèkèllum.

Speed, *s.* کیدش ghìdish, سرعت sùr"àt; —, *v.a.* صاغلق ویرمك sàgh-lik-vèrmek; —, *v.n.* کتمك ghìt-mek, چابك کتمك chàbik-ghìt-mek; full — (of a horse) طولو دیزکین dòlu-dìzghin.

Speedily, *ad.* چابك chàbik.

Speedy, *a.* چابك chàbik.

Spell, *s.* بوکو bùghu *or* بویو bùyu, افسانه èfsāné, افسون èfsūn; —, *v.a.* املاسنی سویلمك ìmlāssini-sùwèy-lémek, املاسنی یازمق ìmlāssini-yàzmāk; هجالمك hèjélémek.

Spend, *v.a.* خرج ا khàrj-et, صرف ا sàrf-et, مصرف ا màssraf-et, بذل ا bèzl-et; (time) کچورمك ghèchirmek, امرار ا ìmrār-et; — itself, حزینی المق hìzini-ȁlmak, قوتی قالمامق kùvvèti-kȁlmamak; —, *v.n.* بلی کلمك bèli-ghèlmek, نفسی کلمك nèfssi-ghèl-mek, منی انزال ا mèny-ìnzāl-et.

Spendthrift, *s.* مسرف mùssrif, میراث یدی mīrȁss-yèdi. [nùtfé.

Sperm, *s.* منی mèny, نفس nèfss, نطفه

Spermaceti, *s.* بالق نفسی bȁlik-nèfssi.

Sphere, *s.* کره kyùré; فلك fèlek; دائره

Spherical, *a.* کروی kyùrévī. [dā'iré.

Spherics, *s. pl.* کرویات kaùrévìyyȁt.

Spice, *s.* بهار bàhār; (touch) مایه māyé, قوقو kòku.

Spider, *s.* اورمجك ùrumjèk, عنکبوت "ànkébūt; —'s web, اورمجك اغی

ùrumjèk-àghi, تارعنكبوت. tāri-"ànkébūt.

Spike, *s.* انكسر ènkser; —, *v.a.* انكسرچاقمق ènkser-chàkmak.

Spill, *v.a.* دوكمك dùkmek; —, *v.n.* دوكلمك dùkyulmek.

Spin, *v.a.* اكرمك èghirmek, اغزال ا ìghzāl-et; —, *v.n.* دونمك dùnmek, فرلدانمق fìrìldanmak; (silkworms) ايپك حاصل ا ìpèk-hāssil-et.

Spinach, *s.* اسپناك isspànāk, اسفناج issfināj.

Spindle, *s.* ايك ìgh; ميل mīl.

Spine, *s.* ارقه‌كميكی àrka-kèmighi, اوكرغه òngurgha (òmurgha).

Spinning-wheel, *s.* چقرق chìkrik.

Spiral, *a.* هلزونی hèlézònī; — line, *s.* هلزون hèlézon.

Spire, *s.* قله kùllé (kùlé), مناره mìnāré; مناره كلاهی mìnāré-kyùlāhi.

Spirit, *s.* روح rūh; spirits, ارواح èrwāh; روح rūh, عرق "àrak, راقی ràki.

Spiritual, *a.* روحانی rūhānī; معنوی mà"névī. [dan.

Spirituous, *a.* عرق نوعندن "àrak-nèv"in-

Spirt, *s.* اتش àtish, فشقرش fìshkirish; —, *v.n.* اتمق àtmak, فشقرمق fìsh-kirmak.

Spit, *s.* كباب شيشی kèbāb-shìshi, سيخ sīkh; (of land) دل dil; —, *v.n.* توكرمك tùkyurmek.

Spite, *s.* نفسانيت nèfsānìyyèt; —, *v.a.* نفسانيت ا nèfsānìyyèt-et; in — of, هيچ باقميه‌رق hìch-bàkmayarak; in — of him, اكا رغماً ànga-ràghman.

Spittle, *s.* توكرك tùkruk.

Splash, *s.* زيفوس zìfoss; —, *v.a.* اوستنه چامورصچراتمق ùsstuna-chàmur-sìchratmak; —, *v.n.* چامور صچراتمق chàmur-sichratmak.

Spleen, *s.* (organ) دلاق dàlak; (passion) قره‌سودا kàra-sèvdā; غضب ghàzab; مراق mèrāk, اوصانج ùssànj, جان صيقنديسی jān-sìkindissi.

Splendid, *a.* رعنا rà"nà, پك اعلا pèk-à"là.

Splendour, *s.* رونق rèvnàk, سلطنت sàltanàt, طنطنه tàntana, دبدبه dèb-débé. [*v.a.* اكلمك èklémek.

Splice, *s.* الك èk, الك يری èk-yèri; —,

Splint, *s.* قيرقجی اغاجی kìrikji-àghaji.

Splinter, *s.* خرده khùrda; اغاج قيرنديسی àghaj-kìrindìssi, خمبره قيرنديسی (kùmbara)-kìrindissi; —, *v.n.* قيرنديسی حاصل او kìrindissi-hāssil-òl; —, *v.a.* خرد ا khùrd-et, خردوخاش ا khùrd-u-khāsh-et.

Split, *s.* يارق yàrik; —, *v.a.* يارمق yàrmak, چاك ا chāk-et; —, *v.n.* يارلمق yàrilmak, چاتلامق chàtlamak.

Spoil, *s.* يغما yàghma, غنيمت ghànī-mèt (*pl.* غنائم ghànā'im), سلب sèleb; —, *v.n.* بوزلمق bòzulmak; —, *v.a.* بوزمق bòzmak; صويمق sòy-mak, يغما ا yàghma-et, غارت ا ghāret-et; نهب ا nèhb-et, سلب ا sèlb-et.

Spoke, *s.* تكرلك پرمغی tèkerlèk-pàrmaghi, پرمق pàrmak; I'll put a — in his wheel, بن اكا براويون بيارم bèn-ànga-bir-òyun-yàpàrim, بن اكابر

طولاب چویررم bèn-ȧnga-bìr-dòlap-chèvirirím.

Spoliate, *v.a.* نهب و غارت ا nèhb-u-ghāret-et, صویمق sòymak.

Spoliation, *s.* صویغون sòyghun.

Sponge, *s.* سونكر sùngher.

Sponsor, *s.* كفيل kèfīl.

Spontaneous, *a.* كندی كندينه ظهور ايدن kèndi-kèndina-zùhūr-èden.

Spoon, *s.* قاشق kȧshik.

Spoonful, *s.* قاشق kȧshik, قاشق طولوسی kȧshik-dòlussu.

Sport, *s.* اويون òyun, اكلنجه èylènja; آو ȧv, شكار shikyār, صيد sàyd, صيادت siyādèt; —, *v.a.* اوينامق òynamak, اويناشمق òynashmak; آوه كتمك ȧva-ghìtmek.

Sportsman, *s.* آوجی ȧvji.

Sportsmanship, *s.* اوجيلق ȧvjilik.

Spot, *s.* لكه lèkè; نقطه nòkta, بنك bènek; یر yèr, محل màhàll, موقع mèvki''; —, *v.a.* لكه ا lèkè-et; —, *v.n.* لكه لنمك lèkèlenmek; on the —, محلنده màhàllinda; اول محلده òl-màhàllda; طورديغی يرده dùrdughu-yèrda; آنيده ānīda, او ساعت ò-sā''àt, هماندم hèmāndèm.

Spotless, *a.* لكه سز lèkèsiz; پاك pāk.

Spotlessness, *s.* لكه سزلك lèkèsizlik; پاكی pākī.

Spotted, *a.* لكه لو lèkèli, بنكلو bènekli.

Spotty, *a.* بنكلو bènekli.

Spouse, *s.* زوج zèvj, قوجه kòja; زوجه zèvjè, قاری kȧri.

Spout, *s.* امزك èmzik, غاغا ghàgha, بورون bùrun, اغز ȧghz; (pipe) اولوق òluk; —, *v.n.* فشقرمق fishkirmak; —, *v.a.* فشقرتمق fishkirt-mak.

Sprain, *s.* بورقلش bùrkulush; —, *v.a.* بورقيتمق bùrkutmak; to be sprained, بورقلمق bùrkulmak.

Sprat, *s.* حمسی بالغی hàmsi-bȧlighi, حمسی hàmsi, *or* خمسی khàmsi.

Spray, *s.* (wood) دال dȧl, اينجه دال ìnja-dȧl; (froth) دكزك يغمور كبی فرلايان كپوكی dèngizing-yàghmur-ghìbi-firlayan-kyùpughu.

Spread, *v.a.* يايمق yàymak; سرمك sèrmek; بسط ا bȧsst-et; نشر ا nèshr-et; —, *v.n.* يايلمق yàyilmak; سرايت ا sirāyèt-et.

Sprig, *s.* اينجه دال ìnja-dāl.

Sprightly, *a.* شنشوخ shènshūkh, فراح fèrāh, مفرح mùferrih.

Spring, *s.* (season) بهار bàhār, اول بهار èvvel-bàhār, الك بهار ìlk-bàhār; (water) پيكار (pùngàr), پيكارباشی (pùngàr)-bȧshi, صوباشی sù-bȧshi, ايازمه àyàzma, سرچشمه sèr-chèshmè, منبع mènbà'', ينبوع yènbū''; (lock) ياى yày; (watch) زنبرك zènbèrek; (jump) صچرايش sichrayish, اتلش ȧtilish; —, *v.n.* صچرامق sichramak; اتلمق ȧtilmak; فرلامق firlamak; نشئت ا nèsh'èt-et, نبع ا nèb''-et; حاصل او hāssil-òl, ترتب ا tèrèttub-et; —, *v.a.* (a mine) اتمق ȧtmak; (a mast) سقط ا sàkat-et; — a leak, صوايتمكه باشلامق sù-ètméghè-bȧshlamak; — up (as plants), سورمك sùrmek, چيقمق chìkmak.

Sprinkle, v.a. and n. سرپمك sèrpmek; —, s. سرپش sèrpish.

Sprout, s. طمروق tòmruk, طمروجق tòmrujuk, فلز fìliz; —, v.n. فلزسورمك fìliz--sùrmek, فلزلنمك fìlizlenmek; چيقمق chìkmak, سورمك sùrmek.

Spun, a. اكرلمش èghirilmish.

Spur, s. مهمز (māhmuz); (mountain) قول kòl; —, v.a. مهمزلمق màhmuzlamak; تشويق ا tèshvīk-et, دورتشدرمك dùrtushdurmek; on the — of the moment, بالبداهه bì-'l-bìdāhé, وهله اولاده vèhlè'i-ūlàda.

Spurious, a. ساخته sàkhta, يلان yàlan.

Spuriousness, s. قالپلق kàlplik.

Spurn, v.a. يوزينه باقميوب حقارتله دفع ا yùzuna-bàkmayup-hàkārètla-dèf''-et.

Spy, s. جاسوس jāssūss (shàshid); —, v.n. جاسوسلق ا jāssūsslùk-et (shàshidlik); — glass, دوربين dūrbīn (dùrbun).

Squabble, s. بوقدن نزاع bòkdan-nìzā''; —, v.n. بوقدن نزاع ا bòkdan-nìzā''-et.

Squad, s. طاقم tàkim.

Squadron, s. (ships) دوننما dònanma, اينجه دوننما ìnja-dònanma; (horse) بلوك bùluk.

Squall, s. (wind) بوره bòra; (child's) كچوك چوجغك فريادى kùchuk-chòjughung-fèryādi; —, v.n. فرياد ا fèryād-et, اغلامق aghlamak.

Squander, v.a. اسراف ا ìssrāf-et, تلف ا tèlef-et.

Square, s. مربع mùrèbbà''; (houses) ميدان mèydān; (carpenter's) كونيه ghyùnya; —, a. طوغرى dòghru, كونيه ghyùnya.; درت كوشه dùrt-kyùshé; —, v.n. اويمق ùymak, طوغرى كلمك dòghru-ghèlmek; — accounts, v.a. حسابلشمك hìssāblashmek; we are —, الوب ويره جكمز قالمدى Alip-vèré-jéghimiz-kalmadi.

Squash, v.a. ازمك èzmek.

Squeeze, s. صيقش sìkish; —, v.a. صيقمق sìkmak. [(satire) هجو hìjv.

Squib, s. (firework) ماهتاب māhitāb;

Squint, s. شاشيلق shàshilik; —, v.n. شاشى او shàshi-òl; — eyed, شاشى shàshi, احول àhvèl.

Squire, s. اغا agha.

Squirrel, s. تيون tèyyūn.

Squirt, s. حقنه hòkna; —, v.a. فشقرتمق fìshkirtmak; —, v.n. فشقرمق fìshkirmak.

Stab, s. خنجر يارەسى khànjar-yàrassi; —, v.a. خنجرايله اورمق khànjar-ila-wūrmak.

Stability, s. متانت mètānèt, ثبات sèbāt, استحكام ìsstìhkyām.

Stable, s. اخور akhir, طوله tàvla, اصطبل ìsstabl; —, a. ثابت sābit, متين mètīn, مستحكم mùsstàhkèm.

Stable-boy, Stable-man, s. سئيس يماغى sè'īss-yàmaghi.

Stack, s. يغين yìghin, كومه kyùmé; —, v.a. يغين ا yìghin-et.

Staff, s. (stick) دينك dèynek, عصا ''assā; (body of assistants) معيت

مأمورلری mà‘‘ìyyèt - mè‘mūrléri ; (army) أركان‌حرب èrkyāni-hàrb.

Stag, *s.* كيك ghèyik.

Stage, *s.* (of a journey) منزل mènzil ; (of transition) حال hāl, كرته kèrté ; (scaffold) اسكله ìsskèlé ; (of a theatre) منصه mànàssé, اويونجيلرك‌يری òyun-julàring-yèri ; (theatres in general) تياترولر tèyàtrolar ; — over, *v.a.* اسكله قوروب دوشمه قاپلمق ìsskèlé-kùrup--dùshémé-kàplamak.

Stage-coach, *s.* منزل عربه‌سی mènzil--‘‘àrabassi.

Stagger, *v.n.* سنده‌لمك sèndélémek, يقلجق‌او yìkìlajak-òl ; —, *v.a.* زده‌لمك zèdélémek ; ثباتنه خلل ويرمك sèbātina-khàlel-vèrmek.

Stagnant, *a.* دورغون dùrghun, راكد rākid ; اركلمش ìrkilmish ; (market) كساد kèssād.

Stagnate, *v.n.* اقمامق àkmamak, اركمك ìrkmek, اركلمك ìrkilmek, دورمق dùrmak, دورغون‌او dùrghun-òl, راكد او rākid-òl ; (market) كساد او kèssād-òl.

Stagnation, *s.* اركمه ìrkmé.

Staid, *a.* تمكينلو tèmkīnli.

Staidness, *s.* تمكين tèmkīn.

Stain, *s.* لكه lèké ; —, *v.a.* لكه‌لمك lèkélémek ; لكه‌ا lèké-et ; —, *v.a.* لكه‌لنمك lèkélenmek.

Stair, *s.* باصه‌مق bàssamak, درجه dèréjé ; —s, *s. pl.* —case, *s.* نردبان nèrdibān (mèrdivèn).

Stake, *s.* (wood) قازق kàzik ; (wager) بحث bàhss ; —, *v.a.* بحث‌ا bàhss--et ; at —, تهلكه‌ده tèhlikédé, مخاطره‌ده mùkhātarada.

Stale, *a.* بيات bàyat ; اسكی èsski ; —, *v.n.* قشانمق kàshanmak.

Stalk, *s.* صاپ sàp ; —, *v.n.* يورومك yùrumek, كزمك ghèzmek ; قورلمق kù-rulmak.

Stall, *s.* خانه khāné, ير yèr.

Stallion, *s.* ات àt, ايغر àyghir.

Stalwart, *a.* قوی البنيان و طويل القامه kàvī-èl-bùnyān-vé-tàvīl-èl-kāmet.

Stamina, *s.* قوت kùvvet.

Stammer, *v.n.* پلتك‌سويلمك pèltèk--sùwèylémek.

Stamp, *s.* تمغا (dàmgha) ; —, *v.a.* تمغا اورمق dàmgha-wùrmak ; (in a mill) دبيكده دوكمك dìbèkda-dùghmek ; (under foot) چينه‌مك chīnémek, اياق‌التنه المق àyak-àltina-àlmak ; —, *v.n.* (with the feet) ديپنمك (tèpin-mek), اياق چالمق àyak-chàlmak.

Stanch, *a.* قوی kàwī, متين mètīn.

Stand, *s.* (pedestal) اياق àyak ; كرسی kyùrsī ; (stall) سركی sèrghi ; (of arms) عدد ‘‘àded, قطعه kìt‘‘à ; (opposition) مقاومت mùkāvémèt ; —, *v.n.* دورمق dùrmak ; (on foot) اياقده دورمق àyakda - dùrmak ; (bear) طيانمق dàyanmak ; چكمك chèk-mek, تحمل‌ا tàhàmmul - et ; (be situated) اولمق òlmak, واقع‌او wākí‘‘--òl ; (a course, a ship) كتمك ghìtmek, يول طوتمق yòl-tùtmak ; (be permanent) سورمك sùrmek, پايدار او pàydār-òl ; — for, دلالت‌ا dèlālet-et ; بدل‌او bèdel-òl, مقامنده‌قائم‌او màkāminda-kāʿim-ôl; معناسندهاو mà‘‘nà-ssinda-ôl; (an office) طالب‌او tālib-ôl; — in, (cost) اولمق òlmak; (a ship) قره‌یه‌یقلاشمق kāraya-yàklashmak; — off, چکلمك chèkilmek; (a ship) أچلمق àchìlmak; — one's ground, — out, ثابتقدم‌او sābit-kādem-ôl, طیانمق dàyanmak; — sentry, نوبت بکلمك nùbèt-bèklémek; — still, دورمق dùrmak, قیملدانمامق kìmīldānmamak; — up, ایاغه‌قالقمق àyagha-kālkmak; طوغری دورمق dòghru-dùrmak; — — for, وقایه‌ا vikāyé-et, تصحب‌ا tàssàhhub-et; استمك ìsstémek; — on end, دیكلمك dìkilmek; to come to a — still, دورمق dùrmak, پوصله‌یی‌شاشرمق pūssulayi-shàshirmak, قالمق kālmak.

Standard, *s.* سنجاق sānjak, علم ‘‘àlem, لوا lìwā, بیراق bàyrak, باندره bàndara; (of weight, &c.) عیار ‘‘àyār, معیار mì‘‘yār, میزان mīzān, قرار kārār; (in machinery) ایاق àyak; (tree) اوزون كتوكلو اغاج ùzun-kyùtuklu-āghaj; — bearer, بیراقدار bàyrakdār.

Standing, *s.* صفت sìfàt; رتبه rùtbé; اعتبار ì‘‘tibār; (in time) قدم kìdèm; —, *a.* ایاقده àyakda, قائم kāʿim; قالقمش kālkmish; (permanent) دائمی dāʿimī, پایدار pàydār; (water) دورغون dùrghun, راكد rākid, اقمیان ākmayan.

Staple, *s.* (iron) كوپری kyùpru; (mart) چارشی chàrshi, قپان kāpan; (of wool, &c.) بوی bòy; —, *a.* بیوك bìyuk, باشلوجه bàshlìja; أصل āssl, انا àna.

Star, *s.* یلدز yìldiz, نجم nèjm, كوكب kèvkèb, ستاره sìtāré; (of knighthood) نشان nìshān; (person of eminence) معتبركمسنه mù‘‘tébèr-kìmèssné.

Starboard, *s.* سنجاق sānjak, كمینك سنجاق طرفی ghèmining-sānjak-tàrafi.

Starch, *s.* نشاسته nìshāssta (نشسته nìshèssté, a deposit ?); —, *v.a.* نشاسته اورمق nìshāssta-wùrmak.

Stare, *v.n.* دیك‌باقمق dìk-bākmak, پك‌باقمق pèk-bākmak; كوزینی چوق اچمق ghyùzunu-chòk-àchmak.

Stark, *ad.* بتون bìtun.

Starling, *s.* صیغرجق sìghirjik.

Start, *s.* صچرایش sìchrayish; قوپش kòpush, چیقش chìkish; میدان mèydān; —, *v.n.* (jump) صچرامق sìchramak; (in motion) چیقمق chìkmak; قوپمق kòpmak; to get the —, ایلرودپرنمك ìléri-dèprenmek (*or* داورانمق dàvranmak); كیروده براقمق ghèrida-bràkmak; —, *v.a.* چیقارمق chìkàrmak; (game) قالدرمق kāldirmak; (water) دوكمك dùkmek, بوشاتمق bòshatmak; (the anchor) اوینانمق òynatmak, دیبدن ایرمق dìbdan-àyrmak.

Startle, *v.a.* تعجب ایتدرمك tà‘‘àjjub-ètdirmek, حیران قیلمق hàyrān-kìlmak; قورقتمق kòrkutmak; بردن بره اویاندرمق bìrdan-bìré-ùyàndirmak.

Starve, *v.a.* اچ براقمق àj-bràkmak, اچ قومق àj-kòmak; —, *v.n.* اجلقدن

اجلق چكمك اولمق àjlikdan-ülmek; اجلق چكمك àjlik-chèkmek; — to death, v.a. اولنجه يه قدراج قومق ülinjéya-kAdar-àj-kòmak; — —, v.n. اجلقدن اولمك àjlikdan-ülmek; — with cold, صوغوقدن اولمك sòghukdan-ülmek.

State, s. (condition) حال hāl; (government) دولت dèvlet, حكومت hùkyūmet; (pomp) سلطنت sAltAnAt, طنطنه tAntAna, دبدبه dèbdébE, الاى Alay; —, v.a. ديمك dèmek, سويلمك sùwèylémek, تقريرا تقرير ا tAkrīr-et, بيان ا bèyān-et, ذكرا zikr-et; تعيين ا tà"yīn-et.

Statesman, s. مدبر امور جمهور mùdèbbiri-ūmūri-jùmhūr.

Station, s. ير yEr, محل màhàll; منزل mènzil, موقف mèvkif; حد hàdd, پايه pāyE, رتبه rūtbE; —, v.a. قومق kòmak, براقمق bràkmak, تعيين ا [tà"yīn-et.

Stationary, a. ثابت sābit.

Stationer, s. كاغدجى kyāghidji.

Stationery, s. كاغد قلم مقوله سى شيلر kyāghid-kàlEm-màkūlEssi-shèylEr.

Statue, s. تصوير tAssvīr, تصوير مجسم tAssvīri-mùjèsssem.

Stature, s. بوى bòy, قامت kAmet, قد kAdd, بالا bālā.

Status quo, s. استاتو قوو isstātū-kuò.

Statute, s. قانون kānūn, نظام nizām.

Stave, s. فوچى تخته سى fichi-tàkhtassi.

Stay, s. دورش dùrush, قالش kAlish, اقامت ikāmet; (prop) دستك dèss-tek, طياق dàyak, پايند̊ه pàyèndE; (moral) ركن rükn; ال El, كوز ghyüz; طوتار قول كورر كوز tòtar-kòl-ghyürur-ghyüz; (of a mast) استراليه isstràlya; —s. s. pl. قورسته kòrsèta; —, v.n. دورمق dùrmak, قالمق kAlmak, اوطورمق òturmak, ايلنمك èylEnmek; (a ship) اورسه الابانده ا òrsa-àlabànda-et; — one's hunger, صفرايى باصدرمق sAfrayi-bAssdirmak.

Stead, s. بدل bèdel; in stead, بدلاً bèdelEn, يرينه yErina.

Steadfast, a. متانتلو mètānètli, ثابتقدم sābitkAdEm, پايدار pàydār.

Steady, a. قوى kàwī, محكم mùhkEm, قرار kArār, بر دوزى يه bìr-dùziyE; دترهمز (titrEmàz), ركاكت كوسترمز rèkyākEt-ghyüsstErmàz; (in character) امين èmīn, معتمد mù"témèd, اوصلو ùsslu, تميز tèmiz; —, v.a. طوتمق tùtmak, اوينامسنى منع ا òynamassini-mèn"-et.

Steak, s. كول باصدى kyül-bAssdi.

Steal, v.a. چالمق chAlmak, سرقت ا sirkAt-et, اوغريلمق òghrulamak; —, v.n. خرسزلق ا khirsizlik-et, سرقت ا sirkAt-et; (move quietly) اصولله حركت ا ùssūlla-hàrékEt-et; — in, اوصولله كيرمك ùssūlla-ghirmek; — out, اوصولله چيقمق ùssūlla-chìkmak; — on, اصولله كچمك ùssūlla-ghèchmek; time steals on, يواش يواش وقت كچيور yāwAsh-yāwAsh-wAkit-ghèchiyor; — away, سيوشمك sivishmek, اصولله صاوشمق ùssūlla-sàwushmak.

Stealth (by), ad. كيزلو كيزلو ghizli-ghìzli, قچامقله kAchamakla, على خفية "àla-khùfyétin.

Steam, *s.* بوغی bŭgh*u*, بخار bŭkhār, واپور vàpor; — engine, واپور چرخی vàpor-chàrkh*i*; — boat, — ship, واپور vàpor, چرخ‌کمیسی chàrkh-ghèmissi; locomotive — engine, واپور عربه‌سی vàpor-"àrabass*i*; —, *v.n.* بوغیسی چیقمق bŭgh*u*ssu-chìkmak; چرخ‌ایله کتمك chàrkh-il*a*-ghìtmek; —, *v.a.* بوغی‌یه‌کوسترمك bùgh*u*ya-ghyùsster-mek; بوغی‌ایله‌پشورمك bŭgh*u*-il*a*-pìshirmek.

Steed, *s.* آت ăt, اسب èssb.

Steel, *s.* چلك chèlik; (for striking fire) قاو چقماغی kàv-chàkm*a*gh*i*; (of a flint lock) قارشیلق kàrshilik; —, *v.n.* چلك كسلمك chèlik-kèssil-mek; —, *v.a.* چلك كبی سرت‌ات chèlik-ghìbi-sèrt-et.

Steelyard, *s.* قنطار kăntār.

Steep, *a.* دیك dìk; —, *v.n.* صوده یاتمق sùd*a*-yàtmak; —, *v.a.* صویه براقمق sùy*a*-bràkm*a*k.

Steeple, *s.* كلسه‌قله‌سی kilìssé-kŭléssi.

Steer, *s.* كنج بوغه ghènj-bògh*a*, كنج اوكوز ghènj-ùkyuz; —, *v.a.* قوللانمق kŭl-lănmak; كوترمك ghyùturmek; —, *v.n.* دومن‌قوللانمق dùmèn-kŭllănmak; (as a ship) دومن‌دكله‌مك dùmèn-dìngl*é*mek (dīnémek); (a course) كتمك ghìtmek.

Steersman, *s.* دومنجی dùmènji.

Stem, *s.* كتوك kyùtuk, كوده ghùwdé; (of straw, &c.) صاپ săp; (of a ship) باش بدوسلمه‌سی băsh-bòdossl*a*massi; —, *v.a.* قارشی‌كتمك kàrshi-ghìtmek.

Stench, *s.* فنا قوقو fēn*a*-kòku, تعفن tà"àffun, رائحهٔ كریهه rāʿihàʿi-kèrīhé.

Step, *s.* ادیم ădim, خطوه khătvé; (of a ladder) باصه‌مق băssamak, ایاق àyak; (of a door) اشیك èshik, استان āssitān; (of promotion) رتبه rùtbé, درجه dèréjé; (of a mast) انا دیركك باصدیغی یر àna-dīrèghing-băssdighi-yèr; —, *v.n.* ایاق‌اتمق àyak-ătmak; ایاق‌باصمق àyak-băssmak; (walk) یورومك yùrumek; —, *v.a.* (a mast) یرینه‌اوطورتمق yèrin*a*-òturtmak; — aside, بر طرفه چكلمك bìr-tàrafa-chèkilmek; — back, كیروكتمك ghèri-ghìtmek; كیروكلمك ghèri-ghèlmek; — down, اشاغی‌انمك ăshàghi-ènmek; — forward, ایلرو كلمك ìléri-ghèlmek; — in, ایچرو كلمك ìchèri-ghèlmek; — out, چابك یورومك chàbik-yùrumek; بیوك‌ادیم‌اتلامق biyuk-ădim-ătlamak; — over, اتلامق ătlamak; — up, یوقاری‌چیقمق yŭkàri-chìkmak; — this way, بوطرفه بیورك bù-tàrafa-bŭyurung; —, *a.* اویكی ùwègh*i*; — son, اویكی‌اوغل ùwègh*i*-òghul; — daughter, اویكی‌قیز ùwègh*i*-kìz; — father, اویكی‌بابا ùwègh*i*-băba; — mother, اویكی‌انا ùwègh*i*-àna.

Steppe, *s.* قیر kìr.

Sterile, *a.* (animal) قسیر kìssir; (land) خیرسز khàyrsiz, چول chùl; (plant) محصولسز màhsūlsizz.

Sterility, *s.* قسیرلق kìssirlik; خیرسزلق

khàyrs*i*zl*i*k ; محصولسزلق màhsūl-suzluk.

Sterling, *a.* حقيقى hàkīkī, خالص khāliss.

Stern, *s.* قيچ kìch ; —, *a.* سرت sèrt, سرت خويلو sèrt-khùylu, حديد مزاجلو hàdīd-mìzājl*i* ; — post, قيچ بدوسلمه سى kìch-bòdossl*a*m*a*ss*i*.

Stern-chaser, *s.* قيچ طوپى kìch-tòpu.

Stethoscope, *s.* سينه بين sīné-bīn.

Stew, *s.* يحنى yàhni ; (of fruit) قومپوسته kòmpòsst*a* ; —, *v.a.* پشورمك pìshir-mek ; يحنى ياپمق yàhni - yàpm*a*k ; —, *v.n.* پشمك pìshmek ; to be in a —, قورقمق kòrkm*a*k, قورقوسى او kòrkussu-òl ; —s, *s. pl.* كارخانه kyār-khānɛ́.

Steward, *s.* كتخدا kètkhudā (ky*ā*ya) ; (ship's) خدمتجى khìdmetji (hìz-).

Stick, *s.* دينك dèynek, چبوق chìbùk, عصا ''Assā ; —, *v.a.* بچاق صاپلايوب اولدرمك bìchAk-sAplayup-ùldurmek ; بچاق صاپلايوب يارەلمق bìchAk - sA-playup-yàr*a*l*a*m*a*k ; —, *v.n.* ياپشمق yàp*i*shm*a*k, طوتمق tùtm*a*k ; ياپشوب قالمق yàp*i*ship - kAlm*a*k ; — at, چكنمك chèkinmek, كيرو دورمق ghèri-dùrm*a*k ; — by, ايرلمامق àyr*i*l-m*a*m*a*k ; — in, *v.a.* صوقمق sòkm*a*k ; صاپلامق sAplam*a*k ; — —, *v.n.* صاپلانمق sAplanm*a*k ; — out, طيشارى اوغرامق d*i*shàr*i*-ò*gh*ram*a*k.

Sticky, *a.* ياپشقان yàpishkAn.

Stiff, *a.* اكلمز èghilmàz, قتى kAt*i*, سرت sèrt ; صيرق كبى sìr*i*k-ghìbi, طاش كبى tàsh-ghìbi ; قالقمش kAlkm*i*sh ; (in manner) صوغوق sò*gh*uk.

Stiffen, *v.n.* پكشمك pèkishmek, قتيلاشمق kAt*i*lashm*a*k ; قالقمق kAlk-m*a*k ; طاش كسلمك tAsh-kèssilmek.

Stiffness, *s.* اكلمزلك èghilmàzlik.

Stifle, *v.a.* بوغمق bò*gh*m*a*k.

Stigma, *s.* لكه lèkɛ́.

Stigmatize, *v.a.* تعييب ا tà''yīb - et, تقبيح ا tAkbīh-et, قدح ا kAdh-et.

Stile, *s.* پرمق قپو pàrm*a*k-kAp*i*.

Still, *a.* ساكت sākit ; ساكن sākin ; دورغون dùr*gh*un, سسسزصداسز sèsssiz-sAdāssiz ; حركتسز hàrékètsiz ; راحت rāhat, تك tèk ; —, *s.* انبيق inbīk ; —, *ad.* ينه yìné (ghènɛ́) ; حالا hālā, حالاينه hālā-yìné (ghènɛ́) ; —, *v.a.* تسكين ا tèsskīn-et ; صوصدرمق sùssdurm*a*k. [حركتسزلك hàrékètsizlik.

Stillness, *s.* سسسزلك sessizlik ;

Stimulate, *v.a.* تشويق ا tèshvīk-et.

Sting, *s.* ايكنه ìghnɛ́, ديكن dìkɛn, خار khār ; (pain) اجى Aj*i*, وجع vèjà'' ; —, *v.a.* صوقمق sòkm*a*k ; اجتمق Aj*i*tm*a*k ; —, *v.n.* اجيمق Aj*i*m*a*k.

Stinginess, *s.* طمعكارلق tAma''ky*ā*rlik.

Stingy, *a.* خسيس khàssīss, طمعكار tAma''kyār, جمرى jìmri, چنكانه (chìnghɛ́ni).

Stink, *s.* فنا قوقو fɛ̀na-kòku, تعفن tà''àf-fun, رائحهٔ كريهه rā'ihà'i-kèrīhɛ́ ; —, *v.n.* فنا قوقمق fɛ̀na-kòkm*a*k ; —, *v.a.* فنا قوقوتمق fɛ̀na-kòkutm*a*k ; — out, فنا قوقو ايله قاچرمق fɛ̀na-kòku-ìl*a*-kAchirm*a*k ; — aloud, پك فنا قوقمق pèk-fɛ̀na-kòkm*a*k.

Stinking, *a.* فنا قوقار fɛ̀na-kòkar.

Stint, *v.a.* حدتعيين ا hàdd-tà''yīn-et, حصرا hàssr-et; without—, بلاحصر bìlā-hàssrin.

Stipend, *s.* معاش mà''āsh.

Stipulate, *v.a.* مشروطقيلمق mèshrūt-kìlmak, مقاوله ا mùkàvélé-et, قول ا kàvl-et; —, *v.n.* شرطشروطباغلامق shàrt-shùrūt-bàghlamak.

Stipulation, *s.* شرط shàrt; قول kàvl, مقاوله mùkàvélé.

Stir, *s.* كورلدى ghyùruldu, پاطردى pàtirdi; تلاش tèlāsh; —, *v.n.* قيملدانمق kìmìldanmak, حركت ا hàrékèt-et; —, *v.a.* قارشدرمق kàrishdirmak.

Stirrup, *s.* اوزنكى ùzènghi, ركاب rìkyāb; — leather, اوزنكى قايشى ùzènghi-kàyishi.

Stitch, *v.a.* ديكمك dìkmek.

Stock, *s.* (wood) كتوك kyùtuk, اوطون òdun; (flower) شببوى shèbbùy; (for grafting) انا àna; (of an anchor), چيپو chìpo; (in trade) سرمايه sèrmāyé, بضاعه bìzā''a; (funds) سهيم sèhīm; ايراد īrād; خزينه khàzīné (hàzna); (for the neck) بويون باغى bòyun-bàghi; (race) صوى sòy, سلسله sìlsilé; (store) موجود mèvjūd; ذخيره zàkhīré; احتياط تداركى ìhtiyāt-tèdāruku; (of a gun) قنداق kùndak; —, *v.a.* لوازماتنى ويرمك lèwāzimātini-vèrmek, دوناتمق dònatmak; — out, *v.n.* داللنمق dàllanmak; stocks, *s.pl.* طمروق tòmruk; (for ships) قزاق kìzàk.

Stockade, *s.* شرانپو shàranpò; —, *v.a.* شرانپو چورمك shàranpò-chèvirmek.

Stockbroker, *s.* حصه و سهم سمسارى hìssa-vè-sèhīm-sìmsāri.

Stockholder, *s.* حصه و سهم صاحبى hìssa-vè-sèhīm-sāhibi.

Stocking, *s.* چوراب chòrap.

Stoker, *s.* واپورك اتشجيسى vàporin-àtèshjissi.

Stomach, *s.* قارن kàrn, معده mì''dé, شكم shìkèm; —, *v.a.* يوتمق yùtmak, قبول ا kàbūl-et, تحمل ا tàhàmmul-et.

Stomach-ache, *s.* صانجى sànji.

Stone, *s.* طاش tàsh; حجر hàjar, سنك sènk; (testicle) طاشاق tàshak, خايه khāya; (of fruit) چكردك chèkirdek; —, *v.a.* طاشلامق tàshlamak, رجم ا rèjm-et; (fruit) چكردكلرينى چيقارمق chèkirdeklérini-chìkàrmak; —, horse, آت àt, آيغر àyghir.

Stoning, *s.* رجم rèjm; چكردكلرينك چيقارلمسى chèkirdeklérining-chìkàrìlmassi.

[tàsh-ghìbi.

Stony, *a.* طاشلق tàshlìk; طاش كبى

Stool, *s.* اسكملى ìsskèmni (ìsskèmlé); (of the bowels) عمل ''àmel; to go to —, عمل ا ''àmel-et, طيشارى چيقمق dìshàri-chìkmak.

Stoop, *s.* اكلش èghilish, قانبورلق kànburluk; —, *v.n.* اكلمك èghilmek; قانبور او kànbur-òl; (morally) تنزل ا tènèzzul-et.

Stop, *s.* دورش dùrush, قالش kàlish; كسلش kèssilish, منع mèn''; (in reading) دوراق يرى dùrak-yèri;

—, *v.n.* دورمق dùrmak, قالمق kàlmak, ايلنمك èylenmek; —, *v.a.* دوردرمق dùrdurmak, اليقومق àlikomak; ضبط ا zàbt-et, طوتمق tùtmak; طيقامق tìkamak; منع ا mèn"et, اوكنى المق ùngunu-àlmak, كسمك kèssmek; مانع او māni-"òl.

Stoppage, *s.* مانع māni"; منع mèn"; سدة sùddé, طيقانقلق tìkànìklik.

Stopper, *s.* طيقاج tìkaj, طاپه tàpa.

Store, *s.* (of provisions) ذخيره zàkhīré; (of necessaries) موجود mèvjūd, تداركات tèdārukyāt, احتياط ìhtiyàt; (magazine) انبار ànbār; (shop) دكان dùkkyān; —, *v.a.* لوازماتله طولدرمق lèwāzimātla-dòldurmak; — up, — away, *v.a.* صاقلامق sàklamak, حفظ ا hìfz-et, در انبار ا dèr-ànbār-et; to set — by, سومك sèvmek, عزيز طوتمق "àzīz-tùtmak; —s, *s.pl.* لوازمات lèwāzimāt, مهمات mùhimmāt.

Storehouse, *s.* مخزن màkhzen.

Storekeeper, *s.* انبار امينى ànbār-èmīni.

Storeroom, *s.* انبار ànbār, مخزن màkhzen; (closet) كيلار kìlār [(kìler).

Stork, *s.* لكلك lèghlek.

Storm, *s.* فرطونه fìrtina, بوره bòra; (assault) يورويش yùruyush, هجوم hùjūm; —, *v.a.* يورويش ا yùruyush-et, هجوم ا hùjūm-et; —, *v.n.* دارلمق dàrilmak, باغرمق bàghirmak; to take by —, يورويشله المق yùruyushla-àlmak.

Stormy, *a.* فرطونه‌لو fìrtinali. [-àlmak.

Story, *s.* (tale), مصال màssal, حكايه hìkyāyé, فقره fìkra, منقبه mànkabé; (falsehood) يلان yàlàn, كذب kìzb, دروغ dùrūgh; (of a house) قات kàt. [yàlanji.

Storyteller, *s.* مداح mèddāh; يلانجى

Stout, *a.* قالين kàlin; متين mètīn, قوى kàwī; دنج dìnj; جسور jèssūr; —, *s.* سياه ارپه صويى sìyāh-àrpa-sùyu.

Stove, *s.* صوبه sòba. [المق àlmak.

Stow, *v.a.* استف ا ìsstif-et; (to hold)

Straddle, *v.a.* ابانمق àbanmak.

Straggle, *v.n.* طاغلمق or داغلمق dàghìlmak, طاغنق كتمك dàghinik-ghìtmek. [dan-àyrilan-àdam.

Straggler, *s.* اردودن ايريلان آدم òrdu-

Straight, *v.n.* طوغرى dòghru, مستقيم mùsstakīm; دوز dùz; —, *ad.* اول ساعت òl-sā"at, درعقب dèr-"àkab.

Straighten, *v.a.* طوغرولتمق dòghrultmak.

Straightforward, *a.* طوغرى dòghru. [luk.

Straightforwardness, *s.* طوغريلق dòghru-

Straightness, *s.* طوغريلق dòghruluk.

Straightways, *ad.* درعقب dèr-"àkab, اول ساعت òl-sā"at, هماندم hèmān-dèm.

Strain, *s.* زور zòr; كركيلك ghèrghilik; —, *v.a.* زورلمق zòrlamak; كرمك ghèrmek; (with a strainer) سوزمك sùzmek; —, *v.n.* كيرلمك ghèrilmek; كنديني زورلمق kèndini - zòrlamak; سوزلمك sùzulmek.

Strainer, *s.* سوزكچ sùzghech.

Strait, *s.* بوغاز bòghàz, خليج khàlīj; —, *a.* دار dàr, ضيق zīk, تنك tènk;

—s, *s. pl.* بوغاز bòghâz, خليج khàlīj ; صيقندى sìkindi, ضرورت zàrūrèt.

Straiten, *v.a.* دارالتمق dàrAltmak ; مضايقه‌يه دوشورمك mūzāyakaya-dùshurmek. [دارالمش dàrAlmish.

Straitened, *a.* مضايقه‌ده mūzāyakada,

Strait-laced, *a.* پك صوفى pèk-sòfu.

Strand, *s.* يالى‌كنارى yAli-kènāri, ساحل sāhil, قيى kìyi ; —, *v.a.* قره‌يه اوغراتمق kAraya-òghrAtmak, اوطورتمق òturtmak ; قره‌يه‌چكمك kàraya-chèkmek ; —, *v.n.* قره‌يه اوطورمق kAraya-òturmak.

Strange, *a.* غريب ghàrīb, عجيب "àjīb (*pl.* عجائب "Ajā'ib) ; يبانجى yàbAnji ; — ! *int.* عجائب "Ajā'ib !

Strangeness, *s.* عجائبلق "Ajā'iblik, يكيلك yèngilik.

Stranger, *s.* يبانجى yàbAnji ; (foreigner) اجنبى èjnébī.

Strangle, *s.* بوغمق bòghmak.

Strangury, *s.* سديك زورى sìdik-zòru.

Strap, *s.* قايش kàyish ; (of plaster) اوزون‌ياقى‌پارچه‌سى ùzun-yàki-pàrchassi ; — up, *v.a.* قايشلرينى چكمك kàyishlarini-chèkmek ; ياقى‌پارچه‌لرينى‌ياپشدرمق yàki-pàrchalarini-yàpishdirmak.

Stratagem, *s.* حيله hīlé, خدعه khùd"à, دسيسه dèssīssé.

Stratum, *s.* قات kAt, طبقه tAbAka ; strata, *s. pl.* طبقات tAbAkāt.

Straw, *s.* (whole) صاپ sAp ; (ground) صمان sàmAn.

Strawberry, *s.* چليك chilèyk.

Stray, *a.* صاحبسز كزن sāhibsiz-ghèzen ; دوشمه dùshmé ; —, *v.n.* ايرلمق àyrilmak ; كزمك ghèzmek, طولاشمق dòlashmak.

Streak, *s.* چيزى chìzi ; طمر dàmar.

Stream, *s.* چاى chày, ايرمق ìrmak, دره dèré, صو sù, نهر nèhr ; اقندى Akindi ; —, *v.n.* اقمق Akmak, چوق اقمق chòk-Akmak.

Streamlet, *s.* چاى chày.

Street, *s.* صوقاق sòkAk, زقاق zùkāk, طريق tàrīk ; — door, صوقاق‌قپوسى sòkAk-kApissi.

Street-walker, *s.* روسپى òrosspo.

Strength, *s.* زور zòr, قوت kùvvèt ; متانت mètānèt, استحكام ìsstìhkyām ; شدت shìddèt ; كسكينلك kèsskinlik.

Strengthen, *v.a.* قوت ويرمك kùvvèt-vèrmek ; قويلشدرمك kàvilEshdirmek, متانت ويرمك mètānèt-vèrmek, تقويت‌ا tAkvìyyèt-et ; تقويت ويرمك tAkvìyyèt-vèrmek ; استحكام ويرمك ìsstìhkyām-vèrmek.

Stress, *s.* زور zòr ; — of weather, هوانك‌فرطونه‌لولغى hàwāning-fìrtinalìlighi ; to lay — upon, لقرديده اهميت ويرمك làkirdida-èhèmmìyyèt-vèrmek.

Stretch, *s.* كرش ghèrish, كريلش ghèrilish ; —, *v.a.* كرمك ghèrmek ; قاصمق kAssmak ; —, *v.n.* كرلمك ghèrilmek ; اوزامق ùzamak ; (in relating) مبالغه‌ا mūbāligha-et ; on the —, كركى ghèrghi, كريلو ghèrili, قاصيلو kAssili ; the utmost — of imagination, حوصلهٔ تخیل hàwsalà'i--tàkhàyyul; — out, *v.a.* اوزاتمق ùzÀtmak; — —, — forward, *v.n.* اوزانمق ùzÀnmak.

Stretcher, *s.* دستکاره dèsstkyàrÉ [(tèsskérÉ).

Strew, *v.a.* صاچمق sÀchmak, دوکمك dùkmek, يايمق yàymak, سرمك sèrmek.

Stricken, *a.* اورلمش wùrulmish; مبتلا [mùbtÉlà.

Strict, *a.* صيقى sìki; دقيق dÀkìk; مدقق mùdÀkkìk; مدققانه mùdÀk-[kìkänÉ.

Strictly, *ad.* صيقى sìki.

Strictness, *s.* صيقيلق sìkìlìk; كمال صحت kèmāl-sìhhàt.

Stricture, *s.* (moral) جرح jèrh, اعتراض ì''tìrÀz, فصل fÀssl; (physical) سده sùddÉ.

Stride, *s.* اديم Àdim; اياق àyak; ايلروليش ìlèriléyish; —, — over, *v.n.* اوستندن كچمك ùsstundan--ghèchmek, اتلايوب كچمك Àtlayup--ghèchmek.

Strife, *s.* نفاق nìfÀk; نزاع nìzā'', چكشمه chèkishma, غوغا (kàwgha).

Strike, *v.a.* اورمق wùrmak, ضرب ا dàrb-et; چالمق chÀlmak; (lower) ماينه ا màyna-et, اندرمك èndirmek; (appear) كلمك ghèlmek, كورنمك ghyùrunmek; — a bargain, پازارلق ا pàzarlìk-et; — against a rock, قيايه چاتمق kàyaya-chàtmak; — blind, كور ا kyùr-et, كوزينى كور ا ghyù-zunu-kyùr-et; — down, يره يقمق yèra-yìkmak; — fire, اتش چاقمق Àtèsh - chàkmak, قاو چاقمق kàw--chàkmak; — off, كسمك kèss-mek; اسمنى چيزمك ìssmini-chìz-mek, ترقين ا tèrkīn-et; — out, اسمنى چيزمك ìssmini - chìzmek, ترقين ا tèrkīn-et; چيقارمق chìkàr-mak, دوشورمك dùshurmek; *v.n.* يوزمكه باشلامق yùzméghÉ - bÀsh-lamak; مشته اتمق mùshta-Àtmak; — root, كوك صالمق kyùk-sÀlmak, طوتمق tùtmak; — (a plant) دالدن يتشدرمك dÀldan-yètishdirmek, قلمدن يتشدرمك kàlEmdan-yètish-dirmek, ديكوب يتشدرمك dìkup--yètishdirmek; — terror into, القاى دهشت ا ìlkāyi-dèhshEt-et, ترهيب ا tèrhīb-et; — the hour, —, *v.n.* چالمق chÀlmak; — up, باشلامق bÀshlamak.

Striking, *a.* عجيب ''Àjīb, غريب gharīb; it is a — likeness, پك بكزر pèk-bèngzEr.

String, *s.* ايپ ìp, سجيم sìjim, تل tèl; (of camels, &c.) قطار kÀtār; (of beads, &c.) ديزى dìzi, صره sìra; —, *v.a.* ديزمك dìzmek; كچورمك ghè-chirmek; (an instrument) تللرينى دوناتمق tèllérini-dònatmak. [èkkèd.

Stringent, *a.* صيقى sìki; مؤكد mù''-

Strip, *s.* اوزون انسز پارچه ùzun-ènsiz--pàrcha; —, *v.a.* صويمق sòymak; اچمق àchmak; —, *v.n.* صوينمق sòyunmak; صويلمق sòyulmak.

Stripe, *s.* چبوق chìbùk, پرمق pàrmak, يول yòl, زه zìh; دينك dèynek, ضرب dàrb, ضربه dàrba.

Striped, *a.* يول يول yòl-yòl; پرمق پرمق pàrmak-pàrmak.

Stripling, *s.* نو جوان nèv-jùwān.

Strive, *v.n.* چالشمق chàlishmak, سعی ا sà''y-et; — with, اوغراشمق òghrash-mak, چكشمك chèkishmek, يراشمق yàrashmak.

Stroke, *s.* (of a pen) چیزی chìzi; (of an oar) چكلش chèkilish; (of a sword) ضربه dàrba; thunder—, يلدرم yìldirim, صاعقه sā''ika; —, *v.a.* اوخشامق òkhshamak.

Stroll, *v.n.* كزمك ghèzmek; —, *s.* كزمه ghèzmé.

Stroller, *s.* در بدر dèr-bé-dèr.

Strong, *a.* زورلو zòrlu, قوتلو kùvvètli; قوی kàwī, متين mètīn, طيانقلو dàyà-nìkli, مستحكم mùsstàhkem; سرت sèrt, كسكين kèsskin, دوقناقلو dòku-[nakli.

Stronghold, *s.* قلعه kalé.

Strop, *s.* اوستره قايشی ùsstura-kàyishi.

Structure, *s.* بنا bìnā, بنيان bùnyān, بنياد bùnyād; ترتيب tèrtīb; هيكل hèykèl.

Struggle, *s.* يراشمه yàrashma, اوغراشمه òghrashma, چكشمه chèkishma; غوغا (kàwgha); —, *v.n.* يراشمق yàrashmak, چكشمك chèkishmek; اوغراشمق òghrashmak, چبالمق chàbalamak; — for life, جان چكشمك jān-chèkishmek.

Strumpet, *s.* فاحشه fāhisha, روسپی (òrosspo).

Strychnia, Strychnine, *s.* قارغه بوكن خلاصه‌سی kàrgha-bùken-khùlāssassi.

Stubborn, *a.* عنادجی ''ìnādji, معند mù''ànnid, متمرد mùtémèrrid, عاصی ''āssī.

Stubbornness, *s.* عناد ''ìnād.

Stucco, *s.* الچی àlchi; مرمر mèrmer.

Student, *s.* مكتب شاكردی mèkteb-shāghirdi; (of law and divinity) سوخته sūkhté (sòfta), طالب العلم tālibu-'l-''ìlm (*pl.* طلبه tàlébé, طلبا tùlébā).

Studio, *s.* كارخانه kyār-khāné.

Studious, *a.* چالشقان chàlishkàn.

Studiousness, *s.* چالشقانلق chàlish-kànlìk.

Study, *s.* (mental) مطالعه mùtāla''à; (object of —) درس dèrss; (closet) اوطه òda; (exercise) تعليم tà''līm; —, *v.a.* مطالعه ا mùtāla''à-et; چالشمق chàlishmak; اوقومق òku-mak; تعليم ا tà''līm-et.

Stuff, *s.* قماش kùmāsh; (woollen) صوف sòf; (rubbish) صاچمه sàchma; bread —, ذخيره zàkhīré; household —, اشيا èshyā; —, *v.a.* طولدرمق dòldurmak; طيقامق tìkamak.

Stumble, *v.n.* (horse) قپانمق kàpan-mak; (man) اياغنی چاريمق àyaghini-chàrpmak.

Stump, *s.* كتوك kyùtuk, كوك kyùk.

Stun, *v.a.* سرسم ا sèrsem-et.

Stupefaction, *s.* سرسملك sèrsemlik.

Stupefied, *a.* سرسم sèrsem.

Stupefy, *v.a.* سرسم ا sèrsem-et.

Stupendous, *a.* عظيم ''àzìm.

Stupendously, *ad.* پك pèk.

Stupid, *a.* احمق àhmak, عقلسز "ʌklsiz, اشك èshek, شاشقين shàshkin.

Stupidity, *s.* حماقت hàmākʌt, عقلسزلق "ʌklsizlik, اشككك èsheklik, شاشقينلق shàshkinlik.

Stupidly, *ad.* عقلسزلق ايله "ʌklsizlik-ìla.

Stupidness, *s.* عقلسزلق "ʌklsizlik.

Stupor, *s.* بيهوشلك bīhushluk. [vetli.

Sturdy, *a.* طيانور dàyànir; قوتلو kùv-

Sturgeon, *s.* مورينه بالغى mòrina-bʌlighi.

Stutter, *v.n.* پپكى سويلمك pèpèghi-sùwèylémek.

Sty, *s.* طوكزاخورى dònguz-ʌkhiri (dòmuz); (on the eyelid) اريه جق àrpajik.

Style, *s.* (manner) طرز tàrz, يول yòl, وجه wèjh, صورت sūrèt; (title) لقب làkab (làghab, *pl.* القاب èlkāb), عنوان "ùnwān; (splendour) سلطنت sʌltʌnʌt; (of writing) اغز ʌghz, لسان lìssān, روش rèvish; —, *v.a.* ديمك dèmek, القاب ويرمك èlkāb-vèrmek, القاب قومق èlkāb-kòmak; old —, رومى rūmī; new —, الافرانغه àla-frànghà.

Subacid, *a.* مايخوش màykhòsh.

Subaltern, *s.* ملازم mùlāzim; —, *a.* مادون mā-dūn, مادونده اولان mā-dūnda-òlʌn.

Subdivision, *s.* تقسيم tàksim; تقسيمك تقسيمى tàksīming-tàksīmi.

Subdue, *v.a.* تسخيرا tèsskhīr-et, راما rʌm-et, اطاعته كتورمك ìtā"ata-ghètirmek.

Subject, *a.* (in point of authority) تابع tābi", تحت حكومتده اولان tàhti-hùkyūmètda-òlʌn, امر تحتنده اولان èmir-tàhtinda-òlʌn; (physically or morally) مبتلا mùbtélā, بعضاً كرفتار bʌ"zan-ghìriftār, بعضاً دوچار bʌ"zan-dūchār; (under) محول mùhàvvel, تحتنده tàhtinda; تحتنده اولهرق tàhtinda-òlarak; (under condition of) شرطيله shàrtīla; —, *s.* (politically) تبعه دن برى tèba"àdan-bìri; (of discussion) ماده māddé, مبحوث عنه mèbhūssun-"ành, (of a recital) محكى فيه màhkīyun-fīh; —, *v.a.* (in point of authority) تسخيرا tèsskhīr-et, راما rʌm-et; تحتنه كتورمك tàhtina-ghètirmek; تحتنه قومق tàhtina-kòmak, تحتنه احاله ا tàhtina-ìhālé-et; احاله ا ìhālé-et; تابع ا tābi"-et; (physically or morally) دوچارا dūchār-et, كرفتارا ghìriftār-et, مبتلا ا mùbtélā-et; قوشمق kòshmak. [ìtā"at.

Subjection, *s.* تبعيت tèbà"iyyèt, اطاعت

Subjoin, *v.a.* تذييل ا tezyil-et; علاوه ا "ìlāvé-et. [hàrrèr.

Subjoined, *a.* ذيلده محرر zèylda-mù-

Subjugate, *v.a.* تسخيرا tèsskhīr-et, اطاعته كتورمك ìtā"ata-ghètirmek, امرينه منقادا èmrina-mùnkād-et.

Sublimate (corrosive), *s.* اق سولمن ʌk-sùlémèn.

Sublime, *a.* عالى "ālī, سامى sāmī, رفيع rèfī"; —, *v.n.* اوچمق ùchmak, صعودا sù"ūd-et; —, *v.a.* اوچرمق ùchurmak, صعود ايتدرمك sù"ūd-ètdirmek.

Sublimeness, Sublimity, *s.* علو ''ùlùvv.

Sublunar, Sublunary, *a.* ارضى àrzi.

Submarine, *s.* دكز ديبنده واقع dèngiz-dìbinda-vwāki''. [dȦldirmak.

Submerge, *v.a.* صويه طالدرمق sūyé-

Submersion, *s.* طالمقلق dȦlmaklik; طالدرلمقلق dȦldirilmaklik.

Submission, *s.* اطاعت ìtā''at, انقياد ìnkiyād; تسخير tèsskhīr; (presentation) عرض ''àrz, تقديم tȦkdīm.

Submissive, *a.* مطيع mūtī'', متواضع mùtéwāzi. [-ìla.

Submissively, *ad.* تواضع ايله tèwāzu''-

Submissiveness, *s.* تواضع tèwāzu''.

Submit, *v.a.* عرض ا ''àrz-et, تقديم ا tȦkdīm-et; —, *v.n.* اطاعت ا ìtā''at-et; اطاعته كلمك ìtā''ata-ghèlmek, اطاعته كيرمك ìtā''ata-ghìrmek, منقاد او mūnkād-òl, رام او rām-òl; تسليم او tèsslīm-òl; راضى او rāzi-òl.

Subordinate, *a.* مادون mā-dūn, مادونده mā-dūnda, اشاغى Ȧshàghi.

Subordination, *s.* اطاعت ìtā''at.

Subscribe, *v.a.* امضالمق ìmzālamak; يازمق yàzmak, قومق kòmak; (money) ويرمك vèrmek.

Subscriber, *s.* مشترى mùshtérī.

Subscription, *s.* امضا ìmzā; پاره pārÉ.

Subsequent, *a.* صكره sòngra, صكره دن sòngradan.

Subside, *v.n.* انمك ènmek; چكلمك chèkilmek; ازالمق Ȧzalmak, خفيفلشمك khàfīfleshmek.

Subsidize, *v.a.* اقچه جه اعانه ا Ȧkchajé-ì''anÉ-et.

Subsidy, *s.* اعانه اقچه ì''ānÉ-Ȧkcha.

Subsist, *v.n.* موجود او mèvjūd-òl, كائن او kyā'in-òl, وار او vàr-òl; كچنمك ghèchinmek, تعيش ا tà''àyyush-et, كفاف نفس ا kèfāfi-nèfss-et; —, *v.a.* بسلمك bèsslémek.

Subsistence, Subsistency, *s.* وارلق vwàrlik, كچنمه gèchinma.

Substance, *s.* جسم jìssm; مال māl, واريت vàrìyyèt.

Substantial, *a.* محكم mùhkèm; قارن دويورر kàrn-dòyurur; اساسلو èssāssli; زنكين zènghin.

Substantive, *s.* اسم ìssm; common —, اسم عام ìssmi-''āmm; علم ''àlem, proper —, اسم خاص ìssmi-khāsss.

Substitute, *s.* بدل bèdel; نائب nā'ib, وكيل vèkīl, قائممقام kā'immàkām; —, *v.a.* يرينه قومق yèrina-kòmak, ابدال ا ìbdāl-et. [mùkābilinda-òl.

Subtend, *v.a.* وتر او vètɛr-òl, مقابلنده او

Subterfuge, *s.* بهانه bàhānÉ, عذر ''ùzr.

Subterranean, Subterraneous, *a.* زير زمين zīr-zèmīn.

Subtle, *a.* پك شيطان pèk-shèytān.

Subtract, *v.a.* اخراج ا ìkhrāj-et, چيقرمق chìkàrmak; طرح ا tàrh-et, تنزيل ا tènzīl-et, اشاغى وارمق Ȧshàghi-vàrmak.

Subtraction, *s.* طرح tàrh, تنزيل tènzīl.

Suburb, *s.* واروش vàrūsh, حوالى hàwālī, جواركويى jìwār-kyùyu.

Subvention, *s.* مقرر اعانه پارەسى mūkàrrèr-ì''ané-pārÉssi.

Subversion, *s.* نسنه يى الت اوست ايتمكلك nèssnÉyi-Ȧlt-ùsst-ètmeklik.

Subversive, *a.* الت اوست ايدر Alt-ùsst-èdER.

Subvert, *v.a.* الت‌اوست‌ا Alt-ùsst-et, خراب‌ا khàrāb-et, دیكركون‌ا dīghER-ghyūn-et.

Succeed, *v.n.* (a person) بجرمك bèjER-mek, ايشنى بجرمك ìshini-bèjERmek, نائل‌مرام‌او nā'ili-mèrām-ōl, مظفر او mùzAffER-ōl, موفق‌او mùwàffak-ōl; ايشى طوغرى كتمك ìshi-dòghrU-ghìtmek, ايشى اويمق ìshi-ùymak; (an experiment) اولمق ōlmak; اويمق ùymak; چيقمق chìkmak; ايوكتمك īyi-ghìtmek; (follow) اولمق ōlmak, چيقمق chìkmak, ظهورا zùhūr-et; (to the throne) جلوس‌ا jùlūss-et, مسند حكومته قعود ا mèssnèdi-hùkyūmèta-kù''ūd-et; —, *v.a.* (follow another) تعاقب ا tà''ākūb-et, متعاقب‌او mùta''ākib-ōl; (in power) خلف‌او khàlef-ōl.

Success, *s.* ظفر zAfER, موفقيت mùwàffa-kìyyèt, حصول‌مرام hùssūlU-mèrām; غلبه ghàlébÉ, نصرت nùssrèt.

Successful, *a.* موفق mùwāfik.

Successfully, *ad.* موفقت ايله mùwāfakAt-[-ila.

Succession, *s.* صره sìra, توالى tèwālī, تتالى tètālī, تسلسل tèssèlsul, سلسله silsilÉ, تعاقب tà''ākub, تخالف takhāluf; (to the throne) جلوس jùlūss; نوبت‌جلوس nùbèti-jùlūss; نوبت‌سلطنت nùbèti-sAltAnAt; in —, صره ايله sìra-ila, صره‌وارى sìra-vārī (vàrdi); على التوالى 'àlé-'t-tèwālī; متواليةً mùtéwālìyyétEn, متعاقباً mù-ta''ākiban, بر برينك اردى صره bìr-bìrining-àrdi-sìra.

Successive, *a.* اردى صره àrdi-sìra, متعاقب mùta''ākib, متوالى mùté-wāli, متتالى mùtétālī.

Successor, *s.* خلف khàlef.

Succinct, *a.* قصه kìssa, مختصر mùkh-tAssar, مجمل mùjmèl, اجمالى ìjmālī.

Succinctly, *ad.* قصه kìssa.

Succinctness, *s.* قصه‌لق kìssalik.

Succour, *s.* ياردم yàrdim, امداد ìmdād, عون ''àvn, نصر nàssr; —, *v.a.* ياردم‌ا yàrdim-et; قورتارمق kùrtar-mak.

Succulent, *a.* صولو sùlU, ابدار Abdār.

Succumb, *v.n.* ينلمك yènilmek.

Such, *a.* مثللو missìllU, كبى ghìbi; بويله bùylÉ, شويله shùylÉ, اويله ùylÉ; — a one, فلان filAn, فلان‌ادم filAn-AdAm; — and —, فلان filAn, فلان‌فلان filAn-filAn.

Suck, *s.* سوت *or* سود sùt; —, *v.a.* امزه‌مك èmzémek; to give —, امزرمك èmzirmek, سوت ويرمك sùt-vèrmek, ممه ويرمك mèmÉ-vèrmek.

Sucker, *s.* بقراج bAkraj.

Suckle, *v.a.* سوت‌ويرمك sùt-vèrmek, ممه‌ويرمك mèmÉ-vèrmek, بسلمك bèsslémek, امزرمك èmzirmek.

Sudden, *a.* بديهى‌الظهور bèdīhìyyu-'z-zùhūr, فجائى fùjā'ī, ناكهانى nā-ghèhānī; —ly, *ad.* بردن‌بره bìrdan-bìrÉ, انسز Ansiz, انسزين Ansizin, اپ‌انسز Ap-Ansiz, فجئةً fùj'étEn, بالبداهه bi-'l-bèdāhÉ.

Sue, *v.a.* محكمه‌يه چكمك mèhkéméya-chèkmek ; —, *v.n.* طلب ا tàleb-et.

Suet, *s.* ايچ ياغى ìch-yàghi.

Suffer, *v.n.* زحمت چكمك zàhmet-chèkmek, صيقندى چكمك sıkindi-chèkmek, مشقت چكمك mè-shàkkat-chèkmek ; قتل اولنمق kàtl-òlunmak ; —, *v.a.* چكمك chèk-mek, تحمل ا tàhàmmul-et, متحمل او mùtahàmmil - òl, راضى او rāzi - òl, مساعده ا mùssā''ada-et, تجويزا tèjvīz-et, قومق kòmak, براقمق bràkmak.

Sufferer, *s.* دردمند dèrdmènd.

Suffering, *s.* اذيت èzìyyèt.

Suffice, *v.n.* يتشمك yètishmek, الويرمك èlvermek, كافى او kyāfi-òl, اكتفا ا ìktifā-et.

Sufficient, *a.* يتشر yètishir, يتشه‌جك yètishéjek, الويرر èlvérir, الويره‌جك èlvéréjek, كافى kyāfi, وافى wāfi.

Suffocate, *v.a.* بوغمق bòghmak ; —, *v.n.* بوغلمق bòghulmak.

Suffocating, *a.* آدامى بوغار àdami-bò-ghar.

Suffocation, *s.* بوغلمه bòghulma.

Suffrage, *s.* رأى rè'y.

Sugar, *s.* شكر shèker, سكر sùkker, قند kànd ; — candy, نبات شكرى nèbāt-shèkéri (nùbèt) ; loaf —, كله شكرى kèllé-shèkéri ; moist —, خام شكر khām - shèker ; —, *v.a.* شكر قومق shèker-kòmak ; —, *v.n.* شكر باغلانمق shèker-bàghlanmak.

Suggest, *v.a.* عقل اوكرتمك ''àkl-ùghrètmek, عقل ا ''àkl-et.

Suggestion, *s.* ايما īmā ; عقله قومقلق ''àkla-kòmaklik.

Suicide, *s.* كندى كنديني اولدرمكلك kèndi - kèndini - ùldurmeklik ; كندى كنديني اولدرن kèndi-kèndini-ùlduren.

Suit, *s.* (of clothes) قات kàt ; (request) رجا rìjā ; (cause) دعوى dà''wà ; —, *v.n.* اويمق ùymak, اولمق òlmak ; —, *v.a.* ايشنى بولمق ìshini-bùlmak ; اويدرمق ùydurmak.

Suitable, *a.* مناسب mùnāssib, لايق lāyik. [عاشق ''āshik.

Suitor, *s.* طالب tālib, استكى ìsstèkli ;

Sulk, *v.n.* صومتمق sòmutmak.

Sulky, *a.* كوسمش kyùssmish.

Sully, *v.a.* كيرلتمك kìrletmek.

Sulphur, *s.* كوكورت kyùkyurt, كبريت kìbrīt. [خنكار khùnkyār.

Sultan, *s.* سلطان sùltān, پادشاه pādishāh,

Sultana, *s.* (sultan's concubine) قدين kàdin ; (sultan's daughter) سلطان sùltān ; (sultan's mother) والده سلطان wālidé-sùltān.

Sultry, *a.* سيجاق sìjàk, حار hārr.

Sum, *s.* (total) يكون yèkyūn, مجموع mèjmū'', طوپ tòp, جمع jèm'' ; (question) سؤال sù'āl ; —, — up, طوپلامق tòplamak, جمع ا jèm''-et, يكون ا yèkyūn-et ; خلاصه ا khùlāssa-et, اجمالاً ذكرا ìjmālan - zìkr-et ; خلاصه طوپلامق khùlāssa-tòplamak.

Summary, *s.* خلاصه khùlāssa, اجمال ìjmāl, ذكر اجمالى zìkri-ìjmālī ; —, *a.* اجمالى ìjmālī, مختصر mùkhtassàr ; چابك chàbik ; —rily, *ad.* چارچابك

chàr-chàb*i*k, چابيجك chàb*i*jek *or* چابيجق chàb*i*j*a*k.

Summer, *s.* ياز yàz, صيف sàyf, تابستان tābisstān, كرما ghèrmā.

Summer-house, *s.* كوشك ky*ù*shk.

Summit, *s.* ديه (tèpé), رأس rè'ss, ذروه zirvé, كنكره kyùnghyuré.

Summon, *v.a.* دعوت ا dà''vet-et, جلب ا jèlb-et, احضارا ìhzār-et.

Sumptuous, *a.* مكلف mùkèllef, اغر ꞇgh*i*r, مطنطن mùtàntàn.

Sumptuousness, *s.* تكلف tèkèlluf.

Sun, *s.* كونش ghyùnèsh, كون ghyùn, شمس shèmss, افتاب āfitāb; —beam, *s.* پرتو pèrtev, شعاع shù''ā''.

Sunburnt, *a.* كونشده يانمش ghyùnèshd*a*-yànmish.

Sunday, *s.* پازار pàzār, پازار كونى pàzār-ghyùnu, يوم احد yùvmu-*à*hàd, يكشنبه yèkshenbih.

Sunder, *v.a.* ايرمق àyrm*a*k; in —, دونيم dū-nīm, ايكى پارچه iki-pàrch*a*.

Sun-dial, *s.* كونش ساعتى ghyùnèsh-sā''*a*ti; بسيطه bèssīt*a*. [bꞇtm*a*ssi.

Sundown, *s.* كونش باتمسى ghyùnèsh-

Sun-dried, *a.* كونشده قورودلمش ghyù-nèshd*a*-kūrudulmush.

Sundry, *a.* مختلف mùkhtèlif; برطاقم bìr-tàk*i*m; بشقه بشقه bꞇshk*a*-bꞇshk*a*.

Sunflower, *s.* آى چيچكى ày-chichèghi.

Sunlight, *s.* كونش ghyùnèsh; كونش ايدينلغى ghyùnèsh-*à*yd*i*nl*i*gh*i*.

Sunny, *a.* كونشى چوق ghyùnèshi-chòk.

Sunrise, Sunrising, كون طوغمسى ghyùn-dò*gh*m*a*ssi. [bꞇtm*a*ssi.

Sunset, *s.* كونش باتمسى ghyùnèsh-

Sunshine, *s.* كونش ghyùnèsh.

Sunstroke, *s.* كونش چارپمسى ghyùnèsh-chàrpm*a*ssi. [-yèmèghini-yèmek.

Sup, *v.n.* كيجه يمكنى يمك ghèyjé-

Superannuated, *a.* متقاعد mùtakā''id; —ation, تقاعد tàkā''ud. [رعنا rà''nà.

Superb, *a.* اعلى à''là, كوزل ghyùzèl,

Supercilious, *a.* مغرور màghrūr.

Superficial, *a.* سطحى sꞇthī; يوزده اولان yùzd*a*-òlan.

Superficies, *s.* سطح sꞇth, يوز yùz.

Superfine, *a.* اعلى à''là, على الاعلى ''àlìyyu-'l-à''là. [ارتق àrt*i*k.

Superfluous, *a.* زائد zā'id, فضله fꞇzl*a*,

Superintend, *v.a.* نظارت ا nꞇzārèt-et, باقمق bꞇkm*a*k.

Superior, *a.* دها اعلا dàhà-à''là; فائق fā'ik; باصقين bꞇssk*i*n, غالب ghālib; بيوك bìyuk, ما فوقنده اولان mā-fèvk*i*nd*a*-òlꞇn; —, *s.* بيوك bìyuk; ضابط zābit.

Supersede, *v.a.* يرينه كچمك yèrin*a*-ghèchmek; عزل ا ''ꞇzl-et, چيقارمق ch*i*kàrm*a*k. [صاچمه sꞇchm*a*.

Superstition, *s.* باطل اعتقاد bāt*i*l-i''tikād,

Supper, *s.* كيجه يمكى ghèyjé-yèmè*gh*i; the Lord's —, بادارق bꞇdarak, عشاى ربانى ''*i*shāy*i*-rꞇbbānī.

Supplement, *s.* ضميمه zàmīmé, تتمه tètìmmé.

Supplicate, *v.a.* يالوارمق yꞇlvarm*a*k, رجا ا rìjā-et, نيازا nìyāz-et.

Supply, *s.* موجود mèvjūd, الده اولان èldé-òlan ; يولده اولان yòlda-òlan, كلمكده اولان ghèlmekda-òlan ; مقدار mìkdār ; كلش ghèlish ; حصول hùssūl ; حوائج hàwā'ij, لوازمات làwāzimāt, مهمات mùhìmmāt, ذخيره zàkhìré ; —, *v.a.* ويرمك vèrmek, بولوب ويرمك bùlup-vèrmek ; حوائجنى ويرمك hàwā'ijini-vèrmek.

Support, *s.* اياق àyak, تمل tèmel ; دستك dèsstek, طياق dayak, پاينده pāyèndé ; ياردم yàrdim, امداد ìmdād ; ارقه àrka, تصحب tàssàhhub ; يمك yèmek, قوت ويره جك شيلر kùvvèt-vèréjék-shèyler ; اعانه ì"āné, احسان ìhsān, صدقه sàdaka ; كفاف نفس kèfàfi-nèfss ; نفقه nàfaka ; —, *v.a.* طوتمق tùtmak ; قالدرمق kàldirmak ; طيانمق dàyanmak ; تحمل ا tàhàmmul-et ; ياردم ا yàrdim-et ; ارقه او àrka-òl, تصحب ا tàssàhhub-et ; اعانه ا ì"āné-et ; بسلمك bèsslémek.

Supportable, *a.* تحمل اولنور tàhàmmul-òlunur, چكلور chèkilir, صبر اولنور sàbr-òlunur. [nāssir.

Supporter, *s.* طرفدار tàraf-dār ; ناصر

Suppose, *v.a.* فرض ا fàrz-et, طوتمق tùtmak, صايمق sàymak ; ظن ا zànn-et, صانمق sànmak, ذاهب او zāhib-òl.

Supposition, *s.* فرض fàrz ; ظن zànn.

Suppress, *v.a.* باصدرمق bàssdirmak ; منع ا mèn-"et.

Suppression, *s.* منع mèn".

Suppurate, *v.n.* جراحت اقمق jèrāhàt-àkmak.

Suppuration, *s.* جراحتك اقمسى jèrāhàtin-àkmassi.

Supremacy, *s.* امارت ìmārèt.

Supreme, *a.* عالى "ālī, اعلى à"là, والا vālā ; — council, مجلس والا mèjlissi-vālā ; — office of state, باب عالى bābi-"ālī. [jèzri-àssàmm.

Surd, *a.* اصم àssàmm ; — root, جذر اصم

Sure, *a.* (safe) امين èmīn ; (free from doubt) شبهه سز shùbhéssiz ; to be —, ايو بلمك īyi-bìlmek, يقيناً بلمك yàkīnan-bìlmek, شبهه سز بلمك shùbhéssiz-bìlmek ; to feel —, همان هيچ شبهه سى اولمامق (hèmen)-hìch-shùbhéssi-òlmamak.

Surety, *s.* كفيل kèfīl ; كفالت kèfālèt ; of a —, البته èlbètté.

Surf, *s.* طالغه كپوكى dàlgha-kyùpughu ; كپوكلو طالغه لر kyùpuklu-dàlghalar.

Surface, *s.* يوز yùz, سطح sàth (t-h) ; طيش dìsh, طيشارى dìshàri, خارج khārij, بيرون bīrūn.

Surgeon, *s.* جراح jèrrāh ; (bone-setter) چيققجى chìkìkji, قيرقجى kìrìkji.

Surgery, *s.* جراحلق jèrrāhlik, جراحخانه jèrrāh-khāné.

Surmise, *s.* ظن zànn, صان sàn ; —, *v.n.* ظن ا zànn-et, صانمق sànmak, ذاهب او zāhib-òl.

Surmount, *v.a.* حقندن كلمك hàkkindan-ghèlmek, غالب او ghālib-òl ; اوستندن اتلامق ùsstundan-àtlamak.

Surname, *s.* كنيه kyùnyé.

Surpass, *v.a.* كچمك ghèchmek, فائق او fā'ik-òl.

Surplus, *s.* فضله fàzla. [fā'ik-òl.

Surprise, *s.* تعجب tà''àjjub, حيرت hàyrèt, وله vèlɛh ; باصقين bàsskin, بربنك خوشلنه جغی شبخون shèbkhūn ; شيئك كيزلو ياپلمسی bìrining-khòsh-lanajaghi-shèy'ing-ghìzli-yàpılmassi ; —, *v.a.* تعجب ايتدرمك tà''àjjub-ètdirmek, حيران ا hàyrān-et ; باصمق bàssmak ; طوتمق tùtmak ; —sed, *a.* متعجب mùtà''àjjib, حيران hàyrān ; to be —sed, شاشمق shàshmak, تعجب ا tà''àjjub-et, متعجب او mùta-àjjib-òl, حيرتده قالمق hàyretda-kàlmak, وله كلمك vèlɛh-ghèlmek ; to my surprise, كورنجه شاشدم ghyù-runja-shàshdim.

Surprising, *a.* عجيب ''àjīb.

Surrender, *s.* تسليم tèsslīm ; —, *v.n.* تسليم او tèsslīm-òl ; —, *v.a.* تسليم ا tèsslīm-et.

Surreptitious, *a.* كيزلو ghìzli ; —ly, *ad.* ال التنده ɛl-àltinda.

Surround, *v.a.* چويرمك chèvirmek, قوشاتمق kùshatmak, اطرافنى المق ètrāfini-àlmak, احاطه ا ìhāta-et.

Surrounding, *a.* اطرافده اولان ètrāfda-òlan.

Survey, *s.* باقش bàkish, كوز كزدرش ghyùz-ghèzdirish, نظر nàzar, معاينه mù''āyéné, كشف kèshf, يوقلمه yòklama ; (mental) مطالعه mùtāla''à ; (plan) خريطه khàrīta (khàrta) ; (plan-taking) خريطه استخراجى khàrīta-ìsstikhrāji ; —, *v.a.* باقمق bàkmak, كوزكزدرمك ghyùz-ghèzdirmek, نظرا nàzar-et ; معاينه ا mù''āyéné-et, يوقلمه ا yòklama-et, كشف ا kèshf-et ; مطالعه ا mùtāla''à-et ; خريطه سنى المق khàrītassini-àlmak.

Surveying, *s.* فن مساحه fèni-mèssāha.

Survive, *v.a.* ينه ياشامق yìné-yàshamak (ghèné), اولمامك ùlmamek ; —, *v.a.* برى اولدقده ديكرى اولمامك bìri-ùldukda-dìgheri-ùlmamek ; برفلاكته مبتلا اولوب ينه اولمامك bìr-fèlākèta-mùbtélā-òlup-yìné-ùlmamek (ghèné).

Susceptible, *a.* قابل kābil, قبول ايدر kàbūl-èdɛr ; (in feeling) حساس hàsssāss, چابك دويار chàbik-dùyar ; چابك كوجنور chàbik-ghyùjènir.

Suspect, *v.a.* شبهه ا shùbhé-et, شبهه لنمك shùbhélɛnmek.

Suspend, *v.a.* (hang up) اصمق àssmak, تعليق ا tà''līk-et ; (a functionary) موقتا خدمتدن قالدرمق mùwàkkatan-khìdmetdan-kàldirmak ; (action) كسمك kèssmek, دوردرمق dùrdur-mak, تعطيل ا tà''tīl-et, معطل ا mù''àt-tal-et.

Suspense, *s.* شبهه shùbhé ; انتظار ìntizār ; in —, مشكوك mèshkyūk ; انتظارده ìntizārda.

Suspicion, *s.* شك shèkk, شبهه shùbhé.

Suspicious, *a.* موسوس mùwèsswiss ; شبهه لو shùphéli.

Sustain, *v.a.* (support) طوتمق tùtmak ; بسلمك bèsslémek ; طيانمق dàyan-mak, تحمل ا tàhàmmul-et ; اثبات ا ìssbāt-et ; تأييد ا tè'yīd-et ; (receive) يمك yèmek, مبتلا او mùbtélā-òl.

Sustenance, *s.* يمك yèmek, قوت kūt, غدا ghìdā.

Swaddling-clothes, قونداق kùndAk, ببك قونداغى bèbèk-kùndAghi.

Swallow, *s.* بوغاز bòghāz; (bird) قيرلانغيچ kìrlanghìch; —, *v.a.* يوتمق yūtmak, بلعا bèl''-et; — up, *v.a.* بتوى يوتمق bìtévi-yūtmak, بترمك bìtirmek, يوق ا yòk-et.

Swamp, *s.* بتاق bAtak, بتاقلق bAtaklik; —, *v.a.* صو طولوب باترمق sù-dòlup-bAtirmak; صو باصدرمق sù-bàssdirmak; (a market) بوغمق bòghmak.

Swampy, *a.* بتاقلق bAtaklik.

Swan, *s.* قوغو kùghu.

Swarm, *s.* أرى سوروسى Ari-sùrussu, سورى sùru; —, *v.n.* قايناMق kàynamak.

Sway, *s.* حكومت hùkyūmèt; —, *v.a.* صاللامق sAllamak; چويرمك chèvirmek; اداره ا ìdāré-et.

Swear, *v.n.* (an oath) يمين ا yèmīn-et, قسم ا kAssem-et, اند ايچمك And-ìchmek; (curse) كفر ا kyùfr-et, اغزينى بوزمق Aghzini-bòzmak; (blaspheme) سب ا sèbb-et.

Swearing, *s.* يمين ايتمكلك yèmīn-ètmeklik; كفر kyùfr.

Sweat, *s.* تر *or* تر tèr, عرق ''àrak; —, *v.n.* ترلمك tèrlémek; — out, *v.a.* ترليوب دفع ا tèrléyup-dèf''-et.

Swede, *s.* اسوچ آدمى ìssvèch-AdAmi.

Sweden, *s.* اسوچ ìssvèch.

Swedish, *a.* اسوچلو ìssvèchli; —, *s.* اسوچ لسانى ìssvèch-lìssāni.

Sweep, *s.* اوجاقجى òjakji, اوجاق سپوران òjak-sùpuren; (oar) كورك kyùrèk; —, *v.a.* سپورمك sùpurmek; — away, سلوب سپورمك silip-sùpurmek; — along, حيزلوكتمك hìzli-ghìtmek; — by, حيزلوكچمك hìzli-ghèchmek.

Sweepings, *s. pl.* سپورندى sùpurundu.

Sweet, *a.* طاتلو tAtli, شيرين shīrīn, حلاوتلو hàlāvètli; كوزل ghyùzèl, خوش khòsh, لطيف làtīf; لذيذ lèzīz, خوشكوار khòsh-ghyùwār; — smelling, *a.* كوزل قوقار ghyùzèl-kòkar, خوشبو khòsh-bū, معطر mù''àttar; — heart, *s.* عاشق ''Āshik; معشوقه mà''shūka.

Sweetmeat, *s.* طاتلو tAtli, شكرلمه shèkerlémé.

Swell, *s.* (of the sea) صالندى sAlindi; —, *v.n.* شيشمك shìshmek, قبارمق kAbarmak; —, *v.a.* قبارتمق kAbartmak.

Swelling, *s.* شيش shìsh; —, *a.* قبا kàba, تومسك tùmsèk.

Swift, *a.* چابك chàbik, سريع sèrī'', سرعتلو sùr''àtli, حيزلو hìzli; —, *s.* قرلانغيچ kìrlanghìch.

Swiftly, *ad.* چابك چابك chàbik-chàbik.

Swim, *v.n.* يوزمك yùzmek, سباحت ا sèbāhàt-et.

Swindle, *s.* حيله hīlé, اويون òyūn, طولاب dòlAp; —, *v.a.* طولاندرمق dòlandirmak.

Swindler, *s.* طولاندريجى dòlandiriji.

Swine, *s.* طوكز dònguz (dòmuz), خنزير khìnzīr, خوك khūgh.

Swing, *s.* صالنجق sAlinjàk; —, *v.n.* صاللانمق sAllanmak; —, *v.a.* صاللاندرمق sAllàndirmak.

Swiss, *s.* اسويچرالو ìssvìcherali; —, *a.* اسويچرالو ìssvìcherali.

Switch, *s.* اينجه چبوق ìnja-chìbùk;

سلكش silkish, صاللايش sallayish; —, *v.a.* سلكمك silkmek, چارپمق chàrpmak, صاللامق sallamak.

Switzerland, *s.* اسويچرا issvìchera.

Swivel, *s.* (gun) چقالوس طوپى chàkalòss-tòpu; (for turning) ميل mil; ميللو حلقه milli-halka.

Swoon, *s.* بايلمه bàyilma; —, *v.n.* بايلمق bàyilmak, بيخود اول bikhòd-òl; in a —, بايلمش bàyilmish; to go off in a —, بايلمق bàyilmak.

Sword, *s.* قلج kìlij, سيف sèyf, تيغ tīgh.

Sword-belt, *s.* قليج قايشى kìlij-kàyishi.

Sword-fish, *s.* قليج بالغى kìlij-balighi.

Sycamore, *s.* چنار chìnār.

Sycophant, *s.* كاسه ليس kyāssé-līss, دالقاوق dal-kàwuk.

Syllable, *s.* هجا hèjā (hèjé).

Syllogism, *s.* قياس kìyāss. [``àlāmèt.

Symbol, *s.* اشارت ìshārèt, علامت

Symmetry, *s.* تناسب اعضا tènāssubu-à``zā, انتظام ìntizām. [-hìss.

Sympathy, *s.* اشتراك حس ìshtirāki-

Symptom, *s.* علامت ``àlāmèt.

Synagogue, *s.* حوره hàwra.

Syndic, *s.* كتخدا kètkhùdā (kyāya), اسكى èsski.

Synod, *s.* علما مجلسى ``ùlèmā-mèjlissi, علما شوراسى ``ùlémā-shūrāssi.

Synonym, *s.* مترادفه mùtérādifé.

Synonymous, *a.* مترادف mùtérādif, هممعنا hèm-mà``nà. [-nàhv.

Syntax, *s.* نحو nàhv, علم النحو ``ìlmu-'n-

Syra (island of), *s.* سيره اطه سى sīrà-adassi.

Syria, *s.* شام shām, سوريه sūriyyé.

Syriac, *a.* سريانى sūriānī.

Syrian, *a.* شامى shāmī; —, *s.* شام ادمى shām-adami.

Syringa, *s.* فول بهار fūli-bàhār.

Syringe, *s.* حقنه hòkna; طلومبه tùlum-ba; —, *v.a.* احتقان ا ìhtikān-et; طلومبه باصمق tùlumba-bassmak.

Syrup, *s.* شروب shùrūb.

System, *s.* (practical) اصول ùssūl; (hypothesis) قول kàvl; (physical) منظومه manzūmé; طاقم tàkim.

T.

Tabernacle, *s.* مأوى mè``và, مسكن mèsskèn, خانه khāné, بيت bèyt.

Table, *s.* تربزه trèbézé, ماصه màssa; (set with food) صفره sòfra, مائده mā'idé; (mathematical) جدول jèd-vel; (astronomical) زيج zīj; —land, يايله yàyla, دوز dùz; — cloth, صفره بزى sòfra-bèzi. [linda.

Tabular, *a.* جدول شكلنده jèdvel-shèk-

Tacit, *a.* معنوى mà``névī; —ly, *ad.* معناً mà``nan, لسان حال ايله lìssāni-hāl-ila.

Tack, *s.* (nail) چيوى chìvi, قارفيچه kàrficha; (taste) لذت lèzzèt, طات tat, چاشنى (chèshni); (of a sail) قونطره اسقوت kòntra-skòt; —, *v.a.* چيوى ايله ايلشدرمك chìvi-ila-ilish-dirmek; —, *v.n.* (a ship) چويرمك chèvirmek, دونمك dònmek, اورصه الاباندا ا òrsa-àlabanda-et; to be on the starboard —, to have the starboard —s aboard, روزکارسنجاقدن‌اول rùzghyār-sànjakdan-òl (*or* صاغدن sàghdan); . . . larboard . . , اسکله‌دن ìsskèlédan (or صولدن sòldan).

Tackle, *s.* طاقم tàkim, أوادانلق àwadànlik, الات ālāt, اداوات èdāwāt; (pulley) پلانقه pàlangha.

Tackling, *s.* طاقم tàkim.

Tactics, *s. pl.* تدبير tèdbīr, حركات hàrékyāt.

Tail, *s.* قويرق kùyruk, زنب zèneb, دمباله dùmbālé; (entail) وقف‌مشروط wàkfi-mèshrūt.

Tailor, *s.* درزی (tèrzi), خياط khàyyāt.

Taint, *s.* قوقو kòku, فناقوقو fèna-kòku, تعفن tà''àffun; —, *v.a.* بوزمق bòzmak, قوقتمق kòkutmak.

Take, *v.a.* المق àlmak, اخذ ا àkhz-et; قبول ا kàbūl-et, قبض ا kàbz-et, ضبط ا zàbt-et; —, *v.n.* المق àlmak; مقبوله کچمك màkbūla-ghèchmek; موده‌او mòda-òl; — after, بکزه‌مك bèngzémek; — a leap, صچرامق sìchramak, اتلمق àtilmak; — a turn, کزمك ghèzmek, طولاشمق dòlash-mak; دونمك dùnmek, دکشمك dìghishmek; بشقه صورته کيرمك bàshka-sūrèta-ghìrmek, بشقه حال کسب ا bàshka-hāl-kèssb-et; —, *v.a.* طولاشدرمق dòlashdirmak, ايلشدرمك ìlishdirmek; — away, قالدرمق kàldir-mak, الوب‌کوترمك àlip-ghyùtur-mek; — care, ايوجه‌باقمق īyija-bàkmak, صاقنمق sàkinmak, دقت ا dìkkàt-et, کوزينی اچمق ghyùzunu-àchmak, حذرا hàzer-et; — care of, صقلامق sàklamak, حفظ ا hìfz-et; باقمق bàkmak; خدمتنی ا khìdmètini-et; — down, اشاغی المق àshàghi-àlmak; اندرمك èndirmek; يازمق yàzmak, قيد ا kàyd-et; بورننی قيرمق bùrnunu-kìrmak, قيرمق kìrmak; — hold, طوتمق tùtmak; — in, ايچرو المق ìchèri-àlmak; المق àlmak; دارالتمق dāràltmak; الداتمق àldatmak, اويون ا òyun-et; — in hand, الهالمق èla-àlmak; ال سورمك èl-sùrmek, بولاشمق bùlashmak; — off, قالدرمق kàldirmak; چيقارمق chìkàrmak; کسمك kèssmek; تقليد ا tàklīd-et; — on, *v.n.* کدر ا kèder-et; *v.a.* کيرمك ghìrmek, کسب ا kèssb-et; — — one's self, اوزرينه‌المق ùzèrina-àlmak; — out, چيقارمق chìkàrmak, طيشاری المق dìshàri-àlmak; کزمکه‌کوترمك ghèzméghé-ghyùturmek; — ship, کمی يه بنمك ghèmiya-bìnmek; — to pieces, *v.a.* سوکمك sùkmek, بوزمق bòzmak; *v.n.* سوکلمك sùkyulmek; — to task, دارلمق dàrilmak, ازارلمق àzarlamak, ياپديغنك حکمتنی صورمق yàpdighining-hìkmètini-sòrmak; — up, المق àlmak; قالدرمق kàldirmak; يوقاری المق yùkàri-àlmak; (a position) ضبط ا zàbt-et, داخل او dākhil-òl, کيرمك ghìrmek, کتمك ghìtmek; (an offender) طوتمق tùtmak, اخذ ا àkhz-et, کرفت ا ghìrift-et; (out of the ground) چيقارمق chìkàrmak; (a question) مباحثه‌سنه کيرشمك mùbāhissasina - ghìrishmek ; (a quarrel) کیرشمك ghìrishmek.

Tale, *s.* مصال mÀssAl, حکایه hìkyāyÉ, فقره fìkra, قصه kìsssa, منقبه màukabÉ; (count) صایی sàyi, عدد حسابی "àded-hìssĀbi ; — bearer, غماز ghÀmmĀz.

Talent, *s.* یوك کبی بر مبلغ yùk-ghìbi-bìr-mèblàgh ; استعداد ìssti"dād, هنر hùnEr.

Talented, *a.* هنرلو hùnErli.

Tale-teller, *s.* مداح mèddāh ; غماز ghÀmmĀz.

Talisman, *s.* طلسم tìlìssm *or* tìlsim.

Talk, *s.* لقردی làkirdi, لاف lÀf ; —, *v.n.* لقردی ا làkirdi-et, لاف ا lÀf-et ; تکلم ا tèkèllum - et ; صحبت ا sùhbet - et, قونکشمق kòngushmak ; — over, (a thing) لقردیسنی ا làkirdissini-et ; (a person) عقلنی چلمك "Àklini-chèl-mek, قاندرمق kÀndirmak, الزام ا ìlzām-et, اقناع ا iknā"-et.

Talkative, *a.* کوزه ghèvézÉ, قوال kÀwwĀl, بوش بوغاز bòsh-bòghĀz.

Talkativeness, *s.* کوزه لك ghèvézÉlik.

Tall, *a.* اوزون بویلو ùzun-bòylu, طویل tàwīl ; بالا bālā, یوکسك yùksek.

Tallow, *s.* طوك یاغی dòng-yàghi.

Tallow-chandler, *s.* مومجی mùmji.

Tally, *s.* چتله chètélÉ ; —, *v.n.* اویمق ùymak, مطابق او mùtĀbik-òl.

Tamarind, *s.* تمر هندی tèmri - hìndī (dèmirhìnd).

Tambourine, *s.* دف dèf.

Tame, *a.* الشمش Àlishmish ; او èv (house) ; مظلوم mÀzlūm, یواش yā-wÀsh ; —, *v.a.* الشدرمق Àlishdirmak, تربیه ا tÈrbìyyÉ-et.

Tamper, *v.n.* حیله ا hīlÉ-et ; قارشدرمق kÀrishdirmak ; (with a person) رشوت تکلیف ا rìshvet - tèklīf - et ; رشوت ویرمك rìshvet - vÈrmek ; ایارتمغه باقمق àyartmagha-bÀkmak.

Tan, *s.* دباغت تربیه سی dìbāghàt-tèr-bìyyÉssi ; (of the skin) یانقلق اسمرلکی yànìklik-èssmErlighi ; —, *v.a.* دباغت ا dìbāghàt-et, تربیه ا tÈrbìyyÉ-et ; —, *v.n.* (leather) دباغت قبول ا dìbāghàt-kÀbūl-et ; (the face, &c.) یانمق yànmak, اسمرلنمك èssmErlEnmek ; — yard, دباغ خانه dèbbĀgh-khānÉ (tÀbAk) ; — pit, دباغخانه قویوسی (tÀbAk)-khānÉ-kùyussu.

Tangent, *s.* مماس mùmĀsss, ظل zìll ; log. —, نسبت ظلیه nìssbèti-zìllìyyÉ.

Tangle, *s.* قارشقلق kÀrishiklik ; —, *v.n.* قارشمق kÀrishmak ; —, *v.a.* قارشدرمق kÀrishdirmak.

Tanner, *s.* دباغ dèbbĀgh (tÀbAk).

Tap, *s.* (blow) خفیف اورش khÀfīf-wùrush, دوقنش dòkunush ; (cock) مصلق *or* مصلوق mùsslUk ; (of a tavern) میخانه پیشتخته سی mèykhānÉ-pèsh-tàkhtassi ; (tapped cask) اچلمش فوچی àchilmish-fìchi ; —, *v.a.* (a cask) مصلوق اورمق mùsslUk-wùrmak, اچمق àchmak ; (strike) خفیفجه اورمق khÀ-fīfja-wùrmak.

Tape, *s.* شرید shèrid, قبا شرید kÀba-shèrid.

Taper, *a.* صوبی sùbu, کتدکجه اینجه ghìtdikja-ìnja ; اینجه ìnja ; —, *s.*

ﺔﻌﻤﺷ shèm‘‘à (shàma); — off, *v.n.* ﻚﻤﻠﺠﻧﺍ ﻪﺠﻜﺪﺘﻛ ghìtdikja-ìnjelmek; —, —, *v.a.* ﻚﻤﺘﻠﺠﻧﺍ ﻪﺠﻜﺪﺘﻛ ghìt-dikja-ìnjeltmek.

Tar, *s.* ﻥﺍﺮﻄﻗ kAtrAn; (sailor) ﻰﺠﻴﻤﻛ ghèmiji, ﻰﺠﻧﻮﻴﻠﻗ kàlyonjυ.

Tardy, *a.* ﭻﻛ ghèch.

Tare, *s.* (in weight) ﻩﺭﺍﺩ dàra; —s, *s. pl.* ﻕﺎﭽﺭﻮﺑ bùrchAk (?), ﻪﺠﻴﻟﺩ dèlija (??). [ﻥﺎﻘﻠﻗ kAlkAn.

Target, *s.* ﻥﺎﺸﻧ nìshAn, ﻑﺪﻫ hèdef;

Tariff, *s.* ﻪﻓﺮﻌﺗ tà‘‘rifé; ﺥﺮﻧ nàrkh.

Tarnish, *v.n.* ﻕﺮﻣﺭﺍﺮﻗ kArarmak, ﻚﻤﻨﻠﻜﻟ lèkélenmek; —, *v.a.* ﺍﺕﺍﺪﻴﺳ sìyāh-et, ﻚﻣﺭﺪﻨﻠﻜﻟ lèkélendirmek.

Tarpaulin, *s.* ﻊﻤﺸﻣ mùshèmmà‘‘ (mū-shàmba). [èkshija.

Tart, *s.* ﻚﻟﺭﻮﺑ bùrèk; —, *a.* ﻪﺠﻴﺸﻛﺍ

Tartar, *s.* ﺭﺎﺗﺎﺗ tàtar.

Tartary, *s.* ﻥﺎﺘﺴﺭﺎﺗﺎﺗ tàtarìsstān.

Task, *s.* (lesson) ﺱﺭﺩ dèrss; (duty) ﺶﻳﺍﺶﻤﻠﺴﻛ kèssilmish-ish, ﻪﻨﻴﻌﻣﺖﻳﺭﻮﻣﺄﻣ mè‘mūrìyyèti-mū‘‘àyyéné, ﻒﻴﻠﻜﺗ tèklīf, ﺖﻣﺫﻪﺒﺟﺍﻭ wājibè‘ī-zìmmèt; —, *v.a.* ﻚﻤﺴﻛﺶﻳﺍ ìsh-kèssmek, ﺍﺖﻴﻴﻌﺗﺶﻳﺍ ìsh-tà‘‘yīn-et; ﻕﺮﻣﺭﺪﺸﻟﺎﭼ chAlishdirmak.

Tassel, *s.* ﻝﻜﺴﭘ pùsskyul.

Taste, *s.* (savour) ﺕﺎﻃ tAt, ﻰﻨﺸﭼ chāshnī (chèshni), ﺕﺬﻟ lèzzèt, ﻡﺎﻌﻃ tà‘‘ām; (sense of) ﻪﻘﺋﺍﺫﺕﻮﻗ kùv-vèti-zā‘ika; (artistic) ﺖﻌﻴﺒﻃ tAbī‘‘at; —, *v.a.* ﻕﻤﺗﺎﻃ tàtmak; —, *v.n.* ﻭﺍﻯﺩﺎﻃ tAdi-ol, ﻭﺍﻰﺴﻴﻨﺸﭼ (chèsh-nissi)-ol, ﻭﺍﻰﺘﺬﻟ lèzzèti-ol.

Tasteful, *a.* ﻒﻳﺮﻇ zārif.

Tastefully, *ad.* ﻪﻠﻳﺍ ﺖﻓﺍﺮﻇ zàrāfèt-ìla.

Tastefulness, *s.* ﺖﻓﺍﺮﻇ zàrāfèt.

Tasteless, *a.* ﺯﺴﺗﺎﻃ tAtsiz.

Tastelessness, *s.* ﻕﻠﺰﺴﺗﺎﻃ tAtsizlik.

Tastily, *ad.* ﻪﻠﻳﺍ ﺖﻓﺍﺮﻇ zàrāfèt-ìla.

Tasty, *a.* ﻒﻳﺮﻇ zārif.

Tavern, *s.* ﻪﻧﺎﺨﻴﻣ mèykhāné.

Tax, *s.* ﻮﻛﺮﻳﻭ vìrghyū, vèrghi, ﻢﺳﺭ rèssm (*pl.* ﺕﺎﻣﻮﺳﺭ rùssūmAt); property or income —, ﻮﻛﺮﻳﻭ (vèrghi), ﻒﻴﻠﻜﺗ tèklīf, ﻪﻧﺎﻴﻟﺎﺳ sāliyāné, ﻦﻴﻐﻟﺎﺻ sAlghin; capitation —, ﺝﺍﺮﺧ khàrāj, ﻪﻳﺰﺟ jìzyé; (expense) ﺭﺎﺑ bàr; —, *v.a.* (a thing) ﺍﻦﻴﻴﻌﺗﻢﺳﺭ rèssm-tà‘‘yīn-et; (a person) ﻕﻤﻟﺎﺻ ﻦﻴﻐﻟﺎﺻ sAlghin-sAlmak; ﻕﻤﻼﻏﺎﺑﺝﺍﺮﺧ khàrāj-bAgh-lamak, ﺍﻦﻴﻴﻌﺗ ﻪﻳﺰﺟ jìzyé-tà‘‘yīn-et (*or* ﺍﻊﻄﻗ kAt‘‘et); (accuse) ﻪﻨﻳﺯﻮﻳ ﻕﻣﺭﻭﺍ yùzuna-wūrmak, ﺍﺩﺎﻨﺳﺍ ìssnād-et, ﺍ ﻭﺰﻋ ‘‘àzv-et; — gatherer, ﻰﺠﺟﺍﺮﺧ khàrājji; ﺭﺍﺪﻠﻴﺼﺤﺗ tàhsīldār.

Tea, *s.* ﻯﺎﭼ chày, ﻰﻳﺎﭼ ﻮﻘﺴﻣ mòsskov-chàyi; — tray, ﻰﺴﭙﺗ tèpsi; — spoon, ﻰﻐﺷﺎﻗﻩﻮﻬﻗ kàhwé-kAshighi; — kettle, ﻢﻜﻛﻮﻛ ghyùghum.

Teach, *v.a.* ﻚﻤﺗﺮﻛﻭﺍ ùghretmek, ﺍﻢﻴﻠﻌﺗ tà‘‘līm-et, ﺍﺲﻳﺭﺪﺗ tèdrīss-et.

Teacher, *s.* ﻪﺟﺍﻮﺧ khòja, ﻢﻠﻌﻣ mū‘‘àl-lim, ﺱﺭﺪﻣ mùdèrriss.

Teacup, *s.* ﻰﻧﺎﺠﻨﻓ ﻯﺎﭼ chày-fìljAni.

Tea-dealer, *s.* ﻰﺠﻳﺎﭼ chàyji.

Teapot, *s.* ﻰﻐﻳﺮﺑﺍ ﻯﺎﭼ chày-ìbrighi.

Tear, *s.* ﻰﺷﺎﻳﺯﻮﻛ ghyùz-yàshi, ﻚﺷﺮﺳ

sìrìshk, دمع dèm'', دمعه dèm''à, (*pl.* دموع dùmū'') ; —, *v.a.* يرتمق yìrtmak, چاك ا chāk - et, خرق ا khàrk-et, هتك ا hètk-et.

Teat, *s.* ممه mèmé, پستان pìsstān.

Teaze, *v.a.* طاقلمق tàkilmak, صاتاشمق sàtashmak, اذيت ا èzìyyèt-et, تعجيز ا tà''jīz-et, عذاب ا ''àzāb-et.

Technical, *a.* علمى ''ìlmī ; فنى fènnī ; اصطلاحى ìsstilāhī ; — term, اصطلاح ìsstilāh. [اوصاندرر ùssàndirir.

Tedious, *a.* اوزون ùzun ; اوزار ùzar ;

Teem, *v.n.* قاينامق kàynamak, چوق او chòk-òl.

Telegram, *s.* تلغرافنامه tèlègrāf-nāmé.

Telegraph, *s.* تلغراف tèlègrāf.

Telegraphic, *a.* تلغرافه منسوب tèlègrāfé-mènsūb.

Telegraphy, *s.* تلغراف ايله خبر كوندرمك صنعتى tèlègrāf-ìla-khàbr-ghyùnder-mek-san''ati. [آيينه àyina, جام jām.

Telescope, *s.* دوربين dūrbīn (dùrbun),

Tell, *v.a.* سويلمك sùwèylémek, نقل ا nàkl-et ; (count) صايمق sàymak, تعداد ا tà''dād-et ; —, *v.n.* خبر ويرمك khàber-vèrmek ; (in account) صايلمق sàyilmak ; (produce an effect) تأثيرى او tè'sīri-òl, تأثير ا tè'sīr - et ; (strike) اورمق wùrmak, ديكمك dèghmek, اصابت ا ìssàbet-et. [dèlilik.

Temerity, *s.* جرئت jùr'èt, دليلك

Temper, *s.* (natural) خوى khūy, طبيعت tàbī''àt, خلق khùlk, جبلت jibìllèt, مشرب mèshrèb ; (of steel) صو sù, آب āb ; —, *v.a.* (steel) صو ويرمك sù-vèrmek ; (the cold) ملايم ا mùlà-yim-et.

Temperance, *s.* پرهيزكارلق pèrhīzkyārlik, اعتدال ì''tidāl, افراطدن اجتناب ìfrātdan-ìjtināb.

Temperate, *a.* پرهيزكار pèrhīzkyār, از ير از ايچر àz-yèr-àz-ìcher ; (in quality or in heat), معتدل mù''tèdil ; — zone, منطقهٔ معتدله màntika'i-mù''tèdilé.

Temperature, *s.* حرارت hàrārèt, درجهٔ حرارت dèréjè'i-hàrārèt.

Tempest, *s.* چوق فرطونه chòk-fìrtina, بوره bòra. [fìrtinali.

Tempestuous, *a.* فرطونه fìrtina, فرطونه لو

Temple, *s.* معبد mà''bèd, عبادتكاه ''ìbādet - ghyāh, عبادتخانه ''ìbādet-khāné, (of idols) بتخانه (pùt)-khāné ; — of Jerusalem, مسجد اقصى mèss-jidi-àksà, المسجد الاقصى èl-mèssjidu-'l-àksà ; — of the head, شقق يرى shàkak-yèri, شقق shàkak.

Temporarily, *ad.* موقتاً mùwàkkatan.

Temporary, *a.* موقت mùwàkkàt ; عاريتى ''āriyyètī (èyréti).

Tempt, *v.a.* ايارتمغه چالشمق àyart-magha-chàlishmak, اغوايه سعى ا ìgh-wāya-sà''y-et ; (an object) دعوت ا dà''vet-et ; — successfully, ايارتمق àyartmak, الداتمق àldatmak, اغوا ا ìghwā-et, اغفال ا ìghfāl-et, اضلال ا ìdlāl-et. [ده dèh.

Ten, *a.* اون òn, عشر ''àshar, عشره àshara,

Tenable, *a.* قابل محافظه kābili-mùhāfaza, محافظه سى ممكن mùhàfazassimùmkin ; (assertion) اثباتی ممکن ìssbāti-mùmkin, صالح sàlih.

Tenacious, *a.* براقمز bràkmàz.

Tenacity, *s.* عناد ‘‘ìnād.

Tenant, *s.* کراجی kìrājì, مستأجر mùsstè'jir ; —, *v.a.* کرا ایله طوتمق kìrā-ila-tùtmak ; اوطورمق òturmak.

Tend, *v.a.* باقمق bākmak, خدمتنی ا khìdmetini-et ; —, *v.n.* مائل او mā'il-òl, متمایل او mùtémàyyil-òl ; منتج او mùntij-òl, وارمق vàrmak, طیانمق dàyanmak, نتیجه ویرمك nètījé-vèr-mek, منجر او mùnjèrr-òl.

Tendency, *s.* میل mèyl, تمایل tèmàyyul, أستعداد ìsstì‘‘dād, رکون rùkyūn.

Tender, *a.* نازك nāzik ; یموشاق yìmu-shàk ; —, *s.* (offer) تکلیف tèklīf ; —, *v.a.* تکلیف ا tèklīf-et, عرض ا ‘‘àrz-et ; ویرمك vèrmek.

Tendon, *s.* سکیر sìngir, عصبه ‘‘àssaba.

Tenor, *s.* مآل mà'āl, فحوا fèhwà, معنی mà‘‘nà.

Tense, *s.* زمان zàmān ; —, *a.* کرکی ghèrghi, کریلو ghèrili ; present —, حال hāl ; imperfect —, حال ماضی hāli-māzī ; perfect —, ماضی māzī ; aorist —, مضارع mùzāri‘‘ ; future —, مستقبل mùsstàkbel.

Tent, *s.* چادر chàdir, خیمه khàymé, خرکاه khàrghyāh.

Tenth, *a.* اوننجی ònunju, عاشر ‘‘āshir, دهم dèhum ; —, *s.* عشر ‘‘ùshr.

Tepid, *a.* ایلیجه ìlìja, ایلیجق ìlìjàk.

Term, *s.* (word) تعبیر tà‘‘bīr ; (technical) اصطلاح ìsstìlāh ; (stipulation) شرط shàrt ; (of time) مدت mùddèt ; (delay) مهل mèhl, مهلت mùhlèt, وعده wà‘‘dé ; (price) فی fī, فیأت fī'àt ; —, *v.a.* تعبیرا tà‘‘bīr-et, تسمیه ا tèssmìyé-et, دیمك dèmek, منقطع او mùnktàti‘‘-òl.

Terminate, *v.n.* بتمك bìtmek, منتهی او mùntèhi-òl, انتهابولمق ìntìhā-bùlmak —, *v.a.* بترمك bìtirmek, کسمك kèssmek, قطع ا kàt‘‘-et.

Termination, *s.* صوك sòng, نهایت nìhāyet, انتها ìntìhā.

Terra firma, *s.* قره kàra.

Terrace, *s.* (on hill-side) سد sèdd ; (house-top) سطح sàth (t-h), دام dàm, باجه bàja ; (of houses) صره اولر sìra-èvler.

Terrestrial, *a.* دنیوی dùnyévī ; ارضی àrzī ; — globe, کره ارض kyùré'i-àrz.

Terrible, *a.* مخوف màkhūf, مدهش mùdhìsh, مهیب mùhīb.

Terrify, *v.a.* قورقتمق kòrkutmak, تخویف ا tàkhwīf-et, اخافه ا ìkhāfa-et, ترهیب ا tèrhīb-et.

Territory, *s.* اراضی àrāzi (*pl.* of ارض arz, land), ممالك mèmālik (*pl.* of مملکت country). [دهشت dèhshèt.

Terror, *s.* قورقو kòrku, خوف khàvf,

Testament, *s.* وصیتنامه wàssìyyèt-nāmé, وصیت wàssìyyèt. [nāmé-sāhibi.

Testator, *s.* وصیتنامه صاحبی wàssìyyèt-

Testicle, *s.* طاشاق tàshak, خایه khāya.

Testify, *v.n.* شهادت ا shàhādet-et ; اظهارا ìzhār-et, کوسترمك ghyùsster-mek, ابرازا ìbrāz-et.

Testimonial, *s.* شهادتنامه shàhādet-nāmé.

Testimony, *s.* شهادت shàhādet; افاده ìfādé, تقریر tàkrīr.

Tether, *s.* پایبند pàybènd (pàywand), ایپ ìp; —, *v.a.* باغلامق bàghlamak.

Text, *s.* (of a book) متن mètn.

Texture, *s.* قماش kùmāsh, نسج nèssj.

Thank, *v.a.* تشکرا tèshèkkyur-et; —s, *s. pl.* تشکر tèshèkkyur, شکر shùkr; —ful, متشکر mùtéshèkkir; to give —, to return —, شکرا shùkr-et, تشکرا tèshèkkyur-et.

That, *pron.* شو shù, اول òl *or* او ò; —, *rel. pron.*: see Grammar; —, *c.* که ki.

Thatch, *s.* صاپدن اورتی sàpdan-ùrtu; —, *v.a.* صاپ ایله اورتمك sàp-ila-ùrtmek.

Thaw, *s.* قارلرك اریمسی kàrlaring-èriméssi, بوزلرك چوزلمسی bùzlaring-chùzulmassi; —, *v.n.* اریمك èri-mek; چوزلمك chùzulmek; —, *v.a.* ارتمك èritmek.

The, *art.* See Grammar.

Theatre, *s.* تیاترو tèyàtro.

Theatrical, *a.* تیاترویه متعلق tèyàtroya-mùta''alik.

Theatrically, *ad.* تیاترویه مخصوص طرز ایله tèyàtroya-màkhsūs-tàrz-ìla.

Theatricals, *s. pl.* تیاترو اویونلری tèyàtro-òyunleri.

Theft, *s.* خرسزلق khìrsizlik, سرقت sìrkàt, سرقه sèrika.

Their, *a. pro.* لری lari, انلرك ànlaring; —s, *pro.* انلركکی ànlaringki.

Theist, *s.* موحد mùwàhhid (Unitarian).

Themselves, *pro. pl.* کندیلری kèndiléri.

Then, *ad.* اولوقت òl-wàkit, اولزمان òl-zàmān; (afterwards) صکره sòngra, بعده bà''dahū, پس pèss; —, *c.* اویله ایسه ùylè-issa, بوصورتده bù-sūrètda, امدی ìmdi.

Thence, *ad.* اول محلدن òl-màhàldan; اول وقتدن ol-vwàktden; اول سببدن òl-sèbebden.

Thenceforth, Thenceforward, *ad.* بعده ba''da-hù.

Theology, *s.* علم کلام ''ìlmi-kèlām, حکمت الهیه hikmèti-ìlāhìyyé.

Theorem, *s.* دعوای نظری dà''wàyi-nàzarī.

Theoretical, *a.* علمی ''ìlmī, نظری nàzarī.

Theory, *s.* قول kāvl, یول yòl, مذهب mèzhèb, طریق tàrīk, نظر nàzar.

Therapeutics, *s.* علم طب ''ilmi-tìbb.

There, *ad.* اورا òra; اورایه òraya; اوراده òrada; شورا shùra; شورایه shùraya, شوراده shùrada; انده ànda, ònda; —! *int.* اشته ìshta, نا nà, تها tèhā; — about, — abouts, اورالر òralar, اورالره òralara, اورالرده òralarda; اول صولرده (ò)-sùlarda, اول صولره طوغری ò-sùlara-dòghru; —by, اول مناسبتله òl-mùnāssébètla; — after, اندنصکره àndan-sòngra; — at, اکا ànga, ònga; — from, اندن àndan, òndan; —in, اکا ànga; انده ànda; اندن àndan; —of, اندن àndan; —on, اکا ànga; انده ànda; انك اوزرینه àning-ùzérina; انك اوزرنده àning-ùzérinda; — to, — unto, اکا ànga, اکا طوغری ànga-dòghru; — out, اندن àndan; — under, انك التنه àning-

-Altina ; انك التنده Aning-Altinda ; — upon, انك اوزرينه Aning-ùzérina ; انك اوزرنده Aning-ùzérinda ; —with, انك ايله Aning-ila, انك ايله برابر Aning-ila-bèrābèr ; معاً mà''an ; لفاً lèffAn, ملفوفاً mèlfūfan ; — withal, انك ايله برابر Aning-ila-bèrābèr.

Therefore, c. امدى ìmdi, بوسببدن bū-sèbebdan, بوسببه بناءً bū-sèbéba-bīnā'an, بوسببه مبنى bū-sèbéba-mèbni, بوكا مبنى bùnga-mèbni, بوكا بناءً bunga-bìnā'an, بناءً عليه bìnā'an-''àlèyh, بناءً على ذلك bìnā'an-''àlà-zālìké, بنابرين bìnābérīn.

Thermometer, s. ميزان حرارت mīzAni-hàrārèt, هوا ترازوسى hàwā-tèrāzissi.

Thessaly, s. لواديه lìvādia ; تساليا tèssālia.

They, pro. انلر Anlar, ònlAr.

Thibet, s. تبت tìbbèt.

Thick, a. (in solidity) قالين kAlin ; (in fluidity) قويو kòyu, كثيف kèssīf ; (coarse) قبا kAba ; (close) صيق sìk ; (intimate) صيقى sìki ; —, s. الك قويو يير èng-kòyu-yèr, اورطه or اورته òrta, اورته يرى òrta-yèri, الك فنا ير èng-fèna-yèr.

Thicken, v.n. قالينلشمق kālinlashmak ; قويولشمق kòyulashmak ; صيقلشمق sìklashmak ; فنالشمك fènalèshmek ; —, v.a. قالينلشدرمق kAlinlashdirmak ; قويولتمق kòyulatmak ; صيقلشدرمق sìklashdirmak.

Thief, s. خرسز khìrsiz, سارق sārik, دزد dùzd, اوغرى òghri.

Thieve, v.n. خرسزلك ا khìrsizlik-et, سرقت ا sìrkAt-et.

Thigh, s. بوط bùt, بجاق bAjak, اويلق ùylùk, فخذ fàkhz.

Thimble, s. يوكسوك yùksuk.

Thin, a. (in solidity) اينجه ìnja ; (in flesh) ضعيف zà''īf, زبون zàbun ; (in fluidity) صولو sùlu ; (wide apart) سيرك sèyrèk ; —, v.a. سيرلتمك sèyreltmek ; —, v.n. سيرلمك sèy-relmek.

Thine, pro. a. ك ìng, ng ; سنك sèning ; —, pro. سنككى sèningki.

Thing, s. شى shèy, شىء shèy' (pl. اشيا eshyā), نسنه nèssné, چيز chīz.

Think, v.n. دوشونمك dùshunmek, تفكر ا tèfèkkyur-et ; (ponder) ملاحظه ا mùlāhaza-et ; — over, مطالعه ا mùtāla''a-et ; —of, خاطرلامق khātirlamak, خاطره كتورمك khātira-ghètirmek ; — about, دوشونمك dùshunmek, قورمق kùrmak ; —, v.a. (imagine) صانمق sànmak, ظن ا zànn-et ; (esteem) صايمق sàymak, عد ا ''àdd-et.

Third, a. اوچنجى ùchunju, ثالث sāliss, سيم sìyum ; —, s. اوچده بر ùchda-bìr, ثلث sùlss (sùluss).

Thirst, s. صوسزلق sùssuzluk, عطش ''Atsh ; حرارت hàrārèt ; —, v.n. صوصامق sùssamak, عطشان او ''Atshān-òl, تشنه او tìshné-òl ; —y, a. صوصامش sùssamish, عطشان ''Atshān, تشنه tìshné.

Thirteen, a. اون اوچ òn-ùch.

Thirty, a. اوتوز òtuz, ثلثون sèlāssūn, ثلثين sèlāssīn, سى sī.

This, *pro.* بو bŭ, شو shŭ.

Thistle, *s.* اشك دیكنی èshek-dìkéni, دوه دیكنی dèvé-dìkéni.

Thither, *ad.* اورایه òraya.

Thorn, *s.* دیكن dìkèn, ایكنه ìghné, خار khār, شوك shèvk; —y, *a.* دیكنلو dìkènli.

Thorough, *a.* اصل assl, تام tamm, كامل kyāmil; —bred, جنس jìnss, صوی sòy; —fare, چیقار صوقاق chìkar-sòkak; no —fare, چیقمز صوقاق chìkmàz-sòkak; —ly, *ad.* بتون بتون bìtun-bìtun, تماماً tamā-man, كاملاً kyāmilan, هر وجهله hèr-wèjhla, كركی كبی ghèrèghi-ghìbi.

Thou, *pro.* سن sèn.

Though, *c.* ایسه‌ده ìssa-da, هر نقدر hèr-nàkadar; ینه yìné (ghèné).

Thought, *s.* فكر fìkr (*pl.* افكار èfkyār); مطالعه mùtāla"à.

Thoughtful, *a.* دوشنور dùshunur.

Thoughtless, *a.* دوشنمز dùshunmàz.

Thoughtlessness, *s.* صایغیسزلق sày-ghisizlik. [hèzār.

Thousand, *a.* بیك bìng, الف èlf, هزار

Thraldom, *s.* رقیت rìkkìyyèt.

Thrash, *v.a.* دوكمك dùghmek; (corn) خرمن ا kharman-et; (the enemy) بوزمق bòzmak.

Thrashing, *s.* خرمن ایتمكلك kharman-ètmeklik; طیاق dàyak.

Thrashing-machine, *s.* خرمن چرخی khàrman-chàrkhi.

Thread, *s.* ایپلك ìplik; تیره tìré; تل tèl; رشته rìshté; —, *v.a.* (a needle) ایپلك كچورمك ìplik-ghè-chirmek; (a path) سوكمك sùkmek, چیقارمق chìkàrmak, كچمك ghèch-mek, مرورا mùrūr-et.

Threat, *s.* قورقو ویره‌جك لقردی kòrku-vèréjek-làkirdi, قورقو kòrku.

Threaten, *v.a.* قورقو ویرمك kòrku-vèrmek; قورقولو كوزكمك kòrkulu-ghyùzukmek.

Three, *a.* اوچ ùch, ثلثه sèlāssé, سه sèh.

Threshold, *s.* قپو اشكی kapi-èshighi, استان āssitān, استانه āssitāné, عتبه "àtébé.

Thrice, *ad.* اوچ كره ùch-kèrré, اوچ دفعه ùch-dèf"à, اوچ سفر ùch-sèfer. [ìdāréjilik.

Thrift, *s.* اداره idāré, اداره‌جیلك

Thrifty, *a.* اداره‌جی idāréji.

Thrive, *v.n.* كلشمك ghèlishmek; —ving, *a.* كلشاتلو ghèlishatli.

Throat, *s.* بوغاز bòghaz, حلقوم hùlkūm.

Throb, *s.* یورك اویناماسی yùrek-òynamassi; یاره زونقلاماسی yàra-zònklamassi; —, *v.n.* اوینامق òynamak; زونقلامق zònklamak.

Throne, *s.* تخت tàkht; مسند mèss-ned, صدر sadr; — of God, عرش "àrsh; —, *v.a.* تخته اوطورتمق tàkhta-òturtmak.

Throng, *s.* غلبه‌لق (kalabalik), ازدحام ìzdihām; —, *v.n.* اوشوشمك ùshushmek, قوششمق kòshushmak; غلبه‌لق ا (kalabalik)-et, ازدحام ا ìzdihām-et.

Throttle, *s.* بوغاز bòghāz; —, *v.a.* بوغمق bòghmak, بوغازینی صیقمق bòghāzini-sìkmak.

Through, *pr.* دن dan; ایچندن ìchindan; — and —, یاندن یانه yàndan-yàna; —out, *ad.* باشدن باشه bāshdan-bāsha; اولندن اخرینه قدر èvvelindan-ākhirina-kādar.

Throw, *s.* اتم ātim; —, *v.a.* اتمق ātmak, انداخت ا èndākht-et, رمی ا rèmy-et; — away, اتمق ātmak; اسراف ا ìssrāf-et, تلف ا tèlef-et; — off, چیقارمق chìkàrmak, دفع ا dèf"-et.

Thrust, *s.* قاقش kākish, ایتش ìtish; دورتش dùrtush; صوقش sòkush; اورش wùrush; —, *v.a.* قاقمق kākmak, ایتمك ìtmek; دورتمك dùrtmek; صوقمق sòkmak; اورمق wùrmak; — away, دفع ا dèf"-et, طرد ا tàrd-et.

Thumb, *s.* باش پارمق bāsh-pàrmak; —, *v.a.* یپراقلرینی پرمقله کیرلدوب اورسه‌لمك yàprakIarini-pàrmàkla-kìrlèdup-ùrsélémek.

Thump, *s.* مشته اورشی mùshta-wùrushu; —, *v.a.* مشته ایله اورمق mùshta-ila-wùrmak.

Thunder, *s.* کوك کورلمسی ghyùk-ghyùrlémèssi, رعد rà"d; —, *v.n.* کورلمك ghyùrlémek; — bolt, یلدرم yìldirim, صاعقه sā"ika; —clap, کوکك بر کورلمسی ghyùghing-bìr-ghyùrlémèssi; —stroke, یلدرم yìldirim, صاعقه sā"ika; —struck, یلدرم چارپمش yìldirim-chàrpmish, صاعقه اصابت ایتمش sā"ika-ìssābet-ètmish; متعجب mùta"àjjib, حیران hàyrān, سرسم sèrsèm, شاشه‌قالمش shàsha-kālmish; to be — struck, قالمق kālmak, شاشه‌قالمق shàsha-kālmak.

Thursday, *s.* پنجشنبه pènjshènbìh (pèrshamba), خمیس khàmīss.

Thus, *ad.* بویله bùylé, بویله‌جه bùyléja; بو صورتله bù-sūrètla; بو وجهله bù-wèjhla; بو تقدیرجه bù-tākdīrja; — far, بورایه‌قدر bùraya-kādar, بورایه‌دق bùrayadak.

Thwart, *v.a.* ایشنی‌بوزمق ìshini-bòzmak, سکته ویرمك sèkté-vèrmek.

Thy, *pro. a.* ك ìng, ng; سنك sèning; —self, کندك kènding.

Thyme, *s.* ککك اوتی kèkik-òtu, ککك kèkik.

Tick, *s.* (insect) کنه ghèné; upon —, ویره‌سی‌یه vèréssiyé; —, *v.n.* طیق‌طیق ا tìk-tìk-et.

Ticket, *s.* کاغد kyāghid; یافته yāfta.

Tickle, *v.n.* غیجقمق ghìjìkmak; —, *v.a.* غیجقدرمق ghìjìkdirmak; — one's fancy, خوشنه کتمك khòshina-ghìtmek.

Tide, *s.* جذر و مد jèzr-u-mèdd; high —, مد mèdd; مد کامل mèddi-kyāmil; ebb —, جذر jèzr.

Tidy, *a.* تمیز tèmiz.

Tie, *s.* باغ bāgh; (in architecture) قوشاق kùshāk; (moral) علاقه "àlāka, مناسبت mùnāssèbèt, انتساب ìntissāb; (impediment) عقده "ùkdé,

مانع mānī"; —, *v.a.* باغلامق bAgh-lamak, عقد ا "Akd-et.

Tier, *s.* صره sira; قات kAt.

Tiger, *s.* ببر bübr.

Tight, *a.* صيقى sìki; water—, صوكچمز sù-ghèchmàz; air—, هوا كچمز hàwā--ghèchmàz.

Tighten, *v.a.* صيقشدرمق sìkishdirmak.

Tigris (the river), *s.* دجله dèjlé. [tüghla.

Tile, *s.* كراميد kìrémīd; (flat) طوغله

Till, *s.* پاره‌چكمجه‌سى pAra-chèkméjéssi; —, *v.a.* تيمارا tīmār-et, زراعت ا zìrā"àt-et, حراست ا hìrāssèt-et; —, *pr.* ئه‌قدر a-kAdar, ئه‌دك é-dek, ئه‌دق a-dak.

Tillage, *s.* زراعت zìrā"àt.

Tiller, *s.* زراعتجى zìrā"àtji; (of a rudder) يكه yèké.

Timber, *s.* كرسته kèresstè, احشب àhshàb, احشاب àhshāb; — yard, كرسته‌جى‌دكانى kèresstéji-dùkkyāni.

Time, *s.* وقت wAkit, زمان zàmAn; هنكام hènghyām; period of —, مدت mùddèt, دور dèvr, عصر "Assr, قرن kàrn, ايام èyyām (*pl.* of يوم yùvm, a day); (number in recurrence) كره kèrré, مره mèrré, دفعه dèf"à, سفر sèfer, نوبت nùbèt; —, *v.a.* وقت تعيين ا wAkit-tà'yīn-et; وقتنه‌دقت ا wAktina-dìkkAt-et; there's — enough, دها وقت وار dàhā-wAkit-vàr, وقت چوق wAkit-chòk; from — immemorial, from — out of mind, اوته‌دنبرو ùtédan-bèri, از قديم èz-kAdīm, من القديم mìn-el-kAdīm.

Timid, *a.* قورقاق kòrkàk, اوركك ùrkek; محجوب màhjūb, اوطانور ùtAnir, اوطانغج ùtAnghàch. [hìjāb.

Timidity, *s.* قورقاقلق kòrkàklik, حجاب

Tin, *s.* قلاى kAlay; (in sheets) تنكه tènéké; —, *v.a.* قلايلمق kAlaylamak.

Tincture, *s.* (medicinal) روح rūh; (slight mixture) قوقو kòkü, شائبه shā'ibé; —, *v.a.* جزئيجه بر رنك ويرمك jùz'ījà-bìr-rènk-vèrmek.

Tinder, *s.* قاو kàw *or* kAv; — box, چقماق‌كيسه‌سى chàkmàk-kèysèssi.

Tinge, *v.a.* جزئيجه بر رنك ويرمك jùz'ījà-bìr-rènk-vèrmek, تلوين ا tèlvīn--et, بويامق bòyamak.

Tinker, *s.* چنكانه (chìnghèni, a gipsy); —, *v.a.* قباجه‌تعمير ا kAbaja-tà"mīr-

Tinman, *s.* تنكه‌جى tènékéji. [-et.

Tinsel, *s.* شماته تلى shàmAta-tèli.

Tint, *s.* چشيد chèshid, رنك rènk, لون

Tiny, *a.* اوفاجق ùfAjèk. [lèvn.

Tip, *s.* اوج ūj, دپه (tèpé); بخشش bàkhshish; —, *v.a.* ويرمك vèrmek, اتمق Atmak; —, *v.n.* بخشش ويرمك bàkhshish-vèrmek; — up, براوجنى قالدرمق bir-ùjùni-kAldirmak; — off, — over, *v.n.* دوريلوب دوشمك dèvrilip-dùshmek; —, *v.a.* دويروب دوشورمك dèvirip-dùshurmek.

Tipple, *s.* ايچقى ìchki; —, *v.n.* ايچمك ìchmek, چاقمق chàkmak.

Tippler, *s.* بكرى bèkrī.

Tipstaff, *s.* قواص kAvwAss. [(sàr-).

Tipsy, *a.* كيف kèyf, سرخوش sèrkhòsh

Tire, *s.* (of a wheel) چنبر chènber,

تیمور (dèymir); —, *v.a.* یورمق yòrmak; (in liking) اوصاندرمق ùssÂndirmak; (in patience) صبرینی دوکتمك sÀbrini-dùkètmek; (cause disgust) بزدرمك bèzdirmek; —, *v.n.* یورلمق yòrulmak; اوصانمق ùssÂnmak; بزمك bèzmek; صبری دوکنمك sÀbri-dùkènmek.

Tiresome, *a.* مناسبتسز mùnâssébètsiz; اوصانج ویرر ùssÂnj-vèrir, اوصاندرر ùssÂndirir; ادمك جاننی صیقار Àdam-ing-jānini-sìkar.

Tissue, *s.* قماش kùmāsh, نسج nèssj.

Tithe, *s.* عشر ùshr (*pl.* اعشار à"shār), اونده‌لق òndalìk.

Title, *s.* (of honour) لقب làkab (*pl.* القاب èlkāb), عنوان ùnwān; (right) حق hàkk; (deed) سند sèned, حجت hùjjèt.

Tittle-tattle, *s.* دیدی قودی لاقردیسی dèdi-kòdu-làkirdissi.

To, *pr.* ئه ـه É, *a*; ئه‌قدر *a*-kÀdar; ئه‌طوغری *a*-dòghru; ایچون ìchin; —day, بوكون bù-ghyùn; —night, بوكیجه bù-ghèyjÉ, بو اوكمزده‌كی كیجه bù-ùngumuzdéki-ghèyjÉ; —morrow, یارین yàrin.

Toad, *s.* قره قوربغه kÀra-kùrbAgha, اودلوبغه òdlu-bÀgha; — stool, زهرلو منتار zèhirli-mÀntar.

Toady, *v.a.* مداهنه‌ا mùdāhéné-et.

Toadyism, *s.* مداهنه mùdāhéné.

Toast, *s.* اكمك قزارتمسی èkmek-kìzàrtmassi; عشقنه شراب ایچلان كمسنه "Àshkina-shàrāb-ìchilen-kìmèssnÉ; —, *v.a.* قزارتمق kìzàrt-mak; عشقنه شراب ایچمك "Àshkina-shàrāb-ìchmek. [dùkhān.

Tobacco, *s.* توتن *or* تتون tùtun, دخان

Tobacconist, *s.* توتونجی tùtunju.

Toe, *s.* پرمق pàrmak, ایاق پرمغی àyak-pàrmaghi.

Together, *ad.* برابر bèrābèr, برلكده bìr-likda; بریره bìr-yèra; بریرده bìr-yèr-da; جمعاً jèm"àn; جمیعاً jèmī"àn.

Toil, *s.* ایش ìsh, رنج rènj, كلفت kyùlfèt, مشقت mèshàkkÀt; —s, *s. pl.* طوزاق tùzÀk; —, *v.n.* چالشمق chÀlishmak, چبالمق chàbAlamak, ایشلمك ìshlémek.

Token, *s.* نشان nìshān, اشارت ìshāret, علامت "àlāmèt; (of remembrance) بركذار bèrghyuzār.

Tolerable, *a.* چكلور chèkilir, تحمل اولنور tàhàmmul-òlunur; اب ایوجه èp-īyija.

Tolerance, Toleration, *s.* تحمل tàhàmmul, هضم hÀzm, مساعده mùssā"adÉ.

Tolerate, *v.a.* مساعده‌ا mùssā"adÉ-et, تجویزا tèjvīz-et, قبولا kÀbūl-et, چكمك chèkmek.

Toll, *s.* باج bÀj, قپو ویركوسی kÀpi-vèrghissi, مروریه mùrūrìyyÉ; —, *v.a.* (a bell) چالمق chÀlmak; —, *v.n.* چالنمق chÀlinmak.

Tomato, *s.* طوماته dòmāta.

Tomb, *s.* مزار mèzār, قبر kÀbr, لحد làhd; تربه tùrbÉ; — stone, مزار طاشی mèzār-tÀshi.

Tomfool, *s.* دالقاوق dÀl-kàwuk.

Tomfoolery, *s.* مسخره‌لق mÀsakharalìk.

Ton, *s.* طونلاته tònélàta.

Tone, *s.* سس sèss ; پرده pèrdé ; (of muscle, &c.) قوت kùvvèt.

Tongs, *s. pl.* ماشه màsha.

Tongue, *s.* دل dìl, لسان lìssān, زبان [zàbān.

Tongue-tied, *a.* دلی طوتلمش dìli-tùtul-[mush.

Tonic, *s.* مقوی mùkàvvī.

Tonnage, *s.* كمینك طونلاته‌سی ghèminin--tònélàtassi.

Too, *ad.* (also) دخی dàkhi, ده da, كذلك kèzālik ; (more than needful) حد لزومدن زیاده hàddi-lùzūmdan--zìyādé. (This particle is not in use in Turkish ; the simple adjective fulfils its function. *Vid.* Grammar.)

Tool, *s.* الت ālet (*pl.* الات ālāt) ; —s, *s. pl.* ادوات èdawāt, اداوات èdāwāt, اوادانلق àwadanlik, طاقم tàkim.

Tooth, *s.* دیش dìsh, سن sìnn (*pl.* اسنان èssnān), دندان dèndān, دندانه dèndāné ; —pick, خلال khìlāl, دیش قارشدره‌جق dìsh-kàrishdirajak.

Top, *s.* اوست ùsst, یوقاری yùkàri, فوق fèvk, بالا bālā ; (summit) دپه (tèpé), ذروه zìrvé ; (of a mast) چناقلق chànaklik ; (plaything) فرلداق fìril-dàk ; —, *a.* اوستده‌كی ùsstdèki, اوستنده‌كی ùsstundèki ; — mast, غابیه‌چبوغی ghàbìya-chìbùghu ; — sail, غابیه ghàbiya ; —most, الك یوقاریكی èng-yùkàriki, الك یوقاریده‌كی èng-yùkàridéki.

Topaz, *s.* زبرجد zèberjèd (?), صاری یاقوت sàri-yākūt.

Topgallant, *a.* بابا فنغونك bàba-fìngonin.

Topic, *s.* ماده māddé.

Topography, *s.* خریطه‌تفصیلاتی khàrīta--tàfsīlāti ; تفصیلات زمین tàfsīlāti--zèmìn. [زیروزبر zīr-u-zèber.

Topsy-turvy, *ad.* الت‌اوست ālt-ùsst,

Torch, *s.* مشعله mèsh''àla (màshala).

Torment, *s.* اذیت èzìyyèt ; —, *v.a.* اذیت ا èzìyyèt-et ; اذیت ویرمك èzìyyèt-vèrmek.

Tornado, *s.* قصرغه kàssìrgha.

Torpedo, *s.* تورپیل tòrpīl.

Torpid, *a.* اویشق ùyushuk, اویشمش ùyushmush, جانسز كبی jānsiz-ghìbi.

Torpor, *s.* اویشقلق ùyushukluk.

Torrent, *s.* سیل sèyl (sèl) ; حیزلو اقان صو hìzli-akan-sù.

Torrid, *a.* حار hārr ; — zone, منطقه حاره màntika'i-hārré.

Tortoise, *s.* قاپلو بغه kàpli - bàgha (kàplimbagha) ; — shell, بغه bàgha.

Torture, *s.* اذیت èzìyyèt, شكنجه shìkènjé, اسكنجه ìsskènjé ; —, *v.a.* اذیت ا èzìyyèt-et, اسكنجه ا ìsskènjé--et, اویقوسز براقمق ùykussuz--bràkmak.

Toss, *s.* اتش àtish, فرلادش fìrlàdish ; —, *v.a.* اتمق àtmak, فرلاتمق fìrlat-mak ; —, — about, *v.n.* صیچرامق sìchramak, فرلامق fìrlamak, اتلمق àtilmak ; (waves) قبارمق kàbarmak.

Total, *s.* یكون yèkyūn, طوپ tòp, مجموع mèjmū'' ; —, *a.* كلی kyùllī ; مجموع mèjmū''.

Totter, *v.n.* سندلمك sèndélémek, یقله‌جق‌او yìkilajak-òl.

Touch, *s.* دوقنش dòkunùsh ; (sense

of) قوت لامسه kùvvèti - lāmissé; last —, صوك ال sòng-èl; (tincture) قوقو kòku, شائبه shā'ibé, اثر èsser; —, v.a. دوقنمق dòkunmak, ال سورمك èl-sùrmek, ال اورمق èl-wùrmak; ملاصق او متصل او mùttàssil-òl, mùlāssik-òl; دكمك dèghmek; بتشمك bìtishmek; یاپشمق yàpish-mak; (move the heart) قلبنه رقت كتورمك kàlbina-rìkkàt-ghètirmek, يموشاتمق yìmushatmak; — upon (in speaking) اكدروب كچمك àngdirip-ghèchmek; — hole, فاليه fàlya, فاليه دليكى fàlya-dèlighi; —stone, محك màhèkk (mèhènk, mèhènk-tàshi); —wood, قاو kàw or kàv.

Tough, *a.* سرت sèrt; قوپمز kòpmàz; قتى kàti, كسلمز kèssilmàz; (difficult) كوچ ghyùch, چتين chètin; (of endurance) جانى پك jāni-pèk.

Tour, *s.* جزئى بر سياحت jùz'ī-bìr-sèyāhàt.

Tourist, *s.* ذوق ايچون كيدن سياح zèvk-ìchin-gìden-sèyyāh.

Tournament, *s.* مزراق اويونى mìzrak-òyunu.

Tow, *s.* بياض استوپى bèyāz-ùsstùpu, كتان فضلەسى kètèn-fàzlassi; قتيق kìtik; —, v.a. يدكه المق yèdégha-àlmak, چكمك chèkmek; — rope, پلمار pàlamār; — line, يدك ايپى yèdek-ìpi.

Toward, **Towards**, *pr.* ئە طوغرى a-dòghru, طرفنه طوغرى tàrafina-dòghru, جهتنه طوغرى jìhètina-dòghru.

Towel, *s.* حاولو hàwli; پشتمال pèshta-māl, فوطه fùta.

Tower, *s.* قله kùllé or قوله kùlé; (in town walls) برج bùrj; —, v.n. يوكسلمك yùkselmek.

Town, *s.* قصبه kàssaba, شهر shèhr, مملكت mèmlékèt, محروسه màhrūssa, محميه màhmìyyé, مدينه mèdīné.

Town-clerk, *s.* شهرك دفترامينى shèhirin-dèfter-èmini. [-mùnādìssī.

Town-crier, *s.* شهرك مناديسى shèhirin-

Town-hall, *s.* شهر قوناغى shèhir-kòna-ghi.

Townsman, *s.* همشهرى hèm-shèhrī.

Toy, *s.* اويونجق òyunjàk; —, v.n. اوينامق òynamak, اويناشمق òynash-mak, ايلنمك èylenmek.

Trace, *s.* ايز ìz, نشانه nìshāné, نشان nìshān, اثر èsser; (of harness) قوشم قايشى kòshum-kāyishi; —, v.a. ايزلمك ìzlémek, اثارينه تتبع ā ssārina-tètèbbu''-et; (on paper) چيزمك chìzmek, رسم ا rèssm-et; سلكمك sìlkmek; ياغلو كاغده المق yàghli-kyāghida-àlmak; ايسلو كاغد ايله چيزمك ìssli-kyāghid-ila-chìzmek; جامده چيزمك jàmda-chìzmek.

Track, *s.* ايز ìz; بللو بللوسز پياده يولى bèlli-bèllissiz-pìyāda-yòlu; —, v.a. قره‌دن يدك ايله چكمك kàradan-yèdek-ila-chèkmek.

Tract, *s.* ناحيه nāhìyyé, الكا (ùlké); (book) رساله rìssālé, جزء jùz'.

Tractable, *a.* مظلوم màzlùm, سوزدكلر sùz-(dìner), منقاد mùnkād.

Trade, *s.* صنعت sàn"at, حرفت hìrfèt; الش ویرش ȦlIsh-vÈrish, تجارت tì-jāret, اخذ وعطا àkhz-ʊ-"Ȧtā, داد وستد dād-ʊ-sìtèd; —, *v.n.* الش ویرش ا Ȧlish-vÈrish-et, تجارت ا tìjāret-et; —sman, دکانجی dùkkyānji, بازرکان bȦzirghyān, اصناف èssnāf.

Tradition, *s.* حدیث hàdīss, حدیث شریف hàdīssi-shèrif; روایت rì-wāyet; —al, *a.* منقول mènkūl, مروی mèrvī.

Traffic, *s.* الش ویرش Ȧlish-vÈrish, تجارت tìjāret; (on a road) کلن کچن ghèlɛn-ghèchɛn; اشلکلك ishleklik; having much —, اشلك ìshlèk; —, *v.n.* الش ویرش ا Ȧlish-vÈrish-et; تجارت ا tìjāret-et.

Tragedy, *s.* عاقبتی وخیم اولان وقعه "ākibéti-wàkhīm-òlȦn-wàk"à.

Train, *s.* اوزون اتك ùzʊn-ètek, ذیل zèyl (*pl.* اذیال èzyāl), دامن dāmɛn; (suite) اتباع طاقمی ètbā"-tàkimi, خدم khȦdem, حشم hȦshem; (of powder) یملمه yèmlémé; فتیل fìtil; صجوق sùjʊk; (series) صره sàra, الای Ȧlay, سورو sùru; (of guns) طوپلر tòplar; siege —, محاصره طوپلری mùhȦssara-tòplari; —, *v.a.* تعلیم ا tà"līm-et; تربیه ا tÈrbìyyé-et; (a tree) داللرینی بر رسمه قومق dȦllarini-bìr-rèssma-kòmak; — on, *v.n.* اوزامق ùzamak, سورمك sùrmek, بتمامك bìtmamek.

Traitor, *s.* دولت خائنی dèvlet-khā'ini, دولتنه خائن dèvlètina-khā'in.

Traitress, *s.* خائن قاری khā'in-kȦri.

Trample on, *v.a.* چینهمك chīnémek, ایاق باصمق àyak-bȦssmak; — under foot, ایاق التنه المق àyak-Ȧltina-Ȧlmak.

Tranquil, *a.* راحت rāhat, اسوده āssūdé, ساکن sākin; مأمون mè'mūn.

Tranquillity, *s.* راحت rāhat, اسایش āssāyish, سکونت sùkyūnèt, امنیت èmnìyyèt.

Tranquillize, *v.a.* تأمین ا tè'mīn-et.

Transaction, *s.* وقعه wàk"à, سرکذشت sÈr-ghyùzèsht; معامله mù"āmélé.

Transcribe, *v.a.* عینینی یازمق "àynini-yàzmak, صورتنی یازمق sūrÈtini-yàz-mak, صورتنی المق sūrÈtini-Ȧlmak, صورتنی چیقارمق sūrÈtini-chìkàrmak, نسخهسنی یازمق nùsskhassini-yàzmak, استنساخ ا ìsstinsākh-et.

Transfer, *v.a.* نقل ا nȦkl-et, دور ا dèvr-et, چویرمك chèvirmek, کچورمك ghèchirmek. [hèy'èta-kòmak.

Transform, *v.a.* بشقه هیئته قومق bȦshka-

Transgress, *v.n.* قباحت ا kȦbāhat-et, جنحه ا jùnhà-et; کناه ا ghyùnāh-et; —, *v.a.* تخطی ا tàkhȦtti-et, تجاوز ا tèjāvuz-et; خلافنده حرکت ا khìlȦ-finda-hàrékÈt-et.

Transgression, *s.* خطا khàtā, جنحه jùnhà, جرم jùrm, قباحت kȦbāhat, کناه ghyùnāh, معصیت mà"sìyyèt.

Transient, *a.* سورکسز sùreksiz, قرارسز kȦrārsiz, بیقرار bīkȦrār, زائل zā'il, فانی fānī.

Transit, *s.* مرور mùrūr.

Translate, *v.a.* ترجمه ا tÈrjumé-et, چویرمك chèvirmek, نقل ا nȦkl-et.

Translation, *s.* ترجمه tèrjumé ; نقل nàkl.

Translator, *s.* مترجم mùtèrjim, ترجمان tèrjumān.

Transmigration, *s.* تناسخ tènāssukh.

Transmission, *s.* نقل nàkl, ارسال ìrsāl, ایصال īssāl ; امرار ìmrār ; مرور mùrūr.

Transmit, *v.a.* یوللامق yòllamak, کوندرمك ghyùndermek, ارسال ا ìrsāl-et, ایصال ا īssāl-et ; کچورمك ghèchirmek, امرار ا ìmrār-et, واسطهٔ مروری او wāssita'i-mùrūru-òl. [bèrrāk.

Transparent, *a.* شفاف shèffāf, براق

Transpire, *v.n.* سزلمك sèzilmek, دویلمق dùyulmak, شیوع بولمق shùyū''-bùlmak.

Transport, *s.* (ship) عسکر کمیسی ''àsker-ghèmissi ; (convict) سورکون ادم sùrghyun-àdam ; منفی mènfī ; (excessive sensation) فرط fèrt, افراط ìfrāt ; (ecstasy) وجدان vìjdān ; (carriage) نقل nàkl ; —, *v.a.* (a criminal) سورمك sùrmek, سورکون ا sùrghyun-et, نفی ا nèfy-et ; (carry) طاشیمق tàshimak, کوترمك ghyùturmek, نقل ا nàkl-et ; (cause joy) سوندرمك sèvindirmek.

Transportation, *s.* سورکون sùrghyun, نفی nèfy, جلا jilā, اجلا ìjlā ; place of —, منفی mènfī *or* mènfā.

Transylvania, *s.* اردل ولایتی èrdèl-vilāyèti. [باجه bàja.

Trap, *s.* طوزاق tùzàk, دام dām ; — door,

Trash, *s.* بوق bòk ; صاچمه sàchma ; (idle talk) هرزه hèrzé.

Travel, *s.* سیاحت sèyāhàt ; سفر sèfer, —, *v.n.* سیاحت ا sèyāhàt-et, سفر ا sèfer-et, کزمك ghèzmek, یولجیلق ا yòljuluk-et. [نورد nèvèrd.

Traveller, *s.* سیاح sèyyāh, یولجی yòlju,

Traverse, *v.a.* یاندن یانه کچمك yàndan-yàna-ghèchmek ; باشدن باشه کزمك bàshdan-bàsha-ghèzmek ; (impede) منع ا mèn''-et, مانع او māni''-òl, بوزمق bòzmak, سکته ویرمك sèkté-vèrmek, [tàbla.

Tray, *s.* تپسی tèpsi, سینی sìni, طبله

Treacherous, *a.* (person) خائن khā'in ; (act) خائنانه khā'ināné ; to have a — memory, چابك اونوتمق chàbik-ùnutmak, خاطرده شی طوته مامق khātirda-shèy-tùtamamak. [khā'inlik.

Treachery, *s.* خیانت khìyānet, خائنلق

Treacle, *s.* بکمز bèkmez, پتمز pètmez.

Tread, *v.a.* ایاق باصمق àyak-bàssmak.

Treason, *s.* دولته ایدیلن خیانت dèvlété-èdilen-khìyānèt.

Treasonable, *a.* دولته خیانت نوعندن dèvléta-khìyānèt-nèv''inden.

Treasure, *s.* مال māl, پاره (pàra), اقچه àkcha ; (hidden) دفینه dèfiné, خزینه khàzīné (hàzna) ; (in affection) ایکی کوز ìki-ghyùz, جکر jìgher, جکرکوشه jīgher-kyùshé ; (in estimation) چوق ایشه یرارشی chòk-ìsha-yàrar-shèy ; — up, *v.a.* صاقلامق sàklamak, حفظ ا hìfz-et. [nadār).

Treasurer, *s.* خزینه دار khàzīnédār (hàz-

Treasury, *s.* خزینه khàzīné ; مالیه نظارتی māliyyé-nàzārèti ; مالیه قپوسی māliyyé-kàpissi.

Treat, *s.* ضيافت zìyāfèt; ايلنجه èylenja; —, *v.a.* (use) قوللانمق kùllanmak, معامله ا mü''amélé-et; (a sick person) باقمق bàkmak, معالجه ا mü''āléjé-et; (feast) ضيافت ويرمك zìyāfèt-vèrmek; (pay for) پاره سنى ويرمك pàrassini-vèrmek; —, *v.n.* (on a subject) بحث ا bàhss-et; (negotiate) مكالمه ا mùkyālémé-et.

Treatise, *s.* رساله rìssālé. [mù''āléjé.

Treatment, *s.* معامله mü''āmélé; معالجه

Treaty, *s.* معاهده mü''āhédé, عهد ''àhd; عهدنامه ''àhd-nāmé.

Treble, *s.* اوچقات ùch-kàt; (voice) اينجه سس ìnja-sèss, قارى سسى kàri-sèssi; —, *v.a.* اوچقات ا ùch-kàt-et; —, *v.n.* اوچقات او ùch-kàt-òl.

Tree, *s.* اغاج àghaj, شجر shèjer, درخت dìràkht; — nail, قويليه kàvìlya; cross—, قورچته kùrchèta.

Tremble, *s.* ديتره مه (tìtrémé), لرزه lèrzé, رعشه rà''shé; —, *v.n.* ديتره مك (tìtrémek), لرزان او lèrzān-òl; —bling, لرزان lèrzān, لرزه ناك lèrzénāk, رعشه دار rà''shédār.

Tremendous, *a.* مهيب mùhīb, مدهش mùdhìsh; چوق chòk, پك pèk.

Trench, *s.* خندق (hèndek); مترس mètériss; —, *v.a.* ايكى اوچ بل درينلكنده قازمق ìki-ùch-bèl-dèrinlighinda-kàzmak; — round, خندق چويرمك (hèndek)-chèvirmek; — upon, تجاوز ا tèjāvuz-et, ال اوزاتمق èl-ùzàtmak.

Trespass, *s.* جنايت jìnāyet; جنحه jùnhà, گناه ghyùnāh; —, *v.n.* جنايت ا jìnāyet-et, گناه ا ghyùnāh-et; — on one, — on one's time, اشغال ا ìshghāl-et, تعجيز ا tà''jīz-et, تصديع ا tàssdī''-et, باش اغرتمق bàsh-àghrìtmak.

Trevet, *s.* صاج اياق sàj-àyak.

Trial, *s.* (experiment) دنه يش dènéyīsh, تجربه tèjrubé; (by law) دعوى dà''wà, محاكمه mùhākémé; on —, *a.* مخير mùkhàyyer.

Triangle, *s.* مثلث mùssèllèss.

Triangular, *a.* مثلث شكلنده mùssèllèss-shèkilinda.

Tribe, *s.* قبيله kàbīlé (*pl.* قبائل kàbā'il), عشيرت ''àshīrèt (*pl.* عشائر ''àshā'ir), ايل īl (*pl.* ايلات īlàt); (of Israel) سبط sèbt (*pl.* اسباط èssbàt).

Tribulation, *s.* محنت mìhnèt.

Tribunal, *s.* محكمه màhkémé, حاكم حضورى hākim-hùzūru.

Tributary, *a.* خراجگذار اولان khàrāj-ghyùzār-òlan. [khàràj. جزيه jìzyé.

Tribute, *s.* ويركو vìrghyu *or* vèrghi, خراج

Trick, *s.* اويون òyun; حيله hīlé; (custom) خوى khūy; —, *v.a.* اويون ا òyun-et, الداتمق àldatmak.

Trickery, *s.* حيله hīlé. [-àkmak.

Trickle, *v.n.* اينجه اينجه اقمق ìnja-ìnja-

Trifle, *s.* صاچمه sàchma, اويون òyun, جزئى شى jùz'ī-shèy, لاشى مقوله سى lā-shèy-màkūléssi; —, *v.n.* اوينامق òynamak, صاچمه ا sàchma-et, دليلك ا délilik-et; —fling, *a.* جزئى jùz'ī; —, *s.* صاچمه sàchma, دليلك dèlilik; —fler, دلى dèli.

Trigger, *s.* تتك tètik.

Trigonometry, *s.* علم مثلثات "ìlmi--mùssèllESSāt.

Trim, *s.* (of a vessel) دنك dènk ; (of clothing) قيافت kỳāfèt ; —, *a.* بچملو bìchimli ; —, *v.a.* دوزلتمك dùzèltmek ; دنك ا dènk-et, دنكنى دوزلتمك dèn*gh*ini-dùzèltmek.

Trimming, *s.* خرج khàrj, قيطان (ghày-tĀn); (moral) مواضعه mŪwĀz*a*"à.

Trinity, *s.* اقانيم ثلثه *à*kĀnīmi-sèlàssÉ.

Trip, *s.* (slip) اياق قپانمسى àyak-kĀpAn-*massi* ; (moral) خطا khĀtā ; (excursion) كزمه ghèzm*a*, طولاشمه dòlashm*a* ; —, *v.n.* اياغى قپانمق àyag*hi*-kĀpAnmak ; خطا ا khĀtā-et ; — up, *v.n.* اياغى قپانوب دوشمك àyaghi-kĀpĀnip-dùshmek ; —, *v.a.* دوشورمك dùshurmek.

Tripe, *s.* اشكنبه ìshkĒnbÉ.

Triple, *s.* اوچ قات ùch-kĀt ; —, *v.a.* اوچ قات ا ùch-kĀt-et ; —, *v.n.* اوچ قات او ùch-kĀt-òl.

Tripoli, *s.* (town in Barbary) طرابلوس غرب tàràbàlūsi-ghàrb ; —, (town of Syria) طرابلوس شام tàràbàlūsi-shām.

Triturate, *v.a.* ازمك èzmek, سحق ا sàhk-et.

Triumph, *s.* غلبه ghàlébÉ, نصرت nùssrèt ; (procession) الاى Ālay ; —, *v.n.* غالب او ghālib-òl ; —, — over (exult) اوكنمك u*gh*Ēnmek, تفاخر ا tèfākhur-et.

Triumphant, *a.* غالب ghālib.

Trivial, *a.* صاچمه sĀchm*a*, جزئى jùz"ī.

Triviality, *s.* صاچمه‌لق sĀchm*a*lik ; جزئيلك jùz"ilik.

Troop, *s.* سورى sùru, طاقم tàk*i*m, الاى àlay ; (of cavalry or horse-artillery) بلوك bùluk ; —, *v.n.* طوپلانمق tòplanm*a*k ; —s, *s. pl.* عسكر "ĀsskEr.

Trooper, *s.* سوارى نفرى sùwāri-nèfEri.

Trophy, *s.* ظفرك علامتى zĀfErin-"*à*lāmèti.

Tropic, *s.* مدار mèdār ; — of Cancer, مدار سرطان mèdār*i*-sèratĀn ; — of Capricorn, مدار جدى mèdār*i*-jèdī.

Trot, *s.* لنك lìnk, لنكلمه lìnklémÉ ; —, *v.n.* لنك كتمك lìnk-ghìtmek, لنكلمك lìnklÉmek.

Trotters, *s. pl.* پاچه pàch*a* ; اياق àyak.

Trouble, *s.* صيقندى sìk*i*ndi, زحمت zàhmet, مشقت mèshàkkĀt, اذيت èzìyyèt, (care) درد dèrd, بلا bèlā, باش اغريسى bĀsh-Āg*h*rissi ; — *v.a.* صيقندى ويرمك sìkindi-vèrmek, تعجيز ا tà"jīz-et ; زحمت ويرمك zàhmet--vèrmek ; — one's self, زحمت ا zàhmet-et ; — one's self about . . . , قيد ا kàyd-et ; وظيفه ا wĀzīfÉ-et ; قساوت ا kĀssāvet-et.

Troublesome, *a.* صيقندى sìk*i*nd*i*, صيقنديلو sìk*i*nd*ili*, زحمت وير zàh-met-vÈrir.

Trough, *s.* يكنه tèknÉ ; اولاق Āvlàk.

Trousers, *s. pl.* پانطلون pàntalòn ; شالوار shĀlwar ; پوطور pòtur, چاقشير [chĀksh*i*r.

Trout, *s.* اله بالق Āl*a*-bĀl*i*k.

Trowel, *s.* ماله mĀl*a*.

Truce, *s.* متاركه mùtārékÉ.

Truck, *s.* ال عربه‌سی èl-‘‘àrabassi; (exchange) ترانپه trànpa; (of a mast) شاپقه shÂpka.

True, *a.* (not false) کرچك ghèrchek, صحیح sàhīh; (real) حقیقی hàkīkī; (faithful) صادق sÂdik, وفادار wèfādār; (right) طوغری dòghru, صحیح sàhīh; (well ascertained) محقق mùhÂkkÂk.

Truly, *ad.* واقعا wākì‘‘ā, حقیقت hÂkīkÂt, فی الحقیقه fī-'l-hÂkīka.

Trumpet, *s.* بورو bòru; سورنا sūrnā (zùrna); —, *v.a.* اعلان ا ì‘‘lān-et.

Trumpeter, *s.* بوروزن bòruzèn (-zàn).

Trunk, *s.* صندق sÂndik, چانطه chÂnta; (of a tree) کتوك kyùtuk; (of the body) کوده ghyùwdé; (of an elephant) خرطوم khòrtūm.

Trunnion, *s.* مویلو mùylu.

Trust, *s.* (faith) اعتماد ì‘‘timād, امنیت èmnìyyèt; (charge) امانت èmānèt; on —, ویره‌سی‌یه vèréssiyé; —, *v.a.* امانة تسلیم ا èmānétèn-tèsslīm-et; —, *v.n.* اعتماد ا ì‘‘timād-et, امنیت ا èmnìyyèt-et; (in God) توکل ا tèvèkkyul-et, متوکل او mùtévèkkil-òl.

Trustee, *s.* متولی کبی امانتدار mùté-vèllī-ghìbi-èmānètdār.

Trustworthiness, *s.* صداقت sÂdākÂt.

Trustworthy, Trusty, *a.* صادق sādik.

Truth, *s.* (absolute) حق hÂkk; (of an assertion) صحت sìhhÂt, حقیقت hÂkīkÂt; (true speech) طوغری لاقردی dòghru-làkirdi; to speak the —, طوغری سویلمك dòghru-sùwèylémek.

Truthful, *a.* طوغری dòghru.

Truthfulness, *s.* طوغریلق dòghrulùk.

Try, *v.n.* (endeavour) چالشمق chÂlishmak, سعی ا sà‘‘y-et; غیرت ا ghàyret-et; —, *v.a.* (as an experiment) باقمق bÂkmak, دنه‌مك dènémek, تجربه ا tèjribé-et; (as a proof) امتحان ا ìmtìhān-et; (cause a great exertion) زورلمق zòrlamak; یورمق yòrmak; اوصاندرمق ùssÂn-dirmak; کوجنه کتمك ghyùjuna-ghìtmek.

Trying, *a.* تحملکداز tùhàmmul-ghyùdāz.

Tub, *s.* بادیه bÂdiya, کردل ghèrdèl.

Tube, *s.* بورو bòru, زوانه zìwāné; (of a water-pipe) مارپیچ màrpich.

Tuberose, *s.* تبر tèber.

Tubular, *a.* بورو شکلنده bòru-shèklinda, بوروکبی bòru-ghìbi.

Tuesday, *s.* صالی sÂli, صالی کونی sÂli-ghyùnu, ثلاثا sèlāsā, سه‌شنبه sèh-shènbih.

Tug, *s.* چکش chèkish; (ship) یدك واپوری yèdek-vàporu; —, *v.a.* چکمك chèkmek; یدکه المق yèdéghé-Âlmak.

Tuition, *s.* درس dèrss, تدریس tèdrīss, تعلیم tà‘‘līm; تعلم tà‘‘àllum, تحصیل tàhsīl.

Tulip, *s.* لاله lālé.

Tumble, *s.* دوشش dùshush, یقلش yìkilish; —, *v.n.* (fall) دوشمك dùshmek, یقلمق yìkilmak; (be disarranged) بوروشمق bùrushmak, اورسه‌لنمك ùrsélenmek; —, *v.a.* دوشورمك dùshurmek, یقمق yìkmak; بوروشدرمق bùrushdurmak, اورسەلتمك ùrsélétmek.

Tumbler, *s.* بیوك قدح bìyuk-kàdeh, صو قدحی sù-kàdéhi.

Tumour, *s.* شیش shìsh, چبان chìbàn.

Tumult, *s.* قارشقلق kàrishiklik; كورلدی ghyùruldu, پاطردی pàtirdi, شماته shàmata. [-(òkkalik)-fichi.

Tun, *s.* سكزیوزقیەلق‌فوچی sèkiz-yuz-

Tune, *s.* هوا hàwā; in —, اهنك āhènk, اویغون ùyghun; —, *v.a.* اهنك ا āhènk-et, اویدرمق ùydurmak.

Tunnel, *s.* یرالتی‌یول yèr-àlti-yòl, یرالتی كمر yèr-àlti-kèmer.

Tunny, *s.* پلامید pàlamīd(?), التی‌پرمق àlti-pàrmak(?); (preserved) لاكرده [lākèrda.

Turban, *s.* صارق sàrik.

Turbid, *a.* بولانق bùlànik.

Turbot, *s.* قالقان kàlkan, قالقان‌بالغی kàlkan-bàlighi.

Turbulent, *s.* (person) زوربا zòrba; (meeting) كورلدیلو ghyùruldulu.

Turcoman, *s.* تركمن tùrkmèn.

Turcomania, *s.* تركمن ولایتی tùrkmèn-vìlāyèti.

Turf, *s.* (green) چیم chìm; (peat) یر تزكی yèr-tèzèghi.

Turk, *s.* عثمانلو "òssmānli; ترك tùrk, ترك‌اوشاغی tùrk-ùshàghi, مسلمان mùsslimān.

Turkey, *s.* (fowl) هندطاوغی hìnd-tàwughu; (empire) دولت‌علیه dèv-léti-"àlìyyé, دولت عثمانیه dèvléti-"òssmānìyyé, دولت‌ال‌عثمان dèv-léti-āli-"òssmān; (territory of) ممالك محروسه mèmāliki-màhrūssa, ممالك دولت‌علیه mèmāliki-dèvléti-"àlìyyé, عثمانلومملكتی "òssmānli-mèmlékéti, عثمانلوطپراغی "òssmānli-tòpraghi, عثمانلو ولایتی "òssmānli-vìlāyéti (wilā'ati).

Turkish language, *s.* تركجه tùrkja, عثمانلوجه "òssmānlija, مسلمانجه mùsslimānja.

Turmeric, *s.* زرده‌چاو zèrdéchàv.

Turmoil, *s.* كورلدی ghyùruldu, حارلدی hàrildi, پاطردی pàtirdi.

Turn, *s.* (revolution) دونش dùnush, دور dèvr; (deviation) دونش dùnush, صاپش sàpish, بورغاج bùrghàj, دیرسك dìrsèk; (in rotation) نوبت nùbèt; (change) دونش dùnush, دیكشش dìghishish, تبدل tèbèddul, انقلاب ìnkilāb; فرق fàrk; —, *v.n.* (round) دونمك dùnmek, دورا dèvr-et, دوران ا dèvérān-et; (to one side) دونمك dùnmek; صاپمق sàpmak; (become) كسلمك kèssilmek, لنمك lènmek *or* لنمق lanmak (as a verbal termination), اولمق òlmak; (change) دیكشمك dìghishmek; (as remade clothes) چویرلمك chèvirilmek; —, *v.a.* چویرمك chèvirmek; (cause to become) ایتمك ètmek, لتمك lètmek *or* لتمق latmak (as a verbal termination); a good —, ایولك īyilik; — about, *v.a.* چویرمك chèvirmek; قارشدرمق kàrishdirmak; — —, *v.n.* دونمك dùnmek; — away, *v.a.* قوغمق kòghmak, دفعا dèf"-et, طرد ا

tàrd-et; (the eyes, &c.) چویرمك chèvirmek; — —, *v.n.* بشقه طرفه دونمك bàshka-tàrafa-dùnmek; — back, *v.n.* کیرو دونمك ghèri-dùnmek; عودت ا "àvdet-et; (on a hinge, &c.) اچلمق àchilmak; — —, *v.a.* کیرو چویرمك ghèri-chèvirmek; — down, *v.n.* (a street) صاپمق sàpmak; (a hill) انمك ènmek; (leaves, &c.) اشاغی قیوریلمق àshàghi-kìvrìlmak; — —, *v.a.* صاپتمق sàpitmak; اشاغی کوندرمك àshàghi-ghyùndèrmek; اندرمك èndirmek; قیویرمق kìvirmak, بوکمك bùkmek; — in, *v.n.* یاتمق yàtmak; ایچرو کیرمك ìchèri-ghìrmek, ایچرو کتمك ìchèri-ghìtmek, ایچرو کلمك ìchèri-ghèlmek; — —, *v.a.* ایچرو چویرمك ìchèri-chèvirmek, ایچرو صوقمق ìchèri-sòkmak; ایچرو قیویرمق ìchèri-kìvirmak; —off, *v.a.* اتمق àtmak, دوشورمك dùshurmek; صاپتمق sàpitmak; سکدرمك sèkdirmek; (a cock) قپامق kàpamak; (water) کسمك kèssmek; (a remark) الدرمامق àldirmamak; — —, *v.n.* صاپمق sàpmak; (a projectile) سکمك sèkmek; — out, *v.n.* قالقمق kàlkmak; طیشاری چیقمق dìshàri-chìkmak, طیشاری اوغرامق dìshàri-òghramak; (prove) چیقمق chìkmak; (the weather) لشمك lèshmek (as a verbal termination); — —, *v.a.* چیقارمق chìkàrmak; — over, *v.n.* دونمك dùnmek; دوریلمك dèvrilmek; — —, *v.a.* چویرمك chèvirmek, دویرمك dèvirmek; (in charge) دور ا dèvr-et; (refer) حواله ا hàwālé-et, احاله ا ìhālé-et; (in one's mind) دوشونمك dùshunmek, طاشنمق tàshìnmak, مطالعه ا mùtāla"à-et; (disappoint) امیدینی بوزمق ùmīdini-bòzmak; — up, *v.n.* چیقمق chìkmak, ظهور ا zùhūr-et, پیدا او pèydā-òl; قالقمق kàlkmak; اچلمق àchilmak; یوقاری دونمك yùkàri-dùnmek; — —, *v.a.* یوقاری چویرمك yùkàri-chèvirmek; اشمك èshmek, قازمق kàzmak; قالدرمق kàldirmak; اچمق àchmak.

Turnip, *s.* شلغام *or* شلغم shàlghàm.

Turnkey, *s.* زندانجی zìndānji.

Turnpike, *s.* قپو kàpi.

Turpentine, *s.* ترمنتی tèrmènti; spirits of —, نفت یاغی nèft-yàghi.

Turquoise, *s.* فیروزه طاشی fìrūzé-tàshi.

Turret, *s.* قوله kùlé, قوله جك kùléjik.

Turtle, *s.* دکزقاپلوبغه‌سی dèngiz-kàpli-bàghassi (kàplim-); — dove, قمری kùmru.

Tuscan, *a.* توسقانه‌لو Tòsscànali.

Tuscany, *s.* توسقانه ولایتی Tòsscàna-vìlāyèti.

Tusk, *s.* ازو àzi, دیش dìsh.

Tutor, *s.* خواجه khòja; —, *v.a.* اوکرتمك ùghretmek, تعلیم ا tà"līm-et.

Twaddle, *s.* بوش لاقردی bòsh-làkìrdi.

Tweezers, *s.* جمبز jìmbiz.

Twelve, *a.* اون ایکی òn-ìki; —month, یل yìl, سنه sèné, سال sāl.

Twenty, *a.* یکرمی yìghirmi, عشرون "ìshrūn, عشرین "ìshrīn, بیست bīsst.

Twice, *ad.* ایکی کره ìki-kèrré, ایکی دفعه

ìki-dèf‘‘à, ایکی نوبت ìki-nùbèt, ایکی سفر ìki-sèfer. [چبوق chìbùk.

Twig, *s.* دال dàl, اینجه‌دال ìnja-dàl,

Twilight, *s.* (morning) اورطه‌لق اغارمسی òrtalik-àgharmassi, فجر fèjir, شفق shàfak; (evening) صولر قرارمسی sùlar-kàrarmassi, اورطه‌لق قرارمسی òrtalik-kàrarmàssi. [*pl.* ایکز ìkiz.

Twin, *s.* ایکز ìkiz, توأم tèv‘àm; —s,

Twine, *s.* سجیم sìjim; —, *v.n.* صارلمق sàrìlmak, طولاشمق dòlashmak; —, *v.a.* طولاشدرمق dòlashdirmak, صارمق sàrmak. [بوکلمك bùkyulmek.

Twist, *v.a.* بوکمك bùkmek; —, *v.n.*

Two, *a.* ایکی ìki, اثنین ìssnèyn, دو dù.

Type, *s.* (model) نمونه nùmūné; (for printing) حرف hàrf (*pl.* حروفات hùrūfāt); in —, مرتب mùrèttèb, ترتیب اولنمش tèrtīb-òlunmush.

Typhus, *s.* قره حما kàra-hùmmà, تیفو tīfo.

Typographer, *s.* باصمه‌جی bàssmaji.

Typography, *s.* حروفات باصمه‌سی hù-rūfāt-bàssmassi.

Tyrannical, *a.* ظالمانه zālimāné, ظلمکارانه zùlumkyārāné.

Tyranny, *s.* ظلم zùlm, تعدی tà‘‘àddī, غدر ghàdr, جفا jèfā.

Tyrant, *s.* ظالم zālim, غدار ghàddār, جفاکار jèfākyār; سفاك sèffāk, خونریز khūnrīz.

Tyro, *s.* عجمی ‘‘àjémī, مبتدی mùbtédī.

U.

Udder, *s.* ممه mèmé. [kèrīhu-’l-mànzar.

Ugly, *a.* چرکین chìrkin, کریه‌المنظر

Ulcer, *s.* یاره yàra.

Ultimate, *a.* صوك sòng.

Umbrage, *s.* اغبرار ìghbirār.

Umbrageous, *a.* کولکه‌لك ghyùlghélik.

Umbrella, *s.* شمسیه shèmsìyyé.

Umpire, *s.* حکم hàkem; to act as —, حکم‌ا hùkm-et, دعوایی فصل‌ا dà‘‘wàyi-fàssl-et.

Unable, *a.* الندن‌کلمز èlindan-ghèlmàz, مقتدر دکل mùktèdir-dìghil, عاجز ‘‘ājiz. [mish.

Unaccustomed, *a.* الشمامش àlishma-

Unadvisable, *a.* مناسبتسز mùnāssébètsiz.

Unanimity, *s.* اتفاق‌ارا ìttifāki-ārā.

Unanimous, *a.* متفق mùttèfik, متحد الارا mùttàhidu-’l-ārā, یکزبان yèkzabān.

Unarmed, *a.* سلاحسز sìlāhsiz; (ship or battery) طوپسز tòpsuz. [zàrūrī.

Unavoidable, *a.* ناچار nāchār; ضروری

Unawares, *ad.* علی الغفله ‘‘àlé-’l-ghàflé.

Unbecoming, *a.* یاقشمز yàkishmàz, یاقشقسز yàkishìksiz, بد bèd, چرکین chìrkin. [کفر kyùfr, جهالت jàhālet.

Unbelief, *s.* عدم‌ایمان ‘‘àdémi-īmān,

Unbeliever, *s.* غیرمؤمن ghàyri-mù‘min, کافر kyāfir, کاور ghyàwr, جاحل jāhil.

Unbend, *v.a.* (a bow) یایك کریشنی چیقارمق yàying-kìrishini-chìkàrmak; (sails) اشاغی المق àshàghi-àlmak; —, *v.n.* اچلمق àchìlmak. [àchmak.

Unbind, *v.a.* چوزمك chùzmek, اچمق

Unbounded, *a.* بیحد bīhàdd, حدسز hàddsiz, بیپایان bīpāyān.

Unburthen (one’s self, one’s mind), *v.n.* دردینی سویلمك dèrdini-sùwèylémek.

Unbutton, *v.a.* أچمق àchma*k*.

Uncertain, *a.* بللوسز bèllisiz, بللو دكل bèlli-dì*gh*il, شبهه‌لو shùbhéli, مشكوك mèshky*u*ūk.

Uncertainty, *s.* مشكوكيت mèshky*u*ū-kìyyèt ; مشكوك‌شى mèshky*u*ūk-shèy.

Unchangeable, *a.* دائمى dā'imī, ديكشمز dì*gh*ishmàz.

Uncharitable, *a.* صدقه ويرمز sAda*k*a-vErmàz ; فنا شبهه ايدر fEna-shūbhÉ-èdEr. [sizlik.

Uncharitableness, *s.* انصافسزلق insAf-

Unchaste, *a.* غير عفيف ghàyri-''àfīf.

Uncivil, *a.* ترس tèrss, قبا kAba.

Uncivilized, *a.* وحشى vwàshī.

Uncle, *s.* (father's brother) عموجه ''Amuj*a* (Amj*a*), عم ''àmm, عمى ''Ammī ; (mother's brother) داى dày. [نجس nèjiss.

Unclean, *a.* پس pìss, مردار mūrdār,

Uncleanliness, *s.* پسلك pìsslik.

Uncleanly, *a.* پس pìss.

Uncleanness, *s.* پسلك pìsslik.

Unclose, *v.a.* أچمق àchma*k*. [-sòyma*k*.

Unclothe, *v.a.* روباسنى صويمق rūbassini-

Unclouded, *a.* بلوطسز bùlutsiz.

Uncomfortable, *a.* راحتسز rāh*a*tsiz.

Uncommon, *a.* أز بولنور Az-bùlunur, نادر nādir, ناديده nādīdÉ, نادر كوريلور nādir-ghy*ù*rulur.

Uncommunicative, *a.* كتوم kètūm.

Unconceivable, *a.* تصور أولنه‌مز tàssAvur-ōlun*a*màz. [lā-kàyd.

Unconcerned, *a.* قيدسز kàydsiz, لاقيد

Unconditional, *a.* شرطسز shàrtsiz.

Unconscionable, *a.* انصافسز insAfsiz.

Unconscious, *a.* خبرسز khAbErsiz, بيخبر bīkhAbEr.

Uncorrupt, *a.* طوغرى dò*gh*ru, مستقيم الاطوار mùsstakīmu-'l-Atwār.

Uncover, *v.a.* أچمق àchma*k*, قپاغنى قالدرمق kApA*gh*ini - kAldirma*k*, اورتيسنى چيقارمق ùrtussunu-chì-kàrma*k*.

Uncreate, **Uncreated**, *a.* غير مخلوق ghàyri-màkhlūk, قائم بالذات kā'im-bì-'z-zāt.

Undecided, *a.* قرارسز kArārsiz ; (person) كندى عقلنى بلمز kèndi-''Akl*i*ni-bìlmàz.

Under, *a.* التده اولان Altd*a* - ōlAn ; اشاغى رتبه‌ده اولان Ashà*gh*i-rùtbÉdÉ-ōlan ; اشاغيكى àshà*gh*iki ; —, *pr.* التنه Alt*i*na, التنده Alt*i*nd*a*, التندن Alt*i*ndan ; تحتنه tàhtina, تحتنده tàhtind*a*, تحتندن tàhtindan ; زيرينه zīrina, زيرنده zīrinda, زيرندن zīrindan ; دن اشاغى dan-Ashà*gh*i ; دن اكسك dan-èksik ; — age, چوجق chòjuk, صبى sAbī. [چيك قالمش chì*gh*-kAlmish.

Underdone, *a.* أز پشمش Az-pìshmish.

Undergo, *v.a.* كرفتار او ghìriftār-ōl, دوچار او dùchār-ōl, مبتلا او mùbtélā-ōl ; طوتلمق tùtulmak ; أولمق ōlmak.

Underhand, *a.* كيزلو ghìzli, صاقلو sàkl*i*, خفى khàfī ; —, *ad.* ال التنده Èl-Alt*i*ndA.

Undermine, *v.a.* التنى قازمق Alt*i*ni-kAzma*k* ; (a person) اياغنى قايدرمق àya*gh*ini-kàydirma*k*.

Undermost, *a.* ال التده‌كی èng-altdaki.

Underneath, *pr.* التنه altina, التنده altinda; —, *ad.* التة alta, التده altda.

Under-secretary, *s.* (of state) مستشار mùsstéshār; (of an office) معاون mū‘‘āvin.

Undersign, *v.a.* امضا ا imzā-et.

Undersigned, *a.* زیرده واضع الامضا zīrda-vwazi‘‘-’l-imzā.

Understand, *v.a.* اكلامق ànglamak (ànnamak), تفهم ا tèfèhhum-et, درك ا dèrk-et, ادراك ا idrāk-et, تعقل ا ta-‘‘àkkūl-et.

Understanding, *s.* عقل ‘‘akl; (agreement) قول kavl, مقاوله mūkavélé; شرط shàrt.

Undertake, *v.a.* اوزرینه‌المق ùzérina-almak, درعهده ا dèr-ùhdé-et.

Undertaker, *s.* تابوتجی tābūtju.

Undertaking, *s.* ایش ish.

Underwriter, *s.* كمی ایله كمی یوكنی سیغورته‌یه آلان اصناف ghèmi-ila-ghèmi-yùkunu-sighūrtāya-alan-èssnāf.

Underwriting, *s.* كمی ایله كمی یوكنی سیغورته‌یه المقلق ghèmi-ila-ghèmi-yùkunu-sighūrtaya-almaklik.

Undesignedly, *ad.* لاعن قصد lā-‘‘àn-kassdin; سهواً sèhven; اتفاقا ittifākā.

Undivided, *a.* بتون bitun; (common) مشاع mùshā‘‘.

Undo, *v.a.* بوزمق bòzmak; (a knot, &c.) اچمق àchmak, چوزمك chùz-mek.

Undone, *a.* یاپلمامش yàpilmamish; (ruined) خراب khàrāb; (in reputation) رذیل rèzīl, رسوای rùssvày.

Undoubtedly, *ad.* شبهه‌سز shùbhéssiz; البته èlbètté.

Undress, *v.a.* صویمق sòymak, اوروبه‌سنی چیقارمق ūrūbassini-chìkàrmak; —, *v.n.* صوینمق sòyunmak, دوكلمك dùkyulmek.

Undulation, *s.* طالغه dàlgha; (of ground) بایر bàyir, تومسكلك tùmseklik.

Undutiful, *a.* رعایتسز ri‘‘āyetsiz.

Undying, *a.* لایموت lā-yèmūt.

Uneasiness, *s.* راحتسزلق rāhatsizlik, صیقندی sìkindi; اضطراب iztirāb.

Uneasy, *a.* راحتسز rāhatsiz; (in body or mind) مضطرب mùztàrib.

Unemployed, *a.* ایشسز ishsiz, بوش bòsh, بوشده bòshda, عاطل ‘‘ātil, معطل mū‘‘attal.

Unequal, *a.* بردكل bir-dighil, غیر مساوی ghàyri-mùssāvī; (to a task) عاجز ‘‘ājiz, اربابی دكل èrbābi-dìghil, كوجی یتمز ghyùju-yètmàz, الدن كلمز èlindan-ghèlmàz.

Unequivocal, *a.* صریح sarīh, اچیق àchik, اشكار ashikyār.

Unerring, *a.* صائب sā‘ib. [nā-hèmvār.

Uneven, *a.* دوزدكل dùz-dighil, ناهموار

Unexampled, *a.* كورلمامش ghyùrulma-mish, مثالسز missālsiz, غیرمسبوق ghàyri-mèssbūk.

Unexpected, *a.* اومولمامش ùmulmamish; —ly, *ad.* من غیرمأمول min-ghàyri-mè‘mūlin.

Unexpired, *a.* وعدەسی كلمامش wà‘‘déssi--ghèlmamish. [sAfsiz.

Unfair, *a.* حقسز hàkksiz, انصافسز ìn-

Unfairness, *s.* حقسزلق hàkksizlik.

Unfaithful, *a.* خائن khā‘in. [mùghāyir.

Unfashionable, *a.* مودەيه مغاير mòdàya-

Unfasten, *v.a.* اچمق àchmak.

Unfathomable, *a.* دبسز dìbsiz, ناقعرياب nā-kà‘‘r-yāb.

Unfavourable, *a.* ترس tèrss, مخالف mùkhālif, اويغونسز ùyghunsuz.

Unfeeling, *a.* مرحمتسز mèrhàmetsiz.

Unfeigned, *a.* خالص khāliss, بيريا bī--riyā. [اكسك èksik.

Unfinished, *a.* بتمامش bìtmamish,

Unfit, *a.* اويمز ùymàz, ياقشمز yàkishmàz, الويرمز èlvermàz; (person) نااهل nā-èhl, اربابیدكل èrbābi-dìghil, لياقتسز lìyākAtsiz; —, *v.a.* اهليتنی ازالها èhliyyètini - ìzālé-et; مانعاول māni‘‘-òl, منعا mèn‘‘-et.

Unfold, *v.a.* اچمق àchmak, سرمك sèrmek, نشرا nèshr-et, بسطا bAsst-et.

Unforeseen, *a.* كورنميان ghyùrunmé-yen, دوشنلمامش dùshunulmamish.

Unforgiving, *a.* عفوايتمز ‘‘Afv-ètmàz, اونوتمز ùnutmàz. [mish.

Unforgotten, *a.* اونودلمامش ùnùdulma-

Unfortified, *a.* غير مستحكم ghàyr-mùsstàhkèm. [nàhiss.

Unfortunate, *a.* بختسز bàkhtsiz; نحس

Unfortunately, *ad.* نه فائدە nè-fā‘idé, چەفائدە chì-fā‘idé.

Unfounded, *a.* اصلی يوق Assli-yòk.

Unfrequent, *a.* نادر nādir.

Unfriendliness, *s.* عداوت ‘‘àdāvèt.

Unfriendly, *a.* دشمن dùshmen; دارغين dàrghin. [عقيم ‘‘àkīm.

Unfruitful, *a.* ميوە ويرمز mèyvé-vèrmàz;

Unfurnish, *v.a.* صويمق sòymak, دوشمەسنی قالدرمق dùshéméssini-kAl-dirmak.

Unfurnished, *a.* دوشمەسز dùshémésiz.

Ungainly, *a.* بد bèd; چركين chirkin.

Ungallant, *a.* قاریيه رعايتسز kàrìyyé--rì‘‘āyetsiz.

Ungenerous, *a.* خسيس khàssīss.

Ungodly, *a.* (man) فاسقوفاجر fāssik-u--fājir; (act) فاسقانه fāssikāné, فاجرانه fājirāné.

Ungovernable, *a.* ضبط اولنەمز zAbt-òlu-namàz, سرت sèrt, حديد hàdīd.

Ungrammatical, *a.* قواعد صرف و نحوە مخالف kàwā‘‘idi - sàrf-u-nahvé-mù-khālif.

Ungrateful, *a.* نانكور nānkyūr (nAm-), نمك بحرام nèmek - bùhrām, خائن khā‘in.

Ungrounded, *a.* اصلی يوق فصلی يوق Assli--yòk - fAssli - yòk, بوش bòsh, باطل bātil, بی اساس bī-èssās.

Unguarded, *a.* نوبتجی و قره قول و استحكامدن خالی nùbètji-vé-kAré-kòl--vé-ìsstìhkyāmdan-khāli; غافل ghAfil.

Unguent, *s.* ياغ yàgh, مرهم mèrhèm.

Unhappy, *a.* دردلو dèrdli, دردمند dèrdmènd.

Unhealthy, *a.* (person) چوروك chùruk, عليل ‘‘àlīl; (place) وخيم wàkhīm, وخامتلو wàkhāmetli.

Unheard of, *a.* اشيدلمامش ìshìdilma-mish, غيرمسموع ghàyri-mèssmū".

Unhoped for, *a.* اوملمامش ùmulmamish; مأمولدن زيادە mè'mūldan-zìyādé.

Unhorse, *v.a.* آتندن‌دوشورمك Àtìndan--dùshurmek (*or* آتدن Àtdan).

Unhurt, *a.* اينجنمامش ìnjinmamish.

Uniform, *a.* منتظم mùntazàm, بر سياقدە bìr-sìyākda; —, *s.* اونيفورمە ùni-fòrma, رسم البسەسی rèssm-èlbisséssi, نظام روبەسی nìzām-rùbassi, عسكر روبەسی "Àskɛr-rùbassi.

Uniformity, *s.* مطابقت mùtābakàt.

Uniformly, *ad.* دائما dā'imā; شاشمیەرق shàshmayarak; نظام اوزرە nìzām--ùzérɛ́.

Unimportant, *a.* غير مهم ghàyri-mùhìmm.

Unincumbered, *a.* هر نوع بار و مانعدن خالی hèr-nèv"i-bār-ū-māni"dan--khāli; بورجسز bòrjsiz.

Uninhabitable, *a.* خيرسز khàyrsiz, غير قابل سكنی ghàyri-kābili-sùknà.

Uninhabited, *a.* غيرمسكون ghàyri--mèsskyūn, بوش bòsh. [-mÀssūn.

Uninjured, *a.* ضرردن مصون zàrardan-

Unintelligible, *a.* اكلاشلمز ànglashìl-màz (ànnàsh-). [-nèv"indan.

Unintentional, *a.* قضا نوعندن kÀzā-

Unintentionally, *ad.* عن غير قصد "àn--ghàyri-kÀssdin.

Uninterrupted, *a.* اراسی يوق àrassi-yòk; —ly, *ad.* ارا ويرمیەرك àra-vèrméyé-rek, اردی اراسی اولمیەرق àrdi-àrassi-òlmayarak, بلا فاصلە bìlā-fÀssila, لا ينقطع lā-yànkÀti".

Union, *s.* اتحاد ìttìhād; جمع jèm", تجمع tèjèmmu", اجتماع ìjtimā", برارایە كلش bìr-àraya-ghèlish; قارشش kÀrishish, قاتشمە kÀtishma, مزج mèzj, امتزاج ìmtizāj; تزوج tèzèvvuj, ازدواج ìzdivāj.

Unit, *s.* فرد fɛ̀rd.

Unitarian, *s.* موحد mùwàhhid, اهل توحيد èhli-tèvhīd.

Unite, *v.n.* برلشمك bìrlɛshmek; برلكدە او bìrlikda-òl, اتفاق ا ìttifāk-et; جمع او jèm"-òl, برارایەكلمك bìr--àraya-ghɛ̀lmek; بری برينە قارشمق bìri-bìrina-kÀrishmak, قاتشمق kÀtish-mak; امتزاج ا ìmtizāj-et; بری برينە وارمق bìri-bìrina-vàrmak, تزوج ا tèzèvvuj-et; قاينامق kàynamak, ياپشمق yàpishmak, باغلانمق bÀgh-lanmak; متصل او mùttÀssìl-òl; مربوط او mrɛ̀būt-òl, منتسب او mùn-tèssib-òl; —, *v.a.* برلشدرمك bìr-lɛshdirmek; قارشدرمق kÀrishdirmak, مزج ا mèzj-et; امتزاج ايتدرمك ìm-tizāj-ètdirmek; اولندرمك èvlɛndir-mek, تزويج ا tèzvīj-et, ويرمك vèrmek; قايناتمق kàynatmak; ياپشدرمق yàpishdirmak; باغلامق bÀghlamak, ربط ا rÀbt-et, بتشدرمك bìtish-dirmek.

United States, *s. pl.* جماهير مجتمعە امريقا jèmāhīri-mùjtémi"a-i-Amèrika.

Unity, *s.* برلك bìrlik; (of God) وحدانيت wàhdānìyyèt; اتفاق ìttifÀk, اتحاد ìttihād.

Universal, *a.* كلی kyùllī; عمومی

"ùmūmī; —ly, *ad.* عموماً "ùmūman, على العموم "àlé-'l-"ùmūm. [kyā'ināt.

Universe, *s.* عالم "ālem, كائنات

University, *s.* دارالفنون dāru-'l-fùnūn.

Unjust, *a.* (man) غدار ghàddār, ظالم zālim, انصافسز ìnsāfsiz; (man or act) حقسز hàkksiz. [sèbebsiz.

Unjustifiable, *a.* حقسز hàkksiz, سببسز

Unkind, *a.* (person) جفاكار jèfākyār; (person or act) ترس tèrss, طاتسز tàtsiz, صوغوق sòghuk.

Unknown, *a.* مجهول mèjhūl, نامعلوم nā-mà"lūm; — to me, *ad.* بنم خبرم اولميه رق bènim-khàbérim-òlmayarak.

Unlade, *v.a.* (a ship, &c.) بوشالتمق bòshaltmak, يوكنى بوشالتمق yùkyunu-bòshaltmak; يوكنى چيقارمق yù-kyunu-chìkàrmak; (a horse, &c.) يوكنى اندرمك yùkyunu-èndirmek; —, *v.n.* بوشالمق bòshalmak.

Unlawful, *a.* حرام hàrām; غيرمشروع ghàyri-mèshrū"; ممنوع mèmnū", منهى mènhī, يساق yàssàk; فضولى fùzūlī, ناحق nā-hàkk; —ly, *ad.* بغيرحق bì-ghàyri-hàkkin, فضولى اوله رق fùzūli-òlarak.

Unlearned, *a.* جاهل jāhil.

Unleavened, *a.* خميرسز khàmirsiz.

Unless, *c.* مگركه mègher-ki. (This conjunction is hardly ever used, but the sense is rendered by employing the conditional negative of the verb which follows in English. Ex.—Unless I go, بن كتمسم bèn-ghìt-massam, *if I go not.*)

Unlikely, *a.* اومولمز ùmulmàz, ياقشق المز yàkìshìk-àlmaz; it is very unlikely, دكمه دى dèghmédé, اومم ùmmàm, مأمول ايتمم mè'mūl-ètmàm.

Unlimited, *a.* حدسز hàddsiz, بيحد [bìhàdd.

Unload, *vid.* Unlade.

Unlock, *v.a.* اچمق àchmak; كليدينى اچمق kìlidini-àchmak; —, *v.n.* اچلمق àchìlmak.

Unlooked-for, *a.* اومولميان ùmulmayan; مأمولدن زياده mè'mūldan-zìyādé.

Unloose, *v.a.* اچمق àchmak, چوزمك chùzmek; صاليويرمك sàlìvèrmek.

Unluckily, *ad.* نه فائده nè-fā'idé, چه فائده chì-fā'idé.

Unlucky, *a.* (man) بختسز bàkhtsiz, بدبخت bèd-bàkht; (day) نحس nàhiss; (house, &c.) شئامتلو shà'ā-metli, مشئوم mèsh"ūm.

Unman, *v.a.* چوجق كبى اغلاتمق chòjuk-ghìbi-àghlatmak; to be —ed, چوجق كبى اغلامق chòjuk-ghìbi-àghlamak, يوركى طيانمامق yùrèghi-dàyànmamak, اغلايه جغى كلمك àghlayajaghi-ghèlmek.

Unmanageable, *a.* ضبط اولنه مز zàbt-òlu-namaz; (ship) دومن دكله مز dùmèn-(dīnémàz). [-yàkìshmàz.

Unmanly, *a.* اركگه ياقشمز èrkégha-

Unmannered, Unmannerly, *a.* قبا kàba, خويراط khòyrāt.

Unmarried, *a.* (man) بيكار bīkyār (bèy-kyār), اولودكل èvli-dìghil, مجرد mù-jèrred; (woman) قوجه ده دكل kòjada-dìghil (*or* اولميان òlmayan); قيز kìz.

Unmerciful, *a.* مرحمتسز mèrhàmetsiz; —**ly,** *ad.* فنا fēna.

Unmindful, *a.* دقتسز dikkàtsiz, دقت أيتمز dikkàt-ètmàz, غافل ghāfil.

Unmingled, Unmixed, *a.* خالص khāliss, صاف sāf, صافى sāfī.

Unmoor, *v.a.* باش قيچ باغلرينى چوزمك bàsh-kìch-bàghlarini-chùzmek, يالكز برتيمور ايله براقمق yàlingiz-bir-(dèmir)-ila-bràkmak.

Unnatural, *a.* طبيعتك خلافى tàbī"àting-khilāfi.

Unnecessary, *a.* لزومسز lùzūmsuz, بيلزوم bī-lùzūm.

Unnerve, *v.a.* ثباتنى اخلال ا sèbātini-ikhlāl-et.

Unnumbered, *a.* حسابسز hìssàbsiz, لا يعدولايحصا lā-yù"àdd-vé-lā-yùhsā.

Unobjectionable, *a.* اعتراض اولنەمز i"tirāz-òlunamàz.

Unoccupied, *a.* بوش bòsh, خالى khālī.

Unoffending, *a.* صوچسز sùchsuz, قباحتسز kàbāhatsiz, ضررسز zàrarsiz.

Unopposed, *a.* مانعسز māni"siz, بلامانع bilā-māni"in, بلا مخالفه bilā-mùkhāléfé.

Unowned, *a.* صاحبسز sāhibsiz, صاحبى مجهول sāhibi-mèjhūl.

Unpack, *v.a.* اچمق àchmak; صندقدن چيقارمق sàndikdan-chìkàrmak.

Unpaid, *a.* ويرلمامش vèrilmamish; (officer) معاشسز mà"āshsiz, ايلقسز àylìksiz.

Unpalatable, *a.* اجى àji.

Unparalleled, *a.* مثالسز missālsiz, كورلمامش ghyùrulmamish, اشيدلمامش ìshìdilmamish, نامسبوق nā-mèssbūk.

Unpardonable, *a.* عفواولنمز "àfv-òlun-màz, پك لايقسز pèk-lāyìksiz, پك مناسبتسز pèk-mùnāssébetsiz.

Unpaved, *a.* قالدريمسز kàldirimsiz.

Unperceived, *ad.* كورلميەرك ghyùrul-méyérek, دويولمەرق dùyulmayarak.

Unpleasant, *a.* فنا fénā, طاتسز tàtsiz, بد bèd, كريه kèrīh, ناخوش nā-khòsh; اويغونسز ùyghunsuz; —**ness,** *s.* اويغونسزلق ùyghunsuzluk.

Unpolite, *a.* قبا kàba, خويراط khòyràt.

Unpopular, *a.* خلق بيننده مقبول وپسنديده اولميان khàlk-bèyninda-màkbūl-vé-pèssendīdé-òlmayan.

Unprecedented, *a.* امثالسز èmsālsiz, نامسبوق nā-mèssbūk.

Unprejudiced, *a.* (mind) سالم sālim; (person) غرضسز ghàrazsiz, منصف mùnsif.

Unpremeditated, *a.* لاعن قصد lā-"àn-kàssdin.

Unprepared, *a.* خبرسز khàbersiz; حاضردكل hāzir-dìghil.

Unpretending, *a.* محجوب màhjūb, كندى حالنده kèndi-hālinda.

Unprincipled, *a.* چاپقين chàpkin, ادبسز èdebsiz, عارسز "ārsiz, حياسز hàyāssiz.

Unprofitable, *a.* فائدەسز fā'idéssiz, فائدەدن خالى fā'idédan-khālī, بوش bòsh, نافله nāfilé, بيهوده bīhūdé, لاطائل lā-tā'il.

Unquestionable, *a.* شبهەسز shùbhéssiz, محقق mùhàkkàk; —**bly,** *ad.* البته èlbétté, مطلقا mùtlakā.

Unreasonable, *a.* مناسبتسز mùnāssébet-siz ; انصافسز ìnsāfsiz.

Unremitting, *a.* لاينقطع lā-yànkAti", اردی اراسی اولمیان àrdi - àrassi - òlmayAn.

Unreserved, *a.* بلاکتم bìlā-kètmin.

Unrevenged, *a.* (blood) هدر hèdr ; انتقامسز ìntikāmsiz.

Unrewarded, *a.* مكافاتسز mùkyāfātsiz.

Unrighteous, *a.* (person) كناهكار ghyù-nāhkyār ; (act) كناه ghyùnāh.

Unripe, *a.* خام khām, اولمامش òl-mamish.

Unrivalled, *a.* مثالسز mìssālsiz, بيمثال bīmissāl, يكتا yèktā, بيهمتا bīhèmtā.

Unruly, *a.* زوربا zòrba, عاصی "āssī, متمرد mùtémèrrid. [èmīn-dìghil.

Unsafe, *a.* قورقلور kòrkulur, امين دکل

Unsaid, *a.* دينلمامش dènilmamish, سويلنلمامش sùwèylEnilmamish.

Unsaleable, *a.* صاتلەمز sAtilamàz.

Unsatisfactory, *a.* غيرمرضی ghàyri-mèrzī.

Unsay, *v.a.* سوزندن دونمك sùzundan--dùnmek, انكار ا ìnkyār-et.

Unscrew, *v.a.* اچمق àchmak, ويدەسنی اچمق vìdéssini-àchmak.

Unscriptural, *a.* كتب سماويەنك مألنه مغاير kyùtubu-sèmāvìyyéning-mà-'ālina-mūghāyir. [mùhrunu-àchmak.

Unseal, *v.a.* اچمق àchmak, مهرينی اچمق

Unseasonable, *a.* وقتسز wAkitsiz.

Unseaworthy, *a.* دكز سفرينه غير صالح dèngiz-sèfErina-ghàyri-sālih.

Unseemly, *a.* چركين chìrkin, ياقشمز yàkishmàz, ياقشقسز yàkishìksiz.

Unseen, *a.* كورنميان ghyùrunméyEn ; كورلمامش ghyùrulmamish ; —, *ad.* كورلميەرك ghyùrulméyérek.

Unsettle, *v.a.* قرارينی بوزوب مشوش ا kArārini-bòzup-mùshèvvèsh-et.

Unsheath, *v.a.* چكمك chèkmek, سل ا sèll-et.

Unship, *v.a.* چيقارمق chìkàrmak, يرندن چيقارمق yErindan-chìkàrmak.

Unsightly, *a.* چركين chìrkin, بد bèd, ياقشقسز yàkishìksiz.

Unskilful, *a.* عجمی "Ajémī.

Unslaked, *a.* (lime) سونمامش sùn-mamish ; (thirst) كسلمامش kèssil-mamish. [fāssid.

Unsound, *a.* چوروك chùruk ; فاسد

Unsown, *a.* اكلمامش èkilmamish, غير مزروع ghàyri-mèzrū".

Unsparing, *a.* بول بول bòl-bòl ; —ly, *ad.* اسركميەرك èssirghéméyérek.

Unspeakable, *a.* تعبيراولنەمز tà"bīr--òlunamàz. [sèbātsiz.

Unstable, *a.* قرارسز kArārsiz, ثباتسز

Unsteady, *a.* اوينار òynar ; صاللانور sAllànir ; دترر (tìtrEr) ; (person) حواردە hòwàrda, چاپقين chApkin.

Unsuccessful, *a.* (person) ايشنی بجرەمامش ìshini - bèjEramamish, موفق اولەمامش mùwàffak - òlama-mish ; (attempt) اويمامش ùymamish.

Unsuitable, *a.* ياقشمز yàkishmàz, اويمز ùymàz.

Untaught, *a.* اوكردلمامش ùghrèdilma-mish ; برشی اوكرنمامش bìr - shèy--ùghrEnmamish.

Untenable, *a.* (assertion) باطل bātıl, بوش bòsh; (position) محافظه‌سی محال mùhāfazassi-mùhāl.

Untenanted, *a.* بوش bòsh.

Unthankful, *a.* شکر ایتمز shùkr-ètmàz.

Unthankfulness, *s.* عدم شکر ''àdemi-shùkr.

Unthinking, *a.* دوشونمز dùshunmàz.

Unthought-of, *a.* دوشونلمامش dùshunulmamish, خاطره تخطر ایتمامش khātira-tàkhàttur-ètmamish.

Untidy, *a.* هر شی‌سی پیس و قارشق hèr-shèy-si-pìss-vé-kārishık.

Untie, *v.a.* چوزمك chùzmek, اچمق àchmak, حل‌ا hàll-et.

Until, *pr.* ئه‌قدر a-kādar, ئه‌دك édek, *or* ئه‌دق adak, ئه‌دکین édèghin (*or* a-).

Untimely, *a.* وقتسز wākıtsiz; — end, وقتسزاولم wākıtsiz-ùlum, تلف tèlef, [هلاك hèlāk.

Unto, *pr.* ئه é, a.

Untold, *a.* صایلمامش sàyılmamish; افاده‌اولنمامش ìfādé-òlunmamish.

Untoward, *a.* چرکین chìrkin, فنا fèna, مناسبتسز mùnāssébetsiz.

Untried, *a.* دننلمامش dènenilmamish.

Untrodden, *a.* ایاق‌باصمامش àyak-bāssmamish. [باطل bātıl.

Untrue, *a.* یلان yàlān, کاذب kyāzib,

Untrustworthy, *a.* اعتماد اولنه‌مز ì''timād-ùlunamaz.

Untruth, *s.* یلان yàlān, کذب kìzb, دروغ dùrūgh, بطلان bùtlān.

Unusual, *a.* عادت‌دکل ''ādet-dìghil, خلاف‌عادت khìlāfi-''ādet; —ly, *ad.* سائروقته‌نسبتله sā'ir-wākta-nissbètla.

Unutterable, *a.* تعبیراولنه‌مز tà''bīr-òlunamàz.

Unveil, *v.a.* and *n.* یاشماغنی‌چیقارمق yàshmaghini-chìkàrmak (*or* اچمق àchmak). [-òlunmàz.

Unwarrantable, *a.* تجویزاولنمز téjvīz-

Unwary, *a.* غافل ghāfil.

Unwell, *a.* کیفسز kèyfsiz, مزاجسز mìzājsiz, خسته khàssta.

Unwholesome, *a.* (air) وخیم wàkhīm, وخامتلو wàkhāmetli; (food) مضر mùzìrr.

Unwilling, *a.* استکسز ìssteksiz, رغبتسز ràghbetsiz, کوکلسز ghyùngulsuz; —ly, *ad.* کرهاً kèrhan, مع‌الکراهه mà''a-'l-kèrāhé, استمیه‌رك ìsstéméyérek, چکنه‌رك chèkinérek; —ness, *s.* کوکلسزلك ghyùngulsuzluk, عدم‌رغبت ''àdémi-ràghbet.

Unworthy, *a.* (person) نااهل nā-èhl, استحقاقسز ìsstihkāksiz; (act) لایقسز lāyıksiz.

Up, *a.* قالقمش kālkmish; یوکسلمش yuksèlmish; پهایه‌چیقمش pahāya-chìkmish; —, *ad.* یوقاری yùkāri; یوقاری‌یه yùkāriya, یوقاریده yùkārida (yùkārda); یوقاری‌یه‌طوغری yùkāriya-dòghru; —, *pr.* دن یوقاری dan-yùkāri; —, *int.* دی‌بقالم dè-bākālim! قالق‌بقالم kālk-bākālim; — and down, اشاغی یوقاری āshàghi-yùkāri; اوته‌بری ùté-bèri; — hill, یوقش یوقاری yòkush-yùkāri; کوچ ghyùch, مشکل mùshkil, چتین chètin; — there! هی‌یوقارده hèy-yùkàrda, هی

کیم وار یوقارده hèy-kìm-vàr-yukarda; — with the helm! اورصه òrsa!

Upbraid, *v.a.* یوزینه اتمق yùzuna-Atmak.

Uphold, *v.a.* طوتمق tùtmak, تصحب ا tàssàhhub-et, صحابت ا sàhābet-et, التزام ا ìltizām-et, ارقه او àrka-òl; (a thesis) ادعا ا ìddi''ā-et, تصدیق ا tAss-dīk-et.

Upholsterer, *s.* یورغانجی yùrghAnji, دوشمه جی dùshémėji.

Upland, *s.* یایلا yàyla, یایلاق yàylAk.

Uplift, *v.a.* یوقاری قالدرمق yùkāri-kAldirmak.

Upmost, *a.* الك یوقاری èng-yùkāri.

Upon, *pr.* اوستنه ùsstuna, اوستنده ùsstunda; اوزرینه ùzérina, اوزرنده ùzérinda.

Upper, *a.* یوقاریکی yùkāriki, یوقارده کی yùkàrdéki; اوستده کی ùsstdéki, اوستنده کی ùsstundéki; — hand, غلبه ghàlébé, غالبلق ghālibl k.

Uppermost, *a.* الك یوقاریکی èng-yù-kāriki, الك اوستده کی èng-ùsstdéki.

Upright, *a.* طوغری dòghru, قائم kā'im; (in morals) طوغری dòghru, مستقیم mùsstakīm.

Uproar, *s.* کورلدی ghyùruldu, حارلدی hArīldi, پاطردی pAtirdi, ولوله vèlvélé.

Upset, *v.a.* دویرمك dèvirmek; کیفنی بوزمق kèyfini-bòzmak; —, *v.n.* دویرلمك dèvirilmek; —, *a.* دویرلمش dèvirilmish; کیفی قاچمش kèyfi-kAchmish; —, *s.* دویرلمه dèvirilmé.

Upside-down, *ad.* آلت اوست Alt-ùsst, زیروزبر zīr-u-zèber.

Upstart, *s.* مجهول الاصل اولان نو رسیده mèjhūl-èl-Assl-òlan-nèv-rèssidé.

Upwards, *ad.* یوقاری یه طوغری yùkāriya-dòghru, یوقاری yùkāri; (more) زیاده zìyādé.

Urchin, *s.* پیچ pìch.

Ureter, *s.* ممر البول mèmèrr-ùl-bèvl.

Urge, *v.a.* ابرام ا ìbrām-et, الحاح ا ìlhāh-et, صیقشدرمق sìkishdirmak; (a plea) ایراد ا īrād-et, درپیش ا dèr-pīsh-et; (a horse) سورمك sùrmek, سوق ا sèvk-et.

Urgency, *s.* عجله ''Ajélé.

Urgent, *a.* مستعجل mùsstà''jel.

Urine, *s.* سدیك sìdik, بول bèvl, کچوك صو kùchuk-sù; —, *v.n.* ایشه مك ìshémek, صو دوکمك sù-dùkmek, تبول ا tèbèvvul-et; (a horse) قشانمق kAshAnmak; (a dog) سیمك sīmek.

Us, *pro.* بزی bìzi, بزه bìzé, بزلری bìzléri, بزلره bìzléra.

Usage, *s.* قوللانش kùllAnish, استعمال ìsstì''māl; (treatment) معامله mù''ā-mélé; (custom) عادت ''ādet.

Use, *s.* قوللانش kùllAnish, قوللانمه kùl-lànma, استعمال ìsstì''māl; (benefit) فائده fā'idé, منفعت mènfà''at; —, *v.a.* قوللانمق kùllanmak, استعمال ا ìsstì''māl-et; (treat) معامله ا mù''ā-mélé-et; to be of —, ایشه یرامق ìsha-yàramak, فائده سی او fā'idéssi-òl, فائده سی مشاهده اولنمق fā'idéssi-mùshāhédé-òlunmak; to be used to, آلشق او Alishik-òl, آلشمش ا Alishmish-òl; to become — —, آلشمق Alish-mak; to be used up, بتمك bìtmek, دوکنمك dùkènmek; (a man) بتمك

bìtmek, ایشی بتمك ìshi-bìtmek, بر خیری قالمامق bìr-khàyri-kālmamak.

Useful, a. ایشه یرار ìsha-yàrar, فائده سی وار fā'idéssi-vàr, فائده لو fā'idéli, نافع nāfi'', مفید mùfid.

Useless, a. برایشه یرامز bìr-ìsha-yàramàz, فائده سز fā'idéssiz, بوش bòsh, نافله nāfilé.

Usher, s. (school) خلیفه khàlīfé (kālfa); (at a door) چاوش chàwush, تشریفاتجی tèshrīfātji, محضر mùhzir; — in, v.a. ایچرو کتورمك ìchèri-ghètirmek, ایچرو کوترمك ìchèri-ghyùturmek, دلالت ا dèlālet-et, احضارا ìhzār-et.

Usual, a. عادی ''ādī, عادت اولان ''ādet-òlan; —ly, ad. اکثریا èksérìyyā.

Usufruct, s. غله ghàllé.

Usurer, s. فاحش معامله جی fāhish-mù''āméléji.

Usurp, v.a. فضولی ضبطا fùzùli-zābt-et, غصب ا ghāssb-et.

Usurpation, s. غصب ghāssb.

Usurper, s. غاصب ghāsib; فضولی اوله رق تخت پادشاهی یه جلوس ایدن غاصب تاج و نکین fuzuli-òlarak-tàkhti-pādishāhìyyé-jùlūss-èden-ghāsibi-tāj-u-nìghīn.

Usury, s. ربا rìbā, فاحش معامله fāhish-mù''āmélé; فاحش معامله جیلك fāhish-mù''āméléjilik.

Utensil, s. خانه آلتی khāné-āléti; —s, s. pl. قاب قچاق kāp-kāchak, چناق چوملك chànak-chòmlek.

Uterine, a. (brother or sister) لام lì-ùmm, اناطرفندن àna-tàrafindan.

Utility, s. فائده fā'idé, نفع nèf'', منفعت mènfā''at.

Utmost, a. اك اوزاق èng-ūzāk, صوك sòng, اقصی āksà; نهایت درجه ده nìhāyet-dèréjédé, اك زیاده èng-zìyādé, نهایت nìhāyet, غایت ghàyet; الدن کلدیکی قدر èldan-ghèldighi-kādar, ممکن مرتبه mùmkin-mèrtébé; —, s. الدن کلن èldan-ghèlen; to the —, ad. نهایت درجه ده nìhāyet-dèréjédé, ممکن مرتبه mùmkin-mèrtébé, غایتله ghāyètla.

Utter, v.a. (pronounce) سویلمك sùwèylémek, تلفظا tèlàffuz-et; اغزه المق āghza-ālmak; (coin, &c.) کچورمك ghèchirmek, ویرمك vèrmek, کچورمکه باقمق ghèchirméghé-bākmak; —, a. کامل kyāmil, تام tāmm, کلی kyùllī.

Utterly, ad. بتون بتون bìtun-bìtun, بسبتون bìss-bìtun, کاملاً kyāmilan, تماماً tāmāman, کلیاً kyùllìyyan, بالکلیه bì-'l-kyùllìyyé, هروجهله hèr-vèjhla.

Uttermost, a. اك اوزاق èng-ūzāk, اقصی āksà; صوك sòng.

Uvula, s. دلجك dìljik, کچوك دل kù-chuk-dìl.

V.

Vacancy, s. بوش یر bòsh-yèr, اچق یر àchìk-yèr, خالی یر khālī-yèr; محلول màhlūl.

Vacant, a. بوش bòsh, خالی khālī, اچق àchìk; محلول màhlūl; — look, شاشقین باقشی shàshkin-bākishi.

Vacate, *v.a.* براقمق bràkmak, چیقمق chìkmak, خالی براقمق khālī-bràkmak, ترك ا tèrk-et.

Vacation, *s.* تعطیل وقتی tà''tīl-wàkti.

Vaccinate, *v.a.* اشلاتمق àshlatmak, اینك چیچكی ماده‌سیله اشلاتمق īnek-chìchéghi-māddéssīla-àshlatmak.

Vaccination, *s.* اینك چیچكنك اشلانلمسی īnek-chìchéghinin-àshlanilmassi; تلقیح بقری tèlkīh-bākārī.

Vaccinator, *s.* اینك چیچكنی اشلایان حكیم īnek-chìchéghini-àshlayan-hèkīm.

Vaccine, **Vaccine matter**, *s.* اینك چیچكنك جراحتی ماده‌سی īnek-chìchéghinin-jèrāhàti-māddéssi.

Vacillate, *v.n.* تردد ا tèrèddud-et.

Vacillation, *s.* تردد tèrèddud.

Vacuum, *s.* خلا khàlā, خلای مطلق khàlāyi-mùtlàk.

Vade-Mecum, *s.* مجمعه mèjma''à.

Vagabond, **Vagrant**, *s.* چاپقین chàpkin, كولخانی kyùlkhānī; دربدر dèrbédèr, سرسری sèrsérī; —, *a.* اواره āwāré.

Vague, *a.* مبهم mùbhèm, غیرمحقق ghàyri-mùhàkkàk.

Vain, *a.* مغرور màghrūr, خودپسند khòd-pèssènd; (futile) بوش bòsh, دیبسز dìbsiz, اصلی یوق àssli-yòk, نافله nāfilé, فائده‌سز fā'idéssiz, بیهوده bīhūdé; in —, vainly, *ad.* نافله nāfilé, اصلی یوقدن àssli-yòkdan.

Valance, *s.* سایبان sàybān, *or* سایوان *sàywan* (sàywànt), صاچاق sàchak.

Vale, *s.* دره dèré.

Valerian, *s.* كدی اوتی kèdi-òtu.

Valet, *s.* اوشاق ùshàk, خدمتكار khìd-metkyār (hiz-), اغا àgha.

Valetudinarian, *s.* علیل كمسنه ''àlīl-kìmèssné, علیل ''àlīl, چوروك chùruk, دائما خسته dā'imā-khàssta.

Valiant, *a.* یكیت yìghit, جسور jèssūr, بهادر bàhādir, دلاور dìlāver, مردانه mèrdāné. [tùtar, یرار yàrar.

Valid, *a.* صالح sālih, صحیح sàhīh, طوتار

Valise, *s.* جانطه jànta.

Valley, *s.* دره dèré.

Valorous, *a.* یكیت yìghit.

Valorously, *ad.* جسارت ایله jèssarèt-ìla.

Valour, *s.* یكیتلك yìghitlik, جسارت jèssārèt, جرئت jùr'èt, مردانكی mèrdānéghī.

Valuable, *a.* ذی قیمت zī-kīmèt, قیمتلو kīmètli; عزیز ''àzīz; ایشه‌یرار ìsha-yàrar.

Valuation, *s.* كشف kèshf, تخمین tàkhmīn, تعیین قیمت tè''yīni-kīmèt, بهابچمكلك pàhā-bìchmeklik.

Value, *s.* دكر dèghèr, قیمت kīmèt, بها pàhā; (moral) قدر kàdr; —, *v.a.* صایمق sàymak, اعتبار ا ì''tibār-et, معتبرطوتمق mù''tébèr-tùtmak; عزیز طوتمق ''àzīz-tùtmak; كشف ا kèshf-et, قیمت تقدیر ا kīmèt-tàkdīr-et, بهابچمك pàhā-bìchmek, بهاتعیین ا pàhā-tà''yīn-et; تقدیر ا tàkdīr-et, قدرینی بلمك kàdrini-bìlmek.

Valve, *s.* قپاق kàpak, دل dìl.

Vampire, *s.* وامپیر vàmpīr, جادی jàdi.

Van, *s.* عربه ''àraba; (of an army)

مقدمةالجيش mùkàddimétu-'l-jèysh, قرەغول kàraghòl.

Vane, *s.* يلقوان yèlkowan, بادنما bād-nùmā.

Vanish, *v.n.* غائب او ghā'ib-òl, كوزدن غائب او ghyùzdan-ghā'ib-òl, زائل او zā'il-òl.

Vanity, *s.* غرور ghùrūr; (emptiness, worthlessness) بوشلق bòshluk, ديبسزلك dìbsizlik.

Vanquish, *v.a.* مغلوب ا màghlūb-et, الت ا àlt-et, ينمك yènmek.

Vapour, *s.* بخار bùkhār, دومان dùmàn.

Variable, *a.* اطرادسز ìttirādsiz, قرارسز kàrārsiz, ديكشر dìghishir.

Variance, *s.* اختلاف ìkhtilàf; at —, *a.* بوزشق (persons) bòzushuk; (things) برى برينەاويمز bìri-bìrina-òymàz.

Variation, *s.* اختلاف ìkhtilàf, انحراف ìnhirāf; تبدل tèbèddul, تحول tàhàvvul.

Variegated, *a.* رنك رنك rènk-rènk, رنكارنك rènghyārènk, كوناكون ghyūnāghyùn.

Variety, *s.* (sort) درلو (tùrlu), چشيد chèshid, نوع nèv''; (collection of different sorts) درلودرلو (tùrlu-tùrlu), درلو (tùrlu), انواع درلو ènvā''i-(tùrlu); (not sameness) ديكشمه dìghishma, تخلف tàkhàlluf.

Various, *a.* (several) برقاچ bìr-kàch, بعض bà''zi, برچوق bìr-chòk, چوق chòk; (different) درلودرلو (tùrlu-tùrlu), مختلف mùkhtèlif, متنوع mùténèvvi'', كوناكون ghyūnāghyūn.

Varnish, *s.* روغن rùghàn; —, *v.a.* روغن اورمق rùghàn-wùrmak.

Vary, *v.n.* تخلف ا tàkhàlluf-et, شاشمق shàshmak, ديكشمك dìghishmek; —, *v.a.* تبديل ا tèbdīl-et, ديكشدرمك [dìghishdirmek.

Vase, *s.* قاپ kàp.

Vassal, *s.* قول kùl; چاكر chākèr.

Vassalage, *s.* قوللق kùlluk.

Vast, *a.* بيوك bìyuk, عظيم ''àzīm; چوق chòk, كلى kyùllī, وافر wāfir.

Vastly, *ad.* چوق chòk.

Vastness, *s.* بيوكلك bìyukluk.

Vat, *s.* بيوك تكنه bìyuk-tèknè, بيوك فوچى bìyuk-fìchi.

Vault, *s.* كمر kèmer; قبه kùbbè; (under ground) بودروم dòdrūm; —, *v.n.* صچرامق sìchramak, اتلامق àtlamak.

Vaunt, *s.* لاف làf, تفاخر tèfākhur, تمادح tèmāduh; —, *v.n.* اوكنمك ùghèumek, قورولمق kùrulmak, تفاخر ا tèfākhur-et, تادح ا tèmāduh-et.

Veal, *s.* دانەاتى dàna-èti.

Veer, *v.n.* ديكشمك dìghishmek, دونمك dùnmek; —, *v.a.* موله ا mòla-et.

Vegetable, *a.* نباتى nèbātī; —, *s.* نبات nèbāt; (for food) سبزه sèbzè (*pl.* سبزوات sèbzèwāt, vulg. zèrzèwāt), يشللك yèshillik; —marrow, *s.* قباق kàbak; ساقزقباغى sākiz-kàbàghi.

Vegetation, *s.* نشو و نما neshv-u-nèmā; نبت nèbt.

Vegetate, *v.n.* يشامق yàshamak.

Vehemence, *s.* شدت shìddèt, حدت hìddèt, سرتلك sèrtlik, زور zòr.

Vehement, *a.* شدتلو shìddètli, شديد shèdīd, حدتلو hìddètli, حديد hàdīd, سرت sèrt, زورلو zòrlu.

Vehicle, *s.* عربة "àraba; (fig.) وسيله vèssīlé, واسطه wāssita.

Veil, *s.* (woman's) ياشماق yàshmak, نقاب nìkāb; (curtain) پرده pèrdé, ستر sìtr; (covering) اورتى ùrtu; —, *v.a.* اورتمك ùrtmek, سترا sètr-et; —, *v.n.* ياشمقلنمق yàshmaklanmak.

Vein, *s.* طمر dàmar, عرق "àrk (*pl.* عروق "ūrūk), رك règh; —ed, طمرلو dàmarli.

Vellum, *s.* ترشه tìrshé.

Velocity, *s.* سرعت sùr"àt, حز hìz.

Velvet, *s.* قطيفه (kàdīfé).

Venal, *a.* رشوتيير rìshvet-yèr, رشوتخوار rìshvetkhòr, مرتشى mùrtèshi.

Venality, *s.* ارتشا ìrtishā.

Vend, *v.a.* صاتمق sàtmak, فروختا fùrūkht-et, بيعا bèy"-et.

Veneer, *v.a.* قاپلامق kàplamak; —ed, *a.* قاپلامه kàplama.

Venerable, *a.* محترم mùhtérem; مبارك mùbārek; (ancient) اسكى èsski, كارقديم kyāri-kàdīm.

Venerate, *v.a.* صايمق sàymak, رعايتا rì"āyet-et, حرمتا hùrmet-et.

Venereal disease, *s.* فرنكى fìrènghi, فرنكى علتى fìrènghi-"illèti.

Vengeance, *s.* اوج ùj, انتقام ìntikām.

Venison, *s.* كيك اتى ghèyik-èti, قراجه اتى kàraja-èti.

Venom, *s.* زهر zèhir, سم sèmm; —ous, زهرلو zèhirli.

Vent, *s.* نفس nèfess, هوا hàwā; (hole) نفسلك nèfesslik, منفس mènfèss; (of a gun) فاليه fàlya; to give — to one's feelings, قلبده اولاننى سربستجه اظهارا kàlbda-òlanini-sèrbèsstja-īzhār-et.

Ventilate, *v.a.* هواويرمك hàwā-vèr-mek.

Ventilation, *s.* هوا ويرمكلك hàwā-vèrmeklik.

Venture, *v.n.* جسارتا jèssāret-et; قورقميوب كتمك kòrkmayup-ghìt-mek; —, *v.a.* تهلكه يه قومق tèhli-kéya-kòmak; بخته حواله ا bàkhta-hàwālé-et.

Venus, *s.* شعرجه حسن معبوده نك اسمى shì"rjé-husn-mà"būdénin-ìssmi; زهره يلدزى zùhré-yìldizi; ناحيد nāhīd.

Veracious, *a.* طوغرى dòghru.

Veracity, *s.* طوغرى سويليجيلك dòghru-sùwèyléyijilik, صداقت sàdākàt.

Verb, *s.* فعل fì"l; — active, فعل معلوم fì"li-mà"lūm; — passive, فعل مجهول fì"li-mèjhūl; — neuter, *or* intransitive, فعل لازم fì"li-lāzim, — transitive, فعل متعدى fì"li-mùta"àddī.

Verbal, *a.* (of a word) لفظى làfzī; (of a verb) فعلى fì"lī; (oral) شفاهى shìfāhī, اغزدن àghzdan; —ly, *ad.* لفظاً làfzan; شفاهاً shìfāhan.

Verbatim, *ad.* لفظابلفظ làfz-bé-làfz, لفظاً làfzan.

Verbena, *s.* مينا چيچكى mīnā-chìchéghi.

Verbiage, *s.* حشويات hàshvìyyāt.

Verbose, *a.* الفاظى چوق èlfāzi-chòk.

Verbosity, *s.* كثرت الفاظ kèssreti-èlfāz; اطناب ìtnāb.

Verdict, *s.* قرار kàrār.

Verdigris, *s.* ژنكار زنكار zènghyār, zhènghyār, باقرك يشل پاسى bàkiring--yèshil-pàssi.

Verdure, *s.* يشللك yèshillik ; اوت òt (grass), ييراقلر yàpraklar (leaves).

Verge, *s.* (brink) كنار kènār, لب lèb ; (limit) سرحد sèr-hàdd, حدود hùdūd (*pl.*) ; (vicinity) يقين yàkin, يقينلر yàkinlar, قرب kùrb, جوار jìwār ; —on, *v.n.* چاتمق chàtmak, وارمق vàrmak, يقلاشمق yàklashmak, يقينلاشمق yàkinlashmak, يقيننده اول yàkininda-òl, قريب اول kàrīb-òl, تقرب ا tàkàrrub-et.

Verification, *s.* تحقيق tàhkīk.

Verify, *v.a.* تصديق ا tàssdīk-et ; to be —fied (by examination), تحقيق اولنمق tàhkīk-òlunmak ; (by the event) تحقق ا tàhàkkuk-et, صحيح چيقمق sàhīh--chìkmak.

Verily, *ad.* واقعا wākì''ā, فى الحقيقه fì-'l-hàkīka, علم الله ''àlima-'llāh.

Verjuice, *s.* قوروق kòruk ; قوروق صويى kòruk-sùyu. [rìyyé).

Vermicelli, *s.* شعريه shà''rìyyé (shèh-

Vermin, *s.* (body or bed) كهله پيره مقوله سى kèhlé-pìré-màkūléssi ; (house or barn) صچان صانصار مقوله سى sìchan-sànsàr--màkūléssi.

Vernacular tongue, *s.* انا دلى àna-dìli, بياغى لسان bàyàghi-lìssān, چارشى دلى chàrshi-dìli.

Verse, *s.* (hemistich) فرد fèrd ; مصراع mìssrā'' ; (couplet) بيت bèyt ; (triplet) مثلث mùssèllèss, (quatrain) رباعى rùbā''ī ; &c. &c. ; (poetry) شعر shì''r ; (of a chapter) ايت āyet, ايت كريمه āyéti-kèrīmé (only used in speaking of the Kur'an) ; بند bènd (paragraph).

Versed, *a.* عالم ''ālim, معلوماتلو mà''lù-[màtli.

Versification, *s.* نظم nàzm.

Versify, *v.a.* نظم ا nàzm-et ; —, *v.n.* شعر ياپمق shì''r-yàpmak. [rìwāyet.

Version, *s.* ترجمه tèrjumé ; روايت

Vertical, *a.* (perpendicular) عمودى ''àmūdī ; (angle) رأسده اولان rè'ssda--òlan ; (sun, &c.) سمت رأسده sèmti--rè'ssda ; ديك يوقاريده dìk-yùkàrida ; سمت رأسده اولان sèmti-rè'ssda-òlan.

Very, *ad.* پك pèk, چوق chòk, غايت ghàyet ; —, *a.* ذات zāt.

Vessel, *s.* (utensil) قاب kàb ; (ship) كمى ghèmi, تكنه tèkné, سفينه sèfīné ; blood —, طمر dàmar, عرق ''àrk, رك règh.

Vest, *s.* يلك yèlek. [نشانه nìshāné.

Vestige, *s.* اثر èsser, نشان nìshān,

Veteran, *s.* اسكى èsski ; (soldier) عسكر اسكيسى ''àssker - èsskissi ; —s, *s. pl.* قدما kùdémā.

Veterinary, *a.* بيطارى bàytārī ; — surgeon, *s.* بيطار bàytār.

Vex, *v.a.* كوجندرمك ghyùjèndirmek, قزدرمق kìzdirmak ; كوجه كتمك ghyùjé-ghìtmek.

Vial, *s.* شيشه shìshé.

Vibrate, *v.n.* صاللانمق sàllanmak, اوينامق òynamak ; دترهمك *or* تترهمك (tìtrémek) ; (a pendulum) رقص ا ràkss-et ; (inner particles) حركته كلمك hàrékèta-ghèlmek.

Vice, *s.* شر shèrr, گناه ghyùnāh, سوءعمل sū'i-''āmel, سيئه sèyyi'é; عيب ''àyb, سوء sū', قبح kùbh; (in horses) خوى khùy, فنا خوى fèna-khùy, سقط sàkat; the —s, *s. pl.* معيبات mū''àyyébāt, سيئات sèyyi'āt; (a smith's vice) منكنه mènghéné; (locum tenens) وكيل vèkīl, نائب nā'ib, قائممقام kā'im-màkām; — admiral, پطرونه پاشا pàtrūna-pàsha (*formerly* بك bègh), — admiral of the fleet, بحريه فريقى bàhrìyyé-fèrīkī.

Vicious, *a.* كوتى kyùtu, شرير shèrīr; (horse) سقط sàkat, يرامز yàramàz, (defective) ناقص nākiss, فاسد fāssid, سقط sàkat, سقامتلو sakāmètli.

Vicissitude, *s.* انقلاب ìnkilāb; —s of fortune, انقلابات دهر ìnkilābāti-dèhr.

Victim, *s.* (for sacrifice) قربان kùrbān; (of slaughter) مقتول màktūl; (of fraud) مغدور màghdūr; (of tyranny) مظلوم màzlūm; (in general) كرفتار ghìriftār, دوچار dūchār, مبتلا mùb-[tèlā, اسير èssīr.

Victor, *s.* غالب ghālib.

Victorious, *a.* غالب ghālib.

Victory, *s.* غلبه ghàlébé, نصرت nùssrèt.

Victual, —s, *s.* ييه جك yèyéjek, طعام tà''ām; —, *v.a.* ذخيره ترتيب ا zàkhīré - tèrtīb - et; (a ship) قومانيه سنى المق kūmānyassini-àlmak; قومانيه سنى ويرمك kū-mānyassini-vèrmek.

Victualler, *s.* ييه جك نسنه صاتيجيسى yèyéjek-nèssné-sàtìjissi.

Vide, *v.a.* (Latin) مراجعت اولنه mū-rāja''at-òluna.

Videlicet, *c.* (Latin) يعنى yà''nī.

Vie with, چيقشمق chìkishmak, ياراشمق yàrashmak.

View, *s.* نظارت nàzārèt; (picture) رسم rèssm (rèssim); —, *v.a.* باقمق bàkmak, معاينه ا mū''āyéné - et; كورمك ghyùrmek.

Vigilance, *s.* كوز اچقلغى ghyùz-àchìklighi, تيقظ tèyàkkuz, تقيد tàkàyyud.

Vigorous, *a.* قوتلو kùvvètli, دنج dìnj, صاغ sàgh, صاغلام sàghlàm.

Vigour, *s.* قوت kùvvèt; (energy) غيرت ghàyrèt, اهتمام ìhtimām.

Vile, *a.* (person) الچق àlchàk, رذيل rèzīl, دنى dènī, رسواى rùssvāy; (thing) پس pìss, مردار mùrdār.

Village, *s.* كوى kyùy, كند kènd, قريه [kàrìyyé.

Villager, *s.* كويلو kyùylu.

Villain, *s.* خبيث khàbīss, خنزير khìnzīr, پزونك pèzéwènk.

Villainy, *s.* خباثت khàbāssèt.

Vindicate, *v.a.* حقنى تأييد ا hàkkini-tè'yid-et.

Vindication, *s.* تأييد tè'yīd.

Vindictive, *a.* كين كوديجى kīn-ghyù-[duju.

Vindictiveness, *s.* انتقامه ميل ìntikāmé-mèyl.

Vine, *s.* (trained) اصمه àssma; (pollard) باغ كتوكى bāgh-kyùtughu.

Vine-dresser, *s.* باغجى bāghji.

Vinegar, *s.* سركه sìrké.

Vineyard, *s.* باغ bāgh.

Vintage, *s.* باغ بوزومی bāgh-bòzūmū.

Vintner, *s.* میخانه‌جی mèy-khānéji.

Violate, *v.a.* بوزمق bòzmak, اخلال ا ìkhlāl-et, نقص ا nàkss-et, هتك ا hètk-et; (women) زورلمق zòrlamak; — one's chastity, هتك پردهٔ عفت ا hètki-pèrdè'i-''ìffèt-et.

Violation, *s.* نقص nàkss; هتك hètk.

Violence, *s.* (strength) زور zòr, شدت shìddet; (in forcing) زور zòr, جبر jèbr, عنف ''ùnf, عنوت ''ànvèt.

Violent, *a.* سرت sèrt, شدید shèdīd, شدتلو shìddètli.

Violet, *s.* بنفشه bènèfshé (mènèkshé); —, *a.* مور mòr.

Violin, *s.* کمان kèmān, کمانچه kèmānché.

Violinist, *s.* کمانی kèmānī.

Viper, *s.* انکرك ènghérek.

Virgin, *s.* قیز kìz, قیز اوغلان قیز kìz-òghlan-kìz, باکره bākiré; the Virgin, البتول el-Bètūl (said of the Virgin Mary and of Fātimé, daughter of Múhammed).

Virginity, *s.* قیزلق kìzlìk, بکر bikr, بکارت bèkyārèt.

Virgo, *s.* سنبله sùnbulé.

Virility, *s.* ارککلك èrkeklik.

Virtue, *s.* خیر khàyr, صلاح sàlāh, فضیلت fàzīlèt (*pl.* فضائل fàzā'il), محمدت màhmédet (*pl.* محامد màhāmid).

Virtuous, *a.* اهل خیر èhli-khàyr, صالح sālih; (woman) عفیفه ''àfīfé, عفتمآب ''ìffèt-mà-āb, عصمتلو ''ìssmètlū, عفتلو ''ìffetlū, اهل پرده èhli-pèrdé.

Viscount, *s.* رتبهٔ خامسه بکی rùtbé'i-khāmissa-bèghi.

Visé, *a.* and *s.* ویزه vìzé.

Visible, *a.* کوریئور ghyùrunur, کوزکور ghyùzukyur, میدانده mèydānda, ظاهر zāhir, بدیدار bèdīdār, بدید bèdīd.

Vision, *s.* (sight) بصر bàssar, دیدار dīdār; (dream) رؤیا rù'yā, دوش dūsh, عالم مثال ''ālémi-mìssāl.

Visit, *s.* (of respect) زیارت zìyārèt; (friendly and prolonged) مسافرلك mùssāfirlik; (medical) ویزیته vìzita; (formal — on arrival) رسم خوش آمدی rèssmi-khòsh-āmédī; —, *v.a.* کتمك ghìtmek, زیارت ا zìyārèt-et, زیارتنه کتمك zìyārètina-ghìtmek; کورشمکه کتمك ghyùrushmégha-ghìtmek; استفسار خاطره کتمك ìsstifsāri-khātira-ghìtmek; (on arrival) خوش کلدك دیمکه کتمك khòsh-ghèlding-dèméghé-ghìtmek; (as a physician) ویزیته ا vìzita-et, باقمق bàkmak; (search) تحری ا tàhàrrī-et, باقمق bàkmak, ارامق àramak, یوقلامق yòklamak; — with, مظهر ا màzhar-et; کرفتار ا ghìriftār-et, دوچار ا dūchār-et, مبتلا ا mùbtélā-et; to go on a —, مسافرلکه کتمك mùssāfirlighé-ghìtmek.

Visiter, *s.* مسافر mùssāfir; —or, سیرجی sèyrji; ناظر nāzir.

Vital, *a.* وسیلهٔ حیات vèssīlé'i-hàyāt; (important) الزم èlzèm, اهم èhèmm.

Vitality, *s.* حیات hàyāt.

Vitriol, *s.* (green) زاج قبرس zāji-kìbriss;

(blue) كوزطاشى ghyùz-tAshi; oil of —, زاج ياغى zĀj-yàghi.

Vituperate, *v.a.* دشنام ا dùshnām-et.

Vituperation, *s.* دشنام dùshnām.

Vituperative, *a.* اغزى پيس Aghzi-pìss.

Vivacious, *a.* نشاطلو nìshĀtlu.

Vivacity, *s.* نشاط nìshĀt.

Vivat, *int.* (Latin) ياشاسون yàshasun.

Vocabulary, *s.* مختصر لغات كتابى mùkhtAssàr-lùghĀt-kìtAbi.

Vocation, *s.* ايش ìsh, مشغوليت mèsh-ghūlìyyèt; استعداد ìsstì''dād, دعوت قلبيه dà''vèti-kAlbìyyé.

Voice, *s.* سس sèss; صدا sAdā, اواز āwāz.

Void, *a.* بوش bòsh, خالى khālī, تهى tèhī; باطل bātil, فاسد fāssid; —, *s.* بوش ير bòsh-yèr, خالى ير khālī-yèr; —, *v.a.* ابطال ا ìbtĀl-et; (excrement) تبول ا tèbèvvul-et, صچمق sìchmak, ايشه مك ìshémek.

Volatile, *a.* اوچار ùchar, طيار tàyyār; (in disposition) بردالده دورمز bìr-dAlda--dùrmàz, متلون mùtélèvvin.

Volcano, *s.* ينارطاغ yànar-dAgh.

Volition, *s.* اختيار ikhtiyār, اراده ìrādé.

Volley, *s.* يايلم yàyìlim.

Volume, *s.* بيوكلك bìyukluk, حجم hàjm, قطعه kìt''à, جرم jùrm; (of a book) جلد jìld. [mùfAssAl.

Voluminous, *a.* بيوك bìyuk, مفصل

Voluntary, *a.* اختيارى ìkhtiyārī.

Volunteer, *s.* كوكللوعسكر ghyùngullu--''Asskèr.

Voluptuous, *a.* (person) حظ نفسه مائل hAzzi-nèfsa-mā'il, اهل صفا èhli-sAfā; (thing) نفيس nèfīss.

Vomit, *s.* (emetic) مقيى mùkàyyī; (vomiting) قى kàyy, استفراغ ìssti-frāgh; (thing ejected) قوصلان ماده kùssulAn-māddé; —, *v.n.* and *a.* قوصمق kùssmak, قى ا kàyy-et, استفراغ ا ìsstifrāgh-et.

Voracious, *a.* پك اجقمش pèk-àjìk-mish; چوق ير chòk-yèr.

Vortex, *s.* كرداب ghìrdĀb.

Votary, *s.* عابد ''ābid, پرست pèrèsst.

Vote, *s.* رأى rè'y; —, *v.n.* رأى ويرمك rè'y-vèrmek.

Vouch, *v.n.* كفيل او kèfīl-òl.

Voucher, *s.* سند sèned. [in''ām-et.

Vouchsafe, *v.a.* احسان ا ìhsān-et, انعام ا

Vow, *s.* (of sacrifice) نذر nèzr, اداق AdAk; (oath) يمين yèmin, اند And; —, *v.a.* يمين ا yèmīn-et, اند ايچمك And-ìchmek.

Vowel, *s.* حركه hàréké. [sèfer.

Voyage, *s.* دكزسفرى dèngiz-sèferi, سفر

Vulgar, *a.* قبا kAba; عيب ''àyb; —, *s.* عوام ناس ''àwAmmi-nāss.

Vulgarity, *s.* قبالق kAbalik. [kàrtAl.

Vulture, *s.* اق بابا Ak-bAba (?), قرتال

W.

Wad, *s.* صيقى sìki; (of a cannon) پالاسطروپه pAlasstròpa.

Wadding, *s.* پاموق pAmuk (pAmbuk).

Wade, *v.n.* صوايچنده يوريمك sù--ìchinda-yùrumek.

Wafer, *s.* مكتوب پولی mèktūb-pùlu; (cake) كاغد حلواسی kyāghid-hèlwāssi; —, *v.a.* پول ايله ياپشدرمق pùl-ila-yàpishdirmak; sacred —, بادأراق bàdarak.

Waft, *v.a.* كوترمك ghyùturmek; كتورمك ghètirmek.

Wag, *s.* لطيفه‌جی làtīféji; —, *v.a.* صاللامق sàllamak; —, *v.n.* صاللانمق sàllanmak.

Wage, Wages, *s.* كونده‌لك ghyùndélik, ايلق àylik; يللق yìllik; — war, *v.n.* محاربه‌ا mùhārébé-et, حربا hàrb-et, سفراچمق sèfer-àchmak, محارب‌او mùhārib-òl; عداوت‌ا "àdāvèt-et, خصومت‌ا khùssūmèt-et.

Wager, *s.* بحث bàhss; —, *v.a.* بحث‌ا bàhss-et, بحث طوتمق bàhss-tùtmak, قومق kòmak.

Waggon, *s.* يوك‌عربه‌سی yùk-"àrabassi, عربه "àraba; —er, عربه‌جی "àrabaji.

Wagtail, *s.* قويرق‌صاللان kùyruk-sàllan.

Wailing, *s.* نالش nālish, فغان fìghān.

Wain, *s.* عربه "àraba; Charles's —, دب اكبر dùbbi-èkbèr.

Wainscot, *s.* دوغرامه‌جی‌ايشی dòghramaji-ìshi, دوغرامه dòghrama.

Waist, *s.* بل bèl, ميان mìyān; — band, *s.* كمر kèmer, اوچقورلق ùchkurluk; —coat, يلك yèlek.

Wait, *v.n.* بكلمك bèklémek; (serve) خدمت‌ا khìdmet-et (hìz-); — on, — upon, خدمت‌ا khìdmet-et; (for orders, &c.) كلمك ghèlmek, اوغرامق òghramak.

Waiter, *s.* خدمتجی khìdmetji; (tray) تپسی tèpsi.

Wake (of a ship), *s.* دومنك صويی dùmèning-sùyu; —, *v.n.* اويانمق ùyanmak; —, *v.a.* اوياندرمق ùyàndirmak. [-tayàkkiz.

Wakeful, *a.* اويانق ùyànik, متيقظ mù-

Wales, *s.* وليس ممالكی vèlīs-mèmāliki.

Walk, *s.* كزمه ghèzmé, سير sèyr, تفرج tèfèrruj; (path) يول yòl; (pace) يورويش yùruyush; —s of life, احوال بشريه àhwāli-bèshérìyyé, مراتب بشريه mèrātībi-bèshérìyyé; —, *v.n.* يورومك or يوريمك yùrumek; مشی‌ا mèshy-et; — about, كزمك ghèzmek; — in, ايچرو كيرمك ichèri-ghìrmek; ايچرو كتمك ìchèri-ghìtmek; ايچرو كلمك ìchèri-ghèlmek; — off, *v.n.* كتمك ghìtmek; — —, *v.a.* كوترمك ghyùturmek, دفعا dèf"-et; — off with, الوب كتمك àlip-ghìtmek; قاپمق kàpmak; چالمق chàlmak; — out, *v.n.* چيقمق chìkmak, طيشاری چيقمق dìshàri-chìkmak; —, *v.a.* طيشاری كتورمك dìshàri-ghètirmek, طيشاری كوترمك dìshàri-ghyùturmek; — the rounds, قول كزمك kòl-ghèzmek; — up and down, كزنمك ghèzinmek; اشاغی يوقاری كزنمك àshàghi-yùkàri-ghèzinmek.

Wall, *s.* ديوار dīwàr, جدار jidār, حائط hā'it; —, *v.a.* ديوارچويرمك dīwār-chèvirmek (*or* چكمك chèkmek).

Wallachia, *s.* افلاق ولايتی ìflàk-vìlāyèti.

Wallachian, *s.* افلاقلو ìflÀklu.

Wallet, *s.* توبره tobr*a*, *or* توربه tòrb*a*, چانطه chànt*a*.

Wall-flower, *s.* صاری شببوی sÀr*i*-shèb-[būy.

Wallow, *v.n.* يوارلنمق yìwarlanm*a*k.

Walnut, *s.* جوز jèv*i*z.

Walrus, *s.* دکز ايغری dèn*g*iz-àygh*i*r*i*.

Waltz, *s.* بر نوع رقص اويونی bìr-nèv''i--ràkss-òyunu; والس vàlss; —, *v.n.* مذکور رقص اويوننی اوينامق mèzk*y*ūr--ràkss-òyunu-òynam*a*k.

Wan, *a.* صاری sÀri, بکزی اتمش bèn*g*z*i*--Àtm*i*sh, بکزی قالمامش bèn*g*zi--kÀlm*a*m*i*sh. [عصا ''àssā.

Wand, *s.* چبوق chìbùk, دينك dèynek,

Wander, *v.n.* کزمك ghèzmek, طولاشمق dòlashm*a*k.

Wanderer, *s.* اواره āwārÉ.

Wane, *v.n.* انقراض بولمق ìnk*i*rĀz-bùlm*a*k.

Want, *s.* حاجت hājet (*pl.* حاجات hājāt, *and* حوائج hàwā'ij), احتياج ìhtiyāj; (severe) ضرورت z*à*rūrèt, صيقندی s*ì*kindi; (necessity) لزوم lùzūm; (absence) نقصان nòksān, بولنمامه bùlunmam*a*, عدم ''àdEm; —, *v.a.* استمك ìsstÉmek, ارامق Àram*a*k; اکسك او èksik-òl; —, *v.n.* محتاج او mùhtĀj-òl; to be —ed, لازم او lāz*i*m-òl, لزومی او lùzūmu-òl, اقتضا ìktizā-et, اقتضاسی او ìktizāss*i*--òl, مقتضی او mùktÀzī-òl; —ing, اکسك èksik.

Wanton, *a.* (playful and innocent) پك سونجلو pèk-sèvinjli; قيدسز kÀydsiz; (wicked) کناه ghyùnāh; (shameless) اچق مشرب *à*chik-mèshreb; —, *s.* فاحشه fāhishÉ, روسپی (òrosspo).

War, *s.* حرب hàrb, سفر sèfEr, غوغا (kàwgha), جنك jènk; —, *v.n.* حرب ا hàrb-et, محاربه ا mùhārébé--et; عداوت ا ''àdāvèt-et, خصومت ا khùssūmèt-et; at war, *a.* محارب mùhārib, بوزشق bòzushuk.

Warble, *v.a.* and *n.* اوتمك *ù*tmek.

Ward, *s.* (of a town) محله m*à*hàllÉ; (of a hospital) قوغوش kò*gh*ush; (of a key) چنتك chèntik, کرتك kèrtik; (orphan) يتيم yètīm; — off, *v.a.* صاوشدرمق sàwushdurm*a*k.

Warden, *s.* محافظ mùhĀf*i*z.

Wardrobe, *s.* (clothes) البسه èlbissÉ, البسه موجوداتی èlbissÉ-mèvjūdĀt*i*; (closet) طولاب dòlAp.

Warehouse, *s.* مغازه mà*gh*az*a*.

Wares, *s. pl.* امتعه èmta''à (*pl. of* متعه mAt''à, a piece of goods).

Warfare, *s.* حرب hàrb, معاملات حربيه mù''āmélāt*i*-hàrbìyyÉ.

Warlike, *a.* حربی hàrbī; — stores, مهمات حربيه mùhimmĀt*i*-hàrbìyyÉ.

Warm, *a.* سيجاق sìjĀk, سيجاجق sijĀj*i*k, کرم ghÈrm, حار hārr; ايليجق *ì*lijàk; —, *v.a.* استمق *ì*ss*ì*tmak; —, *v.n.* اسنمق *ì*ss*ì*nmak. [-sìjĀk.

Warm-hearted, *a.* يورکی سيجاق yùre*gh*i-

Warmth, *s.* سيجاق s*ì*jĀk, سيجاقلق s*ì*jĀkl*ì*k, کرمی ghèrmī, کرميت ghèrmìyyèt, حرارت h*à*rārèt.

Warn, *v.a.* خبرويرمك khÀbEr-vèrmek, اخبارا ìkhbār-et; اخطارا ìkhtār-et.

Warning, *s.* خبر khàber, اخبار ìkhbār, اخطار ìkhtār.

War-office, *s.* حربیه نظارتی قپوسی hàr-bìyyé-nàzārèti-kàpissi.

Warp, *s.* (of a tissue) ارغاج àrghàj, تار tār; (rope) پلامار pàlamār; —, *v.n.* چارپلمق chàrpilmak, اکلمك èghil-mek; —, *v.a.* چارپلمسنه سبب او chàrpilmassina-sèbeb-òl; (a ship) چکمك chèkmek.

Warrant, *s.* بیورلدی bùyuruldu, فرمان fèrmān; برات bèrāt; سند sèned, حجت hùjjèt; —, *v.a.* کفیل او kèfīl-òl, تکفل ا tèkèfful-et.

Warranted, *a.* صلاحیتلو sàlāhìyyètli; جائز jā'iz; قصورسزلغنه کفالت ویرلمش kùssūrsizlighina-kèfālèt-vèrilmish.

Warranty, *s.* کفالت kèfālèt.

Warrior, *s.* جنکجی jènkji, غازی ghāzī.

Wart, *s.* نصر nàssir, طاوق کوتی tàwuk-ghyùtu.

Wary, *a.* اویانق ùyànik, بصیرتلو bàssīrètli.

Wash, *s.* (cosmetic) صو sù; (of clothes) چماشیر chàmàshir, چماشیریقانمسی chàmàshir-yìkanmassi; (mess for animals) چوربا chòrba; (of the sea) طالغه لرك یورویوب چکلمسی dàlgha-laring-yùruyup-chèkilmassi; —, *v.a.* یقامق yìkamak, تطهیرا tàthīr-et (t-h); —, *v.n.* یقانمق yìkanmak; (for prayers) ابدست المق àbdesst-àlmak; (for purification) غسل ا ghùssl-et.

Washerman, *s.* چماشیرجی chàmàshirji; —woman, *s.* چماشیرجی قاری chà-màshirji-kàri.

Wash-tub, *s.* چماشیرتکنه سی chàmàshir-tèknéssi.

Wasp, *s.* اشك اریسی èshek-àrissi.

Waste, *s.* تلف tèlef, اسراف ìssrāf; (wilderness) بیابان bèyābān; ویرانه vīrāné; خالی یر khālī-yèr; —, *a.* بوش bòsh; خالی khālī; ویران vīrān, خراب khàrāb; —, *v.a.* تلف ا tèlef-et, اسراف ا ìssrāf-et; —, lay —, خراب ویباب ا khàrāb-et, خراب ویباب ا khàrāb-u-yàbāb-et, ویران ا vīrān-et; —, *v.n.* تلف او tèlef-òl; — away, اریوب کتمك èriyup-ghìtmek.

Watch, *s.* (guard) قول kòl, قره غول kàraghòl; (time of) نوبت nùbèt; (on board ship) وارده vàrda; (time-piece) ساعت sā''at, قوین ساعتی kòyn-sā''ati; —, *v.a.* کوزلمك ghyùzlé-mek, کوزتمك ghyùzètmek, باقمق bàkmak; —, *v.n.* اویومامق ùyuma-mak, تیقظاوزره دورمق tèyākkuz-ùzéré-dùrmak; بکلمك bèklémek, بکجیلك ا bèkjilik-et, نوبت بکلمك nùbèt-bèklémek, وارده بکلمك vàrda-bèklé-mek, وارده جیلق ا vàrdajilik-et; —man, *s.* بکجی bèkji; وارده جی vàrdaji, دیده بان dīdébān; — house, قوللق kòlluk; — maker, ساعتجی sā''atji; — word, پاروله pàrola.

Water, *s.* صو sù, ما mā, اب àb; (on stuffs) منویش mènévish (?), طالغه dàlgha; —, *v.a.* (a horse, &c.) صوارمق sùwarmak; (a garden) صولامق sùlamak; (stuffs) منويش ا mènévish-et (?), طالغه لتمق dàlghalatmak; —, *v.n.* (the mouth) صولنمق sùlanmak, صولری اقمق sùlari-àkmak; (the eyes, &c.) يشارمق yàsharmak; (a ship) صوالمق sù-àlmak; high —, مد mèdd; low —, جزر jèzr; fresh —, soft —, طاتلوسو tàtli-sù; salt —, طوزلوصو tùzlu-sù; sea —, دكزصويى dèngiz-sùyu; hard —. أجى صو àji-sù; — course, *s.* صويك اقديغى ير sùyung-àkdighi-yèr, مجرا mèjrà; صويولى sù-yòlu; — cresses, *s.* صوتره سى sù-tèrèssi; — fall, *s.* صولرك اوچديغى ير sùlaring-ùchdughu-yèr, چغلايان chàghlayan; — gruel, *s.* يوان چوربا yàwan-chòrba; — man, *s.* قايقجى kàyikji; — melon, *s.* قارپوز kàrpuz; — mill, صودكرمنى sù-dèghirmèni; — pipe, *s.* كونك kyùnk; (for smoking) ناركله nàrghilé; — proof, *a.* صوكچمز sù-ghèchmàz; — spout, *s.* قصرغه kàssirgha (sàkirgha); — tight, *a.* اقمز àkmàz, صيزمز sizmàz; — wheel, طولاب dòlab; چرخ chàrkh; to make —, چيش ا chìsh-et, صودوكمك sù-dùkmek, كچوك صودوكمك kùchuk-sù-dùkmek, ايشه مك ìshémek, تبول ا tèbèvvul-et; (a ship) صوايتمك sù-ètmek.

Watering-place, *s.* قدرت حمامى kù-drèt-hàmmàmi, قاپلوجه kàplija, ايليجه ìlija, بانيه bànya; يالى كويى yàli-kyùyu, ساحل برمحل sāhil-bìr-màhàll; — pot, قوغه kògha.

Watery, *a.* صولو sùlu.

Wave, *s.* طالغه dàlgha, موج mèvj; —, *v.a.* صاللامق sàllamak; —, *v.n.* صاللانمق sàllanmak.

Waver, *v.n.* شبهه يه دوشمك shùbhéyé-dùshmek, پوصله يى شاشرمق pùsslayi-shàshirmak, ثباتى بوزلمق sèbāti-bòzulmak, تردد ا tèrèddud-et, ركاكت كوسترمك rèkyākèt-ghyùsstermek.

Wavering, *a.* ترددده tèrèddudda.

Wavy, *a.* طالغه لو dàlghali.

Wax, *s.* بالمومى bàl-mumu, شمع عسل shèm"i-"àssel, موم mūm; (of the ears) قولاق كيرى kùlak-kìri; —, *v.a.* بالمومى سورمك bàl-mūmu-sùrmek; —, *v.n.* اولمق òlmak, كسلمك kèssilmek, لنمك lenmek *or* لنمق lanmak (as a verbal termination); — candle, — light, بالمومى bàl-mumu; — taper, شمعه shèm"à (shàma).

Way, *s.* يول yòl, طريق tàrīk, راه rāh; (manner) درلو (tùrlu) وجه wèjh, اسلوب ùsslūb, صورت sūrèt, طرز tàrz; (custom) عادت "ādet; رسم rèssm; (behaviour) خوى khùy; (side) طرف tàraf; — in, قپو kàpi, كيره جك ير ghìréjek-yèr, مدخل mèdkhàl; — out, قپو kàpi, چيقه جق ير chìkajak-yèr, مخرج màkhrèj; — through, يول yòl, كچه جك ير ghèchéjek-yèr, ممر mèmèrr; high —, جادّه jāddé, شاهراه shāhrāh, طريق عام tàrīki-"āmm; bye—, صاپه يول sàpa-yòl; by the —, يولده yòlda, يول اوستنده yòl-ùsstunda, اثناى راهده èssnāyi-rāhda; ways and means, ايراد īrād, واردات vāridāt.

Wayfarer, *s.* يولجى yòlju.

Wayfaring, *s.* يولجيلق yòljuluk.

Wayward, *a.* ترس tèrss.

Waywardly, *ad.* ترس ترس terss-terss.

Waywardness, *s.* ترسلك tèrsslik.

We, *pr.* بز bìz, بزلر bìzlır.

Weak, *a.* ضعيف zà''īf, قوتسز kùvvetsiz; (in mind) عقلسز ''àklsiz; دلى dèli; مراقلو mèràkli; (in character) متانتسز mètānètsiz, ثباتسز sèbātsiz, خفيف khàfīf; — side, مراق mèrāk.

Weaken, *v.a.* ضعيفلتمق zà''īflatmak, قوتنى كسمك kùvvètini-kèssmek, ضعيف براقمق zà''īf-bràkmak, خلل ويرمك khàlel-vèrmek.

Weakly, *a.* عليل ''àlīl.

Weakness, *s.* ضعف zà''f, ضعيفلق zà''īflik; (of character) مراق mèràk, دليلك dèlilik.

Wealth, *s.* زنكينلك zènghinlik, مال māl, ثروت sèrvèt, غنا ghìnā.

Wealthy, *a.* زنكين zènghin, مالدار māldār, متمول mùtémèvvil, غنى ghànī, صاحب ثروت sāhib-sèrvèt.

Wean, *v.a.* سوددن كسمك sùddan--kèssmek, كسمك kèssmek; واز كچورمك vāz-ghèchirmek.

Weapon, *s.* صلاح silāh (*pl.* اسلحه èsslihà), آلت حرب āléti-hàrb.

Wear, *s.* قوللانش kùllànish; ايپرنش ìprènish; اسكيش èsskiyish; —, *v.a.* (as clothing) كيمك ghīmek; (out) اسكتمك èsskitmek, ايپرتمك ìprèt-mek; (away) يمك yèmek, اشندرمق àshindirmak; —, *v.n.* (well) طيانمق dàyanmak; (not well) طيانمامق dàyànmamak; — out, *v.a.* (clothes) اسكتمك èsskitmek, (ropes, &c.) ايپرتمك ìprıtmek; (a person) يورمق yòrmak; —, *v.n.* (clothes) اسكيمك èsskimek; (ropes, &c.) ايپرنمك ìprınmek; — — one's patience, صبرينى دوكتمك sàbrini-dùkètmek, اوصاندرمق ùssàndirmak; — away, *v.a.* يمك yèmek, اشندرمق àshin-dirmak; —, *v.n.* اشنمق àshinmak; (time) كچمك ghèchmek, مرورا mùrùr--et; — on, (time) كچمك ghèchmek, مرورا mùrūr-et; — off, *v.a.* بوزمق bòzmak, سلمك sìlmek; —, *v.n.* بوزلمق bòzulmak, سلنمك sìlinmek, كتمك ghìtmek; (grief, &c.) اونودلمق ùnùdulmak.

Wearisome, *a.* ادمك جانى صيقلور [àdàmin-jāni-sıkılır.

Weary, *a.* يورغون yòrghun, يورلمش yòrulmush; —, *v.a.* يورمق yòrmak; —, *v.n.* يورلمق yòrulmak.

Weasel, *s.* كلينجك ghèlinjik (?), صانصار sànsār (?).

Weather, *s.* هوانك حالى hàwāning--hāli, هوا hàwā; fine —, كوزل هوا ghyùzèl-hàwā; bad —, فناهوا fènā--hàwā; rough —, سرت هوا sèrt-hàwā; mild —, ملايم هوا mùlāyim-hàwā; —, *a.* روزكارطرفى rùzghyār-tàrafi; *v.a.* (a cape, &c.) كچمك ghèchmek; (a difficulty) كچورمك ghèchirmek; — cock, يلقوان yèlkowan, فرلداق fìrìldàk, بادنما bādnùmā; — gage, روزكاراوستى rùzghyār-ùsstu.

Weave, *v.a.* دوقومق dòkumak, نسجا nèssj-et. [nèsssāj.

Weaver, *s.* دوقوبيجى dòkuyuju, نساج

Web, *s.* قماش kùmash, نسج nèssj; — footed, قازاياقلو kaz-àyakli.

Wed, *v.a.* (take to wife) المق almak, تزوجا tèzèvvuj-et; (accept as husband) وارمق vàrmak; (find a wife for) اولندرمك èvlendirmek; (find a husband for) ويرمك vèrmek, قوجه‌يه‌ويرمك kòjaya-vèrmek; (husband or wife) تزويجا tèzvīj-et; (as a priest) عقدا ''akd-et, نكاحا nìkyāh-et; —ed, *a.* (man) اولو èvli; (woman) نكاحلو nìkyāhli, نكاح تحتنده nìkyāh-tàhtinda, منكوحه mènkyūha, قوجه‌ده kòjada.

Wedding, *s.* (feast) دوكون dùghun, وليمه vèlīmé; (ceremony) عقدنكاح ''akdi-nìkyāh.

Wedge, *s.* قامه kàma, چيوى chìvi, سيل sīl.

Wedlock, *s.* نكاح nìkyāh, ازدواج ìzdiwāj.

Wednesday, *s.* چهارشنبه chìhàrshènbìh (chàrshàmba), اربعا èrba''ā.

Weed, *s.* اوت òt, خيرسزاوت khàyrsiz-òt; —s (widow's) دول قارينك ماتم البسه‌سى dūl-kàrining-mātem-èl-bissèssi; —, *v.a.* خيرسزاوتلرينى يولمق khàyrsiz-òtlarini-yòlmak; — out, *v.a.* سوكمك sùkmek, يولمق yòlmak.

Week, *s.* هفته hàfta, اسبوع ùssbū''; — day, بياغى كون bàyaghi-ghyùn, عادى كون ''ādī-ghyùn.

Weekly, *a.* and *ad.* هفته‌ده بر hàftada-bìr.

Weep, *v.n.* اغلامق àghlamak, كوز ياشى دوكمك ghyùz-yàshi-dùkmek,

Weevil, *s.* قورت kùrt. [بكاا bùkyā-et.

Weigh, *v.a.* طارتمق tàrtmak, وزنا vèzn-et, چكمك chèkmek; (in mind) دوشونمك dùshunmek, مطالعها mùtāla''à-et; —, *v.a.* كلمك ghèlmek, چكمك chèkmek; — upon, كدر ويرمك kèder-vèrmek, اضطراب ويرمك ìztirāb-vèrmek; — anchor, تيمور المق (dèmir)-almak, تيمور قالدرمق (dèmir)-kàldirmak.

Weight, *s.* طارتى tàrti, وزن vèzn; اغرلق àghirlik, ثقلت sìklèt; (personal influence) نفوذ nùfūz, اعتبار i''tibār, خاطر khàtir; (moral influence) تأثير tè''sīr, حكم hùkm.

Weighty, *a.* اغر àghir, ثقيل sàkīl; (important) مهم mùhìmm, اهم èhèmm.

Welcome, *int.* بيورك bùyurung, بيورسونلر bùyursunlar; خوش كلدك khòsh-ghèlding, صفا كلدك sàfā-ghèlding; —, *s.* رسم خوش امدى rèssmi-khòsh-āmédī; —, *a.* باعث مسرت bā''issi-mèssèrrèt; —, *v.a.* خوش كلدك ديمك khòsh-ghèlding-dèmek, رسم خوش امدى‌يى اجراا rèssmi-khòsh-āmédīyi-ìjrā-et; you are — (on arriving), ماشاالله mā-shā-'llāh! بيورك bùyurung! you have been — (on leaving), خوش كلدك صفا كلدك khòsh-ghèl-ding-sàfā-ghèlding; you are — to it, الكرسزنكدر àlingiz-sìzing-dir.

Weld, *v.n.* قاينامق kāynamak, ياپشمق yàpishmak ; —, *v.a.* قايناتمق kàynatmak.

Welfare, *s.* حسن حال hùssnu-hāl, ايولك īyilik, رفاه rèfāh, رفاهيت rèfāhìyyèt, سعادت حال sà''ādéti-hāl.

Well, *s.* قيو *or* قويى kùyu, چاه chāh, بئر bì'r ; —, *ad.* ايو īyi ; —, *int.* اى èy ! افرين (àfèrim) ! ماشاالله mā-shā-'llāh ! very —, پك ايو pèk-īyi, پك كوزل pèk-ghyùzèl, پك اعلا pèk-à''là ; to be —, to become —, ايواو īyi-òl ; —, — up, — out, *v.n.* اقمق ākmak, نبعا نèb''-et ; — and good, فبها fè-bèhā, نه كوزل nè-ghyùzèl.

Well-being, *s.* سعادت حال sà''ādet-hāl.

Well-bred, *a.* تربيه لو tèrbìyyéli.

Well-informed, *a.* معلوماتلو mà''lūmātli.

Well-known, *a.* مشهور mèshhūr.

Well-wisher, *s.* خير خواه khàyr-khāh.

Welsh, *a.* وليس مملكتى اهاليسندن vélìss-mèmlékéti-àhālīsindan ; —, *s.* وليس اهاليسنك لسانى véliss-àhālīsinin-lìssāni.

Wen, *s.* اور ūr.

Wench, *s.* بيومش قيز biyumush-kìz, قارى kāri ; فاحشه fāhisha.

West, *s.* باطى bāti, مغرب màghrib, غرب ghàrb ; south —, لدوس lòdoss ; north —, قره يل kāra-yèl ; —ern, *a.* غربى ghàrbī ; —erly, غربى ghàrbī ; غربدن يانه ghàrbdan-yàna ; —ward, غربه طوغرى ghàrba-dòghru.

Wet, *s.* ياش yàsh ; ياغمور yàghmur ; چامور chàmur ; —, *a.* ياش yàsh, اصلاق ìsslāk, اصلانمش ìsslānmish, صوكسلمش sū-kèssilmish ; (over head) ياغمور yàghmur, ياغمورلو yàghmurlu ; (under foot) چامور chàmur, چامورلو chàmurlu ; —, *v.a.* اصلاتمق ìsslātmak ; —, to get —, *v.a.* اصلانمق ìsslānmak ; — nurse, سودانا sùd-àna, (slave) دايه dàya.

Wether, *s.* قويون kòyun.

Wetness, *s.* ياش yàsh.

Whack, *v.a.* اورمق wùrmak.

Whale, *s.* اطه بالغى āda-bālighi.

Whaler, *s.* اطه بالغى شكارينه كيدن كمى āda-bālighi-shìkyārina-ghìden-ghèmi.

Wharf, *s.* اسكله ìsskèlé.

Wharfage, *s.* اسكله حقى ìsskèlé-hākki.

Wharfinger, *s.* اسكله و مخزن صاحبى اولوب تجار ìsskèlé-vè-màkhzen-sāhibi-òlup-tùjjār.

What ? *pro.* نه nè ? — ! *int.* نه nè ! (For the relative sense of *what*, see the Turkish Grammar.)

Whatever, Whatsoever, *pro.* نه nè, هرنه hèr-nè.

Wheat, *s.* بوغداى bòghday, حنطه hìnta, كندم ghèndum.

Wheedle, *v.a.* اوخشايه رق يالوارمق òkhshayarak-yālvarmak, نازوادا ايله يالوارمق nàz-u-èdā-ila-yālvarmak, جلوه‌ا jìlvé-et.

Wheel, *s.* (carriage) تكرلك tèkerlèk ; (of machinery) چرخ chàrkh ; —, *v.a.* تكرلك اوستنده يوروتمك tèker-lèk-ùsstunda-yùrutmek, يوروتمك

yùrutmek ; كتورمك ghètirmek ; كوترمك ghyùturmek ; —, *v.n.* دونمك dùnmek ; — about, *v.a.* اوته بروكوترمك ùté-bèri-ghyùturmek ; —, *v.n.* دونوب طولاشمق dùnup-dòlash-mak ; دونمك dùnmek ; balance —, رقاص چرخی ràkkāss-chàrkhi ; fly —, پروانه pèrwāné ; turner's —, چرخ chàrkh ; spinning —, چقرق chìkrik ; — barrow, ال عربه‌سی èl-"àrabassi.

Wheelwright, *s.* تكرلكجی tèkerlikji.

When ? *ad.* نه‌زمان nè-zàmān, نه‌وقت nè-wàkit ; —, *rel.* قچان kàchan (also see Grammar) ; —ever, —soever, هرنه‌زمان hèr-nè-zàmān, هرنه‌وقت hèr-nè-wàkit.

Whence ? *ad.* نره‌دن nèrédan (nèrdan) ; —, *rel.* (see Grammar) ; —, *ad.* and *c.* ایمدی or امدی ìmdi, اشته بو سببدن ìshta-bū-sèbebdan ; —soever, *ad.* هرنره‌دن hèr-nèrédan.

Where ? *ad.* نره‌یه nèréya ; نره‌ده nèréda (nèrda) ; —, *rel.* (see Grammar) ; — about ? — abouts ? نره‌لره nèré-léra ; نره‌لرده nèrélerda ; —, *rel.* (see Grammar).

Whereas, *c.* چونكه chùnku, chùnki.

Wherefore, *ad.* نیچون nìchin ; —, *c.* امدی ìmdi. [نره‌ده hèr-nèréda.

Wherever, *ad.* هرنره‌یه hèr-nèréya, هر

Wherry, *s.* پیاده‌قایغی pìyādé-kàyighi.

Whet, *s.* اشتهالق ìshtahālik, راقیجق ràkijik ; —, *v.a.* بیله‌مك bilémek.

Whether, *pro.* قنغی kànghi (hànghi) ; —, *ad.* می mi, mi.

Whey, *s.* ایران àyrān.

Which ? *pro.* قنغی kànghi (hànghi) ; —, *rel.* (see Grammar) ; —ever, —soever, *pro.* هرقنغی hèr-kànghi.

Whiff, *s.* نفس nèfess, چكم chèkim, چكش chèkish.

While, Whilst, *ad.* ایكن ìken ; اثناسنده èssnāssinda ; —, *rel.* (see Grammar) ; worth the —, دكر dègher ; not worth the —, دكمز dèghmaz.

Whim, *s.* مراق mèràk.

Whip, *s.* قامچی kàmchi, قرباچ kìrbàch, تازیانه tāzyāné ; —, *v.a.* قامچیلمق kàmchilamak ; دوكمك dùghmek ; (conquer) غالب‌او ghālib-òl ; (into a froth) چالقامق chàlkamak, كپوك‌ا kyùpuk-et ; — about, *v.n.* فرلامق fìrlamak, صچرامق sìchramak.

Whirl, *v.a.* چویرمك chèvirmek, دوندرمك dùndermek ; —, *v.n.* دونمك dūnmek.

Whirlpool, *s.* كرداب ghìrdāb. [gha).

Whirlwind, *s.* قصرغه kàssirgha (sàkir-

Whiskers, *s. pl.* ایكی یناقده‌اولان صقال ìki-yànakda-òlan-sàkal.

Whisky, *s.* راقی ràki.

Whisper, *s.* فسلدامه fìssildama, فسلدی fìssildi ; —, *v.n.* فسلدامق fìssilda-mak ; —, *v.a.* قولاغه‌سویلمك kùlàgha-sùwèylémek, یواش‌سویلمك yāwàsh-sùwèylémek.

Whistle, *s.* اصلق ìsslik ; —, *v.n.* اصلق چالمق ìsslik-chàlmak ; boatswain's —, دودوك dùduk.

Whit, *s.* ازبرشی àz-bìr-shèy.

White, *a.* and *s.* اق ȧk, بياض bèyȧz, ابيض èbyȧd (*fem.* بيضى bèyzȧ), سفيد sèfīd, سپيد sèpīd; — of an egg, يمورطه‌نڭ‌اقى yìmurtaning-ȧki.

Whitelead, *s.* استوبج ùsstubèj; اسويداج ìssvīdāj.

White-livered, *a.* قورقاق kòrkak.

Whiten, *v.a.* اغارتمق ȧghartmak; بياضلتمق bèyȧzlatmak; —, *v.n.* اغارمق ȧgharmak; بياضلنمق bèyȧzlanmak.

Whiteness, *s.* بياضلق bèyȧzlik.

Whitesmith, *s.* چلنگر chìlinghir.

Whitewash, *s.* بادانه bȧdana; —, *v.a.* بادانه‌اورمق bȧdana-et, بادانه‌ا bȧdana-wùrmak.

Whither? نره‌يه nèréya; —, *rel.* (see Grammar); —soever, هرنره‌يه hèr-nèréya.

Whitlow, *s.* طولامه dòlama.

Whiz, *v.n.* وزلامق wìzlamak, وزوزاوتمك wìz-wìz-ùtmek.

Who? *pro.* كيم kìm; —, *rel.* (see Grammar); —ever, —soever, هركيم hèr-kìm.

Whole, *s.* (quantity) بتون bìtun; (number or quantity) هپ hèp; —, *a.* يكپاره yèkpāré, بتون bìtun, قيرلمامش kìrilmamish (not broken), كسلمامش kessilmamish (not cut), &c.

Wholesale, *ad.* كليت‌اوزره kyùllìyyèt-ùzéré.

Wholesome, *a.* خاصيتلو khāsssìyyètli, شفالو shìfāli.

Wholly, *ad.* بتون‌بتون bìtun-bìtun, كلياً kyùllìyyan, بالكليه bì-'l-kyùllìyyé.

Whore, *s.* روسپى ròsspu (dròsspo), فاحشه fāhishé; —, *v.n.* زنپاره‌لكده‌ كزمك (zàmparalìkda)-ghèzmek.

Whoso, —ever, *pro.* هركيم hèr-kìm.

Why? *ad.* نيچون nìchin; —, *c.* or *int.* اونه ò-né, بونه bù-né.

Wick, *s.* فتيل fìtil.

Wicked, *a.* (thing) كناه ghyùnāh, فنا fèna; — person, كناهكار ghyùnāh-kyār, اثم āssim, عاصى ''āssī.

Wickedness, *s.* كناه ghyùnāh, اثم ìssm, معصيت mà''sìyyèt, فسق‌وفجور fìssk-u-fùjūr.

Wicker, *s.* سپدايشى sèped-ìshi; — basket, سپد sèped.

Wicket, *s.* قپو kȧpi.

Widdin, *s.* ويدن‌شهرى vìdìn-shèhiri.

Wide, *a.* انلو ènli, عريض ''ȧrīz; (spacious) كنش ghènish, واسع wāsi''; (in fullness) بول bòl; far and —, *ad.* اطراف‌واكنافه ètrāf-u-èknāfa, اطراف واكنافده ètrāf-u-èknāfda.

Widow, *s.* دول قارى dùl-kȧri, ارمل èrmèl or ارمله èrmélé (*pl.* ارامل èrāmil), بيوه bìvé; —er, قاريسى‌اولمش‌ادم kȧrissi-ùlmush-ȧdȧm; —hood, ارمللك èrmèllik.

Width, *s.* ان èn, عرض ''àrz.

Wield, *v.a.* قوللانمق kùllȧnmak, صاورمق sàwurmak.

Wife, *s.* قارى kȧri, اهل èhl, اهل‌بيت èhli-bèyt, حليله hàlīlé, منكوحه mènkyūhé, باجى bȧji, ارقه‌داش ȧrkadàsh; حرم hàrem; husband's brother's —, التى or ايلتى èlti.

Wild, Wilderness, *s.* بيابان bèyābȧn, قير kìr, صحرا sàhrà, دشت dèsht.

Wild, *a.* يبانى yàbȧnī, دشتى dèshtī; (mad) دلى dèli.

Wile, *s.* دسيسه dèssīssé.

Wilful, *a.* قصدى kʌssdī, اختيارى ìkhtiyārī; (man) ترس tèrss, معند mū''ànnid, عنادجى ''ìnādji; —ly, *ad.* عمداً ''àmdan, قصداً kʌssdan; مخصوص màkhsūss.

Will, *s.* اختيار ìkhtiyār, اراده ìrādé; (testament) وصيتنامه wʌssìyyèt-nāmé; —, *v.a.* اراده ا ìrādé-et; وصيت ا wʌssìyyèt-et; free— (human) ارادهٔ جزئيه ìrādé'i-jùz'ìyyé; (of God) ارادهٔ كليه ìrādé'i-kyùllìyyé; —, *v. aux.* (see Grammar).

Willing, *a.* راضى rāzī; كوكللو ghyùng-ullu; —ly, *ad.* باش اوستنه bàsh-ùsstuna, ازدل وجان èz-dìl-u-jān.

Willow, *s.* سوكود sùghud.

Wily, *a.* حيله كار hìlékyār, شيطان shèytān.

Wimble, *s.* مثقب (mʌtkʌb).

Win, *v.a.* and *n.* قزانمق kʌzanmak.

Wince, *v.n.* چكنمك chèkinmek.

Winch, *s.* طولاب dòlāb, چرخ chàrkh.

Wind, *s.* روزكار rùzghyār, يل yèl, ريح rīh, باد bād; هوا hàwā; fair —, ايوهوا īyi-hàwā, ايوروزكار īyi-rùzghyār, موافق هوا mùwāfik-hàwā, مساعدروزكار mùssā''id-rùzghyār; foul —, ترس هوا tèrss-hàwa, مخالف روزكار mùkhālif-rùzghyār; high —, سرت هوا sèrt-hàwā, صيقى روزكار sìki-rùzghyār; reigning —, prevailing —, اكثرى اسان روزكار èksérī-èssen-rùzghyār.

Wind, *v.a.* صارمق sʌrmak, طولاشدرمق dòlashdirmak; —, *v.n.* طولاشمق dòlashmak; — round, — about, *v.n.* صارلمق sʌrìlmak; طولاشمق dòlash-mak; — up, *v.a.* (a watch, &c.) قورمق kùrmak; (a string, &c.) طوپلامق tòplamak; (a discourse) ختم ا khʌtm-et.

Windfall, *s.* روزكارك دوشورديغى rùz-ghyāring-dùshurdughu, دوشوك dù-shuk; (of fortune) كله پير kèlépīr, باد اورد bād-āvèrd, باداورده bād-āvèrdé.

Winding-sheet, *s.* كفن kèfen (kèfin).

Window, *s.* پنجره pènjéré; — blind, *s.* كونش پردهسى ghyùnèsh-pèrdéssi.

Windpipe, *s.* غرتلق ghìrtlʌk.

Windsail, *s.* مانيقه mànika.

Windward, *s.* روزكاراوستى rùzghyār-ùsstu.

Windy, *a.* روزكارلو rùzghyārli.

Wine, *s.* شراب shàrāb (shàrap), باده bādé; — merchant, *s.* شراب صاتان بازركان shàrāb-sʌtan-bʌzirghyān; — press, *s.* شراب باصقيسى shàrāb-bʌsskissi.

Wing, *s.* قناد kʌnad, جناح jènāh, پر pèr; (of an army) قول kòl, جناح jènāh; —, *v.a.* (a bird) قناديني قيرمق kʌnadini-kìrmak; — one's flight, اوچمق ùchmak.

Wink, *s.* كوزاشارتى ghyùz-ìshārèti; طرفة العين tàrféti-'l-''àyn; —, *v.n.* كوزقيپمق ghyùz-kìpmak; — at, *v.n.* (a person) كوزايله اشارت ا ghyùz-ila-ìshāret-et; — (any impropriety) كوز قپامق ghyùz-kʌpamak, كورممزلك ا ghyùrmamazlik-et, مسامحه ا mùssāmaha-et, اغماض عين ا ìghmāzi-''àyn-et.

Winnow, *v.a.* صاورمق sàwurmak.

Winter, *s.* قيش kìsh, شتا shìtā, زمستان zìmisstān; —, *v.n.* قيشلامق kìshlamak; the depth of —, قره‌قيش kAra-kìsh, اربعين èrba"īn, زمهرير zèmhérīr.

Wintry, *a.* قيش‌كبى kìsh-ghìbi.

Wipe, *s.* سلش sìlish (fig.) تكمه tèkmé (kick); —, — off, — out, *v.a.* سلمك sìlmek.

Wire, *s.* تل tèl; gold —, سرمه sìrma; silver —, كومش‌سرمه ghyùmush-sìrma; iron —, تيمورتل (dèmir)-tèl; copper —, باقرتل bAkir-tèl; gold — drawer, سرمه‌كش sìrma-kèsh.

Wisdom, *s.* عقل "Akl, عقللولق "Akllìlik; (of an act) حكمت hìkmèt, مناسبت mùnāssèbèt.

Wise, *a.* عاقل "Ākil, عقللو "Aklli; all — (all-knowing) عليم "àlīm, علام "àllām.

Wiseacre, *s.* بوداله bùdAla.

Wish, *s.* (for an event) ارزو àrzu; خواهش khāhish, امل èmel; (to do) مراد mùrĀd, مرام mèrām; (for a thing) استك ìsstek; —, *v.n.* ارزوا àrzu-et, خواهش‌ا khāhish-et, امل‌ا èmel-et; مراد‌ا mùrĀd-et, مرام‌ا mèrām-et; —, *v.a.* استمك isstémek, استك‌ا ìsstek-et; ارزوا àrzu-et, ارزولمق ārzulamak; — joy, تبريك‌ا tèbrīk-et, تهنيه‌ا tèhnìyyé-et; I wish you —, كوزك ايدين ghyùzung-àydin (may thy eyes be brightened), مبارك‌اولسون mùbārek-òlsun (may it be blessed to you).

Wit, *s.* (of mind) ذكا zèkyā; (of a saying) لطافت làtāfèt; (witty person) لطيفه‌كو حاضرجواب hAzir-jéwAb, latìfé-ghyū; to —, يعنى yà"nī.

Witch, *s.* جادى jAdi, بوكوجى‌قارى bughuju-kAri, سحربازقارى sìhrbAz-kAri; (old woman) قوجه‌قارى kòja-kAri; (knowing woman) پيغمبر pèyghAmbèr; (beautiful woman) دلبر dìlbèr, جلوه‌كار jìlvékyār.

Witchcraft, *s.* بوكو bùghu, *or* بويو bùyu, سحر sìhr.

Witchery, *s.* جلوه jìlvé, ناز nāz, ادا èdā.

Witching, *a.* كوزل ghyùzèl, نازك nāzik, دلبر dìlbèr, جلوه‌كارانه jìlvékyārāné.

With, *pr.* ايله ìla (ìlen); ب bi, مع mà"; together —, ايله‌برابر ìla-bèrābèr, معاً mà"an.

Withal, *ad.* بونك ايله برابر bùnun-ìla-bèrābèr.

Withdraw, *v.n.* چكلمك chèkilmek, ايرلمق àyrìlmak, كتمك ghìtmek; —, *v.a.* كيرو المق ghèri-Almak; چيقارمق chìkàrmak; قالدرمق kAldirmak.

Withdrawal, *s.* چكلمكلك chèkilmeklik.

Wither, *v.n.* صولمق sòlmak, قورومق kùrumak; —, *v.a.* قوروتمق kùrutmak.

Withhold, *v.a.* ويرمامك vèrmamek, اليقومق Ali-kòmak, طوتمق tùtmak.

Within, *pr.* ايچنده ìchinda, داخلنده dākhilinda, درونده dèrūnunda; —, *ad.* ايچروده ìchèrida (ìchèrda); (at home) اوده èvda; — reach, ال يتشر èl-yètishir; — ear-reach, قولاق اشيدر kùlAk-ìshìdir; — range, كله يتشر ghyùllé-yètishir, قورشون يتشر kùrshun-yètishir.

Without, *pr.* سز siz, s*i*z, بی bī, بلا b*i*lā; (outside of) طیشاریسنده d*ì*sh*à*r*i*ssind*a*, خارجنده khārijind*a*, بیرونده bīrūnund*a*; —, *ad.* طیشارده d*ì*sh*à*rd*a*, طشره ده t*à*shrad*a*.

Withstand, *v.a.* and *n.* طیانمق d*à*yanm*a*k, تحمل ا t*à*h*ə*mmul-et.

Witness, *s.* (one present) کورن ghy*ù*ren; اشیدن *ì*shìden; (at a trial) شاهد shāhid, کواه ghy*ù*wāh; (testimony) شهادت sh*ə*hādet; —, *v.a.* کورمك ghy*ù*rmek, مشاهده ا m*ù*shāhédé-et; to bear —, شهادت ا sh*ə*hādet-et, شاهد او shāhid-*ò*l; false —, (person) یلان شاهدی y*à*l*a*n-shāhidi, شاهد زور shāhidi-zūr; (testimony) شهادت زور sh*à*hādeti-zūr, یلان y*à*l*a*n.

Wits, *s. pl.* عقل ''*a*kl; he has his wits about him, عقلی باشنده در ''*a*kl*i*-b*a*sh*i*nd*à*-dir.

Wittol, *s.* پزونك p*è*zéw*è*nk, دیوث d*è*yyūss.

Witty, *a.* (person) تحاف سویلر t*ù*h*a*f-s*ù*w*è*yler, نکره لو n*è*kréli; (saying) کوزل ghy*ù*z*è*l, تحاف t*ù*h*a*f.

Wive, *v.n.* اولنمك *è*vl*è*nmek, تأهل ا t*è*'*è*hhul-et, قاری المق k*a*r*i*-*a*lm*a*k.

Wizard, *s.* سحرباز s*ì*hrb*a*z.

Wo! Woe! *int.* ولی w*a*y, واه wāh, ایواه *è*ywāh, یازق y*à*z*i*k; —, *s.* بلا b*è*lā, فلاکت f*è*lāk*è*t, درد d*è*rd, کدر k*è*der.

Woful, Woeful, *a.* کدرلو k*è*derli, دردالود d*è*rd-ālūd, دردناك d*è*rdnāk.

Wolf, *s.* قورت k*ù*rt, کرك ghy*ù*rgh, ذئب zè'b.

Wolfsbane, *s.* قورت بوغان k*ù*rt-b*ò*gh*a*n.

Woman, *s.* قاری k*a*r*i*, عورت ''*à*vret, زن z*è*n, نسا n*ì*ssā; —kind, قاری قسمی k*a*r*i*-k*ì*ssm*i*, طائفهٔ نسا tā'ifè'i-n*ì*ssā.

Womanish, *a.* قاری کبی k*a*ri-gh*ì*bi.

Womb, *s.* دول یتاغی dūl-y*à*tagh*i*, رحم r*à*hm.

Wonder, *s.* (feeling) تعجب t*à*''*à*jjub, حیرت h*à*yret, وله v*è*leh; (thing) عجیب شی (''*a*jā'ib)-sh*è*y, عجیبه ''*a*jībé, غریبه gh*à*rībé, غرائبدن gh*à*rā'ibd*a*n; (miracle) معجزه m*ù*''jizé; —, *v.n.* شاشمق sh*ə*shm*a*k, قالمق k*a*lm*a*k, تعجب ا t*à*''*à*jjub-et, متعجب او m*ù*t*a*''*à*jjib-*ò*l, حیرتده قالمق h*à*yretd*a*-k*a*lm*a*k, حیران او h*à*yrān-*ò*l, متحیر او m*ù*t*a*h*à*yyir-*ò*l, وله کلمك v*è*leh-gh*è*lmek.

Wonderful, Wondrous, *a.* عجیب ''*a*jīb (''*a*jā'ib), غریب gh*à*rīb, عقلدن خارج ''*a*kld*a*n-khārij, شاشله جق sh*ə*sh*i*l*a*j*a*k.

Wont, *s.* عادت ''ādet; —ed, *a.* عادت ایدلمش ''ādet-*è*dilmish, معتاد m*ù*''tād.

Woo, *v.a.* عرض عشق ا ''*à*rz*i*-''*a*shk-et.

Wood, *s.* (material) اغاج *a*gh*a*j; (of trees) اورمان *ò*rm*a*n; (for burning) اوطون *ò*dun, حطب h*a*tab.

Woodbine, *s.* یبان خانم الی y*à*b*a*n-h*à*n*i*m-*è*li.

Woodcock, *s.* چوللق ch*ù*lluk.

Wood-cutter, *s.* بالطه‌جی bàltaji.

Wooden, *a.* اغاج àghaj, اغاجدن àghaj-dan; (of timber) أحشب àhshàb, أحشاب àhshāb.

Woodpecker, *s.* اغاج‌قاقان àghaj-kàkan.

Woof, *s.* أتقی àtki, پود pūd.

Wool, *s.* یون yùn *or* یوك yùng, یپاغی yàpaghi; goat's —, تفتك tìftik.

Woollen, *a.* یون yùn, یوكدن yùngdan; —draper, چوقه‌جی (chòhaji).

Word, *s.* سوز sùz, لقردی làkirdi, لفظ làfz, كلمه kèlimé; تعبیر tà''bīr; كلام kèlām; —, *v.a.* تعبیرات قوللانمق tà''bīrāt-kùllanmak; — of mouth, شفاه shìfāh, مشافهت mùshāféhèt; by — — —, شفاهاً shìfāhan; — of God, كلام‌قدیم kèlāmi-kàdīm (applied to the Kùr'ān); high —s, غوغا (kàwgha), نزاع nìzā''.

Work, *s.* ایش ìsh, ایش‌كوچ ìsh-ghyùch; كار kyār, صنع sùn''; فعل fì''l, عمل ''àmel; —, *v.n.* ایشلمك ìshlémek, ایش‌ایشلمك ìsh-ìshlémek, چالشمق chàlishmak; (a machine) ایشلمك ìshlémek; (in fermentation) قاینامق kàynamak, تخمرا tàkhàm-mur-et, قبارمق kàbarmak; (medicine) عمل‌ویرمك ''àmel-vèrmek; —, *v.a.* (embroider) ایشلمك ìshlémek; (any material) ایشلمك ìshlémek; (a mine) ایشلتمك ìshletmek; (a person) ایشلتمك ìshletmek; یورمق yòrmak, باشنه‌ایش‌چیقارمق bàshina-ìsh-chìkàrmak; — up, (materials) ایشلمك ìshlémek; خرجا khàrj-et, قوللانمق kùllanmak; — one's self up into a passion, قوروب‌قیزمق kùrup-kìzmak, قوردقجه قیزمق kùrdukja-kìzmak; — out, باشارمق bàsharmak, بجرمك bèjermek, وجوده كتورمك vùjūda-ghètirmek; (a problem) حل‌ا hàll-et; — upon, تأثیرا tè'sīr-et; (a person's feelings) مرحمت ایتدرمك mèrhàmet-ètdir-mek.

Workhouse, *s.* محله‌نك فقرا خانه‌سی màhàllénin-fùkarā-khānéssi.

Workman, *s.* ایشجی ìshji.

Workmanship, *s.* ایشجیلك ìshjilik; كار kyār.

Workshop, *s.* دكان dùkkyān (dùkkèn).

Workwoman, *s.* ایشجی قاری ìshji-kàri.

World, *s.* عالم ''ālem; this —, دنیا dùnyā; عالم‌دنیا ''ālémi-dùnyā; the habitable —, ربع مسكون rùb''i-mèsskyūn; — (great quantity) دنیا قدر dùnyā-kàdar.

Worldly, *a.* دنیوی dùnyévī, خاكی khākī.

Worm, *s.* صوغلجان sògh uljàn; (maggot) قورت kùrt; (of a gun) طوكزایاغی (dòmuz) - àyaghi; (of a still) بورو bòru; (of a screw) تل tèl, بورمه bùrma; — out, *v.a.* اكلامق àngla-mak (ànnamak); — one's self in, صوقلمق sòkulmak; — one's self into one's favour, چاتمق chàtmak; to try and . . . , یلتنمك yèltenmek; — eaten, قورت‌یمش kùrt-yèmish.

Wormwood, *s.* پلین pèlin.

Worry, *v.a.* (as a dog) صالدرمق sàldirmak; (teaze) اذيت ويرمك èzìyyèt-vèrmek, راحتسزا rāhatsiz-et.

Worse, *a.* دهافنا dàhā-fèna, دهااشاغی dàhā-àshàghi, بتر bètèr, دهابتر dàhā-bètèr; — and worse, كتدكجه فنا ghitdikja-fèna.

Worship, *s.* عبادت "ìbādet, پرستش pèresstish, طاپنش tàpinish; —, *v.a.* طاپنمق tàpinmak, عبادتا "ìbādet-et, پرستشا pèresstish-et; your —, his —, ذات عطوفيلری zāti-"ùtūfilèri; —ed, معبود mà"būd; —er, عابد "ābid (*pl.* عبده "àbédé).

Worst, *a.* اك فنا èng-fèna; اك اشاغی èng-àshàghi; —, *v.a.* ينمك yènmek, التا àlt-et.

Worsted, *s.* يوك اپلكی yùng-ìplighi; — stockings, يوك جوراب yùng-chòrab.

Worth, *s.* and *a.* دكر dèghèr; —, *s.* قدر kàdr, قيمت kìmet; to be —, دكمك dèghmek, ايتمك ètmek; —less, *a.* براقچه لق bìr-àkchalìk, بر اقچه ايتمز bìr-àkcha-ètmàz.

Worthy, *a.* دكرلو dèghèrli; — (of) شايان shāyān, شايسته shāyèssta, لايق lāyìk, جسبان jùssbān.

Wound, *s.* ياره yàra, جرح jùrh, جرحه jùrha; —, *v.a.* يارهلمق yàralamak, يارها yàra-et, جرحا jùrh-et.

Wrangle, *v.n.* غوغا (kàwgha)-et, نزاعا nìzā"-et, منازعه ا mùnāza"a-et.

Wrap, *v.a.* صارمق sàrmak; — round, *v.a.* صارمق sàrmak, طولاشدرمق dòlashdìrmak; —, *v.n.* صارلمق sàrìlmak, طولاشمق dòlashmak; — up, *v.a.* صارمق sàrmak, اورتمك ùrtmek; —, *v.n.* صارلمق sàrìlmak, اورتنمك ùrtunmek.

Wrapper, *s.* اورتی ùrtu.

Wrath, *s.* دارغينلق dàrghinlìk, أويكه (ùfké), غضب ghàzab.

Wreak, *v.a.* اجراا ìjrā-et.

Wreath, *s.* چيچك باغی chìchek-bàghi, يپراق باغی yàprak-bàghi (*or* اوريسی

Wreathe, *v.a.* اورمك ùrmek. [ùrussu).

Wreck, *s.* بقيه bàkìyyé, دوكندی dùkyundu, خرابه khàràbé, ويرانه vīrāné; —, *v.a.* قضايه اوغراتمق kàzāya-òghràtmak; to be —ed, قضايه اوغرامق kàzāya-òghramak, قضا زده اول kàzā-zèdé-òl; —ed, قضايه اوغرامش kàzāya-òghramish, قضازده kàzāzèdé.

Wren, *s.* بوقلوجه بلبل bòkluja-bùlbul.

Wrench, *s.* بورقلش bùrkulush; زورلايش zòrlayish; —, *v.a.* (a joint) بورقتمق bùrkutmak; (open) زورلامق zòrlamak.

Wrest, *v.a.* زورايله المق zòr-ila-àlmak, سوكوب المق sùkyup-àlmak.

Wrestle, *v.a.* كورشمك ghyùreshmek, كولشمك ghyùleshmek.

Wrestler, *s.* پهلوان pèhliwān.

Wrestling, *s.* كولشمه ghyùleshma.

Wretch, *s.* خبيث khàbìss; (poor) بيچاره bīchāré, زواللو zàwàlli.

Wretched, *a.* فنا حالده fèna-hālda, پريشان pèrīshān, پژمرده pèzhmùrdé; (in mind) پريشان خاطر pèrīshāni-khàtir.

Wring, *v.a.* صيقمق sìkmak; بورمق

bùrmak ; — off, بوكه بوكه قوپارمق bùké-bùké-kòpàrmak.

Wrinkle, *s.* بورشق bùrushuk ; —, *v.n.* بورشمق bùrushmak ; —, *v.a.* بورشدرمق bùrushdurmak ; —led, *a.* بورشق bùrushuk ; بورشقلو bùrushuklu.

Wrist, *s.* بلك bilèk.

Wristband, *s.* يك yèng.

Write, *v.a.* يازمق yàzmak, تحريرا tàhrīr-et, تنميقا tènmīk-et, تسطيرا tèsstīr-et ; — down, قيدا kàyd-et ; ضبطا zàbt-et ; —, *v.n.* يازى يازمق yàzi-yàzmak.

Writer, *s.* (author) مصنف mùssànnif, مؤلف mù'èllif ; (penman) خطاط khàttāt ; (clerk) يازيجى yàziji, كاتب kyātib ; (of a letter) محرر الحروف mùhàrriru-'l-hùrūf.

Writhe, *v.n.* قيورلمق kìvrilmak, پيچ و تاب ا pīch-u-tāb-et.

Writing, *s.* يازى yàzi ; hand—, يازى yàzi, خط khàtt ; —s, *s. pl.* محررات mùhàrrérāt ; كاغدلر kyāghidler.

Written, *a.* يازيلو yàzili ; يازلمش yàzilmish ; مكتوب mèktūb, مسطور mèsstūr, محرر mùhàrrer, مقيد mùkàyyed.

Wrong, *a.* (erroneous) ياكلش yàngilish (yānish) ; (bad) فنا fèna ; —, *s.* حقسزلق hàkksizlik, غدر ghàdr, ظلم zùlm ; —, *v.a.* حقسزلقا hàkksizlik-et, غدرا ghàdr-et, ظلما zùlm-et ; — side, ترس tèrss, ترس طرفى tèrss-tàrafi ; — side outwards, — side up, ترس tèrss.

Wrongful, *a.* —ly, *ad.* ناحق يره nā-hàkk-yèra.

Wroth, *a.* دارغين dàrghin.

Wrought, *a.* ايشلمه ìshlémé, دوكمه dùghmé.

Wry, *a.* چارپق chàrpik.

Y.

Yacht, *s.* سيركميسى sèyr-ghèmissi.

Yankee, *s.* امريقان ادمى àmèrikān-àdami.

Yard, *s.* (measure) يارده yàrda, ارشون àrshin ; (of a house) حولى hàvli ; (of a ship) سرن sèren ; (of a horse) سك sìk, ذكر zèker ; — arm, سرن اوجى sèren-ūju.

Yarn, *s.* ايلك ìplik, تل tèl ; (fig.) مصال màssal.

Yawn, *v.n.* اسنمك èssnémek.

Ye, *pro.* سز sìz, سزلر sìzler.

Yea, *ad.* بلى bèli, اوت èvet, نعم nā''m.

Year, *s.* ييل *or* يل yìl, سنه sèné, سال sāl.

Yearling, *s.* برسنه لك bìr-sènélik.

Yearly, *a.* and *ad.* سنوى sènévī, يلده بر yìlda-bìr.

Yearn, *v.n.* اشتياق چكمك ìshtiyāk-chèkmek, ارزولمق àrzulamak.

Yeast, *s.* ارپه صويى مايه سى àrpa-sùyu-màyassi.

Yell, *s.* حيقرش hàykirish ; —, *v.n.* حيقرمق hàykirmak.

Yellow, *a.* صارى sàri, اصفر àssfèr, زرد

zèrd, زرده zèrdé; —s, s. pl. صاريلق sarilik.

Yellow-fever, s. صارى حما sari-hùmmà.

Yelp, v.n. باغرمق bàghirmak.

Yeoman, s. آغا āgha.

Yes, ad. بلى bèli, اوت èvet.

Yesterday, s. دون dùn, دونكى كون dùnku-ghyùn.

Yesternight, s. دون كيجه dùn-ghèyjé.

Yet, ad. دها dàhā; (still) حالا hālā; (again) ينه yìné (ghène); not —, هنوز hènuz (hèniz); more —, دها dàhā; —, c. لكن lākin, ولكن vè-lākin, اما àmmā, ينه yìné (ghèné).

Yew, s. بورصق اغاجى bòrsuk-aghaji (?).

Yield, s. محصول màhsūl; —, v.a. (give) ويرمك vèrmek, حاصل ا hāssil-et; (give up) تسليم ا tèsslīm-et; —, v.n. تسليم او tèsslīm-òl.

Yoke, s. بويوندروغ bòyundurugh; (pair) چفت chìft; —, v.a. قوشمق kòshmak. [-sarissi.

Yolk, s. يمورطه نك صاريسى yìmurtaning-

Yon, Yonder, a. شو shū, شورادهكى shūradéki; yonder, ad. شورا shūra, شوراسى shūrassi, اورا òra, اوراسى òrassi; شورايه shūraya, اورايه òraya; شورادة shūrada, اوراده òrada.

Yore, s. اسكى زمان èsski-zàmān, ايام ماضى èyyāmi-māzī.

You, pro. سز siz, سزلر sìzler; سزى sìzi, سزلرى sìzléri; سزه sìzé, سزلره sìzléra.

Young, a. كنج ghènj; —, — one, s. ياورى yàvri; —er, كچوك kùchuk; —est, الككچوك èng-kùchuk; —ish, كنجچه ghènjja.

Youngster, s. دليقانلو dèlikanli, جوان jìwān, شاب shābb.

Your, pro. a. كز ngiz, ingiz; سزك sìzing, سزلرك sìzlèring.

Yours, pro. سزك sìzing, سزلرك sìzléring; سزككى sìzingki, سزلرككى sìzléringki.

Yourself, pro. كنديكز kèndingiz; —lves, كنديلريكز kèndiler-ingiz.

Youth, s. كنجلك ghènjlik, جوانلق jìwānlik, شبابت shèbābèt; (lad) اوغلان òghlan, دليقانلو dèlikanli, جوان jìwān, شاب shābb.

Youthful, a. كنج ghènj.

Z.

Zeal, s. غيرت ghàyret, حميت hàmmìyyèt; (blind) تعصب tà"-asssub.

Zealot, s. متعصب كمسنه mùta"asssib-kìmèssné.

Zealous, a. غيرتلو ghàyretli, غيور ghàyūr.

Zealousness, s. غيرت ghàyret.

Zebra, s. يبان اشكى yàban-èshèghi.

Zenith, s. سمت رأس sèmti-rè'ss.

Zephyr, s. بادصبا bādi-sàbā.

Zero, s. صفر sìfr.

Zigzag (of trenches) صچان يولى sìchan-yòlu.

Zinc, s. توتيا tùtya.

Zodiac, *s.* منطقةالبروج mìntakatu-'l--bùrūj (mántik —).

Zone, *s.* قوشاق kùshàk, كمر kèmer; (geographical) منطقه mìntaka (mán-tika); torrid —, منطقهٔ حاره (mán-tika'i)-hārré; temperate —, منطقهٔ معتدله (mántika'i)-mù''tèdilé; frigid —, منطقهٔ منجمده (mántika'i)--mùnjèmidé.

Zoography, Zoology, *s.* علم بحث حيوانات "ìlmi-bàhssi-hày-wānat.

Zoological, *a.* حيواناته متعلق hày-wānata-mùta''àllik.

END OF PART THE FIRST.

REDHOUSE'S DICTIONARY.

PART II.—TURKISH AND ENGLISH.

N.B.—The form of the aorist indicative, which is the same as that of the aorist active participle, of every Turkish simple verb, is given in parenthesis immediately after the verb itself, for the reason that it is not subject to any definite rule, easy of enunciation. The *a*, *p*, or *t*, after each word, denotes it to be of either Arabic, Persian, or purely Turkish origin. All the verbs are Turkish.

ا èlif. First letter of the Turkish alphabet. In chronograms and astronomical tables it has the value of 1. Pronounced as ā, it is a Turkish interjectional affix of affirmation, something of the value of our English *do* in affirmations. It is also a Persian vocative affix, often employed in poetry. It is, further, placed between a repetition of a word, in the sense of *and* or *with*. In the dates of letters, when following one of the characters ذ zèl, ر rè, *or* ج jìm, as جا, را, it indicates the first of the couple in three couples of months with the same name, and those characters alone, without the ا, indicate the second month in each couple (see ذا, را, and جا).

اب āb, *s. p.* Water; juice; lustre; honour, spotlessness; temper (of steel); —, *s. a.* A father, master, possessor. Used in the composition of Arabic words, altering its termination according to its case, having ابو abū in the nominative, ابا aba in the accusative, and ابی abi in the other cases; as, ابوبكر Abubeker.

ابا èbā, *in* اباعن جد èbā-"an-jèddin, *ad. a.* From father to son (*lit.* through the father from the grandfather), hereditarily.

ابا ābā, *s. pl. a.* (*of* ابو èbu) Fathers; ancestors, forefathers.

ابا ìbā, *s. a.* Refusal, rejection, abstaining; ا—, ـــ et, *v.n.* To refuse, reject, abstain from.

اباد ābād, *s. pl. a.* (*of* ابد èbed)

Eternities; —, *a. p.* Cultivated; peopled; populous; flourishing; —, *s. p.* City, town, place of residence.

اباداں àbādān, *a. p.* Cultivated; peopled; populous. [Devils.

ابالیس èbālīss, *s. pl. a.* (*of* ابلیس)

ابانمق ʌbʌnmak (*aor.* ابانور ʌbʌnir), *v.n.* To lean forward over another.

ابتدا ìbtidā (ìp-), *s. a.* Beginning, commencement; —, *ad. t.* First, in the first place.

ابتدار ìbtidār, *s. a.* Setting about any work; ا—, —et, *v.n.* To set about, begin.

ابتسام ìbtissām, *s. a.* Smiling, smile; ا—, —et, *v.n.* To smile.

ابتلا ìbtilā, *s. a.* The being subject or addicted to anything wrong or unpleasant. [cheerfulness.

ابتهاج ìbtihāj, *s. a.* Hilarity, joy,

ابجد ѐbjɘd, *s. a.* The alphabet in its old arrangement, conformable to the order in which the letters are placed in the Hebrew alphabet, with some additions at the end. It is this order which gives the numerical value to the letters, and very useful to be known. This system of notation is called ابجدحسابی Ѐbjɘd - hìssʌbi. The order, mode of reading, and values of the letters are as follows:—

ابجد هوز حطی کلمن سعفص قرشت ثخذ ضظغ Ѐbjɘd-hèwwʌz-hùttī-kèlémèn--sà''fàss-kʌrashʌt-sàkhaz-dʌzagha.

ا 1, ب *or* پ 2, ج *or* چ 3, د 4, ه 5, و 6, ز *or* ژ 7, ح 8, ط 9, ی 10; ك *or* گ *or* ڭ 20, ل 30, م 40, ن 50, س 60, ع 70, ف 80, ص 90, ق 100, ر 200, ش 300, ت 400, ث 500, خ 600, ذ 700, ض 800, ظ 900, غ 1000.

The letters may be arranged regularly or irregularly; they have always the same value, and the addition of the several values gives the value of the whole. This system is much used in chronograms, and in books of astronomical tables, &c.

ابحار èbhār, ابحر èbhùr, *s. pl. a.* (*of* بحر bàhr). Seas, oceans.

ابخره èbkhiré, *s. pl. a.* (*of* بخار bòkhār), Vapours.

ابد èbed, *s. a.* Eternity to come; الی الابد ìlé-'l-èbed, *ad. a.* To all eternity; ابداً èbédɘn, *ad. a.* To all eternity; never.

ابدار ʌbdār, *a. p.* Having water or juice; tempered (steel); lustrous.

ابداع ìbdā'', *s. a.* Invention, production, innovation; ا—, —et, *v.a.* To produce a new thing, invent, innovate.

ابدان èbdān, *s. pl. a.* (*of* بدن bèden), Bodies.

ابدست àbdesst, *s. p.* The smaller ablution before prayer; —المق, —ʌlmak, *v.n.* To perform one's ablution.

ابدی èbédī, *a. a.* Which will endure to all eternity.

ابديت èbédìyyét, *s. a.* Quality of eternal durability.
ابر èbr, *s. p.* A cloud.
ابرا ìbrā, *s. a.* Quittance, acquittal, discharge; ا—, —et, *v.a.* To free, acquit, discharge, exonerate.
ابرار èbrār, *s. pl. a.* (*of* بر bèrr), The good, just, virtuous.
ابراز ìbrāz, *s. a.* Production, manifestation, showing; ا—, —et, *v.a.* To manifest, produce, show, display.
ابرام ìbrām, *s. a.* Importunity, urging; ا—, —et, *v.a.* To importune, urge.
ابرشيم ìbrishim, *s. p.* Double-twisted silk thread.
ابرص èbràss, *a. a.* Leprous; —, *s. a.* A leper; leprosy.
ابرو èbru, *a. t.* Marbled; —, *s. t.* Marbled appearance in colours; —, *s. p.* The eyebrow; —ābrū, *and* ابروى ābrūy, *s. p.* Honour, spotlessness.
ابريق ìbrik, *s. t.* Ewer for washing; a brig; brigantine; sloop of war.
ابصار èbsār, *s. pl. a.* (*of* بصر bāssar), Eyes; penetrations, sagacities.
ابطال èbtāl, *s. pl. a.* (*of* بطال bāttāl), Champions, heroes; —, ìbtāl, *s. a.* Avoiding, abolishing, annulling; ا—, —et, *v.a.* To make void, *or* of no value, annul, abolish.
ابعاد èb''ād, *s. pl. a.* (*of* بعد bù''d), Distances; —, ìb''ād, *s. a.* Removal to a distance; ا—, —et, *v.a.* To remove to a distance.
ابعد èb''àd, *a. a.* More or most distant; very distant.

ابقا ìbkā, *s. a.* A causing to continue, continuance, confirmation; ا—, —et, *v.a.* To confirm, cause to remain or continue (in an office).
ابكار ébkyār, *s. pl. a.* (*of* بكر bìkr), Virgins.
ابلا *or* ابله ābla, *s. t.* Eldest sister.
ابلاغ ìblāgh, *s. a.* A causing to reach, attain, or arrive at; ا—, —et, *v.a.* To cause to reach, arrive at, attain, mount up to.
ابلغ èblàgh, *a. a.* More, most, or very eloquent.
ابلق èblàk, *a. a.* Piebald; —, *s. a.* A piebald horse; (fig.) Time *or* the world, as consisting of night and day; — *or* ايبلق ìblìk (ìmlìk), *s. t.* A capon.
ابله ābilé, *s. p.* A bubble; a pimple; —, ābla, *s. t.* Eldest sister; —, èblèh, *a. a.* More, most, or very stupid.
ابليس ìblīss, *s. a.* Iblis, Satan; a devil.
ابن ìbn, *s. a.* Son of, as احمدابن محمد Ahmed - ìbni - Mùhāmmed, Ahmed, son of Mùhāmmed.
ابنة ìbnèt, *s. a.* A daughter.
ابنا èbnā, *s. pl. a.* (*of* ابن), Sons, children; ابناى سبيل èbnāyi - sèbīl, Sons of the road, travellers.
ابنوس àbanòss, *s. t.* Ebony.
ابنيه èbnìyyé, *s. pl. a.* (*of* بنا bìnā), Buildings, edifices; ابنيهٔ خيريه èbnìyyè'i - khàyrìyyé, Buildings for charitable or benevolent purposes.
ابو èbu, *s. a.* Father of, as ابوسينا èbu-Sīnā, Avicenna.

ابواب èbvāb, *s. pl. a.* (*of* باب), Gates, doors; chapters. [ship.

ابوت ùbùvvet, *s. a.* Paternity, father-

ابوين èbévèyn, *s. dual a.* (*of* ابو èbu, a father), The two parents.

ابه èbé, *s. t.* A midwife; ابه‌كومجى èbè-ghyùmèji, Mallows; geranium.

ابهام ìbhām, *s. a.* Enunciating obscurely and so as to create doubt.

ابهت ùbbéhèt (ùbhèt), *s. a.* Grandeur, glory, magnificence, pomp.

ابيات èbyāt, *s. pl. a.* (*of* بيت), Houses; verses, *or rather* distichs.

ابيض èbyàd, *a. a.* White.

ابين èbyèn, *a. a.* More, most, or very clear, explicit, manifest, evident.

اپ ap. Turkish particle placed before a few adjectives, and there signifying *quite, very, altogether,* as اپ‌اچق ap-àchik, wide open, اپ‌انسز ap-ansiz, all of a sudden, &c.

اپارمق aparmak (*aor.* اپارر aparir), *v.a.* (*provincial*), To bring; to carry away.

اپرتمك ìprètmek (*aor.* اپردر ìprèdir), *v.a.* To wear by use, to make a stuff ragged and rough; اپرنمك ìprèn-mek (*aor.* اپرنور ìprènir), *v.n.* To become rough and worn.

اپسد *or* اپسيد ìpsid, *s. t.* Felloe of a wheel.

اپش apish, *s. t.* The grip of the legs, or that part of the thighs, knees, &c., by which a seat is obtained in a saddle.

اپشمق apishmak (*aor.* اپشور apishir), *v. n.* To open the legs and stand or sit a-straddle.

اپلك ìplik, *s. t.* Thread.

ات èt, *s. t.* Flesh; meat; —, at, *s. t.* A horse; a stallion.

اتا ata, *s. t.* (*old*), Father; اتابك ata-bègh (*lit.* Prince-father), Tutor of the monarch, *or* regent (in some of the old Mussulman dynasties).

اتالق atalik, *s. t.* Tutor, guardian.

اتباع ètbā‘‘, *s. pl. a.* (*of* تبع tèba‘‘, *not in use*), Followers, suite, dependants, servants; —, ìttibā‘‘, *s. a.* A following, complying with, imitating; ا—, —et, *v.n.* To follow, obey, act up to, comply with.

اتحاد ìttihād, *s. a.* Union, concord, friendship; unanimity; ا—, —et, *v. n.* To join one's self to another, act in concert, be unanimous.

اتحاف ìthāf, *s. a.* Presenting, giving; ا—, —et, *v.a.* To give as a present, to present. [*v.a.* To take; to use, adopt.

اتخاذ ìttikhāz, *s. a.* A taking; ا—, —et,

اتش atèsh, *s. p.* Fire; —, atish, *s. t.* Action *or* manner of throwing; اتشپرست atèsh-pèrèsst, *s. p.* A fire-worshipper; اتشكده atèsh-kèdé, *s. p.* A fire temple. [with a quality.

اتصاف ìttissāf, *s. a.* Being endowed

اتصال ìttissāl, *s. a.* Being joined, touching, reaching to.

اتعاب ìt‘‘āb, *s. a.* A fatiguing, a causing fatigue; ا—, —et, *v.a.* To fatigue, wear out.

اتفاق ìttifāk, *s. a.* Union, concord; confederacy, alliance; hazard, chance; ا—, —et, *v.n.* To come to an agreement together, make an alliance; to chance, happen; على الاتفاق "àlé-'l-ìttifāk, *ad. a.* Unanimously; اتفاقا ìttifākā, *ad. a.* By chance, fortuitously; اتفاقى ìttifākī, *a. a.* Fortuitous.

اتقان ìttikān, *s. a.* Certain knowledge.

اتقى ātkī, *s. t.* The woof of cloth carried by the shuttle. [or of mountains.

اتك ètek, *s. t.* The skirts of clothes,

اتكا ìttikyā, *s. a.* A leaning upon or against; a relying on, trusting in; ا—, —et, *v.n.*

اتكال ìttikyāl, *s. a.* A leaving one's matters entirely to another.

اتلاف ìtlāf, *s. a.* A destroying; ا—, —et, *v. a.* To destroy, waste, ruin; kill.

اتلامق ātlamak (*aor.* اتلار ātlar), *v.a.* To spring, or jump over, or across; to omit, leave out.

اتلمق ātilmak (*aor.* اتلور ātilir), *v.n.* To spring or jump up, spring upon; —, *v. p.* To be thrown.

اتلنمق ātlanmak (*aor.* اتلانور ātlànir), *v.n.* To mount on horseback.

اتلو ātli, *a. t.* On horseback; —, *s. t.* A horseman; cavalry.

اتم ètèmm, *a. a.* More, most, or very complete; —, ātim, *s. t.* A cast, a throw; a charge (of powder).

اتمام ìtmām, *s. a.* Action of completing, completion; ا—, —et, *v.a.* To finish, complete.

اتمجه ātmaja, *s. t.* A sparrow-hawk.

اتمق ātmak (*aor.* اتار ātar), *v.a.* To throw, cast, project; to throw away, down, aside, up, &c.; to fire (a gun, &c.); to card (cotton); —, *v.n.* To fade, lose colour (stuffs); turn pale (countenance); grow light (the morning); طوپ اتمق tòp-ātmak, to fire guns, to fire a salute; (*fig.*) to become bankrupt. [livelihood.

اتمك (èkmek), *s. t.* Bread; (*fig.*)

اتهام ìthām, *s. a.* Imputation, accusation; ا—, —et, *v.a.* To impute, to accuse.

اتى ātī, *a. a.* Future, coming, to come; further on, lower down (in writing).

اتيان ìtyān, *s. a.* A bringing forward, mentioning; ا—, —et, *v.a.* To adduce, mention.

اتينا Atina, *s. t.* Athens. [duce, mention.

اثاث èssāss, اثاث بيت èssāssi-bèyt, *s. a.* Household stuff, goods, furniture.

اثار āssār, *s. pl. a.* (*of* اثر èsser), Vestiges, traces, signs, marks; remains; monuments; buildings; books, writings, works; doings; sayings.

اثاره ìssārè, *s. a.* A raising (the dust); an exciting (of troubles).

اثالت èssālet, *s. a.* Nobility of extraction.

اثام āssām, *s. pl. a.* (*of* اثم ìssm), Sins, iniquities, wickednesses.

اثبات ìssbāt, *s. a.* A making firm, fixing; a proving, demonstrating; a proof; ا—, —et, To prove, demonstrate; to fix, stablish, confirm; محو واثبات màhv-u-ìssbāt, A taking away some parts, and leaving or adding others;

alteration (in buildings or in writings).

اثر èsser, *s. a.* A vestige, trace, sign, mark; an effect; a monument (of art); a writing, saying, or doing; اثرطراز èsser-tìrāz, An historian.

اثقال èsskāl, *s. pl. a.* (*of* ثقل *not used*), Baggage, luggage, impedimenta.

اثم ìssm, *s. a.* A sin; —, āssim, *s. a.* A sinner. [Fruits.

اثمار èssmār, *s. pl. a.* (*of* ثمره sèmérē),

اثمان èssmān, *s. pl. a.* (*of* ثمن sèmen), Prices; values.

اثنا èssnā, *s. pl. a.* (*of* ثنى *not used*), Windings, foldings, sinuosities; —, *s. t.* Time or duration of any action; يول اثناسنده yòl-èssnāssìnd*a*, *or* اثناى راهده èssnāy*i*-rāhd*a*, while on the journey, مكالمه اثناسنده mùk*y*āléme-èssnāssìnd*a*, during the conference.

اثنين ìssnèyn, *s. a.* Monday.

اثواب ésswāb (èssbāb), *s. pl. a.* (*of* ثوب sèvb), Clothes.

اج àj, *or* اچ àch, *a. t.* Hungry; fasting, not having eaten; اچ كوزلو àj-ghyùzlu (hungry-eyed), Covetous, insatiate, insatiable; اچ قارننه àj-kàrnìn*a*, *ad.* On an empty stomach, fasting.

اجابت ìjābet, *s. a.* Acceptance of a request, compliance; ا—, —et, *v.n.* To comply.

اجار ājār, *s. pl. a.* (*of* اجر èjr), Recompenses, remunerations; rewards.

اجاره ìjārē, *s. a.* Rent; ground-rent paid for land, &c. in mortmain; اجارهٔ معجله ìjāré'i-mù''àjjélē, the sum or fine paid on first acquiring possession; اجارهٔ مؤجله ìjāré'i-mù'èjjélē, the monthly or yearly quit-rent paid ever afterwards.

اجازت ìjāzet, *s. a.* Permission, authorization; diploma or authority to act as a teacher of the humanities, or of divinity. [circulate.

اجاله ìjālē, *s. a.* A causing to flow, or

اجانب èjānib, *s. pl. a.* (*of* اجنبى èjnébī), Strangers, aliens (in blood, or of race).

اجبار ìjbār, *s. a.* A forcing, compelling; force, compulsion; ا—, —et, *v.a.* To compel.

اجبال èjbāl, *s. pl. a.* (*of* جبل jèbel), Mountains. [selection, election.

اجتبا ìjtiba, *s. a.* A choosing; choice,

اجترا ìjtirā, *s. a.* A daring; audacity; courage; ا—, —et, *v.n.* To dare, have the courage.

اجتماع ìjtimā'', *s. a.* A coming together, being collected, united, gathered together; meeting, conjunction; unanimity of opinion or decision (in matters of faith or discipline).

اجتناب ìjtināb, *s. a.* An abstaining, avoiding; ا—, —et, *v.n.* To abstain from, avoid.

اجتهاد ìjtihād, *s. a.* Exertion, endeavour; a striving to arrive at the true meaning of any point in law or religion.

اجداد èjdād, *s. pl. a.* (*of* جد jèdd), Ancestors, forefathers.

اجر èjr, *s. a.* Recompense, remuneration; reward.

اجرا ìjrā, *s. a.* A causing to flow; a putting in force, in operation; ا—, —et, *v.a.* To cause to flow; to put in force, execute; to perform the formalities of taking up a commission of office.

اجرت ùjrèt, *s. a.* Pay for any service, remuneration.

اجزا èjzā, *s. pl. a.* (*of* جزء jùz'), Parts; particles, atoms; ingredients; drugs, chemicals; sheets (of a book), or parts containing twenty pages; (as a Turkish singular) a chemical composition of any kind; a percussion cap; اجزاجى èjzāj*i*, A chemist or apothecary.

اجقمق àj*i*kmak (*aor.* اجقر àj*i*k*i*r), *v.n.* To become hungry, قارنم اجقدى kàrn*i*m-àj*i*kd*i* (lit. my stomach has become hungry), I am hungry.

اجل ājil, *a. a.* Future, to come, postponed to a future time; —, èjl (èjil), *s. a.* Cause, reason, motive, consideration; —, èjel, *s. a.* An appointed time; the appointed time of death; —, èjèll, *a. a.* More, most, or very great and glorious.

اجلا ìjlā, *s. a.* Banishment, exile; ا—, —et, *v.a.* To banish, exile.

اجلاس ìjlāss, *s. a.* A causing to sit down; ا—, —et, *v.a.* To cause to sit, to seat; to place on (the throne).

اجلال ìjlāl, *s. a.* Praise, glory, honour.

اجله èjìllé, *s. pl. a.* (*of* جليل jèlīl), Those who are very great and noble.

اجماع ìjmā'', *s. a.* A collecting; the unanimity of opinion or decision (of the Fathers of the Church on points of faith or discipline, this being one of the fundamental sources of authority in Muhammedan canon law, in matters where an explicit Divine command or apostolic word or deed cannot be cited: it is called also اجماع امت ìjmā''i-ùmmèt, *the unanimous decision of the Church*).

اجمال ìjmāl, *s. a.* The making a summary, an abbreviating; a summary, abbreviation; ا—, —et, *v.a.* To condense, abbreviate.

اجمتراق aj*i*mtràk, *a. t.* Rather bitter.

اجناد èjnād, *s. pl. a.* (*of* جند jùnd), Troops, legions, cohorts.

اجناس èjnāss, *s. pl. a.* (*of* جنس jìnss), Sorts, kinds; اجناس اقچه èjnāss-akch*a*, Mixed coins, foreign or old, no longer legally current.

اجنبى èjnébī, *s. a.* A foreigner.

اجوبه èjvibé, *s. pl. a.* (*of* جواب jèwāb), Answers.

اجى aj*i*, *a. t.* Bitter; hot (spices, &c.); —, *s. t.* Pain, smart; the word حاجى hājjī (hàj*i*), *a pilgrim to Mecca at a certain season, and with certain rites*, is sometimes thus spelt when applied to non-Muslim pilgrims to Jerusalem.

اجيمق aj*i*mak (*aor.* اجر *or* اجير aj*i*r), *v.n.* To be painful, to hurt, smart, ache; —, *v. a.* To be sorry for, to pity, feel for, compassionate.

اچ **àch**, *a. t.* Hungry; fasting; اچ‌كوزلو àch-ghyùzlu (having hungry eyes), *a. t.* Covetous, insatiable.

اچق **àchik**, *a. t.* Open; clear, serene; plain, clear, explicit; light (colour); اچق‌مشرب àchik-mèshreb; (of an open character), *a. t.* Forward, impudent; —, *s. t.* The open sea, the offing; any open space away from buildings.

اچلق **àchlik**, Hunger.

اچلمق **àchilmak** (*aor.* اچلور àchilir), *v.n.* To open; to become bright and shining, polished; to become clear and serene; to become lively, quick, merry; to acquire cleverness, expertness, experience; to lose one's bashfulness; to quit the shore or the harbour; to commence, begin, be entered upon; —, *v. p.* To be opened.

اچمق **àchmak** (*aor.* اچار àchar), *v.a.* To open; to polish; to begin; to explain clearly; to make explicit; to make a new pen; to unravel, untie, undo; to spread, set (sails), roll out (paste).

احاد **āhād**, *s. pl. a.* (*of* احد àhàd), Units; individuals.

احاديث **àhādiss**, *s. pl. a.* (*of* حديث hàdiss), Events, happenings; traditions of the sayings or doings of Muhammad (These, as a collection, hold a rank among Mussulman divines, corresponding to that of the book of the Acts of the Apostles and the Apostolic Epistles with us: they are a perfectly valid and binding source of authority in the determination of canonical questions), called generally احاديث نبويه àhādissi-nèbéviyyé, the Apostolic Acts.

احاطه **ìhāta**, *s. a.* A surrounding; a comprising, comprehending, containing, holding; ا—, —et, *v.a.* To encircle, surround; to comprise, contain, hold; to comprehend, understand.

احاله **ìhālé**, *s. a.* A giving in charge, committing to the care, referring; ا—, —et, *v.a.* To refer, commit, give in charge, leave.

احبا **àhìbbā**, احباب àhbāb, *s. pl. a.* (*of* حبيب hàbīb), Friends.

احتجاج **ìhtijāj**, *s. a.* A bringing forward proofs and documents; احتجاجه صالح ìhtijāja-sālih, Valid, fit for exhibition as documentary evidence.

احتراز **ìhtirāz**, *s. a.* Taking care, avoiding, using circumspection; ا—, —et, *v.n.* To take care, avoid.

احتراق **ìhtirāk**, *s. a.* A burning, being burnt.

احترام **ìhtirām**, *s. a.* Respect, reverence, veneration.

احتساب **ìhtissāb**, *s. a.* The municipal excise; احتساب اغاسى ìhtissāb-àghàssi (*or* ناظرى nāziri), The superintendant of excise at Constantinople; احتسابيه ìhtissābiyyé, *s. a.* The excise dues.

احتشام **ìhtishām**, *s. a.* Pomp, majesty; the having a large retinue.

احتقان ìhtikān, *s. a.* The using an injection or glyster.

احتكار ìhtiky̆ār, *s. a.* The holding back grain from market in hopes of a time of scarcity and dearth.

احتمال ìhtimāl, *s. a.* Probability, the being probable; —, *a. t.* Possible, probable; —, *ad. t.* It is possible, perhaps, may be.

احتواء ìhtìwā, s. *a.* Comprehending, containing, collecting, protecting, occupation, enjoyment. [wanting, need.

احتياج ìhtiyāj, *s. a.* The being in want,

احتياط ìhtiyāt, *s. a.* Prudence, circumspection; the keeping a reserve; the reserve itself; احتياط عسكرى ìhtiyāt-"àsskéri, the reserve of an army.

احداث ìhdāss, *s. a.* A producing, creating, making, inventing; ا—, —et, *v.a.* To produce, create, make, invent.

احدى ìhdà, *s. a.* (*fem. of* احد), One.

احديت àhàdìyyèt, *s. a.* The quality of being unique; the unity of God.

احرار àhrār, *s. pl. a.* (*of* حر hùrr), Freemen; noblemen.

احراز ìhrāz, *s. a.* An obtaining, gaining, reaching; ا—, —et, *v.a.* To obtain, gain, reach.

احراق ìhrāk, *s. a.* A burning, consuming by fire; ا—, —et, *v.a.* To burn, consume by fire.

احرام ìhrām, *s. a.* Sacred vestment of the pilgrims at Mecca; a kind of woollen tissue, covered on one side with little twisted bullions.

احزان àhzān, *s. pl. a.* (*of* حزن huzn), Griefs, sorrows; —, ìhzān, *s. a.* Vexing, grieving.

احسان ìhsān, *s. a.* A benevolent act; goodness, kindness; a present (to an inferior); ا—, —et, *v.a.* To give, make present; —, *v.n.* To have the kindness, do the favour, be so kind, &c. [bering.

احصا ìhsā, *s. a.* A counting, num-

احضار ìhzār, *s. a.* A bringing into some one's presence, producing; citing to appear, summoning; ا—, —et, To produce, bring into presence.

احفاد àhfād, *s. pl. a.* (*of* حفيد hàfīd), Grandsons; posterity.

احقاق ìhkāk, *s. a.* A rendering justice, righting; ا—, —et, *v.a.* To right, (authoritatively); احقاق حق ا ìhkāki-hàkk-et, *v.n.* To right any one (authoritatively; lit. to right one's rights).

احكام àhky̆ām, *s. pl. a.* (*of* حكم hùkm, not used in this sense). Tenours, meaning; orders, commands, requisitions, ordinances (discoverable in writings); influences (of the stars); —, ìhky̆ām, *s. a.* A strengthening, fortifying, consolidating. [dark.

احمر àhmèr, *a. a.* Red; tawny, swarthy,

احمق àhmàk, *a. a.* Stupid.

احوال àhwāl, *s. pl. a.* (*of* حال hāl), States, conditions, situations.

احيا àhyā, *s. pl. a.* (*of* حى hàyy), Those who are alive, the living; —, ìhyā, *s. a.* A raising to life, animating; a resuscitation, reanimating; a rendering vigorous, powerful, populous, cultivated; ا—, —et, *v.a.* To animate, give life to; to reanimate, restore to life; to give new vigour to, enforce anew; to make populous; to restore from neglect or ruin, renovate; to bring into cultivation, reclaim (waste lands); to pass (the night) watching or in activity.

احيان àhyān, *s. pl. a.* (*of* حين hīn), Times, moments; احياناً àhyān*a*n, *ad. a.* Now and then, from time to time, at times, sometimes.

اخافه ìkhāfé, *s. a.* A frightening; ا—, —et, *v.a.* To frighten, to menace.

اخبار àkhbār, *s. pl. a.* (*of* خبر khàber), News, informations, reports; —, ìkhbār, *s. a.* A giving intelligence, informing; ا—, —et, *v.a.* To communicate (information). [star-fish.

اختپوط àkhtapòt, *s. g.* (οκταποδος), The

اختتام ìkhtitām, *s. a.* The being finished; completion; —بولمق, —bùlmak, *v.n.* To be completed.

اختر àkhter, *s. p.* A star.

اختراع ìkhtirā", *s. a.* An inventing, invention; ا—, —et, *v.a.* To invent.

اختصار ìkhtissār, *s. a.* A shortening, abbreviation; ا—, —et, *v.a.* To abbreviate. [devotion, friendship.

اختصاص ìkhtissāss, *s. a.* Devotedness.

اختفا ìkhtifā, *s. a.* A hiding one's self, concealment.

اختلاط ìkhtilāt, *s. a.* A mixing with, intercourse; ا—, —et, *v.n.* To mix, have intercourse.

اختلاف ìkhtilāf, *s. a.* Difference, want of agreement, variation; ا—, —et, *v.n.* To differ; to vary, اختلاف منظر ìkhtilāfi-mànzàr, (Difference of place of observation) Parallax.

اختلال ìkhtilāl, *s. a.* Trouble, sedition; confusion, derangement.

اختیار ìkhtiyār, *a. t.* Old, aged; —, *s. t.* An old man; —, *s. a.* Choice, option; ا—, —et, *v.a.* To choose; to prefer; to undertake *or* submit to in preference.

اختیاری ìkhtiyārī, *a. a.* Of choice, optional.

اخذ àkhz, *s. a.* A taking; a receiving; ا—, —et, *v.a.* To take, to receive; اخذواعطا àkhz-u-ì"tā, Buying and selling, commerce, trade, traffic.

اخر ākh*i*r, *a. a.* The last; یوم الاخر yùvmu-'l-ākh*i*r, The last day; —, *s. a.* The end; conclusion; —, àkhàr, *a. a.* Other, another; اخرالامر ākhiru-'l-èmr, *ad. a.* At last, at length; lastly, in conclusion.

اخراج ìkhrāj, *s. a.* A putting out, pulling out, extraction; subtraction; a prolonging, producing (in mathematics); expense; ا—, —et, *v.a.* To pull out, extract; to subtract; to prolong, produce; اخراجات ìkhrājāt, *s. pl. a.* Expenses, outgoings.

اخرت ākh*i*rèt, *s. a.* The future state;

اخرتلك اخرت اوغلى ākhirèt-òghlu *or* ākhirètlik, An adopted child.

اخروى ùkhrévī, *a. a.* Relating to the future life. [Other, another.

اخرى ùkhrà, *a. a.* (fem. of آخر àkhàr),

اخشام Akhsham (Ak-), *s. t.* The evening.

اخشاملمق Akshamlamak (*aor.* اخشاملار àkshamlar), *v.n.* To become evening; to pass the evening.

اخص àkhàsss, *a. a.* More, most, or very special, intimate, or pure.

اخضر àkhzàr, *a. a.* Green.

اخطار àkhtār, *s. pl. a.* (*of* خطر khAtar), Dangers; —, ìkhtār, *s. a.* A putting in mind, calling to one's attention; ا—, —et, *v.a.* To recall to one's mind; —, *v.n.* To warn, put upon one's guard, call one's attention.

اخفا ìkhfā, *s. a.* A hiding, secreting, concealing; ا—, —et, *v.a.* To hide, secrete, conceal.

اخگر àkhghèr, *s. p.* Charcoal, a piece of charcoal; a piece of burning charcoal. [devoted attachment.

اخلاص ìkhlāss, *s. a.* Sincere and

اخلاط àkhlāt, *s. pl. a.* (*of* خلط, *not used*), The humours of the body, blood, bile, phlegm, and *black-bile;* —, àkhlAt, *s. t.* A wild pear.

اخلاف àkhlāf, *s. pl. a.* (*of* خلف khàlef), Successors; posterity.

اخلاق àkhlāk, *s. pl. a.* (*of* خلق khùlk), Moral qualities, points of character or disposition; (*of* خلق khAlk), Creatures; human creatures; علم اخلاق "ìlmi-àkhlāk, Ethics, moral science, metaphysics.

اخلال ìkhlāl, *s. a.* A putting in disorder, deranging, spoiling; ا—, —et, *v.a.* To spoil, derange, disorder.

اخوان ìkhwAn, *s. pl. a.* (*of* اخ *not used*), Brethren; comrades, fellows; co-religionists. [brotherhood.

اخوت ùkhùvvet, *s. a.* Fraternity,

اخور (Akhir), *s. p.* A stable; ميراخور mīrì-àkhòr (èmrakhòr), Master of the horse.

اد àd, *s. t.* A name.

ادا èdā, *s. a.* A paying; a fulfilling; a manner; a tone; grace or affectation of manner or tone; ا—, —et, *v.a.* To pay; to fulfil.

اداب ādāb, *s. pl. a.* (*of* ادب èdeb), Manners, modes of behaviour; gentlemanly behaviour.

ادات èdāt, *s. a.* An instrument, implement, tool; a particle (in grammar).

اداره ìdārè, *s. a.* A causing to turn round, revolve, or circulate; the conduct of business, supervision, superintendence; economy; savings; ا—, —et, *v.a.* To cause to turn round, revolve, or circulate; to conduct, or superintend; to save by economy; —, *v.n.* To be economical.

اداق AdAk, *s. t.* A vow; an offering made according to a vow.

اداوات èdāwāt, *s. pl. a.* (*of* ادات èdāt), Instruments, implements, tools; particles.

ادب èdeb, *s. a.* Modesty, politeness, good manners, respectful behaviour; ترك ادب tèrki-èdeb, A want of proper respect; ادب يرلرى èdeb-yèrléri, The privities.

ادبار ìdbār, *s. a.* A going backwards or downwards (in the world); adversity.

ادخال ìdkhāl, *s. a.* An introducing, causing to enter; ا—, —et, *v.a.* To introduce, cause to enter.

اداش àddàsh, *s. t.* A namesake.

ادرار ìdrār, *s. a.* A flowing, or causing to flow, copiously (wine, milk, &c.); a bestowing abundantly.

ادراك ìdrāk, *s. a.* An overtaking, coming up with; an understanding, comprehending; comprehension, intelligence; ا—, —et, *v.a.* To comprehend, understand; to catch, come up with, overtake; to be partly contemporaneous with (one who was born earlier).

ادرنه Edìrné, *s. t.* The town of [Adrianople.

ادعا ìddi‘‘ā, *s. a.* A pretension, claim, pertinacious assertion; ا—, —et, *v.a.* To assert pertinaciously, to maintain; —, *v.n.* To be pertinacious in assertion.

ادعيه èd‘‘ìyyé, *s. pl. a.* (*of* دعا dù‘‘ā), [Prayers; thanksgivings.

ادلامق àdlamak (*aor.* ادلار àdlar), *v.a.* To measure by paces; to step over.

ادله èdìllé, *s. pl. a.* (*of* دليل dèlīl), Guides; indications; proofs, arguments.

ادم ādem (àdam), *s. a.* A man; a human creature; an agent, servant, messenger; a person; somebody; (in negations) nobody; حضرت ادم Hàzréti-Adem, Adam, the father of mankind; بنى ادم bènī-ādem, the sons of men, mankind; — àdim, *s. t.* A step, pace.

ادمان ìdmān, *s. a.* The facility, or power of endurance, gained by long practice.

ادملامق àdimlamak (*aor.* ادملار àdimlar), *v.a.* To measure by paces.

ادمى ādémī, *a. a.* Human; ادميان ādémìyyān, *s. pl. a.* Human beings, [men.

ادنا èdnā, *a. a.* Less; the least.

ادويه èdvìyyé, *s. pl. a.* (*of* دوا dèwā), Medicines, drugs.

ادهم èdhèm, *s. a.* A black horse.

اديان èdyān, *s. pl. a.* (*of* دين dīn), Religions.

اديب èdīb, *a.* and *s. a.* Modest, polite, well-behaved; refined in mind and [manners.

اذا èzā, Molestation, hurt.

اذابه ìzābé, *s. a.* A melting, causing to melt; ا—, —et, To melt, bring into fusion.

اذان èzān, *s. a.* The call to prayer; — اوقومق —, — òkumak, To perform the call to prayer.

اذعاج ìz‘‘āj, *s. a.* A teazing, worrying, urging; ا—, —et, *v.a.* To teaze, worry, urge.

اذعان ìz‘‘ān, *s. a.* A complying, acting in obedience; a comprehending, understanding.

اذكار èzkyār, *s. pl. a.* (*of* ذكر zìkr), Services of prayer and praise.

اذكيا èzkiyā, *s. pl. a.* (*of* ذكى zèkī), Men of intelligence.

اذن ìzn (ìzin), Permission, leave; — ويرمك —, — vèrmek, To give leave, grant permission; to discharge, dismiss. [Minds, intellects.

اذهان èzhān, *s. pl. a.* (*of* ذهن zìhn),

اذيال èzyāl, *s. pl. a.* (*of* ذيل zèyl), Skirts; appendices.

اذيت èzìyyèt, *s. a.* Pain, torture, suffering; ا—, —et, *v.n.* To cause pain; to put to the torture, to torture; ويرمك —, — vèrmek, *v.n.* To cause trouble, or suffering; to teaze. [اكر èghɐr), *c. p.* If.

ار èr, *s. t.* A man; a husband; — (for

ارا àra, *s. t.* The midst; an interval; — ārā, *s. pl. a.* (of رأى rèʿy), Opinions; —, ārā, *a. p.* (*in composition*), Adorning, which adorns.

اراجيف èrājīf, *s. pl. a.* (*of* ارجوفه, *not in use*), Scandal; false rumours.

اراده ìrādé, *s. a.* The will, volition; a rescript, command, injunction; ارادهٔ كليه ìrādéʿi-kyùllìyyé, The Divine, or universal will; ارادهٔ جزئيه ìrādéʿi-jùzʿìyyé, Human, or partial will, free-will; ارادهٔ شاهانه ìrādéʿi-shāhāné, An imperial rescript.

اراذل èrāzil, *s. pl. a.* (*of* ارذل èrzèl), The vilest men. [adorned.

اراسته ārāsstè, *a. p.* Equipped; prepared;

اراشدرمق ʌrashdirmak (*aor.* اراشدرر ʌrashdirir), *v.a.* To cause search or inquiry after to be made.

اراضى àrāzī, *s. pl. a.* (*of* ارض àrz), Lands.

اراقه ìrāka, *s. a.* A shedding, pouring out, spilling; ا—, —et, *v.a.* To shed, spill, pour out; اراقهٔ دما ìrākaʿi-dìmā, A shedding of blood.

ارالق àralɪk, *s. t.* An interval, space; an interval of time; a time.

ارام ārām, ارامش ārāmish, *s. p.* Repose, tranquillity.

ارامق ʌramak (*aor.* ارار ʌrar), *v.a.* To seek, look for, search after, inquire for; to miss, feel the absence or want of; to search (a place, pockets, &c.).

ارايش ārāyish, *s. p.* An adornment, an ornament.

ارباب èrbāb, *s. pl. a.* (*of* رب rʌbb, *not in use in this sense*), Possessors, owners; persons endowed with; people occupied about; competent and fitting persons; people belonging to, or occupied with; (*as a Turkish singular*) a competent and fit person; رب الارباب rʌbbu-'l-èrbʌb, The Lord of Lords, God.

اربع èrbàʿʿ (fem. اربعه èrbaʿʿà), *a. a.* Four. [*a. a.* Forty.

اربعين èrbaʿʿīn (*rarely* اربعون èrbaʿʿūn),

اربه àrpa, *s. t.* Barley; اربه جق àrpajɪk, *s. t.* (*lit.* little barley-corn), A sty on the eye; the dispart or sight-piece placed near the muzzle of fire-arms; اربه صويى àrpa-sùyu, (barley-water) Beer.

اربه‌لق àrpalik, *s. t. Barley-field* or *Barley-money,* The title under which various districts were given to certain functionaries, under the old system, now abolished, and from the revenues of which they were supposed, according to the feudal theory, to supply their horses with barley.

ارتباط ìrtibāt, *s. a.* A being connected, connexion.

ارتجا ìrtijā, *s. a.* An expecting, a wishing for, desiring.

ارتحال ìrtihāl, *s. a.* A change of abode, a journeying, migration; the passing from this life; ـــدار بقا, ìrtihāli-dāri-bākā, The passage to the world (abode) of permanency; ا—, —et, *v.n.* To change one's abode, migrate; to die.

ارتداد ìrtidād, *s. a.* Apostacy, an apostatizing (from isslām).

ارتسام ìrtissām, *s. a.* A being marked or remarkable; مودت ارتسام mèvèddet-ìrtissām, Bearing the stamp of affection.

ارتشا ìrtishā, *s. a.* The receiving a bribe.

ارتفاع ìrtifā", *s. a.* Height, elevation; altitude; غایت ارتفاع ghāyeti-ìrtifā", (astr.) (extreme) meridian altitude.

ارتق àrtik, *a. t.* Over and remaining; —, *ad. t.* (with a negative) no more; never again; (with an affirmative) now, at last; under those circumstances.

ارتقا ìrtikā, *s. a.* A going upwards, rising; advancing in rank; increasing.

ارتکاب ìrtikyāb, *s. a.* The committing any bad act, a stooping to anything base; ا—, —et, *v.a.* To commit, stoop to.

ارتمق àrtmak (*aor.* ارتار àrtar), *v.a.* To augment, increase, become more in quantity or degree.

ارتمك èritmek (*aor.* اریدر èridir), *v.a.* To melt, fuse, liquefy, dissolve.

ارتیاب ìrtiyāb, *s. a.* Doubt.

ارث ìrss, *s. a.* Inheritance; ارثاً ìrssen, *ad. a.* By inheritance.

ارجمند èrjumènd, *a. p.* Noble, worshipful, excellent.

ارحام èrhām, *s. pl. a.* (*of* رحم ràhm), Relatives (on the mother's side, or in general).

ارحم èrhèm, *a. a.* More, most, or very merciful and compassionate; ارحم الراحمین Erhèmu-'r-rāhimīn, The Most Merciful of those who show mercy, God.

ارخا ìrkhā, *s. a.* A loosening, slacking; ارخای عنان ا ìrkhāyi-"ìnān-et, *v.n.* To slack the reins, give a horse his head, to start on a journey.

ارد àrd, *s. t.* The back side of anything; the space behind anything; اردی صره àrdi-sìra, *ad. t.* Immediately following *it* (him or her); اردم صره àrdim-sira, After me; اردك صره àrding-sìra, After thee; &c. &c.

اردج àrdij, *s. t.* Juniper.

اردل *or* اردل مملکتی Erdèl *or* Erdèl-mèmlékèti, *s. t.* Transylvania.

اردو òrdu, *s. t.* A camp; an army.

ارذل èrzèl, *a. a.* More, most, or very vile.

ارزاق èrzāk, *s. pl. a.* (*of* رزق rìzk, *not used in this sense*), Provisions, corn, &c.

ارزان èrzān, *s. p.* Deemed fit and worthy; ارزان بیورمق èrzān-bùyurmak, *v.a.* To deem fit and worthy; ارزانی èrzāni, *s. p.* A deeming fit and worthy.

ارزو àrzu, *s. p.* Wish, desire; ا—, —et, *v.a.* To wish, to desire, to long for; ارزوکش àrzukèsh, ارزومند àrzumènd, *a. p.* Desirous.

ارسال ìrsāl, *s. a.* A sending, forwarding, despatching; ا—, —et, *v.a.* To send.

ارسلان àrsslan (àsslan), *s. t.* A lion; ارسلانلو (àsslanli), ارسلانی àrsslānī, *a. t.* A piastre (*term used only by auctioneers and criers*).

ارشاد ìrshād, *s. a.* A showing the right way, directing truly; a teaching the true religion or tenets; ا—, —et, *v.a.* To put in the right way (moral or physical).

ارشون *or* ارشین àrshin, *s. t.* The Turkish yard, of which there are two; one called معمارارشونی mì''-mār-àrshini, *architect's yard,* of 29½ inches English, the other named چوقه ارشونی (chòha)-àrshini, *cloth yard,* of about 28 inches; the first is divided into 24 پرمق pàrmak, *inches;* the latter into 8 ربع rùb'', *quarters.*

ارض àrz, *s. a.* Land; کرهٔ ارض kyùré'i-àrz, The world, the terraqueous globe; a terrestrial globe.

ارضروم *or* ارض روم Arzi-rūm, *s. t.* The city of Erzeroum.

ارضا ìrzā, *s. a.* A satisfying, contenting, making willing; ا—, —et, *v.a.* To make willing, content, satisfied; to obtain one's consent, or assent.

ارغاج àrghàj, *s. t.* Warp of cloth, the threads stretched lengthwise in weaving.

ارغاد ìrghàt, *s. g.* A labourer.

ارغوان èrghawān, *s. p.* Judas-tree; ارغوانی èrghawānī, *a. p.* Red, as the flowers of the Judas-tree.

ارق àrk, *s. t.* A small water-course for irrigation; —, àrik, *a. t.* Thin, lean.

ارقام èrkām, *s. pl. a.* (*of* رقم ràkam). Arithmetical figures; written characters; diplomas, commands.

ارقوری àrkuri (àykiri), *a.* and *ad. t.* Thwartwise; slantwise; exorbitant, out of bounds or reason.

ارقه àrka, *s. t.* The back; support, protection; a patron, protector.

ارکان èrkyān, *s. pl. a.* (*of* رکن rùkn), Pilasters, pillars, columns; customs, rules; chief men, people of rank and influence, ministers; ارکان حرب èrkyāni-hàrb, The staff of an army.

ارکچ èrghech, *s. t.* A male goat.

ارکك èrkek, *s. t.* A male; a man; —, *a. t.* Male.

ارکمك ìrkmek (*aor.* ارکر ìrker), *v.n.* To stagnate, become stagnant and offensive.

ارکن èrken, *a.* and *ad. t.* Early; —,

èrghèn, *s. t.* A bachelor, unmarried man; اركنلك èrghenlik, *s. t.* Pimples on the face of young people.

ارمغان èrmaghān (ìrmighān), A present, gift.

ارمل èrmel (fem. ارمله èrmélé), *s. a.* A widow; a widower.

ارمنجه Ermènjé, *s. t.* The Armenian language; ارمنستان Ermènisstān, *s. t.* Armenia; ارمنی Ermènī, *s. t.* An Armenian; —, *a. t.* Armenian.

ارمود àrmud, *s. t.* A pear; ارموداغاجی àrmud-àghaji, A pear-tree; التونی —, — altini, A pear-shaped gold medallion, worn by women or children, on the cap, on the forehead, or suspended round the neck.

ارمه àrma, *s. t.* (*of Italian origin*), A coat of arms; the rigging of a ship.

ارن èren, *act. part.* (*of* ایرمك ìrmek *or* ermek, to arrive at), An adept, one initiated into the mysteries of any order or secret society, one who has arrived at the truth; ارنلر èrenler, term used by the old Bèktashī dervishes to designate themselves and those affiliated to their order: they were in reality atheists or pantheists.

ارناود Arnāwd, *a. t.* Albanian; —, *s. t.* An Albanian, Albania.

ارواح èrwāh, *s. pl. a.* (*of* روح rūh), Souls, spirits; spirituous liquors.

اره èrré, *s. p.* A saw; اره‌خانه èrré-khāné, A saw-mill.

اری ari, *s. t.* A bee; یبان‌اریسی yàban-arissi, A drone (bee of the wilds); اشك‌اریسی èshek-arissi, A wasp; اری‌قوانی ari-kòwani, A bee-hive; foxglove.

ارياح èryāh, *s. pl. a.* (*of* ريح rīh), Winds.

اريك èrik, *s. t.* A plum; قوری‌اريك kùru-èrik (dried plum), A prune; موردم‌اريكی mùrdum-èrighi, A damson; جان‌اريكی jan-èrighi, The Orleans plum; برداق‌اريكی bàrdak-èrighi, The egg-plum; &c., &c.

اريكه èrīké, *s. a.* A throne.

اريمك èrimek (*aor.* ارير èrir), *v.n.* To melt, become melted, fused, liquefied.

از az, *a. t.* Little in quantity; few in number; —, *ad. t.* Seldom; little; —, *s. t.* The less part; براز bìr-az, A little; a few; برازدن bìr-azdan, In a little while, shortly, by-and-bye, presently; ازاجق azajìk (*dim.*), A very little in quantity, the least quantity; — az, *s. p.* Vehement lust and desire, avidity, cupidity, covetousness; —, èz, *pr. p.* From; of; by, through, over, under.

ازاد āzād (azad), *a. p.* Free; enfranchised, set at liberty; —, *s. p.* Freedom, enfranchisement; ا—, —et, *v.a.* To give freedom, enfranchise.

ازاده āzādé, *a. p.* Free, exempt.

ازار āzār (azar), *s. p.* Blame, reprimand; —, *a. p.* (in compound words), Which vexes, troubles, pains; دل ازار dil-āzār, Giving trouble to the heart.

ازارش āzārish, *s. p.* Vexation, trouble; anguish, pain.

ازارلمق ȧzarlamak (*aor.* ازارلار ȧzarlar), *v.a.* To scold, reprimand.

ازاله ìzālé, *s. a.* A removing, causing to disappear, obliterating, annihilating; ا—, —et, *v.a.* To remove, extirpate, eradicate, obliterate, annihilate.

ازالمق ȧzȧlmak (*aor.* ازالور ȧzȧlir), *v.n.* To diminish, grow less in number, quantity, or degree.

ازباندید ìzbàndit, *s. t.* (*Italian*), A highwayman, bandit, outlaw.

ازبر èzbèr, *in* ازبردن èzbèrdan, By heart; *and* ازبرلمك èzbèrlémek, *v.a.* To learn by heart.

ازدحام ìzdìhām, *s. a.* A collecting together in crowds; a crowd. [in pairs.

ازدواج ìzdiwāj, *s. a.* Marriage; being

ازدیاد ìzdiyād, *s. a.* An increasing, increase, augmentation; —بولمق, —bùlmak, *v.n.* To increase, be augmented. [tressed.

ازرده āzùrdé, *a. p.* Hurt; afflicted, dis-

ازرق èzrȧk, *a. a.* Blue.

ازغون *or* ازغین ȧzghin, *a. t.* Depraved, rebellious, refusing all restraint; furious; in heat; grown beyond all natural or usual bounds.

ازكیا èzkiyā, *s. pl. a.* (*of* زكی zèkī), The good, pure, virtuous.

ازل èzel, *s. a.* Past eternity; من الازل mìn-el-èzel, *ad. a.* From all eternity; ازلی èzélī, *a. a.* Who has existed from all eternity; ازلیت èzéliyyèt, *s. a.* Quality of having eternally existed.

ازما āzmā, *a. p.* (*in comp.*), Who knows, who has learnt, has had experience.

ازمان èzmān, *s. pl. a.* (*of* زمان zàmān), Times, seasons, epochs; —, ȧzmān, *a. t.* Grown out of all natural or usual bounds.

ازمق ȧzmak (*aor.* ازار ȧzar), *v.n.* To become depraved, rebellious (man); to become furious, *or* in heat (animal); to grow beyond all natural or usual bounds; دوش— dūsh—, To take a lascivious form (a dream) and cause pollution.

ازمك èzmek (*aor.* ازر èzer), *v.a.* To crush, bruise, pound, triturate, smash.

ازمنه èzminé, *s. pl. a.* (*of* زمان zàmān), Times, seasons, epochs.

ازموده āzmūdé, *a. p.* (*in composition*), Who has learnt, experienced.

ازمه ȧzma, *s. t.* A becoming rebellious; furious; a growing beyond all usual bounds; a monster; —, èzìmmé, *s. pl. a.* (*of* زمام zìmām), Reins.

ازو ȧzi, *and* ازودیشی ȧzi-dìshi, *s. t.* A canine tooth; a tusk, tush.

ازواج èzwāj, *s. pl. a.* (*of* زوج zèvj), Couples, pairs; spouses, husbands, wives. [Flowers.

ازهار èzhār, *s. pl. a.* (*of* زهره zèhré),

ازهر èzhèr, *a. a.* More, most, or very shining, splendid, brilliant.

اژدر èzhdĕr, اژدرها èzhdærhā, and اژدها èzhdihā, *s. p.* A dragon.

اس āss, *s. a.* The myrtle; —, ùsss, *s. a.* A foundation, basis.

اسا āssā, *a. p.* (*in composition*), Like, resembling.

اساتذه èssātizé, *s. pl. a.* (*of* استاذ ùsstāz, *for* استاد ùsstād, *s. p.*), Masters (of an art or science).

اسارا ùssārà, *s. pl. a.* (*of* اسیر èssīr), Captives, prisoners of war; slaves on sale.

اساس èssāss, *s. a.* Foundation; basis; fundamental rule or principle.

اساطیر àssātīr, *s. pl. a.* Fables; اساطیر الاولین àssātīr-u'l-èwwèlīna, The fables of the ancients, myths.

اسافل èssāfil, *s. pl. a.* (*of* اسفل èssfèl), The lowest classes, ranks, or places.

اسامه èssāmé, *s. t.* Ticket or document for pay and rations under the old Janissary system.

اسامی èssāmī, *s. pl. a.* (*of* اسم ìssm), Names.

اسان āssān, *a. p.* Easy; اسانلق āssānlìk, *s. t.* اسانی āssānī, *s. p.* Ease, facility.

اسایش āssāyish, *s. p.* Tranquillity.

اسب èssb, *s. p.* A horse.

اسباب èssbāb, *s. pl. a.* (*of* سبب sèbeb), Reasons, motives; materials; means; (*for* اثواب èsswāb, clothes, clothing); مسبب الاسباب mùssèbbibu-'l-èssbāb, The causer of all means, God.

اسبق èssbàk, *a. a.* Former, last but one (in past time), or any former.

اسبوع ùsbū'', *s. a.* (*pl.* اسابیع àssābī''), A week.

اسپاناك *or* اسپناك ìsspànak, *s. t.* [Spinach.

اسپانیا Isspānya, *s. t.* Spain.

اسپانیالو Isspanyali, *a. t.* Spanish; —, *s. t.* A Spaniard. [nationality).

اسپیر ìsspir, *s. t.* A groom (of Roumelian

استاد ùsstād, *s. p.* استاذ ùsstāz, *s. a.* A master in any profession or calling.

استاده ìsstādé, *a. p.* (*in composition*), Standing.

استار èsstār, *s. pl. a.* (*of* ستر sìtr), Vails, curtains; —, àsstar, *s. t.* Lining; coarse cloth fit only for linings or for clouts. [lobster.

استاقوس ìsstàkoss, *s. t.* (*Greek*), A

استان āssitān, *s. p.* A threshold; a royal court or hall; استانه āssitāné, *s. p.* A threshold; a royal court or hall; the capital, Constantinople.

استانبول Isstànbòl, *s. t.* Constantinople; Stamboul.

استاوروس ìsstàvross, *s. t.* (*Greek*), A cross, crucifix; sign of the cross.

استبداد ìsstibdād, *s. a.* Absolute and independent power.

استبدال ìsstibdāl, *s. a.* A changing, giving one thing and receiving another; the regular discharge of soldiers who have served their time, and the enlistment of fresh recruits by ballot in the new system.

استثقال ìsstisskāl, *s. a.* A deeming anyone a bore, and showing it; ا—, —et, v.a. To show anyone that you deem him a bore.

استثنا isstissnā, *s. a.* An excepting; an exception; ا—, —et, *v.a.* To except.

استج ùsstuj (ùsstùnj), Case of mathematical instruments (or surgical).

استجلاب isstijlāb, *s. a.* An attracting, drawing to one; ا—, —et, *v.a.* To attract, draw to *or* upon one's self.

استحسان isstìhsān, *s. a.* An approving; approval, approbation; ا—, —et, *v.a.* To approve.

استحصال isstìhsāl, *s. a.* An acquiring, obtaining, gaining; acquisition; ا—, —et, *v.a.* To acquire.

استحقار isstìhkār, *s. a.* A treating with contempt; ا—, —et, *v.a.* To treat with contempt.

استحقاق isstìhkāk, *s. a.* A right, just claim, merit.

استحکام isstìhky̆ām, *s. a.* Strength, solidity; استحکامات isstìhkyāmāt, *s. pl. a.* Fortifications; the science of fortification; استحکام ويرمك isstìhkyām-vèrmek, *v.n.* To fortify; to make strong, give solidity.

استخاره isstikhārè, *s. a.* A looking for some dream, sign, or portent, which may serve as a guide in some business on hand.

استخبار isstikhbār, *s. a.* A demanding *or* a receiving intelligence; ا—, —et, *v.a.* To receive intelligence; to demand intelligence.

استخدام isstìkhdām, *s. a.* An employing in one's service; ا—, —et, *v.a.* To employ as a servant or in an office.

استخراج isstìkhrāj, *s. a.* An extracting; a deducing; ا—, —et, *v.a.* To extract; deduce.

استخفاف isstìkhfāf, *s. a.* A looking upon as of no account; contempt, disdain; ا—, —et, To despise, make no account of.

استدامه isstidāmè, *s. a.* Perpetuity, a being perpetual.

استدانه isstidānè, *s. a.* A borrowing.

استدراج isstidrāj, *s. a.* A gradual descent in wickedness, through a gradually increasing apparent success, but real temptation.

استدعا isstid''ā, *s. a.* A demanding; a demand; ا—, —et, *v.a.* To demand.

استدلال isstidlāl, *s. a.* A concluding or deducing by means of indications; ا—, —et, *v.a.* To deduce, to conclude.

استراحت isstirāh*a*t, *s. a.* Rest, repose.

استراق isstirāk, *s. a.* A stealing, thieving; ا—, —et, *v.a.* To steal, thieve.

استرجا isstirjā, *s. a.* A begging, praying, soliciting; ا—, —et, *v.a.* To ask for, solicit.

استرداد isstirdād, *s. a.* A demanding restitution; a making restitution, a giving back; ا—, —et, *v.a.* To demand restitution; to restore, give back.

استريديه isstrìdiy*a*, *s. t.* (*Greek*), An oyster.

استرقاق isstirkāk, *s. a.* A reducing to slavery, an enslaving.

استسقا **ìsstisskā**, *s. a.* The dropsy; an offering of prayers for rain in time of drought.

استشاره **ìsstishārĕ**, *s. a.* A consulting, or deliberating with; ا—, —et, *v.n.* To consult, or deliberate with.

استشمام **ìsstishmām**, *s. a.* A perceiving by the smell; a perceiving, comprehending in a slight degree.

استصحاب **ìsstisshāb** (ss-h), *s. a.* A taking with one; an acquiring, acquisition; ا—, —et, *v.a.* To take with one; to acquire possession of.

استصواب **ìsstisswāb**, *s. a.* An approving, approval.

استطاعه **ìsstitā''a**, *s. a.* Power, ability.

استطراد **ìsstitrād**, *s. a.* A digression.

استظهار **ìsstizhār**, *s. a.* A seeking for protection.

استعاره **ìssti''ārĕ**, *s. a.* A borrowing, taking for temporary use; a kind of metaphor.

استعانه **ìssti''āné**, *s. a.* A demand for assistance; ا—, —et, *v.n.* To ask for assistance.

استعجال **ìsstì''jāl**, *s. a.* A hasting, haste.

استعداد **ìsstì''dād**, *s. a.* A state of preparedness; an inclination, tendency, predisposition; natural disposition, genius, ability, talent.

استعفا **ìsstì''fā**, *s. a.* A request to be superseded in office, a resignation; ا—, —et, *v.n.* To beg to be allowed to quit office.

استعلام **ìsstì''lām**, *s. a.* An official demand for information from inferior functionaries, an official inquiry; ا—, —et, *v.n.* To address an official demand for information; to seek for information in general.

استعمال **ìsstì''māl**, *s. a.* A using, making use of, employing (things); ا—, —et, *v.a.* To use, make use of, employ.

استغراب **ìsstighrāb**, *s. a.* A being struck with surprise, surprise, wonder.

استغفار **ìsstìghfār**, *s. a.* The addressing to God a prayer or ejaculation for pardon of sin by saying استغفرالله èsstàghfirū-'llāh, *I ask pardon of God!*

استغنا **ìsstìghnā**, *s. a.* The not being in want; an accounting one's self free from want and therefore contemning things.

استف **ìsstif**, *s. t.* (*Italian*), A packing or stowing; ا—, —et, *v.a.* To pack or stow.

استفاده **ìsstifādĕ**, *s. a.* A reaping some advantage; a gain; a learning; a comprehending, gathering; ا—, —et, *v.a.* To derive benefit, reap an advantage; to learn, to gather, comprehend, understand.

استفتا **ìsstiftā**, *s. a.* An application to a jurist (mufti) for a legal opinion on a case.

استفراغ **ìsstifrāgh**, *s. a.* A vomiting; ا—, —et, *v.n.* To vomit.

استفسار **ìsstifsār**, *s. a.* An inquiring

after; استفسارخاطرا ìsstifsāri-khātir-et, v.n. To ask after one's health.

استفهام ìsstifhām, s. a. An effort or question made in order towards understanding anything; an interrogation.

استقامت ìsstikāmet, s. a. Rectitude, uprightness, integrity, probity; straightness; a straight direction.

استقبال ìsstikbāl, s. a. A going forth to meet one; a meeting face to face; future time; ا— —et, v.a. To go forth to meet; to meet face to face.

استقرار ìsstikrār, s. a. Permanency, a not being liable to change, firmness, fixedness.

استقراض ìsstikrāz, s. a. A borrowing; a loan (of money); ا—, —et, v.a. To borrow.

استقصا ìsstiksā, s. a. Minute attention.

استقلال ìsstiklāl, s. a. Independency, absolute authority; independent sovereignty.

استك ìsstek, s. t. Desire; استكلو ìsstekli, a. t. Desirous; desirous to become purchaser.

استكبار ìsstikbār, s. a. Pride.

استكراه ìsstikrāh, s. a. A loathing, looking upon as filthy.

استكشاف ìsstikshāf, s. a. An effort or question made to elucidate a matter.

استكمال ìsstikmāl, s. a. A completing.

استكناه ìsstiknāh, s. a. Minute attention in investigation.

استماع ìsstimā'', s. a. A hearing; ا—, —et, v.a. To hear.

استمداد ìsstimdād, s. a. The demanding succour or help; ا—, —et, v.n. To demand help.

استمرار ìsstimrār, s. a. Uninterrupted continuance in duration; استمراراً ìsstimrāran, Without ceasing.

استمق ìssitmak (aor. اسيدر ìssìdir), v.a. To warm, to heat, make warm or hot.

استمك ìsstémek (aor. استر ìsster), v.a. To wish, wish for, desire; to take, require; to demand, ask for; to ask a price.

استمه ìssitma, s. t. The ague, intermittent fever.

استمهال ìsstimhāl, s. a. The asking for a delay, term, or respite.

استناد ìsstinād, s. a. A relying on for support, taking as a basis of operations.

استنباط ìsstinbāt, s. a. A deducing, inferring; ا—, —et, v.a. To deduce, infer.

استنتاج ìsstintāj, s. a. The drawing a conclusion; ا—, —et, v.a. To draw (a conclusion).

استنساخ ìsstinsākh, s. a. The taking a copy in writing (of a book); ا—, —et, v.a. To copy.

استنطاق ìsstintāk, s. a. An interrogating; interrogatory; ا—, —et, v.a. To interrogate.

استنكاف ìsstinkyāf, s. a. A refusing, rejecting, disdaining.

استوا ìsstiwā, s. a. Equality, evenness; خط استوا khātti-(ùsstuwā), The equinoctial line, the equator.

استوار ùsstuwār, *a. p.* Firm, strong; استواری ùsstuwārī, *s. p.* Firmness, strength.

استوپی ùsstùpu, *s. t.* (*Italian*), Oakum.

استهزا ìsstihzā, *s. a.* A ridiculing; derision; ا—, —et, *v.a.* To ridicule, deride.

استیجار ìsstījār, *s. a.* A taking on hire; ا—, —et, *v.a.* To take on hire.

استیذان ìsstīzān, *s. a.* An asking for permission; ا—, —et, *v.n.* To ask for permission.

استیصال ìsstīssĀl, *s. a.* An extirpating, eradicating.

استیعاب ìsstī‘‘Āb, *s. a.* A filling, covering, occupying; ا—, —et, *v.a.* To take up, occupy, fill, cover.

استیفا ìsstīfā, *s. a.* A paying completely (debts, or values); ا—, —et, *v.a.* To pay completely.

استیلا ìsstīlā, *s. a.* An overrunning, conquering (countries); ا—, —et, *v.a.* To overrun, conquer.

استیمان ìsstīmān, *s. a.* A demand by an alien for safe-conduct and immunity in a foreign or hostile country (especially by non-Musslims in a Musslim country).

استین āssitīn, *s. p.* A sleeve.

اسد èssed, *s. a.* A lion.

اسر èssr, *s. a.* The taking prisoner of war, making captive; —, ùssr, *s. a.* Captivity.

اسرا ùsséra, *s. pl. a.* (*of* اسیر èssīr), Prisoners of war, captives; —, ìssrā, *s. a.* A sending; ا—, —et, *v.a.* To send.

اسرار èssrār, *s. pl. a.* (*of* سر sìrr), Secrets; mysteries; (*Turk. singular*) the narcotic preparation of hemp, &c., known as *bang*.

اسراف ìssrāf, *s. a.* A wasteful expenditure.

اسرکمك èssirghémek (*aor.* اسرکر èssirghɛr), *v.a.* To spare, to be chary of.

اسره èsséré, *s. t.* The vowel-point for the vowels i and *i*.

اسطوانه ùsstuwāné, *s. a.* A column; a cylinder.

اسعار èss‘‘ār, *s. pl. a.* (*of* سعر, *not used*), Prices of commodities shown in a market roll.

اسعاف ìss‘‘āf, *s. a.* A granting, conceding, complying with (a suit or request).

اسف èssef, *s. a.* Regret, sorrow.

اسفار èssfār, *s. pl. a.* (*of* سفر sèfɛr), Travels, voyages; campaigns; books.

اسفل èssfèl, *a. a.* More, most, or very low; —, *s. a.* The lowest place; the anus.

اسفیداج ìssfīdāj (ùsstubèch), *s. p.* White lead, ceruse.

اسقاره ìsskĀra, *s. t.* Gridiron; the bars of a grate; a grill, grilled or broiled food; ا—, —et, *v.a.* To grill, broil.

اسقاط ìsskĀt, *s. a.* A causing to fall, *or* drop down, *or* off; ا—, —et, *v.a.* To cause to fall; اسقاط جنین ا ìsskĀti-jìnīn-et, *v.n.* To have a miscarriage.

اسقندیل ìsskĀndil, *s. t.* A sounding lead and line; ا—, —et, *v.a.* To sound the depth of anything; sound a person's thoughts.

اسقوچيا Isskòchia, *s. t.* Scotland;

اسقوچیالو Isskòchiali, *a. t.* Scotch; —, *s. t.* A Scotchman. [mackerel.

اسقومری ùsskùmru, *s. t.* (*Greek*), A

اسقونه ùsskùna, *s. t.* (*Italian*), A schooner.

اسکات ìsskyāt, *s. a.* A causing to be silent, a silencing; a convincing, a satisfying; ا—, —et, *v.a.* To silence; to convince, satisfy.

اسکان ìsskyān, *s. a.* A causing to inhabit; an inhabiting; ا—, —et, *v.a.* To cause to inhabit; —, *v.n.* To inhabit, dwell, live, settle.

اسکتمك èsskitmek (*aor.* اسکیدر èsskidir), *v.a.* (*causal of* اسکیمك èsskimek), To wear out.

اسکدار Uskùdār, *s. t.* Town of Scutari.

اسکله ìsskèlé, *s. t.* (*Italian*), A port, harbour; a landing-place, stairs, wharf; a scaffold; a platform. [A stool.

اسکمله ìsskèmlé, اسکمنی ìsskèmni, *s. t.*

اسکنجه ìsskènjé, *s. t.* The torture; ا—, —et, *v.a.* To put to the torture, to torture.

اسکندرون Isskènderūn, *s. t.* Alexandretta in Syria (Scanderoon), اسکندریه Isskèndèriyyé, *s. t.* Alexandria in Egypt.

اسکی èsski, *a. t.* Old (not new), ancient, of long-standing; اسکیلر èsskiler, *s. pl.* Old clothes; old members of any corps; اسکیجی èsskiji, *s. t.* Dealer in old clothes; a cobbler.

اسکیمك èsskimek (*aor.* اسکر èsskir), *v.n.* To wear out; to become old in service, to be of long standing.

اسلاف èsslāf, *s. pl. a.* (*of* سلف sèlef), Predecessors.

اسلام ìsslām, *s. a.* The Muhammedan religion, Islamism; the Muhammedan Church or community; اهل اسلام èhli-ìsslām, a member of the Muhammedan Church, a Mussulman, a Muhammedan; شیخ الاسلام shèykhu-'l-ìsslām (the Elder of the Muhammedan Church), the chief legist and jurist of the Turkish Empire; اسلامی ìsslāmī, *a. a.* Of, or pertaining to, the Mussulman faith.

اسلحه èssliha, *s. pl. a.* (*of* سلاح sìlāh), Arms, weapons. [method, manner.

اسلوب ùsslūb, *s. a.* Fashion, form;

اسم ìssm (ìssim), *s. a.* A name; a noun, A noun substantive; اسم خاص ìssmi-khāsss, A noun proper; اسم عام ìssmi-''āmm, A noun common; اسم تفضیل ìssmi-tàfdīl, A noun or adjective of the superlative degree, being of the form افعل èf''àl; اسم تصغیر ìssmi-tàssghīr, A diminutive, being of the form فعیل fù''èyl; اسم فاعل ìssmi-fā''il, The active participle, name of the actor; اسم مفعول ìssmi-mèf''ūl, The passive participle, name of the receiver of the action; بسم الله bì-'ssmi-'llāh, *or* bì-'ssmi-'llāhi, In the name of God! (an ejaculation used whenever any work is about to be entered upon, and at the beginning of most books, as of every chapter of the Kur'ān. It is rendered more complete by adding the terms, الرحمن

الرحيم, the compassionate, the very merciful, when it is pronounced, bì-'ssmi-'llāhi-'r-Ràhmāni-'r-Ràhīm; and to this is also sometimes appended ولاحول ولاقوة الابالله العلى العظيم và-lā-hàvla-vè-lā-kùvvéta-illā-bì-'llāhi-'l-"àlìyyi-'l-"ᴧzīm, and there is no power or strength but through God, most high, most great).

اسما èssmā, *s. pl. a.* (*of* اسم ìssm), Names, attributes of God; —, èssmà, *a. a. fem.* Very exalted (*proper name*).

اسمان āssimān, *s.p.* The sky; heaven; a sphere; اسمانه āssimānɛ́, A cieling.

اسمر èssmèr, *a. a.* Dark of complexion, tawny.

اسمك èssmek (*aor.* اسر èssɛʀ), *v.n.* To blow (the wind).

اسمير Essmìr, *s. t.* Smyrna.

اسناد ìssnād, *s. a.* A causing to lean or bear upon; an imputing, casting upon; ا—, —et, *v.a.* To cause to lean, stand, or bear upon; to impute, to cast upon.

اسنمك èssnɛ́mek (*aor.* اسنر èssnɛʀ), *v.n.* To gape, yawn; to give, be elastic.

اسواق èsswᴀ̄k, *s. pl. a.* (*of* سوق, *not used*), Streets; streets of shops.

اسود èssvèd, *a. a.* Black.

اسوده āssūdɛ́, *a. p.* Tranquil, undisturbed, at rest; اسودكى āssūdéghī, *s. p.* Tranquillity, quiet, rest, repose.

اسويداد ìssvīdād, *s. a.* Blackness.

اسهال ìsshāl, *s. a.* Diarrhœa, looseness of bowels.

اسهام èsshām, *s. pl. a.* (*of* سهم sèhm, *or* سهيم sèhīm), Shares, portions; shares or assignments of stock, issued by the treasury at Constantinople, and bearing interest as a life annuity, but formerly transferable to any new life.

اسهل èsshèl, *a. a.* More, most, or very easy.

اسيا āssyā, *s. p.* A mill; —, *s. t.* Asia.

اسير èssīr (yèssīr), *s. a.* A prisoner of war, a captive; a galley-slave (formerly); a slave while in the market for sale, or on the road to a market.

اش ᴧsh, *s. t.* (*old*), Food; اشجى ᴧshji, *s. t.* A cook; اش يرمك ᴧsh-yɛ̀rmek, *v.n.* To long for things to eat (a pregnant woman); —, èsh, *s. t.* A fellow, similar one, the second of a pair.

اشارت ìshāret, *s. a.* A sign; a signal; a mark; ا—, —et, *v.n.* To make a sign, signal, or mark; —چكمك, —chekmek, To hoist a signal.

اشاعه ìshā"a, *s. a.* A divulging, promulgating; ا—, —et, *v.a.* To divulge; to promulgate.

اشاغى ᴧshàghi, *s. t.* The lower part or portion; —, *a. t.* Lower in position, or rank; —, *ad. t.* Down lower; down.

اشبو ìshbù, *pron. dem. t.* This.

اشتباه ìshtibāh, *s. a.* Doubt; doubtfulness.

اشتداد ìshtidād, *s. a.* A becoming or being violent, vehement; violence, vehemency.

اشتر ùshtùr, *s. p.* A camel.

اشترا ìshtirā, *s. a.* A buying, purchasing; ا—, —et, *v.a.* To buy, purchase.

اشتراك ìshtirāk, *s. a.* A possessing or acting in common.

اشتعال ìshti''āl, *s. a.* A breaking out into flame, burning with flame; ا—, —et, *v.n.* To break out in flames; to catch fire; to burn with flame.

اشتغال ìshtighāl, *s. a.* A being occupied; an occupying one's self; ا—, —et, *v.n.* To be occupied; to occupy one's self.

اشتقاق ìshtikāk, *s. a.* A being derived, [derivation.

اشتكا ìshtikyā, *s. a.* A complaining; ا—, —et, *v.n.* To complain, make complaint.

اشتكاك ìshtikyāk, *s. a.* A being [doubtful.

اشتمال ìshtimāl, *s. a.* A comprehending, holding, containing.

اشتمك ìshitmek (*aor.* اشيدر ìshidir), *v.a.* [To hear.

اشته ìshtĕ, *int. t.* Here! Lo! Behold.

اشتها ìshtihā, *s. a.* An appetite; the feeling an appetite or desire for.

اشتهار ìshtihār, *s. a.* A becoming known or famous; celebrity, fame.

اشتياق ìshtiyāk, *s. a.* A longing for; a longing to see.

اشجار èshjār, *s. pl. a.* (*of* شجر shèjer), [Trees.

اشخاص èshkhāss, *s. pl. a.* (*of* شخص shàkhss), Persons.

اشرا èshìrrā *s. pl. a.* (*of* شرير shèrīr), The mischievous, malignant persons.

اشراب ìshrāb, *s. a.* A giving information; ا—, —et, *v.a.* To communicate (information).

اشرار èshrār, *s. pl. a.* (*of* شرير), Mischievous, malignant persons; (*of* شر shèrr), Ills, evils.

اشراف èshrāf, *s. pl. a.* (*of* شريف shèrīf), The noble; nobles; the descendants of Muhammed; نقيب الاشراف nàkību-'l-èshrāf, *The chief of the nobles,* title of an officer of high rank who is charged at Constantinople with a certain jurisdiction in matters relating to the pedigree and privileges of the descendants of Muhammed.

أشرف èshrèf, *a. a.* More, most, or very noble or sacred.

اشعار èsh''ār, *s. pl. a.* (*of* شعر shì''r), Pieces of poetry; —, *s. a.* A notifying; ا—, —et, *v.a.* To notify, communicate.

اشعال ìsh''āl, *s. a.* A lighting, causing to flame; ا—, —et, *v.a.* To light, to make blaze.

اشغال èshghāl, *s. pl. a.* (*of* شغل shŭghl), Occupations; —, ìshghāl, *s. a.* A giving occupation, occupying; ا—, —et, *v.a.* To give occupation, to occupy.

اشفته āshùftĕ, *a. p.* Bewildered, confounded, astonished; beside one's self with love.

أشق àshik, *s. t.* A knuckle-bone (which children play with).

اشقيا èshkiyā, *s. pl. a.* (*of* شقى shàkī), Ruffians, rascals; rebels.

اشك èshk, *s. p.* A tear; —, èshek, *s. t.* An ass, donkey; jackass; a fool, stupid fellow; —, èshik, *s. t.* A threshold; a lintel; الت اشيكى àlt-èshighi, A threshold; اوست اشيكى ùsst-èshighi, A lintel.

اشكار āshikyār, *a. p.* Manifest, evident, plain. [cult matter.

اشكل ìshkil, *s. a.* A dubious or diffi-

اشكين èshkin, *s. t.* The amble; —, *a. t.* An amber, ambling; —كتمك —ghitmek, *v.n.* To amble, to go the amble. [*v.a.* To graft, engraft, bud.

اشلامق ʌshlamak (*aor.* اشلار ʌshlar),

اشمق ʌshmak (*aor.* اشار ʌshar), *v.a.* To go beyond, to pass over or beyond; —, *v.n.* To cover (a stallion, a mare, &c.)

اشمك èshmek (*aor.* اشر èshɪʀ), *v.n.* To go to the wars on horseback; to amble, go the amble; —, *v.a.* To scratch or dig holes in the earth.

اشنا āshinā, *a. p.* Knowing, acquainted with, accustomed to; اشنالق āshinālɪk (ʌshnalɪk), *s. t.* A bow, salutation, sign of friendly recognition, acquaintance, knowledge (of a person); ا—, —et, *v.n.* To bow, to make any sign of friendly recognition.

اشنمق ʌshɪnmak (*aor.* اشنور ʌshɪnɪr), *v.n.* To wear away, be worn by friction.

اشوب āshūb, *s. p.* Confusion, tumult.

اشورمق ʌshɪrmak (*aor.* اشورر ʌshɪrɪr), *v.a.* (*causal of* اشمق), To carry, or cast over or beyond, to send, project, to pass. [bounds.

اشورى ʌshɪrɪ, *a.* and *ad. t.* Beyond

اشهاد èshhād, *s. pl. a.* (*of* شاهد shāhid), Witnesses; —, ìshhād, *s. a.* To cite or bring forward as a witness.

اشيا èshyā, *s. pl. a.* (*of* شى shèy), Things; goods, chattles; merchandize.

اشيان āshyān; اشيانه āshyānɛ, *s. p.* A nest.

اصابت ìssābet, *s. a.* A hitting the mark, attaining the object; a striking, hitting, or falling upon; —, *int. t.* I am glad of it, that is as it should be; ا—, —et, *v.n.* To hit, strike, attain, fall upon; to do what should be; —او, —òl, *v.n.* To be as it should be.

اصالت ʌssālèt, *s. a.* Nobility of extraction; the quality of being the real officer, and not the temporary substitute; اصالتلو ʌssālètlū, *a. t.* Noble; اصالةً ʌssālétɛn, *ad. a.* As the real and permanent officer, not as a substitute. [An inch.

اصبع ùssbū", *or* اصبوع ùssbū", *s. a.*

اصحاب ʌsshāb, *s. pl. a.* (*of* صاحب sāhib), Possessors; companions; the companions of Muhammed in his lifetime.

اصدار ìssdār, *s. a.* A causing to go forth or emanate, an issuing, giving out (orders, &c.); ا—, —et, *v.a.* To issue, give forth, cause to emanate.

اصرار ìssrār, *s. a.* A being pertinacious, a persisting; ا—, —et, *v.n.* To persist.

اصرغان ìssɪrghʌn, *or* اصرغان اوتى ìssɪrghʌn-òtʋ, *s. t.* A stinging nettle, a nettle. [*v.a.* To bite.

اصرمق ìssɪrmak (*aor.* اصرر ìssɪrɪr),

اصطبل ìsstʌbl, *s. a.* A stable, mews;

اصطبل عامره ìsstÀbli-‘‘āmirÉ, the royal mews.

اصطلاح ìsstilāh, s. a. A technical mode of term; a technical expression.

اصغا ìssghā, s. a. A listening to; a consenting to; ا—, —et, v.a. To accede to.

آصف Āssef, s. a. Asaph (reputed in the East to have been Solomon's vizier); the Grand Vizier; a pasha having the rank of Grand Vizier; آصفانه āséfānÉ, a. p. and آصفی āséfī, a. a. Vizirial.

اصفر Àssfèr, a. a. Yellow; pale-faced, [white-faced.

اصفرار ìssfirār, s. a. Yellowness.

اصفهان Issfâhān, s. t. The town of Ispahan, in Persia.

اصفیا Àssfiyā, s. pl. a. (of صفی sÀfī), The pure, the virtuous.

اصقی Àsski, s. t. Anything suspended to or over another thing as an ornament; a string, cord, or strap, by which anything is suspended, as braces, sword-belt, &c.; a state of suspension; a state of suspense, of uncertainty.

اصل Àssl, s. a. A root; an origin; foundation; —, s. t. Real, true; original; فی الاصل fī-’l-Àssl, ad. a. Originally, at the commencement, at first; اصلزاده Àssl-zādÉ, s. p. A person of good or noble family; اصلی فصلی یوق Àssli-fÀssli-yòk, There is no truth in it, it is altogether unfounded.

اصلا Àsslā, ad. a. Never, not at all.

اصلاتمق ìsslÀtmak (aor. اصلادر ìsslÀdir), v.a. To wet.

اصلاح ìsslāh, s. a. A correcting, improving; ا—, —et, v.a. To improve, ameliorate, set right, correct; اصلاح ذات البین ìsslāhi-zāté-’l-bèyn, An adjusting differences, removing causes of quarrel.

اصلاق ìsslÀk, a. t. Wet, wetted.

اصلانمق ìsslÀnmak (aor. اصلانور ìsslÀnir), v.n. To get wet, to be wetted.

اصلی Àsslī, a. a. Original, primitive, fundamental.

اصمارلمق ìssmàrlamak (aor. اصمارلار ìssmàrlar), To order or request that a thing may be made or done.

اصمق Àssmak (aor. اصار Àssar), To hang, hang up, suspend.

اصمه Àssma, s. t. A vine, grape-vine; اصمه قباغی Àssma-kÀbÀghi, A kind of pumpkin or vegetable-marrow, the plant of which is usually trained as a vine, and which grows itself to the length of three feet and more.

اصناف èssnāf, s. pl. a. (of صنف sìnf), Classes; sorts, kinds; trades, corporations; (as a Turkish singular), a tradesman, artisan, shopkeeper; an artificer in the army or navy.

اصول ùssūl, s. pl. a. (of اصل Àssl), Roots; origins; principles; (as a Turkish singular) a method, way, manner, custom; اصولله ùssūlla, ad. t. Gently; براصول ایله bìr-ùssūl-ila, ad. t. Somehow or other.

اضائه ìzā'É, *s. a.* The throwing light upon; elucidation; ا—, —et, *v.a.* To elucidate.

اضاعه ìzā''*a*, *s. a.* A wasting; ا—, —et, *v.a.* To waste.

اضافت ìzāfet, *s. a.* Construction of noun with noun; an incidental quality.

اضحا (*for* اضحی) Àdhà, *s. pl. a.* (*of* اضحاة, *not in use*), Sacrifices; عید اضحا ''ìdi-Àdhà, The feast of sacrifices, called usually قربان بیرامی kŭr-bān-bàyrām*i*.

اضطراب ìzt*i*rāb, *s. a.* Agitation; pain; tribulation, grief, anxiety; —چکمك, —chèkmek, *v.n.* To be in pain; to be under anxiety; —ویرمك, —vèr-mek, *v.n.* To give pain; to cause anxiety.

اضطرار ìzt*i*rār, *s. a.* Necessity.

اضعاف èz''āf, *s. pl. a.* (*of* ضعف z*i*''f), Twice or more quantities; —, ìz''āf, *s. a.* An enfeebling, weakening.

اضلاع Àdlā'', *s. pl. a.* (*of* ضلع d*i*l''), Sides of a figure; متساوی الاضلاع mùtéssāvìyyu-'l-Àdlā'', Equilateral.

اضلال ìdlāl, *s. a.* A leading astray, a causing to go astray, a perverting; ا—, —et, *v.a.* To lead astray, cause to wander from the right path; to pervert.

اضمار ìzmār, *s. a.* Concealing in one's mind or heart; ا—, —et, *v.a.* To conceal in one's mind or heart.

اضمحلال ìzmìhlāl, *s. a.* A total disappearing, dispersing.

اطاعت ìtā''*at*, *s. a.* An obeying; obedience, submission; ا—, —et, *v.n.* To obey; to submit.

اطاله ìtālÉ, *s. a.* A stretching forth; اطالهٔ ید ا ìtālé'i-yèd-et, To stretch forth the hand; اطالهٔ لسان ا ìtālé'i--lìssān-et (*lit.* To stretch forth the tongue) to speak ill of.

اطبا àt*i*bbā, *s. pl. a.* (*of* طبیب tàbīb), Physicians, doctors of medicine; سر اطبا sèri-àt*i*bbā, The chief of the physicians.

اطراد ìtt*i*rād, *s. a.* Regularity, subjection to rule.

اطراف ètrāf, *s. pl. a.* (*of* طرف tàraf), Sides, parts; districts; every side, all sides; اطرافیله ètrāfīl*a*, *ad. t.* In a properly detailed manner, with all its circumstances.

اطفا ìtfā, *s. a.* An extinguishing; ا—, —et, *v.a.* To put out, extinguish.

اطلاع ìtt*i*lā'', *v.a.* A becoming aware, informed; —کسب ا, —kèssb-et, *v.n.* To become aware, acquire a knowledge or information.

اطلاق ìtlāk, *v.a.* A setting free; a divorcing; the applying (a name or term); ا—, —et, *v.a.* To set free, to set at liberty; to divorce; to apply (a term); اطلاق عنان ا ìtlāk*i*-''ìnān-et, *v.n.* To let go the reins, give a horse his head; to set out on a journey; علی الاطلاق ''àlé-'l-ìtlāk, *ad. a.* Generally, in a general manner or sense.

اطلس Àtlàss, *a. a.* Plain, unornamented; فلك اطلس fèléki-Àtlàss, The empyrean or primum-mobile, the sphere beyond that of the fixed stars, being without the ornament of stars; called also فلك الافلاك fèléku-'l-èflāk, *the sphere of spheres;* —, *s. a.* Satin; an atlas of geography.

اطماع ìtmā'', *s. a.* An exciting to cupidity, a causing to long for possession; ا—, —et, *v.a.* To cause one to be desirous of possessing or acquiring, to tempt, to raise expectations.

اطمينان ìtmīnān, *s. a.* A sense of safety and security. [bombast.

اطناب ìtnāb, *s. a.* Sublimity of style;

اطوار àtwār, *s. pl. a.* (*of* طور tàvr), Manners, the outward indicative active signs of inward feelings towards other people.

اطه àda, *s. t.* An island, isle, islet.

اظهار ìzhār, *s. a.* A showing, manifesting, making visible, causing to be seen; ا—, —et, *v.a.* To manifest, show.

اعاده ì''ādé, *s. a.* A causing to return; ا—, —et, *v.a.* To cause to return, to send back, drive back, bring back; to return, restore, give back. [Enemies.

اعادى à''ādī, *s. pl. a.* (*of* عدو ''àdùvv),

اعانه ì''āné, *s. a.* An assisting, helping; help, assistance; ا—, —et, *v.n.* To help, assist.

اعتبار ì''tibār, *s. a.* Esteem, consideration; mercantile credit; ا—, —et, *v.n.* To hold in esteem.

اعتدال ì''tidāl, *s. a.* The being of a mean, average, or moderate degree.

اعتذار ì''tizār, *s. a.* The begging to be excused, the offering an excuse; ا—, —et, *v.n.* To offer an excuse or apology; to beg to be excused.

اعتراض ì''tirāz, *s. a.* The offering an objection; finding fault; ا—, —et, *v.n.* To offer objections; to find fault; —, *v.a.* To allege (an objection).

اعتراف ì''tirāf, *s. a.* An admission, an avowal; ا—, —et, *v.a.* To admit, avow.

اعتساف ì''tissāf, *s. a.* Oppression, tyranny.

اعتقاد ì''tikād, *s. a.* A believing in, holding to be true; belief; religious belief; ا—, —et, *v.n.* To believe in, to hold to be true.

اعتماد ì''timād, *s. a.* A placing trust or confidence in; trust, confidence; ا—, —et, *v.n.* To place trust, to put confidence, to put faith.

اعتنا ì''tinā, *s. a.* A taking pains, a paying great attention; ا—, —et, *v.n.* To take great pains, pay great attention.

اعتياد ì''tiyād, *s. a.* The contracting a habit; ا—, —et, *v.a.* To adopt as a habit. [Enemies.

اعدا à''dā, *s. pl. a.* (*of* عدو ''àduvv),

اعداد à''dād, *s. pl. a.* (*of* عدد ''àded), Numbers; —, ì''dād, *s. a.* A preparing, making ready; ا—, —et, *v.a.* To make ready, prepare.

اعدام ì''dām, *s. a.* An annihilating; a killing, putting to death; ا—, —et, *v.a.* To annihilate; to kill, put to death.

اعزا à"ìzzā, *and* اعزه à"ìzzé, *s. pl. a.* (*of* عزيز "ʌzīz), The dearest, most honoured.

اعزاز ì"zāz, *s. a.* A raising to dignity and glory; ا—, —et, *v.a.* To dignify, glorify. [Tithes.

اعشار à"shār, *s. pl. a.* (*of* عشر "ùshr),

اعضا à"zā, *s. pl. a.* (*of* عضو, *not used*), Members (of the body, or of a council or assembly); (*as a Turkish singular*) a member; اعضالق à"zālik, *s. t.* Membership. [*v.a.* To give.

اعطا ì"tā, *s. a.* A giving; ا—, —et,

اعظم à"zàm, *a. a.* Greater, greatest, or very great; صدراعظم sʌdri-à"zàm (sàdrāzàm), The Grand Vizier.

اعلا (*for* اعلى) à"là, *a. a.* Higher, highest, most or very high; the best; good, excellent, admirable; —, *ad. t.* Well; —, ì"lā, *s. a.* A raising up, elevating; ا—, —et, *v.a.* To raise, raise up, set up, to elevate.

اعلام à"lām, *s. pl. a.* (*of* علم "àlem), Signs, signals; flags, standards; —, ì"lām, *s. a.* A declaring, making known; a declaration; an official report given in answer to an official inquiry; a judicial sentence in writing; ا—, —et, *v.a.* To report officially in answer to an official inquiry.

اعلان ì"lān, *s. a.* A publishing, making publicly known; an advertisement; ا—, —et, *v.a.* To publish, to make publicly known; to advertise; اعلاننامه ì"lān-nāmé, A manifesto; an advertisement.

اعلم à"lem, *a. a.* More, most, or very knowing; الله اعلم ʌllāhu-à"lem (ʌllā'lem) (God is He who knows best) *int. a.* I am not sure, but I think so; I am very much inclined to believe so, &c. [—, *s. a.* A blind man.

اعما (*for* اعمى) à"mà, *a. a.* Blind;

اعمار à"mār, *s. pl. a.* (*of* عمر "ùmr), Lives; life-times; —, ì"mār, *s. a.* A rendering cultivated, populous, full of life; ا—, —et, *v.a.* To reclaim (waste lands); to people, populate.

اعمال à"māl, *s. pl. a.* (*of* عمل "ʌmel), Acts, actions; —, ì"māl, *s. a.* A making, manufacturing; ا—, —et, *v.a.* To make, prepare, manufacture.

اعوام à"wām, *s. pl. a.* (*of* عام "ām), Years.

اعيان à"yān, *s. pl. a.* (*of* عين "àyn), Persons of note; (*as a Turkish singular*) a mayor; an alderman; اعيان باشى à"yʌn-bʌshi, the mayor.

اغ ʌgh, *s. t.* A net; اورمجك اغى ùrumjèk-ʌghi, A spider's web, a cobweb.

اغا ʌghʌ, *s. t.* A country gentleman; a master (of servants); the eldest brother; a superior servant, officer of a household; the title of military or naval officers from the bing-bʌshi (mayor or chef-de-bataillon) downwards; the title of various chief officers in the civil service; يكيچرى اغاسى yèngichéri-ꜧghꜧssi, The Aga or chief of the janissaries; اغا قپوسى ꜧghꜧ-kꜧpissi, The office and official residence (formerly) of the Aga of the janissaries, now changed into that of the Shèykhu-'l-ìsslām; قيزلر اغاسى kìzlar--ꜧghꜧssi, The chief eunuch of the imperial household; حرم اغاسى hàrem-ꜧghꜧssi, A eunuch in a private family.

اغاج ꜧghꜧj, *s. t.* A tree; a shrub; a bush; wood; — قره kꜧra —, An elm-tree; elm-wood; قاونى —, — kàwunu, A citron; قاقان —, — kꜧkꜧn, A woodpecker.

اغارمق ꜧgharmak (*aor.* اغارر ꜧgharir), *v.n.* To become white or grey (the hair, beard; or the morning).

اغاز ꜧghꜧz, *s. p.* A beginning, commencing; ا—, —et, *v.n.* To begin, set about, commence.

اغبرار ìghbirār, *s. a.* A becoming dusty; خاطر —, ìghbirāri-khꜧtir, A taking offence, a being offended.

اغتنام ìghtinām, *s. a.* A seizing prey, making booty; ا—, —et, *v.a.* To seize as booty.

اغر ꜧghir, *a. t.* Heavy; slow in motion; hard to digest, indigestible; ill-savoured, bad-smelling, fetid; hard to be borne, insupportable; high (price); —, *s. t.* Serious, or stately demeanour; اغريتى طاقنمق ꜧghirini--tàkinmak, *v.n.* To put on a serious countenance, assume a formal manner.

اغرا ìghrā, *s. a.* An exciting, inciting; ا—, —et, *v.a.* To excite, incite.

اغرتمق ꜧghritmak (*aor.* اغريدر ꜧghridir), *v.a.* (*causal of* اغريمق), To cause to ache; — باش bàsh —, *v.n.* To cause one's head to ache, give the headache; to importune, teaze.

اغرلق ꜧghirlik, *s. a.* Weight, heaviness; luggage, baggage, impedimenta; a girl's bridal dower or trousseau; the nightmare; a burden (on one's purse).

اغرى ꜧghri, *s. t.* A pain, ache; باش اغريسى bꜧsh-ꜧghrissi, The headache; an importunate, tiresome bore; قارن اغريسى kàrn-ꜧghrissi, The belly-ache, gripes; a peevish child; اغرى طاغى ꜧghri-dꜧghi, Mount Ararat on the confines of Georgia and Armenia.

اغريمق ꜧghrimak (*aor.* اغرر ꜧghrir), *v.n.* To ache, to be painful.

اغز ꜧghz, *s. t.* The mouth; the mouth or opening into anything; the special place at a stairs where passengers get into boats, or out of them; نهر اغزى nèhr-ꜧghzi, The mouth of a river; قويو اغزى kùyu-ꜧghzi, The mouth of a well; اغز جوابى ꜧghz-jèwꜧbi, A verbal answer; اغزاوتى ꜧghz-òtu, The priming of a gun; درت يول اغزى dùrt-yòl--ꜧghzi, The place where four roads meet; اغزلق ꜧghzlik, A mouthpiece (of a pipe, or of a musical instrument).

اغسامق ꜧghsamak (*aor.* اغسار ꜧghsar), *v.n.* To limp in walking.

اغستوس àghosstoss, *s. t.* The month of August.

اغضاب ìghzāb, *s. a.* A moving to anger, an angering; ا—, —et, *v.a.* To anger.

اغفال ìghfāl, *s. a.* A putting off one's guard; ا—, —et, *v.a.* To put off one's guard, to lull into security, to deceive.

اغل àghl, *s. t.* A fold, or pound for sheep.

اغلامق àghlamak (*aor.* اغلار àghlar), *v.n.* To weep, cry, shed tears; —, *v.a.* To weep for, mourn over, deplore the loss of.

اغماز ìghmāz, *s. a.* A speaking ill of; tale-bearing.

اغماض ìghmāz, *s. a.* A shutting the eyes; اغماض عين ا ìghmāzi-"àyn-et, *v.n.* To shut the eyes (to faults or improper conduct).

اغمق àghmak (*aor.* اغار àghar), *v.n.* To rise in the air (dust, &c.); to be preponderant and sink (one side of a balance).

اغنام àghnām, *s. pl. a.* (*of* غنم, *seldom used*), Sheep.

اغنيا àghniyā, *s. pl. a.* (*of* غنى ghànī), [The rich.

اغوا ìghwā, *s. a.* A seducing, a turning from rectitude; ا—, —et, *v.a.* To seduce, pervert, lead from rectitude, cause to do wrong.

اغوش āghūsh, *s. p.* Lap, bosom, em- [brace.

اغيار àghyār, *s. pl. a.* (*of* غير ghàyr), Others, strangers, rivals.

افاته ìfātè, *s. a.* An allowing to escape out of one's power or possession, a losing; ا—, —et, *v.a.* To lose, allow to escape.

افاده ìfādè, *s. a.* An explaining, representation, relation; ا—, —et, *v.a.* To explain, represent, relate.

افاضه ìfāzè, *s. a.* A pouring out abundantly.

افاق āfāk, *s. pl. a.* (*of* افق ŭfŭk), Horizons; districts (as being bounded by their horizons); افاقى āfākī, *a. a.* Common to the whole world, public, spread through all lands; wandering, vagabond.

افاقت ìfākàt, *s. a.* Convalescence; — بولمق —, — bŭlmak, To get well, be relieved from sickness.

افت āfet, *s. a.* A calamity; —, ìft, A prodigy; a fruitful she-camel; a portent; extraordinary calamity; a lie.

افتا īftā, *s. a.* The giving a positive legal opinion (on a supposed case), well known by the name *fetwa*.

افتاب āfitāb, *s. p.* The sun.

افتاده ùftādè, *a. p.* Fallen; fallen into; fallen into the power of; a prisoner to the beauty, wiles, or charms of; which has happened, taken place.

افتان ìftān, *s. a.* A leading into some improper practices, a perverting; —, ùftān, *ad.* or *a. p.* Falling, falling down; — وخيزان —, —u-khīzān, Falling and rising (as a drunken or wounded person).

افتحاص ìftihāss, *s. a.* Diligence in inquiry, in searching into.

افتخار ìftikhār, *s. a.* Well-founded pride; ا—, —et, *v.n.* To pride one's self; — نشان nìshāni —, *or* نشانی —, — nìshāni, The former decoration of the order of merit, founded by Mahmud the Second.

افترا ìftirā, *s. a.* A calumniating; a calumny; ا—, —et, *v.n.* To calumniate.

افتراق ìftirāk, *s. a.* A being separated (from friends.)

افتقار ìftikār, *s. a.* Poverty, the being poor.

افراد èfrād, *s. pl. a.* (*of* فرد fèrd), Individuals.

افراز èfrāz, *a. p.* (*in composition*), Which raises, lifts up; —, ìfrāz, *s. a.* A separating, dividing; ا—, —et, *v.a.* To separate, divide.

افراط ìfrāt, *s. a.* Excess; ا—, —et, *v.n.* To exceed due bounds.

افراغ ìfrāgh, *s. a.* A casting in a mould; a putting into order, shape, or form; ا—, —et, *v.a.* To pour into a mould; to reduce to order, shape, or form.

افروخته èfrūkhté, *a. p.* Lighted, on fire, burning.

افروز èfrūz, *a. p.* Which lights, sets on fire, or illuminates.

افریدگار āférīdéghyār, *s. p.* The Creator.

افریده āférīdé, *a. p.* Created; —, *s. p.* A creature.

افرین āférīn, *a. p.* (*in composition*), Who creates; —, *int. p.* (āfèrim), Well done!

افریقا Afrika, *s. t.* Africa.

افرینش āférīnish, *s. p.* A creating, creation.

افزا èfzā, *a. p.* (*in composition*), Which augments.

افزون èfzūn, *a. p.* More in number or quantity; (*in composition*), Augmented; much, many; افزونی èfzūnī, *s. p.* The being augmented; the being much or many, abundance.

افساد ìfsād, *s. a.* A corrupting; a throwing into disorder; a leading into bad practices; ا—, —et, *v.a.* To corrupt; to throw into disorder; to introduce abuses into; to lead into bad practices.

افسانه èfsāné, *s. p.* A tale, fiction, romance.

افسر èfsèr, *s. p.* A crown, diadem.

افسون èfsūn, *s. p.* A spell, incantation.

افشا ìfshā, *s. a.* A divulging, revealing; ا—, —et, *v.a.* To divulge, reveal.

افشان èfshān, *a. p.* (*in composition*), Who sheds or spreads abroad.

افضال èfdāl, *s. pl. a.* (*of* فضل fazl), Favours, graces.

افضل èfdal, *a. a.* More, most, or very worthy (person), or advantageous (thing).

افطار ìftār, *s. a.* The breaking of the fast in times of abstinence; the food with which the fast is broken; ا—, —et, *v.n.* To partake of meat and drink after a religious fast.

افعی èf'à, *s. a.* A viper.

افق ùfuk, *s. a.* The horizon; افقی ùfukī, *a. a.* Horizontal.

افك ìfk, *s. a.* A lie, a falsehood.

افكار èfkyār, *s. pl. a.* (*of* فكر fikr), Ideas, thoughts.

افكن èfkèn, *a. p.* (*in composition*),

Which throws, throws down, throws out.

افلاس ìflāss, *s. a.* The becoming poor and bankrupt; bankruptcy; poverty.

افلاق Iflak, *s. t.* Wallachia.

افلاك èflāk, *s. pl. a.* (*of* فلك fèlek), Skies, heavens, spheres.

افنا ìfnā, *s. a.* An annihilating, destroying; ا—, —et, *v.a.* To annihilate, destroy.

افندی èfèndi, *s. t.* (*Greek*), A gentleman of education; a man of polished manners; a master (of servants); a patron, protector, benefactor; a prince of the blood; افندم èfèndim! (my master) Sir! افندیمز èfèndimiz (our master), Our sovereign, the Sultan; our lord, his excellency, his worship, his grace, &c. &c.; شوكتلوافندیمز shèvkètli-èfèndimiz, Our imperial master (the Sultan).

افواه èfwāh, *s. pl. a.* (*of* فم fèm), Mouths.

افول ŭfūl, *s. a.* A setting or decreasing in altitude; ا—, —et, *v.n.* To descend in altitude towards the horizon; to set, go down.

افیون ǎfyòn, *s. t.* Opium.

آق ǎk, *a. t.* White; —, *s. t.* The white part of certain things; كوزك اقی ghyùzung-ǎki, The white of the eye; یمورطه نك اقی yìmurtaning-ǎki; اق جكر ǎk-jìgher, The lungs, the lights; اق صقاللو ǎk-sàkalli, One with a white beard, an old man; an elder; the chief man *or* petty magistrate of a village; اق بابا ǎk-bàba, A kind or vulture; اق دكز ǎk-dèngiz, The Mediterranean; یوزی اق yùzu-ǎk, (whose face is white) metaphor meaning one who has performed his duty well and honourably, who has cause to feel a just pride; اقلق ǎklik, *s. t.* Whiteness; یوزاقلغی yùz-ǎklighi, (whiteness of face) metaphor meaning the having no cause to feel ashamed, but every cause to feel proud of one's self.

اقالیم àkālīm, *s. pl. a.* (*of* اقلیم ìklīm), Climes (in geography, the world being supposed to be divided into seven such sections, whence اقالیم سبعه àkālīmi-sèb‘‘à, *the seven climes,* means the whole world).

اقامت ìkāmet, *s. a.* A staying in a place, stay, residence; ا—, —et, *v.n.* To stay (in a place), to live, dwell, reside.

اقامه ìkāmé, *s. a.* (*identic originally with the preceding word*), A setting a thing up, establishing it, fixing it upright; a producing (proofs or indications); a performing (prayers); ا—, —et, *v.a.* To set (a thing) in its place; to set up; to produce, adduce, bring forward; to perform (prayers).

اقانیم àkānīm, *s. pl. a.* (*of* اقنوم ŭknūm), The persons of the Trinity; اقانیم ثلثه àkānīmi-sèlāssé, The three Persons of the Trinity.

اقبال ìkbāl, *s. a.* Good luck; a turning the face or the mind towards any object; a desiring; a slave-girl taken into the imperial favour, but not yet advanced as one of the Sultan's seven acknowledged state concubines.

اقتار Aktār, *s. pl. a.* (*of* قتر, *not used*), Districts, regions; —, *s. t.* (*for* عطار "àttār, *s. a.* A seller of perfumes), a kind of druggist, grocer, perfumer, and toyman, in one, and in a small way.

اقتارمق Aktarm*a*k (*aor.* اقتارر Aktar*i*r), To shift (things) from one vessel to another; to turn over.

اقتباس ìktibāss, *s. a.* A borrowing (phrases or arguments from the works of another author), a citing (the words of another); ا—, —et, *v.a.* To borrow, to cite, to use (words or arguments).

اقتحام ìkt*i*hām, *s. a.* An attacking courageously; an embarking heart and soul in any affair; ا—, —et, *v.n.* To attack; to embark in heart and soul.

اقتدا ìktidā, *s. a.* A taking as one's ensamplar, following the teaching, and imitating the actions of; ا—, —et, *v.n.* To follow as a guide and example. [puissance, capacity.

اقتدار ìkt*i*dār, *s. a.* Power, might,

اقتران ìkt*i*rān, *s. a.* Conjunction (of the heavenly bodies).

اقتضا ìktizā, *s. a.* A being needful, requisite, or necessary; ا—, —et, and اقتضاسی او ìktizāss*i*-òl, *v.n.* To be needful, requisite, or necessary.

اقتفا ìktifā, *s. a.* A following after, (physically or morally); ا—, —et, To follow after.

اقچه Akch*a*, *a. t.* Rather white, whitish; —, *s. t.* Money in general, coin, cash; a small monetary value (formerly a coin), one-third of a pàr*a*, and consequently the $\frac{1}{120}$ of a piastre, or the $\frac{1}{55}$ of a penny; it is frequently mentioned under the name of *asper*, a corruption of the Greek equivalent for the proper Turkish word.

اقدام Akdām, *s. pl. a.* (*of* قدم kAdEm), Feet; —, ìkdām, *s. a.* Perseverance; ا—, —et, *v.n.* To persevere.

اقدم AkdEm, *a. a.* Prior, anterior; —, *ad. t.* Before, anterior, prior; بوندن اقدم bùnd*a*n-AkdEm, Some time ago; بوندن اقدمجه bùnd*a*n-AkdEmj*a*, Some little time ago, a few days since.

اقرار ìkrār, *s. a.* A confessing, avowing, admitting; ا—, —et, *v.a.* To confess, avow, admit.

اقران Akrān, *s. pl. a.* (*of* قرن kìrn, *not in use*), Equals (in rank or age); (*as a Turkish singular*) an equal (in rank or age). [Near relatives.

اقربا Akr*a*bā, *s. pl. a.* (*of* قريب kArīb),

اقسامق *or* اقصامق Aksam*a*k (*aor.* اقصار), *v.n.* To lean over to one side in walking, from one leg being longer than the other, the person having this infirmity being called اقصاق *or* اقساق Aks*a*k.

اقسرمق *or* اقصرمق ʌksɪrmak (*aor.* اقصرر ʌksɪrir), *v.n.* To sneeze.

اقصا *or* اقصى ʌksà, *a. a.* More or most remote, ultimate; —, *s. a.* The ultimate point or degree.

اقطار ʌktār, *s. pl. a.* (*of* قطر kŭtr), Countries, districts; (*of* قطره kʌtra), Drops.

اقعاد ìk''ād, *s. a.* A causing to sit, placing on a seat; ا—, —et, *v.a.* To place on a seat.

اقل àkàll, *a. a.* The least in number or quantity; اقلى àkàlli, *ad. t.* At least, at the very least.

اقلام ʌklām, *s. pl. a.* (*of* قلم kàlɛm), Pens; offices, rooms of clerks under government.

اقليم ìklīm, *s. a.* A clime.

اقمشه ʌkmishé, *s. pl. a.* (*of* قماش kŭmāsh), Stuffs, cloths.

اقمق ʌkmak (*aor.* اقار ʌkar), *v.n.* To run, flow.

اقناع ìknā'', *s. a.* A contenting, satisfying; ا—, —et, *v.n.* To content, satisfy.

اقندى ʌkɪndi, *s. t.* A current, flow of water, stream, rapid.

اقنوم ŭknūm, *s. a.* A Person of the Trinity.

اقين ʌkin, *s. t.* Predatory incursion in an enemy's country.

اك èk, *s. t.* A joint, joining of two parts or pieces; —يرى, —yèri, A joint of the members; —, èng, *ad. t.* The most.

اكابر èkyābir, *s. pl. a.* (*of* اكبر èkbɛr), The greatest persons.

اكارم èkyārim, *s. pl. a.* (*of* اكرم èkrèm), The most noble or generous persons.

اكاه āghyāh, *a. p.* Aware, on one's guard; informed.

اكبر èkbɛr, *a. a.* More, most, or very great; greater; the greatest.

اكترا ìktirā, *s. a.* A taking on hire; ا—, —et, *v.a.* To take to one's self on hire.

اكتساب ìktissāb, *s. a.* An acquiring to one's self; ا—, —et, To acquire.

اكتفا ìktifā, *s. a.* A being sufficient; ا—, —et, *v,n.* To suffice, to be sufficient.

اكتنا ìktinā, *s. a.* A being surnamed.

اكتناه ìktināh, *s. a.* The striving to understand a thing thoroughly.

اكثر èksɛr, *a. a.* More or most in number or quantity; اكثرى èksèrī, *ad. t.* and اكثريا èksèrìyyā, *ad. a.* For the most part, most generally.

اكر ègher, *c. p.* If.

اكرام ìkrām, *s. a.* Deference, respect, a receiving well; a present; ا—, —et, *v.n.* To receive well, treat with respect; —, *v.a.* To give as a present.

اكراه ìkrāh, *s. a.* The feeling an utter aversion and disgust.

اكرچه èghèrché *or* èghèrchi, *c. p.* If; although; true it is that.

اكرلمك èghrilmek (*aor.* اكريلور èghrilir), *v.n.* To bend, to become bent; to become leaning, out of the perpendicular.

اكرم èkrèm, *a. a.* More, most, or very noble or generous.

اكرمق ʌngirmak (*aor.* اكرر ʌngirir), *v.n.* To bray (an ass).

اكرمك èg*h*irmek (*aor.* اكرر èg*h*irir), *v.a.* To spin (thread).

اكرى èg*h*ri, *a. t.* Bent, crooked; slanting, out of the perpendicular; اكرى بوكرى èg*h*ri-bùg*h*ri, Very crooked, devious, tortuous.

اكسك èksik, *a. t.* Incomplete, wanting in number, quantity, or part; —, *s. t.* A defect; a number, quantity, or part which is wanting.

اكسلمك èksilmek (*aor.* اكسلور èksilir), *v.n.* To become less in number or quantity, to diminish, decrease.

اكسه èn*g*sé, *s. t.* The back of the head or upper part of the neck; the back or hind part of an object.

اكسير ìksīr, *s. a.* An elixir, liqueur; the philosopher's stone or philtre.

اكشى èkshi, *a. t.* Sour, acid, tart; unfavourable, unpromising, menacing (countenance).

اكشيمك èkshimek (*aor.* اكشير èkshir), *v.n.* To become sour; to put on an unfavourable or menacing aspect (a countenance).

اكل èkl, *s. a.* An eating; —وشرب —u-shùrb, Eating and drinking; ا—, —et, *v.a.* To eat.

اكلامق ànglamak (*aor.* اكلار ànglar) (ànnamak, *aor.* ànnar), *v.a.* To understand, comprehend; سوزاكلار sùz-ànnar (understanding fully what is said to him), intelligent; tractable; reasonable (person).

اكلمك èklémek (*aor.* اكلر èklér), *v.a.* To join (two pieces together, or one to another); to add; —, ìn*g*lémek, *v.n.* To groan, to moan.

اكليل ìklīl, *s. a.* A diadem.

اكمال ìkmāl, *s. a.* A completing, finishing, perfecting; ا—, —et, *v.a.* To complete, finish, perfect, fill up.

اكمق ȧn*g*mak (*aor.* اكار ȧn*g*ar), *v.a.* To think of, call to mind, or pronounce the name of.

اكمك èkmek (*aor.* اكر èkér), *v.a.* To sow (seed); to sprinkle (salt, &c.); — (*for* اتمك), *s. t.* Bread; —, èg*h*mek, *v.a.* To bend.

اكندى *or* اكنتى èg*h*enti, *s. t.* Filings.

اكه èg*h*é, *s. t.* A file (steel instrument for filing metals). [*v.a.* To file with a file.

اكه‌لمك èg*h*élémek (*aor.* اكه‌لر èg*h*élér),

اكى èg*h*i, *or* اكى كموكى ég*h*i-kèmig*h*i, *s. t.* A rib, rib-bone.

اكيد èkīd, *a. a.* Very strong.

اكين èkin, *s. t.* Seed-sowing; sown seed; cereal crops; —وقتى, —wȧkt*i*, seed-time; —اكمك, —èkmek, To sow corn; —بچمك, —bìchmek, To cut down the corn.

ال èl, *art. a.* The Arabic definite article, placed equally before nouns and adjectives: it is found in many Turkish adverbial and qualifying expressions. When preceded by the Arabic preposition ل (lì, for, &c.), the ا is suppressed, and the two letters ل are joined, as, للتأديب lì-'t-tè'dib, *for punishment*; and the word الله Allāh,

God, in that case becomes لله lì-'llʌh, *for God, for God's sake.* The case of suppressing the sound of the ل of this article is explained in our prefatory remarks; —, ɛl, *s. t.* The hand, a hand; a stranger in blood; another person; ال ايشى ɛl-ìshi, Work of hand; ال يازيسى ɛl-yàzissi, Writing, manuscript; ال التندہ ɛl-ʌltinda, Underhand, in secret; الده در ɛlda-dir, It is in hand, in course of preparation; it is not beyond control, it is in man's power; المده در ɛlimda-dir, It is in my power, it is at my option; الهويرمك ɛla-vɛrmek, To betray; to give up to the authorities; الهكتورمك ɛla-ghètirmek, To acquire possession of; to catch, take, make prisoner; ال چكمك ɛl-chèkmek, To withdraw one's assistance or cooperation; to have nothing more to do with a thing; الدن كلمك ɛldan-ghɛlmek, To be in (one's) power (to do), as, المدن كلمز ɛlimdan-ghɛlmàz, It is not in my power, I am not able (to do it); —, ʌl, *a. t.* Scarlet; red, rosy; —, *imper. of* المق ʌlmak, Take, take thou; as, ال سنا ʌl-sɛn-a! There, take that! there's for you! —, āl, *s. a.* A family, race, dynasty, as, ال عثمان āli-"òssmʌn, The Ottoman dynasty; —, *s. p.* Fraud, deceit, stratagem.

الا ālā, *s. pl. a.* (*of* الا èlā, *not used*), Graces, favours; —, *a. p.* (*in composition*), Which defiles, pollutes; —, èlā, *int. a.* Ho! —, ʌla, *a. t.* Spotted, diversified with large bright or white spots on a dark ground; الابالق ʌla-bʌlik, A trout; الاقارغه ʌla-kàrgha, A jack-daw; الاتنلو ʌla-tɛnli, A leper, leprous; الاجه ʌlaja, Somewhat diversified by spots; —بولاجه, —bùlaja, Very grossly diversified with colours; —illā, *c. a.* Unless, but, except; or otherwise; only that, saving that.

الارغه àlàrgha, *s. t.* (*Italian*), A certain distance from shore, or from any object; —, *a.* and *ad. t.* At a distance from shore, or from any object; —, *int. t.* Be off! keep away! keep your distance! [actually, presently.

الآن èl-ān, *ad. a.* Now, at this moment,

الاه *or* آلہ ìlāh, A god; God; الاهى *or* آلهى ìlāhī, *a. a.* Divine, godly; —, *s. t.* An anthem or carol; الاهيت *or* آلهيت ìlāhìyyèt, *s. a.* Divineness, divinity, Godhead.

الاى ʌlay, *s. t.* A procession; a regiment; a line deployed; a set, lot, parcel; الاى مالاى ʌlay-mʌlay, *ad. t.* One over the other, all together as when a crowd rushes; ميرالاى mīri-ʌlày (mìrʌlày), A colonel, commandant of a regiment; —, ālāy, *a. p.* (*in composition*), Which defiles, pollutes.

الايش ālāyish, *s. p.* Defilement, pollution, filthiness; —, *s. t.* Pomp, parade.

البته ɛlbèttɛ, *ad. a.* Assuredly, certainly; without fail.

البسه èlbissé, *s. pl. a.* (*of* لباس libāss), Clothes, garments, raiment.

الت ālt, *s. t.* The under part or side; the space underneath; اوست —, —ùsst, Upside down, topsy-turvy; —يانى, —yàni, —طرفى, —tàrafi, The next place lower down; the remainder, the sequel; ا—, —et, *v.a.* To vanquish, overcome; —او, —ōl, *v.n.* To be vanquished, conquered, overcome; —, ālet, *s. a.* An instrument, tool, implement; an organ; الت تناسل āléti-tènāssul, The organ of generation.

التباس ìltibāss, *s. a.* The wearing an appearance calculated to create doubt.

التجا ìltijā, *s. a.* A taking refuge, seeking an asylum; ا—, —et, *v.n.* To take refuge, seek an asylum.

التحاق ìltihāk, *s. a.* The joining one's self or becoming joined to; adhesion; ا—, —et, *v.n.* To join one's self on to.

التحام ìltihām, *s. a.* The heat of battle.

التزام ìltizām, *s. a.* The taking upon one's self, undertaking; the taking a great interest in, protecting, giving one's influence; the taking the public revenues on farm; ا—, —et, *v.a.* To undertake; to take (the public revenues) on farm; to protect or support actively.

التفات ìltifāt, *s. a.* A turning one's face towards; taking notice of (persons or things); showing attentions to (persons); ا—, —et, *v.n.* To take notice of; to show attentions.

التماس ìltimāss, *s. a.* The making a request, begging a favour; a request; ا—, —et, *v.a.* To request.

التمش āltmish, *a. t.* Sixty. [money.

التون āltin, *s. t.* Gold; a piece of gold

التهاب ìltihāb, *s. a.* Inflammation.

التى ālti, *a. t.* Six; —, èlti, The wife of the brother of one's husband, a sister-in-law (of a woman).

التيام ìltiyām, *s. a.* A being healed (a wound).

الچق ālchàk, *a. t.* Low; mean, base; —كوكللو, —ghyùngullu, Meek, low in spirit; —طبيعتلو, —tābi''àtli, Of a mean, low, base disposition.

الچى ālchi, *s. t.* Plaster of Paris.

الحاح ìlhāh, *s. a.* A soliciting with importunity.

الحاد ìlhād, *s. a.* A departing from the true doctrine in religion; heresy.

الحاصل èl-hāssil, *ad. a.* In fine, in short, to sum up all.

الحاق ìlhāk, *s. a.* The adjoining one thing to another; ا—, —et, *v.a.* To adjoin, annex.

الحال èl-hāl, *ad. a.* Now, at the present time; فى الحال fi-'l-hāl, At once, immediately; الحالةهذه èl-hālétu-hāzihi, *ad. a.* Now, at present.

الحق èl-hākk, *ad. a.* In sooth, in truth, truly, verily.

الداتمق āldatmak (*aor.* الدادر āldàdir), *v.n.* To deceive; to cheat; to disappoint.

الدانمق aldanmak (*aor.* الدانور aldànir), *v.n.* To be deceived; to make a mistake.

الدوان èldivèn, *s. t.* A glove.

الزام ìlzām, *s. a.* A convincing; ا—, —et, *v.a.* To convince.

الزام èlzèm, *a. a.* More, most, or very necessary.

السنه èlsiné, *s. pl. a.* (*of* لسان lìssān), Tongues, languages; السنه شرقيه اشنا èlsiné-shàrkìyyé-āshinā, An Orientalist.

الش alish, *s. t.* A taking; a mode of taking; —ويرش, —vèrish, Trade, commerce.

الشمق alishmak (*aor.* الشور alishir), *v.n.* To grow used, become accustomed; to get into a habit; to grow tame; to grow easy in action (a machine).

الغا ìlghā, *s. a.* An abolishing, annulling; ا—, —et, *v.a.* To abolish, to annul.

الغار ìlghàr, *s. t.* A canter or gallop; ا—, —et, *v.n.* To go at a canter or gallop; to make an incursion or military reconnaissance on horseback.

الغرض èl-ghàraz, *ad. a.* In short, what we want to explain is this.

الف èlf, *s. a.* A thousand; —, èlif, Name of the first letter of the alphabet; the upright figure of a handsome young person.

الفت ùlfet, *s. a.* Acquaintanceship, a knowledge of; ا—, —et, *v.n.* To become acquainted; to cultivate one's friendship; to become accustomed (to a thing).

الفته ālùfté, *a. p.* Beside one's self; miserable.

القا ìlkā, *s. a.* A throwing, casting out of the hand before one, a merely dropping a thing without projecting it to a distance; ا—, —et, *v.a.* To cast, throw, drop; to impute, cast upon.

القشلمق alkishlamak (*aor.* القشلار alkishlar), *v.a.* To greet with applause.

القصه èl-kìssa, *ad. a.* In fine, in short; the fact of the matter is this.

الك èlek, *s. t.* A sieve; —, ìlk, *a. t.* First; الك بهار ìlk-bàhār, Spring, early spring; الك ابتدا ìlk-ìptidā, First and foremost, first of all, in the first place; الكين ìlkin, *ad. t.* First and before doing anything else; —, ìlik, *s. t.* Marrow; a loop for a button to pass into; an eye for a hook to pass into.

الكا ùlkyā (ùlké), *s. t.* Country, territory, land.

الكلمك ìliklémek (*aor.* الكلر ìlikler), *v.a.* To button; to hook; to fasten with hooks or buttons.

اللمك èllémek (*aor.* اللر èller), *v.a.* To touch, finger, handle; to turn out of doors.

الله allāh, *s. a.* God; —كريم, —kèrīm! God is beneficent, never mind! ماشاالله mā-shā-'llāh! Well! Wonderful! (*lit.* What things God wills!) ان شاالله ìn-shā-'llāh! God willing! If God so wills! Let us hope so! اللهى سورسك allāhi-sèvèrsen! If you love God! For God's sake! —راضى اوله, —rāzi-

-òla! May God be satisfied (and reward you)! مقلاسون—, —sàklassin! كوسترمسون—, —ghyùsstɪrmassin! God forbid! May God preserve us! ويره—, —vèré (or ويرسون vèrsin)! God grant it! اللهه‌اصمارلدق ɪllāha-ìssmàrladik! Good bye! we commend you to God! والله wɪ-'llāhi! بالله bì-'llāhi! تالله tɪ-'llāhi! By God! (These three expressions are used, either the first alone and most frequently, or with the second after it pretty commonly, or with the third following them as a very solemn oath). اللهالله ɪllɪh-ɪllɪh! (O God! O God!) Wonderful! What a shame! What a pity! What's all this!

اللى èlli, *a. t.* Fifty; اللنجى èllinji, Fiftieth; اللیشر èllishèr, Fifty a-piece.

الم ɪlim, *s. t.* A taking, a buying; the quantity taken at once; كوزالمى ghyùz-ɪlimi, The space the eye can take in; صاتم—, —sɪtim, Purchase and sale, transfer; —, èlem, *s. a.* Pain, suffering; grief, anguish.

الما ɪ̀lma, *s. t.* An apple; قزل— kìzil—, Rome; صویى— —sùyu, Cider.

الماس ɪ̀lmɪss, *s. a.* A diamond; a rose diamond.

المق ɪlmak (*aor.* الور ɪlir), *v.a.* To take; to receive; to buy; to hold, contain, take; —, *v.n.* To take, catch (a fire); to take fire, to go off (fire-arms); نفس—, nèfess—, *v.n.* To breathe; to take breath; to have a hole whence air or water escapes (any vessel, pipe, or reservoir that should be air-tight).

الملك ìlmek, *s. t.* A noose, slip-knot.

الن ɪlin, *s. t.* The forehead.

الود ālūd (*in composition*), الوده ālūdé, (*in composition or alone*), *a. p.* Soiled, polluted, stained, smeared over.

الوهیت ùlūhìyyèt, *s. a.* Godhead, the quality of being God, divinity.

الويه èlviyé, *s. pl. a.* (*of* لوا lìwā), Flags, standards; provinces.

آله ìlāh, *s. a.* A god; God; الهى ìlāhī, *a. a.* Divine, godly; —, *s. a.* A hymn, anthem, carol; الهیت ìlāhìyyèt, *s. a.* The quality of being divine.

الهام ìlhām, *s. a.* (God's) inspiring or revealing (divine truths to his prophets); ا—, —et, *v.a.* To inspire into the mind, to reveal.

الهجق ɪlajak, *fut. pass. part.* (*of* المق ɪlmak), Anything which is to be taken or received; a debt receivable; الهجقلو ɪlajakli, A creditor, one who has debts to receive.

الهمك èlémek (*aor.* الر èlɪr, *v.a.* To sift, pass through a sieve; الهمه èlémé, Anything which has been sifted and freed from dust or broken parts.

الى ìlà, *p. a.* (ilé before the definite article ال), To, towards (*used in Turkish adverbial expression*), ماشا— الله, —mā-shā-'llāh, To *or* until (the time) which God wills; —اخره, —ākhirihi, To the end, and so forth, &c.; الى الابد ìlé-'l-èbed, To all eternity.

اليقومق Alìkòmak (*aor.* اليقور Alìkor), *v.a.* To keep, retain, detain, stop.

اليم èlīm, *a. a.* Painful. [present day.

اليوم èl-yèvm, *ad. a.* Now, at the

اليويرمك Alìvèrmek (*aor.* اليويرر Alìvèrir), *v.a.* To take, reach, or obtain, and then hand or give to another.

ام Am, *s. t.* The female organ of generation; —, ùmm, *s. a.* A mother; ام الولد ùmmu-'l-vèled, A slave who has borne an acknowledged child to her owner.

اما àmmā, *c. a.* But.

اماثل èmāssil, *s. pl. a.* (*of* امثل, *not used*), Equals, persons of like rank.

اماده āmādé, *a. p.* Ready, prepared.

امارت ìmārèt, *s. a.* Commandership, chieftainship.

اماره èmāré, *s. a.* Sign, trace; sign, signal, indication; —, èmmāré, *a. a.* (*fem. of* امار èmmār, *not used*), Which commands and will be obeyed; —نفس nèfsi— (the commanding spirit), the uncontrolled passions, (one of the three states of the passions in Mussulman ethics, the two others being نفس لوامه nèfsi-lèvwāmé (the reproaching spirit), when the passions are controlled, but still struggle for mastery, and نفس مطمئنه nèfsi-mùt-ma''ìnné, (the resigned spirit), when the passions are completely subdued).

اماله ìmālé, *s. a.* A causing to incline; —ا, —et, *v.a.* To cause to incline; to turn, to bend.

امام ìmām, *s. a.* A chief, leader; a leader in the ritual performance of prayer; امامت ìmāmèt, *s. a.* امامليق ìmāmlìk, *s. t.* The office of imam.

امامه ìmāmé, *s. a.* The longish and somewhat pear-shaped ornament at the end of the tassel of prayer-beads; the similarly shaped, but much larger, mouthpiece of a smoking-pipe.

امان èmān, *s. a.* Safety, security; safe-conduct, protection; quarter, mercy; —, Amān! *int. a.* Oh! O dear me! Mercy!

امانت èmānèt, *s. a.* Anything placed in trust, either to be returned to the giver, or to be given to a third party; an office of trust under government, and conducted on government account, not on farm; اللهه امانت اوله Allāha-èmānet-òla (Allā'mānet-òla), Thank you! (used when anyone wishes us health after we drink or have been shaved, by saying عافيت اوله "āfiy-yèt-òla, *or* صحتلر اوله sìhhàtlar-òla; it means literally, *may that* (or *may you*) *be left in trust with God's providence*), امانتدار èmānetdār, *s. p.* One who holds something in trust.

امت ùmmèt, *s. a.* The church, the whole body of the followers of a religion; —محمد, ùmmèti-Mùhàmmed, The Muhammedan Church;

—عیسی, ùmmèti-‘‘Īssà, The Church of Jesus; —ناجیه, ùmmèti-nājìyyé, The body of those who will be saved (from hell).

امتثال ìmtissāl, *s. a.* A conforming to, obeying, following, imitating; ا—, —et, *v.n.* To conform.

امتحان ìmtihān, *s. a.* A trying, putting to the proof; examination; ا—, —et, *v.n.* To prove, try; to examine (scholastically); —او, —òl, To submit to a formal examination; بری‌ایله —او bìri-ìla —òl, *v.n.* To be examined competitively with another. [(in time).

امتداد ìmtidād, *s. a.* Duration; length

امتزاج ìmtizāj, *s. a.* A combining or agreeing with; ا—, —et, *v.n.* To agree well (with anyone), get on well together. [Goods, merchandise.

امتعه èmti‘‘à, *s. pl. a.* (*of* متاع màtā‘‘),

امتلا ìmtilā, *s. a.* Indigestion, oppression of the stomach.

امتناع ìmtinā‘‘, *s. a.* A refusing, drawing back; ا—, —et, *v.n.* To draw one's self back and refuse.

امتنان ìmtinān, *s. a.* A taunting one with the favours you have done him; the being under obligations for a favour; ا—, —et, *v.n.* To taunt one with favours bestowed. [vilege.

امتیاز ìmtiyāz, *s. a.* Distinction; pri-

امثال èmsāl, *s. pl. a.* (*of* مثل mìssl), Similar things; precedents; (*as a Turkish singular*) a precedent; ضروب امثال zūrubu-èmsāl, Proverbs, proverbial expressions; امثال‌کثیره‌سنی میسرایلیه èmsāli - kèssīréssini - mùyèssɛr-èyléyé, May (God) grant (you) many such (happinesses)! *equivalent to our* Many happy returns of the day! *and used on any occasion of rejoicing.*

امد āmed, *s. p.* Coming, arrival; امدی āmédī, *s. p.* امدجی āmedj*i*, *s. t.* The title of one of the higher functionaries of the Turkish government; to him are delivered all papers and reports *coming* from the provinces and departments, which are to be submitted to the grand vizier and sultan; —شد, —shùd, Coming and going; ا— —, — —et, *v.n.* To come and go, backwards and forwards; —, èmed, *s. a.* Space of time.

امداد ìmdād, *s. a.* Assistance, helping, succouring; ا—, —et, *v.a.* To give assistance.

امدی ìmdi, *c. t.* Now, then, therefore; wherefore, —, āmédī (*see* امد āmed).

امدیه āmédìyyé, *s. t.* Import duty on merchandise.

امر āmir, *s. a.* A commander, one who commands, the competent authority; امرانه āmirāné, *a. p.* Suitable or proper for a commander; imperative; —, èmr (èmir) *s. a.* A command, order, injunction; a matter, affair, business; من‌له‌الامر mèn-làhū-'l-èmr, He to whom the right of commanding belongs, *i.e.* the competent authority; *also, by implication,* you yourself;

امرعالى èmri-"ālī, The supreme command, a firman, imperial rescript or edict; يول امرى yòl-èmri, A passport or order for post-horses; امرسزك èmir-sìzing, It is for you to say, to order, to command; امرنامه èmir-nāmé, Any letter received from a superior; ا—, —et, v.a. To order, command (a thing to be done): *it is intransitive as to the person to whom the order is addressed;* بكاامرايتدى he commanded it *to me*.

امرا ùmérā, *s. pl. a.* (*of* امير èmīr), Commanders, lords, officers.

امرار ìmrār, *s. a.* A causing to pass, through, by, over, &c.; ا—, —et, *v.a.* To cause to pass; امرار وقت ا ìmrāri-wàkt-et, To procrastinate, lose time, [gain time.

امروز ìmrūz, *s. p.* To-day.

امزرمك èmzirmek (*aor.* امزيرر èmzirir), *v.a.* To suckle, give suck to.

امزك èmzik, *s. t.* The spout of a vessel.

امزه مك èmzémek (*aor.* امزر èmzer), *v.a.* To suck (as a lozenge, &c.).

امساك ìmsāk, *s. a.* An abstaining; a restraining one's self; economy, parsimony, avarice; the putting away food and entering on a fast; ا—, —et, *v.n.* To enter on a fast by putting away food; to practise abstinence, to restrain one's self.

امضا ìmzā, *s. a.* The signing a paper; a signature; ا—, —et, *v.a.* To sign, زيرده واضع الامضا zīrda-wāzi"u-'l-ìmzā, The undersigned.

امعان ìm"ān, *s. a.* The regarding very attentively, giving great attention.

امك èmek, *s. t.* Labour, pains, trouble, work; امكدار èmekdār, An old servant; — صرف ا —, — sarf-et, To bestow labour, take pains.

امكان ìmkyān, *s. a.* Possibility, the being possible; امكانى وارمى ìmkyāni-vàr-mi? Does the (its) possibility exist? Is there a possibility?

امل èmel, *s. a.* A desire, wish (to obtain); ا—, —et, *v.a.* To covet, desire, wish for, seek after.

املا ìmlā, *s. a.* A writing, penning; spelling, orthography; ا—, —et, *v.a.* To write.

املاك èmlāk, *s. pl. a.* (*of* ملك mùlk), Lands; freehold properties.

امم ùmèm, *s. pl. a.* (*of* امت ùmmèt), Churches, religious aggregations of mankind. [suck, draw by suction.

اممك èmmek (*aor.* امر èmer), *v.a.* To

امن ùmn, *s. a.* Safety, security.

امنيت èmnìyyèt, *s. a.* Safety, security, confidence.

امنيه ùmnìyyé, *s. a.* Hope, wish, desire.

اموات èmvāt, *s. pl. a.* (*of* ميت mèyyit), The dead. [Waves.

امواج èmvāj, *s. pl. a.* (*of* موج mèvj),

اموال èmwāl, *s. pl. a.* (*of* مال māl), Possessions, properties, goods.

امواه èmvāh, *s. pl. a.* (*of* ما mā), Waters.

امور ùmūr, *s. pl. a.* (*of* امر èmr), Affairs, matters, businesses; (*as a Turkish singular*) an affair of importance; ا—,

—et, *v.n.* To make a fuss, as though it were an affair of importance; امورمده دكل ùmūrumda-dìghil, I don't care a fig about it.

امهال ìmhāl, *s. a.* A putting off for a term, deferring; granting a delay; ا—, —et, *v.a.* To put off, defer; to grant a delay.

اميد ùmīd (ùmut), Hope; ا—, —et, *v.a.* To hope for, expect, build upon; —ويرمك, —vèrmek, To give some hope; —كسمك, —kèssmek, *and* قطع اميد ا kat'i-ùmīd-et, To give up all hope, to despair; اميدوار ùmīdvār, *a. p.* Hopeful, hoping still, in expectation. [Cape of Good Hope.

اميد بورونى ùmīd-būrunu, *s. t.* The

امير èmīr, *s. a.* A commander; a prince, chief, chieftain; a descendant of Muhammed. [with, containing.

اميز āmīz, *a. p.* (*in composition*), Mixed

امين āmīn! *int. a.* Amen! —, èmīn, *a. a.* Sure, safe, secure; (a man) who may be trusted, honest, upright; —, *s. a.* A high civil functionary, having charge of government property, a superintendant; الاى امينى Alay-èmīni, A military officer of the new regular army, ranking next to the lieutenant-colonel, who had charge of the stores and accounts of the regiment; the title and rank are now abolished; ترسانه امينى tèrsānè-èmini, The (former) superintendant of the imperial dockyard at Constantinople.

ان ān, *s. a.* Time; a moment, instant; الان èl-ān, *ad. a.* Now, at present; الى الان ìlé-'l-ān, *ad. a.* Until the present time, hitherto; من الان mìn-el-ān, *ad. a.* Henceforward, henceforth; انيده ānida, *ad. t.* Instantly, in an instant, immediately; —, *s. p.* Beauty, grace, gracefulness; —, ān, *pron. p.* That; اين وان īn-u-ān, This and that; this world and the world of spirits *or* the world to come; all things; —, èn, *s. t.* Width, breadth; —, ìn, *c. a.* If; ان شا الله ìn-shā-'llāh! If God wills it!

انا àna, *s. t.* A mother; the principal or chief kind or part of some things; انا ديرك àna-dìrèk, A *lower* mast; انا لغم àna-làghim, A *main* drain or sewer; دميرك اناسى قيرلدى dèmiring-ànassi-kìrìldi, The *shank* of the anchor has broken; بيوك انا bìyuk-àna, A grandmother; اويكى انا ùwèghi-àna, A stepmother; قاين انا kàyn-àna, A mother-in-law, the mother of one's wife; انا بابا كونى àna-bàba-ghyùnu, An uproar.

انابت ìnābet, *s. a.* A repenting, repentance; ا—, —et, *v.n.* To repent, to feel repentance for sin.

اناث ìnāss, *s. pl. a.* (*of* انثى, *not used*), Women, womankind.

اناختار ànakhtàr, *s. t.* A key.

انار ènār (nār), *s. p.* A pomegranate.

اناس ùnāss, *s. pl. a.* (*of* انسان ìnsān), Men, mankind.

اناطولی Anadoli, *s. t.* Asia Minor.

انافور ànafòr, *s. t.* (*Greek*), A counter-current, up-current in bays, &c., near the shore.

انام ènām, *s. a.* Mankind.

اانمق ìnanmak (*aor.* انانور ìnànır), *v.a.* To believe (an assertion); —, *v.n.* To believe in, to believe (anything other than an assertion).

انانیت ènānìyyèt, *s. a.* Egotism.

انبا ìnbā, *s. a.* The communicating intelligence; ا—, —et, *v.a.* To communicate.

انبار ànbar, *s. t.* A granary, storehouse, room, or chest; a gun-deck in a man-of-war; the hold of a ship; اوچ‌انبارلو ùch-ànbarlı, A three-decker.

انباز āmbāz, *s. p.* A companion, partner.

انبساط ìnbissāt, *s. a.* An unfolding, opening itself out; —خاطر, ìnbissātı-khātır, Pleasure, an opening out of the heart. [copious, large.

انبوه ènbūh, *a. p.* Numerous, bountiful,

انبیا ènbiyā, *s. pl. a.* (*of* نبی nèbī), The prophets. [alembic.

انبیق ìnbīk, *s. a.* A still, a retort, an

انتاج ìntāj, *s. a.* The producing as a consequence, a causing; ا—, —et, *v.a.* To produce, cause.

انتباه ìntibāh, *s. a.* The being on one's guard, vigilance, circumspection.

انتخاب ìntıkhāb, *s. a.* A choosing, selecting, electing; ا—, —et, *v.a.* To choose, select, elect.

انتزاع ìntizā'', *s. a.* A plucking out or off; ا—, —et, *v.a.* To pluck out or off.

انتساب ìntissab, *s. a.* A being related to, in relations with.

انتظار ìntizār, *s. a.* A waiting for, waiting in expectation; الانتظاراشدمن‌النار èl-ìntizārυ-èshèddun-mìn-en-nār, Expectancy is worse than fire (*Arabic proverb*).

انتظام ìntizām, *s. a.* The being ranged in order; order, regularity.

انتفاع ìntifā'', *s. a.* The being benefited, deriving a profit or advantage; ا—, —et, *v.a.* To derive, gain; —, *v.n.* To reap a benefit, derive a profit, gain an advantage.

انتقال ìntikāl, *s. a.* The changing one's place or residence; the passing from this life to the future state; the passing from in thought, and comprehending, one subject after another; ا—, —et, *v.n.* To pass from one place to another; from one subject to another, mentally, and so to comprehend fully; from this life; —داربقا, ìntikālı-dāri-bākā-et, *v.n.* To die; سریع‌الانتقال sèrī''υ-'l-ìntikāl, *a. a.* Quick in comprehending subjects.

انتقام ìntikām, *s. a.* Vengeance, revenge; —المق, —àlmak, *v.n.* To take vengeance, to take revenge, to avenge one's self.

انتما ìntimā, *s. a.* The being connected, or having a relation with, a growing out of.

انتها ìntihā, *s. a.* The coming to an end, finishing; a reaching to, terminating at.

انتهاز ìntihāz, *s. a.* The taking or seizing (an opportunity); ا—, —et, *v.a.* To take, seize (an opportunity).

انجاز ìnjāz, *s. a.* The fulfilment (of a promise); ا—, —et, *v.a.* To fulfil, perform (a promise).

انجام ènjām, *s. p.* The end, upshot, conclusion; انجامپذير ènjām-pèzīr, *a. p.* Ending, being finished, coming to an end.

انجق ànjak, *ad. t.* Only, just, hardly; —, *c. t.* But, however, still.

انجك ìnjik, *s. t.* The bone of the leg below the knee (in men) or the hough (in animals); the instep of the foot.

انجم ènjum, *s. pl. a.* (*of* نجم nèjm), Stars.

انجماد ìnjimād, *s. a.* The becoming congealed, frozen, solid.

انجمن ènjumèn, *s. p.* An assembly, society; —دانش, ènjumèni-dānish, The Scientific Institution of Constantinople.

انجير ìnjir, *s. t.* A fig; قورو انجير kūru-ìnjir, A dried fig; قوطی انجيری kūtu-ìnjiri, Figs in drums or boxes; الدمه انجيری èlémé-ìnjiri, Picked figs (this very likely should be اللمه èllémé, *picked by hand*); انجيردلن ìnjir-dèlen, The becafico.

انجيل ìnjīl, *s. a.* The gospel, the book of the gospel.

انحراف ìnhirāf, *s. a.* A turning away, swerving; —خاطر, ìnhirāfi-khātir, An unfriendly or unpleasant state of mind; —مزاج, ìnhirāfi-mìzāj, An ailment, indisposition in health; —ابره, ìnhirāfi-ìbré, —پوصله, ìnhirāfi-pūssla, The variation of the compass.

انحصار ìnhissār, *s. a.* A being surrounded, bounded, restricted (in action, number, &c.); monopoly.

انحطاط inhitāt, *s. a.* A descending from on high; —ابره, ìnhitāti-ìbré, The dip of the magnetic needle; —افق, ìnhitāti-ūfuk, The dip of the horizon.

انحنا ìnhinā, *s. a.* A being bent, deflected, curved.

انختار ànakhtàr, *s. t.* A key.

اند ànd, *s. t.* An oath; —ایچمك, ànd-ìchmek, *v.n.* To take an oath.

انداخت èndākht, *s. p.* A casting, throwing, projecting; a firing (of guns); ا—, —et, *v.a.* To cast, throw, project; to fire (a gun).

انداخته èndākhté, *a. p.* Cast, thrown, projected; fired (a gun).

انداز èndāz, *a. p.* (*in composition*), Which throws, casts, projects; who fires (a gun); لنكرانداز lèngher-èndāz, *a. p.* At anchor, anchored.

اندازه èndāzé, *s. p.* Measure (in general); بی— bī—, beyond measure; —, *s. t.* A Turkish ell of 26 English inches, used for measuring linens, silks, &c.

اندام èndām, *s. p.* Stature, figure, form; symmetry of shape, proportion.

اندرون èndérun, *s. p.* The inside; the

inner, private, or women's apartments; —همایون, èndérūnu-hùmāyun, The more private apartments of the Sultan's court; —اغالری, èndérūn-àghalari, The superior attendants attached to the more private apartments of the Sultan's court.

اندفاع ìndifā'', s. a. The being repelled, expelled, repulsed.

اندود èndūd, a. p. (*in composition*), Covered, plated, or plastered over with.

اندوه èndūh, s. p. Grief, affliction, sadness.

اندیش èndīsh, a. p. (*in composition*), Who thinks.

اندیشه èndīshé, s. p. Thought, care, anxiety.

انزال ìnzāl, s. a. A causing to descend, sending down; emission of seed (*in coitu*); ا—, —et, v.a. To cause to descend; ا—, —et, v.n. To emit seed (*in coitu*).

انزوا ìnziwā, s. a. A going into retirement; retirement.

انس ìnss, s. a. Mankind, the human species; a man, a creature of the human species.

انساب ènsāb, s. pl. a. (*of* نسب nèsseb), Relatives, kindred; (*of* نسبت nìssbèt) logarithms, proportional numbers.

انسان ìnsān, s. a. A man, a human being; —العین, ìnsānu-'l-''àyn, The pupil of the eye; انسانی ìnsānī, a. a. Human; انسانیت ìnsānìyyèt, s. a. Humanity; انسانیتسز ìnsānìyyètsiz, a. t. Inhuman, brutal.

انسز ānsiz, انسزین ānsizin, اپ‌انسزین àp-ānsizin, ad. t. Suddenly, all on a sudden; —, ànsiz, ad. t. Without that; —, ènsiz, a. t. Narrow.

انسیت ùnsìyyèt, s. a. More or less intimate acquaintanceship; ا—, —et, v.n. To be more or less intimately acquainted with (any one).

انشا ìnshā, s. a. A making; a building, constructing, erecting; the art of epistolary or literary composition; ا—, —et, v.a. To make, build, construct, erect.

ان‌شاالله ìn - shā -'llāh, int. a. God willing! If God wills it! Let us hope so!

انشته ènishta, s. t. A brother-in-law, husband of one's sister.

انشراح ìnshirāh, s. a. A being open, expanded; joy, pleasure.

انصار ànsār, s. pl. a. (*of* ناصر nāssir, *not used in this sense*), Helpers, viz. those inhabitants of Medina who joined Muhammed's standard, and *assisted* him in his struggles until the conquest of Mecca.

انصاف ìnsāf, s. a. Conscience, a sense of justice; ا—, —et, v.n. To have a conscience, to act with consideration and a sense of justice.

انصراف ìnsirāf, s. a. A turning aside from the road; a desisting from continuing to advance; a turning back; ا—, —et, v.n. To desist form advancing straight on, to turn on one side or back.

انضمام ìnzimām, *s. a.* A being added, appended, affixed; —رأى, ìnzimāmi-rè'y, The addition of some one's approval or favourable opinion.

انطفا ìntifā, *s. a.* The being extinguished, being put *or* going out.

انعام èn''ām, *s. pl. a.* (*of* نعمت nì''met), Favours, benefits, graces; —, ìn''ām, *s. a.* The bestowing (a gift, a favour); a gift (from a superior); ا—, —et, *v.a.* To bestow, give (a superior to an inferior).

انعطاف ìn''itāf, *s. a.* A being turned aside, deflected.

انعقاد ìn''ikād, *s. a.* The becoming tied or bound (a knot, a contract).

انغاريه ànghārìyyé, *s. t.* Any work which brings in no return, forced labour.

انف ènf, *s. a.* The nose; رغماًلانفه ràghman-lì-ènfihi, *ad. a.* In spite of him, in order to vex and mortify him (*lit.* so as to strip the skin off his nose), —, ānif, *a. a.* Going before, preceding (*in* انف الذكر ānifu-'z-zìkr, *a. a.* the afore-mentioned); انفا ānifā, *ad. a.* Before, above.

انفاذ ìnfāz, *s. a.* A causing an order to have weight, to be respected, to be put in execution; ا—, —et, *v.a.* To cause to be executed, respected, or put in force.

انفراد ìnfirād, *s. a.* The being single, alone; على الانفراد ''àlé-'l-ìnfirād, By himself, &c., separately; one by one.

انفراق ìnfirāk, *s. a.* A being separated.

انفس ènfùss, *s. pl. a.* (*of* نفس nèfss), Persons; souls; —, ènfèss, *a. a.* More, most, or very exquisite.

انفصال ìnfissāl, *s. a.* The leaving an office (either by resignation, dismissal, or appointment to something else); the being judged and determined (a cause).

انفصام ìnfissām, *s. a.* The being cut or broken in two (a thread, &c.).

انفعال ìnfi''āl, *s. a.* A being displeased, hurt, vexed, grieved.

انفيه ènfìyyé, *s. t.* Snuff; —قوطيسى, —kùtussu, A snuff-box.

انقباض ìnkibāz, *s. a.* A being seized, laid hold of; costiveness.

انقراض ìnkirāz, *s. a.* The being cut off; coming to an end, totally failing (in succession.)

انقسام ìnkissām, *s. a.* The being divided into parts, division.

انقضا ìnkizā, *s. a.* The coming to an end, being terminated.

انقطاع ìnkitā'', *s. a.* The being cut off, the being interrupted, discontinued.

انقلاب ìnkilāb, *s. a.* A being reversed; a reverse, a change in circumstances.

انقياد ìnkiyād, *s. a.* Obedience, submission; ا—, —et, *v.n.* To yield obedience, to submit.

انكار ìnkyār, *s. a.* A denial, negation; ا—, —et, *v.a.* To deny.

انكبين ènghyubīn, *s. p.* Honey.

انكرك ènghérek, *s. t.* A viper.

انكسار ìnkissār, *s. a.* A being broken, smashed to pieces; a being put out of all temper; a cursing; ا—, —et, *v.n.* To be heart-broken and to curse in consequence.

انكسر ènksɛr, *s. t.* A nail (for nailing).

انكشاف ìnkishāf, *s. a.* A clearing up, brightening up.

انكشت ènghyùsht, *s. p.* A finger.

انكشتر ènghyushtɛr, *s. p.* A finger-ring.

انكل ènghèl, *s. t.* A rival.

انكلتره Inghilterra, *s. t.* England.

انكليز Inghliz, *a. t.* English; —, *s. t.* An Englishman.

انكور ènghyūr, *s. p.* A grape, grapes.

انكيز ènghīz, *a. p.* (*in composition*), Which excites, raises.

انكين ènghin, *s. t.* The open sea, far from shore.

انمك ènmek (*aor.* انر ènɛr), *v.n.* To descend, come *or* go down; to subside; to flow downwards (as humours are supposed to do in some diseases).

انها ìnhā, *s. a.* A reporting, communicating; ا—, —et, *v.a.* To report, communicate.

انهدام ìnhidām, *s. a.* A being demolished, falling *or* being pulled down.

انهزام ìnhizām, *s. a.* A being routed, defeated; defeat.

انهماك ìnhimāk, *s. a.* Diligent application, setting heart and soul about a thing.

انيس ènīss, *s. a.* A familiar and intimate friend.

انيق ènīk, *a. a.* Graceful, elegant, beautiful.

انى‌قونى èni-kònʊ, *ad. t.* In detail and at leisure.

انين ènīn, *s. p.* A moan.

او ò (*or* اول òl), *pron. t.* He, she, it; that; —, èv, *s. t.* A house; —, ʌv, *s. t.* The chase, field sport of any kind, as hunting, shooting, fishing, &c.; game; اوبارق èv-bàrk, *s. t.* House and household; wife, children, and attendants; اوصاحبى èv-sāhibi, The master of the house; a house-keeper, householder; او اوشاقلرى èv-ʊshʌklari, The family, the wife and attendants, or wife, children, and attendants; اولو èvli, *a. t.* Married, having a wife; اولولك èvlilik, *s. t.* The married state.

اواخر èwākhir, *s. pl. a.* (*of* آخر akhir), The last (decade or ten) days of a month.

اوادانلق àwadànlik, *s. t.* A workman's set of tools.

اواره āwārɛ́, *a. p.* Vagabond, errant.

اواز āwāz, اوازه āwāzɛ́, *s. p.* A voice, sound; rumour, fame.

اواسط àwāssit, *s. pl. a.* (*of* اوسط èvsāt, *not used in this sense*), The middle (decade or ten) days of a month.

اوامر èwāmir, *s. pl. a.* (*of* امر emr), Commands.

اوان āwān, *s. pl. a.* (*of* ان ān), Moments, instants, times.

اوانى èwāni, *s. pl. a.* (*of* انا ina, *rarely used*), Vases, vessels.

اوائل àwā'il, *s. pl. a.* (*of* اول ɛvvɛl), The first (decade or ten) days of a month.

اوبا òba, *s. t.* A tartar tent or hut.

اوباش èvbāsh, *s. pl. a.* (*of* وبش, *not used*), Low fellows, rascals.

اوپمك ùpmek (*aor.* اوپر ùpER), *v.a.* To kiss.

اوت òt, *s. t.* Grass; a herb: قورواوت kùrυ-òt, Hay, dry grass; —, èvet, *ad. t.* Yes.

اوتارمق òtarmak (*aor.* اوتارر òtarir), To lead to pasture (provincial). [tent.

اوتاغ òtāgh, اوتاق òtāk, *s. t.* A large

اوتانغج ùtànghàch *a. t.* Modest, timid, bashful.

اوتانمق ùtànmak (*aor.* اوتانور ùtànir), *v.n.* To be ashamed, abashed.

اوتری ùturu, *ad. s.* Concerning, about, on the subject, on account of; name of the vowel point ـُ.

اوتلاق òtlàk, *s. t.* Pasture; —یری, —yèri, A place of pasture, a pasturage, pasture-ground.

اوتلامق òtlamak (*aor.* اوتلار òtlar), *v.n.* To graze, pasture.

اوتلق òtlυk, *s. t.* Grass; a place abounding in grass, or from whence grass or hay is procured.

اوتمك ùtmek (*aor.* اوتر ùtER), *v.n.* To sound, to echo, to ring; to sing (birds).

اوتوری ùturu, *s. t.* The vowel-point ـُ, corresponding to o, u, υ, or *u*.

اوتوز òtυz, *a. t.* Thirty.

اوته ùtÉ, *s. t.* The space beyond or farther off; —, *ad. t.* far off, farther off; —برو, —bèri, Hither and thither; —برى‌ا, —beri-et, *or* اوته برى‌ا ùtÉ-bèri-et, *v.n.* To try all manner of ways; اوته‌دن برو ùtÉden-bèri, Always, ever.

اوتى ùtu, *s. t.* An iron for ironing, a tailor's goose.

اوتلمك ùtulémek, (*aor.* اوتيلر ùtulER), *v.a.* To iron, to press with a hot iron.

اوج àwυj, *s. t.* The palm of the hand; the inside of the hand held so as to contain anything; a handful; —طولوسى, —dòlυssυ, a handful; —, ùj, *s. t.* Revenge, vengeance; —, ūj, *s. t.* The end, extremity; —, èvj, *s. a.* The highest pinnacle; the perigee, or perihelion.

اوجاق òjak, *s. t.* A fireplace, hearth; a chimney; a family; a dynasty; a corps, and especially *the Corps of Janissaries;* a colony, and especially the *Colonies* (or *regencies*) *of Tripoli, Tunis, and Algiers;* اوجاغمز سونمسون òjaghimiz-sùnmassin, May our hearth (family *or* corps) never be extinguished!

اوجوز ùjùz, *a. t.* Cheap, low-priced.

اوچ ùch, *a. t.* Three. [lips.

اوچق ùchυk, *s. t.* A pimple on the

اوچقور ùchkυr, *s. t.* The string or riband with which drawers or trousers are fastened round the waist like the mouth of a bag; اوچقورلق ùchkυr-lυk, the waistband or broad hem through which the string passes all round so as to tie drawers or trousers about the body.

اوچمق ŭchmak (*aor.* اوچار ŭchar), *v.n.* To fly; to fall down (a precipice, &c.), be precipitated.

اوچوروم ŭchurum, *s. t.* A precipice; —, *a. t.* Precipitous, like a precipice.

اوچیوز ŭchyuz, *a. t.* Three hundred.

اوخ ŏkh! *int. t.* Oh! I am glad of it! I am delighted!

اوخشامق ŏkhshamak (*aor.* اوخشار ŏkhshar), *v.a.* To caress, stroke, pat.

اود ŭd, *s. t.* The gall, the gall-bladder; اودى قوپمق ŭdu-kŏpmak, *v.n.* (Anyone's) gall-bladder to burst (through fear), to have any great or sudden fright; —, (ŏt), *s. t.* (*almost obsolete itself*), Fire; poison; a depilatory mixture used in baths; اغزاودى ăghz-ŏtu, the priming of a gun; اوديرلرى (ot)-yĕrlĕri, those parts of the body which require the application of depilatory substances; اودلوبغه ŏtlu-băgha (the poisonous batrachian), the toad.

اودنج ŭdunj, *s. t.* Money which has to be repaid, borrowed money.

اوده‌مك ŭdémek (*aor.* اودر ŭder), *v.a.* To pay (a debt).

اور āvĕr, *a. p.* (*in composition*), Which brings; which possesses; —, ūr, *s. t.* A wen.

اورا ŏra, *s. t.* That place, that spot; اورام ŏram (my that place) there, that part of my body; اوراك ŏrang, there, that part of thy body; اوراسى (its that place) there, that part of him, her, or it, &c.; اورايه ŏraya, to that place, there; اوراده ŏrada, at that place, there; اورالره óralara, to those places, thereabouts; اورالرده ŏralarda, at those places, thereabouts.

اوراق ŏrak, *s. t.* A sickle, reaping-hook; —وقتى, —wăkti, Harvest-time.

اورپرمك ŭrpermek (*aor.* اورپرر ŭrpérir), *v.n.* To stand on end (the hairs of the head or body).

اورتاق ŏrtak, *s. t.* A partner, sharer; —او, —ŏl, *v.n.* To be a partner, *or* partners; to take part with.

اورتالق ŏrtalik, *s. t.* The general term for which we say in English "*the world,*" and meaning two different things, viz. *the inanimate world,* or *nature,* and *the public;* in the first sense they say اورتالق اغاردى ŏrtalik-ăghardi (*the world became bright*), daylight dawned (or قراردى *darkened, i.e.* the shades of evening fell on nature); and in the second, اورتالقده نه خبر وار what news is there abroad (among the public)?

اورتانجه ŏrtănja, *a. t.* The middle in age or size.

اورتمك ŭrtmek (*aor.* اورتر ŭrter), *v.a.* To cover, cover up.

اورته ŏrta, *s. t.* The middle; the midst; a regiment (of Janissaries); —, *a. t.* Of a middling degree or quality; ايلچى —, —ĕlchi, A diplomatic minister of the second class, an envoy extraordinary, or a minister plenipotentiary (though these have each their special designations). [covering.

اورتى ùrtu, *s. t.* A cover, a cloth for

اورد āvèrd, *s. p.* Battle, fight, combat; —, àwurd, *s. t.* The inner or lower part of the cheek, used as a bag by monkeys; the jowl.

اوردك ùrdek, *s. t.* A duck; a urinal.

اورده āvèrdé, *a. p.* Brought; related, narrated; carried away.

اورس ùrss, *s. t.* An anvil.

اورسه‌لمك ùrsélémek (*aor.* اورسه‌لر ùrsélir), *v.a.* To handle roughly and rumple; to treat roughly.

اورصه òrsa, *s. t.* (*Italian*), A going near the wind; luffing; —, *int.* Luff! ا—, —et, *v.n.* To luff; —كتمك, —ghìtmek, *v.n.* To be on a wind, to go on a wind; اورصه‌الابانده òrsa-àlabànda! Down with the helm! Helm's a-lee! ا— —, — —et, *v.n.* To put the helm hard a-lee; to tack, to go about. [camel's back.

اوركج ùrghyuj, *s. t.* The hump on a

اوركك ùrkek, *a. t.* Shying, which shies (a horse).

اوركمك ùrkmek (*aor.* اوركر ùrker), *v.n.* To shy, to be frightened, to take fright.

اوركه ùréké, *s. t.* A distaff.

اورمان òrmān, *s. t.* A wood, forest.

اورمجك ùrumjèk, *s. t.* A spider.

اورمق (wùrmak) (*aor.* اورر wùrur), *v.n.* To strike, beat, knock, hit, rap; —, *v.a.* To pop (anything) into its place; to attack and pillage (a town, &c.) to take (an adverse piece at chess, &c.); —ال èl—, *v.n.* To put a hand (to work), to take in hand, to set to work upon; —باش bàsh—, *v.n.* To apply to, have recourse to for assistance, &c.; to pitch (a ship, boat, &c.); بويوننى— bòyununu—, To decapitate (a person); —يوزينه yùzuna—, To taunt with, reproach with, cast in one's teeth; —طيشارى dìshàri—, *v.n.* To come out, make its appearance on the surface (an eruption, &c.); بريولدن— bìr-yòldan—, *v.n.* To strike into, to take a road; —بويا bòya—, *v.n.* To paint with paint; —اير èyer—, *v.n.* To put on a saddle (&c.), to saddle; —كوزه ghyùzé—, To be very conspicuous, striking; —قولاق kùlak—, *v.n.* To give ear, to listen; —تيموره (dèymira)—, *v.a.* To put in irons.

اورمك ùrmek (*aor.* اورر ùrer), *v.a.* To knit; to net; to tress, braid; to fine-draw; to build up (a wall, &c.); —, èvermek (*aor.* اورير èvérir), *v.a.* To give in marriage.

اورنك ùrnek, *s. t.* A pattern; a sample; —, èvrèngh, *s. p.* A throne.

اوروپا Urupa, *s. t.* Europe.

اوروج ùruj, *s. t.* A fasting, observation of total abstinence from earliest dawn to sunset; —طوتمق, —tùtmak, *v.n.* To fast (in that manner).

اورومك ùrumek (*aor.* اورور ùrur), *v.n.* To howl (a dog).

اوره‌مك ùrémek (*aor.* ا ، ùrer), *v.n.*

To multiply, increase in numbers (a race of animals).

اوز **ùz**, *s. t.* The heart, pith, sap, marrow, or essence of anything; قرنداشی—, —(**kàrdashi**), One's own brother (of the same father and mother); اوزلو **ùzlu**, *a. t.* Being charged with sap, unctuous and tough.

اوزاتمق **ùzàtmak** (*aor.* اوزادر **ùzàdir**), *v.a.* To stretch out *or* forth; to lengthen out; to delay, put off, procrastinate; to make many words, much ado, a fuss.

اوزادی **ùzādi**, *in* اوزون اوزادی‌یه **ùzun-ùzàdiya**, *ad.* In detail, with all details, at great length.

اوزاق **ùzàk**, *a. t.* Distant, far off; —, *s. t.* The distance, a distance off.

اوزامق **ùzamak** (*aor.* اوزار **ùzar**), *v.n.* To go away to a distance; to be long (time); to take a long time.

اوزانمق **ùzànmak** (*aor.* اوزانور **ùzānir**), *v.n.* To lie at full length, to lie down; to stretch, become longer.

اوزر **ùzer**, *s. t.* The space (*or* degree) over anything; اوزرم **ùzérim**, The space over *me*; اوزرك **ùzéring**, The space over *thee*; اوزری **ùzéri**, The space over *him, her,* or *it*; اوزریمه **ùzérima**, Over or *on to* me; اوزرمده **ùzérimda**, Over *or upon* me; اوزرلرینه **ùzerlerina**, Over *or* on to them; اوزرلرنده **ùzerlerinda**, Over *or* upon them.

اوزره **ùzéré**, *pr. t.* Upon, by, according to.

اوزلاشمق **ùzlashmak** (*aor.* اوزلاشور **ùzlashir**), *v.n.* To come to terms together.

اوزلمك **ùzulmek** (*aor.* اوزیلور **ùzulur**), *v.n.* or *p.* To be much pulled down (by grief or illness).

اوزمك **ùzmek** (*aor.* اوزر **ùzer**), *v.a.* To pull down, to render weak and feeble.

اوزنکی **ùzenghi**, *s. t.* A stirrup.

اوزنمك **ùzènmek** (*aor.* اوزنور **ùzènir**), *v.n.* To take great pains, and use one's best endeavour (over any work).

اوزوم **ùzum**, *s. t.* A grape; grapes; قورو— **kùru—**, Raisins, plums, dried grapes; قوش اوزومی **kùsh-ùzumu**, (Bird-grapes) currants (of Corinth); فرنك اوزومی **firènk-ùzumu**, (European grapes) Currants (red, white, or black); بکطاشی اوزومی **bèktāshi-ùzumu**, (from its resemblance to the striped cap worn by the Bektashi dervishes) Gooseberries.

اوزون **ùzun**, *a. t.* Long; tall (man); اوزون بویلو **ùzun-bòylu**, *s. t.* Tall (man).

اوس **ùvèss**, *s. t.* An insipid wild fruit (the berry of the sorb or service tree ?).

اوست **ùsst**, *s. t.* The upper part; — یانی —**yàni**, The upper side, the place next above; اوستم باشم **ùsstum-bàshim**, (My head (*for* my head-gear) and what is on me) my clothes; اوستمه **ùsstuma**, To the upper part of me, to what is on me, *i.e.* on to me, on to my clothes; اوستکده **ùsstungda**, At the upper part of thee, upon thee, upon thy clothes; اوستندن ùsstundan, From the upper part of him, her, it, from it, off from it, off of it, &c.; اوستهچيقمق ùssta-chìkmak, v.n. To get the upper hand, to get uppermost.

اوستريا Avstria, s. t. Austria.

اوستره or اوستوره ùsstura, s. t. A razor.

اوستون ùsstun, s. t. The vowel-point َ, designating one or other of the five vowel-sounds A, a, a, É, or é.

اوشاق ŭshAk, s. t. A boy, lad; a man-servant; او اوشاقلری èv-ŭshAklari, The household, the family, or the women and children.

اوشمك ùshmek (aor. اوشر ùsher), and اوششمك ùshushmek (aor. اوششور ùshushur), v.n. To run together crowdingly, to collect, be collected in flocks and crowds.

اوشنمك ùshĕnmek (aor. اوشنور ùshĕnir), v.n. To be too idle or indifferent to do a thing, to leave a thing undone from want of inclination.

اوشيمك or اوشومك ùshumek (aor. اوشور ùshur), v.n. To feel cold, to be cold (a man or beast).

اوصاف èvsAf, s. pl. a. (of وصف, not used in this sense), Moral qualities.

اوصانج ŭssAnj, s. t. The losing all relish for, or pleasure in anything.

اوصانمق ŭssAnmak (aor. اوصانور ŭssAnir), v.n. To lose all relish or pleasure.

اوصلنمق ŭsslanmak (aor. اوصلنور ŭsslanir), v.n. To behave better in future, to become docile, quiet, and well-behaved. [behaved.

اوصلو ŭsslu, a. t. Docile, quiet, well-

اوصورق òssuruk, s. t. A fart.

اوصورمق òssurmak (aor. اوصورر òssurur), v.n. To fart, break wind.

اوضاع èvzā", s. pl. a. (of وضع wAz"), Postures; gestures; actions, conduct, behaviour.

اوطوراق òturAk, s. t. A seat; a stool or chair, with pan, for invalids; stationary troops, local, reserve, or militia forces in garrison.

اوطورمق òturmak (aor. اوطورر òturur), v.n. To sit down; to sit up, not go to bed, keep up a meeting, not separate; to sink (the foundations of a building); to get ashore, touch the bottom (a ship, &c.)

اوطون òdun, s. t. Firewood.

اوطه òda, s. t. A room; an office, bureau; a counting-house.

اوغراشمق òghrashmak (aor. اوغراشر òghrashir), v.n. To strive, struggle.

اوغرامق òghramak (aor. اوغرار òghrar), v.n. To call in at, to pass by or through, to touch at; بلايهاوغرارسن bèlāya-òghrarsin, you will meet with some accident (judgment or punishment).

اوغری òghru, s. t. (old), A thief, robber.

اوغشمق òghushmak (aor. اوغشور òghushur), v.n. (recip. of اوغمق òghmak), To rub each (hand) with the other.

اوغل òghl, *s. t.* A son.

اوغلاق òghlak, *s. t.* A kid.

اوغلان òghlan, *s. t.* A boy, lad; ايچ اوغلانى ìch-òghlani, (Formerly) a lad studying in a special school with a view to future admission as an officer of the Sultan's palace; دل اوغلانى dìl-òghlani, A student attached to any one of the European embassies at Constantinople to learn the language; قپو اوغلانى kapi-òghlani, A kind of clerk, or under-agent of an embassy, acting under the dragomans or interpreters to call at the various offices of the Porte, and receive such papers and documents as may have been in course of preparation, &c. &c.; قيزاوغلان قيز kìz-òghlan-kìz, A maid, a virgin.

اوغمق òghmak (*aor.* اوغار òghar), *v.a.* To rub with the palm of the hand or inside of the fingers.

اوغور òghur, *s. t.* (*Latin ?*), A good augury, a good presage; اوغورلو òghurlu, *a. t.* Of good augury, auspicious, lucky; اوغورلراوله òghurlar-òla! May (your journey) be auspicious! Happy journey to you! وطن اوغورندە اولمك wàtan-òghurunda-ùlmek, To die for the good of one's country; براوغوردن bìr-òghurdan, *ad.* All at once, all together.

اوفاتمق ùfàtmak (*aor.* اوفادر ùfàdir), *v.a.* To make small; to break small.

اوفاق ùfàk, *a. t.* Small, little; —, *s. t.* Crumbs, or the small pieces of anything.

اوفلمك ùflémek (*aor.* اوفلر ùfler), *and* اوفورمك ùfurmek (*aor.* اوفورر ùfurur), *v.a.* To blow upon *or* into, with the mouth, *or* a bellows.

اوق òk, *s. t.* An arrow; a fiddlestick; the pole (of a waggon or carriage); تاتاراوقى tàtar-òku, A cross-bow.

اوقاف èvkāf, *s. pl. a.* (*of* وقف wàkf), Properties in mortmain.

اوقلاغى òklaghi, *s. t.* A rolling-pin.

اوقومق òkumak (*aor.* اوقور òkur), *v.a.* To read; to say or repeat solemnly; ميدان— mèydān—, *v.n.* To challenge, to make a challenge.

اوقه òkka, *s. t.* (*written generally* وقيه), An oke (the Turkish pound, being equal to about 2¾ lbs. avoirdupois).

اوك ùng, *s. t.* The front, fore part; the space in front of anything.

اوكتمك ùghutmek (*aor.* اوكودر ùghudur), *v.a.* To grind (corn to flour) in a mill.

اوكجه ùngjé, *ad. t.* in الك اوكجه ìlk-ùngjé, First, first of all, before all other things.

اوكچه ùkché, *s. t.* The heel of the foot, *and especially* the back of the heel; the heel part of the upper leather of a shoe or boot.

اوكدل ùngdul, *s. t.* The *cup* or prize to be won at a race, &c.

اوكرتمك ùghrètmek (*aor.* اوكردر ùghrèdir), *v.a.* To teach (a thing to anyone), cause to learn.

اوكرغه òngurgh*a* (òmurgh*a*), *s. t.* The spine, back-bone; the keel of a ship.

اوكرنمك ù*gh*rɛnmek (*aor.* اوكرنور ù*gh*rɛ̀nir), *v.a.* To learn.

اوكسرك ùksuruk, *s. t.* A cough.

اوكسرمك ùksurmek (*aor.* اوكسرر ùksurur), *v.n.* To cough.

اوكسز ùksuz, *s. t.* An orphan.

اوكسه ùksɛ́, *s. t.* Birdlime on twigs.

اوكندره ù*gh*èndérɛ́, *s. t.* A goad.

اوكنمك ù*gh*unmek (*aor.* اوكنور ù*gh*unur), (ù*gh*ɛ̀nmek, *aor.* ù*gh*ɛ̀nir), *v.n.* To praise one's self, sound one's own trumpet.

اوكوت ù*gh*ut, *s. t.* Advice, counsel.

اوكوز ùk*y*uz, *s. t.* An ox.

اول òl (ò), *pron. t.* He, she, it; that; اول بر òl-bir (ò-bir), The other, not this one; —, ɛvvɛl, *a. a.* The first; —, *s. a.* The first, beginning, commencement; the first day (of a month); —, *ad. t.* Firstly; before; earlier; بركون اول bìr-gh*y*ùn-ɛvvɛl, One day earlier; برساعت اول bìr-sā‘‘*a*t-ɛvvɛl, بران اول bìr-ān-ɛvvɛl, As early as possible, with the greatest possible dispatch; اولسى كون ɛvvɛlsi-gh*y*ùn, The day before yesterday; —الك èn*g*—, First of all, in the very first place; —بهار, —bàhār, Spring, the early spring; اولكى ɛv-vɛlki, *pron. a.* The first.

اولا (*for* اولى) ūlà, *a. a.* (*fem. of* اول ɛvvɛl), The first; — (*for* اولى), èvlà, Better, more advantageous, preferable; —, ɛvvɛ́lā, *ad. a.* In the first place, firstly.

اولاد èvlād, *s. pl. a.* (*of* ولد vèled), Sons; children, offspring; (*as a Turkish singular*) a child.

اولاشمق ùl*a*shm*a*k (*aor.* اولاشور ùlàshir), *v.n.* To reach, come up to, attain, join on.

اولامق àvlamak (*aor.* اولار àvlar), *v.a.* To take, *or* try to take, by hunting, fishing, &c. [*v.a.* To measure.

اولچمك ùlchmek (*aor.* اولچر ùlchɛr),

اولچى ùlchu, *s. t.* A measure.

اولسى ɛvvɛlsi, *a. t.* Before yesterday; —كون, —gh*y*ùn, The day before yesterday.

اولطه òlt*a*, *s. t.* A fishing line; a fish-hook; —, vòlt*a*, A tack, a board (in sailing); a time, a turn (in repetition); —اورمق, —wùrm*a*k, *v.n.* To beat, to sail to and fro.

اولم ùlum, *s. t.* A mode or manner of dying; death.

اولمق òlm*a*k (*aor.* اولور òlur), *v.n.* To become, to acquire or enter upon any state; to be, to possess any state; to acquire any fitting or required state, to become ripe, cooked, sufficient, &c.

اولمك ùlmek (*aor.* اولور ùlur), *v.n.* To die. [*v.n.* To marry, take a wife.

اولنمك èvlɛnmek (*aor.* اولنر èvlɛ̀nir),

اولو èvli, *a. t.* Married, having a wife; —, ùlu, *a. t.* Dead; —, *s. t.* A dead body, a corpse; —, ūlu, *a. t.* (*old*) Large, great; —, ūlu, *s. pl. a.* (*of*

ذو zu), Lords, possessors, people connected with; اولوالامر ūlu-'l-èmr, Those in authority, who have a right to command. [rain pipe.

أولوق òluk, s. t. A gutter; a spout; a

اولویت èvléviyyèt, s. a. Superiority in advantageousness, preferableness.

أولى èvlà, a. a. (fem.) Superior, preferable; —, ūlà, a. a. (fem.) First; —, ūlī, s. pl. a. (accus. of اولو), Lords, possessors, people connected with; —, ùlu, a. t. Dead; —, èvli, a. t. Married (man).

اوليا èvliyā, s. pl. a. (of ولى vèlī), The next of kin; people intimately connected with; saints, holy men (as being in more intimate relation with God); (as a Turkish singular) a saint, a holy man. [To hope, expect, look for.

أومق ùmmak (aor. أومار ùmar), v.a.

اوموز òmuz, s. t. The shoulder.

أون òn, a. t. Ten; —, ūn, s. t. Flour, meal; —, ùn, s. t. Fame; a voice; أوندەبر ònda-bir, A tenth, the tenth part; أوندەلق òndalik, s. t. A tithe; tithes. [v.a. To forget.

أونوتمق ùnùtmak (aor. أونودر ùnùdur),

اوه òva, s. t. A plain, a field.

أويالمق òyalamak (aor. أويالار òyalar), v.a. To put (a person) off with vain promises or excuses.

اويانمق ùyanmak, (aor. اويانر ùyànir), v.n. To wake from sleep. [up.

أويخته āvīkhté, a. p. Suspended, hung

اويدرمق ùydurmak (aor. اويدرر ùydurur), v.a. To cause to suit, fit, or be adapted; to arrange; to manage; to bring into submission; to invent (tales or stories); to deceive, pervert, seduce; to have carnal connection with. [suspends.

اويز āvīz, a. p. (in composition), Which

اويزه āvīzé, s. t. A chandelier.

اويشمق or اويوشمق ùyushmak (aor. أويشور ùyushur), v.n. To be benumbed; to become favourable, compliant, accommodating.

اويغون ùyghun, a. t. Favourable; fitting, appropriate; good, proper; اويغونسز ùyghunsuz, a. t. Unfavourable; bad, unbeseeming, improper; اويغونسزلق ùyghunsuzluk, s. t. Unfavourableness; impropriety; badness; abuse.

اويقو ùyku, s. t. Sleep; اويقومكلدى ùykum-ghèldi, or اويقوموار ùykum-vàr, I am sleepy; اويقوسز ùykussuz, a. t. Sleepless; اويقوسز براقمق ùykussuz-bràkmak (or قومق kòmak), v.a. To torture by depriving of sleep.

اويكه (ùfké), s. t. Anger, passion, rage.

اويكى ùvèghi, a. t. Step; —بابا, —bàba, A step-father; &c. [inner part of it.

اويلق ùyluk, s. t. The thigh, or the

اويله ùylé, s. t. Noon; noon prayer; —, pron. t. Such, that sort, that kind; —, ad. t. So, in that manner, in that way.

اويمق òymak (aor. اويار òyār,), v.a. To carve or dig out, to make hollow;

to cut out, to cut into a stuff so as to form ornamental patterns; to carve (wood, stone, &c.); —, ŏymak (*aor.* اويار ŏyar), *v.n.* To adapt one's self, *or* be adapted; to follow, submit, fall in with, be led by; to fit, suit, do.

اويمه ŏyma, *s. t.* Carving, carver's work; scalloping, pinking (the edges of stuffs).

اويناق ŏynak, *a. t.* Fresh, playful, skittish (horse); inconstant, capricious (person); —يرى, —yèri, The joints of the body.

اوينامق ŏynamak (*aor.* اوينار ŏynar), *v.n.* To play; to dance; to move on a joint; —, *v.a.* To play (a game).

اويوز ŏyuz, *s. t.* The mange; the scab; the itch; —, *a. t.* Mangy (beast); itchy (person). [dug or scraped out.

اويوق ŏyuk, *a. t.* Hollow, cavernous,

اويوقلمق ŏyuklamak (*aor.* اويوقلار ŏyuklar), *v.n.* To doze, be sleepy, to fall asleep. [sleep; go to sleep.

اويومق ŏyumak (*aor.* (اويور), *v.n.* To

اويون ŏyun, *s. t.* Play; a game; fraud, deceit, a trick, a stratagem; —, ăyun, *s. t.* A meal.

اويونجق ŏyunjak, *s. t.* A toy, a plaything.

اويه ŏya, *s. t.* The hem or border of a garment (if scalloped?).

آه āh! *int. t.* Ah! O! —, *s. t.* A sigh; ا—, —et, *and* —چكمك, —chèkmek, *v.n.* To sigh.

اهار àhar, *s. t.* A glazing used for writing paper, commonly made of the white of egg rubbed up with alum till it coagulates. [habitants.

اهالى àhālī, *s. pl. a.* (*of* اهل èhl), In-

اهانت ìhānet, *s. a.* The doing anything to a person which shows you do not love or esteem him; ا—, —et, *v.n.* To insult, to show an utter want of respect for.

اهتزاز ìhtizāz, *s. a.* The trembling or vibrating of long flexible things; vibratory motion.

اهتمام ìhtimām, *s. a.* A bestowing of every care; ا—, —et, *v.n.* To bestow care.

اهدا ìhdā, *s. a.* A conducting in the right road; a presenting, giving a present; ا—, —et, *v.a.* To conduct in the right road, bring into the fold of the true church; to present, give.

اهرام èhrām, *s. pl. a.* (*of* هرم *not used*), The pyramids of Egypt; —, ìhrām, *s. t.* A pyramid. [low in sound.

آهسته āhèsstè, *a. p.* Slow in motion;

اهل èhl, *s. a.* A person connected with anything; a wife; a proper, competent, suitable person; اهل بيت èhli-bèyt, A wife; اهل اسلام èhli-ìsslām, A Musslim, Muhammedan believer; اهل عرض èhli-ʻìrz (èhlìriz), An honourable, honest man *or* woman; اهل كتاب èhli-kìtāb, People of the dispensations which have revealed books of religion, as the Jews and Christians.

اهليت èhlìyyèt, *s. a.* The quality of

being a fit, proper, and competent person. [urgent *or* important.

اهم èhèmm, *a. a.* More, most, *or* very

اهمال ìhmāl, *s. a.* A neglecting; ا—, —et, *v.a.* To neglect, not pay due attention to.

اهن āhĕn, *s. p.* Iron; اهنربا *à*hènrùbā, *s.p.* The loadstone; a magnet.

اهنك āhènk, *a. p.* Properly prepared for any action; properly tuned (a musical instrument).

اهنكر āhènghèr, *s. p.* A blacksmith.

اهنين āhénīn, *a. p.* Of iron, iron.

اهو āhū, *s. p.* The gazelle.

اهون èhvèn, *a. a.* More, most, or very trifling, unimportant, or easy; cheap.

اى èy, *int. t.* O! eh! holloa! —, ày, *s. t.* The moon; a crescent or figure of a crescent; a month; a lunation; اى ايله يلديز ày-(*lan*)-y*ì*ld*iz*, The star and crescent (symbol of the Turks); ايلق àyl*ì*k, *s. t.* Monthly wages or salary; —, *a.* A month old; sufficient for a month; —باشى, —b*à*sh*i*, The first of a month; a woman's monthly courses; —چيچكى, —chìchèghi, The sunflower; —طوتلمسى, —tùtul-m*à*ss*i*, A lunar eclipse.

ايا àya, *s. t.* The inside or palm of the hand; —, àyā, *ad. t.* I wonder whether, let us see whether; —, èyā, *int. a.* O! اياصوفيه Àya-Sòfiy*a*, The mosque (originally the cathedral church) of Saint-Sophia (or of *the Divine Omniscience*) at Constantinople.

اياب ìyāb, *s. a.* The returning, coming back; ذهاب و اياب zìhāb-u-ìyāb, A going forth and a returning, a coming and going.

ايادى èyādī, *s. pl. a.* (*of* يد yèd), Hands.

ايارتمق àyartm*ak* (*aor.* اياردر àyard*ì*r), *v.a.* To pervert, seduce, lead astray.

اياز àyaz, *s. t.* Frost, clear bright weather with frost.

ايازل àyazil, *s. t.* (*corruption from* خيال ظل khàyālī-zìll), *called also* خيال khàyāl, A kind of puppet-show, or exhibition of shadows behind a cloth screen.

ايازمه àyàzm*a*, *s. t.* (*Greek*), A sacred spring or source of water.

اياق àyak, *s. t.* The foot; the whole leg and foot; the leg of any piece of furniture; the tail-stream of any water, by which it flows away, as the head-water is called باش b*à*sh, and water which has not these two appendages is esteemed unfit for drinking or washing; —يولى, —yòlu, *s. t.* A privy, water-closet; —طاقمى, —tàk*i*m*i*, *s. t.* The common people, lower classes; سوز اياغه دوشمك s*ù*z-àyag*ha*-dùshmek, *v.n.* To be in a state of anarchy, so that the lower classes rule the day; اياق قابى àyak-k*à*b*i*, A shoe, boot, slipper; اياقداش àyakd*a*sh, *s. t.* A fellow, companion; اياقلو àyakl*i*, *a. t.* Footed, having a foot or feet; اياقلنمق àyaklanm*ak*, *v.n.* To rise into action, *or* into sedition, rebellion, &c., *or* to remonstrate ; ایاغه قالقمق àyagha-kàlkmak, v.n. To rise and stand, to get up on one's feet ; to rise in sedition or rebellion ; ایاقده‌دورمق àyakda-dùrmak, v.n. To stand, to remain standing ; ایاق باصمق àyak-bàssmak, v.n. To tread, place the foot on.

ایالت èyālèt, s. a. A province governed by a والی wālī, a government-general.

ایام èyyām, s. pl. a. (of یوم yèvm), Days ; (as a Turkish singular) a space of time ; —باحور, èyyāmi-bāhūr, The dog-days.

ایبك ìbik, s. t. The comb (of a cock, &c.) ; خروس ایبکی khòross-ìbighi, Cock's-comb (a flower).

ایپ ìp, s. t. A cord, string ; a rope ; —اوجی, —ūjʊ (the end of the string), A clue (to any secret matter).

ایت āyet, s. a. A verse, phrase, or sentence of the Kur'an, generally mentioned as —كریمه, āyéti-kèrīmé, A sacred verse ; —, īt, s. t. A dog ; ایت اوغلی ایت īt-òghlʊ-īt, Dog, son of a dog.

ایتالیا Italia, s. t. Italy.

ایتالیالو Italiali, a. t. Italian ; —, s. t. An Italian.

ایتام èytām, s. pl. a. (of یتیم yètīm), [Orphans.

ایتشمك ìtishmek (aor. ایتشر ìtishir), v.n. (recip. of ایتمك ìtmek), To push one another about, to teaze one another, plague one another, quarrel with one another, bother with one another.

ایتلامق àytlamak (aor. ایتلار àytlar), v.a. To clean out (a pipe, &c.) ; to pick (the teeth, &c.) ; to clean or pick (rice, raisins, &c., clear of stones, dirt, &c.).

ایتمك ètmek (aor. ایدر èdʀʀ), v.a. To do ; to render, cause to become, make ; —, ìtmek (aor. ایتر ìtʀʀ), v.a. To push.

ایثار īssār, s. a. A giving, bestowing ; ا—, —et, v.a. To give, bestow.

ایجاب ījāb, s. a. A being necessary, requisite; ا—. —et, v.n. To be requisite, necessary.

ایجاد ījād, s. a. A bringing into existence ; an inventing ; an invention ; ا—, —et, v.a. To invent.

ایجار ījār, s. a. A giving for hire, a hiring ; ا—, —et, v.a. To hire.

ایجاز ījāz, s. a. A shortening, abbreviating.

ایچ ìch, s. t. The inside ; ایچ یاغی ìch-yàghi, Suet, fat of the inside ; ایچ اوغلانی ìch-òghlani, A young man (in former times) preparing by training and study to become an officer of the Sultan's palace ; ایچ اغاسی ìch-aghassi, A personal attendant, who waits on his master and the guests in person.

ایچرو or ایچری ìchèri, s. t. The inside, space contained inside.

ایچقی ìchki, s. t. Wine, spirits, and such like drink.

ایچم ìchim, s. t. Enough for one drink.

ایچمك ìchmek (aor. ایچر ìchʀʀ), v.a. To drink ; to smoke (pipes or tobacco).

ایچون ìchin, pr. t. For ; as ; on account of ; by reason of ; for the sake of.

ایداع īdā'', *s. a.* A depositing in trust; ا—, —et, *v.a.* To deposit in trust.

ایدنمك èdinmek (*aor.* ایدنور èdinir), *v.a.* (*indet. of* ایتمك ètmek), To procure for one's self, provide one's self with, gain for one's self.

ایدی èydī, *s. pl. a.* (*of* ید yèd), Hands.

ایدین àydin, ایدینلق àydinlik, *s. t.* Light, daylight, firelight, &c.; كوزك ایدین ghyùzung-àydin! (May) your eyes (be *as bright as*) light! This is the usual mode of wishing anyone joy.

ایر èyer, *s. t.* A saddle; —اورمق, —wùrmak, *v.n.* To put the saddle on; ایرلمك èyerlémek, *v.a.* To saddle.

ایراث īrāss, *s. a.* A causing, a bringing about; ا—, —et, *v.a.* To cause.

ایراد īrād, *s. a.* A putting forward, bringing forward (arguments); revenue, income; ا—, —et, *v.a.* To put or bring forward, adduce, cite.

ایراق ìràk, *a. t.* Distant, far off;—, *s. t.* A distance, a distant place.

ایران Irān, *s. t.* Persia.

ایرانی Irānī, *a. p.* Persian.

ایرته èrté *or* ìrté, *s. t.* The day after, the next day; پازار ایرتسی pàzār-èrtéssi, Monday (the day after Sunday); جمعه ایرتسی jùm''à-èrtéssi, Saturday (the day after Friday); ایرتسی èrtéssi, *or* ایرتسی كون èrtéssi--ghyùn, The day after that (its next day).

ایرشمك èrishmek *or* ìrishmek (*aor.* ایریشر èrishir), *v.n.* To reach, attain.

ایرك ìring, *s. t.* Pus, matter of sores.

ایركمك ìrkmek (*aor.* ایركر ìrker), *or* ایركلمك ìrkilmek (*aor.* ایركلور ìrkilir), *v.n.* To collect in pools and stagnate (water).

ایركورمك ìrghyurmek (*aor.* ایركورر ìrghyurur), *v.a.* (*old*), To cause to reach or attain.

ایرم *or* ایریم èrim, *s. t.* The range, the distance to which a thing can reach.

ایرمق (*or* ایرماق) ìrmak, *s. t.* A river; —, àyrmak (*aor.* ایریر àyrir), *v.a.* To separate, disjoin, put asunder; to choose, select, pick.

ایرمك èrmek (*aor.* ایرر èrer), *v.n.* To reach, arrive, attain; عقل— ''àkl —, *v.n.* To understand, comprehend, عقلم ایرمیور ''àklim-èrmiyor, I do not understand, my mind does not go so far as to comprehend; عقل ایررشی دكل ''àkl-èrer-shèy-dìghil, It is an incomprehensible thing (it is not a thing which the mind can reach).

ایری àyri, *a. t.* Separate, apart; غیری —, —ghàyri, Separate things; ایریمز غیریمز یوق àyrimiz-ghàyrimiz-yòk, We have no separate interests; —, ìri, *a. t.* Large.

ایز ìz, *s. t.* A footmark, track, trace; ایزلمك ìzlémek (*aor.* ایزلر ìzler), *v.a.* To follow by the traces.

ایس ìss, *s. t.* Soot; lampblack.

ایش ìsh, *s. t.* Work, business, occupation; service; action; a matter, affair; workmanship; the work of one's hands, handiwork; the thing worked, made, or done; —كوچ, —ghyùch, Business, occupation; —ایشلمك, —ishlémek, To be occupied with work; كورمك —, —ghyùrmek, To do business, to finish a business; to be of use, to be useful in any work or business; ایشكذار ìsh-ghyùzār, *a. t.* Diligent, clever, enterprising, energetic; —كورمش, —ghyùrmush, *a.* (A person) of experience, who has had a hand in many and various affairs; (a thing) old and worn, which has done service; ایشهیرامق ìsh*a*-yàram*a*k, *v.n.* To be useful, serviceable; برایشه یرامامق bìr-ish*a*-yàramam*a*k, *v.n.* To be of no use whatever; ایشمه یرار ìshim*a*-yàrar, It will be (*or* is) useful to me; ایشی اویمق ìshi-ùym*a*k (*or* بتمك bìtmek, *or* دوزلمك dùzèlmek, *or* طوغرلمق dò*gh*r*u*lm*a*k), Anyone's affairs to be in good train, or settled to his satisfaction; ایشجی ìshji, *s. t.* A workman; ایشجیلك ìshjilik, *s. t.* Workmanship.

ایشتمك ìshìtmek (*aor.* اشیدر ìshìdir), *v.a.* To hear; —, ìshetmek (*aor.* ایشدر ìshèdir), *v.a.* (*caus. of* ایشهمك ìshémek), To cause or allow one to make water.

ایشق ìsh*i*k, *s. t.* Light, daylight, fire-light, candle-light, &c.

ایشلتمك ìshletmek (*aor.* ایشلدر ìshlédir), *v.a.* (*caus. of* ایشلمك ìshlémek), To cause, *or* to allow to work, *or* to be worked; to cause (an ulcer, &c.) to suppurate; to work (a mine, quarry, forest, &c.); to cause to be embroidered, carved, illuminated, &c.

ایشلك ìshlek, *a. t.* (A thing) which works easily or quickly; (a road) which has much traffic on it; (handwriting) which is easy and flowing; (a pipe) which is free from stoppage, or from an accumulation of the oil of tobacco.

ایشلمك ìshlémek (*aor.* ایشلر ìshler), *v.a.* To work at; to work up; to embroider, carve, illuminate, or ornament with work; —, *v.n.* To go, to work, to perform (a machine); to have much traffic on it (a road); to be free from stoppage (a pipe, &c.); to suppurate (a sore).

ایشهمك ìshémek (*aor.* ایشر ìsher), *v.n.* To piss, to make water, pass urine.

ایصال īssāl, *s. a.* A causing to reach, join, arrive; ا—, —et, *v.a.* To bring or send.

ایضاً èyz*a*n, *ad. a.* As above, in the same manner, also, likewise.

ایضاح īzāh, *s. a.* A making clear and explicit; ا—, —et, *v. a.* To make clear and explicit.

ایغدش ì*gh*dish, *s. t.* A gelding.

ایغر àygh*i*r, *s. t.* A stallion, stone-horse.

ایفا īfā, *s. a.* A duly performing, accomplishing, *or* paying; ا—, —et, *v.a.* To perform, accomplish, or pay.

ایق àyik, *a. t.* Sober, not intoxicated.

ایقاد īkād, *s. a.* A lighting, setting fire to; ا—, —et, *v.a.* To light, set on fire.

ايقاظ īkāz, *s. a.* A waking, rousing, making vigilant; a rousing from torpor or inaction; an exciting to any action; ا—, —et, *v.a.* To wake, to rouse; to excite, stir up.

ايك ī*gh*, *s. t.* A spindle; a small spindle and wheel for spinning yarn by hand.

ايكرنمك ì*gh*rɛnmek (*aor.* (ايكرنور)), *v.n.* To feel an abhorrence for (anything nasty).

ايكلمك ìnglḗmek (*aor.* (ايكلر)), *v.n.* To moan, to groan; ايكلدى ìn*g*ildi, A moaning.

ايكندى ìkindi, *s. t.* The prayer, or prayer-time, of the middle of the afternoon.

ايكنه ì*gh*nɛ́, *s. t.* A needle; a pin; a prickle, thorn; a sting; ايكنه‌جك ìghnɛ́jik, *dimin. t.* (a little needle) A pintle of a rudder.

ايكو è*gh*i, *or* ايكو كموكى è*gh*i-kèmi*gh*i, *s. t.* A rib, a rib-bone.

ايكى ìki, *a. t.* Two; —قات, —kàt, Twofold, double; ايكيمز ìkimiz, The two of us, both of us; ايكيكز ìkin*g*iz, Both of you; ايكيسى ìkissi, Both of them; ايكيده بر ìkid*a*-bìr, *ad. t.* Now and then, once (in fact) for every twice (that should be); —يوزلو, —yùzlu, *a. t.* Double-faced, treacherous, false, hypocritical; ايكنجى ìkinji; *a. t.* Second. [a twin.

ايكيز ìkiz, *s. t.* Twins; one of twins,

ايكيوز ìkiyuz, *a. t.* Two hundred.

ايل īl *or* èyl, *s. t.* A country; a wandering pastoral tribe; روم ايلى rūm-èyli, The land of the Romans, Rumelia; ايلات īlāt (*Arabic plural of the word*), The wandering pastoral tribes of the mountains between Turkey and Persia.

ايلتمك ìlɛtmek (*aor.* ايلدر ìlɛ̆dir), *v.a.* To send forward, forward, send.

ايلتى èlti, *s. a.* The wife of the brother of one's husband, a sister-in-law (of a woman).

ايلچى èlchi, *s. t.* An ambassador, an envoy (literally *the agent of his country* or *tribe*).

ايلخان īlkhān, *s. t.* The Sultan (literally *the prince of the tribe*).

ايلرو ìléri, *s. t.* The space further in advance; —, *ad.* Further on, in advance.

ايلشك ìlishik, *s. t.* A scruple, doubt, dislike, anything that holds one from acting; —, *a. t.* Slightly caught or tacked on.

ايلشمك ìlishmek (*aor.* ايلشر ìlishir), *v.n.* To catch, adhere to, or be hooked slightly on to anything; to pause in doubt; to feel a scruple or a dislike.

ايلق àylɪk, *s. t.* Monthly wages or salary; quantity (of anything) sufficient for a month; —, *a. t.* A month old.

ايلك ìlik, *s. t.* A loop for a button; an eye for a hook; ايلكلمك ìliklḗmek, *v.a.* To button; to hook (a dress, &c.).

ايلمق àyilmak (*aor.* ايلور àyilir), *v.n.* To become sober (from drunkenness); to regain one's senses (from fainting, or from being stunned).

ايلمك èylémek (*aor.* ايلر èyler), *v.a.* To do; to make, render, cause to become; —, ìlmek, *s. t.* A noose, a slip-knot; —, ìlmik, *s. t.* Semoule, a preparation of paste in small grains, semolina.

ايلنجه èylenja, *s. t.* Amusement, pastime, fun.

ايلنمك èylenmek (*aor.* ايلنور èylénir), *v.n.* To amuse one's self; to be amused; to stay, stop, wait.

ايلول èylūl, *s. t.* September.

ايله ìla (*often pronounced* ìlen *or* ilan, *and contracted in writing to* له la, *which is also frequently pronounced* len *or* lan), *p. t.* With.

ايليجق ìlijàk, *a. t.* Tepid.

ايليجه ìlija, *s. t.* A natural tepid spring.

ايما īmā, *s. a.* An allusion, a slight mention; a hint; ا—, —et, *v.a.* To allude to *or* mention slightly; to hint at.

ايمان èymān, *s. pl. a.* (*of* يمين yèmīn), Oaths; —, īmān, *s. a.* A believing, holding as a creed or faith; religious faith or belief; the Muhammedan faith; ا—, et, *and* —كتورمك, —ghètirmek, *v.n.* To believe in; ايمانه‌كلمك īmāna-ghèlmek, *v.n.* To be converted, to receive the faith; to become a Muhammedan; ايمانه‌كتورمك īmāna-ghètirmek, *v.a.* To convert, bring to the faith.

ايمپراطور ìmpèratūr, *s. t.* An emperor.

ائمه è'immé, *s. pl. a.* (*of* امام ìmām), Pontiffs; fathers of the church; imams. [therefore, wherefore.

ايمدی (*or* امدی) ìmdi, *c. t.* Now, then,

ايمرنمك ìmrenmek (*aor.* ايمرنور ìmrènir), *v.n.* To have a longing for (anything nice).

ايمن èymèn, *a. a.* More, most, *or* very safe, secure, or fortunate.

اين īn, *s. t.* A cave, cavern, grotto; a den; —, *pron. p.* This; —(*or* ان), èn, *s. t.* Width, breadth.

اينجتمك ìnjitmek (*aor.* اينجدر ìnjidir), *v.a.* To hurt, injure, cause pain, sorrow, or injury to.

اينجنمك ìnjinmek (*aor.* اينجنور ìnjinir), *v.n.* To be hurt, injured, or pained.

اينجو ìnji, *s. t.* A pearl.

اينجه ìnja, *a. t.* Thin, fine, small.

اينده āyèndé, *a. p.* Coming, to come, [future.

اينك ìnèk, *s. t.* A cow.

اينه (*for* ايينه) àyna, *s. t.* A looking-glass, a mirror.

ايو àyi, *s. t.* A bear; —, īyi, *a. t.* Good; —, *ad. t.* Well; پك‌ايو pèk-īyi, Very good; very well; اپ‌ايو èp-īyi, Pretty good; pretty well; ايوجه īyija, Rather good, rather well, rather better; ايولك īyilik, *s. t.* Goodness; kindness.

ايوا àywa, *s. t.* A quince.

ايوان èywān, *s. p.* A court, a large state apartment.

ايواه èywāh! *int. t.* Alas!

ايوب èyyūb, *s. t.* Job.

ایهام īhām, *s. a.* Ambiguous language, amphibology; ا—, —et, *v.a.* To hint darkly, or disguise in ambiguous language. [formal method.

آیین āyīn, *s. t.* A rite, ceremonial,

آیینه āyīnᴇ́, *s. p.* A looking-glass, mirror; a telescope; a reflector.

ب

ب bā (bᴇ́). Second letter of the Turkish alphabet, having the value of *b* in English, though in some cases taking the sound of *p*, when placed before or after any of the sharp sounding letters, and at the end of the first gerund of verbs. It is sometimes interchanged, in Persian words, with پ pē, and و wāw; as, بستر bìsstᴇr, or پستر, pìsstᴇr; تاب tāb, or تاو tāv; also, but much less frequently, with ف fé and م mìm. In chronograms and astronomical tables it has the numerical value of 2. In the dates of letters it stands for the month رجب Rèjeb; —, bᴇ́, *pr. p. (in composition)*, With; by, in, for; —, bì, *pr. a. (in composition)*, With; by; in; on.

با bā, *s. a.* Name of the letter ب; —, *pr. p. (in composition)*, With; by; in.

باب bāb, *s. a.* A door; a gate; a chapter; a matter, subject, category; a house of government, a ministerial official residence or place of business; —عالی, bābi-ʻʻālī, The chief office of the Ottoman government (the so-called *Porte* or *Sublime Porte*, a perverted French translation of the original, which merely means "the High House" as we say the High Court of Chancery), otherwise called پاشاقپوسی pàsha-kᴧpìssi, "*the House of the Pasha*," or simply قپو kᴧpi, *the Office;* these two latter terms being also applied, in the provinces, to the residence of the governor. The extravagant and unmeaning term "*Sublime Porte*," or rather its original, is never applied by the Turks to the Sultan or to the government, but simply to the premises where the general business of the government is carried on; —سرعسکری, bābi-sᴇrʻʻᴧsskérī, "The Horse-Guards" of Constantinople, or its War-Department; —فتوا پناهی, bābi-fètvà-pènāhī, The offices of the Shèykhᴜ-'l-ìsslām; —همایون, bābi-hùmāyūn, The principal gate of entrance to the premises of the old imperial residence, opening near the mosque of St. Sophia.

بابا bᴧbᴀ, *s. t.* A father; —, *a.* Fatherly, old and kind or respectable; آق بابا ᴧk-bᴧbᴀ, A kind of vulture; بابالق bᴧbᴀlɪk, A sort of father, a second father, one who takes care of a child; an old man, one who can be looked upon as a father; باباقوری bᴧbᴀ-kòrᴜ, A kind of hard stone; an agate(?).

بابل Bàbèl, *s. t.* Babylon.

باترمق bᴀtirmak (*aor.* باترر bᴀtirir), *v.a.* (*causal of* باتمق) To dip, plunge, submerge; to cause to sink, to sink, send to the bottom.

باتمق bᴀtmak (*aor.* باتار bᴀtar), *v.n.* To sink, go to the bottom; to set, go down (stars, &c.); to be lost to the owner (money).

باتی *or* باطی bᴀti, *s. t.* The west; the west wind; —لدوس, —lòdoss, west-south-west; —قره يل, —kᴀra-yel, west-north-west.

باج bᴀj, *s. p.* A toll; black-mail.

باجاق *or* باجق bᴀjak, *s. t.* The thigh; the whole leg; باجاقسز bᴀjaksiz, A person with very short legs; باجاقلو bᴀjakli, A person with long legs, all legs; a Dutch ducat, so called from the figure of a man on one side of it, in armour, with his legs rather open and long.

باجناح bājénāh, (*or* باجناخ bājénākh, *or* باجناق bājénak, *or* باجيناق bàjinᴀk), *s. t.* (bᴀjanᴀk), A brother-in-law, husband of one's wife's sister, fellow sharer in two sisters as wives.

باجه bᴀja, *s. t.* A chimney; an air-shaft; a loop-hole, *or* small opening for light or air in towers or dungeons; the flat terraced roof of a house; قپو باجه kᴀpi-bᴀja, Door and roof, *or* door and chimney, saying used to signify a house, a home; all over the house.

باجی bᴀji, *s. t.* A sister; a wife.

باحور bāhūr, *s. a.* The heat of the dog-days; —ايام èyyāmi-bāhūr, The dog-days.

باخصوص bā-khùssūss, *ad. p.* In particular, particularly, especially, above all.

باد bād, *s. p.* Wind; a wind, breeze; —صبا, bādi-sàbā, The gentle, cool, and delicious breeze that usually blows in spring and early summer, the zephyr; —هوا, bàdi-hèvā (bèdāwā), Gratis, without money and without price; —فنا, bādi-fènā, The cold wind of death or annihilation.

بادبان bādbān, *or* bādibān, *s. p.* A sail.

بادم bādem (*or* بادام bādām), *s. p.* An almond. [purple egg-plant.

بادنجان bādinjᴀn (pᴀtlijᴀn), *s. t.* The

بادنه bᴀdana, *s. t.* Whitewash; —اورمق, —wūrmak, *v.n.* To whitewash.

باده bādé, *s. p.* Wine.

بادی bādī, *s. a.* One who begins, brings about, or causes anything; a cause; بادیٔ نظر bādi'i-nᴀzar, The first glimpse or look.

باديه bādiyé, *s. a.* A desert, a wilderness, unreclaimed country; —, bᴀdya, *s. t.* A tub.

بار bār, *s. p.* A load, burthen; fruit (as the burthen of the tree); a time; —, *a. p.* (*in composition*) Which rains, pours forth; —اولمق, —òlmak, *v.n.* To be at charge, to be a burthen; برك وبار bèrgh-u-bār, Leaves and fruit; هربار hèr-bār, Every time, always; كهربار ghyùher-bār, Which sheds precious stones; بارخانه bār-khāné, The baggage and baggage horses of a grandee.

باران bārān, *s. p.* Rain. [unpleasant.

بارد bārid, *a. a.* Cold; disagreeable,

بارداق bàrdak, *s. t.* A drinking cup, a mug.

بارز bāriz, *a. a.* Apparent, conspicuous.

بارش bārish, *s. t.* Peace, cessation of hostilities; —كورش, —ghyùrush, Peace and friendship; —او —, ——ol, To make peace and see each other on friendly terms.

بارشق bārishik, *a. t.* At peace; بارشقلق bārishiklik, *s. t.* Peace.

بارشمق bārishmak (*aor.* بارشور bārishir), *v.n.* To make friends with one another, make it up again, make peace, to be reconciled to each other.

بارگاه bārghyāh, *s. p.* A royal court, or hall of audience.

باركير bārghīr (bèghir), *s. p.* A gelding; a hack; a pack-horse. [or tower.

بارو bārū, *s. p.* A castle wall, battlement,

باروت bārūt (bārit), *s. t.* (*from ar.* بارود saltpetre, the salt used for cooling), Gunpowder; باروتخانه bārit-khānè, A powder-mill, powder-mills; باروتجى باشى bāritji-bāshi, The director of the imperial powder-works.

باره bārè, *s. p.* A time; دوباره dū-bārè, (Two times) twice; deuces (of the dice at backgammon); a trick, piece of trickery or knavery.

بارى bārī, *s. a.* The Creator, God; —, *s. p.* One time, once; —, (*and* bārim) *ad. t.* At least, if nothing else, just, only, anyhow, at all events, at any rate.

باز bāz, *s. p.* A falcon; a time, return, repetition; —, *a. p.* Open; (*in composition*) who plays; —, *ad. p.* Again, anew.

بازار bāzār (*also* پازار pāzār), *s. p.* A fair, a movable market; Sunday; —ايرتسى, —èrtéssi, Monday (day after Sunday); —ا, —et, *v.n.* To make a bargain; بازارلشمق pàzarlashmak, *v.n.* To talk over a bargain, and perhaps conclude it.

بازخاست bāz-khāsst, *s. p.* The resurrection, a rising again (from the dead).

بازركان bāzirghyān (bèzirghèn), *s. p.* A merchant; a shopkeeper; a pedlar; a Jew.

بازو bāzū, *s. p.* The arm; strength, power, might; —, (bāzi), *s. t.* The upper arm; وار قوتنى بازويه ويرمك vàr-kùvvètini-bāzūya-vèrmek, To put forth one's whole strength (to give one's existing strength to the arm); بازوبند bāzubènd, *s. p.* An armlet.

بازى bāzī, *s. p.* Play, playing, a game; بازيچه bāzīchè, *dim. p.* A plaything.

بأس bè'ss, *a. a.* Harm, injury, injuriousness, ill; بأس يوق bè'ss-yòk, No matter, it does not signify.

باستون bāsstūn, *s. t.* A jibboom.

باسور bāssūr, *s. a.* Hemorrhoids, the piles; hemorrhoidal or scrofulous humours.

باش bāsh, *s. t.* The head; a chief; a

commencement; an end; a spring, source; a summit, top; the head of a ship or boat, the bows; صوباشی sù-bAshi, A spring, source, head-water; a kind of rural mayor of a village; an equal; agio; discount; dress, clothes; باشی بوزق bAshi-bòzuk, One whose clothes are not uniform; باش اوستنه bAsh-ùsstuna, *ad. t.* (Upon the head) with pleasure, your command shall be obeyed; باش اوجنده bAsh-ùjunda, *and* یانی باشنده yàni-bAshinda, *ad. t.* Close by, near at hand; یکی باشدن yèngi - bAshdan, *ad.* Anew, over again; باشدن اياغه قدر bAshdan-àyagha - kAdar, *ad.* From head to foot; بر باشدن او برباشه bìr-bAshdan-ò-bir-bAsha, From one end to the other; باشلو bAshli, *a. t.* Headed; بللو باشلو bèlli-bAshli, *a.* One who is well known; باشلو باشنه bAshli-bAshina, *ad. t.* Separately, apart, independently; باشلق bAshlik, *s. t.* A cowl; a bridle; the capital of a column or cross-piece over a post or pillar; چاوش باشی chàwush-bAshi, The chief pursuivant, herald, or messenger of state, now in some respects a minister of justice; the title of باشی bAshi added to the name of any follower of a trade or occupation, is often a mere mark of courtesy; thus every medical man is called هكيم باشی hèkim-bAshi, every tailor درزی باشی (tèrzi)-bAshi, &c., though strictly these titles belong only to the tradesmen, &c., of the Sultan, they being, as it were, the heads of their several professions; اربباشی èr-bAshi, A leader of his fellows; a ringleader; سوز باشی sùz-bAshi, A spokesman; اون باشی òn-bAshi, A decurion, a corporal, a second-class petty naval officer; يوز باشی yùz-bAshi, A centurion, a captain of the army, a lieutenant of the navy; بيكباشی bìng-bAshi, A chiliarch, a chef-de-bataillon, major, or lieutenant-colonel in the army, a commander in the navy; باشبوغ bAsh-bògh, A commodore, a commander of an army or division; باش اولمق bAsh-òlmak, *v.a.* To be one's peer or equal; باشه کچمك bAsha - ghèchmek, *v.n.* To become chief, to take the lead; باشه چيقمق bAsha - chìkmak, *v.n.* To strive to equal, to emulate, to rival; باشدن چيقمق bAshdan - chìkmak, *v.n.* To become undutiful, rebellious, disobedient, to cast away restraint; باشدن چيقارمق bAshdan-chìkàrmak, *v.a.* To entice to disobedience; باش قالدرمق bAsh - kAldirmak, *v.n.* To raise the head; to revive, regain one's strength, courage, or spirits; to appear, show one's self, come into active being; باشك ايچون bAshing-ìchin! By your head! For your head's sake! باشك صاغ اولسون bAshing-sàgh-òlsun, May your head be in health! (said when a misfortune has happened to anyone, as though we should say: "Well, you have your health, and this misfortune can be remedied"); باشدن قره یه اورمق bàshdan-kàraya-wùrmak, *v.n.* To run straight ashore; عقلی باشنده در "àkli-bàshindā-dir, (His senses are in his head), he has not lost his senses, he knows what he is about; عقلی باشنده دکل "àkli-bàshinda-dìghil, *or* عقلی باشندن کتدی "àkli-bàshindan-ghìtdi, He has lost his wits, he does not know what he is about; بالق باشدن قوقار bàlik-bàshdan-kòkar, *Fish first stink at the head,* proverbial expression to signify that *the bad example of the upper classes causes their inferiors to become similarly infected with vice.*

باشارمق bàsharmak (*aor.* باشارر bàsharir), *v.a.* To accomplish, to manage to bring to the desired end or state.

باشاق bàshak, *s.* The ear or spike of corn. [*v.n.* To commence, begin.

باشلامق bàshlamak (*aor.* باشلار bàshlar),

باصامق bàssamak, *s. t.* A step in a ladder, a stair.

باصره bàssira, *s. a.* The sight; —, *a. a. fem.* Seeing, which sees; قوت باصره kùvvèti-bàssira, The sight, the seeing faculty.

باصقی bàsski, *s. t.* A press for pressing.

باصقین bàsskin, *s. t.* A military surprise; a seizure *or* entry by the police, generally for affairs of gallantry; —, *a.* Preponderant, overbearing, irresistible.

باصمه جی bàssmaji, *s. t.* A printer.

باصمق bàssmak (*aor.* باصار bàssar), *v.n.* To press, weigh upon; to tread; —, *v.a.* To print; to attack suddenly, to surprise; to make a seizure or domiciliary visit; to take in the act; —ایاق àyak—, *v.n.* To tread, set the foot; باصدرمق bàssdirmak (*aor.* باصدرر bàssdirir), *v.a. causal.* To press *or* beat down; to put down; to put out, extinguish (a conflagration); to get under, to hold down, prevent from rising.

باطل bātil, *a. a.* Vain, unfounded, untrue, false, groundless.

باطن bātin, *s.* and *a. a.* Interior; باطنی bātinī, *a. a.* Internal; mystical.

باطی bàti, *s. t.* The west; the west wind (see باتی).

باع bā", *s. a.* A fathom, the length to which the two arms can stretch.

باعث bā"iss, *s. a.* A cause, a causer.

باغ bāgh, *s. p.* A vineyard; (*in poetry*) a garden; —بوزمق, —bòzmak, *v.n.* To gather the grapes of a vineyard; —bàgh, *s. t.* A tie, binding, string, &c.; a knot;

باغبان bāghbān, *s. p.* A gardener;

باغلق bàghlik, *s. t.* Land appropriate to vineyards; باغلو bàghli, *a. t.* Tied, bound; dependent on; بوکی— bùghu—, *a. t.* Bound by some charm.

باغچه bàghcha, *s. p. dim.* A garden (*lit.*

a little garden); باغچوان bāghchawān, *s. p.* A gardener.

باغرمق bàghirmak (*aor.* باغرر bàghirir), *v.n.* To call out, cry out, cry, cry aloud.

باغشلامق bāghishlamak (*aor.* باغشلر bāghishlar), *v.a.* (*for* بخشلامق bàkhshlamak), To forgive, to pardon (a fault); to spare, spare the life of (a person).

باغلامق bāghlamak (*aor.* باغلار bāghlar), *v.a.* To tie, bind, fasten, make fast; —بوكى bùghu—, To make a charm, use some kind of sorcery; —صلح sùlh—, *v.n.* To make peace, conclude a peace; —نكاح nikyāh—, *v.n.* To assign a dower, on marriage, in case of separation; —ايراد īrād—, To assign a revenue or income.

باغى bāghī, *a. a.* A rebel; a sinner.

بافته bāftē, *a. p.* Woven, wove.

باقر bākir, *s. t.* Copper (metal); a piece of copper money; copper sheathing of ships; *pl.* باقرلر bàkirlar, Copper utensils, pots and pans, kettles and cans.

باقمق bākmak (*aor.* باقار bākar), *v.a.* To look; to regard; to consider; to superintend; to attend; to treat medically; to face, be opposite to; to depend, be dependent; to hope.

باقى bākī, *a. a.* Permanent, durable; remaining; —, *s. a.* The remainder, the rest; —, *ad. t.* As to anything else; —قالمق, —kālmak, *v.n.* To remain.

باك bāk, *s. p.* Fear; —وپروا, —u-perwā, Fear and dread; بى باك bī-bāk, Fearless.

باكره bākirē, *s. a.* A virgin.

بال bāl, *s. t.* Honey; —, bāl, *s. a.* The heart; the mind; —, *s. p.* A wing; بال يماز bāl-yèmàz, *a. t.* The common long kind of cannon, neither carronade nor chambered; كومج بالى ghyùmèj-bāli, Honey in the comb; بالمومى bāl-mùmu, Bees'-wax, wax; a wax-candle; —, bì-'l (at the beginning of many Arabic adverbial expressions), in, with, by, &c. (it is the *prep.* ب, and the *def. art.* ال).

بالا bālā, *a. p.* High; —, *s. p.* Height, stature; the top, summit; رتبهٔ بالا rùtbé'i-bālā, The highest civil grade after which the holders are generally made mushirs, and take the title of pasha; some ministers hold this rank.

بالچق bālchik, *s. t.* Tenacious clay; the cross-piece or guard of a sword-handle.

بالجمله bì-'l-jùmlē, *a. a.* All, every one.

بالدر bāldir, *s. t.* The calf of the leg; بالدرى چيلاق طاقمى bāldiri-chìplāk-tàkimi, The rabble (those who go bare-legged).

بالدز bàldiz, *s. t.* A man's sister-in-law, the sister of his wife.

بالذات bì-'z-zāt, *ad. a.* In person, personally.

بالطه bālta, *s. t.* An axe; a battle-axe; بالطه جى bāltaji, A woodcutter, one who cuts up firewood; one of a former corps of guards to the Sultan.

بالغ bāligh, *a. a.* Reaching, arriving; amounting, mounting up to; arrived at years of puberty (also expressed عقله بالغ "àkla-bāligh, *arrived at* (years of) *discretion*).

بالفعل bì-'l-fi"l, *ad. a.* Actually, really, in act and deed.

بالق bàlìk, *s. t.* A fish; —اوى, —àvi, fishing; —اولامق, —àvlamak, To fish; —يمورطهسى, —yìmurtassi, the roe or spawn of fish; botargo, the dried roe of the grey mullet; —اغى, —àghi, A fishing-net.

بالقان bàlkan, *s. t.* A mountain covered with forests.

بالين bālīn, *s. p.* A cushion, bolster, pillow; —, *s. t.* A round long bolster.

باليوس bàlyoss, *s. t.* (*Italian*), A consul (*formerly* an ambassador).

بام bām, *s. p.* The dawn, early morn; the terraced roof of a house.

باندره bàndara, *s. t.* (*Italian*), A foreign flag, colours, or ensign.

بانك bānk, *s. p.* A voice, a cry.

بانى bànī, *s. a.* A builder, founder.

باور bāvɛr, *s. p.* Truth; credit, belief; —قيلمق, —kìlmak, *v.a.* To credit, believe.

باه bāh, *s.a.* Sexual intercourse.

باهر bāhir, *a. a.* Manifest, evident.

باى bày, *s. p.* A rich or great man.

بايات bàyat, *a. t.* Stale, old, not fresh.

باى حال bì-èyyi-hāl, *ad. a.* In any case, under whatever circumstances it may be.

باير bàyìr, *s. t.* A rising, sloping ground.

بايع bāyi", *s. a.* A seller, vendor.

بايغين bàyghìn, *a. t.* Faint, fainting, swooning; drooping.

بايقوش bàykush, *s. t.* An owl.

بايلمق bàyìlmak (*aor.* بايلور bàyìlìr), *v.n.* To faint, swoon; to droop.

ببر bìbɛr, *s. t.* Pepper; —, bùbr, *s. p.* A tiger; قرمزى ببر kìrmizi-bìbɛr, Red pepper, cayenne, and the like; ببريه bìbérìyyé, *s. t.* Rosemary.

ببك bèbek, *s. t.* An infant, child in swaddling-clothes; كوزببكى ghyùz-bèbèghi, The pupil of the eye.

بت bìt, *s. t.* A louse; —, (pùt), *s. p.* An idol, object of false worship; a mistress, sweetheart; —بازارى, bit-pāzāri, A market for old clothes (*and lice*); تخته بتى tàkhta-bìti, A bug; قاصق بتى kàssìk-bìti, A crab-louse; بتلنمك bìtlɛnmek, *v.n.* To louse one's self; بتخانه (pùt)-khāné, An idol-temple; بتپرست (pùt)-pèrèsst, An idolater, worshipper of idols.

بتاق bàtak, *s. t.* A morass, a slough, a slime-pit; a quick-sand; a place where travellers sink in; a bad business where money is lost; a cut-throat's den where people are secretly made away with; بتاقجى bàtakji, A secret cut-throat who entices people to his house, and then makes away with them; a swindler, who sinks people's money or goods.

بتر bètɛr, *a. p.* Worse.

بترمك bìtirmek (*aor.* بترر bìtirir), *v.a.* (*caus. of* بتمك bìtmek), To finish, conclude, bring to an end, make an end of.

بتمك bìtmek (*aor.* بتر bìtER), *v.n.* To end, be finished, come to an end, be all used up, or spent; to grow, sprout (as plants).

بتون bìtun, *a. t.* Whole, entire; —, *s. t.* The whole, the entire; — *or* بتون بتون bìtun-bìtun, *ad. t.* Wholly, entirely.

بتوى bìtévī, *s. a.* and *ad. t.* Same meanings as بتون.

بجا bè-jā, *a. p.* Which is in its place, worthy, suitable; نابجا nā-bè-jā, *a. p.* Unworthy, improper; بجايش bè-jāyesh (bèjàyish), *s. t.* (in its place, in lieu, *ad. p.*) An exchange of places or offices; ا—, —et, *v.n.* To exchange offices with one another.

بجالت bèjālèt, *s. a.* Beauty and portliness combined.

بچ Bèch, *s. t.* Vienna.

بچاق bìchAk, *s. t.* A knife; a cutter; بچاقجى bìchAkj*i*, A knife cutler.

بچقى bìchk*i*, *s. t.* A cross-cut saw, a sawyer's saw; بچقيجى bìchk*i*j*i*, A sawyer.

بچم bìchim, *s. t.* Cutting; a mode of cutting, cut, shape, form; harvest, reaping.

بچمك bìchmek (*aor.* بچر bìchER), *v.a.* To mow; to reap; to saw into planks; to cut out (clothes); to estimate (the value).

بچوق bŭchuk, *s. t.* A half over any whole numbers, as بربچوق bìr-bŭchŭk, One and a half, ايكى بچوق ìki-bŭchuk, Two and a half, &c.

بچه bèchE, *s. p.* The young of an animal; a child.

بحار bìhār, *s. pl. a.* (*of* بحر bàhr), Seas.

بحث bàhss, *s. a.* A dissertation, discourse; a wager; ا—, —et, *v.n.* To discourse, treat, enlarge upon; —, *v.a.* To wager, bet, lay.

بحر bàhr, *s. a.* The sea; any great water; —محيط, bàhr*i*-mŭhīt, The ocean (as formerly supposed to surround the habitable part of the world); —ابيض, bàhr*i*-èbyàd, The Mediterranean; —اسود, bàhr*i*-èssvèd, The Black Sea; —احمر, bàhr*i*-àhmEr, *or* —قلزم, bàhr*i*-kŭlzŭm, *or* —سويس, bàhr*i*-Sŭwèyss, The Red Sea; —خزر, bàhr*i*-hàzER, The Caspian; —لوط, bàhr*i*-Lūt, The Dead Sea; بحرين bàhrèyn, *s. a. dual.* The two seas, *i.e.* the Black Sea and the Mediterranean; بحرى bàhrī (*fem.* بحريه bàhrìyyE), *a. a.* Maritime; marine; naval; nautical.

بحران bŭhrAn, *s. a.* The crisis of a fever.

بخار bŭkhār, *s. a.* Vapour, exhalation.

بخارا Bŭkhārā, *s. t.* Bokhara.

بخت bàkht, *s. p.* Luck, fortune; good luck, good fortune; بختلو bàkhtl*i*, *a. t.* بختيار bàkht-yār, بختاور bàkht-āvER, *a. p.* Lucky, fortunate; بختسز bàkhtsiz, *a. t.* بدبخت bèd-bàkht, *a. p.* Unfortunate, unlucky.

بخش bàkhsh, *and* بخشا bàkshhā, *a. p.* (*in composition*), Who gives, a giver.

بخشش bàkhshish, *s. p.* A giving; a present in money (from a superior).

بخل bŭkhl *or* bàkhl, *s. a.* Stinginess, avarice.

بخور bŭkhūr, *s. a.* Incense; بخوردان bŭkhūrdān (*or* بخوردانلق bŭkhurdanlik), *s. p.* A censer, pan or box in which incense is burnt.

بخيل bàkhīl, *s. a.* A miser; a stingy, avaricious man. [improper.

بد bèd, *a. p.* Bad, ill; ugly, shocking,

بدء bèdʻ, *s. a.* A beginning, commencing; a commencement; ا—, —et, *v.n.* To begin, commence.

بداهت bèdāhèt, *s. a.* A sudden appearance or effusion; بالبداهه bì-'l-bèdāhé, Suddenly, unexpectedly, unpreparedly, extemporarily.

بدايت bìdāyet, *s. a.* A beginning, commencement.

بدر bèdr, *s. a.* The full moon.

بدرقه bèdraka, *s. a.* A guide; a fellow-traveller; an escort.

بدعت bìd"àt, *s. a.* An innovation; —حسنه, bìd"àti-hàssana, A praiseworthy *or* useful innovation, a reform, an opportune departure from routine.

بدل bèdel, *s. a.* Anything set in lieu of another; money paid instead of rations; a substitute given for a person drawn by ballot for the army.

بدن bèdɛn, *s. a.* The body; the trunk of the body; the main body of a building; the walls (of a castle or town); قلعه بدنى kàl"a-bèdéni, The walls of a (the) castle.

بدوح bèdūh, Mystical word usually written under the address of letters, and sometimes represented by the numeral equivalents of its component letters, thus ٨٦٤٢, as an invocation for its safe arrival.

بدوى bèdévī, *a. a.* Inhabiting, *or* growing in the desert or unreclaimed wilderness (*pl.* بدويون bèdévìyyūn, and *accus.* بدويين bèdévìyyīn; this latter word, in which the *v* is pronounced *w* by the Arabs, is the original of the French *bedouin*, adopted by us also).

بديدار bèdīdār, *a. p.* Visible, apparent, manifest.

بديع bèdī", *a. a.* New, never seen or heard of before, beautiful, wonderful, astonishing; (*fem.* بديعه bèdī"à, A wonderful, *or* beautiful thing, act, *or* quality).

بديهه bèdīhé, *s. a.* A witty impromptu, a spiritual saying or remark.

بديهى bèdīhī, *a. a.* Which happens suddenly; self-evident, manifest.

بذل bèzl, *s. a.* A bestowing profusely; ا—, —et, *v.a.* To bestow.

بر bèr, *pr. p.* On, upon; over; according to; —, *s. p.* The breast, bosom; fruit; —, *a. p.* (*in composition*), Who carries, brings, or carries away; —, bìr, *a. t.* One; the same; equal; a, an; —, bèrr, s. a. Land; mainland; a just man; —, bìrr, s. a. Virtue; —طرف, bèr-tàraf, a. p. Aside, on one side, out of the way; ا— —, — —et, v.a. To get rid of, dispose of, put out of the way; برمنوال محرر bèr-mìnvāli-mŭhàrrer, According to the manner described, as above-mentioned; سیمین بر sīmīn-bèr, a. p. Silver-breasted; نامه بر nāmé-bèr, Who carries a letter; بری bìri, or بریسی bìrissi, One, a person, a man; one (of them); بریکی bìr-ìki, One or two; ایکیده بر ìkida-bìr, Every now and then; برده bìrda, c. t. And also, moreover; —او, bìr-òl, v.n. To act together, be as one; بربرینی bìr-bìrini, or بری برینی bìri-bìrini, pron. acc. One another; بربرینه bìr-bìrina, To one another; بربرندن bìr-bìrindàn, From one another, بربریله bìr-bìrīla, With one another; &c.; بربر bìr-bìr, One by one; برلك bìrlik, s. t. Unity; concord; برلکده bìrlikda, (In unity) together.

برء bùr', s. a. A being healed, a cure; —الساعه, bùr'u-'ss-sā''a, An instantaneous cure.

برابر bèrābèr, a. p. Equal, on a footing of equality, on a line, breast and breast; —, ad. p. Together, at the same time, along with.

برات bèrāt, s. t. A warrant, or letters-patent of the second class; a diploma; a consul's exequatur; براتلو bèràtli, A merchant, or other, holding a patent of privilege.

برادر bìrāder, s. p. A brother; a friend, comrade, companion, fellow; برادرانه bìrādérāné, a. p. Brotherly (thing).

براعت bèrā''at, s. a. Elegance, perfection of beauty; —استهلال, bèrā''àti-ìsstihlāl, The beauty of symbolic literary composition, by which the technical terms of any science are used (for example, in a preface) and symbolized.

براغه bràgha, s. t. (Italian), The breeching of a cannon on board ship.

براق bèrrāk, a. t. Clear, limpid (liquid), free from mistiness, cloudiness, or turbidity; —, bŭrāk, s. a. Name of the celestial steed said to have carried Muhammed to the highest heaven, and variously explained by the commentators.

براقمق bràkmak (aor. براقر bràkir, or براغر bràghir, or bràghàr), v.a. To leave, quit, forsake, abandon; to let go, loose; to let, permit; to leave, not meddle with, let alone; to put down, lay down.

بران bùrrān, a. p. Sharp, keen, cutting.

برای bèrāyi, pr. p. For, for the sake of, on account of.

برایا bèrāyā, s. pl. a. (of بریه, not used), Creatures; men; Musslim subjects of the Sultan, free from tribute; رعایاو برایا rì''āyā-u-bèrāyā, The subjects of the Sultan, free and protected.

براءت bèrāʿat, s. a. Freedom, a being free from any defect or blemish.

برباد bèrbād (bĕrbāt), a. p. Gone to the winds, destroyed, ruined; spoilt, dirtied. [aboriginal of Barbary.

بربر bèrbĕr, s. t. A barber; a Berber,

بربط bìrbèt, s. p. A lute, a harp.

برتر bèrtĕr, a. p. Higher; برترين bèr-térīn, a. p. The highest.

برج bùrj, s. a. A round or square tower at intervals in old castle walls; a sign of the zodiac.

برچاق bùrchāk, s. t. A lupin? a vetch?

برخوردار bèrkhòrdār, a. p. Prosperous, fortunate, happy.

برد bèrd, s. a. Cold, coldness.

بردار bèrdār, a. p. On the gibbet, gibbeted; ا—, —et, v.a. To hang, to gibbet; —او, —òl, v.n. To be hung.

برزخ bèrzàkh, s. a. An unfathomable gulf; the great gulf between this world and heaven, or between this life and the eternal future.

برف bĕrf, s. a. Snow.

برق bĕrk, s. a. Lightning; —, bàrk, s. t. Always follows the word او èv, *a house*, and corroborates it; اوبرق èv-bàrk, House and home, wife and family; اولو برقلو èvli-bàrkli, Who possesses house and home, wife and family; برقلنمق bàrklanmak (aor. برقلنور bàrklanìr), v.n. To become possessed of home and family.

برك bèrgh, s. p. A leaf of a tree.

بركت bèrékĕt, s. a. (pl. بركات bè-rékyāt), God's blessing; increase; plenty; بركتلو bèrékĕtli, a. t. Plentiful, abundant (year); blessed as the widow's cruse, and yielding much increase, prolific (plant or animal); بركت ويرسون bèrékĕt-vĕrsin! int. t. May it be returned to you a hundred-fold! (lit. May it bring you a blessing of increase). [souvenir.

بركذار bèr-ghyùzār, s. p. A keepsake,

برله bìrla, pr. t. With, in, by.

برنا bèrnā, s. p. A young person, a young man.

برنجق bùrunjuk, s. t. Gauze, crape.

برو bèri, s. t. The space on the hither side of any object; —, ad. t. Hither; hitherwards; بروسى bèrissi, The space on the hither side of it; بروسنه bèrissina, To the hither side, to this side of it; بروسنده bèrissinda, On or at this side of it; —دن برو, or —دنبرو, —dan-bèri, From — till now, ever since —.

برودت bùrūdèt, s. a. Coldness, frigidity; coolness of feeling, interruption of friendship.

بروز bùrūz, s. a. Evidence, the being evident, manifest, clear, palpable.

بره brĕ! int. t. Sirrah! Fellow! —, bĕrĕ, s. t. A bruise; برهلنمك bè-rélĕnmek, v.n. To be bruised, become bruised; ا—, —et, v.n. To bruise, make a bruise. [demonstration.

برهان bùrhān, s. a. A proof, evidence,

برهنه bìrèhnĕ, a. p. Naked, bare.

برى bèrī, a. a. Free, exempt (from ill or

defect); —, bèrrī, *a. a.* Wild, growing wild.

بریان bùryān, *s. p.* Roast meat, a roast.

بریزولیه brìzòly*a*, *s. t.* A mutton chop.

بریه bèrrìyyé, *s. a.* A wilderness, unreclaimed tract of country.

بریق brìk (ìbrik), *s. t.* A brig.

برین bèrīn, *a. p.* Highest, most high; —, bèrrèyn, *s. a. dual.* Two lands or continents.

بز bèz, *s. t.* Cotton or linen cloth; —, bìz, *pron. t.* We; صوغوق بز sòg*h*ʊk-bèz, (Cold cloth) Linen cloth; بزی bèzi, The cloth; its cloth; —, bìzi, Us; بزم bìzim, Our; ours; بزه bìzé, To us; بزده bìzdé, At *or* in us; بزدن bìzd*a*n, From us; بزمله bìzimla, With us; بزسز bìzsiz, Without us; بزجه bìzj*a*, Our fashion; according to us.

بزر (bèzir), *s. a.* Seed; linseed; بزر تخمی bèzir-tòkhʊmʊ, Linseed; بزر یاغی bèzir-yàg*hi*, Linseed-oil.

بزرك bùzùrgh, *a. p.* Great, large; بزركوار bùzurghvār, *a. p.* Great in esteem.

بزم bèzm, *s. p.* A banquet, feast; —, bìzim (*gen. of* بز), *pron. t.* Our; ours.

بزمك bèzmek (*aor.* بزر bèzer), *v.n.* To become tired of, lose one's taste for.

بزنمك bèzenmek (*aor.* بزنور bèzénir), *v.n.* To adorn one's self, put on one's fine clothes and ornaments.

بساط bìssāt, *s. a.* A cloth *or* carpet for spreading.

بست bèsst, *s. p.* A tying, binding; —وبند ا—, bèsst-u-bènd-et, *v.n.* To bind, tie.

[a cushion.

بستر bìsster, *s. p.* A mattrass or bed,

بستان bòsstan, *s. p.* A large market-garden; a melon-garden; melons; بستانجی bòstanj*i*, A soldier of one of the corps of guards of the Sultan's palace in the time of the Janissaries; a soldier of the foot-guards in the early days of the new system; بستانجی باشی bòsstanj*i*-bàsh*i*, The commander of the Bosstanji guards, and superintendent of police in the Bosphorus.

بسته bèssté, *a. p.* Tied, bound.

بسط bàsst, *s. a.* A spreading out, extending; a laying down, explaining at length; —ا—, —et, *v.a.* To spread out, lay, extend; to lay down, declare, *or* explain at length.

بسلمك bèsslémek (*aor.* بسلر bèssler), *v.a.* To feed, nourish, keep, maintain, support; to fatten; بسلمه bèsslémé, *s. t.* A maid or woman servant; a child fed in the house for charity; بسلو bèssli, *a. t.* Fed, fattened.

بسم الله bì-'ssmi-'llāh! *int. a.* In the name of God! (*Invocation used before commencing any kind of work*).

بسیار bìssyār, *a. p.* Many in number; much in quantity.

بسیط bàssīt, *a. a.* Spread out, extended; simple, uncompounded.

بسیم bèssīm, *a. a.* Smiling.

بسیطه bèssīté, *s. a.* A sun-dial.

بش bèsh, *a. t.* Five; بشنجى bèshinji, *a. t.* Fifth; بشلك bèshlik, *s. t.* A five-piastre piece.

بشارت bèshārèt, *s. a.* Joy caused by any happy event; the announcement of a happy event.

بشاشت bèshāshèt, *s. a.* Hilarity, brightness of conntenance.

بشر bèshER, *s. a.* A human being, a man; mankind; —, *a. t.* Five a-piece; بشرى bèshérī, *a. a.* Human; بشريت bèshérìyyèt, *s. a.* Humanity, the quality of being human, human nature.

بشرا (*for* بشرى) bùshrà, *s. a.* Good news, joyful intelligence.

بشقه bAshka, *pr. t.* Other; بشقه‌سى bAshkassi, Another of them; —دن بشقه —dan-bAshka, Other than —, beside —.

بشك bèshik, *s. t.* A cradle.

بصر bàssar, *s. a.* The sight.

بصره Bàssra, *s. t.* Bassora (town of).

بصيرت bAssīrèt, *s. a.* Foresight; circumspection.

بضاعت bìzā''at, *s. a.* Capital, stock in trade.

بطال bAttĀl, *a. a.* Of no further use; large; —, *s. a.* A letter, paper, or document which has been answered, or which does not require answering, or which is laid aside as of no further use; a champion, man of valour.

بطائت bAtā'àt, *s. a.* Slowness, heaviness, sluggishness; indigestibleness; stupidity of intellect; tiresomeness, wearisomeness of manner.

بطش bAtsh, *s. a.* Martial strength and impetuosity.

بطلان bŭtlĀn, *s. a.* A being unfounded, futile, vain; absurdity, futility.

بطمان bAtmĀn, *s. t.* A weight of six okes, or about 16lbs: it varies in different places.

بطن bAtn, *s. a.* The belly, inside; a sept, a tribe; a generation, or degree of relationship; an interior or mystical sense of a writing.

بطى bAtī, *a. a.* Slow in motion; difficult of digestion.

بعث bà''ss, *s. a.* A sending; a deputing; a resuscitating, raising from the dead; ا—, —et, *v.a.* To send.

بعد bù''d, *s. a.* Distance; —, bà''da, *pr. a.* After; بعده bà''da-hŭ, *ad. a.* Afterwards, then; بعدالسلام bà''da-'ss--sèlām, After salutation; من بعد mìn--bà''d, *ad. a.* (Never) more, (never) again, (never) afterwards; فيما بعد fī-mā-bà''d, *ad. a.* Henceforward, thenceforward, henceforth; بعد بعد bà''da-bù''din, *ad. a.* After a while, after a certain length of time; وبعد vè-bà''du, اما بعد amma-ba''d, *c. a.* And now then (an introductory formula to the proper matter of any discourse or treatise, after the customary prayers and praises); مابعد mā--bà''d, *s. a.* The word or words next after, or the place occupied by them.

بعض bA''zi, *a. a.* Some, certain; —كره, —kÉrrÉ, *ad. t.* Sometimes.

بعيد bà''īd, *a. a.* Distant, far off.

بعينه bì-''àyni-hi, *ad. a.* As though it were the very self, exactly.

بغات bùghāt, s. pl. a. (of باغى bāghī), Rebels; wicked sinners.

بغتة bàghtétɛn, ad. a. Suddenly, all of a sudden.

بغداد Bàghdād, s. t. Bagdad (town of).

بغدادى bàghdādī, s. t. Lath and plaster work.

بغدان Bòghdān, s. t. Moldavia.

بغداش bàghdàsh, s. t. A tailor's mode of sitting cross-legged; —قورمق, —kùrmak, v.n. To sit cross-legged as tailors do.

بغداى bòghdày, s. t. Wheat; a grain weight; مصربغدايى mìssir-bòghdàyi, Indian corn.

بغر bàghir (*little used*), بغرصاق bàghir-sàk, s. t. The guts, bowels, intestines.

بغض bùghz, s. a. Hatred, enmity, ill-will; ا—, —et, v.n. To bear malice.

بغل bàghl, s. a. A mule; s. p. The arm-pit; رسم بغلكيرى rèssmi-bàghl-ghīrī, The ceremony of supporting persons of rank as they walk, by holding them by the arm close to the arm-pits, like crutches.

بغه bAgha, s. t. The generic name for animals of the frog and tortoise kinds; tortoise-shell; قوربغه kùr-bAgha (or قوروبغه kùru-bAgha, The naked batrachian) the frog; اودلوبغه (òtlu)-bAgha, قره قوربغه kAra-kùr-bAgha, The toad; توسبغه tòssbAgha, قاپلوبغه kàpli-bàgha (kàplimbAgha), The tortoise; دكزقاپلوبغه سى dèngiz-kàpli-bAghassi, The turtle.

بغير bì-ghàyri, pr. a. Without; بغيرحق bì-ghàyri-kAkkin, Without right or justice, unjustly.

بقا bAkā, s. a. Permanency, a remaining without change; داربقا dāri-bAkā, The mansion of permanency, the future life.

بقال bAkkāl (bAkAl), s. a. A grocer, a chandler.

بقايا bAkāyā, s. pl. a. (of بقيه bAkìyyé), Remnants; outstanding deficits of revenue due to government or to farmers by the people, arrears.

بقراج bAkraj, s. t. A leather bucket; the piston of a pump.

بقلوا bAklawā, s. t. A dish of flaky pastry, sweetened with syrup or honey, and cut up in rhomboidal pieces; hence بقلوابقلوا bAklawā-bAklawā means, *divided into rhomboidal figures.*

بقله bAkla, s. a. A broad bean, a horse bean; —قيرى, —kìri, a. t. Dapple grey (horse).

بقم bAkam, s. t. Brazil-wood, log-wood.

بقمق bìkmak (aor. بقار bìkar), v.n. To become cloyed, disgusted, tired (of anything).

بقيه bAkìyyé, s. a. A remnant.

بك bègh, s. t. A bey; a prince; a lord; a squire; the son of a pasha or high functionary; the style of colonels, lieutenant-colonels, post-captains, and commanders; the style of ambassadors, and of the governors of Moldavia, Wallachia, and Samos; the style often given abusively to sons of private individuals, embassy interpreters, consuls, and even to servants; بكزاده bègh-zādé, Son of a bey, a Christian whose father held the title of bey; a European gentleman; بكلربكی bèghler-bèghi, Bey of beys, style formerly given to the viceroys or governors-general of Rumelia and Anatolia; —, bèng, s. t. A mole on the skin.

بك اوغلی Bègh-òghlu, s. t. Pera (a suburb of Constantinople).

بكجی bèkji, s. t. A watchman, watcher.

بكر bìkr, s. a. Virginity; a virgin; ازالهٔ بكرا ìzālé'i-bìkr-et, v.n. To deflower.

بكرش Bùkrèsh, s. t. The town of Odessa.

بكری bèkrī, a. a. An habitual drunkard.

بكز bèngz, s. t. Countenance, complexion.

بكزهمك bèngzémek (aor. بكزر bèngzer), v.n. To resemble.

بكلك bèghlik, s. t. The rank of bey, beyship; a principality, state under the rule of a bey; government property of any kind; بكلكجی bèghlikji, Title of one of the principal functionaries of the Ottoman government, who is at the head of the imperial chancery, from which all letters patent, commissions, treaties, &c. &c. emanate.

بكلمك bèklémek (aor. بكلر bèkler), v.n. To wait; to act as watchman; —, v.a. To wait for; to watch over, act as guard or watchman over.

بكمز bèkmaz (pètmaz) s. t. Grape-treacle.

بكنمك bèghenmek (aor. بكنور bèghènir), v.a. To like, approve.

بل bèl, s. t. The waist; a fork, a pronged spade for digging; a passage over a range of mountains where the heads of two opposite valleys meet and the ridge is lower than elsewhere; —ويرمك, —vèrmek, v.n. To droop in the middle, as a horse's back, when the two ends are supported (a beam, &c.); —صوغوغی, —sòghughu, Gonorrhea.

بلا bèlā, s. a. A misfortune, plague, trouble; —, bìlā, pr. a. Without; بلايه اوغرامق bèlāya-òghramak, To meet with irretrievable misfortune, to be utterly ruined; اللهك بلاسی Allāhing-bèlāssi, A plague sent by God; الله بلاكی ويرسون Allāh-bèlāngi-vèrsin! God damn you! الله بلاسنی ويرسون Allāh-bèlāssini-vèrsin! God damn him (her, it)!

بلابان bàlabàn, a. t. Big, large, huge.

بلاد bìlād, s. pl. a. (of بلد bèled), Cities, towns; countries. [Persian Irak.

بلاد الجبل Bìlād-u'-l-jèbel, s. t. Media,

بلادت bèlādèt, s. a. Stupidity.

بلازك bìlāzik (bìlèzik), s. t. A bracelet.

بلاغت bèlāghàt, s. a. The eloquence which fully explains one's meaning.

بلاهت bèlāhèt, s. a. Extreme stupidity.

بلايا bèlāyā, s. pl. a. (of بلا bèlā), Evils, misfortunes, plagues.

بلبل bùlbul, s. p. The nightingale; —بوقلوجه bòkluja—, The wren (?).

بلد bèled, *s. a.* A city, town, village; a country.

بلدان bùldān, *s. pl. a.* (*of* بلد bèled), Cities, towns; countries.

بلده bèldé, *s. a.* A city, town, village.

بلغار Bùlgār, *s.* and *a. t.* Bulgarian; a Bulgarian; بلغارستان Bùlgārisstān, *s.t.* Bulgaria.

بلغاری bùlghārī, *s. t.* A kind of Russia leather, very thick and coarse; a kind of small lute strung with wires.

بلغراد Bèlègràd, *s. t.* The town of Belgrade.

بلغم bàlghàm, *s. a.* Phlegm; بلغمی bàlghàmī, *a. a.* Phlegmatic; —, *or* —يشم, —yèshem, Veined jasper, of the colour of phlegm.

بلغور bùlghur, *s. t.* Wheat grains prepared like rice or like pearl-barley.

بلكه bèlki, *ad. t.* Perhaps, may be, by chance.

بلكى *or* بلكو bilèghi, *s. t.* A hone; a grind- or whet-stone; ياغ بلكيسى yàgh-bilèghissi, A hone used with oil.

بللمك bèllémek (*aor.* بللر bèller), *v.a.* To dig with a fork or spade; to learn by heart so as to remember again.

بللو bèlli, *a. t.* Known; بللو باشلو bèlli-bàshli, *a.t.* (A person) publicly known, whose person and physiognomy are generally known.

بللور bìllūr, *s. a.* Crystal, cut-glass.

بلمجه bìlméjé, *s. t.* A riddle, an enigma.

بلمك bìlmek (*aor.* بلور bilir), *v.a.* To know; to guess; to recognize; to know as, or suppose to be; (*in composition with the root of any verb increased by the syllable* ه *or* يه) to be able, as: كله بلمك ghèlé-bilmek, To be able to come.

بلند bùlènd, *a. p.* High; loud.

بلوت *or* بلوط bùlut; *s. t.* A cloud; بلوتلو bùlutlu, *a. t.* Cloudy, clouded.

بلوغ bùlūgh, *s. a.* Maturity, puberty.

بلوك bùluk, *s. t.* A division, subdivision; a piece; a company of infantry; a squadron of horse; a number of persons.

بلهمك bilémek (*aor.* بلر biler), *v.a.* To whet, set, sharpen.

بلى bèli, *ad. a.* Yes.

بليه bèliyyé, *s. a.* A misfortune, plague, visitation.

بليد bèlīd, *a. a.* Stupid.

بليغ bèlīgh, *a. a.* Eloquent in expressing ideas; copious, plentiful; strenuous.

بن bèn, *pron. t.* I; بنم bènim, My; mine; بنى bèni, Me; بكا bànga, To me; بنده bènda, At *or* in me; بندن bèndan, From me; بنمله bènimla, With me; بنسز bènsiz, Without me; بنجه bènja, My fashion; according to me; —, bin, *s. a.* Son of, as احمد بن محمود Àhmed bin Màhmūd, Ahmed, son of Mahmud; —, bùn, *s. p.* The foot, stock, bottom, lower end or base of anything.

بنا bìnā, *s. a.* A building; the building of buildings; the *voice* of verbs in grammar; —ا, —et, *v.a.* To build; —امينى, —èmīni, A clerk of the works and paymaster; بناء bìnā'an, *ad. a.* Consequently; as بوكابناء bùn*ga*-bìnā'*an*, *or* بناءعليه bìnā'*an*-"àlèyh, In consequence thereof.

بند bènd, *s. p.* A sentence, a paragraph, an article, a verse of literary composition; a band, ligature, tie; a dam shutting up a valley so as to form a reservoir of water or artificial lake; —, *a. p.* (*in composition*), Which ties, binds, makes fast. [A seaport.

بندر bènder *or* بندرگاه bènderghiāh, *s. t.*

بنده bèndé, *s. p.* (*pl.* بندگان bèndé-ghyān), A servant, bondsman; بندگی bèndéghī, *s. p.* بنده‌لك bèndélik, *s. t.* Servitude, service; بنده‌خانه bèndé--khāné, *s. p.* The house of your humble servant (used in polite conversation instead of "*my house*," as دولتخانه dèvlet-khāné, *the house of prosperity*, is instead of "*your house*").

بنفشه bènefshé (mènèkshé), *s. p.* A violet.

بنك bènek, *s. t.* A spot; —, bìnek, *s.* and *a. t.* A saddle-horse, horse for riding; بنكلو bènekli, *a. t.* Spotted, speckled.

بنم bènim, *pron. t.* (*gen. of* بن bèn, I), My, of me; mine; بنمكى bènimki, *pron. t.* Mine.

بنمك bìnmek (*aor.* بنر bìner), *v.n.* To mount, get upon; to get into (a carriage or boat); to ride (on a horse, in a carriage, or boat).

بنى bènī, *s. pl. a.* (*of* بن bìn), Sons, children; —ادم, —Adem, Sons of Adam, children of men, men, mankind. [sical constitution.

بنياد bùnyād, *s. p.* A foundation; phy-

بنيان bùnyān, *s. a.* The building, constructing; construction; physical constitution.

بو bū, *pron. t.* This; —, bū, *s. p.* Smell, odour; —, *a. p.* (*in composition*), Smelling, having an odour; —, bū, *s. a.* Father; خوشبو khòsh-bū, Sweet-smelling; بوالفضول bū-'l-fūzūl, (The father of presumption), presumptuous.

بواب bèwwāb, *s. a.* A door-keeper, gate-keeper, porter; a chamberlain; سربوابين sèr-bèwwābīn, A chief chamberlain (title of dignity something like our knight-bachelor).

بوار bèvār, *s. a.* Destruction; دارالبوار dāru-'l-bèvār, (The house of destruction) hell.

بوبرك bùbrek, *s. t.* A kidney.

بوت bùt, *s. t.* A thigh of an animal, a leg (of mutton, &c.).

بوجاق bùjàk, *s. t.* A distant out-of-the-way corner; Bessarabia.

بوجك bùjek, *s. t.* Any creeping animal, as a slug, silkworm; a crayfish; سموكلو بوجك sùmuklu-bùjek, A slug or snail; قوندز بوجكى kùnduz-bùjè-*ghi*, Cantharides. [gnarl in a tree.

بوداق bùdāk, *s. t.* A knot in wood; a

بوداله bùdala, *s. t.* A simpleton, idiot.

بوداموق bùdamak (*aor.* بودار bùdar), *v.a.* To prune, thin out, lop.

بودور bòdur, *a. t.* Dwarf, short in stature amounting to deformity.

بودین Būdìn, *s. t.* The town of Buda.

بورا bùra, *s. t.* This place, this spot; بورام bùram, (my this place) here, this place in my body; بوراك bùrang, Here, this place in thy body; بوراسی bùrassi, Here, this place in it; &c.; بورایه bùraya, Here, to this place; بورامه bùrama, Here, to this place in my body; &c.; بوراده bùrada, Here, in this place; بورادن bùradan, Hence, from hence; &c. &c.; بورالر bùralar, Hereabouts, these parts or places; &c. &c.

بورج bòrj, *s. t.* A debt; duty incumbent; —, bùrj, *s. t.* The misletoe; بورجلو bòrjlu, In debt; indebted; a debtor; بورجه کیرمك bòrja-ghìrmek, *v.n.* To get in debt.

بورده bòrda, *s. t.* (*Italian*), A ship's side; a board, tack (in sailing); بورده بوردهیه bòrda-bòrdaya, Side by side, porthole to porthole.

بورسمق bùrushmak (*aor.* بورشور bù-rushur), *v.n.* To become wrinkled, rumpled, ruffled.

بورغو or بورغی bùrghu, *s. t.* A gimlet; a screw.

بورقتمق bùrkutmak (*aor.* بورقودر bùrku-dur), *v.a.* To sprain (a joint); بورقلمق bùrkulmāk (*aor.* بورقلور bùrkulur), *v.n.* To be sprained.

بورك bùrek, *s. t.* A pie, tart, pasty.

بورمق bùrmak (*aor.* بورار bùrar), *v.a.* To twist (with strength, *e.g.* A bar of iron, a person's arm); بورمه bùrma, *s. t.* A twist; a screw; —, *a. t.* Twisted.

بورون bùrun, *s. t.* The nose; the point of anything; a cape, promontory, point; the snuff (of a candle).

بورنمك bùrunmek (*aor.* بورنور bùrunur), *v.n.* To wrap one's self, cover one's self up (in a scarf, mantle, &c.)

بورو or بوری bòru, *s. t.* A horn, trumpet; بوروزن bòruzèn, *s. t.* A trumpeter.

بوره bòra, *s. t.* Borax (?), Sal-ammoniac (?); a storm of wind, a squall; a good scolding; بوره یمك bòra-yèmek, *v.n.* To be exposed to a squall; to get a good scolding.

بوز bùz, *a. t.* Ice; بوزکبی bùz-ghìbi, Like ice; very white; very smooth; —, bòz, *a. t.* Dark iron grey.

بوزاغی bùzaghi, *s. t.* A young calf.

بوزجه اطه‌سی Bòzché-Adassi, The island of Tenedos.

بوزطغان bòz-dàghān, *s. t.* A mace of arms.

بوزشمق bòzushmak (*aor.* بوزشور bòzu-shur), *v.n.* To quarrel, fall out with each other; بوزشق bòzushuk, *a. t.* At variance, not on good terms together; بوزشقلق bòzushukluk, *s. t.* Variance, bad terms.

بوزغون bòzghun, *a. t.* Defeated, routed; troubled, cast down; —, *s. t.* Defeat, rout; بوزغونلق bòzghunluk, *s. t.* Defeat, rout; troubled, broken-spiritedness.

بوزق bòzuk, *a. t.* Spoilt, bad; changed

into a small coin; بوزق پاره bòzuk--pàra, Small change.

بوزلمك bùzulmek (*aor.* بوزيلور bùzulur), *v.n.* To become contracted, to contract.

بوزمق bòzmak (*aor.* بوزار bòzar), *v.a.* To spoil; to take to pieces; to rout, defeat; to contradict (one) to a third person, to put to the blush by saying something; to deflower (a virgin); to violate, act in contrariety to, infringe; to change (money), give change (for it).

بوزه bòza, *s. t.* A kind of thick white drink made of millet fermented.

بوس būss, *s. p.* A kissing; —, *a. p.* (*in composition*), Who kisses; ا—, —et, *v.a.* To kiss; بوسى būssī, *s. p.* The act or quality of a kisser.

بوستان bòsstān, *s. p.* See بستان

بوسنه Bòssna, *s. t.* Bosnia.

بوسه būssé, *s. p.* A kiss, a buss.

بوش bòsh, *s. t.* Empty; vain, useless, void of sense, meaning, or utility; idle, unemployed; loose, not tied, not tight; loosened, let go; divorced; —لاقردى, —làkirdi, Nonsense; —وقت, —wàkit, Leisure time; —بوكر, —bùghur, The part of the side of the belly just below the ribs; —بوغاز, —bòghàz, A babbler; —كزمك, —ghèzmek, *v.n.* To wander about without employment; to be without a place, out of service.

بوشاتمق bòshatmak (*aor.* بوشادر bòshàdir), *or* بوشالتمق bòshaltmak (*aor.* بوشالدر bòshaldir), *v.a.* To empty (a vessel of anything, or anything from a vessel).

بوشامق bòshamak (*aor.* بوشار bòshar), *v.a.* To divorce, repudiate, put away (one's wife).

بوشانمق bòshanmak (*aor.* بوشانور bòshà-nir), *v.n.* To empty itself; to become loose, loosened; to burst forth, break loose from restraint (people, a horse, a spring, a bow, &c.); to be divorced (a wife).

بوغ bògh, *s. t.* (*in* باشبوغ bàsh-bògh, A commodore (at sea); a commander (of a corps on land).

بوغا bògha, *s. t.* A bull.

بوغاز bòghàz, *s. t.* The throat, gullet, windpipe; a defile, pass; a strait, channel; the mouth of a river; the quinzy, a sore-throat; the Bosphorus, and particularly the middle portion of it; بوش— bòsh—, A babbler; —او, —òl, To have a sore-throat or the quinzy; بوغازلمق bòghàzlamak, *v.a.* To kill (any animal) by cutting open its throat.

بوغچه bòghcha, *s. t.* A square shawl; a large square piece of stuff used as a wrapper for bundles or parcels; a bundle, a parcel in a wrapper.

بوغق bòghuk, *a. t.* Hoarse, stifled (voice).

بوغم bòghum, *s. t.* A joint in a reed; a knot in wood; a constricted place in any channel or pipe.

بوغمجه bòghmaja, *a. t.* Which chokes;

ـــاوکسرك, bòghmaja-ùksuruk, *s. t.* The whooping-cough.

بوغمق bòghmak (*aor.* بوغار bòghar), *v.a.* To stifle, strangle, drown, suffocate; بوغلمق bòghulmak (*aor.* بوغلور bòghulur), *v.n.* and *p.* To be stifled, strangled, drowned, suffocated; to be ready to burst (with rage, laughter, &c.).

بوغو or بوغی bùghu, *s. t.* Steam, reek [of hot water.

بوق bòk, *s. t.* Excrement, dung, turd, shit; scoria of ores; anything bad or disagreeable; —, *a. t.* Bad; disagreeable; شیطان بوقی shèytAn - bòku, (Devil's dung) assafœtida.

بوقاغی bùkAghi, *s. t.* Fetters, hobbles.

بوکالمق bùngAlmak (*aor.* بوکالور bùngAlir), *v.n.* To become stupified.

بوکر bùghur, *s. t.* (*in* بوش بوکر bòsh-bùghur, The side part of the belly just below the ribs).

بوکرتلن bùghurtlÈn, *s. t.* A blackberry.

بوکرك bùghrek (bùbrek), *s. t.* A kidney.

بوکرلجه bùghrulja, *s. t.* A small white [French bean.

بوکری bùghru, *a. t.* (*in* اکری بوکری èghri-bùghru), Very crooked, tortuous, devious.

بوکلم bùklum, *s. t.* A curl (in any-[thing), a twist.

بوکمك bùkmek (*aor.* بوکر bùkEr), *v.a.* To twist between the fingers; to fold double; to bend.

بوکو or بوکی bùghu, *s. t.* A charm, spell, sorcery; بوکوجی bùghuju, *s. t.* A sorcerer, sorceress.

بول bòl, *a. t.* Plentiful, abundant; ample; wide, loose, in folds (clothing, &c.); —, bèvl, *s. a.* Dung; urine; بوللق bòlluk, *s. t.* Abundance, plenty; looseness (of clothes, &c.).

بولاشق bùlàshik, *a. t.* Daubed, besmeared, contaminated.

بولاشمق bùlàshmak (*aor.* بولاشور bùlàshir), *v.n.* To become irregularly spread upon in daubs (as paint, tar, mud, &c.); to pass by contagion (disease); to set (about any business); to meddle.

بولاماج bùlamaj, *s. t.* Grape-juice boiled to the consistency of honey.

بولانق bùlànik, *a. t.* Turbid, not clear (water, &c.); cloudy and foggy (weather); sick, nauseated (the stomach).

بولانمق bùlànmak (*aor.* بولانور bùlànir), *v.n.* To become turbid, thick, cloudy; to become sick (the stomach).

بولدر bùldur (bìldir), *s. t.* Last year.

بولدرجین bùldurjin, *s. t.* A quail.

بولمق bùlmak (*aor.* بولر bùlur), *v.a.* To find.

بولمك bùlmek (*aor.* بولر bùlEr), *v.a.* To divide, parcel out, partition off.

بولنمق bùlunmak (*aor.* بولنور bùlunùr), *v.n.* To be found, to be present; —, *v. p.* To be found.

بولوط or بولوت bùlut, *s. t.* A cloud; بولوتلو bùlutlu, *a. t.* Cloudy; بولوتلنمق bùlutlanmak, *v.n.* To become cloudy.

بومبار bùmbār (*for* مومبار mūmbār), The large gut of sheep; fresh sausage made in the fresh gut.

بونجق bònjuk, *s. t.* A small shell, a bead, a bugle (with which certain ornaments are made); قاطر بونجغی kàtir-bònjughu, The small shell used as coin in some parts of Africa.

بونجه bùnja, *a. t.* (This is simply another *case* of the demonstrative pronoun بو bū), After this fashion, thus; thus long, thus much, so much, so many; بونجه‌لین *or* بونجلین bùnjaleyin, *ad. t.* Thus long.

بوی bòy, *s. t.* Length; height of stature; —, būy, *s. p.* Smell, scent, odour; بوی بوص bòy-bòss, Stature and general appearance; بویلو bòylu, *a. t.* Having stature; tall; اوزون بویلو ùzun-bòylu, Tall in stature; اورته بویلو òrta-bòylu, Of a middling stature; قصه بویلو kìssa-bòylu, Short in stature.

بویا bòya, *s. t.* Paint; dye; اشی بویاسی àshi-bòyassi, Ochre; یاغلو بویا yàghli-bòya, Oil-paint; قوندره بویاسی kùndura-bòyassi, Blacking; بویاجی bòyaji, A dyer.

بویار bòyàr, *s. t.* A Wallachian noble.

بویامق bòyamak (*aor.* بویار bòyar), *v.a.* To dye; to paint; بویاتمق bòyatmak, *v. caus.* To give to be dyed, to cause to be painted; بویانمق bòyanmak, *v. p.* To be dyed; to be painted; —, *v.n.* To take the dye.

بویله bùylé, *a. t* This kind, this sort; —, *and* بویله‌جه bùyléja, *ad.* Thus, so, in this manner, way, or fashion.

بوین *or* بویون bòyn *or* bòyun, *s. t.* The neck; بویون باغی bòyun-bàghi, A neck-tie; کناهی بویونکه ghyùnāhi-bòynunga! May the sin be on thy neck!

بویندروغ bòyndurugh, *s. t.* A yoke-tree, the yoke (for oxen).

بوینوز bòynuz, *s. t.* A horn (of an animal); horn; کچی بوینوزی kèchi-bòynuzu, The fruit called the locust, a kind of sweet pod.

به bé, *ad. p.* To, for, in; —, bìh, *a. p.* Good, excellent, safe, sound; —, bìhi, (*mas.*) بها bìhā (*fem.*) *pron. a.* (*in composition*), To *or* with him, her, it.

بها bàha (pàha), *s. p.* Price in money, money value; —, bàhā, *s. a.* Beauty; فبها fè-bàhà, Well and good! That will do very nicely! بهالو pàhali, Dear, high-priced.

بهادر bàhādir, *s. p.* A brave man, a hero.

بهار bàhār, *s. p.* The spring; —, *s. a.* Spice; — اول èvvel—, — الك ìlk—, Spring, early spring; — صوك sòng—, Autumn; بهارات bàhārāt, *s. pl. a.* Spices; بهارلو bàhàrli, *a. t.* Spiced, spicy.

بهانه bàhāné, *s. p.* A pretext; an idle excuse; a finding fault; —بولمق, —bùlmak, *v.n.* To find an excuse; to find fault (with a thing).

بهتان bùhtān, *s. a.* Calumny, false accusation.

بهجت bèhjèt, *s. a.* Beauty and cheerful pleasing look of countenance.

بهر bèhèr (ب bè, *for* هر hèr, *each*), *ad. p.* Each; بهرينه bèhèriné, Each, a-piece, for each one of them; بهرماه bèhèr-māh, Each month, monthly.

بهره bèhré, *s. p.* A lot, share, portion; بهره‌دار bèhrédār, بهره‌مند bèhrémènd; بهره‌ور bèhrévèr, *a. p.* Sharing, having a share.

بهشت bìhìsht, *s. p.* Heaven, paradise.

بهی bèhèy! *int. t.* O! Ho! بهی‌اشك bèhèy-èshek, Ass that thou art! —, bèhī, *a. a.* Beautiful.

بی bī, *prep. p.* (*in composition*), Without; بيباك bī-bāk, *a. p.* Without fear, fearless.

بيابان bèyābān, *s. p.* The desert, a wilderness, the wilds.

بيات bàyat, *a. t.* Stale, not new or fresh.

بياض bèyāz, *s. a.* Whiteness; —, *a. t.* White; —, *s. t.* A fair copy of a writing; unwritten paper; بياض اوزرنده اراده bèyaz-ùzérinda-ìrādé, An imperial command given *propriâ motu*, and not on any petition or ministerial report; بياضه چكمك bèyaza-chèkmek, *v.a.* To copy out fairly.

بياغی bàyaghi, *a. t.* Mere, sheer; common, ordinary, every-day; —, *ad. t.* Neither more nor less, simply, in good sooth.

بيان bèyān, *s. a.* A setting forth, explaining, expounding; ا—, —et, *v.a.* To set forth, declare, expound; آتی البيان ātìyyu-'l-bèyān, The following, the hereinafter mentioned.

بيت bèyt, *s. a.* A house; a couplet, a distich; بيت الله الحرام bèytu-'llāhi-'l-hàrām, (The holy house of God) the Temple of Mecca; بيت المال bèytu-'l-māl, *or* بيت مال المسلمين bèytu-māli-'l-mùsslimīn, (The house of the treasure of the Muslim community) the public treasury; بيت المالجی bèytu-'l-mālji (bèytamālji), An officer who takes cognizance of the estates of deceased persons, or of spoils of war, assesses them for succession dues, &c.

بيتوتت bèytūtèt, *s. a.* A passing the night in any abode; ا—, —et, *v.n.* To pass the night in any abode.

بيچاره bī-chāré, *s.* and *a. p.* Poor, helpless, forlorn.

بيخ bīkh, *s. p.* A root.

بيخود bī-khòd, *a. p.* Insensible, swooned, fainted; insane, beside one's self.

بيدار bīdār, *a. p.* Awake; vigilant; —بخت, —bàkht, *a. p.* One whose good fortune is awake and active, slumbering not.

بيدق (pàytak), *s. a.* A peon, or pawn at chess.

بئر bi'r, *s. a.* A well.

بيراق bàyrak, *s. t.* A flag, banner, standard; بيراقدار bàyrakdàr, *s. p.* A standard-bearer.

بيرام bàyram, *s. p.* A holy feast, a holy day, festival; شكربيرامی shèker-bàyrami, (The feast of sugar), the feast of three days next after the close of Ramazan; قربان بيرامی kùrbān-bàyrami, The feast of sacrifice, in commemoration of Abraham's intended offering of Ishmael (according to the Kur'an), held on the tenth day of the last month of the Muslim year, Zī-'l-hijjé (the month of pilgrimage); قامش بیرامی kàmish-bàyrami, The Jewish feast of tabernacles.

بیرون **bīrūn**, *s. p.* The outside; —, *ad. p.* Out of; beyond.

بیز **bìz**, *s. t.* An awl.

بیزار **bīzār**, *a. p.* Tired, weary, annoyed.

بیش **bīsh**, *a. p.* More in number or quantity.

بیضی **bèyzī**, *a. a.* Egg-shaped, oval, elliptical; —, *s. t.* An oval, ellipse.

بیطار **bàytār**, *s. a.* A farrier, veterinary surgeon; بیطارلق bàytārlìk, *s. t.* بیطاری bàytārī, *s. p.* بیطرت bàytaret, *s. a.* The veterinary art or profession.

بیع **bèy‘‘**, *s. a.* A selling; بیع وشرا bèy‘‘-u-shìrā, Buying and selling, trade.

بیعت **bī‘‘àt**, *s. a.* The ceremony of swearing allegiance; ا—, —et, *v.n.* To declare one's self a loyal subject or vassal.

بیق **bìyìk**, *s. t.* The mustachio.

بیك **bìng**, *a. t.* A thousand, one thousand; بیکباشی bìng-bàshi, (A chiliarch, chief of a thousand), A major or *chef de bataillon* in the army; a commander in the navy.

بیکار **(pùngar)**, *s. t.* A spring, source of water; بیکار باشی pùngar-bàshi, The head water or spring of a stream; —, **bī-kyār** (bèkyar), *s. p.* A bachelor.

بیکانه **bīghyāné**, *s. p.* A stranger.

بیلك **bìlek**, *s. t.* The wrist.

بیله **bìlé**, *ad. t.* Even; together.

بیم **bīm**, *s. p.* Fear.

بیمار **bīmār**, *a. p.* Sick, ill, diseased; بیمارخانه bīmār-khāné, *s. p.* A hospital; a mad-house.

بین **bèyn**, *s. a.* The interval between two things; the relation between two things; the midst of several or many things; بینلری bèynléri, Their interval *or* relation; بینلرینه bèynlérina, To their interval, between them, among them; بینلرنده bèynlérinda, In their interval, between them, among them; بینلرندن bèynlérindan, From between them, from among them; &c. &c.; —, **bīn**, *a. p.* (*in composition*), Who sees, perceives; دوربین dūrbīn, (Far-seeing), A telescope; خرده بین khùrda-bīn (Small-seeing) a microscope; —, **bèyn**, *s. t.* The brain.

بینش **bīnish**, *s. p.* A seeing, viewing; an old ceremony of court, a kind of levee; a kind of outer and very full robe in the old costume.

بینه **bèyyiné**, *s. a.* A proof, evidence, conclusive fact. [Houses.

بیوت **bùyūt**, *s. pl. a.* (*of* بیت bèyt),

بیورلدی **bùyuruldu**, *s. t.* A governor's written order.

بیورمق **bùyurmak** (*aor.* بیورر bùyurur),

v.n. To exercise authority, act as master, give orders; to say, to do (anything, used when speaking of a superior); نه بیوردیکز nè-bùyurdun*g*uz, What did you say? ایچرو بیوریکز ìchĕri-bŭyurun*g*uz, Pray walk in; بیورك bŭyurun*g*! I beg you! Do me the favour!

بیوك bìyuk, *a. t.* Great, large, big, vast; high in rank.

بیومك bìyumek (*aor.* بیور bìyur), *v.n.* To grow, increase in size; to grow up; to become an adult; to rise in rank.

بیوه bīvĕ, *s. p.* A widow.

بیهوده bīhūdĕ, *a. p.* Vain, fruitless, useless; —, *ad. p.* In vain.

بیهوش bīhush, *a. p.* Senseless, swooned.

پ

پ pĕ *or* pā'i-fārsī. Third letter of the Turkish alphabet, having the value of *p* in English. In old manuscripts, as in many modern writings from the pens of pedantic or ignorant students of Arabic, this letter is ignored, and its place supplied by the ب, so that sometimes words written with that letter will be found ranged in the present chapter, want of space forbidding the repetition in each place. It is sometimes interchangeable with ف fĕ; as, فیل fīl, *or* پیل pīl. In chronograms this letter has the same numeral value with ب, and is never used in astronomical tables, or in the dates of letters, by reason that it is not of Arabic origin.

پا pā, *s. p.* A foot. (Abbreviated from پای pày, and entering into the composition of many words, sometimes in the one form, sometimes in the other).

پاپادیه pApAdiy*a*, *s. t.* Camomile.

پاپاس pApAss, *or* پاپاز pApAz, *s. t.* A priest (Christian or Pagan).

پابوس pā-būss, *s. p.* Foot-kissing.

پاپوش pā-pūsh (pAbuch), *s. p.* Any covering for the feet, particularly a kind of slipper worn out of doors.

پاتردی pAt*i*rd*i*, *s. t.* Noise.

پاترونه pàtrūn*a*, *s. t.* (*Italian*), The vice-admiral, formerly entitled a Bey, now a Pasha.

پاتلامق pAtlam*a*k (*aor.* پاتلار pAtlar), *v.n.* To crack or explode with a great noise; to burst without noise.

پاتلیجان pAtlijAn, *s. t.* The egg-plant; فرنك پاتلیجانی firĕnk-pAtlĭjAn*i*, The love-apple or tomata.

پاتەدق pAtad*a*k, *ad. t.* Suddenly, unexpectedly.

پاچارز pàchàriz, *s. t.* A thing likely to give trouble, as a ship coming athwart hawse.

پاچاوره pàchàvr*a*, *s. t.* A rag, clout; یاغلو پاچاوره yà*gh*l*i*-pàchàvr*a*, (A greased rag), a fire-ball thrown against ships or towns by the enemy.

پاچه pàch*a*, *s. p.* Sheep's trotters; trotter jelly; any dish made to imitate trotter jelly; the lower part of the legs of trousers; the feet and leg parts of furs.

پادشاه pādishāh, *s. p.* The Sultan; an emperor; پادشاهی pādishāhī, *s. p.* The imperial dignity or function; —, *a. p.* Imperial; پادشاهانه pādishā-hānē, *a. p.* Imperial.

پارچه pàrcha, *s. p.* A piece, fragment, morsel; a whole individual thing; پارچه پارچه ا pàrcha-pàrcha-et, *v.a.* To cut, pull, or knock to pieces.

پارس Paris, *s. t.* Paris.

پارلاق pàrlàk, *a. t.* Bright, shining, clear; handsome; promising, talented.

پارلامق pàrlamak (*aor.* پارلار pàrlar), *v.n.* To shine, to be bright; to break out in flame; to acquire a conspicuous station and reputation; to get in a rage.

پارمق pàrmak, *s. t.* A finger; a toe; an inch; a rail, a bar; a spoke of a wheel; a stripe (in stuffs, &c.); پارمقلق pàrmaklík, *s. t.* Railings; a grating, a grate; التی پارمق Alti--parmak, *s. t.* The tunny-fish (?); a kind of striped stuff. (See پرمق).

پاره pārē (pàra), *s. p.* A piece, fragment; a whole individual thing; money; a small coin, the fortieth of a piastre, about $\frac{1}{20}$ of a penny; اوچ پاره تکنه ùch-pārē-tèknē, Three individual ships; پاره پاره pārē-pārē, *ad. p.* Piecemeal, in pieces, یکپاره yèk-pārē, *a. p.* Of one single piece; پارهلمك pārēlémek (*aor.* پارهلر pārē-ler), *v.a.* (pàralamak, *aor.* pàralar), To cut or knock to pieces; پارهلنمك (pāralanmak), *v.n.* To be broken in pieces.

پازی pAzi, *s. t.* White beet, of which the leaves are used as a vegetable.

پاس pāss, *s. p.* A sentry's round, guard, watch; —, pAss, *s. t.* Rust; پاسلنمق pAsslanmak (*aor.* پاسلنور pAsslanir), —طوتمق, —tùtmak, *and* —باغلامق, —bAghlamak, *v.n.* To become rusty, to contract rust; پاسبان pāssbān, *or* پاسوان pāsswān, *s. p.* A watchman, guard, sentry.

پاش pāsh, *a. p.* (*in composition*), Which sprinkles, scatters, diffuses.

پاشا pàsha, *s. t.* The highest title in the civil or military hierarchy in Turkey. There are now many grades of pashas. 1st. The grand-vizier and those who rank with him; 2d. Those who have filled that office; 3d. Those connected by marriage with the imperial family; 4th. The general class of ministers or secretaries of state, and those to whom the rank is given; 5th. Simple mùshīrs not ministers of state; these are governors-general of large provinces, or generals commanding corps-d'armée, &c.; 6th. Vèzīrs, also governors-general; 7th. Fèrīks or lieutenants-general; 8th. Mīri-Mīrān, or civil fèrīks, governors of smaller provinces; 9th. Mīri-Lìwā, or generals of brigade; and 10th. Mīru-'l-

-Umérā, or civil liwās, governors of small provinces also. All these functionaries, and all those who have ever received the grades, retain the title of pasha for life, unless degraded for some offence. This title is sometimes given to children and young men by their family or companions. پاشا قپوسی pàsha-kàpissi, The official place of business of the government in Constantinople, and of the governor in a province. پاشالق pàshalik, s. t. The grade or functions of a pasha; a government held by a pasha; پاشالو pàshali, a. t. (Suitable for a pasha) name of a certain style of clothing.

پاك pāk, پاكيزه pākīzé, a. p. Clean, pure, undefiled.

پالاسطروپه pàla-strùpa, s. t. (*Italian*), A rope wad for a gun. [tridge-box.

پالاسقه pàlasska, s. t. A soldier's car-

پالان pàlan, s. t. A kind of soft-cushioned saddle or pillion.

پاموق pàmuk, s. t. Cotton.

پانطلون pàntalòn, s. t. Trousers.

پای pāy, s. p. The foot. (This word, sometimes contracted into پا pā, enters into the composition of many words, either at the beginning or end; as, پانهاده pā-nìhādé, Who has placed his foot, چارپا chār-pā, Four-footed); —, pày, s. t. A share, part, portion; پایلاشمق pàylashmak, v.a. To share (anything) with others; پای بچمك pày-bìchmek, v.n. To draw comparisons from an instance given. [limit, term.

پایان pāyān, s. p. The end, extremity,

پایبند pāy-bènd (pàywànt), s. p. Ligatures with which the feet of horses are bound in stable, or at picket.

پایتخت pāyitàkht, s. p. (Foot of the throne) the capital city, the seat of government. [blished.

پایدار pāydār, a. p. Permanent, sta-

پایدوس pàydoss, s. t. A cessation from work; —, *int. t.* All hands knock off work! ا—, —et, v.n. To knock off working; —, v.a. To cause work to be suspended.

پایمال pàymāl, a. p. Trodden under foot; ا—, —et, v.a. To tread under foot. [support.

پاینده pàyèndé, s. p. A prop, stay,

پایه pāyé, s. p. Footing, grade, rank, dignity; the footstool or platform of a throne; a step, a stair.

پپکی pèpèghi, s. t. A stammerer, stutterer; —سویلمك, —sùwèylémek, پپه‌لمك pèpélémek, v.n. To stammer, to stutter.

پخته pùkhté, a. p. Cooked; ripe; experienced in worldly wisdom.

پختی pùkhti, s. p. Jelly.

پداوره pàdàvra, s. t. A shingle, split lath, or rough thin board.

پدر pèder, s. p. A father; پدرانه pèdérāné, a. p. Fatherly, paternal.

پذير pézīr, a. p. (*in composition*), Which receives or has received.

پر pùr, *a. p.* Full; filled with, replete with; —, pĕr, *s. p.* A feather.

پرازوانه pìrāzwāna, *s. t.* The ferrule usually placed at the bottom of sticks, scabbards, &c.

پراكندہ pèrakèndé, *a. p.* Scattered, dispersed, not collected together.

پران pèrān, *a. p.* Flying, which flies.

پرانغه prànghа, *s. t.* The convict's chain; the galleys, the convict's punishment of imprisonment and forced labour.

پرتاب pĕrtāb, پرتاو pĕrtàv, *s. p.* A cast, a throw, a launch; a jump; a precipitating; a summerset.

پرتو pĕrtev, *s. p.* A ray of light; —انداز, —èndāz, *a. p.* Throwing rays of light, shining, sparkling; —سوز, —sūz (pèrtevsiz), *s. p.* (Burning by rays), a lens, a burning-glass, a magnifier.

پرچم pĕrchem, *s. p.* The tuft of hair left on the summit of the head in the East, when the rest of the hair is shaved off.

پرچين pĕrchin, *s. p.* The clenching of a nail; ا—, —et, *v.a.* To clench (a nail). [contention.

پرخاش pùrkhāsh, *s. p.* Strife, battle,

پرداخت pĕrdākht (pĕrdāh), *s. p.* Polish, burnish; ا—, —et, *v.a.* To polish, burnish.

پرداخته pĕrdākhté, *a. p.* Worked with great pains, finished and polished off.

پرداز pĕrdāz, *a. p.* (*in composition*), Who makes, works at, completes, finishes and polishes off.

پرده pĕrdé, *s. p.* A curtain, a veil; a musical key; a cataract in the eye; تخته پرده tàkhta-pĕrdé, *s. t.* Palings, a partition of boards; اهل پرده èhli-pĕrdé, A chaste, modest, honest woman; پرده نشين pĕrdé-nìshīn, *a.p.* Who sits behind a curtain; پرده دار pĕrdé-dār, *s. p.* The keeper of the curtain, the waiter at the door, who lifts the curtain for those who enter, and refuses admittance to improper people.

پرست pèrèsst, *s. p.* (*in composition*), A worshipper, adorer.

پرستار pèresstar, *s. p.* A servant.

پرستش pèresstish, *s. p.* Worship, adoration. [quiry.

پرسش pùrsish, *s. p.* An asking, in-

پركار pĕrghyār (pĕrghel), *s. p.* A pair of compasses.

پرلانتی pìrlànti, *s. t.* A brilliant.

پرمق pàrmak, *s. t.* (See پارمق), باش— bāsh—, The thumb; اياق باش پرمغی àyak-bāsh-pàrmaghi, The great toe; شهادت پرمغی shàhādet - pàrmaghi, The fore-finger; اورته پرمق òrta-pàrmak, The middle finger; يوزك پرمغی yùzuk-pàrmaghi, The fourth finger; سرچه پرمغی sĕrché-pàrmaghi, The little finger.

پرمقلق pàrmaklik, *s. t.* Railings, rails, banisters, a grating.

پرنده pèrendé, *a. p.* Flying, which flies;

s. p. A summerset; پرنده باز pèrèndé-bāz, *s. p.* A thrower of summersets in the air. [sion.

پروا pèrvā, *s. p.* Fear, fright, apprehen-

پرواز pèrwāz, *s. p.* A raised border or cornice; the act of flying, flight by wing; —, *a. p.* (*in composition*), Which flies, soars.

پروانه pèrwāné, *s. p.* A moth, night moth which flies round lights; the fly-wheel of a machine.

پروردكار pèrvèrdighyār, *s. p.* God the nourisher.

پرورده pèrvèrdé, *a. p.* Nourished, cherished, brought up, educated.

پرورش pèrvèrish, *s. p.* Care, the care bestowed in feeding, protecting, and teaching one's children or dependants, kind care.

پرهيز pèrhīz, *s. p.* Regimen, diet; a Christian fast; abstaining, abstinence; —ا, —et, *v.n.* To abstain; to keep a regimen, be careful what we eat; —طوتمق, —tùtmak, *v.n.* To keep a fast (as Greeks and Catholics do); —كار, —kyār, *s. p.* One who abstains.

پرى pèri, *s. p.* A fairy.

پريشان pèrishān, *a. p.* In disorder; in ruin; پريشانلق pèrishānlik, *s. t.* پريشانى pèrishānī, *s. p.* پريشانيت pèrishānìyyet, *s. a.* Disorderedness; ruin. [a bawd.

پزونك pèzéwènk, *s. t.* A pimp, a pander,

پژمرده pèzhmùrda, *a. p.* Shabby, in sad plight, old and faded.

پژوه pùzhūh (pù-zhūh), *a. p.* (*in composition*), Who diligently seeks after.

پس pèss, *c. p.* Then, after that, after which, moreover; —, *s. p.* The hind, or after part; the bass of music; —, *ad. p.* Behind; after; —, pìss, *a. t.* Dirty, filthy, unclean. [bass in music.

پست pèsst, *a. p.* Low; —, (pèss), The

پستان pìsstān, *s. p.* A teat, pap, dug.

پسقپوس pìsskaposs, *s. t.* (*Greek*), A bishop.

پسند pèssènd, *a. p.* (*in composition*), Approving; approved; خودپسند khòd--pèssènd, *a. p.* Self-approving, vain; عوام پسند "àwāmm-pèssènd, Approved by the common people, popular.

پسنديده pèssendīdé, *a. p.* Approved, liked.

پسى pìssi, *s. t.* A sole or dab (flat-fish).

پسين pèssīn, *a. p.* The hindermost, the last.

پشت pùsht, *s. p.* The back; پشت پاى pùshti-pāy, The sole of the foot; پشت پاى زن pùshti-pāy-zèn, *a. p.* Who walks or runs (striking the soles of his feet on the ground).

پشتمال pùshtmāl (pèshtamāl), *s. p.* A coarse large towel and an apron.

پشكين pìshkin, *a. t.* Crisp, well baked (bread); thoroughly baked (bricks, &c.); ripe and well hardened (reeds used in writing, &c.); well broken into business, thoroughly acquainted with the roughs of life and service (man).

پشم pèshm, *s. p.* Wool; down.

پشمك pìshmek (*aor.* پشر pìshER), *v.n.* To cook, be cooked (whether baked, roasted, or boiled, &c.); to become properly ripened, hardened, or prepared; to become thoroughly acquainted with the roughs and requirements of life and service.

پشورمك pìshirmek (*aor.* پشورر pìshirir), *v.a.* To cook, to prepare by cooking; to boil, to roast, to stew, to bake; to harden, make hardy in matters of life and service.

پشيمان pèshīmān (pìshMAN), *a.p.* Sorry, regretting an action or omission; —او, —ŏl, *v.n.* To repent, be sorry, regret.

پصدرمه pÀssdirma, *s. t.* Jerked beef, hung beef, ham, bacon, dry, salt, smoked, &c.

پصطال pÀsstAl, *s. t.* A whole piece of broad-cloth.

پطريق pÀtrik, *s. t.* (*Greek*), A patriarch (title of the spiritual chiefs of the several Christian nationalities subject to the Sultan).

پف pùf, *s. p.* A puff of breath; پفكرده pùf-kèrdÉ, *a. p.* Blown out.

پك pèk, *a. t.* Hard; —, *ad. t.* Very.

پكسمات pèksémāt (pèksémèt), *s. t.* Bread, twice baked, or biscuit for provisions.

پكشمك pèkishmek, (*aor.* پكشور pèkishir), *v.n.* To become hard, to harden.

پلاز pÀlAz, *s. t.* A gosling, a duckling; a young pigeon.

پلاسقه pÀlasska, *s. t.* A cartridge-box.

پلامار pÀlamar, *s. t.* A hawser or stream cable.

پلاموت pÀlamud, *s. t.* An acorn; acorn husks, vallonea.

پلاميد pÀlamīd, *s. t.* A kind of very large mackerel.

پلاو pìlaw, *s. p.* Rice prepared by boiling, with the addition of flesh or scalded butter or oil; —زرده, —zèrdÉ (yellow pilaw), The same with saffron and sugar or honey added.

پلتك pèltek, *s. t.* A stutterer, stammerer.

پلته pèltÉ, *s. t.* A kind of jelly of wheat sweetened with honey.

پلج pìlij, *s. t.* A chick, chicken.

پلسقه pÀlAsska, *s. t.* A soldier's cartridge-box.

پلنقه (pÀlAngha), *s. t.* A small fort or stockade; a tackle or double pulley.

پلنك pèlenk, *s. p.* A leopard or panther.

پلين pèlin, *s. t.* Absinthe, wormwood.

پناه pènàh, *s. p.* An asylum, refuge.

پناير pÀnàyir, *s. t.* (*Greek*), A country fair.

پنبه pènbÉ, *s. p.* Cotton; —, *a. t.* Rose-colour, light-pink.

پنتالومبه pàntalòmba, *s. t.* Gamboge.

پنتى pìnti, *a. t.* Dirty, ragged, and miserable-looking; miserly.

پنج pènj, *a. p.* Five; پنجم pènjum, *and* پنجمين pènjumīn, *a. p.* The fifth; پنجاه pènjāh, *a. p.* Fifty.

پنجار pÀnjar, *s. t.* Beet-root.

پنجره pènjérÉ, *s. t.* A window.

پنجشنبه pènjshènbih (pèrshembÉ), *s. p.* Thursday.

پنجك pènjik, *s. t.* A kind of title-deed

to a slave, given to the first purchaser by Government when the duty is paid, and passed on to each successive owner.

پنچه pènché, *s. p.* The hand of man, or foot of birds or beasts, viewed as an instrument of prehension; a kind of official signature for ministers of state or governors, something like the *tughra* of the Sultan.

پند pènd, *s. p.* Counsel, advice, admonition.

پنهان pìnhān, *a. p.* Hidden, concealed, secret.

پنیر pènir, *s. p.* Cheese.

پو pŭ, *s. p.* A running about; —, *a. p.* (*in composition*), Who runs about.

پوته pŭté, *s. p.* A crucible.

پوجه pòj*a*, *s. t.* (*Italian*), An easing of the helm, a bearing up; ا—, —et, *v.n.* To ease the helm; to bear up.

پود pūd, *s. p.* The woof or weft in cloth, the thread *which goes to and fro* with the shuttle.

پوس pūss, *s. t.* Fogginess, thickness of weather.

پوست pòsst, *s. p.* The fell or furry skin of an animal, tanned or not; the same tanned and used as a cushion to sit on; a special seat; a seat of office, an office under Government.

پوستکی pòsstéki, *s. p.* A sheepskin, tanned or not.

پوسته pòssta, *s. t.* (*Italian*), The post for letters; a watch or relay of workmen.

پوستین pòsstīn, *s. p.* A fur or sheepskin cloak.

پوسکورمك pùsskyurmek (*aor.* پوسکورر pùsskyurur), *v.a.* To blow (water) out of the mouth in a fine shower.

پوسکی pùsskyu, *iterative of* اسکی èsski, *a. t.* اسکی‌پوسکی èsski-pùsskyu, Rags and tatters.

پوش pūsh, *a. p.* (*in composition*), Who wears, clothes himself with; which clothes.

پوشیده pūshīdé, *a. p.* Covered, hidden, concealed, kept secret.

پوصله pŭssl*a*, *s. t.* A short note or letter; a short account or bill; a mariner's compass.

پوصو *or* پوصی pùssu, *s. t.* An ambush, ambuscade.

پوطور pòtur, *s. t.* A kind of trousers, full to the knee, but fitting tight below with hooks and eyes, and garters above the calf of the leg.

پوغاچه pò*gh*àcha, *s. t.* A kind of pastry like pie-crust.

پوفله pŭfl*a*, *s. t.* The down used in pillows.

پول pùl, *s. p.* A bridge; a small piece of money, or money in general; a spangle; a fish-scale; a thin disc of ivory or bone placed over a seal in wax to preserve the impression; a wafer.

پولاد pūlād, *s. p.* An imaginary metal, after the nature of our word *adamant*, the characteristic of which is hardness.

پولیچه pòlich*a*, *s. t.* (*Italian*), A bill of exchange.

پوی pūy. The same with پو pū; پویان pūyān, *a. p.* Who runs to and fro.

پویراز pòyraz, *s. t.* (*Greek boreas*), The north-east wind or quarter.

پهلو pèhlu, *s. p.* The side of the body.

پهلوان pèhluwān, *s. p.* A wrestler.

پهن pèhn, *and* پهنا pèhnā, *s. p.* Width; —, —, *a. p.* Wide.

پى pèy (*for* پاى pay), *s. p.* A foot; a step; —, *s. t.* Earnest-money; پياپى pèyā-pèy, *and* پيدرپى pèy-dər-pèy, *ad. p.* By degrees, by instalments; successively; continuously.

پياده piyādé, *s. p.* A man on foot; a boat built for only one pair of oars; infantry. [or bowl.

پياله piyālé, *s. p.* A drinking-cup, glass,

پيام pèyām, *s. p.* A message; پيامبر pèyambèr, پيامرس pèyamrèss, A messenger.

پيانقو piyànko, *s. t.* A lottery, a raffle.

پيچ pìch, *s. t.* A bastard; a sucker from the root of a plant; —, pīch, *s. p.* A twisting, convulsion, contortion; پيچاپيچ pīchāpīch, *a. p.* Twisted fold on fold.

پيچيده pīchīdé, *a. p.* Twisted, contorted.

پيدا pèydā, *a. p.* Existing, forthcoming, present, visible; ا—, —et, *v.a.* To find, to manage and have in one's possession, to get; او—, —òl, *v.n.* To spring up, come, come into existence, become visible or present.

پيده pīdé, *s. t.* A flat, thin cake of bread, something like a muffin.

پير pīr, *s. p.* An old man; the patron saint or superior of any order or guild.

پيرا pīrā, *a. p.* (*in composition*), Who adorns, decks out.

پيراسته pīrāssté, *a. p.* Adorned, decked out. [inclosure or environs of a place.

پيرامن pīrāmèn, *s. p.* The circuit or

پيرايش pīrāyish, پيرايه pīrāyé, *s. p.* An ornament, adornment. [panion.

پيرو pèy-rèv, *s. p.* A follower; a com-

پيره pīré, *s. t.* A flea; —زن, —zèn, *s. p.* An old woman.

پيش pīsh, *s. p.* The front, fore part of anything, the space in front of anything.

پيشانى pīshāni, *s. p.* The forehead.

پيشتخته pīsh-tàkhta (pèsh—), *s. p.* The counter of a shop, shop-board.

پيشرو pīsh-rèv (pèsh—), *s. p.* A guide, forerunner; grape-shot.

پيشگاه pīsh-ghyāh, *s. p.* The space in front of anything.

پيشكش pīsh-kèsh (pèsh—), *s. p.* A gift offered to a superior as homage.

پيشكير pīsh-ghīr (pèshkir), *s. p.* A napkin for use at table.

پيشنهاد pīsh-nìhād, *s. p.* A model, thing placed to be copied or followed.

پيشوا pīsh-vā, *s. p.* A leader.

پيشه pīshé, *s. p.* An art, trade, occupation, profession, calling.

پيشين pīshīn (pèshin), *a. p.* Foremost; former; foregoing; old, antique, ancient; ready (money); —, *ad. t.* Before proceeding further in the matter; —, *s. t.* Ready money.

پيغام pèyghām, پيغم pèygham, پيام pèyām, *s. p.* A message; پيغامبر pèyghāmbèr, پيغمبر pèyghambèr, پيامبر pèyāmbèr, *s. p.* A messenger, bearer

of a message; a prophet, bearer of God's message to man.

پیغوله pèyghūlé, *s. p.* A corner; a retired nook or spot; any narrow, retired place. [messenger; a satellite.

پیك pèyk, *s. p.* A valet, footman, foot-

پیكار pèykyār, *s. p.* Battle, fight, combat, action; —, pìngàr (pŭnàr), *s. t.* A spring, fountain.

پیكر pèykĕr, *s. p.* The face, countenance.

پیل pīl (*for* فیل fīl), *s. p.* An elephant.

پیما pèymā, *a. p.* (*in composition*), Who measures; who paces, paces over.

پیمان pèymān, *s. p.* A promise, undertaking, treaty, agreement.

پیوست pèyvèsst, *a. p.* (*in composition*), Reaching, touching, joining, attaining.

پیوسته pèyvèsstĕ, *a. p.* Reaching, touching, joining, attaining; —, *ad. t.* Always, continually, without interruption.

پیوند pèyvènd, *s. p.* See پایبند; (*also, in composition*), *a. p.* Reaching, touching, joining.

ت

ت *or* ة tĕ *or* tā. Fourth letter of the Turkish alphabet, having the value of *t* in English. At the end of many words and roots, this letter is changed, both in writing and pronouncing, into د dàl, having the value of our *d*. Compared with the letter ط tì, which is also an equivalent to our *t*, the ت tĕ is a soft consonant, and is followed *in preference* by soft vowels in words of Turkish origin, though in this respect there are but too many exceptions in practice. In chronograms and astronomical tables, this letter has the numerical value of 400, but is not used in the dates of letters. In the Arabic asseveration تالله tà-'llàhì (By God!), it is a preposition, which is used in no other case, and the asseveration is generally placed third in the series of corroborative import واللهبااللهتاالله, wà-'llàhī, bì-'llâhi, tà-'llàhi, the most solemn form of asseveration employed. In the case of verbs of Turkish origin, the roots of which, being of more than one syllable, end in a vowel, or in one of the letters ر rì *or* ل làm quiescent, their causatives are formed by adding to the root this letter ت in the quiescent form also, instead of the usual causative increment در dir. Ex. سویلمك sùwèylĕmek, To say, سویلتمك sùwèylĕtmek, To cause to say; اوكسرمك ŭksurmek, To cough, اوكسرتمك ŭksurtmek, To cause to cough; قصالمق kìssàlmak, To become shorter, قصالتمق kìssàltmak, To shorten. At the end of many Arabic nouns this letter is interchangeable with the ه vowel, the word being sometimes written with the one letter, sometimes with the other. When the form ة is used (at the end of Arabic feminine nouns only) it is read either as tin or tɪn. (See تنوين).

تا tā, *s. a.* Name of the letter ت ; —, *s. p.* (*in composition*), Fold (in number), as يكتا yèk-tā, Onefold, single ; دوتا dū-tā, Twofold, double, &c. ; —, *ad. p.* Even as far, even until you arrive (at such a place or time).

تاب tāb, *s. p.* Strength, power, might ; power of resistance ; a twisting, contortion, writhing ; brightness ; splendour ; heat ; burning, ardour ; the required degree of temper, hardness, softness, lustre, &c., in any manufactured article ; —, *a. p.* (*in composition*), Which illumines ; which warms or burns.

تابان tābān, *a. p.* Shining, bright, brilliant.

تابع tābi'', *a. a.* Subject, under subjection ; following, depending upon.

تابوت tābūt (tᴧbut), *s. a.* A bier or coffin ; the ark.

تابه tābé (tᴧwa), *s. p.* A frying-pan.

تأبيد tè'bīd, *s. a.* A causing to endure, a causing to be everlasting ; ا—, —et, *v.a.* To cause to endure ; to make everlasting.

تاتار tàtar, *s. t.* A courier ; a Tartar ; تاتارجق tàtarjɪk, *s. t. dim.* A little insect that gets under people's skin and causes itching. [grieved, vexed.

تأثر tè'èsssur, *s. a.* A being affected,

تأثير tè'sīr, *s. a.* An affecting, producing an effect ; an effect ; ا—, —et, *v.n.* To produce an effect.

تاج tāj (tᴧj), *s. a.* A crown ; a sort of turban worn by some dervishes.

تاجر tājir, *s. a.* A merchant.

تأخر tà'àkhkhur, *s. a.* A being too late or too slow.

تأخير tà'khīr, *s. a.* A causing to be late or slow ; a delaying, deferring ; a putting after ; ا—, —et, *v.a.* To delay, defer ; to put after.

تأديب tè'dīb, *s. a.* Correctional punishment ; ا—, —et, *v.a.* To punish correctionally.

تأديه tè'dìyyé, *s. a.* A paying, payment ; ا—, —et, *v.a.* To pay (debts).

تار tār, *s. p.* A thread, string, yarn, wire ; the warp of woven textures, or threads stretched lengthwise ready to receive the woof ; —, *a. p.* Dark, sombre, obscure ; —عنكبوت, tāri-''ànkébūt, A spider's web, cobweb ; تارمار tār-mār, *or* تارومار tār-u-mār, *a. p.* Scattered, dispersed, disordered, in shreds.

تاراج tārāj, *s. p.* Pillage, plunder, rapine.

تارة tārétɪn, *ad. a.* Once, one time, now (and then).

تاريخ tārīkh, *s. a.* The date of an event or letter, including the year, month, and day ; the date of an event or year only ; an era ; a style of computing dates ; a history, annals, chronicles ; a chronogram, or piece of literary composition of one or more words, so arranged and chosen that the numeric value of each letter contained therein, when added into one sum, shall represent the date of the year in which any specific event occurred; sometimes the letters with dots, and sometimes those without dots, are alone taken into the computation, leaving out the values of the others; تاريخ هجرى tārīkhi-hijrī, The year of the Hejira, the emigration, or, as commonly called, Flight of Muhammed; تاريخ رومى tārīkhi-rūmī, The Roman, *i.e.* Greek, or Old Style; الافرانغه تاريخى àlafràngha-tārīkhi, The Frank, *i.e.* European, or New Style.

تاريك tārīk, *a. p.* Dark, sombre, obscure.

تاز tāz, *a. p.* (*in composition*), Who runs, rushes.

تازه tāzé, *a. p.* Fresh, new, young; تازه‌لمك tāzélémek, *v.a.* To make fresh again; to refill (a pipe).

تازى tàzi, *s. t.* A greyhound; —, tāzī, *a. p.* Arabian.

تازيانه tāziyāné, *s. p.* A whip.

تأسف tè''èsssuf, *s. a.* Regret, sorrow; ا—, —et, *v.n.* To regret, be sorry.

تاسه (tàsssa), *s. p.* Grief, sorrow, care, disquietude; تاسه‌لنمق tàsssalanmak, *v.n.* To become sorrowful, to entertain grief.

تأسيس tè'sīss, *s. a.* A founding, placing on a firm basis; ا—, —et, *v.a.* To found; to base.

تاقمق tàkmak (*aor.* تاقار tàkar), *v.a.* To stick or fasten (anything on to another; to put on (any ornament); تاقلمق tàkilmak (*aor.* تاكلور tàkilir), *v. p.* To be stuck, fastened, or put on; —, *v.n.* To tease, worry, meddle with, make game of, skylark with (a person); to attach one's self to, stick to as a burr; تاقنمق tàkinmak (*aor.* تاقنور tàkinir), *v.a.* To put on one's self; اغريني— àghirini—, *v.n.* To put on a formal demeanour.

تأكيد te''kīd, *s. a.* A strengthening, confirming; repeating, making peremptory; ا—, —et, *v.a.* To strengthen, confirm, consolidate; to repeat, to make peremptory.

تالان tālān, *s. p.* Plunder, pillage, rapine.

تاليقه tàlika, *s. t.* A light four-wheeled Turkish carriage.

تالى tālī, *s. a.* A consequent.

تأليف tè'līf, *s. a.* The writing a book; a book; ا—, —et, *v.a.* To write, compose, compile; تأليفات tè'līfāt, *s. pl. a.* Books, works.

تام tàmm, *a. a.* Complete, perfect, finished, entire; —چرخ, —(chàrk), *s. t.* A patent lathe with improvements.

تأمل tè'èmmul, *s. a.* A deliberate weighing and consideration.

تأمين tè'mīn, *s. a.* The giving a feeling of confidence and security; ا—, —et, *v.a.* To impart full confidence.

تأنى tè'ènni, *s. a.* A slowness in commencing or in carrying on work, arising from care or caution.

تأنيث tè'nīss, *s. p.* The giving a feminine form to a word; ا—, —et, *v.a.* To put into the feminine form.

تأنيس tè'nīss, *s. a.* A rendering familiar, tame, domesticated.

تاو tāw, *s. t.* A proper degree of hardness, or other requisite quality, in manufactures; the proper degree of heat in a furnace; تاولنمق tāwlanmak, *v.n.* To grow fat, get into condition (animals); تاو ويرمك tāv-vèrmek, *v.a.* To give the proper degree of hardness, &c.; to anneal glass.

تأويل tè'vīl, *s. a.* The putting a peculiar meaning or construction on words, explaining differently; ا—, —et, *v.a.* To explain in a peculiar manner.

تأهل tè'èhhul, *s. a.* The taking a wife; ا—, —et, *v.n.* To take a wife, become a married man, to marry.

تائب tā'ib, One who repents, vows to forsake sin.

تأييد tè'yīd, *s. a.* A giving strength, strengthening, supporting, backing; ا—, —et, *v.a.* To give strength, support, back.

تب tèb, *s. p.* Fever, burning heat.

تبار tèbār, *s. a.* Ruin, destruction, perdition; —, *s. p.* Family, race, stock, lineage.

تباشير tèbāshīr, *s. pl. a.* (*of* تبشير tèbshīr), Happy tidings; the cheering signs of approaching dawn; —, *s. t.* Chalk.

تباعد tèbā''ud, *s. a.* A going to a distance; a being at a distance; ا—, —et, *v.n.* To go away, go to a distance.

تباه tèbāh, *a. p.* Spoilt, ruined, destroyed.

تباين tèbāyun, *s. a.* A being separate, distinct from one another.

تبت Tìbbèt, *s. t.* Thibet.

تبجيل tèbjīl, *s. a.* A rendering illustrious or noble; an honouring; treating with great respect.

تبخير tèbkhīr, *s. a.* A fumigating; ا—, —et, *v.a.* To fumigate with incense.

تبدل tèbèddul, *s. a.* A change of any kind; ا—, —et, *v.n.* To change, become altered or replaced; تبدلات tèbèddulāt, *s. pl. a.* Changes in office.

تبر tèber, *s. p.* A battle-axe; —, *s. t.* A tuberose; تبردار tèberdār, *s. p.* A battle-axe man; a kind of royal bodyguardsman.

تبرع tèbèrru'', *s. a.* An act of donation, or of attaching something to any property in mortmain, without an intention of claiming payment for it; تبرعاًللوقف tèbèrru''an-li-'l-wākf, *ad. a.* As a voluntary free service done to the property in mortmain.

تبرك tèbèrruk, *s. a.* Accounting or receiving, or doing anything as sacred, holy, or likely to draw down blessings; تبركاً tèbèrrukèn, *ad. a.* As a sacred, or holy act, as a blessing or as a means of blessing.

تبريد tèbrīd, *s. a.* A making cool or cold.

تبريك tèbrīk, *s. a.* A congratulating; congratulation, felicitation; ا—, —et, *v.n.* To congratulate.

تبريه tèbrìyyé (for تبرئه tèbri'é), *s. a.* A freeing, making free or exempt; تبريۀ ذمت tèbrìyyè'i-zìmmèt, *s. a.* A freeing from any charge or imputation.

تبسم tèbèssum, *s. a.* A smiling; a smile; ا—, —et, *v.n.* To smile.

تبشير tèbshīr, *s. a.* A giving good news; ا—, —et, *v.a.* To communicate (good news to a person); تبشيرنامه tèbshīr-namé, *s. p.* A letter of good news.

تبصبص tèbàssbùss, *s. a.* Insinuating, flattering words and actions.

تبعيت tèb''ìyyèt *or* tèbà''ìyyèt, *s. a.* The being, *or* the becoming a subject.

تبعيد tèb''īd, *s. a.* A removing (anything) to a distance; ا—, —et, *v.a.* To remove (anything) to a distance.

تبليغ tèblīgh, *s. a.* The causing (a thing) to reach or attain; the communication (of intelligence); ا—, —et, *v.a.* To communicate (a message or intelligence to a person); to cause (a thing) to reach or attain.

تبول tèbèvvul, *s. a.* The act of easing nature by passing urine or fæces; ا—, —et, *v.n.* To ease nature, to make water or go to stool.

تبويب tèbvīb, *s. a.* Arranging by chapters; ا—, —et, *v.a.* To arrange in chapters.

تبيان tibyān, *s. a.* A manifesting, exposition, declaration.

تبين tébèyyun, *s. a.* A becoming manifest; ا—, —et, *v.n.* To appear, to become manifest.

تبييض tèbyīz, *s. a.* A copying out fairly; a fair copy; ا—, —et, *v.a.* To copy fairly.

تپسى tèpsi, *s. t.* A tray, salver, waiter.

تپمك tèpmek (*aor.* تپر tèpér), *v.a.* and *n.* To kick; —كيرو ghèri—, *v.n.* To return (a disease, fever, &c.)

تپنمك tèpinmek (*aor.* تپنور tèpinir), *v.n.* To stamp with the feet as children in a rage; to jump about in an agitated manner.

تتبع tètebbu'', *s. a.* A studying diligently; ا—, —et, *v.a.* To study diligently (books).

تترهمك titrémek (*aor.* تترر titrér *or* titirir), *v.n.* To shiver and shake, to quake.

تتك tètik, *a. t.* Quick, sharp, wide-awake; nice, delicate, requiring to be managed with great care; —, *s. t.* The trigger of a gun or pistol; the notches in the tumbler of a gun-lock; —اوست ùsst—, The last notch which makes the hammer ready for firing; —الت Alt—, The first notch, at which the trigger will not pull; اوست تتكه المق ùsst-tètighé-Almak, *v.a.* To cock a gun full cock; الت تتكه المق Alt-tètighé-Almak, *v.a.* To half-cock a gun from the hammer being down; الت تتكه اندرمك Alt-tètighé-èndirmek, *v.a.* To half-cock a gun from full-cock; —دورمق, —dùrmak, *v.n.* To be on one's guard, to keep one's eyes well open, to be vigilant.

تتمه tètìmmé, *s. a.* Any necessary appendage to a thing without which it is not complete; a complement, supplement, appendix. [—et, *v.a.* To complete.

تتميم tètmīm, *s. a.* A completing; ا—, [please.

تتويج tètvīj, *s. a.* A crowning; a coronation; ا—, —et, *v.a.* To crown with a crown.

تتيز tìtiz, *a. t.* Peevish, cross, difficult to

تثبيت tèssbīt, *s. a.* A rendering firm, fixed, stable.

تثليث tèsslīss, *s. a.* A doing anything in threes; a tripling; a dividing into three equal parts; a boiling down to one-third; an avowal of belief in the Trinity; ا—, —et, *v.a.* To triple; to divide into three equal parts; —زاويه tèsslīssi-zāvìyyé, The tri-section of an angle.

تثنيه tèssnìyyé, *s. a.* The dual form of nouns, pronouns, and verbs.

تجار tùjjār, *s. pl. a.* (*of* تاجر tājir), Merchants; (*as a Turkish singular*), a merchant.

تجارت tìjāret, *s. a.* Commerce, trade; —ناظرى, tìjāret-nāziri, *s. t.* The minister of commerce.

تجاسر tèjāssur, *s. a.* A daring, hardihood; ا—, —et, *v.n.* To dare, have the hardihood. [ness.

تجانس tèjānùss, *s. a.* Homogeneous-

تجاوز tèjāvuz, *s. a.* A passing beyond a limit in space, time, number, &c.; being transitive (*a verb*), governing; an offensive act, an infringement; ا—, —et, *v.n.* To pass beyond; to infringe; to invade; to govern (*a verb*).

تجاوزى tèjāvuzī, *a. a.* Offensive (treaty); —وتدافعى, —vè-tèdāfu‘‘ī, Offensive and defensive.

تجاهل tèjāhul, *s.a.* A feigning ignorance; ا—, —et, *v.a.* To feign ignorance of.

تجبر tèjèbbur, *s. a.* Pride, haughtiness.

تجدد tèjèddud, *s. a.* A becoming new, a being renewed.

تجديد tèjdīd, *s. a.* A renewing, renewal; ا—, —et, *v.a.* To renew.

تجربه tèjribé, *s. a.* An experiment, trial; ا—, —et, *v.a.* To try.

تجريد tèjrīd, *s. a.* Asceticism.

تجريم tèjrīm, *s. a.* The condemning to pay a fine; ا—, —et, *v.a.* To condemn to pay a fine.

تجسس tèjèsssuss, *s. a.* Diligent search by examination and inquiry; ا—, —et, *v.a.* To inquire into, search into.

تجسم tèjèsssum, *s. a.* A taking a solid form; appearing a solid body; ا—, —et, *v.n.* To take a bodily form; appear a solid body.

تجلى tèjèlli, *s. a.* A being manifested in full glory; lot, fate, luck, fortune.

تجليد tèjlīd, *s. a.* The binding up, *or* causing to be bound up, of a book; ا—, —et, *v.a.* To bind (a book); to cause (a book) to be bound.

تجمع tèjèmmu‘‘, *s. a.* A congregating, assembling together.

تجمل tèjèmmul, *s. a.* Any handsome or

pleasant incidental thing; تجملات tèjèmmulāt, *s. pl.* Embellishing accessories.

تجنن tèjènnun, *s. a.* A going mad, a being possessed; ا—, —et, *v.n.* To go mad.

تجنيس tèjnīss, *s. a.* A figure of speech [like a trope.

تجويز tèjvīz, *s. a.* A granting permission; ا—, —et, *v.a.* To permit, authorise.

تجهيز tèjhīz, *s. a.* A fitting out; ا—, —et, *v.a.* To fit out; equip; rig.

تحاشى tàhāshi, *s. a.* A withdrawing, an abstaining from; ا—, —et, *v.n.* To keep one's self clear of, to avoid.

تحاف tùhāf, *a. t.* Funny, curious.

تحت tàht, *s. a.* The under or lower part of a thing; the space beneath it; —, tàht*a*, *pr. a.* (*in composition*), Under, beneath.

تحتانى tàhtānī, *a. a.* (A letter) which has its dot or dots beneath it; the ground or basement (story of a house).

تحجر tàhàjjur, *s. a.* A being changed into stone.

تحدث tàhàdduss, *s. a.* An arising, springing into existence (events); ا—, —et, *v.n.* To arise, spring into being, happen in consequence of something else.

تحديد tàhdīd, *s. a.* The assigning limits; ا—, —et, *v.a.* To assign limits (either by description, by maps, or on the spot).

تحرى tàhàrri, *s. a.* Inquest, search, examination; ا—, —et, *v.a.* To search, examine, inquire into.

تحرير tàhrīr, *s. a.* A writing; an enrolling, enlisting; an enregistering; ا—, —et, *v.a.* To write; to enrol, enlist; to register; تحريرات tàhrīrāt, *s. pl.* Despatches, official letters; (*as Turkish singular*) a despatch; تحريراً tàhrīran, *ad. a.* In writing, by letter.

تحريض tàhrīz, *s. a.* An exciting, encouraging; ا—, —et, *v.a.* To excite, encourage.

تحريف tàhrīf, *s. a.* A changing the sense of any writing by slight literal or verbal alterations; a tampering with writings; an anagram; ا—, —et, *v.a.* To tamper with writings, and alter the sense by making literal or verbal changes.

تحريك tàhrīk, *s. a.* A setting in motion; an exciting, instigating; ا—, —et, *v.a.* To set in motion; to excite, instigate.

تحسر tàhàsssur, *s. a.* A longing and pining after an absent object of affection.

تحسين tàhsīn, *s. a.* An approving, esteeming a thing to be worthy of approval; ا—, —et, *v.a.* To approve.

تحصن tàhàsssun, *s. a.* A shutting one's self up in a stronghold; ا—, —et, *v.n.* To shut one's self up in any strong place.

تحصيل tàhsīl, *s. a.* A gathering (things) into one's own possession; acquisition; collecting (dues, &c.); study, acquisition of learning; ا—, —et, *v.a.* To acquire; to collect; to study;

تحصيلدار tàhsīldār, *s. p.* A collector.

تحفه tùhfé (*pl.* تحف tùhàf), *s. a.* Any elegant thing fit for a present.

تحفظ tàhàffuz, *s. a.* A guarding one's self, preserving one's self (from contagion, &c.); —خانه, —khānė, A place of quarantine, a lazaretto.

تحقق tàhàkkuk, *s. a.* A turning out to be true; —ا, —et, *v.n.* To turn out true.

تحقير tàhkīr, *s. a.* A treating with contempt and insult; —ا, —et, *v.a.* To contemn and insult.

تحقيق tàhkīk, *s. a.* An ascertaining; —ا, —et, *v.a.* To ascertain: تحقيقاً tàhkīkan, *aä. a.* (To know) for certain, of a certainty.

تحكم tàhàkkyum, *s. a.* An excessive or unwarrantable assumption of authority.

تحمل tàhàmmul, *s. a.* A power or act of bearing, supporting; patience, longanimity; —ا, —et, *v.n.* To bear, support; to be patient in enduring.

تحميل tàhmīl, *s. a.* A placing (a load) on anything; —ا, —et, *v.a.* To place (a load) on or in anything.

تحول tàhàvvul, *s. a.* A changing, being changed from one state to another.

تحويل tàhvīl, *s. a.* The changing (anything) from one state to another; a passage from sign to sign of the zodiac; a cheque or promissory note; —ا, —et, *v.a.* To change, to reduce from state to state; —, *v.n.* To pass from sign to sign of the zodiac.

تحير tàhàyyur, *s. a.* A being astonished, bewildered.

تحيه tàhiyyé, *s. a.* A salutation, a greeting.

تخت tàkht, *s. p.* A throne; —روان, tàkhti-rèwān, *s. p.* A palanquin carried between two mules on poles, one leading, the other following; پاى تخت or پايتخت pāyi-tàkht, *s. p.* (The foot of the throne) the capital city of a state.

تخته tàkhta, *s. p.* A plank, board; a board used for any special purpose; a sheet (of metal, &c.); half the quantity of fur required for a robe; —, *s. t.* Made of boards: جدول تختهسى jèdvel-tàkhtassi, A flat ruler for drawing lines; ربع تخته rùb'u-tàkhta, A small astronomical quadrant of wood, with lines and circles on either side, and a plummet, used for taking the sun and computing time; تخته پوش tàkhta-pòsh, A kind of flooring fixed above the roof of a house, and used for drying linen and for taking the air; تخته بتى tàkhta-bìti, A bug; تخته پرده tàkhta-pèrdé, Palings; تخته بولمه tàkhta-bùlmé, A partition of planks.

تخديش tàkhdīsh, *s. a.* A grating, scratching, excoriating; —ا, —et, *v.a.* To grate, graze, scratch, excoriate.

تخريب tàkhrīb, *s. a.* A laying waste, desolating; —ا, —et, *v.a.* To lay waste, to desolate, waste, destroy.

تخصيص tàkhsīss, *s. a.* A making or being made special to anything; ا—

—et, *v.a.* To make (anything) special to a purpose; to consecrate, assign; to designate, determine, name, appoint, point out; بالتخصيص bì-'t-tàkhsīss, بتخصيص bì-tàkhsīss, *ad.-a.* Specially; تخصيصات tàkhsīssāt, *s. pl.* Funds of government assigned to special purposes.

تخفيف tàkhfīf, *s. a.* A making light or lighter, a lightening in weight; a soft mode of sounding a letter in pronunciation ا—, —et, *v.a.* To lighten, make lighter in weight or severity.

تخلف tàkhàlluf, *s. a.* A getting out of agreement, differing, varying; ا—, —et, *v.n.* To differ, vary, change.

تخليص tàkhlīss, *s. a.* A making, or being made, free and exempt from any impurity, ill, or defect); ا—, —et, *v.a.* To free (from impurity, ill, or defect). [adulterating.

تخليط tàkhlīt, *s. a.* A mixing or adding;

تخليف tàkhlīf, *s. a.* A making (some one) successor to another.

تخليه tàkhlìyyé, *s. a.* An emptying, evacuation; ا—, —et, *v.a.* To empty, [to evacuate.

تخم tòkhm, *s. p.* Seed.

تخمير tàkhmīr, *s. a.* A causing (wine, &c.) to ferment; a compounding of the dough or materials of any object.

تخمين tàkhmīn, *s. a.* A guess, approximation; ا—, —et, *v.a.* To guess approximately (number or value); تخمينا tàkhmīna, *ad. a.* About, approximately.

تخويف tàkhwīf, *s. a.* A frightening; ا—, —et, *v.a.* To frighten.

تخيل tàkhàyyul, *s. a.* An imagining, forming an idea; imagination; ا—, —et, *v.a.* To imagine, to conceive in idea.

تداخل tèdākhul, *s. a.* Action of interpenetration; a getting into arrears (pay, salary, &c.); تداخله بنمك tèdākhul*a*-bìnmek, *v.n.* To get into arrears (payments) so that the payment of one term is not made before the next is due or overdue.

تدارك tèdāruk (tèdārik), *s. a.* A procuring anything wanted; ا—, —et, *v.n.* To procure (anything wanted); تداركات tèdārik*y*āt, *s. pl. a.* Preparation and laying in of various necessaries; تداركاتنى كورمك tèdārik*y*ātini-ghy*ù*rmek, *v.n.* To make one's preparations; تداركلو tèdārikli, *a. t.* In a state of preparedness with respect to necessaries; تداركلو بولنمق tèdārikli-bùlunm*a*k, *v.n.* To be prepared with what is required.

تدافع tèdāfu'', *s. a.* Defence; تدافعى tèdāfu''ī, *a. a.* Defensive; تجاوزى و تدافعى tèjāvuzī-vè-tèdāfu''ī, Offensive and defensive.

تداول tèdāvul, *s. a.* A passing current from hand to hand (money or books); ا—, —et, *v.n.* To pass current, be in common use.

تداوى tèdāvi, *s. a.* The treatment of disease with medicine.

تدبير tèdbīr, *s. a.* Any measure, plan, or design, adopted after mature deliberation, for the accomplishment of an object; the ruling, governing or ordaining, business by fit measures; ا—, —et, *v.a.* To conceive or lay down a plan of action; —ملك, tèdbīri-milk, The art of governing, political economy, politics; تقدير تدبيرى بوزار tàkdīr-tèdbīri-bòzar, The Divine decree (often) sets at nought the designs of man.

تدريج tèdrīj, *s. a.* Progress by successive steps; تدريجى tèdrījī, *a. a.* Progressive and successive; على التدريج ‘‘àlé-’t-tèdrīj, Little by little, by degrees. [or lectures.

تدريس tèdrīss, *s. a.* A giving lessons

تدقيق tèdkīk, *s. a.* Very minute inquiry; ا—, —et, *v.a.* To inquire into.

تدمير tèdmīr, *s. a.* A ruining, destroying, destruction.

تدوين tèdvin, *s. a.* A collecting into a volume; ا—, —et, *v.a.* To collect into a volume (an author's works).

تدهين tèdhīn, *s. a.* An anointing, oiling; ا—, —et, *v.a.* To oil, anoint.

تذكار tèzkyār, *s. a.* A recalling to memory by name.

تذكر tèzèkkyur, *s. a.* A talking (any matter) over; the private study of any subject explained in public lecture.

تذكره tèzkéré, *s. a.* A note, missive, billet; a memoir; a passport, permit, pass; تذكره جى tèzkéréji, *s. t.* A functionary of the Ottoman Government (or rather two, one being called بيوك تذكره جى biyuk-tèzkéréji, and the other كچوك تذكره جى kùchuk-tèzkéréji).

تذكير tèzkīr, *s. a.* A mentioning by name; a calling to memory; a putting into the masculine form; ا—, —et, *v.a.* To mention, to call to memory.

تذلل tèzèllul, *s. a.* A becoming abased, abject.

تذليل tèzlīl, *s. a.* An abasing, making abject; ا—, —et, To abase, make abject. [—et, *v.a.* To gild with gold.

تذهيب tèzhīb, *s. a.* A gilding; ا—,

تذييل tèzyīl, *s. a.* The adding a supplement or appendix.

تر tèr, *s. t.* Sweat, transudation; —, *a. p.* Fresh; —, Comparative affix of Persian adjectives, answering to our English syllable *er* in similar use; as بد bèd, *bad,* بدتر bèdtèr (*badder*) *worse;* ترُوتازه tèr-u-tāzé, Fresh and young; quite fresh; اياق ترى àyak-tèri (Foot-sweat), a doctor's or foot-messenger's fee for coming.

تراب tùrāb, *s. a.* Earth.

تراطور *or* تراتور tèrātòr, *s. a.* A condiment of nuts pounded with garlic, oil, and curdled milk, esteemed to be cooling.

تراخى tèrākhī, *s. a.* A want of zeal, neglect.

ترازو tèrāzi, *s. p.* A balance, pair of scales; ترازونك كوزى tèrāzining-ghyùzu, One pan, scale, or side of a balance; صو ترازوسی sū-tèrāzissi, *s. t.* A device in hydraulics for carrying water across a valley without losing the level, and so as to allow the easy escape of air from the pipes: it consists in a small tower with a small reservoir at top, the pipes being led up one side to the reservoir, and down the other from it.

تراش tìrāsh (trȦsh) *a. p.* (*in composition*), Which shaves; —, *s. p.* The state of hair or beard which requires shaving; ا—, —et, *v.a.* To shave (another's head or beard); to cut or shave away a little of any substance; او—, —òl, To shave one's self; to be shaved by another; تراشم کلدی tràshim-ghèldi, I require shaving; قلمتراش kàlem-tràsh, A pen-knife (*Turkish*).

تراضی tèrāzī, *s. a.* Mutual satisfaction.

ترافع tèrāfu'', *s. a.* A mutual appealing to a tribunal.

تراکم tèrākyum, *s. a.* A becoming collected in heaps; ا—, —et, *v.n.* To become collected in great quantities.

تربزه tìrèbézé, *s. t.* (*Greek*), A table.

ترانه tèrāné, *s. p.* Melody, symphony.

تراویح tèrāvīh, *s. pl. a.* (*sing.* not used), The long prayers or litanies peculiar to the nights of Ramazan; the literal meaning is *recreations*.

تربه tùrbé, *s. a.* (*Originally* one portion of earth, *then* a grave), A mausoleum or chapel built over a tomb; تربه‌دار tùrbédār, A keeper of a tùrbé.

تربیه tèrbìyyé, تربیت tèrbìyyèt, *s. a.* The doing something to a thing in order to improve its quality; education; sauce for meats; preparation for stuffs; good and polite manners; punishment; ا—, —et, *v.a.* To educate; to punish; to prepare or ameliorate by any special treatment; تربیه‌سنی ویرمك tèrbìyyéssini - vèrmek, *v.n.* To punish.

تربیع tèrbī'', *s. a.* A squaring; ا—, —et, *v.a.* To square; —دائره, tèrbī''i-da'iré, The squaring of the circle; تربیعی tèrbī''ī, Square (measurement).

ترتب tèrèttub, *s. a.* A taking form, proceeding, resulting, coming into being; ا—, —et, *v.n.* To take form and being, to proceed, result.

ترتیب tèrtīb, *s. a.* An arranging; arrangement; order; a set, series; a row, line; a system, method; a disposition, plan of action; a prescription, recipe; ا—, —et, *v.a.* To arrange, dispose; to prescribe.

ترجمان tèrjumān, *a. a.* An interpreter; —افندی, —èfèndi, *and* —دیوان همایون tèrjumānì - dīwānì - hùmāyūn, The Chief Interpreter of the Ottoman Government; سفارت ترجمانی sèfāret-tèrjumānì, An interpreter to an embassy.

ترجمه tèrjumé, *s. a.* A translating, an interpreting; translation; interpretation; a translation; ا—, —et, *v.a.* To translate; to interpret.

ترجى tèréjji, *s. a.* Hope, expectation.

ترجيح tèrjīh, *s. a.* A preferring; ا—, —et, *v.a.* To prefer.

ترحم tèràhhum, *s. a.* Commiseration, compassion, pity.

ترحيب tèrhīb, *s. a.* A giving the salutation مرحبا mèrhabā! May you be prosperous!

ترخانه tàrkhānέ, *s. t.* A preparation of dry curds.

ترخون tàrkhòn, *s. t.* Tarragon (herb).

ترخيص tèrkhīss, *s. a.* A granting permission; ا—, —et, *v.a.* To give permission.

تردد tèrèddud, *s. a.* A going to and fro; a vacillation in purpose, hesitation.

ترديف tèrdīf, *s. a.* A sending (anyone) as companion to another, or as an escort; ا—, —et, *v.a.* To send (anyone) as a companion or escort (to another).

ترذيل tèrzīl, *s. a.* A humbling, humiliating, mortifying; ا—, —et, *v.a.* To humble, humiliate, mortify.

ترزى tèrzi, *s. t.* A tailor.

ترس tèrss, *s. t.* The reverse or wrong side or way of anything; dung, excrement; —, *a. t.* Cross, peevish, ill-tempered, obstinate; contrary; ترسلمك tèrsslémek, *v.a.* To scold severely; —, tùrss, *s. a.* A shield, buckler; —, tèress, *s. t.* A cuckold.

ترسانه tèrsānέ, *s. t.* (*Italian, darsena,* an inner harbour), Dockyard.

ترش tùrsh, *a. p.* Sour; ترشرو tùrsh-rū, *a. p.* Sour-faced.

ترشح tèrèshshuh, *s. a.* A percolation, exudation.

ترشه tìrshέ, *s. t.* Parchment; —, *a. t.* Of a very light bluish-green colour.

ترشى tùrshu, *s. t.* Pickles in vinegar or with leaven.

ترصيص tèrsīss, *s. a.* A firmly joining or clamping together.

ترصيع tèrsī", *s. a.* An adorning with precious stones.

ترضيه tàrzìyyέ, *s. a.* A giving satisfaction or begging pardon.

ترغيب tèrghīb, *s. a.* The making (anyone) desirous; ا—, —et, *v.a.* To make desirous, excite to emulation.

ترفنده tùrfànda, *s. t.* The first of the season of any fruits or vegetables.

ترفيع tèrfī", *s. a.* An elevating, raising on high; ا—, —et, *v.a.* To raise, elevate.

ترفيه tèrfīh, *s. a.* The procuring (for others) ease and prosperity.

ترقب tèràkkub, *s. a.* A waiting in expectation.

ترقى tèràkki, *s. a.* An increasing in quantity or in dignity; بولمق—, —bùlmak, *v.n.* To increase, be increased, be raised.

ترقيم tèrkīm, *s. a.* A writing down; ا—, —et, *v.a.* To write, pen down.

ترقين tèrkīn, *s. a.* A running the pen through, an effacing, defacing; ا—, —et, *v.a.* To run the pen through, efface, blot out.

ترك tèrk, *s. a.* A leaving, abandoning, quitting, forsaking knowingly and intentionally; —, tùrk, *s. t.* An Asiatic provincial Turk; a rustic, clod-hopper; ا—, tèrk-et, *v.a.* To leave, abandon, quit, forsake; ترکجه tùrkj*a*, *s. t.* The Turkish language.

ترکمن Tùrkmèn, *s.* and *a. t.* Turcoman; ترکمن ولایتی Tùrkmèn-vìlāyèti, *s. t.* Turcomania.

ترکه tèrikė (tèrékė), *s. a.* The estate or movable effects of a deceased person.

ترکی tùrkyu, *s. t.* A song; —, tùrkī, *a. a.* Turkish.

ترکیب tèrkīb, *s. a.* A compounding, composing; a composition; ا—, —et, *v.a.* To compound; to compose; ترکیبی tèrkībī, *a. a.* Appertaining to composition; composite; وصف ترکیبی wassf*i*-tèrkībī, A composite qualificative epithet, as بادبانکشا bādbān-kyùshā, Sail-opening, which spreads its sails. [or leather.

ترلك tèrlik, *s. t.* House slippers of cloth

ترلمك tèrlémek (*aor.* ترلر tèrlèr), *v.a.* and *n.* To sweat; to perspire.

ترمیم tèrmīm, *s. a.* A repairing, patching; ا—, —et, *v.a.* To repair, patch up.

ترنج tùrunj, *s. a.* The bitter or Seville orange; ترنجی tùrunjī, *a. p.* Of the reddish colour peculiar to the Seville orange.

ترنکت trìnkèt, *s. t.* (*Italian*), The fore-sail; ترنکتین trìnkétīn, The fore-stay-sail.

ترنم tèrènnum, *s. a.* Any melodious and continued sound, as chanting, warbling, humming, praying, or reading.

ترویج tèrvīj, *s. a.* A giving currency and briskness to markets or business; ا—, —et, *v.a.* To promote, advance, assist, make brisk (commerce or business).

تره tèrė, *s. t.* Cress; صوترهسی sū-tèrėssi, Water-cresses; ترهیاغی tėrė-yàghi, Fresh butter. [words.

ترهات tùrréhāt, *s. pl. a.* Nonsense, vain

ترهیب tèrhīb, *s. a.* A frightening, terrifying; ا—, —et, *v.a.* To terrify, frighten.

تریاق tìryāk, *s. a.* A kind of electuary, theriaca, of various kinds, one of which is eaten with opium, and hence opium-eaters are called تریاقی tìryākī (tìrākī), A theriaca-man. [with gravy or broth.

ترید tìrid, *s. t.* A dish of bread stewed

تزاید tèzāyud, *s. a.* An increasing, becoming augmented; augmentation.

تزك tèzek, *s. t.* Dung in cakes and dried as fuel.

تزکیه tèzkìyyė, *s. a.* A man's character as known by inquiry; an inquiring about a person's character; a giving of a tenth of one's possessions as alms, and so rendering the rest blessed.

تزلزل tèzèlzul, *s. a.* The shaking of an earthquake.

تزوج tèzèvvuj, *s. a.* The taking a wife to one's self; ا—, —et, *v.a.* To marry, to take as a wife, to espouse.

تزویج tèzvīj, *s. a.* A causing to marry, a giving in marriage; ا—, —et, *v.a.* To procure a wife for a man, or a husband for a wife, and cause them to marry.

تزویر tèzvīr, *s. a.* Any fraudulent act or assertion.

تزیین tèzyīn, *s. a.* An ornamenting; ا—, —et, *v.a.* To beautify, adorn, ornament.

تسالیا Tèssàlia, *s. t.* Thessaly.

تساوی tèssāvi, *s. a.* A being mutually equal; تساوی لیل ونهار tèssāviyi-lèyl-u-nèhār, The equinox.

تسبیح tèssbīh, *s. a.* A rosary of beads; a litany of praises said by tale, for which the beads are used as counters; — بوجکی, —bùjèghi, The wire-worm (?).

تسبیل tèssbīl, *s. a.* A consecrating (anything) to pious or charitable uses.

تستر tèssèttur, *s. a.* A covering or hiding one's self behind a vail.

تستی tèssti, *s. t.* A jug, a pitcher.

تستیر tèsstīr, *s. a.* A covering (anything), hiding it; ا—, —et, *v.a.* To hide, cover.

تسجیل tèssjīl, *s. a.* An enregistering in the public records of a court.

تسخیر tèsskhīr, *s. a.* A subjugation, conquest; ا—, —et, *v.a.* To conquer, take, subjugate, subdue.

تسخین tèsskhīn, *s. a.* A making warm; ا—, —et, *v.a.* To warm, to heat.

تسطیر tèsstīr (tàss—), *s. a.* A writing down line by line; ا—, —et, *v.a.* To write.

تسع tùss", *s. a.* A ninth; —tìss", *and* تسعة tìss"a, *a. a.* Nine; تسعون tìss-"ūn, *and* تسعین tìss"īn, *a. a.* Ninety.

تسکین tèsskīn, *s. a.* A quieting, calming, appeasing; ا—, —et, *v.a.* To calm.

تسلسل tèssèlsul, *s. a.* A concatenation; a passing by pedigree; a series of promotions when one high office is vacated.

تسلط tèssàllut, *s. a.* An assumption of sovereign power; an arbitrary assumption of power and authority; a vexatious exercise of power or physical force.

تسلم tèssèllum, *s. a.* A receiving possession or into charge when another delivers (anything) over.

تسلی tèssèlli, تسلیت tèssliyyèt, *and* تسلیه tèssliyyé, *s. a.* Consolation; تسلی ویرمك tèssèlli-vèrmek, *and* تسلیت ا tèssliyyèt-et, *v.a.* To console; تسلی بولمق tèssèlli-bùlmak, *v.n.* To find consolation.

تسلیم tèsslīm, *s. a.* A salutation; a giving up; a delivery; a conceding a point in reasoning, submitting; ا—, —et, *v.a.* To give up, deliver over; او—, —òl, *v.n.* To give one's self up.

تسمیه tèssmìyyé, *s. a.* A naming; a name; ا—, —et, *v.a.* To name, call.

تسوید tèssvīd, *s. a.* A foul copy of a letter.

تسویه tèssvìyyé, *s. a.* An arranging, setting straight, putting to rights; a smoothing, rendering even and regular; ا—, —et, *v.a.* To arrange, put to rights; to smooth, make even, straight, and regular.

تسهيل **tèsshīl,** *s. a.* **A facilitating ; ا—, —et,** *v.a.* **To facilitate, make easy.**

تسيار **tèssyār,** *s. a.* **A sending, forwarding ; ا—, —et,** *v.a.* **To send, forward.**

تسيب **tèssèyyub,** *s. a.* **A neglecting important affairs, either through sloth, indifference, or the pursuit of pleasure.**

تسيير **tèssyīr,** *s. a.* **A sending, forwarding ; ا—, —et,** *v.a.* **To send, to forward.**

تشبث **tèshèbbuss,** *s. a.* **A setting about, a taking in hand ; ا—, —et,** *v.n.* **To take in hand ; to set about, to begin ; to apply one's self to.**

تشبيه **tèshbīh,** *s. a.* **A comparing or likening (one thing or another), a comparison ; ا—, —et,** *v.a.* **To compare, to liken.**

تشتت **tèshèttut,** *s. a.* **A being dispersed, scattered, separated.**

تشخيص **tèshkhīss,** *s. a.* **A distinguishing individually, making out, recognising, seeing, perceiving ; ا—, —et,** *v.a.* **To distinguish, make out, recognise.**

تشديد **tèshdīd,** *s. a.* **A making strong, severe, or violent ; the pronunciation of a letter twice following, as with our** ***d*** **in** ***mid-day*****, or as** ***l*** **in** ***full lips*** **; the name of the orthographical mark ـّ, used to denote this mode of pronunciation by being placed over the reduplicated letter.**

تشريح **tèshrīh,** *s. a.* **A dissecting, anatomizing ; anatomy ; a skeleton, or anatomical drawing or preparation ; ا—, —et,** *v.a.* **To dissect, anatomize ; علم تشريح "ìlmi-tèshrīh, The science of anatomy.**

تشريف **tèshrīf,** *s. a.* **A making honourable, rendering noble, conferring honour ; ا—, —et,** *v.a.* **To make honourable, confer honour, render noble ; to do the honour of visiting ; تشريفات tèshrīfāt,** *s. pl. a.* **Court ceremonies, with the order of precedence ; تشريفاتجى tèshrīfātji,** *s. t.* **The Master of Ceremonies to the Ottoman Court ; خارجيه تشريفاتجيسى khārijìyyé - téshrīfātjissi, The Master of Ceremonies for the Foreign Department ; تشريفساز tèshrīfsāz,** *a. p.* **Who confers honour.**

تشريك **tèshrīk,** *s. a.* **The making (one) a partner or associate (with another) ; ا—, —et,** *v.a.* **To associate, make a partner.**

تشرين **tèshrīn,** *s. a.* **Name of two Syro-Roman months, corresponding with October and November ; one is distinguished as تشرين اول tèshrīni-ÈVVEL, The first Teshrin ; the other as تشرين ثانى tèshrīni-sānī, The second Teshrin.**

تشكر **tèshèkkyur,** *s. a.* **A feeling thankful ; a giving thanks ; thanks ; ا—, —et,** *v.n.* **To be thankful ; to express gratitude.**

تشكى **tèshèkki,** *s. a.* **A complaining ;**

تصحيح tàsshīh (ss-h), *s. a.* A correcting, rectifying; ا—, —et, *v.a.* To correct, to rectify; تصحيح مزاج‌ا tàsshīhi-mizāj-et, *v.n.* To regain one's health.

تصدق tàssàdduk, *s. a.* The giving of [alms.

تصدى tàssàddī, *s. a.* A setting about (any work): ا—, —et, *v.n.* To set about.

تصدير tàssdīr, *s. a.* A causing to emanate.

تصديع tàssdī'', *s. a.* The giving a headache; plaguing, importuning; ا—, —et, *v.a.* To give the headache; to plague, annoy, importune.

تصديق tàssdīk, *s. a.* A confirming, corroborating, affirming; ا—, —et, *v.a.* To confirm, corroborate, affirm; to ratify (a treaty); تصديقنامه tàssdīk-nāmé, *s. p.* The ratifications (of a treaty).

تصرف tàssàrruf, *s. a.* The possession, disposal, or using of anything; the using economy, in endeavouring to curtail expense; the having carnal connexion (with a woman) viewed as an exercise of physical power.

تصريح tàssrīh, *s. a.* An explicit declaration; ا—, —et, *v.a.* To express, declare explicitly.

تصفيه tàssfīyyé, *s. a.* A purifying, clarifying, cleansing; ا—, —et, *v.a.* To purify, clarify, cleanse.

تصليت tàsslīyyèt, *s. a.* A benediction (on Muhammed, by saying صلى الله عليه sàlla-'llāhu-''àlèyh! May God be propitious unto him!)

ا—, —et, *v.n.* To complain, make complaint.

تشكيل tèshkīl, *s. a.* A giving form and shape, a shaping, forming; ا—, —et, *v.a.* To shape, to form.

تشمير tèshmīr, *s. a.* A tucking up (skirts or sleeves) in order to work; ا—, —et, *v.a.* To tuck up (skirts or sleeves).

تشنه tìshné, *a. p.* Thirsty, athirst; تشنكى tìshnéghī, *s. p.* Thirst.

تشويش tèshvīsh, *s. a.* A confusing, putting in confusion.

تشويق tèshvīk, *s. a.* A stimulating, exciting, stirring up, urging on; ا—, —et, *v.a.* To stimulate, excite, stir up, urge on (to action).

تشهير tèshhīr, *s. a.* A making publicly known; an exposing (a false witness, &c.) to public ignominy by parading through the streets.

تشييد tèshyīd, *s. a.* A building, constructing; ا—, —et, *v.a.* To found, build, construct.

تشييع tèshyī'', *s. a.* The accompanying a person a short distance on his road when he sets out.

تصادف tèssādüf, *s. a.* An accidental or undesigned meeting; chance; ا—, —et, *v.n.* To meet accidentally; to happen, to chance.

تصادم tèssādum, *s. a.* The shock of two bodies against each other.

تصارلمق tàssarlamak (*aor.* تصارلر tàssarlar), *v.a.* To arrange (any scheme) in one's mind.

تصمة **tAssma**, *s. t.* A strap or latchet.

تصميم **tAssmīm**, *s. a.* An intending, a resolving; intention, resolution; ا—, —et, *v.a.* To intend, resolve.

تصنيف **tAssnīf**, *s. a.* A compiling, composing, writing (a book); a book, work, compilation, composition; ا—, —et, *v.a.* To write, compose.

تصور **tàssAvvur**, *s. a.* The forming an idea, picturing to one's self; ا—, —et, *v.a.* To form an idea of, picture to one's self.

تصوف **tàssAvvuf**, *s. a.* Mystical philosophy.

تصويب **tAssvīb**, *s. a.* An approving, approbation; ا—, —et, *v.a.* To approve.

تصوير **tAssvīr**, *s. a.* A drawing, designing, painting; a picture; a statue; a portrait.

تضرع **tàzàrru"**, *s. a.* A humbling one's self; humility.

تضعيف **tAz"īf**, *s. a.* A doubling in number or quantity; ا—, —et, *v.a.* To double.

تضمين **tAzmīn**, *s. a.* A making reparation for injury, repaying damages; ا—, —et, *v.a.* To make reparation, indemnify; تضمينات **tAzmīnĀt**, *s. pl.* Damages, indemnity.

تضييع **tAzyī"**, *s. a.* A wasting; ا—, —et, *v.a.* To waste, lose, throw away.

تضييق **tAzyīk**, *s. a.* A pressing, squeezing; an importuning; a using gentle violence; a pressing sorely, a driving to extremities; ا—, —et, *v.a.* To press.

تطاول **tètāvul**, *s. a.* Rapacity, oppression.

تطبيق **tAtbīk**, *s. a.* The applying (one thing to another) so as to touch and fit, or to see whether it accords, either physically or morally; ا—, —et, *v.a.* To apply; to compare; —مهرى, —mùhuru, *s. t.* An impression of a seal left with an agent or banker for comparison in case of doubt of forgery.

تطليق **tAtlīk**, *s. a.* A repudiating, divorcing a wife; ا—, —et, *v.a.* To divorce, put away, repudiate (a wife).

تطويل **tAtvīl**, *s. a.* Prolixity of discourse.

تطهير **tAthīr**, *s. a.* A cleansing, cleaning; ا—, —et, *v.a.* To cleanse, clean.

تطييب **tAtyīb**, *s. a.* A making pleased and happy; ا—, —et, *v.a.* To make pleased and happy.

تظلم **tàzàllum**, *s. a.* A plaint against oppression; —حال ا—, tàzàllumu-hāl-et, *v.n.* To complain of one's oppressed condition.

تعاقب **tà"ākub**, *s. a.* A following in succession; ا—, —et, *v.n.* To follow (one another) in succession.

تعالى **tà"ālà**, *int. t.* May (His name) be glorified! حق تعالى Hakk-tà"ālà! (God) the Truth, may His name be glorified! This is as common a designation of God as when we say *Our heavenly Father*.

تعب **tà"b**, *s. a.* Fatigue, trouble.

تعبير **tà"bīr**, *s. a.* A naming, calling; an explaining; a word, an expression; ا—, —et, *v.a.* To apply (a name to a thing); to explain (a dream).

تعجب tà‘‘àjjub, *s. a.* A being surprised; astonished; ا—, —et, *v.n.* To be astonished, surprised; to wonder.

تعجيز tà‘‘jīz, *s. a.* A teasing, annoying; ا—, —et, *v.a.* To tease, annoy, worry.

تعجيل tà‘‘jīl, *s. a.* A hurrying, hastening; ا—, —et, *v.a.* To expedite, hasten.

تعداد tà‘‘dād, *s. a.* A counting; ا—, —et, *v.a.* To count.

تعدى tà‘‘àddi, *s. a.* An injuring, vexing, oppressing.

تعديل tà‘‘dīl, *s. a.* A changing slightly, a modifying; ا—, —et, *v.a.* To modify.

تعرض tà‘‘àrruz, *s. a.* A meddling without a right, an injuring; ا—, —et, *v.n.* To meddle with wrongfully, to offer injury. [a reproaching.

تعريض tà‘‘rīz, *s. a.* A finding fault with,

تعريف tà‘‘rīf, *s. a.* An explaining; a describing; description; ا—, —et, *v.a.* To describe; to explain; حرف تعريف hàrfi-tà‘‘rīf, *and* لام تعريف lāmi-tà‘‘rif, The Arabic definite article ال

تعزير tà‘‘zīr, *s. a.* A reprimanding; a legal punishment of less than eighty stripes; ا—, —et, *v.a.* To reprimand; to punish legally with less than eighty stripes.

تعزيه tà‘‘zìyyé, *s. a.* An expression of condolence; a letter of condolence.

تعسف tà‘‘àssuf, *s. a.* Violent tyranny and oppression.

تعشق tà‘‘àshshuk, *s. a.* A falling in love; ا—, —et, *v.n.* To fall in love (with).

تعشير tà‘‘shīr, *s. a.* A collecting of tithes; ا—, —et, *v.a.* To tithe.

تعصب tà‘‘àssub, *s. a.* Bigotry, fanaticism, a being bigoted; ا—, —et, *v.n.* To be a bigot. [sing (juice).

تعصير tà‘‘sīr, *s. a.* A pressing, expres-

تعطف tà‘‘àttuf, *s. a.* Condescending kindness.

تعطيل tà‘‘tīl, *s. a.* A causing (any thing or body) to remain idle or unemployed; a remaining, being caused to remain idle; a holiday; ا—, —et, *v.a.* To stop from work, hinder, cause to remain inactive. [ness.

تعظم tà‘‘àzzum, *s. a.* Pride, false great-

تعظيم tà‘‘zīm, *s. a.* A respecting, revering, treating with consideration and honour; a deeming and treating as important; ا—, —et, *v.a.* To honour, respect, revere, venerate; to treat with great consideration; to deem and treat as important, to give importance to.

تعفن tà‘‘àffun, *s. a.* A stink of putrefaction; ا—, —et, *v.n.* To stink.

تعقل tà‘‘àkkul, *s. a.* A finding out (a method) by thought; ا—, —et, *v.a.* To find out by thinking, to think of.

تعقيب tà‘‘kīb, *s. a.* A following, pursuing; ا—, —et, *v.a.* To pursue, follow.

تعلق tà‘‘àlluk, *s. a.* A being attached to, or depending on (anything), being related to, in relations with, having anything to do with; ا—, —et, *v.n.* To become attached to, affixed to; to regard, become dependent on, or connected with; تعلقات tà"àllukāt, *s. pl. a.* Things or persons dependent on, or connected with.

تعلل tà"àllul, *s. a.* A delaying under various pretences, or an alleging pretexts so as to avoid or delay doing something.

تعلم tà"àllum, *s. a.* A learning (any art or science).

تعليق tà"līk, *s. a.* A suspending, hanging up (anything); the making (anything) dependent (on another); a fixing (the eye on anything); the Persian mode of writing the Arabic character; ا—, —et, *v.a.* To hang up, suspend; to fix (the eye on anything); to give (a thing) some relation (to some other).

تعليم tà"līm, *s. a.* A teaching, instructing, exercising; practice, exercise; military exercise, drill; a specimen copy of scholar's writing; ا—, —et, *v.a.* To teach, instruct; ا—ايتدرمك, —ètdirmek, *v.n.* To cause one to practice or do exercise; تعليمات tà"līmāt, *s. pl. a.* Instructions; تعليمجى tà"līmji, *s. t.* A military instructor.

تعمير tà"mīr, *s. a.* A repairing, mending; reparation; ا—, —et, *v.a.* To repair, mend.

تعميم tà"mīm, *s. a.* A making general or common; ا—, —et, *v.a.* To make general.

تعهد tà"àhhud, *s. a.* An undertaking to perform, rendering the performance (of something) obligatory to one's self; ا—, —et, *v.n.* To undertake, to make one's self responsible for (the performance of something).

تعيش tà"àyyush, *s. a.* A maintaining one's self, living, maintenance; ا—, —et, *v.n.* To live, maintain one's self.

تعين tà"àyyun, *s. a.* A becoming conspicuous, remarkable.

تعييب tà"yīb, *s. a.* A reproaching, finding fault with, blaming, shaming; ا—, —et, *v.a.* To reproach, blame, shame.

تعيين tà"yīn, *s. a.* A pointing out, designating to the eye; a naming, appointing; a fixing, allotting, allowing; a ration; ا—, —et, *v.a.* To point out, designate; to name, appoint; to fix, allot, allow; تعيينات tà"yīnāt, *s. pl. a.* Rations of all kinds.

تغلغه tŭghulgha, *s. t.* A helmet.

تغليط tàghlīt, *s. a.* A leading into error, causing to make a mistake; ا—, —et, *v.a.* To mislead.

تغنى tàghànni, *s. a.* A singing, chanting, warbling.

تغير tàghàyyur, *s. a.* An undergoing change, becoming changed; ا—, —et, *v.n.* To change, become different.

تغيير tàghyīr, *s. a.* A changing, altering; ا—, —et, *v.a.* To change, to alter, make different.

تفاخر tèfākhur, *s. a.* An ostentatious boasting of talents or superiority over others (usual, and considered quite proper among poets).

تفاضل tèfāzul, *s. a.* A superiority (in number or quantity) over another; a remainder, a difference; علم تمامی وتفاضلی "ilmi-tāmāmi-vè-tèfāzulī, The integral and differential calculus.

تفأل tèfè' 'ul. (See تفوّل, the correct orthography).

تفاوت tèfāvut, *s. a.* A surpassing another; the surplus, remainder, difference.

تفتك tiftik, *s. t.* The wool of Angora goats.

تفتیح tèftīh, *s. a.* An opening, causing to open; a breaking the wind off the stomach, causing eructation.

تفتیش tèftīsh, *s. a.* A diligent searching and examining; ا—, —et, *v.a.* To search and examine.

تفحص tèfàhhuss, *s. a.* Inquiry, investigation; تفتیش و تفحص ا tèftīsh-u-tèfàhhuss-et, *v.a.* To investigate, inquire into.

تفخیم tèfkhīm, *s. a.* An honouring; a giving honour to; ا—, —et, *v.a.* To honour, to give honour to.

تفرج tèfèrruj, *s. a.* The taking a walk or ride for recreation.

تفرد tèfèrrud, *s. a.* A separating one's self; an acting rebelliously.

تفرس tèfèrruss, *s. a.* A judging sagaciously from physiognomy or appearance.

تفرقه tèfrika, *s. a.* Separation, separateness, dispersion.

تفریح tèfrīh, *s. a.* A cheering, exhilarating; ا—, —et, *v.a.* To cheer, to make glad.

تفریط tèfrīt, *s. a.* A doing less than necessary; افراط و— ìfrāt-u—, Exaggeration and shortcoming, the doing more than necessary and the doing less.

تفریق tèfrīk, *s. a.* A separating, dividing; a distinguishing; ا—, —et, *v.a.* To separate, divide, put asunder; to distinguish, make out.

تفسیر tèfsīr, *s. a.* A commenting on the Kur'an word by word; a commentary on the Kur'an.

تفصیل tāfsīl, *s. a.* A going into details; ا—, —et, *v.a.* To detail; تفصیلاً tāfsīlan, *ad. a.* In detail; تفصیلات tāfsīlāt, *s. pl. a.* Details.

تفقد tèfàkkud, *s. a.* An inquiring after an absent person.

تفکر tèfèkkyur, *s. a.* A thinking, pondering, turning over in one's mind; ا—, —et, *v.n.* To think, to ponder.

تفنك tùfènk (tùfèk), *s. t.* A gun (not a cannon), musket, fowling-piece, rifle, carbine; —طولدرمق, —dòldurmak, *v.n.* To load a gun; —آتمق, —àtmak, *v.n.* To fire off a gun; او تفنکی àv-tùfèghi, A fowling-piece; چفته تفنك chiftè-tùfèk, A double-barrelled gun; ششخانه‌لو تفنك shèsh-khānèli-tùfèk (*or* ششخانه shèsh-khānè *simply*), A rifle; آتلو تفنکی àtli-tùfèghi, A carbine; فتیللو تفنك fitilli-tùfèk, A match-lock; چاقمقلو تفنك chàkmakli-tùfèk, A flint musket, &c.; اجزالو تفنك èjzāli-tùfèk, A percussion gun; تیموری—, —dèmiri, A gun-barrel; قونداغی—, —kùndàghi, A gunstock; چاقمغی—, —chàk-maghi, A gunlock; چبوغی—, —chì-bughu, A ramrod; تفنکجی tùfèkji, s. t. A musketeer; an infantry soldier; a soldier on police duty; a kind of irregular police soldier; a kind of rural police soldier; a marine (*called also more especially* بحریه تفنگجیسی bàhrìyyé-tùfèkjissi, *a naval musketeer*); a gunsmith.

تفوق tèfèvvuk, *s. a.* Superiority over another.

تفؤل tèfè''ul, *s. a.* The drawing an augury; an appeal to the *sortes Virgilianæ*; ا—, —et, *v.a.* To take (any conclusion) from an omen or augury; to appeal to the *sortes Virgilianæ.*

تفوه tèfèvvuh, *s. a.* An uttering from the mouth; ا—, —et, *v.a.* To utter, mention.

تفویض tèfvīz, *s. a.* A dispensing (favours, honours, &c.); ا—, —et, *v.a.* To dispense, confer (honours, &c., upon a person).

تفهم tèfèhhum, *s. a.* A comprehending, understanding; ا—, —et, *v.a.* To comprehend, to understand.

تفهیم tèfhīm, *s. a.* An explaining, giving to understand, causing to be comprehended; ا—, —et, *v.a.* To explain, to cause (a person) to understand (something).

تقاص tàkāsss, *s. a.* A mutual exercise of the law of reprisal (*lex talionis*); a mutual exchange of employment or the like.

تقاضا (*for* تقاضی) tàkāzà, *s. a.* A dunning, an importuning, a worrying for anything due.

تقاطع tàkātu'', *s. a.* Intersection.

تقاعد tàkā''ud, *s. a.* The state of an old servant pensioned off; the pensioning off of old servants; ا—, —et, *v.a.* To pension off, to dismiss from service with a pension.

تقبیح tàkbīh, *s. a.* A looking upon and stigmatizing as bad and improper; ا—, —et, *v.a.* To stigmatize as bad and improper.

تقبیل tàkbīl, *s. a.* A kissing in respect; ا—, —et, *v.a.* To kiss in respect.

تقدس tàkàddéssé, *int. a.* May (He) be glorified and hallowed! حق تعالی و تقدس Hàkk-tà''āla-vè-tàkàddéssé, God, may He be glorified and hallowed!

تقدم tàkàddum, *s. a.* A taking precedence; ا—, —et, *v.n.* To take precedence.

تقدیر tàkdīr, *s. a.* The Divine predestination or foreknowledge of events; an appreciation of worth or value; the supposing or understanding any word implied in a sentence; a supposition, not arbitrary but implied; a case supposed by implication; ا—, —et, *v.a.* To appreciate the worth, to value highly; تقدیر تدبیری بوزار tàkdīr-tèdbīri-bòzar, The Divine prescience overrules the counsels of man; بوتقديرده bŭ-tʌkdīrd*a*, In this case; تقدمى تقديرنده tàkʌddumu-tʌkdīrind*a*, In the case of his taking the precedence; تقديرجه tàkdīrj*a*, *ad. t.* According to the supposition in the case.

تقديس tʌkdīss, *s. a.* A consecrating, making holy.

تقديم tʌkdīm, *s. a.* A bringing forward; a causing to precede; a presenting; ا—, —et, *v.n.* To present, lay before.

تقرب tàkàrrub, *s. a.* A drawing nigh, approaching; a being near; ا—, —et, *v.n.* To approach, to draw near.

تقريب tʌkrīb, *s. a.* A means, a consideration; برتقريب ايله bìr-tʌkrīb-il*a*, *ad. t.* Somehow or other; بو تقريب ايله bŭ-tʌkrīb-il*a*, By these means, through this consideration; تقريبا tàkrība, *ad. a.* About, approximatively.

تقرير tʌkrīr, *s. a.* A making permanent and stable, an establishing; a formal declaration, an affidavit; an official report or diplomatic note; ا—, —et, *v.a.* To establish; to declare, depone; to represent in an official note or report.

تقريض tʌkrīz, *s. a.* A peculiar kind of approbatory criticism of any book by a person supposed to be an excellent judge of the subject, and which is always prefixed to the work to which it relates; ا—, —et, *v.a.* To approve (a book in this peculiar critical form).

تقسيم tàksīm, *s. a.* A dividing; division; a division; a mark of division; the arithmetical rule of division; ا—, —et, *v.a.* To divide.

تقصير tʌksīr, *s. a.* A making short or shorter; a shortcoming, failing, fault; ا—, —et, *v.a.* To shorten; —, *v.n.* To fail in point of duty; تقصيرات tʌksīrʌt, *s.pl. a.* Faults, failings.

تقطر tàkʌttur, *s. a.* A dripping, falling by drops; ا—, —et, *v.n.* To fall by drops.

تقطير tʌktīr, *s. a.* A distillation; a causing to fall by drops; ا—, —et, *v.a.* To distil; to cause to fall by drops.

تقطيع tʌktī'‘, *s. a.* A cutting in pieces; a scanning (of verses); ا—, —et, *v.a.* To cut in pieces; to scan (verses).

تقلدامق tàkıldamak (*aor.* تقلدار tàkıldar), *v.n.* To make a noise (by one thing striking against another, as a loose thing in a box on a porter's back).

تقلاق tàklʌk, *s. t.* A turning head over heels; —قيلمق, —kılmak, *v.n.* To tumble, to turn head over heels; بر اقچه‌يه بيك تقلاق قيلار bìr-ʌkch*aya*-bìn*g*-tàklʌk-kılar, He does, will, would tumble over head and heels a thousand times for one farthing; *i.e.* he is a mean, sordid fellow.

تقليد tʌklīd, *s. a.* A placing round one's own neck like a necklace, or over one shoulder as a baldric; a becoming obedient to, following, imitating; an imitation; a mimicking; ا—, —et, *v.a.* To imitate, to mimic; to follow and obey; —سيف, tāklīdi-sèyf, The investiture with the sword (the parallel ceremony to crowning the Sultan).

تقليل tāklil, *s. a.* A lessening in number or quantity. [God, piety.

تقوا (*for* تقوى) tākwà, *s. a.* The fear of

تقويت tākvìyyèt, *s. a.* A strengthening; ا—, —et, *v.a. and* —ويرمك, vèrmek, *v.a.* To strengthen; —بولمق, —bùlmak, *v.n.* To become strengthened.

تقويم tākvīm, *s. a.* A making straight or upright; a setting in order; an almanack; ا—, —et, *v.a.* To make straight or upright; to set in order, arrange properly; to rectify.

تقيد tàkàyyud, *s. a.* An employing one's whole attention, taking great care and pains; ا—, —et, *v.n.* To take great care and pains.

تقيه tàkyé, *s. t.* A small linen cap worn under the turban.

تك tèk, *a. t.* Odd (not even); quiet (alone, to one's self); —دورمق, —dùrmak, To be quiet, keep still, keep one's self to one's self; —, *ad. t.* Merely, only, but once; تك تك tèk-tùk, *ad. t.* Now and then; here and there one; —, *s. p.* A running about. [puffed up.

تكابر tèkyābur, *s. a.* Pride, a being

تكاثر tèkyāssur, *s. a.* An increasing in number, becoming numerous.

تكاسل tèkyāssul, *s. a.* Negligence.

تكاليف tèkyālīf, *s. pl. a.* (*of* تكليف), Government dues, taxes; propositions, [proposals.

تكبر tèkèbbur, *s. a.* Pride.

تكبير tèkbīr, *s. a.* A making great; a saying الله اكبر allāhu-èkbèr! God is very great.

تكثير tèksīr, *s. a.* A making numerous; ا—, —et, *v.a.* To make numerous, increase the number of.

تكدير tèkdīr, *s. a.* A reprimanding, a causing grief; ا—, —et, *v.a.* To reprimand; to cause grief, to hurt one's feelings.

تكذيب tèkzīb, *s. a.* A contradicting flatly, telling one he lies; ا—, —et, *v.a.* To contradict flatly.

تكر tèkir, *s. t.* The red mullet; —, tèker, *s. t.* A wheel.

تكرار tèkrār, *s. a.* A repetition; —, *ad. t.* Again, anew, once more; ا—, —et, *and* تكرارلمق tèkrārlamak (*aor.* تكرارلار tèkrārlar), *v.a.* To repeat, do or say again; —بتكرار, —bé-tèkrār, *ad. p.* Again and again.

تكرك tèghèrk, *s. p.* Hail.

تكرلنمك tèkerlenmek (*aor.* تكرلنور tèkerlénir), *v.n.* To roll over and over; to fall down and roll.

تكرى tàngri, *s. t.* God.

تكرير tékrīr, *s. a.* A repeating, doing again. [and respect.

تكريم tèkrīm, *s. a.* A showing honour

تكسر tèkèssur, *s. a.* A being broken or damaged.

تكسنمك tìksinmek (*aor.* تكسنور tìksinir), *v.n.* To loathe, feel a disgust at, an aversion for.

تكفل tèkèfful, *s. a.* A standing surety, making one's self responsible, standing bail; ا—, —et, *v.n.* To stand surety, stand bail, be answerable, make one's self responsible.

تكفور tèkfūr (tèkir), *s. t.* (*Greek τοῦ Κυρίου*), The Greek Emperor of old.

تكفين tèkfīn, *s. a.* A wrapping in a winding-sheet; ا—, —et, *v.a.* To wrap in a winding-sheet.

تكلتى tè*gh*elti (tèlti), *s. t.* The straps behind the saddle with which a cloak, &c., may be bound.

تكلف tèkèlluf, *s. a.* Expensive and ceremonious observances, preparations, or decorations; تكلفلو tèkèlluflu, *a. t.* Sumptuous.

تكلم tèkèllum, *s. a.* A speaking, conversing; ا—, —et, To speak, talk.

تكليف tèklīf, *s. a.* The making a proposal, proposing; a proposal; the casting any charge or duty (upon one); a tax, a due, an impost; ceremony, ceremonious behaviour; ا—, —et, *v.a.* To propose; to offer; to cast (any duty) upon (some one); خام— khām—, An unduly-weighed proposal; تكليفسز tèklīfsiz, *a.* and *ad. t.* Without ceremony.

تكمه tèkmé, *s. t.* A kick; اتمق—, —ʌtmak, *v.n.* To kick, give a kick.

تكميل tèkmīl, *s. a.* A making complete, perfecting; —, *a. t.* Finished; complete; ا—, —et, *v.a.* To finish, perfect, complete.

تكنه tèkné, *s. t.* A trough; a washing-tray; the hull of a ship; a ship.

تكوين tèkvīn, *s. a.* A calling into existence, creating.

تكه tèké, *s. t.* A he-goat; a shrimp, a prawn.

تكيه tèkyé, *s. a.* A convent of dervishes, as asylum, place of repose.

تل tèl, *s. t.* A thread; a wire; a rope-yarn; شماته تلى shàmʌta-tèli, Tinsel.

تلاتين tèlātīn, *s. t.* Russia leather.

تلاش tèlash, *s. t.* A fuss; a hurry; ا—, —et, *v.n.* To make a fuss, be alarmed.

تلاشى tèlāshī, *s. a.* A being alarmed, in a fuss.

تلاطم tèlātum, *s. a.* The heaving of the waves.

تلافى tèlāfi, *s. a.* A making up (for lost time or opportunity).

تلاقى tèlāk*i*, *s. a.* The mutual meeting of two or more.

تلامذه tèlāmizé, *s. pl. a.* (*of* تلميذ tèlmīz), Disciples, pupils.

تلاوت tìlāvet, *s. a.* The decorous reading aloud or intoning of a holy book.

تلبس tèlèbbuss, *s. a.* A wearing (of apparel).

تلبيس tèlbīss, *s. a.* Fraud, deceit, lies.

تلخ tèlkh, *a. p.* Bitter.

تلخيص tèlkhīss, *s. a.* The customary report laid by the grand vizier before the Sultan daily on current affairs.

تلذذ tèlèzzuz, *s. a.* A being pleased in point of taste, an enjoying; ا—, —et, *v.n.* To be pleased, to enjoy.

تلطف tèlàttuf, *s. a.* A manifestation of kindness, friendship, and favour.

تلطيف tAltīf, *s. a.* (A superior's) making (some one) feel that he is an object of favour, a treating with marked kindness and condescension.

تلف tèlef, *s. a.* A wasting; a killing; ا—, —et, *v.a.* To waste; to kill.

تلفظ tèlAffuz, *s. a.* A pronouncing; pronunciation; ا—, —et, *v.a.* To pronounce.

تلقيب tèlkīb, *s. a.* The giving a name [or title.

تلقيح tèlkīh, *s. a.* An inoculating, *or* vaccinating.

تلقين tèlkīn, *s. a.* An instructing or prompting *vivâ voce* (especially as done to the dead, when first buried, by an imam, on the subjects of their creed); ا—, —et, *v.a.* To explain or communicate *vivâ voce, or* generally.

تلكى tìlki, *s. t.* A fox.

تلميذ tèlmīz, *s. a.* A student, scholar, [pupil.

تلوث tèlèvvuss, *s. a.* A becoming soiled, polluted.

تلون tèlèvvun, *s. a.* Capriciousness or inconstancy of disposition, versatility of character.

تلوه tèlvé, *s. t.* Grounds, dregs, sedi-[ment.

تلويث tèlvīss, *s. a.* A soiling, polluting; ا—, —et, *v.a.* To soil, pollute.

تليين tèlyīn, *s. a.* A softening, emolliating; a loosening (the bowels); ا—, —et, *v.a.* To soften, emolliate; to loosen (the bowels).

تم tèmma, *3rd pers. sing. pret. a.* It was finished (the *Finis* of Eastern books).

تمارض tèmāruz, *s. a.* A feigning sickness; ا—, —et, *v.n.* To feign sickness.

تماس tèmāsss, *s. a.* A mutual contact; ا—, —et, *v.n.* To touch each other.

تماشا tèmāshā (tA—), *s. a.* A sight-seeing, surveying, viewing (any spectacle) on a promenade.

تمام tAmām, *s. a.* A being complete, completed, finished; a being correct, right, just, accurate; a state of completeness; the arriving at completion; the complement (of any trigonometrical quantity); —, *a. t.* Complete; finished; correct, accurate, right; —, *int. t.* That's right! I dare say! تماماً tAmāman, *ad. a.* Completely, entirely; تمامى tAmāmī, *a. a.* Relating to completeness; حساب تمامى وتفاضلى hìssābi-tAmāmī-vè-tèfāzulī, The integral and differential calculus.

تمايل tèmāyul, *s. a.* A leaning, an inclination.

تمتع tèmèttu", *s. a.* A deriving some pecuniary or equivalent profit or advantage from the possession of anything.

تمثال tìmsāl, *s. a.* A figure, comparison; a representation; a drawing or statue.

تمثيل tèmsīl, *s. a.* The comparing or likening (one thing to another); a comparison; an illustrating by comparison or by an example; ا—, —et, *v.a.* To liken; to illustrate by comparison or example.

تمجيد tèmjīd, *s. a.* An acknowledging as most glorious, a glorifying; a special prayer of praise sung at early dawn from the minarets; ا—, —et, *v.a.* To glorify, attribute glory to; —وقتى, —wàkt*i*, The time of earliest dawn.

تمدن tèmèddun, *s. a.* Settling in a town; ا—, —et, *v.n.* To settle (in a town).

تمديد tèmdīd, *s. a.* A making extensive or extended in space or time; ا—, —et, *v.a.* To extend.

تمر tèmr, *s. a.* A date (fruit); —هند, tèmri-hìnd (dèmir-hìnd), *or* —هندى, tèmri-hìndì, (The Indian date) A tamarind.

تمرد tèmèrrud, *s. a.* Obstinacy, stiff-neckedness; rebellion; wickedness.

تمزيق tèmzīk, *s. a.* A tearing, rending.

تمساح tìmsāh, *s. a.* A crocodile.

تمسك tèmèsssuk, *s. a.* A keeping fast hold, not quitting one's grasp; a document; a title-deed; a promissory note.

تمشيت tèmshìyyèt, *s. a.* A causing to move on, a giving motion; ا—, —et, *v.a.* To cause to make progress, to push forward (affairs).

تمغا (dàmgh*a*), *s. t.* A stamp; a mark made by a stamp; تمغالو dàmghal*i*, *a. t.* Stamped, bearing a stamp mark; —اورمق, dàmgh*a*-wùrm*a*k, *v.n.* To stamp, mark with a stamp.

تمكن tèmèkky*u*n, *s. a.* The becoming fixed or resident.

تمكين tèmkīn, *s. a.* A making fixed or resident; a being dignified in rank or demeanour.

تمل tèmel, *s. a.* A foundation; تمللو tèmèlli, *a. t.* Having a foundation; founded, grounded; permanent.

تمليك tèmlik, *s. a.* A causing (anything) to belong (to some one); ا—, —et, *v.a.* To cause to belong (to some one).

تمنا (*for* تمنى) tèmènnà, *s. a.* A begging, praying for, entreating for (some favour); a salutation of thanks or respect, consisting in carrying the inner portion of the fingers, joined together, to the lips, kissing them, and then carrying them to the top of the forehead or head; ا—, —et, *v.n.* To salute in this fashion; تمنىا tèmènni-et, *v.a.* To beg, pray, or entreat for (some favour).

تموج tèmèvvuj, *s. a.* A rising in waves.

تموز tèmmuz, *s. a.* The Syro-Roman month of July.

تمهيد tèmhīd, *s. a.* A making the foundations broad and solid; ا—, —et, *v.a.* To establish on broad and solid foundations.

تمهير tèmhīr, *s. a.* A sealing; ا—, —et, [*v.a.* To seal.

تميز tèmiz, *a. t.* Clean; pure; honourable, respectable, estimable, loveable; good; desirable; considerable; ا—, —et, تمیزلمك tèmizlémek, *v.a.* To clean; to clean up; تمیزلك tèmizlik, *s. t.* Cleanness; purity; cleanliness; —, tèmèyyuz, *s. a.* A becoming distinguished; distinction.

تمییز tèmyīz, *s. a.* A distinguishing; ا—, —et, *v.a.* To distinguish, see or point out a distinction, make a distinction.

تن tèn, *s. p.* The body.

تن صویی Tèn-sūyu, *s. t.* The river Don.

تناسب tènāssub, *s. a.* The being in mutual proportion; gracefulness of proportion.

تناسخ tènāssukh, *s. a.* The transformation of bodies, or transmigration of souls, metempsychosis.

تناسل tènāssul, *s. a.* A generating one another, or being generated one from another; الت— āléti—, The organ of generation.

تناقض tènākuz, *s. a.* A mutually contradicting and destroying the validity of each other.

تناوب tènāvub, *s. a.* A doing things by turns, alternating.

تناول tènāvul, *s. a.* A taking, partaking, eating; ا—, —et, *v.a.* To eat.

تنباكو *or* تنبكی tùnbéki, *s. t.* Persian tobacco, used for smoking through water.

تنبل tènbel, *a. t.* Lazy, slothful.

تنبه tènèbbuh, *s. a.* The being aroused to attention and carefulness.

تنبیه tènbīh, *s. a.* The calling to attention; a giving orders; issuing injunctions or proclamations; a public notice, injunction, or proclamation; a *nota bene* in a book; ا—, —et, *v.a.* To recommend or give orders to (a person) to do or leave undone something.

تنته tènta, *s. t.* (*Italian*), An awning.

تنجره tènjéré, *s. t.* A saucepan.

تنجیس tènjīss, *s. a.* A making foul, impure, or unclean; ا—, —et, *v.a.* To make unclean.

تند tùnd, *a. p.* Swift, impetuous, violent.

تنزل tènèzzul, *s. a.* A condescending; condescension; ا—, —et, *v.n.* To condescend.

تنزه tènèzzuh, *s. a.* A being exempt, free from; —, tènèzzéhé! He (God) is free and exempt (from any defect)!

تنزیل tènzīl, *s. a.* A reducing in height, degree, or quantity; a subtracting; the Kur'an; ا—, —et, *v.a.* To reduce in height, degree, or quantity; to subtract.

تنسخ tènsùkh, *s. t.* Amulets or stamped cakes of odoriferous paste, used for making bracelets, brooches, &c.

تنسم tènèsssum, *s. a.* A gentle blowing or breathing of wind.

تنسیب tènsīb, *s. a.* A deeming fit and proper, approving; ا—, —et, *v.a.* To deem fit and proper, to approve.

تنسیق tènsīk, *s. a.* A ranging in regular order; ا—, —et, *v.a.* To range in order; تنسیقات عسکریه tènsīkāti-

-ʻAsskèrìyyé, The new regulations for the army as to time of service, recruiting, pensions, pay, promotion, &c.

تنصيف tAnsīf, *s. a.* A dividing into two equal portions; ا—, —et, *v.a.* To divide equally into two; to bisect.

تنظيف tànzīf, *s. a.* A cleaning, cleansing; ا—, —et, *v.a.* To clean, cleanse.

تنظيم tànzīm, *s. a.* A putting in order; ا—, —et, *v.a.* To put in order; تنظيمات tànzīmAt, *s. pl. a.* The new regulations in financial, civil, criminal, and political affairs.

تنفر tènèffur, *s. a.* Aversion, avoiding [from dislike.

تنفس tènèffuss, *s. a.* A breathing, respiration; a taking breathing time, reposing a short while for refreshment; ا—, —et, *v.n.* To breathe; to repose a little after labour.

تنفيذ tènfīz, *s. a.* The causing (anything) to penetrate (into another); a giving effect (to commands), causing them to have weight and be respected; ا—, —et, *v.a.* To give effect, execute, or cause to be executed (orders).

تنفير tènfīr, *s. a.* The causing of fright or dislike, and so driving away.

تنقيح tènkih, *s. a.* A revising and trimming up literary compositions, removing any obnoxious forms or expressions.

تنقيه tènkìyyé, *s. a.* A cleaning, cleansing; ا—, —et, *v.a.* To clean, cleanse.

تنك tènk *or* tèngh, *a. p.* Narrow, pinched or cooped up.

تنكار tènékyār, *s. t.* Borax (?).

تنكرى tànghri, *s. t.* God.

تنكناى tènknāy, *s. p.* A narrow, close place; تنكناى دنيا tènknāyi-dùnyà, The world, this nether vale.

تنكه tènéké, *s. t.* Tin in sheets; any vessel of tin; صارى— sAri—, Sheet-brass.

تنكيل tènkīl, *s. a.* A punishing, chastising, putting down.

تنميق tènmīk, *s. a.* A writing down, inditing; ا—, —et, *v.a.* To write, pen, indite.

تنميه tènmìyyé, *s. a.* A causing to grow, to flourish.

تنور tènnūr (tAndir), *s. a.* An oven, or hole dug in the ground and used as an oven; an Eastern arrangement of a pan of charcoal placed under a small table and covered with a large carpet or quilt which hangs to the ground and confines the warmth, so that, when sitting round this table, the legs and feet are kept warm.

تنوير tènvīr, *s. a.* A making bright, luminous, light; ا—, —et, *v.a.* To illuminate, light up.

تنوين tènvin, *s. a.* The addition of a letter *n* at the end of the word in pronouncing Arabic nouns, which is denoted by doubling any one of the three vowel-points; thus كتابٌ is read kìtAbun, كتابٍ kìtAbin, and كتاباً kìtāban, the third case generally requiring the addition of an ا as well as the double vowel-point. The first form is never used in Turkish; the second is seldom used, and then generally in the case of an indefinite noun feminine ending in ت or ة, and preceded by a preposition, when, to denote this peculiar pronunciation, the ت or ة is converted into ةٍ, as in على خفية ‟àla - khùfyétin. The third form is very frequently used in Turkish, and by it a noun or adjective of Arabic origin becomes converted into a Turkish adverb. In the case of nouns feminine ending in ت or ة, these letters become changed into ةً, the distinction between this form and the second being, that here the noun is not preceded by a preposition. Ex. امانةً èmānétEN, On trust.

تنها tènh*a*, *a. p.* Solitary; alone; —, *s. p.* Solitude.

توابع tèwābi‟, *s. pl. a.* (*of* تابعه tābi‟*a*), Dependent things or persons.

تواتر tèwātur, *s. a.* Public rumour, notoriety; ا—, —et, *v.a.* To publish abroad by mentioning to one person after another.

توارث tèvāruss, *s. a.* A succeeding to possession by inheritance.

توارد tèwārud, *s. a.* An arriving; a successive arriving; ا—, —et, *v.a.* To arrive.

تواريخ tèwārīkh, *s. pl. a.* (*of* تاريخ tārīkh), Histories, chronicles; dates; chronograms.

تواضع tèwāzu‟, *s. a.* Humility.

توافق tèwAfuk, *s. a.* A coinciding with, an agreeing with.

توالى tèwāli, *s. a.* A succeeding, following one another; على التوالى ‟àlé-'t--tèwāli, *ad. a.* Successively, in succession.

توأم tèv'àm, *s. a.* A twin; بصرت توأم nùssret - tèv'àm, *a. p.* Which is the twin-brother of victory, *i.e.* victorious.

توان tèwān, *s. p.* Power, strength, might.

توانا tèwānā, *a. p.* Strong, powerful; توانايى tèwānāyī, *s. p.* Strength.

توانكر tùwānghèr, *s. p.* A rich man.

توبره tòbr*a* (tòrb*a*), *s. t.* A bag.

توبه tèvbÉ (tùbÉ), *s. a.* A renunciation (of any particular sin), vow of renunciation so as never to do it again; ا—, —et, *v.n.* To renounce sin, to vow renunciation; توبه اولسون tùbÉ--òlsun, توبه‌لر اولسون tùbÉlEr - òlsun! May it be a vow! I repent me of it! I am sorry for it, and will never do it again; توبه‌لو tùbÉli, *a. t.* Who has made a vow of renunciation.

توبيخ tèvbīkh, *s. a.* A finding fault with, reproaching, blaming; ا—, —et, *v.a.* To blame, reproach.

توت tùt, *s. a.* A mulberry, white mulberry; قره توت kAr*a*-tùt, *s. t.* A black mulberry.

توتسى tùtsu, *s. t.* A fumigation; —, —ويرمك vèrmek, *v.n.* توتسيلمك tùtsulÉmek, *v.a.* To fumigate.

توتمك tùtmek (*aor.* توتر tùter), To smoke, to give out smoke.

توتن *or* توتون tùtun, *s. t.* Tobacco; smoke.

توتيا tùtya, *s. a.* A fabulous mineral, a kind of philosopher's stone, but said also to be good for the eyes; —, *s. t.* Zinc, zinc ore.

توثيق tèvsīk, *s. a.* Confirming, ratifying; ا—, —et, *v.a.* To confirm, ratify.

توج tùj (tùnj), *s. t.* Bronze, gun-metal.

توجه tèvèjjuh, *s. a.* A turning the face, attention, or favour towards any object; ا—, —et, *v.n.* To turn the face, prepare to advance towards; توجهات tèvèjjuhāt, *s. pl. a.* Favours, indications of favour.

توجيه tèvjīh, *s. a.* A turning (anything) towards (any object), a pointing, directing; a conferring (any office); ا—, —et, *v.a.* To turn (anything) in a certain direction, point, direct; to give, confer (an office or dignity); توجيهات tèvjīhāt, *s. pl. a.* New appointments to office or dignity by the sovereign, and mentioned in the gazette.

توحيد tèvhīd, *s. a.* A declaration of a belief in the unity of God.

توده tūdé, *s. p.* A heap, hill.

توديع tèvdī'', *s. a.* A consigning (anything) to the care or custody (of some one), a depositing for safe keeping; ا—, —et, *v.a.* To consign, deposit.

تورات tèvrāt, *s. a.* The Pentateuch of [Moses.

توربه tòrba, *s. t.* A bag.

توربی tùrpu, *s. t.* A rasp; تورپيلمك tùrpulémek, *v.a.* To rasp.

تورهمك tùrémek (*aor.* تورر tùrer), *v.n.* To breed and increase and multiply in a prolific manner; تورتمك tùretmek, *v.a.* To cause to breed greatly. [herit.

توريث tèvrīss, *s. a.* A causing to in-

توز tòz, *s. t.* Powder; dust; —, *a. t.* Dusty; توزأتمق tòzatmak (*aor.* توزأدر tòzadir), *v.n.* To make a dust, raise a dust; توزلق tòzluk, *s. t.* Gaiters.

توزيع tèvzī'', *s. a.* A distributing; distribution; ا—, —et, *v.a.* To distribute.

توسط tèwassut, *s. a.* A being, going, or coming between; intervention; mediation; ا—, —et, *v.n.* To go or come between; to intervene; to mediate.

توسل tèvèsssul, *s. a.* A drawing nigh (unto God). [charger.

توسن tèvsèn, *s. a.* A steed, horse,

توسيخ tèvsīkh, *s. a.* A making filthy.

توسيع tèvsī'', *s. a.* A making wide or wider, a widening, making spacious; ا—, —et, *v.a.* To enlarge, widen, make spacious.

توشه tūshé, *s. p.* Provisions.

توشيح tèvshīh, *s. a.* An ornamenting with a band of any kind, or with lines of writing.

توصيه tavsiyyé, *s. a.* A recommendation; a letter of recommendation; a recommending; ا—, —et, *v.a.* To recommend (a person).

توصيف tavsīf, *s. a.* A describing, mentioning the qualities; mentioning the good qualities, praising; ا—, —et, *s. a.* To describe; to praise.

توصيل **tȧvsīl**, *s. a.* A causing (one thing) to reach or join (to another).

توطن **tèwȧttun**, *s. a.* The settling one's self in a place, and making it one's home and country; ا—, —et, *v.n.* To settle (in a country).

توغ **tùgh**, *s. t.* The special kind of banner or insignia (*tail*) of a pasha in the old system, as the fasces were of the lictors in Rome, or the spurs of a knight with us. There were one, two, or three of these (*tails*) given to pashas according to rank, the greater number to the higher functionary.

توغل **tèvàghghul**, *s. a.* The busying one's self seriously (with anything) as a study or occupation.

توفير **tèvfīr**, *s. a.* A making numerous; ا—, —et, *v.a.* To increase numerously.

توفيق **tèvfīk**, *s. a.* The making (one thing) accord (with another); God's favour by which He makes success attend upon endeavours, or endeavours and wishes accord with His prescient resolves; ا—, —et, *v.a.* To make (one thing) agree (with another); الله توفيق ويرسوں **Allāh-tèvfīk-vèrsin!** May God grant you (*or* him) success!

توق **tòk**, *a. t.* Full, satiated (the stomach); قارنم توق **kàrnim-tòk**, My belly is full, I am not hungry; كوزى توق **ghyùzu-tòk**, His eye is satiated, he is not covetous, he is as rich as he wishes to be.

توقع **tèvàkkuʿ**, *s. a.* Hoping, expecting.

توقف **tèwȧkkuf**, *s. a.* A stopping, staying, halting, tarrying, lingering; a waiting for, being dependent on; ا—, —et, *v.n.* To stop, rest, stay; to wait for, or be dependent on.

توقير **tèvkīr**, *s. a.* An honouring, treating with respect; ا—, —et, *v.a.* To treat with great respect and consideration.

توقيع **tèvkīʿ**, *s. a.* The cypher of the Sultan, called also طغرا **tùghra** (q. v.) and نشان **nishān**; the imperial letters-patent or rescript (called also فرمان **fèrmān**) bearing this cypher; توقيعى **tèvkīʿī**, *s. a.* An officer of state, called also نشانجى **nishānji** in old times, and طغراكش **tùghra-kèsh** at present, in whose office this cypher is apposed to muniments.

توقيف **tèvkīf**, *s. a.* An arresting, stopping, detention, causing to stop or stand still; ا—, —et, *v.a.* To arrest, stop, hold, keep, detain.

توكرك **tùkruk**, *s. t.* Spittle.

توكرمك **tùkyurmek** (*aor.* توكرر **tùkyurur**), *v.a.* and *n.* To spit.

توكل **tèvèkkyul**, *s. a.* A depending upon and trusting in God for the working of His divine will in all our affairs; ا—, —et, *v.a.* To trust entirely (in God); توكللو (**tèvékelli**), *ad. t.* (*with a negative verb*) Without good reason.

توكيل **tèvkīl**, *s. a.* The appointing (some one) as one's agent; ا—, —et, *v.a.* To appoint agent.

تولد tèvèllud, *s. a.* A being born; —ا, —et, *v.n.* To be born.

تولیت tèvlìyyèt, *s. a.* The appointing (some one) to certain offices.

تومار tòmār, *s. p.* A roll, scroll (of paper).

تومان tūmān, *s. p.* A body of ten thousand men, a legion; تومان پاچه tūmaɴ-pàcha, *a. t.* (Trousers) having the legs very wide, and not fastened at the bottom in any way; —, *ad. t.* (To be dressed) in loose, wide trousers or drawers, *en négligé.*

تومباز tòmbàz, *s. t.* A pontoon.

تونس Tùnùs, *s. t.* Tunis.

توهم tèvèhhum, *s. a.* A doubting, surmising, or fearing.

توی tùy, *s. t.* A feather; a downy soft hair; down; —قلم, —kàlɛm, A hair pencil; قوش تویی kùsh-tùyu, A bird's feather; feathers; دوه تویی dèvé-tuyu, Camel's down; the colour of camel's down (resembling that of grated nutmeg); تویلو tùylu, *a. t.* Feathered; downy; hairy.

تهدید tèhdīd, *s. a.* A menacing, threatening, frightening; —ا, —et, *v.a.* To menace by words, threaten, try to frighten; to frighten.

تهران Tèhrān, *s. t.* Teheran.

تهذیب tèhzīb, *s. a.* A correcting, amending, beautifying; —ا, —et, *v.a.* To correct, amend, polish, beautify; —اخلاق, tèhzīb*i*-àkhlāk, A correcting the defects of one's character or disposition.

تهلکه tèhliké, *s. a.* Danger, peril; تهلکه یه صوقمق tèhlikéyé - sòkmak, To put in danger; تهلکه لو tèhlikéli, *a. t.* Dangerous.

تهلیل tèhlīl, *s. a.* The utterance of the formula لااله الاالله lā-ìlāh*a*-illā-'llāh, *There is no god but God.*

تهمت tùhmet, *s. a.* A fault, a blameable action; تهمتلو tùhmetli, *a. t.* Culpable.

تهنیت tèhnìyyèt, تهنیه tèhnìyyé, *s. a.* A congratulating; congratulations; —ا, —et, *v.a.* عرض تهنیه ا "àrz*i*-tèhniyé-et, *v.n.* To congratulate, offer congratulations.

تهور tèhèvvur, *s. a.* Impetuosity, inconsiderate violence.

تهی tèhi, *a. p.* Empty; vain, futile;

تهی دست tèhi-dèsst, *a. p.* Empty-handed.

تهیه tèhìyyé, *s. a.* A preparing, making ready, disposing; —ا, —et, *v.a.* To prepare, dispose, make ready.

تهییج tèhyīj, *s. a.* A causing (dust) to get in motion and blow about.

تیر tīr, *s. p.* An arrow, a bolt; تیرکش tīr-kèsh, *s. p.* A quiver for arrows.

تیره tīré, *a. p.* Dark, gloomy; —, *s. t.* Sewing cotton thread.

تیز tīz (tèz), *a. p.* Quick, swift; hasty; —, *ad. t.* Quickly, quick.

تیزاب tīzāb (kèzzàb-sūyu), *s. p.* Aqua-fortis, nitric acid.

تیزه tèyzé, *s. t.* A maternal aunt, mother's own sister.

تیشه tīshé, *s. p.* An axe, a hatchet.

تيغ tīgh, *s. p.* A sword; a dagger; a sunbeam; a pointed summit; the long prow of a kayik.

تيقظ tèyàkkuz, *s. a.* A being awake and vigilant.

تيقن tèyàkkun, *s. a.* A knowing for certain, the acquiring a knowledge (of any fact) entirely void of doubt or uncertainty.

تيمار tīmār, *s. p.* The care and culture bestowed on any object, a tending (a sick person, a horse, a garden); a military fief in the now obsolete feudal system of Turkey, the value of which was under 20,000 (or 3,000?) Akcha in the Doomsday Book of the empire, and the holder of which was held to go to the wars on horseback, equipped at his own expense on certain special contingencies arising; —خانه, tīmār-khānè, *s. p.* A madhouse.

تيمم tèyèmmum, *s. a.* The ceremonial act of ablution with the dry hands, when water cannot be had, merely touching some object with the open palm instead of taking up water.

تيمن tèyèmmun, *s. a.* A being the receptacle of good fortune and happiness; تيمناً tèyèmmunan, *ad. a.* Happily, fortunately.

تيمور tīmūr (dèmir) *s. t.* Iron; any iron instrument; an anchor; —اتمق, dèmir-àtmak, *v.n.* To cast anchor; تيمورباش (dèmir)-bàsh, (Iron-head), The stock-in-trade of cattle, seed, and implements belonging to a farm, and let with it; an old servant or pensioner. (This is the term which was applied to Charles XII. of Sweden, and meaning "*an established pensioner*," but translated by his biographers, "iron-headed" or "obstinate.")

تيون tèyyūn, *s. t.* A squirrel.

تيها tèyhā! *int. t.* Lo yonder!

تيهو tīhū, *s. p.* A smallish grey partridge (?).

ث

ث sè or sā'i-mùssèllèss. (The three-pointed sā.) Fifth letter of the Turkish alphabet, having the sharp value of s or ss in English. In Arabic it is properly of the sharp value of our *th* in *thin* (the θ of the Greek), but is generally pronounced as a *t* by the nations who speak Arabic. This has, however, no influence in Turkish. Its numeral value in chronograms, &c., is 500.

ثا sā, *s. a.* Name of the letter ث.

ثابت sābit, *a. a.* Fixed, firm, immovable; proved, proven, demonstrated, incontrovertible; ثابته sābitè, *s. a.* (*pl.* ثوابت sèwābit), A fixed star.

ثار (*for* ثأر sè'r) sār, *s. a.* Revenge, vengeance; اخذ— àkhzi-sār, The taking vengeance, using reprisals.

ثاقب sākib, *a. a.* Penetrating.

ثالث sāliss, *a. a.* The third; ثالثه

sālissé, *s. a.* A third, $\frac{1}{60}$ of a second; ثالثا sālissā, *ad. a.* Thirdly.

ثامن sāmin, *a. a.* The eighth; ثامنا sāminā, *ad. a.* Eighthly.

ثانى sāni, *a. a.* The second; ثانيه sāniyyé, *s. a.* A second, $\frac{1}{60}$ of a minute; ثانيا sāniyyā, *ad. a.* Secondly.

ثبات sèbāt, *s. a.* Firmness, steadiness, immovableness.

ثبت sèbt, *s. a.* A fixing; a writing down; ا—, —et, *v.a.* To fix; to write down.

ثبوت sùbūt, *s. a.* A being incontrovertible, certainty in point of fact; ثبوتى sùbūtī, *a. a.* Affirmative, positive; صفات ثبوتيه sifāti-sùbūtiyyé, The positive attributes (of God, as power, knowledge, will, &c.).

ثروت sèrvèt, *s. a.* Opulence, wealth.

ثريا sùrèyyā, *s. a.* The Pleiades.

ثغور sùghūr, *s. pl. a.* (*of* ثغر sàghr), Frontier towns, passes, and places by which an enemy may penetrate into the country.

ثقات sìkāt, *s. pl. a.* (*of* ثقة *not used*), The faithful friends and companions (of Muhammed).

ثقب sàkb, *s. a.* A piercing, boring through or into; a hole pierced or bored; ا—, —et, *v.a.* To pierce, to bore.

ثقلين sàkalèyn, *s. dual a. oblique case.* The two material worlds, or the two grosser races of intelligent and responsible creatures, mankind and genii, to both of whom Muhammed's mission was addressed, and from whence he is styled رسول الثقلين rèssūlu-'ss-sàkalèyn, The apostle of the two gross or material races.

ثقلت sìklet, *s. a.* Weight, heaviness; heaviness, oppression; gravity; —ذاتيه, sìkléti-zātiyyé, Specific gravity; —ويرمك, —vèrmek, *v.n.* To oppress one's spirits, worry, annoy.

ثقيل sàkīl, *a. a.* Heavy, weighty, ponderous; oppressive, unpleasant; ugly, disagreeable, unbecoming, unseemly.

ثلاثا sèlāssā, *s. a.* Tuesday, the third day of the week.

ثلاثى sùlāssī, *s. a.* The triliteral root of any congeries of co-derivative Arabic words.

ثلث sùlss, *s. a.* A third, a third part; ثلثان sùlsān, *s. dual a.* Two-thirds.

ثلثه sèlāssé, *a. a.* Three; ثلثون sèlāssūn, *and* ثلثين sèlāssīn, *a. a.* Thirty.

ثلثى sùlussī (sùluss), *a. a.* A kind of Arabic handwriting, corresponding to our *large text.*

ثلج sèlj, *s. a.* Snow.

ثم sùmma, *c. a.* And then, and afterwards.

ثمان sèmān, *and* ثمانيه sèmāniyyé, *a. a.* Eight; ثمانون sèmānūn, *and* ثمانين sèmānīn, *a. a.* Eighty.

ثمره sèmeré, *s. a.* Fruit; result, consequence.

ثمن sèmen, *s. a.* Price, value; —, sùmn, *s. a.* An eighth, eighth part.

ثمين sèmīn, *a. a.* Of price, valuable.

ثنا sènā, *s. a.* Praise; a praising; ا—, —et, *v.a.* To praise, speak well of.

ثواب sèwāb, *s. a.* A meritorious action in the sight of God; a reward or degree of merit attached to actions by God.

ثوب sèvb, *s. a.* A garment.

ثور sèvr, *s. a.* The sign Taurus.

ثيب sèyyib, *s. a.* (*fem.* ثيبه sèyyibé) *m.* and *f.* One who is no longer a virgin.

ج

ج jìm. Sixth letter of the Turkish alphabet, having the value of *j* in English, though sometimes acquiring the sound of *ch* in *church*. It has the numeral value of 3 in astronomical tables, and in chronograms; and in the dates of letters it is the sign of the month جمادى الآخر Jèmāzìyyu-'l-ākh*i*r.

جا jā. In dates of letters this is an abbreviation of the name of the month جمادى الاول Jèmāzìyyu-'l-èvvel; —, *s. p.* Place, spot, station; جابجا jā-bè-jā, *ad. p.* Here and there.

جابلوسى jābilūssī, *s. p.* Flattery, adulation.

جابى jābi, *s. a.* The collector of rents to property in mortmain.

جادو jādū, *and* جاذو jāzū (jādi), *s. p.* A witch; a charmer; an old woman; a vampire (dead person supposed to rise from its grave by night and feed on the blood of living people); witchery.

جاده jāddé, *s. a.* A highway, public road.

جاذب jāzib, *a. a.* Attractive, attracting;

جاذبه jāzibé, *s. a.* Attractive power, attraction.

جار jār, *s. a.* A neighbour; —, jārr, *a. a.* Which draws, pulls; (a noun, particle, or preposition) which causes its dependent noun to be read with its last consonant followed by the vowel *i* or syllable *in*; —, *s. a.* A preposition, particle, or preceding noun in construction with a noun; —, *s. p.* A single whole shawl; a square shawl.

جاروب jārūb, *s. p.* A broom, besom; —زن, —zèn, *s. p.* A sweeper.

جارى jārī, *a. a.* Flowing, running (water, &c.); current (time, custom, &c.).

جاريه jārìyyé, *s. a.* A female slave, a white female slave.

جاسوس jāssūss (shàshid), *s. a.* A spy.

جالب jālib, *a. a.* Which attracts, draws from a distance.

جالس jāliss, *s. a.* A seated person, one who is sitting.

جام jām (jàm), *s. p.* Glass; a drinking glass; a mirror; a telescope.

جامع jāmi', *a. a.* Which collects, assembles; which assembles and contains within itself; comprehensive, containing much; (a mosque) which has ceremoniously been consecrated, and may no more be converted to secular purposes; —, *s. a.* A public mosque; a collector or compiler of writings.

جامكان jāmékyān, *s. p.* The outer hall of a bath used for dressing and undressing.

جاموس jāmūss (jàmish), *s. a.* A buffalo.

جامه jāmé, *s. p.* Clothing, apparel; —شوى, jāmé-shūy, *s. p.* A washer of linen; linen itself, wash-linen; the washing of linen.

جان jān, *s. p.* The soul; the life; a soul, individual; جانم jānim! My soul! My life! My dear! My good fellow! My dear sir! &c.; جانم صيقلدى jānim-sìkìldi, My soul is oppressed; my feelings were hurt; I was sorry (for what occurred); I was tired and disgusted; جانسز jānsiz, *a. t.* Lifeless, inanimate; wanting in animation; جان اتمق jān-ātmak, *v.n.* To give one's life (for a thing), throw it away; —چكشمك, —chèkishmek, *v.n.* To be in the agonies of death; —ويرمك, —vèrmek, *v.n.* To give life, animate; از دل و جان èz-dil-u-jān, *ad. p.* also جان وكوكلدن jān-u-ghyùnguldan, *ad. t.* With all (my, &c.) heart and soul; جان صيقلمق jān-sìkìlmak, *v.n.* To be weary at heart, to be vexed or sorry at heart (*with a pronoun affixed to* جان).

جانان jānān, *s. p.* The beloved object, a mistress.

جانب jānib, *s. a.* A side; a direction; لين الجانب lèyyinu-'l-jānib, *a. a.* Kind, compassionate.

جانباز jānbāz (jàmbàz), *s. p.* (One who risks his life) A breaker of horses; a horse-dealer; a rope-dancer.

جانفس jānfèss (jànfèss), *s. t.* Plain silk stuff, gros de Naples.

جانلنمق jānlanmak (*aor.* جانلنور jānlanir), *v.n.* To come to life; to become lively.

جانوار jānvār (jànavàr), *s. p.* An animal; a disagreeable or noxious animal; a pig, hog, swine.

جاود jāvid, جاويد jāvīd, جاودان jāvidān, جاويدان jāvīdān, جاودانه jāvidāné, جاويدانه jāvīdāné, جاودانى jāvidānī, *a. p.* Eternal.

جاه jāh, *s. p.* Rank, dignity.

جاهل jāhil, *a. a.* Ignorant; inexperienced in life; جاهليت jāhiliyyèt, *s. a.* The state of ignorance, the pre-Muhammedan pagan state of Arabia.

جاى jāy, *s. p.* A special spot, station.

جائز jā'iz, *a. a.* Licit, allowed, not improper, permissible; possible, probable, feasible.

جايگاه jāy-ghyāh, *s. p.* A special place.

جايگير jāy-ghīr, *a. p.* Which occurs, takes place.

جبا jàba, *a. t.* Gratis, for nothing.

جبار jèbbār, *s. a.* A tyrant, oppressor; an excessively proud man; God, the curber of the proud and of oppressors.

جبال jibāl, *s. pl. a.* (*of* جبل jèbel), Mountains.

جبانت jèbānèt, *s. a.* Cowardice, want of courage.

جبایت jìbāyet, *s. a.* The office and functions of collector of rents to property in mortmain.

جبخانه jèb-khānÉ, *s. t.* A powder-magazine; gunpowder in store.

جبر jèbr, *s. a.* A constraining; force, constraint; a binding up (of broken or sprained bones); algebra; ا—, —et, *v.a.* To constrain, force; to bind up (broken bones); جبر و مقابله jèbr-u-mŏkābélÉ, Algebra; جبراً jèbr*an*, *ad. a.* By force, not willingly.

جبروت jèbérūt, *s. a.* God's quality of being the irresistible Ruler and Constrainer.

جبره jìbrÉ, *s. t.* The lees of any fruit, &c., from which the juice has been drawn off.

جبل jèbel, *s. a.* A mountain.

جبل الشیخ Jèbel-u-shèykh, Mount Hermon; جبل موسی Jèbel-i-Mūssà, Mount Sinai.

جبلت jìbìllèt, *s. a.* Nature, character, disposition; جبلتسز jìbìllètsiz, *a. t.* Ungenerous, disagreeable in character.

جبلقوم jèbèll*a*kūm, *s. t.* The amethyst (?).

جبلی jèbéli, *a. a.* Pertaining to mountains; —, jìbìllī, *a. a.* Natural, inherent in one's nature.

جبن jùbn, *s. a.* Cowardice, want of courage.

جبندانلق jìbind*a*nl*i*k *and* جبنلك jìbinlik, *s. t.* A mosquito net.

جبه jèbÉ, *s. p.* Arms, armour; —, jùbbÈ, *s. a.* A kind of light cloak; جبه‌لو jèbÈli, *s. t.* A kind of irregular horse patrol; جبه‌جی jèbÉji, *s. t.* A kind of soldier in the old system, who had charge of the spare arms, ammunition, tents, &c.; جبه‌خانه jèbÉ-khānÉ, An arsenal, armoury, store of warlike muniments; (also جبخانه jèb-khānÉ), a powder-magazine; gunpowder in store.

جبهه jèbhÉ, *s. a.* The forehead.

جبین jèbīn, *s. a.* The forehead; —سای, jèbīn-sāy, *a. p.* Who rubs his forehead (on the ground, &c., out of respect).

جثه jùsssÉ, *s. a.* The body; the size of body; جثه‌لو jùssÉli, *a. t.* Large-bodied.

جحیم jàhīm, *s. a.* Hell.

جد jèdd (*fem.* جده jèddÉ), *s. a.* A grandfather; a forefather, ancestor; —اعلی, jèddì-à''là, The most remote ancestor, origin of a family; ابا عن جدن èbā-''àn-jèddin, *ad. a.* (Through the father from the ancestors) from father to son; —, jìdd, *s. a.* A strenuous persevering effort, a real endeavour; جدی jìddī, *a. a.* Real, serious, not in fun or in mockery.

جدا jùdā, *a. p.* Separate, separated, divided, asunder.

جدار jìdār, *s. a.* A wall.

جدال jìdāl, *s. a.* A disputing, contesting; a fighting, quarrelling; battle.

جدری jùdérī, *s. a.* The small-pox; جدری بقری jùdérī'i-bÀkarī, The cow-pox.

جدول jèdvel, *s. a.* A canal; a mathematical or statistical table; —تختهسى, —tàkhtassi, *s. t.* A flat ruler.

جدى jèdi, *s. a.* The sign Capricorn; —, jùdèy, *s. a.* (diminutive), The pole-star.

جديد jèdīd, *a. a.* New.

جذب jèzb, *s. a.* An attracting; ا—, —et, *v.a.* To attract.

جذر jèzr, *a.* A root; an arithmetical root of a number; —مربع, jèzri-mùrèbbà'', A square root; —مكعب, jèzri-mùkyà'' ''àb, A cube root; دردنجى جذر dùrdinji-jèzr, A fourth root, &c., &c.; جذرتام jèzri-tāmm, A perfect root; —اصم, jèzri-āssàmm, A surd root.

جر jèrr, *s. a.* A drawing, pulling, training; a causing the last consonant of Arabic words to be pronounced with the vowel *i* or the syllable *in* after it; —اثقال, jèrri-èsskāl, The art or science of mechanics or of the power of moving heavy bodies.

جراح jèrrāh, *s. a.* A dresser of wounds; a surgeon. [pus, matter.

جراحت jèrāhàt, *s. a.* A wound; a sore;

جرار jèrrār, *a. a.* Who ravishes, carries off booty, slaves, &c.; bold, valorous; impudent, importunate; —, *s. a.* A brave warrior, adventurous soldier; an impudent beggar.

جربزه jèrbézé, *s. a.* Ready wit and facility of argument, the gift of the gab.

جرح jèrh, *s. a.* A wounding; a controverting; —, jùrh, *s. a.* A wounding; a wound; ا—, jèrh-et, *v.a.* To wound; to controvert; — —, jùrh-et, *v.a.* To wound; جرحه jùrh*a*, *s. a.* A wound.

جرع jèr'', *s. a.* A drinking; ا—, —et, *v.a.* To drink; جرعه jùr''*a*, *s. a.* A draught.

جرم jìrm, *s. a.* A body, solid body; size (of a body); —, jùrm, *s. a.* A fault, culpability; لاجرم la-jèrem, *ad. a.* Without fail, in any case.

جرمانيا Jèrmāni*a*, *s. t.* Germany.

جروف jùrūf, *s. t.* The scoriæ of metals.

جرى jèrī, *a. a.* Brave, bold, adventurous.

جريان jèrēyān, *s. a.* A flowing; a being current; a happening, taking place; ا—, —et, *v.n.* To flow; to be current; to happen, take place. [hardihood.

جرئت jùr'et, *s. a.* Boldness, courage,

جريد jèrīd, *s. a.* A stick used as a dart in a peculiar kind of military exercise or game on horseback.

جريده jèrīdé, *s. a.* A register, roll, ledger. [misdemeanour.

جريمه jèrīmé, *s. a.* A fine paid for any

جزء jùz', *s. a.* A part, portion; a small book of a few pages; a portion of twenty pages in a large written book, or of a sheet in a printed book;

جزئى jùz'ī, *a. a.* Partial; small, insignificant; ارادهٔ جزئيه ìrādé'i-jùz'-ìyyé, The partial free-will of man (which is but a portion of the ارادهٔ كليه ìrādé'i-kyùllìyyé, the universal will of God); ذكرجزءوارادهٔ كل zìkri-jùz'-vé-ìrādé'i-kyùll, The mention of a part instead of the whole, as *a sail* when we mean *a ship*.

جزا jèzā, *s. a.* Retribution; punishment; روز جزا rūzi-jèza, The day of judgment; اللهجزاسنی ویرسون Allāh-jèzāssini-vèrsin! May God give him retribution!

جزائر jèzā'ir, *s. pl. a.* (*of* جزیره jèzīré), Islands; Algiers in Barbary; —بحرسفید, jèzā'iri-bàhri-sèfīd, The islands of the Grecian Archipelago; —سبعه, jèzā'iri-sèb''à, The seven Ionian islands.

جزدان jùzdān (jùzdànlik), *s. p.* A portfolio; a pocket-book; a kind of book or thin cushion held in the hand under a sheet of paper when writing, so as to keep it flat and unbending.

جزر jèzr, *s. a.* The ebb-tide, low water.

جزع jèz'', *s. a.* A crying, lamenting.

جزم jèzm, *s. a.* A deciding in one's mind that a thing must be so and so, a deducing very positively (though still liable to mistake); the orthographical sign—ْ, which, placed over a consonant, shows that a syllable ends with that consonant, or that it is not followed by a vowel in the syllable; ا—, —et, *v.a.* To decide, deduce very positively.

جزو jùzv *or* جزوْ jùz' (*for* جزْ jùz', *which see*); جزوی jùzvī, *for* جزئی (*see* جزْ jùz'). [without a cover.

جزوه jèzvé, *s. t.* A small coffee-pot

جزئی jùz'ī, *a. a.* Partial; trifling, insignificant; جزئیات jùz'ìyyāt, *s. pl. a.* Partial things; special sciences; trifles, insignificant things.

جزیه jìzyé, *s. a.* The special tax or tribute paid by non-Muslim subjects to a Muslim state for safety and protection. It is also called خراج khàrāj.

جزیره jèzīré, *s. a.* An island; جزیرةالعرب jèzīrétu-'l-''àrab, The Arabian peninsula.

جزیل jèzīl, *a. a.* Copious, abundant.

جسارت jèssāret, *s. a.* Valour, courage, boldness, hardihood; ا—, —et, *v.n.* To dare, to have the courage.

جسامت jèssāmèt, *s. a.* Great size of body; importance (of affairs) in respect of the vastness of the interests they affect. [fitting, meet.

جسبان jùssbān, *a. p.* Worthy, suitable,

جستوجو jùsst-u-jū, *s. p.* A seeking, looking for; ا—, —et, *v.a.* To seek.

جسد jèssed, *s. a.* The body (of man or animals).

جسر jìssr, *s. a.* A bridge; a viaduct; a causeway through a morass, or along the low banks of a river.

جسم jìssm, *s. a.* A body; a solid body; a mathematical solid figure. [terial.

جسمانی jìssmānī, *a. a.* Corporeal; ma-

جسور jèssūr, *a. a.* Brave, bold, valorous, courageous. [important.

جسیم jèssīm, *a. a.* Large, great, vast;

جغرافیا jàghrāfiya, *s. t.* Geography.

جفا jèfā, *s. a.* Ill-treatment, ill-usage; جفاكار jèfā-kyār, A cruel person.

جكر jìghᴇr, *s. p.* The pluck; the liver; the lungs; —اق Ak-jìghᴇr, The lungs, lights; —قره kAra-jìghᴇr, The liver; جكرجى jìghᴇrji, A seller of plucks; a cat's-meat man; جكرم jìghèrim! (My liver!) My darling! جكركوشهم jìghᴇr-kyùshém! (Corner of liver!) My ducky darling!

جل jèlla, *int. a.* May He (*or* His name) be magnified! — jùll, *s. a.* The totality, or principal portion (of anything); a horse-cloth.

جلا jìlā, *s. a.* A polishing, burnishing; polish; —, jèlā, *s. a.* Exile; ا—, —et, jìlā-et, *v.a.* —ويرمك, jìlā-vèrmek, *v.n.* To polish, burnish.

جلاب jèllāb, *s. a.* A factor who imports cattle or slaves from distant places.

جلاد jèllād, *s. a.* An executioner, headsman, hangman.

جلادت jèlādèt, *s. a.* Bravery, intrepidity.

جلال jèlāl, *s. a.* Greatness, grandeur; a great passion; ذو الجلال zū-'l-jèlāl, God of greatness; جلاللنمق jèlāllanmak, *v.n.* To get into a great passion.

جلالت jèlālèt, *s. a.* Human greatness.

جلب jèlb, *s. a.* A sending for and causing to come from a distance; importing; ا—, —et, *v.a.* To send for and cause to come or to be brought; to draw (anything) towards one's self; — (*for* جلاب jèllāb), jèleb, *s. a.* A drover of cattle or slaves, one who brings them from their native place to the place of sale.

جلد jìld, *s. a.* The hide of an animal; a volume; the binding of a book.

جلدلمك jìldlémek, *v.a.* To bind (a book); جلدلتمك jìldlᴇtmek, *v.a. causal,* To cause (a book) to be bound, to give (it) to be bound.

جلسه jìlsé, *s. a.* A sitting, one interval of sitting.

جلق jèlk, *a. t.* Rotten (egg).

جلوس jùlūss, *s. a.* The accession of a sovereign to the throne; ا—, —et, *v.n.* To ascend the throne, become sovereign.

جلوه jìlvé, *s. a.* The airs, manners, coquetries, blandishments of beauties; the natural graces and beauties of various objects.

جلى jèlī, *a. a.* Conspicuous, patent; a kind of handwriting, something similar to that used in firmans called ديوانى dīwAnī.

جليس jèlīss, *s. a.* A social companion, one who sits much with another.

جليل jèlīl, *a. a.* Great, grand.

جم jèmm, *s. a.* A multitude; جم غفير jèmmi-ghāfīr, A great multitude.

جمادات jèmādāt, *s. pl. a.* (*of* جماد jèmād), Inanimate objects, the mineral world.

جمازى jèmāzī, *s. a.* Name of two consecutive lunar months in the Muhammedan year; one, called جمازى الاول jèmāziyyu-'l-èvvᴇl (The first Jemazi), is the fifth, and in the dates of letters is represented by the abbreviation حا (*for* جا); the other, named جماذى الآخر jèmāzìyyu-'l-ākh*i*r (the latter Jemazi), is the sixth, and is represented in dates by ح (*for* ج).

جماع jìmā'', *s. a.* Copulation, sexual intercourse; ا—, —et, *v.n.* To copulate, have sexual intercourse.

جماعت jèmā''at, *s. a.* A congregation.

جمال jèmāl, *s. a.* Severe beauty.

جماهير jèmāhīr, *s. pl. a.* (*of* جمهور jùmhūr), Republics, commonwealths.

جمره jèmrᴇ́, *s. a.* A live coal; an astronomical or meteorological term used to signify the infusion of vital heat into the elements in spring, or rather at the end of winter. According to the theory there are three jèmrᴇ́; one, the infusion of heat into the air, occurs thirty days before the vernal equinox; the second, affecting the waters, seven days later; and the third, vivifying the earth, sixteen days before the equinox. They are said to fall into or upon their elements, as بوكون جمرەهوايەدوشدى bù-ghyun-jèmrᴇ́-hàwāy*a*-dùshdu, To-day the *vital heat* has fallen on the air.

جمرى jìmri, *s. t.* A miserable, avaricious [fellow.

جمشيد Jèmshīd, *s. p.* Name of a Persian king.

جمع jèm'', *s. a.* A collecting together, aggregating; a collection, assembly, congregation; an adding up, adding together; addition in arithmetic; an adding something more; the plural number; ا—, —et, *v.a.* To collect, bring together; to add up, add together; to add something more; —او, —òl, *v.n.* To collect together, come together; —اولنمق, —òlunm*a*k, *v. p.* To be collected, brought together; —صحيح, jèm''*i*-sàhīh, The regular form of plural; —مكسر, jèm''*i*--mùkèssser, An irregular form of plural in Arabic nouns; —الجمع, jèm''u-'l-jèm'', A plural of a plural (frequently used in Arabic words).

جمعه jùm''à, *s. a.* Friday, the Day of Congregation; —ايرتەسى, —èrtéssi, Saturday, the morrow of the Day of Congregation.

جمعيت jèm''ìyyèt, *s. a.* An assembly, a party; a state of tranquillity or collectedness (of mind).

جمله jùmlé, *s. a.* The whole, totality; a whole, a totality; all; a sentence, phrase, paragraph, proposition; a category, class; بالجمله bì-'l-jùmlᴇ́, *a. a.* All, every one; فى الجمله fì-'l-jùmlᴇ́, *ad. a.* In a summary manner, concisely; بو جملەدن bù-jùmlᴇ́d*a*n, Of this class, in this category; جملة jùmlét*ᴇ*n, *ad. a.* Totally, all, altogether; جملەسى jùmléssi, All of it; all of them.

جمهور jùmhūr, *s. a.* A republic; the commonwealth; anarchy; جمهوريت jùmhūrìyyèt, *s. a.* A republican form of government; anarchy.

جميع jèmīʻʻ, *s. a.* All, every one; جميعاً jèmīʻʻan, *ad. a.* All together.

جميل jèmīl, *a. a.* Beautiful, handsome.

جن jìnn, *s. a.* The Genii, a race of material intelligent beings, whose bodies are similar to the essence of fire or smoke; جنى jìnnī (ìjinni), One of the Genii; جن طائفه‌سى jìnn-tāʻifési, The race of Genii; ايچنده جنلر طوپ اوينار ìchinda-jìnnlær-tòp-òynar, (The Genii play at bowls in it) It is quite empty and deserted (a house, &c.).

جناب jènāb, *s. a.* Presence, dignity; a sense of pride and honour; a title of respect of universal signification, from Godhead, Majesty, Highness, Grace, Excellency, &c., down to simple Worship, Honour, and Respectability. In the case of God, and of all exalted personages of the Muslim hierarchy, this title precedes the word indicative of office; whereas, in cases of non-Muslim personages the title follows that word, or the mere name of the person (man or woman), and takes the pronominal affix of the third person, singular or plural according to the degree of respect shown: there was, therefore, a combination of disrespect in the application of this title; or better, it should be considered as a compromise between national or sectarian pride and the natural kindly feelings entertained for friends; جناب حق jènābi-hākk, His Divine Majesty the Essence of Truth; جناب رسالتپناهى jènābi-rèssālet-pènāhī, His Holiness the Refuge of the Apostolic office (Muhammed); جناب شهريارى jènābi-shèhriyārī, His Majesty the Sultan; جناب وكالتپناهى jènābi-vèkyālet-pènāhī, His Excellency the Refuge of the Lieutenancy (the grand vizier); انكلتره قراليچه‌سى جنابلرى ìnghiltèra-kìrālìchassi-jènāblari, Her Majesty the Queen of England; ايلچى بك جنابلرى èlchi-bègh-jènāblari, His Excellency the Lord Ambassador; ارمنى پطريقى جنابلرى èrméni-pàtriki-jènāblari, His Reverence the Armenian Patriarch; &c. &c. The Armenian practice of addressing people by this title followed by the pronominal affix of the second person is not used by the Turks, either among themselves or with people of other nationalities. (See حضرت hàzret) عاليجناب ʻʻālī-jènāb, *a. p.* Magnanimous, high-principled, proud in honour.

جنابت jènābèt! *int. t.* You beast! you polluted fellow!

جناح jènāh, *s. a.* A wing; a wing of an army; جناحين jènāhèyn, *s. dual a.* The two wings.

جنازه jènāzé, *s. a.* A dead human body; [a funeral.

جناس jìnāss, *s. a.* A double-entendre, play upon words.

جنايت jìnāyet, *s. a.* A trespass, offence; a trespassing; ا—, —et, *v.n.* To trespass (against).

جنب jènb, *s. a.* The side; ذات الجنب zātu-'l-jènb (sʌtlijʌn), The pleurisy.

جنبان jùnbān, *a. p.* Which moves, [plays.

جنبز jìnbiz, جنبستره jìnbìsstra, *s. t.* Tweezers.

جنبش jùnbush, *s. a.* Motion, play; fun, amusement, play.

جنت jènnèt, *s. a.* Heaven, paradise; جنتمكان jènnʌt-mèkyān, *a. p.* Whose place is in paradise, the late (Sultan); —, jìnnet, *s. a.* Madness.

جنحه jùnha, *s. a.* An offence, crime; —صاحبى, jùnha-sāhibi, A criminal, offender.

جند jùnd, *s. a.* A troop, body of troops.

جندره jèndéʀ, *s. p.* A press for pressing.

جندى jìndi, *s. t.* A perfect military [horseman.

جنس jìnss, *s. a.* A genus, kind, sort; —, *a. t.* Of race, of blood.

جنك jènk, *s. p.* Battle; war; ا—, —et, *v.n.* To do battle, fight; جنكجى jènkji, *s. t.* A warrior, one skilful in war.

جنوب jènūb, *s. a.* The south; جنوبى [jènūbī, *a. a.* South, southern.

جنود jùnūd, *s. pl. a.* (*of* جند jùnd), Bodies of troops.

جنون jùnūn, *s. a.* Madness.

جنويز Jènvìz, *s. t.* Genoa.

جو jèv, *s. p.* Barley; —, jū, *a. p.* (*in composition*), Who seeks, looks for; —, jèvv, *s. a.* The vacant space (of air); جو سما jèvvi-sèmā, The vacant space of air towards the sky.

جواب jèwāb, *s. a.* An answer; ا—, —et, *v.a.* To say in answer; — ويرمك jèwāb-vèrmek, *v.n.* To give an answer.

جوار jìwār, *s. a.* The vicinity, neighbourhood.

جوارح jèwārih, *s. pl. a.* (*of* جارحه jāriha), Those members of the body with which necessities are supplied.

جوارى jèwāri, *s. pl. a.* (*of* جاريه jārìyyé), Female slaves.

جواز jèwāz, *s. a.* Permission given; —ويرمك, —vèrmek, —كوسترمك, —ghyùsstʌrmek, *v.n.* To give permission, to allow.

جوان jùwān, *s. p.* A young man, a youth; —بخت, —bàkht, *a. p.* Whose fortune or star is on the ascendant, like a young man's progress.

جوانمرد jùwānmèrd (jùmèrd), *a. p.* Generous, liberal.

جواهر jèwāhir, *s. pl. a.* (*of* جوهر jèvhèr), Jewels, precious stones; atoms; جواهرجى jèwāhirji, *s. t.* A dealer in precious stones, a jeweller.

جوجه jùjé, *s. t.* A dwarf.

جود jūd, *s. a.* Goodness, kindness, beneficence.

جودت jèvdèt, *s. a.* Goodness, excel- [lence.

جور jèvr, *s. a.* Unkind and unjust treatment, tyranny; ا—, —et, *v.n.* To treat tyrannically, unkindly, and unjustly.

جوز jèvz (jèviz), *s. a.* A walnut; walnut-tree-wood; —بوا, jèvzi-bèvwà, *and*

هندستان جوزى hìndisstān - jèvizi, A nutmeg; هندستان جوزى قبوغى hìndisstān - jèvizi - kʌbʊghʊ (cuticle of nutmeg), Mace.

جوزا jèvzā, *s. a.* The sign Gemini.

جوش jūsh, *s. p.* A boiling; a rushing; a violent motion; جوش وخروش ا jūsh-ʊ-khʊrūsh-et, *v.n.* To rush; to be in violent commotion.

جوشان jūshān, *a. p.* Which boils, boiling; which rushes; which is in violent motion.

جوشش jūshish, *s. p.* A boiling up; a rushing; a violent motion.

جوشقون jòshkʊn, *a. t.* Full, high, overflowing (water of streams).

جوع jū‘, *s. a.* Hunger.

جوف jèvf, *s. a.* A hollow, hollow place, [cavity.

جولان jèvélān, *s. a.* Motion; agitation; circulation; ا—, —et, *v.n.* To be in motion, to circulate.

جومرد jùmèrd (*for* جوانمرد jùwānmèrd), *a. p.* Generous, liberal.

جوى jūy, *s. p.* A stream, canal.

جويبا jūybār, *s. p.* A great river; a place abounding in springs or running streams.

جوهر jèvhʊr, *s. a.* A precious stone, a jewel; the essence of any being; mineral ore, especially if in the form of sand; the lines and marks on Damascus blades; —فرد, jèvhéri-fèrd, An atom, a primitive particle of matter.

جه jé *or* ja, *pr. t.* or *inseparable particle.* When joined to a noun or pronoun substantive it signifies *manner* or *style,* as ادم ʌdʌm, Man; ادمجه ʌdʌmja, In a manly way, like a man; when joined to an adjective it forms a kind of diminutive, corresponding to our *rather* or *ish,* though this is still an expression of the primitive value of *manner* or *style,* as طاتلو tʌtli, Sweet; طاتلوجه tʌtlija, Sweetish; يواشجه سويله yāwʌshja-sùwèylé, Speak rather gently; when joined to an adjective of nationality it implies *language,* still without losing the idea of manner, *manner of speaking,* as ترك tùrk, A Turk; تركجه tùrkja, The Turkish language, *or* the Turkish manner. This particle is sometimes followed by the syllables لين léyin, but then the ه of جه is suppressed as redundant, and the whole particle becomes جلين jéléyin. This form is of the same value as the simple جه, or it adds to it the idea of affection or regard; it may be likened to the difference between Tom and Tommy.

جهاد jīhād, *s. a.* A zealous striving; a fighting the good fight, either against wicked inner lusts, or against outward enemies of the faith.

جهاز jīhāz (chèhiz), *s. a.* A bride's marriage portion of clothes, jewels, furniture, &c.

جهالت jàhālet, *s. a.* Ignorance, lack of knowledge or information.

جهان jìhān, *s. p.* The world, this world; a world; جهنبان jìhān-bān, جهاندار jìhān - dār, جهانپناه jìhān - pènāh, جهانکشا jìhān-kyùshā, جهانگیر jìhān--ghīr, A sovereign, the Sultan, keeper, possessor, asylum, conqueror, holder, of the world; جهانیان jìhānīyān, *s. pl. p.* The inhabitants of the world.

جهت jìhèt, *s. a.* A direction, side, quarter; respect, relation, head, cause.

جهد jèhd (jàhd), *s. a.* A strenuous endeavour; —ا, (jàhd)-et, *v.n.* To try very hard.

جهر jèhr, *s. a.* A speaking aloud, openly; جهراً jèhran, *ad. a.* Aloud.

جهری jèhri, *s. t.* Yellow berries.

جهل jèhl, *s. a.* Ignorance; —مرکب, jèhli-mùrèkkeb, Compound ignorance, which is not even aware of being ignorant.

جهنم jihànnam, *s. a.* Hell; —اول, jìhànnam-òl! Go and be d—d!

جی ji *or* j*i*, A Turkish particle, which, added to any noun, expresses the person who sells or makes the thing denoted by the noun, or who has some constant relation with that thing, as شکرجی shèkérji, A seller of sugar or sweetmeats; قایقجی kàyìkj*i*, A boatman; یلانجی yàlànj*i*, A liar.

جیب jèyb, *s. a.* The breast or bosom, or breast-pocket of a garment; the sine of an arc; (jèb) a pocket; —همایون, jèybi--hùmāyun, The Sultan's privy purse; تمام جیب tàmāmi-jèyb, A cosine; نسبت جیبیه nìssbèti - jèybìyyé, A log. sine; تمام نسبت جیبیه tàmāmi--nìssbèti-jèybìyyé, A log. cosine.

جاجی jìji, *s. t.* Any pretty little plaything; جیجیلومیجیلو jìjili-mìjili, *a. t.* Ornamented so as to please children.

جیران jèyrān (jèylàn), *s. t.* A gazelle; —, *s. pl. a.* (*of* جار jār), Neighbours.

جیش jèysh, *s. a.* An army.

جیفه jīfé, *s. a.* A carrion carcase.

جیم jīm, *s. a.* Name of the letter ج.

جیوش jùyūsh, *s. pl. a.* (*of* جیش jèysh), Armies.

جیوه jìwa, *s. t.* Quicksilver, mercury.

چ

چ chīm *or* jīmi-fārsī. Seventh letter of the Turkish alphabet, having the value of the English *ch* in *church*. Like ج it has the numeral value of 3 in chronograms, but is not used elsewhere as a numeral.

چابك chàbik, *a. p.* Quick; *ad. t.* Quickly; soon.

چاپ chàp, *s. t.* The bore or calibre of guns, or size of balls and bullets.

چاپقون *or* چاپقین chàpk*i*n, *a. t.* Which runs fast, a good runner; —, *s. t.* A blackguard; good-for-nothing, low fellow.

چاپمق chàpmak (*aor.* چاپار chàpar), [*v.n.* To run.

چاپوت chàpūt, *s. t.* A clout, cloth, rag.

چاپول chàpul, *s. t.* A predatory incursion.

چاپه chàpa, s. t. A hoe; چاپه‌لمق chàpalamak, v.a. To hoe.

چات‌پات chàt-pàt, ad. t. Now and then, but rarely.

چاتردامق chàtirdamak (aor. چاتردار chàtirdar), v.n. To chatter (the teeth); to creak, make a loud noise (as the timbers of a ship in a storm).

چاتردى chàtirdi, s. t. A noise of crushing, bumping, creaking.

چاتره پاتره chàtara-pàtara, ad. t. (To be able to say a few words of a language) in a broken manner. [Cracked, split.

چاتلاق chàtlak, s. t. A crack; —, a. t.

چاتلامق or چاتلمق chàtlamak (aor. چاتلار chàtlar), v.n. To crack, split, become cracked; to burst (with rage, &c.).

چاتمق chàtmak (aor. چاتار chàtar), v.n. To knock against, run against, run foul of; to meet with; to become thick or intimate with, make great friends with; to come (time); —, v.a. To baste (needle-work preparatory to sewing); قاش— kàsh—, v.n. To frown. [a house.

چاتى chàti, s. t. The skeleton roof of

چادر chàdir, s. t. A tent; —قورمق, —kùrmak, To pitch a tent.

چار chār, a. p. Four; —, s. p. Rescue, remedy; چاروناچار chār-u-nā-chār, ad. p. Whether there be a remedy or not; will ye, nill ye; —, s. t. The Czar of Russia; چارپا chārpā, s. p. A quadruped; چارپاره chār-pārè (chàlpara), s. p. The castanets (four pieces);

چارطاق chār-tàk, Any little arbour or building with posts or columns.

چارپلمق chārpilmak (aor. چارپلور chàrpilir), v.n. To become warped or crooked; —, v. p. To be struck.

چارپمق chàrpmak (aor. چارپار chàrpar), v.a. To strike (with any long thing, as the hand, the tail, &c.); to strike or dash (anything against another); to strike (with palsy or other affliction); to strike (anything, as lightning does).

چارداق chàrdak, s. t. A kind of terrace on a housetop, or in a garden, provided with trellis-work for drying linen, or for training vines, &c.

چارسو chārsū (چارشو or چارشى chàrshi), s. p. A street of shops; the (by Europeans so called) bazaars of towns in the Levant.

چارشب chār-shèb (چارشف chàrshaf), s. p. A sheet for a bed.

چارق chàrik, s. t. Sandals such as shepherds and peasants wear in the East, as also soldiers on a march.

چارميخ chàrmīkh (chàrmik), s. p. A full size cross for criminals; the shrouds of a mast. [avoiding.

چاره chārè, s. p. A remedy, a means of

چاريك chār-yèk (chèyrek), s. p. A quarter of an hour; a quarter, fourth part.

چاسار chāsār, s. t. Cæsar, emperor.

چاشنى chāshni (chèshni), s. p. The

taste, savour (of food); چاشنیگیر chāshnighīr, s. p. An officer whose duty it is to taste the food of his master.

چاغرمق chàghirmak (aor. چاغرر chàghirir), v.a. To call; to sing (a song); —, v.n. To call out; ترکی— tùrkyu—, v.n. To sing songs.

چاغلدامق chàghildamak (aor. چاغلدار chàghildar), چاغلامق chàghlamak (aor. چاغلار chàghlar), v.n. To make a murmuring, splashing, or rippling noise in running over rocks or stones (water); چاغلدی chàghildi, s. t. The noise of water running over a cascade; چاغلیان chàghlayan, s. t. A cascade which murmurs.

چاغنوس chàghanoss, s. t. A crab, sea crab.

چاقشر chākshir, s. t. A kind of wide trousers which tie round the ankle.

چاقل chàkil, s. t. A pebble, round smooth stone.

چاقمق chàkmak, s. t. A steel to strike fire with; the lock of a gun; —, v.a. (aor. چاقار chàkar), To strike (fire); —, v.n. To drink, to use intoxicating drinks; —طاشی, —tāshi, s. t. A flint, or agate to strike fire with, or for a gunlock; —شمشك shimshek—, v.n. To lighten, flash with lightning.

چاقی chàki, s. t. A pocket-knife, clasp-knife, pocket pen-knife.

چاك chāk, s. p. A rent; —, a. p. Rent, torn; —, chāng, s. t. A large bell.

چاکر chākèr, s. p. A servant; چاکریکز chākèringiz, I, your servant.

چالاك chālāk, a. p. Quick, agile, nimble.

چالشقان chālishkān, a. t. Industrious, assiduous.

چالشمق chālishmak (aor. چالشور chālishir), v.n. To work, be busy, occupy one's self.

چالغی chālghi, s. t. Any instrument of music; چالغیجی chālghiji, s. t. A musician.

چالق chālik, a. t. Cracked, half-witted, crazy.

چالقامق chālkamak (aor. چالقار chālkar), v.a. To shake violently; to shake up; to beat up (eggs, &c.); to rinse; چالقانمق chālkanmak (aor. چالقانور chālkanir), v.n. or p. To be violently shaken or agitated.

چالمق chālmak (aor. چالار chālar), v.a. To strike, beat, knock; to steal; to play (any musical instrument), sound, beat, strike, blow; to strike (the hours, a clock); —, v.n. To draw or approach (to any shade of colour).

چالی chāli, s. t. A briar, any prickly bush.

چام chàm, s. t. Deal or pine, or firwood; —اغاجی, —āghāji, A pine or fir tree; —ساقزی, —sàkizi, Resin, rosin.

چامور chàmur, s. t. Mud, mire; clay.

چانته or چانطه chānta, s. t. A knapsack.

چاوش chàwush, s. t. A serjeant in the army; a herald or serjeant at arms in olden times; —باشی, chàwush-bāshi, Formerly the Grand Usher and

Marshal of the Empire, now a kind of Chief Baron of the Court of Chancery.

چاه chāh, *s. p.* A well; a pit; —زنخدان, chāhi-zènakhdàn, The dimple of the chin.

چای chày, *s. t.* A river, rivulet, brook, stream, streamlet; tea (the herb, or an infusion); مسقو چایی mòsskov-chàyi, (Russian tea) Tea (the herb); اطه چایی ada-chàyi, Sage (the herb).

چایر chàyir, *s. t.* A field, meadow, pasture-land; چایر چایر chàyir-chàyir, *ad. t.* (To burn) vehemently with flame and a crackling noise; —پنیری, chàyir-pèniri, Cream cheese, new cheese; —قوشی, chàyir-kūshu, The lark.

چایلاق chàylak, *s. t.* The kite (bird).

چبالمق chàbalamak (*aor.* چبالار chàbalar), *v.n.* To strive, struggle, make efforts.

چبوق chìbùk, *s. t.* A stick, wand; a pipe for smoking; a bar (of metal); a stripe (in stuffs).

چپ chèp, *s. p.* The left-hand side; — (*in* چپ چوره chèp-chèvrè, All round, quite round), a Turkish particle of completeness.

چپاق chàpak, *s. t.* The gum of the [eyes.

چپراز chàpraz, *s. t.* The frogs or braidings across the breast of some military coats, with their loops and buttons.

چپکن chèpken, *s. t.* A kind of coat or jacket, like that worn by hussars.

چپلاق chìplak, *a. t.* Naked, bare.

چتال chàtal, *s. t.* A fork; the forking of a branch or road; —, *a. t.* Forked; —طرناقلو, chàtal-tìrnakli, *a. t.* Cloven-hoofed; چتاللانمق chàtallanmak, *v.n.* To fork, become forked; چتاللاشمق chàtallashmak, *v.n.* To become intricate or complicated (any question or business).

چتر chètr, *s. p.* A tent; a vail, a veil.

چتله chètélé, *s. t.* A tally-stick, tally-[score.

چتین chètin, *a. t.* Difficult.

چدیك or چدك chèdik, *s. t.* A kind of light boot.

چرا chìrā, *ad. p.* Why? بی چون و چرا bī-chūn-u-chìrā, *a. p.* (God) Who is without a why or a wherefore, unaccountable for what He wills; —, chèrā, *s. p.* Pasturage; —, chìra, *s. t.* The resinous part of pine-wood.

چراغ chìrāgh, *s. p.* A lamp, candle, flambeau; an apprentice, pupil; a client; a pensioner, protégé, one who owes his station to another (the idea of a *lamp* or *candle lighted and made visible*, being the prevailing figure in all these secondary meanings).

چرب chèrb, *a. p.* Fat and smooth, plump.

چرپمك chìrpmek (*aor.* چرپر chìrper), *v.a.* To mark (timber) with a tight cord and chalk or ruddle; to bleach (linen or wax).

چرپی chìrpi, *s. t.* The cord with which carpenters mark timber with straight lines; a straight line.

چرپیجی chìrpìji, *s. t.* A bleacher.

چرچوه chèrchivé, *s. t.* A frame; the sash of a window.

چرخ chàrkh (chàrk), *s. p.* A wheel (of any machinery); a turner's lathe; an engine, a machine; the sphere, the firmament, the universe; fate, fortune.

چرخه chàrkha, *s. t.* A wheeling about and skirmishing; *in* چرخه طوپی chàrkha-tòpu, A fieldpiece, light gun for campaigning; چرخه جی chàrkhaji, *s. t.* A skirmisher; چرخه جیلر غوغاسی chàrkhajilar-kàwghassi, A skirmish.

چرز chèrez, *s. t.* Condiments served on small saucers as relish.

چرك chìrk, *s. p.* Dirt, filth; چركاب chìrkyāb, *s. p.* Dirty water, water which has been used for washing; (chirghèf) a sink, a drain.

چركین chìrkin, *a. p.* Nasty; ugly; disagreeable or unsuitable (act).

چرنده chèrèndé, *a. p.* Which pastures, grazes; —, *s. p.* A grazing animal.

چریش chìrish, *s. t.* A peculiar kind of paste used in the East; the powder of which this is made; —اوتی, chìrish-òtu, The plant, from the dried roots of which the paste-powder is prepared by pounding.

چزمك chìzmek (*aor.* چیزر chìzer), *v.a.* To mark with lines; to draw, design; to efface by a mark with the pen; to scratch, make scratches.

چزمه chìzma, چزی chìzi. See چیزمه and چیزی.

چشم chèshm, *s. p.* The eye.

چشمه chèshma, *s. p.* A fountain; a spring, source.

چشید chèshid, *s. t.* A shade of colour.

چغرتمه chìghirtma, *s. t.* A small kind of fife or pipe.

چغرمق chìghirmak (*aor.* چغرر chìghirir), *v.a.* To call (anyone).

چفت chìft, *s. p.* A pair; a pair of oxen at the plough; an even number; چفتجی chìftji, *s. t.* A farmer; a ploughman; چفتلشمك chìftlishmek, *v.n.* To have sexual connexion (animals); چفت سورمك chìft-sùrmek, *v.n.* To drive the oxen at the plough, to follow the plough; چفتلك chìftlik, *s. t.* A farm.

چفته chìfté, *s. p.* A pair (of some special things; as, oars, gun-barrels, kicks with the hind legs of a horse); برچفته bìr-chìfté, A boat with only one pair of oars, called also پیاده pìyādé; ایکی چفته ìki-chìfté, A boat with two pairs of oars, &c. &c.; چفته تفنك chìfté-(tùfèk), A double-barrelled gun; چفته اتمق chìfté-atmak, *v.n.* To kick with both hind legs at once (a horse, &c.); چفته لو chìftéli, *a. t.* Sly, deceitful, not to be trusted.

چفوت chìfut, *s. t.* A Jew; a mean, sordid fellow.

چقارمق chìkàrmak (*aor.* چقارر chìkàrir), *v.a.* To take out, pull out, put out, push out; to take off, pull off, put off; to get out or off, cause to come or go out or off; to make out, decipher, read; to cause to go up, cause to ascend, make go up, cause to rise; to cause to go or come out, leave or abandon, to expel, to turn out; to extract; to invent or introduce to use; to have (any eruptive disease); —باشدن bàshdan —, *v.a.* To render disobedient and unruly, to pervert; —اقچه‌دن àkchadan—, *v.a.* To put to expense, cause to spend money; —چیچك chìchek—, *v.n.* To have the small-pox.

چقال chàkal, *s. t.* A jackall.

چقرق chìkrik, *s. t.* A spinning-wheel.

چقشمق chìkishmak (*aor.* چقشور chìkishir), *v.n.* To display one's skill, ability, or courage; to try to do so; to try to show off; to try to equal, strive, compete (with another).

چقلوس chàkaloss, *s. t.* A wall-piece, small swivel-gun.

چقمق chìkmak (*aor.* چقار chìkar), *v.n.* To go or come forth, out, off, up; to come out of joint, be dislocated; to arise, proceed, result; to come into season, or into use; to ascend, rise, mount; to emanate; to leave, set out, depart, start, set sail, sail; to prove, be found, be; to mount to, make, cost; to be visible; to be published (a book or paper), be out; to be paid (salary); —صاحب sàhib —, *v.n.* To declare one's self the owner (of anything found) or protector (of any person in trouble); —پهايه pàhàya—, *v.n.* To rise in price; —پاره‌دن pàradan —, *v.n.* To lose or be obliged to spend money; —باشدن bàshdan, *v.n.* To become rebellious or unruly; —, chàkmak, *s. t.* and *v.a.* and *n.* See چاقمق.

چقين chìkin, *s. t.* A small muslin packet of money corresponding to a rouleau.

چقور chùkur, *s. t.* A cavity, hollow place; —, *a. t.* Sunk and hollow.

چك chìgh, *a. t.* Raw, uncooked; —, *s. t.* Dew; —, chìng, *a. t.* Early (*in* چك صباح chìng-sàbàh, Early dawn); —, chùk, *s. p.* Penis (in speaking to a child).

چكترمه *or* چكدرمه chèktirma, *s. t.* A galley (in bye-gone days).

چكردك chèkirdek, *s. t.* A pip or stone in fruit; a weight among druggists.

چكغراق chìnggharak, *s. t.* A small bell, a hand or house bell.

چكركه chèkirghé, *s. t.* A grasshopper; a locust.

چكشمك chèkishmek (*aor.* چكشور chèkishir), *v.n.* To quarrel, pull one another about; —جان jàn—, *v.n.* To be in the throes of death.

چكلمك chèkilmek (*aor.* چكلور chèkilir), *v.n.* To retire; withdraw, draw one's self back; to shrink (cloth, &c.); to be low (water), to dry up, totally or partially disappear; —, *v. p.* To be drawn; to be borne, supported; to be supportable; — (*or* چكلده‌مك), chìnglémek (*aor.* چكلر chìngler), *v.n.* To ring (as metals do).

چكمجه chèkméjé, *s. t.* A portable writing-desk, a jewel or money-box; a bureau, escritoire, chest of drawers; a drawer (in a table, box, or cupboard); a drawbridge.

چكمك chèkmek (*aor.* چكر chèkER), *v.a.* To pull, draw, drag, haul; to attract; to draw (as a blister); to bring out (a horse or carriage for riding); to bear, support; to suffer, endure; to tolerate; —اذيت èzìyyèt—, *v.n.* To suffer pain or ill-treatment; —كورك kyùrek—, *v.n.* To row, pull at the oar; —ال èl—, *v.n.* To pull away the hand, have nothing more to do with; —عسكر "Asskèr—, *v.n.* To lead troops, lead an army (against a place); —آخوره Akhira—, *v.a.* To put into the stable; بنى چكه‌ميور bèni-chèkémiyor, He cannot bear me, he is envious of me.

چكنمك chèkinmek (*aor.* چكنور chèkinir), *v.n.* To be unwilling, loth; to scruple, have scruples; to hang back, be bashful; to be afraid to speak out.

چكه chèké, *in* چكه‌دوزن‌ويرمك chèké-dùzen-vèrmek, *v.n.* To put on fine clothes and ornaments, attire in full fig; —, chèngé, *s. t.* The chin; چكه‌يورمق chèngé-yòrmak, *v.n.* (To tire the chin) To talk very much; to cause to talk very much; چكه‌يارش‌ا chèngé-yārish-et, *v.n.* (To have a chin-race) To dispute tenaciously (with anyone).

چكى chèki, *s. t.* A horse-load, a weight of 180 okkas or about 500 lbs.

چكيج chèkij, *s. t.* A hammer.

چل chìl, *s. t.* A freckle; —, *a. t.* New and bright (money); —قوشى, chìl-kùshu, *s. t.* A bird good for eating, a francolin (?), grey partridge (?), wood-hen (?).

چلاب chAlAb, *s. t.* Jalap; (obsolete) God.

چلبور chìlbìr, *s. t.* Eggs with butter.

چلبى chèlébi, *s. t.* A Greek or European gentleman; (formerly) a prince of the blood; a gentleman; —, *a. t.* Gentlemanly, polite.

چلتك chèltik, *s. t.* A rice-field, rice-ground.

چلدرمق chìldirmak (*aor.* چلدرر chìldirir), *v.n.* To go mad.

چلك chèlik, *s. t.* Steel.

چلمك chèlmek (*aor.* چلر chèlER), *v.a.* To change (one's mind).

چلنك chèlenk, *s. t.* A kind of ornament worn on the head-dress.

چلنكر chìlinghir, *s. t.* A locksmith.

چله chìllé, *s. p.* A period of forty days devoted to ascetic practices, either as a noviciate or as an expiation; any period of suffering; suffering itself (chìlé) a bowstring.

چليك chìlèk, *s. t.* A strawberry; اغاج چليكى Aghaj-chìlèghi, A raspberry.

چماشير chàmAshir, *s. t.* Body-linen; wash-linen; a washing (of linen); —برقات bìr-kAt—, A suit of body-linen; —يقامق, —yìkamak, To wash linen ; ا—, —et, *v.n.* To have a wash (of clothes in the house) ; چماشیرجی chàmàshirji, A man who washes clothes.

چمچاق *or* چامچاق chàmchak, *s. t.* A wooden cup, bowl, or water-vessel.

چمدك chìmdik, *s. t.* A pinch with the thumb and finger ; چمدكلمك chìmdiklémek, *v.a.* To pinch with the thumb and finger. [tree ; dwarf box.

چمشیر chìmshir, *s. t.* Boxwood ; box-

چمن chìmèn, *s. p.* A green grass-field ; a grass-plot.

چمندر chìmendèr, *s. p.* An ass, donkey.

چنار chìnār, *s. t.* A plane tree, a sycamore.

چناق chànak, *s. t.* An earthen bowl, plate, or saucer ; —چوملك, —chùmlek, Pots and pans ; باش‌چناغی bàsh-chànaghi, The skull. [Dardanelles.

چناق قلعه‌سی Chànak - kàléssi, The

چناقلق chànaklìk, *s. t.* The top (scaffold aloft on board ship, round the foot of the topmast) ; باش‌چناقلغی bàsh (*or* پرووه prùwa)-chànaklighi, The fore-top ; غراندی‌چناقلغی ghràndi-chànaklighi, The main-top.

چنان chùnān, *ad. p.* As, even as.

چنتك chèntik, *a. t.* Notched ; —, *s. t.* A notch ; چنتمك chèntmek (*aor.* چنتر chènter), *v.a.* To notch.

چند chènd, *pron. p.* How many? several ; هرچند hèr-chènd, *c. p.* Although ; how many soever, how much soever.

چندان chèndān, *ad. p.* In a certain degree, to a certain point, so much, so many, as much, as many.

چنك chèngh, *s. p.* A harp ; چنكی chènghi, *s. p.* A public dancer.

چنكل chènghel, *s. p.* A hook, large iron hook. [manner.

چنین chùnīn, *ad. p.* So, thus, in this

چو chū, *ad. p.* Like, as.

چوال chùwal, *s. p.* A sack ; چوالدوز chùwāldūz (—diz), *s. p.* A large needle for sewing sacks.

چوب chòb, *s. p.* A stick, a wand ; wood, a piece of wood. [clownish fellow.

چوبان chòban, *s. t.* A shepherd ; a

چوپ chùp, *s. t.* A small splinter or fragment of wood ; the sweeping of houses ; چوپجی chùpju, *s. t.* A dustman ; چوپلك chùpluk, *s. t.* A heap or place where dust and rubbish is thrown. [bottle or flask.

چوتره chòtra, *s. t.* A wooden travelling

چوجق chòjuk, *s. t.* A child ; چوجقلق chòjukluk, *s. t.* Childhood ; childishness. [Sticks and stakes.

چور chòr, *in* چورچوپ chòr - chòp,

چوراب chòrab, *s. p.* A stocking, a sock.

چوراق chòrak, *a. t.* Saltish, brackish (water) ; desert because salt (land).

چوربا chòrba, *s. t.* Soup ; چورباجی chòrbaji, *s. t.* The master of a household, the master of a shop ; (formerly) the colonel of a regiment of Janissaries.

چورك chùrek, *s. t.* A kind of cake or bun ; —, chùruk, *a. t.* Rotten, decayed ;

proud (flesh); bruised (flesh); vain or stupid (reasoning).

چورومك *or* چوريمك chùrumek (*aor.* چورور chùrur), *v.n.* To rot, decay, putrefy, decompose.

چوره chèvré, *s. p.* The circuit, contour, circumference; a muslin handkerchief; —چپ chèp—, *or* —چپه chèpé, *ad. t.* All round.

چوريش chèvrish (*or* چرويش chèrvish), *s. t.* (*in* چوريش ياغى chèvrish-yàghi, A kind of fat or butter used in cooking).

چوزلمك chùzulmek (*aor.* چوزيلور chùzulur), *v.n.* To melt or break up (ice on ponds, rivers, &c.); —, *v.p.* To be or become untied. [*v.a.* To untie (a knot).

چوزمك chùzmek (*aor.* چوزر chùzer),

چوغالمق chòghalmak (*aor.* چوغالور chòghalir), *v.n.* To increase in number or quantity.

چوغان chòghan (chùghen), *s. t.* The plant saponaria or soap-wort.

جوق chòk, *a. t.* Much; many; great; long (time or while); —, *s. t.* The majority, greater part or number; —, *ad. t.* Very; چوقلق chòkluk, *s. t.* A great quantity, abundance; —, *ad. t.* Often (*used with a negative verb only*); —شى, —shey! How odd! That's very surprising! چوقدن chòkdan, A long while ago, for a long while.

چوقه (chòha), *s. t.* Broad-cloth; چوقه‌دار chòhadār, *s. p.* (Formerly) a kind of upper personal attendant, who walked by the side or before his master's horse in the street, and waited upon him at home or at his office. [used in playing at hockey.

چوكان chèvghyān, *s. p.* A crooked stick

چوكمك chùkmek (*aor.* چوكر chùker), *v.n.* To give way, settle down (a wall), to fall in (a well, &c.); —ديز dìz—, *v.n.* To kneel, bend the knee; —دبيه dìbé—, *v.n.* To be precipitated, settle, depose (lie, sediment). [naria or soap-wort.

چوكن chùghen, *s. t.* The plant sapo-

چول chùl, *s. t.* A desert, unproductive land; —, chūl, *s. t.* A horsecloth.

چولاق chòlak, *s. t.* A man who has lost an arm.

چوللق chùlluk, *s. t.* A woodcock.

چوماق chòmak, *s. t.* A club, mace, or beetle.

چوملك chùmlek, *s. t.* An earthenware pot, jar, or vase; —چناق chànak—, Pots and pans.

چوملمك chùmulmek (*aor.* چوملور chùmulur), *v.n.* To crouch down.

چون chūn, *ad. p.* As; when, as soon as; since; چونكه chùnku, *c. t.* Since, as, because; بيچون bī-chūn, *a. p.* Who is without a *why*, who is not to be asked His reasons for His acts (God).

چوى (*or* چيوى) chìvi, *s. t.* A nail; a wooden peg; a wooden wedge; چويلمك chìvilémek, *v.a.* To nail, fix with a nail or pegs.

چويد chìvid, *s. t.* Indigo, blue.

2 N 2

چویرمك chèvirmek (*aor.* چویرر chèvirir), *v.a.* To turn, turn round, turn over, turn back; to change into, turn into; to surround, hem in, inclose.

چه Ché, *or* چه ولایتی Ché-vilāyèti, Bohemia; —, chi, *pron.p.* What? چه فائده chi-fāʿidé, What is the use? unfortunately, as bad luck would have it; —, chī, *s. t.* Dew; —, chèh (*for* چاه chāh), *s. p.* A well.

چهار chàhār, *a. p.* Four; درت چهار dùrt-chàhār, All fours (at dice).

چهار شنبه chàhār-shènbih (chàrshanba), *s. p.* Wednesday.

چهره chèhré, *s. p.* The face, visage, countenance, physiognomy.

چیت chìt, *s. p.* Chintz, printed cotton; a fence of cut brushwood and brambles.

چیچك chìchek, *s. t.* A flower; a blossom, bloom; the small-pox; —چیقارمق, —chìkàrmak, To have the small-pox.

چیده chīdé, *a. p.* Gathered, gathered up, picked, picked up.

چیز chīz, *s. p.* A thing; ناچیز nā-chīz, Nothing; ناچیزانه nā-chīzāné, *a. p.* Of no account, insignificant, poor.

چیزمك chìzmek (*aor.* چیزر chìzer), *v.a.* To draw, mark with lines, &c. (See چزمك).

چیزمه chìzma, *s. t.* A boot.

چیزی chìzi, *s. t.* A line, a mark, a scratch.

چیش chìsh, *s. t.* The want of relief, and the relief itself of nature, either by stool or urine; —بیوك bìyuk—, The stool; —كچوك kùchuk—, Urine (or their passing); چیشم وار chìshim-vàr, *or* چیشم كلدی chìshim-ghèldi, I want to go to the water-closet; ا—, —et, *v.a.* To pass urine, *or* to go to stool.

چیغ chìgh, *s. t.* An avalanche.

چیقمق chìkmak. (See چقمق).

چیك chīgh, *a. t.* Raw, uncooked; underdone; —, *s. t.* Dew; —, chìng, *a. t.* Early; —صباح, —sàbāh, Early dawn.

چیل chìl. (See چل chìl).

چیم chìm, *s. t.* Turf, greensward; a grass-plot; name of the letter ج.

چین chìn, *a. p.* (*in composition*), Who gathers, picks up; —, *s. p.* A plait, fold, wrinkle; China; چین وماچین chīn-u-māchīn, The Chinese Empire.

چینمك chīnémek (*aor.* چینر chīner), *v.a.* To chew, masticate; to trample upon; ایاق التنده چینمك àyak-àltìnda-chīnémek, *v.a.* To trample under foot.

چینی chìni, *s. t.* China-ware; Dutch tiles.

چیوی chìvi, *s. t.* A nail; a wooden peg; a wooden wedge.

ح

ح hà. Eighth letter of the Turkish alphabet, having the value of an aspirated *h* in English, with this difference, that it is always aspirated, in whatever position it may occupy, whether at the beginning, in the middle, or at the end of words. Compared with ه, which is also an *h*, it is a hard consonant, and is consequently associated with hard vowels. In chronograms, and in astronomical tables, it has the numeral value of 8. In the dates of letters, the ج takes this form by the omission of its diacritical point, but is still read jìm, and stands for the month of Jèmāzìyyu-'l-ākhir, the sixth of the Muhammedan year.

حا hā, *s. a.* Name of the letter ح; in the dates of letters, this form is used, by the omission of the diacritical point, instead of جا, but is still read jā, and denotes the month of Jèmāzìyyu-'l-èvvel, the fifth of the Muhammedan year.

حاج hājj, *s. a.* One who has duly performed the pilgrimage to Mecca, with all its attendant ceremonies; the word is generally written with the Arabic definite article الحاج èl-hājj, but is commonly pronounced Hàji.

حاجب hājib, *s. a.* A door-keeper, usher, chamberlain; —العين, hājibu-'l-'àyn, The eyelid.

حاجت hājet, *s. a.* A want; want, need; اكاحاجت يوق ànga-hājet-yòk, There is no need of that; نه حاجت nè-hājet, What necessity is there?

حاجى hàji, *s. p.* One who has duly performed the pilgrimage to Mecca; a Jew or Christian who has religiously visited Jerusalem.

حاج hàch, *s. t.* A cross; a crucifix; حاجه كرمك hàcha-ghèrmek, *v.a.* To crucify, stretch on a cross.

حاد hādd (*fem.* حاده hāddè), *a. a.* Sharp, acute; زاويهٔ حاده zāvìyyè'i-hāddè, An acute angle; مثلث حاد الزوايا mùssèlléssi-hāddu-'z-zèwāyā, An acute-angled triangle.

حادث hādiss, *a. a.* Recently come into being, recently happened; not having eternally existed; حادثه hādissè, *s. a.* An event; an accident; حادث او hādiss-òl, *v.n.* To happen, come to pass; to take rise, originate, come into being.

حاده hāddè, *s. a.* A wire-drawer's guage; a rolling machine for making wire, bars, plates, &c., of metal; حاده خانه hāddè-khānè, A rolling-mill house.

حاذق hāzik, *a. a.* Sagacious and clever physician.

حار hārr (*fem.* حاره hārrè), *a. a.* Hot; منطقهٔ حاره màntikà'i-hārrè, The torrid zone.

حارطوج hàrtuj, *s. t.* A cartridge for a cannon; حارطوج پلاسقه‌سی hàrtuj-pàlasskassi, A cartridge-box (on board a ship).

حاسه hāssa (*pl.* حواس hàwāss), *s. a.* A sense, faculty of perceiving.

حاشا hāshā, *int. a.* God forbid!

حاشلمق hàshlamak (*aor.* حاشلار hàshlar), *v.a.* To boil, cook by boiling; to ice, cool with ice.

حاشيه hāshiyyé, *s. a.* A border, margin; a marginal note; a postscript.

حاصل hāssil, *a. a.* Produced, resulting; —, *s. a.* Produce, proceeds, result, fruit; ا—, —et, *v.a.* To produce; او—, —ŏl, *v.n.* To result, come, proceed; حاصلات hāssilāt, *s. pl. a.* The produce or fruit, or revenue of land, &c.; ضرب—, hāssili-zàrb, The product (in multiplication); الحاصل èl-hāssil, *ad. a.* or حاصل كلام hāssili-kèlām, *ad. p.* In short, in fine, to sum up all.

حاضر hāzir, *a. a.* Present in person; ready, prepared; ا—, —et, *and* حاضرلمق hāzirlamak, *v.a.* To make ready, get ready, prepare; او—, —ŏl, *v.n.* To be present in person; to be ready, to make one's self ready; اول—, —ŏl! *int. t.* Make ready! جواب—, hāzir-jèwāb, *a. p.* Quick at repartee, quick in replying; امر حاضر èmri-hāzir, The second person imperative of an affirmative verb active.

حافظ hāfiz, *s. a.* God the guardian; a guardian; one who knows the Kur'an by heart; كتب—, hāfizi-kyùtub, A librarian; حافظه hāfiza, *a. a.* (*fem. of* حافظ), Which guards, keeps; قوت حافظه kùvvéti-hāfiza, The retentive faculty of the mind, memory.

حاكم hākim, *s. a.* One who gives decrees, a judge, a ruler, a king; مطلق—, hākimi-mŭtlāk, God the absolute Ruler; حاكمانه hākimāné, *a. p.* Royal, princely, rulerlike, judgelike (act, word, or thing).

حال hāl, *s. a.* The present moment; the present tense (in grammar); a state, condition, case, position, situation; —, *a. a.* The present, current (month); حال بوكه hāl-bŭ-ki, *c. t.* Whereas, whereas at the same time, and all the while; درحال dèr-hāl, *ad. p.* In the same instant, instantly, immediately; بهرحال bè-hèr-hāl, بهمه حال bè-hèmé-hāl, *ad. p.* In any case, however things may be, without fail; عرضحال 'àrzi-hāl (àrzuhāl), A petition, a declaration of one's case; كندى حالنده kèndi-hālinda, *a. t.* Who is quiet and contented with his condition, and gives trouble to no one, inoffensive and quiet; لسان حال lìssāni-hāl, (The tongue of one's state) the language that may be supposed to be addressed to one's mind by the circumstances or condition of any other person or thing; حالا hālā, *ad. a.* At the present moment, still; حالاً hālan, *ad. a.* By, *or* as regards, the state or condition (in which a thing is); حالى hālī, *a. a.* Pertaining to a state; pertaining to the present time; حاليا hāliyā, *ad. a.* At present.

حالت hālet, *s. a.* One single time, state, or condition; الحالة هذه èl-hālétu-hāzihi, *ad. a.* Now, at this present time.

حالی hàlı, *s. t.* A large, thick carpet; —, hālī, *a. a.* Pertaining to a state; pertaining to the present time.

حامل hāmil, *s. a.* A bearer, carrier; حامله hāmilé (*fem.*), *a. a.* Big with child.

حامی hāmi, *s. a.* A protector, defender.

حاو hàw, *s. t.* The nap of cloth, the pile of velvet.

حاویار hàvyār, *s. t.* Caviar. [contains.

حاوی hāvi, *a. a.* Containing, which

حائز hā'iz, *a. a.* Possessing, who possesses, who has acquired.

حائط hā'it, *s. a.* A wall; any fence which encloses a space.

حائل hā'il, *s. a.* Anything which intercepts, obstructs, or hinders sight or communication between two objects or persons.

حب hàbb (hàp), *s. a.* A grain, a berry; a pill; —, hùbb, *s. a.* Love, affection; —الوطن, hùbbu-'l-wàtan, Love of one's country.

حباب hàbāb (*and* حبابه hàbābé), *s. a.* A bubble on water; —, hìbāb, *s. a.* Love, affection.

حبائل hàbā'il, *s. pl. a.* (*of* حباله, *not used*), Nets, snares, gins; —الشيطان, hàbā'ilu-'sh-shèytān, The snares of Satan; women.

حبس hàbss, *s. a.* An imprisoning, detaining, shutting up; imprisonment; (hàpiss) a prisoner, man in prison; —ا, —et, *v.a.* To imprison, incarcerate, lock up; to hold (the breath); to hoard (money); کوزحبسی ghyùz-hàpsi, The being a prisoner in charge, but without being locked up.

حبش Hàbsh, *s. t.* Abyssinia.

حبل hàbl, *s. a.* A rope, tendon, vein; حبل الورید hàbl-ul-wèrīd, The jugular vein.

حبوبات hùbūbàt (*pl. of* حبوب hùbūb, *the pl. of* حب hàbb), The various kinds of pulse.

حبور hùbūr, *s. a.* Joy, gladness.

حبه hàbbé, *s. a.* One grain, one berry; حبه‌یی قبه‌ا hàbbéyi-kùbbé-et, *v.n.* To make domes of berries, *i.e.* to make mountains of molehills; —حبة hùbbétan—, *ad. a.* For the love, for the sake; حبة‌لله hùbbétan-li-'llāh, For the love of God, for God's sake.

حبیب hàbīb, *s. a.* A dearly-beloved friend; —الله, hàbību-'llāh, The dearly-beloved of God, Muhammed.

حتف انفه hàtfa-ènfi-hī, *ad. a.* Of a natural death.

حتی hàttà, *c. a.* So much so that, to such a degree that; and, in proof of it, I may as well mention that . . . .

حج hàjj, *s. a.* The pilgrimage to Mecca, including all its formalities.

حجاب hìjāb, *s. a.* A vail, veil, curtain; modesty, shame; —ا, —et, *v.n.* To feel ashamed, be ashamed; to feel timid. [Pilgrims to Mecca.

حجاج hùjjāj, *s. pl. a.* (*of* حاج hājj),

حجامت hìjāmet (hÀjamÀt), *s. a.* The application of cupping-glasses or horns; ا—, —et, *v.n.* To apply cupping, to cup. [proof, a title-deed.

حجت hùjjet, *s. a.* A document, a

حجر hÀjar, *s. a.* A stone; stone.

حجره hùjrÉ, *s. a.* A small retired chamber, a cell; a niche in a wall.

حد hàdd (*pl.* حدود hùdùd), *s. a.* A limit, term, boundary; a point or degree (reached or defined); a definition; one's proper place, station, and behaviour; a legal punishment of eighty stripes; حاددن زياده hàdd*a*n-ziyādÉ, *ad. t.* More than the usual limit; حد ذاتنده hàddi-zātind*a*, *ad. t.* Originally, in reality; نه حدى nÈ-hÀddi! I should like to see him dare to do it! حدم يوق hàddim-yòk, I dare not, my station is not high enough for that; برينه حدينى بلدرمك bìrin*a*-hàddini-bìldirmek, To teach one, by punishment or admonition, to know how to behave according to his station, to teach one his place; حديمى بلورم hàddimi-bilirim, I know my place and the behaviour it requires.

حداثت hàdāssèt, *s. a.* Youth, youngness; —سن, hàdāssèti-sìnn, Youth in point of years.

حدت hìddèt, *s. a.* Impetuosity, violence; sharpness (of temper, &c.).

حدوث hùdūss, *s. a.* A coming into existence, happening; the being recent, not being from everlasting.

حدود hùdūd, *s. pl. a.* (*of* حد hàdd), Limits; boundaries, borders, frontiers; definitions; legal punishments by stripes.

حديث hàdīss, (*pl.* احاديث) *and* حديث شريف hàdīssi-shèrīf, A sacred tradition (of Muhammed), a saying, proverb, or sentence uttered by Muhammed, considered of secondary authority and holiness to the divine words of the Kur'an alone, and constituting the second basis of Muhammedan canon law; احاديث نبويه àhādīssi-nèbéviyyÉ, The sayings of the prophet. [violent, impetuous.

حديد hàdīd, *s. a.* Iron; —, *a. a.* Sharp;

حديقه hàdīk*a*, *s. a.* A garden.

حذا hìz*a*, *s. t.* The space opposite to anything. [cleverness in a physician.

حذاقت hìzākÀt, *s. a.* Sagacity and

حذر hàzɛr, *s. a.* Care, caution in avoiding or keeping free from any evil.

حذف hàzf, *s. a.* Elision; ا—, —et, *v.a.* To cut off or out (a letter from a word, or a word from a sentence).

حر hùrr, *s. a.* A freeman. [ture.

حراثت hìrāssèt, *s. a.* Tillage, agricul-

حرارت hàrārèt, *s. a.* Heat, warmth; fever; thirst.

حراست hìrāssèt, *s. a.* A guarding, taking care of; tillage, agriculture.

حرام hàrām, *a. a.* (Anything) the use or doing of which is specially forbidden by God, unlawful; حرامزاده hàrām-zādÉ, An illegitimate child; a rascal; حرامی hàrāmī, *s. a.* A thief; a robber.

حرب hàrb, *s. a.* War; battle; دار الحرب dāru-'l-hàrb, The whole world which is not subject to the Muslim power, the enemy's country; حربی hàrbī, *s. a.* An enemy, a person belonging to the enemy's country, an alien; — (*fem.* حربیه hàrbìyyé), *a. a.* Pertaining to war; مهمات حربیه mùhìmmāt*i*-hàrbìyyé, Muniments of war; حرباً hàrb*an*, *ad. a.* By war.

حربه hàrb*a*, *s. a.* A halberd, javelin.

حرص hìrss, *s. a.* Avidity; cupidity; —الشان, hìrssu-'sh-shān, Avidity for fame, ambition; حرص جاه hìrss*i*-jāh, Avidity for place, ambition.

حرف hàrf (*pl.* حروف hùrūf, *and* حروفات hùrūfāt), *s. a.* A letter of the alphabet; a grammatical particle, other than a noun or a verb; حرف بحرف hàrf-bé-hàrf, Literatim, letter by letter; حرف انداز hàrf-èndāz, *a. p.* Who reproaches, reviles; —, hìref, *s. pl. a.* (*of* حرفت hìrfet), Trades, arts.

حرفت hìrfet, *s. a.* A trade, an art; اهل— èhli-hìrfet, An artisan.

حرق hàrk, *s. a.* A burning with fire; —ا, —et, *v.a.* To consume by fire, to burn.

حرکت hàrékèt, *s. a.* Motion, movement; behaviour, conduct, action, act, proceeding; —ا, —et, *v.n.* To move, be in motion; to conduct one's self, behave, act, proceed; حرکته کلمک hàrékèté-ghèlmek, *v.a.* To get into motion, begin to move; —ارض, hàrékèti-àrz, An earthquake.

حرکه hàréké, *s. a.* The Arabic vowel-points, of which there are three simple and three complex. (See Grammar.)

حرم hàrem, *s. a.* A sacred place; the women's apartments in a house; the female part of a family; a wife or concubine; حرمین hàréméyn, *s. a. dual.* The two sacred territories of Mecca and Medina.

حرمان hìrmān, *s. a.* Disappointment of one's hopes, utter disappointment.

حرمت hùrmet, *s. a.* Respect, reverence; unlawfulness, prohibitedness; —ا, —et, *v.n.* To respect, to hold in reverence.

حروانی hàrwāni, *s. t.* A half, three-quarter, or full circle cloak.

حرون hàrūn, *a. a.* Restive, refractory (a horse). [manship.

حریت hùrrìyyèt, *s. a.* Freedom, free-

حریر hàrīr, *s. a.* Silk.

حریص hàrīss, *a. a.* Greedy, covetous.

حریف hàrīf (hèrif), *s. a.* A man, a fellow. [of houses, &c.

حریق hàrīk, *s. a.* A fire, conflagration

حزب hìzb, *s. a.* A body of men; a portion of the Kur'an, resulting from its division into 120 parts.

حزم hàzm, *s. a.* Wariness and circumspection in acting.

حزن hùzn, *s. a.* Sadness, melancholy.

حزيران hàzīrān, *s. a.* The Syro-Roman month of June. [acting.

حزيم hàzīm, *a. a.* Cautious, prudent in

حزين hàzīn, *a. a.* Sad, melancholy.

حس hìss (*pl.* أحساس àhsāss), A perceiving, being sensible of, feeling, seeing, hearing, smelling, tasting; a sense, power of perception; a perception, sensation; the instinct of animals; ا—, —et, *v.a.* To perceive, be sensible, feel, see, hear, smell, taste; to be sensible of intellectually, feel pretty sure; to know by instinct; حسى hīsssī, *a. a.* Pertaining to sense or instinct.

حساب hìssāb (hèssap), *s. a.* A calculating; calculation; arithmetic; an account, bill; ا—, —et, *v.a.* To calculate; to reckon, count, include in a calculation; —طوتمق, —tùtmak, *v.n.* To keep an account; —كورمك, —ghyùrmek, To reckon, go over accounts; to settle an account, pay an account; حسابلشمك hìssābléshmek, *v.n.* To settle accounts mutually; حسابسز hìssābsiz, *a. t.* Innumerable, uncounted, untold, of which no account is kept.

حسب hàssb, *s. a.* A portion, a share, a lot, what falls to one's share by calculation of heads; a requirement; a reason; —, hàsseb, *s. a.* Personal condition, rank, quality; a requirement; a reason; حسب ونسب hàsseb-u-nèsseb, (A person's) rank and family connexions; —, hàssba, *ad. a. and* برحسب bèr-hàssbi, *ad. p.* According to, in accordance with; حسب الاشارة hàssba-'l-ìshāré, According to the order given; برحسب فرمان bèr-hàssbi-fèrmān, According to the requirements of the command; خرسزى كورمامسى حسبيلة khìrsizi-ghyùrmamassi-hàssébīla, By reason of his not having seen the thief; حسبحال ا hàssbi-hāl-et, *v.n.* To tell one's tale, confide one's sorrows, recount one's difficulties.

حسد hàssed, *s. a.* An envying; envy; ا—, —et, *v.n.* To be envious.

حسرت hàssret, *s. a.* The feeling of regret for the absence of anything, with a desire for its return; —چكمك, hàssret-chèkmek, *v.n.* Sorrowfully to sigh for the return or presence of anything.

حسن hùssn, *s. a.* Beauty, fairness, agreeableness, loveliness, goodness; —, hàssan (*fem.* حسنة hàssana), *a. a.* Beautiful, lovely, good; —تعبير, hùssnu-tà''bīr, A beautiful expression; —ظن, hùssnu-zànn, A favourable opinion entertained (of anyone); —خط, hùssnu-khàtt, A beautiful handwriting; أخلاق حسنة àkhlāki-hàssana, Good moral qualities; —ويرمك, hùssà-vèrmek, *v.n.* To set off to advantage, cause to look well.

حسنا hàssnà, *s. a.* A beautiful woman; —(*for* حسنى) hùssnà, *a. a.* (*fem. of*

أحسن àhsĕn), More, most, or very beautiful; the best.

حسنة hàssana (pl. حسنات hàssanāt), s. a. A good action, charitable deed; صاحب الخيرات والحسنات sāhibu-'l--khàyrāt-vè-'l-hàssanāt, (The possessor or author of these good and charitable works) The charitable and benevolent founder.

حسنيات hùssnìyyāt, s. pl. a. (no sing.) Good qualities, praiseworthy points of quality or character. [person.

حسود hàssūd, a. a. Envious; an envious

حشر hàshr, s. a. A causing the dead to arise from their graves and assemble to be judged; ا—, —et, v.a. To assemble the dead for judgment.

حشرات hàsharāt, s. pl. a. (no sing.), Reptiles and insects; vile, contemptible people.

حشم hàshem, s. pl. a. (no sing.), Attendants, retinue, suite.

حشمت hàshmet, s. a. The being attended by a crowd of servants, grandeur, pomp, magnificence, majesty; حشمتلو hàshmetlu, a. a. Majestic or Magnificent (the title usually given to European sovereigns in Turkish state papers, the Sultan being styled شوكتلو shèvketlū, &c. &c. &c.).

حشويات hàshvìyyāt, s. pl. a. (no sing.), Words or phrases used merely to fill up space and make any literary composition appear of a decent or proper length.

حصاد hàssād, s. a. A reaping the harvest; —وقتى, wàkti, Harvest-time.

حصار hìssār, s. a. A castle, fort; a besieging, shutting in.

حصانت hàssānet, s. a. A being strong and impregnable; the chastity or virtue of women.

حصر hàssr, s. a. A confining, limiting, shutting in; ا—,—et, v.a. To confine, limit, bound, shut up or in.

حصن hìssn, s. a. A castle, fort, stronghold, fastness.

حصول hùssūl, s. a. A coming into existence, forthcoming, proceeding, realization, accomplishment, taking a form and a being; —مرام, hùssūlu--mèrām, The fruition of one's wishes; حصوله كلمك hùssūla-ghèlmek, v.n. To come into existence, to be realized; حصولپذير hùssūl-pèzīr, a. p. Realized, accomplished, done.

حصه hìsssa, s. a. (pl. حصص hìssàss), A share; حصه‌دار hìsssa-dār, s. p. A sharer, participator; a shareholder; حصه‌مند hìsssamènd, s. p. A sharer, participator; —صاحبى, hìsssa-sāhìbi, A shareholder; حصه‌لشمك hìsssa-lèshmek, v.n. To share together.

حصير hàssir, s. t. A mat, matting; — سپوركه‌سى — sùpurghéssi, A broom for sweeping indoors.

حصين hàssīn, a. a. Strong, fortified.

حضر hàzar, s. a. A state of peace and repose (opposed to سفر sèfèr, A state of travelling or campaigning).

حضرت hàzrèt, *s. a.* Presence, dignity; a title of respect of universal signification from Godhead, Majesty, &c., down to simple Worship, Honour, and Respectability. (See جناب jènāb). This title may either precede or follow the official title of any personage respected by the Muslim church: in the former case it stands alone in the singular number, or without any pronominal affix; as, حضرت خدا hàzrètī-khùdā, God, His Divine Majesty; حضرت رسالتپناهی hàzrèti--rèssālèt-pènāhī, His Holiness the Prophet, &c., &c.; in the latter case, and whenever the name of the person (man or woman) is mentioned, this title takes after it the pronominal affix of the third person plural; as, حق تعالی حضرتلری hàkk-tà‘‘ālà-hàzrètléri, His Divine Majesty the God of Truth, whose name be sanctified; شوكتمأب افنديمز حضرتلری shèvket--mà‘āb-èfèndimiz-hàzrètléri, His Majesty our Imperial Master; دولتلو فؤاد پاشا حضرتلری dèvletlū-Fū‘ād-Pàsha--hàzrètléri, His excellency the very noble Fu‘ad Pasha, &c., &c. Until thirty or forty years ago this title was never given to non-Muslim personages; but since then it has been applied to the Sovereigns of the greater powers; and after the Crimean war it was extended to some of the Generals of the Allies. It is now often given to European private gentlemen. It is to be hoped that such puerile distinctions will be utterly discontinued, and the two words جناب *and* حضرت used quite synonymously, or with a distinction according to rank only, not according to religion. The Armenian practice of addressing people by this title, followed by the pronominal affix of the second person, is never used by the Turks in any case; عاليحضرت ‘‘ālī-hàzrèt, *a. p.* High in dignity.

حضور hùzūr, *s. a.* Presence; a being present; the imperial presence; tranquillity.

حضون hùzūn, *s. a.* Sitting on eggs, incubation.

حضيض hàdīd, *s. a.* The apogee; the aphelion; the lowest point.

حط hàtt, *s. a.* A casting down, throwing on the ground; ا—, —et, *v.a.* To throw on the ground, throw off, cast down.

حطب hàtab, *s. a.* Firewood.

حظ hàzz (*pl.* حظوظ hùzūz), *s. a.* Enjoyment, pleasure; ا—, —et, *v.n.* To be pleased, derive pleasure, be glad (of anything); —نفس, hàzzi-nèfss, Sensual pleasure.

حفر hàfr, *s. a.* A digging, excavating; ا—, —et, *v.a.* To dig out, excavate.

حفره hùfrè, *s. a.* A pit, hollow, cavity dug out.

حفظ hìfz, *s. a.* A preserving; a guarding; a keeping; a learning the Kur‘an by heart, *or* the knowing it by heart; ا—, —et, *v.a.* To preserve; to keep safely; to put safely away; to learn (the Kur'an) by heart; حفظه چالشمق hìfza-chàlìshmak, To be busily engaged in learning the Kur'an by heart.

حفيد hàfīd, *s. a.* A grandson.

حق hàkk, *s. a.* The truth, the pure verity; God, the essence of truth; (*pl.* حقوق hòkūk) right, a person's rights or due; —, *a. a.* True; ا—, —et, *v.a.* To do justice to, to right; حق تعالى hàkk-tà''ālà, God, may (His name) be glorified; حقك وار hàkkìng-vàr, You are right, the right is on your side; حقمدر hàkkìm-dìr, It is my right, my due; حقدر hàkk--dìr, It is true, it is the pure verity; حق دين hàkk-dīn, The true religion; دينك حقى ايچون dīning - hàkkì - -ìchin! For the truth of your religion! برينك حقندن كلمك bìrining--hàkkìndan-ghèlmek, *v.n.* To master or overcome anyone; برينك حقنى حق ا bìrining-hàkkìnì-hàkk-et, To right a person, obtain justice for him, do justice to him. With the locative preposition and a pronominal affix, this noun is equivalent to our preposition *against*, or adverb *in respect of*; as, حقمده hàkkìmda, Against me, *or* in respect of me; &c., &c.; الحق èl-hàkk, *and* حقا hàkkā, *ad. a.* *and* حقاكه hākkā-ki, *ad. p.* Truly, verily.

حقارت hàkārèt, *s. a.* Contemptuous treatment, insulting treatment; ا—, —et, *v.n.* To treat insultingly or with contempt.

حقانيت hàkkānìyyèt, *s. a.* Justice, equity; حقانيتلو hàkkānìyyètli, *a. t.* Just (person); equitable (manner, &c.).

حقائق hàkā'ik, *s. pl. a.* (*of* حقيقت hàkīkàt), True things, true words.

حقد hìkd, *s. a.* Hatred, enmity.

حقنه hòkna, *s. a.* A clyster-pipe; a squirt; an injection. [Rights, dues.

حقوق hòkūk, *s. pl. a.* (*of* حق hàkk),

حقه hòkka, *s. a.* An inkstand, or any small pot or vessel for containing a little jam, electuary, or the like; حقه باز hòkka-bāz, *s. p.* A juggler, conjuror.

حقير hàkīr, *a. a.* Low in station, humble, poor, abject, vile (used in speaking of people's own selves).

حقيقت hàkīkàt, *s. a.* A true thing; a true saying; the truth; truth; —, *ad. t.* Indeed, really; حقيقة hàkīkàtan *and* فى الحقيقه fī-'l-hàkīka, *ad. a.* Truly, really, in effect; حال — hàkīkàtì-hāl, The truth of the case; حقيقتلو hàkīkàtlì, *a. t.* Sincere (in friendship). [*a. a.* True, real.

حقيقى hàkīkī (*fem.* حقيقيه hàkīkìyya),

حك hàkk, *s. a.* A graving, engraving, cutting in; a scraping, scratching, erasing; ا—, —et, *v.a.* To engrave (a seal); to scratch out (writing).

حكاك hàkkyāk (hèkkyāk), *s. a.* An engraver of seals, amulets, &c.

حكام hùkkyām, *s. pl. a.* (*of* حاكم hākim), Judges ; rulers.

حكايه hìkyāyé, *s. a.* A narration, narrative, tale, story, history ; a narrating ; ا—, —et, *v.a.* To narrate, recount, tell, relate.

حكم hàkem, *s. a.* An arbitrator, umpire ; —, hìkem, *s. pl. a.* (*of* حكمت hìkmet), Portions of wisdom, sound reasons ; —, hùkm (hùkyum), A decreeing ; (*pl.* احكام àhkyām), A decree ; a requirement ; authority, weight, power, influence ; ا—, —et, *v.a.* To make (a decree) ; give (a sentence) ; —, *v.n.* To rule, govern, exercise authority ; حكمى كچمك hùkmu--ghèchmek, To pass or be received as an authoritative decree, as an authority ; حكمدار hùkmdār, حكمران hùkmrān, *s. p.* A ruler, a sovereign.

حكما hùkémā, *s. pl. a.* (*of* حكيم hàkīm), Sages, doctors, philosophers.

حكمت hìkmet, *s. a.* Wisdom ; a determining reason influencing the mind of an actor, good and sufficient reason ; hidden, mysterious cause or reason ; philosophy ; —طبيعه, hìkméti-tàbī‘-ìyyé, Natural philosophy ; a natural cause ; —الهيه, hìkméti-ìlāhìyyé, Metaphysics ; a cause arising out of God's will and determination.

حكومت hùkyūmèt, *s. a.* The exercise of rulership ; the office of sovereign, ruler, or judge ; the sphere of a jurisdiction ; a state ; —مركز mèrkézi—, The seat of jurisdiction, seat of government ; ا—, —et, *v.n.* To rule, govern.

حكيم hàkīm (*pl.* حكما hùkémā), *s. a.* A sage, a philosopher ; —, *a. a.* Very wise in decision ; —مطلق, hàkīmi--mùtlàk, God, the absolutely wise.

حل hàll, *s. a.* A melting ; an untying ; a solving, resolving, dissolving, analyzing ; ا—, —et, *v.a.* To melt, dissolve, to untie ; to solve, resolve ; to analyse.

حلاج hàllāj (hàlach), *s. a.* A carder of [cotton.

حلاط hàlat, *s. t.* A rope.

حلال hàlāl (hèlāl), *a. a.* Permitted by God's law, (anything) the use of which is expressly permitted and consequently free from sin ; حلاللشمق hàlāllashmak, *v.n.* To forgive mutually any trespass or unlawful advantage taken of each other (usual between persons who are bidding each other a long adieu) ; ا—, —et, *v.a.* To declare lawful, to renounce any claim one might possibly have to a thing possessed by another, and say : "Be it thy lawful property."

حلاوت hàlāvèt, *s. a.* Sweetness.

حلقه hàlka, *s. a.* A ring, a link of a chain.

حلقوم hùlkūm, *s. a.* The throat, the gullet ; راحت الحلقوم rāhatu-'l--hùlkūm (rāhat-lòkūm), A celebrated sweetmeat prepared from wheat-starch, sugar, and perfume, with blanched almonds sometimes bedded in it.

حلو hùlu (hùru), *s. p.* A choice kind of melting peach.

حلوا hèlwā, *s. a.* Name of various kinds of sweetmeats or sweet dishes; as, اون حلواسی ūn - hèlwāssi, made with flour; ایرمك حلواسی ìrmik-hèlwāssi, made with semolina; نشاسته حلواسی nìshàssta-hèlwāssi, made with wheat-starch; which are all dishes and appear at table as such; قار حلواسی kàr--hèlwāssi, made with snow, a frolicking winter dish; کاغد حلواسی kyāghid--hèlwāssi, made of two large wafers; کتان حلواسی (kètæn)-hèlwāssi, made to look like hanks of unspun flax; طحن حلواسی tàhan (tàyn)-hèlwāssi, made of honey and saponaria root; —فندق fìndìk—, —جوز jèviz—, —بادم bādem—, made respectively with nuts, walnuts, and almonds, which are all eaten as sweetmeats or with bread for lunch, &c.; —قدرت kŭdrèt-hèlwāssi, Manna. Helwā is always a standing dish at feasts among the people, and may be likened, in that respect, to our plum-pudding.

حلول hùlūl, *s. a.* A passing into (as the soul into the body); a coming (as time does); ا—, —et, *v.n.* To pass (into); to come; حلوليون hùlūlìyyūn, Those who hold that God passes into man's body. [wife or concubine.

حليله hàlīlé, *s. a.* A legitimate consort,

حليم hàlīm, *a. a.* Kind, gentle, long-suffering, slow to anger.

حليه hìlyé, *s. a.* An ornament, a jewel.

حما hùmmà, *s. a.* Burning fever.

حمار hìmār, *s. a.* An ass, donkey.

حمارات hàmāràt, *a. t.* Hard-working and industrious (woman).

حماست hàmāssèt, *s. a.* Courage, valour, bravery.

حماقت hàmākàt, *s. a.* Stupidity.

حمال hàmmāl (hàmal), *s. a.* A porter; carrier; برکیر حمالی (bèghir)-hàm-mali, A town carrier who employs pack-horses; صیرق حمالی sìrìk-hàm-mali, A porter who works in a pair or in gangs, with poles, to carry heavy loads; حماليه hàmmālìyyé, Carriage, porter's hire.

حمام hàmmām (hàmam), *s. a.* A bath; bathing-place; a bathing; قدرت حمامی kŭdrèt-hàmàmi, A natural hot-spring or bath; —, hìmām, *s. a.* Death; حمامی hàmmāmi, *s. a.*, حمامجی hàmamji, *s. t.* A bath-keeper. [dove.

حمامه hàmāmé, *s. a.* A pigeon or

حمایت hìmāyet, حمایه hìmāyé, *s. a.* Protection; a protecting; ا—, —et, *v.a.* To protect, guard from harm or oppression.

حمائل hàmā'il, *s. pl. a.* (*as a Turkish sing.*), The cord or belt by which the sword is slung over the shoulder.

حمد hàmd, *s. a.* Thanks, praise, glory offered in prayer; لله الحمد lì-'llāhi--'l-hàmd! *or* الحمدلله èl-hàmdu-lì--'llāh! Praise be to God! praise is due to

God alone! حمد اولسون hàmd-òlsun!
Thank God! حمداً hàmdan, *ad. a.* Thanks; حمداً ثم حمداً hàmdan-sùmmé-hàmdā, Thanks upon thanks.

حمدله hàmdélé, *s. a.* The pronouncing the formula الحمدلله èl-hàmdu-lì-'llāh.

حمرت hùmret, *s. a.* Redness; a colouring up from shame or modesty.

حمق hùmk, *s. a.* Stupidity.

حمل hàml, *s. a.* A bearing, carrying; a loading; a load; pregnancy, or the fœtus; an imputing, casting upon the shoulders; —, hàmel, *s. a.* The sign Aries; ا—, hàml-et, *v.a.* To attribute, impute, cast upon; to load, place (in or upon something) as a load; وضع حمل ا wàz''*i*-hàml-et, *v.n.* To bear, bring forth (a child or young).

حمله hàml*a*, *s. a.* An effort; a pull; a charge; an attack; حمله جى hàmlaj*i*, *s. t.* The strokesman or chief boatman of a row-boat.

حموله hàmūlé, *s. a.* A load; a cargo.

حميت hàmmìyyèt, *s. a.* Zeal, jealous feeling of honour.

حميد hàmīd (*fem.* حميده hàmīdé), *a. a.* Very praiseworthy; —, *s. a.* God.

حميه hìmyé, *s. a.* Abstinence, diet.

حنا hìnnā (kìn*a*), *s. a.* The herb henna.

حنث hìnss, *s. a.* The violation of an oath.

حنجقرق hìnchkirik, *s. t.* The hiccup; حنجقرمق hìnchkirmak, *v.n.* To hiccup.

حنطه hìnt*a*, *s. a.* Wheat.

حوادث hàwādiss, *s. pl. a.* (*of* حادثه hādissé), Events; news; (*as a Turkish sing.*), a piece of news.

حوارده hòwàrd*a*, *s. t.* A wild, unsteady fellow, a scamp.

حوارى hàwārī (*pl.* حواريون hàwārìyyūn), *s. a.* An apostle, *or* a companion of a prophet, especially those of our Lord.

حواس hàwāsss, *s. pl. a.* (*of* حاسه hāsss*a*), Senses, faculties of sense; حواس خمسهٔ ظاهره hàwāsssi-khàmsa'i-zāhiré, The five external senses.

حواشى hàwāshi, *s. pl. a.* Servants, attendants.

حواله hàwālé, *s. a.* A referring, trusting, confiding (the execution of any matter to a person); a cheque, money order; overhanging height; ا—, —et, *v.a.* To refer, trust, confide (business to a person); حوالهلو hàwāléli, *a. t.* High and overhanging.

حوالى hàwāli, *s. pl. a.* (*no sing.*), Environs, vicinity; اول حواليلرده òl-hàwālilerd*a*, In that neighbourhood, thereabouts; in those parts.

حوائج hàwā'ij, *s. pl. a.* (*of* حاجت hājet), Wants, necessities; necessaries.

حوپا hòppa, *s. t.* An affected coxcomb.

حوت hūt, *s. a.* The sign Pisces.

حور hūr, *a. pl. a.* Black-(eyed); حورالعين hūru-'l-''àyn, *and* حور عين hūru-''àyn, Those (damsels of Paradise) who have black eyes, the houris; حورى hūrī, *s. p.* One of the black-eyed damsels of Paradise.

حورة hàvr*a*, *s. t.* A Jewish synagogue.

حوزة hÂvz*a*, *s. a.* A containing fold, circle, or circuit; حوزهٔ اسلام hÂvz*a*'i-ìsslām, The fold or church of Islamism.

حوصله hàvs*a*l*a*, *s. a.* The crop or stomach of an animal; intellectual capacity in man; solid capacity for containing. [water, pond, tank.

حوض hàvz (hàwuz), *s. a.* A reservoir of

حول hàvl, *s. a.* Change, mutation; a year; strength, power, might; لاحول ولاقوة الا بالله lā-hàvl*a*-vè-lā-kùvvét*a*-illā-bì-'llāh, There is no power, neither is there any strength, unless in God.

حولامق hàvlam*a*k (*aor.* حولار hàvlar), *v.n.* To bark (a dog).

حولی hàvl*i* (hàvlu), *s. t.* A court-yard, a yard; a towel. [bottles, &c.

حونی hùni, *s. t.* A funnel for filling

حویار hÂvyàr, *s. t.* Caviar.

حی hàyy, *a. a.* Alive, living; حی القیوم hàyyu-'l-kàyyūm, The living and self-existent God; —, hàyy*a*! *int. a.* Come! hasten! حی علی الصلاح حی علی الفلاح hàyy*a*-"àlé-'ss-sÂlāh! Hàyy*a*-"àlé-'l-fèlāh! Come to what is a solid advantage! hasten to what is truly profitable! (This is a part of the call to prayer.)

حیا hàyā, *s. a.* A feeling of shame, bashfulness, modesty; بی حیا bī-hàyā, *a. p.* Shameless (person), impudent.

حیات hàyāt, *s. a.* Life; life-time; اب حیات Âb*i*-hàyāt, The water of life; حیات اولسون hàyāt-ölsun! May it be life (to you)! (said to a person when he has drunk).

حیثیت hàysìyyèt, *s. a.* Status, station, dignity, consideration.

حیدود hàydūd, *s. t.* A brigand, robber.

حیران hàyrĀn, *a. a.* Bewildered, confounded, astounded.

حیرت hàyret, *s. a.* Bewilderment, confusion, utter astonishment.

حیز hàyz, *s. a.* A containing fold, court, or circuit. [charge.

حیض hàyz, *s. a.* The menstrual dis-

حیف hàyf, *s. a.* Harm, injury; —! *int. a.* Alas!

حیقرمق hàyk*i*rm*a*k (*aor.* حیقرر hày-k*i*r*i*r), *v.n.* To call out, cry out.

حیلاز hàylÂz, *s. t.* An idler, idle fellow.

حیله hīlé, *s. a.* A trick, fraud, deceit; —, —et, *v.n.* To play tricks, to use fraud; حیله باز hīlé-bÂz, حیله کار hīlé-kyār, *s. p.* A cheat; knave.

حین hīn, *s. a.* Time, a small indefinite space of time, a moment.

حیوان hàywĀn, *s. a.* Life; (*pl.* حیوانات hàywĀnĀt) a living creature, an animal; a horse; a brute; a boor, clown; —ناطق, hàywĀn*i*-nĀt*i*k, A talking (rational) animal; حیوانلق hàywĀnl*i*k, *s. t.* حیوانیت hàywĀnìyyèt, *s. a.* Stupidity; boorishness, clownishness; حیوانی (*fem.* حیوانیه hàywĀnìyyé) hàywĀnī, *a. a.* Animal, pertaining to animals, or to animal life.

حیوت hàyāt (an Arabic form of حیات hàyāt), *s. a.* Life.

حیه hàyyé, *s. a.* A serpent, snake.

خ

خ khì (*or* خاءسخذ khā'i-sàkhaz, the letter *kh* in the word sàkhaz). Ninth letter of the Turkish alphabet, having no equivalent value in English, but corresponding with the *ch* of the German, Scotch, &c. It is better for the learner to pronounce this letter as an *aspirated h* until he can acquire the correct sound from a teacher, and he should *never sound it as a* k. In chronograms this letter has the numeral value of 600.

خا khā, *s. a.* The letter خ; —, *a. p.* (*in composition*), Which eats.

خاتم khātem, *s. a.* A seal, signet, signet-ring; —, khātim, *s. a.* The last of a series, that which closes or finishes; —الانبیا, khātimu-'l-ènbiyā, The last of the prophets, Muhammed; خاتمه khātimé, The conclusion, concluding phrase or prayer of a book, epilogue.

خاتون khātun, *s. t.* A woman; a lady; [a wife.

خاج khāj, *s. p.* A cross.

خادم khādim, *s. a.* A servant, servitor; (khādim) an eunuch; —الحرمین الشریفین khādimu-'l-hàréméyni-'sh-sheriféyn, Servitor of the two sacred spots at Mecca and Medina (one of the titles of the Sultan).

خار khār, *s. p.* A thorn, prickle; a sting.

خارا khārā, *a. p.* Hard (stone).

خارج khārij, *s. a.* The outside; —, *a. a.* Outside, beyond, exceeding, not included, excluded; خارجی khārijī, *s. a.* A rebel, outlaw; — (*fem.* خارجیه khārijìyyé), *a. a.* Pertaining to the outside; external, exterior; foreign; provincial; خارجیه ناظری khārijìyyé-nāziri, *or* ناظر امور خارجیه nāziri-ùmūri-khārijìyyé, The Minister for Foreign Affairs.

خارق khārik, *a. a.* Which rends; خارق العاده khāriku-'l-'ādé, *a. a.* Extraordinary, strange.

خاسته khāssté, *a. p.* Risen.

خاسر khāssir, *a. a.* Who is completely disappointed, and has lost all hope of success in his undertaking.

خاشاك khāshāk, *s. p.* Sticks and straws blown about.

خاص khāss (*fem.* خاصه khāssa), *a. a.* Special, peculiar, proper; pure, unalloyed, unadulterated; white (bread or flower); fixed (dye); public (buildings); royal or imperial (guard, &c.); —, *s. a.* (*pl.* خواص khàwāss), A person of note, of mark; a royal domain or due.

خاصه khāssa, *s. a.* A peculiar property, virtue, or quality; a virtue, power, beneficial property; خاصةً khāssétan, *ad. a.* Especially, specially.

خاصکی khāsséki, *s. t.* Certain special

officers of the Sultan's court in the olden time.

خاصيت khāssìyyèt, *s. a.* A nutritive or sanative virtue, wholesomeness; خاصيتلو khāssìyyètli, *a. t.* Wholesome, nutritive, or sanative.

خاطر khātir, *s. a.* The memory; the heart or mind, or the faculty of being vexed or pleased; خاطرده طوتمق khātirda-tùtmak, *v.a.* To bear in mind, not to forget; خاطری قالمق khātiri-kālmak (*the pron. affix being changed as required*), *v.n.* To be vexed, hurt, angry; خاطرده قالمق khātirda-kālmak, *v.n.* To remain in the memory, not be forgotten; خاطرینی یاپمق khātirini-yàpmak (*varying the affix*), To make one feel satisfied or pleased (by promises, presents, &c.); خاطرینی قیرمق khātirini-kìrmak (*or* یقمق yìkmak), *v.n.* To make one feel vexed, hurt, or angry (by refusing his request, by rudeness, &c.); خاطرینی صایمق khātirini-sàymak, To have regard for one, hold him as worthy of consideration, esteem him, love him; خاطره كلمك khātira-ghèlmek, *v.n.* To come into one's mind, be recalled to memory, occur to one; خاطره كتورمك khātira-ghètirmek, *v.a.* To call to mind, recall to mind, remember; برینك خاطرینه كتورمك bìrining-khātirina-ghètirmek, *v.a.* To recall to one's mind, put him in mind of; خاطردن چیقمق khātirdan-chìkmak (*with pron. affixes as required*), *v.n.* To be forgotten, be out of memory; خاطرم ایچون khātirim-ìchin, For my sake, for love of me, out of consideration for me; صفای خاطر ایله sāfāyi-khātir-ila! (Go) in peace of mind! (said to anyone who takes leave); خاطر صورمق khātir-sòrmak, *v.n.* To ask after anyone, ask how one is; خاطرلمق khātirlamak, *v.a.* To remember, call to mind; خاطرلو khātirli, *a. t.* (A person) of consideration; خاطرخواه khātir-khāh, *s. p.* The wish of one's heart; خاطرمانده khātir-mānde, *a. p.* Hurt, vexed, grieved.

خاطره khātira, *s. a.* A thought, an idea.

خاقان khākān, *s. t.* (*pl.* خواقين khàwākīn), The Sultan; a sovereign; خاقانى khākānī, *a. a.* Imperial, sovereign, pertaining to the khākān.

خاك khāk, *s. p.* Earth; the ground; the earth; خاكى khākī, *a. p.* Earthy, earthly; خاكپاى khāki-pāy, *s. p.* The ground under the foot (as we say "*the feet*") of a superior; a superior himself.

خاكستر khākisstèr, *a. p.* Ashes.

خال khāl, *s. p.* A mole on the skin.

خالص khāliss, *a. a.* Pure, unmixed; sincere, true, real.

خالق khālik, *s. a.* The Creator.

خاله khāle, *s. a.* A maternal aunt, mother's own sister. (The corrupted form of this word, حاله hāla, signifies in Turkish a paternal aunt, a father's own sister).

خالی khāli, *a. a.* Empty; free, exempt.

خام khām (khȃm), *a. p.* Unripe, green (fruit); unprepared, rough (material); stupid, unreasonable (proposal); inexperienced, raw (person); unseasoned, untrained (for travelling); brown (sugar).

خامس khāmiss, *a. a.* The fifth; خامسا khāmissā, *ad. a.* Fifthly.

خاموش khāmūsh, *a. p.* Silent; dead (person); out, extinguished (fire).

خامه khāmé, *s. p.* A pen *or* reed for writing.

خان khān, *s. p.* The Sultan; a lord (in Persia); (khȃn) an inn, a public building for the accommodation of travellers or merchants.

خاندان khānédān, *s. p.* A noble family; a person belonging to a noble family.

خانقاه khānkāh, *s. p.* A convent for dervishes. [tame.

خانکی khānéghī, *a. p.* Domestic, house,

خانم khȃnim, *s. t.* A Turkish lady.

خانمان khānumān, *s. p.* A family (of distinction).

خانه khāné, *s. p.* A house, dwelling; (*in composition*) a manufactory, a special house *or* room; a place of figures (in arithmetic); a place, partition, pigeon-hole, square (on a chess-board), stall, hole, &c.; a family; ادبخانه èdeb-khāné, ابدستخانه àbdesst-khāné, A privy, water-closet; کتبخانه kyùtub-khāné, A library; بندهخانه bèndé-khāné, (The house of a servant) My house; دولتخانه dèvlet-khāné, (The house of prosperity) Your house; (*with the pron. affix of the third pers. plur.*) his *or* their house; خانهزاد khāné-zād, *a. p.* Born in the house, home-bred.

خائب khā'ib, *a. a.* Utterly disappointed and deceived in his hopes.

خائن khā'in, *s. a.* A perfidious, treacherous fellow.

خایه khāyé, *s. p.* An egg; a testicle.

خباثت khàbāssèt, *s. a.* Turpitude; a villainous act; villainousness of disposition.

خبائث khàbā'iss, *s. pl. a.* (*no sing.*), Vices; ام الخبائث ùmmu-'l-khàbā'iss, (The mother of the vices) Wine.

خبر khȃber, *s. a.* Information possessed or imparted; intelligence, news; historical information; the attribute or predicate in grammar or logic; ا—, —et, —ویرمك, —vèrmek, *v.n.* To give notice, to give information, to inform; —المق, —ȃlmak, *v.n.* To receive intelligence, to hear, to be informed; خبریکزوارمی khȃbéringiz-vàrmi? Do you know? Are you aware? خبرم یوق khȃbérim-yòk, I do not know, I am not aware, I have no information on the subject; علم وخبر 'ìlm-u-khȃber, Information and intelligence; an invoice sent with goods, or a letter of advice on business; خبردار khAberdār, a. p. Informed, aware; خبرلشمك khAberlsshmek, v.n. To correspond, send mutual information.

خبره khìbrÉ, s. a. Experimental or practical knowledge; اهل خبره èhli-khìbrÉ, (èhli-kìbla), An adept, a person well and practically acquainted with any subject to whom disputes are referred.

خبيث khàbīss, s. a. A villain, a rascal; —(fem. خبيثه khàbīssÉ), a. a. Depraved, villainous, infamous.

خبير khàbīr, a. a. Informed, aware.

ختام khìtAm, s. a. An ending, completion; —بولمق, —būlmak, v.n. To be completed, finished; ختامپذير khìtām-pèzīr, a. p. Finished, completed; حسن ختام hùssni-khìtAm, A happy conclusion.

ختان khìtān, s. a. A circumcising, circumcision.

ختم khAtm, s. a. The bringing any discourse to an end; a finishing the complete reading of the Kur'an; a sealing; ا—, —et, v.a. To finish (reading the Kur'an through); to bring to an end (a discourse); to seal; —, khAtémÉ! May (God) finish and complete!

ختمى khAtmī, s. t. The hollyoak, hollyhock; اغاج ختميسى Aghaj-khAtmīssi, s. t. The gum-cistus (?) or hollyhock tree.

خجالت khìjālet, s. a. A sense of shame; bashfulness.

خجسته khùjèsstÉ, a. p. Lucky, blessed, fortunate, auspicious.

خخام khàkhAm, s. t. A Jewish rabbi; —باشى, —bAshi, The chief rabbi.

خد khàdd, s. a. The cheek.

خدا khùdā, s. p. God; خداداد khùdā-dād, Theodore or Theodosius, the gift of God.

خدام khŭddAm, s. pl. a. (of خادم khĀdim), Servants, servitors.

خداوند khùdāvènd, خداوندكار khùdāvèndighyār, s. p. A lord, a master; a sovereign; God.

خدشه khàdshÉ, s. a. A scratching, itching; خدشۀ خاطر khàdshé'i-khAtir, An uneasiness of mind, apprehension, misgiving.

خدعه khŭd''a, s. a. A trick, piece of deceit, stratagem.

خدم khàdem, s. pl. a. Servants, suite, train, retinue.

خدمت khìdmet (hìzmet), s. a. Service, ministry; a servant's place, a situation; a government situation; mission, commission, employ, employment; a fee; ا—, —et, v.n. To do service, act as servant; —كورمك, —ghyùrmek, To be of essential service, to do good service; خدمتده قوللانمق khìdmetda-kŏllAnmak, To employ in one's service; خدمتجى (hìzmetji), s. t. خدمتكار (hìzmetkyār), s. p. A servant.

خدنك khàdengh, s. p. An arrow.

خديو khìdīv, s. p. A prince, a lord.

خذلان khìzlān, s. a. Abandonment, the being without friends or means.

خذله khàzélé, *s. pl. a.* (*no sing.*), Wretched fellows, poor wretches.

خر khàr, *s. p.* An ass, donkey.

خراب khàrāb, *s. a.* A making desolate, laying waste; desolation, ruin; —, *a. t.* Desolate, ruined, in ruins; —ا, —et, *v.a.* To ruin, lay waste; to do a great injury to; —أو, —ôl, *v.n.* To be ruined or greatly injured.

خرابه khàrābé (*pl.* خرابات khàrābāt), *s. a.* A ruin, heap of ruins; خراباتی khàrābātī, *s. a.* A confirmed drunkard.

خراج khàrāj, *s. a.* Tribute paid to the government, either by a subject country, or by subject individuals in the governing country; this latter is also called جزیه jìzyé; خراجكذار khàrāj-ghyùzār, *s. p.* A tributary; خراججی khàrājji, *s. t.* A collector of individual tribute.

خراسان khòrāssān, *s. p.* Name of a country in the east of Persia; powdered brickdust for making cement when mixed with lime; —قره kàra—, One of the most esteemed kinds of Damascus sword-blades.

خراش khìrāsh, *a. p.* (*in composition*), Which irritates, scratches, pricks, annoys.

خرام khìrām (*in composition*), and خرامان khìrāmān, *a. p.* Who walks, carries himself.

خرج khàrj, *s. a.* A spending, expending; expense; materials for any work; braid or lace on clothes; mortar, cement; —ا, —et, *v.a.* To spend, expend; خرجراه khàrji-rāh, *s. p.* Money for travelling expenses and outfit; وكيل خرج vèkīl-khàrj, A domestic whose duty it is to go to market and buy provisions, &c.; خرجلق khàrjlìk, *s. t.* Pocket-money, money for necessary expenses; —, khòrj, *s. a.* A large saddle-bag, put in pairs upon pack-horses.

خرد khìrèd, *s. p.* Intelligence, sagacity; باخرد bā-khìrèd, *and* خردمند khìred-mènd, *a. p.* Intelligent; —, khùrd, *a. p.* A fragment, piece; —, *a. p.* Small, little; خردسال khùrd-sāl, *a. p.* Young in years.

خردل khàrdʌl, *s. t.* Mustard or cress seed used as mustard at table.

خرده khùrdé, *a. p.* Small, little; —, *s. p.* A small piece or fragment; a crumb; (*pl.* خردوات khùrdawʌt), Small things, small wares; —فروش, khùrda-fùrūsh, *s. p.* A chapman, small dealer; خرده بین khùrda-bīn, *s. p.* A microscope; a person who takes notice of trifles.

خرسز khìrsiz, *s. t.* A thief; a robber; an embezzler; دكز خرسزی dèngiz-khìrsizi, A pirate; خرسزلق khìrsizlìk, *s. t.* Theft; robbery; embezzlement, peculation; خرسزلق‌ا khìrsizlìk-et, *v.n.* To commit theft; to commit robbery; to commit embezzlement or peculation.

خرطوم khòrtūm, *s. a.* The trunk of an elephant, proboscis; the hose of a fire-engine. [ا—, —et, *v.a.* To rend, tear.

خرق khàrk, *s. a.* A rending, tearing;

خرقه khìrk*a*, *s. a.* A kind of quilted jacket; a ragged garment.

خرگاه khàrghyāh, *s. p.* A tent, pavilion; a royal court.

خرگوش khàrghyush, *s. a.* (donkey's ears) A hare; —خواب khābi—, (hare's sleep) Vigilance under seeming carelessness, sleeping with one eye open.

خرلدامق khìrìldamak (*aor.* خرلدار khìrìldar), *and* خرلامق khìrlamak (*aor.* خرلار khìrlar), *v.n.* To snarl or growl (a dog); to snore; خرلدى khìrìldi, *s. t.* A snarling, growling; a snoring; خرلاشمق khìrlashmak, *v.n.* To growl at each other. [pleasant.

خرم khùrrem, *a. p.* Cheerful, smiling,

خرما khùrma, *s. a.* A date (fruit).

خرمن khàrmen (hàrmàn), *s. p.* The threshing and winnowing of corn after harvest; the threshing-floor or circular space where this is performed; the produce of the operation.

خروات Khìrvāt, *s.* and *a. t.* Croatian; a Croat; خروات مملكتى Khìrvāt-mèmlékèti, Croatia.

خروار khàrvār, *s. p.* A donkey-load; a horse-load.

خروب khàrrūb (khārub), *s. a.* The locust fruit; —شربتى, —shèrbéti, A drink prepared from that fruit.

خروج khùrūj, *s. a.* A going out, coming out, exit, passing out; a rebelling, rebellion; صاحب خروج sāhib-khùrūj, A great conqueror; خروج على السلطان khùrūj-'àlé-'ss-sùltān, Rebellion against the sovereign.

خروس khòross, *s. t.* A cock (fowl); the cock or hammer of a gun-lock.

خروش khùrūsh, *s. p.* A noise, row, tumult, tumultuous motion.

خريد khìrīd, *s. p.* A buying; فروخت وخريد fùrūkht-u-khìrīd, Buying and selling; — (*in composition*), *a. p.* Bought; زرخريد zèr-khìrīd, *a. p.* Bought with gold.

خريدار khìrīdār, *s. p.* A buyer, purchaser.

خريده khìrīdé, *a. p.* Bought.

خريستان khrīsstiyān, *s. t.* (*Greek*), A Christian man. [chart, plan.

خريطه khàrīt*a* (hàrt*a*), *s. a.* A map,

خريف khàrif, *s. a.* The autumn.

خزان khìzān, *s. p.* The autumnal cold wind which causes the leaves to fall.

خزائن khàzā'in, *s. pl. a.* (*of* خزينه khàzīné), Treasuries; treasures.

خزينه khàzīné (hàzn*a*), *s. a.* A treasury; a treasure; public treasure, or treasure being conveyed over the country; a special fund for administering a department of state; a sum of 36,000 purses (about £150,000); a reservoir for water above ground and covered in; the chamber (of a gun or mine); buried treasure, treasure-trove; خزينه دار (hàzn*a*dār), *s. p.* A treasurer.

خس khìss, *s. p.* Rubbish, sticks and straws.

خسار khàssār, خسارت khàssārèt, *s. a.* A doing damage; injury; — ا, khàssāret-et, *v.n.* To do damage.

خست khìsssèt, *s. a.* Avarice, avariciousness.

خسته khàssta, *a. p.* Sick, ill; خانه—, —khānè, *s. p.* A hospital; a sick-ward; a sick-bay; خستەلق khàsstalìk, *s. t.* Sickness, illness, malady, disease, the plague.

خسرو khùssrev, *s. p.* A prince, monarch; خسروانه khùssrévānè, *a. p.* Princely, royal.

خسوف khùssūf, *s. a.* A lunar eclipse, eclipse of the moon.

خسيس khàssīss, *s. a.* A miser; a sordid, parsimonious fellow.

خشت khìsht, *s. p.* A brick.

خشخاش khàshkhāsh, *s. a.* A poppy from which opium is extracted.

خشك khùshk, *a. p.* Dry, dried.

خشم khìshm, *s. p.* Anger, rage, fury; الود—, khìshm-ālūd, *a. p.* Angry, furious; خشمناك khìshmnāk, *a. p.* Angry, easily angered.

خشنود khòshnūd, *a. p.* Satisfied, content, contented, pleased.

خشوع khùshū", *s. a.* Humility.

خشونت khùshūnèt, *s. a.* Severity, hardness, harshness, sharpness.

خشيان khàshéyān, خشيت khàshyet, *s. a.* Fear, terror, fright.

خشين khàshīn, *a. a.* Severe, harsh, sharp (in disposition).

خصال khìssāl, *s. pl. a.* (*of* خصلت khàsslet), Points of character, moral qualities. [Qualities, properties.

خصائص khàssā'iss, *s. pl. a.* (*of* خصيصه),

خصائل khàssā'il, *s. pl. a.* (*of* خصيله), Points of character, moral qualities.

خصلت khàsslet, *s. a.* A quality of the heart, a point of character.

خصم khàssm, *s. a.* (*pl.* خصما khùssémā), An adversary; an enemy; —, khìssm, *s. t.* A relative, relation; خصملق khìssmlìk, *s. t.* Affinity or consanguinity, relationship.

خصوص khùssūss, *s. a.* Any particular subject, matter, affair, business; speciality; devotedness, love, friendship; خصوصا khùssūssā, على الخصوص "àlé-'l-khùssūss, *ad. a.* Especially, particularly, more particularly, above all, more than all; خصوصى khùssūssi (*fem.* خصوصيه khùssūssiyyè), *a. a.* Special, particular; خصوصيت khùssūssìyyèt, *s. a.* The quality of being special; the quality of being devoted, devotedness, love, friendship.

خصومت khùssūmèt, *s. a.* Enmity, ill-will; contention, litigation, adversary-[ship.

خصى khàsi, *s. a.* A eunuch.

خصيتين khùssyétèyn, *s. a. dual* (*of* خصيه), The two testicles.

خضاض khìdād, *s. a.* Ink.

خضرا khàzrā, *s. a.* The sky; —, *a. a. fem.* Green, verdant.

خضوع khùzū", *s. a.* Humility.

خط khàtt, *s. a.* A fine hair or down; (*pl.* خطوط khùtūt), A line drawn;

a line, row; writing, handwriting; the Sultan's autograph commands; — مستقيم khAtti-mùsstakīm, A straight line; منحنى—, khAtti-mùnhàni, A curveline; مختلط—, khAtti-mùkhtèlit, A mixed line; موازى—, khAtti-mùwāzī, A parallel line; خطين متوازيين khAt-tèyni-mùtévāzìyyèyn (*dual*), Two lines reciprocally parallel; خطوط متوازيه khùtūti-mùtévāzìyyé (*plur.*), Lines parallel to each other; استوا—, khAtti-ìsstiwā (ùsstuwā), The equator, equinoctial; نصف النهار—, khAtti-nìssfu-'n-nàhār, The meridian; حسن خط hùssnu-khAtt (Beauty of handwriting), Beautiful handwriting; شريف—, khAtti-shèrīf, همايون—, khAtti-hù-māyūn, The gracious *or* august autograph commands.

خطا khAtā, *s. a.* A fault, mistake, error; ا—, —et, *v.n.* To make a mistake, commit a fault, an error.

خطاب khìtAb, *s. a.* The addressing one's speech to a person; ا—, —et, *v.n.* To address one's speech; خطاباً khìtAban, *ad. a.* خطابله khìtAbla, *ad. t.* By way of address, as an address (of speech).

خطاط khAttAt, *s. a.* A calligrapher, professed writer of calligraphy.

خطايا khAtāyā, *s. pl. a.* (*of* خطا khAtā), Faults, faulty actions.

خطبه khùtbé, *s. a.* The public prayer for the life and prosperity of the sovereign.

خطر khAtar, *s. a.* Danger, peril.

خطوه khAtvé, *s. a.* A step, pace, foot.

خطور khùtūr, *s. a.* A coming into the mind; ا—, —et, *v.n.* To come into the mind. [Lines.

خطوط khùtūt, *s. pl. a.* (*of* خط khAtt),

خطه khìtté, *s. a.* A district, region, country, tract.

خطيب khàtīb, *s. a.* The officiating clerk or priest who pronounces the خطبه or public prayer for the sovereign.

خطير khàtīr, *a. a.* Grave, important.

خفاف khàffāf (kàwwAf), *s. a.* A shoemaker or seller.

خفت khìffèt, *s. a.* Lightness; volatileness of character, want of stability.

خفقان khàfakān, *s. a.* A palpitation of the heart through disease or fear.

خفى khàfī, *a. a.* Hidden, concealed, secret.

خفيف khàfīf (hAfif), *a. a.* Light of weight, volatile, unstable in character; slight, not severe; light, gentle (wind).

خلا khàlā, *s. a.* A vacuum, empty space; a privy, water-closet; خلاوملا khàlā-u-mèlā, Vacuum and plenum.

خلاص khàlāss, *s. a.* A being saved, delivered; salvation, deliverance; بولمق—, —būlmak, *v.n.* To be saved, delivered; —, khàllāss, *s. a.* A saviour, redeemer.

خلاصه khùlāssa, *s. a.* The extract or quintessence of anything; a summary.

خلاف khìlāf, *s. a.* A being contrary, or in opposition (to anything); a lie, untruth.

خلافت khĭlāfĕt, *s. a.* The Caliphate, office of Caliph; the being Caliph; —ا, —et, *v.n.* To be Caliph, reign as Caliph.

خلاق khàllāk, *s. a.* God, the continual Creator.

خلال khĭlāl, *s. a.* A toothpick, an ear-pick; a time, point of time; a grammatical conjugation, or paradigma of derivation; friendship; the centre, bottom.

خلائق khàlā'ik, *s. pl. a.* (*no sing.*), Creatures; (*as a Turkish sing.*), a female slave.

خلجان khàléjān, *s. a.* A tremor, agitation.

خلط khàlt, *s. a.* A mixing, mingling; any one of the four elementary humours of an animal body; —ا, —et, *v.a.* To mix, mingle; —, *v.n.* To be quite wrong and be d—d; —يمك, —yèmek, *v.n.* (To eat humour) To mean, to pretend; to make a great mistake (an insulting expression).

خلع khàl'', *s. a.* A dethroning; —ا, —et, *v.a.* To dethrone; —, khĭlà'', *s. pl. a.* (*of* خلعت khĭl''àt), Robes of honour.

خلعت khĭl''àt, *s. a.* A robe of honour.

خلف khàlef, *s. a.* A successor; ناخلف nā-khàlef, *a. p.* Unworthy to be a successor, degenerate; —, khŭlf, *s. a.* An acting contrary to (a promise); —ا, khulf-et, *v.a.* To act contrary to (a promise); —وعد ا, khŭlfu-và''d-et, *v.n.* To break a promise, act contrary to promise.

خلفا khŭléfā, *s. pl. a.* (*of* خليفه khàlīfĕ), Caliphs, successors of Muhammed in ruling the empire, pontiffs; assistants, ushers (in schools); assistant clerks (in public offices).

خلق khàlk, *s. a.* A creating; (khàlk) people, men; the public; —ا, —et, *v.a.* To create, bring into being; قبا— kàba-khàlk, Common people; —, khŭlk, *s. a.* A point of natural disposition; خلقى khĭlkī, *a. a.* Natural, innate.

خلقت khĭlkàt, *s. a.* A creating; a being created; natural disposition.

خلل khàlĕl, *s. a.* Injury, damage, detriment; —كلمك, —ghèlmek, *v.n.* To be received (injury); —ويرمك, —vèrmek, *v.n.* To damage, spoil, hurt, destroy.

خلوت khàlvet, *s. a.* Retirement, solitude, privacy; a private room; a private room in a bath.

خلود khŭlūd, *s. a.* The being eternal.

خلوص khŭlūss, *s. a.* Sincere friendship, devotion; —چاقمق, —chàkmak, *v.a.* To make protestations of friendship, to show a zeal in performing little services as a proof of devotion.

خليج khàlīj, *s. a.* A gulf, a bay, a strait or arm of the sea.

خليع khàlī'', *a. a.* (*in* خليع العذار khàlī''u-'l-''ìzār, *a. a.* Barefaced, shameless).

خليفه khàlīfĕ, *s. a.* A successor to Muhammed in governing the community of believers, a Caliph; the Sultan; (kȁlfa) a school-usher; a clerk in a public office; (قالفه kȁlfa) a builder, an architect; an elder female slave who has others under her, and directs a department; a journeyman artisan who has duly served his apprenticeship.

خليل khàlīl (*fem.* خليله khàlīlé, A wife), *s. a.* An intimate friend; الله—, khàlīlu-'llȁh, The patriarch Abraham.

خم khàm, *a. p.* Crooked, bent; —, *s. p.* A bend, a curl, a fold, a wrinkle; —, khùm, *s. p.* A jar; a drum; the sky.

خمار khŭmār, *s. a.* The headache or nervous feeling caused by a debauch.

خماسى khŭmāssī, *s. a.* A word containing *five* radical letters.

خمبره khùmbara (kùmbara), *s. p.* A bombshell; a child's money-box made of earthenware and round like a bombshell, with only a slit in it, so that the money cannot be got out unless the toy be broken; خمبره‌جى (kùmbaraji), *s. t.* A bombardier; ال خمبره‌سى ĕl-(kùmbarassi), *s. t.* A hand-grenade.

خمر khàmr, *s. a.* Wine.

خمس khŭmss, *s. a.* A fifth part; —, khàmss, *a. a. fem.* Five.

خمسه khàmsa, *a. a. mas.* Five.

خمسى khàmsi, *s. t.* A sprat.

خمسين khàmsīn, *s. a.* The fifty days preceding the vernal equinox; (in Egypt) a sultry noxious wind; (*or* خمسون khàmsūn), *a. a.* Fifty.

خمود khŭmūd, *s. a.* Extinction or lowness (of fire, life, or action).

خمول khŭmūl, *s. a.* Obscurity, neglectedness, low estate.

خميازه khàmyāzé, *s. p.* A gape, a yawn.

خميده khàmīdé, *a. p.* Bent.

خمير khàmīr (khȁmur), *s. a.* Dough (of bread); clay (of which men are made); any plastic material (of which any ware is made).

خميس khàmīss, *s. a.* Thursday.

خناق khùnnȁk, *s. a.* The quinzy.

خنثى khùnsà, *s. a.* An hermaphrodite.

خنجر khànjær (hȁnchar), *s. p.* A large curved dagger.

خند khànd, (*in composition*) خندان khàndān, *a. p.* Who laughs, laughing, smiling.

خندق (hèndek), *s. a.* A ditch; a fosse, a moat.

خنده khàndé, *s. p.* Laughter; a smile; —, *a. p.* Laughing, smiling.

خنزير khìnzīr, *s. a.* A swine, pig, hog.

خنكار khùnkyār, *s. p.* A sovereign, the Sultan.

خو khū (*in composition*), *s. p.* Character, disposition.

خواب khāb, *s. a.* Sleep; a dream, vision.

خواجه khājé (khòja), *s. p.* A gentleman, an esquire in the civil service; (*pl.* خواجكان khòjaghyān); a schoolmaster, teacher, professor; a respectable tributary banker or man of business; خواجكانلق khòjaghyānlĭk, *s. t.* The rank and dignity of an officially recognised civil servant of the government.

خوار khār, *a. p.* Low, vile, abject, despised; (*in composition*), Who eats, drinks, smokes, or receives.

خواص khàwāsss, *s. pl. a.* (*of* خاص khāsss), Special, select people, people of quality; intimate friends; confidential or personal attendants; (*of* خاصه khāsssa), properties, qualities; remarkable objects.

خوان khān, *s. p.* A table or cloth set with food; —, (*in composition*) *a. p.* Who reads, recites, sings, chants; who invites.

خوانده khāndé, *a. p.* Called, invited.

خواننده khānèndé, *s. p.* A singer; a reader; an inviter.

خواه khāh (*in composition*), Who desires, wishes; —, *s. p.* (*in composition*) A wish; —, *c. p.* Either, or; whether, or; —, *ad. p.* Willingly; —وناخواه, —u-nā-khāh, Willingly or unwillingly, voluntarily or forcedly; خاطر خواه khātir-khāh, The mind's desire; خیرخواه khàyr-khāh, *s. p.* A well-wisher; بدخواه bèd-khāh, *s. p.* An evil-wisher.

خواهر khāhèr, *s. p.* A sister.

خواهش khāhish, *s. p.* A wish, desire, longing, inclination.

خوب khòb, khūb, *a. p.* Good; pretty; خوبان khūbān, *s. pl. p.* The beautiful, pretty women.

خود khòd, *s. p.* Self; —, *ad. p.* Even, though; خودبخود khòd-bé-khòd, *ad. p.* Alone, by one's self, of one's own self; خودبین khòd-bin, *a. p.* Self-seeking, egotistical, selfish; —پسند, —pèssènd, *a. a.* Vain, in love with himself, self-admiring.

خور khòr, *a. p.* (*in composition*), Who eats, drinks, smokes, or receives; —, *a. p.* Low, vile, abject, despised; —باقمق, —bàkmak, *v.n.* To look upon with contempt.

خوراته khòrata, *s. t.* A noise of loud voices.

خورد khūrd, *s. p.* Anything to eat or drink, nourishment, food.

خورشید khūrshīd, *s. p.* The sun.

خوره khòra, *s. t.* (*Greek*), Dancing; —دپمك, —(tèpmek), *v.n.* To dance.

خوش khòsh, *a. p.* Agreeable; —, *int. p.* Well, well! —كلدك, —ghèlding! I have been happy to see you! —بولدق, —bùlduk! I have been well received! —كورمك, —ghyùrmek, *v.a.* To admire, see with pleasure and satisfaction; خوشه كچمك khòsha-ghèchmek, *v.n.* To please, give pleasure, give joy and satisfaction, be liked; خوشه كلمك khòsha-ghèlmek (*with a pronoun after* خوش), *v.n.* To appear charming or funny (to some one).

خوشه khūshé, *s. p.* A bunch (of grapes, &c.); an ear (of corn, &c.)

خوف khàvf, *s. a.* Fear, fright, terror; —ا, —et, *v.n.* To fear.

خوك khūgh, *s. p.* A hog, pig, swine.

خون khūn, *s. p.* Blood; خوناب

khūnāb, *s. p.* (Blood mixed with water) hot tears; خون‌آلود khūn-ālūd, *a. p.* Mixed or smeared with blood; خونبار khūnbār, *a. p.* From which blood falls as rain; خونبها khūn-bàhā, *s. p.* The price of blood, blood-money.

خوى khūy, *s. p.* A point of character, disposition; a way, trick; خويلنمق khūylanmak, *v.n.* To be out of temper, sulky, or obstinate; خويلو khùylu, *a. t.* Sulky, obstinate, or passionate.

خيار khìyār, *s. a.* A cucumber; —شنبر, —shènber (shènbé), *s. p.* Cassia.

خيال khàyāl, *s. a.* A kind of puppet-show of the shadows of figures projected on a white screen; the imagination; a chimera.

خياله khàyālé, *s. a.* A spectre.

خيانت khìyānèt, *s. a.* Perfidiousness, treachery; —, *s. t.* A perfidious person; خيانتلك khìyānètlik, *s. t.* Perfidy; a treacherous trick.

خير khàyr, *ad. a.* No; —, *s. a.* Good; —, *a. a.* Good; خيرلو khàyrli, *a. t.* Good, beneficial, bringing advantage, advantageous; خيرات khàyrāt, *s. pl. a.* Good works, charitable or benevolent institutions; خيرخواه khàyr-khāh, *s. p.* A well-wisher; خيرسز khàyrsiz, *a. t.* Good for nothing; uninhabitable (island).

خيره khīré, *a. p.* Dark, sombre.

خيز khīz, *a. p.* (*in composition*), Who rises, gets up.

خيزاب khīzāb, *s. p.* A wave, billow.

خيزان khīzān, *a. p.* Who rises, gets up; —وافتان, —vé-ùftān, Rising and falling.

خيط khàyt, *s. a.* A thread.

خيف khàyf, *s. a.* A fearful, dreadful state of things; —, *int. a.* Alas!

خيل khàyl, *s. a.* Horses, cavalry.

خيلى khàyli, *a. t.* A good deal, much, many; highly.

خيمه khàymé, *s. a.* (*pl.* خيم khìyèm), A tent.

د

د dāl. Tenth letter of the Turkish alphabet, having the value of *d* in English, though sometimes acquiring the sharp sound of *t*. In chronograms and astronomical tables it has the numerical value of 4. In the dates of letters it stands for ذ, and represents, when alone, the month ذى الحجه Zī-'l-hìjjé; but when followed by ا, as دا, the month ذى القعده Zī-'l-kà''dé.

داء dā', *s. a.* A malady, distemper, disease.

دأب dè'b, *s. a.* A custom, usage.

دابه dābbé, *s. a.* A saddle-beast; an animal; دابة الارض dābbétu-'l-àrz, (The beast of the earth) the beast of the Apocalypse, which is to appear in power in the latter days.

داخل dākhil, *s. a.* The interior, inside; داخلى dākhilī, *a. a.* (*fem.* داخليه dākhilìyyé) Relating to the interior; امور داخليه ùmūru-dākhilìyyé, Domestic affairs, home affairs; داخلیه ناظری dākhilìyyé - nāziri, A home minister, Secretary for the Home Department; —او, —ōl, *v.n.* To enter, get in; to be in; to be included.

داد dād, *s. p.* Justice; redress; lamentation; a gift; — (*for* طات tAt), *s. t.* Taste, savour.

دادا dAda, *s. t.* A nursery servant, a nurse for children.

دادانمق dAdanmak (*aor.* دادانور dAdanir), *v.n.* To acquire a great relish or desire for, from having had a slight [taste of.

دادر dāder, *s. p.* A brother.

داده dādé (*in composition*), *a. p.* Which is given; to which is given; —, dAda, *or* دادی dAdi, *s. t.* A nurse for children.

دار dàr, *a. t.* Narrow; —, *ad. t.* Narrowly; —, *s. a.* A house; a town; a country; a world; —, *s. p.* A gallows; — (*in composition*), *a. p.* Who has, possesses, holds, keeps; —الاسلام, dāru-'l-ìsslām, The Mussulman's land; دارالحرب dāru-'l-hàrb, The enemy's country; —بقا, dāri-bākā, The world which fades not; —فنا, dāri-fènā, The world of decay; دارین dārèyn, *s. a. dual,* The two worlds, present and future; —الشفا, dāru-'sh-shìfā, A hospital; —السعادةالشریفه, dāru-'ss-sà''ādéti-'sh-shèrīfé, The female establishment of the Sultan, from which the Chief Eunuch derives his title of دارالسعادةالشریفهاغاسی dāru-'ss-sà''ādéti-'sh-shèrifé-Āghassi; آبدار Āb-dār, *a. p.* Juicy; watered; tempered (steel); lustrous (diamond); خزینه‌دار khàzīné-dār, *s. p.* A treasurer (treasury-keeper); داروکیر dār-u-ghīr, *s. p.* (Have and hold) Battle; دار اغاجی dār-Aghaji, *s. t.* A gibbet, a gallows; a masting machine, shears. [nificence.

دارات dārāt, *s. p.* State, pomp, magdارالمق

دارالمق dàrAlmak (*aor.* دارالور dàrAlir), *v.n.* To grow narrow, shrink, become too narrow. [mon.

دارچین dàrchīn (tàrchin), *s. p.* Cinna-

دارغین dàrghin, *a. t.* Passionate, easily provoked; angry; دارغینلق dàrghinlik, *s. t.* Anger.

دارلمق dArīlmak (*aor.* داریلور dArīlir), *v.n.* To be angry; to become angry; دارلتمق dArīltmak (*aor.* داریلدر dArildir), *v.a.* To anger, put in a passion.

دارمه‌داغین dàrma-dAghin, *a. t.* Very much scattered, dispersed; all to pieces.

دارنده dārendé, *s. p.* A bearer, holder, possessor (of a note, pass, &c.).

دارو dārū, *s. p.* A drug; a medicine; —, *or* داری dàri, *s. t.* Millet; ارناوددارو سی àrnàwut-dàrissi, (Albanian millet) Panicum miliaceum (?); داریسی باشکزه dàrissi-bAshingiza! (May the millet thereof be on your head!) May happiness accrue to you therefrom! (a form of wish expressed at wedding feasts to the parents of the new-married couple). [goods sold by weight).

دراه dàra, *s. t.* (*Italian*), The tare (of

داس dāss, *s. p.* A sickle, reaping-hook.

داستان dāssitān, *s. p.* A tale, story.

داش dàsh, as a Turkish particle, placed at the end of any word, has the signification of our word *fellow*, as, ارقه داش àrk*a*-dash, A fellow-companion, يولداش yòld*a*sh, A fellow-traveller, *or* one in the same line of life; قرنداش kàrn-d*a*sh, A brother or sister (womb-fellow); &c. &c.

داعی dā‘‘ī, *s. a.* (*fem.* داعيه dā‘‘ìyyé), One who prays (for another); a cause, incentive, inviting agent; داعيلرى dā‘‘īléri, (I *or* he) who prays for you, your servant.

داغ dāgh, *s. p.* A branding or cauterising iron; a mark branded by a hot iron; a cautery by iron; —درون, dāghi-‑dèrūn, Inward grief; the black spot in the bottom of the cup of the tulip.

داغتمق dà*ghi*tmak (*aor.* داغيدر dà*ghi*d*i*r), *v.a.* To scatter, disperse; to distribute; to deal, serve out, give out; to disseminate, spread (reports, &c.).

داغلمق dà*ghi*lmak (*aor.* داغلور dà*ghi*l*i*r), *v.n.* To become scattered, dispersed; to fall to pieces, go piecemeal; to separate (an assembly); to become healed without coming to a head (a gathering); to be dissipated (clouds, &c.); to be disseminated, to spread.

داغنق dà*ghi*n*i*k, *a. t.* Scattered, wide apart, not held together.

دافع dāfi‘, *a.* and *s. a.* (*fem.* دافعه dāfi‘*a*), Who repels, expels.

دال dāl (dàl), *s. a.* Name of the letter د; —, dàl, *s. t.* A branch, twig, slip; —, dāll, *a.* and *s. a.* (*fem.* داله dāllé), Who conducts, guides, points out, signifies; دال قلج dàl-k*i*lij, *s. t.* A kind of militia swordsman in olden times; دالقاوق dàl-kàwuk, A buffoon, a willing butt for jokes; دال طبان dàl-t*a*bàn, *s. t.* A great walker. (In these three terms, the word دال dàl is the imperative of دالمق dàlmak, [q.v.)

دالاق dàlak, *s. t.* The spleen.

دالغج dàlgh*ij*, *s. t.* A diver.

دالمق dàlm*a*k (*aor.* دالار dàlar), *v.n.* To dive, plunge (in the water, into business, &c.); to doze; to be in a fit of abstraction, to be absorbed in thought, in study, in reading, &c.; اويقويه— ùykuy*a*—, *v.n.* To go fast asleep; —باشنى bàshini—, *v.n.* To duck down or flinch by stooping the head; دالدرمق dàld*i*rmak (*aor.* دالدرر dàld*i*r*i*r), *v.a. causal*, To plunge or bury, by pushing (one thing into another); to lay (a twig or branch so as to root); to speak ill of, traduce, backbite.

دام dàm, *s. t.* The roof of a house; a house (as a unit and as we say *a hearth*); —, dām, *s. p.* A trap, snare, gin; —, dāmé (*fem.* دامت dāmet), *int. a.* May he (she *or* it) endure!

داماد dāmād, *s. p.* Son-in-law (*or* brother-in-law, in the case of the Sultan's sister's husband) by marriage.

دامن dāmen, *s. p.* The skirt (of

a garment, of a mountain, &c.); دامنبوس dāmen-būss, *a. p.* Who kisses one's skirt; دامنبوسی dāmen--būssī, The ceremony of kissing the skirt of a superior.

دامه dāma, *s. t.* The game of draughts; —طاشی, —tāshi, A draughtsman, man at draughts.

دان dān, *a. p.* (*in composition*), Who knows, understands; —, *s. p.* (*in composition*), A holder, case, sheath, &c.

دانا dānā, *s. p.* A person of great learning, a sage; —, dāna, *s. t.* A calf.

دانش dānish, *s. p.* Knowledge, learning; —انجمن ènjumèni-dānish, The Imperial Academy of Science of Constantinople; دانشمند dānishmènd, *s. p.* A scholar, learned person.

دانشمق dānishmak (*aor.* دانشور dānishir), *v.n.* To apply to for advice or permission.

دانه dāné (tānē), *s. p.* A separate grain or berry; a separate unit of any sort; a cannon or musket ball; the grain which baits a trap for birds; دانه‌لو (tānéli), *a. t.* Grainy, gritty, composed of grains; —, dāna, *s. t.* A calf.

دانیمارقا Dànimàrka, *s. t.* Denmark.

داور dāver, *s. p.* A prince, ruler, judge; a sovereign, monarch; God.

داورانمق dàvranmak (*aor.* داورانور dàvrànir), *v.n.* To start from a state of repose or inattention, and become guarded or vigilant; to put one's self in an attitude of defence; to stir one's self, be active, move; to regain one's footing after a slip, one's health after illness, one's position after a misfortune.

داول dàwul, *s. t.* A big drum; a common drum of any kind except a military drum; a drum (in machinery).

داولمباز dàwlumbāz, *s. t.* The paddle-box of a steamer. [misfortune.

داهیه dāhìyyē, *s. a.* A calamity, great

دای dày, *s. t.* A maternal uncle, mother's own brother; a friendly title formerly given to middle-aged or old people, especially among the Janissaries; and hence, in Algiers, consecrated at length to the commanding officer of that corps, who frequently became afterwards pasha or regent of the colony: hence our misnomer of Dey, as applied to the latter officer.

دائر dā'ir, *a. a.* Concerning, relating to, about; دائراً ما دار dā'iran-mā-dār, *s.* and *ad. a.* All round, all the parts surrounding.

دائره dā'irē, *s. a.* A circle; a tambourine; a suite of apartments; a sphere of duty; a suite of attendants; —نصف nìssfi-dā'irē (nìssif—), A semicircle; —تربیع tèrbī'i-dā'irē, The quadrature of the circle.

دائم dā'im (*fem.* دائمه dā'imē), *and* دائمی dā'imī (*fem.* دائمیه dā'imiyyē), *a. a.* Enduring, incessant, constant, lasting, permanent, fixed, established, eternal; دائما dā'imā, *ad. a.* Always, for ever; continually, incessantly.

داءن dāʿin, *s. a.* A creditor.

دايه dāyé, *s. t.* A nursing slave-woman, bought with her infant to act as wet-nurse to her owner's infant.

دب dùb, *s. a.* A bear; دب اكبر dùbbi-ekbèr, The great bear.

دباغ dèbbāgh (tàbak), *s. a.* A tanner; دباغخانه (tàbak)-khāné, A tannery, tan-yard.

دباغت dìbāghàt, *s. a.* The tanner's art; tannery; a being tanned, tanning.

دبدبه dèbdébé, *s. a.* Pomp, state.

دبر dùbr, *s. a.* The backside.

دبستان dèbisstān, *s. p.* A school.

دبوس dèbbūss, *s. a.* (*t.* طوپوز tòpuz), A club, mace of arms.

دبير dèbīr, *s. a.* An administrator.

دپرنمك dèprenmek (*aor.* دپرنور dèprè-nir), *v.n.* To move; to get up; to show signs of life.

دپه (tèpé), *s. t.* The summit of anything; the crown of the head; a hill, hillock, mound, heap; دپه‌لمك (tè-pélémek), *v.a.* To kill by knocking on the head; دپه‌لنمك tèpélenmek, *v.n.* To be killed, be knocked on the head.

دتمك dìtmèk (*aor.* ديتر dìter), *v.a.* To pull linen cloth into lint or the like, to shred by pulling.

دجال dèjjāl, *s. a.* The false prophet or Antichrist who is to appear in the latter days.

دجله Dèjlé, *s. t.* The river Tigris.

دجيل Dùjèyl, *s. t.* The Little Tigris, a branch of the Tigris.

دخان dùkhān, *s. a.* Smoke; tobacco.

دختر dùkhter, *s. p.* A girl; a daughter; —رز dùkhtéri-rèz, Wine (the daughter of the grape).

دخل dàkhl, *s. a.* Intervention, meddling; influence.

دخمه dùkhmé, *s. p.* A grave, tomb.

دخول dùkhūl, *s. a.* An entering, entrance; a commencing, commencement; an entering into one's presence; the consummation of marriage; the positive act of sexual intercourse; ا—, —et, *v.n.* To enter.

دخی dàkhi, *c. t.* Also; and; even; —, (*for* دها dàhā), *ad. t.* More.

دده dèdé, *s. t.* A grandfather; title given to dervishes.

در dèr, *s. p.* A door; a gate; —, *pr. p.* In; into; on the subject of, about; —سعادت, dèri-sàʿʿādet, (The gate of felicity) Constantinople; دربدر dèr-bé-dèr, (From door to door), *s. p.* A vagabond, a mendicant; —, (tèr), *s. t.* Sweat, perspiration; transpiration; —, dir *or* dir, The Turkish *vinculum* of grammar or logic, signifying *is*, or *it is*; —, dùrr, *s. a.* A pearl; ا . . . . . —, dèr- . . . . . -et, *v.a.* To get (something) into (something else, as custody, bosom, store, &c.).

دراج dùrrāj, *s. p.* A francolin, a kind of partridge (?)

دراز dìrāz, *a. p.* Long; —دورو dūr-u-dìrāz, *ad. p.* Far and away; in great detail.

دراقى dùrrākī, *s. p.* A nectarine.

درايت dìrāyet, *s. a.* Intelligence; درايتلو dìrāyetli, *a. t.* درايتكار dìrāyetkyār, *s. p.* Intelligent.

دربار dèrbār, *s. p.* The court of a sovereign.

دربان dèrbān, *s. p.* A porter, door-[keeper.

دربند dèrbend (dèvrent), *s. p.* A place easily guarded, as a bridge, mouth of a valley, pass, &c.; a guard-house in the country, usually in some such position; دربندجى (dèvrentchi), *s. t.* A rural guard, coast-guardsman; ا—, dèr-bènd-et, *v.a.* To bind in fetters.

درپيش ا dèr-pīsh-et, *v.a.* To introduce, bring forward, advance, say.

درت dùrt, *a. t.* Four; دردنجى dùrdinji, *a. t.* The fourth.

دراچ Dìrāch, *s. t.* Durazzo in Albania.

درج dèrj, *s. a.* The placing anything in a casket; the introducing any word or phrase in a written paper, inserting; —, dùrj, *s. a.* A casket; ا—, dèrj-et, *v.a.* To insert, introduce.

درجه dèréjé, *s. a.* (*pl.* درجات dèréjāt), A step of a ladder or stairs; a degree of a circle; a degree or rank in dignity; a degree or mansion in heaven; the relative degree of any quality; درجه درجه dèréjé-dèréjé, *ad. t.* By degrees, little by little; in degrees; into degrees.

درخت dìrakht, *s. p.* A tree.

درخشان dìrakhshān, *a. p.* Brilliant, effulgent, shining, glittering.

درخواست dèr-khāsst, *s. p.* A prayer, request.

درد dèrd, *s. p.* Ailment, pain; sickness; grief, trouble, anxiety; —, dùrd, *s. p.* Lie, dregs, sediment, grounds; دردلشمك dèrdleshmek, *v.n.* To confide mutually to one another each other's griefs; دردلو dèrdli, *a. t.* دردمند dèrdmènd, دردناك dèrdnāk, *a. p.* One in pain or in grief and trouble.

دردست dèr-dèsst, *a. p.* In hand, in [course of preparation.

درر dùrer, *s. pl. a.* (*of* در dùrr), Pearls; دررباز dùrer-bār, *a. p.* From which pearls drop as rain.

درز dèrz, *s. t.* The pointing with mortar or cement the joints of masonry or brickwork; ا—, —et, *v.a.* To point.

درزى (tèrzi), *s. p.* A tailor; —, dùrzī, *s.* and *a. a.* A Druze, Druze; درزى طاغى dùrzī-dāghi, Mount Lebanon.

درس dèrss, *s. a.* A lesson; a lecture; درسعام dèrssi-ʻāmm, *s. a.* A public lecture; —المق, —almak, *v.n.* To take a lesson; to have a lesson assigned; —ويرمك, —vèrmek, *v.n.* To give a lesson; to set a lesson; —اوقومق, —okumak, *v.n.* To study; to study a lesson.

درست dùrusst, *a. p.* Right, true; healthy; correct, exact, as it should be; نادرست nā-dùrusst, *a. p.* Bad, as it should not be; false; incorrect

درستی dùrussti, *s. p.* Rightness; تندرست tèndùrùsst, *a. p.* Right in body.

درشت dùrùsht, *a. p.* Rough, gross.

درك dèrk, *s. a.* A reaching, attaining; a comprehending; comprehension; ا—, —et, *v.a.* To reach, attain; to comprehend; to have lived long enough ago to have seen (some person).

دركات dèrékyāt, *s. pl. a.* (*of* دركه dèréké), The degrees of hell or perdition, the one lower than the other.

دركار dèr-kyār, *a. p.* Evident, manifest; acting, in action, in operation.

دركاه dèr-ghyāh, *and* دركه dèrghèh, *s. p.* A gateway, doorway, porch, portico; the court of a sovereign, of God.

درلو dùrlu (tùrlu), *s. t.* A sort, kind, manner, species; a dish of mixed meats and vegetables; — —, tùrlu-tùrlu, *a. t.* Of various kinds.

درمان dèrmān, *s. p.* Strength of body; physic, medicine; a remedy.

درميان dèr-mìyān, *a. p.* In the midst; on the tapis; ا—, —et, *v.a.* To introduce a subject.

درن جبلی Dèrn-jèbeli, *s. t.* The Atlas mountains.

درنده dìrendé, *a. p.* (A beast of prey) which tears its victims.

درنك dìrèngh, *s. p.* Delay, procrastination.

درواز dèrvāz, دروازه dèrvāzé, *s. p.* A door, a gate.

درود dùrūd, *s. p.* Greeting, salutation, praise.

دروغ dùrūgh, *s. p.* A lie, falsehood, untruth.

درون dèrūn, *s. p.* The inside, inner part; the heart, mind.

درويش dèrvish, *s. p.* A poor man; a kind of monk or friar, of which there are many sorts.

دره dèré, *s. t.* A valley; a stream of water.

درهم dìrhèm, *s. a.* A drachm, of which 400 make one *okka*, and about 140 a pound avoirdupois; general name for silver money; —, dèr-hèm, *a. p.* Together; —برهم, dèr-hem-bèr-hem, *a. p.* Jumbled together, confused, in confusion.

دری dèri, *s. t.* The skin of animals, the hide, fell.

دريا dèryā, *s. p.* The sea, ocean.

دريچه dèrīché, *s. p.* A window; a loop-hole; a wicket.

دريغ dìrīgh, *s. p.* A refusal; —, and دريغا dìrīgha, *int. p.* Alas! بيدريغ bī-dìrīgh, *a. p.* Who never refuses a request; ا—, —et, *v.a.* To refuse, to withhold, not to grant (a request).

درين dèrin, *a. t.* Deep, profound.

دزد dùzd, *s. p.* A thief; a robber.

دزكين dìzghin, *s. t.* The reins, a rein; طولو دزكين dòlu-dìzghin, *ad. t.* At full gallop.

دست dèsst, *s. p.* The hand; دستدرازی dèsst-dìrāzī, *s. p.* The stretching out of the hand for oppression or rapine.

دستار dèsstār, *s. p.* The cloth which, wound round the head, forms the turban.

دسترس dèsst-rèss, *a. p.* Whose hand reaches (the desired object), successful.

دستره (tèsstérÉ), *s. p.* A hand-saw.

دستگاه dèsst-ghyāh (tèzghyāh), *s. p.* A place for handiwork, a bench, a loom, a frame, a slip (for building ships), &c., &c. [another by the hand.

دستگیر dèsst-ghīr, *s. p.* One who takes

دستور dèsstūr, *s. p.* A minister of state; permission, leave; —العمل, dèsstūru-l-''ĀmEl, *s. a.* An exemplar, guide for conduct; —, —! With your permission! Get out of the way! Clear the road!

دسته dèsstÉ, *s. p.* A quire (of paper); a packet, a dozen or any number in which goods are usually made into packets; a bunch; a pestle.

دستی (tèssti), *s. p.* A pitcher, a jug.

دستیار dèsst-yār, *s. p.* A friend, helper; دستیاری dèsst-yārī, *s. p.* Assistance.

دسیسه dèssīssÉ, *s. a.* A stratagem; a trick, piece of knavery.

دشت dèsht, *s. p.* The uncultivated open country.

دشمك dèshmek (*aor.* دشر dèshEr), *v.a.* To open an abscess with a lancet.

دشمن dùshmEn, *s. p.* An enemy.

دشنام dùshnĀm, *s. p.* An invective; ا—, —et, *v.n.* To revile.

دشوار dùshvār, *a. p.* Difficult.

دعا dù''ā, *s. a.* A prayer; خیر— khàyri-dù''ā, A blessing, or prayer for one's good; بد— bèd-dù''ā, A curse, malediction, prayer against one; دعالرله dù''ālErla! Good bye! With (our) prayers! دعالرایدیکز dù''ālEr-èdingiz, Pray present my compliments! باقی الدعا bākī-èd-dù''ā, We say nothing more, but offer prayers (for you)! (*a usual way of finishing a letter*); ا—, —et, *v.n.* To offer a prayer (to God); to pray (for anyone by way of thanks);

دعاجی dù''āji, *s. t.* One who prays for another. [pillar.

دعامت dì''āmet, *s. a.* A prop, support,

دعاوی dà''āvī, *s. pl. a.* (*of* دعوی dà''wà), Lawsuits, causes; —ناظری, dà''āvī-nāzìri, *s. t.* The Minister of Justice (whose old title was چاوش باشی chàwush-bĀshi, q. v.).

دعوا *and* دعوی dà''wà, *s. a.* An assertion, thesis, proposition; a pretension, claim; a lawsuit, cause; دعواجی dà''wàji, *s. t.* A claimant, plaintiff, suitor, complainant; دعوالو dà''wàli, *a. t.* (A person) with great pretensions; ا—, —et, *v.n.* To claim; to open a lawsuit; to raise a pretension.

دعوت dà''vet, *s. a.* An inviting, an invitation; a courting, seeking (harm, &c.); ا—, —et, *v.a.* To invite; to court, seek. [care, bother.

دغدغه dàghdagha, *s. a.* Turmoil, trouble,

دف dèf, *s. p.* A tambourine.

دفتر dèftEr, *s. p.* (*pl.* دفاتر dèfātir), A register, note-book, account-book; a list, note, inventory; دفتردار dèftEr-dār, Title formerly of a kind of Finance Minister; now, of the highest class finance agents of a whole province; دفترخانه dèftɛr-khānɛ́, The archives, especially of the finance department; دفاترخاقانيه dèfātiri-khākānìyyɛ́, The imperial registers of fiefs, a kind of Doomsday-book, showing the value and possessor of every fief in the empire, with all other necessary particulars.

دفع dèf'', s. a. A repelling, driving away; ا—, —et, v.a. To drive away, repel.

دفعه dèf''à, s. a. (pl. دفعات dèf''āt), A time of repetition; بودفعه bù-dèf''à, This time; بر دفعه bìr-dèf''à, Once; چوق دفعه chòk-dèf''à, Many times; دفعةً dèf''àtan, ad. a. At once.

دفن dèfn, s. a. A burying; burial; ا—, —et, v.a. To bury.

دفنه dèfnɛ́, s. t. (Greek, δαφνη), The bay-tree.

دفينه dèfīnɛ́, s. a. Buried treasure.

دق dàkk, s. a. A knocking; ا—, —et, v.n. To knock (at the door).

دقت dìkkàt, s. a. Care, attention; ا—, —et, v.n. To be attentive, take pains.

دقيق dàkīk, a. a. Thin, fine; subtle; nice, fine-drawn, delicate; —, s. a. Flour.

دقيقه dàkīka, s. a. A minute of time or of an arc; a delicate point, subtle question.

دك dèk, s. t. A trick, piece of deceit; —, a Turkish particle of the nature of an adverb of space or time, following the dative preposition, the two together having the signification of *till, until, as far as*; it sometimes becomes دكين dèghin. Ex. يارينه‌دك yàrinɛ́-dek, *or* يارينه‌دكين yàrinɛ́dèghin, Until to-morrow, by to-morrow.

دكان dùkkyān (dùkɛ̀n), s. a. (pl. دكاكين dèkyākīn), A shop; دكانجى dùkky-ānji, s. t. A shopkeeper.

دكرمن dèghirmɛn, s. t. A mill; a mill worked by horses; صو دكرمنى sù-dèghirmɛ́ni, A water-mill; ال دكرمنى ɛ̀l-dèghirmɛ́ni, A hand-mill; دكرمنجى dèghirmɛ̀nji, s. t. A miller.

دكرمنلك Dèghirmɛnlik, s. t. Milo, an island of the Archipelago.

دكرمى dèghirmi, a. t. Round, circular.

دكز dèngiz, s. t. The sea.

دكش dìghish, s. t. An exchanging; —, dìkish, s. t. Sewing, needle-work; a seam; ا—, dìghish-et, v.a. To exchange; —يرى, dìkish-yɛ̀ri, s. t. A dream.

دكشمك dìghishmek (aor. دكشر dìghishir), v.n. To change, become altered, or different, or other than before; دكشدرمك dìghishtirmek (aor. دكشدرر dìghishtirir), v.a. To change, make different, alter, substitute another in lieu of.

دكل dìghil, ad. t. Not; not only, not merely.

دكلمك dìkilmek (aor. ديكلور dìkilir), v.n. To stand bolt upright; —, v. p. (see دكمك); — *or* دكله‌مك dìnglɛ́-mek (aor. دكلر dìnglɛr) (dīnɛ́mek, aor. dīnɛ́), v.a. To listen to, give ear to; to obey, to mind.

دكلنمك dìnglɴnmek (*aor.* دكلنور dìng-léɴir) (dīɴɴnmek, *aor.* dīɴèɴir), *v.n.* To rest one's self, take breath.

دكلو dìnglʊ, *s. t.* A kind, sort, manner.

دكلهمك dìngléɴmek (see دكلمك dìngléɴmek).

دكمك dìkmek (*aor.* ديكر dìkɛʀ), *v.a.* To sew, stitch; to plant; to set, set up; —, dèghmek (*aor.* دكر dèghɛʀ), *v.n.* To touch; to hit, strike, attain; to be worth; —, dīngmek (*aor.* ديكر dīngɛʀ), *v.n.* To cease (rain, &c.).

دكمه dèghmé, *a. t.* Not every one, especially if of no particular account; دكمه‌حال‌ايله dèghmé-hāl-ila, Not easily, not readily; دكمه‌ده dèghmédé, *ad. t.* Not very likely, hardly.

دكنك dèghnek, دينك dèynek, *s. t.* A stick, staff, wand; قولتق‌دكنكى kòl-tʊk-dèghnéghi, A crutch (staff for the armpit).

دكورمك dèghirmek (*aor.* دكورر dèghirir), *v.a.* To cause to reach.

دل dìl, *s. t.* The tongue; language; a spit of land or sand, an isthmus; intelligence (got by spies, prisoners, or reconnoitering); —, *s. p.* The heart; ترازونك دلى tèrāzining-dìli, The tongue of a pair of scales; دل بالغى dìl-bʌlighi, A sole, a small flat-fish; دل التى dìl-ʌlti, A complaint in which the tongue becomes inflamed underneath; دل اوغلانى dìl-òghlʌni, A student of languages attached to an embassy or consulate in Turkey; طاتلو دل tʌtli-dil, Soft words; طاتلو دللو tʌtli-dìlli, Who uses soft or kind words; دل المق dìl-ʌlmak, To gain intelligence (of the enemy's state and movements); دلنى طوتمق dìlini-tʊt-mak, To hold one's tongue or peace; دلمك اوجنده‌در dìliming-ʊ̃jʊnda-dir, It is at the end of my tongue; دلسز dìlsiz, *a.* and *s. t.* Dumb, mute; a dumb person; از دل و جان èz-dìl-u-jān, *ad. p.* With all my heart and soul.

دلاك dèllāk (tèllāk), *s. a.* A servant in a bath who shampoos, scrubs, soaps, and wipes the bathers.

دلال dèlāl, *s. a.* Coquetry, blandishments; —, dèllāl, *s. a.* One who guides or points out the way in any business; (tèllāl) a broker, an auctioneer, a public crier; دلاليه dèllā-lìyyé, *s. a.* A broker's fee.

دلالت dèlālet, *s. a.* A pointing out, showing; an indication; ا—, —et, *v.n.* To act as a guide, to point out things; to be indicative, significative.

دلاور dìl-āvèr, *s. p.* A man of heart and courage. [fragrant.

دلاويز dìl-āwīz, *a. p.* Heart-ravishing;

دلبر dìlbɛʀ, *a. p.* Pretty, beautiful.

دلبند dùlbend (tùlbent), *s. t.* Muslin.

دللشمك dìllɛshmek (*aor.* دللشور dìllè-shir), *v.n.* To communicate with each other by letter, message, or conversation.

دللنمك dìllɛnmek (*aor.* دللنور dìllènir),

v.n. To set to and begin talking and grumbling.

دلمك dèlmek (*aor.* دلر dèlɪʀ), *v.a.* To make a hole in *or* through; to pierce, bore, open; — *or* دلهمك dìlémek (*aor.* ديلر dìlɪʀ), *v.a.* To wish for; to ask for.

دلنمك dèlinmek (*aor.* دلينور dèlinir), *v.n.* or *p.* To be pierced with a hole; to get a hole.

دلو dèlv, *s. a.* The sign Aquarius.

دلورمك dèlirmek (*aor.* دلورر dèlirir), *v.n.* To go mad (*provincial*).

دلى dèli, *s. t.* A madman; a kind of irregular trooper in olden times; —, *a. t.* Mad, insane, foolhardy, imprudent, queer, foolish, strange, original, &c.; دليقانلو dèli-kanli, *s. t.* A lad, young man (whose blood is not yet cooled down).

دليجه dèlija, *a. t.* Somewhat mad or extravagant; —, *s. t.* A kind of wild darnel (?).

دلير dìlīr, *s. p.* A brave man, hero.

دليك dèlik, *s. t.* A hole; —, *a. t.* Having a hole in it.

دليل dèlīl, *s. a.* (*pl.* دلائل dèlā'il, *and* ادله èdìllé), Anything indicative or which serves to guide; a symptom; a proof; an argument.

دليم *or* دلم dìlim, *s. t.* A slice; a quarter (of an orange).

دم dèm, *s. a.* (*pl.* دما dìmā), Blood; —, *s. p.* A moment, instant; a breath; a word; —, dùm, *s. p.* The tail (of animals).

دمار dèmār, *s. a.* Perdition, destruction, ruin.

دماغ dìmāgh, *s. p.* The palate, roof of the mouth; —, *s. a.* The brain.

دمت dèmet, *s. t.* (*Greek*, δεματι), A bunch, a bundle; چيچك دمتى chìchek-dèméti, A nosegay.

دمدمه dèmdémé, *s. p.* The buzz or murmuring noise of a number of people speaking or moving.

دمساز dèmsāz, *s. p.* A friend, confidant, companion of the same mind.

دمشق Dàmàshk, *s. t.* Damascus.

دموع dùmū'', *s. pl. a.* (*of* دمع), Tears.

دموى dèmévī (*fem.* دمويه dèméviyyé), *a. a.* Sanguine (temperament).

دمياط Dìmyàt, *s. t.* Damietta.

دمير *or* دمور *or* دمر (*for* تيمور tīmūr) démir, *s. t.* Iron; a ship's anchor; fetters; an iron instrument; دميرلو dèmirli, *a. t.* Anchored, at anchor; دميرلمك dèmirlémek, دمير آتمق dèmir-àtmak, *v.n.* To anchor, cast anchor.

دمين dèmin, *ad. t.* Just now, but a minute ago.

دن dan, *pr. t.* Of, from, out of, by, for, through.

دنائت dènā'àt, *s. a.* Lowness, vileness, baseness, meanness.

دنبلك dùnbélek, *s. p.* A tom-tom, small kettle-drum.

دنج dìnj, *a. t.* Hale, hearty (old man).

دندان dèndān, *s. p.* A tooth.

دندانه dèndāné, *s. p.* Anything like a tooth, as those of a wheel, a saw, of writing.

دنك dènk, *s. t.* A half-load of a pack-horse, a bale, a pack; the trim of a boat or ship; an equipoise, counter-balance; —, *a. t.* Equipoised, balanced, trimmed, in trim.

دنگل dìnghil, *s. t.* An axle-tree.

دنی dènī, *a. a.* Mean, base, low, vile.

دنیا dùnyā, *s. a.* This *lower* world, the world; —قدر, dùnyā-kādar, Ever so much; عالم دنیا "ālémi-dùnyā, The nether world, this world; ینگی— yèngi-dùnyā, (The new world) America; a particular size of timber.

دنیوی dùnyévī, *a. a.* Worldly, pertaining to this world, temporal.

دو dù, *a. p.* Two; دوم dùwum, *a. p.* The second.

دوا dèvā, *s. a.* (*pl.* ادویه èdvìyyé), Physic, medicine, a remedy.

دوات dèwāt (dìvit), *s. a.* An inkstand (with a tube for pens attached).

دوار dèvwār, *a. a.* Which turns round, rotates, revolves continually.

دوازده dùvāzdeh, *a. p.* Twelve.

دوام dèwām, *s. a.* Uninterrupted duration; uninterrupted application or attendance, assiduity; علی الدوام "ālé-'d-dèwām, *ad. a.* In an uninterrupted manner; دوامسز dèwāmsiz, *a. t.* Inconstant, not constant in attendance, not assiduous.

دواهی dèwāhi, *s. pl. a.* (*of* داهیه dā-hìyyé), Calamities.

دوباره dù-bāré, *s. p.* Deuces at dice; —, *s. t.* A trick, piece of knavery;

دوباره جی dùbāraji, *s. t.* A knave, trickster.

دوت dùt, *s. t.* A mulberry.

دوچار dūchār, *a. p.* Who is a prey to, subject, exposed; —او, —òl, To be a prey (to anything disagreeable), to suffer, be subject, exposed.

دوحه dèvha, *s. a.* A garden.

دوخته dūkhté, *a. p.* Sewed; embroidered, worked.

دود dūd, *s. a.* A worm; a caterpillar; —, *s. p.* Smoke; —الحریر, dūdu-'l-hàrīr, The silk-worm; —دل, dūdi-dìl (Smoke of the heart), A sigh.

دوداق dùdak, *s. t.* A lip.

دودك dùduk, *s. t.* A fife, flute, pipe, pandean pipe; دودکجی dùdukju, A fifer.

دودمان dūdmān, *s. p.* A house, family, race, dynasty.

دودو dùdu, *s. t.* An Armenian lady.

دور dèvr, *s. a.* A revolving; a revolution; a period, time; —ا, —et, *v.n.* To revolve; —, *v.a.* To turn round; to turn over; to give over, make over, deliver (into the charge of another); —دائم, dèvri-dā'im, Perpetual revolution (motion); دوریه dèvrìyyé, *a. a. fem.* Name of certain jurisdictions and the judges thereof, who remove from the one to the other without further promotion; —, dūr, *a. p.* Distant, far off; دورادور dūr-ā-dūr, *a. p.* Very distant; far apart.

دوراق dùrak, *s. t.* A staying, stopping, *in* دوراق یری dùrak-yèri, *s. t.* A stop, a place where a pause can be made in reading or writing.

دوران dèvérān, *s. a.* Circular motion, rotation, revolution; —, dèvrān, *s. p.* Time, fortune, the world, age.

دورباش dūr-bāsh (Be distant), *s. p.* A staff or mace.

دوربين dūr-bīn (dùrbun), *s. p.* A telescope; —, *a. p.* Far-seeing, far-sighted.

دورتمك dùrtmek (*aor.* دورتر dùrter), *v.a.* To push, jog; دورتشدرمك dùrtushdurmek, *v.a.* To push or jog (one's mind), stir up to action, remind.

دورلمق dūrulmak (*aor.* دورولور dūrulur), *v.n.* To stand so as to depose its sediment.

دورمق *or* طورمق dùrmak (*aor.* دورر dùrur), *v.n.* To stay, remain; to stop, halt; to hesitate; to stand, stand up; to keep still, quiet, motionless; to cease from any action; to be in any posture; to remain steadfast; to continue in existence.

دورمك dèvirmek (*aor.* دويرر dèvirir), *v.a.* To upset, capsize; to pass (any term of life), be more than, be older than, to turn; to turn over (to anyone's charge); دوريلمك *or* دورلمك dèvrilmek (*aor.* دوريلور dèvrilir), *v.n.* To be upset, turned over.

دوز dùz, *a. t.* Smooth, flat, even, straight, level, horizontal; —, *s. t.* A level spot among mountains; —, dūz, *a. p.* (*in composition*), Who or which sews or stitches or embroiders.

دوزتمك dùzètmek (*aor.* دوزدر dùzèdir), دوزلتمك dùzèltmek (*aor.* دوزلدر dùzèldir), *v.a.* To set straight, put in order; to correct, touch up, finish off.

دوزجه dùzja, *a. t.* Pretty smooth; —, *ad. t.* Flatly (to refuse, &c.).

دوزخ dūzakh, *s. p.* Hell; دوزخى dūzakhī, *s. p.* Anyone doomed to hell.

دوزكون dùzghyun, *s. t.* Paint for the face, rouge or blanc; —, *a. t.* In fit order; دوزكونجى dùzghyunju, A woman who paints the faces of brides.

دوزلتمك dùzèltmek. See دوزتمك.

دوزلمك dùzèlmek (*aor.* دوزلور dùzèlir), *v.n.* To become as it should be, nice, fit, orderly, clean, &c.

دوزمك dùzmek (*aor.* دوزر dùzer), *v.a.* To invent (stories); to have sexual connexion with; دوزمه dùzmé, *a. t.* False, invented, fictitious.

دوزن dùzen, *s. t.* Proper order and adornment (of person or place).

دوست dòsst, *s. p.* A friend; a lover; دوستلق dòsstluk, *s. t.* دوستى dòsstī, *s. p.* Friendship; دوستانه dòsstāné, *a. p.* Friendly (thing).

دوستدار dòsstdār, *s. p.* A friend.

دوش dūsh, *s. p.* The shoulder; —, *s. t.* A dream; nocturnal involuntary pollution; —ازتمق, dūsh-àzitmak, *v.n.* To have a lascivious dream and become polluted; دوش ا dūsh-et, *v.n.* To fall upon, meet.

دوشاخ dūshākh, دوشاخه dūshākha, *s. p.* A kind of pillory.

دوشتمك dùshᴇtmek (*aor.* دوشه‌در dù-shᴇ̀dir), *v.a.* To lay down (carpets, floors, &c.); to furnish (apartments).

دوشرمك dùshurmek (*aor.* دوشورر dù-shurur), *v.a.* (*causal of* دوشمك), To cause to fall, to throw down, trip up.

دوشك dùshèk, *s. t.* A bed; —, dùshuk, *s. t.* An abortion, abortive child.

دوشكون dùshkyun, *a. t.* Fallen in circumstances, in bad circumstances.

دوشمك dùshmek (*aor.* دوشر dùshᴇr), *v.n.* To fall, fall down; to happen; to fall to the lot (of anyone), to be a part of the duty of anyone, be incumbent; —برينك سوزى يره bìrining-sùzu-yèra--dùshmek, To fall to the ground, to be of no use or effect (the words of any person); —, *or* دوشه‌مك dù-shémek (*aor.* دوشر dùshᴇr), *v.a.* To spread, lay, put down (mats, carpets, &c.); to lay down (flooring).

دوشمه *or* دوشه‌مه dùshémé, *s. t.* Flooring, paving, pavement; furniture.

دوشنبه dūshènbih, *s. p.* Monday.

دوشنمك dùshᴇ̀nmek (*aor.* دوشنور dù-shᴇ̀nir), *v.n.* To be or become furnished *or* laid with flooring or pavement; —, dùshunmek (*aor.* دوشونور dùshunur), *v.n.* To be thoughtful, absorbed in thought, melancholy, depressed; to think, reflect; —, *v.a.* To think over, turn over in one's mind, reflect upon.

دوغرامق dòghramak (*aor.* دوغرار dògh-rar), *v.a.* To cut up, cut in pieces or slices, carve (meat).

دوغرامه dòghrama, *s. t.* Joiners' work;

دوغرامه‌جى dòghramaji, *s. t.* A joiner.

دوقشمق dòkʊshmak (*aor.* دوقشور dò-kʊshʊr), *v.n.* To knock mutually against each other (especially heads, and hard-boiled eggs).

دوقنمق dòkʊnmak (*aor.* دوقنور dòkʊ-nʊr), *v.a.* To touch; to affect, to hurt.

دوقومق dòkʊmak (*aor.* دوقور dòkʊr), *v.a.* To weave.

دوكتمك dùkᴇ̀tmek (*aor.* دوكدر dù-kᴇ̀dir), *v.a.* To use up entirely, to make an end of, to finish, to have none left.

دوكش dùghush, *s. t.* A fight, battle; a mode of striking.

دوكلمك dùkyulmek (*aor.* دوكلور dùkulur), *v.n.* To run over (water in a vessel), be spilt; to flow (into anything), discharge itself; to cast themselves, rush pell-mell (into anything); to fall to pieces; to fall (as leaves, hair, &c.); —, *v.p.* To be cast (in a mould); to be poured out; to be scattered about; —, dùghulmek (*aor.* دوكلور dùghulur), *v.p.* To be beaten; to be forged, hammered (iron).

دوكم *or* دوكوم dùghum, *s. t.* A knot.

دوكمك dùkmek (*aor.* دوكر dùkᴇr), *v.a.* To pour, pour out, pour in, pour on; to spill; to shed; to cast (metals); —, dùghmek (*aor.* دوكر dùghᴇr), *v.a.* To beat, thrash, punish with blows; to beat, forge, hammer, work (iron,

&c.); to cannonade, bombard (with artillery).

دوكمه dùkmé, *a. t.* Cast (metal, &c.); —, dùghmé, *a. t.* Wrought, hammered (metal); —, dùghmé (dùymé), *s. t.* A button; دوكمه‌جی dùkméji, *s. t.* A brassfounder; دوكمه‌لمك dùymé-lémek, *v.a.* To button, button up.

دوكندی dùkyundu, *s. t.* Anything spilt or scattered about; a reef of rocks.

دوكنمك dùkènmek (*aor.* دوكنور dù-kènir), *v.n.* To be finished, exhausted, all used up, to come to an end, to expire (a term); —, dùkyunmek (*aor.* دوكنور dùkyunur), *v.n.* To undress, throw off one's clothes, be *en déshabille* after having been dressed; —, dùghunmek (*aor.* دوكنور dùghunur), *v.n.* To beat one's breast or head (in grief, rage, &c.).

دوكون dùghun, *s. t.* A merry-making, a marriage-feast, wedding-feast, a circumcision-feast.

دول dūl, *s. t.* A fœtus in the womb; a widow; دول قاری dūl-kāri, دول عورت dūl-'àvret, A widow-woman; دول یتاغی dūl-yàtàghi, The womb; —, dù-vèl, *s. pl. a.* (*of* دولت dèvlet), States, kingdoms, empires, governments.

دولاب dòlab, *s. p.* Anything which turns round, a wheel, water-wheel, the heavens, a turning cupboard; a common cupboard or closet; a trick, piece of cunning or knavery; the whole affairs of a state, household, or mercantile concern; —قورمق, —kūrmak, *v.n.* To prepare a snare, lay a plot; — چویرمك —chèvirmek, *v.n.* To turn a wheel; to work a plot; to manage affairs.

دولت dèvlet, *s. a.* A state, government, kingdom, empire; prosperity, felicity; —علیه, dèvléti-'àlìyyé (The very high *or* supreme state), The Ottoman Government; (this title of "very high" or "supreme," mistranslated into "*Sublime*" in Europe, is given to no other State); —بهیه‌ء ایران, dèv-léti-bèhìyyé'i-Irān, The "very beautiful" State of Persia: all other governments are entitled —فخیمه, dèvléti-fàkhīmé, The "high ranking" State. This is one of the senseless distinctions remaining from the olden time which require to be abolished in Turkey; in the treaty of Erzeroom, 1847, the title of علیه "àlìyyé," "*very high*," was given to Persia through the management of the author; دولتلو dèvlètlū, *a. t.* The official style by which a Mùshīr, or Pasha of the first class, is addressed in letters; — *or* دولتلی dèvlètli, *a. t.* A familiar style of addressing persons of a certain standing, something equivalent to our "my dear fellow;" دولتخانه dèvlet-khāné, *s. p.* (The house of prosperity) Your house, your honour's house; دولتجه dèvlètcha, *ad. t.* On the part of government and officially.

دولكر dùlgher, *s. t.* A carpenter; —بالغى, dùlgher-bàlìghi, The saw-fish (?).

دومان dùmàn, *s. t.* Smoke; a fog, mist; a cloudiness in the eye injuring the sight; the fumes of wine; the bloom of freshness on fruits; قفا دومان او kàfa-dùmàn-òl, *v.n.* To be fuddled, tipsy.

دومن dùmèn, *s. t.* A rudder; دومنجى dùmènji, *s. t.* A helmsman, steersman, coxswain; دومن نفرى dùmèn-nèféri, *s. t.* The last or lowest man in a squad, or boy in a class; —قوللانمق, dùmèn-kùllànmak (*or* طوتمق tùtmak), *v.n.* To steer, hold the helm.

دون dūn, *a. a.* Inferior, lower; low (price); —, dùn, *s. t.* Yesterday; دون اخشام dùn-àkhsham, Last evening; دون كيجه dùn-ghèyjé, Last night; دون دكل اولسى كون dùn-dìghìl-èvvelsi-ghyùn, The day before yesterday; مادون mā-dūn, *a. a.* Inferior in rank; —, *s. a.* Inferiority of rank, lower rank.

دوناتمق dònatmak, (*aor.* دونادر dònàdir), *v.a.* To equip, rig, fit out; to adorn; to man (a boat); دونانمق dònanmak (*aor.* دونانور dònànir), *v.n.* or *p.* To be equipped, fitted out, rigged; adorned; manned.

دونش dönush, *s. t.* A turning round; a turning back, a return.

دونم dönum, *s. t.* A Turkish land measure of about a quarter of an English acre, being 40 arshins (100 feet) long and broad.

دونمك dönmek (*aor.* دونر döner), *v.n.* To turn round, revolve; to turn, turn over, turn about, turn back, turn away, turn from; to turn into, be changed into; to change one's mind, turn from one idea to another; to change (from any religion); —ادمك باش àdàming-bàshì-dönmek, To swim, feel giddy (a person's head).

دونمه dönmé, *s. t.* One who has changed his religion to become a Mussulman, a renegade.

دونما dònanma, *s. t.* A fleet, squadron; —, *or* قنديل دونماسى kàndīl-dònanmassi, An illumination.

دونيم dū-nīm, *a. p.* In two, in two pieces, in halves.

دوه dèvé, *s. t.* A camel; دوه‌جى dèvéji, *s. t.* A camel-driver; دوه‌تويى dèvé-tùyu, *s. t.* The down of camels, of which stuffs are made; the peculiar yellowish or dun colour of the same; دوه قوشى dèvé-kùshu, The ostrich; دوه ديكنى dèvé-dìkéni, The thistle; دوه‌دن قولاق dèvéden-kùlak, Out of the whole camel, only the ear (a proverb to say that very little has been saved in any disaster; since, when a hired beast of burden dies, the ears are carried to the owner in proof of the death).

دويت dìvìt (dīvit), *s. p.* An inkstand with a tube for pens.

دويرمك dèvirmek (*aor.* دويرر dèvirir),

v.a. To upset, overturn; to pass (any certain year in age); to turn over (anything into another's charge).

دویست dùvīsst, *a. p.* Two hundred.

دویمق dùymak (*aor.* دویار dūyar), *v.a.* To feel, be sensible of; to hear, become aware of, gain intelligence of, learn; —, dòymak (*aor.* دویار dòyar), *v.n.* To become satisfied, appeased, satiated; دویورمق dūyurmak (*aor.* دویورر dūyurur), *v.a. caus.* To cause to feel, or to be felt; to cause to hear, or to be heard; —, dòyurmak (*aor.* دویورر dòyurur), *v.a. caus.* To cause to be satiated, to satisfy, appease.

ده da, dé, *pr. t.* In, at, within the limit of space or possession of; —, *c. t.* And, also (it follows the word like a preposition); —, dèh, *a. p.* Ten; —dih, *s. p.* A village; *a. p.* (*in composition*), Who *or* which gives.

دها dàha, *ad. t.* More.

دهان dìhān, *s. p.* The mouth.

دهر dèhr, *s. a.* Time; the world; دهری dèhrī, *s. a.* One who believes there is no future state, and that this life is all there is.

دهشت dèhshèt, *s. a.* Fear, fright, terror.

دهقان dìhkān, *s. p.* A villager, peasant, [farmer.

دهلیز dèhlīz, *s. a.* A porch, portico, entry, passage.

دهن dìhèn, *s. p.* The mouth.

دهیم dèhīm, *s. p.* A crown, diadem.

دی dè *or* dì! *int. t.* دی بقالم dè-bàkàlim! دی امدی dè-imdi (dè-indik)! Now then! Well! Go on!

دیار dìyār, *s. a.* A country.

دیانت dìyānèt, *s. a.* Piety, exemplary observance of religious duties.

دیب dìb, *s. a.* The bottom of anything.

دیبا dībā, *s. p.* Brocade. [book.

دیباجه dībājé, *s. p.* The preface of a

دیبك dībèk, *s. t.* A large trough or mortar in which things are pounded in quantities.

دیت dìyyèt, *s. a.* The compensation for manslaughter paid to the heirs of the slain person.

دیجور dèyjūr, *a. a.* Very dark (night).

دید dīd, *a. p.* (*in composition*), Which is seen, which is looked upon as (something); صوابدید sàwāb-dīd, What is looked upon as proper, approved; an approval.

دیدار dīdār, *s. p.* The sight of anyone after absence; the face, visage.

دیدنه dèydéné, *s. a.* A custom, usage.

دیده dìdé, *s. p.* The eye; —, *a. p.* (*in composition*), Who has seen, experienced, received, or suffered; نادیده nā-dīdé, *a.p.* Rarely or never seen.

دیده بان dīdé-bān, *s. p.* A watchman, a looker-out for smugglers, &c.

دیدی قودی dèdi-kòdu, *s. t.* Talk, any piece of scandal or gossip.

دیر dèyr, *s. a.* A Christian church, convent, or monastery; a temple; a wineshop.

دیرسك dirsek, *s. t.* The elbow; a knee-piece of timber or metal; a bend; a turn (in a road, river, &c.).

دیرك dīrèk, *s. t.* A post, pillar, column; a mast; انا — *àna*—, A lower-mast; پرووه دیركی prūwa-dìrèghi, The foremast; غراندی دیركی gràndi-dìrèghi, The mainmast; قونطره مجانه دیركی kòntra-màjāna-dìrèghi, The mizenmast; the upper masts are called چبوق chìbùk, *Sticks*.

دیرلك dīrlik, *s. t.* Means or manner of living, livelihood, life.

دیرلمك dīrilmek (*aor.* دیریلور dīrilir), *v.n.* To come to life; to come to life again; to recover one's strength and faculties.

دیروز dīrūz, *s. p.* Yesterday.

دیری dìri, *a. t.* Alive.

دیرین dīrīn, دیرینه dīrīné, *a. p.* Old, ancient, long established.

دیز dìz, *s. t.* The knee; دیز باغی dìz-bàghi, A garter; دیزچوكمك dìz-chùkmek, *v.n.* To kneel, kneel down.

دیزلك dìzlik, *s. t.* Knee-breeches.

دیزمان dìzmàn, *a. t.* Large, big; tall and corpulent.

دیزمك dìzmek (*aor.* دیزر dìzer), *v.a.* To range, draw up in a line; to thread (beads, &c.).

دیزی dìzi, *s. t.* A row, rank, file.

دیش dìsh, *s. t.* A tooth; a cog; a notch; —, dèyish, *s. t.* What is said, assertion; دیش بوداق اغاجی dìsh-bùdàk-àghàji, *s. t.* The ash-tree; دیشجی dìshji, *s. t.* A dentist; دیشلمك dìshlémek, *v.a.* To give a gentle bite.

دیشی dìshi, *a.* and *s. t.* A female (animal); a male or fruitless plant; a female (key or screw, &c.).

دیك dìk, *a. t.* Steep, perpendicular; —, dīgh, *s. p.* A cauldron.

دیكر dīgher, *a. p.* Other, different; another; — كون, dīgher-ghyūn, Altered in appearance or in circumstances.

دیكمك. See دكمك.

دیكن dìken, *s. t.* A thorn, prickle, prick; a sting.

دیلنجی dìlenji, *s. t.* A beggar.

دیلنمك dìlenmek (*aor.* دیلنور dìlènir), *v.n.* To beg as a beggar, go about begging.

دیمك dìmek *or* dèmek (*aor.* دیر dér), *v.a.* To say; to call, to name; to mean, signify.

دیمومت dèymūmet, *s. a.* Continued duration, permanency.

دین dīn, *s. a.* Religion; —, dèyn, *s. a.* Debt; دیندار dīn-dār, *a. p.* Religious, pious; دینسز dīnsiz, *a. t.* Irreligious; دینی dīnī, *a. a.* (*fem.* دینیه dīnìyyé), Pertaining to religion.

دینار dīnār, *s. a.* A gold coin, a sequin.

دینمك dìnmek, dènmek (*aor.* دینور dènir), *and* دینلمك dènilmek (*aor.* دینلور dènilir), *v.n. or p.* To be said, spoken, pronounced; to be given as a name, used as a name.

دیو dèyu (*in conversation* dèyé, *a gerund of* دیمك dèmek, *To say*), Saying;

intending; —, dīv (dèv), *s. p.* A kind of monster or demon.

ديوار dīwār (dŭwAr), *s. p.* A wall; —چكمك, dīwār-chèkmek, To build a wall (along or about a place); ديوارجى dīwārji, *s. t.* A brick-layer.

ديوان dīwAn, *s. p.* A court held in state either by the sovereign, by the Grand Vizier, or by a governor in his province; a complete book of poetry with poems ending in every rhyme by one author, the whole arranged in alphabetical order by rhymes; ديوانخانه dīwAn-khānÉ, A large room or hall where a court is sometimes held; a large hall or antichamber where the servants remain assembled; — افنديسى dīwAn-èfendissi, The official secretary of a governor; —دورمق, dīwān-dŭrmak, *v.n.* To shoulder or order arms (in military exercise); to stand with the arms folded, or one over the other, as a mark of respect; ديوانى dīwānī, *a. a.* Pertaining to a dīwAn; —, *s. p.* A kind of bold, official handwriting used in firmans.

ديوانه dīwānÉ, *s. p.* A madman, lunatic.

ديوث dèyyūss, *s. a.* One who panders to his own wife.

ديوشرمك dèvshirmek (*aor.* ديوشرر dèvshirir), *v.a.* To gather, gather up, collect. [Debts.

ديون dŭyūn, *s. pl. a.* (*of* دين deyn),

ديهيم dīhim, *s. p.* A crown, diadem.

ذ

ذ zāl (zèl), Eleventh letter of the Turkish alphabet, having the value of *z* in English. In chronograms it has the numeral value of 700; and, in the dates of letters, it stands, deprived of its dot, for the month ذى الحجه Zi-'l-hijjÉ.

ذا zā, In the dates of letters, stands, without the dot over the ذ, for the month ذى القعده Zī-'l-kà''dÉ; —, *a. a.* (*in composition, acc. of* ذو zū), Possessing, lord or owner of, endowed with.

ذات zāt, *s. a.* A person's own self; a person or personage of distinction; the essence or identity of any matter; —, *a. a. fem.* Possessing, owner of, endowed with; بالذات bì-'z-zāt, *ad. a.* In person, personally; حد ذاتنده hàddi-zātinda, *ad. t.* In reality, essentially, really; originally; ذات الله zātu-'llAh, God's own self, person, or essence; ذات الجنب zātu-'l-jènb (sAtlijAn), The pleurisy; ذاتى zātī (*fem.* ذاتيه zātiyyÉ), *a. a.* Pertaining to the person or essence of anything, personal, essential, original.

ذال zāl, *s. a.* Name of the letter ذ.

ذاهب او zāhib-ŏl, *v.n.* To fancy, imagine, presume, be led to suppose, infer.

ذائق zā'ik (*fem.* ذائقه zā'ika), *a. a.* Who tastes; قوت ذائقه kŭvvéti-

-zā'ika, or simply ذائقه zā'ika, The sense or faculty of taste.

ذبح zèbh, s. a. A killing (of animals) in sacrifice by fairly cutting their throats; ا—, —et, v.a. To kill in sacrifice.

ذخيره zàkhīré, s. a. (pl. ذخائر zàkhā'ir), Provisions of corn, &c.

ذرارى zèrārī, s. pl. a. (of ذريت zùrrìyyèt), Descendants, progeny, posterity.

ذراع zìrā'', s. a. The Arabic name for the Turkish yard of thirty inches.

ذره zèrré, s. a. An atom, a mote in the sunbeams. [peak of anything.

ذروه zìrvé, s. a. The summit, top, or

ذريت zùrrìyyèt, s. a. Progeny.

ذريعه zèrī''à, s. a. A means, pretext, handle, excuse (in a good sense).

ذكا zèkyā, ذكاوت zèkyāvèt, s. a. Quickness of intellect, intelligence.

ذكر zìkr, s. a. A reciting, mentioning, relating; a repeating, saying (prayers or praises); —, zèker, s. a. The penis; (pl. ذكور zùkyūr) A male, a man; ا—, zìkr-et, v.a. To recite, mention, make mention of, relate: مارالذكر mārru-'z-zìkr, سالف الذكر sā-lifu-'z-zìkr, a. a. The above-mentioned; اتى الذكر ātìyyu-'z-zìkr, The hereinafter-mentioned; ذكرسابق وجهيله zìkri-sābìk-véjhīlé, ad. t. As above mentioned, according to what has already been stated.

ذكى zèkī, a. a. Quick, intelligent.

ذل zùll, ذلت zìllèt, s. a. Dishonour, indignity.

ذلك zālikè, pron. a. This; كذلك kè-zālik, ad. a. Likewise, in like manner, also, furthermore; بناءعلى ذلك bìnā'an-''àla-zālikè, ad. a. For this reason, based upon this consideration.

ذليل zèlīl, a. a. Low in estate, abject.

ذم zèmm, s. a. Blame bestowed; censure; a blaming, censuring, speaking in disparagement of; ا—, —et, v.a. To dispraise, speak in disparagement of, condemn, censure.

ذمت zìmmèt, s. a. The debtor side of one's account, financial or moral; any moral or social duty; tributariship; —اهل èhli-zìmmet, s. t. A tributary; —تبريهٔ tèbrìyyè'i-zìmmet, The clearing one's self of any charge or imputation. [paying non-Muslim subject.

ذمى zìmmī, s. a. A tributary; tribute-

ذنب zènb (pl. ذنوب zùnūb), s. a. A sin; —, zèneb, s. a. A tail.

ذو zū, s. a. (in composition, pl. ذوى zèvī; acc. sing. ذى zī; fem. sing. ذات zāt; fem. pl. ذوات zèwāt), An owner, possessor; ذو اربعة الاضلاع zū-èrba''atu-'l-àzlā'', A quadrilateral figure; ذوذوابه zū-zù'ābé (zū-zèwābé) (Owner of flowing forelocks), A comet.

ذوابه zù'ābé (zèwābé), s. a. A forelock, a dangling tuft of hair.

ذوات zèwāt, s. pl. a. (of ذات zāt), Persons, personages; female possessors.

ذوق zèvk, *s. a.* Fun, amusement, pleasure; ا—, —et, *v.n.* To have pleasure and amusement, to enjoy one's self in pleasure; ذوقلنمك zèvklɴnmek (*aor.* ذوقلنور zèvklɴnir), *v.a.* To mock, laugh at, ridicule; ذوقيات zèvkìyyɑt, *s. pl. a.* (*no sing.*), Pleasures of various kinds.

ذوى zèvī (*in composition*), *s. pl. a.* (*of* ذو zū), Owners, possessors; ذوى العقول zèvī-'l-"ŭkūl, *s. pl. a.* People of intelligence, sane persons.

ذهاب zèhāb, *s. a.* A going forth; a mode of conduct.

ذهب zèheb, *s. a.* Gold. [the memory.

ذهن zìhn, *s. a.* The mind, intellect;

ذهول zùhūl, *s. a.* Neglect, oblivion.

ذى zī (*acc. of* ذو zū, *in composition*), *s. a.* An owner, possessor; ذى القعده zī-'l-kà"dé (Possessor of rest), The eleventh month of the Muhammedan year; ذى الحجه zī-'l-hìjjé (Possessor of the pilgrimage), The twelfth month of the year, in which the ceremonious performance of the pilgrimage takes place at Mecca; ذى قيمت zī-kīmèt, *a. a.* Precious, valuable.

ذيل zèyl, *s. a.* (*pl.* اذيال èzyāl), A skirt; foot of a mountain; an appendix.

ر

ر rā (rì), Twelfth letter of the Turkish alphabet, having the value of *r* in English. In chronograms it has the numeral value of 200, and in the dates of letters it stands, by abbreviation, for the month of ربيع الاخر Rèbī"ʊ-'l-ākhir.

را rā, *s. a.* Name of the letter ر; in dates of letters it stands, by abbreviation, for the month of ربيع الاول Rèbī"ʊ-'l-èvvɛl.

رابطه rɑbita, *s. a.* A bond of union; system, regularity; رابطه لو rɑbitali, *a. t.* Good, capital, excellent; رابطه سز rɑbitassiz, *a. t.* Bad, not as it should be; رابطه ويرمك rɑbita-vèrmek, *v.n.* To put in order, arrange, systematize.

رابع rābi", *a. a.* The fourth; رابعا rābi"ā, *ad. a.* Fourthly.

راتبه rātibé, *s. a.* Fixed salary or allowance; —خوار, rātibé-khōr, *s. p.* One who receives a fixed allowance.

راجح rājih, *a. a.* Better, preferable; superior, perponderant.

راجع rāji", *a. a.* Relative, related, dependent, pertaining; —اول, —ōl, *v.n.* To regard, concern; to affect, touch; to revert to, return to, fall to; to depend, pertain, be related.

راجل rājil, *a. a.* One on foot; راجلا rājilan, *ad. a.* On foot.

راحت rāhat, *s. a.* Repose, ease, tranquillity; —, *a. t.* Comfortable, cosy, convenient, commodious; comfortable, at ease; comfortable, well off, in easy circumstances; —, *ad. t.* Comfortably; quietly; easily, cosily, nicely; ا—, —et, *v.n.* To rest one's self; —او,

—ȯl, *v.n.* To be at ease; ـــبورمق, —dùrmak, *v.n.* To keep quiet; ـــاوطورمق, —ȯturmak, *v.n.* To sit still; to sit comfortably; to live comfortably (in a house); راحت الحلقوم rāhatu-'l-hùlkūm (rāhat-lòkum), A well-known Turkish sweetmeat; راحتسز rāhatsiz, *a. t.* Uneasy, restless; inconvenient.

رادّه rāddé, *s. a.* A rank, point, or degree (of any quality).

راز rāz, *s. p.* A secret.

رأس rè'ss, *s. a.* The head; a summit; the end, extremity; the beginning; a chief man or officer; ـــالمال, rè'ssu-'l-māl, Capital, stock in trade.

راست rāsst, *a. p.* Right (hand); right, true, correct; ـــكلمك, rāsst-ghèlmek, *v.n.* To meet by chance; to happen by chance; ـــكتورمك, rāsst-ghètirmek, *v.a.* To manage so as to meet (some one); راستى rāsstī, *s. p.* Rectitude.

راستق rāsstik, *s. t.* A preparation of copper or antimony, used for blackening the eyebrows of women and children.

راسخ rāssikh, *a. a.* Firm, immovable.

راسم rāssim, *s. a.* Who draws, figures, traces, writes.

راشد rāshid, *a. a.* Sound in judgment; orthodox in belief; خلفاى راشدين khùléfā'i-rāshidīn, The orthodox caliphs.

راشى rāshi, *s. a.* One who gives a bribe to a government officer.

راضى rāzi, *a. a.* Well-pleased, satisfied, content; الله راضى اوله Allāh-rāzi-ȯla! May God be well-pleased! Thank you! God reward you.

راعى rā''ī, *s. a.* A shepherd, pastor; a guardian, protector of subjects.

راغب rāghib, *a. a.* Who has a wish, desire, or longing; desirous.

راف rāf, *s. t.* A shelf.

رأفت rè'fet, *s. t.* The kindness of disposition which leads to pity or clemency; رأفتلو rè'fetlū, *a. t.* Kind, benignant.

رافضه rāfiza, *s. a.* (*pl.* روافض rèwāfiz), The sectators of Ali; رافضى rāfizī, *s. a.* One belonging to the Rafiza sect.

رافع rāfi'', *s. a.* One who lifts up, raises; the bearer, holder up (of a letter, &c.); one who takes away, drives away, does away.

راقم rākim, *s. a.* The writer (of any paper).

راقى rāki, *s. t.* Brandy or spirits for drinking.

راكب rākib, *a. a.* On horseback, or in a carriage, boat, or ship; راكباً rākiban, *ad. a.* Same meanings.

راكد rākid, *a. a.* Stagnant (water or business).

رام rām, *a. p.* Obedient, submissive, submitting.

ران rān, *a. p.* (*in composition*), Who gives course to anything; حكمران hùkm-rān, *s. p.* Who gives course to commands, a commander, a sovereign.

راوند rāvend, *s. p.* The drug rhubarb.

راوى rāvī, *s. a.* A narrator, relater.

راه rāh, *s. p.* A road, way, path; a method, system, custom; شاهراه shāh--rāh, *s. p.* A royal road, a public road, highway.

راهب rāhib, *s. a.* A Christian priest or monk.

رهوان rāhwān, *a. p.* Amble-paced (hack for travelling); *ad. t.* In an amble.

رأى rèʼy, *s. a.* An opinion, manner of seeing, thinking, or judging.

رايت rāyet, *s. a.* A flag, standard.

رائج rāʻij, *a. a.* Which is current among the public.

رائحه rāʻiha, *s. a.* Odour, smell.

رايكان rāyghyān, رايكانه rāyghyānÉ, *s. p.* Anything acquired without an equivalent given.

رب rÀbb, *s. a.* The Lord God (this expression is never used alone); يا ربى yā-rÀbbī, O my God! ربم حقى ايچون rÀbb*i*m-hÀkk*i*-ìchin! (For the verity of my God) As surely as that God truly exists!

ربا rìbā, *s. a.* Interest on money, usury; —, rùbā, *a. p.* (*in composition*), Who carries off or away; اهنربا āhÈn--rùbā, (The iron-snatcher) The magnet; كهربا kèhrùbā, Amber.

رباب rèbāb (rùbāb), *s. a.* A kind of lute, rebeck, or guitar.

رباح rèbāh, *s. a.* Gain, profit in business.

رباط rìbāt, *s. a.* A strong and secure place, formerly always fortified, where travellers, caravans, or military expeditions can take up their quarters on their journey, or on an enemy's frontier.

رباعى rùbāʻʻī, *s. a.* A quatrain; a word containing four radical letters.

ربانى rÀbbĀnī, *a. a.* Divine, pertaining [to God.

رباه rùbāh, *s. p.* A fox.

ربح rìbh, *s. a.* Gain, profit, interest on money.

ربط rÀbt, *s. a.* A fastening, binding, tying; an arranging, regulating, ordering; ا—, —et, *v.a.* To fasten, bind, tie; to arrange, regulate, order.

ربع rùbʻʻ, *s. a.* A quarter, one-fourth; —دائره, rùbʻʻi-dāʻirÉ, A quadrant, the quarter of a circle; —تخته, rùbʻʻi--tàkht*a*, A wooden quadrant marked with lines, for taking the sun's altitude and calculating the time of day; —مسكون, rùbʻʻi-mèssky*ū*n, The inhabited quarter (of the world); orbis pars veteribus notus; ربعيه rùbʻʻìyyÉ, A kind of old gold coin (the *rupee* of India, as to the name).

ربقه rìbk*a*, *s. a.* A halter; ربقهٔ اطاعت rìbk*a*ʻi-ìtāʻʻ*a*t, The halter (yoke) of submission. [ished, carried off.

ربوده rùbūdÉ, *a. p.* Carried away, rav-

ربيع rèbiʻʻ, *s. a.* The spring season; name of the third and fourth months of the Muhammedan year, the third being distinguished as *the first*, and the fourth as *the latter*, ربيع الاول rèbīʻʻu-'l-ÈvvEl, ربيع الاخر rèbīʻʻu--'l-ākh*i*r.

رتبه rùtbÉ, *s. a.* (*pl.* رتب rùteb), A

degree of rank or dignity; a point or degree of quality.

رتق rètk, *s. a.* A closing; رتق وفتق امور rètk-u-fètki-ùmūr, The conduct and management (closing and opening) of public business.

رتيمه rètīmé, *s. a.* A piece of thread wound on a finger as a reminder, like our knotting a handkerchief.

رجا rìjā, *s. a.* A request; —ا, —et, *v.a.* To make a request about.

رجال rìjāl, *s. pl. a.* (*no sing.*) People on foot; the grandees of the empire; (*as a Turkish singular*) a grandee, high civil functionary.

رجب rèjeb, *s. a.* Name of the seventh month of the Muhammedan year.

رجحان rèjéhān, *s. a.* Superiority, preponderance.

رجحانيت rùjhānìyyèt, *s. a.* Preferableness, superior advantage.

رجعت rìj''at, *s. a.* The apparent retrograde motion of a planet.

رجم rèjm, *s. a.* Lapidation, stoning; —ا, —et, *v.a.* To stone; stone to death.

رجيم rèjīm, *a. a.* Epithet applied to the devil as accursed, or driven from heaven by missiles, or as having stones cast at him intentionally by the pilgrims to Mecca. [sugar.

رچل rèchel, *s. t.* A preserve of fruit in

رحلت rìhlet, *s. a.* A journey of emigration. [for holding books.

رحله ràhlé, *s. t.* A kind of reading-desk

رحم ràhm, *s. a.* The womb; the collective body of one's relatives; صلهٔ رحم sìla'i-ràhm, A visit to one's home and relatives after an absence; —, ràhima! May (God) admit (someone) to His mercy! (said of a dead person).

رحمت ràhmet, *s. a.* God's mercy in a future state; rain; —اوقومق, rāhmet-òkumak, *v.n.* To offer the ejaculation, *May God admit him to mercy!*

رحمن (*for* رحمان,) ràhmān, *s. a.* The God of mercy to us in a future state; رحمانى ràhmānī, *a. a.* Divine, pertaining to the God of mercy.

رحموت ràhmūt, *s. a.* The quality of being the God of mercy.

رحيق ràhīk, *s. a.* Wine. [migration.

رحيل ràhīl, *s. a.* Departure, journey,

رحيم ràhīm, *s. a.* The very compassionate God.

رخ rùkh, *s. p.* The cheek; the castle or rook at chess; the fabulous bird *roc.*

رخام rùkhām, *s. a.* Marble. [pineness.

رخاوت ràkhāvèt, *s. a.* Relaxation, su-

رخت ràkht, *s. p.* A horse; goods, traps, furniture of any kind.

رخسار rùkhsar, رخساره rùkhsāré, *s. p.* The cheek; the face.

رخش ràkhsh, *s. p.* A horse. [ing.

رخشان ràkhshān, *a. p.* Brilliant, flash-

رخصت rùkhsat, *s. a.* Permission, authorization, leave; power, authority (to act); —ويرمك, rùkhsat-vèrmek, *v.n.* To give permission; رخصتنامه rùkhsat-nāmé, Letters of authority, full powers; ـــكامله, rùkhsAti-kyāmilé, Full power.

رخنه ràkhné, s. p. A rent, breach, tear, hole; ـــدار, ràkhné-dār, a. p. Rent, breached, torn; wounded, pierced.

رخيص ràkhīss, a. a. Of little value, cheap, low-priced, not in demand.

رد rèdd, s. a. A giving back, rendering, returning, restoring, sending back; refusing, not receiving, not complying with, rejection; ـــا, —et, v.a. To give back, send back, render, return, restore; to refuse, reject; رد جوابـا rèddi-jèwAb-et, v.n. To return an answer. [tle.

ردا rìdā, s. a. A kind of cloak or man-

ردى rèdī, a. a. Bad.

رديف rèdīf, s. a. A veteran who has served five years in the army or navy, and placed in the reserve, but liable to be called out again in case of necessity. [a shameful act.

رذالت rèzālèt, s. a. Ignominy, shame;

رذيل rèzīl, a. a. Dishonoured, dishonourable, shameful.

رز rèz, s. p. A vine; grapes.

رزاق rèzzAk, s. a. God, who provides sustenance for his creatures.

رزانت rèzānèt, s. a. Sedateness, gravity of reflexion.

رزق rìzk, s. a. Our daily bread.

رزم rèzm, s. p. A battle, fight, action, combat.

رزه rèzé, s. t. A rough kind of hinge composed of two slight eye-bolts.

رزين rèzīn, a. a. Sedate, well weighed, grave, maturely deliberated.

رس rèss, a. p. (*in composition*), Who brings, who causes (anything) to reach its destination; نامه‌رس nāmé-rèss, An envoy who brings a letter.

رسالت rèssālèt, s. a. The prophetic office and function.

رساله rìssālé, s. a. (*pl.* رسائل rèssā'il), A small treatise, a tract, pamphlet.

رسام rèsssām, s. a. A painter, draughtsman. [tion.

رستاخيز rèsstākhīz, s. p. The resurrec-

رسم rèssm (rèssim), s. a. A drawing, picture, design, draught, sketch, painting, print; a ceremony, an official observance; a tax, due; رسمى rèssmī, a. a. Official; formal, merely ceremonious; رسمًا rèssmEn, ad. a. In an official manner; in a purely formal manner.

رسن rèssen, s. p. A cord, rope.

رسواى rùssvāy, a. p. Dishonoured, disgraced.

رسوخ rùssūkh, s. a. Firmness, well-groundedness (of opinion), stability.

رسول rèssūl, s. a. A messenger, prophet, apostle, one sent.

رسوم rùssūm, s. pl. a. (*of* رسم rèssm), رسومات rùssūmAt (*pl. of pl.*) Ceremonies; taxes, dues.

رسيد rèssīd, s. p. A note of receipt; ـــا, —et, v.a. To note or mark as having been paid or received (an account).

رسیده rèssīdé, *a. p.* Arrived; matured.

رشته rìshté, *s. p.* Thread, yarn.

رشحه rèshha, *s. a.* Sweat, perspiration, transpiration, transudation.

رشد rùshd, *s. a.* Rectitude of thought, correctness of thinking.

رشك rèshk, *s. p.* Envy; a thing envied.

رشوت rìshvet, *s. a.* A bribe; —يمك, rìshvet-yèmek, *v.n.* To receive bribes.

رشيد rèshīd, *a. a.* Whose opinions and judgment are correct. [observer.

رصاد ràsssād, *s. a.* An astronomical

رصاص ràssāss, *s. a.* Lead; tin.

رصانت ràssānèt, *s. a.* Strength, firmness, solidity.

رصد ràssad, *s. a.* An observing (the heavenly bodies); ا—, —et, *v.a.* To observe; رصدخانه ràssad-khāné, *s. p.* An observatory.

رضا rìzā, *s. a.* Consent, acquiescence; satisfaction, the being pleased, satisfied; —ويرمك, rìzā-vèrmek, *v.n.* To consent, acquiesce, give consent.

رضوان rìzwān, *s. a.* Consent, acquiescence; satisfaction; paradise.

رضى ràdiya! May (God) be pleased (with him)! [ture.

رطوبت rùtūbèt, *s. a.* Dampness, mois-

رعايا rì"āyā, *s. pl. a.* (*of* رعيت rà"ìyyèt). Tributary non-Muslim subjects of Turkey (*vulg.* Rayahs).

رعايت rì"āyet, *s. a.* Respect, deference, reverence, consideration; ا—, —et, *v.n.* To show respect or consideration; to observe, keep, follow, hold sacred; رعاية rì"āyéten, *ad. a.* Out of respect or consideration; رعايتسز rì"āyetsiz, *a. t.* Wanting in respect, disrespectful; رعايتسزلك rì-"āyetsizlik, *s. t.* عدم رعايت "àdémi--rì"āyet, *s. p.* Want of respect, disrespect; رعايتكار rì"āyetkyār, *a. p.* One who shows respect or deference; رعايتكارانه rì"āyetkyārāné, Pertaining to one who shows respect or deference.

رعب rà"b, *s. a.* Terror.

رعد rà"d, *s. a.* Thunder.

رعشه rà"sha, *s. a.* A trembling, shivering. [upon.

رعنا rà"nā, *a. p.* Beautiful, fair to look

رغبت ràghbet, *s. a.* Inclination, wish, desire; ا—, —et, *v.n.* To feel an inclination or desire; رغبتلو ràghbètlū, *a. t.* Dear, for whom friendly feelings exist.

رغماً ràghman, *ad. a.* Out of spite to, so as to vex; —لانفه, ràghman-li-ènfihī, *ad. a.* (So as to rub his nose in the dirt), As a source of vexation to him.

رفاقت rèfākàt, *s. a.* Companionship; the being a companion; ا—, —et, *v.n.* To go in company, act together.

رفاه rèfāh, رفاهت rèfāhèt, رفاهيت rèfāhìyyèt, *s. a.* Ease, comfort, good circumstances.

رفت rèft, *s. a.* A going, departure; رفتيه rèftìyyé, *s. a.* Export dues.

رفتار rèftār, *s. p.* A mode of walking; a manner of conduct. [poached egg.

رفدان ràfadān, *s. t.* A soft-boiled or

رفع rèf", *s. a.* A lifting up, raising; a taking away; ا—, —et, *v.a.* To lift up, raise; to take away.

رفعت rìf"at, *s. a.* Height; elevation; رفعتلو rìf"atlū, *a. t.* Exalted, illustrious. [benignity.

رفق rìfk, *s. a.* Kindness, gentleness,

رفقا rùfakā, *s. pl. a.* (*of* رفيق rèfīk), Companions, comrades, fellows.

رفيع rèfī", *a. a.* High.

رفيق rèfīk, *s. a.* A fellow, comrade, companion.

رفيه rèfīh, *a. a.* Easy or comfortable in circumstances.

رقاب rìkāb, *s. pl. a.* (*of* رقبه ràkabé), Backs of necks where the yoke bears in oxen, emblematic of submission and obedience or subjection. [tition.

رقابت ràkābèt, *s. a.* Rivalry, compe-

رقاص ràkkāss, *s. a.* A dancer; the pendulum or balance-wheel of a watch.

رقبه ràkabé, *s. a.* The back of the neck where the yoke presses in oxen, emblematic of submission and obedience or subjection.

رقت rìkkàt, *s. a.* Thinness, slightness; pity; compassion felt inwardly; —قلب, rìkkatì-kàlb, Tenderness of heart.

رقص ràkss, *s. a.* Dancing, a dance; ا—, —et, *v.n.* To dance; to spin round as the Mevlevi dervishes do.

رقعه rìk"à, *s. a.* The common handwriting used in letters and business; a piece of paper, parchment, or cloth.

رقم ràkam, *s. a.* The Arabian cyphers of arithmetic; arithmetic; writing.

رقيب ràkīb, *s. a.* A rival. [slavery.

رقيت rìkkìyyèt, *s. a.* Servitude,

رقيق ràkīk, *a. a.* Thin, slender; tender.

رك règh, *s. p.* A vein.

ركاب rìkyāb, *s. a.* A stirrup; the place near the stirrup of a prince on horseback, which is taken by his chief attendant who hands things to him when presented (this is a parallel term to our word "footstool"); a kind of levee of the sovereign; ركاب عرضحالى rìkyāb-"àrzuhālì, *s. t.* A petition presented to the Sultan publicly when going in state on horseback.

ركاكت rèkyākèt, *s. a.* Weakness (of intellect or argument); want of firmness; shakiness (of handwriting).

ركز rèkz, *s. a.* A planting, a setting up; ا—, —et, *v.a.* To plant, set up.

ركعت rìk"àt, *s. a.* A prostration in prayer.

ركن rùkn, *s. a.* (*pl.* اركان èrkyān), A column or solid part of a house-wall, or corner part; a principal and fundamental element in any composite matter or subject.

ركون rùkyūn, *s. a.* A leaning, inclination.

ركيك rèkīk, *a. a.* Weak, shaky; puerile, futile.

ركين rèkīn, *a. a.* Firm, solid, strong.

رماح rìmāh, *s. pl. a.* (*of* رمح rùmh), Lances.

رماد rèmād, *s. a.* Ashes, wood-ashes.

رمان rùmmān, *s. a.* A pomegranate.

رمانى rùmmānī, *s. a.* A ruby.

رمد rèmed, *s. a.* The ophthalmia.

رمز rèmz, *s. a.* A sign, wink, nod; an enigmatical phrase or puzzling circumstance.

رمضان ràmazān, *s. a.* The ninth month of the Muhammedan year, and month of abstinence.

رمق ràmak, *s. a.* The last spark or breath of life; سد رمق sèddi-ràmak, The administration of food in time or quantity just sufficient to save life. [Geomancy.

رمل rèml, *s. a.* Sand; —, rèmel, *s. a.*

رمه rèmé, *s. p.* A flock of sheep.

رمى rèmy, *s. a.* A casting, throwing, projecting; ا—, —et, *v.a.* To cast, throw, project. [gusted.

رميده rèmìdé, *a. p.* Frightened, dis-

رنج rènj, رنجش rènjish, *s. p.* Trouble; رنجبر rènj-bèr (rènchpèr), *s. p.* A labourer, navvy.

رنجيده rènjīdé, *a. p.* Troubled, vexed, annoyed, molested, hurt, injured.

رند rìnd, *s. p.* A free-thinking free-liver; one, on the contrary, whose thoughts and motives being pure, is careless of appearances and speech.

رنده rèndé, *s. p.* A carpenter's plane; a grater (for spice, cheese, &c.); رنده لمك rèndélémek, *v.a.* To plane; to grate.

رنك rèngh (rènk), *s. p.* Colour, hue; —ويرمك, rènk-vèrmek, *v.n.* To explain, give a colouring; رنكارنك rènghyārèngh, *a. p.* Variegated, various, varied in hue.

رنكين rènghīn, *a. a.* Coloured; capital, funny, fun to tell or hear.

رو rū, *s. p.* A face, visage, countenance; —, rèv, *a. p.* (*in composition*), Who or which goes, walks, runs, moves, marches; which grows, springs up.

روا rèwā, *a. p.* Fit to pass, allowable, just, proper.

رواج rèwāj, *s. a.* Currency, a passing current; briskness of markets.

روان rèwān, روانه rèwāné, *a. p.* Flowing; moving; the soul, spirit. [cake.

روانى rèwāni, *s. t.* A kind of sponge-

روايت rìwāyet, *s. a.* A legend, tale, relation, story, rumour, *on dit;* a relating; ا—, —et, *v.a.* To relate.

روبا rùba, *s. t.* Clothes, dress.

روباه rūbāh, *s. p.* A fox.

روح rūh, *s. a.* The soul, spirit; spirit, essence; —الله, rūhu-'llāh (The spirit of God), Jesus Christ; —القدس, rùhu-'l-kùduss, The Holy Ghost (among Christians); Gabriel (with Muslims).

روحانى rūhānī, *a. a.* Spiritual, pertaining to the soul or spirit; روحانيت rūhānìyyèt, *s. a.* Spirituality.

رودوس Ròdòs, *s. t.* Rhodes.

روز rūz, *s. p.* Day; روزنامه rūz-nāmé (jùznāmé), *s. p.* An almanack; a day-book or register; روزنامچه rūz-nāmcha, *s. p.* A kind of register at public offices.

روزكار rūzghyār, *s. p.* Time, fortune, or

the world; —, rùzghyar, *s. t.* The wind. [dow.

روزن rèvzèn, روزنه rèvzénɛ́, *s. p.* A window.

روزه rūzɛ́, *s. p.* A fast, abstinence.

رؤس rūʿūss, *s. pl. a.* (*of* رأس rèʾss), Heads; (*as a Turkish sing.*) a diploma.

رؤسا rūʾessā, *s. pl. a.* (*of* رئيس rèʾiss), Chiefs, chief people.

روسپی ròsspi (òrosspo), *s. t.* A whore, prostitute, harlot.

روستپوللو ròsstopòllu (òrosstopòllu), *s. t.* A knavish fellow, sly rogue.

روسیه Rūssìyya, *s. t.* Russia.

روش rèvish, *s. p.* The way things (or persons) go on; conduct.

روشن rūshèn, روشنا rūshénā, *a. p.* Bright, luminous; clear, manifest, plainly seen.

روغن rùghàn, *s. p.* Any kind of fat or oil; —, rùghàn, *s. t.* Varnish.

روف rèʿūf, *a. a.* Benign, tender, compassionate. [salad.

روقه ròka, *s. t.* A kind of plant used for

روم rūm, *s. p.* A Roman; the Eastern empire, Turkey; —, (ūrum), *s. t.* A Greek; —, rùm, *s. t.* Rum; روم ايلی rùm-èyli (The country of the Greeks), Roumelia; Turkey in Europe; رومی rūmī, *a. a.* (Roman) Greek; Turkish.

روما Ròma, *s. t.* Rome. [going.

رونده rèvèndɛ́, *s. p.* One who goes, is

رونق rèvnak, *s. p.* A flourishing condition, pride, beauty, glory, splendour.

روی rūy, *s. p.* The face, visage, countenance.

رويا rūyā, *s. a.* A dream, vision.

رويت rèvìyyèt, *s. a.* Uprightness, correctness, straightforwardness of character; —, rūʿyet, *s. a.* Supervision, care, conduct, guidance, direction; careful consideration. [or bronze.

رويين rūyīn, روينه rūyīnɛ́, *a. p.* Of brass

ره rèh, *s. p.* (*for* راه rāh), A road.

رها ràhā, *s. a.* Deliverance, escape, safety; — بولمق, —būlmak, *v.n.* To escape.

رهب rèhb, *s. a.* Fear, fright, terror.

رهبان rùhbān, *s. a.* A Christian priest or monk; رهبانيت rùhbānìyyèt, The quality, state, or functions of a Christian priest or monk, especially his celibacy and the indissolubility of his vows.

رهبر rèhbèr, *s. p.* A guide, conductor.

رهن rèhn, *s. a.* A pawning, pledging; —ا, —et, رهنه قومق rèhnɛ́-kòmak, *v.a.* To pawn, to pledge.

رهين rèhīn, *s. a.* A thing given in pledge; a thing which may be looked upon as a pledge. [*s. p.* A hypocrite.

ريا rìyā, *s. a.* Hypocrisy; رياكار rìyākyār,

رياح rìyāh, *s. pl. a.* (*of* ريح rīh), Winds.

رياست rìyāssèt, *s. p.* The presidency, presidentship. [Gardens.

رياض rìyāz, *s. pl. a.* (*of* روضه ràvza),

رياضت rìyāzàt, *s. a.* Mental or bodily discipline; رياضی rìyāzī (*fem.* رياضيه rìyāzìyyɛ́), *a. a.* Pertaining to discipline; علوم رياضيه ʿūlūmu-rìyāzìyyɛ́, The disciplinary sciences of mathematics, &c.

رياله rìyāla, *s. t.* A rear-admiral, formerly a bey, now a pasha.

ریب rèyb, *s. a.* Doubt, incertitude.

ریباس rībāss, *s. a.* Garden rhubarb growing wild.

ریح rīh, *s. a.* The wind; rheumatism; flatulency.

ریختم rīkhtim, *s. p.* A quay on the sea, faced with cut stone, and filled in with rubble.

ریخته rīkhtĕ, *a. p.* Spilt, poured out; scattered, shed.

ریز rīz, *a. p.* (*in composition*), Who or which sheds.

ریزان rīzān, *a. p.* Shedding; shed, dropping, falling.

ریزه rīzĕ, *s. p.* A dropping, portion dropped, piece.

رئس rè'ss, *s. a.* A chief; a sailor; a merchant captain.

ریسمان rīssmān, *s. p.* A rope, cord.

ریش rīsh, *s. p.* The beard; —, *a. p.* (*in composition*), Wounding; wounded.

ریشه rīshĕ, *s. p.* A wound.

ریك rīgh, *s. p.* Sand; the peculiar sand used for drying the ink of writing; ریكدان rīghdān, *s. p.* A sand-box.

رئیس rè'īss, *s. a.* A chief; —افندی, rè'īss-èfèndi (*abbreviation of* رئس الكتاب افندی rè'īssu-'l-kyùttāb-èfèndi, Chief of the scribes, clerks, or secretaries), The Chief Secretary of State in the old system: when this was changed, that officer received the present title of خارجیه ناظری khārijìyyĕ-nāziri, Minister of Foreign Affairs.

ز

ز zā (zĕ, also كسكین زه kèsskin-zè, *sharp z*). Thirteenth letter of the Turkish alphabet, having the value of *z* in English. In chronograms and astronomical tables, it has the numeral value of 7; —, zì, *pr. p.* From.

زا zā, *s. a.* Name of the letter ز.

زاج zāj (zāch), *s. a.* Vitriol; زاج قبریس zāchi-(kìbriz), *s. t.* Green vitriol, sulphate of iron; زاج یاغی zāch-yāghi, *s. t.* Oil of vitriol, sulphuric acid.

زاد zād, *s. a.* Provisions for a journey or voyage; —, *a. p.* (*in composition*), Born, born of; —, zādĕ! *int. a.* May (God) augment . . . ! مادرزاد mā-dɛr-zād, *a. p.* Possessed from birth, innate, inborn.

زاده zādé, *s. p.* (*in composition*), Son; شهزاده shèh-zādĕ, An Ottoman prince of the blood; شاهزده shāh-zādĕ, A Persian prince; بكزاده bègh-zādĕ, Son of a Bey (this title is very usually given to European gentlemen: it means no more than our word *esquire*); زادكان zādĕghyān, *s. pl. p.* (*of* زاده zādĕ), The nobility, people of family and consequence.

زار zār, *s. t.* A membrane, pellicle; a die (for playing); —, *s. p.* A groan, a plaint; —, *a. p.* Despised, contemned; —, *s. p.* (*in composition*), A bed or plot of ground where anything particular grows; زاری zārī, *s. p.* One groan or plaint; abjectness.

زاغ zāgh, *s. p.* A crow, rook, raven.

زانو zānū, *s. p.* The knee.

زانی zānī (*fem.* زانیه zānìyyé), *s. a.* An adulterer; a fornicator.

زاویه zāvìyyé, *s. a.* (*pl.* زوایا zàwāyā), A corner; an angle; a convent or cell; زاویهٔ قائمه zāvìyyè'i-kā'imé, A right angle; زاویهٔ حاده zāvìyyè'i-hāddé, An acute angle; زاویهٔ منفرجه zāvìyyè'i-mùnfèrijé, An obtuse angle; زاویهٔ مجسمه zāvìyyè'i-mùjèssémé, A solid angle; قائم الزاویه kā'imu-'z-zāvìyyé, Right-angled; منفرج الزاویه mùnfèriju-'z-zāvìyyé, Obtuse-angled; حادالزوایا hāddu-'z-zàwāyā, Acute-angled.

زاهد zāhid, *s. a.* An ascetic.

زاهر zāhir, *a. a.* Shining, bright; clear.

زایچه zāyché, *s. a.* A horoscope.

زائد zā'id, *a. a.* Redundant, more than enough; plus (in algebra).

زائل zā'il, *a. a.* Fading away, about to fade, which has faded, the nature of which is to fade away, evanescent.

زبان zèbān (zàbān), *s. p.* The tongue; speech, language, idiom; زبانزد zàbānzèd, Commonly used in speaking.

زبانه zèbāné, *s. p.* Anything tongue-shaped; a flame.

زبانی zèbānī, *s. p.* A demon, tormenting imp of hell.

زبده zùbdé, *s. a.* The essence or choicest of anything.

زبر zèber, *s. p.* The up side; زیرو زبر zīr-u-zèber, *ad. p.* Topsy-turvy, up-side-down, in confusion, in complete ruin.

زبرجد zèberjèd, *s. a.* A topaz(?), a chrysolite(?).

زبقین zìbkìn, *s. t.* A harpoon, a grains for spearing fish.

زبور zèbūr, *s. a.* The Psalms of David.

زبون zèbūn (zàbun), *a. p.* Weak, feeble; lean, thin, meagre.

زجر zèjr, *s. a.* A restraining, preventing; a prohibiting; a using active measures of prevention; —ا, —et, *v.a.* To restrain, prevent; زجریه zèjrìyyé, A tax on wine, spirits, and public-houses, as though it were a prohibitory tax.

زحل zùhàl, *s. a.* The planet Saturn.

زحمت zàhmet, *s. a.* Trouble, bother; pain, fatigue, anxiety; disease; — چکمك zàhmet-chèkmek, *v.n.* To suffer inconvenience; —ا, —et, *v.n.* To give one's self trouble, to trouble one's self.

زخار zàkhkhār, *a. a.* Raging (sea).

زخم zàkhm, *s. p.* A wound.

زخمه zàkhmé, *s. p.* The plectrum with which a lute is played.

زده zèdé, *a. p.* (*in composition*), Struck; قضازده kàzā-zèdé, (Struck by fate) Wrecked (a ship); زده لمك zèdélé-mek, *v.a.* To knock about, ill-use.

زر zèr, *s. p.* Gold; زرگر zèr-ghèr, A goldsmith; زرکش zèr-kèsh, A gold-wire drawer; embroidered with gold.

زراعت zìrā'àt, *s. a.* Agriculture; —ا, —et, *v.a.* To cultivate.

زرافه zùrāfé (zùrāfā), *s. a.* A giraffe.

زرد zèrd, *a. p.* Yellow.

زردالو zèrd-ālu (zèrdāli), *s. p.* A wild apricot; a kill-John.

زرده zèrdé, *s. p.* A sweet dish of rice with saffron; زردهچوب zèrdé-chòb (zèrdéchàw), Turmeric.

زرشك zìrìshk, *s. p.* Barberries.

زرع zèr'', *s. a.* Seed-sowing; ا—, —et, *v.a.* To sow.

زرق zèrk, *s. p.* Hypocrisy.

زرنيخ zìrnikh, *s. p.* Orpiment; realgar.

زره zirh, *s. p.* Defensive armour, mail.

زرين zèrīn, *a. p.* Of gold, golden; — قدح zèrīn-kàdeh (zèren), *s. p.* The [narcissus.

زشت zìsht, *a. p.* Ugly.

زعامت zì''āmet, *s. a.* A major fief, one entered in the archives as above a certain yearly value.

زعفران zà''férān (sàfràn), *s. a.* Saffron.

زعم zù''m, *s. a.* An unfounded idea or opinion.

زعما zù''amā, *s. pl. a.* (*of* زعيم zà''īm), Possessors of major fiefs.

زغر zà*gh*ar, *s. t.* A pointer; a spaniel.

زفت zift, *s. a.* Pitch.

زقاق zùkkāk (صوقاق sòkak), *s. a.* A street; a street of shops.

زقوم zàkkūm, *s. a.* The oleander; an infernal tree bearing demons' heads.

زكا zèkyā, *s. a.* Purity; piety, devotion.

زكات zèkyāt, *s. a.* Canonical alms, the proper bestowal of which purifies the enjoyment or possession of the remainder of one's property.

زكام zùkyām (zùkkyām), *s. a.* A cold in the head, rheum. [devout.

زكى zèkī, *a. a.* Pure of spirit; pious,

زل zil, *s. t.* A cymbal; a little bell, a tympanum of a clock.

زلال zùlāl, *s. a.* Pure, sweet, good water.

زله zèllé, *s. a.* A slip; a fault. [quake.

زلزله zèlzélé (zèrzélé), *s. a.* An earth-

زلف zùlf, *s. p.* A ringlet; —عروس, zùlfu-''àrūss, (Bride's ringlets) The caracalla-bean flower and plant.

زمام zìmām, *s. a.* A rein, a bridle or head-stall; guidance (of affairs).

زمان zèmān (zàmān), *s. a.* Time; circumstances.

زمانه zèmāné, *s. p.* Time; the world; circumstances, fortune.

زمره zùmré, *s. a.* A body (of men), set.

زمرد zùmùrrud (zùmrùd), *s. a.* An emerald. [voices.

زمزمه zèmzémé, *s. a.* Soft murmur of

زمستان zìmisstān, *s. p.* The winter.

زمهرير zèmhérīr, *s. a.* The severest cold of winter; the forty days following the winter solstice.

زمين zèmīn, *s. p.* The surface of the earth; the ground on which any other colours are worked.

زن zèn, *s. p.* A woman; a wife; —, *a. p.* (*in composition*), Who strikes; who sounds, plays; زندوست zèn-dòsst, *s. p.* A lover of women; لافزن lāf-zèn (làfazàn), *s. p.* A boaster, talker.

زنا zìnā, *s. a.* Adultery, fornication;

ولدالزنا vèlédu-'z-zinā, *s. a.* A bastard; (vèlédiznā), a cunning rogue.

زنپاره zèn-pārÉ (zàmpara), *s. p.* A gallant; a frequenter of harlots.

زنبرك zènberèk, *s. p.* A watch-spring; زهرزنبرك zèhir-zènberèk, *ad. t.* Very cold with high wind and drifting snow or sleet.

زنبق zànbAk, *s. a.* A lily; an iris.

زنبور zènbūr, *s. p.* A bee.

زنبيل zènbīl, *s. p.* A rush-basket, a tool-basket.

زنجبيل zènjébīl (zènjéfīl), *s. a.* Ginger; a river in Paradise.

زنجير zinjir, *s. p.* A chain.

زنخدان zènakhdān, *s. p.* The chin; —چاه chāhi—, The dimple of the chin.

زندان zindān, *s. p.* A prison.

زندكانى zindéghyānī, *s. p.* Life, livelihood, living.

زنده zindÉ, *a. p.* Alive, living; (a night) passed without sleep, and in occupation of some kind.

زنديق zindīk, *s. a.* An atheist.

زنكين zènghin, *a. t.* Rich, affluent, opulent.

زنهار zinhār! *int. p.* Look to it! Look out! Take care! Beware!

زواد zèwād, *s. a.* Provisions for a journey.

زوار zùvwār, *s. pl. a.* (*of* زائر zāʿir, *not used*), Pilgrims to any other sacred places than Mecca; visitors.

زوال zèwāl (zàwāl), *s. a.* The instant after the sun has attained the meridian when he begins to decline; a declining from any high position; —, *s. t.* Poor fellow! Poor thing.

زواللو zàwAlli! *int. t.* Poor fellow! Poor thing.

زوانه zìwĀnÉ, *s. t.* Any pin or long centre-piece on which a thing turns, or on which the parts of a whole are strung together, as the wooden middle of a mouthpiece on a Turkish pipe.

زوايا zèwāyā, *s. pl. a.* (*of* زاويه zāvìyyÉ), Angles.

زوج zèvj, *s. a.* (*fem.* زوجه zèvjÉ), One of a pair; a spouse.

زود zūd, *a. p.* Quick; soon.

زور zòr, *s. p.* Force, active strength; stress, violence; a disease; —, *a. t.* Difficult, hard; —, zūr, *s. a.* False-witness; شاهد زور shāhidi-zūr, A bearer of false-witness; زورلمق zòrlamak (*aor.* زورلار zòrlar), *v.a.* To force, break, bend, or violate by force.

زوربا zòrba, *s. t.* A rebel.

زورق zèvrAk, *s. p.* A boat, state barge; —, *s. t.* The curved-up part of the stern of a Turkish boat.

زوزك zèvzèk, *s. t.* An inconsiderate, foolish, talkative person.

زوكورت zùghurt, *a. t.* Poor, penniless.

زونقه zònka, *s. t.* A fish-hook.

زه zìh, *s. a.* A bowstring; a line drawn round a page as a border; a cord sewn to the edge or near the border of clothing or furniture; a corresponding ornament on wood-work, masonry, &c.

زهد zùhd, زهادت zèhādet, *s. a.* Asceticism, religious rigidity.

زهر zèhir, *s. p.* Poison; —, zèhr, *s. a.*

A flower; زهرلمك zèhirlémek, *v.a.* To poison.

زهرا zèhrā, *a. a. fem.* Beautiful, brilliant.

زهراب zèhrāb, *s. p.* Gall-water, bitter water; bitter cup; tears.

زهره zèhré, *s. p.* The gall-bladder; courage, pluck; —, *s. a.* A flower; —, zùhré, *s. a.* The planet Venus.

زهی zèhī! *int. p.* O worthy of admiration!

زی zìy, *s. p.* Dress, costume; form, figure.

زیاده zìyādé, *s. a.* An increase, augmentation; a surplus, remainder; —, *a. and ad. t.* More.

زیارت zìyārèt, *s. a.* A visit of ceremony, of devotion, or of friendship.

زیان zìyān, *s. p.* Harm, damage, injury, loss.

زیب zīb, *s. p.* Anything which gives beauty.

زیبا zībā, *a. p.* Beautiful.

زیبق zībàk, *s. p.* Mercury, quicksilver.

زیت zèyt, *s. a.* Olive-oil; روغن زیت rùghàn*i*-zèyt, The oil called olive-oil.

زیتون zèytūn (zèytin), *s. a.* An olive; زیتونی zèytūnī, *a. a.* Of an olive colour.

زیج zīj, *s. a.* An astronomical table, or a book containing such.

زیر zīr, *s. p.* The under part of, or space beneath, anything.

زیرا zīra, *c. p.* For, because.

زیردست zīr-dèsst, *s. p.* A subject, anyone subject to another.

زیرك zīrèk, *a. p.* Quick, intelligent, clever, sharp.

زین zīn, *s. p.* A saddle.

زینت zīnèt, *s. a.* An ornament.

زیور zīvèr, *s. p.* An ornament.

زیوف zùyūf, *s. pl. a.* (*of* زیف, *not used*) *as a Turkish adj.* Bad, base (coin).

ژ

ژ zhè *or* zāʿi-fārsī. Fourteenth letter of the Turkish alphabet, having the value of the English *s* in *pleasure, treasure,* &c., which we have represented by *zh*. In chronograms it has the same value as j, that is, 7.

ژاژ zhāzh, *s. p.* Dung; ژاژخای zhāzh-khāy, *s. p.* (Eater of dung) A fool, a stupid ass.

ژاله zhālé, *s. p.* A dew-drop; dew; hoar-frost; a small icicle.

ژرف zhèrf, *a. p.* Deep, profound.

ژنك zhènk, *s. p.* Rust.

ژنكار zhènghyār, *s. p.* Verdigris.

ژورنال zhūrnāl, *s. t.* (*French*), A journal, daily register, log-book; daily, weekly, or monthly *state* (of regiments, &c.).

ژولیده zhūlīdé, *a. p.* Dishevelled (hair).

ژیان zhìyān, *a. p.* Furious, raging (animal).

ژیوه zhīvé (jìwa), *s. p.* Mercury, quick-silver.

س

س sīn (sìn). Fifteenth letter of the Turkish alphabet, having *always* the sharp sound of *s* in English, which never degenerates into that of *z*. In chronograms and astronomical tables it has the numeral value of 60. In the dates of letters it stands, instead of ش, for the month Sha‘‘ban.

سا sā, *a. p.* (*in composition*), Who or which rubs, has rubbed, or is as though it had rubbed.

سابع sābi‘‘, *a. a.* The seventh; سابعا sābi‘‘ā, Seventhly.

سابق sābik, *a. a.* The former, prior; سابقا sābikā, *ad. a.* Formerly; سابقه sābika, *s. a.* A former act of crime, former conviction; سابقه‌لو sābikali, *a. t.* Who has before committed some offence, or been convicted.

ساحر sāhir, *s. a.* A magician.

ساحل sāhil, *s. a.* The seashore, a river-bank; ساحلخانه sāhil-khānė, *s. t.* A house on the Bosphorus or seashore; ساحلسرای sāhil-sàrāy, A palace on the shore of the Bosphorus or sea.

ساحه sāhė, *s. a.* A level space; a place, square, court.

ساخته sākhtė, *a. p.* Simulated, false, forged; ساخته‌کار sākhtė-kyār, A forger.

سادس sādiss, *a. a.* The sixth; سادسا sādissā, *ad. a.* Sixthly.

ساده sādė, *a. p.* Plain, unadorned, unmixed; —كوزل, sādė-ghyùzèl, *a. t.* Neat, plain, simple; ساده‌دل sādė-dil, *s. p.* A greenhorn, simpleton.

سار sār, *s. p.* (*in composition*), Country, land (where anything is found).

سارده‌له sàrdèlė, or سارده‌له‌بالغی sàrdèlė-bàlighi, *s. t.* A sardine.

سارق sārik, *s. a.* A thief, a robber.

سارنج sàrnij, *s. t.* An underground reservoir for water.

ساری sārī (*fem.* ساریه sārìyyė), *a. a.* Contagious.

ساز sāz, *s. t.* A rush, bulrush; a reed; a lute; —, *s. p.* Paraphernalia; —, *a. p.* (*in composition*), Who makes, does, performs, accomplishes; ناساز nā-sāz, *a. p.* Good for nothing.

سازان sāzan, *s. t.* A carp (?).

سازنده sāzèndė, *s. p.* A musician.

ساطور sātūr (sàtir), *s. p.* A large knife, chopper, or cutter.

ساعت sā‘‘at, *s. a.* A moment of time; any appointed time (as that of death, &c.); an hour; a timepiece of any kind; a league, or hour's distance قوم‌ساعتی kūm-sā‘‘ati, An hour or minute glass; قوین‌ساعتی kòyn-sā‘‘ati, A watch; چكمجه ساعتی chèkméjė-sā‘‘ati, A timepiece, chimney-clock; قوله ساعتی kùlė-sā‘‘ati, A tower-clock; تام‌ساعت tāmm-sā‘‘at, A chronometer; ساعتجی sā‘‘atji, A watch and clock maker.

ساعی sā‘‘iy, *s. a.* One who endeavours, does his best, works at (anything); a foot-messenger, foot postman.

ساغر sāgher, *s. p.* A drinking-cup.

ساق sāk, *s. a.* The leg or thigh; the trunk of a tree, a pole; تشمیرساق tèshmīri-sāk, The tucking up one's trousers (when going about in the dirt or water), preparing for business; ساقین sākàyn, The two legs of a triangle ; متساوى الساقين mùtéssāvìyyu--'ss-sākàyn, Isosceles (triangle).

ساقز sàkiz, s. t. The island Chio ; gum mastic ; gum resin ; چام ساقزى chàm--sàkizi, Pine resin, rosin.

ساقط sākit, a. a. Fallen into disuse, no longer valid.

ساقى sākī, s. a. A cupbearer.

ساكت sākit, a. a. Mute, not speaking ; not spoken.

ساكن sākin, a. a. Who dwells, lives, inhabits ; dwelling, living, inhabiting ; quiet, gentle, tranquil ; not followed by a vowel in the same syllable (a consonant) ; —, —اُو —ὸl, v.n. To dwell, live, inhabit, stay.

سال sāl, s. p. A year ; سالنامه sāl--nāmé, An almanack.

سالار sālār, s. p. A general, commander, captain of a post.

سالف الذكر sālifu-'z-zìkr, a. a. The above-mentioned, the forenamed.

سالك sālik, a. a. Who treads a path, follows a road or example.

سالم sālim, a. a. Free from hurt, vice, disease, defect.

ساله sālé, a. p. (*following Persian numeral adjectives*), Years old, years [of age.

ساليار sàlyār, s. t. Saliva.

ساليان sālyān, ساليانه sālyāne, s. p. Income-tax.

سام sāmm, a. a. Poisonous ; the poisonous wind of the desert, called in Turkish سام يلى (sàm)-yèli.

سامان sāmān, s. p. All or any necessary things, material or mental ; سامانسوز sāmān-sūz, a. p. Which burns (destroys) any or all of one's needful havings.

سامع sāmī'' (*fem.* سامعه sāmi''a), a. a. Who hears ; قوت سامعه kùvvéti--sāmi''a, The auscultative faculty ; sense of hearing ; سامعين sāmi''īn, s. pl. a. Hearers, an audience.

سامى sāmī, a. a. High, exalted ; vizirial ; مكتوب سامى mèktubu-sāmī, A vizirial letter.

سانح sānih, a. a. Emanating ; سانحه sānīha, s. a. An event, occurrence.

ساى sāy, a. p. (*in composition*), Who rubs, has rubbed, or is as though he had rubbed. [Other.

سائر sā'ir, a. a. Who travels ; —, a. t.

سائسخانه sa'iss-khāné, s. t. A baggage-horse, bât-horse, sumpter-horse ; a great man's baggage. [drives.

سائق sā'ik, a. a. Who pushes, urges,

سائل sā'il, s. a. A beggar ; a questioner ; an asker ; a plaintiff.

سايه sāyé, s. p. A shadow, shade ; protection, auspices ; سايه بان sāyébān, s. p. A kind of pavilion or tent for shade ; a canopy ; a parasol.

سب sèbb, s. a. Blasphemy, reviling anything sacred ; ا—, —et, v.n. To utter blasphemy. [ming.

سباحت sèbāhàt, s. a. Natation, swim-

سباع sèbā'', s. pl. a. (*no sing.*), Wild beasts, beasts of prey.

سباق sìbāk, s. a. What precedes (in

discourse); سياق‌سباق sìyāk-sìbāk, What follows and what precedes, the context, the general sense and structure (of a writing).

سبايا sèbāyā, *s. pl. a.* Captives, prisoners of war, slaves.

سبب sèbeb, *s. a.* (*pl.* اسباب èssbĀb), A cause, reason, motive; a means; سببسز sèbebsiz, *a. t.* Without cause; سببلنمك sèbeblɪnmek, *v.n.* To obtain a means of gaining a livelihood; سببيت sèbébìyyèt, *s. a.* The quality of being the cause.

سبت sèbt, *s. a.* Saturday.

سبحان sùbhāna, *s. a.* (*oblique case*) in سبحان‌الله sùbhāna-'llĀh! (I sing) the praises of God! O God! O God! حق‌سبحانه‌وتعالى hĀkk-sùbhānahū-vĒ-ta''ālà, (God) the Very Truth, to whom be praise, and whose name be exalted! سبحانى sùbhānī (*fem.* سبحانيه sùbhānìyyĒ), *a. a.* Divine, pertaining to God.

سبز sèbz, *a. p.* Green.

سبزه sèbzĒ, *s. p.* (*pl.* سبزوات sèbzéwĀt, *vulg.* zèrzéwĀt), Any green vegetable for table.

سبع sèb'', سبعه sèb''à, *a. a.* Seven; —, sùb'', A seventh part; سبعون sèb''ūn, سبعين sèb''īn, Seventy.

سبق sàbak, in ماسبق mā-sàbak, *s. a.* What has been said, what precedes, and in سبقخوان sàbak-khān, *s. p.* One who learns a lesson.

سبقت sàbkAt, *s. a.* A preceding in narration, or in point of time; ا—, —et, *v.n.* To precede; to happen.

سبك sèbuk, *a. p.* Light, volatile; not heavy; not grave or sedate; —, sèbk, *s. a.* Order of words in phrases; سبك و ربط sèbk-u-rĀbt, The order and construction (of phrases); سبكبار sèbuk-bār, *a. p.* Whose load is light; سبكپاى sèbuk-pāy, *a. p.* Light of foot; سبكمغز sèbuk-màghz, *a. p.* Volatile, foolish, light-witted.

سبو sèbu, *s. p.* A pitcher or jar.

سبى sèby, *s. a.* A taking captive, carrying into captivity; ا—, —et, *v.a.* To carry into captivity. [cast metal.

سبيكه sèbīkĒ, *s. a.* An ingot, a bar of

سبيل sèbīl, *s. a.* A road; (zèbil) a building where cups of water are kept ready for thirsty passers-by; ابناى‌سبيل ebnāyi-sèbīl, Travellers; فى‌سبيل‌الله fī-sèbīli-'llāh, In the cause and for the love of God.

سپا (sìpa), *s. p.* A three-legged stool.

سپارش sìpārish, *s. p.* A request, order, or command; a thing made to order; ا—, —et, *v.a.* To recommend, leave, request, order, command (anything to be done). [giving.

سپاس sìpāss, *s. p.* Praise or thanks-

سپاه sìpāh, *s. p.* An army; سپاهى sìpāhī (the *sepoy* of India and Spahi of Turkey, as misspelt and mispronounced by Europeans), *s. p.* A soldier, a feudal soldier serving under military tenure.

سپد sèped, *s. t.* A small open-mouthed basket; سپد ایشی sèped-ìshi, *s. t.* Basket-work; سپدصندیغی sèped--sàndighi, A trunk or box made on a frame of basket-work covered with leather; مترس سپدی mètériss-sèpédi, *s. t.* A gabion.

سپر sìpᴇʀ, *s. p.* Any kind of protection; a shield; a parapet; a peak (of a cap).

سپکن sèpken, *s. t.* Drizzle, sleet; صولو سپکن sùlu-sèpken, Mixed sleet and drizzle. [spit, drizzle, sleet.

سپمك sèpmek (*aor.* سپر sèpᴇʀ), *v.n.* To

سپورکه sùpurghé, *s. t.* A broom.

سپورمك sùpurmek (*aor.* سپورر sùpurur), *v.a.* To sweep.

سپورندی sùpurundu, *s. t.* Sweepings; سپورندیلك sùpurunduluk, *s. t.* A dust-heap, a dust-hole.

سپه sìpeh, *s. p.* Abbreviation of سپاه sìpāh; سپهسالار sìpehsālār, *s. p.* A captain or commander-in-chief of an army.

سپهر sipìhr, *s. p.* The sphere, the sky; fate as ruled by the planets. [White.

سپید sèpīd (*for* سفید sèfīd), *a. p.*

ست sìtt, ستّه sìttÉ, *a. a.* Six.

ستاره sìtārÉ, *s. p.* A star.

ستان sìtān, *a. p.* (*in composition*), Who or which takes possession; —, isstān, *s. p.* (*in composition*), A country.

ستایش sìtāyish, *s. p.* Praise, eulogy; ا—, —et, *v.a.* To praise, eulogize.

ستر sètr, *s. a.* A covering over; — *or* sìtr, *s. a.* A cover; a vail, veil, curtain; ا—, sètr-et, *v.a.* To cover, to conceal. [walking coat.

ستری sètri, *s. t.* A military or undress

ستم sìtem, *s. p.* Violence, ill-treatment; hard words; ا—, —et, *v.n.* To ill-treat; to use hard words; ستمدیده sìtem-dīdÉ, *a. p.* Who has been hardly used. [termittent fever.

ستمه sìtma, *s. t.* An ague, common in-

ستوده sùtūdÉ, *a. p.* Praiseworthy.

ستون sùtūn, *s. p.* A column, pillar, post, mast; —, sìttūn, *and* ستین sìttīn, *a. a.* Sixty. [affliction, anxiety.

ستوه sùtūh, *s. p.* Trouble, sorrow, grief,

سجاده sèjjādÉ, *s. a.* A prayer-carpet.

سجده sèjdÉ, *s. a.* Adoration, prostration of the head; ا—, —et, *v.n.* To prostrate the head in sign of adoration.

سجع sèj‘‘, *s. a.* A rhyming of the ends of members of a prose phrase.

سجل sìjìll, *s. a.* A register or book of records in a court of law.

سجم sìjim, *s. t.* Packthread, string.

سجن sìjin, *s. a.* A prison.

سجود sùjūd, *s. a.* Adoration, prostration in adoration.

سجوق sùjuk, *s. t.* A dried sausage; a train of powder in a hose for firing a mine.

سچان sìchᴀɴ, *s. t.* A mouse; a rat; فندق سچانی fìndik-sìchᴀɴi, A mouse; کمر سچانی ghèmᴇʀ-sìchᴀɴi, A rat; سچان یولی sìchᴀɴ-yòlᴜ, *s. t.* The zigzag or covered way for communication between parallels in sieges.

سچمك sèchmek (*aor.* سچر sèchER), *v.a.* To select, pick, pick out; سچمه sèchma, *a. t.* Selected, picked.

سحاب sàhāb, *s. a.* A cloud. [enchanter.

سحار sàhhār, *s. a.* A magician, sorcerer,

سحر sìhr (sìhir), *s. a.* Magic, enchantment, sorcery; —, sàhr, *s. a.* The early part of the morning; سحراً sàhran, *ad. a.* Early in the morning; سحرباز sìhir-bāz, *s. p.* A magician.

سحق sàhk, *s. a.* A bruising, pounding, triturating; ا—, —et, *v.a.* To bruise, pound, triturate.

سحور sàhūr, *s. a.* The meal taken in Ramazan a short time before the earliest dawn when fast-time begins.

سخا sàkhā, سخاوت sàkhāvèt, *s. a.* Liberality, generosity, munificence.

سخت sàkht, *a. p.* Hard; rough; severe. [leather; calf leather.

سختيان sàkhtiyān, *s. p.* Morocco

سخن sùkhàn, *s. p.* A word; speech, talk, discourse. [munificent.

سخى sàkhī, *a. a.* Liberal, generous,

سد sèdd, *s. a.* A stopping, shutting, blocking up (any passage); a wall, &c., by which a passage is blocked up; a terrace supported by a wall or bank; a bank or dyke for turning the stream of a river; ا—, —et, *v.a.* To shut, stop up, block up.

سداد sèdād, *s. a.* Uprightness, integrity, rectitude of faith or morals.

سده sùddé, *s. a.* Any obstruction in any part of the body; a threshold; سدهٔ سعادت sùddé'i-sà''ādet, (The threshold of felicity) The seat of empire. [part.

سدس sùdss (sùduss), *s. a.* A sixth

سدف sèdef, *s. t.* The herb rue.

سدك *or* سديك sìdik, *s. t.* Urine.

سديد sèdīd, *a. a.* Right (in faith or morals).

سر sÈr, *s. p.* The head; the extremity, end or beginning; the tip; the top, summit; a chief; —, sìrr, *s. a.* A secret; —طوتمق, sìrr-tūtmak, *v.a.* To keep secret, keep as a secret; — —, *v.n.* To keep a secret; —كاتبى, sìrr-kyātibi, *s. t.* A secretary, private or confidential secretary; سراً sìrràn, *ad. a.* In secret.

سرا sèrā, *s. p.* (*or* سراى sàrāy), A palace; —, sìrā, *a. p.* (*in composition*), Who sings.

سراب sìrāb, *s. p.* The mirage.

سراج sìrāj, *s. a.* A lamp, any artificial light; —, sèrrāj (sàraj), *s. a.* A saddler.

سراخى sùrākhī, *s. p.* A decanter.

سرادق sèrādik, *s. a.* (*pl.* سرادقات sèrādikĀt), A pavilion. [Concubines.

سرارى sèrārī, *s.pl.a.* (*of* سريه sùrrìyyÉ),

سراسمه *or* سراسيمه sèrāsimÉ, *a. p.* Stupefied, bewildered.

سراى sàray, *s. p.* A palace; a mansion; سرايلو sàrayli, *a. t.* Any person, especially a woman, who belongs, or has belonged, to the Sultan's palace.

سرايت sìrāyet, *s. a.* Contagion, a contagious communication; ا—, —et, *v.a.* To be communicated, spread contagiously.

سرب Sèrp, *a.* and *s.t.* Servian; a Servian.

سربست sèr-bèsst (sèr-bèss), *a. p.* Free, independent; سربستی ser-bèsstī, *s. p.* سر بستیت sèr-bèsstiyyèt, *s. a.* سر بستلك ser-bèsstlik (sèr-bèsslik), *a. t.* Liberty, freedom, independence.

سربستان Sèrpìsstān, *s. t.* Servia.

سرپمك sèrpmek (*aor.* سرپر sèrper), *v.a.* and *n.* To sprinkle.

سرت sèrt, *a. t.* Strong, pungent; violent, vehement; angry, severe.

سرچه sèrché, *s. t.* A sparrow; —پرمغی, sèrché - pàrma*ghi*, *s. t.* The little finger.

سرحد sèr-hàdd, *s. p.* A border, frontier.

سرخ sùrkh, *a. p.* Red; —, *s. t.* Red ink. [intoxicated.

سرخوش sèr-khòsh (sàrhòsh), *a.p.* Drunk,

سرد sèrd, *a. p.* Cold; —, *s. a.* A laying down, setting forth, reciting; ا—, —et, *v.a.* To lay down, set forth, recite. [chief.

سردار sèrdār, *s. p.* A commander-in-

سررشته sèr-rìshté, *s. p.* (The end of a clue or thread) A handle or pretext.

سرزنش sèr-zènish, *s. p.* A knock on the head, a rebuff, a rebuke. [giddy.

سرسام sèrsām (sèrsem), *a. p.* Stupefied,

سرسری sèrsérī, *s. p.* A vagabond.

سرشت sìrìsht, *s. p.* Nature, natural disposition.

سرشك sìrìshk, *s. p.* A tear, tears.

سرطان sèratān, *s. a.* The sign Cancer.

سرعت sùr"àt, *s. a.* Speed, velocity, swiftness, quickness.

سرعسكر sèr-"àsskér, *s. p.* A military commander-in-chief; the Minister of War.

سرقت sirkàt, سرقه sèrika, *s. a.* Theft; a thieving, stealing; ا—, —et, To thieve, steal.

سرگذشت sèr-ghyùzèsht, *s. p.* An adventure, what happens to anyone.

سركرده sèr-kèrdé, *s. p.* A commander, chief, head.

سركش sèr-kèsh, *a. p.* Disobedient, intractable, unruly, rebellious.

سركه sìrké, *s. t.* Vinegar.

سرگی sèrghi, *s. t.* A stall at a fair; a paymaster's office or temporary stall when paying troops; an order or bill on a paymaster.

سرما sèrmā, *s. p.* Winter.

سرمایه sèr-māyé, *s. p.* Capital, stock; original, prime cost; original material of which a thing is made; سرمایه‌دار sèrmāyé-dār, *s. p.* A capitalist.

سرمد sèrmèd, سرمدی sèrmédī, *a. a.* Everlasting, eternal.

سرمك sèrmek (*aor.* سرر sèrer), *v.a.* To spread (cloths or stuffs).

سرمو sèr-mū, *s. p.* A hair's-tip (a hair's-breadth).

سرمه sìrma, *s. t.* Gold thread; gold lace; gold embroidery; —, sùrmé, *s. t.* Collyrium for tinging the eyelashes, or for improving the sight;

ـــكش, sìrma-kèsh, *s. t.* A gold-wire drawer.

سرنا sùrnā (zùrna), *s. p.* A kind of horn or trumpet; a stupid fool.

سرو sèrv (sèlvi), *s. p.* A cypress; ـــازاد, sèrvi-āzād, ـــروان, sèrvi-rèwān, (A free, a walking cypress), سروقد sèrv-kàdd, (Cypress-statured), A tall, slim, graceful person.

سرور sèrvèr, *s. p.* A chief; —, sùrūr, *s. a.* Joy, delight, happiness.

سروش sùrūsh, *s. p.* An angel.

سره sèrè, *s. t.* The distance spanned by the thumb and *fore*-finger.

سرير sèrīr, *s. a.* A throne.

سريع sèrī'', *a. a.* Quick, swift; سريعاً sèrī''*an*, *ad. a.* Quickly; swiftly.

سرين sèrin, *a. t.* Cool (air); سرينلشمك sèrinleshmek, *v.n.* To grow cool or fresh.

سريه sèrìyyè, *s. a.* An expeditionary army; —, sùrrìyyè, *s. a.* A concubine.

سز sìz, *pron. t.* Ye, you; —, siz *or* siz, The Turkish privative particle placed like the prepositions at the end of a noun, and has the meaning of our *less* or *without;* سزك sìzing, Your; yours; سزى sìzi, Ye, you (*acc.*); سزه sìzè, To you; سزده sìzdè, At *or* in you; سزدن sìzdan, From you; سزكله sìzing*la*, With you; سزسز sìzeiz, Without you; سزجه sìzj*a*, Your fashion; according to you.

سزا sèzā, سزاوار sèzāvār, *a. p.* Worthy.

سزمك sèzmek (*aor.* سزر sèzer), *v.a.* To penetrate, see through (a concealed design); —, sìzmek (*aor.* سيزر sìzer), *v.n.* To percolate, filter (through a rock, jar, &c.).

سس sèss, *s. t.* Sound; voice; ـــا, —et, *v.n.* To call out, speak; ـــويرمك, sèss-vèrmek, *v.n.* To sound, give a sound.

سست sùsst, *a. p.* Weak, feeble, relaxed, languid.

سطح sàth (t-h), *s. a.* A surface, superficies; a flat-terraced roof; ـــمستوى, sàth*i*-mùsstèvī, A plane, plane surface; ـــمستدير, sàth*i*-mùsstèdīr, A globular surface.

سطر sàtr, *s. a.* A line of writing; a line drawn on which to write straight.

سطوت sàtvet, *s. a.* Might, warlike power.

سعادت sà''ādet, *s. a.* Happiness, good-luck, prosperity, felicity; سعادتلو sà''ādetlū, *a. t.* Title given to lieutenants-general and their equals in the civil service; دارالسعادت dāru-'ss-sà''ādet, (The house of felicity) The Sultan's gyneceum; سدهٔ سعادت sùddè i - sà''ādet, (The threshold of felicity) The court of government.

سعايت sì''āyet, *s. a.* Calumny; back-biting; ا—, —et, *v.n.* To backbite, calumniate.

سعه sì''à, *s. a.* Amplitude; سعهٔ مشرق sì''à'i - mèshrik, Eastern amplitude; سعهٔ مغرب sì''à'i - màghrib, Western amplitude.

سعد sà''d, *s. a.* Favourable aspect of the planets; سعدين sà''dèyn, *s. a. dual.*

The two fortunate planets, Jupiter and Venus. [modity in the market.

سعر sì‘‘r, *s. a.* Price current of any com-

سفارت sèfārèt, *s. a.* An embassy, legation, mission; ambassadorship; سفارتخانه sèfārèt-khānè, *s. p.* An ambassadorial residence.

سفاك sèffāk, *a. a.* Bloodthirsty, sanguinary, shedder of blood.

سفالت sèfālèt, *s. a.* Lowness of rank and condition.

سفاهت sèfāhàt, *s. a.* Senseless and inconsiderate conduct, especially in ostentatiously spending money.

سفته sùftè, *a. p.* Bored, drilled through; ناسفته nā-sùftè, Not drilled or bored.

سفر sèfer, *s. a.* A journey, trip, voyage; a campaign, a cruise; war; travel; time; —ا, —et, *and* —ويرمك, —vèrmek, *v.n.* To go on a journey, voyage; —اچمق, sèfer-àchmak, *v.n.* To commence war or hostilities; بو سفر bū-sèfer, This time, this once; قاچ سفر kAch-sèfer? How many times?

سفرا sùfèrā, *s. pl. a.* (*of* سفير sèfīr), Ambassadors, envoys.

سفره sòfra, *s. a.* A table (or substitute) prepared with food, &c., ready for a meal; —بزی, sòfra-bèzi, *s. t.* A tablecloth. [casuistic argumentation.

سفسطه sèfsata (sAfsAta), *s. a.* Sophisms,

سفك sèfk, *s. a.* A shedding (of blood); —دما ا, sèfki-dìmā-et, *v.n.* To shed blood. [fellows.

سفله sèfèlè, *s. pl. a.* (*of* سافل sāfil), Low

سفلی sùflī (*fem.* سفلیه sùfliyyè), *a. a.* Low. [Ships.

سفن sùfun, *s. pl. a.* (*of* سفينه sèfīnè),

سفيد sèfīd, *a. p.* White; بحر— bàhri-sèfīd, The Mediterranean.

سفير sèfīr, *s. a.* An ambassador, envoy.

سفينه sèfīnè, *s. a.* A ship; the ark (Noah's). [spendthrift.

سفيه sèfīh, *s. a.* A foolish, inconsiderate

سقا sàkkā (sàka), *s. a.* A water-carrier; —قوشی, sàka-kùshu, *s. t.* A pelican; a goldfinch.

سقامت sàkāmèt, *s. a.* Harm, hurt; hurtfulness.

سقط sàkAt, *s. a.* A defect, defectiveness, damage; —, *a. t.* Defective, damaged, injured; dangerous; infirm, mutilated, invalided; سقطلق sàkAtlik, *s. t.* Danger of harm; —ا, —et, *v.a.* To hurt, injure, damage, make infirm, mutilate.

سقف sAkf, *s. a.* A roof; a ceiling.

سقنغور sàkanghūr, *s. t.* A square or half-square piece of muslin used as an envelope for letters and official papers.

سقوط sùkūt, *s. a.* A falling downwards.

سك sègh, *s. p.* A dog; —, sìk, *s. t.* The penis.

سكان sùkkyān, *s. a.* A ship's or boat's rudder or helm; —, *s. pl. a.* (*of* ساكن sākin), Inhabitants.

سكبان sèghbān (sèymen), *s. p.* Formerly a soldier of a particular corps of the Janissaries, next a soldier of some regiments organised in the European style, and latterly a kind of irregular police soldier.

سكته sèktÉ, *s. a.* An impediment; — ويرمك sèktÉ-vèrmek, *v.n.* To impede, hinder, be a source of impediment.

سكر sèkr, *s. a.* Drunkenness, ebriety, inebriety; —, sùkkER, *s. a.* Sugar; —, *or* سكير sìngir, *s. t.* A nerve; a tendon; a muscle.

سكرتمك sèghirtmek (*aor.* سكردر sèghirdir), *v.n.* To run.

سكردم sèghirdim, *s. t.* The raised way or platform on which soldiers stand behind a parapet.

سكز sèkiz, *a. t.* Eight; سكزنجى sè-kizinji, *a. t.* The eighth.

سكسان (sèksEN), *a. t.* Eighty.

سكشمك sìkishmek (*aor.* سكشور sìki-shir), *v.n.* To copulate together.

سكك. See سينك.

سكمك sèkmek (*aor.* سكر sèkER), *v.n.* To glance off, ricochet (a projectile); —, sìkmek, *v.a.* To act the male in copulation, to tread, line, cover, &c.

سكنات sèkénāt, *s. pl. a.* (*of* سكنت, *not used*), Quiescent states; حركات و— hàrékyāt - u —, Active and quiescent states, uprisings and lyings down.

سكنه sèkénÉ, *s. pl. a.* (*of* ساكن sākin), Inhabitants.

سكنى *or* سكنا sùknà, *s. a.* A habitation; قابل— kābili-sùknà, *a. p.* Habitable.

سكوت sùkyūt, *s. a.* Silence, holding one's tongue; ا—, —et, *v.n.* To re-frain from speaking.

سكون sùkyūn, *s. a.* A remaining motion-less; a remaining, staying in a place; the quiescent state of a consonant or the not being followed by a vowel in same syllable.

سكونت sùkyūnèt, *s. a.* Tranquillity of deportment, freedom from hurry or disturbance.

سكه sìkkÉ, *s. a.* The impression on coins; the coin itself; the die with which coins are struck; —كسمك, sìkkÉ--kèssmek, *v.n.* To strike money.

سكير sìngir, *s. t.* A nerve; a tendon; a muscle.

سكين sìkkīn, *s. a.* A knife.

سكينه sèkinÉ, *s. a.* The glory of God in the ark of the covenant.

سل sèll, *s. a.* The drawing (a sword) from its scabbard; سل سيف ا sèlli--sèyf-et, *v.n.* To draw the sword.

سلاح sìlāh, *s. a.* Any kind of offensive arm; سلاحلو sìlāhli, *a. t.* Armed; سلاحلنمق sìlāhlanmak, *v.n.* To arm one's self, take up arms; سلاحشور sìlāh-shòr (sÀlahòr), *s. p.* A kind of knight in dignity.

سلاست sèlāssèt, *s. a.* Facility (of dic-tion); —لسان, sèlāssèti-lìssAn, An easy flowing manner of speech.

سلاله sùlālÉ, *s. a.* Children, descendants, posterity, descending race or stock.

سلام sèlām, *s. a.* Peace; the saying, Peace be to you! a salutation, a motion or signal of courtesy equiva-lent to taking off the hat, and con-sisting in kissing the finger ends of the right hand and carrying it to the head; ويرمك—, sèlām-vèrmek, *v.n.* To make (as a superior) the signal of courtesy to anyone; المق—, sèlām-ālmak, *v.n.* To receive and render (as an inferior) this salute; to receive by letter the salutation of a person; كوندرمك—, sèlām-ghyùndermek, *or* ا—, —et, *v.n.* To send compliments or salutations; دورمق—, sèlām-dùrmak, *v.n.* To present arms; سلامه دورمق sèlāma-dùrmak, *v.n.* To stand ready to receive and salute a superior; سلام عليكم sèlāmun (*or* sèlām)-"àlèykyum! Peace be upon you! (*to which is replied*) عليكم سلام "àlèykyum-sèlām (*or* —وعليكم vè-"àlèykyum—) Upon you be peace! (It is not usual for Turkish Mussulmans to give or receive this salutation from people of another religion, though the Arabs do so).

سلامت sèlāmet, *s. a.* Safety, freedom from harm or danger; سلامتله sèlāmètla! In safety! (said to anyone on his taking leave).

سلاملك sèlāmlik, *s. t.* The men's part of a Turkish house; a public appearance of the Sultan every Friday when he goes in state to a place of worship.

سلانيك Sèlànik, *s. t.* Salonica.

سلب sèlb, *s. a.* A taking away, seizing, spoiling; —, sèleb, *s. a.* Arms and other spoils taken from an enemy; ا—, sèlb-et, *v.a.* To take, seize, carry off; سلبى sèlbī (*fem.* سلبيه sèlbiyyé), *a. a.* Privative or negative; صفات سلبيه sifāti-sèlbiyyé, The privative or negative attributes of God, as, *deathless, fellowless,* &c.

سلحدار silahdār (silihdār), *s. p.* An esquire or arms-bearer to his lord.

سلخ sèlkh, *s. a.* A skinning; the skin or fell of an animal; the thirtieth day of a lunar month (always so used in dating letters).

سلسله silsilé, *s. a.* A chain; a series; a race, family, dynasty; an hierarchy; يوريمك—, silsilé-yùrumek, *v.n.* To take place through the whole of the grades of an hierarchy (promotion when a superior post becomes vacant).

سلطان sùltān, *s. a.* (*pl.* سلاطين sèlātīn), The Sultan; a daughter of the Sùltan; a proof; dominion; والده— wālidé-sùltān, The mother of the Sultan. (In naming the Sultan this title precedes his name, as, سلطان محمود Sùltān-Màhmūd; but in the case of his daughters, the name stands first, as, اسما سلطان Essmà-Sùltān; سلطانى sùltānī (*fem.* سلطانيه sùltāniyyé), *a. a.* Imperial, Sultanic.

سلطنت sāltanāt, *s. a.* The sultanate; empire, sovereignty; pomp, magnificence, grandeur; سنيه—, sāltanāti-sèniyyé, The imperial Ottoman Government.

سلف sèlef, *s. a.* (*pl.* اسلاف èsslāf), A predecessor in office.

سلك silk, *s. a.* A series, order, row (of

beads, words, &c.); a career or line of public life.

سلكمك sìlkmek (*aor.* سلكر sìlkER), *v.a.* To shake (a thing) so as to free it from something on or in it, as a mat, a tablecloth, a pipe; to trace (a drawing, &c.) by pricking holes in the outlines, and then shaking charcoal dust through it on to another paper or cloth; سلكنمك sìlkinmek, *v.n.* To shake itself (as a dog when it comes out of the water); سلكمه sìlkm*a*, *s. t.* A kind of toss-up dish of fried food.

سلم sèllèm! May (God) grant (him) eternal peace! (said in speaking of Muhammed, in the phrase صلى الله عليه وسلم sALLA-'llāhu-"àlèyhi-vè-sèllèm); —, sùllem, *s. a.* A ladder; a staircase.

سلمك sìlmek (*aor.* سيلر sìlER), *v.a.* To wipe; to wipe out; to scrub and wash (floors).

سلمن sùlumèn, *s. t.* Name of two preparations of mercury; آق— Ak—, Corrosive sublimate, hydro-chlorate of mercury; طاتلو— tATl*i*—, Calomel.

سلوك sùlūk, *s. a.* The taking, turning into, keeping, or following a road, a line of life, a rule of conduct; ا—, —et, *v.n.* To take or keep (a road, &c.).

سلوى sèlvà, The quails sent to feed the Israelites.

سله sìllÉ (*for* سيلى sìlī, *s. p.*), *s. t.* A smack on the face, box on the ear.

سليقه sèlīk*a*, *s. a.* Natural genius.

سليم sèlīm, *a. a.* Free from defect, as it should be, proper.

سليمان Sùlèymān, *s. t.* Solomon.

سليمانى sùlèymĀnī, *s. t.* A kind of precious agate. [sèmm, *s. a.* Poison.

سم sùm, *s. p.* The hoof of a horse; —,

سما sèmā, *s. a.* (*pl.* سماوات sèmāvāt), The sky.

سمات sìmāt, *s. a.* A mark made on anything to distinguish it; a characteristic.

سماحت sèmāhàt, *s. a.* Beneficence, liberality, generosity; سماحتلو sèmā-hatlū, *a. t.* Beneficence (title given to high dignitaries of the law).

سماط sùmāt, *s. a.* A table (or its substitute) ready prepared with food for a meal.

سماع sèmā", *s. a.* Hearing; the dance of the dervishes; سماعى sèmā"ī (*fem.* سماعيه sèmā"ìyyÉ), *a. a.* Founded on general hearsay; irregular (in grammar).

سماق sùmmāk, *s. a.* Sumach; سماقى sùmmākī (sòmāk*i*), *s. t.* Porphyry.

سماك sìmāk, *s. a.* Name of two stars; سماك اعزل sìmāki-*à*"zèl, (The unarmed Simak) Spica Virginis (?) *and* سماك رامح sìmāki-rāmih, (The spearholding Simāk) Arcturus (?); بين السماك والسمك bèyné-'ss-sìmāki-vÈ-'ss-sèmèk, The distance between the stars (Sìmāk) and the fish (Sèmèk) on which the universe used to be said to be supported. [*a. a.* Celestial.

سماوى sèmāvī (*fem.* سماويه sèmāviyyÉ),

سمپاره sùmpārÉ (zìmp*a*r*a*), *s. p.* Emery.

سمت sèmt, *s. a.* A quarter, tract, country; a parish, neighbourhood; a house, dwelling; a direction, course; —رأس, sèmti-rèʿss, The zenith; سمت قدم sèmti-kʌdɪm, The Nadir.

سمر sèmɪr, *s. t.* A pack-saddle.

سمرمك sèmirmek (*aor.* سميرر sèmirir), *v.n.* To grow fat.

سمسار sìmsār, *s. a.* A broker.

سمع sèmʿʿ, *s. a.* A hearing; the ear; سمعاً وطاعه sèmʿʿan-vè-tāʿʿa, *ad. a.* No sooner heard than obeyed (an answer to a command or request).

سمك sèmek, *s. a.* A fish.

سمكورمك sùmkyurmek (*aor.* سمكورر sùmkyurur), *v.n.* To blow one's nose.

سمن sèmen, *s. p.* Jessamine; —, sìmèn, *s. a.* Fatness, stoutness of body.

سمند sèmènd, *s. p.* A horse.

سمندر sèmendèr, *s. p.* A salamander.

سمو sùmùvv, *s. a.* Elevation, exaltedness, eminence.

سمور sèmmūr (sāmur), *s. a.* The sable.

سموك sùmuk, *s. t.* Snot, mucus; سموكلو sùmuklu, *a. t.* Snotty, mucous; سموكلو بوجك sùmuklu-bàjek, *s. t.* A snail, a slug. [The poisonous wind.

سموم sèmūm, *a. a.* Poisonous; —, *s. a.*

سميت *or* سميد sìmit, *s. t.* A kind of breakfast cake made like a large ring.

سمير sèmīr, *s. a.* Evening conversation.

سميز sèmiz, *a. t.* Fat, well-fed; —اوت, sèmiz-ɔt, *s. t.* Purslain.

سميع sèmīʿʿ, *s. a.* The all-hearing God.

سمين sèmīn, *a. a.* Fat, well-fed.

سن sɛn, *pron. t.* Thou; سنك sɛning, Thy; thine; سنى sɛni, Thee; سكا sànga, To thee; سنده sɛndɛ́, At *or* in thee; سندن sɛndan, From thee; سنكله sɛningla, With thee; سنسز sɛnsiz, Without thee; سنجه sɛnja, Thy fashion, according to thee; —, sìnn, *s. a.* A year of age; age; (*pl.* اسنان èssnān), A tooth.

سنا sɛnā, *s. a.* Brightness, splendour; —, *or* —مكى, sɛ́nā-mèkkī, Senna (the most esteemed coming from Mecca).

سنان sìnān, *s. a.* The point or head of a lance. [water.

سنبكى sùnbéki, *s. t.* A diver in deep

سنبل sùnbul (zùnbul), *s. p.* A hyacinth; سنبلى sùnbulī, *a. a.* Hyacinthine in colour, overcast (summer sky).

سنبله sùnbulɛ́, *s. a.* A head *or* ear of corn; the sign Virgo. [Sleep.

سنه sɛnɛ́, *s. a.* A year; —, sìnɛ́, *s. a.*

سنت sùnnèt, *s. a.* Any religious practice founded on an imitation of the actions of Muhammed, especially circumcision; the whole body of practices so founded, constituting the third basis of Muhammedan canon law; سنتجى sùnnètji, *s. t.* A circumciser; سنتلو sùnnètli, *a. t.* Circumcised; سنتسز sùnnètsiz, *a. t.* Uncircumcised; —او, sùnnèt-ɔl, *v.n.* To undergo circumcision; ا—, sùnnèt-et, *v.a.* To circumcise.

سنتنه sèntina, *s. t.* (*Italian*), The bilge of a ship; —صويى, —sùyu, Bilge-water.

سنج sènj, *a. p.* (*in composition*), Who weighs, measures, esteems, values, considers.

سنجاب sìnjāb (zìnjèf), *s. p.* The grey squirrel ; سنجابی sìnjābī, *a. a.* Of the colour of the grey squirrel's fur.

سنجاق sànj*a*k, *s. t.* A flag, banner, ensign, standard; a minor province, of which several may be included in one ایالت èyālèt, or government-general ; سنجاقدار sànj*a*kdār, An ensign-bearer ; —شریف, sànj*a*k*i*-shèrīf, The sacred banner of Muhammed preserved at Constantinople.

سند sèned, *s. a.* A document (as being a thing on which one can lean with confidence).

سندروس sèndérūss (sàndaloss), *s. t.* Gum copal(?), gum sandarac(?).

سندس sùnduss, *s. a.* A kind of rich silk [stuff.

سنسی sìnsi, *s. t.* A sly fellow.

سنك sènin*g*, *pron. t.* Thy; thine; —, sèngh, *s. p.* A stone; سنکبار sènghbār, سنکسار sènghsār, سنکلاخ sènghlākh, *s. p.* A stony place.

سنکسار sènghsār, *s. p.* The punishment of lapidation or stoning to death.

سنکین sènghīn, *a. p.* Heavy.

سنمك sìnmek (*aor.* سینر sìnER), *v.n.* To shrink to nothing (in a corner), to huddle one's self up, to hide one's self as it were from shame, modesty, or confusion.

سنوح sùnūh, *s. a.* A becoming manifest, appearing; ا—, —et, *v.n.* To appear, come forth, be made manifest.

سنور sìnir, *s. t.* A limit, boundary, frontier, coast ; —کسمك, sìnir-kèssmek, *v. n.* To appoint, mark out, lay down, define a frontier or boundary.

سنوی sènévī (*fem.* سنویه sènévìyyÉ), *a. a.* Annual.

سنی sèni, *pron. t. acc.* Thee ; —, sènī (*fem.* سنیه sènìyyÉ), *a. a.* Splendid, brilliant ; —, sùnnī, *a. a.* Conforming to the practices of Muhammed in all religious observances; a Sunnite or orthodox Mussulman.

سنین sènīn, *s.pl.a.* (*of* سنه sènÉ), Years.

سو sū, *s. p.* A side ; سوبسو sū-bè-sū, Side by side ; on all sides.

سؤ sù', *s. a.* Evil ; badness ; —حال, sù'i-hāl (Badness of condition or circumstances), Bad circumstances ; سؤظن sù'i-zànn (Badness of conjectural opinion), A bad opinion, suspicion.

سواحل sèwāhil, *s.pl. a.* (*of* ساحل sāhil), Shores, coasts.

سواد sèwād, *s.a.* Blackness; a dark body easily seen at a distance, *and hence* a town, city.

سوار sùwār, *a. p.* Mounted, riding.

سواری sùwāri, *s. p.* A cavalry soldier ; cavalry; —, *s.t.* The captain of a man-of-war.

سؤال sù'āl, *s. a.* A questioning, asking ; begging ; a question ; ا—, —et, *v.a.* To ask. [crushed pips, kernels, &c.

سوبیه sùbiyÉ, *s. t.* Any drink made from

سوپرمك sùpurmek, سوپرکه sùpurghÉ, سوپرندی sùpurundu, See سپورمك, &c.

سوخته sūkhtÉ, *a.p.* Burnt; —, *s.p.* (sòft*a*), One whose heart or mind is burnt or inflamed with the love of God, religion, or science; a student of law and divinity.

سود sūd, *s. p.* Profit, gain; —أور, sūd-āvÈr, *a. p.* Which brings profit; — (*or* سوت sùt), *s. t.* Milk; —انا, sùt-àna, A wet-nurse; foster-mother; —قرنداشی, sùt-(kàrdashi), A foster-brother; سودن کسمك sùtd*a*n-késsmek, *v.a.* To wean.

سودا sÈvdā, *s. a. Black bile* (a supposititious humour of the body); melancholy; any fixed idea, wish, or monomania; قره— kAra-sÈvdā, *s. t.* The spleen or monomania of melancholy; سوداوی sÈvdāvī, *a. a.* Pertaining to *black bile* or melancholy.

سوده sūdÉ, *a. p.* Rubbed.

سور sūr, *s.a.* A rampart, city wall, castle wall; —, *s. p.* A feast, merry-making.

سوراخ sūrākh, *s. p.* A hole. [attack.

سورت sÈvrÈt, *s. a.* The violence of an

سورتمك sùrtmek (*aor.* سورتر sùrtEr), *v.a.* To draggle (one's clothes) in the dirt; سورتنمك sùrtunmek (*aor.* سورتنور surtunur), *v.n.* To crawl, drag one's self along in the dirt; to grub one's self in the dirt; to frequent improper places.

سورچمك sùrchmek (*aor.* سورچر sùrchEr), *v.n.* To slip (the foot).

سورك sùrek, *s. t.* Duration, durability.

سوركلمك sùruklémek (*aor.* سوركلر sùruklEr), *v.a.* To drag, drag along; سوركلنمك sùruklEnmek (*aor.* سوركلنور sùruklEnir), *v.n.* and *p.* To trail *or* be dragged along.

سوركون sùrgh*y*un, *s. t.* Exile; a place of exile; an exiled person. [a lock.

سوركی sùrghu, *s. t.* A bolt; the bolt of

صورمك sùrmek (*aor.* سورر sùrEr), *v.a.* To exile (a person); to drive (cattle, &c.); to rub in, on, *or* against (ointment, &c.); to plough (land); to live (a life); to shoot out (roots or branches); —, *v.n.* To travel quickly; to last (a while); to require time, take time; to shoot (seeds, plants), spring up, take root, send forth shoots, grow; to be purged or very much relaxed (the belly); عمر— ʿùmr-sùrmek, *v.n.* To lead an agreeable life; چفت— chìft-sùrmek, *v.n.* To drive the plough; يوز— yùz-sùrmek, *v.n.* To rub the face (on the ground) as a sign of humility.

سورنمك sùrunmek (*aor.* سورينور sùrunur), *v.n.* To rub one's self (against anything); to drag one's self along.

سوره sūrÉ, *s. a.* A chapter of the Kurʿan.

سوری *or* سورو sùru, *s.t.* A flock (as being driven by a drover); a considerable number of individuals of any live thing, a flock, crowd, group, herd; —, sivri, *a. t.* Sharp-pointed; سوریجی sùruju, *s. t.* A postilion.

سوریه Sùrrìyy*É*, *s. a.* Syria.

سوریوس Sūrrìyyūs, *s. a.* Nimrod.

سوز sùz, *s. t.* A word; a saying, what one says; a promise; a word to say against anything; an objection;

سوزی كچر sùzu-ghèchER, *a. t.* One whose word, command, or request has great weight; اكاسوزم يوق Anga-sùzum-yòk, I have nothing to say against that; برينه سوز اتمق bìrina-sùz-Atmak, *v.n.* To talk at one; برنيك سوزينى طوتمق bìrining-sùzunu-tûtmak, To keep some one's commandments; —دكلەمك, sùz-dīnĕmek, To give ear to advice; برنيك سوزندن چقمق birining-sùzun-dan-chìkmak, Not to follow what some one has recommended or requested; سوزندن دونمك sùzundan - dùnmek *with the necessary change of pronoun*), To go away from one's word, retract a promise or assertion; سوزم يبانه sùzum-yàbAna (my word to the wilderness), I beg your pardon for using the term, but it does not apply to you (the *Italian: con rispetto parlando*, said when the speaker uses any vulgar epithet); —, sūz, *a. p.* (*in composition*), Which burns, ignites, destroys by burning; —, *s. p.* A burn, a burning; grief, sorrow, regret.

سوزان sūzān, *a. p.* Burning. [der, filter.

سوزكچ sùzghech, *s. t.* A strainer, cullen-

سوزلمك sùzulmek (*aor.* سوزيلور sùzulur), *v.n.* To have the appearance seen in those of a drunken or sleepy person (the eyes); to droop down on the spot (a drunken man); —, *v.p.* To be strained, filtered. [To strain, filter.

سوزمك sùzmek (*aor.* سوزر sùzER), *v.a.*

سوزن sūzèn, *s. p.* A needle.

سوس sùss, *s. t.* Any superficial embellishment; the *shading* of pencil or water-colour drawings; سوس ويرمك sùss-vèrmek, *v.n.* To set off with any embellishment; سوسنى اورمق sùssunu-wûrmak, To shade (a drawing); سوس ا sùss-et, *v.n.* To strut and show one's self off.

سوسن sūsèn, *s. p.* A lily; an iris.

سوق sèvk, *s. a.* A driving, pushing forward, urging, causing to go or march, sending; an instigating; ا—, —et, *v.a.* To drive, push, urge, send, cause to go; to instigate, incite; —, sūk, *s. a.* A street of shops. [seam.

سوكك sùkuk, *a. t.* Ripped open at the

سوكلون sùghlun, *s. t.* A pheasant.

سوكمك sùkmek (*aor.* سوكر sùkER), *v.a.* To rip up (a seam), unsew; to take to pieces; to pull up by the roots; to make one's way (through obstacles of any kind); to read, decipher; —, *v.n.* To make its way to the surface (any internal disease), discharge itself, and be healed; —, sùghmek, *v.n.* To call names, revile, curse, swear; سوكلمك sùkyulmek, *v.n.* To come unsewn; to run, rove out (any knitted work); —, *v.p.* To be ripped or unsewn or unrove, taken to pieces; to be got through, got over; to be read or deciphered.

سوكند sèvkènd, *s. p.* An oath.

سوكيلو sèvghili, *s. t.* The beloved object of one's affection; a gallant; a sweetheart.

سولپك **sùlpuk,** *a. t.* **Limp, hanging loose and flaccid, flabby.**

سولك **sùluk,** *s. t.* **A leech.**

سولمن **sùlumèn,** *s. t.* **Calomel.**

سومك **sèvmek** (*aor.* سور **sèver**), *v.a.* **To love; to like.**

سونج **sèvinj,** *s. t.* **Joy, gladness.**

سوندرمك **sèvindirmek** (*aor.* سوندرر **sèvindirir**), *v.a.* **To make happy, cause to rejoice; —, sùndurmek** (*aor.* سوندورر **sùndurur**), *v.a.* **To put out, extinguish.**

سونكر **sùngher,** *s. t.* **A sponge.**

سونكى **sùnghu,** *s. t.* **A bayonet.**

سونمك **sèvinmek** (*aor.* سوينور **sèvinir**), *v.n.* **To rejoice, be glad, be pleased; —, sùnmek** (*aor.* سونر **sùner**), *v.n.* **To go out, become extinguished.**

سويه **sèvìyyé,** *s. a.* **Equality (in** على السويه **"àlé-'ss-sèvìyyé,** *ad. a.* **Equally, alike).**

سوبجى **sèviji,** *s. t.* **A woman who loves to excite herself with another woman.**

سويدا **sùwèydā,** *s. a.* **A small black spot, the speck of original sin.**

سويلجه *or* سيويلجه **sìvilja,** *s.t.* **A pimple.**

سويلمك **sùwèylémek** (*aor.* سويلر **sùwèyler**), *v.a.* **To say; to tell, communicate; to pronounce, utter; to speak; to confess;** سويلتمك **sùwèyletmek,** *v.a.* **To cause to speak; to allow to speak; to force to speak; to torture and extort a confession from (a person);** سويلنمك **sùwèylenmek,** *v.n.* **To speak or murmur to one's self, to grumble; —,** *or* سويلنلمك **sùwèylénilmek,** *v.p.* **To be said, pronounced, spoken;**

سويلشمك **sùwèyleshmek,** *v.a.* **To confer together, talk (some matter over) together.**

سويندرمك **sùyundurmek (sùndurmek);** سوينمك **sùyunmek (sùnmek).** **See** سوندرمك *and* سونمك.

سه **sèh,** *a. p.* **Three;** سه‌شنبه **sèh-shènbih,** *s. p.* **Tuesday; —, sa, sé, Turkish conditional termination, contracted from** ايسه **ìssé,** *if it be, though it be.*

سهام **sìhām,** *s. pl. a.* (*of* سهم **sèhm**), **Arrows.**

سهر **sèhr,** *s. a.* **Restlessness, sleeplessness.**

سهل **sèhl (sèhil),** *a. a.* **Easy, not difficult; level, plain (country).**

سهم **sèhm,** *s. a.* **An arrow; (sèhim) a share, portion (of an inheritance); a kind of transferable life annuity payable by the treasury; a kind of exchequer bill, bank-note, or assignat (afterwards called** قائمه **kā'imé).**

سهو **sèhv,** *s. a.* **A mistake;** ا—, **—et,** *v.n.* **To make a mistake.**

سهولت **sùhūlèt,** *s. a.* **Facility, ease; gentleness, caution;** سهولتلو **sùhūlètli,** *a. t.* **Easy, not difficult.**

سى **si,** *a. p.* **Thirty; —, si** *or* **si, Turkish pronominal affix of the third person singular when the word to which it is added ends with a vowel; as** باباسى **bābassi, His father,** دده‌سى **dèdéssi, His grandfather.**

سيا **sìya,** *s. t.* **The backing a boat with one or both oars, so as to turn her or make her go astern; —!** *int. t.* **Back** your boat! ا—, —et, *v.a.* To back (a boat); —, *v.n.* To back astern (with a boat).

سیاح sèyyāh, *s. a.* A traveller.

سیاحت sèyāhàt, *s. a.* Travel; سیاحتنامه sèyāhàt-nāmé, *s. p.* A book of travel.

سیادت siyādèt, *s. a.* The quality of being a سید sèyyid, *descendant of Muhammed.*

سیار sèyyār (*fem.* سیاره sèyyāré, A planet), *a. a.* Who or which moves about, wandering.

سیاست siyāssèt, *s. a.* The government or administration of public affairs; capital punishment; ا—, —et, *v.a.* To subject to capital punishment; to govern, rule as a magistrate.

سیاق siyāk, *s. a.* What follows in a sentence; the grammatical or logical construction of a phrase; a mode, manner, way; سیاق وسباق siyāk-u-sìbāk, The context; بوسیاقده bū-sìyākda, According to this, thus, in this manner.

سیاقت sìyākàt, *s. a.* The peculiar hand-writing used in the finance department.

سیال sèyyāl (*fem.* سیاله sèyyālé), *a. a.* Flowing, liquid.

سیان siyān, *s. a. dual* (*of* سی *not used*), Two like or equal things; (*as a Turkish adjective*) equal, alike, all the same.

سیاه siyāh, *a. p.* Black; —, *s. p.* A black spot; blackness, of a black colour; سیم سیاه sìm-siyāh, Quite black; سیاهلاتمق siyāhlatmak, *v.a.* To blacken, make black; سیاهلنمق siyāhlanmak, *v.n.* To become black.

سیب sīb, *s. p.* An apple.

سیجاق sìjāk, *a. t.* Warm, hot; —, and سیجاقلق sìjāklik, *s. t.* Heat, warmth.

سیخ sīkh, *s. p.* A spit or skewer.

سید sèyyid, *s. a.* (*fem.* سیده sèyyidé), *s. a.* A prince; a descendant of Muhammed.

سیر sèyr, *s. a.* Motion, change of place, a wandering; a show, sight, anything to look at, a spectacle; a looking at anything; سیریری sèyr-yèri, *s. t.* A place where people collect for enjoyment; سیرجی sèyrji, *s. t.* A spectator, looker-on, a promenader, a lounger; ا—, —et, *v.a.* To look at, look on (anything as an object of pleasure or curiosity); —, *v.n.* To move, travel, change its locality; —, siyèr, *s. pl. a.* (*of* سیرت sīrèt), The characteristic acts of a person's life, particularly those of Muhammed or other celebrated men; کتب سیر kyù-tubu-siyèr, Historical books, biographical works relating to the lives of Muhammedan worthies; —, sīr, *s. p.* Garlic; *a. p.* Full, satiated.

سیران sèyrān, *s. a.* A promenading, walking about for pleasure; سیرانگاه sèyrān-ghyāh, A place for a promenade.

سیرت sīrèt, *s. a.* The general tenour of a person's life and deeds.

سیره sìra, *s. t.* Syra (island of).

سیرك sèyrèk, *a. t.* Wide apart, open, not close; not close woven; *ad. t.* Not frequently, seldom.

سیس sìss, *s. t.* A fog, a mist.

سیغورته sìghùrta, *s. t.* Insurance.

سیف sèyf, *s. a.* A sword, sabre.

سیل sèyl (sèl), *s. a.* سیلاب sīlʌb, *s. p.* A torrent; the overflowing of water.

سیلان sèyélān, *s. a.* A flowing, running; ا—, —et, *v.n.* To flow, run.

سیلی sīlī, *s. p.* A smack on the face; a box on the ear. [The thirtieth.

سیم sīm, *s. p.* Silver; —, sìyum, *a. p.*

سیما sīmā, *s. p.* The features, visage, physiognomy; لاسیما lā-sìyyémā, *ad. a.* Especially, principally, above all.

سیماب sīmʌb, *s. p.* (Silver-water) Quicksilver, mercury.

سیمك sīymek (*aor.* سیر sìyer), *v.n.* To urine (said only of a dog).

سیمیا sīmyā, *s. a.* A kind of occult science, magic, necromancy.

سیمین sīmīn, *a. p.* Of silver.

سینك sìnek, *s. t.* A fly; اتسینكی ʌt--sìnè*gh*i, *s. t.* A gad-fly; سوری‌سینك sìvri-sìnek, *s. t.* A musquito; a gnat; سینكلك sìneklik, *s. t.* A whisp for driving flies away with, a fly-flapper.

سینه sīné, *s. p.* The breast, bosom.

سینی sìni, *s. t.* A large brass or copper tray.

سیوشمك sìvishmek (*aor.* سویشور sìvi-shir), *v.n.* To slip away quietly.

سیوف sùyūf, *s. pl. a.* (*of* سیف sèyf), Swords, sabres.

سیولجه *or* سیویلجه sìvilj*a*, *s. t.* A pimple.

سیه sìyèh (*contracted from* سیاه sìyāh), *a. p.* Black. [keeper.

سئیس sè'īss, *s. a.* A groom, horse-

سیئه sèyyi'é, *s. a.* A sin; an evil consequence; سیئه‌سنی چكمك sèy-yi'éssini-chèkmek, *v.n.* To be exposed to the evil consequences (of any act).

ش

ش shīn (shìn), Sixteenth letter of the Turkish alphabet, having always the value of the English *sh* in *sharp, rash.* In chronograms it has the numeral value of 300, and in the dates of letters it stands, deprived of its points, as the abbreviation for the month شعبان Shà''bʌn.

شا shā, *or* شاء shā'*a*, (God) wills (in the Arabic adverbial locution ان‌شاءالله ìn-shā-'llāh, *If God wills, God willing,* used instead of the English term, *I hope, let us hope*).

شاب (shʌp), *s. t.* Alum; —, shʌbb, *s. a.* A young man, youth. [bravo!

شاباش shābʌsh! *int. p.* Well done!

شاپقه shʌpk*a*, *s. t.* A hat, a European cap of any kind; the truck of a mast; شاپقه‌لو shʌpk*a*li, *a. t.* A man wearing a hat or cap of European form.

شاخ shākh, *s. p.* A branch.

شاد shād (shʌz), شادان shādān, شادمان shādmān, *a. p.* Happy, joyful, merry, delighted.

شادروان shād-rèwān, *s. p.* (Which flows merrily), a kind of reservoir for water in the court of mosques, having a roof and conveniences for the performance of ablution. [annotator.

شارح shārih, *s. a.* A commentator,

شارق shārik, *in* شارق الانوار shāriku-'l-ènvār, *a. a.* Light-diffusing, luminous, glorious, brilliant.

شاشرمق shàshirmak (*aor.* شاشرر shàshirir), *v.n.* To be confused, not know what to say or do; —, *v.a.* To lose (one's way), take the wrong (road); to lose (one's place in reading or writing).

شاشقين shàshkin, *s. t.* A stupid fellow, one who does not know what he is about.

شاشمق shàshmak (*aor.* شاشار shàshar), *v.n.* To be surprised, astonished; to be bewildered, confounded; to miss (*generally used in the negative form*).

شاشى shàshi, *a. t.* Squinting (eye).

شاطر shAtir, *s. t.* A kind of running footman in the olden time.

شاعر shā''ir, *s. a.* A poet.

شاقول shākūl (shāghol), *s. t.* A mason's plummet and line; a mason's or carpenter's plumb level.

شاكر shākir, *s. a.* One who gives thanks.

شاكرد shāghird, *s. p.* A pupil, schoolboy, scholar; an apprentice, learner of any kind.

شاكى shākī, *a. a.* One who complains.

شال shāl (shAl), *s. p.* A shawl; a Cashmere shawl; the stuff of a Cashmere shawl. [merino.

شالاكى shAlāki, *s. t.* The best French

شالى shAli, *s. t.* A kind of camlet made of goat's hair.

شام shām, *s. p.* The evening; —, shāmm (*fem.* شامه shāmmé), *s. t.* Syria; —, *a. a.* Which perceives odours; قوت شامه kùvvéti-shāmmé, The sense of smelling.

شآمت *or* شئامت shà'āmet, *s. a.* The being inevitably unlucky to its possessor (a house, horse, estate, employ).

شامخ shāmikh, *a. a.* High (mountain, &c.). [which contains; comprehensive.

شامل shāmil, *a. a.* Which includes,

شان shAn, *s. t.* (*for* شأن shè'n, *s. a.*) Honour, glory, reputation.

شانه shāné, *s. p.* A comb.

شاه shāh, *s. p.* The king of Persia; the Sultan; شاهانه shāhāné, *a. p.* Pertaining to the Shah of Persia or to the Sultan; royal; imperial.

شاهباز shāh-bāz, *s. p.* The royal falcon.

شاهد shāhid, *s. a.* An eye-witness; a legal witness in a court of justice; —, *s. p.* A beautiful youth or woman.

شاهراه shāh-rāh, *s. p.* A royal road, public road.

شاهزاده shāh-zādé, *s. p.* A Persian prince of the blood; an Ottoman prince of the blood.

شاهنشاه shāhinshāh, *s. p.* (King of kings) The Sultan.

شاهنشين shāhnishīn, *s. p.* A kind of

projecting covered balcony or bow-window in a house.

شاهين shāhin, *s. t.* A royal falcon.

شايان shāyān, *a. p.* Worthy, meriting.

شائبه shā'ibé, *s. a.* A semblance, small tincture, least appearance.

شايد shāyed, *c. p.* Lest; perhaps, peradventure.

شايسته shāyèssté, *a. p.* Proper, fitting.

شايع shāyi'', *a. a.* Diffused, divulged, rumoured, spread.

شايقه shāyika, *s. t.* A kind of Levantine lugger.

شايكان shāyghyān, *a. p.* Great, abundant (riches); —, *s. p.* A treasury or treasure.

شب shèb, *s. p.* The night.

شباب shèbāb, شبابت shèbābèt, *s. a.* Youth, youthfulness; عنفوان شبابت ''ùnfuvāni-shèbābèt, The flower of youth.

شباط shùbāt, *s. a.* February.

شبانروز shèbānrūz, *ad. p.* By night and by day.

شببوى shèb-būy, *s. p.* (Night-smelling), The stock; the wall-flower.

شبپره shèb-pèré, *s. p.* A bat (bird).

شبخون shèb-khūn, *s. p.* A night attack.

شبلك shèbek, *s. t.* A baboon.

شبكه shèbéké, *s. a.* Anything formed in meshes like a net, network.

شبنم shèb-nèm, *s. p.* Dew.

شبه shibh, *s. a.* A resemblance; —معين, shibhi-mà''īn, A rhomboid.

شبهه shùbhé (shùp—), *s. a.* A doubt, incertitude; a doubt, suspicion; ا—, —et, *v.n.* To doubt, to feel uncertain; to have a suspicion; شبهه‌لنمك shùphélènmek, *v.n.* To become suspicious, to have one's suspicions or doubts awakened; شبهه‌لو shùphéli, *a. t.* Doubtful, uncertain (thing); شبهه‌جى shùphéji, *s. t.* A doubting person.

شبيكه shèbīké, *s. a.* Any kind of net-work.

شبيه shèbīh, *a. a.* Similar, resembling, like.

شتا shitā, *s. a.* The winter; —, shèttà, *a. a.* Various, many, different.

شتاب shitāb, *s. p.* A running, making haste; ا—, —et, *v.n.* To run, hasten.

شتابان shitābān, *a. p.* Who runs, who makes haste.

شتر shùtur, *s. p.* A camel; شترمرغ shùtur-mùrgh, *s. p.* (Camel-bird), The ostrich; شتركاوپلنك shùtur--ghyāw-pèlènk, (Camel, cow, leopard) A cameleopard; شتربان shùturbān, *s. p.* A camel-driver.

شتم shètm, *s. a.* A vilifying, abusing, scolding; ا—, —et, *v.n.* To call names.

شجاعت shèjā''àt, *s. a.* Courage, bravery, valour.

شجر shèjer, *s. a.* A tree, plant, bush.

شجره shèjéré (sèjéré), *s. a.* A genealogical tree, scheme of descent.

شجون shùjūn, *s. pl. a.* (*of* شجن, *not used*), Different ways of solution, relation, or explanation, *in* ذوشجون zū--shùjūn, *a. a.* Differently explained by different people (a tradition, &c.).

شجيع shèjī'', *a. a.* Courageous, brave, bold.

شحامت shàhāmet, *s. a.* Fatness, plumpness of body.

شحنه shàhné, *s. p.* A magistrate, governor.

شخص shàkhss, *s. a.* A person; the person, individual body; any object set up or fixed upon as a mark by surveyors.

شد shèdd, *s. a.* A tightening, making tight, firm, strong; ا—, —et, *v.a.* To tighten; to make firm, strong; to strengthen; —, shùd, *s. p.* A going, going away, departing; آمدشد āmed-shùd, آمدوشد āmed-u-shùd, *s. p.* A coming and going, traffic of passengers, &c.; ا— — —, āmed-u-shùd-et, *v.n.* To come and go to and fro.

شدت shiddèt, *s. a.* Violence, force, strength, vehemence; شدتلو shìddètli, *a. t.* Violent, vehement.

شدگان shùdéghyān, *s. pl. p.* (*of* شده shùdé, *not used*), The dead, those who were.

شديد shèdīd, *a. a.* Violent, vehement, severe.

شر shèrr, *s. a.* Evil; mischief; خيروشر khàyr-u-shèrr, Good and evil.

شرا shìrā, *s. a.* A buying, purchasing; بيعوشرا bèy''-u-shìrā, Sale and purchase.

شراب shèrāb (shàrab), *s. a.* Wine.

شرار shirār, *s. pl. a.* (*of* شر shèrr), Evils; mischiefs; (*of* شراره shìrārē), Sparks.

شراره shìrārē, *s. a.* A spark.

شراع shìrā'', *s. a.* A sail; شراعكشا او shìrā''-kyùshā-òl, *v.n.* To set sail, spread sails.

شرانپو shàranpo, *s. t.* A palisade; a stockade.

شرائر shèrā'ir, *s. pl. a.* (*of* شريره shèrīrē), Evils, mischiefs.

شرائط shèrā'it, *s. p. a.* (*of* شريطه shèrīta), Conditions, stipulations; indispensable previous accessories.

شرب shùrb, *s. a.* A drinking; ا—, —et, *v.a.* To drink.

شربت shèrbèt, *s. a.* A drink, either sweet and agreeable, or medicinal as a purgative draught, &c.; the water of twice-boiled coffee; the water obtained by steeping anything, as liquid manure, &c.

شرت shìrrèt, *s. a.* Malice, evil-mindedness; —, *s. t.* A mischievous person.

شرح shèrh, *s. a.* A cleaving and laying open; a commenting, glosing, paraphrasing; a commentary, glose, paraphrase; a marginal or interlineary note; ا—, —et, *v.a.* To explain by way of comment, glose, paraphrase, or marginal or interlineary note; to cleave and lay open.

شرحه shèrha, *s. a.* A slice; a gash, cut, cleft.

شرذمه shèrzimē, *s. a.* A body of people, congregation, troop.

شرط shàrt, *s. a.* An indispensable previous accessory, a condition, stipulation, proviso; شرطنامه shàrt-nāmē, *s. p.* A paper of conditions, an agreement; ا—, —et, *v.n.* To stipulate, lay down stipulations; شرط اولسون shàrt-òlsun, *int. t.* (I will really do so, or) be it a condition (that I divorce my wife)!

شرطه **shùrta**, *s. a.* A kind of beadle or officer; —, *a. p.* Favourable (wind).

شرع **shèr‘‘**, *s. a.* God's sacred law, as educed from the Kur‘an, the sayings or acts of Muhammed, and the unanimous opinions of the Church in the earliest times; شرعی shèr‘‘ī (*fem.* شرعیه shèr‘‘ìyyé), *a. a.* Pertaining to God's law; agreeable to God's law; شرعاً shèr‘‘*an*, *ad. a.* Agreeably with God's law.

شرف **shèref**, *s. a.* Honour, of which a person may feel proud; honour, or sanctity, which others respect; شرفیاب او sheref-yāb-òl, *v.n.* To be honoured, receive honour.

شرفا **shùréfā**, *s. pl. a.* (*of* شریف shèrīf), Princes, descended from Muhammed.

شرفه **shùrfé** (shèrifé), *s. a.* The gallery of a minaret; شرفه لو (shèriféli), *s. t.* Possessed of a gallery or galleries (a minaret).

شرق **shàrk**, *s. a.* The east; شرقی shàrkī (*fem.* شرقیه shàrkìyyé), *a. a.* Eastern.

شرك **shìrk**, *s. a.* The sin of professing that God is not one but has associates; polytheism.

شركا **shùrékyā**, *s. pl. a.* (*of* شریك shèrīk), Partners, associates.

شركت **shìrkèt**, *s. a.* Partnership; an association, company.

شرلغان **shìrlaghàn** (*for* شیرروغن shīr-rūghān, *s. p.* Milk-oil), *s. t.* (Oil) of sesame.

شرم **shèrm**, *s. p.* Shame; bashfulness; modesty; شرمسار shèrmsār, شرمكین shèrmghīn, شرمناك shèrmnāk, شرمنده shèrmèndé, شرمیده shèrmīdé, *a. p.* [Ashamed.

شروب **shūrup**, *s. t.* Syrup.

شرور **shùrūr**, *s. pl. a.* (*of* شر shèrr), Evils; mischiefs, misdeeds, troubles.

شروط **shùrūt**, *s. pl. a.* (*of* شرط shàrt), Conditions, provisos, stipulations, points.

شروع **shùrū‘‘**, *s. a.* A beginning, commencing, entering upon; ا—, —et, *v.n.* To begin, commence, enter.

شره **shèreh**, *s. a.* Avidity, greediness.

شریان **shìryān**, (*s. a.* A pulse-vein, an artery) *in* شریان طمری shìryān-dàmari, *s. t.* The aorta, jugular vein, or carotid artery (?). [tape.

شرید **shèrīd**, *s. t.* A piece of braid or

شریر **shèrīr**, *s. a.* A malignant.

شریعت **shèrī‘‘àt**, *s. a.* The same as شرع shèr‘‘, which see.

شریف **shèrīf** (*fem.* شریفه shèrīfé), *a. a.* Honourable, honoured, noble, sacred, holy; —, *s. a.* A prince, descendant of Muhammed. [associate, a fellow.

شریك **shèrīk**, *s. a.* A partner, an

شست **shùsst**, *s. p.* A washing; شست وشوا shùsst-u-shū-et, *v.a.* To wash.

شسته **shùssté**, *a. p.* Washed; نا شسته nā-shùssté, Unwashed.

شش **shèsh**, *a. p.* Six.

ششخانه **shèsh-khāné** (shìsh-hāné), *s. p.* A rifle; ششخانه لو (shìsh-hānéli), *a. t.* Rifled (gun).

ششمان shìshmʌn, *a. t.* Corpulent.

ششمك shìshmek (*aor.* شيشر shìshɪr), *v.n.* To swell, swell out.

شصت shʌsst, *a. p.* Sixty.

شطارت shʌtārèt, *s. a.* Alacrity, activity, sharpness.

شطرنج shʌtrènj (sʌntrànj), *s. p.* The game of chess; a check *or* chequer (on any stuff or surface); شطرنجلو (sʌntrànjli), *a. t.* Checked, chequered.

شعار shì"ār, *s. a.* A distinctive mark or sign. [sunbeam.

شعاع shù"ā", *s. a.* A ray of light, a

شعبان shà"bʌn, *s. a.* The eighth month of the Muhammedan year.

شعبده shù"bédé, *or* شعبذه shù"bézé, *s. p.* Any trick of legerdemain or conjuring; شعبده باز shù"bédé-bʌz, *s. p.* A conjurer, trickster.

شعبه shù"bé, *s. a.* A ramification; a subdivision; a branch of a clan or tribe.

شعر shì"r, *s. a.* Poetry; the poetical fire or vein; —, shà"r, *s. a.* Hair; —سويلمك, shì"r-sùwèylémek, *v.n.* To indite poetry; —اوقومق, shì"r-òkumak, To read, recite, repeat poetry; شعرى shì"rī (*fem.* شعريه shì"rìyyé), *a. a.* Pertaining to poetry.

شعرا shù"arā, *s. pl. a.* (*of* شاعر shā"ir), Poets. [Vermicelli.

شعريه shà"rìyyé (shèhrìyyé), *s. t.*

شعشعه shà"sha"a, *s. a.* A glittering, flashing, gleaming.

شعله shù"lé, *s. a.* Flame.

شعور shù"ūr, *s. a.* Intelligence, intellect, understanding.

شعير shà"īr, *s. a.* Barley.

شغب shàghab, *s. a.* A turmoil.

شغف shàghf, *s. a.* Violent love, passion.

شغل shùghl, *s. a.* An occupation.

شفا shìfā, *s. a.* A state of health; a return to health, a cure; a remedy, means of cure, or wholesome thing conducive to health; شفالو shìfāli, *a. t.* Wholesome, beneficial to health; —بولمق, shìfā-bùlmak, *v.n.* To be cured, get well; —ويرمك, shìfā-vèrmek, *v.n.* To grant health (God); شفالر اولسون shìfālɪr-òlsun! *int. t.* May it be health to you! (*said to one after he has drunk, bathed, or been shaved*); دارالشفا dāru-'sh-shìfā, An hospital.

شفاعت shìfā"àt (shè—), *s. a.* Intercession; ا—, —et, *v.n.* To make intercession. [transparent.

شفاف shèffāf, *a. a.* Diaphanous, clear,

شفاه shìfāh, *s. pl. a.* (*of* شفه shèfé), Lips; شفاهى shìfāhī, *a. a.* Verbal, oral; شفاهاً shìfāhan, *ad. a.* Verbally, orally, by word of mouth.

شفتالو shèftāli, *s. p.* A peach; a kiss; —يارمه yàrma—, A melting peach; اتشفتالوسى èt-shèftālissi, كباد شفتالوسى kèbād-shèftālissi, A clingstone peach; تويسز شفتالو tùysuz-shèftāli, (*a downless peach*) A nectarine.

شفته shìfté, *a. p.* Mad; distracted with love; —, *s. p.* A lover.

شفق shàfak, s. a. The evening twilight; the break of day.

شفقت shàfakat, s. a. The tendency of feeling which leads to commiseration; شفقتلو shàfakatlū, a. t. Kind (*used in addressing letters*).

شفوى shèfévī, a. a. Labial.

شفه shèfé, s. a. A lip; شق شفه ا shàkki-shèfé-et, v.n. To open one's lips or mouth and speak.

شفيع shèfī'', s. a. An intercessor; the great intercessor (Christ with Christians, Muhammed with Muhammedans).

شفيق shèfīk, a. a. Kind, commiserating.

شق shàkk, s. a. A splitting open, rending, severing; —, shìkk, s. a. A part, a subdivision of any matter under consideration, a case; شقين shìkkàyn, s. a. *dual*, The two cases (supposed or shown); ا—, shàkk-et, v.a. To rend.

شقا shàkā, s. a. Wickedness, ill-doing; —, s. t. Fun, a joke; ارباب— èrbābi-shàkā, Wicked people, evil-doers; ا—, —et, v.n. To speak or act in joke; —سويلمك, shàka-sùwèylémek, To speak in joke.

شقاق shìkāk, s. a. Contention, quarrelling, discord.

شقاوت shàkāvèt, s. a. Evilness, wickedness, badness.

شقايق shàkāyik, s. t. The peony.

شقه shùkka, s. a. A note, short letter.

شقى shàkī (*fem.* شقيه shàkìyyé), a. a. Wicked, evil-minded, bad; —, s. a. A wretch, villain.

شك shèkk, s. a. A doubt; a doubting; ا—, —et, v.n. To have a doubt, to doubt.

شكار shìkyār, s. p. The chase, hunting, fowling, fishing; anything caught in the chase, prey; —, a. p. (*in composition*), Who or which catches as prey.

شكاف shìkyāf, s. p. A crack, fissure, cleft; —, a. p. (*in composition*), Who cleaves; موشكاف mū-shìkyāf, a. p. Who splits hairs; موشكافانه mū-shìkyāfāné, a. p. After the manner of one who splits hairs.

شكال shìkyāl, s. p. Trammels for a horse.

شكان shìkyān, s. p. A curl; a twist; a plait; a wrinkle; —, a. p. Curly; folded; wrinkled.

شكايت shìkyāyet, s. a. A complaint, doleance; ا—, —et, v.n. To make a complaint; شكايتجى shèkyāyetji, s. t. A complainant.

شكر shèker, s. t. Sugar; sweetmeats made with sugar; كل بشكر ghyùl-bé-shèker, Conserve of roses; شكرجى shèkerji, s. t. A confectioner; شكرلمه shèkerlémé, s. t. Sweetmeats of sugar, confectionery; —, shùkr (shùkyur), s. a. Thanks, thankfulness; ا—, —et, v.n. To give thanks; —, shùkr! —اولسون, shùkr-òlsun! شكرلراولسون shùkyurler-òlsun! Thanks be (to God)!

شكران shùkrān, a. a. Thankful, grateful; شكرانيت shùkrānìyyèt, s. a. Gratitude, thankfulness.

شکرانه shùkrānÉ, *s. p.* A thanks-offering, anything done as a mark of gratitude. [much.

شگرف shìghèrf, *a. p.* Good; abundant,

شکست shìkèsst, *s. p.* A breaking; ا—, —et, *v.a.* To break.

شکسته shìkèsstÉ, *a. p.* Broken; —, *s. p.* The common running writing of Persia. [open (a flower).

شکفته shùkyùftÉ, *a. p.* Blown, opened,

شکل shèkl (shèkil), *s. a.* A form, figure; a kind, sort.

شکم shìkèm, *s. p.* The belly.

شکمبه shìkèmbÉ (ìshkèmbÉ), *s. p.* Tripe.

شکن shìkèn, *a. p.* (*in composition*), Who breaks.

شکنجه shìkènjÉ (ìshkènjÉ), *s. p.* Torture; ا—, —et, *v.a.* To torture, put to the torture.

شکوا (*for* شکوی) shèkwà, *s. a.* A complaint; ا—, —et, *v.n.* To make a complaint. [som.

شکوفه shùghyūfÉ, *s. p.* A flower, blos-

شکوه shùkyūh, *s. p.* Majesty of appearance, dreadness, awe-inspiringness.

شکیب shèkīb, شکیبا shèkībā, *a. p.* Patient; شکیبائی shèkībā'ī, *s. p.* Patience. [cushion for sitting on.

شلته shìltÉ, *s. t.* A thin quilted upper

شلغم shàlgham, *s. t.* A turnip.

شلوار shàlwar, *s. t.* Loose and long trousers.

شم shèmm, *s. a.* A smelling, examining, or perceiving odours; ا—, —et, *v.a.* To smell.

شماتت shèmātèt, شماته shèmātÉ (shàmAta), *s. a.* A noise, loud noise; ا—, shàmAta-et, *v.n.* To make a great noise; شماته‌تلی shàmAta-tèli, *s. t.* Tinsel. [fellow.

شماته‌جی shèmātÉji, *s. t.* A noisy

شمار shàmar, *s. t.* A smack on the face, a box on the ear; —, shŭmār, *s. p.* A counting; count, tale; —, *a. p.* (*in composition*), Who counts, tells.

شمال shìmāl, *s. a.* The north; the left side; شمالی shìmālī, *a. a.* Northern.

شمائل shèmā'il, *s. pl. a.* (*of* شمال shìmāl, *not used in this sense*), The qualities of heart or mind *contained* in one; the features *contained in one's countenance*.

شمدی shìmdi (shìndi), *s. t.* The present time; —, *ad. t.* Now, at present; presently, immediately, directly, in a minute; just now, a minute ago; همان— hèmEn-shìndi, *ad. t.* Almost directly; just this moment; شمدیلك shìmdilik, *ad. t.* For the present; شمدیجك shìmdijik, *ad. t.* Almost directly; just this moment; شمدیکی shìmdiki, *a. t.* The present.

شمرده shùmùrdÉ, *a. p.* Counted, told.

شمس shèmss, *s. a.* The sun; شمسی shèmsī (*fem.* شمسیه shèmsìyyÉ), *a.a.* Pertaining to the sun, solar; شمسیه shèmsìyyÉ, *s. t.* An umbrella; parasol; pavilion; حروف شمسیه hŭrūfu-shèmsìyyÉ, (The solar letters) Those letters which, when in Arabic phrases they commence a noun or adjective having the definite article ال el, *the,* before them, require that, in pronunciation, the sound of the ل should be omitted, and their own sound reduplicated, as is the case in the word الشمس èsh--shèmss, *the sun.* Those letters are ت, ث, د, ذ, ر, ز, س, ش, ص, ض, ط, ظ, and ن; the others being styled حروف قمريه hùrūfu-kàmèrìyyé, *lunar letters.* [of lightning.

شمشك shìmshek, *s.t.* Lightning, a flash

شمشير shìmshīr, *s. p.* A sword, sabre.

شمع shèm'', *s. a.* A candle; —عسل, shèm''*i*-''àssel, Bees'-wax; a wax-candle, wax-light; شمعدان shèm''idan (shàmdan), *s. p.* A candlestick.

شمعه shèm''*a* (shàma), *s.a.* A wax-taper.

شمول shùmūl, *s. a.* A comprehending; including; comprehensiveness; شمولى او shùmūlu-òl, *v.n.* To comprehend, include, embrace.

شمه shèmmé, *s. a.* A single whiff or sniff of odour; a slight tinge. [perfumed.

شميم shèmīm, *a. a.* Smelling, odorous,

شن shèn, *a. t.* Lively, gay; populous, cultivated, inhabited; شنلك shènlik, *s. t.* Liveliness, gaiety; a populous place, showing signs of man's presence by buildings, cultivation, traffic, &c.; a merry-making, public rejoicings and illuminations.

شناس shìnāss, *a. p.* (*in composition*), Who knows, understands.

شناعت shènā''àt, *s. a.* A being bad, odious, shameful; a bad, odious, shameful act.

شناور shìnāver, *s. p.* A swimmer.

شنائع shènā'i'', *s. pl. a.* (*of* شنيعه shènī''*a*), Bad, odious actions.

شنبه shènbih (shènbé), *s. p.* Saturday.

شنشنه shìnshiné, *s. a.* Natural disposition, character.

شنيد shènīd, *s.p.* A hearing; گفت وشنيد ghyùft-u-shènīd, Speaking and hearing.

شنيده shènīdé, *a. p.* Heard, heard of; who has heard.

شنيع shènī'', *a. a.* Bad, odious, shameful; شنيعه shènī''*a, a. a. fem.*; —, *s. a.* One bad, odious act. [ing.

شو shū, *pron. t.* That; —, *s. p.* A wash-

شوال shèvwāl, *s. a.* Name of the tenth month of the Muhammedan year.

شوخ shūkh, *a. p.* Free in manners, forward, pert.

شور shòr, *a. p.* Saltish, brackish; bad, evil; —, *s. p.* Evil, trouble, disorder.

شورا shùra, *pron. t.* This place, this spot; — (*for* شورى), shùrà, *s. a.* A council.

شوربا shòrba (chòrba), *s. p.* Soup.

شورش shòrish, *s. p.* Trouble, confusion, sedition, contention, disorder.

شورى shùrà, *s. a.* A council.

شوريده shūrīdé, *a. p.* In confusion, confused, disordered.

شوط shàvt, *s. a.* A course or round (in running, especially in the ceremonious running performed by the pilgrims to Mecca).

شوق shèwk, *s. a.* Alacrity, cheerfulness and spirit in acting; inclination, eagerness.

شوك shèvk, *s. a.* A thorn; a spur, a goad.

شوكت shèvkèt, *s. a.* Imperial majesty; شوكتلو shèvkètlū, *a.t.* شوكتمآب shèvkèt-mà'āb, *a. p.* Majestic (the title most specially assumed by and given to the Sultan).

شول shòl, *or* شو shū, *pron. t.* That.

شوم shūm, *a. a.* Unlucky, bringing bad luck.

شؤون shù''ūn, شؤونات shù'ūnāt, *s. pl. a.* (*of* شأن shè'n, *not used*), States, conditions, aspects of being.

شوهر shèvhèr, *s. p.* A husband.

شوى shūy, *a. p.* (*in composition*), Who washes; جامه‌شوى jāmé-shūy, *s. p.* A washer of linen.

شويله shùylé, *ad. t.* So, in that manner; —بويله, shùylé-bùylé, *ad. t.* Middling, not too well.

شه shèh (*abbreviated form of* شاه shāh), *s. p.* The Sultan; the Shah; a king.

شهاب shìhāb, *s. a.* A shooting or falling star; a fiery meteor.

شهادت shàhādet, *s. a.* Valid legal testimony; martyrdom; the profession of the Mùhammedan faith; all things visible; —پرمغى, shàhādet-pàrmaghi, *s. t.* The fore-finger.

شهامت shàhāmet, *s. a.* Courage, valour.

شهپر shèh-pèr, *s. p.* The (royal *or*) pinion feather of a bird's wing.

شهبندر shèh-bèndèr, *s. p.* A consul or commercial magistrate.

شهد shèhd, *s. a.* Honey.

شهدا shùhédā, *s. pl. a.* (*of* شهيد shèhīd), [Martyrs.

شهر shèhr, *s. a.* A lunar month; a calendar month; —, (shèhir), *s. p.* A city, town; شهرلو shèhirli, *a. t.* A townsman (not a rustic); شهرى shèhrī (*fem.* شهريه shèhrìyyé), *a. a.* Pertaining to a month, monthly; شهريه shèhrìyyé, *s. a.* Monthly allowance, pay, or salary.

شهريار shèhriyār, *s. p.* A monarch; the Sultan; شهرياري shèhriyārī, *s. p.* The quality of being a monarch, empire, sovereignty; —, *a. p.* Royal, imperial; شهريارانه shèhriyārāné, *a. p.* Pertaining to a monarch, to the Sultan.

شهزاده shèh-zādé, *s. p.* A prince of the [blood.

شهلا shèhlā, *a. a.* Grey (eye).

شهنشاه shèhinshāh, *s. p.* The king of kings, the Sultan. [for a king's use.

شهوار shèhvār, *a. p.* Good, excellent, fit

شهوانى shèhwānī (*fem.* شهوانيه shèhwānìyyé); *a. a.* Pertaining to the appetites and passions, sensual.

شهوت shèhvèt, *s. a.* Sensual desire.

شهود shùhūd, *s. a.* The being visible; all that is visible; —, *s. pl. a.* (*of* شاهد shahid), Eye-witnesses; witnesses before a judge; —عالم ''ālémi —, The visible world.

شهور shùhūr, *s. pl. a.* (*of* شهر shèhr), Lunar months; calendar months.

شهيد shèhid, *s. a.* A martyr, one who

dies for the faith, either in battle or in any other manner; ـــاو, shèhīd-òl, To be killed in the cause of religion.

شهير shèhīr, *a. a.* Commonly known.

شی (*for* شیء) shèy, *s. a.* A thing; هرشی hèr-shèy, Everything; هیچ بر شی hìch-bir-shèy, Nothing; چوق شی chòk-shèy! Astonishing! Wonderful.

شیاطین shèyàtīn, *s. pl. a.* (*of* شیطان shèytān), Devils, demons.

شیبا shèybā, *a. a.* (*in* لیلهء شیبا lèylé'i-shèybā), The bridal night.

شیخ shèykh, *s.a.* An old man; a mature aged man; an elder; a chief of an Arab tribe; a chief of a community of dervishes; a kind of ecclesiastical dignitarian equivalent to our *dean* or *canon*; a prince (in Arabia); ـــالاسلام, Shèykhu-'l-ìsslām, The chief doctor-of-law in Turkey (his office being at once equal to those of the Lord Chancellor and Archbishop of Canterbury in England); ـــالحرم, Shèykhu-'l-Hàrem, The Prince or Governor of Medina.

شیخوخت shèykhūkhàt, *s. a.* Old age.

شیدا shèydā, *a. p.* Mad, insane; crazed with love. [rānÉ, *a. p.* Lion-like (act).

شیر shīr, *s. p.* Milk; a lion; شیرانه shī-

شیرازه shīrāzÉ, *s. p.* The band at the top and bottom of the back of a book, which is usually ornamented.

شیردان shīrdān, *s. p.* The rennet stomach of an animal.

شیره shīrÉ (shìra), *s. p.* The must or newly-expressed juice of grapes or [fruit.

شیرین shīrīn, *a. p.* Sweet.

شیش shìsh, *s. t.* A skewer; a spit; a small-sword or any similar weapon; a swelling. [(man).

شیشقو shìshko, *a. t.* Fat, corpulent

شیشقین shìshkin, *a. t.* Swoln, swelled.

شیشمك shìshmek (*aor.* شیشر shìshER), *v.n.* To swell; to become fat; to be inflated; شیشرمك shìshirmek (*aor.* شیشرر shìshirir), *v.a.* To cause to swell.

شیشه shīshé (shìshÉ), *s. p.* Common glass; a glass bottle; a bottle of any kind; a lath; a cupping-glass.

شیطان shèytAn, *s. a.* The devil; a cunning fellow; شیطانی shèytAnī, *a. a.* Pertaining to the devil, diabolic, devilish. [ishness, mischief, malice.

شیطنت shèytAnàt, *s. a.* Devilry, imp-

شیعه shī''a, *s. a.* Heresy in religion, particularly the Mussulman heresy prevalent in Persia principally; شیعی shī''ī, *a. a.* Pertaining to the Shi''a sect; a Shiite.

شیفته shīftÉ, *a. a.* Enamoured; mad.

شیم shìyèm, *s. pl. a.* (*of* شیمه shīmÉ), Qualities of the heart, points of natural or moral character.

شین shīn (shìn), *s. a.* Name of the letter ش; —, shèyn, *s. a.* Disgrace, shame, dishonour.

شیو (shèv), *s. p.* A slope, talus, inclined plane, bevel; —, *a. t.* Inclined;

levelled; —صحرا, shèvi-sàhrā, The glacis.

شيوخ shùyūkh, *s. pl. a.* (*of* شيخ shèykh), Old man; elders; chiefs of tribes.

شيوع shùyū'', *s. a.* A being rumoured abroad; —بولمق, shùyū''- būlmak, *v.n.* To be publicly spoken of, to be noised abroad.

شيوه shīvé, *s. a.* Grace, any graceful act, look, or motion; coquetry; شيوهٔ لسان shīvé'i-lìssān, A delicate point in language.

ص

ص sĀd (sĀt), Seventeenth letter of the Turkish alphabet, having the value of the letter *s* or *ss* in English, though occasionally becoming more guttural. Compared with the س, it is the hard letter of the pair, and takes the hard vowels after it. In chronograms and astronomical tables it has the numeral value of 90; and in the dates of letters it is the abbreviation of the name of the month صفر SĀfer.

صابر sĀbir, *s. a.* A patient person.

صابون (sàbun), *s. a.* Soap; صابونلمق sàbunl*a*m*a*k, *v.a.* To soap.

صاپ sĀp, *s. t.* The stalk of anything; a long handle; straw (in its natural untriturated state); صاپلو sĀpl*i*, *a. t.* Having a handle, handled.

صاپلامق sĀplam*a*k (*aor.* صاپلار sĀplar), *v.a.* To stick (any long or pointed thing into any other thing); صاپلانمق sĀplanm*a*k (*aor.* صاپلانور sĀplan*i*r), *v.n.* To stick in, become stuck, stick fast.

صاپمق sĀpm*a*k (*aor.* صاپار sĀpar), *v.n.* To leave a straight course and take a lateral direction.

صاپه sĀp*a*, *a. t.* Not in a straight line of road, out of the road, out-of-the-way; —دوشمك, sĀp*a*-dùshmek, *v.n.* To lie out of the road, to be out of the way.

صاتاشمق sĀt*a*shm*a*k (*aor.* صاتاشر sĀt*a*-sh*i*r), *v.n.* To touch, meddle, have anything to do with (by word or deed).

صاتمق sĀtm*a*k (*aor.* صاتار sàtar), *v.a.* To sell, vend, debit; to talk, prate about (anything), narrate, relate with an air of confidence; to talk with the air of possessing (any particular quality).

صاتون sàt*i*n, *ad. t.* By way of purchase; —المق, sĀt*i*n-Ālm*a*k, *v.a.* To buy, acquire by purchase.

صاتيجى sĀt*i*j*i*, *s. t.* A seller.

صاتيلق sĀt*i*l*i*k, *a. t.* For sale, on sale.

صاج sĀj, *s. t.* Sheet iron; —اياق, sĀj--àyak, *s. t.* A trevet.

صاچ sĀch, *s. t.* The hair of the head, a hair from the head.

صاچاق *or* صاچق sĀch*a*k, *s. t.* The eaves of a house; a fringe.

صاچمق sĀchm*a*k (*aor.* صاچار sĀchar), *v.a.* To scatter, to throw (seed, money, &c.) so as to fall in a scattered manner.

صاچمه sĀchm*a*, *s. t.* Anything thrown

scatteredly; a cast-net; small shot for fowling; foolish talk, nonsense; any foolish act; any valueless thing.

صاچی sàchi, s. t. Small money scattered at weddings, &c.

صاحب sāhib (sāʻab), s. a. An owner, possessor; a friend, protector; صاحبسز sāhibsiz (sāʻabsiz), a. t. Without an owner; friendless; او صاحبی èv-sāhibi (sāʻabi), خانه‌صاحبی khānė-sāhibi, The master of the house; a landlord; صاحب‌فراش sāhib-firāsh, a. p. Sick, ill in bed; طبیعت‌صاحبی tàbiʻʻàt-sāhibi, A man of refined taste; —چیقمق, sāʻab-chìkmak, v.n. To come forward and claim (anything) as the owner or protector; —قران or صاحبقران sāhib-kìrān, (Lord of the age) A Mussulman monarch of mark (such as is said to have been promised in every century for the protection of the faith); —خروج, sāhib-khùrùj, A great but unlawful conqueror, such as Timur the Lame, Jenghiz-Khan, &c.

صاد sàd, s. a. Name of the letter ص.

صادر sàdir, a. a. Emanating, coming forth; —او, —òl, v.a. To emanate, to spring, arise, take its being.

صادق sàdìk, a. a. Truthful, true, truth-speaking, true-spoken; faithful.

صارپ sàrp, a. t. Difficult of ascent, steep; difficult of access; violent, vehement.

صارصمق sàrssmak (aor. صارصار sàrsar), v.a. To shake violently and suddenly.

صارغی sàrghi, s. t. A bandage.

صارق sàrìk, s. t. The shawl or muslin used in forming a turban.

صارقمق sàrkmak (aor. صارقار sàrkar), v.n. To hang loosely down, to dangle; صارقتمق sàrkìtmak (aor. صارقیدر sàrkìdìr), v.a. To cause or leave (anything) to hang down, to let down danglingly (the end of a rope, &c.); صارقق sàrkìk, a.t. Pendulous, dangling, hanging down.

صارقندیلق sàrkìndìlìk, s. t. Any lawless, oppressive, or vexatious act of spoliation or damage. [A sharp sword.

صارم sārim, a. a. Sharp (sword); —, s. a.

صارماشق sàrmàshìk, s. t. Ivy.

صارماشمق sàrmàshmak (aor. صارماشر sàrmàshìr), v.n. To twine mutually round and about each other.

صارمتراق sàrìmtràk, a. t. Yellowish.

صارمساق sārìmsàk, s. t. Garlic.

صارمق sàrmak (aor. صارار sàrar), v.a. To bind, bind up (a thing with some other thing); to bind or twine (a thing) round or about (another thing); صارلمق sàrìlmak (aor. صاریلور sàrìlìr), v.n. To twine, to embrace; —, v. p. To be bound up; to be twined or bound round something.

صاری sàri, a. t. Yellow; red, carrotty (hair); —, s. t. The yolk or yellow (of an egg); صاریلق sàrìlìk, s. t. Yellowness; the jaundice.

صاعقه sāʻʻika, s. a. A thunderbolt.

صاغ sàgh, a. t. Right (hand or side);

alive; well, in good health; whole, not broken, cracked, or injured; صاغلق sàghlik, s. t. Health; a direction given as to any road to be followed; صاغليجق sàghlijàk, s. t. dim. Good little health; صاغليجقله sàghlijàkla! (Go) with a good little health! (*said to friends who are taking leave, generally by ladies*); صاغلقله اولمسه sàghlikla-òlmassa (*or some other verb*)! (O! that he were not, in health!) I wish he had been anything else! صاغلق ويرمك sàghlik-vèrmek, v.n. To direct (anyone as to the road he is to follow); to grant health (God); صاغلق اولسون sàghlik-òlsun! Never mind so long as health remains!

صاغالمق sàghalmak (*aor.* صاغالور sàghalir), v.n. To get well, be healed, cured.

صاغر sàghir, a. t. Deaf; dead, dull, surd (sound).

صاغرى sàghri, s. t. The crupper (of a horse); shagreen.

صاغمق sàghmak (*aor.* صاغار sàghar), v.a. To milk.

صاغناق sàghanak, s. t. A heavy summer shower, storm of rain.

صاف sâf, a. p. Pure unmixed, unadulterated; guileless, simple-minded.

صافى sâfī, a. a. Pure, unmixed; mere, sheer.

صاقسى sâksi, s. t. A flower-pot.

صاقلامق or صاقلمق sàklamak (*aor.* صاقلار sàklar), v.a. To hide, hide away; to save, keep; to protect, guard, preserve.

صاقنمق sàkinmak (*aor.* صاقنور sàkinir), v.n. To keep one's self free, safe; to get out of harm's way; to flinch; to be careful, have a care; to refrain from speaking, be afraid to speak, not to like to speak; to avoid; صاقن sàkin! Take care, now! Mind what you're about!

صاقلو sàkli, a. t. Hidden, secret.

صال sâl, s. t. A raft.

صالت sâlt, ad. t. Only, nothing but, merely.

صالح sālih, a. a. (*fem.* صالحه sāliha), Fit, valid, efficient; righteous (man); —, s. a. A righteous man.

صالدرمق sâldirmak (*aor.* صالدرر sâldirir), v.n. To fly at and attack (as a dog or wild beast); —, v.a. (*caus. of* صالمق sâlmak), To cause to rush, or to make a push; to urge.

صالغون or صالغين sâlghin, s. t. A personal, property, or income tax.

صالقم sâlkim, s. t. A bunch (of grapes, currants, &c.); grape-shot.

صاللامق sâllamak (*aor.* صاللار sâllar), v.a. To swing, shake, wag, wave, or brandish to and fro; to nod or shake (the head).

صاللانمق sâllànmak (*aor.* صاللانور sâllànir), v.n. To swing, wag, shake; to be loose in a socket and move when touched.

صالمق sâlmak (*aor.* صالار sâlar), v.n. To rush, make a push; —, v.a. To cast, throw, heave, pitch; to send; to put, place.

صالنجق **sàlinjàk**, *s. t.* A swing, a seesaw.

صالندى **sàlindi**, *s. t.* The swell of the sea after a storm, the ground-swell.

صالى **sàli**, *s. t.* Tuesday.

صاليويرمك **sàlivèrmek** (*aor.* صاليويرر sàlivèrir), *v.a.* To let go, let loose, set at liberty; —صقال **sàkal-sàlivèrmek**, *v.n.* To let one's beard grow.

صامت **sāmit**, *s. a.* Any kind of property which has no voice.

صامسون **sàmsun**, *s. t.* A mastiff or bull-dog; صامسونجى **sàmsunju**, *s. t.* *Keeper of the mastiffs*, title of certain of the Sultan's guards in the olden time.

صانجى **sànji**, *s. t.* A colic, the gripes, pain in the stomach; صانجيلنمق **sànjilanmak**, *v.n.* To have a colic, to be attacked with the gripes.

صانجيمق **sànjimak** (*aor.* صانجر sànjir), *v.a.* (*old*) To thrust or stick (a lance, &c., into something).

صانصار *or* صانسار **sànsār**, *s. t.* A pole-cat(?); a weasel(?).

صانع **sāni'**, *s. a.* A maker; the Creator.

صانمق **sànmak** (*aor.* صانور sanir), *v.a.* To take for by mistake; —, *v.n.* To think, suppose, imagine; صانكه **sàn-ki**, *c. t.* As if, as though, supposing it were. [respect or consideration.

صاورق **sàvrik**, *a. t.* Who speaks without

صاورمق **sàwurmak** (*aor.* صاورر sàwurur), *v.a.* To winnow, to throw (grain) scatteringly and circularly against the wind; to brandish (a sword).

صاوشمق **sàwushmak** (*aor.* صاوشور sàwushur), *v.n.* To get out of the way; to go away; to leave, quit; صاوشدرمق **sàwushturmak** (*aor.* صاوشدرر sàwushturur), *v.a.* To cause (any evil, or trouble) to pass or go away; to cause to pass by, allow to pass by; to escape from.

صاوصه **sàwsa**, صاوصەجى **sàwsaji**, *s. t.* A sworn or professed seducer.

صاولمق **sàwulmak** (*aor.* صاولور sàwulur), *v.n.* To clear the road, get out of the way.

صاومق **sàwmak** (*aor.* صاوار sàwar), *v.n.* To pass and be at an end, to pass over, pass away (any evil); —, *v.a.* To dismiss, send away, get rid of (visitors, suitors, &c.); صاودرمق **sàwdirmak** (*aor.* صاودرر sàwdirir), *v.a.* To cause to pass away; to dismiss, send away.

صائب **sā'ib**, *a. a.* Which hits the mark.

صايغى **sàyghi**, *s. t.* A consideration, matter taken into consideration, a scruple, a point of caution; صايغيلو **sàyghili**, *a. t.* Cautious, scrupulous.

صايقلمق **sàyiklamak** (*aor.* صايقلار sàyiklar), *v.n.* To be in a delirium and talk nonsense, to wander in mind.

صائم **sā'im**, *a. a.* Fasting, who fasts.

صايمق **sàymak** (*aor.* صايار sàyar), *v.a.* To count, tell; to enumerate; to esteem, consider; to hold in esteem, in consideration.

صايى **sàyi**, *s. t.* A number, count, tale.

صبا sàbā, *or* بادصبا bādi-sàbā, A zephyr, gentle spring breeze.

صباح sàbāh, *s. a.* The morning; to-morrow; صباحليين sàbāhléyin, *ad. t.* In the morning; early, betimes; چيكصباح ching-sàbāh, The time just after daybreak; صباحلمق sàbāh-lamak (*aor.* صباحلار sàbāhlar), *v.n.* To become morning, to begin to be day; to be, to remain *or* to arrive (in any place) on the morrow; صباحكز خيراولسون sàbāhingiz-khàyr-òlsun! Good morning to you! (*said on first meeting*); صباح الخير sàbāhu-'l-khàyr, A round white spot (on a horse's forehead); صباحجى sàbāhji, *s. t.* A person who rises early to business.

صباحت sàbāhàt, *s. a.* Beauty, comeliness.

صبان sàban, *s. t.* A plough.

صباوت sàbāvèt, *s. a.* Childhood; minority of age.

صبح sùbh, *s. a.* The morning.

صبر sàbr, *s. a.* Patience; gum aloes; the American aloe; ا—, —et, *v.n.* To be patient, have patience.

صبغ sìbgh, *s. a.* A dye; Christian baptism.

صبغت sìbghat, *s. a.* Any particular distinctive religious rite, as baptism or circumcision; a religious dispensation.

صبوح sàbūh, *s. a.* Wine drunk in the morning.

صبور sàbūr, *a. a.* Patient.

صبى sàbī (*fem.* صبيه sàbìyyé, and *pl.* صبيان sìbyān), *s. a.* A child, a minor.

صبيح sàbīh (*fem.* صبيحه sàbīha), *a. a.* Beautiful, comely.

صپا sìpa, *s. t.* An ass-colt; a three-legged stool or pair of steps.

صپان sàpan, *s. t.* A sling for throwing stones.

صچان sìchan, *s. t.* A mouse; a rat; فندق صچانى fìndik-sìchani, A mouse; كمرصچانى ghèmer-sìchani, A rat; صچان يولى sìchan-yòlu, The zigzag or covered way or trench for communicating between parallels in sieges.

صچرامق sìchramak (*aor.* صچرار sìchrar), *v.n.* To jump; to jump, spring, or fly up; to splash (water); صچراتمق sìchratmak (*aor.* صچرادر sìchradir), *v.a.* To cause to spring or fly up; to cause (water, mud, &c.) to splash up.

صچمق *or* صيچمق sìchmak (*aor.* صيچار sìchar), *v.n.* To dung, shit, mute.

صح sàhh, *s. a.* A special kind of official signature (equivalent to our initialing); صحلمق sàhhlamak, *v.a.* صح چكمك sàhh-chèkmek, *v.n.* To sign in that special manner.

صحابت sàhābet, *s. a.* Protection or assistance given by influential persons.

صحابه sàhābé, *s. pl. a.* (*of* صاحب sāhib, *not used in this sense*), The companions or personal disciples of Muhammed.

صحارا *or* صحارى sàhārà, *s. pl. a.* (*of* صحرى sàhrà), Deserts, wilds, wildernesses.

صحاف sàhhāf, *s. a.* A vendor of books, especially of Kur'ans.

صحائف sàhāʿif, *s. pl. a.* (*of* صحيفه sàhīfé), Pages of paper or writing.

صحب sàhb, *s. pl. a.* (*of* صاحب sāhib, *not used in this sense*), Personal companions or disciples of Muhammed.

صحبت sùhbèt (sòhpet), *s. a.* Conversation, chit-chat, friendly talk or intercourse; ا—, —et, *v.n.* To talk, converse.

صحت sìhhàt, *s. a.* Truth, correctness, exactitude; (sà'at) health of body; صحتلر اولسون sìhhàtlar (sàʿatlɪr)-òlsun! May it be health to you! (*said to a person when he has been shaved, bathed,* &c.).

صحرا *or* صحری sàhrà, *s. a.* A desert, wild, wilderness, unreclaimed land, a plain, moor, moorland, heath, heathland.

صحف sùhuf, *s. pl. a.* (*of* صحيفه sàhīfé), Pages; the smaller prophetical writings.

صحن sàhn, *s. a.* A metal dish for food; the nave or central interior of an edifice; صحنلق sàhnl*ɪ*k, *s. t.* A landing-place on a staircase.

صحيح sàhīh (sàhīh), *a. a.* True; correct, exact; without defect or ailment, in an effective state.

صحيفه sàhīfé, *s. a.* A page on a leaf; صحيفهٔ زمين sàhīféʿi-zèmīn, The surface of the earth.

صد sAd, *a. p.* A hundred; صدبرك sAd-bèrk (sAbbèrk), The hundred-leaved or cabbage rose.

صدا sAdā, *s. a.* A sound; a noise.

صدارت sAdārèt, *s. a.* The office of the Grand Vizier.

صداع sùdāʿʿ, *s. a.* The headache.

صداقت sAdākAt, *s. a.* Fidelity.

صدد sAded, *s. a.* Intent, purpose, idea, design, wish.

صدر sAdr, *s. a.* The breast, bosom, chest; the first hemistich in a poem; the chief seat in an Eastern room, the seat of honour; the occupier of the chief seat; the office and title of two legal officers in Turkey, who administer the ecclesiastical or canon law, the one over all Turkey in Europe, the other over all Turkey in Asia, and known as *Cadilesker*, the corruption of KAzìyyu-'l-ʿʿAsskɪr; their dignity is similar to that of our archbishops; (sèdir) the slightly-raised platform on which ottomans are arranged in Eastern rooms; صدراعظم sAdr*i*-àʿʿzam (sàdrāzàm), *s. p.* The Grand Vizier or Prime Minister; صدری sAdrī (*fem.* صدريه sAdrìyyé), *a. a.* Pertaining to the breast or chest; a person troubled with a chest complaint.

صدف sAdef (sèdef), *s. a.* Mother-of-pearl; a mother-of-pearl shell; the herb rue.

صدق sìdk, *s. a.* Truth, truthfulness; [fidelity; sincerity.

صدقه sAd*aka*, *s. a.* Alms, charity.

صدمه sAdémé, *s. a.* A shock, violent collision.

صدور sùdūr, *s. a.* A coming or going

forth, emanating; —, *s. pl. a.* (*of* صدر sAdr), Breasts, bosoms, chests; the actual and past chief legal officers of Turkey immediately under the *Sheykhu-'l-isslam*; —ا, —et, *v.n.* To emanate.

صديق sìddīk, *s. a.* A true and sincere friend; the special appellative of Ebu-Bekir, the firm friend of Muhammed.

صراجه sAraja, *s. t.* The scrofula or king's evil.

صراحت sArāhàt, *s. a.* Explicitness of declaration; صراحةً sArāhatan, *ad. a.* Explicitly, in the most explicit manner.

صراحى sùrāhī, *s. p.* A decanter.

صرارمق sArarmak (*aor.* صرارر sArarir), *v.n.* To turn yellow, become yellow; to become sere (leaves); to turn pale, become pale.

صراط sìrAt, *s. a.* A path, way; —مستقيم, sìrAti-mùsstakīm, The straight and narrow way to salvation; —كوپريسى, sìrAt-kyùprussu, The allegorical *bridge* over which souls are to pass to heaven.

صراف sàrrāf (sàraf), *s. a.* A money-changer; a banker; صرافيه sàrrāfìyyÉ, A banker's charges.

صرت sìrt, *s. t.* The back (of any animal or man); a ridge (of hills or mountains); بالق‌صرتى bAlik-sìrti, *s. t.* A ridge, *and a. t.* Ridged like the back of a fish or roof of a house with a slope on each side.

صرتلان sìrtlAn, *s. t.* A hyena.

صرچه sìrcha, Rock-crystal; glass; any vitrified mineral; the glazed or vitrified cubes or parallelopipeds used in mosaic work.

صرح sàrh, *s. a.* A castle; a palace.

صرصر sàrsàr, *s. a.* The violent wind which is to sweep the earth at the end of days; a hurricane.

[fits.

صرعه sAr''a, *s. a.* The epilepsy, epileptic

صرف sàrf, *s. a.* A turning (anything) out of the direction it was taking; the grammar, accidences, or etymology of a language; —, sìrf, *a. t.* Sheer, mere; —ونحو, sàrf-u-nàhv, (Etymology and syntax) Grammar in general; —ا, sàrf-et, To turn (anything) out of its road into another direction; to spend, expend; صرفى sàrfī (*fem.* صرفيه sàrfìyyÉ, *a. a.* Pertaining to etymology or grammar; صرفيون sàrfìyyūn, *s. pl. a.* Grammarians; etymologists.

صرة sùrrÉ, *s. a.* A money-bag or purse; the treasure sent to Mecca and Medina each year by the Sultan and various functionaries for the support of various officers or pensioners attached to the sacred places; —, sìra, *s. t.* A series; a row; a turn; proper order; صرةايله sìrà-ila, *ad. t.* By turns, one at a time; صرةسيله sìrassīla, In its proper order, time, or place; apropos; صرةسنه قومق sìrassìna-kòmak, *v.a.* To put (a thing) into proper order, to reform, to arrange or re-arrange; صرةوارى sìra-vāri (sìra-vàrdi), *a. p.* Successive, consecutive, following; —, *ad. t.* Along; قيى صره kìyi - sìra, Along shore, following the line of coast; اردم صره àrdim-sìra (*changing the pronoun as occasion requires*), Along behind me (thee, him, &c.).

صريح sArīh, *a. a.* Clearly expressed; clear, explicit.

صزلامق sìzlamak (*aor.* صزلار sìzlar), *v.n.* To ache (a wound, or sore).

صزمق sìzmak (*aor.* صزار sìzar), *v.n.* To transude, to exude, percolate.

صزندی sìzindi, *s. t.* Leakage, transudation, exudation.

صزی sìzi, *s. t.* An ache, a shooting pain.

صعب sà''b, *a. a.* Difficult.

صعوبت sù''ūbet, *s. a.* Difficulty.

صعود sù''ūd, *s. a.* A rising, mounting; going up; ا—, —et, *v.n.* To mount, go up.

صغار sìghār, *s. pl. a.* (*of* صغير sàghīr), Small, little; small people; little people.

صغامق sìghamak (*aor.* صيغار sìghār), (sìwamak, sìwar), *v.a.* To tuck up (skirts, sleeves, &c.).

صغائر sàghā'ir, *s. pl. a.* (*of* صغيره sàghīrė), Minor sins.

صغر sìghàr, *s. a.* Smallness, littleness, youngness; —سن, sìghàri-sìnn, *s. p.* Youngness of years, youth; —, *or* صيغر sìghir, *s. t.* An ox.

صغرا *or* صغرى sùghrà, *s. a. fem.* The smaller or smallest.

صغير sàghīr, *a. a.* Little, small; young.

صف sAff, *s. a.* A row, a rank.

صفا sAfā, *s. a.* Purity, pureness; clearness, brightness; freedom from sorrow, pleasure, enjoyment; صفاى خاطر sAfāyi-khAtir, Peace of mind, freedom from any misgiving or scruple; اهل صفا èhli-sAfā, A person occupied only with pleasure; —سورمك, sAfā--sùrmek, *v.n.* To enjoy one's self in pleasure; —كلدك, sAfā-ghèlding! You have been welcome! (*said to a friend when he is going away after a visit*).

صفاف sìfĀf, *s. a.* A going into the order of battle; a battle, fight, action.

صفت sìfAt (*pl.* صفات sìfĀt), *s. a.* An attribute, a moral quality; an adjective; صفات ثبوتيه sìfĀti - sùbūtìyyė, The affirmative or positive attributes (of God), as *power, seeing, hearing, knowing*, &c.; صفات سلبيه sìfĀti-sèlbìyyė, The negative attributes, as, *fellowlessness, illimitability in time or space*, &c.; صفت رسميه sìfĀti-rèssmìyyė, An official quality.

صفح sAfh, *s. a.* A pardoning, overlooking.

صفحه sAfha, *s. a.* A surface; a plain, an open place or space of ground.

صفدرانه sAff-dèrānė, *a. p.* Pertaining to a hero *who rends the ranks* of the foe.

صفر sAfer, *s. a.* Name of the second month of the Muhammedan year; —, sìfr, *s. a.* A cypher, nought, zero; —اليد, sìfru - 'l - yèd, Penniless, in whose hands there is nought.

صفرا sAfrā (sAfra), *s. a.* The bile; سفراسی قبارمق sAfrāssi-kAbarmak, To rise *or* overflow (the bile of any person, *the pronoun changing accordingly*).

صفروی sAfrévī, *a. a.* Pertaining to the bile; bilious. [ship.

صفره sAfra, *s. t.* (*Italian*), Ballast of a

صفوت sAfvet, *s. a.* Purity, clearness, clearness, pureness. [Rows, ranks.

صفوف sŭfūf, *s. pl. a.* (*of* صف sAff),

صفه sòffa, *s. a.* An open room or alcove in an antechamber, usually where the windows are placed, and generally fitted up with cushions for seats: it is used by the servants and minor visitors when waiting to be admitted to the rooms; *hence our word* sofa.

صفی sAfī, *s. a.* A pure, righteous man; name of the founder of the modern Persian dynasty called صفوی SAfévī; صفی الله sàfìyyu-'llāh, Adam, the pure man before God. [blast; a sapphire.

صفیر sAfīr, *s. a.* A loud shrill sound, a

صقال sàkAl, *s. t.* The beard and whiskers; صقاللو sàkAlli, *a. t.* Bearded; اق صقاللو Ak-sàkAlli, *s. t.* A grey-beard; an elder; a kind of rural magistrate; برینك صقالنه کولمك bìrining - sàkAlina - ghyùlmek, *v.n.* (To laugh at one's beard) To deceive anyone with trumped-up stories.

صقصغان sAksaghān, *s. t.* A magpie.

صك sàkk, *s. a.* A legal document issued from a court of justice.

صکره sòngra, *s. t.* The time after the end of any term, the future; by-and-bye; —, *ad. t.* Afterwards; later; صکره سی نصل اولدی sòngrassi - nàssl - òldu? (How was its future?) How did things go with it after that? صکره یه قالمق sòngraya - kAlmak, *v.n.* To be postponed; صکره یه براقمق sòngraya-bràkmak, *v.a.* To postpone; صکره کی sòngraki, *pron. t.* The latter, the one of the after-time; صکره دن اولمق sòngradan - òlmak, *v.n.* To happen afterwards; to be of more recent occurrence; الك صکره èng-sòngra, At the very last, last of all.

صکوك sŭkyūk, *s. pl. a.* (*of* صك sàkk, *which see*), Legal documents.

صلابت sAlābèt, *s. a.* Firmness.

صلات *or* صلاة *or* صلوة sAlāt, *s. a.* (*pl.* صلوات sAlawāt), The ritual performance of prayer.

صلاته sAlAta, *s. t.* (*Italian*), A salad, certain salad plants; طوپ صلاته tòp-sAlAta, The cabbage-lettuce; فرنك صلاته سی firènk-sAlAtassi, Endive.

صلاح sAlāh, *s. a.* The best and most fitting state of anything; rectitude, virtue (in worldly or religious affairs); peace, harmony (between men); advantage, welfare, interest (worldly or spiritual).

صلاحیت sAlāhìyyèt, *s. a.* Fitness, right, validity, authority (to act). [pickle.

صلامورہ sAlamūra, *s. t.* (*Italian*), Brine,

صلب sAlb, *a. a.* A hanging; a crucifying; ا—, —et, *v.a.* To hang; to crucify; —, sùlb, *s. a.* The loins; صلبی sulbī (*fem.* صلبیه sùlbìyyé), *a. a.* Pertaining to the loins; issued from the loins.

صلح sùlh, *s. a.* Peace, cessation of war; —او, sùlh (sùlf)-òl, *v.n.* To come to a compromise; —ا, sùlh-et, *v.n.* To make peace; صلحاً sùlhan, *ad. a.* In a pacific manner without recourse to hostilities; in time of peace.

صلحا sùlahā, *s. pl. a.* (*of* صالح sālih), Virtuous men.

صلعم. An abbreviation in writing of the ejaculation صلى الله عليه وسلم sàlla-'llāhu-''àlèyhi-vé-sèllem! May God look favourably upon him (Muhammed) and grant him peace! Like our &c., this abbreviation is to be read in full.

صلوات sàlawāt, *s. pl. a.* (*of* صلوت sàlāt), Prayers or ascriptions of praise.

صلوة sàlāt (*so written and so pronounced*), *s. a.* A ritual performance of prayer, or ascription of praise.

صله sìla, *s. a.* A meeting, junction; the antecedent of a relative pronoun (in Arabic or other language); —, *or* صلهٔ رحم sìla'i-ràhm, A visit to one's home and kindred, a soldier's furlough.

صلى sàlla! May (God) look with favour (upon Muhammed), in the ejaculation صلى الله عليه sàlla-'llāhu-''àlèyh.

صليب sàlīb, *s. a.* A crucifix.

صماخ sìmākh, *s. a.* An ear.

صمان sàman, *s. t.* Straw ground to a coarse consistency like chaff in the operation of rubbing out the corn; صمان التندن صو يوروتمك sàman-altindan-sù-yùrutmek, *v.n.* (To cause water to flow under bruised straw) To do things in an underhand manner (*sub rosâ*); صمانلق sàmanlìk, *s. t.* A barn or store for triturated straw.

صمد sàmad, *a. a.* Sempiternal, eternal in the past and in the future (God); صمدانی sàmadānī, *a. a.* Pertaining to the sempiternal God; صمدانیت sàmadānìyyèt, *s. a.* The divine quality of being sempiternal.

صمصام sàmsām, *s. a.* A sword, a sabre.

صمغ sàmgh (zàmk), *s. a.* Gum; gum-arabic; صمغ عربی (zàmkì) - ''àrébī, Gum-arabic.

صمون sòmun, *s. t.* A loaf of bread; bread in loaves; the nut of a screw-bolt.

صميم sàmīm, *s. a.* The bottom or interior (of the heart); عن صميم القلب ''àn-sàmīmi-'l-kàlb, *ad. a.* From the very bottom of the heart; صميمی sàmīmī, *a. a.* Cordial, sincere.

صناديد sànādīd, *s. pl. a.* (*of* صنديد sìndīd), Chiefs, princes, leaders.

صنائع sànā'i'', *s. pl. a.* (*of* صنعت sàn''àt), Arts, handicrafts.

صندال sàndal, *s. t.* A large boat, a ship's boat; —, *or* صندل sàndal, *s. t.* Sandal-wood; a kind of silk stuff.

صندالی sàndālī, *s. t.* A throne or chair of state (said of European thrones).

صنداليه sàndālìyyé, *s. t.* A chair.

صندوق sàndūk (sàndìk), *s. a.* A chest,

coffer, box, trunk, case; سپدصندوق sèped-sAndik, s. t. A coffer of basket-work covered with leather; صندوقچه sAndūkcha, s. p. A small chest or case; صندوقه sAndūka, s. t. A kind of wooden or stone construction erected over graves (generally when under the cover of a mausoleum), and covered over with shawls, carpets, silks, &c. [leader.

صندید sìndīd, s. a. A chief, prince,

صنع sün", s. a. Handiwork, work, the thing made; —الهی, sün"u-ìlāhī, The work of God.

صنعت sàn"àt (zànāt), s. a. An art, handicraft, craft; skill, cunning in any art; any stroke of art, craft, or skill; a rhetorical embellishment in literary composition; صنعتلو sàn"àtli, a. t. Skilful; —, ad. t. Skilfully, with skill; with tact; with deep cunning.

صنف sìnf, s. a. A class; (pl. اصناف èssnāf, Classes; trades corporations; sorts, kinds); (*as a Turkish sing.*) a tradesman; an artificer in the army or navy; اصنافلق èssnāflik, s. t. Trade, tradesmanship.

صنم sànem, s. a. An idol.

صنو sìnv, s. a. A brother.

صنوبر sànevbèr, s. p. A cone, the fruit of any cone-bearing tree; the tree itself.

صنوف sünūf, s. pl. a. (of صنف sìnf), Kinds, sorts.

صنیعه sànī"a, s. a. An act, deed, work.

صو sū, s. t. Water; a stream, brook, rivulet, river; water (of a diamond); temper (of steel); صو باشی sū-bAshi, s. t. A spring, fountain-head; a kind of village mayor; اربه صویی àrpa--sùyu, Beer, ale, porter; — —بیاض bèyAz— —, Ale; — —سیاه sīyāh— —, Porter; کل صویی ghyùl-sùyu, Rose-water; کول صویی kyùl-sùyu, Lie, lixivium of wood-ashes; صو دوکمك sū-dùkmek, v.n. To ease nature; — —کچوك kùchuk— —, To make water; — —بیوك bìyuk— —, To go to stool; صو ویرمك sū--vèrmek, v.n. To temper (steel); صولو sūlu, a. t. Watery; juicy; صوسز sūssuz, a. t. Dry, thirsty; صوسزلق sūssuzluk, s. t. Thirst, drought; صولر sūlar, s. pl. t. Approximate time of day; ساعت برصولرنده sā"at-bìr-sū-larinda, About one o'clock.

صوا sīwa, s. t. Plaster; a coat of plaster or cement; صوامق sìwamak (aor. صوار sìwar), v.a. To plaster, coat over with plaster or cement.

صواب sàwAb (sèwAb), s. a. The fit, proper, or correct state of anything; a good or charitable action; the merit due to a good action, the reward promised for it hereafter; the correct word or orthography in a table of errata; خطا صواب khAtā-sàwAb, Errata; صوابدید sàwAb-dīd, s. p. That which is esteemed proper; a deeming proper, approval.

صوارمق sùwarmak (*aor.* صوارر sùwarir), *v.a.* To take (cattle) to drink, to give water, to water (cattle).

صواش sàwash, *s. t.* Battle, strife.

صواشمق sàwashmak (*aor.* صواشر sàwashir), *v.n.* To strive, to struggle, fight, combat; to strive, endeavour, buckle to. [direction.

صوب sàvb, *s. a.* A side, coast, place,

صوبه sòba, *s. t.* A stove, close stove; a hothouse.

صوپه sòpa, *s. t.* A thick stick.

صوت sàvt, *s. a.* A sound; a voice.

صوچ sùch, *s. t.* A fault, a crime, a sin.

صور sūr, *s. a.* A trumpet; —, sùwèr, *s. pl. a.* (*of* صورت sūrèt, *which see*).

صورت sūrèt, *s. a.* A form, figure; a mode, manner; a face, visage, countenance; a formula; a copy (of a writing); a drawing of any animal form; a statue; a case, supposed case, supposition; an appearance, external show; صورتا sūrétā, *ad. a.* As a matter of external appearance; apparently; for form's sake; in appearance, externally; صورتپذیر sūrèt-pèzīr, *a. p.* Which has taken a definite form, been put into shape, been accomplished.

صورغج sòrghuj, *s. t.* A tuft of feathers worn as an ornament on the head.

صورمق sòrmak (*aor.* صورار sòrar), *v.a.* To ask a question; to ask for, after, or about (any person or thing); —, *v.n.* To suck (as a pump, especially when the air penetrates and makes a sucking noise); — خاطر khātir—, *v.n.* To ask after one's health and welfare.

صوری sūrī (*fem.* صوریه sūriyyé), *a. a.* Formal, apparent.

صوصامق sùssamak (*aor.* صوصار sùssar), *v.n.* To feel thirst, to be thirsty; صوصاتمق sùssatmak (*aor.* صوصادر sùssadir), *v.a.* To make thirsty, cause to feel thirsty.

صوصمق sùssmak (*aor.* صوصار sùssar), *v.n.* To hold one's tongue, hold one's peace, be silent, refrain from speaking, cease speaking, leave off speaking or talking; صوص sùss! Hold your tongue! [a tuber.

صوغان sòghan, *s. t.* An onion; a bulb;

صوغلجان sòghuljàn, *s. t.* A worm.

صوغوق sòghuk, *a. t.* Cold; —, *s. t.* The cold; a cold.

صوغومق sòghumak (*aor.* صوغور sòghur), *v.n.* To become cold or cool; to grow cold or cool; to lose one's first warmth of feeling, become lukewarm; صوغوتمق sòghutmak (*aor.* صوغودر sòghudur), *v.a.* To cause to grow cold, to cool.

صوف sūf (sòf), *s. a.* Wool; goats' wool; a kind of camlet or homespun linsey-woolsey; صوفی sōfī, *s. a.* Of wool; woollen; wearing woollen or linsey-woolsey; —, *s. a.* (*pl.* صوفیون sòfiyyūn), A kind of Muhammedan ascetic rationalist; —, (sòfu), *a. t.* Scrupulously devout and stiff-starched;

صوفيلك (sòfuluk), *s. t.* Exaggerated piety.

صوفيه Sòfiya, *s. t.* Sophia (town of, in Bulgaria).

صوق sūk, *s. a.* A street of shops; a market.

صوقاق sòkAk, *s. t.* A street; an alley of trees; a corridor.

صوقلغان sòkulghAn, *a. t.* One who intrudes or pushes himself into company where he is not wanted.

صوقمق sòkmak (*aor.* صوقار sòkar), *v.a.* To push in; to sting (a bee, &c.), to bite (a snake, &c.); صوقلمق sòkulmak (*aor.* صوقلور sòkulur), *v.p.* To be pushed in; to be stung or bitten; —, *v.n.* To push one's self forward, intrude one's self, press one's self (near a person or into a company, place, or business); صوقشمق sòkushmak (*aor.* صوقشور sòkushur), *v.n. recip.* To push forwards together; crowd together; صوقشدرمق sòkushdurmak (*aor.* صوقشدرر sòkushdurur), *v.a. caus.* To push in (a number of things) together, *or* (one thing) with several others.

صوڭ sòng, *s. t.* The end (of any time or succession).

صول sòl, *a. t.* Left; the left hand.

صولاق sòlAk, *s. t.* A left-handed man; name of certain officers of the Sultan's palace in the olden time; —, sūlAk, *a. t.* Abounding in water, springs, rivers, marshes, &c.

صولامق sūlamak (*aor.* صولار sūlar), *v.a.* To water (a garden, plants, &c.).

صولت sAvlet, *s. a.* A determined attack, rush, assault.

صولجان sAvléjān, *s. a.* A hockey stick.

صولق or صولوق sòluk, *s. t.* The breath, a breath; —المق, sòluk-Almak, *v.n.* To breathe.

صولمق sòlmak (*aor.* صولار sòlar), *v.n.* To fade (colour).

صولومق sòlumak (*aor.* صولور sòlur), *v.n.* To breathe hard (as when out of breath), to pant.

صوم sàvm, *s. a.* A fasting, abstaining from food as a rite.

صومتمق or صوموتمق sòmutmak (*aor.* صومودر sòmudur), *v.n.* To pout and be sulky.

صومردانمق sòmurdAnmak (*aor.* صومردانور sòmurdAnir), *v.n.* To talk sulkily.

صومعه sAvma"a, *s. a.* A church or monastery; any religious or conventual edifice.

صون sàvn, *s. a.* Active protection.

صوندرمه sūndurma, *s. t.* A shed, penthouse, lean-to.

صونمق sūnmak (*aor.* صونار sūnar), *v.a.* (*provincial*) To push forward (towards anyone as in the act of presenting).

صوی sòy, *s. t.* A race, stock, family; a kind, sort; a good race; a good sort; —, *a. t.* Of a good race; of a good sort.

صویش sūyush, *s. t.* Plain boiled meat.

صويغون sòyghun, *s. t.* Pillage, plunder, sack, rapine; wholesale theft or robbery; a stripping; —قاریلری, sòyghun-kArilari, Hired women at wedding-feasts who assist the lady visitors to uncloak, &c.

صويمق sòymak (*aor.* صويار sòyar), *v.a.* To strip; to strip off clothes; to plunder, sack, rob; صوينمق sòyunmak (*aor.* صوينور sòyunur), *v.n.* To undress one's self.

صهباء sàhbā, *s. a.* Wine, the expressed juice of white grapes.

صهر sìhr, *s. a.* A son *or* brother-in-law, he who has taken to wife the daughter or sister of some one; صهريت sìhrìyyèt, *s. a.* The quality of being son or brother-in-law.

صهيل sàhīl, *s. a.* The neighing of a horse.

صياد sàyyād, *s. a.* A hunter or fisher of any kind.

صيادت sìyādèt, *s. a.* A chase, hunting, fowling, fishing of any kind; huntsmanship of any kind. [religious fast.

صيام sìyām, *s. a.* The act of fasting; a

صيانت sìyānèt, *s. a.* Active protection; ا—, —et, *v.a.* To protect, guard.

صيت sīt, *s. a.* A sound, a noise; a voice; rumour; reputation, fame.

صيحه sàyha, *s. a.* A loud cry.

صيد sàyd, *s. a.* A hunting, chasing, fowling, trapping, fishing, taking, catching in any manner; the chase, &c., of any kind; prey taken in any manner; ا—, —et, *v.a.* To take, catch as prey in any manner.

صيدا Sàyd*a*, *s. t.* Sidon in Phœnicia.

صيرق sìrìk, *s. t.* A small pole, a perch, a long thick stick. [leather or hide.

صيرم sìrìm, *s. t.* A strip, lace or thong of

صيرمق sìyìrmak (*aor.* صيرر sìyìrir), *v.a.* To strip (the skin off of anything), to pull off (any covering of anything) after the fashion used in skinning eels; صيرلمق sìyìrilmak (*aor.* صيريلور sìyìrilir), *v.p.* To be pulled or stripped off like an eel-skin; —, *v.n.* To slip away quietly, to get away by slipping off a coat, &c., which someone has hold of. [To ache.

صيزلامق sìzlamak (*aor.* صيزلار sìzlar), *v.n.*

صيزمق sìzmak (*aor.* صيزار sìzar), *v.n.* To transude, exude, percolate.

صيزى sìzi, *s. t.* An ache, a pain.

صيغ sìgh, *a. t.* Shallow (water).

صيغامق sìghamak (*aor.* صيغار sìghar), *v.a.* To tuck up (skirts, sleeves, &c.).

صيغه sīgh*a*, *s. t.* The peculiar termination of a word in a grammatical view, its form as indicative of case, mood, tense, &c.; a conjugation.

صيغر sì*ghi*r, *s. t.* An ox; صو صيغرى sū-sì*ghi*ri, A buffalo. [herdsman.

صيغرتماج sì*ghi*rtmàj, *s. t.* A drover,

صيغرجق sì*ghi*rjìk, *s. t.* A starling.

صيغمق sì*gh*mak (*aor.* صيغار sì*gh*ar), *v.n.* To go in, to be in such quantity or of such a size as to admit of being contained in any given receptacle; صيغنمق sì*ghi*nmak (*aor.* صيغنور sì*ghi*nìr), *v.n.* To go in for shelter, to take refuge; صيغشمق sì*ghi*shmak (*aor.* صيغشور sì*ghi*shir), *v.n.* To manage to get in (several people), to find room.

صيف sàyf, *s. a.* The summer; صيفى sàyfī, *a. a.* Pertaining to summer;

صيفيه sàyfîyyé, *s. a.* A country-house, inhabited during summer.

صيق sìk, *a. t.* Thick, close together, not far apart, of a close texture; —, *ad. t.* Often.

صيقل sàykàl, *s. a.* A polish, burnish; —ويرمك, sàykàl-vèrmek, *v.n.* To give a polish or burnish.

صيقمق sìkmak (*aor.* صيقار sìkar), *v.a.* To squeeze, press, subject to pressure; to express (juice); to subject to an unpleasant degree of importunity or trial of patience; to fire off (a pistol); صيقلمق sìkìlmak (*aor.* صيقلور sìkìlir), *v.p.* To be squeezed; to be pressed; to be expressed (juice); to be fired off (a pistol); —, *v.n.* To be annoyed; to feel dull; ادمك جانى صيقلمق àdàming-jāni-sìkìlmak, *v.n.* To be vexed, grieved, annoyed; to feel in low spirits, feel dull; صيقشمق sìkìsh-mak (*aor.* صيقشور sìkìshir), *v.n.* To crowd, to be crowded, pressed, jammed in together; صيقشدرمق sìkìshdìrmak (*aor.* صيقشدرر sìkìshdìrir), *v.a.* To crowd (many things), press together; to screw up tight, make (a thing) quite tight and close; to press (a person), importune, to subject to the strictest oral examination, to use threats.

صيقندى sìkìndi, *s. t.* Any unpleasantness which weighs on one; want, penury; a bodily want, want to ease nature; an unpleasant feeling, heaviness; trouble.

صيقى sìki, *a. t.* Tight; —, *s. t.* A moral screw or necessity applied to make a person exert himself; صيقى يى كورمك sìkiyi-ghyùrmek, *v.n.* To be placed under some kind of moral pressure or necessity.

صيوا or صيوه sìwa, *s. t.* Plaster, a coat of plaster; صيوامق sìwamak (*aor.* صيوار sìwar), *v.a.* To plaster.

ض

ض dàd (dàt). Eighteenth letter of the Turkish language, having two different powers. It is sometimes sounded as an English *d*, at other times like a *z*; but in either case it has generally a more guttural and harder sound than the د or ز. In chronograms it has the numeral value of 800.

ضابط zābit, *s. a.* An officer; a magistrate; one's immediate chief in an official capacity; —بيوك bìyuk—, A commissioned officer; —كچوك kùchuk—, A warrant or non-commissioned officer.

ضاد dàd, *s. a.* Name of the letter ض.

ضال dàll, *s. a.* One who is in error, out of the right path.

ضامن zāmin, *s. a.* A surety, bail, guarantee (person).

ضايع zāyi'', *a. a.* Going to waste, being uselessly spent, being lost; او—, —òl, *v.n.* To be lost; to go to waste; ا—, —et, *v.a.* To lose; to waste.

ضبط zàbt, *s. a.* A holding firmly; a holding together; a holding in, restraining, governing; a conquering; a seizing; a taking possession; ا—, —et, *v.a.* To hold; to hold together; to hold in, restrain; to conquer; to seize; to take possession of, enter into possession of; to assume the functions of; to rule, govern, exercise authority over; to take down, pen down (notes of oral communications); ضبطی zÀbtī (*fem.* ضبطیه zÀbtìyyÉ), *a. a.* Pertaining to the police; ضبطیه zÀbtìyyÉ, ضبطیه قواصی zÀbtìyyÉ - kÀwwÀssi, *s. t.* A policeman; ضبطیه ناظری zÀbtìyyÉ--nāziri, *s. t.* The Minister of Police.

ضجر dàjar, *and* ضجرت dàjrèt, *s. a.* Sorrow, chagrin.

ضحا dàhā, *s. a.* The morning when the sun is high up.

ضحك dàhk, *s. a.* A laughing; a laugh.

ضحوه dàhvÉ, *s. a.* The morning when the sun is high up.

ضد zìdd, *s. a.* The contrary or opposite to anything; a thing very much disliked; a person who opposes anyone; برینك ضدینه یاپمق bìrining-zìddina--yàpmak, *v.a.* To do (anything) to vex someone; برینك ضدینه كتمك bìrining - zìddina - ghìtmek, *v.n.* To annoy, be distasteful to someone.

ضر zàrr, *s. a.* Harm, damage, detriment; hurtfulness; noxiousness; سراً و ضراً sèrrᴇn-vè-zàrran, *ad. a.* In weal and in woe, for better for worse.

ضراعت dàrā''àt, *s. a.* Humility.

ضرب dàrb, *s. a.* A striking in any manner; a stroke, blow; —, zàrb (*the same word differently pronounced*), *s. a.* The force or violence of a blow; multiplication (in arithmetic); —, dùriba (on coins), It was struck; ا—, dàrb-et, *v.a.* To strike; to set up (tents, &c.); ا—, zàrb-et, *v.a.* To multiply arithmetically; ضرب سكه dàrbi-sìkkÉ, *s. p.* The coining of money; ضرب مثل zàrbi-mèssel, *s. p.* A proverb, a common expression; ضرباً dàrban, *ad. a.* By force of arms; ضربخانه zàrb-khānÉ, *s. p.* A royal mint; ضربخانه ناظری zàrb-khānÉ-nā-ziri, *s. t.* The master of the mint (a cabinet minister).

ضربه dàrba, *s. a.* A single stroke, a blow.

ضرر zàrar, *s. a.* Harm, damage, detriment, injury; loss (in business); hurtfulness, noxiousness; ضرر یوق zàrar-yòk! *int. t.* No matter! Never mind! ضرری یوق zàrari-yòk, There is no harm in that; ا—, —et, *v.n.* To hurt, injure, harm; to lose (in business); ضررلو zàrarli, *a. t.* Who has suffered loss; ضررسز zàrarsiz, *a. t.* Harmless, not hurtful; harmless, free from harm or loss; not bad, pretty good considering.

ضرطه zàrta, *s. a.* A fart.

ضروب zùrūb, *s. pl. a.* (*of* ضرب zàrb, *seldom used in this sense*) Kinds, sorts; —امثال, zùrūbu-èmsāl (*pl. of* ضرب مثل zārbi-mèssel), Proverbs.

ضرورت zàrūrèt, *s. a.* Necessity, pressing need; indigence, want, poverty;

بالضروره bì-'z-zàrūré (*and* بالضرور bì-'z-zàrūr), *ad. a.* Necessarily, forcedly, obligedly; ضروری zàrūrī, *a. a.* Indispensable, pressingly needful; obligatory, forced.

ضعف zà''f, *s. a.* Weakness, feebleness, debility; —, zì''f (*pl.* اضعاف èz''āf), *s. a.* The double *or* any multiple (of a quantity).

ضعفا zū''afā, *s. pl. a.* (*of* ضعيف zà''īf), The weak, the infirm; the poor. (This is the original of the now celebrated French word *zouave*, the term being applied by the Arabs to those who from weakness, sickness, poverty, or loss of arms or horses, cannot be considered effective warriors).

ضعيف zà''īf, *a. a.* Weak, infirm, not strong, not powerful; thin, not fat; poor; ضعيفلق zà''iflik, *s. t.* Weakness, debility; ضعيفلنمق zà''iflanmak, *v.n.* To grow weak; to grow thin, to lose flesh; ضعيفلتمق zà''iflatmak, *v.a.* To make weak, to weaken; to cause to lose flesh.

ضلال dàlāl, *and* ضلالت dàlālèt, *s. a.* Error, deviation from the right path.

ضلع dìl'' (*pl.* اضلاع ɅdlɅ''), A side (of a triangle); —معلوم, dìl''i-mà''lūm, A known or given side; a base-line (in surveying).

ضم zàmm, *s. a.* An adding; the pronouncing a letter with one of the vowels o, u, ʊ, *or* *u*, after it; ا—, —et, *v.a.* To add (something more).

ضمان zàmān, *s. a.* Suretiship, bail, guaranteeship.

ضمائر zàmā'ir, *s. pl. a.* (*of* ضمير zàmīr), Hearts, minds; thoughts.

ضمائم zàmā'im, *s. pl. a.* (*of* ضميمه zàmīmé), Addenda, appendices, additions, supplements; things of any kind added.

ضمن zìmn, *s. a.* The interior (of any containing exterior); the design (contained in any act); the implied sense (contained in any expression); ضمننده zìmnında (*an apparent Turkish adverb or conjunction*), In order to, with a view to, with a design to; ضمناً zìmnan, *ad. a.* In an implied manner; ضمنی zìmnī, *a. a.* Implied, contained.

ضمير zàmīr, *s. a.* The heart or mind; a pronoun; ما فی الضمير mā-fì-'z-zàmīr, That which is (or was) on the mind, one's thoughts.

ضميمه zàmīmé, *s. a.* Anything added (to another thing); an appendix, supplement.

ضيا zìyā, *s. a.* Light; ضيادار zìyādār, *a. p.* Luminous; lighted, illuminated; —ويرمك, zìyā-vèrmek, *v.n.* To give light.

ضياع zìyā'', *s. pl. a.* (*of* ضيعه zì''a, *not used*), Estates, farms, lands, and villages; —, zàyā'', *s. a.* Destruction, ruin.

ضيافت zìyāfèt, *s. a.* A banquet, a feast, [a set dinner or supper.

ضيف zàyf, *s. a.* A guest.

ضيق zīk, *a. a.* Narrow, straitened,

close ; النفس—, zīku-'n-nèfess, *s. a.* An asthmatic person ; نفس—, zīk--nèfess (tìk-nèfess), The asthma.

ضیوف zūyūf, *s. pl. a.* (*of* ضیف zàyf), Guests.

ط

ط tā''i-hòttī (tà). Nineteenth letter of the Turkish alphabet, having two different values. It is generally sounded as an English *t*, but sometimes, at the beginning of words of Turkish origin, as a *d*, and is always more harsh and guttural than the corresponding letters ت and د. In chronograms and astronomical tables it has the numeral value of 9.

طا tā, *s. a.* Name of the letter ط.

طاب tāba! *int. a.* May (his tomb) be pleasant (to him), in طاب‌ثراه tāba--sùrāhu, *and* طاب‌سره tāba-sirruhu.

طابور tàbur, *s. t.* A battalion ; a column (of march or attack) ; a certain large number (of people).

طابیه tàbiya, *s. t.* A battery ; a bastion ; an earthwork, fleche, redoubt, redan, or fort.

طاپمق tàpmak, *and* طاپنمق tàpinmak, [*v.n.* To worship, adore.

طاپو tàpi *or* tàpu, *s. t.* A kind of title-deed for lands held on the old feudal system, by tenants of low degree : it is also called طاپو تذکره‌سی tàpu-tèz-kéréssi.

طاپه tàpa, *s. t.* A cork *or* stopper to a [bottle.

طات tàt, *s. t.* Taste, savour ; طاتلو tàtli, *a. t.* Sweet ; savoury ; pleasant, agreeable ; —, *s. t.* Any sweet dish or sweetmeat ; طاتسز tàtsiz, *a. t.* Unsavoury, tasteless ; unpleasant, disagreeable ; طاتلولق tàtlilik, *s. t.* Sweetness ; pleasantness ; طاتسزلق tàtsizlik, *s. t.* Unpleasantness.

طاتمق tàtmak (*aor.* طادار tàdar), *v.a.* To taste, try the taste of ; perceive the taste of.

طارتمق tàrtmak (*aor.* طارتار tàrtar), *v.a.* To weigh ; to try the weight ; to try the strength, or to sound the ideas (of a person).

طارتی tàrti, *s. t.* A weight for weighing ; the weighing weight of anything.

طارم tārim, *s. p.* A dome ; the sky *or* a sphere.

طاره tàra *or* dàra, *s. t.* (*Italian*), The tare (of goods sold by weight).

طاری tāri, *a. a.* Which comes (upon one), happens disagreeably ; او—, —ōl, *v.n.* To come upon, overtake, happen disagreeably.

طاس tàss, *s. p.* A bowl of metal, glass, or earthenware ; —, *a. t.* Bald (head); یاپشدرمق—, tàss-yàpishdirmak, *v.n.* (To apply a bowl) To torture by application of heated bowls of metal to the bare head.

طاش tàsh, *s. t.* A stone, a rock ; stone ; a millstone ; a draughtsman, piece at draughts ; دیکیلو طاش dìkili-tàsh, An obelisk (while standing) ; طاشجی

tAshji, *s. t.* A stone-cutter, worker in stone; طاشلمق tAshlamak, *v.a.* To stone with stones. [(in a male animal).

طاشاق tAshak, *s. t.* A testicle, a stone

طاشمق tAshmak (*aor.* طاشار tAshar), *v.n.* To overflow; طاشرمق tAshirmak, (*aor.* طاشرر tAshirir), *v.a. caus.* To cause to overflow; to allow one's words or acts to go beyond the bounds of due respect.

طاشيمق tAshimak (*aor.* طاشر tAshir), *v.a.* To carry; to carry about; طاشنمق tAshinmak, *v.n.* To move, to carry one's effects and furniture to another house.

طاصلاق tAsslAk, *a. t.* In an unfinished state, rough, unworked; —, *s. t.* A sketch, an outline; anything just roughly brought into shape.

طاصمه tAssma, *s. t.* A strap or lachet by which anything is held or fastened.

طاعت tā''at, *s. a.* Active devotion or piety, active conformity with God's ordinances. [tagious pest.

طاعون tā''ūn, *s. a.* The plague, the con-

طاغ dAgh, *s. t.* A mountain, mount, hill; طاغلو dAghli, *s. t.* A mountaineer.

طاغتمق dAghitmak (*aor.* طاغدر dAghidir), *v.a.* To scatter; to distribute.

طاغلمق dAghilmak (*aor.* طاغلور dAghilir), *v.n.* To disperse, be dispersed; —, *v.p.* To be distributed.

طاغى tAghi, *s. a.* A rebel; a sinner; —, dAghī, *s. t.* A mountaineer.

طاق tAk, *s. p.* Any vaulted or domed construction; a vault; an arch; a dome; an arched window; a sphere; the sky; a single one, an odd one; a single fold; —, *a. p.* Curved, vaulted, bent; odd; single.

طاقت tākAt (tākAt), *s. a.* Strength, power to do or bear; —كتورمك, tākAt--ghètirmek, *v.n.* To be able, to find strength sufficient. [ing or rattling.

طاقردى tàkirdi, *s. t.* A noise of knock-

طاقلاق tàklak, *s. t.* A tumble heels over head; —قيلمق, tàklak-kìlmak, *v.n.* To tumble, to throw one's self heels over head.

طاقلدامق tàkildAmak (*aor.* طاقلدار tà-kildar), *v.n.* To make a rattling noise.

طاقم tàkim, *s. t.* A set (of anything, of people, of tools, &c.); a mouth-piece (of a pipe); a squad, sub-division, or detachment (of soldiers); a crew (of a boat); tools, implements, necessaries, furniture; utensils.

طاقمق tàkmak (*aor.* طاقار tàkar), *v.a.* To fix (anything on to something else), to append; —قلج kìlìj-tàkmak, To put on a sword; —اد àd-tàkmak, To give a name; طاقلمق tàkilmak, *v.p.* To be fixed on or attached to anything; —, *v.n.* To attach one's self to anything, lay hold of, meddle with, make game of, chaff, skylark with; طاقنمق tàkinmak, *v.a.* To attach (something) to one's self; —اغرينى Aghrini-tàkinmak, *v.n.* To assume an air of gravity.

طاقیه tàkyé; *s. t.* A small linen cap.

طاك dàng, *s. t.* The dawn; ——یری, dàng-yèri, The place where the light of morning first appears; ——اتمق, dàng-àtmak, *v.n.* To begin to show signs of light (the dawn), to brighten.

طال tàlé! May (his elevation, &c.) long endure! (*used in firmans after the names of honourable personages*).

طالب tālib, *s. a.* A wisher, seeker for, inquirer after; a student; ——او, tālib-òl, *v.n.* To desire, ask for.

طالح tālih, *s. a.* A sinner.

طالع tāli", *s. a.* The ascendant (in astrology); fate, fortune, luck.

طالغه dàlgha, *s. t.* A wave; a ripple; طالغه‌لنمق dàlghalanmak, *v.n.* To rise in waves; to be wavy.

طالیان dàlyan, *s. t.* A fishing station erected on poles in the water.

طانه dàna, *s. t.* A calf.

طانیمق tànimak (*aor.* طانور tànir), *v.a.* To know again, to recognise; طانشمق tànishmak, *v.n.* To know or recognise one another; طانشق tànishik, *s. t.* An acquaintance.

طاوس tāwuss, *s. a.* A peacock.

طاوشان tàwshan, *s. t.* A hare; a Greek from certain of the isles; a cabinet-maker; اطه‌طاوشانی àda-tàwshani (A hare of the isles), a rabbit.

طاوق tàwuk, *s. t.* A fowl, a hen; ——ماوق, tàwuk-màwuk, Poultry of various kinds; طاوق کومسی tàwuk-kyümèssi, *s. t.* A fowl-house; طاوقجی tāwukju, A poulterer; a dealer in live fowls; ——کوتی, tàwuk-ghyütu, *s. t.* A wart.

طاوه tàwa, *s. t.* A frying-pan; any fried food; the pan of a gun-lock.

طاهر tàhir, *a. a.* Clean, lawfully clean.

طای tày, *s. t.* A colt; half a horse-load; (a bale, &c.) equal in weight to another.

طائر tā'ir, *s. a.* A bird, a fowl, any flying [animal; the soul.

طائف tā'if, *s. a.* A patrol, anything that goes round; name of a town in Arabia; a spectre, vision.

طائفه tā'ifé, *s. a.* A set of men, body of men; a people, nation, tribe; a ship's crew.

طائل tā'il, *in* لاطائل, lā-tā'il, *ad. a.* With-[out any beneficial result.

طب tìbb, *s. a.* The science of medicine; طبی tìbbī (*fem.* طبیه tìbbìyyé), *a. a.* Medical, pertaining to the science of medicine.

طبابت tìbābèt, *s. a.* The practice of medicine, the medical profession.

طباع tìbā", *s. pl. a.* (*of* طبع tàb"), Natures; dispositions; minds.

طباق tàbak, *s. t.* A plate; a dish; a saucer; طباقجی tàbakji, *s. t.* A dealer in china and earthenware.

طبان tàban, *s. t.* The sole of the foot; firmness, courage, intrepidity; ——تیموری, tàban-(dèymiri), One of the kinds of Damascus steel; دال——, dàl-tàbàn, *s. t.* A quick or continual runner; ——قالدرمق tàban-kàldirmak, *v.n.* To ply the foot, to take to one's heels, run.

طبانجه tàbAnja, s. t. A pistol.

طبائع tAbā'i", s. pl. a. (of طبيعت tAbī"àt), Natures; dispositions; characters; natural qualities.

طبخ tAbkh, s. a. A cooking; —ا, —et, v.a. To cook.

طبع tAb", The printing or impressing an impression of any kind; the nature, natural quality impressed by nature; natural health or state of body; taste, liking; disposition, character; —ا, —et, v.a. To print; to imprint.

طبق tìbk, s. a. Conformity, exact similarity of form.

طبقه tAbAka, s. a. A stratum; a sheet (of paper); a rank or degree (in a series); a floor (in a house).

طبل tAbl (dàwul), s. a. A drum.

طبله tAbla, s. a. Any flat tray with a high rim; those which are large are of wood, and the small ones of brass or silver; طبله‌كار tAbla-kyar, s. t. A baker's retailer who carries bread about on a tray.

طبيب tAbīb, s. a. A doctor of medicine [a physician.

طبيعت tAbī"àt, s. a. Nature; natural quality, disposition, or character; taste, delicacy of taste in matters of elegance.

طبيعى tAbī"ī, (fem. طبيعيه tAbī"ìyyE), a. a. Natural, not artificial.

طپراق tòprAk, s. t. Earth, soil; territory; عثمانلو طپراغى "òssmAnli-tòprAghi, s. t. Turkey, the Ottoman territory; طپراق ايشى tòprAk-ìshi, Any work made of clay, or of earth.

طپو tApu, s. t. See طاپو.

طحن tàhn, s. a. A grinding in a mill; —ا, —et, v.a. To grind in a mill.

طحين tàhīn, s. a. Ground sesame, being an oily paste used for food by Eastern Christians in Lent, and of which *helwa* is also made.

طرار tàrrār, s. a. A cutpurse, pickpocket, scamp, vagabond, rogue, rascal.

طراز tìrāz, a. p. (*in composition*), Who embroiders; who weaves the web of refined diction; an embroidered hem or border.

طراق tàrak, s. t. A comb; a card; a rake; a harrow; a limpet or cockle.

طرامق tàramak (aor. طرار tàrar), v.a. To comb; to card; to rake; to harrow. [flowers, &c.).

طراوت tàrāvèt, s. a. Freshness (of fruit,

طرب tàreb, s. a. Joy, joyousness, joyfulness, mirth, glee.

طربزون tàràbizūn (trAbzAn), s. t. Trebizond in Pontus; (or طربزان) a portcullis; the arm of a sofa, or rather the railing or slab which terminates a Turkish sofa when it does not reach to a wall; طربزان باباسى trAbzAn-bAbassi, The post which supports this railing in front of the sofa, the other end of the rail being fixed in the wall at the back of the sofa.

طرابلوس Tàrābalūs, s. t. Tripoli; طرابلوس غرب Tàrābalùs-i-gharb, Tripoli in Africa; طرابلوس شام Tàrābalūs-i-Shām, Tripoli in Syria.

طرپان tìrpan, *s. t.* A scythe.

طرتل tìrtìl, *s. t.* A caterpillar, especially the smaller kinds which destroy leaves and flowers; the velvet fringe called *chenille*; the bullions of gold-lace or epaulettes.

طرح tàrh, *s. a.* A casting, throwing, laying, or placing on the ground; a laying (foundations); a casting away; a subtracting; subtraction in arithmetic; —ا, —et, *v.a.* To cast, throw, lay, or place on the ground; to lay (foundations); to cast away; to subtract.

طرخون tàrkhūn, *s. t.* Tarragon (herb).

طرد tàrd, *s. a.* To drive away, send away, reject, repel.

طرز tàrz, *s. a.* A way, manner, fashion.

طرف tàraf, *s. a.* A side; a tract, district; a direction; a party; طرف طوتمق tàraf-tùtmak, *v.n.* To espouse a cause, side with a party or person; طرفدار tàraf-dār, *s. p.* A partisan; طرفين tàrafèyn, *s. a. dual,* The two sides or parties (in a question, suit, quarrel, &c.).

طرفانده tùrfanda, *s. t.* Fresh fruit or vegetables being the first fruits of a season.

طرفه tàrfa, *s. a.* A twinkling (of an eye); —, tùrfé, *s. a.* Anything fresh, new, rare; طرفةالعين tàrfétu-'l-"àyn, The twinkling of an eye.

طرق tùruk, *s. pl. a.* (*of* طريق tàrīk), Roads, paths, ways.

طرلا tàrla, *s. t.* Plough-land, arable land; one field of arable land.

طرماشمق tìrmashmak (*aor.* طرماشر tìrmashir), *v.n.* To climb up (trees, &c.) by using the claws (as cats, &c., do); to scratch one another, claw each other.

طرمالامق tìrmalamak (*aor.* طرمالار tìrmalar), *v.a.* To scratch with the claws.

طرمنتی tìrmenti, *s. t.* Turpentine.

طرناق or طرنق tìrnak, *s. t.* A nail, claw, talon, hoof; طرناقلو tìrnakli, *a. t.* Having a nail or nails, claws, hoofs; چتال‌طرناقلو chàtal-tìrnakli, *a. t.* Having a cloven hoof, cloven-hoofed.

طره tùrré, *s. p.* A lock of hair, a curl, a ringlet; a leather strap or a handkerchief twisted into a rope by children in certain games, a cob.

طرياق tìryāk, *s. a.* Theriaca, an opiate electuary.

طريان tàrayān, *s. a.* A happening, affecting (disagreeably).

طريد tàrīd, *s. a.* Any thing or person rejected, refused, cast away.

طريف tàrīf, *a. a.* Any object newly acquired possession of.

طريق tàrīk, *s. a.* A road, way, path; a mode, manner; a fashion; a quality; —عام, tàrīki-"āmm, A public road; —خاص, tàrīki-khāss, A private road; —حق, tàrīki-hàkk, The way of truth.

طريقت tàrīkat, *s. a.* A hierarchy; an order (of dervishes or monks).

طست tàsst, *s. a. and* طشت tàsht, *s. p.* A basin; a tray.

طشره tȧshra, *and* طشری dìshāri, *s. t.* The exterior, outer part (of anything); any provincial place away from the capital; —, *ad. t.* Beyond, out.

طعام ta‘‘ām, *s. a.* Food; a meal; taste, savour; ا—, —et, *v.n.* To breakfast or dine.

طعم ta‘‘m, *s. a.* Taste, savour; food.

طعمه tù‘‘mé, *s. a.* Food; prey; طعمهٔ شمشیر tù‘‘mé‘i-shìmshīr, Prey to the sword.

طعن ta‘‘n, *s. a.* A wounding, stabbing; a reproving, blaming, reproaching, speaking ill of; ا—, —et, *v.n.* To wound with any kind of stab; to reprove, reproach, blame, speak ill of.

طعنه ta‘‘né, *s. a.* A wound, a stab.

طغات tùghȧt, *s. pl. a.* (*of* طاغی tȧghī), Rebels; sinners.

طغرا tùghra, *s. t.* The cypher of the Sultan in an ornamental shape, used for inscribing over firmans, on coins, and on public buildings; it contains the name of the Sultan, and of his father, with the title Khān, and the epithet "*always successful.*"

طغرجق dògharjik, *s. t.* A wallet.

طغوا (*or* طغوی) tàghwà, طغوان tùghwȧn, طغی tàghy, *s. a.* Sin, wickedness; rebellion.

طغیان tùghìyyān, *s. a.* Being rebellious; exceeding bonds, overflowing.

طفره tȧfra, *s. t.* A proud careless insolence.

طفل tìfl, *s. a.* A child, an infant; طفلیت tìfliyyèt, *s. a.* Childhood, infancy.

طفلان tȧflȧn, *s. t.* (*Greek* δαφνη), The true laurel, different from *the bay*.

طفولت tùfūlèt, *and* طفولیت tùfūliyyèt, *s. a.* Childhood, infancy.

طفیل tùfèyl, *s. a.* A parasite, feast-hunter, lick-spittle, trencher-fly.

طقسان dòksan, *a. t.* Ninety; طقسانجی dòksaninji, *a. t.* The ninetieth.

طقوز dòkuz, *a. t.* Nine; اون‌طقوز òn-dòkuz, Nineteen; طقوزنجی dòkuzunju, *a. t.* Ninth.

طلا tìlā, *s. p.* Gold; a gold coin, piece of gold, gold piece; طلادوز tìlādūz, *s. p.* An embroiderer in gold thread.

طلاش tȧlash, *s. t.* Wood shavings.

طلاق tȧlāk, *s. a.* A divorce.

طلاوت tȧlāvèt, *s. a.* Beauty, grace, loveliness.

طلائع tȧlā‘i‘‘, *s. pl. a.* (*of* طلیعه tȧlī‘‘a), Scouts, the first indications of an approaching army.

طلب tàleb, *s. a.* A demanding, asking for, perquisition, seeking; ا—, —et, *v.a.* To demand, ask for, require, seek.

طلبا tùlébā, *and* طلبه tȧlébé, *s. pl. a.* (*of* طالب tālib), Demanders, askers for, requirers, seekers; students, seekers after learning.

طلسم tìlsim, *s. a.* A talisman.

طلعت tàl‘‘àt, *s. a.* An appearing, coming in sight; an aspect.

طلوع tùlū‘‘, *s. a.* A rising above the horizon; ا—, —et, *v.n.* To rise.

طلوم tùlum, *s. t.* A whole sheep's or goat's skin, used as a vessel for holding wine, oil, butter, &c.; a bagpipe;

the bag of a bagpipe; the quantity of fur in commerce ready prepared in form for a long cloak.

طلومبه **tùlumba,** *s. t.* A pump; a fire-engine; a glyster-pipe; a waterspout.

طليعه **tàlī‘‘à,** *s. a.* A scout of an army, the most advanced patrols which are first seen by the enemy.

طمر **dàmar,** *s. t.* A vein, artery, nerve; the grain of wood; a vein in stone or in mines; شاه‌طمر shāh-dàmar, *s. t.* An artery; قان‌طمری kān-dàmari, A blood-vessel, vein or artery; اق‌طمر àk-dàmar, A nerve.

طمروق **tòmruk,** *s. t.* A bud, leaf-bud; a stocks or pillory or billet of wood to which criminals are fastened; a police prison; طمروقلنمق tòmruklanmak, *v.n.* To form buds (a tree); طمروغه اورمق tòmrugha-wùrmak, *v.a.* To put into prison, *or* into the stocks.

طمطراق **tòmturàk,** *s. t.* Pomp, magnificence, grandeur, show.

طمع **tàma‘‘,** *s. a.* A coveting; covetousness; ا—, —et, *v.n.* To be covetous; طمعكار tàma‘‘kyār, *s. p.* An avaricious person, a miser.

طملامق **dàmlamak** (*aor.* طملار dàmlar), *v.n.* To drop, fall drop by drop; طملاتمق dàmlatmak (*aor.* طملادر dàmlàdir), *v.a.* To drop, to pour out by drops, to cause to fall by drops.

طمله **dàmla,** *s. t.* A drop (of fluid); the apoplexy.

طنبور **tànbūr,** *s. a.* طنبوره tànbura, *s. t.* A sort of guitar.

طنطنه **tàntana,** *s. a.* Pomp, magnificence, the being attended with many servants and every incident of state and grandeur.

طنمق **tìnmak,** *used only in the negative* طنمامق tìnmamak (*aor.* طنمز tìnmàz), *v.n.* Not to make any observation by speech or by notice, apparently; to keep quite quiet, apparently.

طنين **tìnīn,** *s. a.* A ringing, sounding, echoing noise.

طوار **dàvar,** *s. t.* (*provincial*), Sheep, animals, cattle.

طواشى **tàwāshī,** *s. pl. a.* (*sing. not used*), Eunuchs; (*as a Turkish singular*) a eunuch.

طواف **tàwāf,** *s. a.* A circumambulation; a processional circumambulation; ا—, —et, *v.n.* To circumambulate; —, tàwwāf, *s. a.* One who performs a circumambulation, a circumambulator.

طوان **tàwan,** *s. t.* A ceiling; —اراسى, tàwan-àrassi, *s. t.* A cockloft, the space among the rafters of a roof.

طوائف **tàwā‘if,** *s. pl. a.* (*of* طائفه tā‘ifé), Peoples, nations, tribes, sets of people.

طوب *or* طوپ **tòp,** *s. t.* A cannon, gun; a lump; a ball; a piece (of stuff); the whole (of anything), all; a wholesale quantity; طوپدن tòpdan, All together; in the lump; wholesale; —, *ad. t.* in طوپ‌طولو tòp-dòlu, Quite full; طوپجى tòpjυ, *s. t.* An artilleryman; a gunner; طوپخانه tòp-khāné, *s. t.* An arsenal of artillery.

طوپارلمق **tòparlamak** (*aor.* طوپارلار tòparlar), *v.a.* To roll or collect together and take away.

طوپال tòpAl, *s. t.* A lame man; —, *a.t.* Lame; طوپاللمق tòpAllamak, *v.n.* To walk lamely, to limp in walking.

طوپالق tòpalàk, *a. t.* Roundish, short and plump.

طوپلامق tòplamak (*aor.* طوپلار tòplar), *v.a.* To collect, to gather; طوپلانمق tòplanmak (*aor.* طوپلانور tòplanir), *v.n.* and *p.* To collect, to gather (of itself); to be collected, to be gathered; طوپلاتمق tòplatmak (*aor.* طوپلادر tòpladir), *v.a.* To cause or allow (one) to gather, to cause or allow (things) to be collected or gathered.

طوپوز tòpuz, *s. t.* A mace of arms, a club.

طوپوق tòpuk, *s. t.* The ankle bone; the back of the heel.

طوپلو tòplu, *s. t.* A pin.

طوتام tùtAm, *s. t.* A handful, as much as can be grasped at once.

طوتساق tùtsak, *s. t.* A prisoner of war, [a captive.

طوتقال tùtkAl, *s. t.* Glue; بالق طوتقالی bàlik-tùtkAli (Fish glue), Isinglass.

طوتمق tùtmak (*aor.* طوتار tùtar), *v.a.* To hold, keep hold of; to catch, lay hold of; to take prisoner, make prisoner; to arrest, stop, intercept; to hold, suppose; to keep, observe; —, *v.n.* To have the power of holding; to have the power of performing its natural functions (any limb); اوروج— ùruj—, *v.n.* To keep a fast canonically; معذور— mà‘‘zūr—, *v.a.* To hold excused, to excuse on account of some valid obstacle; سوز— sùz—, To take or follow advice; یاس— yàss—, ماتم— mātem—, *v.n.* To be in mourning; یوز— yùz—, *v.n.* To begin to show signs (of decay, &c.); خاطرده— khātirda—, *v.a.* To remember, not to forget, to hold in one's memory; هیچ بریری طوتمز hìch-bìr-yèri-tùtmàz, He is quite decrepit, all his limbs, his whole body is disabled; طوتلمق tùtulmak (*aor.* طوتلور tùtulur), *v.p.* To be held; to be seized; to be kept; to be rendered powerless in function by disease (any limb or organ); to be eclipsed (the sun or moon); to be observed or kept (a fast or ordinance of any kind); طوتنمق tùtunmak (*aor.* طوتینور tùtunur), *v.a.* To hold to one's self, apply to one's self or to any part of one's own body; طوتشمق tùtushmak (*aor.* طوتشور tùtushur), *v.n.* To hold to each other; to seize hold of each other; to quarrel together; to take fire, catch fire; to fly into a passion; طوتشدرمق tùtushturmak (*aor.* طوتشدرر tùtushturur), *v.a.* To cause (others) to quarrel, to set by the ears; to set fire to.

طور tàwr, *s. a.* A manner of acting, speaking, treating, or conducting one's self; a haughty or supercilious manner, superciliousness; —, tòr, *ad. t.* in طورطوب tòr-tòp, Quite round, quite like a ball.

طورانمق dàwranmak (*aor.* طورانور dàwrànir), *v.n.* To start into a posture of defence or vigilance; to regain one's health, footing, or position.

طوروپ tùrp, *s. t.* A radish. [grounds.

طورطی tòrtu, *s. t.* Sediment, lie, lees,

طورغون dùrghun, *a. t.* Motionless, stagnant. [fellow.

طورلاق tòrlàk, *s. t.* A foolish, careless

طورلمق dùrulmak (*aor.* طوریلور dùrulur), *v.n.* To stand so as to become clear by deposing its sediment; —, *v.p.* To be such that things can stand in, on, &c.

طورلەصویی Tūrla-sūyu, *s. t.* The river Dniester.

طورمق dùrmak (*aor.* طورر dùrur), *v.n.* To stay, remain; to stop, halt; to hesitate; to stand, stand up; to keep still, quiet, motionless; to cease from any action; to be in any posture; to remain steadfast (in any idea, to any promise); to continue in existence.

طورنه tùrna, *s. t.* A crane (bird).

طورو *or* طوری dòru, *a. t.* Bay (horse).

طوره (*for* طره tùrré), tùra, *s. t.* Anything twisted or bound up into a rope shape; a cob (used in play by children).

طوز tùz, *s. t.* Salt; طوزلو tùzlu, *a. t.* Salt, saltish; طوزسز tùzsuz, *a. t.* Insipid; طوزلامق tùzlamak (*aor.* طوزلار tùzlar), *v.a.* To salt.

طوزاق tùzàk, *s. t.* A trap, a snare; —قورمق, —kùrmak, To set a trap; طوزاغەطوتلمق tùzagha-tùtulmak, To be caught in a trap.

طوزله tùzla, *s. t.* A salt-works, salt-pans.

طوس dòss, *ad. t. in* طوس‌طوغری dòss-dòghru, Quite straight; —, tòss, *s. t.* The butting of rams or sheep; —اورمق, tòss-wùrmak, *v.n.* To butt; —اورشمق, tòss-wùrushmak, *v.n.* To butt at each other; طوسبغه tòss-bàgha, *s. t.* A tortoise. [woman.

طوطی tūtī, *s. p.* A parrot; a beautiful

طوع tàv'', *s. a.* Willing submission; طوعاً tàv''an, *and* بالطوع bì-'t-tàv'', *ad. a.* With submissive willingness.

طوغان dòghan, *s. t.* A hawk (?); a falcon (?).

طوغری dòghru, *a. t.* Straight; upright; true, exact, correct; honest.

طوغریلمق dòghrulmak (*aor.* طوغریلور dòghrulur), *v.n.* To become straight, upright, correct; to be directed, pointed, turned (towards a thing); to take the road, way, or direction (for any place); طوغرلتمق dòghrultmak (طوغریلدر dòghruldur), *v.a.* To make straight, upright, correct; to direct, turn, point (a thing towards an object).

طوغله tùghla, *s. a.* A brick.

طوغمق dòghmak (*aor.* طوغار dòghar), *v.n.* To be born; to rise (the sun, &c.); طوغرمق dòghurmak (*aor.* طوغرر dòghurur), *v.a. caus.* To give birth to, bring forth; to litter, pup, &c.; طوغرتمق dòghurtmak (*aor.* طوغردر dòghurdur), *v.a. double causal,* To attend in childbirth, to assist in giving birth to a child or to young, to act as midwife.

طوغی dòghʊ, s. t. in کون‌طوغیسی ghyùn-dòghussʊ, The east, sunrising.

طوف tàwf, s. a. A circumambulation; ا—, —et, v.n. To circumambulate.

طوفان tūfān, s. a. A deluge; —نوح, tūfāni-Nūh, The deluge of Noah.

طوق tàwk, s. a. A collar; a necklace; a pillory; power, strength, ability; —, tòk, a. t. Full, satiated; قارنم‌طوق kàrnim-tòk, My belly is full; کوزم‌طوق ghyùzum-tòk, (My eyes are satiated) I have nothing to wish for, I have no desires for wealth.

طوقشمق dòkushmak (aor. طوقشور dòkʊshʊr), v.n. To play with another person at knocking hard-boiled eggs together to see which will crack the other.

طوقمق tòkmak, s. t. A mallet; a knocker of a door; a hammer of a percussion cannon-lock.

طوقنمق dòkunmak (aor. طوقنور dòkʊnʊr), v.n. To touch; to meddle; to interfere; to hurt; to injure; to affect, to regard; طوقندرمق dòkundʊrmak (aor. طوقندرر dòkundʊrʊr), v.a. To cause or allow to touch, &c.

طوقومق dòkumak (aor. طوقور dòkʊr), v.a. To weave.

طوقه tòka, s. t. A buckle.

طوك dòng, s. t. Frost, hard frost; drawers or inner trousers; the coat (of a horse); —یاغی, dòng-yàghi, s. t. Tallow.

طوكدرمه dòngdʊrma, s. t. Ice-cream or water-ice.

طوكز dònguz (dòmuz), s. t. A pig, hog, swine; a beast, a wretch; a ruffian; a bold, brave fellow; —ایاغی, (dò-mʊz)-àyaghi, A worm for drawing wads from a gun; a dentist's instrument for drawing teeth; —قیلی, (dòmʊz)-kìli, Pigs' bristles; یبان طوكزی yàbʌn-(dòmʊzʊ), A wild pig or boar.

طوكمق dòngmak (aor. طوكار dòngar), v.n. To freeze; to become congealed; to harden, to set; طوكدرمق dòng-dʊrmak (aor. طوكدرر dòngdʊrʊr), v.a. To freeze, cause to become congealed, hardened, or set.

طول tūl, s. a. Length; longitude; طولاً tūlan, ad. a. In length; in longitude.

طولاب dòlʌb, s. t. Anything which turns round, a wheel, water-wheel, the heavens, a turning cupboard; a common cupboard or closet; a trick, piece of cunning or knavery; the whole affairs of a state, household, or mercantile concern; —قورمق, —kʊrmak, v.n. To prepare a snare, lay a plot; —چویرمك chèvirmek, v.n. To turn a wheel; to work a plot; to manage affairs. [about.

طولاشق dòlàshik, a. t. Circuitous, round-

طولاشمق dòlashmak (aor. طولاشر dòlashir), v.n. To go round, walk round; to be circuitous, go round about; طولاشدرمق dòlashdirmak (aor. طولاشدرر dòlàshdirir), *v.a.* To cause to go round; to cause to make a circuit; to cause to twine, wrap, or cling round.

طولامه dòlam*a*, *s. t.* A whitlow; a kind of garment of the olden time.

طولاندرمق dòlàndirmak (*aor.* طولاندرر dòlandirir), *v.a.* To cheat, swindle; طولاندريجى dòlàndiriji, *s. t.* A cheat, a swindler.

طولانمق dòlanmak (*aor.* طولانور dòlanir), *v.n.* To go wandering or meandering about.

طولايى dòlay*i*, *ad. t.* On account of, by reason of, concerning, relatively to.

طولمق dòlmak (*aor.* طولر dòlar), *v.n.* To fill, become filled, become full; to run, flow, or go in (to any receptacle so as to fill it); طولمش dòlmush, *part. past.* (Which has become full) Filled; any vehicle which takes many passengers at once; طولمه dòlm*a*, *s. t.* Several kinds of food made by stuffing various things; —, *a. t.* Anything filled in artificially; طولدرمق dòldurmak (*aor.* طولدرر dòldurur), *v.a.* To fill; to stuff; to fill in; to put (things) into any receptacle.

طولو dòlu, *s. t.* Hail; the fill (of anything); —, *a. t.* Full; —ياغمق, dòlu-yàghmak, *v.n.* To hail.

طوله tàwl*a*, *s. t.* A great man's stable; a tethering rope to which horses are fastened in the fields; the game of backgammon.

طولى dòlu. See طولو.

طومار tòmār, *s. a.* A roll or scroll of paper. [coat (of a horse).

طون dòn, *s. t.* Inner drawers; trousers;

طوى tòy, *s. t.* The greater bustard.

طويت tàvìyyèt, *s. a.* Intention, design, inward thoughts.

طويل tàvīl, *a. a.* Long; tall. [stable.

طويله tàvīlé (tàvl*a*), *s. a.* A great man's

طويمق dòymak (*aor.* طويار dòyar), *v.n.* To become satiated, satisfied with food; طويورمق dòyurmak (*aor.* طويورر dòyurur), *v.a.* To satiate, satisfy.

طهارت tàhāret, *s. a.* Purity, cleanliness; legal cleanliness.

طى tàyy, *s. a.* The folding or rolling up (a carpet, scroll, &c.); a travelling (over space); ا—, —et, *v.a.* To roll or fold up; to travel over and leave behind.

طيار tàyyār, *a. a.* Which flies about; ريح طيار rīh*i*-tàyyār, Flying rheumatic pains.

طياق dàyak, *s. t.* A prop, stay, support; a thrashing, beating; the bastinado, corporal punishment; —يمك, dàyak-yèmek (To eat a thrashing), To be beaten; —اتمق, dàyak-àtmak, To give a thrashing, to beat. [thing.

طيالو dàyāl*i*, *a. t.* Leaning against any-

طيامق dàyamak (*aor.* طيار dàyar), *v.a.* To press or lay anything against another for the support of either, or as an obstacle; to present or place anything in a resolute or offensive manner; طيانمق dàyanmak (*aor.*

طيانور dàyànir), *v.n.* To lean against anything; to be based upon anything; to lead to anything; to bear, support, resist; to last, to resist wear and tear.

طيب tàyyib (*fem.* طيبه tàyyibé), *a. a.* Good; pleasant; —, tīb, *s. a.* Perfume, scented cosmetics.

طيران tàyarān, *s. a.* A flying, flight; ا—, —et, *v.n.* To fly.

طيش dìsh, *s. t.* The outside, exterior part of anything; the space outside of anything.

طيشارى dìshàri, *s. t.* Equivalent to طيش; *also,* Any foreign country; any place away from Constantinople; —, *ad. t.* Out; abroad; away from Constantinople. [for plugging a hole.

طيقاج tìkaj, *s. t.* A plug, anything used

طيقامق tìkamak (*aor.* طيقار tìkar), *v.a.* To plug, stop up (a hole, a pipe, &c.); to push (into anything) as a plug; طيقانمق tìkanmak (*aor.* طيقانور tìkanir), *v.n.* To become plugged or stopped up; to be pushed into anything as a plug.

طيلسان tàylèssān, *s. a.* The end of a turban hanging down over the back or shoulder.

طين tīn, *s. a.* Earth, clay; مختوم—, tīni-màkhtūm, A kind of earth formerly used as a medicine, and marked with a seal.

طينت tīnèt, *s. a.* Nature, natural disposition, as though proceeding from the earth of which we are formed.

طيور tùyūr, *s. pl. a.* (*of* طائر tā'ir), Birds.

ظ

ظ zā (zì), Twentieth letter of the Turkish alphabet, having the value of *z* in English, though essentially more harsh and guttural. In chronograms its numeral value is 900.

ظا zā, *s. a.* Name of the letter ظ.

ظالم zālim, *a. a.* Tyrannical, oppressive (person); —, *s. a.* A tyrant; ظالمانه zālimāné, *a. p.* Tyrannical (thing or act).

ظاهر zāhir, *a. a.* Apparent, visible; —, *s. a.* The outer or visible portion of anything; —, *ad. t.* Of course, to be sure; ظاهرى zāhirī, *a. a.* Pertaining to the outer or visible portion; ظاهرا zāhirā, *ad. a.* Apparently, according to outward appearances.

ظبى zàby, *s. a.* A gazelle.

ظرافت zàrāfèt, *s. a.* A combination of elegance, wit, and tact.

ظرف zàrf, *s. a.* Any containing receptacle or cover; an envelope for a letter; an outer cup used in the East in lieu of a saucer; a noun of time or place.

ظرفا zùréfā, *s. pl. a.* (*of* ظريف zàrīf), Those who combine elegance, wit, and tact.

ظروف zùrūf, *s. pl. a.* (*of* ظرف zàrf), Envelopes, containing receptacles.

ظريف zàrīf (zārif), *a. a.* Elegant, witty, and possessed of tact; pretty looking.

ظفر zàfer, *s. a.* Success; victory; —,

zìfr, *s. a.* A nail, claw, talon, hoof; ظفریاب zàfer-yāb, *a. p.* Who has been successful, who has found a way to accomplish his wish; بولمق—, zàfer-bōlmak, *v.n.* To be successful, to find a way to accomplish a wish.

ظل zìll, *s. a.* A shadow, shade; protection; a tangent; ظل الله zìllu-'llāh, (The shadow of God) *or* ظل الله فی الارض zìllu - 'llāhi - fì - 'l - àrz (The shadow of God upon earth) The Sultan; نسبت ظلیه nìssbèti-zìllìyyé, A log. tangent; ظلیت zìllìyyèt, *s. a.* The (Sultan's) quality of being (God's) shadow; حضرت ظلیت پناه hàzréti--zìllìyyèt - pènāh, His Majesty (the abode of the quality of being God's shadow) the Sultan. [Shadows.

ظلال zìlāl, *s. pl. a.* (*of* ظل zìll),

ظلام zìlām, *s. a.* Darkness; —, zàllām, *s. a.* A persevering tyrant; —, zùllām, *s. pl. a.* (*of* ظالم zālim), Tyrants, oppressors.

ظلم zùlm (zùlum), *s. a.* Oppression, tyranny; injustice; —, zùlèm, *s. pl. a.* (*of* ظلمت zùlmet), Darknesses.

ظلمانی zùlmānī, *a. a.* Dark.

ظلمت zùlmet, *s. a.* Darkness.

ظلمه zàlémé, *s. pl. a.* (*of* ظالم zālim), Oppressors, tyrants.

ظلیل zàlīl, *a. a.* Shady, umbrageous.

ظن zànn, *s. a.* (*pl.* ظنون zùnūn), A conjecture, surmise, opinion, suspicion; any impression on the mind short of positive knowledge; ا—, —et, *v.a.* To opine, surmise, conjecture, think, fancy, imagine; to take for, suppose; حسن ظن hùssni-zànn, A good opinion (formed without experience of the person); سوء ظن sū'i-zànn, A bad opinion, a doubt or suspicion (about any person).

ظهر zàhr, *s. a.* The back; the back or outside of a book or paper; the letter or outward meaning of a word, phrase or discourse; —, zùhr, *s. a.* Noon.

ظهور zùhūr, *s. a.* A coming forth, coming out, becoming visible; a happening, coming into being, springing, arising; ا—, —et, *v.n.* To come forth, become visible; to happen, spring, arise; ظهوره كلمك zùhūra-ghèlmek, *v.n.* To happen, come to pass; صاحب ظهور sāhib-zùhūr, *s. p.* A conspicuous personage. [assists, protects.

ظهیر zàhīr, *s. a.* One who backs, aids,

ع

ع 'àyn. Twenty-first letter of the Turkish alphabet, having no real equivalent in English. In Turkish it is very usually silent like *h*, *l*, or *r*, in many English words; but as no one has ever called those letters vowels in consequence, so also is it absurd to call the ع a vowel in Turkish as some writers have done. When sounded it is a strong guttural hiatus. Its numeral value in chronograms and astronomical tables is 70.

عابد "ābid, *s. a.* A servant; a worshipper; عابدانه "ābidānè, *a. p.* Humble, servantlike. [over.

عابر "ābir, *s. a.* A passer by, a passer

عاج "āj, *s. a.* Ivory.

عاجز "ājiz, *a. a.* Unable, not sufficiently powerful, unequal to any task; worn out, tired out; —قالمق, "ājiz-kālmak, *v.n.* To be or become unable, unequal to, or worn out; عاجزانه "ājizānè, *a. p.* عاجزى "ājizī, *a. a.* Relating to a poor, weak, humble fellow (myself).

عاجل "ājil, *a. a.* Present (not future); ready (not deferred); عاجلاً "ājilan, *ad. a.* At once, down, on the spot.

عادت "ādet, *s. a.* A custom; a habit; the menses (of women); عادتا "ādétā, *ad. a.* In a common, customary manner; as usual; just; downright; خارق العاده khāriku -'l-"ādè, *s. a.* Any uncommon occurrence, any surprising thing or event; عادت ايدنمك "ādet-èdinmek, *v.a.* To contract (anything) as a habit; عادت بلده "ādéti-bèldè, *s. p.* The custom of the place or country; عادتدر "ādèt-dir, It is a (*or* the) custom; عادتمدر "ādétìm-dir, It is my custom or habit.

عادل "ādil, *a. a.* Just (person); legal, competent, fit, proper (witness); عادلانه "ādilānè, *a. p.* Just (thing, act, or word).

عادى "ādī (*fem.* عاديه "ādìyyè), *a. a.* Common, of every-day occurrence.

عار "ār, *s. a.* The feeling of shame; any cause of shame; ا—, —et, *v.n.* To be ashamed, feel ashamed; عارسز "ārsiz, *a. t.* Shameless, impudent; pertinacious; what there is no getting rid of (any unpleasantness); عارلنمق "ārlanmak, *v.n.* To become ashamed.

عارض "āriz, *a. a.* Which comes upon, lights upon, happens; —اول, "āriz-òl, *v.n.* To seize, happen, overtake (any calamity); عارضى (*fem.* عارضيه "āriz-ìyyè), *a. a.* Accidental, incidental, casual (not essential).

عارضه "ārizа, *s. a.* An accident, any fortuitous event; a misfortune.

عارف "ārif, *s. a.* A person well versed in knowledge; عارفانه "ārifānè, *a. p.* Pertaining to a person of knowledge; —, *s. p.* A share, subscription, contribution towards any payment in common; —, *ad. t.* By way of equal shares of contribution, by subscription. [defect).

عارى "ārī, *a. a.* Naked; free (from any

عاريت "ārìyyèt, *s. a.* The quality of being merely borrowed and temporary; عاريتى "ārìyyètī (èyréti), *a. t.* What is makeshift, temporary, borrowed; jury (mast); عارية ārìyyétan, *ad. a.* In a temporary, makeshift manner.

عازم "āzim, *a. a.* Who sets out, undertakes a journey (or other act).

عاشر "āshir, *a. a.* The tenth; —, *s. a.* A tithe-gatherer.

عاشق "āshik, *s. a.* A lover; one rapt in love towards God; عاشقانه "āshikāné, *a. p.* Pertaining to a lover; —او, "ăshık-ōl, *v.n.* To fall in love.

عاشورا "ăshūrā, *s. a.* A kind of sweet pottage made of ten kinds of pulse and grains, on the tenth of Muharrem, in commemoration of Noah's coming out of the ark and having a feast with the remains of his provision.

عاصف "ăssif, *a. a.* Violent, high (wind).

عاصم "ăssim, *a. a.* Chaste, pure from sin.

عاصى "ăssi, *s. a.* A rebel; a sinner.

عاطر "ătir, *a. a.* Sweet-smelling, perfumed.

عاطف "ătif (*fem.* عاطفه "ătifé), *a. a.* Affable, kind; copulative (conjunction); واو عاطفه wāwi-ātifé, The copulative و. [ness.

عاطفت "ătifet, *s. a.* Affability, kind-

عاطل "ătil, *a. a.* Idle, useless, not in use, not at work.

عافيت "āfiyyèt, *s. a.* Health, immunity from sickness; —أولسون, "āfiyyèt-ōlsun! May it be health to you! (*said to anyone who has drunk, been shaved, or bathed; or who is eating, and invites you to join him, when you do not accept the invitation*).

عاقبت "ākıbèt, *s. a.* The end (of any affair, person, or time); عاقبتكز خيراولسون "ākıbètingiz-khàyr-ōlsun! May your end be good! (*generally said by Turks to non-Mussulmans in answer to their salutation of* Good morning, &c.; *and implying*, May you ultimately embrace the true faith and be saved); —, *ad. t.* At last, at length.

عاقل "ăkil, *s. a.* A person of sense; a person endowed with reason; a reasonable being; عاقلانه "ăkılāné, *a. p.* Pertaining to a person of sense.

عالم "ālim, *a. a.* A learned man; one who knows much; —, "ālem, *s. a.* A world; a state of being; the public in general, everybody; ربالعالمين Ràbbu-'l-"ālémīn, The Lord of all worlds; عالمغائب "ālémi-ghā'ib, The invisible world; —شهادت, "ālémi-shàhādet, The visible world; —جبروت, "ālémi-jèbérūt, —ملكوت "ālémi-mèlékyūt, —لاهوت, "ālémi-lāhūt, The world of the Godhead (under various qualifications); —منام, "ālémi-mènām, —مثال, "ālémi-mìssāl, &c., The world of dreams seen in sleep; —صباوت, "ālémi-sàbāvèt, The age of childhood, childhood; &c. &c.; عالمانه "ālimāné, *a. p.* Pertaining to a learned man; عالمپناه "ālem-pènāh, *s. p.* (The asylum of the world) The Sultan; عالميان "ālémìyyān, *s. pl. p.* The inhabitants of this world.

عالى "ālī, *a. a.* High; high up, exalted, elevated; superior, supreme; باب عالى bābi-"ālī, (The Supreme Office) The house or office of Government at Constantinople, so needlessly misnomered "*the Sublime Porte.*"

عام "ām, *s. a.* A year; —, ămm (*fem.*

عامّه "Ammé), *a. a.* Common, universal; عامّه "Ammé, *s. a.* The public in general; خاص وعام khāsss - u- -"Amm, (The special and the common) People of all grades, high and low.

عامر "āmir (*fem.* عامره "āmirē), *a. a.* (A place) Busy, full of life and kept in good order. (An epithet applied to public establishments.)

عامل "āmil, *s. a.* Who acts; a governor; a governing word (in grammar).

عائد "A'id (*fem.* عائده "A'idē, *pl.* عائدات "A'idAt *and* عوائد "àwā'id), *a. a.* Which returns, comes back; which results; which comes in (as revenue); which affects, regards, falls to; (in the *pl.*) fees, perquisites, pickings, profits; —او, "ā'id-ol, *v.n.* To return, come *or* go back; to result, come in as revenue; to affect, regard, fall, pertain.

عبا "àba, *s. t.* A thick kind of woollen cloth for cloaks, &c.; a cloak made of this cloth.

عباد "ìbād, *s. pl. a.* (*of* عبد "àbd), Servants; worshippers; —الله, "ìbādu- -'llAh, Men, God's servants.

عبادت "ìbādet, *s. a.* Worship, service; ا—, —et, *v.n.* To worship; عبادتگاه "ìbādet-ghyāh, *s. p.* Any place where worship is performed; عبادتخانه "ìbā- det-khānē, *s. p.* A house of worship, a temple, church, mosque.

عبارت "ìbāret, *s. a.* A compound thing; *or a. a.* Compounded, composed; —او, "ìbāret-òl, *v.n.* To consist, to be composed, to be.

عباره "ìbārē (*originally identic with the preceding word*), *s. a.* A sentence, phrase.

عبث "àbess, *s. a.* A vain trifle, a futility, nonsense, trifling, a thing of no use.

عبد "àbd, *s. a.* A servant; الله —, "Abdu-'llAh, (The servant of God) Abdallah.

عبده "àbédé, *s. pl. a.* (*of* عابد "ābid), Worshippers; عبدهٔ اوثان "àbédè'i- -èvsān, Idolaters, worshippers of idols.

عبرانی "ìbrānī, *a. a.* Hebrew.

عبرت "ìbret, *s. a.* Any punishment or occurrence which may serve as a warning example to other people; عبرةً للسائرين "ìbrétEn-lì-'ss - sā'irīn, *ad. a.* As a warning example to others.

عبوديت "ùbūdìyyèt, *s. a.* Humble service, respectful service; عرض عبوديت ا "àrzi-"ùbūdìyyèt-et, *v.n.* To present one's respectful service.

عبور "ùbūr, *s. a.* A passing through or over; ا—, —et, *v.n.* To pass (through *or* over).

عبوس "àbūss, *a. a.* Sour, crabbed, austere-looking.

عبوست "ùbūssèt, *s. a.* Sourness, crabbedness, austerity of countenance.

عبير "àbīr, *s. a.* Ambergris.

عتاب "ìtāb, *s. a.* Reproach, blame, scolding; ا—, —et, *v.n.* To address in terms of blame.

عتاق "àtāk, *s. a.* Emancipation, freeing

a slave; ا—, —et, *v.a.* To set free, emancipate. [age.

عتاه "àtāh, *s. a.* The imbecility of old

عتبه "àtébé, *s. a.* A threshold; عتبهٔ عليه "àtébé'i-"àllìyyé, The imperial *threshold (equivalent to our "footstool.")*

عتق "àtk, *s. a.* A freeing, emancipating a slave; ا—, —et, *v.a.* To set free, emancipate. [insolence.

عتو "ùtùvv, *s. a.* Excessive pride and

عتوه "àtūh, *a. a.* Imbecile from age.

عته "àtah, *s. a.* Imbecility from old age.

عتيق "àtīk, *a. a.* Old, ancient.

عثمان "òssmān, *s. a.* Osman (*prop. name*); عثمانى "òssmānī (*fem.* عثمانيه "òssmānìyyé), *a. a.* Ottoman, Turkish; عثمانلو "òssmānli, *s. t.* A Turk, an Ottoman; ممالك عثمانيه mèmāliki-"òssmānìyyé, *and* عثمانلو طپراغى "òssmānli-tòprAghi, Turkey, the Ottoman dominions; ال عثمان āli-"òssmān, The house, family, or dynasty of Osman, the Ottoman dynasty; عثمانلولق "òssmanlilik, *s. t.* The kind of life essentially peculiar to the Ottoman, *i.e.* serving the Government, armed and on horseback, either in the provinces or against the enemy.

عجاله "ìjālé, *s. a.* Any thing or act ready or done off-hand; عجالةً "ìjālétén, *ad. a.* Quickly, in an off-hand way.

عجائب "àjā'ib (*pl.* عجائبات "àjā'i-bāt), *s. pl. a.* (*of* عجيبه "àjībé), Curious, astonishing, wonderful things, wonders, marvels; dear me! (*as a Turkish adj.*) curious, astonishing, wonderful, marvellous; singular, odd, funny, queer; —! *int. t.* How very singular!

عجب "àjab, *ad. t.* (*and* عجبا "àjabā, *ad. a.*), I wonder whether . . . ., I wonder if . . . .; that remains to be seen! —, "ùjb, *s. a.* Pride, self-conceit.

عجز "àjz, *s. a.* Inability, want of strength or means to accomplish, bear, or overcome; poverty.

عجزه "àjézé, *s. pl. a.* (*of* عاجز "ājiz), The poor, people of small means.

عجله "àjélé, *s. a.* Haste; a hurry; a pressing necessity; على العجله "àlé-'l-"àjélé, *ad. a.* In haste, hastily; ا—, "àjélé-et, *v.n.* To haste, to make haste, to be in a hurry.

عجم "àjem, *s. a.* A Persian; Persia; a barbarian, *i.e.* not an Arabian; عجمى "àjémī, *s. t.* A tyro, beginner, learner; عجمى اوغلان "àjémi-òghlan, A lad newly received into the service of the Sultan's person (in olden times); عجمستان "àjémisstān, *s. p.* Persia.

عجوز "àjūz, *and* عجوزه "àjūzé, An old woman (ninety-six meanings are noted against this word in Arabic lexicons, but this alone is used in Turkish); برد العجوز bèrdu-'l-"àjūz, (Old woman's cold, called also in common Turkish قوجه قارى صوغوغى kòja-kāri-sòghu-ghu), A noted return of cold weather, esteemed to last a week, from about the 7th to the 14th of March every year.

عجيب "àjīb (*fem.* عجيبه "àjībé), *a. a.* Astonishing, wonderful, marvellous, rare, curious, singular; عجيبه "àjībé, *s. a.* A curious thing.

عد "àdd, *s. a.* A reckoning, esteeming, counting; ا—, —et, *v.a.* To reckon, esteem, account.

عدا "àdā, *v.n.a.* Is beyond (*in* ماعدا mā-"àdā, *ad. a.* Besides, what is more).

عداد "ìdād, *s. a.* A number; a numbering.

عدالت "àdālèt, *s. a.* Justice, equity; competency (in a legal sense).

عداوت "àdāvèt, *s. a.* Enmity, hatred, ill-will, malevolence, spite, grudge, persecution; ا—, —et, *v.n.* To persecute, pursue with ill-will.

عدت "ìdet *or* "ìddet, *s. a.* The space of time during which a woman may not lawfully have connection with a man to whom she has newly become lawfully bound either by marriage or by purchase, so that it may be ascertained that she is not pregnant.

عدد "àded, *s. a.* A number; —صحيح, "àdédi-sàhīh, A whole number. (*It is usual to introduce this word* عدد *after any number and before the name of the thing numbered, when some other special term is not so introduced, e.g.* ایکی عدد عربه ìki-"àded-"àraba, *Two carriages*).

عدل "àdl, *s. a.* Justice, equity; عدلی "àdlī (*fem.* عدلیه "àdlìyyé), *a. a.* Pertaining to justice or equity; the poetical name of Sultan Mahmud the Second, the *fem.* being now applied to the Turkish Privy Council, instituted by that monarch.

عدم "àdem, *s. a.* Naught, nothingness, non-existence, nothing; as a component part of privative expressions this word is equivalent to our addition of one of the syllables *un*, *in*, *dis*, &c., before, and *ness*, or other corresponding syllable after, or of the syllables *lessness* after a word; ex. عدم وفا "àdémi-wèfā, *faithlessness* or *inconstancy*.

عدو "àdùvv, *s. a.* An enemy; —, "ùdùvv, *s. a.* A passing beyond, going beyond.

عدوان "ùdwān, *s. a.* Hatred, enmity.

عدول "ùdūl, *s. a.* A deviating; deviation; ا—, —et, *v.n.* To deviate.

عدید "àdīd, (*fem.* عدیده "àdīde), *a. a.* Numerous.

عدیل "àdīl, *s. a.* An equal; an equivalent.

عدیم "àdīm, *a. a.* Non-existent; not endowed with.

عذاب "àzāb, *s. a.* Pain, punishment.

عذار "ìzār, *s. a.* The cheek; خلیع العذار khàlī"u-'l-"ìzār, Barefaced, shameless.

عذب "àzb, *s. a.* Sweet water; عذب البیان "àzbu-'l-bèyān, *a. a.* Sweet and smooth in utterance as the flowing of a stream of water.

عذبه "àzébé (àssaba), *s. a.* The upper-leather of a shoe ; عذبه‌لو ‟àssabali, a. t. High in the upper-leather (a shoe).

عذر ‟ùzr, s. a. Any valid impediment, obstacle, excuse, or reason for not acting; —دیله‌مك, ‟ùzr-dilémek, v.n. To beg to be excused.

عذرا ‟àzrā, s. a. A virgin.

عراق ‟ìrāk, s. a. Babylonia, Chaldea; عراق عجم ‟ìrāki-‟àjàm, Persian Irak or Media; عراق عرب ‟ìrāki-‟àrab, Arabian Irak or Babylonia, Chaldea.

عراقان ‟ìrākānī, s. a. The cities of Bassora and Kufa.

عرائس ‟àrā'iss, s. pl. a. (of عروس ‟àrūss), Brides.

عرب ‟àrab (pl. عربان ‟ūrbān), s. a. An Arab; عربی ‟àrébī, s. a. عربجه ‟àrabja, s. t. The Arabic language; عربی ‟àrébī (fem. عربیه ‟àrébìyyé), a. a. Arabic, Arabian; عربیات ‟àrébìyyāt, s. pl. a. The rules of Arabic grammar and rhetoric.

عربده ‟àrbédé, s. a. A row, quarrel.

عربستان ‟àrabìsstān, s. p. Arabia.

عربه ‟àraba, s. t. A cart or carriage of any kind; ال‌عربه‌سی èl-‟àrabassi, A hand-barrow or wheel-barrow; عربه‌جی ‟àrabaji, A coach or cart-maker; a coach-hirer; a coach or cart-driver.

عرش ‟àrsh, s. a. The throne of God.

عرصه ‟àrsa, s. a. A space of ground, a plot of ground; a plain, a field; عرصهٔ‌عرصات ‟àrsa'i-‟àrsāt, The plain of plains, where all mankind will assemble at the resurrection; عرصه‌گاه ‟àrsa-ghyāh, s. p. A battle-field.

عرض ‟àrz, s. a. Breadth, width; latitude; a presenting, offering to view or for acceptance; a representing by speech or writing; a petition; —, ‟ìrz, s. a. Honour; that which honour compels us to defend from harm or suspicion, the sense of honour; —, ‟àraz, s. a. An accident, an incidental state or quality (in logic); عرضاً ‟àrzan, ad. a. In width; in latitude; ا—, —et, v.a. To offer, present, lay before; to represent by speech or writing; عرضحال ‟àrzi-hāl (àrzuhāl), A petition; a letter from an inferior; عرضی ‟àrazī (fem. عرضیه ‟àrazìyyé), a. a. Accidental, incidental, not essential.

عرف ‟ùrf, s. a. The temporal administration of the affairs of a nation (*in contradistinction to* شرع shèr‟, *the ecclesiastical or canonical administration*); equity (*as opposed to* law) violence, injustice, oppression (*because of the abuses suffered under the name*) عرفاً ‟ùrfan, ad. a. By the temporal law or will of the sovereign or his delegates; violently, unjustly, oppressively; اهل‌عرف èhli-‟ùrf, An exerciser of temporal law; an unjust oppressor; عرفی ‟ùrfī (fem. عرفیه ‟ùrfìyyé), a. a. Pertaining to the temporal mode of administration; violent, oppressive, unjust.

عرفان "ìrfān, s. a. A general knowledge of polite and scientific matters.

عرفه "àréfé, s. a. The last day of Ramazan, before Bayram day, Bayram-eve.

عرق "àrak, s. a. Sweat, perspiration; (ràkı) any distilled spirit; —, "ìrk, s. a. A vein; عرق النسا "ìrk-u-nìssā, Sciatica; عرقيه "àrakìyyé, s. a. عرقچين "àrak-chīn, s. p. A small linen cap worn under the turban to prevent soiling from sweat. [leader.

عرنين "ìrnīn, s. a. A prince, chieftain,

عروت "ùrvet, s. a. A handle; عروة الوثقى "ùrvétu-'l-vùskā, (The firmest of all handles) The Muhammedan religion.

عروج "ùrūj, s. a. An ascent; ا—, —et, v.n. To ascend, go up.

عروس "àrūss, s. a. A bride; a bridegroom; نو عروس nèv-"àrūss, s. p. A new-married bride; زلف عروس zùlfu-"àrūss, (Brides' ringlets) The snail-plant or Caracalla-bean; عروسی "àrūssī, s. p. A wedding.

عروض "àrūz, s. a. Prosody; the last foot in the first hemistich of a verse; —, "ùrūz, s. pl. a. (of عرض "àraz), Accidents, incidents. [Veins.

عروق "ùrūk, s. pl. a. (of عرق "ìrk),

عريان "ùryān, a. a. Naked, bare.

عريض "àrīz, a. a. Wide, broad.

عز "àzzé! May (he, she, or it) be respected; —, "ìzz, s. a. Respect, or the quality which commands deference and consideration, as power, grandeur, &c.

عزب "àzeb, s. a. A bachelor, a distinct body of troops in the old system.

عزبت "ùzbet, s. a. An unmarried life, single blessedness.

عزت "ìzzèt, s. a. Power and glory; consideration, dearness, prizedness.

عزل "àzl, s. a. A dismissing any functionary from office; dismissal; the act of Onan, spilling the seed expressly at the end of coition, so as to avoid the procreation of children; ا—, —et, v.a. To dismiss from office; —, v.n. To spill the seed.

عزلت "ùzlet, s. a. Retirement from the busy affairs of life, seclusion of life.

عزم "àzm, s. a. Purpose, firm intention, resolution; a setting out, undertaking a journey or expedition; اولو العزم ūlū-'l-"àzm, Those endowed with firmness of purpose in publishing God's will.

عزيز "àzīz, a. a. Dear, beloved; rare, highly prized; powerful, grand; عبد العزيز "àbdu-'l-"àzīz (The servant of the Powerful God), A proper name.

عزيمت "àzīmèt, s. a. A departure, setting forth on a journey; ا—, —et, v.n. To start, leave, set out, set sail, sail.

عساكر "àssākir, s. pl. a. (of عسكر "àsskèr), Troops, soldiers; —خاصه, "àssākiri-khàsssa, The guards; — نظاميه "àssākiri-nìzàmìyyé, The line;

—ردیفه, ʻʻàssākiri-rèdīfé, The reserve of veterans. [matter.

عسر ʻʻùssr, *s. a.* A difficulty, difficult

عسرت ʻʻùssrèt, *s. a.* Difficulty, difficultness.

عسس ʻʻàssess, *s. a.* A watchman, policeman.

عسکر ʻʻàsskεr, *s. a.* A soldier; an army; a body of men, a gang, a crew; عسکری ʻʻàsskérī (*fem.* عسکریه ʻʻàsskérìyyé), *a. a.* Military.

عسل ʻʻàssel, *s. a.* Honey; شمع عسل shèmʻʻ*i*-ʻʻàssel, Bees'-wax; عسلبند ʻʻàssel-bènd, Gum benjamin(?).

عسیر ʻʻàssīr, *a. a.* Difficult, hard.

عشا ʻʻìshā, *s. a.* The evening; the time of night prayer; —, ʻʻàshā, Supper, the evening meal; عشای ربانی ʻʻàshāy*i*-ràbbāni, The Lord's Supper.

عشائر ʻʻàshāʻir, *s. pl. a.* (*of* عشیرت ʻʻàshīrèt), Tribes, clans, septs.

عشر ʻʻùshr, *s. a.* A tenth part, a tithe; —, ʻʻàshar, *and* عشره ʻʻàshara, *a. a.* Ten.

عشرت ʻʻìshret, *s. a.* A pleasant life; a merry life; indulgence in strong drink; ا—, —et, *v.n.* To indulge in drink. [*a. a.* Twenty.

عشرون ʻʻìshrūna, *and* عشرین ʻʻìshrīna,

عشق ʻʻàshk, *s. a.* Love.

عشوه ʻʻìshvé, *s. a.* Coquetry, blandishments; عشوه کار ʻʻìshvé-kyār, *s. p.* A coquette.

عصا ʻʻàssā, *s. a.* A staff, stick, wand; a crutch; a sceptre; a crozier; شق عصا ا shàkk*i*-ʻʻàssā-et, *v.n.* (To break one's staff) To go away.

عصابت ʻʻìssābet (ʻʻàssābet), *s. a.* Sticklishness, nicety, tenacity on points of honour; pride of family and descent.

عصابه ʻʻìssābé, *s. a.* (*originally identic with the preceding word*), The bandage which forms the turban.

عصات ʻʻùssāt, *s. pl. a.* (*of* عاصی ʻʻāssī), Rebels; sinners.

عصاره ʻʻùssāré, *s. a.* The expressed juice of any fruit or plant.

عصبه ʻʻàssaba, *s. a.* A nerve, or tendon; a person's relatives and connexions other than parents and children.

عصر ʻʻàssr, *s. a.* An age, a space of several years; (*also* عصراول ʻʻàssri-èvvεl) the time of afternoon prayer.

عصفور ʻʻùssfūr, *s. a.* A sparrow.

عصمت ʻʻìssmèt, *s. a.* Chastity; purity of life, innocence; عصمتلو ʻʻìssmètlū, *a. t.* عصمتمآب ʻʻìssmet-màʻāb, *a. p.* Chaste, virtuous (woman).

عصیان ʻʻìssyān, *s. a.* Rebellion, revolt; sin and wickedness; ا—, —et, *v.n.* To rebel, revolt. [juice of anything.

عصیرت ʻʻàssīrèt, *s. a.* The expressed

عضاده ʻʻìzādé, *s. a.* The *alhidade* or movable part of a quadrant, sextant, &c.

عضد ʻʻàzud, *s. a.* The upper arm from the shoulder to the elbow.

عضله ʻʻàzàlé, *s. a.* A muscle; عضله ناك ʻʻàzàlénak, *a. p.* Muscular.

عضو ʻʻùzv, *s. a.* (*pl.* اعضا àʻʻzā), A member (of the body; in speaking of the members of a *council*, &c., the plural only is used; and if the singular is required, they say *one of the members*, اعضادن بری à''zādan-bìri).

عطا ''ʌtā, *s. a.* A giving; اخذوعطا àkhz-u-''ʌtā, Commerce, trade, business.

عطار ''ʌttār (ʌktār), *s. a.* A perfumer, seller of perfumes; a combination, in a small way, of druggist, grocer, stationer, and toyman.

عطارد ''ʊtārid, *s. a.* The planet Mercury.

عطالت ''ʌtālèt, *s. a.* Inertia, idleness, supineness.

عطایا ''ʌtāyā, *s. pl. a.* (*of* عطیه ''àtìyyé), Gifts, presents (from superiors).

عطر ''ìtr, *s. a.* Perfume; the scented-leaved geranium; عطر شاهی ''ìtri-shāhī, *s. p.* A sweet-pea, the sweet-smelling pea of gardens; عطر یاغی ''ìtr-yàghi, *s. t.* Essential oil of roses (the so-called *otto*). [*v.a.* To sneeze.

عطسه ''ʌtsé, *s. a.* A sneeze; —ا, —et,

عطش ''ʌtsh, *s. a.* Thirst; thirstiness.

عطشان ''ʌtshān, *a. a.* Thirsty, parched with thirst.

عطف ''ʌtf, *s. a.* A turning in any direction; a conjoining (in grammar); —بیان, ''ʌtfi-bèyān, The adding one noun, adjective, or verb, after another, joining them by the conjunction *and*, so as to express a different matter; as, *land and water*; —تفسیر, ''ʌtfi-tèfsīr, The adding a second noun simply corroborative and determinative of the first; as, *kindness and favour*; —عنان ا, ''ʌtfi-''ìnān-et, *v.n.* (To turn the rein) To go in the direction.

عطوفت ''ʊtūfet, *s. a.* Kindness, favour, condescension; عطوفتلو ''ʊtūfetlū, *a. t.* Kind, benevolent. [superior.

عطیه ''ʌtìyyé, *s. a.* A present from a

عظام ''ìzām, *s. pl. a.* (*of* عظم ''ʌzm), Bones; (*of* عظیم ''ʌzīm), Great men.

عظما (*for* عظمی) ''ʊzmà, *a. a. fem.* Greater; the greatest.

عظمت ''ʌzamèt, *s. a.* Greatness, grandeur; pride; عظمتلو ''ʌzamètlū, *a. t.* Grand.

عظیم ''ʌzīm, *a. a.* Great, large, big; great, grand; great, considerable.

عفت ''ìffèt, *s. a.* Chastity, purity of life, virtue and honour in women; عفتلو ''ìffetlū, *a. t.* Chaste, virtuous (woman).

عفریت ''ìfrīt, *s. a.* A genie of the most hideous kind; —کسلمك, ''ìfrīt-kèssilmek, *v.n.* To look a very demon from rage.

عفو ''ʌfv, *s. a.* A pardoning, forgiving; —ا, —et, *v.a.* To pardon, forgive; to let off, to excuse; to exempt.

عفونت ''ʊfūnèt, *s. a.* A malignant state, bad state, inflammation, tendency to mortification or putrefaction.

عفیف ''ʌfīf (*fem.* عفیفه ''ʌfīfé), *a. a.* Chaste, virtuous, honest.

عقاب ''ìkāb, *s. a.* Punishment, chastisement; —, ''ʊkāb, *s. a.* An eagle.

عقار "ʌkār, *s. a.* Real property in general. ["àkreb), Scorpions.

عقارب "ʌkārib, *s. pl. a.* (*of* عقرب

عقارت "ʌkārèt, *s. a.* Any single piece of real property; sterility, barrenness (of animals).

عقائد "ʌkā'id, *s. pl. a.* (*of* عقيده "ʌkīdé), Points of religious belief.

عقب "àkab, *s. a.* The time or space immediately after a thing; درعقب dèr-"àkab, *ad. p.* Immediately afterwards, immediately, instantly. [life.

عقبا (*for* عقبى) "ùkbʌ, *s. a.* The future

عقد "ʌkd, *s. a.* A tying of a knot; a concluding (of a treaty); a marrying, giving in marriage, tying (a woman to her husband) by the performance of the marriage ceremony; a holding (a meeting); —ا, —et, *v.a.* To tie; to conclude; to marry; to hold.

عقده "ùkdé, *s. a.* A knot; a difficulty.

عقرب "àkreb, *s. a.* A scorpion; the sign Scorpio; the hour-hand of a watch or clock.

عقل "ʌkl, *s. a.* The reasoning faculty, reason; sense, intelligence, quickness; judgment; prudence; memory; عقلده طوتمق "ʌklda-tùtmak, *v.a.* To remember, not to forget, to keep in mind, bear in mind; عقلمده در "ʌklimda-dir, I have (it) in mind, I have not forgotten; عقلى باشنده او "ʌkli-bʌshinda-òl, *v.n.* To have one's wits about one, to know what one is about; عقلى باشنه كلمك "ʌkli-bʌshina-ghèlmek, *v.n.* To recover one's senses, to have one's senses return, be restored to reason, to gain a right perception of things; برينك عقلنه كتورمك bìrining-"ʌklina-ghétìrmek, To recall (something) to a person's memory; عقلى "ʌklī (*fem.* عقليه "ʌklìyyé), *a. a.* Pertaining to reason; عقليات "ʌklìyyāt, *s. pl. a.* Things pertaining to reason, objects of the reasoning faculty; عقللو "ʌklli, *a. t.* Wise, prudent, sage; عقلسز "ʌklsiz, *a. t.* Foolish; عقلا "ʌkl:et, *v.a.* To think of, suggest, invent, find out; علوم عقليه "ùlūmu-"ʌklìyyé, The humanities, or sciences depending upon human reason.

عقلا "ùkalā, *s. pl. a.* (*of* عاقل "ākil), People of intelligence; عقلالق "ùkalālik, *s. t.* A presumptuous show of superior intelligence.

عقوبت "ùkūbèt, *s. a.* Punishment, chastisement. [dience

عقوق "ùkūk, *s. a.* Perversity, disobe-

عقول "ùkūl, *s. pl. a.* (*of* عقل "ʌkl), Intelligences, reasons; ذوى العقول zèvi-'l-"ùkūl, Beings endowed with reason.

عقيب "àkīb, *s. a.* The time or space immediately following anything.

عقيده "àkīdé, *s. a.* A point of religious belief; a kiss *or* bull's-eye (of sugar).

عقيق "àkīk, *s. a.* Cornelian stone.

عقيم "àkīm, *a. a.* Barren, childless.

عكا *or* عكه "Akkā, *s. t.* St. Jean d'Acre.

عكام "àkkyām, *s. a.* A tent-pitcher and palanquin attendant.

عكس "àkss, *s. a.* An echo, reverberation; reflection; report; whispering; being talked about, or being heard; the reverse, or contrary (of anything); ا—, —et, *v.n.* To be talked about; to be heard talk of, to reach anyone's ears; —, *v.a.* To reflect (light, sound, &c.); عكسى "àksī, *a. a.* Contrary, reverse; برعكس bèr-("àkiss), *ad. p.* بالعكس bì-'l-("àkiss), *ad. a.* On the contrary.

علا "àlā, *s. a.* Elevation, sublimity, highness; علاالدين "àlā'u-'d-dīn (The sublimity of religion), Proper name (Aladdin); —! May (God) be exalted!

علاج "ìlāj, *s. a.* A medicine, remedy; a remedying, curing, treating medically.

علاقه "àlāka, *s. a.* Any kind of connexion, business, or relation; love; ا—, —et, *v.n.* To fall in love, become enamoured.

علام "àllām, *s. a.* The Omniscient God.

علامت "àlāmèt, *s. a.* A sign, signal, symbol, symptom; a wonder; a phenomenon.

علامه "àllāmé, *s. a.* A very learned man.

علاوه "ìlāvé, *s. a.* An adding, superadding, appending; anything added, superadded, appended; ا—, —et, *v.a.* To add, append.

علائق "àlā'ik, *s. pl. a.* (*of* علاقه "àlāka), Connexions, things connected, business, relations.

علائم "àlā'im, *s. pl. a.* (*of* علامت "àlāmèt), Signs, signals, symptoms; wonders, phenomena; —السما, "àlā'imu-'ss-sèmā (èlèym-sāmā), (The signs of the sky) The rainbow.

علت "ìllèt, *s. a.* A cause, means; a disease, complaint, malady.

علف "àlef, *s. a.* Provender, forage.

علل "ìlèl, *s. pl. a.* (*of* علت "ìllèt, q. v.)

علم "àlem, *s. a.* A flag, ensign, standard; the half-moon and star usually placed over mosques and other public buildings in Turkey; a common name; —, "ìlm (ìlim), *s. a.* Knowledge sure and perfect knowledge; science a science; علم وخبر "ìlm-ū-khāber, Knowledge and information; a letter of advice, an invoice; علم اليقين "ìlma-'l-yàkīn, *ad. a.* For certain, of certain knowledge; طالب علم tālibi-"ìlm, A student; العلم عندالله èl-"ìlmu-"ìnda-'llāh, Perfect knowledge is with (God) alone; علمى "ìlmī (*fem.* علميه "ìlmìyyé), *a. a.* Pertaining to science, scientific; pertaining to the learned body; علمدار "àlemdār, *s. p.* A standard-bearer.

علما "ùlémā, *s. pl. a.* (*of* عالم "ālim), Doctors of law and theology, men learned in the law.

علناً "àlénan, *ad. a.* Publicly, openly, avowedly; علنى "àlénī (*fem.* علنيه "àléniyyé), *a. a.* Public, open, avowed; علنيت "àléniyyèt, *s. a.* The quality of being done in public, openly and avowedly.

علو ''àlev, *s. t.* Flame; a flash; —, ''ùlùvv, *s. a.* Highness, exaltedness, sublimity; علوجناب ''ùlùvvu-jènāb, Magnanimity, high-mindedness; علولنمك ''àlevlanmek (*aor.* علولنور ''àlevlénir), *v.n.* To burst into flame; to burst into a passion.

علوفه ''ùlūfé, *s. a.* Pay, salary.

علوم ''ùlūm, *s. pl. a.* (*of* علم ''ìlm), Sciences; علوم نقليه ''ùlūmu-nāklìyyé, The sciences which depend upon tradition, as theology, canonical law, &c.; علوم عقليه ''ùlūmu-''āklìyyé, The sciences resulting from human reason; علوم رياضيه ''ùlūmu-rìyāzìyyé, The exact sciences, the sciences of discipline, the mathematical sciences.

علوى ''ùlvī (*fem.* علويه ''ùlvìyyé), *a. a.* Pertaining to the higher regions; علويان ''ùlvīyān, *s. pl. p.* Angels; planets, stars.

على ''àlī, *s. a.* Ali (*prop. name*); —, (*fem.* عليه ''àlìyyé), *a. a.* Very high, very exalted (*This is the title always given exclusively to the Ottoman Government*); دولت عليه dèvléti-''àlìyyé, The Very Exalted State; *Persia is called* دولت بهيهٔ ايران dèvléti-bèhìyyè'i-Īrān, The Beautiful State of Persia; and all European States are designated as دولت فخيمهٔ سى —, — dèvléti-fàkhīméssi, The high-ranking State of——. It is one of those instances of an assumed exclusiveness, the practice of which requires to be abrogated; —, ''àla (*or* ''àlé *when placed before the definite article,* ال, *and* ''àlèy *when followed by an Arabic pronoun*), *pr. a.* On, upon; against; according to; in; to, towards; *joined to Arabic nouns, with or without the article, &c., it is much used to form adverbs or adverbial expressions*; as, على الاطلاق ''àlé-'l-ìtlāk, In a general sense; على العموم ''àlé-'l-''ùmūm, Generally, commonly, universally; على التحقيق ''àlé-'t-tàhkīk, Verily, assuredly, really; على وجه التفصيل ''àla-vèjhi-'t-tāfsīl, In a detailed manner; على التوالى ''àlé-'t-tèvāli, Successively, uninterruptedly; على اى حال àla-èyyi-hālin, In whichever way; على كلا التقديرين ''àla-kèlā-'t-tàkdīrèyn, In either of the two cases.

عليا ''ùlyā, *a. a. fem.* (*of* اعلى à''la), The highest.

عليك ''àlèyké, *comp. a.* (على ''àlèy *and* ك ké), Upon thee; عليكم ''àlèykyum, (على àlèy *and* كم kyùm), Upon you; عليك البيان ''àlèyké-'l-bèyān! It is for you to demonstrate or explain that! عليكم سلام ''àlèykyum-sèlam! Upon you be peace!

عليل ''àlīl, *a. a.* Infirm, invalid, suffering under some bodily infirmity or defect.

عليم ''àlīm, *a. a.* Very knowing, very [learned.

عليه ''àlèyh (*or* ''àlèyhi *if followed by*

any other word in an Arabic phrase), *comp. a.* (على "àlèy, *and* ه h *or* hi), On, towards, *or* against him (*or* it); —, *s. t.* The abstract state or position of what is against a person; عليهمه "àlèyhim*a* *or* عليهمده "àlèyhimd*a*, Against me; عليهنه "àlèyhin*a*, عليهنده "àlèyhind*a*, Against him, her, it; &c. &c.; عليها "àlèyhā (على *and* ها hā, *her, it*), On, towards, *or* against her, it; عليهما "àlèyhimā (على *and* هما himā, *The two of them*), On *or* against them both; عليهم "àlèyhim (على *and* هم him, *them*) (*mas.*) On them all; عليهن "àlèyhìnna (على *and* هن hìnn*a*, *them*) (*fem.*), On them all.

عمّ "àmm, *s. a.* A paternal uncle, father's own brother; —, abbreviation for the words عليه السلام "àlèyhi-'ss--sèlām! *Peace be upon him!* —, "àmma! *int. a.* May (God's favours, &c.) be universal!

عما "àmā, *s. a.* Blindness, cecity.

عماد "ìmād, *s. a.* A prop, support, post, column.

عمارت "ìmārèt, *s. a.* The bearing the signs of man's presence and industry, being cultivated, populated, in a state of good repair; an inhabited or cultivated district or place; any public building; a kitchen for the poor.

عمامه "ìmāmé, *s. a.* A turban; a particular kind of turban worn by the doctors of the law.

عمان "ùmman, *s. a.* The ocean, a sea.

عمد "àmd, *s. a.* Design and premeditation; عمداً "àmdan, *ad. a.* Designedly, premeditatedly.

عمده "àmdet, *s. a.* A pillar, prop, stay; a chief, a person of distinction.

عمر "ùmr, *s. a.* The duration of life, lifetime; real and true living, fun; —سورمك, —sùrmek, *v.n.* To live comfortably and happily; —كچورمك, —ghèchirmek, *v.n.* To live, pass one's time or life; عمريكز چوق اولسون "ùmrunguz-chòk-òlsun! *int. t.* (May your life be long!) I thank you! (*vulgar*) الله عمرلرو يرسون Allāh-"ùmrlar-vèrsin! May God grant you (or him) many ordinary lifetimes! —, "ùmer, Omar.

عمرت "ùmret, *s. a.* One of the obligatory ceremonies performed at Mecca as a part of the pilgrimage, that of visiting certain places.

عمرو "àmru, *s. a.* Amru (*proper name* much used in law books, with زيد Zèyd, as we do the letters A and B).

عمق "ùmk, *s. a.* Depth; thickness; عرض وطول وعمق "àrz-u-tūl-u-"ùmk, The three dimensions, length, breadth, and thickness or depth; عمقاً "ùmkan, *ad. a.* In depth.

عمل "àmel, *s. a.* An acting, doing; an act, action; a stool, going to stool; عمل ا "àmel-et, *v.n.* To act, perform actions; عمل ويرمك "àmel-vèrmek, *v.n.* To purge, give a stool; عمل مانده "àmel-mandé, *a. p.* Incapacitated for any kind of work by age or infirmity; عملی "àmélī (*fem.* عملیه "àmélìyyé), Practical; artificial.

عمله "àmélé, *s. pl. a.* (*singular not used in this sense*), Workmen, labourers.

عموجه "àmuja (àmja), *s. t.* A paternal uncle, father's own brother. [dicular.

عمود "àmūd, *s. a.* A column; a perpen-

عموم "ùmūm, *s. a.* The being general or universal, the generality or universality of anything (not any particular portion of it); عمومی "ùmūmī (*fem.* عمومیه "ùmūmìyyé), *a. a.* General, universal; عمومیت "ùmūmìyyèt, *s. a.* The quality of being general or universal; علی العموم "àlé-'l-"ùmūm, *and* عموماً "ùmūman, *ad. a.* Generally, universally.

عمی "àmmī, *s. a.* A paternal uncle, father's own brother.

عمیا "ìmmìyyā (ìmyā), *s. a.* Blindness, want of mental vision; *in* علی العمیا "àlé-'l-"ìmmìyyā, *ad. a.* Blindly, without understanding or thinking of the consequences, ignorantly.

عمیق "àmīk, *a. a.* Deep, profound.

عمیم "àmīm, *a. a.* General, universal, common to all; —الاحسان, "àmīmu-'l-ìhsān, *a. a.* Whose favours are universal and common to all.

عن "àn, *p. a.* Of, from, out of; عنه "ànhu *or* "ành, From him, it; عنها "ànhā, From her, it; عن قصد "àn-kàssdin, *ad. a.* On purpose, with malice prepense; لاعن قصد lā-"àn-kàssdin, *ad. a.* Accidentally, without malice prepense; عن قریب "àn-kàrībin (*or* kàrīb), *ad. a.* Soon, in a short time, before long.

عنا "ànā, *s. a.* Fatigue, wearisome work, forced labour, molestation.

عناب "ùnnāb, *s. a.* The jujube fruit; عنابی "ùnnābī, *a. a.* Of a nut-brown colour.

عناد "ìnād, *s. a.* Obstinacy; perversity; —ا, —et, *v.n.* To be obstinate; to contend obstinately.

عنادل "ànādil, *s. pl. a.* (*of* عندلیب "àndélīb), Nightingales.

عناصر "ànāssir, *s. pl. a.* (*of* عنصر "ùnsur), The elements; —اربعه, "ànāssiri-èrba"à, The four elements.

عنان "ìnān, *s. a.* The reins of a horse's bridle; عطف عنان ا "àtfi-"ìnān-et, *v.n.* (To turn the rein), To go in any direction.

عنایت "ìnāyet, *s. a.* Favour, grace, kindness; بعنایته تعالی bì-"ìnāyètihi-tà"ālà, *or* بعنایة الله تعالی bì-"ìnāyéti-'llāhi-tà"ālà, *ad. a.* By the grace of God, (whose name) be exalted; عنایت اوله "ìnāyet-òla! May (God's) favour be (upon you)! (*usually said to beggars by way of refusing them an alms*).

عنب "ìneb, *s. a.* A grape, grapes.

عنبر "ànbèr, *s. a.* Ambergris; the yellow-flowered, sweet-smelling, dwarf acacia; عنبریه "ànbèrìyyé, *s. t.* Rosaglio, liqueur; عنبربارس "ànbèrbāriss, *s. t.* Barberries; عنبرين "àn-bérīn, *a. p.* Perfumed, scented with ambergris, sweet-smelling as ambergris.

عند "ìnd, *s. a.* The space near the side of any object; the faculty of appreciation; —, "ìnda, *pr. a.* Near, by the side of, at the time of; بنم عندمده bènim-"ìndimda, In my estimation; عندالوصول "ìnda-'l-vùssūl, At the time of (his, her, its) arrival; عندى "ìndī (*fem.* عنديه "ìndìyyé, *pl.* عنديات "ìndìyyāt), *a. a.* Pertaining to mere idea and private appreciation.

عندليب "àndélīb, *s. a.* A nightingale.

عنصر "ùnsur, *s. a.* An element, one of the four elements.

عنف "ùnf, *s. a.* Violence, force; عنفى "ùnfī (*fem.* عنفيه "ùnfìyyé), *a. a.* Pertaining to force and violence.

عنفوان "ùnfuwān, *s. a.* The prime or time of greatest beauty; —شبابت, "ùnfuwāni-shébābèt, The flower of youth, the prime of youth.

عنق "ùnk ("ùnuk), *s. a.* The neck or throat; ضرب عنق dàrbi-"ùnuk, A decollation, decapitation, beheading.

عنقا "ànkā, *s. a.* A fabulous bird.

عنكبوت "ànkébūt (*pl.* عناكب "ànākib), *s. a.* A spider; تار عنكبوت tāri-"ànkébūt, A spider's web.

عنوان "ùnvwān, *s. a.* A title of dignity.

عنوت "ànvet, *s. a.* Force, violence; عنوةً "ànvéten, *ad. a.* By force, by violence.

عنيف "ànīf (*fem.* عنيفه "ànīfé), *a. a.* Violent, tyrannical, cruel, vexatious.

عنين "ìnnīn, *s. a.* An impotent man; عنينت "ìnnīnet, *or* عنينيت "ìnnīnìyyèt, *s. a.* Impotency as to the generative function.

عوارض "àwāriz, *s. pl. a.* (*of* عارضه "āriza), Accidents, misfortunes, betidings.

عوارف "àwārif, *s. pl. a.* (*singular not used*), Kindnesses, favours, good actions.

عواطف "àwātif, *s. pl. a.* (*of* عاطفت "ātifet), Kindnesses, favours.

عواقب "àwākib, *s. pl. a.* (*of* عاقبت "ākibet), Latter ends, conclusions.

عوام "àwāmm, *s. pl. a.* (*of* عامه "āmmé), The common people.

عوامل "àwāmil, *s. pl. a.* (*of* عامل "āmil), Governing words (in grammar).

عوائد "àwā'id, *s. pl. a.* (*of* عائده "ā'idé), Fees, dues, pickings.

عوائق "àwā'ik, *s. pl. a.* (*of* عائق "ā'ik), Obstacles, impediments.

عود "àvd, *s. a.* A return; —, "ùd, *s. t.* The gall; the gall-bladder; —, "ūd, *s. a.* A kind of lute; عود اغاجى "ùd-aghaji, Wood of aloes; عودم پاتلادى "ùdum-pātladi, (My gall burst) I was very much frightened.

عودت "àvdet, *s. a.* A returning, coming *or* going back; return; ا—, —et, *v.n.* To return, to come *or* go back.

عورت "àvret, *s. a.* Any part of the body, or of a frontier, or any part of a man's family, which requires protection from exposure or from insult; a wife; —يرلرى, "àvret - yèrléri, The privities; عورتنى سكديكم "àvrétini--sìkdighim! (àvradini) O man whose wife I have had carnal connexion with! O dear me! Oh, what shall I do! Well, that is singular! (*ejaculation of anger or surprise*, in which, for decency, they often say صاتديغم sàtdighim, *I have sold;* or صاللاديغم sàlladighim, I have swung *or* rocked, instead of the common expression first given).

عوض "ìvaz, *s. a.* Any equivalent, reward, compensation.

عوق "àwk, *s. a.* An impeding, hindering, letting.

عون "àvn, *s. a.* Aid, help, assistance.

عهد "àhd, *s. a.* (*pl.* عهود "ùhūd), A solemn promise; a covenant, agreement, convention; an age, the time when anyone was alive; ا—, —et, *v.a.* To covenant, promise solemnly, undertake; عهدنامه "àhd-nāmé, *s. p.* A written treaty, covenant, convention.

عهده "ùhdé, *s. a.* A charge or responsibility resulting from a promise or from an acceptance of office; درعهدءا dèr-ùhdé-et, *v.a.* To take into one's charge, take charge of, receive in charge; عهدهسندن كلمك "ùhdéssindan-ghèlmek, *v.n.* To accomplish or discharge completely (the functions of any responsible office).

عيادت "ìyādet, *s. a.* A visiting the sick; ا—, —et, *v.a.* To visit (a sick person).

عياذ "ìyāz, *s. a.* A taking refuge; عياذاًبالله "ìyàzan - bì - 'llāhi! *or* العياذبالله èl-"ìyāzu-bì-'llāhi! (Refuge can only be taken in God!) God forbid!

عيار "àyyār, *s. a.* An impudent cheat, rogue, impostor, knave; —, "ìyār ("àyār), *s. a.* The standard of the precious metals, or of time and timepieces; the regulator of a watch; —, *a. t.* Of the standard degree of fineness (gold or silver); true, correct (a watch or clock); ا—, —et, *v.a.* To regulate (a watch, &c.); to assay (gold or silver); صاحب عيار sāhib-"àyār, The assay-master of a mint.

عياش "àyyāsh, *s. a.* A drunkard, one who passes his time in sensual pleasures.

عيال "ìyāl ("àyāl), *s. pl. a.* (*sing. not used*), Family dependants; wife, children, slaves, and servants; (*as a Turkish sing.*) a wife; كثيرالعيال kèssīru--'l-"àyāl, *a. a.* Having a large family.

عيان "àyān, *a. a.* Manifest, evident, clear; عياناً "àyānan, *ad. a.* Clearly.

عيب "àyb ("àyp), *s. a.* Anything which may cause shame; a defect, a vice; —, *int. t.* Shame! What a shame! It is a shame! —, *a. t.* Shameful; عيبلمق "àyplamak (*aor.* عيبلار "àyplar), *v.a.* To blame.

عيد ‘‘īd, *s. a.* A religious festival, of which the Mussulmans have but two; viz. the عيدفطر ‘‘īdi-fitr, *or* عيدالفطر ‘‘īdu-’l-fitr, The festival of the breaking of fasts, called also شكر بيرامى shèkær-bàyrami, The festival of sugar, immediately following the end of Ramazan; and the عيداضحى ‘‘īdi-àdhà, *or* قربان بيرامى kùrbān-bàyrami, The festival of sacrifices, on the 10th of Zī-’l-hìjjé; عيدشريفكز سعيداولسون ‘‘īdi-shèrīfingiz-sà‘‘īd-òlsun! May your sacred festival be happy! (*equivalent to our* Merry Christmas!) عيدى ‘‘īdī (*fem.* عيديه ‘‘īdìyyé), *a. a.* Pertaining to a festival; عديه ‘‘īdìyyé, *s. a.* A present given at festival time.

عيسى ‘‘īssà, *s. a.* Jesus; حضرت عيسى Hàzréti-‘‘*I*ssà, Jesus Christ; عيسوى ‘‘īssévī, *a. a.* Christian, pertaining to Jesus; —, *s. a.* A Christian.

عيش ‘‘īsh, *s. a.* The living a joyous life; عيش وعشرت ‘‘īsh-u-‘‘ìshrèt, Life and pleasure, fun and frolic, wine and women.

عين ‘‘àyn, *s. a.* The eye; a spring, fountain, source; anything’s own self; anything very much like another, a second self; kind (*as opposed to* money *or to* equivalent); the letter ع; the second radical letter of any Arabic word; a copy (of a paper); a similar number or quantity; عيننى المق ‘‘àynini-àlmak, *v.n.* To take a copy; عيننى چيقارمق ‘‘àynini-chìkàrmak, *v.n.* To extract a copy (from a book or register); عين الشمس ‘‘àynu-’sh-shèmss, The opal; عين اليقين ‘‘àyna-’l-yàkīn, *ad. a.* As of positive knowledge; عين الكمال ‘‘àynu-’l-kèmal, The eye of perfection, called also *the evil eye*, because when it admires perfection in anything it is supposed to bring calamity on the thing admired; عينى ‘‘àyni, *a. t.* Very like, quite like, so much resembling as to leave no difference perceptible; عيناً ‘‘àynan, *ad. a.* In kind; the very thing itself; عبدالعين ‘‘àbdu-’l-‘‘àyn, An eye-servant; صديق العين sìddīku-’l-‘‘àyn, A friend to one’s face, but not a true one; انسان العين ìnsānu-’l-‘‘àyn, The pupil of the eye.

عيوب ‘‘ūyūb, *s. pl. a.* (*of* عيب ‘‘ayb), Faults, defects, vices.

عيوق ‘‘àyyūk, *s. a.* A certain bright star proverbially cited for its elevation; عيوقه چيقارمق ‘‘àyyūka-chìkàrmak, *v.a.* To praise to the skies.

عيون ‘‘ùyūn, *s. pl. a.* (*of* عين ‘‘àyn), Eyes; springs, fountains, sources.

غ

غ ghàyn, Twenty-second letter of the Turkish alphabet, having radically the sound of *g hard*, or *gh*, or *gu*, in English, though sometimes softened down, as is *gh* in English, till nearly or quite inaudible, and sometimes taking (also as *gh* in English) the incidental sound of *y* and of *w*. Its numeral value is 1000.

غابن ghābin, *s. a.* A cheater, deceiver, impostor. [thicket.

غابه ghābé, *s. a.* A forest, a jungle, a

غابيه ghàbiya, *s. t.* (*Italian*), A top-sail; غابيه پرووه ghàbiya-prùwa, The fore top-sail; غابيه غراندى ghàbiya--ghràndi, The main top-sail; غابيه چبوغى ghàbiya-chìbùghu, A top-mast; غابيه سرنى ghàbiya-sèréni, A topsail-yard.

غار ghār, *s. a.* A cave, cavern, grotto; يارغار yārì-ghār (The cave-friend), A faithful friend and companion in trouble (in allusion to Ebu-Bekr's having been Muhammed's companion in a cave during his flight from Mecca).

غارت ghāret, *s. a.* Pillage, plunder, spoiling; ا—, —et, *v.a.* To take as plunder.

غازى ghāzī, *s. a.* A champion of religion, one who has fought for the faith.

غاشيه ghāshiyyé, *s. a.* A covering, wrapper of any kind; (hàsha) an embroidered or plain saddle-cloth.

غاغه ghàgha, *s. t.* The bill or beak of a bird; غاغه لمق ghàghalamak, *v.a.* To peck, bite with the beak.

غافل ghāfil, *a. a.* Negligent, careless, inattentive (to events); unaware, ignorant (of an event); غافلانه ghāfilāné, *a. p.* Pertaining to a negligent, inattentive person.

غالب ghālib, *a. a.* Preponderant; victorious; غالبا ghālibā, *ad. a.* Most likely, according to appearances, if I judge rightly, if I am not mistaken.

غالى ghālī (*fem.* غاليه ghāliyyé), *a. a.* Dear, valuable, high-priced, expensive.

غاليه ghāliyé, *s. p.* Perfume, musk.

غانم ghānim, *a. a.* Laden with plunder, rich with spoil; غانماً ghāniman, *ad. a.* Same meaning adverbially.

غانى ghānī (*fem.* غانيه ghāniyyé), *a. a.* Rich, well off, independent of other people's pecuniary assistance; (*fem.*) a beautiful woman who has no need of artificial embellishment.

غائب ghā'ib, *a. a.* Absent; lost; lost to sight; the third person (in grammar); —او, —òl, *v.n.* To disappear; to be lost; ا—, —et, (kàyb-ĕt—), *v.a.* To lose; غائبانه ghā'ibāné, *ad. p.* In the absence of anyone, behind one's back.

غايت ghāyet, *s. a.* The extreme limit of anything, the extremity, end; —, غايتده ghāyetda, غايتله ghāyetla, *ad. t.*, بغايت bè-ghāyet, *ad. p.* Extremely, very, very much; غاية الغايه ghāyétu-'l-ghāyé, *s. a.* The extreme extremity, extreme end; —, —, *ad. a.* Extremely, in the very extremest degree.

غائله ghā'ilé, *s. a.* Any cause of anxiety or painful solicitude.

غب ghìbbé, *p. a.* After.

غبار ghùbār, *s. a.* Dust.

غباوت ghàbāvèt, s. a. Weakness of intellect, stupidity.

غبطه ghìbta, s. a. Desire to possess, longing; an object of desire, anything longed for.

غبغب ghàbghàb, s. p. The under part of the chin, the space between the chin, cheeks, and throat; غبغب مینا ghàbghàbi-mīnā, The under part of the lip of a bottle or decanter.

غبن ghàbn, s. a. Unfairness in relations of business, taking an unfair advantage, cheating.

غبی ghàbī, a. a. Weak in intellect, stupid.

غبین ghàbīn, s. a. A gull, dupe.

غدا ghìdā, s. a. Food, nutriment, aliment; a dose; a usual quantity (of anything) for any particular purpose.

غدار ghàddār, s. a. An iniquitous, unjust dealer; a cruel, unconscionable person.

غدر ghàdr, s. a. Injustice, unconscionableness in dealing; ا—, —et, v.n. To act with injustice, to cause a loss (of some kind to anyone) iniquitously; to treat with injustice.

غدو ghùdùvv, s. a. The morning; بالغدو والاصال bì-'l-ghùdùvvi-vè-'l-āssāl, ad. a. Morning and evening.

غدیر ghàdīr, s. a. A pool, a pond.

غذا ghìzā, s. a. Food, aliment.

غرا ghàrrā, a. a. fem. Bright, shining, splendid.

غراب ghùrāb, s. a. A crow, rook, or raven.

غرابت ghàrābèt, s. a. Strangeness, oddness, marvellousness.

غرار ghàrār (hàrer), غرارهٔ ghàrārè, s. a. A sack of hair-cloth; hair-cloth prepared for sacking, sometimes used as stair-carpets.

غرامت ghàrāmèt, s. a. Debt, indebtedness.

غرائب ghàrā'ib, s. pl. a. (of غریبه ghārībè), Strange things, marvellous things.

غرب ghàrb, s. a. The west; غربی ghàrbī, a. a. Western, westerly, west; غرباً ghàrban, ad. a. To or towards the west, in a westerly direction.

غربا ghùrébā, s. pl. a. (of غریب ghàrīb), Strangers; a special corps of troops in the olden time.

غربال ghìrbāl, s. a. A seive.

غربت ghùrbèt, s. a. A sojourning away from home in a strange place; — چکمك —chèkmek, v.n. To suffer or undergo a sojourning in a strange place.

غرتلاق ghìrtlak, s. t. The windpipe, the throat.

غرر ghùrèr, s. pl. a. (of غره ghùrré), The choice, select ones of any kind of things.

غرس ghàrss, s. a. A planting, setting (of plants); ا—, —et, v.a. To plant, to set.

غرض ghàraz, s. a. A motive, object in view in doing anything; a spite; ا—, —et, v.n. To have a spite, hold a grudge; الغرض èl-ghàraz, ad. a. In short, in one word; بیغرض bī-ghàraz, *a. p.* Disinterested, having no motive for partiality; بیغرضانه bīghàrazānĕ, *a. p.* Pertaining to a disinterested person.

غرغره ghàrghar*a*, *s. a.* A gurgling sound in the throat; the death-rattle; a gargle; ا—, —et, *v.a.* To gargle; —, *v.n.* To make a rattling or gurgling noise in the throat.

غرق ghàrk, *s. a.* A drowning in water; a flooding; ا—, —et, *v.a.* To drown, in or with anything; —اولنمق, —òlunmak, *v.p.* To be drowned; غرقاب ghàrk-āb, *s. p.* Any water threatening one with drowning.

غرما ghùrĕmā (ghùramā), *s. pl. a.* (*of* غریم ghàrīm), Creditors, the body aggregate of a bankrupt's creditors; —, *s. t.* A division of a bankrupt's effects among his creditors *pro rata*; غرمایه کیرمك ghùramày*a* - ghìrmek, *v.n.* To be one of a body of creditors; to be part of a bankrupt's estate divided among his creditors.

غرنده ghùrrèndĕ, *a. p.* Roaring fiercely.

غروب ghùrūb, *s. a.* The setting (of stars, &c.); ا—, —et, *v.n.* To set, go down.

غرور ghùrūr, *s. a.* Vanity, presumption.

غروش ghùrūsh, *s. t.* A piastre (value about 2*d.*); —قره kāra—, A Spanish dollar.

غره ghùrrĕ, *s. a.* The first day in any lunar month; a large white spot on a horse's forehead, esteemed an ornament; the choicest, best of any things.

غریب ghàrīb, *a. a.* Strange, singular, curious, wonderful, marvellous; —, *s. a.* A stranger in any place; غریب یکیت ghàrīb-yìghit (kāripīt), *s. t.* A poor person.

غریر ghàrīr, *s. a.* One who is deceived with false ideas, fed with false hopes.

غریق ghàrīk, *s. a.* A drowned person; —, *a. a.* Drowned, flooded, submerged. [a creditor.

غریم ghàrīm, *s. a.* A debtor; an offender;

غریو ghìrīv, *s. p.* A cry, plaint, lamentation; غریوان ghìrīvān, *a. p.* Crying, lamenting.

غزا ghàzā, *s. a.* Holy warfare, crusade, war for religion.

غزات ghùzāt, *s. pl. a.* (*of* غازی ghāzī), Champions of religion, holy warriors.

غزال ghàzāl, *s. a.* The gazelle.

غزته ghàzèt*a*, *s. t.* A newspaper.

غزل ghàzèl, *s. a.* A short ode.

غزوات ghàzéwāt, *s. pl. a.* (*of* غزا ghàzā), Expeditions in defence of one's religion.

غزه Ghàzz*a*, *s. t.* Gaza in Palestine.

غساق ghàsssāk, *s. a.* The horrible sweat and putrefaction which is to exude in hell from the bodies of the damned.

غسل ghùssl, *s. a.* The greater ablution when the whole body is bathed; ا—, —et, *v.n.* To perform the greater ablution; —, *v.a.* To wash a dead body canonically.

غش ghìshsh, *s. a.* Alloy in precious metals; deceit in a show of friendship.

غشيان ghàshéyān, *s. a.* A fainting fit.

غصب ghAssb, *s. a.* A seizing by force, a taking unlawfully; ا—, —et, *v.a.* To seize by force and unlawfully.

غصن ghùssn, *s. a.* A branch of a tree.

غصه ghùsssa, *s. a.* Sorrow, grief.

غضب ghAzAb, *s. a.* Wrath, indignation, anger; ا—, —et, *and* غضبه كلمك ghAzAba-ghèlmek, *v.n.* To get in a passion, be angry.

غضبان ghAzbAn, *a. a.* Angry, furious, exasperated; passionate.

غضنفر ghAzAnfèr, *s. a.* A lion; a brave man, a hero. [angered.

غضوب ghAzūb, *a. a.* Passionate, easily

غفار ghAffār, *s. a.* God the continual pardoner of sin. [our sins.

غفران ghùfrān, *s. a.* God's pardon of

غفلت ghAflet, *s. a.* A want of care and circumspection, want of vigilance, negligence, carelessness; ا—, —et, غفلتده بولنمق ghAfletda - bùlunmak, *v.n.* To be without vigilance, to be asleep at one's moral post, to be caught napping. [of sin.

غفور ghAfūr, *s. a.* God the pardoner

غفول ghùfūl, *s. a.* Neglect, negligence.

غفير ghàfīr, *a. a.* Numerous, *in* جم غفير jèmmi-ghàfīr, A great multitude.

غل ghìll, *s. a.* Deceit in professed friendship; —, ghùll, *s. a.* A yoke; a pillory. [provisions.

غلا ghàlā, *s. a.* Dearth, scarcity of

غلاظت ghìlāzèt, *s. a.* Coarseness.

غلاف ghìlāf (kìlìf), *s. a.* A bag-shaped cover for anything; a bed-ticking.

غلام ghùlām, *s. a.* A lad; a slave; a courier (in Persia); غلامپاره ghùlām--pārÉ (kùlAmbara), A sodomite.

غلبه ghàlébÉ, *s. a.* Preponderance; a thronging; victory; ا—, —et, *v.n.* To gain the victory; غلبه‌لق ghAlé-bÉlìk (kAlabAlìk), A crowd, a throng; confusion; a litter; ا—, kAlabAlìk-et, *v.n.* To form a crowd, assemble in crowds; to create confusion; to make a litter.

غلط ghAlAt, *s. a.* A great and stupid mistake, an error; an erroneous expression.

غلطان ghAltAn, *a. p.* Rolling; او—, —òl, *v.n.* To roll; ا—, —et, *v.a.* To make roll. [Constantinople).

غلطه Ghàlàta, *s. t.* Galata (a suburb of

غلطيده ghàltīda, *a. p.* Which has rolled, rolled.

غلظت ghìlzèt, *s. a.* Coarseness.

غلغله ghùlghulÉ, *s. a.* A noise of many voices or sounds mixed.

غلمان ghìlmAn, *s. pl. a.* (*of* غلام ghù-lām), Boys, youths; young male slaves.

غلو ghùlùvv, *s. a.* An assault, attack.

غله ghàllÉ, *s. a.* The fruits or produce of agriculture, corn; the income arising from any property in mortmain or in tail.

غليان ghàléyān, *s. a.* A boiling, ebullition; active fermentation, working;

the excitement or fermentation of a mob ; —, ghàlyān, *s. p.* A hooka or water-pipe for smoking.

غليظ ghàlīz, *a. a.* Coarse.

غم ghàmm (ghàm), *s. a.* (*pl.* غموم ghūmūm), Grief, sorrow, care, regret; غمخوار ghàm-khār, *s. p.* A person in sorrow ; a friend in need, a sympathizing friend ; غمكسار ghàm-kyùssār, *s. p.* A sympathizing friend.

غماز ghàmmāz, *s. a.* A tale-bearer.

غمزه ghàmzé, *s. p.* A wink, a sign with the eye, a look.

غنا ghànā, *s. a.* Sufficiency, comfortable circumstances ; —, ghìnā, *s. a.* A singing.

غنائم ghànā'im, *s. pl. a.* (*of* غنيمت ghànīmèt), Spoils, plunder.

غنچه ghòncha, *s. p.* A rose-bud or rose just opening.

غنم ghànem, *s. a.* A sheep.

غنوده ghùnūdé, *a. p.* Asleep, sleeping.

غنه ghùnné, *s. a.* A nasal twang in pronunciation.

غنى ghànī, *a. a.* Rich, possessing a sufficiency, comfortably off ; plentiful, abundant ; in want of no assistance or embellishment.

غنيمت ghànīmèt, *s. a.* Spoil, plunder; any advantage that can be realised.

غواص ghàvwāss, *s. a.* A diver, a plunger.

غوانى ghàwānī, *s. pl. a.* (*singular not used*), Songs.

غوائل ghàwā'il, *s. pl. a.* (*of* غائله ghā'ilé), Cares, causes of anxiety or preoccupation.

غور ghàvr, *s. a.* The bottom of any deep water, well, &c.

غوص ghàvss, *s. a.* A plunging, a diving.

غوطه ghàvta, *s. a.* A ducking, a dipping; غوطه‌خوار ghàvta-khòr, *s. p.* One who gets a ducking.

غوغا ghàwgha (kàwgha), *s. t.* A quarrel; a fight ; a battle ; ا—, —et, *v.n.* To quarrel ; to fight.

غول ghūl, *s. p.* A kind of demon or goblin, *commonly termed* غول يبانى ghūlυ-yàbānī (kùlυyabānī), *The goblin of the wilds.*

غومنه ghòmana, *s. t.* (*Italian*). A ship's cable.

غياب ghìyāb, غيابت ghìyābet, *s. a.* Absence ; غيابت جب ghìyābéti-jùbbi, The bottom of the well (into which Joseph was cast).

غياصت ghìyāssèt, *s. a.* A plunging, diving, dipping deeply.

غيب ghàyb, *s. a.* Absence ; any absent thing ; all absent and all invisible things, all things past or future, not actually existing or present ; عالم غيب "ālémi-ghàyb, The invisible world, the past or future state of things, the unknown ; غيبى ghàybī (*fem.* غيبيه ghàybìyyé), *a. a.* Pertaining to the invisible world.

غيبت ghàybèt, *s. a.* Absence ; backbiting ; ا—, —et, *v.n.* To backbite.

غيبوبت ghàybūbèt, *s. a.* Absence.

غيث ghàyss, *s. a.* Rain.

غيجقمق ghìjìkmak (*aor.* غيجقر ghìjikir), *v.n.* To be ticklish, or tickled ;

غيجقدرمق ghìjìkdirmak (*aor.* غيجقدرر ghìjìkdirir), *v.a.* To tickle.

غير ghàyr, *s. a.* Any other or others than self; —, *a. a.* Not, non (*this word before any Arabic adjective has the same privative effect as the syllables* un, in, dis, &c., *with us; as,* غير متساوى ghàyri-mùtéssāvī, *unequal to each other;* غيرمعلوم ghàyri-mà''lūm, *unknown,* &c.); بغير bì-ghàyri, *ad. a.* Without; وغيره vè-ghàyrihi, Et cetera; الى غيرالنهايه ilà - ghàyri -'n - nìhāyé, *ad. a.* Ad infinitum.

غيرت ghàyrèt, *s. a.* Zeal; earnest endeavour; honest jealousy, jealousy of one's honour; ا—, —et, *v.n.* To strive zealously, to do one's best.

غيرى ghàyri, *a. t.* Other, another; —, *ad. t.* Besides; —(kàyri), *ad. t.* No more, never again; at length, after all.

غيطان ghàytan, *s. t.* Narrow braid or square cord.

غيظ ghàyz, *s. a.* Anger, wrath; كاظم الغيظ kyāzimu-'l-ghàyz, *a. a.* One who subdues his rising anger.

غيم ghàym, *s. a.* A cloud.

غين ghàyn, *s. a.* Name of the letter غ.

غيور ghàyur, *a. a.* Zealous (man); غيورانه ghàyūrāné, *a. p.* Pertaining to a zealous person.

ف

ف fā (fè). Twenty-third letter of the Turkish alphabet, having the value of *f* in English. Its numeral value is 80. In Persian words it is sometimes interchangeable with ب, پ, and و.

فا fā, *s. a.* Name of the letter ف; the first radical letter of any Arabic word.

فاتح fātih, *s. a.* A conqueror; فاتح سلطان محمد fātih-sùltan-Mèhémed, Mahomed the Second, conqueror of Constantinople.

فاتحه fātiha, *s. a.* The *opening* chapter of the Kur'an, generally used as the concluding prayer at devotions, and repeated over people's graves.

فاتر fātir, *a. a.* Weak, worn out, unable [to proceed.

فاجر fājir, *s. a.* A sinner.

فاحش fāhish, *a. a.* Infamous; passing the bounds of decorum; فاحشه fāhishé, *s. a. fem.* A prostitute, whore.

فاخته fākhté, *s. p.* A pigeon.

فاخر fākhir (*fem.* فاخره fākhiré), *a. a.* Glorious (apparel, &c.).

فارسى fārsī, *a. a.* Persian (language); —, *s. a.* The Persian language; فارسيات fārsìyyāt, *s. pl. a.* Persian idioms or grammatical rules.

فارغ fārigh, *a. a.* Who desists, leaves off, or reposes from any action; free from action or anxiety; —او, —òl, *v.n.* To finish, have done, leave off, rest; فارغ البال fārighu-'l-bāl, Easy at heart, free from care.

فاره fāré, *s. a.* A mouse.

فاسد fāssid (*fem.* فاسده fāssidé), *a. a.* Bad, spoilt, corrupt, false.

فاسق fāssik, *s. a.* A sinner.

فاش fāsh, *a. p.* Which has transpired,

oozed out, got wind; ا—, —et, *v.a.* To betray (a secret), make public; او—, —òl, *v.n.* To become known, ooze out, transpire.

فاصل fāssil (*fem.* فاصله fāssila), *a. a.* Which divides, separates; فاصله fāssila, *s. a.* A division, partition, separation; intermission; بلافاصله bìlā-fāssila, *ad. a.* Unceasingly, uninterruptedly, incessantly, without intermission.

فاضل fāzil, *s. a.* One who excels others [in virtue, learning, &c.

فاطر fātir, *s. a.* God the impresser of natural qualities, the Creator.

فاطن fātìn, *a. a.* Intelligent, quick.

فاعل fā''il, *s. a.* An actor, doer; اسم فاعل ìssmi-fā''il, The active participle; فاعلی fā''ilī (*fem.* فاعليه fā''ilìyyé), *a. a.* Pertaining to an actor; فاعليت fā''ilìyyèt, *s. a.* Quality of being an actor.

فاقه fāka, *s. a.* Poverty, indigence.

فاكهه fākiha, *s. a.* A fruit.

فال (*for* فأل fè'l), fāl (fàl), *s. a.* Anything taken as an omen, particularly in the nature of the *Sortes Virgilianæ*; فال باقمق fàl-bàkmak, *v.n.* To open any one of certain books and take the first word of the page as an augury; or to use any other kind of augury.

فالج fālij, *s. a.* Paralysis, the palsy.

فاليه fàlya, *and* فاليه دليكى fàlya-dèlighi, *s. t.* The touch-hole of a gun.

فام fām, *s. p.* (*in composition*), Coloured.

فانوس fānūss, *s. a.* A glass shade.

فانى fānī (*fem.* فانيه fānìyyé), *a. a.* Perishable; ready to perish.

فائح fā'ih, *a. a.* Which exhales (perfumes); which pervades the air (perfume).

فائده fā'idé, *s. a.* A use, an advantage; a moral (of a tale); فائده لو fā'idéli, *a. t.* Useful, beneficial; فائده سز fā'idéssiz, *a. t.* Useless, of no avail; فائده ا fā'idé-et, *v.n.* To avail, be of use, benefit; فائده كورمك fā'idé-ghyùrmek, *v.n.* To derive benefit; برفائده يى مفيداو bìr-fā'idéyi-mùfīd-òl, To be of some use; فائده مند fā'idé-mend, *a. p.* Benefited.

فائز fā'iz, *a. a.* Who obtains.

فائض fā'iz, *a. a.* Who or which gives forth abundantly; —, *s. t.* Interest on money.

فائق fā'ik, *a. a.* Excelling, superior, sur- [passing.

فبها fè-bèhā, *ad. a.* Then all is well; in that case all is right.

فت fìt, *s. t. in* فت ويرمك fìt-vèrmek, *v.n.* To put (a person) up to something, inspire with a mischievous idea.

فتاح fèttāh, *s. a.* God *the opener* of the means of welfare.

فتاده fùtādé, *a. p.* Fallen; fallen captive.

فتان fèttān, *s. a.* A plotter, intriguer, mischief-maker; Satan.

فتح fèth (t-h), *s. a.* An opening; a broaching; a conquering; a pronouncing with the *a* or *e* vowel; ا—, —et, *v.a.* To open; to broach; to conquer; to pronounce (a consonant) with the *a* or *e* vowel following it; فتح كلام fèth*i*-kelām-et, *v.n.* To begin a discourse; فتحنامه fètihnāmé, *s. p.* A letter giving news of some victory or conquest.

فتحه fètha, *s.a.* The vowel point ـَ, equivalent to one of the vowels A, a, *a*, E *or* e.

فترت fìtrèt, *s. a.* A time of general revolt; an interregnum; an interval.

فتق fètk, *s. a.* A bursting, breaking asunder; a rupture, *or* hernia; رتق وفتق امور rètk-u-fètk*i*-ùmūr, The general management of public business.

فتنه fìtné, *s. a.* Temptation; any tempting thing; a conspiracy, plot, treason; public trouble, sedition, disorder, riot; ـــانكيز, fìtné-ènghīz, ـــكار, fìtné-kyār, ـــجو, fìtné-jū, *s. p.* فتنه‌جى fìtnéji, *s. t.* A causer of sedition.

فتوا (*for* فتوى) fètvà, *s. a.* A legal opinion delivered by the proper legal functionary (the Muftī) upon any supposed case submitted to him; حضرت فتوا پناهى hàzréti - fètvà - -pènāhī, (H. E. the Asylum of legal opinions) The Shèykhu-'l-ìslām.

فتوت fùtùvvet, *s. a.* Generosity of character, magnanimity.

فتوح fùtūh (*pl.* فتوحات fùtūhāt), *s. pl. a.* (*of* فتح fèth), Victories, successes.

فتور fùtūr, *s. a.* Lassitude, inability to proceed with work, lack of spirit; ـــكتورمك, fùtūr-ghètirmek, *v.n.* To lose spirit; ـــكلمك, fùtūr-ghèlmek, *v.n.* To seize (a loss of spirit for work).

فتوى fètvà. See فتوا.

فتى fètà, *s. a.* A lad.

فتيل fìtil, *s. a.* The wick of a lamp or candle; a quick-match; a plug or pledget for deep wounds; a seton.

فج fèjj, *s. a.* An open and easy way between mountains.

فجأة fùj'étεn, *ad. a.* Suddenly, unexpectedly.

فجاج fìjāj, *a. a.* Open and easy (a way between mountains).

فجائى fèjā'ī, *a. a.* Sudden; unexpected.

فجر fèjr, *s. a.* The dawn, daybreak; ـــكاذب, fèjri-ky*ā*zib, The false daybreak, after which darkness is said to fall again; فجر صادق fèjri-sĀd*i*k, The true dawn, the break of day.

فجور fùjūr, *s. a.* Sin, iniquity, wickedness, the lust of the flesh.

فحص fàhss, *s. a.* An inquiring after or into, inquiry, search.

فحل fàhl, *s. a.* A stallion; a man distinguished for learning.

فحم fàhm, *s. a.* Charcoal.

فحوا (*for* فحوى) fàhwà, *s. a.* The sense, signification, meaning contained in a phrase.

فخام fìkhām, *s. pl. a.* (*of* فخيم fàkhīm), The very high in rank and station.

فخامت fàkhāmet, *s. a.* Exalted rank and station; فخامتلو fàkhāmetlū, *a. t.* The exalted in rank and station (second title of the Grand Vizier, to whom Europe accords the princely title of Highness).

فخذ fàkhz, *s. a.* The thigh.

فخر fàkhr, *s. a.* A glorying; a cause of just pride; فخرعالم fàkhri-"ālem, (The pride of the world) Muhammed; فخری fàkhrī (*fem.* فخریه fàkhrìyyé), *a. a.* Pertaining to pride and glorying; فخریه fàkhrìyyé, *s. a.* The latter part of a poem, in which it is usual for the poet to speak of himself in terms of glorification, which we should call boasting.

فخیم fàkhīm (*fem.* فخیمه fàkhīmé), *a. a.* Very high in rank and station (The feminine is the title hitherto given to all European States in distinction to علیه "àlìyyé, *the very exalted,* assumed for Turkey alone).

فدا fèdā, *s. a.* The sacrificing or giving up anything in order to obtain some end; a sacrifice, a ransom; ا—, —et, *v.a.* To give up, to sacrifice; فداکار fèdākyār, *a. p.* One who makes sacrifices, who sacrifices his own interests; فداکارلق fèdākyārlìk, *s. t.* The quality of sacrificing one's interests; فدائی fèdā'ī, *s. p.* One who voluntarily risks his life in any perilous but praiseworthy enterprise.

فدان fìdan, *s. t.* (*Greek* φιτανη), A young plant; تازه فدان tāzé-fìdan (*fig.*), A young person.

فدیه fìdyé, *s. a.* Anything sacrificed or given up in order to attain some good end; a sacrifice; a ransom.

فذلکه fèzléké, *s. a.* The sum and substance of any train of reasoning.

فر fèr, *s. p.* Pomp, splendour, magnificence.

فرات Fùrāt, *s. t.* The river Euphrates.

فراجه fèrrājé (fèrājé), *s. a.* An over-cloak worn out of doors by women (formerly applied also to a cloak worn by doctors of the law).

فراح fèrāh, *s. a.* Cheerfulness, gladness; —, *a. t.* Cheerful, open (a place, house, &c.); —, *and* فراح فراح fèrāh-fèrāh, *ad. t.* Amply; easily; and to spare.

فراخ fèrakh, *a. p.* Wide, ample, spacious; abundant; فراخی fèrākhī, *s. p.* Ampleness, abundance.

فرادیس fèrādīss, *s. pl. a.* (*of* فردوس firdèvss), Paradises; gardens or parks.

فرار fìrār, *s. a.* A running away; a deserting; ا—, —et, *v.n.* To run away; to desert.

فراز fìrāz, *s. p.* An ascent; فرازونشیب fìrāz-u-nèshīb, Up-hill and downdale; —, *a. p.* (*in composition*), High, uplifted; سرفراز sèr-fìrāz, *a. p.* Who holds up his head and is not ashamed, or who feels a just pride.

فرازنده fìrāzendé, *s. p.* One who lifts up on high, who raises.

فراست fèrāssèt, *s. a.* Sagacity, judgment, penetration; equitation, horsemanship; the science of physiognomy.

فراش fàrash, *s. t.* A dust-pan; —, fèrāsh, *s. a.* A moth which flies round a candle; —, fìrāsh, *s. a.* A bed; —, fèrrāsh, *s. a.* An attendant whose duty it is to spread carpets, &c., especially one attached to the temple at Mecca (this last office is held by a certain number of the highest people, as an honour, and as meritorious, the duties being performed by persons on the spot paid by the titular officers); صاحب— sāhib-fìrāsh, *a. p.* Sick in bed.

فراشت fèrāshèt, *s. a.* The office of carpet-spreader (to the temple of Mecca).

فراعنه fèrā''inÉ, *s. pl. a.* (*of* فرعون fìr''àvn), Pharaohs; proud, rebellious men.

فراغ fìrāgh, *s. a.* Ease, freedom from work or care.

فراغت fèrāghAt, *s. a.* The giving up, ceding; a ceasing from work; ا—, —et, *v.a.* To cede.

فراق fìrAk, *s. a.* Separation, the being separated one from the other, absence from one another.

فراموش fèrāmūsh, *s. p.* A forgetting; ا—, —et, *v.a.* To forget; فراموشی fèrāmūshī, *s. p.* Oblivion.

فرانجله fìrànjìla, *s. t.* White wheaten bread in rolls.

فرانسز Frànsìz, *s.* and *a. t.* French; a Frenchman.

فرانسه Frànsa, *s. t.* France.

فراوان fèrāwān, *a. p.* Copious, abundant.

فراهم fèrāhèm, *a. p.* Accumulated, heaped up.

فرائد fèrā'id, *s. pl. a.* (*of* فریده fèrīdÉ), Separate, single, unique things, single pearls or precious stones, beads, &c.

فرائض fàrā'iz, *s. pl. a.* (*of* فریضه fàrīza), Things incumbent and not to be omitted; the indispensable parts of worship; the portions allotted by the canonical law to the relatives of a deceased person; the science of apportioning property among the relatives of deceased persons.

فرتوت fÈrtūt, *a. a.* Decrepid.

فرج fÈrj, *s. a.* The female organ of generation; —, fèrej, *s. a.* Joy, happiness; الصبرمفتاح الفرج èss-sAbru-mìftāhu-'l-fèrèj, Patience is the key of happiness.

فرجام fèrjām, *s. p.* The end, conclusion; نافرجام nā-fèrjām, بدفرجام bèd-fèrjām, *a. p.* Ending ill, not ending as could be wished.

فرجه fùrjÉ, *s. a.* An opening, an opportunity; فرجه‌یاب fùrjÉ-yAb, *a. p.* Who finds an opportunity; او—, fùrjÉ-yAb-òl, *v.n.* To find an opportunity.

فرچه fìrcha, *s. t.* A brush.

فرح fèrah, *s. a.* Joy, gladness; فرحناك fèrahnāk, *a. p.* Joyful, glad.

فرحان fÈrhān, *a. a.* Rejoicing, glad, joyful.

فرحه fÈrha, *s. a.* Joy, gladness.

فرخ fèrrùkh, فرخنده fÈrkhùndÉ, *a. p.* Happy, fortunate.

فرد fÈrd, *s. a.* An individual; a single one; anything unique sui generis;

جوهرفرد jèvhĕri-fĕrd, An atom (in the atomic theory); فرداًفردا fèrdan-fèrdā, *ad a.* فردافرد fĕrdafĕrd, *ad. p.* One by one, singly, individually.

فردا fĕrdā, *s. p.* The following day, the morrow.

فردوس firdèvss, *s. a.* Paradise; a garden [or park.

فرز fĕrz, *s. p.* The queen at chess.

فرزانه fèrzānĕ, *a. p.* Distinguished, remarkable (person); فرزانه‌لك fèrzānĕlik, *s. t.* فرزانكى fèrzānéghī, *s. p.* Distinction (of a person).

فرزند fĕrzènd, *s. p.* A son.

فرس fèress, *s. a.* A horse.

فرسا fĕrsā, *a. p.* (*in composition*), Which rubs against; فلك‌فرسا fèlek-fĕrsā, *a. p.* Rubbing against, high as and touching the sky.

فرستاده firisstādĕ, *a. p.* Sent.

فرسخ fĕrsàkh, *s. p.* A parasang, an hour's journey on horseback at a walk.

فرسوده fĕrsūdĕ, *a. p.* Rubbed; worn.

فرسى fùrsī, *s. a.* The Persian language; فرسيات fùrsìyyāt, *s. pl. a.* Persian idioms and rules.

فرش fĕrsh, *s. a.* The spreading (carpets, &c.) on the floor; ا—, —et, *v.a.* To spread on the ground.

فرشته firishtĕ (*pl.* فرشتكان firishtéghyān), *s. p.* An angel.

فرصت fùrsat (fìrsànt), *s. a.* An opportunity.

فرض fàrz, *s. a.* An indispensable rite; a supposing, a taking for granted; ا—, —et, *v.a.* To set down as supposed or granted; فرضا fàrzā (fàrazā), *ad. a.* By supposition, let us suppose, let it be granted; فرض محال fârzi-mŭhāl, The admission of an impossibility for argument's sake.

فرط fàrt, *s. a.* A superabundant quantity, or degree.

فرطونه fìrtina, *s. t.* (*Italian*), A storm at sea, a rough sea; فرطونه‌لو fìrtinali, *a. t.* Stormy (sea or weather).

فرع fèr‘‘, *s. a.* A secondary branch, a ramification; a subdivision; فرعى fèr‘‘ī (*fem.* فرعيه fèr‘‘ìyyĕ), Secondary, derivative.

فرعون fìr‘‘àwn, *s. a.* Pharaoh; any excessively proud and refractory man.

فرق fàrk, *s. a.* The crown of the head; a distinguishing; a distinction, difference; ا—, —et, *v.n.* To change, alter, vary; —كورمك, fàrk-ghyùrmek, To see a difference; —, fìrak, *s. pl. a.* (*of* فرقه fìrka), Bodies, troops of men.

فرقان fùrkàn, *s. a.* The Kŭr‘‘an, in its quality of distinguishing between good and evil.

فرقتين fìrkatèyn, *s. t.* A frigate.

فرقه fìrka, *s. a.* Any detached part; a body, troop; a sect; a division (of an army).

فرقد fèrkàd, *s. a.* A certain brilliant star used figuratively; فرقدساى fĕrkàd-sāy, *a. p.* Touching or reaching in height to the star Ferkad.

فركنده fĕrkèndĕ, *a. p.* Old, worn.

فرلامق fìrlamak (*aor.* فرلار fìrlar), *v.n.* To

fly (as splinters, &c.); to chip, to splinter (as glass, steel, &c.); فرلاتمق fırlatmak (*aor.* فرلادر fırlàdır), *v.a.* To cause to fly; to throw; to cause to chip.

فرما fèrmā, *a. p.* (*in composition*), Who commands; فرمانفرما fèrmān-fèrmā, *s. p.* One who gives commands, a commander, a sovereign.

فرمان fèrmān, *s. p.* A command, order, injunction; an imperial rescript, commission, or letters-patent; فرمانبر fèrmān-bèr, فرمانبردار fèrmān-bèrdār, *s. p.* One who is obedient to his sovereign's commands; فرمانده fèrmān-dìh, *s. p.* A giver of orders, a sovereign.

فرموده fèrmūdé, *a. p.* Ordered, commanded; —, *s. p.* An order, command.

فرنك firènk, *s. t.* A man of any European nation; فرنكستان firènghisstān, *s. p.* Europe, or the whole country inhabited by non-Turkish Europeans; فرنكی firènghi, *s. t.* The venereal disease.

فرو fùru, *ad. p.* Down, downwards; —, *a. p.* Low; فرومايه fùru-māyé, *a. p.* Low bred.

فروخت fùrùkht, *s. p.* A selling; a sale; ا—, —et, *v.a.* To sell.

فروخته fùrùkhté, *a. p.* Sold.

فرود fùrùd, *s. p.* The lower part, bottom; a hollow place, valley.

فروز fùrūz, *a. p.* (*in composition*), Who or which lights or illuminates.

فروزان fùrūzān, *a. p.* Shining, bright, alight, blazing.

فروزنده fùrūzèndé, *a. p.* Who or which illuminates, makes light.

فروست fùrūssèt, فروسيت fùrūssìyyèt, *s. a.* Equitation, horsemanship.

فروش fùrūsh, *s. p.* (*in composition*), A seller, vender; خودفروش khòd-fùrūsh, (A self-seller) A brag; كندم نمای جو فروش ghèndum-nùmāyi-jèv-fùrūsh, (A barley-selling wheat-shower) A cheat.

فروع fùrū'' (*pl.* فروعات fùrū''āt), *s. pl. a.* (*of* فرع fèr''), Branches, ramifications.

فروغ fùrūgh, *s. p.* A ray, sunbeam; splendour.

فرومانده fùru-māndé, *a. p.* Who lags, straggles, remains behind; worn out with fatigue and weakness.

فرون fırın, *s. t.* An oven; a bakehouse; فرونجی fırınji, *s. t.* A baker; a constructor of ovens.

فروه fèrvé, *s. a.* A fur coat or cloak.

فرياد fèryād, *s. p.* A cry, scream; ا—, —et, *v.a.* To cry, call out, scream; فريادرس fèryād-rèss, *s. a.* Anyone who runs to help at a call for succour.

فريب firīb, *a. p.* (*in composition*), Who or which deceives.

فريد fèrīd (*fem.* فريده fèrīdé), *a. a.* Alone; single; unique; فريده fèrīdé, *s. a.* A single or unique pearl, precious stone, bead, person, &c.

فريفته firīfté, *a. p.* Deceived, taken in, cajoled, seduced.

فريق fèrīk, *s. a.* A class, body, or sect of men; a lieutenant-general, or general of division; بحريه فريقى bàhrìyyé--fèrīki, An officer of corresponding rank in the naval service.

فزا fèzā, *a. p.* (*in composition*), Who or which increases, augments.

فزع fèz'', *s. a.* A lamenting; lamentation, plaint.

فزون fùzūn, *a. p.* Augmented, increased; فزونى fùzūnī, *s. p.* Increasedness; فزونىءعمر fùzūnī'i-''ùmr, Length of life.

فس fèss, *s. t.* The red cap worn all over Turkey.

فساد fèssĀd, *s. a.* Disorder; an abuse of any kind, a wrong practice; sedition, trouble; villainy; intrigue; corruption, bad state of anything; معدهء فسادى mì''dé-fèssĀdi, The stomach's being disordered; فسادهوارمق fèssĀ-da-vàrmak, *v.n.* To get disordered, to become vitiated by abuses; فساد قورمق fèssād-kùrmak, To plot, devise any intrigue or villainy; فساد چيقارمق fèssād-chìkàrmak, To put any plot or villainy into execution.

فسانه fèssānė, *s. p.* An idle tale.

فستاكيز fìsstākīz, *s. t. in* فلان فستاكيز fīlĀn-fìsstākīz, So and so, and so forth.

فستان fìsstĀn, *s. t.* A woman's gown; a man's kilt; ايچ فستانى ìch-fìsstĀni, *s. t.* A petticoat.

فستق fìsstik, *s. a.* A pistachio; فستقى fìsstìkī, *a. t.* Of a certain shade of lightish green, of a pistachio green colour.

فسحت fùsshat, *s. a.* Spaciousness, vastness, roominess; فسحتسراى fùss-hat-sàrāy, *s. p.* A palace of great extent.

فسخ fèsskh, *s. a.* A disuniting, pulling to pieces; an annulling, abolishing; ا—, —et, *v.a.* To pull to pieces; to annul.

فسرده fùssūrdé, *a. p.* Congealed, set.

فسق fìssk, *s. a.* Sin, wickedness, iniquity, the lusts of the flesh.

فسقه fèssaka, *s. pl. a.* (*of* فاسق fāssik), Sinners.

فسقيه fìsskìyyé, *s. t.* A jet d'eau, a fountain which throws its water up in a jet.

فسكه fìsské, *s. t.* A fillip; —اورمق, fìsské-wùrmak, *v.n.* To give a fillip.

فسلدامق fìssìldamak (*aor.* فسلدار fìssìldar), *v.n.* To whisper, make a whispering noise; فسلدى fìssìldi, *s. t.* A whispering, whispering noise.

فسلكن fèsslégh**è**n, *s. t.* Sweet basil.

فسون fùssūn, *s. p.* An idle tale.

فسيح fèssīh (*fem.* فسيحه fèssīha), *a. a.* Spacious, vast, roomy.

فشان fìshān, *a. p.* (*in composition*), Who or which sheds, spreads, scatters.

فشقرمق fìshkìrmak (*aor.* فشقرر fìshkìrìr), *v.n.* To spout out, spirt out.

فشقى fìshki, *s. t.* The dung of animals, stable manure.

فشنك fìshenk (fìshek), *s. t.* A cartridge; a squib; a sky-rocket; fireworks in general; فشنكلك fisheklik, *s. t.* A kind of receptacle for cartridges worn on the breast; هوائی فشنك hàwā'ï-fishek, *s. t.* A sky-rocket; فشنكجی fishekji, *s. t.* A maker of fireworks.

فص fAsss, *s. a.* The bezel of a finger-ring, in which the stone is fixed.

فصاحت fAssāhàt, *s. a.* Flowingness and clearness of discourse.

فصال fAsssAl, *s. a.* A habitual criticiser or disparager; —, fìssāl, *s. a.* Mutual separation.

فصحا fŭssahā, *s. pl. a.* (*of* فصيح fAssïh), Discoursers with ease and clearness.

فصل fAssl, *s. a.* A dividing, separating; a deciding (disputes); a criticising, disparaging; a division, section, chapter, act, paragraph; a season of the year; —ا, —et, *v.a.* To divide, separate; to decide, judge and terminate (a quarrel); to criticise, find fault with, disparage; in the phrase اصلی فصلی یوق Assl*i*-fAssl*i*-yòk, *There is no foundation for it* (*a report*) فصل is merely an imitative sequent of اصل; فصول اربعه fŭssūlu-èrba"a, The four seasons.

فصوليه fAssūly*a*, *s. t.* A French bean, a kidney-bean, a haricot bean.

فصيح fAssïh (*fem.* فصيحه fAssïh*a*), *a. a.* Clearly expressed, pure and free from outlandish expressions.

فضا fAzā, *s. a.* An open space of ground.

فضاحت fAzāhàt, *s. a.* Villainy, villainousness.

فضائل fAzā'il, *s. pl. a.* (*of* فضيلت fAzïlèt), Virtues, eminent qualities.

فضل fAzl, *s. a.* Virtue, any eminent quality; grace, favour, kindness.

فضلا fŭzalā, *s. pl. a.* (*of* فاضل fĀzïl), Men of virtue; men of eminent qualities.

فضله fAzl*a*, *s. a.* A surplus, residue; a residuum; any excrementitious productions of the body.

فضول fŭzūl, *s. a.* An exceeding the bounds of propriety or right; بوالفضول bū-'l-fŭzūl, *a. a.* A talkative babbler; فضولی fŭzūlī, *ad. t.* Without right, without right or title.

فضه fìdda, *s. a.* Silver.

فضيح fAzïh (*fem.* فضيحه fAzïh*a*), *a. a.* Villainous, bad, infamous; فضيحه fAzïh*a*, *s. a.* A villainous act, bad, infamous action.

فضيلت fAzïlèt, *s. a.* A virtue; a good, eminent quality, eminence, excellence; فضيلتلو fAzïlètlū, *a. t.* Excellent, eminent (a title given to the "ulémā).

فطانت fAtānèt, *s. a.* Quickness of intelligence.

فطر fìtr, *s. a.* The breaking of a fast at the expiry of its legal term; عيدالفطر "ïdu-'l-fìtr, The festival of cessation from fasting, called also شكربيرامی shèkær-bàyram*i*, *The festival of sugar.*

فطرت fìtret, *s. a.* The natural constitution of creatures; فطری fìtrī (*fem.* فطريه fìtrìyyé), *a. a.* Natural, constitutional.

فطنت fìtnèt, *s. a.* Quickness of intelligence.

فطين fàtīn, *a. a.* Quick, intelligent.

فظاظت fàzāzàt, *s. a.* Coarseness, grossness of speech and manners.

فعال fà‘‘‘āl, *s. a.* God the constant actor.

فعل fì‘‘l, *s. a.* An act, action; a verb (in grammar); the word which is used as the paradigm of triliteral roots of Arabic words; —متعدی, fì‘‘li-mùta‘‘àddī, A verb transitive; —لازم, fì‘‘li-lāzim, A verb intransitive; —معلوم fì‘‘li-mà‘‘lūm, A verb active or neuter, of which the actor is made *known* by the verb itself; —مجهول, fì‘‘li-mèjhūl, A verb passive, the actor of which is left *unknown* by the verb; —ماضی, fì‘‘li-māzī, A verb in the past tense; —مضارع, fì‘‘li-mùzāri‘‘, A verb in the aorist, having either a present or future sense; فاء الفعل fā‘u-’l-fì‘‘l, The first radical letter of an Arabic word; عين الفعل ‘‘àynu-’l-fì‘‘l, The second, *and* لام الفعل lāmu-’l-fì‘‘l, The third radical letter;

فعلاً fì‘‘lan, *ad. a.* In act, indeed, by deed; بالفعل bì-’l-fì‘‘l, *ad. a.* In actuality, really; فعلی fì‘‘lī (*fem.* فعليه fì‘‘lìyyé), *a. a.* Pertaining to action, or to a verb; فعله كتورمك fì‘‘la-ghètirmek, فعله چيقارمق fì‘‘la-chìkàrmak, فعله اخراج fì‘‘la-ìkhrāj-et, *v.a.* To do, execute, perform, bring into a state of active performance; قوه دن فعله چيقارمق kùvvédan-fì‘‘la-chìkàrmak, To raise from *posse* to *esse*, from a state of possibility or mere project to one of actuality.

فغان fìghān, *s. p.* Plaint, lamentation, cry of distress. [China; china-ware.

فغفور fàghfūr, *s. a.* The Emperor of

فقاهت fàkāhèt, *s. a.* Intelligence, aptness of mind; quality of being versed in law.

فقدان fìkdān, *s. a.* A state of desertion, abandonment by friends, separation from friends.

فقر fàkr, *s. a.* Poverty, indigence.

فقرا fùkarā, *s. pl. a.* (*of* فقير fàkīr), The poor, poor people; (*Turkish singular*) a poor man.

فقره fìkra, *s. a.* An anecdote, a tale; a paragraph, an article.

فقط fàkat, *ad. a.* Only; but still, still, yet, and yet. [prudence.

فقه fìkh (k-h), *s. a.* The science of juris-

فقها fùkahā, *s. pl. a.* (*of* فقيه fàkīh), Lawyers, legists.

فقير fàkīr, *s. a.* A poor man; your humble servant, I; فقيرانه fàkīrāné, *a. p.* Pertaining to a poor man; to your humble servant, to me.

فقيه fàkīh, *s. a.* A person versed in the law, a lawyer, legist.

فك fèkk, *s. a.* A separating, detaching.

فكار fìkyār, *a. p.* (*in composition*), Sore, galled; دل فكار dìl-fìkyār, *a. p.* Sore at heart.

فكر fìkr (fìkir), *s. a.* The reflective or

actively commemorative power of the mind; thought, reflection, meditation; —ا, —et, *v.a.* To think of, to call to mind; فكرسز fìkirsiz, *a. t.* Stupid, irreflective.

فكن fìkèn, *a. p.* (*in composition*), Who casts down, throws on the ground.

فلاجرم fè-lā-jèrem, *ad. a.* Without fail, absolutely.

فلاح fèlāh, *s. a.* A state of virtue, happiness, or prosperity; —بولمق, fèlāh-bùlmak, *v.n.* To attain a state of virtue, happiness, or prosperity; حی علی الفلاح hàyya-''àlé-'l-fèlāh ! Come to (what will lead to) happiness ! (*paragraph in the call to prayer*); —, fèllāh, *s. a.* An Arab peasant.

فلاحت fèlāhət, *s. a.* Agriculture.

فلاخن fèlākhòn, *s. p.* A sling for throwing stones.

فلاسفه fèlāssifé, *s. pl. a.* (*of* فيلسوف fèylésòf), Philosophers.

فلاكت fèlākèt, *s. a.* Adversity, misfortune, an effect of the adverse influence of the spheres.

فلامور fìlāmūr (ìkhlāmūr), *s. t.* The lime-tree, linden-tree.

فلان filan, *a. t.* Such a one, so-and-so, a certain; —ادم, filan-adam, Such a person, a certain person; —شی, filan-shèy, Such a thing, a certain thing.

فلج fèlj, *s. a.* Paralysis, the palsy.

فلذه filzé, *s. a.* A lobe; فلذهٔ كبد filzé'i-kèbed, (The lobe of the liver) A dearly-beloved person.

فلز fìliz, *s. t.* A shoot, young branch; —, fillìzz (fìliz), *s. a.* Mineral ore.

فلس filss, *s. a.* A mite, a farthing; —احمر, fìlssi-àhmər, (A red farthing) The smallest piece of copper money; فلس احمرهٔ محتاج او fìlssi - àhméra--mùhtāj-òl, *v.a.* To be reduced to sheer beggary, to be penniless, without a farthing.

فلفل fìlfìl, *s. a.* Pepper; دارفلفل dāri-fìlfìl, Red pepper in pods.

فلقه fàlaka, *s. t.* A stout pole, with two holes about six inches asunder in the middle of its length, through which the two ends of about two feet of rope are passed and knotted. This is used for the infliction of the bastinado, the feet being passed through the loop of rope, and the pole being then turned round till the slack of the rope is wound up, the pole becomes pressed against the back of the leg near the ankle, and the soles of the feet are firmly held up to view.

فلك fèlek, *s. a.* The sky, the firmament; a sphere (according to the Ptolemaic system of astronomy), of which there are nine; fortune, or the influence of the spheres; فلك الافلاك fèléku-'l--èflāk, (The sphere of spheres) The primum mobile; —, fùlk, *s. a.* A ship, boat, craft; فلكزده fèlek-zèdé, *a. p.* Struck by the adverse influence of the spheres.

فلمنك filémènk, *s. t.* A Fleming, a Dutchman; the Dutch nation.

فلنته or فلنطه filìnta, s. t. A fowling-piece.

فلوری fìlūrī, s. t. A ducat, a sequin.

فلوقه fìlìka, s. t. A ship's boat, barge, cutter; a pleasure boat. [of a gun.

فم fèm, s. a. The mouth; the muzzle

فن fènn, s. a. An art; هزارفن hèzār-fènn (hèzārifend), s. t. A jack-of-all-trades, a person clever at many things.

فنا fèna, a. t. Bad; dangerous; grave; —, fènā, s. a. Corruption, destruction, annihilation, death; دارالفنا dāru-'l-fènā, The world of change; فنابولمق fènā-bùlmak, v.n. To be annihilated, destroyed; فنالشمك fènāleshmek, v.n. To become bad, dangerous, grave; to grow worse, more dangerous.

فنار fènār (fènər), s. t. A lantern; a lighthouse; a pinion (on the shaft of a wheel). [coffee cup.

فنجان fìnjān (fìnjan), s. t. A tea or

فند fènd, s. t. A trick, piece of deceit.

فندق fìndik, s. t. A nut, filbert, cob, or Barcelona nut; —صچانی, fìndik-sìchānì, A mouse.

فنون fùnūn, s. pl. a. (of فن fènn), Arts; kinds, sorts, species. [the affections.

فؤاد fù'ād, s. a. The heart, the seat of

فواره fèvwārè, s. a. A *jet d'eau*, a fountain which throws its water up in a jet.

فواكه fèvākih, s. pl. a. (of فاكهه fākihè), Fruits.

فوائد fèwā'id, s. pl. a. (of فائده fā'idè), Uses, useful results, benefits.

فوت fèvt, s. a. To lose, to neglect, not to seize, to allow to go by and be lost; —فرصت ا, fèvti-fùrsat-et, v.n. To lose an opportunity; —او, —òl, v.n. To die.

فوج fèvj, s. a. A troop of men, a cohort.

فوچی fìchì, s. t. A cask, barrel.

فودله fòdula, s. t. A kind of better bread-cake, served out at colleges and poor-kitchens, &c.

فور fèvr, s. a. Extreme quickness, hurry; فوراً fèvran, على الفور 'àlé-'l-fèvr, ad. a. In extreme haste, quickly, hurriedly.

فوران fèvérān, s. a. A boiling, bubbling; spirting like a *jet d'eau*.

فوز fèvz, s. a. Success in an undertaking.

فوطه fūta, s. a. A kind of apron.

فوق fèvk, s. a. The top or space above the top of anything; any superior degree of rank; فوقانی fèvkānī, a. a. Upper (storey of a house); —, fèvka, ad. a. Above; فوق العاده fèvka-'l-"ādè, Extraordinary, extraordinarily; فوق الغايه fèvka-'l-ghāyè, More than extremely, exceedingly.

فونده fònda, s. t. The branches of the vine pruned away; —كومری, —kyùmuru, Vine-charcoal (used by blacksmiths, &c.); ا—, —et, v.a. To let go (the anchor).

فهرس fihriss, s. a. فهرست fihrisst, s. p. The index of a book.

فهم fèhm, s. a. The comprehending power of the mind; comprehension;

ـــ ا, —et, *v.a.* To comprehend, seize the meaning of. [ing.

فهيم fèhīm, *a. a.* Quick in comprehend-

فى fi, *pr. a.* In; into; about, relating to; among, between; فى الجمله fi-'l-jùmlé, *ad. a.* Generally; abstractedly, in a general sense; فى الحال fi-'l-hāl, *ad. a.* Instantly, at once; فى الحقيقه fi-'l-hàkīka, *ad. a.* In truth, in sooth, really. This preposition is always placed before the date of letters and papers, and also before the price of things in accounts, in the following shape, and without the dot over the ف, thus ڡى. [goods.

فيات fi'àt, *s. a.* The price *per article* of

فياض fèyyāz, *s. a.* God who abundantly pours out blessings.

فيافى fèyāfī, *s. pl. a.* (*sing. not used*), Deserts, uncultivated districts.

فيروز fīrūz, فيروزمند fīrūzmènd, فيروزى fīrūzī, *a. p.* Victorious, successful, fortunate.

فيروزه fīrūzé, *s. p.* A turquoise.

فيصل fèysàl, *s. a.* A discontinuance, interruption, cessation; a decision (of a trial or dispute), a terminating; ـــ ويرمك, fèysàl-vèrmek, *v.n.* To decide, terminate (a trial or dispute); ـــ بولمق, fèysàl-būlmak, *v.n.* To be decided, terminated.

فيض fèyz, *s. a.* Abundance; any peculiar gift of God, eminence; ـــ بولمق, fèyz-būlmak, *v.n.* To become eminent.

فيضان fèyézān, *s. a.* A plentiful outpouring.

فيل fīl (fil), *s. a.* An elephant; the bishop in chess; فيل ديشى fil-dìshi, *s. t.* Ivory.

فيلسوف fèylàssòf, *s. a.* A philosopher.

فيلو fīlo, *s. t.* (*Italian*), A squadron, or line of ships of war.

فيمابعد fi-mā-bà''d, *ad. a.* Henceforward, henceforth.

فيوضات fùyūzāt, *s. pl. a.* (*of* فيوض fùyūz, *not used, which is itself the pl. of* فيض fèyz), Peculiar and abundant gifts of Providence.

فئه fi'è, *s. a.* A troop of men.

فيه fīh, *or* fīhi, *comp. a.* In or about him, it; فيها fīhā, In or about her, it.

ق

ق kāf. Twenty-fourth letter of the Turkish alphabet, having the value of *k* in English, but is always followed by a hard vowel, in contradistinction to ك, which is also a *k* but softer in sound. The numeral value of ق is 100.

قاب kàb (*or* قاپ kàp), Any containing vessel, comprising even certain cases, covers, or envelopes; قاب قجاق kàb-kàchak, Pots and pans, kettles and cans; اياق قابى àyak-kàbi, Any kind of shoe, boot, or slipper; كورك قابى kyùrk-kàbi, The outer material of a fur cloak or coat; —, kàb, *s. a.* The length of a bow, or of a bow-shot; قاب قوسين kāba-kāvsèyn, Two bow-shots, *or* the length of two bows (an expression of the Kŭr'ān indicative of Muhammed's near approach to God on the occasion of his night-journey and ascent to heaven); قابلو (kāpli), *a. t.* Cased, covered.

قابض kābiz, *s. a.* Who seizes, lays hold of; —ارواح, kābizi-èrwāh, The soul-taking angel of death.

قابل kābil, *a. a.* Capable, possible; accepting, receiving, taking; قابليت kābiliyyèt, Capacity, ability, genius; قابليتلو kābiliyyètli, *a. t.* Capable, clever.

قابلمق *or* قاپلمق (kāplamak), *v.a.* See قپلامق; —قاپلوجه. See قپلوجه.

قاپ kāp, *ad. t. in* قاپ قره kāp-kāra, All black, quite black, very black.

قاپلو kāpli, *a. t.* Cased, covered; قاپلو بغه kāpli-bāgha (kāplimbāgha), A tortoise; a turtle. [To seize, snatch.

قاپمق kāpmak (*aor.* قاپار kāpar), *v.a.*

قات kāt, *s. t.* A fold (of any stuff); a fold (of any number or quantity); a change (of linen); a suit (of clothes); a storey or floor of a house; opinion, estimation (in which one holds things or persons); the vicinity or presence (of a person); برقات bir-kāt, One single fold; of one single fold, plain; of a single storey, consisting of only a ground floor; برقات دخی bir-kāt-dākhi, *or* برقات دها bir-kāt-dāha, *ad. t.* Still more, doubly; ايكى قات iki-kāt, Double, twofold; two-storied, consisting of a ground floor and upper storey; &c. &c.; اوست قات ŭsst-kāt, The upper storey; الت قات ālt-kāt, The lower storey; قات قات kāt-kāt, In folds, layers, strata, stories; قات اندر قات kāt-èndεr-kāt, Fold upon fold; by many degrees; بنم قاتمده bènim-kātimda, In my estimation; with me, near me, by me; &c. &c.; برقات روبا bir-kāt-rūba, A suit of clothes; ايكى قات چماشير iki-kāt-chāmāshir, Two changes of linen.

قاتق kātik, *s. t.* Anything eaten with bread to give it a relish.

قاتل kātil, *a. a.* Which kills, deadly; —, *s. a.* A homicide, man-slayer, murderer; قانلو قاتل kānli-kātil, A murderer, assassin.

قاتلنمق kātlanmak (*aor.* قاتلنور kātlanir), *v.n.* To get admitted into the service or companionship of (someone).

قاتمر kātmèr, *a. t.* Double (flower).

قاتمق kātmak (*aor.* قاتار kātar), *v.a.* To add, superadd; to send in company, send by the side (of some person); اوکه قاتمق ŭnga-kātmak (*with a pronominal affix added to* اوك ŭng), *v.a.* To cause to walk before or in front of one's self.

قاچ kāch, *interrog. t.* How many?

قاچنجى kāchinji, *a. t.* The how-manyeth? Which one in point of order in the row or series?

قاچاق kAchak, قاچامق kAchamak, *s. t.* A pretext, excuse, means of escape.

قاچق kAchik, *a. t.* Foolish, cracked, queer, half-witted, crazy. [deserter.

قاچقين kAchkin, *s. t.* A runaway; a

قاچمق kAchmak (*aor.* قاچار kAchar), *v.n.* To run away; to desert; قاچرمق kAchirmak (*aor.* قاچرر kAchirir), *v.a.* To drive away; to allow to escape; to aid to escape; to run away with; to smuggle away; —, *v.n.* To go crazy, lose one's wits; قاچرمه kAchirma, *or* كمركدن قاچرمه ghyùmrukdan - kAchirma, *a. t.* Smuggled (goods); قاچنمق kAchinmak (*aor.* قاچنور kAchinir), *v.n.* To avoid, to keep or get out of the way.

قادر kādir, *a. a.* Able, having the power; God the able One; —اول, kādir-òl, *v.n.* To be able, to have the power or ability; to have power enough.

قادم kādim, *s. a.* A person newly arriving or newly arrived at a place; القادم يزار èl-kādimu-yùzār, The newly arrived person is visited (by the older inhabitants).

قاديس Kàdiss, *s. t.* Cadiz (town of, in Spain).

قادى كوى Kādīkyùyi, *s. t.* Kadikeuyi (a town in Asia Minor, the ancient Calcedonia).

قادين kAdin, *s. t.* A genteel or respectable woman; one of the seven state concubines of the Sultan.

قار kAr, *s. t.* Snow; قارياغمق kAr-yàghmak, *v.n.* To snow; قارلق kArlik, *s. t.* A large bottle used for icing water.

قارپوز kàrpuz, *s. t.* A water-melon.

قارت kàrt, *a. t.* Old (man); tough meat; قارتلشمق kàrtlashmak (*aor.* قارتلاشور kàrtlashir), *v.n.* To grow old; to grow tough.

قارس Kàrss, *s. t.* The town of Kars.

قارش kArish, *s. t.* A span; قارشلمق kArishlamak, *v.a.* To measure by spanning; قارش مورش kArish - mùrush, *s. t.* Utter confusion; قارمه قارش kàrma - kArish, *a. t.* In utter confusion.

قارشق kArishik, *a. t.* Mixed; confused; in disorder; قارشقلق kArishiklik, *s. t.* Confusion; disorder; a row, tumult.

قارشمق kArishmak (*aor.* قاريشور kArishir), *v.n.* To mix, mingle, combine; to become confused, or disordered; to meddle, have to do, interfere; to exercise authority; قارشدرمق kArishdirmak (*aor.* قارشدرر kArishdirir), *v.a.* To add; to mix, mix up, stir up, stir about; to put in disorder; to cause or allow to meddle or interfere.

قارشو *or* قارشى kàrshi, *s. t.* The opposite side (of a street, river, &c.); the space opposite (to anything); —, *ad. t.* Opposite; قارشى قومق kàrshi-kòmak, *v.n.* To oppose, resist; قارشى چيقمق kàrshi-chikmak, *v.n.* To go forth to meet; قارشيلمق kàrshilamak, *v.a.* To meet, to advance and meet intentionally; to answer in an adverse manner, oppose in argument; قارشیلاشمق kàrshilashmak, v.n. To meet one another face to face; to correspond, balance one another (the debtor and creditor sides of an account, or income and expenditure); قارشیلاشدرمق kàrshilashdirmak, To bring (two people) face to face; to compare, collate (papers); to make balance, to balance (income and expenditure); قارشیلق kàrshilik, s. t. The steel (of a flint gun-lock); any retort, answer; tit for tat, quid pro quo; equivalent, complete set-off; a fund or means (in finance); قارشیم kàrshim, The space opposite to me; قارشیکه kàrshinga, Opposite to thee, to the space opposite to thee; قارشیسنده kàrshissinda, Opposite to him, her, it; in the space opposite to him, her, it; &c. &c.

قارغشالق kàrghashalik, s. t. A noise as of crows cawing; a noise of tumult and squabbling.

قارغه kàrgha, s. t. A crow; a rook; الاقارغه ala-kàrgha, (The black and white spotted crow) The jackdaw (?); قارغه‌بوکن kàrgha-bùken, s. t. Nux vomica.

قارن kàrn, s. t. The belly; the womb; قارن اجقمق kàrn-àjikmak (*with pronominal affixes to* قارن), v.n. To be hungry; قارن اغریمق kàrn-aghrimak, v.n. To have the belly-ache; قارن اغریسی kàrn-aghrissi, s. t. The belly-ache; a peevish child; (*as an interj.*) O you belly-ache! you peevish thing!

قارنداش kàrn-dàsh (Womb *or* belly-fellow, usually written قرنداش), s. t. A brother; a sister.

قارنجه karinja, s. t. An ant, pismire, emmet; honeycomb (in cast metals); قارنجه‌لو karinjali, a. t. Honeycombed (metal).

قارون kārūn, s. a. A person proverbial for his wealth, supposed to be the same as Korah; the river Karoon.

قاری kari, s. t. A woman; a wife; —, kārī, s. a. A reader (especially of the Kūr'ān); an inhabitant of a town.

قاریوط Kàriot, s. t. The island of Nicaria.

قاز kaz, s. t. A goose; قازکبی باقمق kaz-ghibi-bakmak, v.n. To stand and stare stupidly without doing anything.

قازق kazik, s. t. A stake (of wood); قازقلمق kaziklamak, v.a. To impale.

قازمق kazmak (*aor.* قازار kazar), v.a. To dig; to dig out, scoop out; to engrave, to sink.

قازمه kazma, s. t. A pick-axe, a pick.

قازمیر kāzmīr, s. t. Kerseymere.

قازیمق kazimak (*aor.* قازر *or* قازیر kazir), v.a. To scratch out (writing with a knife).

قاش kash, s. t. The eyebrow; ایرقاشی èyer-kashi, s. t. The pommel, *also* the cantle, of a saddle (*or* the curved pieces of wood which form the front and back part of the frame of a saddle); قاشلو kashli, a. t. Eyebrowed, having eyebrows; دورت قاشلو dùrt-kAshli, a. t. (Having four eyebrows) Having the moustache, from youth, no thicker than the eyebrows; قاش چاتمق kAsh-chàtmak, v.n. To frown; چاتق قاشلو chàtik-kAshli, a. t. Having the eyebrows joined or meeting over the nose.

قاشاغى kAshàghi, s. t. A currycomb.

قاشق kAshik, s. t. A spoon.

قاشنمق kAshinmak (aor. قاشينور kAshinir), v.n. To itch; to scratch (an itching place on one's own body).

قاشيمق kAshimak (aor. قاشر kAshir), v.a. To scratch (an itching place on any other person); to curry (a horse).

قاصد kAssid, s. a. One who definitively intends to do something or to go somewhere, and is acting or preparing to act accordingly; a foot-messenger.

قاصر kAssir, a. a. Deficient, defective, wanting, not up to the mark.

قاصق kàssik, s. t. The groin; —بتى, kAssik-biti, A crab-louse.

قاصمق kAssmak (aor. قاصار kAssar), v.a. To stretch tight (an extended rope).

قاصنق kAssnak, s. t. A hoop, rim, or other contrivance for tightening or holding together.

قاضى kAzī (kAdi), s. a. A judge according to the canonical law; a putter of an end (to matters); قاضى الحاجات kAzìyyu'l-hājāt, God who satisfieth the wants of His creatures; قاضى عسكر kAzi-''àsskER (kAz'-''àsskER), قاضى العسكر kAzìyyu-'l-''àsskER, (Judge of the army) Title of two high legal functionaries of Muhammedan canon law in Turkey, one for Rumelia and the other for Anatolia, ranking next to the Shèykhu-'l-ìsslām, and exercising the office of Supreme Judges in Constantinople, though formerly they were the judges of the army.

قاطبة kAtibétEN, ad. a. Not at all, never, in قطعاً وقاطبة kAt''an-vè-kAtibétEN, By no means whatever, in no case.

قاطر kAtir, s. t. A mule; an impudent little upstart.

قاطرجى kàtirji, s. t. A muleteer.

قاطع kAti'', a. a. Which cuts; —, s. a. A secant; قاطع الطريق kAti''u-'t-tàrīk, A highwayman, brigand.

قاعده kA''idé, s. a. A rule; the base (of a mathematical figure); قاعدهٔ كليه kA''idé'i-kyùlliyyÉ, A general rule.

قاف kAf, s. a. Name of the letter ق; name of the Caucasian chain; ازقافتاقاف èz-kAf-tā-kAf, From east to west (the Caucasus being imagined to surround the whole habitable world).

قافله kAfilÉ, s. a. A caravan of travellers.

قافيه kAfìyyÉ, s. a. Rhyme in poetry; the syllables which compose the rhyming of words together.

قاقله kākulÉ, s. a. The cardamum.

قاقم or قاقوم kākum, s. t. The ermine; the ermine fur.

قاقمق kAkmak (aor. قاقار kAkar), v.a. To give a tap; to drive in by tapping; to push; to emboss (designs in metal);

باشه‌قاقمق bÂsh*a*-kÂkmak, *v.n.* To cast (former favours) in one's teeth, to upbraid, reproach, twit (with former benefits conferred); قاقمه kÂkma, *s. t.* An embossed design on metal; the art of embossing metals.

قال kÂl, *s. a.* Word of mouth; قالاً kÂl*a*n, *ad. a.* In word; قيل وقال kīl-ʊ-kÂl, People's remarks, talk, whisperings, grumblings (*These two words are originally verbs in Arabic, third pers. sing. pret.*, قال *is active*, he said, قيل *is passive*, it was said); —, kÂl, *s. t.* The action of melting and refining (ores and metals); —ا, kÂl-ètmek, *v.a.* To melt and refine; قالجى kÂlj*i*, *s. t.* A refiner, a smelter.

قالب kÂl*i*b, *s. a.* A mould; the body; — *or* قالپ (kÂlp), *a. t.* Bad, false (money); قالپزن (kÂlp*a*z*à*n), *s. t.* A false-coiner, forger of coin; a fellow of great pretension and no intrinsic value.

قالبور kÂlbur, *s. t.* A screen, a riddle; قالبوردن كچورمك kÂlburd*a*n-ghèchirmek, *v.a.* To screen, to riddle, to sift.

قالتق kÂlt*à*k, *s. t.* A slut, wench (term of reproach among women only).

قالچه kÂlch*a*, *s. t.* The hip, hip-bone.

قالچين kÂlch*i*n, *s. t.* A kind of shoe.

قالدرم kÂld*i*r*i*m, *s. t.* A causeway; pavement; پياده‌قالدريمى pìyÂdé-kÂld*i*r*i*mi, A foot pavement.

قالدرمق kÂld*i*rmak (*aor.* قالدرر kÂldirir), *v.a.* To raise, lift; to take up, off, away; to suppress, abolish; to cause to get up from sleep or rest, to rouse; to raise (troops).

قالع kÂl*i*", *s. a.* Who pulls up or out, extirpates.

قالفه kÂlf*a*, *s. t.* (*from* خليفه khÂlīfé), A builder, architect; a workman (in any trade), journeyman; an upper female servant or slave.

قالقان kÂlkʌn, *s. t.* A shield, buckler, target; —بالغى, kÂlkʌn-bÂl*ighi*, A turbot.

قالقمق kÂlkmak (*aor.* قالقار kÂlkar), *v.n.* To rise, to get up; اياغه قالقمق *à*ya*gha*-kÂlkmak, *v.n.* To get up on one's feet, to rise; to rise in rebellion; to set out on a journey.

قالمق kÂlmak (*aor.* قالور kÂl*i*r), *v.n.* To rest, stay, remain; to stop, leave off; to stop short; to be altogether surprised, astonished, confounded; to wait; to be put off (in time), deferred; to be left; to be left at the option or discretion (of anyone); بكاقالسه bÂn*g*a-kÂlsa, If it were me, if I had to decide, if it were left to my option, I think, I am inclined to think, I am of opinion; يانكده‌قالمز yàn*i*ngda-kÂlmàz, (It will not stay with thee), You will not retain possession of it.

قاله KÂlé, *s. t.* Calais (town of).

قالى kÂlī (hÂl*i*), *s. p.* A large carpet; قاليچه kÂlīché, *s. p.* A small carpet, a rug.

قالين kÂl*i*n, *a. t.* Thick (through); قالينلق kÂl*i*nl*i*k, *s. t.* Thickness.

قاليون kàlyòn, *s. t.* A man-of-war; a ship of the line; قاليونجى kàlyònji, *s. t.* A man-of-war's-man, sailor of the navy.

قالیه kAlya, s. t. Rough potash; قالیه طاشی kAlya-tAshi, Rough vitrified potash.

قامت kAmet, s. a. Stature.

قامچی kAmchi, s. t. A whip; قامچیلمق kAmchilamak (aor. قامچیلار kAmchilar), v.a. To whip; to whip up, spur up, stir up to action.

قامره kàmara, s. t. (Italian), A ship's [cabin.

قامش kAmish, s. t. A reed; penis.

قامع kAmi'', s. a. A subduer, breaker down, striker down.

قاموس kAmūss, s. a. A sea, ocean; name of a celebrated Arabic lexicon.

قامه kAma, s. t. An iron wedge; a long and broad Georgian dagger.

قان kAn, s. t. Blood; —او, —ol, v.n. To be bloody, or bloodshot; قان تر kAn-tèr, A sweat of blood, a profuse perspiration; —المق, kAn-Almak, To bleed, take blood; —دوکمك, kAn-dùkmek, v.n. To shed blood; —اغلامق, kAn-àghlamak, v.n. To shed tears of blood; —توکرمك, kAn-tùkyurmek, v.n. To spit blood; برینك قاننه کیرمك bìrining-kAnina-ghìrmek, v.n. To take one's life, be guilty of his blood; قانه بولاشمق kAna-bùlashmak, v.n. To become soiled with blood; قانه بولاشدرمق kAna-bùlashdirmak, v.a. To soil with blood, to steep in gore; قانلو kAnli, a. t. Bloody; blood-guilty; قان قورودان kAn-kūrUdAn, s. t. The mandrake (?); قان بهاسی kAn-(pAhAssi), s. t. Blood-money, a deodand, price paid to the heir of a slain man by the homicide; دلی قانلو dèli-kAnli, s. t. (One whose blood is mad) A young lad.

قانامق kAnamak (aor. قانار kAnar), v.n. To bleed, flow with blood; قاناتمق kAnAtmak (aor. قانادر kAnAdir), v.a. To draw blood, cause to bleed, make bleed.

قانبور kAnbūr, a. t. Crooked, bent; hunchbacked; hogged (a ship); —, s. t. A hunchback, hunchbacked person; a hunched back, hunch.

قانت kānit, s. a. Pious, devout.

قانجق kAnjik, s. t. A bitch.

قانجه kAnja, s. t. A boat-hook; a hook; a grappling-iron; —باش, kAnja-bAsh, A kind of large boat with high hooked prow.

قانده kAnda, ad. t. Where? In what place? In what place soever.

قانع kāni'', a. a. Satisfied, content, contented with what he possesses.

قانمك kAnmak (aor. قانار kAnar), v.n. To satisfy one's thirst, one's desire for riches, one's doubts; to have one's doubts or objections removed and be fully satisfied; قاندرمق kAndirmak (aor. قاندرر kAndirir), v.a. To satisfy; to persuade, remove one's doubts or objections, to satisfy one's mind.

قانون kānūn, s. a. A law, canon; a statute, regulation, bye-law; a psaltery; قانوننامه kānūn-nāmé, A code of laws, a set of statutes, regulations, or bye-laws; قانونى kānūnī, *s. a.* قانونجى kānūnj*i*, *s. t.* A lawgiver, maker of laws and regulations.

قانى kàn*i* (hàn*i*), *ad. t.* Where? In what place? قانى‌يا kàn*i*-yā (hàn*i*-yā)! Where then! Where is it, then? Where are you, then!

قاو kàw, *s. t.* Touchwood, tinder, German tinder; اغاج‌قاوى ʌghʌj-kàw*i*, Touchwood; منطارقاوى mʌntār-kàw*i*, German tinder; بزقاوى bèz-kàw*i*, Tinder.

قاورامق kàwramak (*aor.* قاورار kàwrar), *v.a.* To seize, gripe, lay tight hold of with the whole hand.

قاورمق kàwʊrmak (*aor.* قاورر kàwʊrʊr), *v.a.* To fry; to torrefy; roast (coffee).

قاورمه kàwʊrm*a*, *s. t.* Mutton or beef fried in small lumps, and either eaten fresh, or potted and preserved in jars or skins by pouring the dripping over it.

قاوشمق kàwʊshmak (*aor.* قاوشور kàwʊshʊr), *v.n.* To come together, meet, join; قاوشدرمق kàwʊshdʊrmak (*aor.* قاوشدرر kàwʊshdʊrʊr), *v.a.* To bring together.

قاوق kàwʊk, *s. t.* Several kinds of cap, of various shapes, but all stuffed with cotton; سديك‌قاوغى sìdik-kàwʊghʊ, The bladder.

قاون kàwʊn, *s. t.* A musk melon; اغاج‌قاونى ʌghʌj-kàwʊnʊ, A citron.

قاهر kāhir (*fem.* قاهره kāhirĕ), *a. a.* Irresistibly subjugating.

قائد kā'id, *s. a.* A conductor, a leader.

قايرمق kàyirmak (*aor.* قايرر kàyirir), *v.a.* To take care of the interests of, push the interests of, take care he shall not come to want, to patronize actively.

قايش kàyish, *s. t.* A leather strap, a belt; a mode or act of slipping; sliding; ا—, —et, *v.a.* To steal, prig, bone (*slang*).

قايق kàyik, *s. t.* A boat or ship with sharp prow and stern; پياده‌قايغى pìyādĕ-kày*ighi*, A common row-boat of Constantinople, usually with only one pair of oars; برچفته‌قايق bìr-chìftĕ-kàyik, A boat with one pair of oars (ايكى ìki, two; اوچ ùch, three; درت dùrt, four; بش bèsh, five; beyond which none are used; the last are peculiar to the ministry, the next to councillors of state, &c., and the others are used by all who can afford them); طولمش‌قايق dòlmush-kàyik, A kind of omnibus-boat, taking several passengers independently; پازارقايغى pàzar-kày*ighi*, A very large passage-boat going to distant villages and taking fifty or more passengers; آتش‌قايغى ʌtèsh-kày*ighi*, اطه‌قايغى ʌda-kày*ighi*, Large kinds of row-boats, the latter from the Princes' Islands; بالقجى‌قايغى bʌlìkji-kày*ighi*, A fisherman's boat; اوطون‌قايغى òdʊn-kày*ighi*, A boat with firewood (كومر kyùmur, charcoal; شراب shàrāb, wine; &c., &c.); تبديل‌قايغى tèbdīl-kàyighi, The Sultan's private boat; سلاملق‌قايغى sèlāmlik-kàyighi (or سلطنت sAltAnAt-), The Sultan's state boat; ايلچى‌قايغى èlchi-kàyighi, An ambassador's state boat; قايقجى kàyikji, A boatman; قايقخانه kàyik-khānÉ, A boathouse.

قائل kā'il, a. a. Consenting; —, — او ôl, v.n. To consent, to give consent; to be satisfied (that a thing should be done).

قائم kā'im (fem. قائمه kā'imÉ), a. a. Upright; standing; existing; right (angle); قائمه kā'imÉ, s. a. An official letter on a full-sized sheet of paper; a treasury bill; a bank-note or assignat; قائممقام kā'im-màkām (kày-makAm), A lieutenant, deputy, vice, substitute; the grand vizier's lieutenant when the former leaves Constantinople; the lord-lieutenant or governor of a secondary government or county; a lieutenant-colonel in the army; a second-class post-captain in the navy; a kind of registrar-general of property in mortmain in each of the subdivisions or departments among which the administration of that kind of property is distributed.

قايمق kàymak, s. t. Clotted cream, similar to that made in Devonshire; — (aor. قايار kàyar), v.n. To slide, slip; قايدرمق kàydirmak, v.a. To cause to slip; to manage underhand to make a person lose his office; قايمق‌كبى kàymak-ghìbi, a. t. Cream-like, white and smooth.

قاين kàyn, s. a. A brother-in-law, own brother to one's wife; قاين‌اتا kàyn-àta, or قاين‌پدر kàyn-pèdEr, A father-in-law, father to one's wife; قاين‌انا kàyn-àna, قاين‌والده kàyn-wālidÉ, A mother-in-law, wife's own mother; قاين‌اغاجى kàyn-Aghaji, A birch tree.

قاينامق kàynamak (aor. قاينار kàynar), v.n. To boil, be in ebullition; to well up, break out at the surface of the earth (water); to swarm (insects, &c.); to sink, go down (a ship, boat); to weld (as iron); قايناتمق kàynatmak, v.a. To cause (water, &c.) to boil (over the fire); to weld (iron).

قاينق or قايناق kàynak, s. t. The cheek of the bottom, the breech, the buttock; a place where iron has been welded.

قبا kAba, a. t. Coarse, rough; open, loose, not closely packed (any fibrous substance); —, s. t. Coarse or rough part; —, kAbā, s. p. Clothing, apparel, garment; قباچه kAbāchÉ, s. p. A small garment.

قباب kìbāb, s. pl. a. (of قبه kùbbé), Domes, cupolas; domed edifices.

قباحت kAbāhat, s. a. A fault, a bad action, a crime.

قبارجق kAbarjik, s. t. A pimple.

قبارمق kAbarmak (aor. قبارر kAbarir), v.n. To swell, become puffed; to rise in blisters; to raise or rise in fermenting (dough); to get up, rise, swell, become rough (the sea); to become loose, open, not closely packed, ruffled (hair, feathers, &c.); to become serious, important, extensive; any quarrel or trouble; قبارتمق kàbartmak (*aor.* قبـاردر kàbard*i*r), *v.a.* To cause to swell and be puffed; to ruffle; to cause (any unpleasant matter) to become serious; قولتوق قبارتمق kòltʋk--kàbartmak, *v.n.* (To puff up the armpits) To strut, walk pompously sticking out the elbows; to become proud; قبارتمه kàbartm*a*, *s. t.* Any design in relief.

قباق kàbak, *s. t.* Any plant or fruit of the gourd kind; بال قباغى bàl-kàbàgh*i*, The yellow squash, calabash, or pumpkin; قنطارقباغى kàntār--kàbàgh*i*, The large round gourd or pumpkin; ساقزقباغى sākiz-kàbàgh*i*, The vegetable marrow; اصمه‌قباغى àssm*a* - kàbàgh*i*, A long vegetable marrow, growing over trellises like a vine; باشى قباق bàsh*i*-kàbak, One whose head is bald like a gourd.

قبائح kàbā'ih, *s. pl. a.* (*of* قبيحه kàbīhà), Vices, defects, bad actions or qualities.

قبائل kàbā'il, *s. pl. a.* (*of* قبيله kàbīlé), Tribes, clans.

قبب kʋbeb, *s. pl. a.* (*of* قبه kʋbbé), Domes, cupolas; domed edifices.

قبح kʋbh, *s. a.* Badness, reprehensibleness.

قبر kàbr, *s. a.* A grave, tomb, sepulchre; قبرستان kàbrisstān, *s. p.* A burial-ground, grave-yard, place of interment, cemetery, churchyard.

قبرس Kìbris, *s. t.* The island of Cyprus.

قبض kàbz, *s. a.* A taking hold of, a taking with the hand; a receiving into possession or custody; constipation; —ا, —et, *v.a.* To take; to receive.

قبضه kàbz*a*, *s. a.* The gripe of the hand; the handle (of a sword); برقبضه‌قلج bìr-kàbz*a*-kìlij, One sword (*and so on for any number, as when we say:* ten *head of cattle*, &c.).

قبطى kìbtī, *s. a.* A Copt; a gypsy; a kind of stuff; —, *a. a.* Coptic.

قبل kàbl, *s. a.* The space in front of anything, or before anything in succession; —, kàbl*a*, *pr. a.* Before; —, kʋbl, *s. a.* A kiss.

قبله kìbl*a*, *s. a.* The spot towards which men turn their faces to pray, formerly the temple at Jerusalem, now the kyà''bé (cubical temple) at Mecca; the south; the south wind; قبله‌لدوس kìbl*a*-lòdoss, South-south-west; قبله كششلمه kìbl*a*-kèshishlémé, South-south-east; قبلهٔ عالم kìblé'i-''àlem, (The point to which the whole world directs its look) The sovereign; قبله نما kìblé-nùmā, *or* قبله‌نامه kìblé--nāmé, A small compass showing the direction of the *kibla*; اهل قبله èhli--kìblé (*for* اهل خبره èhli-khìbré), An expert (to whose examination and decision disputes are referred); قبلتين **kìblétèyn,** *s. a. dual,* The ancient and present *Kiblas.*

قبور **kŭbur,** *s. t.* A long cylindrical pen-case, or any long case; —, **kŭbūr,** *s. pl. a.* (*of* قبر kàbr), Graves, sepulchres.

قبورغه **kàburgha,** *s. t.* A rib; a timber (in a ship's frame).

قبوق **kàbuk,** *s. t.* A shell, pod, cod, seed-vessel; bark, peel; a scab; a shell (of a shell-fish, eggs, &c.); crust (of bread); قبوقلو **kàbuklu,** *a. t.* Covered with a crust, a shell, bark, or a scab; قبوقسز **kàbuksuz,** *a. t.* Free from crust, shell, bark, or scab; قبوقلنمق **kàbuklanmak,** *v.n.* To become covered with a scab (a sore); قبوق باغلامق **kàbuk-bàghlamak,** *v.n.* To pod, form pods.

قبول **kàbūl,** *s. a.* An accepting or receiving; an admitting; a permitting; ا—, —et, *v.a.* To accept, receive; to admit; to permit.

قبه **kŭbbé,** *s. a.* A dome, cupola; a domed edifice.

قبيح **kàbīh** (*fem.* قبيحه **kàbīha**), *a. a.* Ugly, unsightly; bad, naughty; قبيحه **kàbīha,** *s. a.* A bad action or quality.

قبيل **kàbīl,** *s. a.* A class, category.

قبيله **kàbīlé,** *s. a.* A tribe, clan, sept.

قپ **kìp,** *ad. t. in* قپ قرمزی **kìp-kìrmizi,** Quite red, very red.

قپاق **kàpak,** *s. t.* A lid, cover; a line-of-battle ship, liner, two-decker; مزه‌قپاق **mèza-kàpak,** A rasee, a liner cut-down, a double-bank frigate; لومبارقپاغی **lùmbar-kàpaghi,** A port, port of a port-hole; كوزقپاغی **ghyùz-kàpaghi,** The eyelid.

قپالو **kàpali,** *a. t.* Shut, closed, covered.

قپامق **kàpamak** (*aor.* قپار **kàpar**), *v.a.* To shut, close, cover; قپاتمق **kàpatmak,** *v.a. caus.* To cause, force, or allow one to shut, close, or cover (something), or to cause, force, or allow (something) to shut of itself; قپانمق **kàpanmak,** *v.n.* To shut (of itself); to stumble (a horse), trip; —, *v.p.* To be shut, closed, or covered (by someone); يوزی قوين قپانمق **yùzu-kòyn-kàpanmak,** *v.n.* To throw one's self flat on the ground, face to the earth.

قپان **kàpan,** *s. t.* A trap; a kind of mart or market-place, wharf, custom-house, or bonded warehouse in one; قپانجه **kàpanja,** *s. t.* A trap; a board that tips or trips over when anything heavy is placed upon it; قپان قاپانه **kàpan-kàpana,** The mart is for him who can take possession (proverbial expression).

قپلامق **kàplamak** (*aor.* قپلار **kàplar**), *v.a.* To cover over or line (with something that can form an extended surface, as, with planks, with clouds, with fur, with silver, with an outer cover, &c.); قپلانمق **kàplanmak,** *v.n.* To become covered; —, *v.p.* To be covered; to be lined; قپلاتمق **kàplatmak,** *v.a.* To cause (someone) to cover or line (something with some other thing); قپلامه kàplama, Covered; plated; كومش قپلامه ghyùmush-kàplama, Silver-plated.

قپلان kàplan, s. t. A leopard.

قپلوبغه kàpli-bàgha (kàplimbagha), s. t. A tortoise; a turtle; دكزقپلوبغه سی dèngiz-kàpli-bàghassi, A turtle.

قپلوجه kàplija, s. t. A hot spring, a bath supplied from a hot spring.

قپمق kìpmak (aor. قیپار kìpar) in كوزقپمق ghyùz-kìpmak, v.a. To close the eye and open it again quickly, to wink, to blink.

قپو kàpi, s. t. A door, gate, wicket; a turnpike; a house; a public office; (or پاشاقپوسی pàsha-kāpissi), the government house (*wherever there is a governor, and especially the office of the central Government at Constantinople*); a place, employment, service; قپوجی kàpiji, s. t. A porter, door-keeper, gate-keeper, turnpike-keeper; قپوجی باشی kàpiji-bàshi, (Head porter) A chamberlain (title of rank and office); قپوباجه kàpi-bàja, (Door and loop-hole) All over the house, in every corner; قپواوغلانی kàpi-òghlani, A kind of under-clerk attached to embassies at Constantinople, and whose business it is to receive such permits, letters, and other documents, as are sent to the embassy; قپوكتخداسی kàpi-kètkhùdāssi (kàpi-kyāyassi), An official agent which each governor, tributary prince, and department of Government having a separate office, is obliged to maintain at Constantinople for the purpose of transacting business at the central office of Government; قپوطاقمی kàpi-tàkimi, The general body of government agents and clerks; قپویولداشی kàpi-yòldashi, A fellow-servant; قپولنمق kàpilanmak, v.n. To get one's self into employment, procure a place; قپولندرمق kàpilandirmak, v.a. To get (some other person) into employment, to find a place, to get employed.

قپودان kàpudān (kàptan), s. t. (*Italian*), A sea-captain, naval captain; any European; —دریا, kàpudāni-dèryā, —پاشا, (kàptan) - pàsha, The lord high-admiral of Turkey.

قپودانه kàpudāna (kàptana), s. t. (*Italian*), The admiral's ship (*old*); —بك, —bègh, or —پاشا, —pasha, A full admiral.

قپوط kàput, قپود kàpud, s. t. A kind of cloak with sleeves and a hood.

قت kàt, See قات; —, kìt, See قیت.

قتال kìtāl, s. a. A fight, battle, mutual slaughter.

قتر kùtr, s. a. A district, country.

قتل kàtl, s. a. A killing; manslaughter, homicide, murder; —ا, —et, v.a. To kill, put to death, slay; to murder; قتل نفس kàtli-nèfss, A slaying, putting to death; قتل نفس بغیرحق kàtli-

-nèfss-bì-ghàyri-hʌkk, Unjustifiable homicide.

قتلا (*for* قتلى) kʌtlà, *s. pl. a.* (*of* قتيل kʌtīl), The slain.

قتلانمق (*or* قاتلنمق) kʌtlanmak, *v.n.* To squat down (with a view of waiting for someone).

قتولك kàtolik, *s. t.* A Roman Catholic, [a papist.

قتى kʌti, *a. t.* Hard; —, *ad. t.* Very (*old*); قتيلاشمق kʌtilashmak, *v.n.* To become hard, to harden.

قتيل kʌtīl, *s. a.* A slain person.

قجردامق kìjirdʌmak (*aor.* قجردار kìjirdar), *v.n.* To gnash or grind together so as to make a noise (the teeth); قجرداتمق kìjirdʌtmak, *v.a.* To grind or gnash (the teeth) and make a noise; قجردى kìjirdi, *s. t.* The grinding noise made by the teeth.

قجقمق kìjìkmak (*aor.* قجيقر kìjìkir), *v.n.* To be ticklish, to be tickled; قجقمه kìjìkma, *s. t.* Ticklishness; a tickling sensation.

قچان kʌchʌn, *ad. t.* When, at the time [when.

قحبه kàhbé, *s. a.* A harlot, whore; —! There's a fine fellow! قحبه اوغلى kàhbé-òghlu (kàhpòghlu)! You ass! you son of a b—ch!

قحط kàht, *s. a.* Scarcity, dearth, famine.

قد kʌdd, *s. a.* Stature.

قدح kʌdeh, *s. a.* A drinking cup or glass; a wine-glass or tumbler; —, kʌdh, *s. a.* A reviling, reproaching, calling names; ا—, —et, *v.a.* To revile, reproach, call bad names.

قدر kʌdr, *s. a.* The real value or just estimation in which a thing or person is or should be held; —, kʌder, *s. a.* The predestination or fore-arrangement of Providence; —, kʌdar, *s. a.* Quantity; number; length of time; بوقدر bū-kʌdar, Thus much, so much; اولقدر òl(ò)-kādar, شو قدر shū-kʌdar, That much, so much; نقدر nàkʌdar? How much? how many? how long (in time)? how much; how much soever; قدركيجهسى kʌdr-ghéyjéssi, The 27th night of Ramazan; براولقدردها bìr-ò--kʌdar-dàhā, As much again as that; —, kʌdar, *ad. t.* As much as; as many as; as long as.

قدرت kūdret, *s. a.* Power, ability, might; wealth, riches, pecuniary ability, omnipotence; يد قدرت yèdi--kūdrèt, (The hand of omnipotence) Nature (in its producing quality); قدرت حمامى kūdrèt-hʌmmʌmi, A natural hot-spring, or bath fed by one; قدرت حلواسى kūdrèt-hèlwàssi, Manna; قدرتلو kūdretlū, *a. t.* Puissant; —, kūdrètli, *a. t.* Wealthy, pecuniarily able.

قدرغه kʌdirgha, *s. t.* A galley.

قدس kūdss, *s. a.* A holy place; paradise, heaven; Jerusalem; —شريف, kūdssi-shèrīf, Jerusalem; روح القدس rūhu-'l-kūdss, (The spirit of paradise) The angel Gabriel (*according to Muhammedans*); The Holy Ghost (*according to Christians*); —, kʌddéssé (*fol-*

lowed by الله) ! May God sanctify ! —, kŭddissé ! May (—) be sanctified !

قدسی kŭdsī (*fem.* قدسیه kŭdsìyyé), *a. a.* Holy, sanctified ; قدسیت kŭdsìyyèt, *s. a.* Holiness, sanctity.

قدم kadem, *s. a.* A foot (limb, *or* measure) ; —, kìdèm, *s. a.* Precedence, seniority ; قدملو kademli, *a. t.* One whose foot or approach brings good luck ; lucky, fortunate ; وضع قدم vwaz"*i*-kadem-et, *or* قدم باصمق kadem-bassm*a*k, To tread, place the foot ; ثابتقدم sābit-kadem, *a. p.* Firm of purpose ; firm of foot.

قدما kŭdémā, *s. pl. a.* (*of* قدیم kadīm), Seniors, old or superior officers.

قدمه kadémé, *s. a.* A step (of a ladder, stairs, or rank).

قدوت kìdvet, *s. a.* A person of mark.

قدورمق kŭdurm*a*k (*aor.* قدورور kŭdurur), *v.n.* To go mad (a dog), be seized with hydrophobia.

قدوز kŭduz, *s. t.* Hydrophobia ; —, *a. t.* Mad, seized with hydrophobia.

قدوم kŭdūm, *s. a.* The approach, or arrival (of a person near to us).

قدید kadīd, *a. a.* Dried, junked.

قدیر kadīr, *a. a.* Almighty ; الله علی کل شیء قدیر allāhu-"àla-ky*ù*lli-shèy'in-kadīr, God is able to do all things, is almighty.

قدیم kadīm, *a. a.* Old, ancient, antique ; —, *s. a.* The olden time ; من القدیم mìn-el-kadīm, *ad. a.* Ab antiquo, time out of mind ; قدیماً kadīm*a*n, *ad. a.* Of old ; قدیمی kadīmī, *a. a.* Pertaining to the olden time. [tery.

قذف kazf, *s. a.* An accusation of adul-

قرا (*for* قری) kŭrà, *s. pl. a.* (*of* قریه karìyyé), Villages ; —, kŭrrā, *s. pl. a.* (*of* قاری karī), Readers of the Kŭr'an.

قرابت karābèt, *s. a.* Nearness, relationship.

قرابین karabīn, *s. pl. a.* (*of* قربان kŭrbān), Sacrifices, beasts sacrificed or for sacrifice.

قرابیه kŭrābìyyé, *s. t.* A small crisp cake, an almond cake ; —ساعتی, kŭrābìyyé-sā"*ati*, A hunting-watch, rather small and thick. [Rather black, blackish.

قراجه karaj*a*, *s. t.* A roebuck ; —, *a. t.*

قرار karār, *s. a.* A state of repose ; a state of changelessness ; permanency ; a decision, resolution ; the usual quantity, size, time, or quality (of anything) ; —ویرمق, karār-vèrmek, *v.n.* To come to a decision, to decide, determine ; —بولمق, karār-bŭlm*a*k, قرارلشمق kararl*a*shm*a*k, *v.n.* To be settled, decided ; قرارلشدرمق karār-lashd*ì*rm*a*k, *v.a.* To arrange, settle definitively ; دارالقرار dāru-'l-karār, The world of changelessness, the future world ; قرارگیر karārghīr, *a. p.* Decided, settled, definitively arranged ;

برقرار bèr-karār, *a. p.* In a state of changelessness, without change ; —, bèr-karār, *ad. t.* In an equable manner, without augmentation or diminution ;

قرارداده karār-dādé, *a. p.* To which

a definitive arrangement has been given; —, *s. p.* A definitive resolution; دوزخ قرار dūzākh-kārār, *a. p.* Whose place of duration is hell, damned; قرارسز kārārsiz, *a. t.* Variable; inconstant, volatile; ephemeral; قرارگاه kārār-ghyāh, *s. p.* A place of permanent stay.

قرارتی kārarti (kāralti), *s. t.* Any dark object or group of objects seen at a distance.

قرارمق kārarmak (*aor.* قرارر kārarir), *v.n.* To become black, dark, lowering; قرارتمق kārartmak (*aor.* قراردر kārardir), *v.a.* To cause to become black or dark.

قراغول kāraghol, *s. t.* A guard; an outpost, picket; a sentry; قراغول خانه kāraghol-khānē, *s. t.* A guard-house.

قراغی kirāghi, *s. t.* Frost; hoar-frost.

قرال kiral, *s. t.* (*Slavonic*), A king, sovereign, emperor (title applied contemptuously to the sovereigns of Europe); یدی قرال yèdi-kiral, The seven kings of Christendom, *i.e.* all the kings; قرالیچه kiralicha, *s. t.* A European queen or empress, consort or regnant; قراللق kirallik, *s. t.* The regal quality and functions; a kingdom.

قرامان kāramān, *s. t.* Caramania; a big-tailed sheep, the Caramanian or Anatolian sheep.

قران kirān, *s. a.* Approach; junction; conjunction of planets; صاحبقران sāhib-kirān, *s. p.* (Lord of the conjunction) A successful monarch; صاحبقرانی sāhib-kirāni, *a. p.* Royal, imperial, august.

قرآن kür'ān, *s. a.* A reading; a book; The Book, the Coran, the Muhammedan Bible; قرآن کریم kür'āni-kèrīm, قرآن عظیم الشان kür'āni-"azīmu-'sh-shān, The noble Book, the glorious Book.

قرانته krànta, *s. t.* A middle-aged man.

قرانتینه kārantina, *s. t.* (*Italian*), Quarantine. [Dark.

قرانلق kāranlik, *s. t.* Darkness; —, *a. t.*

قراوله kāravèla, *s. t.* (*Italian*), A man-of-war, ship of the line.

قرائت kirā'at, *s. a.* A reading aloud; ا—, —et, *v.a.* To read aloud.

قرائن kārā'in, *s. pl. a.* (*of* قرینه kārīnē), Indications from whence inferences are drawn; inferences.

قرب kürb, *s. a.* Nearness, vicinity.

قرباچ kirbach, *s. t.* A riding whip.

قربان kürbān, *s. a.* An approaching near; sexual connexion; a means of approach, *i.e.* a sacrifice, a beast sacrificed or for sacrifice; قربان واقع او kürbān-wāki"-ol, To take place (sexual connexion); قربان بیرامی kürbān-bàyrami, The festival of sacrifices on the 10th of Zī-'l-hijjē.

قربه kirba, *s. a.* Two kinds of large leathern bottle or vessel for carrying water, one borne by men, the other by horses.

قرت kùrret, *s. a.* Coolness (of the eye, freedom from the redness caused by grief and weeping); قرت العين kùr-rétu-'l-''àyn, (Coolness of the eye) Joy, freedom from grief.

قرتال kàrtàl, *s. t.* A kind of vulture (*or* a kind of carrion-eating eagle?).

قرح kàrh, *s. a.* A wounding; ا—, —et, *v.a.* To wound; قرحه kàrha, *s. a.* A wound, sore.

قرص kùrss, *s. t.* A round cake; a pastile for fumigation.

قرض kàrz, *s. a.* A borrowing; a loan, any money lent; ا—, —et, *v.a.* To lend; to borrow.

قرطاس kìrtāss, *s. a.* Paper.

قرع kàr'', *s. a.* Knocking (at a door for admittance); ا—, —et, *v.a.* To knock for admittance.

قرعه kùr''à, *s. a.* A casting or drawing lots; the ballot; —چكمك, kùr''à--chèkmek, *v.n.* To draw lots; قرعه‌يه كيرمك kùr''àya-ghìrmek, *v.n.* To be one of those balloted for.

قرق kìrk, *a. t.* Forty; قرقنجی kìrkinji, *a. t.* The fortieth; قرق اياق kìrk-àyak, *s. t.* A millipede; قرق نردبان kìrk--(mèrdivèn), *s. t.* (Forty steps) An excellent kind of Damascus-steel sword-blade.

قرقمق kìrkmak (*aor.* قرقار kìrkar), *v.a.* To clip; to shear (sheep); قرقندی kìrkindi, *s. t.* Clippings.

قرلانغيچ kìrlanghìch, *s. t.* A swallow; a martin; —بالغی, —bàlighi, The flying fish.

قرمز kìrmiz, *s. a.* Cochineal; kermes, alkermes; قرمزی kìrmizi, *a. a.* Red.

قرن kàrn, *s. a.* An age, an indefinite period of time, ten, twenty, fifty years; a horn (of an animal); ذوالقرنين zū--'l-kàrnèyn, (The lord of two horns) An imaginary hero, based upon Alexander the Great, on account of the horns marked upon his coins.

قرنا kùrénā, *s. pl. a.* (*of* قرين kàrīn), Associates, companions; the personal suite of the sovereign.

قرناس kùrnāss, *a. p.* Subtle, sly.

قرنبيت kàrnabìt (*usually written* قرين بهار kàrīni-bàhār, *Near to spring*), *s. t.* A cauliflower.

قرنداش (*for* قارنداش) kàrndàsh (kàrin-dàsh, *vulg.* kàrdash), *s. t.* A brother; a sister; قيزقرنداش kìz-kàrdash, A sister; اركك قرنداش èrkek-kàrdash, A brother; سوت قرنداشی sùt-kàr-dashi, A foster-brother; اوز قرنداشی ūz-kàrdashi, An own brother or sister; اويكی قرنداش úwèghi-kàrdash, A step-brother or sister.

قرنستاد Krònstād, *s. t.* Cronstadt.

قرنفل kàrenfil (kàremfil), *s. a.* A clove (spice); a pink, carnation, picotee (flower).

قرنه (*or* قورنه) kùrna, *s. a.* A sink, or rather a kind of fixed marble basin in Turkish baths, in which the cold and boiling waters are mixed for use.

قرون kùrūn, *s. pl. a.* (*of* قرن kàrn), Ages, spaces of time.

قروی kùrévī (*fem.* قرویة kùrévìyyé), *a. a.* Rustic, pertaining to a village.

قره kArа, *a. t.* Black; dark-coloured; swarthy; —, *s. t.* Land (in distinction to water); قره اغاج kАra-Аghaj, An elm; elm-wood; یوزی قره yùzu-kАra, One who has reason to be ashamed; قره باش kАra-bАsh (Black head) A Christian bishop; قره بتاق kАra-bАtak, A cormorant; قره جکر kАra-jìghur, The liver; قره حما kАra-hùmmà, The black fever; قره طاوق kАra-tāwuk, The blackbird; قره قوش kАra-kùsh, The eagle; قره قوربغه kАra-kùrbАgha, The toad; قره قوللقجی kАra-kùllukju, (Formerly) a private in the janissary corps, stationed at a guard-house; قره قونجلوس kАra-kònjaloss, A hobgoblin; قره قیش kАra-kìsh, The coldest part of winter, mid-winter; قره کوز kАra-ghyùz, (Black-eye) The parallel of our *Punch* in Turkish puppet-shows; قره قولاق kАra-kūlАk, (Black ear) The lynx, *or* the jackal, *called also* the lion's provider; title of an officer attached to the Grand Vizier, and sent on important missions to other functionaries; قره جمله kАra-jùmlé, Addition (in arithmetic); قاپ قره kАp-kАra, Quite black; قره دن کتمك kАradan-ghitmek, To go by land; قره جه kАraja (See قراجه), *a. t.* Blackish, rather black.

قره لمق kАralamak (*aor.* قره لار kАralar), *v.a.* To write over as an exercise in caligraphy; to scribble over (paper); قره لمه kАralama, *s. t.* A copy, exercise in caligraphy; careless writing, scribbling. Villages, hamlets.

قری kùrà, *s. pl. a.* (*of* قریه kАrìyyé),

قریب kАrīb, *a. a.* Near; —, *s. a.* A near relative; عن قریب *or* عنقریب ʻʻàn-karib, *ad. a.* Soon, before long.

قریحه kАrīha, *s. a.* The initiative unprompted thought from which actions spring.

قریر kАrīr, *a. a.* Cool, free from redness and signs of grief (the eye); قریرالعین kАrīru-'l-ʻʻayn, *a. a.* (Whose eyes are free from all redness of grief), Happy.

قریم Kìrìm, *s. t.* The Crimea.

قرین kАrīn, *a. a.* Quite close, quite near; —, *s. a.* An associate, companion; سؤقرین sùʻi-kАrīn, A bad companion, evil associate; سعادتقرین sàʻʻādet-kАrīn, *a. p.* Whose companion is fortune, happiness, or prosperity; قرین قبول او kАrīni-kАbūl-òl, *v.n.* (To be the associate of acceptance) To be accepted.

قرینه kАrīné, *s. a.* An indication which, with reflection, points to some inference; قرینه ایله بولمق kАrīnè-ila-bùlmak, To infer, to judge from indications.

قریه kАrìyyé, *s. a.* A village; a hamlet.

قزارمق kìzàrmak (*aor.* قزارر kìzàrir), *v.n.* To become red, or brown; to grow red in the face, to flush; to become toasted or grilled brown; قزارتمق

kızàrtmak, *v.a.* To toast or grill; to cause to become red. [chant.

قزاز kAzzĀz (kAzez), *s. a.* A silk-merchant.

قزاق kızĀk, *s. t.* A sledge, sleigh; the ways on which ships are built; a wooden frame placed under boats for the purpose of hauling them up out of the water; a Cossack. [scarletina.

قزامق kızāmuk, *s. t.* The measles, or scarletina.

قزانج kAzAnj, *s. t.* Gain, profit; earnings.

قزانمق kAzAnmak (*aor.* قزانور kAzAnır), *v.a.* To gain; to earn.

قزح kūzàh, *s. a. in* قوس قزح kAvsi-kūzàh, (The bow of Kuzah) The rainbow.

قزغان kAzghĀn (kAzAn), *s. t.* A boiler, cauldron; قزغانجی (kAzAnjı), *s. t.* A boiler-maker.

قزقانج kızkAnj, *a. t.* Jealous; envious; —, *s. t.* Jealousy; envy.

قزقانمق kızkAnmak (*aor.* قزقانور kızkAnır), *v.n.* To be jealous; to be envious.

قزل kızıl, *a. t.* Red; —الما, kızıl-èlma, (Red apple) The (legendary) city of Rome; —يمورطه, kızıl-yımurta, (Red egg) The eggs, died red and hard-boiled, eaten by Christians in the East at Easter. [its tree, and its wood.

قزلجق kızıljık, *s. t.* The cornel-berry, its tree, and its wood.

قزلجه kızılja, *a. t.* Reddish; —, *s. t.* Rouge (cosmetic).

قس kıss, *v.a. imper.* Be (it) judged, *in* وقس علی هذا vè-kıss-"àlà-hāzā, *ad. a.* (And be (the others) judged by this) And so forth, and so on, et cetera.

قسام kAsssām, *s. a.* A distributor; an officer of the ecclesiastical court, whose duty it is to apportion the property of deceased persons among the heirs.

قساوت kAssāvèt, *s. a.* Grief, regret; —ا, —et, *and* —چکمك, kAssāvèt--chèkmek, *v.n.* To grieve, feel regret.

قسراق kıssrAk, *s. t.* A mare.

قسط kısst, *s. a.* Justice, equity; a share, portion; يوم القسط yùvma-'l-kısst, *or* قسط اليوم kıssta-'l-yùvm, *ad. a.* According to the portion falling to each day. [balance, pair of scales.

قسطاس kısstAss, *s. a.* Justice, equity; a balance, pair of scales.

قسطنطنيه Kòsstantanıyyé, *s. a.* Constantinople.

قسم kAssem, *s. a.* An oath; the taking an oath; ا—, —et, *v.n.* To swear, take an oath; —, kıssm, *s. a.* A part, portion; a kind, the generality of any sort of thing; as, قاری قسمی kAri--kıssmi, Womankind, عرب قسمی "àrab-kıssmi, Arabs in general.

قسمت kıssmet, *s. a.* Division, apportioning, distributing; a lot; خارج قسمت khāriji-kıssmet, The quotient of arithmetical division.

قسوت kAssvet, *s. a.* Hardness or want of moral feeling; قسوت قلب kAssvèti-kàlb, Hardness of heart.

قسيس kAssīss, *s. a.* A Christian priest or monk.

قشاغی kAshaghi, *s. t.* A currycomb.

قشانمق kAshAnmak (*aor.* قشانور kAshAnır), *v.n.* To stale (a horse); —, *v.p.* To be groomed, curried (a horse).

قشر kìshr (kÀshr), *s. a.* Bark, peel.

قشلا kìshla, قشلاغ kìshlāgh, قشلاق kìsh-lÀk, *s. t.* A winter quarters; winter pasturage for cattle; a barracks for troops. [*v.n.* To winter.

قشلامق kìshlamak (*aor.* قشلار kìshlar),

قصاب kÀsssāb (kÀssAb), *s. a.* A butcher; قصابيه kÀssAbìyyÉ, *s. t.* Butcher's fee.

قصار kÀsssār, *s. a.* A fuller; a bleacher.

قصاج kìssAj, *s. t.* A pair of pincers, pliers, forceps, or blacksmith's tongs.

قصارت kìssāret, *s. a.* The fuller's or bleacher's art.

قصاص kìssAss, *s. a.* The application of the *lex talionis*, especially in the precept of "life for life;" ا—, —et, *v.a.* To punish according to the *lex talionis*, especially in putting to death.

قصالمق kìssAlmak (*aor.* قصالور kìssA-lìr), *v.n.* To shrink in length, become shorter, be made shorter, be shortened; قصالتمق kìssAltmak, *v.a.* To shorten, make shorter.

قصائد kÀssā'id, *s. pl. a.* (*of* قصيده kÀssīdÉ), Long poems.

قصب kÀssAb, *s. a.* A cane, a reed.

قصبه kÀssAba, *s. a.* A town, borough, burgh.

قصد kÀssd, *s. a.* A determination, resolution, fixed purpose, design; an evil intent; an evil attempt; ا—, —et, *v.a.* To resolve, to purpose; —, *v.n.* To make an evil attempt (against some one's life); قصداً kÀssdan, عن قصد "àn-kÀssdin, *ad. a.* Designedly; with malice prepense.

قصر kÀssr, *s. a.* A shortening, a pulling in or back; a castle; a palace; a royal pavilion; ا—, —et, *v.a.* To shorten, to pull in or back; قصر يدا kÀssri-yèd-et, *v.n.* (To draw back the hand) To withdraw (from any business or possession); —, kìssr, *a. t.* Barren (animal). [tornado, hurricane.

قصرغه kÀssìrgha, *s. t.* A whirlwind,

قصص kìssass, *s. pl. a.* (*of* قصه kìsssa), Anecdotes, short histories, tales.

قصعه kÀss"a, *s. a.* A platter; ارباب قصعه èrbÀbì-kÀss"a, Trencher-friends.

قصق kìssìk, *a. a.* Pinched up or in, not loose and free (the voice, &c.).

قصمق kìssmak (*aor.* قصار kìssar), *v.a.* To pinch (with anything but the fingers), to squeeze violently, to jam; قصلمق kìssìlmak, *v.n.* To be hoarse (the voice); —, *v.p.* To be pinched or jammed.

قصور kùssūr, *s. a.* Want, deficiency; a fault; a defect; a surplus, remainder; —, *s. pl. a.* (*of* قصر kÀssr), Castles; palaces; pavilions; ا—, —et, *v.n.* To fail (in points of duty), to be wanting.

قصه kìssa, *a. t.* Short; —, kìsssa, *s. a.* An anecdote, short history, tale; an event, occurrence; القصه èl-kìsssa, *ad. a.* In fine, to make short of a long story; قصه‌دن حصه چيقارمق kìsssa-dan-hìsssa-chìkàrmak, To derive a moral from a tale; قصه‌جق kìssajìk, a. t. (A) short little (thing); قصه‌جه kìssaja, a. t. Shortish; قصه‌خوان kìsssa-khān, s. p. A narrator.

قصیده kàssīdé, s. a. A long poem.

قصیر kàssīr, a. a. Short.

قضا kàzā, s. a. The charge and functions of a judge; the separate district subject to a judge's jurisdiction; God's decree or fiat; an accident; a fulfilling, or paying (duty or debt); a paying up, squaring up (of arrears); ا—, —et, v.a. To fulfil, pay (a duty or debt); pay up, make up; square up (arrears); قضای حاجت ا kàzāyi-hājet-et, v.n. To ease nature, do one's jobs; قضاوقدر kàzā-u-kàder, Fate and destiny; قضای مبرم kàzāyi-mùbrèm, A fatal accident; کورینور کورنمز قضالر ghyùrunur-ghyùrunmàz-kàzālar, Accidents which can and which cannot be foreseen; واجب القضا vwājibu-'l-kàzā, a. a. Which must or ought to be paid or fulfilled; قضاایله kàzā-ila, ad. t. قضارا kàzārā, ad. p. By accident, by chance.

قضات kùzāt, s. pl. a. (of قاضی kàzī), [Judges.

قضایا kàzāyā, s. pl. a. (of قضیه kàzìyyé), Propositions (in logic); matters.

قضیه kàzìyyé, s. a. A proposition (in [logic); a matter.

قطار kàtār, s. a. A string (of mules, horses, or camels).

قطاع kìtā'', or قطاع دائره kìtā''i-dā'iré, s. a. A sector of a circle, comprised between two radii and the intervening portion of the circumference; —, kùttā'', s. pl. a. (of قاطع kàti''), They who cut, in قطاع الطریق kùttā''ù-'t-tàrīk, Brigands, highwaymen.

قطائف kàtā'if, s. pl. a. (of قطیفه kàtīfé), Velvets; —, (kàdā'if), s. t. Several sweet dishes, or the principal material of them; تل قطائفی tèl-kàdā'ifi, A preparation like fresh-made vermicelli; یصی قطائف yàsssi-kàdā'if, A kind of crumpet; اتمك قطائفی (ekmek)-kàdā'ifi, Pain-perdu.

قطب kùtb, s. a. A pole (of a circle, the earth, the heaven); a man of mark, leader of a religious community; قطب شمال kùtbu-shìmāl, The north pole; قطب جنوب kùtbu-jènūb, The south pole.

قطر kùtr, s. a. The diameter (of a circle).

قطران kàtrān, s. a. Tar.

قطره kàtra, s. a. A drop (of fluid).

قطع kàt'', s. a. A cutting; a section; ا—, —et, v.a. To cut; to cut off; to cut out; to intersect; to stop, put a stop to, interrupt; to do away with; a passing over (distances in travelling); to decide, to determine, to fix; قطع زائد kàt''i-zā'id, The hyperbola; قطع مكافی kàt''i-mùkyāfi, The parabola; قطع ناقص kàt''i-nākiss, The ellipse; قطع طریق ا kàt''i-tàrīk-et, v.n. To act the highwayman; قطع امید ا kàt''i-ùmīd-et, v.n. To lose all hope, to despair; قطع علاقه ا kàt''i-''àlāka-

-et, *v.n.* To cease from all relation, intercourse, or affection; قطع مسافه ا kAt"*i*-mèssāfé-et, *v.n.* To pass over distance; قطعا kAt"ā, *ad. a.* Not at all; never.

قطعه kìt"à, *s. a.* A piece, portion; a segment of a circle; a single one (of many things); ایکی قطعه سفینه ìki--kìt"à-sèfìné, Two *sail* of ships; بش قطعه طوب bèsh-kìt"à-tòp, Five *pieces* of artillery. [and cotton.

قطنى kŭtnī, *s. a.* A kind of stuff of silk

قطیفه (kAdīfé), *s. a.* Velvet; قطیفه چیچکی kAdīfé-chìchè*gh*i, The French or African marigold.

قعده kà"dé, *s. a.* Repose by sitting down, *in* ذى القعده Zī-'l-kà"dé, (The month of repose) The eleventh month of the Arabian year.

قعر kà"r, *s. a.* The bottom of anything deep; ناقعریاب nā-kà"r-yāb, *a. p.* Unfathomable, bottomless, of which the bottom cannot be found.

قعود kŭ"ūd, *s. a.* A sitting down; —ا, —et, *v.n.* To sit down; to rise to a sitting posture. [of fire.

قغلجم *or* قغلجیم kìghìljìm, *s. t.* A spark

قفا kAfā, *s. a.* The back of the head; the head, skull, pate; برینك قفاسنى یارمق bìrining-kAfassin*i*-yàrm*a*k, To break one's skull; قفادار kAfadār, *s. p.* A friend, comrade, companion, associate.

قفتان kAftAn, *s. t.* A kind of robe formerly worn; a robe of honour.

قفس kAfess, *s. a.* A cage; a wire or lattice-work; a kind of window-blind of lattice-work; anything quite full of holes; a suite of apartments in the Sultan's palace, allotted to the younger princes of the blood. [bolt, latch.

قفل kŭfl, *s. a.* (*pl.* قفول kŭfūl), A lock,

ققرداق kìkirdAk, *s. t.* Gristle.

ققنس kAknuss, *s. a.* The phœnix.

قلاب kŭllAb, *s. a.* A hook.

قلابدان kìlAbd*a*n, *s. t.* Gilt, silver, or copper wire.

قلاده kìlādé, *s. a.* A necklace.

قلاش kAllāsh, *s. p.* A rogue, rascal.

قلاع kìlā", *s. pl. a.* (*of* قلعه kàl"a), Forts, castles, fortresses, fortified places.

قلاغوز kìlà*gh*uz, *s. a.* A guide; a pilot; a small gimlet, wimble, or auger; a grooved surgical instrument for guiding the point of a cutting instrument; قلاغوزلق kìlà*gh*uzluk, *s. t.* The functions of a guide or pilot; قلاغوزلق ا kìlà*gh*uzluk-et, *v.n.* To act as guide or pilot. [(of a sharp instrument).

قلاغى kìlà*ghi*, *s. t.* The edge, fine edge

قلان (*for* قالان) kAlAn, *act. part.* (*of* قالمق kAlm*a*k), Which rests, remains; باقى قلان bAk*i*-kAlAn, *a. t.* Which remains over.

قلاى kAlay, *s. t.* Tin (metal, not tin in sheets; this latter is called تنكه tènékè); قلایجى kAlayj*i*, *s. t.* A tinner of copper vessels; قلایلمق kAlayla-m*a*k, *v.a.* To tin; قلایلنمق kAlayl*a*n-m*a*k, *v.p.* To be tinned.

قلب kàlb, *s. a.* The heart; the centre or main body (of an army); a reversing; a changing; ا—, —et, *v.a.* To reverse; to change; — (*for* قالپ), kàlp, *a. t.* False, forged; insincere, untrue; قلباً kàlb*an*, *ad. a.* At heart; from the heart, cordially; قلبی kàlbī (*fem.* قلبیه kàlbìyyé), *a. a.* Pertaining to the heart; قلبزن kàlbzèn (kàlpazàn), *s. p.* A forger of money; a [knave.

قلبه kùlubé, *s. t.* A hut.

قلپاق kàlpak, *s. t.* Various kinds of cap formerly worn in Turkey.

قلت kìllèt, *s. a.* Smallness of number or quantity, scarcity. [cuckold.

قلتبان kàlt*a*bān, *s. p.* A contented

قلج kìlìj, *s. t.* A sabre, sword; دال قلج dàl-kìlìj, *s. t.* A kind of bravo or adventurous trooper; قلجدن کچورمك kìlìjd*a*n-ghèchirmek, *v.a.* To put to the sword, slay with the sword, massacre; قلج چکمك kìlìj-chèk-mek, *v.n.* To draw a sword; قلج بالغی kìlìj-bàl*ighi*, The sword-fish; قلجلمه kìlìjl*ama*, *s. t.* The edgewise position of a flat substance; قلجلمهسنه kìlìj-l*amassina*, *ad. t.* Edgewise; قلججی kìlìjji, *s. t.* A sword-cutler; قلجخانه kìlìj-khāné, *s. p.* A government sword-manufactory; قلجلو kìlìjli, *a. t.* Armed with a sword.

قلچق (*for* قیلچق) kìlch*i*k, *s. t.* The very small bones in fish; قلچقلو kìlch*i*kl*i*, *a. t.* Having many small hair-like bones (a fish).

قلع kàl'', *s. a.* A pulling up or out; ا—, —et, *v.a.* To pull up or out, eradicate.

قلعه kàl''a, (kàlé), *s. a.* A castle, fort, fortress, fortified place; a square (of infantry). [outer cover.

قلف kìl*i*f, *s. t.* Any long bag-shaped

قلفات or قلفت kàl*a*fàt, *s. t.* A caulker; the caulking (of ships); ا—, —et, *v.a.* To caulk; —یری, —yèri, *s. t.* A place were ships are hauled down and caulked. [Peaks; spires, towers.

قلل kùlèl, *s. pl. a.* (*of* قله kùllé),

قلم kàlem, *s. a.* A pen; a reed pen; a pencil; a camel-hair brush; a chisel; a cutting (for a graft or planting); a public office where many clerks assemble; an item; توی قلم tùy-kàlem, A quill-pen; قیل قلم kìl-kàlem, A hair-pencil; قورشون قلم kùrshun-kàlem, A lead-pencil; طاش قلم tàsh-kàlem, A slate-pencil; دیوان قلمی dīwān--kàlémi, The office of the Imperial chancery; &c.; قلمه کلمك kàléma--ghèlmek, To be written or described; قلمه المق kàlém*a*-àlm*a*k, *v.a.* To write, compose in the first instance; قلمکار kàlem-ky*ā*r, A jeweller's engraver; a painter of handkerchiefs; ornamental engraving on gold, &c.; —, *a. t.* Hand-painted (handkerchief, &c.); قلمدان kàlemdān, *s. p.* A pencase; قلمتراش kàlemtràsh, *s. p.* A Turkish penknife; قلمرو kàlemrèv, *s. p.* The limit of jurisdiction; قلمزن kàlem-zèdé, *a. p.* Written; قلميه kàlémìyyé, *s. a.* Office fees.

قلمق (*for* قيلمق) kìlmak (*aor.* قلور kìlir, قيلار kìlar), *v.a.* See قيلمق.

قلندر kAlendèr, *s. p.* A kind of Muhammedan friar. [Hearts.

قلوب kùlūb, *s. pl. a.* (*of* قلب kAlb),

قلوچقه kùlùchka, *s. a.* A hen sitting on eggs or tending chickens; قلوچقه‌يه اوطورمق kùlùchkaya-òturmak, *v.n.* To sit (a hen on eggs).

قله kùllé (kùlé), *s. a.* A tower; a spire; a mountain peak.

قليل kālīl, *a. a.* Little (in number, quantity, or duration), few; قليلاً kAlīlan, *ad. a.* Little, a little; seldom.

قمار kùmAr, *s. a.* Gambling of any kind; —اويناميق, kùmār-òynamak, *v.n.* To gamble; قمارباز kùmār-bAz, *s. p.* قمارجى kùmārji, *s. t.* A gambler.

قماش kùmAsh, *s. a.* Any cotton, linen, or silk textile fabric; the texture (of any such stuff).

قماشمق kàmAshmak (*aor.* قمشور kAmAshir), *v.n.* To be dazzled (the eyes); to be set on edge (the teeth); قماشدرمق kàmAshdirmak (*aor.* قماشدرر kàmAshdirir), *v.a.* To dazzle (the eyes); to set on edge (the teeth).

قمر kAmer, *s. a.* The moon; قمرى kAmérī, *a. a.* Lunar; قمريه kAmérìyyé, *s. a.* An arbour, summer-house in trellis-work.

قمرى kùmru, *s. t.* A dove.

قمع kAm", *s. a.* A felling, striking to the ground; ا—, —et, *v.a.* To fell, knock down.

قمقمه kùmkuma, *s. a.* A squat round bottle with a long neck.

قمل kAml, *s. a.* A louse.

قملدامق kìmildamak (*aor.* قملدار kìmildar), *and* قملدانمق kìmildAnmak (*aor.* قملدانور kìmildAnir), *v.n.* To move, to have, or be in, motion; قملداتمق kìmildAtmak (*aor.* قملدادر kìmildAdir), *v.a.* To move, cause to move.

قمو kAmu, *s. t.* (*old*), The whole, all, all things. [shift.

قميص kAmīss, *s. a.* A shirt, chemise,

قناد kAnAd, *s. t.* A wing; a fold (of a door, window, or shutter); قنادلو kAnAdli, *a. t.* Winged.

قناديل kAnādīl, *s. pl. a.* (*of* قنديل kAndīl), Lamps. [bird.

قناريه kànàriya, *s. t.* A canary, canary-

قناطر kAnātir, *s. pl. a.* (*of* قنطره kAntara), Arches, bridges, viaducts, aqueducts.

قناعت kAnā"at, *s. a.* Content, contentment; ا—, —et, *v.n.* To be contented, satisfied. [bark (drug).

قناقنا kìna-kìna, *s. t.* Peruvian bark,

قنامق kìnamak (*aor.* قنار kìnar), *v.a.* To blame, find fault with (a person).

قنب kùnnèb, *s. a.* Hemp.

قند kànd, *s. a.* Sugar, sugar-candy; قندى kàndī, *a. a.* Of sugar; pertaining to sugar.

قنداق kùndAk, *s. t.* Swaddling-clothes; the stock (of any portable fire-arms); the carriage (of a cannon on board ship); a bundle of incendiary rags, oakum, &c.; قنداقده‌اول kùndakda-òl, To be in swaddling-clothes (equivalent to our being in long-clothes); — صوقمق kùndak-sòkmak, To introduce a prepared bundle of incendiary substances.

قندرمق kìndirmak (*aor.* قندرر kìndirir), *v.a.* (*provincial*), To excite to anger or discontent.

قندز kùnduz, *s. t.* The beaver(?); the otter(?); —بوجكی, kùnduz-bùjèghi, Cantharides; —خایه‌سی, kùndūz--khàyassi, A musk-bag, castoreum.

قنده kànda, *ad. t.* (*old*), Where? wherever, wheresoever.

قندهار Kàndàhār, *s. p.* Kandahar.

قندیل kàndīl, *s. a.* A lamp.

قنطار kàntār, *s. a.* A steelyard; a quintal or hundredweight, varying in different places, that of Constantinople being 44 okes, or about 126 lbs. avoirdupois. [bridle).

قنطارمه kàntarma, *s. t.* A bit (of a

قنطره kàntara, *s. a.* An arch; a bridge; a viaduct or aqueduct.

قنغال kànghal, *s. t.* A coil.

قنغی kànghi (hànghi), *pron. t.* Which? which one? whichever; قنغیمز kànghimiz, Which of us? whichever one of us; قنغیكز kànghingiz, Which of you? whichever of you; قنغیسی kànghissi, Which? which of them? whichever one of them; قنغیلر kànghilar, Which ones?

قنی kàni (hàni), *ad. t.* Where? where is it?

قوا kùwā, *s. pl. a.* (*of* قوت kùvvet), Powers, strengths, mights; senses, faculties.

قواص kàvwàss, *s. t.* A kind of policeman.

قواطه kàwata, *s. t.* A round wooden platter; an unripe, exceedingly bitter kind of love-apple or tomata.

قواعد kàwā‘‘id, *s. pl. a.* (*of* قاعده kā‘‘idé), Rules; bases.

قواق kàwak, *s. t.* A poplar tree.

قوال kàvwāl, *s. a.* A very talkative person. [Turkey).

قواله Kàvālla, *s. t.* Cavalla (town of, in

قوام kìwām, *s. a.* The proper state in which a thing should be; قوامه كلمك kìwāma-ghèlmek, *v.n.* To acquire the proper state.

قوان kòwan, *s. t.* A hive; an outer mould or case (as for squibs, rockets, &c.); اری قوانی àri-kòwani, A bee-hive; the flower fox-glove; يلقوان (*for* يلقوغان), yèlkowan (*for* yèlkoghan), A swift-flying sea-bird which passes in flocks up and down the Bosphorus close to the water, and called by Europeans "souls of the damned"; the minute-hand (of a watch, &c.).

قوانوس kàwanòss, *s. t.* A jar, pot, gallipot. [kānūn), Laws.

قوانين kàwānīn, *s. pl. a.* (*of* قانون

قوپارمق kòparmak (*aor.* قوپارر kòpàrir), *v.a.* To tear or break off or away; to pluck, gather; to obtain by pertinacity; قیامت قوپارمق kỳāmèt-kòparmak, *v.n.* To make a great fuss (*lit.* to bring the resurrection about).

قوپچه kòpch*a*, *s. t.* A large hook and eye, a clasp.

قوپمق kòpm*a*k (*aor.* قوپار kòpar), *v.n.* To break (as a rope, branch, &c.); to start (from a spot in great haste); برینك عودی قوپمق bìrining-"ùdu--kòpm*a*k, To burst (any one's gall-bladder), to be extremely frightened; قیامت قوپمق kỳāmèt-kòpm*a*k, *v.n.* To take place (the resurrection); to be (a great row, fuss, confusion).

قوت kǔvvet, *s. a.* Strength, power, might; a sense, faculty; vigour; —, kūt, *s. a.* Food; قوت لایموت kūti-lā--yèmūt, Food just sufficient to keep body and soul together; قوت باصره kùvvéti-bāssiré, The faculty of sight; —شامه, kǔvvéti-shāmmé, The power of smelling; —سامعه, kǔvvéti-sāmi"*a*, The hearing; —ذائقه, kǔvvéti-zā'ika, The tasting faculty; —لامسه, kǔvvéti--lāmissé, The power of touch; — حافظه kǔvvéti-hāfiz*a*, The power of memory.

قوتارمق kàwtarm*a*k (*aor.* قوتارر kàwtàrir), *v.a.* To shift (anything) from one vessel to another.

قوجاق kǔjàk, *s. t.* The space or quantity embraced by the two arms; the embrace; a double armful; the lap, or bosom (as though encircled by the two arms); قوجاقلمق kǔjàkl*a*m*a*k, *v.a.* To take into one's arms (either to embrace or to carry); to encircle with the arms, to reach round (anything) with both arms.

قوجامق kòjam*a*k (*aor.* قوجار kòjar), *v.n.* To become old in years or in appearance.

قوجمان kòj*a*man, *a. t.* Large, immense.

قوجه kòj*a*, *s. t.* A husband; —, *a. t.* Old in age; large in size; ای قوجه حریف āy-kòj*a*-hèrif! There's a good fellow! There's a trump! قوجه یه وارمق kòj*aya*-vàrm*a*k, *v.n.* To be married (a girl or woman), to get married; قوجه سی اول kòj*assi*-òl, *v.n.* To be married (a woman), to have or possess a husband; قوجه یه ویرمك kòj*aya*-vèrmek, *v.a.* To marry (a girl) to a husband, give in marriage; قوجه قاری kòj*a*-kāri, An old woman, قوجه یمشی kòj*a*-yèmishi, *s. t.* (Old man's fruit) The arbutus, or tree-strawberry. [Odessa.

قوجه بك Kòj*a*-Bè*gh*, *s. t.* The town of

قوچ kòch, *s. t.* A ram.

قوچاچ kòch*a*ch, *s. t.* A coachman.

قوچی kòchu, *s. t.* A kind of large carriage.

قودورمق kǔdurm*a*k (*aor.* قودورر kǔ-durur), *v.n.* To go mad, be seized with hydrophobia (a dog); —, kòdur-m*a*k (*aor.* kòdurur), *v.a.* To cause or allow to place. [Mad (a dog).

قودوز kǒduz, *s. t.* Hydrophobia; —, *a. t.*

قور kòr, *s. t.* Clear, bright, live coal of

fire; —, *a. t.* Clear, bright, smokeless fire.

قوراق kùrʌk, *a. t.* Dry (weather); parched (soil); قوراقلق kùrʌklik, *s. t.* Drought.

قوربغه kùrbʌgha (*for* قوروبغه kùrʋ-bʌgha, The naked tortoise or batrachian), *s. t.* A frog; قره قوربغه kʌra-kùrbʌgha, The toad.

قورت kùrt, *s. t.* A wolf; a maggot; قورت بهاری kùrt-bàhàri, *s. t.* The privet; اسکی قورت èsski-kùrt, (An old wolf) A well-known rascal; ایپك قوردی ìpèk-kùrdʋ, The silk-worm; قورتلنمق kùrtlanmak, *v.n.* To become maggoty or worm-eaten.

قورتارمق kùrtarmak (*aor.* قورتارر kùrtarir), *v. a.* To save, deliver, obtain the salvation of (anything from danger or any unpleasantness); to save (a dealer) from loss, to repay, pay (for expense and trouble).

قورتلمق kùrtʋlmak (*aor.* قورتلور kùrtʋlʋr), *v.n.* To be saved, delivered; to escape; قورتلش kùrtʋlʋsh, *s. t.* A mode or way of escape, deliverance, salvation.

قورساق kùrsak, *s. t.* The craw or crop (of a fowl).

قورشون kùrshʋn, *s. t.* Lead (metal); a [bullet.

قورصان kùrsān, *s. t.* A man-of-war; a piratical ship; a letter-of-marque ship, privateer.

قورطو Kòrto, *s. t.* The town of Corinth.

قورفه Kòrfa, *s. t.* Corfu.

قورق kòrʋk, *s. t.* Sour grapes, green grapes; —صویی, kòrʋk-sʋyʋ, Ver-[juice.

قورقاق kòrkak, *s. t.* A coward.

قورقمق kòrkmak (*aor.* قورقار kòrkar), *v.n.* To be afraid, to fear; قورقتمق kòrkʋtmak (*aor.* قورقودر kòrkʋdʋr), *v.a.* To frighten; to threaten.

قورقنج kòrkʋnj, *a. t.* Fearful, frightful, terrible, dreadful, causing fear, dangerous.

قورقو kòrkʋ, *s. t.* Fear, fright; any fearful thing; a threat, a menace; an alarm; danger, peril; —ویرمك, kòrkʋ-vèrmek, *v.n.* To frighten; to alarm; to menace, threaten (by words); قورقولق kòrkʋlʋk, *s. t.* A scarecrow; a balustrade, railings, banister, guard, parapet; قورقولو kòrkʋlʋ, *a. t.* Fearful, frightful; dangerous.

قورمق kùrmak (*aor.* قورار kùrar), *v.a.* To place anything in working order; to set (a trap, &c.); to wind up (a watch, &c.); to lay (foundations); to pitch (a tent); to erect (a scaffold, &c.); to plan (in thought); —, *v.n.* To be pensive, moody, melancholy; قورلمق kùrʋlmak, *v.n.* To set one's self up, assume airs; —, *v.p.* To be set, wound up, laid, pitched, planned, &c.

قورندی kùrʋndʋ, *s. t.* Vain fears or imaginations.

قورنه kùrna, *s. t.* See قرنه.

قورو *or* قوری kùrʋ, *a. t.* Dry (not wet); dry (not fresh, fruit, &c.); mere, sheer, unaccompanied with anything to add to the value or agreeableness, as, قورو اتمك kŭrŭ-(èkmek), Dry bread, bread with no condiment; —لاف, kŭrŭ-lāf, Mere words; —, kòru, *and* قورولق kòruluk, *s. t.* A preserve, any wood or forest in which wood must not be cut, or meadow kept for hay into which cattle must not be turned by the public generally.

قوروت kŭrvèt, *s. t.* (*Italian*), A corvette; —, kŭrut, *s. t.* A kind of dried curds.

قوروم kŭrum, *s. t.* Soot.

قورومساق kŭrumsàk, *s. t.* A contented cuckold.

قورومق *or* قوريمق kŭrumak (*aor.* قورر *or* قورور kŭrur), *v.n.* To dry, become dry; to dry up; to be parched; —, kòrumak, *v.a.* To preserve (from injury of any kind), to shield, protect; قوروتمق kŭrutmak (*aor.* قورودر kŭrudur), *v.a.* To dry, cause to become dry; to parch; —, kòrutmak, *v.a.* To manage so that something shall be shielded from any injury.

قوز kòz, قوزاق kòzak, *s. t.* A cone or apple (of any cone-bearing tree).

قوزغون kŭzghun, *s. t.* The raven; قوزغونى سياه kŭzghunī-sīyāh, *a. t.* Raven black.

قوزه kòza, *s. t.* The ball spun by the silkworm, the cocoon.

قوزى kŭzu, *s. t.* A lamb; قوزيم kŭzum! My lamb! My dear! My dear sir! Kind sir! (term of request); قوزى قولاغى kŭzu-kŭlāghi, (Lamb's ear) Sorrel (plant).

قوس kāvss, *s. a.* A bow; an arc of a circle; —قزح, kāvssi-kŭzàh, The rainbow.

قوسقون kŭsskun, *s. t.* The crupper strap of a saddle or harness.

قوش kŭsh, *s. t.* A bird; دوه قوشى dèvé-kŭshu, (Camel-bird) The ostrich; قوش قونمز kŭsh-kònmàz, (Birds do not perch on it) A kind of wild prickly asparagus; قوش اوزومى kŭsh-ùzumu, Small dried currants (for puddings, &c.); قوشباز kŭshbāz, *s. t.* A bird-catcher, bird-seller, bird-fancier.

قوشاتمق kŭshātmak (*aor.* قوشادر kŭshādir), *v.a.* To surround; to wind or fasten round the waist; قوشانمق kŭshānmak (*aor.* قوشانور kŭshānir), *v.a.* To wind or fasten round one's own waist; —, *v.n.* To dress or arm one's self; —, *v.p.* To be wound or fastened round the waist; to be surrounded.

قوشاق kŭshàk, *s. t.* Any sash, shawl, or belt, worn round the waist; any diagonal piece of timber or iron which gives firmness to posts or beams, a brace.

قوشلق kŭshluk, *s. t.* (Bird-time) The morning about breakfast-time; قبا قوشلق kāba-kŭshluk, *s. t.* The time when the sun is drawing towards the meridian.

قوشمق kòshmak (*aor.* قوشار kòshar), *v.n.* To run (an animal or man); —, *v.a.* To put (horses, &c.) to (carriages,

&c.); to appoint as a guide, escort, &c.; قوشلمق kòshulmak, *v.p.* To be such that one may run; to be put to (horses); to be appointed as guide, escort, &c.; قوششمق kòshushmak, *v.n. recip.* To run all together towards one place.

قوشى kòshu, *s. t.* A race.

قوصره kAwsara, *s. a.* A kind of large mat basket, generally sent with rice from Egypt.

قوصمق kùssmak (*aor.* قوصار kùssar), *v.n.* and *a.* To vomit, spue.

قوطور Kòtūr, *s. p.* The town of Kotur.

قوطى kùtu, *s. t.* A small box or case; انفيه قوطيسى ènfìyyé - kùtussu, A snuff-box.

قوغالمق kòghAlamak (*aor.* قوغالار kòghAlar), *v.a.* To pursue.

قوغش kòghush, *s. t.* A ward, a general sleeping-room; a beam for supporting a floor.

قوغمق kòghmak (*aor.* قوغار kòghar), *v.a.* To drive away.

قوغو kùghu, *s. t.* A swan.

قوغوق kùghuk, *s. t.* A cuckoo.

قوغه kògha, *s. t.* A bucket.

قوف kòf, *s. t.* Dried up and hollow inside (fruit).

قوقلامق kòklamak (*aor.* قوقلار kòklar), *v.a.* To smell at, sniff at; قوقلاتمق kòklatmak, *v.a.* To cause or allow to smell or sniff at.

قوقله kùkla, *s. t.* A doll.

قوقمق kòkmak (*aor.* قوقار kòkar), *v.n.* To smell, have a smell, to stink; to become putrid or stinking; قوقوتمق kòkutmak (*aor.* قوقودر kòkudur), *v.a.* To cause to emit a smell, especially a bad smell; to cause to be pervaded with a smell.

قوقو kòku, *s. t.* A smell, odour; a scent, a perfume; a stink; a taint; a smack, a tack, the slightest degree of anything; قوقولو kòkulu, *a. t.* Having a smell (good or bad); scented, perfumed, sweet-smelling.

قوقونه kòkona, *s. t.* (*Greek*), A Greek lady or woman; the lady of the house, the mistress.

قوكشمق kòngushmak (*aor.* قوكشور kòngushur), *v.n.* To hold converse, to chat; to associate; قوكشدرمق kòngushdurmak, *v.a.* To cause or allow to converse or associate; to introduce (persons to one another).

قوكشى kòngshu (kòmshu), *s. t.* A neighbour; قونى قوكشى or قوكى قوكشى kònu - kòmshu, Friends and neighbours, near and distant neighbours.

قول kAvl, *s. a.* An assertion; one's words, what one says; a compact, agreement, understanding; a system, or view (in science); —, kòl, *s. t.* The arm; a branch (of anything which has ramifications, but not of trees or plants); a patrol; —, kùl, *s. t.* A servant, slave, bondsman; a janissary (in bye-gone days); man, mankind (God's servant); ا—, kAvl-et, *v.a.* To agree, make an agreement; قولى kAvlī (*fem.* قوليه kAvlìyyé), *a. a.* Verbal, pertaining to words, or opinions; قوليات kAvlìyyAt, *s. pl. a.*

Mere verbal assertions; قول کزمك kòl-ghèzmek, *v.n.* To go the rounds, to patrol; قره قول kàra-kòl, قراغول kàraghol, *and* قراول kàradl, *s. t.* A guard of several soldiers or policemen; قره قولخانه kàra-kòl-khānè, *s. t.* A guardhouse; قول تیموری kòl-dèmiri, *s. t.* A bar of iron used for closing a door or gate; قولکز kùlunguz, Your servant, I; قوللق kùlluk, *s. t.* Servantship; a guardhouse.

قولاچ kūlach, *s. t.* A fathom.

قولاق kūlak, *s. t.* The ear; a dwarf handle; a small piece of paper tacked on to the corner of a document with any little note relating thereto; قوزی قولاغی kūzu-kūlaghi, (Lamb's-ear) Sorrel (plant); —اصمق, kūlak-àssmak, —ویرمك, kūlak-vèrmek, *v.n.* To give ear, lend an ear, listen; برینك قولاغنه سویلمك bìrining-kūlaghina-sùwèylémek, *v.a.* To whisper in one's ear; قولاغنه قومق kūlaghina-kòmak, *v.a.* To put (some tale) into one's head.

قولان kòlan, *s. t.* A saddle-girth.

قولای kòlay, *a. t.* Easy, not difficult; —, *s. t.* A means, way (to do or obtain anything); قولایلق kòlaylik, *s. t.* Easiness, facility; convenience; قولایلقلو kòlaylikli, *a. t.* Convenient, handy; قولای کله kòlay-ghèlé, May (your work) come easy (to you)! قولایلنمق kòlaylanmak, *v.n.* To become easy, to draw near to being accomplished.

قولبه kùlubé, *s. t.* A hut.

قولپ kùlp, *s. t.* An arched handle.

قولتق kòltuk, *s. t.* The armpit; the end of a sofa or ottoman, the arm of an arm-chair; قولتقلو kòltuklu, *s. t.* An arm-chair; —, *a. t.* Having arms (a chair); —دینکی, kòltuk-dèynéghi, *s. t.* A crutch; برینك قولتغنه کیرمك bìrining-kòltughuna-ghìrmek, *v.n.* To support anyone under the arms in walking; قولتقجی kòltukju, *s. t.* A pedlar, hawker.

قوللانمق kùllanmak (*aor.* قوللانور kùllanir), *v.a.* To use; to employ; قوللاندرمق kùllandirmak, *v.a. caus.* To cause or allow to employ or be employed; قوللانلمق kùllanilmak, *v.n.* To be such as can be used; قوللانلش kùllanilish, *s. t.* A manner of being used or employed; قوللانلشلو kùllanilishli, *a. t.* Convenient, fit or apt for use.

قولنج kùlunj, *s. t.* The gripes, colic, or spasms in the belly.

قوله kùlé, *s. t.* A tower, a steeple; —, kūla, *a. t.* A kind of bay colour (in a horse).

قوم kūm, *s. t.* Sand; —, kòm, *s. t.* A kind of roadside inn or stables; —, kàvm, *s. a.* A people.

قوماندە kòmànda, *s. t.* (*Italian*), The military word of command; a military command; !—, —et, *v.n.* To command; to give the word of command.

قومپانیه kòmpànya, *s. t.* (*Italian*), A commercial company.

قومرال kŭmràl, *a. t.* Auburn.

قومصال kŭmsal, *s. t.* A sand in the sea; a sandy beach; sandy land or soil.

قومق kòmak (*aor.* قور kòr), *v.a.* To put, place, lay; to leave, allow, permit, suffer, let; —آد àd—, *v.n.* To name, give a name, christen; —بشقه bàsh-*ka*—, —ايرى àyri—, *v.a.* To put apart, place separately; —ميدانه mèydana—, *v.a.* To produce, show, exhibit; —رهين rèhīn—, *v.a.* To pledge, pawn, give in pledge; قونمق kònmak, قونلمق kònulmak, *v.p.* To be placed.

قومناستق kòmnàsstik, *s. t.* (*French*), [India-rubber.

قومه kŭma, *s. t.* A fellow-wife, either of two or more wives of one sole husband (in respect of the other or others).

قوناق kònak, *s. t.* A large house, mansion; a station, or resting place (on a journey); a day's journey; a guest, a lodger, one quartered or billeted in a house; the scurf (of the head); —ا, —et, *v.n.* To make a station, halt for the night or for a space.

قونت kŭnt, *a. t.* Thick and strong, solid.

قونج kònj, *s. t.* The upper leather (of [boots or shoes).

قونداق kŭndak, *s. t.* See قنداق.

قوندره kŭndura, *s. t.* A shoe, shoes; قوندره‌جى kŭnduraji, *s. t.* A European shoemaker.

قونسلوس kònsoloss, *s. t.* (*Italian*), A consul; قونسلوسخانه kònsoloss-khāné, *s. t.* The consular residence or office.

قونمق kònmak (*aor.* قونار kònar), *v.n.* To perch, to alight (a bird); to alight for rest (on a journey), to halt, camp, or bivouac; to fall upon anything (dust, &c.).

قونو or قونى kònu, *ad. t.* in انى قونى èni-kònu, *ad. t.* In full detail and at ease (to converse).

قونيه Kònìyya, *s. t.* The town of Iconium.

قوه kŭvvé (*for* قوت kŭvvet, *q.v.*), قوه‌دن فعله چقارمق kŭvvédan - fi''la--chìkàrmak, *v.a.* To change from *posse* to *esse*, to accomplish.

قوى kàvī, *a. a.* Strong; firm; robust; —kòy, *s. t.* A small bay or inlet.

قويتى kŏytu, *a. t.* Sheltered, secluded; قويتى ير kŏytu-yèr, A sheltered nook.

قويرق kŏyruk, *s. t.* A tail; —ياغى, kŏyruk-yàghi, (Tail fat) Dripping obtained from the large tails of the Asiatic sheep; —صالان, kŏyruk-sàlan, The water-wagtail; قويرقلو kŏyruklu, *a. t.* Tailed; —يلدز, kŏyruklu-yìldiz, A comet.

قويمجى kŏyumju, *s. t.* A gold and silver-smith and jeweller.

قويمق kòymak *or* قومق kòmak. See [قومق.

قوين kòyn, *s. t.* The bosom or breast-pocket of one's dress, the fob; — ساعتى kòyn-sā''ati, A watch; —, kòyun, *ad. t. in* يوزى قوين yùzu-kòyun, With the face to the earth, flat on one's belly; يوزى قوين ياتمق yùzu-

-kòyun-yàtmak, To lie flat on one's belly.

قویو kŭyu, s. t. A well; a pit; —, kòyu, a. t. Thick (any fluid, semi-fluid; a forest, &c.); dark (a shade of colour).

قویون kòyun, s. t. A sheep.

قویویرمك kòyuvermek (aor. قویویرر kòyuvèrir), v.a. (*facile form of* قومق kòmak, *To let, allow, not hinder*), To let loose, let go. (*It has also every meaning of the original verb*).

قهار kàhhār, s. a. God the curber or queller of the proud.

قهر kàhr, s. a. A subduing, curbing, or quelling by violence; power, might; violent grief; ا—, —et, v.a. To subdue, curb, or quell by force; v.n. To be violently grieved; قهراً kàhran, ad. a. By force, by violence. [queror.

قهرمان kàhramān, s. p. A victorious con-

قهقری kàhkarà, s. a. A moving backwards, walking backwards; رجوع قهقری rùjū'i - kàhkarà, An ignominious retreat.

قهقهه kàhkaha, s. a. A burst of laughter; —کولمق, kàhkaha-ghyùlmek, v.n. To laugh aloud.

قهوه kàhwé, s. a. Coffee (either the raw berry, the roasted powder, or the beverage); a coffee-house; قوری قهوه kŭru-kàhwé, (Dry coffee) Coffee in the berry or in powder, not prepared as a beverage; قهوه دانه سی kàhwé-(tānéssi), A coffee-berry; قهوه پاره سی kàhwé-(pàrassi), Coffee - money, a small present in money, a tip; قهوه رنکی kàhwé-rènghi, Coffee-brown (colour); قهوه جی kàhwéji, A coffee-maker in a gentleman's house; a keeper of a coffee - shop; قوری قهوه جی kŭru--kàhwéji, A dealer in coffee berries or powder.

قی kày', s. a. A vomiting; ا—, —et, v.a. To vomit; —کلمق, kày'-ghèlmek, v.n. To feel sick; to vomit; —کتورمك, kay'-ghètirmek, v.n. To cause to vomit.

قیا kàya, s. t. A rock (either in the sea or in the strata of the earth); قیا پارچه سی kàya-pàrchassi, A rough fragment of rock; قیابالغی kàya--bàlighi, Rock-fish (black - skinned, but with very white delicate flesh, especially recommended for persons recovering from severe illness).

قیاس kìyāss, s. a. A measuring or judging one by comparison with another; a syllogism (in logic); ا—, —et, v.a. To liken, compare; —, v.n. To think, suppose, judge; قیاسی kìyāssī, a. a. Regular (in grammar), founded upon comparison; بی قیاس bī-kìyāss, a. p. Without measure.

قیاصره kàyāsséré, s. pl. a. (*of* قیصر kàyser), Cæsars, emperors of Rome or Constantinople.

قیافت kìyāfèt, s. a. External appearance; physiognomy; dress, costume.

قیام kìyām, s. a. A rising and standing on foot; application, assiduity, perseverance; a departure, starting, setting out; ا—, —et, *v.n.* To rise and stand on foot; to apply one's self diligently; to depart, start, set out; يوم القيام yùvmu-'l-kìyām, The day of the resurrection.

قيامت kìyāmèt, *s. a.* The resurrection; any noise, confusion, scolding, or press, hurry, and crowding; —قوپمق kìyāmèt-kòpm*a*k, *v.n.* To happen suddenly (the resurrection); to take place (a great noise or confusion); —قوپارمق, kìyāmèt-kòparm*a*k, *v.n.* To make a great noise of scolding.

قيت kìt, *a. t.* Scarce, not plentiful; قيتلق kìtlìk, *s. t.* Scarcity.

قيچ kìch, *s. t.* The stern of a ship or boat; قيچين قيچين kìch*i*n *or* kìch*i*n - kìch*i*n, *ad. t.* Backwards, stern-foremost; قيچينليه قيچينليه kìch*i*nlay*a* - kìch*i*nlay*a*, *ad. t.* By dint of a repeated or continuous moving backwards.

قيد kàyd, *s. a.* Any fastening with a rope, chain, or similar instrument; a rope, a chain, or any similar instrument of binding; a taking notice, fixing the attention (on anything unpleasant); an enregistering, entering; an entry in a register; a restriction, or restrictive word in a phrase (logic); ا—, —et, *v.a.* To bind, fasten (with a rope, chain, &c.); to enter (in a register), to enregister; to restrict the application of a term (in logic); —, *v.n.* To care, take notice, pay attention (*generally used in the negative*); قيدنده دكل kàydìnd*a* - dìghil (*changing the pronoun as required*), He (&c.) does not care (about it); قيدى بيله دكل kàyd*i* - bīlé - dìghil, He does not take even the slightest notice (of it); قيد حيات شرطيله kàyd*i*-hàyat-shàrtīl*a*, For life (*lit.* under condition of a restriction to the period of his natural life); بيقيد bī-kàyd, *a. p.*, لاقيد lā-kàyd, *a. a.* Careless, thoughtless.

قير kìr, *s. t.* The uncultivated plain; heathland, moorland; —, *a. t.* Grey, black and white mixed.

قيراچ kìrach, *a. t.* Of the nature of sterile parched moorland.

قيراط kīrāt, *s. a.* A carat.

قيرغين kìrgh*i*n, *a. t.* Hurt in one's feelings, somewhat grieved and angry, vexed.

قيرق kìr*i*k, *a. t.* Broken; —, *s. t.* A broken place; قيرقلق kìr*i*klìk, *s. t.* A feeling unwell, feeling of indisposition; كوكل قيرقلغى ghyùngul-kìr*i*k-l*ighi*, A being wounded in spirit, feeling hurt, grieved and sorrowed; قيرقجى kìr*i*kj*i*, *s. t.* A setter of broken bones.

قيرم kìr*i*m, *s. t.* Wholesale slaughter; wholesale death from disease.

قيرمق kìrmak (*aor.* قيرار kìrar), *v.a.* To break; to hurt a person's feelings; to fold, plait, crimp; to discount (a bill of exchange); to slaughter, massacre, cause wholesale death; قيرلمق kìrīl-mak, *v.n.* To break (of itself); to become folded; to have one's feelings hurt, to feel hurt; to die in great numbers; —, *v.p.* To be broken; to be folded or plaited; to be slaughtered wholesale.

قيرمه kìrma, *s. t.* A fold, a plait.

قيرندى kìrìndi, *s. t.* A broken piece, a fragment.

قيز kìz, *s. t.* A maid, maiden, virgin, girl; حانم قيز hànìm-kìz, A young lady; قيز اوغلان قيز kìz-òghlan-kìz, A virgin; قيزقرنداش kìz-(kàrdash), A sister; قيزلق kìzlìk, *s. t.* Virginity, maidenhead, maidenhood; قيزك قيزلغنى بوزمق kìzìng-kìzlìghìnì-bòz-mak, To deflower a virgin.

قيزغين kìzghìn, *a.t.* Hot; red-hot; very angry; in heat (an animal).

قيزمق kìzmak (*aor.* قيزار kìzar), *v.n.* To become hot; to become red-hot; to become very angry; to get in heat (an animal); قيزدرمق kìzdìrmak, *v.a.* To heat, to make hot; to vex, enrage, put in a passion; قيزشمق kìzìshmak, *v.n.* To become hot on all sides (a battle, &c.).

قيسى kàysì, *s. t.* An apricot.

قيش kìsh, *s. t.* The winter; قره قيش kàra-kìsh, The depth of winter; قيشين kìshìn, *ad. t.* In winter, during winter.

قيشلا kìshla, قيشلاغ kìshlagh, قيشلاق kìshlak, *s. t.* See قشلا.

قيشلامق kìshlamak, *v.n.* See قشلامق.

قيصر kàysır, *s. a.* Cæsar, the emperor of Rome or Constantinople.

قيصريه Kàyseriyyé, *s. a.* Cesarea.

قيغنه kàyghana, *s. t.* An omelet.

قيغى kàyghì, *s. t.* Care, anxiety, solicitude; قيغيسز kàyghìssiz, *a. t.* Free from care.

قيل kìl, *s. t.* A hair; a bristle; —, kīl, *s. a. in* قيل وقال kīl-u-kāl, Public remarks and criticisms; قيل قلم kìl-kàlım, A hair-pencil, a small painting brush.

قيلچق kìlchìk, *s. t.* The small hair-like bones of fishes.

قيلمق kìlmak (*aor.* قيلار kìlar), *v.a.* To do, perform (*This verb is not much used excepting as an active auxiliary, and even as such not very frequently*); نمازقيلمق namaz-kìlmak, To perform one's devotions; تاقلق قيلمق tàklak-kìlmak, To tumble heels over head.

قيلوله kàylūlé, *s. a.* The siesta, the noon-day nap.

قيمت kīmet, *s. a.* Value, price; ذيقيمت zī-kīmet, *a. a.* Valuable, precious; — (*for* قيامت kìyāmèt), *s. a.* The resurrection.

قيمق kìymak (*aor.* قيار kìyar), *v.a.* To chop up fine; to mince; —, *v.n.* To bring one's self to make a sacrifice.

قيمه kìyma, *s. t.* Mince-meat.

قين kìn, *s. t.* A sheath, scabbard.

قيود kùyūd (*pl.* قيودات kùyūdāt), *s. pl. a.* (*of* قيد kàyd), Entries; registries; restrictions.

قیوراق kìvràk, *a. t.* Crisp, frizzly (hair); tight-twisted (yarn, thread, &c.).

قیورجق *or* قویرجق kìvìrjìk, *s. t.* The thin, long-tailed sheep of Europe.

قیورم *or* قیوریم *or* قوریم kìvrim, *s. t.* A single twist in a hair or thread.

قیورمق *or* قیویرمق kìvìrmak (*aor.* قیویرر kìvìrir), *v.a.* To twist; to frizzle; قیورلمق kìvrìlmak, *v.n.* To twist, become frizzly; —, *v.p.* To be twisted or frizzled.

قیوم kàyyūm, *s. a.* God the self-existing.

قیه kìyyé, *s. a.* An oke or oka, Turkish weight of 2¾lbs. avoirdupois.

قیی kìyi, *s.t.* The shore, coast, sea-shore; یالی قیییسی yàli-kìyissi, The sea-side; قیی یه چقمق kìyiya-chìkmak, *v.n.* To land, get to the shore; قیی صره kìyi--sìra, *ad. t.* Along the shore, close in land.

ك

ك kyāf (kèf). Twenty-fifth letter of the Turkish alphabet, having three distinct values, for the discrimination of which no generally recognized method has been adopted, and consequently none used in printed books or in current writing. In the first of these values, that of a true and pure English *k*, the letter receives the appellative of کاف عربی kyāfi-ʻàrébī (*the Arabic* kèf *or k*), and in this value it is always left in its original forms, without any addition. In the second value, that of a *g hard*, *gh*, or *gu*, in English, the letter is called کاف فارسی kyāfi - fārsī (*the Persian* kèf). And in the third value, that of our final *ng* in the word *sing* (which, however, is always, in the mouth of educated city-bred people, sounded like a plain *n*), the letter is called صاغر کاف sà*gh*ir-kyāf (*surd k*) *or* صاغر نون sà*gh*ir-nūn (*surd n*). These two latter cases are, in some books where the vowel-points are marked, distinguished from the first by the addition of three dots over the letter; but this method does not distinguish between the two cases themselves. It has therefore been imagined, that if the three points were confined to the *ng* sound of the letter, the *hard g* value might be shown by doubling the dash, and adding this double dash even to the letter when final, though then it usually has no dash at all. In chronograms and astronomical tables the letter has the numeral value of 20. In pronouncing this letter in either of its two first values, when followed by one of the vowels a, o, u, ū, or *u*, the incipient sound of a *y* must be inserted between the letter and the vowel, and this peculiarity we have denoted by putting the inserted letter in italics. Compared with ق as a *k*, or with غ as a *gh*, ك is a soft letter, and is always followed, when possible, by a soft vowel.

ك kè (at the beginning of some compounds), *ad. a.* As, like; —, k or KÉ (at the end of a few compounds), *prep. a.* Thy; thee.

كابل Kābul, *s. p.* The town of Cabul.

كابوس kyābūs, *s. a.* Nightmare, an incubus. [a dower.

كابين kyābīn, *s. p.* A marriage portion;

كاتب kyātib, *s. a.* One who writes; a clerk in a public office; سركاتبي sìrr-kyātibi, A secretary; كاتب الحروف kyātibu-'l-hùrūf, *s. a.* The writer of the present letter.

كاخ kyākh, *s. p.* A palace or pavilion.

كاذب kyāzib, *a. a.* False, lying.

كار kyār, *s. p.* Work, occupation, business; the fruit or result of work; profit, advantage; sexual intercourse; combat, fight, battle; —, (*in composition*), *a. p.* Who does or performs; who works with (some instrument or material); worked (with some instrument or material); ا—, —et, *v.n.* To make a profit, to gain, be a gainer; كارخانه kyār-khānÉ (kèr-khānÉ), *s. p.* A manufactory; a brothel.

كارد kyārd, *s. p.* A knife.

كارزار kyārzār, *s. p.* A battle, conflict, fight, combat, action, engagement.

كاركير kyārghīr (kyàvghir), *a. p.* Built of brick or stone.

كاروان kyārwān, *s. p.* A caravan, a company of travellers or of horses laden with merchandise; —سراى, kyārwān-sàrāy, A caravanserai.

كاست kyāsst, *s. p.* A deficit, a deficiency; بى كم و كاست bī-kèm-u-kyāsst, *ad. p.* Exactly, with no deficiency.

كاسه kyāssÉ, *s. p.* A basin; كاسه ليس kyāssÉ-līss, *s. p.* A parasite, lick-trencher. [ment or hall.

كاشانه kyāshānÉ, *s. p.* A large apart-

كاشف kyāshif, *s. a.* One who discovers or uncovers a hidden thing; a kind of mayor in Egypt.

كاشكه kyāshké (kèshkÉ), *c. p.* O that, I would that; —, *int. p.* I wish it were so.

كاظم kyāzim, *s. a.* One who restrains his anger; كاظمين الغيظ kyāziminu-'l-ghàyz, They who restrain their anger.

كاغد kyāghid, *s. p.* Paper; a written paper; a card; playing cards; كاغد خانه kyāghid-khānÉ, *s. p.* A paper mill, paper manufactory.

كاف kyāf, *s. a.* Name of the letter ك; —, (*in composition*), *a. p.* Which cleaves, splits; كاف ونون kyāf-u-nūn, The mysterious letters ك and ن of the Arabic imperative كن kyùn (*Be thou, exist thou*), being all that God had to pronounce in order to create; كاف لولاك kyāfi-lèv-lāk, The ك (thee) of the expression لولاك lèv-lā-KÉ (*were it not for thee*), mentioned in the Kùr'ān, and indicating Muhammed.

كافر kyāfir, *s. a.* A denier; an infidel or a denier of God's unity and Muhammed's divine mission; (*in joke*) A rogue, a saucy chap; (*in anger*) A brute, a beast; كافرالنعمه kyāfiru-'n--nì''mé, An ungrateful person, who denies the benefit he has received; كافرانه kyāfirāné, *a. p.* Pertaining to an infidel.

كافور kyāfūr, *s. a.* Camphor; كافوريه kyāfūrìyyé, *s. t.* Southernwood.

كافه kyāffé, *s. a.* The whole of them; كافةً kyāffétun, *ad. a.* Altogether, wholly.

كافى kyāfī, *a. a.* Sufficient; —, *s. a.* God the all-sufficient. [lock.

كاكل kyākyul, *s. p.* A ringlet, curl, fore-

كالا kyālā, *s. p.* Rich silk stuff.

كالبد kyālbud, *s. p.* A form, mould; a body.

كام kyām, *s. p.* Wish, desire; بكام bè--kyām, *a. p.* Successful, having his desire fulfilled; نابكام nā-bè-kyām, *a. p.* Unsuccessful, disappointed. (*Many adjectives are composed with this word, almost all meaning successful*).

كامل kyāmil, *a. a.* Complete, perfect; honest, well-behaved, good-tempered.

كان kyān, *s. p.* A mine; —, kyāné, *a. verb subst. third pers. sing. masc. pret.* He (she, it) was; —, kè-ènna, As if, as though (*in* كان لم يكن kè-ènna-lèm--yèkyùn, As though it exist not; كان لم يكن حكمنه قومق kè-ènna-lèm--yèkyùn-hùkmuna-kòmak, *v.a.* To esteem as though it exist not, to regard as *non avenu*).

كانون kyānūn, *s. a.* A fireplace; name of two Syro-Roman months, of which the first, كانون اول kyānūni-èvvel, is our December, and the second, كانون ثانى kyānūni-sānī, our January.

كانه kè-ènnahū (kè-ènna), *comp. a.* As though, as if. [cow.

كاو ghyāw, *s. p.* An ox, bull, bullock, or

كاور ghyàwur, *s. t.* A non-Muhammedan, unbeliever, infidel.

كاه kyāh (*in composition*), *a. p.* Which diminishes or takes away; —, ghyāh, *s. p.* A place; a time; a fitting or seasonable time; —, *ad. p.* Sometimes; كاه كاه ghyāh-ghyāh, *ad. p.* Now and then; كاه وناكاه ghyāh-u-nā--ghyāh, Seasonable or not.

كاهل kyāhil, *a. a.* Lazy, slow, slothful, indolent.

كاهن kyāhin, *s. a.* A diviner, soothsayer, augur.

كاهى ghyāhi, *ad. p.* كاهيجه ghyāhījé, *ad. t.* Sometimes, at one time; at another time.

كائن kyā'in, *a. a.* Being, existing, extant; كائن مطلق kyā'ini-mùtlàk, God, the absolute Being; كائنات kyā'ināt, *s. pl. a.* All existing things.

كباب kèbāb (kèwab), *s. a.* Roast (meat or other substance).

كباد kèbād, *s. t.* A clingstone peach.

كبار kibār, *s. pl. a.* (*of* كبير kèbīr), The great, grandees; (*as a Turkish singu-*

lar) a grandee; a gentleman or great lady. [Great sins.

كبائر kèbā'ir, *s. pl. a.* (*of* كبيره kèbīré),

كبد kèbd, *s. a.* The liver.

كبر kìbr, *s. a.* Pride, haughtiness; —, kìbèr, *s. a.* Oldness, greatness (of age); —, ghèbr, *s. p.* A fire-worshipper. [Great people, grandees.

كبرا kyùbérā, *s. pl. a.* (*of* كبير kèbīr),

كبرمك ghèbermek (*aor.* كبرر ghèbérir), *v.n.* To die as a dog.

كبره ghébéré, *s. t.* A caper.

كبرى kyùbrà, *a. a. fem.* (*of* اكبر èkbèr), The greatest; —, *s. a.* The major proposition of a syllogism.

كبريا kìbriyā, *s. a.* The greatness and majesty of God.

كبريت kìbrīt, *s. a.* Sulphur, brimstone; small brimstone tapers or matches; —احمر, kìbrīti-àhmèr, (Red sulphur) The philosopher's stone; كبريتى kìbrītī, *a. a.* Brimstone coloured.

كبش kèbsh, *s. a.* A ram; a chief, a leader.

كبك kèbk, *s. p.* A partridge.

كبوتر kèbūtèr, *s. p.* A pigeon.

كبه kèbé, *s. t.* A kind of felt or very thick coarse woollen cloth; —, ghèbé, *a. t.* Big with child or young, pregnant.

كبى ghìbi, *a. t.* Like, similar (*is never used absolutely, but always accompanied by the indication of the thing compared with*); —, *ad. t.* As soon as, immediately on, *or* after.

كبير kèbīr (*fem.* كبيره kèbīré), *a. a.* Large, great; كبيره kèbīré, *s. a.* A great sin. [sextile.

كبيسه kèbīssé, *s. a.* Leap-year, the bis-

كپازه kèpāzé, *s. p.* A weak bow for aspiring toxophilites; a foolish trifler.

كپچه kèpché, *s. p.* A ladle, a skimmer.

كپك kèpek, *s. t.* Bran.

كپنك kèpenk, *s. t.* A window-shutter; —, kèpénèk, *s. t.* A butterfly; a moth.

كپوك kyùpuk, *s. t.* Froth; foam; suds; lather; كپورمك kyùpurmek, *v.n.* To froth; to foam, lather.

كتاب kìtāb, *s. a.* A book; كتابجى kìtābjì, *s. t.* A seller of foreign or common books; كتابخانه kìtāb-khāné, A library; كتاب الله kìtābu-'llāh, (God's book) The Kur'ān; اهل كتاب èhli-kìtāb, (People of a book) Jews, Christians (as having revealed Scriptures); —, kyùttāb, *s. pl. a.* (*of* كاتب kyatib), Secretaries, clerks in Government offices; رئيس الكتاب rè'īssu-'l-kyùttāb, (Chief of the Secretaries) Former title of the Ottoman Secretary of State, who also officiated as Minister for Foreign Affairs; he was commonly called رئيس افندى rè'īss-èfèndi; the title is now abolished.

كتابت kìtābet, *s. a.* The art of literary or epistolary composition; style.

كتابه kìtābé, *s. a.* (*originally identic with the preceding*), An inscription in a regularly formed frame, shield, or cartouche, on a public building, &c.

كتان kètān (kètèn), *s. p.* Flax; كتان بزى (kètèn)-bèzi, *s. t.* Linen.

كتب kyùtub, *s. pl. a.* (*of* كتاب kìtāb), Books; كتبخانه kyùtub-khānè, *s. p.* A library. [Secretaries, clerks.

كتبه kètébè, *s. pl. a.* (*of* كاتب kyātib),

كتخدا kètkhudā (kyāya), *s. p.* A steward, administrator of affairs or of a large household; the master or warden of a trade corporation; قپوكتخداسى kàpi-(kyāyassi), *s. t.* The official agent at the chief office of government at Constantinople of any of the various departments of State, of a governor in the provinces, the Danubian Principalities, &c.; كتخدابك (kyaya)-bègh, *s. t.* (Formerly) the official steward of the Grand Vizier (now abolished).

كتف kètf, *s. a.* The shoulder-blade.

كتم kètm, *s. a.* A concealing, not revealing by words or signs; ا—, —et, *v.a.* To conceal, not to reveal.

كتمان kìtmān, *s. a.* The non-revelation of anything on one's mind.

كتمك ghitmek (*aor.* كيدر ghìder), *v.n.* To go; —يبانه yàbana-ghìtmek, *v.n.* To go to the winds, go to waste; كيدەرك ghìdérek, *gerund* (By dint of going) By degrees, in time, by little and little; كتدكجه ghìtdikja, *gerund* (In proportion as — goes), By degrees, by little and little.

كتورمك ghètirmek (*aor.* كتورر ghètirir), *v.a.* To bring with one, to fetch; to cause to come; كتورتمك ghètirtmek (*aor.* كتورتدر ghètirdir), *v.a.* To cause to be brought or fetched; يرينه كتورمك yèrina-ghètirmek, *v.a.* To bring or get (a thing) into its proper place; to accomplish, fulfil, perform, execute, carry out; وجوده كتورمك vùjūda-ghètirmek, To bring about, cause to exist, do, accomplish, call into existence; ايمانه كتورمك īmāna-ghètirmek, *v.a.* To convert to the faith; خاطره كتورمك khātira-ghètirmek, To call to mind.

كتوم kètūm, *a. a.* Who conceals his thoughts and does not divulge them.

كتيبه kètībè, *s. a.* A troop or body of soldiers.

كثافت kèssāfèt, *s. a.* The being thick together, dense (trees, hair, atoms), density; opacity; coarseness, grossness.

كثرت kèssret, *s. a.* Multiplicity, multitude, numerousness, great number; great quantity; frequency; —اوزره, kèssret-ùzèrè, *ad. t.* Frequently, often; in great numbers or quantity.

كثير kèssīr (*fem.* كثيره kèssīrè), *a. a.* Much (in quantity); many (in number); frequent (in recurrence).

كثيف kèssīf (*fem.* كثيفه kèssīfè), *a. a.* Thick, dense, close; opaque, not transparent; coarse, gross.

كج kèj, *a. p.* Oblique, awry, crooked;

كج رفتار kèj-rèftār, *a. p.* Whose gait is awry; whose conduct is not straightforward; كج‌رأى kèj-rè'y, *a. p.* Who has strange and unsuitable opinions.

كچكمك ghèjikmek (*aor.* كچكور ghèjikir), *v.n.* To be late; to become late, grow late; to be behindhand.

كچكول kèjkyūl, *s. p.* A kind of long basket or receptacle formed of a half cocoa-nut shell cut lengthwise, and suspended by chains, carried by mendicant dervishes.

كچ ghèch, *a. t.* Late.

كچكين ghèchkin, *a. t.* Past, over (the prime, or some particular age or state); oldish; rather too tipsy, half-seas over; overripe (fruit).

كچمك ghèchmek (*aor.* كچر ghècher), *v.n.* To pass (over, by, through, in, into, out, &c.), to go (by, through, in, &c.); to pass current (money, &c.); to pass away, not endure, not last, to finish, come to an end; to surpass (in number, quantity, or quality); to beat, leave behind, get before (in a race); to penetrate (into or through a substance); to do without, to manage without, to relinquish, give up; يانندن— yànin-dan-ghèchmek, To pass by *or* near; ايچندن— ìchindan-ghèchmek, To pass through; اوستندن— ùsstundan-ghèchmek, To pass over, above; آلتندن— àltindan-ghèchmek, To pass under; يره كچمك yèra-ghèchmek, To sink into the earth (for shame); يرينه كچمك yèrina-ghèchmek, To pass or go into (its) proper place; وازـــ vwāz-ghèchmek, To give up, leave, abandon, relinquish; وازكچ vwāz-ghèch! Leave off! Be quiet! Don't say that! سوزىـــ sùzu-ghèchmek, To have great weight and influence (one's words); كچمش اولسون ghèch-mish-òlsun! May (worse than this trial) have been (thus) averted! (*said to anyone by way of condolence after sickness or any accident*); كچن ghè-chen, *acc. part.* Who or which passes, passed, or will pass; the past; كچنلرده ghèchenlerda, *ad. t.* Latterly, a short time back, during one or some of the days of a week or month ago.

كچمه ghèchma, *a. t.* Anything which is composed of two or more pieces which fit into (*pass into*) each other; —, *s. t.* A portable pipe for smoking, which takes to pieces.

كچنمك ghèchinmek (*aor.* كچنور ghè-chinir), *v.n.* To pass *or* hold a station among men, to be held as, to be ac-counted; to pass one's life, *or* obtain the means of living, to live, subsist, maintain one's self, exist; (*as a reci-procal*) to pass time or life (with one another), to agree.

كچورمك ghèchirmek (*aor.* كچورر ghè-chirir), *v.a. caus.* To cause or allow to pass (by, in, through, &c.); عمر كچورمك "ùmr-ghèchirmek, *v.n.* To spend one's life; وقتـــ (wàkit)-ghèchirmek, *v.n.* To lose time; to gain time; to spend time; to pass time ; —قلجدن kìlijdan-ghèchirmek, *v.a.* To slay with the sword (many people) ; —كوزدن ghyùzdan-ghèchirmek, *v.a.* To take a cursory view or survey.

كچوك kùchuk, *a. t.* Small, little (in size) ; young, *or* younger (in years) ; كچوك دوشمك kùchuk-dùshmek, *v.n.* To appear small or mean in other people's eyes.

كچولمك kùchulmek (*aor.* كچولور kùchulur), *v.n.* To become smaller, grow smaller ; كچولتمك kùchultmek, *v.a.* To lessen in size, make smaller.

كچه kèché, *s. t.* Felt ; a coarse carpet.

كچى kèchi, *s. t.* A goat ; —بوينوزى, kèchi-bòynuzu, (Goat's-horn) The carob or locust-fruit (a kind of sweet pod).

كچيد ghèchid, *s. t.* A ford ; a ferry ; a pass, defile, gorge.

كحل kyùhl, *s. a.* A kind of collyrium used in the East for the eyes or for blackening the eyelids or eyelashes.

كد kèdd, *s. a.* Work, real hard work ; كديد kèddi-yèd, *s. a.* The work of one's hands.

كدا ghèdā, *s. p.* A beggar, mendicant, a poor person.

كداز ghyùdāz, *a. p.* (*in composition*), Which melts, softens, takes away all power of endurance.

كدر kèdeʀ, *s. a.* Grief, sorrow ; harm, injury ; vexation, annoyance ; ا—, —et, *v.n.* To grieve, mourn ; —ويرمك, kèdeʀ-vèrmek, *v.n.* To cause sorrow, harm, or annoyance.

كدك ghèdik, *a. t.* Notched ; —, *s. t.* A notch ; a patent office or shop (*i.e.* office or shop established by patent, charter, or deed) ; a place held on any foundation or establishment of a limited number ; the right or title by which such an office or place is held, or such a shop is opened ; كدكلو ghèdikli, *a. t.* On the establishment, on the foundation, held by deed or charter (a shop, office, or place).

كدمك ghèdmek (*aor.* كدر ghèdeʀ), *v.a.* To notch.

كدو kèdū, *s. p.* A gourd, pumpkin, calabash.

كدورت kyùdūrèt, *s. a.* Harm, injury ; vexation, annoyance.

كده kèdé, *s. p.* (*in composition*), A house (devoted to something special).

كدى kèdi, *s. t.* A cat ; —اوتى, kèdi-òtu, Valerian ; مسك كديسى mìssk-kèdissi, The musk-cat, civet-cat ; —, ghìdi ! *int. t.* What a fellow ! What a thing ; (*used both in praise and blame*).

كذا kè-zā, *comp. a.* (*lit.* like that), *in* وكذا vè-kè-zā, *c. a.* Also, and in like manner.

كذاب kèzzāb, *s. a.* A liar ; كذاب صويى kèzzāb-sùyu (*for* تيزاب tīzāb), Aqua-fortis.

كذار ghyùzār, *s. p.* A passing ; —, *a. p.* (*in composition*), Who passes or causes to pass ; who fulfils ; خراج كذار kharāj-ghyùzār, *a. p.* Tributary, who pays tribute ; مصلحتكذار mässlāhat-ghyùzār, *s. p.* A *chargé d'affaires*.

agent; ايشكذار ìsh-ghyùzār, *a. t.* Clever and diligent in business.

كذارنده ghyùzārèndé, *a. p.* Who or which passes; who or which bears, carries part.

كذاشته ghyùzāshté, *a. p.* Past, which has passed; which has been passed.

كذاف ghyùzāf, *s. p.* Talk, chat; لافوكذاف lāf-u-ghyùzāf, Chit-chat, conversation.

كذب kìzb, *s. a.* A lie, falsehood.

كذر ghyùzèr, كذران ghyùzérān, *s. p.* A passing, passage; كذران ايدن ghyù-zérān-èden, *a. t.* Last (month), last part. [of passing.

كذرش ghùzèrish, *s. a.* The act or mode

كذشت ghyùzésht, *s. p.* The act of having passed; سر كذشت sèr-ghyùzèsht, *s. p.* An adventure (what has passed over one's head).

كذشته ghyùzèshté, *a. p.* Past; —, *s. p.* Interest on money. [wise.

كذلك kèzālik, *comp. a. conj.* Also, like-

كر ghèr, *c. p.* (*for* اكر èghèr), If; —, *p. particle* (*at the end of some words*), Maker of *or* worker in; —, kèrr, *s. a.* The act of charging or assaulting the enemy; آهنكر āhenghèr, A blacksmith, worker in iron; كروفر kèrr-u-fèrr, The charge and retreat (of combatants, especially horsemen, in the ancient mode of warfare).

كرا kìrā, *s. a.* Rent or hire paid for the use of a house or other object; ديش كراسى dish-kìrāssi, (Tooth-rent) Money exacted in olden times by janissaries, &c., who *honoured* you by becoming your guest; كرايه ويرمك kìrāya-vèrmek, To let out for hire or rent; كراايله طوتمق kìrā-ila-tùtmak, To take upon rent or hire; كراجى kìrāji, *s. t.* A tenant on rent; a lodger.

كرات kèrrāt, *s. pl. a.* (*of* كره kèrré); Times (of repetition); — جدولى, kèrrāt - jèdvéli, The multiplication-table.

كرار kèrrār, *a. a.* Impetuous in assault, bold and constant in attack.

كراز kìrāz, *s. t.* A cherry; —, ghyùrāz, *s. p.* A boar, hog, pig; an iron mace.

كراس kìrāss, *s. t.* A cherry.

كرام kìrām, *s. pl. a.* (*of* كريم kèrīm), The noble, great, well-bred.

كرامت kèrāmèt, *s. a.* A wondrous work, a sign, a wonder, a marvel; any word or deed which proves the actor to be especially under divine guidance; nobility, greatness; كرامتلو kèrāmetlū, *a. t.* Noble, great; wonder-working.

كران kèrān, *s. p.* A side, margin, shore, limit; —, ghìrān, *a. p.* Heavy, weighty; dull, stupid; difficult, slow (of digestion, motion, &c.); dear, high (priced); بيكران bī-kèrān (bī-ghìrān), *a. p.* Boundless; كران پاى ghìrān-pāy, *a. p.* Heavy-footed, slow; كران بار ghìrān-bār, *a. p.* Whose baggage is much and heavy. [seed.

كراويه kèrāvìyyé, *s. a.* The caraway-

كراهت kèrāhet, *s. a.* The being abominable ; an abominating; كراهة kèrā-hétᴇɴ, *ad. a.* With great repugnance.

كرب kèrb (*pl.* كروب kyùrub), *s. a.* Sorrow, affliction.

كرباس kìrbāss, *s. a.* Cotton or linen cloth.

كربال kìrbāl, *s. a.* A sieve ; a screen.

كربه ghyùrbé, *s. p.* A cat.

كرپيج kìrpij, *s. p.* A sun-dried brick.

كرپك kìrpik, *s. t.* An eyelash.

كرپى kìrpi, *s. t.* A hedgehog ; a porcupine.

كرتك kèrtik, *s. t.* A notch.

كرتمك kèrtmek (*aor.* كرتر kèrtᴇʀ), *v.a.* To notch.

كرتنكلر kèrten-kèlér (kèrtenkélé), *s. t.* A lizard.

كرته kèrté, *s. t.* A degree (as marked on a circle) ; a point (of the compass) ; a degree (of any quality, especially of physical or moral condition).

كرچك ghèrchèk, *a. t.* True ; real ; —, *s. t.* Truth, reality ; —, *ad. t.* Truly, really.

كرچه ghèrchi *or* ghèrché, *c. p.* It is true that . . . . ; although.

كرد kèrd, *s. p.* Work ; an act ; a deed ; —, ghèrd, ghìrd, *a. p.* (*in composition*), Who or which revolves round ; revolves.

كرداكرد ghìrd-ā-ghìrd, *ad. p.* Round and round, all round.

كرد Kùrd, *s. a.* (*pl.* اكراد èkrād), A Kurd.

كرداب ghìrdāb, *s. p.* A whirlpool.

كردار kìrdār (kèrdār), *s. p.* Work, deed, act ; بدكردار bèd-kìrdār, *a. p.* Whose deeds are evil.

كردان ghèrdān, *a. p.* Which turns round,

كردباد ghìrd-bād, *s. p.* A whirlwind.

كردستان Kùrdìsstān, *s. p.* Kurdistan.

كردش ghìrdish, *s. p.* Rotation, revolution.

كردك ghèrdek, *s. t.* The bridal chamber or canopy (as used in the East).

كردكار kìrdighyār, *s. p.* God, the absolute actor.

كردل ghèrdel, *s. t.* A bucket.

كردن ghèrdᴇɴ, *s. p.* The neck ; كردنلك ghèrdᴇɴlik (ghèrdᴀnlik), *s. t.* A necklace ; كردن بسته ghèrdᴇɴ - bèssté, *a. p.* Fastened by the neck ; a slave ;

كردنكش ghèrdᴇɴ-kèsh, *a. p.* Refractory.

كردون ghèrdūn, *s. p.* The world ; the spheres.

كردونه ghèrdūné, *s. p.* A coach.

كرده kèrdé, *a. p.* Made, done ; —, *s. p.* An act, deed; —, *a. p.* (*in composition*), Which is or has been effected, done, worked out, accomplished, acted.

كرديده ghèrdīdé, *a. p.* Who or which has gone round, or been gone round ; which has turned or been turned ; who has returned.

كرز ghyùrz, كرزه ghyùrzé, *s. p.* A mace.

كرسته kèressté, *s. t.* Timber (for building) ; materials in general.

كرسى kyùrsī, *s. a.* A stool ; a preacher's or professor's chair or throne ; the throne of God ; the base of a column ; the bottom edge of a line of writing, which should be even ; كرسىء مملكت kyùrsī'i- mèmlékèt (*or* حكومت hùkyūmèt), The chief town or capital ;

كرسيلو kyùrsulu, *a. t.* Written straight in a line (writing).

كرش kìrish, *s. t.* Catgut; a bowstring; a joist (of timber).

كرشمه kìrishma, *s. t.* Coquetry, blandishments.

كرفت ghìrìft, *s. p.* A taking, seizing; —ا, —et, *v.a.* To take, seize, catch.

كرفتار ghìriftār, *a. p.* Seized, taken; troubled with, afflicted with.

كرفته ghìriftè, *a. p.* Seized, taken, caught.

كرك ghèrek, *a. t.* Fitting, beseeming, opportune; —, *c. t.* Whether, or whether; كركى كبى ghèrè*gh*i-ghìbi, (As is beseeming to it) Well, properly, thoroughly; —, ghyùrgh, *s. p.* A wolf.

كركف kèrghèf, *s. t.* An embroidering frame.

كرم kèrem, *s. a.* Kindness, favour; —, —ا, —et, *v.a.* To give *or* do as a favour; — —, *v.n.* To be so kind, be so good, to do the favour; —, kèrm, *s. a.* A grape-vine; —, ghèrm, *a. p.* Warm, hot, sultry; swift; —, kìrm, *s. p.* A worm.

كرما kyùrémā, *s. pl. a.* (*of* كريم kérīm), The noble, the great, the generous; —, ghèrmā, *s. p.* Hot weather, heat of summer.

كرمان kìrmān, *s. t.* A town; —, Kèrmān, *s. p.* Kerman (the town of, in Persia).

كرمانشاه Kèrmānshāh, *s. p.* Kermanshah (the town of, in Persia).

كرمك ghèrmek (*aor.* كرر ghèrer), *v.a.* To stretch, extend forcibly; —حاچه hàcha-ghèrmek, *v.a.* To crucify (extend on a cross).

كرمل طاغى Kèrmèl-dà*gh*i, *s. t.* Mount Carmel.

كرميت ghèrmìyyèt, *s. a.* Warmth; heat; zealousness; activity.

كرميد kīrémīd, *s. t.* A tile.

كرو ghìrèv, *s. p.* A pawn, pledge; a hostage.

كروان kèrwān, *s. p.* A caravan or company of travellers or merchants on the road; كروان سراى kèrwān-sèrāy, *s. p.* A caravanserai.

كروب kyùrūb, *s. pl. a.* (*of* كرب kèrb), Sorrows, afflictions, griefs, cares.

كروبيون kèrūbìyyūn, *s. pl. a.* The cherubim.

كروت kèrévèt, *s. t.* A bedstead or platform for a bed or sofa.

كروه ghyùrūh, *s. p.* A body of people.

كرويز kèréviz, *s. t.* Celery.

كره kèrh, *s. a.* Aversion, distaste, repugnance; —, kèrré, *s. a.* One time (in repetition); كرهاً kèrhan, *ad. a.* Repugnantly, with distaste; —, kyùré, *s. a.* A globe; —, ghìrih, *s. p.* A knot; a button; a difficulty; كرةً kèrréten, *ad. a.* Once; كرةً بعد كرة kèrréten - bà‘‘da - kèrrétin, *ad. a.* Time after time, repeatedly, often; بركره bìr-kèrré, Once; ايكى كره ìki-kèrré, Twice; اوچ كره ùch - kèrré, Thrice, three times; درت كره dùrt-kèrré, Four times; &c. &c.; بعض كره bà‘‘zi--kèrré, Sometimes; برقاچ كره bìr-kàch--kèrré, Several times; قاچ كره kàch--kèrré, How many times? how many times soever; كرهٔ ارض kyùré‘i-àrz, The terrestrial globe; the world; كروى kyùrévi (*fem.* كرويه kyùrévìyyé), *a. a.* Globular, spherical; كرويات kyùrévìyyāt, *s. pl. a.* Spherics.

كريان ghìryān, *a. p.* Weeping.

كريد Ghìrìd, *s. t.* The island of Crete.

كريز ghìrīz, *s. p.* Flight, running away.

كريزان ghìrīzān, *a. p.* Who takes flight, fugitive.

كريم kèrīm, *a. a.* Noble; worthy of respect; generous; kind; كريم الشيم kèrīmu-'sh-shìyèm, *a. a.* Of a noble and generous disposition; اللهكريم Allāh-kèrīm! God is good! كريمانه kèrīmāné, *a. p.* Pertaining to a noble, generous, or kind person.

كريمه kèrīmé, *s. a.* A daughter; —, *a. a.* (*fem. of* كريم), Noble, worthy of respect; آيت كريمه āyéti-kèrīmé, (A wonder worthy of respect) A phrase or verse of the Kur'ān. [hostage.

كريو ghìrīv, *s. p.* A pawn, pledge; a

كريه kèrīh, *a. a.* Ugly, displeasing, unpleasant, disagreeable, disgusting; —, ghìryé, *s. p.* Tears, weeping.

كز ghèz, *s. p.* An ell, the length of an arrow; —, ngiz, *pron. t.* Your (joined to the end of a substantive; as بابا bāba, Father, باباكز bābangiz, Your father). [edge of a sabre.

كزلك ghìzlik, *s. p.* A penknife; the curved

كزمك ghèzmek (*aor.* كزر ghèzer), *v.n.* To walk about, take a walk, promenade; to go about; to be at large; كزدرمك ghèzdirmek (*aor.* كزدرر ghèzdirir), *v.a. caus.* To cause or allow to walk about; to show (anyone) over (a place as a sight to be seen); كزنمك ghèzinmek, *v.n.* To walk up and down without any exterior object; كزمكه كتمك ghèzméghé-ghìtmek, *v.n.* To go for a walk. [harm.

كزند ghèzènd, *s. p.* Loss, damage, injury,

كزيده ghèzīdé, *a. p.* Bitten; —, ghyùzīdé, *a. p.* Choice, chosen, select.

كزين ghyùzīn, *a. p.* (*in composition*), Who seeks, chooses, prefers. [scorpion.

كژدم kèzhdùm, *s. p.* (Crooked-tail) A

كس kèss, *s. p.* (*pl.* كسان kèssān), A person; هركس hèr-kèss, *pr. t.* Everybody; —, kyùss, *s. p.* The female organ of generation. [of commerce.

كساد kèssād, *s. a.* Heaviness, stagnation

كسافت kèssāfèt, *s. a.* Obscuration.

كسالت kèssālèt, *s. a.* Sloth.

كسب kèssb, *s. a.* An acquiring, gaining, obtaining; —, kìssb, *s. a.* An occupation of profit, trade, business; —ا, kèssb-et, *v.a.* To acquire, gain, obtain.

كستاخ kyùsstākh, *a. p.* Bold, impudent, insolent; كستاخانه kyùsstākhāné, *a. p.* Pertaining to a bold, impudent person.

كستانه kèsstāné, *s. t.* A chestnut.

كستر ghyùsstèr, *a. p.* (*in composition*), Who or which diffuses or scatters.

كسر kèssr (kèssir), *s. a.* A breaking, smashing; a defeating, routing; a mortifying, subduing; the pronouncing a consonant with the vowel i or *i* following it in the same syllable; a vulgar fraction (in arithmetic); —, kèssɪʀ, s. t. A small adze; ا—, kèsser-et, v.a. To break; to rout; to mortify; كسرنفس kèssri-nèfss, The mortifying the flesh; كسراعشارى kèssri-āʿʿshārī, s. p. A decimal fraction; كسورات kyùssūrāt, s. pl. a. (of كسور kyùssūr, pl. of كسر kèssr), Vulgar fractions; fractions (in arithmetic). [equivalent to i or i.

كسرة kèssrɛ́, s. a. The vowel-point ـِ,

كسرى kèssrà, s. a. General name for a king of Persia, as Cæsar for a Roman emperor. [snapped.

كسسته kyùssissté, a. p. Broken,

كسك kèssik, a. t. Cut; cut off; having a part cut off; terminating abruptly; separate, detached (words or ejaculations).

كسكين kèsskin, a. t. Sharp (cutting); strong, sharp, pungent; violent; swift; intelligent.

كسل kèssel, s. a. Sloth, sluggishness; neglectfulness, negligence.

كسلان kèsslān, s. a. Slothful, sluggish; neglectful, negligent. [charge, or tax.

كسم kèssim, s. t. A determined price,

كسمك kèssmek (aor. كسر kèssɪʀ), v.a. To cut; to cut off, chop off, slice off, amputate; to determine, decide, fix, conclude; to interrupt, prevent; to bring to an end, finish, put a stop to; اميدينى— ùmīdini-kèssmek (changing the pronoun as required), v.n. To lose all hope; بريندك عقلى— bʿrining-ʿʿākli-kèssmek, v.a. To think in the affirmative, to hope (generally used in the negative, as عقلم كسمز ʿʿāklim-kèssmàz, I think not, I cannot venture to hope it); سوتدن— sūtdan-kèssmek, To wean; فيأت— fiʿàt-kèssmek, To fix a price; كسلمك kèssilmek (aor. كسيلور kèssilir), v.p. To be cut, cut off; determined, fixed, concluded; interrupted; finished, ended, put a stop to; —, v.n. To break, snap, become broken (a rope, &c.); to end, stop, finish; to become, turn into, be changed into; كسشمك kèssishmek (aor. كسشور kèssishir), v.a. To fix or conclude mutually.

كسمه kèssma, s. t. A soft kind of rock or shale which disintegrates on exposure to the weather. [anything.

كسندى kèssindi, s. t. Pieces cut off from

كسوت kìssvet, s. a. Costume, dress.

كسوف kyùssūf, s. a. A solar eclipse.

كسيجى kèssiji, s. t. One who cuts as an occupation; يول— yòl-kèssiji, A highwayman; يان— yàn-kèssiji, A pickpocket.

كش kèsh, a. p. (in composition), Who or which bears, supports, or draws, pulls; —, kùsh, a. p. (in composition), Who or which kills, slays; —, kìsh! int. p. Check to your king!

كشا kyùshā, a. p. (in composition), Who or which opens; who or which conquers, subdues; who or which makes bright or joyful.

کشاد kyùshād, *s. p.* The act or manner of opening; a special method of beginning the game of backgammon.

کشاده kyùshādé, *a. p.* Open; opened.

کشاف kèshshāf, *s. a.* An officer whose business it is to examine and report upon something, as a valuer or a coroner.

کشاکش kèsh-ā-kèsh, *s. p.* A state of discord; pull here, pull there.

کشان kèshān, *a. p.* Who or which bears, supports; draws, pulls; drags itself along.

کشایش kyùshāyish, *s. p.* Openness, [brightness.

کشت ghèsht, *s. p.* A passing by; —, kìsht, *s. p.* Seed-sowing; sown seed; growing corn; کشت وکذار ghèsht-u-ghyùzār, A promenade, a travel; کشتزار kìsht-zār, *s. p.* A field of arable land, sown or to be sown.

کشته ghèshté, *a. p.* (*in composition*), Become; —, kìshté, *a. p.* Sown; —, kyùshté, *a. p.* Slain, killed.

کشتی kèshtī, *s. p.* A ship, boat, vessel; the ark (of Noah); کشتیبان kèshtībān, *s. p.* A sailor, boatman.

کشش kèshish, *s. p.* An act or manner of bearing, supporting; or of pulling; or of fighting; —, kyùshish, *s. p.* Slaughter.

کششلمه (*for* کشیشلمه kèshīshléma, *The wind or quarter of Mount Olympus*) kèshishléma, *s. t.* The south-east wind or quarter; قبله کششلمه kìbla-kèshishléma, S.S.E.; کون طوغیسی کششلمه ghyun - (doghrussu) - kèshishléma, E.S.E.

کشف kèshf, *s. a.* The uncovering anything covered; the discovering anything existing but unknown; the examining and valuing any property; the making an estimate; the estimate itself; the examining into the condition and circumstances of any thing or act; ا—, —et, *v.a.* To uncover; to discover; to examine, survey, value, estimate; to examine into the circumstances of a thing or fact.

کشکك kèshkek, *s. t.* A kind of porridge.

کشکول kèshkyūl, *s. p.* A mendicant's begging-basket, generally of cocoa-nut shell, hung by chains.

کشمش kìshmish, *s. p.*, *or* کشمش اوزومی kìshmish-ùzumu, *s. t.* Common raisins, plums. [squabble, battle.

کشمکش kèsh-mékèsh, *s. p.* A fight,

کشنش kìshnish, کشنیج kìshnīj, *s. p.* The coriander. [*v.n.* To neigh.

کشنمك kìshnémek (*aor.* کشنر kìshner),

کشوده kyùshūdé, *a. p.* Opened.

کشور kìshver, *s. p.* A country, region; کشورکشا kìshver - kyùshā, *s. p.* A monarch, subduer of regions.

کشی kìshi, *s. t.* A person, individual; کشیزاده kìshi-zādé, *s. p.* A gentleman by birth, person of gentle extraction.

کشیده kèshīdé, *a. p.* Borne, supported; pulled, drawn; who has borne; who has drawn; —, kyùshīdé, *a. p.* Killed, slain.

کشیش kèshīsh, *s. p.* A Christian monk or priest; —طاغی, —dàghi, The Bithynian Olympus.

کظم kyàzm, *s. a.* A subduing (one's own rising anger); —ا, —et, *v.a.* To subdue (one's rising anger).

کعب kyà''b, *s. a.* The ankle-joint or projecting bone; a cube.

کعبه kyà''bé, *s. a.* The sanctum sanctorum, or *square-house* at Mecca, towards which Muhammedans turn, when praying, in all parts of the world; کعبتین kyà''bétèyn, *s. a. dual.* The two kyà''bés, the present one at Mecca and the former one at Jerusalem.

کف kèf, *s. p.* Foam, froth; —, kèf, *s. a.* The palm (of the hand); the sole (of the foot); —, kèff, *s. a.* The act of drawing back, withdrawing; —یدا, kèffi-yèd-et, *v.n.* To withdraw the hand from possession, to relinquish, or give up one's hold.

کفار kyùffār, *s. pl. a.* (*of* کافر kyāfir), Infidels, unbelievers, non-Muhammedans.

کفارت kèfārèt, *s. a.* A kind of voluntary deodand or expiatory alms-giving.

کفاف kèfāf, *and* کفاف نفس kèfāfi-nèfss, *s. a.* Subsistence, maintenance.

کفال kèfal, and کفال بالغی kèfal-bàlighi, *s. t.* (*Greek*) The grey mullet (fish).

کفالت kèfālèt, *s. a.* Guaranteeship; bailship; —ا, —et, *v.n.* To be bail or guarantee.

کفالونیا Kèfalōnia, *s. t.* Cephalonia.

کفایت kìfāyet, *s. a.* The being enough, ample, sufficient; the being competent; the being anyone's equal in position; —ا, —et, *v.n.* To be enough; —مرتبه, kìfāyet-mèrtébé, *a.* or *ad. t.* Enough.

کفت ghyùft, *s. p.* A word, saying, talk, speech; کفت وکو ghyùft-u-ghyū, Chit-chat, talk, conversation; discussion; — — —ا, ghyùft-u-ghyū-et, *v.n.* To converse, talk, chat; to discuss, have a discussion.

کفتار ghyùftār, *a. p.* Talk, conversation.

کفته ghyùfté, *a. p.* Said, spoken; —, *s. p.* The words (of a song).

کفتین kèffétèyn, *s. a. dual* (*of* کفه kèffé), The two basins of a balance.

کفچه kèfché (kèpché), *s. p.* A ladle.

کفر kèfr, *s. a.* An expiating (any sins by alms-giving, &c.); —, kyùfr, *s. a.* Unbelief, misbelief, denial of the unity of God or of the apostleship of Muhammed; swearing, cursing; —ا, —et, *v.n.* To say anything smacking of misbelief; to curse and swear; کفر نعمت kyùfru-nì''mèt, *or* کفران نعمت kyùfrāni-nì''mèt, Ingratitude, denial of benefits (in word or deed).

کفره kèféré, *s. pl. a.* (*of* کافر kyāfir), Misbelievers, non-Muhammedans.

کفش kèfsh, *s. p.* A shoe or slipper.

کفکیر kèf-ghīr, *s. p.* A skimmer; the strainer of a sink-hole.

کفن kèfen (kèfin), *s. a.* A winding-sheet.

كفو **kyùfv**, *s. a.* A peer, an equal in position.

كفه **kèffé**, *s. a.* One basin of a balance.

كفيل **kèfīl** (kèyfil), *s. a.* A person who is bail or guarantee, or answerable.

كگرمك **ghèghirmek** (*aor.* كگرر ghèghirir), *v.n.* To belch.

كگز **ghèngz**, *s. t.* The opening of the nostrils into the mouth.

ككك **kèkik**, *s. t.* Wild thyme.

ككلك **kèklik**, *s. t.* A partridge.

كل **kèl**, *s. t.* The ringworm, tetterworm, scald (of the head); —, *a. t.* Affected with the ringworm, tetter, or scald; —, **ghyùl**, *s. p.* A rose; a flower; —, **kyùll**, *s. a.* The whole, all; —, **ghil**, *s. p.* Clay; —, **kil**, *s. t.* Fullers' earth; bole; كل صويى **ghyùl-sùyu**, Rose-water; كل بشكر **ghyùl-bé-shèker**, Conserve of roses; كل اغاجى **ghyùl-aghaji**, A rose-bush; rosewood.

كلا **kilā**, *pr. a.* Both (*in* على كلاالتقديرين "àla-kilā-'t-takdīrèyn, In both cases).

كلاب **kilāb**, *s. pl. a.* (*of* كلب kèlb), Dogs; —, **ghyùlab**, *s. p.* Rose-water; —, **kyùllab**, *s. a.* A hook for pulling and reaching things with.

كلاج **ghyùllàj**, *s. t.* A sweet dish made from very white and thin skin-like cakes, composed of some farinaceous substance.

كلاغ **kèlāgh**, *s. p.* A crow, rook, or raven.

كلال **kèlāl**, *s. a.* Lassitude, fatiguedness.

كلام **kèlām**, *s. a.* A saying, a word, speech; —قديم, **kèlāmi-kadīm**, The eternally existing word (of God, *i.e.* the Kur'ān); ميركلام **mīri-kèlām**, (A lord of speech) A fluent or eloquent speaker; رد كلام ا **rèddi-kèlām-et**, *v.a.* To answer one in conversation; خلاصهٔ كلام **khùlāssé'i-kèlām**, محصل كلام **màhsali-kèlām**, نتيجهٔ كلام **nètījè'i-kèlām**, *ad. t.* In short, in fine, to sum up all.

كلاه **kyùlāh**, *s. p.* A felt cap; the spire of a minaret or steeple.

كلب **kèlb**, *s. a.* A dog.

كلبانك **ghyùl-bāngh**, *s. p.* The Muhammedan call to prayer or to battle.

كلبتان **kèlbétān** (kèrpédèn), *s. a. dual.* Pincers, pliers, forceps.

كلبرو *or* كلبرى **ghèl-béri**, *s. t.* A long iron hook for stirring the fire in an oven.

كلبك **kèlébèk**, *s. t.* A butterfly.

كلبه **kyùlbé**, *s. p.* A hut; a cell.

كلخان **kyùlkhān**, كلخن **kyùlkhàn**, *s. p.* The fireplace of a bath, the stove; the ash-pit of a fireplace; كلخانى **kyùlkhānī**, *s. p.* A little blackguard (as usually to be found at night in the fire-rooms of public baths).

كلدسته **ghyùl-dèssté**, *s. p.* A nosegay, bouquet.

كلر **kèler**, *s. t.* Shagreen (skin of some kinds of fish, &c.).

كلستان **ghyùlisstān**, *s. p.* A flower-garden.

كلش **kèlesh**, *s. t.* A ringwormy, mangy fellow.

كلشن **ghyùlshèn**, *s. p.* A flower-bed, flower-garden.

كلفت **kyùlfet**, *s. a.* The care and trouble attending work; ا—, —et, *v.n.* To be at the trouble, to put one's self out of the way.

كلك kèlek, *s. t.* A kind of raft in the Tigris and Euphrates, &c., supported by inflated sheep-skins; —, kilk, *s. p.* A reed-pen.

كلكشت ghyùlghèsht, *s. p.* A place of promenade among flowers.

كلكون ghyùlghyūn, كلكونه ghyùlghyūné, *a. p.* Rose-coloured; —, *s. p.* Rouge.

كلمه kèlimé, *s. a.* (*pl.* كلمات kèlimāt), A word; كلمة الله kèlimétu-'llāh, (The word of God) Jesus Christ.

كلمك ghèlmek (*aor.* كلور ghèlir), *v.n.* To come; to arrive; —ايمانه īmāna-ghèlmek, *v.n.* To receive, embrace the true faith; —حقندن hàkkindan-ghèlmek, *v.n.* To overcome; to manage; —راست ràsst-ghèlmek, *v.n.* To meet by hazard; —الدن èldan-ghèlmek, *v.n.* To be possible, in one's power; (*joined to the fifth gerund of any verb, it forms a new class of verbs signifying* to be usual to ——, *as;*) اوله كلمك òla-ghèlmek, To be, in a customary manner; ويريله كلمك vèrila-ghèlmek, To be customarily given; كلنمك ghèlinmek, *v.p.* To be arrived at.

كلنك kyùlunk, *s. t.* A stone-cutter's hammer-pick for shaping stones.

كلو ghyùlu, *s. p.* The throat; كلوكير ghyùlu-ghīr, *a. p.* Which seizes the throat, chokes.

كلور ghèlir, *s. t.* Income, revenue, receipts.

كليبولى Ghèliboli, *s. t.* The town of Gallipoli.

كله kèllé, *s. p.* The head, the pate (detached from the body); a sheep's head (cooked); a loaf (of sugar); a head (of a cabbage, &c.); —, ghyùllé, *s. t.* A cannon-ball, a shot; —, ghèlé! (*In backgammon, said when the adversary has a man on the bar and throws such points as are covered; it means literally*) (wait patiently in order) that (a favourable point) may come! —, ghèlé, *s. p.* A flock, herd; —, ghilé, *s. p.* Plaint, lament; —, kyùlèh (*abb. from* كلاه kyùlāh), *s. p.* A cap; a spire; كله پوش kèllé-pòsh, *s. p.* (Head-cover) A cap.

كله پير kèlépir, *s. t.* A prize obtained by chance.

كلى kyùllī (*fem.* كليه kyùllìyyé), *a. a.* Pertaining to all, to the whole; general, universal; much, great (in number or quantity); كليات kyùllìyyāt, *s. pl. a.* Generalities, universalities; the general sciences; the whole works of an author; كليت kyùllìyyèt, *s. a.* Universality; greatness (of number or quantity); كليت اوزره kyùllìyyèt-ùzré, In great quantity; كلياً kyùllìyyan, بالكليه bi-'l-kyùllìyyé, *ad. a.* Altogether, quite, totally.

كليچه kyùlīché, *s. p.* A disk; a bar, ingot of metal.

كليد kìlid, *s. t.* A lock; اصمه كليد àssma-

-kìlid, A padlock; كليدلمك kilidlémek (kitlémek), v.a. To lock. [church.

كليسا kèlìssa, s. t. (Greek), A Christian

كليم kìlim, s. t. A Turkey carpet (of various kinds); —, kèlīm, s. a. An interlocutor; كليم الله kèlīmu-'llāh, Moses, the interlocutor of God.

كلين ghèlin, s. t. A bride; a newly-married daughter-in-law; كلينلك ghèlinlik, s. t. The quality of being a bride; —, a. t. Nubile (girl), marriageable; كلينجك ghèlinjik, s. t. dim. A little bride; a weasel(?); a ferret(?); كلينجك چيچكی ghèlinjik-chìchéghi, The wild red corn-poppy.

كم kèm, a. p. Few in number, small in quantity; insignificant, trifling; bad (*always used in the negative*, as كم دكل kèm-dìghil, It is not so very bad); —, kèm *and* kèmm, s. a. Quantity (in number or substance); —, ghèm, s. t. A snaffle; —, ghyùm, a. p. Lost; —, kyùmm, s. a. A sleeve.

كما kèma, ad. a. As; كما فی الاول kèmā-fi-'l-èvvel, As at first; كما فی السابق kèmā-fi-'ss-sābik, As before; كما كان kèmā-kyān, As it was; كما ينبغی kèmā-yènbàghi, As is fitting, as is proper.

كمات kyùmāt, s. pl. a. (*sing. not used*), Warriors, heroes, champions.

كماشته ghyùmāshté, s.p. (pl. كماشتكان ghyùmāshtèghyān), A person in any public office or employ.

كمال kèmāl, s. a. Perfection of any state or quality; completeness; كمال مرتبه kèmāli-mèrtébé, In a supreme degree; كمال بولمق kèmāl-bùlmak, كماله ايرمك kèmālé-èrmek (كلمك ghèlmek, وارمق vàrmak), v.n. To arrive at perfection; كمالات kèmālāt, s. pl. a. Perfections of various qualities.

كمان kèmān, كمانه kèmāné, s. p. A bow (for shooting); a violin; —, ghyùmān, s. p. A doubt; a suspicion; كمانچه kèmānché, s. p. dim. A small violin; كمانكش kèmān-kèsh, s. p. An archer, bowman; a toxophilite.

كمتر kèmtèr, a.p. compar. Less; smaller; very little; very small; humble; كمترانه kèmtérāné, a. p. Pertaining to a humble individual; كمترين kèm-térīn, a. p. sup. The least, smallest; most humble. [brocade.

كمخا kèmkhā, s. p. A kind of Oriental

كمر kèmer, s. p. A girdle, waist-belt, sash; an arch; (pl. كمرلر kèmerler), An aqueduct on arches; —, ghèmer, s. t. A gnawing noise of rats; كمر صيچانی ghèmer-sìchani, A rat; كمر بسته kèmer-bèssté, a. p. Girded, ready.

كمراه ghyùmrāh, a. p. Lost, erring from the road; corrupt, depraved; rebellious.

كمرك ghyùmruk, s. t. (Greek κομερκι), A custom-house; an export or import duty; قره كمركی kara-ghyùmrughu, A land custom-house; رسم كمرك rèssmi-ghyùmruk, An export or import customs duty; كمركدن قاچيرمق ghyùmrukdan - kàchirmak, v.a. To smuggle.

كمرمك ghémirmek (aor. كمرر ghèmirir), v.a. To gnaw.

كمسنه kìmèssné (kìmsé), s. t. A person; (*with a negative*) Nobody, no one; (*with an interrogation or a verb in the conditional*), Anyone.

كمند kèmènd, s. p. A noose, slip-knot; [a halter.

كمور or كومر kyùmur, s. t. Charcoal; معدن كموری mà"dɛn - kyùmuru, Mineral coal, mine coal, fossil coal, coal; فونده كموری fùnda-kyùmuru, Charcoal made from vine-branches(?), or heather, furze, &c.(?), used by blacksmiths, coppersmiths, tinners, &c.

كمون kèmmūn (kìmiyon), s. a. Cummin; —, kyùmūn, s. a. A hiding one's self, laying wait, lying in ambush.

كمی ghèmi, s. t. A ship; كميجی ghèmiji, s. t. A sailor; چرخ كميسی (chàrk)-ghèmissi, A steamer; اتش كميسی àtèsh-ghèmissi, A fire-ship; جنك كميسی jènk-ghèmissi, A man-of-war; بكلك كميسی bèghlik-ghèmissi, A government ship, man-of-war or otherwise; تجار كميسی tùjjār-ghèmissi, A merchantman.

كميت kèmmìyyèt, s. a. Quantity; —, kyùmèyt, s. a. A bay horse.

كميك or كموك kèmik, s. t. A bone.

كمين kèmīn, s. a. An ambush, ambuscade; —, *and* كمينه kèmīné, a. p. Very small; very few; very humble.

كن kɛ̀n, a. p. (*in composition*), Who digs, undermines; —, kyùn, a. p. (*in composition*), Who makes, does; —, kèn (*for* ايكن ìken), *gerund of the fragmentary verb substantive*, While being; —, kyùn, v. *imperat.* a. Be thou, exist thou (the word with which God created all things).

كنار kɛ̀nār, s. p. An edge, margin, border, shore; a marginal note; a postscript; دركنارا dɛ̀r-kɛ̀nār-et, v.a. To write as a marginal note, or as a postscript.

كنان kyùnān, a. p. (*in composition*), Who makes, does.

كناه ghyùnāh, s. p. A sin; كناهكار ghyùnāh-kyār, s. p. A sinner; —ا, —et, v.n. To commit sin; كناهی بوينكزه ghyùnāhi - boynunguza! May the sin thereof (light) upon your neck!

كنايه kināyé, s. a. Metonymy, the giving to understand one's meaning by parallel, and not direct, explanation.

كنائس kɛ̀nā'iss, s. pl. a. (*of* كنيسه kɛ̀nīssé), Christian churches.

كنبد kyùnbed, s. p. A dome, cupola; a domed building.

كنت kìnet, s.t. A clamp or cramp-iron; كنتلمك kìnetlémek, v.a. To join with clamps or cramps.

كنج ghènj, a. t. Young; —, s. p. A hidden treasure; —, kyùnj, s. p. A corner.

كنجايش ghyùnjāyish, s. p. Measure, capacity; كنجايشپذير ghyùnjāyish-pèzīr, a. p. Measured.

کنجشك kyùnjishk, *s. p.* A sparrow.

کنجلمك ghènjelmek (*aor.* کنجلور ghènjèlir), *v.n.* To become young again in appearance or activity.

کنجور ghènjvèr, *s. p.* A treasurer.

کنجیده ghyùnjīdé, *a. p.* Measured as to capacity. [magazine, store.

کنجینه ghyùnjīné, *s. p.* A treasury,

کند kènd, *s. p.* A village; —, kyùnd, *a. p.* Blunt; stupid.

کندر kèndir, *s. t.* Hemp.

کندم ghèndum, *s. p.* Wheat; کندم نما وجوفروش ghèndum-nùmā-vè-jèv-fùrūsh, A cheat, one who shows wheat and sells barley.

کندو and کندی kèndi, *s. t.* Self; —, *a. t.* Own; کندم kèndim, Myself; کندك kèndin*g*, Thyself; کندیسی kèndissi, His, her, its, self, himself, itself; کندیمز kèndimiz, Ourselves; کندیکز kèndin*g*iz, Yourselves; کندیلری kèndiléri, Theirselves, themselves; کندی بابام kèndi-bābam, My own father; کندی پاره کز kèndi-pàran*g*iz, Your own money, &c.; کندی حالنده kèndi-hālind*a*, *a. t.* (A person) who minds his own business without meddling in the affairs of others.

کندیده ghèndīdé, *a. p.* Putrid, stinking.

کنز kènz, *s. a.* Hidden treasure.

کنش ghènish, *a. t.* Wide; full, ample; large, bountiful; کنشلتمك ghènishlitmek, *v.a.* To make wide, full, or ample. [a privy.

کنف kènef, *s. a.* A side, coast, region;

کنك kyùnk, *s. p.* Pipes for water, &c., of earthenware or of trees bored out.

کنکره kyùnghyuré, *s. p.* The crenelated battlements of a castle, or a small tower or spire of any building; a hill-top, peak; the summit of anything high. [Who makes, does.

کننده kyùnendé, *a. p.* (*in composition*),

کنوز kyùnūz, *s. pl. a.* (*of* کنز kènz), Hidden treasures.

کنویر kènévīr, *s. t.* Hemp (as a plant ?).

کنه ghèné, *s. t.* A tike; —, kyùnh, *s. a.* The inward reality of anything; —, ghyùnèh (*contr. from* کناه), *s. p.* Sin, wickedness.

کنیه kyùnyé, *s. a.* A surname composed by calling anyone the father or mother, or the son or daughter, of someone else, thus "*The father of lies,*" "*The Son of man,*" are of this class, as also, and more correctly, "*The sons of Zebedee.*"

کنیز kènīz (*dim.* کنیزك kènīzek), *s. p.* A girl, maid, maiden, maid-servant.

کنیسه kènīssé, *s. a.* A Christian church.

کو ghyù, *s. p.* Speech, talk; کفت وکو ghyùft-u-ghyù, Conversation; —, ghèv, *s. t.* The cud; کو کتورمك ghèv-ghètirmek, *v.n.* To chew the cud (*lit.* to bring the cud).

کوار ghyùwār, *s. p.* Taste, savour.

کواکب kèwākib, *s. pl. a.* (*of* کوکب kèvkeb), Stars. [testimony.

کواه ghyùwāh, *s. p.* A witness; witness,

کوب kyòb, *a.p.* (*in composition*), Who or which beats, strikes.

کوبره ghyùbré, *s. t.* (*Greek* κοπριας), Stable manure, dung.

کوبك ghyùbek, *s. t.* The navel; the heart (of any plant); a degree of descent, a generation in a line.

کوپ kyùp, *s. t.* A large jar for oil, water, or wine.

کوپرمك kyùpurmek (*aor.* کوپرر kyùpurur), *v.n.* To froth; to foam; to lather.

کوپری kyùpru, *s. t.* A bridge; an iron staple; a cross-strap behind a buckle.

کوپك kyùpek, *s. t.* A dog; کوپك اوغلی کوپك kyùpek-òghlu-kyùpek (kyùp-òghlu-kyùpek), Dog, son of a dog (term of insult or of fun, and even admiration).

کوپه kyùpé, *s. t.* An ear-ring; the fuchsia; خاصکی کوپه‌سی khàsséki-kyùpéssi, *s. t.* Columbine, aquilegia (flower).

کوت ghyùt, *s. t.* The backside, breech; anus; (*vulg.*) courage; طاوق کوتی tàwuk-ghyùtu, *s. t.* A wart.

کوتاه kyùtāh, *a. p.* Short.

کوتردی kyùturdu, *s. t.* A noise as of knocking or falling substances.

کوترمك ghyùturmek (*aor.* کوترر ghyùturur), *v.a.* To take or carry off or away; to bear, carry.

کوترم kyùturum, *s. t.* A bed-ridden, paralytic person.

کوتری ghyùturu, *ad. t.* In the lump (bargaining or contracting); —, *s. t.* A bargain in the lump.

کوتك kyùtek, *s. t.* A thrashing with a stick; — یمك kyùtek-yèmek, *v.n.* To receive a thrashing; *or* کتوك kyùtuk, *s. t.* The stump of a tree or grape-vine; a block (on which to cut things), a billet (for burning); (*vulg. for* کتب kyùtub) The official register of a court of law.

کوتمك ghyùtmek (*aor.* کودر ghyùdær), *v.a.* To watch, lead to pasture; *in* کین کوتمك kīn-ghyùtmek, *v.n.* To bear malice, to keep a malicious remembrance of a wrong.

کوته kyùtèh (*contr. from* کوتاه), Short.

کوتی kyùtu, *a. t.* Bad; کوتیلتمك kyùtulætmek, *v.a.* To give a bad name, speak ill of.

کوجنمك ghyùjænmek (*aor.* کوجنور ghyùjènir), *v.n.* To be hurt, vexed, angry; کوجندرمك ghyùjèndirmek, *v.a.* To vex, make angry, hurt the feelings of.

کوچ ghyùch (*in oblique cases* کوج ghyùj), *s. t.* Work, occupation, business; strength of body; —, *a. t.* Difficult; —, ghyùch, *s. t.* Migration, change of abode; death; the whole of one's traps and effects in moving; ایش کوچ ìsh-ghyùch, Business and occupation; ایشلوکوچلو ìshli-ghyùchlu, *a. t.* Occupied in business regularly; ایشسز کوچسز ìshsiz-ghyùchsuz, *a. t.* Having no regular business;

قاچ كوچ kÀch-kyùch, The retirement of women from the presence or society of men, as practised in the East; ـــا, ghyùch-et, *v.n.* To change one's residence, move one's family and furniture; to die; كوچ‌ايله ghyùj-ila, *ad. t.* With difficulty; hardly; كوچ‌بلا ghyùch-bèlā, *ad. t.* Hardly (in point of time), only just, at most, with the greatest difficulty; كوجم‌يتمز ghyùjum-yètmàz, I am not able, I have not strength sufficient; بريننك كوجنه كتمك bìrining-ghyùjuna-ghìtmek (كلمك ghèlmek *is generally substituted in the first persons*), *v.n.* To go against one's grain, not to be liked, to displease, vex, ruffle.

كوچبه ghyùchébé, *s. t.* A nomade, wandering man; ـــطاقمى, ghyùchébé-tàkimi, The nomade or wandering tribes.

كوچك kyùchek, *s. t.* A dancing boy; —, *or* كچوك kùchuk, *a. t.* Small, little (in size); young, younger, or youngest in age; كچوكلك kùchukluk, *s. t.* Smallness; infancy; littleness, little-mindedness.

كوچمك ghyùchmek (*aor.* كوچر ghyùchɪr), *v.n.* To migrate, change one's abode; to die (*familiar*).

كوچه kyùché, *s. p.* Any public place, street, or square. [or buckskin.

كودرى ghyùdéri, *s. t.* Chamois leather

كودە ghyùwdé, *s. t.* The trunk of an animal, man, or tree, distinct from the limbs or branches; كودەلو ghyùwdéli, *a. t.* Corpulent.

كور kyùr, *a. t.* Blind; blunt; —, *s. t.* A blind man; كوراول kyùr-òl! Be thou blind! كوزك كوراولسون ghyùzung-kyùr-òlsun! May thy eyes become blind! (*Imprecations*); اغزى كور Àghzi-kyùr, Its edge is blunt; —, kyòr, *s. p.* A grave, tomb, sepulchre; كورستان kyòrisstān, *s. p.* A graveyard, burial-ground, cemetery; كورا kyùr-et, *v.a.* To blind, make blind, strike blind; كورلنمك kyùrlɪnmek, *v.n.* To become blunt; to be deprived of vitality (any project); كورلتمك kyùrlɪtmek, *v.a.* To make blunt, to blunt; to deprive of vitality (any growing scheme).

كورجستان Ghyùrjìsstān, *s. t.* Georgia; كورجى Ghyùrji, *s.* and *a. t.* Georgian; a Georgian.

كورش ghyùresh, *or* كولش ghyùlesh, *s. t.* Wrestling; كورشمك ghyùreshmek, كولشمك ghyùleshmek, *v.n.* To wrestle.

كورفز kyùrfez, *s. t.* A gulf, bay, cove, inlet; the island of Corfu.

كورك kyùrk, *s. t.* A fur; any fur clothing; —, kyùrèk, *s. t.* A wooden shovel; an oar; a shoulder blade-bone; the galleys (as a punishment); —, kyùruk, *s. t.* A pair of bellows; —, ghèvrèk, *a. t.* Brittle; crisp; —, *s. t.* Various kinds of crisp cakes; ـــ چكمك, kyùrèk-chèkmek, *v.n.* To pull at the oar, to row, to pull;

کورکه کوندرمك kyùrègha - ghyùn-dermek, *v.a.* To send to the galleys.

کورکن kyòr-kèn, *s. p.* A grave-digger.

کورلدی or کورلتی ghyùruldu, *s. t.* A loud noise ; کورلدمك ghyùruldémek, *v.n.* To make a rumbling noise.

کورلمك ghyùrlémek (*aor.* کورلر ghyùrlɪr), *v.n.* To make the noise of thunder ; کوك کورليور ghyùk-ghyùr-liyor, It thunders, it is thundering ; کوك کورلمسی ghyùk-ghyùrléméssi, Thunder ; —, or کوریلمك ghyùrul-mek, *v.p.* To be seen.

کورمك ghyùrmek (*aor.* کورر ghyùrur), *v.a.* To see; to suffer, bear, be subjected to, pass through; to do, perform; to provide for or bear (expenses); to esteem, consider, see; ایش— ìsh-ghyùrmek, *v.n.* To be useful; to be effective; to do, perform, accomplish; to work, act; مناسب— mùnāssib-ghyùrmek, *v.a.* To consider fit and proper; کوره يم سنی ghyùrèyim-sèni! Let me see what you can do, what you are made of! —, or کویرمك ghèvirmek, *v.n.* To chew (the cud); کیو کویرمك ghèv-ghèvirmek, To chew the cud; کورلمك or کوریلمك ghyùrulmek, *v.p.* To be seen; to be suffered, borne; to be done, performed; to be provided for; to be esteemed or considered; کورنمك ghyùrunmek, *v.n.* To be seen, be in sight, appear; to seem; کورشمك ghyù-rushmek, *v.n. recip.* To see one another, visit, be on terms of friendly visiting; to be introduced to each other; کورشدرمك ghyùrushdurmek, *v.a.* To cause or allow (two people) to see each other; to introduce to each other.

کورومك kyùrumek (*aor.* کورور kyùrur), *v.a.* To shovel away; to blow with a bellows.

کوره kyùré, *s. p.* A district, region, country; —, ghyùré, *5th gerund of* کورمك, *used like an adverb,* According; بکاکوره bànga-ghyùré, According to me; انك لاقرديسنه کوره àning-làkirdissina-ghyùré, According to his account, to what he says.

کوز ghyùz, *s. t.* The eye; the eye (of a needle); a compartment or pigeon-hole (in a box or desk); a mesh (in a net); any small hole (in a porous substance); —, ghyùz, *s. t.* Autumn; —, kyūz, *s. a.* A jug, pitcher; —, ghèvz, *s. p.* A walnut; کوزقولاق او ghyùz-kùlàk-òl, *v.n.* To be all eyes and ears, all attention; کوزك ببکی ghyùzung-bèbéghi, The pupil of the eye; کوزك اقی ghyùzung-àki, The white of the eye; کوزقپاغی ghyùz-kàpàghi, An eyelid; کوزقیپمق ghyùz-kìpmak, *v.n.* To wink, blink; کوز یوممق ghyùz-yùmmak, *v.n.* To shut the eyes tight; کوزیاشی ghyùz-yàshi, Tears; کوزیشارمق ghyùz-yàshar-mak, *v.n.* To have water run from the eyes; کوزحبسی ghyùz-hàbsi, A prisoner on parole or under surveillance; the quality of being under surveillance and without leave to go out unless under escort; کوز دیکمک ghyùz-dìk-mek, *v.n.* To fix the eyes (upon a thing), to stare (at a thing); — —, ghyùz-dèghmek, *v.n.* To produce an evil effect of fascination (the eyes, on anything); کوز باغی ghyùz-bàghi, (A knot in the eye) A charm, enchantment, sorcery; کوز باغیجی ghyùz-bàghiji, A sorcerer; کوز کزدرمك ghyùz-ghèzdirmek, *v.n.* To give a cursory look all over; کوزدن کچورمق ghyùzdan - ghèchirmek, *v.a.* To examine cursorily; کوزاچمق ghyùz-àchmak, *v.n.* To open the eyes; to be vigilant, attentive, sharp; کوز اچدرمق ghyùz-àchdirmak, *v.n.* To make or allow (one) to open his eyes, to become vigilant and attentive, or sharp; کوز اچدرمامق ghyùz-àchdir-mamak, *v.n. neg.* Not to give time or opportunity to take any precaution; کوزك ایدین ghyùzung-àydin! (May) thy eyes (be) radiant! (*equivalent to our* "I wish you joy!") کوزیمك نوری ghyùzumung - nūru! Light of my eyes! اچ کوزلو àch - ghyùzlu, *a. t.* Covetous, insatiable; اچق کوز àchik-ghyùz (Open-eye) *and* کوزی اچق ghyùzu-àchik (Whose eye is open), *a. t.* Having his wits about him, quick, intelligent; کوزین ghyùzun, *ad. t.* In autumn, during autumn.

کوزتمك ghyùzetmek (*aor.* کوزدر *or* کوزهدر ghyùzèdir), *v.a.* To look after, keep one's eye upon (from regard or from fear); —, *v.n.* To mind, take care, look after one's self.

کوزکمك ghyùzukmek (*aor.* کوزیکور ghyùzukyur), *v.n.* To be visible, be in sight; to come in sight, appear, become visible.

کوزل ghyùzèl, *a. t.* Pretty, fine, handsome, nice, good, excellent, pleasant; نه کوزل nè-ghyùzèl! How pretty! how nice? how pleasant? پك کوزل pèk-ghyùzèl, Very well! کوزل اولور ghyùzèl-òlur! That will be excellent! that will do very nicely! کوزللنمك ghyùzèllenmek, *v.n.* To become pretty (from what has been done to it); کوزللشمك ghyùzèlleshmek, *v.n.* To become pretty (of itself and without anything being done to it).

کوزلك ghyùzluk, *s. t.* Spectacles, barnacles; an eye-glass.

کوزلمك ghyùzlémek (*aor.* کوزلر ghyùzler), *v.a.* To eye, watch with the eye.

کوزلمه ghyùzlémé, *s. t.* A species of pancake or fritter.

کوزه ghèvézé, *s. t.* A babbler, a blab; —, kyūzé, *s. p.* A jug, pitcher.

کوس kyūss, *s. a.* A drum or kettle-drum.

کوساله ghyūsālé, *s. p.* A calf.

کوسپند ghyòsspènd (*for* کوسفند ghyòssfènd), *s. p.* A sheep.

کوستبك kyùsstébek, *s. t.* A mole (animal).

کوستریش ghyùsstèrish, *s. t.* Show, showiness ; کوسترشلو ghyùsstèrishli, *a. t.* Showy. [ghyùsstèrir), *v.a.* To show.

کوسترمک ghyùsstèrmek (*aor.* کوستر

کوستک kyùsstèk, *s. t.* A watch-guard or chain; any short chain, rope, or cord for securing anything, if used lengthwise only. [(town of).

کوستنجه Kùstènjé, *s. t.* Kustendje

کوسفند kyòssfènd, *s. p.* A sheep.

کوسکون kyùsskyun, *a. t.* In a pet, vexed, angry; —, *s. t.* The sensitive plant; کوسکونلك kyùsskyunluk, *s. t.* A pet, a fit of pettishness against anyone.

کوسکی kyùsskyu, *s. t.* An iron implement, a poker or crowbar.

کوسله kyùssélé, *s. t.* Sole leather, pump-leather; the sole of a shoe or boot.

کوسمك kyùssmek (*aor.* کوسر kyùsser), *v.n.* To become disgusted or to fall out with any thing or any person hitherto liked; to wish to break off a bargain after having desired it.

کوسه kyùssé, *s. p.* A person with little or no beard naturally.

کوش ghyūsh, *s. p.* The ear; —, kyùsh, *a. p.* (*in composition*), Who exerts himself, who labours at; —, *or* کیوش *or* کویش ghèvish, *s. t.* The cud, a chewing of the cud.

کوشت ghyūsht, *s. p.* Flesh, meat.

کوشتره kyùshtéré, *s. t.* A sort of long plane for forming straight edges to boards.

کوشش kyūshish, *s. p.* A diligent striving, exertion, application, effort.

کوشك kyùshk, *s. t.* A summer-house, small pleasure house, pavilion; a belvedere or look-out room in some high position; —, ghèvshek, *a. t.* Loose, slack (not tight); lukewarm (not zealous); heavy, dull (weather); کوشکلك ghèvsheklik, *s. t.* Looseness; lukewarmness; heaviness; dulness; a feeling of fatigue or indisposition. [ear; a reprimand.

کوشمال ghyūshmāl, *s. p.* A box on the

کوشوار ghyūshvār, کوشواره ghyūshvāré, *s. p.* An ear-ring or drop.

کوشه kyùshé, *s. p.* A corner; a place of retreat from the world; کوشه‌کیر kyùshé-ghīr, *a. p.* Who has taken up a place of retreat; درت کوشه dùrt-kyùshé, *a. t.* Four-cornered.

کوشه‌مك ghèvshémek (*aor.* کوشر ghèvshér), *v.n.* To become loose, slack (a knot or fastening, &c.); to become lukewarm (in one's endeavours); to give (frost, ice, &c.); to become less severe; کوشتمك ghèvshètmek, *v.a.* To loose, loosen, slacken.

کوف kyùf, *s. t.* Mouldiness, mould; کوفلنمك kyùflènmek, کوف باغلامق kyùf - bāghlamak, *v.n.* To become mouldy. [to damson cheese.

کوفتر kyùftèr, *s. t.* A preparation similar

کوفتن kyùftun, *s. t.* Oil-cake.

کوفته kyùfté, *s. t.* Mincemeat balls.

کوفه kyùfé, *s. t.* A large open basket of one, two, or three bushels, with two handles.

كوك kyùk, *s. t.* A root; —, ghyŭk, *s. t.* The sky; heaven; —, *a. t.* Sky-blue; كوك يوزى ghyùk-yùzu (Face of heaven), The sky; كوك كورلمك ghyùk-ghyùrlémek, *v.n.* To thunder; كوك مائيسى ghyùk-mā'īssi (māvissi), *s. t.* A sky-blue colour; كوك بويا kyùk-bòya, Madder-roots; كوكجى kyùkju, *s. t.* A herbalist.

كوكب kĕvkeb, *s. a.* A star.

كوكبه kĕvkébé, *s. a.* Pomp, grandeur, splendour.

كوكچ ghyùghèch, *s. t.* A baking-dish.

كوكرته ghyùghèrté, *s. t.* (*Italian* coperta), The deck or upper deck of a ship.

كوكرجين ghyùghèrjin, *s. t.* A pigeon; كوكرجينلك ghyùghèrjinlik, *s. t.* A pigeon-house, dove-cote.

كوكرمك ghyùghermek (*aor.* كوكرر ghyùghèrir), *v.n.* To put on the blue or green colour of the first sprouting of corn, &c.

كوكس ghyùkss, *s. t.* The breast, chest; طاوق كوكسى tàwuk-ghyùkssu (fowls'-breasts), A sweet dish of pounded rice and fowls' breasts.

كوكل ghyùngul, *s. t.* The heart or seat of the affections; كوكل بولانمق ghyùngul-bŭlanmak, *v.n.* To feel sick, have a nausea; كوكل بولانتيسى ghyùngul-bùlàntissi, Sickness, nausea; كوكلنى ياپمق ghyùngulunu-yàpmak (*or* ايتمك ètmek), To persuade (one), obtain his consent (*changing the pronoun as required*); كوكلنى خوش طوتمق ghyùngulunu-khòsh-tùtmak, *v.n.* To keep one's heart or mind free from anxiety or vexation; كوكل قالمق ghyùngul-kàlmak, *v.n.* To be angry, vexed, dissatisfied; كوكل طيانمق ghyùngul-dàyanmak, *v.n.* To bear to see or hear of (the heart); كوكل اچلمق ghyùngul-àchilmak, *v.n.* To become pleased, rejoiced, freed from anxiety or restraint; كوكل اچمق ghyùngul-àchmak, To open one's heart or mind; كوكلى اولمق ghyùngulu-òlmak (*or* اولمامق òlmamak *in the negative*), To have a desire, a heart, an inclination; جان و كوكلدن jān-u-ghyùnguldan, *ad. t.* With all one's heart and soul; الچق كوكللو alchak-ghyùngullu, *and* كوكلسز ghyùngulsuz, *a. t.* Meek, lowly of heart.

كوكم ghyùghum, *s. t.* A kind of tall water-kettle.

كوكنار ghyùknār, *s. p.* A poppy.

كوكنمك ghyùghènmek (*aor.* كوكنور ghyùghènir), *v.n.* See كونمك ghyùwènmek.

كوكورت kyùkyurt, *or* كوكورد kyùkyurd, *s. t.* Sulphur.

كول kyùl, *s. t.* The ashes of wood or charcoal; —, ghyùl, *s. t.* A lake, a pond, a pool, a puddle; كول او kyùl-òl, *v.n.* To be ruined (in property); كول رنكى kyùl-rènghi, Ash-coloured, colour of ashes; كول كسلمك ghyùl-kèssilmek, *v.a.* To be all afloat, inundated, like a lake; كولباصدى kyùl-bàssdi, *s. t.* A steak or chop grilled (done in the ashes).

كولچه **kyùlché**, *s. t.* A bar or ingot of metal.

كولخن **kyùlkhàn**, *s. p.* An ashpit; a place from whence the fire is fed in large establishments. (See كلخان).

كـولشمك **ghyùleshmek**, *v.n.* (See كورشمك), To wrestle; —, ghyù-lushmek, *v.n.* To laugh together.

كـولكن **gyùlghèn**, *s. t.* The beech-tree.

كولكه **ghyùlghé**, *s. t.* A shadow; shade; كولكه لك ghyùlghélik, *s. t.* A shady place; anything which creates a shade.

كولمسيمك **ghyùlumsumek** (*aor.* كولمسر ghyùlumser), *v.n.* To smile derisively.

كولمك **ghyùlmek** (*aor.* كولر ghyùler), *v.n.* To laugh; to smile; —پك pek-ghyùlmek, To laugh out; —خفيف khàfif-ghyùlmek, To smile; ادمك صقالنه— adaming-sàkalina-ghyùlmek, *v.n.* To try and make a fool of anyone, to deceive (*lit.* To laugh at one's beard); —بيق التنده bìyik-altinda-ghyùlmek, *v.n.* To laugh in one's sleeve (*lit.* To laugh under one's moustache).

كوله **kyùlé**, *s. t.* A male slave, bondsman; كوله كز kyùléngiz, Your slave, your humble servant.

كولهمن **kyùlémèn**, *s. t.* An old Egyptian [Mameluke.

كومچ **ghyùmèch**, *s. t.*(?) كومچ بالى ghyù-mèch-bali, Honey in the comb; ابه كومجى èbé-ghyùmèji, *s. t.* The marsh-mallow; the common geranium.

كومر **kyùmur**, *s. t.* Charcoal. See كمور.

كومس **kyùmèss**, *s. t.* A fowl-house, hen-coop.

كومش **ghyùmish**, *s. t.* Silver; كومشى ghyùmishī, *a. t.* Silver-grey.

كومك **ghèvmek** (*aor.* كور ghèver), *v.a.* To chew (the cud).

كوملك **ghyùmlek**, *s. t.* A shirt; a coat (of paint).

كومك **ghyùmmek** (*aor.* كومر ghyùmer), *v.a.* To bury, inter; كوملمك ghyù-mulmek, *v.n.* To bury one's self; —, *v.p.* To be buried.

كومه **kyùmé**, *s. t.* A heap; a group.

كون **ghyùn**, *s. t.* A day; the sun; —, ghyūn, *s. p.* (*in composition*), Colour; —, *a. p.* Coloured; —, kyūn, *s. p.* The backside, breech; —kèvn, *s. a.* Being, existence; كون طوغيسى ghyùn-dòghussu (dòghrussu), *s. t.* The east point of the horizon; the east wind; اولسى كون èvvelsi-ghyùn, The day before yesterday; اولبر كون (ò)-bìr-ghyùn, The day after to-morrow; دها اولبر كون dàhā-ò-bìr-ghyùn, The third day from this; بوكون bū-ghyùn, To-day, this day; بركون اول bìr-ghyùn-èvvél, *ad. t.* As soon as possible, as early as possible; one day before; هركون hèr-ghyùn, Every day; ايكى كونده بر ìki-ghyùndé-bìr, Every other day, every second day, every alternate day; كون بكون ghyùn-bè-ghyùn, كوندن كونه ghyùndan-ghyùné, From day to day, daily; بركون bìr-ghyùn, كونلردن بركون ghyùnlerdan-

-bìr-ghyun (*or* بریسنده bìrissinda), Once upon a time; one day.

کوناکون ghyūn-ā-ghyūn, *a. p.* Of various colours, many-coloured; of various kinds and sorts.

کوندر ghyùndεr, *s. t.* A staff (of a boat-hook, a flag-staff, &c.).

کوندرمك ghyùndεrmek (*aor.* کوندرر ghyùndεrir), *v.a.* To send.

کوندوز ghyùnduz, *s. t.* The daytime; کوندوزین ghyùnduzun, *ad. t.* In the daytime, during the daytime, by day; کیجه‌کوندوز ghèjέ-ghyùnduz, Day and night.

کونده‌لك ghyùndέlik, *s. t.* A day's pay or wages; کونده‌لکجی ghyùndέlikji, *s. t.* A day-labourer, workman hired by the day.

کونش ghyùnèsh, *s. t.* The sun.

کونلك ghyùnluk, *s. t.* Frankincense; a quantity relating to a day; —, *a. t.* A day old, of a day's standing.

کونمك ghyùwènmek (*aor.* کونور ghyùwènir), *or* کوکنمك ghyùghènmek (*aor.* کوکنور ghyùghènir), *or* کوینمك ghyùyεnmek (*aor.* کوینور ghyùyènir), *v.n.* To trust, place one's faith in (as a support, protection, or assistance).

کونه ghyūnέ, *s. p.* A kind, sort, species, manner.

کونین kèvnèyn, *s. a. dual* (*of* کون kèvn), The two worlds, spiritual and material.

کونیه ghyùnyέ, *s. t.* (*Greek* γονῆ), A carpenter's or mason's square; —, *a. t.* Square (a figure or corner).

کوه ghyùwέ, *s. t.* The moth or maggot in cloth, furs, &c.; —, kyūh, *s. p.* A mountain, a hill; —, ghyūh, *s. p.* Human dung; —, ghyùwèh (*contr. from* کواه ghyùwāh), A witness, witness, testimony.

کوهر ghèvhèr *and* ghyùhèr, *s. p.* A pearl or precious stone; the matter or substance of which things are made, especially lumps of steel for Damascus blades; کوهربار ghyùhèr-bār, *a. p.* Who or which pours out pearls and precious stones.

کوی kyùy, *s. t.* A village or hamlet; کویلو kyùylu, *s. t.* A villager, rustic, peasant; —kyūy, *s. p.* A street or lane; —, ghyūy, *a. p.* (*in composition*), Who speaks or says.

کویا ghyūyā, *a. p.* Speaking; having the faculty of speech; —, *ad. t.* As though, as if, as it were.

کویکو *or* کویکی ghyùwèghi, *s. t.* A son-in-law, husband to one's daughter; a bridegroom; ایچ‌کویکی ìch-ghyùwèghi (Interior son-in-law), *s. t.* A son-in-law who goes and lives with his wife at her parents' house.

کوینده ghyùyèndέ, *a. p.* Speaking; endowed with speech.

کوینمك ghyùyεnmek, *v.n.* See کونمك.

که ki, *conj. t.* That; for, because; —, kèh (*contr. from* کاه kyāh), *s. p.* A bit of straw; —, ghèh (*contr. from* کاه ghyāh), *s. p.* A place; —, kìh, *a. p.* Small in size, young in years.

کهانت kìhānet, *s. a.* Divination, soothsaying, augury.

کهتر kìhtèr, *a. p.* Smaller in size; younger in age; کهترین kìhtérin, *a. p.* The smallest; the youngest.

کهر ghyùhèr, *contr. from* کوهر, q.v.

کهربا kèh-rùbā (kèhlibār), *s. p.* Yellow amber (*lit.* Straw-snatcher). [nitre.

کهرچله ghyùhèrchilé, *s. p.* Saltpetre,

کهف kèhf, *s. a.* A cave, cavern, grotto; اصحاب کهف Asshābi-kèhf, The seven sleepers (*lit.* Men of the cave).

کهکشان kèh-kèshān, *s. p.* The milky way (*lit.* The straw-stealers).

کهله kèhlé, *s. t.* A louse; تخته کهله سی tàkhta-kèhléssi, A bug (*lit.* a plank-louse); کهله لنمق kèhlélenmek, *v.n.* To louse one's self; to become lousy.

کهن kyùhèn, *a. p.* Old, ancient.

کهنه kèhéné, *s. pl. a.* (*of* کاهن kyāhin), Soothsayers, augurs, seers, diviners; —, kyùhné, *a. p.* Old, worn out.

کهواره kèhwāré, *s. p.* A cradle.

کهیلان kyùhèylān, *s. a.* An Arab horse of pure blood.

کی ki, *Turkish relative particle,* signifying, according as it is joined to a noun or pronoun by the genitive preposition, or by the locative, *that which belongs to,* or *that which is held by or attached to*; as, بابامڭکی bàbamingki, That which belongs to my father, my father's; بابامده کی bàbamdéki, That which is held by my father: it is joined directly to nouns of time; as, صباحکی sàbāhki, The one of the morning; دونکی dùnku, The one of yesterday; —, ghī, *Persian particle,* joined to adjectives terminated in ه vowel, which is then suppressed and equivalent to our terminations *ment, ness,* &c.; as, مردانکی mèrdānéghī, Manliness; ستودکی sùtūdéghī, Praiseworthiness.

کیاست kèyāssèt, *s. a.* Soundness of understanding and judgment.

کیان Kèyyān, *s. p.* Surname of the second dynasty of Persian kings.

کیاه ghìyāh, *s. p.* Grass, herbage; hay.

کیتی ghītī, *s. p.* The world; کیتی ستان ghītī-sìtān, *s. p.* A monarch, as conqueror of the world; کیتی ستانی ghītī-sìtānī, *s. p.* Sovereignty; —, *a. p.* Pertaining to a monarch, royal, imperial, sovereign.

کیجشمك ghìjishmek (*aor.* کیجشور ghìjishir), *v.n.* To itch.

کیجك ghìjik, *s. t.* An itching.

کیجه ghèyjé, *s. t.* The night; last night; —, *ad. t.* By night, in the night; last night; کیجه لین ghèyjéléyin, *ad. t.* By night, during the night; کیجه لك ghèyjélik, *s. t.* Night-clothes; the quantity special to a night; —, *a. t.* Special to the night; کیجه لمك ghèyjélémek, *v.n.* To become night; to pass the night, spend the night; کیجه اول ghèyjé-òl, *v.n.* To become night; یاری کیجه yàri-ghèyjé *or* کیجه یارسی ghèyjé-yàrissi, Midnight.

کیخ kīkh, *s. p.* The gum of the eyes.

کید kèyd, *s. a.* A trick, stratagem, plot, ruse.

کیدش ghìdish, *s. t.* Departure, mode of going.

کیر kìr, *s. t.* Any dirt collecting on bodies; the scurf which may be rubbed off the body; the wax of the ear; —, ghìr, *a. p.* (*in composition*), Who takes, holds, conquers; —, *s. p.* A taking, seizing; داوركير dār-u-ghīr, *s. p.* Fight, battle; كيرلو kìrli, *a. t.* Dirty, dirtied; كيرلنمك kìrlɛnmek, *v.n.* To become soiled, dirtied; كيرلتمك kìrlɛtmek, *v.a.* To dirt, make dirty, soil.

کیرچ kìrèch, *s. t.* Lime; كيرچ اوجاغى kìrèch-òjaghi, A lime-kiln; سونمامش كيرچ sùnmamish-kìrèch, Quick-lime.

كيرمك ghìrmek (*aor.* كيرر ghìrɛr), *v.n.* To enter, go in, penetrate; كناهه— ghyùnāha-ghìrmek, *v.n.* To do wrong, to sin; برينك كناهنه— bìrining-ghyùnāhina-ghìrmek, *v.n.* To accuse or suspect falsely, to sin against by so doing; ارايه— àraya-ghìrmek, *v.n.* To interpose; mediate; يوله— yòla-ghìrmek, *v.n.* To get into proper train, to get to rights, in a regular way, be rectified, be reformed; كيرشمك ghìrishmek, *v.n.* To come into any understanding (with others), to act (with others); to enter into (any affair).

كيرو ghèri, *s. t.* The space further and further away from the back of any one or thing; —, *a. t.* Slow (a watch); —, *ad. t.* Back; backwards (in space); forwards (in time); —كتمك, ghèri-ghìtmek, To go back; —قالمق, ghèri-kàlmak, To go too slow (a watch); كيروده قالمق ghèrida-kàlmak, To remain behind; برايشدن كيرو قالمق bìr-ìshdan-ghèri-kàlmak, To be remiss in the execution of any business (*generally used in the negative, and then meaning*, To be as good as one's word); كيرو استمك ghèri-ìsstémek, *v.a.* To demand back again, demand the restitution; شمديدن كيرو shìmdidan-ghèri, From this time forwards.

كيزلمك ghìzlémek (*aor.* كيزلر ghìzlɛr), *and* كيزلتمك ghìzlɛtmek (*aor.* كيزلدر ghìzlèdir), To hide, secrete; كيزلنمك ghìzlɛnmek (*aor.* كيزلنور ghìzlénir), *v.n.* To hide one's self; كيزلندرمك ghìzlèndirmek (*aor.* كيزلندرر ghìzlèndirir), *v.a.* To cause one to hide himself.

كيزلو ghìzli, *a. t.* Secret, covert, hidden, underhand.

كيس kīss, *s. a.* A purse, money-bag.

كيسو ghèysū, *s. p.* A curl, ringlet of hair, tresses.

كيسه kèysé, *s. a.* A bag or purse; a sum of 500 piastres; a small hair-bag used in baths for scrubbing the body without soap; كيسه اقچه kèysé-àkcha, 500 piastres; كيسه سورنمك kèysé-sùrunmek, *v.n.* To be scrubbed with a hair-bag at a bath; كيسه‌دار kèysé-

-dār, *s. p.* A purse-bearer; title of several functionaries of distinction, being a kind of chief clerk in certain offices of Government; (*fam.*) the state of one's own finances.

کیش kīsh, *s. p.* Faith, religion, sect.

کیف kèyf, *s. a.* The *quomodo* of anything, the how, in what way, what sort or kind; the state of one's health; the hilarity produced by joy, pleasure, or wine; joy, pleasure, happiness; good humour; —, *a. t.* Tipsy, drunk; —او, —òl, *v.n.* To get tipsy; —ا, —et, *v.n.* To be amused, to enjoy one's self; *v.a.* To get into one's head and inebriate (liquor); —یتشدرمك, kèyf-yètish-dirmek, *v.n.* To make one's self cosy, with all the appliances; کیفی وار kèyfi-vār, He is in a good humour; کیفی یوق kèyfi-yòk, He is unwell; کیفی یرنده kèyfi-yèrinda, He is in good health; کیفی قاچدی kèyfi-kàchdi, His joy vanished; کیف ویرمك kèyf-vèrmek, *v.n.* To cause pleasure; to inebriate (liquor); کیفسز kèyfsiz, *a. t.* Unwell; out of spirits; کیفسزلك kèyfsizlik, *s. t.* Illness, sickness; a being out of spirits; —, kèyfa, *ad. a.* How? howsoever; کیفما kèyfamā, *ad. a.* In what way soever.

کیفیت kèyfìyyèt, *s. a.* A circumstance, event, matter; a quality, state, mode or manner of being; the exhilarating effect of wine, &c.

کیك ghèyik, *s. t.* A stag, buck.

کیل kèyl, *s. a.* A measuring (grain, &c.); a bushel.

کیلار kīlār (kìlær), *s. t.* A pantry, store-room, store-closet; کیلارجی kìlærji, *s. t.* One who has charge of the pantry or store-closet.

کیلوس kèylūss, *s. a.* (*Greek*), The chyle.

کیله kìlé, *s. a.* A bushel.

کیم kìm, *pron. t.* Who? whosoever; some individuals; کیمی kìmi, Some of them (those persons); کیممز kìmimiz, Some of us; کیمکز kìmingiz, Some of you.

کیمك ghìymek (*aor.* کیر *or* کییر ghìyær), *v.a.* To wear; to put on (clothes); کینمك ghìyinmek (*aor.* کینور ghìyinir), *v.n.* To dress one's self; to put on one's clothes; —, *v.a.* To put on (one's clothes); کیدرمك ghìdir-mek, *v.a.* To cause or allow to wear; to cause or allow to put on; to cause or allow to be worn; گیندرمك ghìyindirmek, *v.a.* To cause or allow to dress one's self; to cause or allow one to put on (some article of clothing).

کیموس kèymūss, *s. a.* (*Greek*), The chyme.

کیمیا kìmiyā, *s. a.* (*Greek*), Alchymy, the art of making gold, of transmutation; the philosopher's stone; کیمیای جدید kìmiyāyi-jèdīd, (The new alchymy) Modern chemistry; کیمیاکر kìmiyā-ghær, A chemist; an alchymist.

کین kīn, *s. p.* Malice, rancour, ill-will;

كين كودمك kīn-ghyùdmek, *v.n.* To bear ill-will; —, ghīn, *Persian termination, changing nouns into adjectives like our ful, ish,* or *y; as,* غمكين ghàm-ghīn, *sorrowful.*

كينونت kèynūnèt, *s. a.* Being, existence.

كينه kīné, *s. p.* Malice, ill-will, rancour; كينه‌خواه kīné-khāh, *and* كينه‌خوار kīné-khār, *a. p.* Malevolent, vindictive (person).

كيو ghèv, *s. t.* The cud of ruminating animals; كيو كتورمك ghèv-ghètirmek, *v.n.* To chew the cud, to ruminate.

كيوان kèywān, *s. p.* Saturn.

كيه ghìyèh (*contracted from* كياه ghìyāh), *s. p.* Grass, herbage; hay.

ل

ل lām. Twenty-sixth letter of the Turkish alphabet, having the value of *l* in English. It has the numeral value of 30 in chronograms and astronomical tables; and, in the dates of letters, stands for the month of شوال shèwwāl.

ل lì, *prep. a.* (*in composition*), For; لاب lì-èb, *a. a.* On the father's side, paternal; لام lì-ùmm, *a. a.* On the mother's side, maternal; لاجل lì-èjl, *ad. a.* In order to, on account of; (*with this preposition the* ا *of the Arabic definite article* ال *is omitted, as in* لله lì-'llāhi, For God).

لا lā, *ad. a.* (*in composition*), No; not; there is not; لاابالى lā-ùbāli, *a. a.* Careless, free and easy (*lit.* I care not); لابأس lā-bè'ss, *a. a.* Harmless, innocuous; لابد lā-bùdd, *a. a.* Indispensable, necessary; —, *ad. a.* Absolutely, without fail; لاجرم lā-jèrem, *ad. a.* Absolutely, without fail; لازال lā-zālé! May (his glory, &c.) never fade away! لايحدولايحصا lā-yùhàdd-vè-là-yùhsà, *a. a.* Unlimited and innumerable; لايموت lā-yèmūt, *a. a.* Immortal.

لاپ làp, *and* لاپادق làpadak, *ad. t.* All at once, suddenly.

لاپه làpa, *s. t.* Porridge; a poultice; —اورمق, làpa-wùrmak, *v.n.* To put on a poultice; to poultice.

لاتين lātīn, *a. t.* A man of Roumelian origin and Romanist by religion.

لاپه‌جى làpaji, *s. t.* (A porridge-man) A coward, a simpleton.

لاجورد lājivèrd, *s. p.* Lapis-lazuli; —, *a. t.* Deep indigo-blue colour; لاجوردى lājivèrdī, *a. p.* Azure, light-blue, sky-blue. [actually in office.

لاحق lāhik, *a. a.* Joined, touching;

لاحنه lāhana, *s. t.* A cabbage.

لادن lādèn, *s. t.* A precious gum or balsam.

لازب lāzib, *a. a.* Adherent.

لازق lāzik, *a. a.* Adhesive.

لازم lāzim (làzim), *a. a.* Necessary, wanted, required, requisite; neuter, intransitive (a verb); never leaving, inseparable; —او, —ōl, *v.n.* To be wanted, necessary, requisite; لازملو lāzimli, *a. t.* Useful, necessary.

لازمه lāzimé, *s. a.* An inseparable, necessary duty or consequence.

لاشه lāshé (lèsh), *s. p.* An unclean carcase; carrion. [a nothing.

لاشیٔ lā-shèy', *s. a.* A thing of naught,

لاغ lāgh, *s. p.* A joke, fun, pleasantry.

لاغر lāghır, *a. p.* Thin, emaciated, lean.

لاف lāf, *s. p.* Chit-chat; conversation; boasting words; لافزن lāfzèn (làfazàn), *s. p.* A talkative person; a vain boaster; لاف وگذاف lāf-u-ghyùzāf, Chit-chat, conversation, talk.

لاقردی làkirdi, *s. t.* A word; talk, speech, saying; conversation; consultation; an assertion; ا—, —et, *v.n.* To talk; to speak, converse; لاقردیسنی ا làkirdissini-et, *v.n.* To talk about; to consult about, talk over; بوش لاقردی bòsh-làkirdi, Nonsense, idle talk; لاقردی قارشمق làkirdi-kārish-mak, To become confused (one's words); —قارشدرمق, làkirdi-kārish-dirmak, To create a confusion of words by interfering and mixing with what is said.

لال lāl, *a. p.* Dumb; dumbfounded.

لالا lāla, *s. t.* A man who has charge of a child, like a nurse.

لاله lāla, *s. p.* A tulip; لاله‌زار lālé-zār, *s. p.* A bed of tulips.

لآلی la'ālī, *s. pl. a.* (*of* لؤلؤ lu'lu'), Pearls.

لام lām, *s. a.* Name of the letter ل; the symbol of crookedness or of being bent; —, li-ùmm, *a. a.* On the mother's side, maternal.

لامحاله lā-màhālé, *ad. a.* Absolutely, inevitably, without fail.

لامس lāmiss (*fem.* لامسه lāmissé), *a. a.* Which touches, feels with the fingers; قوت لامسه kùvvéti-lāmissé, The faculty of touch, tact.

لامع lāmi'', *a. a.* Throwing forth rays, shining, sparkling.

لانه lāné, *s. p.* A nest. [lute.

لاوته *or* لاوطه làwuta, *s. t.* A kind of

لاهوت lāhūt, *s. a.* Divinity, the Divine nature or quality, the Godhead; عالم لاهوت "ālémi-lāhūt, The Divine nature; the universe peculiar to the Godhead.

لائح lā'ih, *a. a.* Clear, evident, manifest.

لائحه lā'iha, *s. a.* A written project, report, scheme.

لایپسقه Làypsìka, *s. t.* Leipsic (town of).

لایزال lā-yèzāl, *a. a.* Unfading, permanent, eternal. [supportable.

لایطاق lā-yùtāk, *a. a.* Unbearable, in-

لایق lāyik, *a. a.* Fitting, proper, worthy; —, *s. a.* That which is worthy of anything, that which is merited; الله لایقنی ویرسون Allāh-lāyikini-vèrsin! May God give him what he deserves! لایق کورمك lāyik-ghyùrmek, *v.a.* To esteem or see fit; لایقیله làyikila, *ad. t.* As he (she, it) deserves or merits.

لائك lā'ik, *s. a.* A cynic, a seeker of faults; a critical person.

لب lèb, *s. p.* The lip; an edge, brink; a shore; —, lùbb, *s. a.* A kernel; the heart; the mind, understanding;

لبالب lèb-ā-lèb, *a. p.* Brimful; lip to lip; لبريز lèb-rīz, *a. p.* Overflowing.

لباچه lìbāché, *s. p.* A mantle, garment, robe.

لباده lèbādé, *s. p. or* lùbbādé, *s. a.* A coarse outer cloak or wrapper.

لباس lìbāss, *s. a.* Clothing, a garment, clothes, raiment.

لبلبى lèblébī, *s. t.* Indian corn parched [in grains.

لبن lèben, *s. a.* Milk; —, lèbin, *s. a.* A brick.

لبنان Lìbnān, *s. t.* The Lebanon.

لبيب lèbīb, *a. a.* Possessed of a heart, mind, and understanding.

لبيك lèbbīk! *int. a.* Here I am! What are your commands? Holloa!

لت lètt, *s. a.* A striking, beating; ا—, —et, *v.a.* To beat, strike.

لتم lètm, *s. a.* A striking; a wounding; ا—, —et, *v.a.* To strike; to wound.

لثم lèssm, *s. a.* A kissing.

لج lèjj, *s. a.* A contending; contention; [obstinacy.

لجاج lìjāj, *s. a.* Mutual contention.

لجام lìjām, *s. a.* The bridle and reins.

لجه lùjjé, *s. a.* The sea.

لحاف lìhāf, لحافه lìhāfé, *s. a.* A quilted counterpane; a quilted jacket.

لحظه làhza, *s. a.* A glance of the eye, a [look.

لحم làhm, *s. a.* Flesh, meat.

لحن làhn, *s. a.* A sound, note, or tone of voice; an error in pronouncing the vowels.

لحنه làhana, *s. t.* A cabbage.

لحوق lùhūk, *s. a.* The reaching to, joining, arriving (of one thing to another).

لحيه làhyé, *s. a.* The beard and whiskers.

لدن lèdun, *s. a.* The presence (of God).

لدوس lòdoss, *s. t.* (*Greek νότος*), The south-west wind or quarter; قبله لدوس kìbla - lòdoss, S.S.W.; باطى لدوس bàtì-lòdoss, W.S.W.

لدى lèda (*before the definite article* ال lèdé), *pr. a.* Immediately near to (in space); immediately after (in time); لدى السؤال lèdé-'ss-sùʿāl, On the question being put, when asked.

لذائذ lèzāʿiz, *s. pl. a.* (*of* لذيذه lèzīzé), Agreeable things, joys, pleasures, delights.

لذت lèzzèt, *s. a.* (*pl.* لذات lèzzāt), Taste, savour; the pleasure felt in enjoyment; المق—, lèzzèt-ālmak, *v.n.* To become fond of (any pleasure); بولمق—, lèzzèt-bùlmak, *v.n.* To feel, derive a pleasure; to find a taste;

لذتلو lèzzètli, *a.t.* Tasty, flavoursome;

لذتسز lèzzetsiz, *a. t.* Insipid; هادم اللذات hādimu-'l-lèzzāt, *s. a.* Death, the destroyer of all pleasures.

لذلك lì-zālìké, *ad. a.* For this reason, therefore.

لذيذ lèzīz, *a. a.* Tasty, savoury, sweet, [pleasant.

لرزان lèrzān, *a. p.* Trembling.

لرزه lèrzé, *s. p.* A trembling, shaking, shivering; لرزه ناك lèrzénāk, *a. p.* Seized with trembling.

لرستان Lùrisstān, *s. p.* Name of a district [in Persia.

لزوم lùzūm, *s. a.* Necessity, want, requisiteness, a being wanted, required; a being in want, need; inseparability.

لسان lìssān (lìssAn), *s. a.* The tongue; speech; language, idiom; لسان حال lìssān*i*-hāl, *s. a.* The mute language of circumstances; لسانه کلمك lìssānɛ́-ghèlmek, *v.n.* To be generally ill-spoken of; لسانه کتورمك lìssānɛ́-ghètirmek, *v.a.* To cause (anyone) to be talked about; لساناً lìssān*an*, *ad. a.* Verbally.

لشکر lèshkɛr, *s. p.* An army.

لشمق l*a*shm*a*k, لشمك lèshmek (*for soft verbs*), *Turkish terminations of infinitives, which, added to many nouns or adjectives, form verbs neuter.* [breaker.

لص lùsss, *s. a.* A thief; a robber, house-

لصوق lùssūk, *s. a.* Junction, adhesion.

لطافت l*à*tāfèt, *s. a.* Grace, gentleness, loveliness, elegance; fineness, pleasantness.

لطائف l*à*tā'if, *s. pl. a.* (*of* لطیفه l*à*tīfɛ́), Agreeable things; agreeable, pleasing sayings.

لطف lùtf, *s. a.* Goodness, kindness, grace, favour, amiability; ا—, —et, *v.n.* To have the goodness, or kindness, to be so good or kind, to do the favour; —, *v.a.* To give, hand, do, &c., out of kindness; لطفاً lùtf*an*, *ad. a.* As a kindness, as a favour.

لطمه l*à*tmɛ́, *s. a.* A blow, a slap, smack, box, cuff. [pleasant, fine, lovely.

لطیف l*à*tīf, *a. a.* Graceful, agreeable,

لطیفه l*à*tīfɛ́, *s. a.* A joke; an agreeable act or saying; ا—, —et, *v.n.* To joke; لطیفه سز l*à*tīfɛ́ssiz, *ad. t.* Really, without joking; لطیفه جی l*à*tīfɛji, *s. t.* A joker; لطیفه کو l*à*tīfɛ́-ghyū, *s. p.* A wit, sayer of witty things.

لعاب lù''āb, *s. a.* A jelly, juice and sugar reduced to a jelly; slaver; لعاب الشمس lù''ābu-'sh-shèmss, (Sun's slaver) Fine cobwebs floating in the air.

لعان lī''ān, *s. a.* A formal bearing witness upon oath in cases of adultery, coupled with self-execration if the testimony be false. [diversion.

لعب là''b, *s. a.* Play, amusement,

لعبتباز lù''betbāz, *s. p.* An exhibitor of *fantoccini* or *ombres chinoises*.

لعبه lù''bɛ́, *s. a.* Any game of amusement; a plaything; a doll.

لعل là''l, *s. a.* The garnet (a stone); carmine (colour); لعل مذاب là''li-mùzAb (Melted garnet), Wine.

لعن là''n, *s. a.* A cursing.

لعنت là''net (*vulg.* nālèt), *s. a.* A curse, malediction; ا—, —et, *and* لعنت اوقومق là''net-òkumak, *v.n.* To curse, utter a curse; لعنت اولسون là''net-òlsun! May he (she, *or* it) be accursed; لعنة الله علیه là''nétu-'llāhi-''àlèyh! (May) the malediction of God (be) upon him!

لعین là''īn, *a. a.* Accursed; اللعین èl-là''īn, *s. a.* The devil, Satan.

لغت lughàt (*pl.* لغات lùghAt), *s. a.* Language, idiom; a word; a lexicon, dictionary; لغات کتابی lùghAt-kìtAb*i*, *s. t.* A dictionary.

لغز làghz, *s. p.* A slip, trip, stumble; —, lùghàz, *s. a.* An enigma, a riddle; an ambiguous phrase.

لغزان làghzān, *a. p.* Sliding, slipping, tripping, stumbling.

لغزیده làghzīdé, *a. p.* Who has slipped, tripped, stumbled.

لغم là*ghi*m, *s. t.* A sewer, drain; a military mine; لغمجی là*ghi*mj*i*, *s. t.* A sapper and miner; a sewerman, a nightman; لغم قازمق là*ghi*m-kAzm*a*k, To construct (dig) a mine; لغم اتمق là*ghi*m-Atm*a*k, To fire, or spring a mine.

لغو làghv, *s. a.* A blunder; nonsense; an abolishing, suppressing (an office); ا—, —et, *v.a.* To abolish, suppress.

لغوفت lòghofèt, *s. t.* (*Greek* λογοθέτης), Title of a high political functionary of the subject Greek nation, acting between the synod and the community; also that of a functionary in Wallachia and in Moldavia, who is a kind of home secretary of state.

لغوی lŭghavī (*fem.* لغویه lùghavìyyé), *a. a.* Literal, etymological (sense of a word).

لغویات làghvìyyāt, *s. pl. a.* (*no sing.*), Foolish talk, nonsensicalities.

لف lèff, *s. a.* An enveloping, folding in something, inclosing in a letter; ا—, —et, *v.a.* To envelop, fold in, enclose.

لفظ lAfz, لفظه lAfza, *s. a.* A word; لفظاً lAfzan, *ad. a.* Verbally; verbatim; لفظابلفظ (lAfiz)-bè-(lAfiz), *ad. p.* Word by word; لفظی lAfzi (*fem.* لفظیه lAfzìyyé), *a. a.* Verbal; اضافت لفظیه ìzāféti-lAfzìyyé, A verbal relation or construction of noun with noun in a sentence. [Nicosia, in Cyprus.

لفقوشه Lèfkōsha, *s. t.* The town of

لق l*i*k (لك lik in soft words), A Turkish terminal syllable with various meanings. 1st. When added to the word denoting any kind of trader, artisan, officer, or functionary, it denotes *the abstract trade, art, office, function*, or *quality*; as, فوچیجی fìch*i*j*i*, a cooper, فوچیجیلق fìch*i*j*i*l*i*k, the cooper's trade or art; یوزباشیلق yùz-bAsh*i*l*i*k, the rank of captain; کاتبلك kyātiblik, the office of secretary; پادشاهلق pādi-shāhl*i*k, the regal or imperial office or function. 2nd. Added in the same way to any noun, it denotes the *abstract essential quality* or *function* of the thing named; as, قلملك kàlEm-lik, the peculiar quality or function of a pen; قلجلق k*i*l*i*jl*i*k, the quality or function of a sword; آدملك ādEmlik (AdAml*i*k), The quality of man; &c. 3rd. Added to the name of anything made of any material, if accompanied with a noun of number and the name of the material, it denotes *the quantity of material necessary* for the number of things designated; as, برستریلك چوقه b*i*r-sètrilik-(chòha), the quantity of cloth necessary for one coat; if the noun of number be wanting, then this syllable denotes *a quantity of the material* fit for the object named; as, ستريللكچوقه sètrilik-(chòha), cloth fit for coats. 4th. Joined to a noun of time, it denotes a thing that has required or would require the time named for its production, accomplishment, or being due; as, برايلق‌چوجق bìr-àylik-chòjuk, A child one month old; اوچ‌كونلك‌يول ùch-ghyùnluk--yòl, three days' journey; ايلق àylik, monthly pay; هفته‌لق hAftalik, weekly pay. 5th. Joined to the name of any natural object which creates a distinction between different kinds of land, it designates land where those objects abound; as, اورمانلق òrmAnlik, a country of forests, طاشلق tAshlik, stony ground, rocky country; طاغلق dAghlik, mountainous, hilly country. 6th. Joined to many nouns it forms a name of a thing special to what the simple noun indicates; as, چبوقلق chìbūkluk, a cupboard where pipes are kept; يازلق yàzlik, clothes, &c., peculiar to summer; توزلق tòzluk, gaiters, as especially designed to protect the legs from dust; طوزلق tùzlūk, a salt-cellar; بشلك bèshlik, a five-piastre piece. 7th. Added to an adjective, it denotes the abstract quality of the same; as, ايولك īyilik, goodness; بياضلق bèyAzlik, whiteness. 8th. Joined to the infinitives of verbs, it forms an abstract verbal noun; as, باقمقلق bAkmaklik, the act of looking, looking in the abstract; كتمكلك ghìtmeklik, the act of going.

لقا lìkā, *s. a.* The face, countenance, physiognomy.

لقب làkab (*pl.* القاب èlkāb), *s. a.* A title of honour. [See لاقردى.

لقردى *or* لاقردى làkirdi, *s. t.* Talk, &c.

لقطه làkta, *s. a.* Any kind of found or stray property. [A stork.

لقلاق làklāk, لقلق làklàk (lèylek), *s. a.*

لقلقيات làklàkìyyāt, *s. pl. a.* (*no sing.*), Senseless chattering, vain babbling, arguments devoid of sense.

لقمه lòkma, *s. a.* A mouthful; a kind of globular fritter.

لقوم lùkūm (lòkum), *s. pl. a.* (*of* لقمه lòkma), Mouthfuls; (*as a Turkish singular*), a kind of small round cake-nut, and various kinds of small cake.

لقه lìka, *s. t.* Refuse silk used for filling inkstands before pouring in the ink.

لقيط làkīt, *s. a.* A foundling.

لك lik, *Turkish termination.* See لق lik.

لكام lìghyām, *s. p.* A bridle and reins.

لكد lèked, *s. p.* A kick; a blow, slap, box, cuff; لكدزده lèked-zèdé, *and* لكدكوب lèked-kyūb, *a. p.* Kicked, beaten, trodden under foot.

لكن lākin, *c. a.* (*also* ولكن vè-lākin), But; —, lèghen, *s. t.* An ewer.

لكنت lùknet, *s. a.* Impediment; لكنت لسان lùknéti-lìssān, Impediment of speech.

لكه lèké, *s. t.* A spot, soil, stain, blemish;

لكه‌دار lèkédār, *a. p.* لكه‌لو lèkéli, *a. t.* Soiled, stained, spotted, blemished; —ا, —et, *v.a.* To spot, soil, stain, blemish; —, *v.n.* To make spots, stains, blemishes; لكه‌لتمك lèkélɪt-mek, *v.a.* To spot, soil, stain, blemish; لكه‌لنمك lèkélɪnmek, لكه‌او lèké-òl, *v.n.* To become spotted, soiled, stained, blemished; لكه‌جى lèkéji, *s. t.* A scourer of stained clothes.

لم lèm, *ad. a.* (*in composition*), Not; لم‌يزل lèm-yèzìl, *a. a.* Which fades not away, eternal; لم‌يزلى lèm-yèzilī, *a. a.* Pertaining to the Eternal (God).

لمحه lèmha, *and* لمحة‌العين lèmhatu-"àyn, *s. a.* A look, glance; a moment.

لمس lèmss, *s. a.* Touching, feeling.

لمعان lèm"ān, *a. a.* Shining, sending forth rays of light.

لمعه lèm"a (*pl.* لمعات lèm"āt), *s. a.* A ray of light, flash.

لمق lamak, لمك lémek with soft verbs, *Turkish termination of infinitives*, which, added to many nouns, form verbs active or neuter.

لنك lènk, *a. p.* Lame; —, lìnk, *and* لنكلمه lìnklama, *s. t.* A horse's trotting pace.

لنكر lènghɪr, *s. p.* A ship's anchor; لنكرانداز lènghɪr-èndāz, *a. p.* Anchored, at anchor; —— او, lènghɪr-èndāz-òl, *v.n.* To anchor, to cast anchor.

لنمق lanmak, لنمك lɪnmek for soft words, *Turkish terminations of infinitives*, which, added to many nouns or substantives, form verbs neuter.

لو lèv, *c. a.* If, even though, though; ولو wè-lèv, And even though; —, li, lɪ, lū, Turkish termination for forming adjectives from nouns, with the sense of *possessing*, or being somehow *related to*, the thing named.

لوا lìwā, *s. a.* A flag, banner, standard; a brigade of soldiers; ميرلوا mīri-lìwā, *s. t.* A brigadier or major-general in the army or a vice or rear admiral in the navy.

لواحق lèwāhik, *s. pl. a.* (*of* لاحقه, *not used*), Appurtenances.

لواديه Lìvādia, *s. t.* Thessaly.

لوازم lèwāzim (*pl.* لوازمات lèwāzimāt), *s. pl. a.* (*of* لازمه lāzimé), Necessaries, needful things, requisites; inseparable accompaniments.

لواطه liwāta, *s. a.* Sodomy, the act of the people to whom Lot (لوط Lūt) preached.

لوام lèvwām (*fem.* لوامه lèvwāmé), *a. a.* Reproaching, upbraiding; نفس لوامه nèfssi-lèvwāmé, The flesh, the carnal spirit, in the middle stage between utter rebellion and complete subjection, when it is forced to submit to the will, but not without an effort to domineer.

لوامع lèvāmi", *s. pl. a.* Rays, flashes; [bright, shining things.

لوائح lèwā'ih, *s. pl. a.* Manifest things; written reports, projects.

لوبيه lūbiya, *s. p.* The haricot bean.

لوث lèvss, *s. a.* Dirt, filth, pollution.

لوح lèvh, لوحه lèvh*a*, *s. a.* A flat surface, plate, board, table, tablet, &c., which can be written over; لوح محفوظ lèvh*i*-màhfūz, (The preserved tablet) The tablet on which God has inscribed the decrees of His providence, the tablet of God's omniscience and prescience.

لوز lèvz, *s. a.* An almond.

لوغسه *or* لوغوسه lò*gh*ussa, *s. t.* A woman newly delivered in childbed.

لوقانده lòkànd*a*, *s. t.* (*Italian*), An eating-house, a lodging-house, an inn, a hotel, a tavern.

لوكن lù*ky*un, *s. t.* A peculiar kind of oil cement, used for water-pipes, cocks, &c.

لولاك lèv-lāk, *comp. a.* If thou hadst not existed, had it not been for thee (said to have been addressed by God to Muhammed, with the addition, "Verily the heavens had not been created." The ك is the Arabic pronoun, *thee* or *thy*; consequently Muhammed is styled كاف لولاك kyāfi-lèv-lāk, the ك (*thou*) of the phrase or address لولاك).

لؤلؤ lù'lù', *s. a.* A pearl; لؤلؤپاش lù'lù'-pāsh, *a. p.* Pearl scattering.

لوله lùlé, *s. t.* A bowl of a smoking-pipe; a large water-pipe or spout; a certain measure for water-pipes in the hydraulic system.

لوم lèvm, *s. a.* Blame, reproach, reprimand; ا—, —et, *v.n.* To speak blamingly.

لون lèvn, *s. a.* Colour; a kind, sort, species.

لونجه lònj*a*, *s. t.* A place for a lounge, for meeting.

لوند lèvend, *s. t.* A volunteer in a certain corps in days of old.

لوندره Lòndr*a*, *s. t.* London.

له l*a*, lé, *pr. t.* (*contracted from* ايله il*a*), With; —, lèh, *s. t.* Poland; —, làhū, lèh, *comp. a.* For him or it; —, làhū,. *s. a.* (An acting or speaking in) favour (or for someone); لهمه *or* لهمه làhūm*a*, لهمده *or* لهمده làhūmd*a*, In my favour; لهسنه *or* لهسنه làhūssin*a*, لهسنده *or* لهسنده làhūssind*a*, In his, or her favour, &c.; لهلو lèhli, *a. t.* A Pole, Polish.

لها làhā, *comp. a.* For her *or* it.

لهجه lèhjé, *s. a.* The tongue; a language, idiom; the face, countenance, visage; —, *s. t.* The Polish language; Polish manner.

لهذا lìhāzā, *comp. a.* For this, for this reason.

لهو lèhv, *s. a.* A playing, romping, diverting, amusing one's self.

لهيم lèhim, *s. t.* Solder; لهيملمك lèhimlémek, *v.a.* To solder.

لى li, *Turkish termination for adjectives, generally written* لو, which see.

لياقت liyākAt, *s. a.* Merit, worthiness.

ليال lèyāl, ليالى lèyālī, *s. pl. a.* (*of* ليل lèyl), Nights.

لئام lì'ām, *s. pl. a.* (*of* لئيم lè'īm), Wretches, reprobates.

ليت lèyté! *int. a.* Oh, that it were! Would to God!

ليث lèyss, *s. a.* A lion.

ليزبون Lìzbon, *s. t.* Lisbon (town of).

ليسى lèysa, *a. negative,* It is not, there is not, is not; ليس الخبر كالعيان lèysa-'l-khàbɛr-kè-'l-''ìyān, Hearsay is not like eye-witness. (Dogma of jurisprudence); —, līss, *a. p.* (*in composition*), Who licks; كاسه ليس kyāssé-līss, A lick-trencher, parasite.

ليف līf, *s. a.* A fibrous mass obtained from the palm and used for lathering soap in baths.

ليك līk (*contr. for* لكن lākin), *c. p.* But.

ليل lèyl, *s. a.* The night; ليلاً lèylan, *ad. a.* By night; ليل ونهار lèyl-u-nàhār, Day and night; تساوى ء ليل و نهار tèssāvī'i-lèyl-u-nàhār, The equinox.

ليلاك lèylāk, *s. t.* The lilac tree or flower.

ليله lèylɛ, *s. a.* A night; ليلة القدر lèylétu-'l-kàdr (The night of power, the night of destiny), The night before the 27th day of Ramazan, being that in which Muhammed's first revelation occurred; ليلهٔ رغائب lèylé'i-ràghā'ib (The night of desirabilities), The night before the first Friday in the month Rèjeb, being that of the conception of Muhammed; ليلهٔ معراج lèylé'i-mī''rāj, (The night of the ascension) The night before the 26th day of Rèjeb, in which Muhammed's ascension to the presence of God took place; ليلهٔ برات lèylé'i-bèrāt, The night of the diploma, being that before the 15th day of Shà''bān, in which it is supposed the recording angels close the register of the year; ليلهٔ مولد lèylé'i-mèvlèd (mèvlūd), The night of (Muhammed's) birth, being that before the 12th day of Rèbī''u-'l-èvvɛl; ليلهٔ زفاف lèylé'i-zìfāf, The bridal night.

ليمان līmàn, *s. t.* (*Greek* λιμὴν), A harbour, port; ليمانلق līmànlìk, *s. t.* State of calm of air and water; ليمان رئيسى līmàn-rè'īssi, *s. t.* A harbour-master; ليمان رئيسى پاشا līmàn-rè'īssi-pàsha (*formerly* بك bègh), The port-admiral.

ليمو līmū, *s. p.*, ليمون līmōn, *s. t.* A lemon.

ليموناته līmonāta, *s. t.* Lemonade.

لين lèyyin (*fem.* لينه lèyyinɛ), *a. a.* Gentle, mild, soft, yielding; —, lèyin, *prep. t.* During, during the time of; according to, after the manner of; لين الجانب lèyyinu-'l-jānib, *a. a.* Of a mild disposition.

لينت līnèt, *s. a.* Softness, emolliency; easiness of the bowels.

ليورپول Lìvèrpūl, *s. t.* Liverpool (town of).

ليونه Lìona, *s. t.* Lyons (town of, in France).

لئيم lè'īm, *a. a.* Worthy of blame and reproach.

م

م mīm. Twenty-seventh letter of the Turkish alphabet, having the value of *m* in English. Its numeral value in chronograms and astronomical tables is 40, and in the dates of letters it stands for the month محرم Muharrem. Added to a noun, it is the possessive pronoun of the first person singular, and if the noun ends in a consonant, that consonant takes an èssérÉ (ـِ), for vowel; as بابام bÂbAm, My father, قلمم kàlÉmim, My pen. Added to a verb in the *third pers. sing.* (with the same rule as to the vowel), it is the sign of the *first pers. sing.* سورم sèvÈrim, I love; باقيورم bÂkiyorim, I am looking; كتسهم ghìtsEm, If I go, that I were to go. Interposed between the root of a verb and its conjugational inflexions, or added to the root in the imperative singular (with the addition of ا or ه as a vowel, if required), it constitutes the negative voice; as سومه sÈvma, Do not love; كلمدى ghÈlmadi, He did not come. Either alone, at the end of a phrase, or in the form of يم *or* ايم im, it is the first person singular present of the fragmentary verb substantive, and signifies *I am;* تميزادمم tèmiz-ÂdAmim, I am a respectable person.

ما mā, *s. a.* Water; juice; humour; —, *pron. a.* What, that which, whatever, so long as; (*added to interrogatives*) Soever.

مآب mà'āb, *s. a.* A resort, focus, place to which one returns; شوكتمآب shèvkEt-mà'āb (Focus of autocracy), The Sultan. [mains.

ماباقى mā-bÂkī, *s. a.* That which re-

مأبون mè'būn, *s. a.* A passive sodomite.

مابين mā-bèyn, *s. a.* The interval between two things, the midst of several things; —, mā-bèyna, *pr. a.* Between; amongst; مابين اوطهسى mābèyn-òdassi, *s. t.* A room between the women's and men's apartments, communicating with both, and capable of being used as part of both on occasions; مابين همايون mābeyni-hùmāyūn, The Sultan's ordinary reception-rooms or palace.

مات māta, *a. verb.* Obit, died (*used in chronologies*); —, mÂt, *s. p.* Checkmate; ا—, —et, *v.a.* To checkmate (in chess); to frustrate.

ماتقدم mā-tàkÂddEm, *s. a.* The words or time preceding; ماتقدمدنبرو mā-tàkÂddEmdan-bèri, Ab antiquo, from times of old.

ماتم mātEm, *s. p.* Mourning for the dead; ا—, —et, To mourn for the dead.

مآثر mà'āssir, *s. pl. a.* (*sing. not used*), Traces, signs, vestiges; any things worthy of being accounted monuments, as books, buildings, acts, &c.

مآثم mà'āssim, *s. pl. a.* (*sing. not used*), Sins, evil deeds. [or spoken of.

مأثور mè'sūr, *a. a.* Traditionally related

ماجد mājid, *a. a.* Glorious, glorified.

ماجرا mā-jèrā, *s. a.* That which happened, an event, adventure.

مأجوج mè'jūj, *s. a.* Magog, name of a northern tribe behind Caucasus.

ماجور mè'jūr, *a. a.* Rewarded, recompensed; having a recompense attached to it.

ماچین māchīn (māchʊn), *s. p.* Some indefinite part of China; چین وماچین chīn-u-māchīn, China in general.

ماحصل mā-hʌssal, *s. a.* That which exists, which has been collected.

ماحضر mā-hàzar, *s. a.* That which is present or ready. [nihilates.

ماحی māhi, *s. a.* Who obliterates, an-

مأخذ mè'khàz (*pl.* مآخذ mà'ākhiz), *s. a.* A place from which anything is taken or derived, a source, derivation, origin.

مأخوذ mè'khūz, *a. a.* Taken, derived.

مادام mā-dāma, *verb. a.* As long as —— endures; مادامکه mādām-ki, *c. t.* Since, as.

مادر mādʌr, *s. p.* A mother; مادرزاد mādʌrzād, *a. p.* Innate, inborn; مادری màdérī, *s. p.* Maternity, motherhood; —, *a. p.* Maternal; مادرانه mādérānʀ, *a. p.* Pertaining to a mother, maternal.

مادرید Màdrid, *s. t.* Madrid.

ماده māddʀ, *s. a.* Matter; an article, paragraph; —, mādé, *a. p.* She, female. [*a. a.* Material.

مادی māddī (*fem.* مادیه māddìyyʀ),

مادیان mādiyān, مادیانه mādiyānʀ, *s. p.* A mare.

مأذون mè'zūn, *a. a.* Having leave, having permission; permitted.

مار mār, *s. p.* A snake, serpent; —, *Syriac*, Lord (title given to saints and bishops); —, mārr (*fem.* ماره mārrʀ), *a. a.* Which passes (through or by); مارالذکر mārru-'z-zìkr, *a. a.* The aforementioned. [month of March.

مارت màrt, *s. t.* The Syro-Roman

مارد màrid, *s. a.* An obstinate, refractory, rebellious person.

مارسلیا Màrsìlia, Marseilles.

مارطی màrti, *s. t.* A sea-gull. [fish).

مارماهی mār-māhi, *s. p.* An eel (snake-

مارول màrʊl, *s. t.* A lettuce, cos-lettuce.

ماریه màriya, *s. t.* A ewe.

مازغال mʌzghʌl, *s. t.* An embrasure.

مازو *or* مازی màzi, *s. t.* A nut-gall, gall-nut. [cedes; preceding time.

ماسبق mā-sèbak, *s. a.* That which pre-

ماسك māssik (*fem.* ماسكه māssikʀ), *a. a.* Who or which holds fast, retains.

ماسوا mā-sèwā, *s. a.* That which is besides (anything, particularly God; hence), the world, the flesh, and the devil. [tive.

مأسور mè'sūr, *a. a.* Captive, taken cap-

ماسوره màssʊra, *s. p.* A small water-pipe or spout; a small measure of water-pipe in the system of hydraulics.

ماسه màssa, *s. t.* (*Italian*), A table, a dining-table.

ماشطه māshita, *s. a.* A tire-woman; a woman who decks out brides.

ماشه mʌsha, *s. p.* Tongs or pincers.

ماشی māshi, *s. a.* Anything walking; a pedestrian; ماشیاً māshiyʌn, *ad. a.* On foot, by way of walking.

ماصدق mā-sàdak, *s. a.* That which proves a saying to be true; a proof, a corroborative fact.

ماضى māzī (*fem.* ماضيه māzìyyé), *a. a.* Which has gone by, former; —, *s. a.* The preterite, the past tense; فعل ماضى fi''li-māzī, A verb in the preterite; حال ماضى hāli-māzi, The imperfect tense, the past condition, or *past present.*

ماعدا mā-''àdā, *s. a.* Whatever is other; —, *ad. t.* Other; دن ماعدا dan-mā''àdā, Besides, else, further; اندن ماعدا andan-mā''àdā, بوندن ماعدا bündan-mā''àdā, *c. t.* Furthermore.

ماغون màghun, *s. t.* Mahogany.

مافات mā-fāt, *s. a.* That which has been lost (time or opportunity).

مافى البال mā-fi-'l-bāl, مافى الضمير mā-fi-'z-zàmīr, *comp. a.* That which is in the heart or mind.

ماقبل mā-kàbl, *s. a.* The word (or words) or letter preceding, or the place thereof.

ماكان mā-kyān, *s. a.* That which is, was, or has been.

مأكل mè'kèl (*pl.* مآكل mà'ākil), *and* مأكول mè'kyūl (*pl.* مأكولات mè'kyūlāt), *s. a.* An eatable, food.

ماكيان mākiyān, *s. p.* A hen, a fowl.

مال māl, *s. a.* Anything that can be accounted property; money, effects; (*in the provinces*) sheep; —, māl, *a. p.* (*in composition*), Who rubs; مالى mālī (*fem.* ماليه māliyyé), *a. a.* Pertaining to the treasury, to the public finances; امور ماليه ùmūru-māliyyé, Financial affairs; ماليت māliyyèt, *s. a.* Value, valuableness, quality of being valuable; بيت المال bèytu-'l-māl, *or* بيت مال المسلمين bèytu-māli-'l-mùsslimīn, The public treasury; بيت المالجى bèytu-'l-mālji, *s. t.* An officer whose duty it is to calculate and collect the share of the public treasury from the estates of defunct persons, and from the spoils of war.

مآل mà'āl, *s. a.* The place to which one returns, a resort; the sense, meaning (of a sentence); مآلسز mà'ālsiz, *a. t.* Meaningless; trifling, inconsiderable.

مالاكلام mā-lā-kèlām, *a. a.* Beyond all expression; beyond controversy.

مالامال mālāmāl, *a. p.* Brimful, quite filled, full.

مالايعنى mā-lā-yà''nī, *a. a.* Vain, useless, worthless, trifling.

ماليخوليا mālikhūlyā, *s. a.* (*Greek* μέλαγχολη), Any vain idea.

مالزم *and* مالزمه mā-lèzimé, *s. a.* The needful, that which is necessary.

مالطه Màlta, *s. t.* The island of Malta.

مالك mālik, *s. a.* A possessor, owner, a king; — اول, —ōl, *v.n.* To own, possess, to be possessed, in possession; مالك ملك māliki-milk, مالك يوم الدين māliku-yèvmi-'d-dīn, God, the possessor of all sovereignty, king of the day of judgment.

مالكانه mālikyāné, *a. p.* Pertaining to a possessor; pertaining to a king; —, *s. t.* A manor, of which the tithes are paid to the lord, but of which the arable land is owned by separate proprietors.

مألوف mèʿlūf (*fem.* مألوفه mèʿlūfé), *a. a.* Accustomed, usual, habituated, habitual.

ماله mà*la*, *s. p.* A mason's trowel.

ماليده mālidé, *a. p.* Rubbed.

ما مضا mā-mʌzā, *s. a.* What is past; مضا ما مضا mʌzā-mā-mʌzā, What is past is past; let bye-gones be bye-gones.

ما ملك mā-mèlek, *s. a.* What is possessed, one's possessions.

مأمن mèʿmèn, *s. a.* A place of safety; a person in whom trust is placed.

مأمور mèʿmūr, *a. a.* Under orders, under authority; —, *s. a.* A public functionary, a commissioner; مأموريت mèʿmūriyyèt, *s. a.* Any employ, office, or commission under government.

مأموره mèʿmūré, *s. a.* An order, command; حسب المأموره hàssb*a*-'l-mèʿmūré, *ad. a.* In accordance with the orders received (or given).

مأمول mèʿmūl, *a. a.* Hoped for, expected; —, *s. a.* Expectation; ا—, —et, *v.a.* To hope, expect, look for.

مأمون mèʿmūn, *a. a.* Made safe and secure, free from fear.

ماندره màndr*a*, *s. t.* A farm-yard for cows, calves, and oxen.

مانده mʌnd*a*, *s. t.* A buffalo; —, māndé, *a. p.* (*in composition*), Remaining, resting, left; —, *s. p.* Arrears of pay or rations (of the Janissaries); فرومانده fūru-māndé, *a. p.* Tired out, knocked up with fatigue.

مانع māniʿʿ, *a. a.* Impeding; —, *s. a.* An obstacle, impediment, difficulty; —او, —ōl, *v.n.* To impede, prevent, obstruct, hinder.

مانند mānènd, *a. p.* Life.

مانوس mèʿnūss, *a. a.* Familiarized with, accustomed to.

مانى (*for* معنى) mān*i*, *s. t.* A song; مانى چاغرمق mān*i*-chà*ghi*rmak, *v.n.* To sing a song.

مأوا (*for* مأوى) mèʿvà, *s. a.* A habitation, place of abode.

ماورا mā-vèrā, *s. a.* That which is behind or beyond; the space behind; ما وراءالنهر mā-vèrāʿu-'n-nèhr, Transoxiania.

ما وقع mā-vàka*ʿʿ*a, *s. a.* That which has happened.

ماوى màvi (*for* مائى māʿī), *a. t.* Light blue.

مأوى (*or* مأوا) mèʿvà, *s. a.* A habitation, place of abode.

ماه māh, *s. p.* The moon; a month, a solar or calendar month; ماه بماه māh-bè-māh, *ad. p.* Monthly, from month to month, once every month; ماهيه māhìyyé, *s. a.* Monthly pay, salary, wages.

ماهتاب māh-tāb (màhitʌb), *s. p.* Moonlight, moonshine; a squib, slow match, a port-fire.

ماهچه māhché, *s. p. dim.* A small moon, moonlet; figure of a crescent used to be placed on spires, cupolas, flagstaffs, &c.

ماهر māhir, *a. a.* Well versed in any science or art.

ماهی māhī, *s. p.* A fish.

ماهیت māhìyyèt, *s. a.* The quiddity of anything, the essence.

مائت mā'it, *a. a.* Dying; dead.

مائتین mi'atèyn, *s. a. dual* (*of* مائة mi'*a*), Two hundred.

مایخوش māykhòsh, *a. p.* Sourish, acidulous, tart, sub-acid.

مائده mā'idé, *s. a.* A table or tray ready set with food for eating.

مایس māyiss, *s. t.* The Syro-Roman month of May; (in Armenia) fresh made cakes of dung for fuel.

مایستره màyisstra, *s. t.* (*Italian*), The main-sail; مایسترهسرنی màyisstra-sèréni, The main-yard, مایستره دیرکی màyisstra-dīrèghi, The main-mast.

مایع māyi'', *a. a.* Fluid, liquid.

مائل mā'il, *a. a.* Leaning, inclined.

ماینه màyna! *int. t.* (*Italian*), Lower away; ا—, —et, *v.a.* To lower (sails, masts, flags, &c.), to strike, haul down.

مأیوس mè'yūss, *a. a.* Desperate, hopeless, who hopes no more; مأیوسیت mè'yūssìyyèt, *s. a.* Despair, hopelessness, lack of all hope.

مایه māyé, *s. p.* The substance of which anything is made, the material; leaven, ferment; مایهسز māyéssiz, *a. t.* Unleavened.

مائة mi'*a*, *a. a.* One hundred.

مایهسیل māyéssīl, *s. p.* (Flood of the humours), The piles, hemorrhoids; any scrofulous appearance or affection of the skin or flesh.

مباح mùbāh, *a. a.* Lawful, not sinful to do or to use.

مباحث mèbāhiss, *s. pl. a.* (*of* مبحث mèbhàss), Subjects treated of; paragraphs.

مباحثه mùbāhéssé, *a. a.* A treating, discoursing; a discussing, disputing, controversy; ا—, —et, *v.n.* To treat, discourse; to discuss, to dispute, hold a controversy.

مباد mèbād, مبادا mèbādā, *int. p.* Be it not! God forbid!

مبادرت mùbādérèt, *s. a.* A setting about (any work), beginning; ا—, —et, *v.n.* To set about, set to work.

مبادله mùbādélé, *s. a.* A mutual exchanging; ا—, —et, *v.a.* To exchange.

مبادی mèbādi, *s. pl. a.* (*of* مبدأ mèbdè'), Sources, origins, beginnings.

مبارز mùbāriz, *s. a.* A fighter, champion, warrior.

مبارزه mùbārézé, *s. a.* Conflict, fight, battle.

مبارك mùbārek, *a.a.* Blessed; —اولسون, mùbārek-òlsun! May it be blessed! (*equivalent to our* "I wish you joy!")

مباشر mùbāshir, *s. a.* A kind of official agent charged to see any business or lawsuit carried through and to help the same.

مباشرت mùbāshérèt, *s. a.* A setting one's self to work; ا—, —et, *v.n.* To set to.

مباعدت mùbā''adèt, *s. a.* A withdrawing, going to a distance.

مبالات mùbālāt, *s. a.* Consideration, regard, deference.

مبالغ mèbāligh, *s. pl. a.* (*of* مبلغ mèblagh), Sums (of money).

مبالغه mùbālagha, *s. a.* Exaggeration; ـا, —et, *v.n.* To exaggerate.

مبانی mèbānī, *s. pl. a.* (*singular not used*), Structures, edifices.

مباهات mùbāhāt, *a. a.* A feeling proud, honoured; ـا, —et, *v.n.* To feel justly proud. [justly proud.

مباهی mùbāhī, *a. a.* Who feels proud,

مبايعه mùbāya''a, *s. a.* A buying; buying up largely; ـا, —et, *v.a.* To buy largely; to buy up old and foreign coins for the mint at their intrinsic value, less the mint profit (one of the most crying evils in Turkey, as the agents in one stage or other invariably pass off, at their nominal value, the coins so bought); مبايعه جی mùbāya''aji, *s. t.* An agent appointed to buy up old and foreign coins for the mint. [unlike, different.

مباين mùbāyin, *a. a.* Separate, distinct,

مباينت mùbāyénèt, *s. a.* Separation, becoming widely separated in distance, quality, or affections.

مبتدا mùbtédà, *s. a.* The grammatical or logical subject of a phrase, sentence, or proposition. [ginner.

مبتدی mùbtédi, *s. a.* A novice, be-

مبتذل mùbtézèl, *a. a.* Little esteemed.

مبتغا mùbtéghà, *a. a.* Desired; —, *s. a.* The thing desired.

مبتلا mùbtélà, *a. a.* Subject to, exposed to, in prey to; addicted, given.

مبتنی mùbténi, *a. a.* Built, founded, based.

مبتهج mùbtèhij, *a. a.* Rejoicing, joyful.

مبجل mùbèjjel, *a. a.* Honoured, to whom honour is paid.

مبحث mèbhàss, *s. a.* A matter of discussion; a section of any treatise, a paragraph, article.

مبدأ mèbdè', *s. a.* An origin, source, commencement, beginning.

مبدل mùbèddel, *a. a.* Changed for or into something else. [given.

مبذول mèbzūl, *a. a.* Abundant, largely

مبرا mùbèrrā, *a. a.* Free, exempt.

مبرد mìbrèd, *s. a.* A file (for filing metals); a rasp.

مبرم mùbrèm, *a. a.* Urgent, which will not be put off; قضای مبرم kAzAyi-mùbrèm, Irresistible fate.

مبرور mèbrūr (*fem.* مبروره mèbrūrÉ), *a. a.* Accounted good; خدمات مبروره khAdémāti-mèbrūrÉ, Good and faithful services. [strated by proofs.

مبرهن mùbèrhèn, *a. a.* Proved, demon-

مبسوط mèbsūt, *a. a.* Spread, extended.

مبشر mùbèshshir, *s. a.* The bringer of good news, of glad tidings.

مبعوث mèb''ūss, *a. a.* Sent; deputed; raised from the dead; —, *s. a.* A deputy, a messenger.

مبغوض mèbghūz, *a. a.* Hated, detested, the object of enmity.

مبلغ mèblagh, *s. a.* A sum of money; —, mùbèlligh, *s. a.* One who communicates (intelligence, information).

مبلق mèblAk (mAb—), *s. a.* A spatula.

مبلول mèblūl, *a. a.* Wetted, drenched.

مبنى mèbnī, *a. a.* Built, founded, based.

مبهم mùbhèm, *a. a.* Doubtful, obscure in meaning.

مبهوت mèbhūt, *a. a.* Reduced to silence, stultified. [the night.

مبيت mèbīt, *s. a.* A place for passing

مبيض mùbèyyiz, *s. a.* A fair-copier; —, mùbèyyez, *a. a.* Copied out fairly.

مبين mùbīn, *a. a.* Which distinguishes truth from error; clear, manifest; declaratory, explanatory; —, mùbèyyin, *a. a.* Which declares, makes manifest; —, mùbèyyen, *a. a.* Declared, made manifest.

متابعت mùtāba"àt, *s. a.* A following, conforming to; ا—, —et, *v.n.* To follow, to conform.

متأثر mùté'èssir, *a. a.* Affected; grieved.

متأخر mùta'àkhkhir, *a. a.* Recent; modern; متأخرين mùta'àkhkhirīn, *s. pl. a.* The moderns.

متأذى mùté'èzzī, *a. a.* Pained, hurt, annoyed, vexed.

متاركه mùtārékĕ, *s. a.* A truce, suspension of hostilities, armistice.

متأسف mùté'èsssif, *a.a.* Sorry, grieved.

متاع mAtā", *s. a.* Any object of merchandise, a piece of goods.

متاعب mAtā"ib, *s. pl. a.* (*singular not used*), Fatigues, fatiguing things.

متألم mùté'èllim, *a. a.* Grieved, pained, afflicted. [strength, solidity.

متانت mètānèt, *s. a.* Firmness, passive

متأهل mùté'èhhil, *a. a.* Married, having a wife.

متبادل mùtébādil (*fem.* متبادله mùtébādilĕ), *a. a.* Interchangeable, interchanged; alternate (angles in geometry).

متبحر mùtébàhhir, *a. a.* Profound as the sea in erudition and learning.

متبوع mètbū", *a. a.* Obeyed, followed, conformed to; —, *s. a.* One's sovereign.

متتالى mùtétāli, *a. a.* Following each other in succession.

متجاسر mùtéjāssir, *a. a.* Daring, having the courage. [ous.

متجانس mùtèjĀniss, *a. a.* Homogene-

متجاوز mùtéjāviz (—jāwuz), *a. a.* Exceeding; passing; more (than any number).

متجسس mùtéjèsssiss, *a. a.* Who pries into, inquires into minutely.

متحاب mùtahābb (*fem.* متحابه mùtahābbĕ), *a. a.* Mutually friendly, mutually loving.

متحاشى mùtahĀshi, *a. a.* Avoiding, abstaining from, keeping clear of.

متحتم mùtahAttim, *a. a.* Indispensable, absolutely necessary. [one.

متحد mùttahid, *a. a.* United, joined in

متحرك mútahàrrik, *a. a.* Moving, in motion; (a letter) followed by a vowel in the same syllable.

متحصن mùtahAsssin, *a. a.* Who fortifies or shuts himself up in a stronghold or fortress.

متحلى mùtahàllī, *a. a.* Ornamented with trinkets and jewels, adorned.

متحمل mùtahàmmil, *a. a.* Bearing, supporting, enduring. [tonished.

متحير mùtahàyyir, *a. a.* Astounded, as-

متحيز mùtahàyyiz, *a. a.* Collected, comprehended, included; possessing, containing; —, *s. a.* A member, fellow (of a grade).

متخشع mùtakhàshshi", متخضع mùtakhàzzi", Endowed with humility, who humbles himself.

متخطى mùtakhàttī, *a. a.* Passing, overstepping (bounds), venturing (too far).

متخلص mùtakhàlliss, *a. a.* Bearing a literary surname.

متخيل mùtakhàyyil (*fem.* متخيله mùtakhàyyilé), *a. a.* Figuring to one's self, imagining; قوت متخيله kùvvéti-mùtakhàyyilé, The imaginative faculty.

متداول mùtédāvil, *a. a.* Passing current from hand to hand (money, books, &c.). [pious.

متدين mùtédèyyin, *a. a.* Religious,

متذكر mùtézèkkir, *a. a.* Calling to mind, remembering. [self, abasing himself.

متذلل mùtézèllil, *a. a.* Humbling him-

مترادف mùtérādif (*fem.* مترادفه mùtérādifé), *a. a.* Joined together in travel, in point of time (events), in meaning (words); synonymous.

متراكم mùtérākim, *a. a.* Collected together in quantities.

مترتب mùtérèttib, *a. a.* Which enters into any series or category; which enters into any shape, form, or mode of being, formed, composed, consisting.

مترجم mùtèrjim, *s. a.* A translator; —, mūtèrjèm, *a. a.* Translated from one language into another; مترجم اول mùtèrjimi-èvvel, Chief translator (title of the principal assistant of the Interpreter of State).

مترجى mùtérèjjī, *a. a.* Hoping, wishing, anxiously looking. (man).

مترحم mùtéràhhim, *a. a.* Compassionate

متردد mùtérèddid, *a. a.* Doubtful, leaning first to one opinion and then to another, hesitating which to choose; coming and going, going to and fro.

مترس mètèriss, *s. t.* Works of circumvallation, field-works round a camp, trenches, breast-works. [exuding.

مترشح mùtérèshshih, *a. a.* Transuding,

مترصد mùtéràsssid, *a. a.* Watching, observing, looking out for.

مترقب mùtéràkkib, *a. a.* Looking for, expecting, hoping, wishing.

مترقى mùtéràkki, *a. a.* Increasing, rising, augmenting by degrees (in quantity or in rank); reaching, attaining.

متركب mùtérèkkib, *a. a.* Composed, consisting (of several things).

متروك mètrūk, *a. a.* Abandoned, left, neglected; متروكات mètrūkyāt, *s. pl. a.* Property left behind at death.

متزاحف mùtézāhif, *a. a.* Drawn up and advancing in order of battle.

متزاحم mùtézāhim, *a. a.* Collected in crowds, crowding, flocking.

متزايد mùtézāyid, *a. a.* Increased, augmented (in number or quantity).

متساوى mùtèssāvī, *a. a.* Reciprocally equal to one another.

متسرى mùtèssèrri, *a. a.* Having a slave concubine.

متسلط mùtéssAllit, *a. a.* Arrogating to himself the exercise of power (over any person or thing).

متسلم mùtéssèllim, *s. a.* A governor of a single town or district.

متسلى mùtéssèlli, *a. a.* Consoled, who derives consolation.

متشابه mùtéshābih, *a. a.* Mutually resembling one another; metaphorical, allegorical, parabolical (expressions).

متشاعر mùtéshā‘‘ir, *s. a.* A person who pretends to be a poet, a writer of doggerel.

متشبث mùtéshèbbiss, *a. a.* Taking hold of, taking in hand; having recourse to; setting to work.

متشبه mùtéshèbbih, *a. a.* Mutually resembling each other.

متشرع mùtéshèrri‘‘, *a. a.* Versed in the canon law.

متشرف mùtéshèrrif, *a. a.* Deriving honour, esteeming himself honoured.

متشعب mùtéshà‘‘‘ib, *a. a.* Derived (as a branch of a family, a ramification, &c.)

متشكر mùtéshèkkir, *a. a.* Thankful, grateful.

متشكل mùtéshèkkil, *a. a.* Formed, figured, put in form.

متشكى mùtéshèkkī, *a. a.* Complaining, lamenting.

متصادف mùtÉssAdif, *a. a.* Who meets, lights upon, finds.

متصادم mùtèssAdim, *a. a.* Mutually dashing against each other.

متصبر mùtÉssAbbir, *a. a.* Patient through reflection, long-suffering.

متصدى mùtÉssAddī, *a. a.* Setting about, occupying one's self with (any work).

متصرف mùtÉssàrrif, *s. a.* An absolute governor of a large province; —, *a. a.* Disposing absolutely of things, being absolute master and possessor; declinable (in grammar).

متصف mùttAssif, *a. a.* Qualified, endowed with, possessing (a general quality).

[—, *ad. t.* Continually.

متصل mùttAssil, *a. a.* Joined, touching;

متصور mùtÉssAvvEr, *a. a.* Imagined, conceived; imaginable, conceivable.

متصوف mùtÉssAvvif, *s. a.* One who studies, pursues, or follows out the science of mystical philosophy and religion.

متضاعف mùtézā‘‘if, *a. a.* Doubled or increased manifold.

متضرر mùtazàrrir, *a. a.* Suffering loss or damage.

متضرع mùtÉdàrri‘‘, *a. a.* Acting with humility, as a supplicant.

متضع mùttAzi‘‘, *a. a.* Low, abject, humble.

متضمن mùtazàmmin, *a. a.* Contained, included; containing, including, comprehending; —, *s. a.* Surety, guarantee, bail.

متطابك mùtétAbik, *a. a.* Mutually conformable, agreeing, corresponding, similar. [behind each other.

متطارق mùtétārik, *a. a.* Following closely

متطاهر mùtétāhir, *a. a.* Canonically cleansed and purified by ablution.

متطارق mùtétàrrik, *a. a.* Contending, opposing, assaulting, striking repeatedly. [clean.

متطهر mùtétàhhir, *a. a.* Cleansed, made

متظلل mùtazàllil, *a. a.* Protected, or taking protection under the shade.

متظلم mùtazàllim, *a. a.* Who complains of injury or wrong.

متظهر mùtazàhhir, *a. a.* Who leans his back against any support.

متعاقب mùta''ākib, *a. a.* Following each other in succession.

متعال mùta''āl, *a. a.* (God) Most High.

متعاهد mùta''āhid, *a. a.* Mutually stipulating and covenanting with each other.

متعبد mùta''àbbid, *a. a.* Devout, practically devotional. [wondering.

متعجب mùta''àjjib, *a. a.* Surprised,

متعدد mùta''àddid, *a. a.* Numerous.

متعدی mùta''àddī, *a. a.* Transitive (a verb). [beset with valid obstacles.

متعذر mùta''àzzir, *a. a.* Impossible,

متعرض mùta''àrriz, *a. a.* Meddling, injuriously interfering.

متعسر mùta''àsssir, *a. a.* Surrounded with difficulty. [ing.

متعفن mùta''àffin, *a. a.* Putrid; stink-

متعلق mùta''àllik, *a. a.* Suspended, attached, dependent; related, connected (from, to, on, with); متعلقات mùta''àllikāt, *s. pl. a.* Dependants and relatives; appurtenances.

متعه mùt''a, *s. a.* A temporary marriage (practised in Persia).

متعهد mùta''àhhid, *a. a.* Who has undertaken (to do or manage something).

متعين mùta''àyyin, *a. a.* Distinguished, notable (person); متعينان mùta''àyyinān, *s. pl. p.* Distinguished, principal persons.

متغلب mùtéghàllib, *a. a.* Exercising an illegal and violent authority; —, *s. a.* A rebel or enemy successful for a time. [altered; spoilt, ruined.

متغير mùtéghàyyir, *a. a.* Changed,

متفاوت mùtéfāvit, *a. a.* Unequal in quantity, differing.

متفحص mùtéfàhhiss, *a. a.* Curious, minute and dilligent in inquiry.

متفرج mùtéfèrrij, *s. a.* (*pl.* متفرجين mùtéfèrrijīn), A promenader.

متفرد mùtéfèrrid, *a. a.* Isolating one's self; rebellious, declaring one's self independent.

متفرع mùtéfèrri'', *a. a.* Derived as a branch or ramification; متفرعات mùtéfèrri''āt, *s. pl. a.* Details; ramifications, branches.

متفرق mùtéfèrrik (*fem.* متفرقه mùtéfèrrika), *a. a.* Separate.

متفرقه mùtéfèrrika, *s. a.* Title of a corps of officers in the olden time, who used to be sent on missions by the Sultan.

متفق mùttéfik, *a. a.* United (in any moral manner); —, *s. a.* An ally, confederate; الرأی —, mùttéfiku-'r--rè'y, *a. a.* United in opinion, agreed; unanimous; — عليه, mùttéfiku-''àlèyh, *s. a.* That upon which different people are agreed.

متفقد mùtéfàkkid, *a. a.* Inquiring after, or longing after, any absent thing.

متفقه mùtéfàkkih, *a. a.* Studious of, or versed in, the canon law.

متفكر mùtéfèkkir, *a. a.* Thoughtful, thinking.

متفوق mùtéfèvwik, *a. a.* Superior (to anything).

متقابل mùtékābil, *a. a.* Opposite to each other.

متقاضی mùtakāzī, *a. a.* Who duns, presses for payment.

متقاعد mùtakā''id, *a. a.* Pensioned off, allowed to retire with a pension.

متقدم mùtakàddim, *a. a.* Preceding, going before; متقدمين mùtakàddimīn, The ancients.

متقرب mùtakàrrib, *a. a.* Approaching.

متقلد mùtakàllid, *a. a.* Who wears round the neck; who obeys, follows.

متقن mùttakin, *a. a.* Who knows for certain, is perfectly convinced.

متقی mùttakī, *a. a.* Pious, devout, God-fearing.

متكا mùttékyà, *s. a.* Anything on which one may lean or recline.

متكبر mùtékèbbir, *a. a.* Proud, puffed up.

متكفل mùtékèffil, *a. a.* Who stands surety, becomes answerable.

متكلف mùtékèllif, *a. a.* Prepared with great cost and care.

متكلم mùtékèllim, *a. a.* Who speaks; نفس — nèfssi - mùtékèllim (The speaker's self), *s. a.* The first person singular of verbs and pronouns in grammar; نفس متكلم مع الغير nèfssi--mùtékèllim - mà''é -'l - ghàyr, (The speaker's self with others) The first person plural.

متكی mùttékī, *a. a.* Leaning against on the elbow.

متكيف mùtékèyyif, *a. a.* Possessing a quality.

متلاطم mùtélātim, *a. a.* Rough (the sea), agitated.

متلافی mùtélāfī, *a. a.* Catching up, making up for (lost time, &c.).

متلاقی mùtélākī, *a. a.* Meeting, coming together.

متلالی mùtélālī (*for* متلألی mùtélè'li'), *a. a.* Glittering, resplendent.

متلذذ mùtélèzziz, *a. a.* Enjoying (anything pleasant), deriving pleasure.

متلفظ mùtélàffiz, *a. a.* Pronounced.

متلقب mùtélàkkib, *a. a.* Taking or bearing a title or surname.

متلون mùtélèvvin, *a. a.* Inconstant, capricious, changeable.

متمادی mùtémādī, *a. a.* Extended in duration, continued; continual; —, *or* متمادياً mùtémādiyyan, *ad. a.* Continually, uninterruptedly.

متمتع mùtémètti'', *a. a.* Reaping a profit or benefit, profiting (by the use or possession of anything).

متمثل mùtémèssil, *a. a.* Conforming to anything.

متمدن mùtémèddin, *a. a.* Established, settled (in some country).

متمرد mùtémèrrid, *a. a.* Perversely obstinate, rebellious.

متمسك mùtémèssik, *a. a.* Miserly, niggardly (person).

متمكن mùtémèkkin, *a. a.* Established (in any place).

متملك mùtémèllik, *a. a.* Possessed of (anything), possessing.

متمم mùtèmmim, *a. a.* Who finishes, completes; —, *s. a.* The supplement (of an arc or angle in trigonometry).

متمنی mùtémènnī, *a. a.* Desiring, asking, praying (for something); —, *or* متمنا mùtémènnà, *a. a.* Asked for, desired, wished for.

متموج mùtémèvvij, *a. a.* Rough with waves (the sea, &c.).

متمول mùtémèvvil, *a. a.* Rich, possessing much property.

متن mètn, *s. a.* The text of any work commented upon.

متناسب mùténāssib, *a. a.* Mutually proportionate, inter-proportionate; well-proportioned in shape; اربع متناسبه èrbà"i-mùténāssébé, (The four proportionals) The rule of three, the rule of proportion.

متناظر mùténāzir, *a. a.* Mutually regarding each other; opposite to each other.

متنافی mùténāfī, *a. a.* Mutually repulsive; inconsistent, incongruous.

متناقض mùténākiz, *a. a.* Mutually demolishing; contradictory.

متناوب mùténāvib, *a. a.* Alternating, taking turns.

متناول mùténāvil, *a. a.* Taking, eating or drinking, partaking.

متناهی mùténāhī, *a. a.* Finite, ending; نا متناهی nā-mùténāhī, Infinite, endless.

متنبع mùténèbbi", *a. a.* Rising, taking rise (a spring, river, &c.).

متنبه mùténèbbih, *a. a.* Aware, advised; on his guard; better aware and conducted in future (after punishment or reprimand).

متنعم mùténà"""im, *a. a.* In the enjoyment of some good.

متنفر mùténèffir, *a. a.* Disgusted; in flight, running away.

متنفس mùténèffiss, *a. a.* Who or which breathes, breathing.

متنکر mùténèkkir, *a. a.* Incognito, not recognisable.

متنوع mùténèvvi", *a. a.* Various, different.

متواتر mùtéwātir, *a. a.* Publicly known, generally spoken of.

متوارث mùtéwāriss, *a. a.* Inheriting in succession.

متوارد mùtéwārid, *a. a.* Successively arriving.

متواری mùtéwāri, *a. a.* Getting behind anything and so being lost from sight.

متوازی mùtéwāzī, *a. a.* Parallel to each other.

متواضع mùtéwāzi", *a. a.* Humble, self-humbling.

متوالی mùtéwālī, *a. a.* Successive, in uninterrupted succession; متوالیة mùtéwālìyyétæn, *ad. a.* In uninterrupted succession, one after the other.

متوجه mùtéwèjjih, *a. a.* Turning the face (towards an object); pointed, directed; travelling in the direction (of a place).

متورع mùtévèrri", *a. a.* Pious, devout.

متوسط mùtéwAssit, *a. a.* Intervening; middling (quality).

متوسل mùtévèssil, *a. a.* Trusting solely [(in God).

متوطن mùtawAttin, *a. a.* Settled (in a country as a home).

متوفی *or* متوفا mùtéwèffà, *a. a.* Dead, [defunct.

متوقع mùtéwàkki", *a. a.* Waiting in expectation.

متوقف mùtéwàkkif, *a. a.* Waiting for the decision, depending on the decision.

متوقی mùtéwàkkī, *a. a.* Cautious, timid.

متوکل mùtévèkkil, *a. a.* Relying, trusting, depending; متوکلاً علی الله mùtévèkkilan-"àla-'llāh, *ad. a.* Putting his trust in God.

متولد mùtévèllid, *a. a.* Born.

متولی mùtévèllī, *a. a.* Turning away (from anything); —, *s. a.* A trustee of property in mortmain.

متهالك mùtahālik, *a. a.* Casting himself precipitately (into danger or trouble).

متهم mùttéhim, *a. a.* Culpable, guilty, convicted of a fault.

متهور mùtéhèvvir, *a. a.* Headstrong, violent, inconsiderate.

متهیج mùtéhèyyij, *a. a.* Set in motion (dust, troops, &c.).

متهیی mùtéhèyyī, *a. a.* Prepared, equipped, in readiness.

متیسر mùtéyèsssir, *a. a.* Facilitated, made easy of accomplishment; becoming accomplished without difficulty.

متیقظ mùtéyàkkiz, *a. a.* Awake; on his guard, watchful.

متین mètīn, *a. a.* Strong, firm.

مثابرت mùssābéret, *s. a.* Setting to (at work), turning to.

مثابه mèssābÉ, *s. a.* Place or degree (of [estimation).

مثال mìssāl, *s. a.* An example, an illustration; a similar thing, counterpart; a command, order; عالم مثال "ālÉmi--mìssāl, The world of counterparts, in which everything occurs, immaterially, in exactly the same time and order as here below materially; a dream.

مثبت mùssbit, *a. a.* Which confirms; —, mùssbèt, *a. a.* Confirmed, proved.

مثقال mìsskāl, *s. a.* A weight for pearls, &c., equal to about 3 dwts. troy.

مثل mèssel, *s. a.* A parable, proverb; —, mìssl, *s. a.* A like thing or quantity; ایکی مثلی ìki-mìssli, Twice the quantity; مثلا mèssélā, *ad. a.* For example; as for example; if, for example; ضرب مثل zàrbi-mèssel, A proverb.

مثلث mùssèllEss, *a. a.* Threefold. composed of three parts; —, *s. a.* A triangle; a preparation of wine boiled with spices and sweetened; مثلثات mùssèlléssāt, *s. pl. a.* Trigonometry, trigonometrics; مثلثات کرویه mùssèlléssāti - kyùréviyyÉ, Spherical trigonometry; مثلث متساوی الاضلاع mùssèlléssi - mùtéssāvìyyu - 'l - AdlĀ", An equilateral triangle; —متساوی الساقین mùssèlléssi - mùtéssāvìyyu -

-'ss-sākàyn, An isosceles triangle; —مختلف الاضلاع, mùssèlléssi-mùkhtèlifu-'l-àdlā'', A scalene triangle; —قائم الزاويه, mùssèlléssi-kā'imu-'z-zāvìyyé, A right-angled triangle; —منفرج الزاويه, mùssèlléssi-mùnfèriju-'z-zāvìyyé, An obtuse-angled triangle; —حاد الزوايا, mùssèlléssi-hāddu-'z-zèwāyā, An acute-angled triangle.

مثللو mìssìlli, *a. t.* Like, similar, of a kind, of a sort; بومثللو bū-mìssìlli, Of this kind; اول مثللو (ò)-mìssìlli, Of that kind.

مثمر mùssmir, *a. a.* Fruitful.

مثمن mùssèmmen, *s. a.* An octagon.

مثنوى mèssnévī, *s. a.* Poetry, every two successive lines or hemistichs of which rhyme with each other.

مثوبت mèssūbet, *s. a.* A promised reward (for good actions).

مثول mùssūl, *s. a.* The standing respectfully in waiting for orders.

مثوى *or* مثوا mèsswà, *s. a.* A place of rest or habitation.

مثيب mùssèyyeb, *a. a.* No longer a virgin, depucelated.

مجاب mùjāb, *a. a.* Answered, accepted; acceptable (prayer).

مجادله mùjādélé, *s. a.* Controversy, contention, dispute; ا—, —et, *v.n.* To contend, dispute.

مجار màjar, *s. t.* A Hungarian; Hungary; —آلتونى, màjar-àltini, A ducat.

مجارى mèjārī, *s. pl. a.* (*of* مجرى mèjrà), Beds (of rivers), courses; the tracks in which things move.

مجاز mèjāz, *a. a.* Permitted, lawful; —, *s. a.* A metaphor; —, mùjāz, *a. a.* Permitted, licit, lawful; مجازى mèjāzī, *a. a.* Metaphorical, figurative.

مجازات mùjāzāt, *s. a.* Punishment; ا—, —et, *v.n.* To punish.

مجال mèjāl, *s. a.* Power, strength, ability (to do anything).

مجالس mèjāliss, *s. pl. a.* (*of* مجلس mèjliss), Assemblies; councils.

مجالست mùjālèssèt, *s. a.* A sitting down in company (with anyone).

مجامعت mùjāma''àt, *s. a.* Sexual intercourse.

مجامله mùjāmélé, *s. a.* A good, kind, honourable treatment.

مجاناً mèjjānan, *ad. a.* Gratis, gratuitously (received or acquired).

مجانبت mùjānébèt, *s. a.* An avoiding, keeping away (from); ا—, —et, *v.n.* To avoid, keep away.

مجاوبه mùjāvébé, *s. a.* An answering each other; altercation.

مجاور mùjāvir, *a. a.* Neighbouring.

مجاهد mùjāhid, *s. a.* One who strives earnestly; a champion of the faith.

مجاهده mùjāhédé, *s. a.* A zealous striving; fighting for the faith.

مجبور mèjbūr, *a. a.* Constrained; put in its place and bound up (a broken bone or sprained joint); obliged (by force or by favour); مجبوريت mèjbūrìyyèt, *s. a.* Constraint; necessity; obligation.

مجبول mèjbūl, *a. a.* Innate, inborn, natural. [selected, chosen.

مجتبا *or* مجتبى mùjtébà, *a. a.* Elected,

مجتمع mùjtèmi'', *a. a.* Collected together, gathered together.

مجتنب mùjtènib, *a. a.* Who avoids, keeps away.

مجتهد mùjtèhid, *s. a.* One who studies the original authorities in matters of religion and law, and founds thereon tenets and doctrine.

مجد mèjd, *s. a.* Majesty ; —, mùjìdd, *s. a.* One who earnestly endeavours.

مجدد mùjèddid, *s. a.* A renewer ; —, mùjèddèd, *a. a.* Renewed, renovated ; new ; مجدداً mùjèddédan, *ad. a.* Anew, afresh, again.

مجذوب mèjzūb, *a. a.* Attracted ; crazy.

مجرا *or* مجرى mèjrà, *s. a.* The bed (of a river), channel, course.

مجرب mùjèrreb, *a. a.* Tried, known by experience ; experienced.

مجرد mùjèrred, *a. a.* Mere, sheer ; naked ; sole, alone ; unmarried ; —, *ad. t.* Only, merely, for nothing else but.

مجرم mùjrim, *s. a.* A culprit, an offender.

مجروح mèjrūh, *a. a.* Wounded.

مجرى mèjrà, *s. a.* See مجرا.

مجزوم mèjzūm, *a. a.* Decided, decided upon ; fully believed, considered as quite substantiated ; marked with the sign ــْـ (a letter), which indicates that it is not to be followed with a vowel in the same syllable when pronounced ; —, *s. a.* The decision or determination taken in any case ; a determined opinion.

مجسم mùjèsssem, *a. a.* Solid (not hollow or superficial) ; زاويهٔ مجسمه zāvìyyé'i--mùjèsssémé, A solid angle.

مجلا *or* مجلى mùjèllà, *a. a.* Polished, burnished ; rubbed up, enlightened.

مجلد mùjèllid, *s. a.* A bookbinder ; —, mùjèlled, *a. a.* Bound (a book) ; —, *s. a.* A volume.

مجلس mèjliss, *s. a.* An assembly, meeting ; a council ; a picture or illustration in Persian books of poetry.

مجمر mìjmer, مجمره mìjméré, *s. a.* A censer.

مجمع mèjmà'', *s. a.* Any place in which things are collected together ; —, *and* مجمعه mèjma''à, *s. a.* A note-book, memorandum-book, album, scrap-book, pocket-book. [summary.

مجمل mùjmèl, *s. a.* Concise, abstract,

مجموع mèjmū'', *a. a.* Collected ; —, *s. a.* The whole.

مجند mùjènned, *a. a.* Collected as troops or regiments, embodied, called out.

مجنون mèjnūn, *a. a.* Mad (possessed with a devil).

مجوز mùjèvvèz, *a. a.* Permitted, tolerated (in grammar).

مجوزه mùjèvvézé, *s. t.* A kind of tall turban worn on state occasions in the olden time by various functionaries.

مجوسى mèjūssī, *s. a.* A fire-worshipper, a magian. [inside.

مجوف mùjèvwèf (mùjèvf), *a. a.* Hollow

مجوهر mùjèvhĕr, *a. a.* Ornamented with pearls and precious stones.

مجهز mùjèhhèz, *a. a.* Equipped, fitted out; rigged and armed (a ship).

مجهود mèjhūd, *s. a.* One's utmost ability.

مجهول mèjhūl, *a. a.* Unknown; passive (*a verb, so called because, in using a verb passive, the actor is not necessarily declared or pointed out*).

مجى mèjī, *s. a.* Arrival, a coming.

مجيب mùjīb, *s. a.* One who answers or grants a request.

مجيد mèjīd, *a. a.* Most glorious, clothed in great majesty; المجيد èl-Mèjīd, *s. a.* God; عبدالمجيد ʻʻabdu-'l-Mèjīd, The servant of God the Most Glorious (*name of a Sultan of Turkey*).

مچ mèch, *s. t.* A small sword, rapier.

محابا mŭhābā, محابات mŭhābāt, *s. a.* Respect of persons, consideration; بى محابا bī-mùhābā, *ad. p.* Without any respect of persons, off-hand.

محاذات mŭhāzāt, *s. a.* Being opposite and parallel; *or* being on the same line. [parallel; equal.

محاذى mŭhāzī, *a. a.* In the same line;

محارب mŭhārib, *a. a.* At war, in a state of warfare.

محاربه mŭhārébé, *s. a.* Warfare; war; a battle, fight, action, engagement.

محاسبه mŭhāssébé, *s. a.* A settling of accounts; an auditing of accounts; محاسبه‌جى mŭhāssébéji, *s. t.* An auditor or accountant-general; — قلمى mŭhāssébé-kàlémi, *s. t.* An audit-office or accountants' office of the treasury.

محاسن màhāssin, *s. pl. a.* (*sing. not used*), Praiseworthy acts or qualities; the beard, whiskers, and mustaches.

محاصر mŭhāssir, *s. a.* A besieger.

محاصره mŭhāssara, *s. a.* A siege; a blockade; ا—, —et, *v.a.* To besiege; to blockade.

محاط mŭhāt, *a. a.* Surrounded, encircled; محاطعلم *or* محاطعلم mŭhāti-ʻʻilm, Embraced in the knowledge, known.

محافظ mŭhāfiz, *s. a.* The governor of a fortified town.

محافظه mŭhāfaza, *s. a.* The guard, keeping, protection, defence; ا—, —et, *v.a.* To guard, keep, protect, defend.

محافل màhāfil, *s. pl. a.* (*of* محفل màhfil, *not used in this sense*), Assemblies, places where people assemble; society.

محاق màhak, *s. a.* Total disappearance of the moon at the end of a lunation.

محاكمه mŭhākémé, *s. a.* The trial (of a person by a judge); ا—, —et, *v.a.* To try, to bring to a trial, to put upon his trial.

محال màhāll, *s. pl. a.* (*of* محل màhàll), Places; —, mŭhāl, *a. a.* Impossible.

محاله màhālé, *s. a.* Fraud, deceit, trick; لامحاله lā-màhālé, *ad. a.* Without fail.

محامد màhāmid, *s. pl. a.* (*of* محمدت màhmédet), Acts or qualities worthy of praise and glory.

محاوره mŭhāvéré, *s. a.* Common conversation; noisy talk.

محب mŭhibb, *s. a.* An affectionate friend; محبانه mŭhibbāné, *a. p.* محبی mŭhibbī, *a. a.* Pertaining to a friend.

محبت màhàbbet, *s. a.* Affection, friendship.

محبس màhbèss, *s. a.* A prison, place of confinement.

محبوب màhbūb (*fem.* محبوبه màhbūbé), *a. a.* Beloved. (*The masculine generally bears a filthy meaning*).

محبوس màhbūss, *a. a.* Imprisoned.

محتاج mŭhtāj, *a. a.* Needing, in need, in want; needy, poor.

محترق mŭhtèrik, *a. a.* Burnt by a conflagration.

محترم mŭhtérèm, *a. a.* Honoured, held in honour, respected, venerated.

محتسب mŭhtèssib, *s. a.* A chief officer of excise, having a supervision over merchants and shop-keepers, at present called احتساب ناظری ihtissāb-nāziri.

محتکر mŭhtèkir, *s. a.* One who keeps back provisions from market in hopes of creating a scarcity and selling dear.

محتمل mŭhtémèl, *a. a.* Possible, probable.

محتمی mŭhtèmī, *a. a.* Who avoids hurtful articles of food, or diet.

محتوی mŭhtèvī, *a. a.* Comprehending, containing, embracing.

محجوب màhjūb, *a. a.* Ashamed; bashful.

محدب mŭhàddeb, *a. a.* Convex.

محدث mŭhàddiss, *s. a.* An author who treats of the acts and words of Muhammed; —, mŭhdèss, *a. a.* Created (not eternal); new, recent (not ancient).

محدد mŭhàddid, *s. a.* A tracer of limits and boundaries.

محدود màhdūd, *a. a.* Limited, bounded; few (in number), small (in extent).

محذور màhzūr, *s. a.* A defect to be guarded against, an objection.

محذوف màhzūf, *s. a.* Understood, not expressed (a word); elided (a letter).

محراب mihrāb, *s. a.* A niche or mark of any kind in the wall of a mosque to show in which direction to turn in prayer.

محرر mŭhàrrir, *s. a.* One who writes, the writer; —, mŭhàrrèr, *a. a.* Written; محررات mŭhàrrérāt, *s. pl. a.* Writings.

محرف mŭhàrref, *a. a.* Corrupted, tampered with, erroneous (texts, books, &c.).

محرك mŭhàrrik, *s. a.* A seditious person, mover of sedition; who causes things to move.

محرم màhrèm, *s. a.* A confidant, one admitted into a secret; one who legally had admission into the society of one of the other sex; —, mŭhàrrem, *s. a.* Name of the first month of the Muhammedan year; —, *a. a.* Prohibited, unlawful (in religion); محرمات mŭhàrrémāt, *s. pl. a.* Unlawful things; نامحرم nā-màhrem, *a. p.* To whom the society of one of the other sex is not legally permitted.

محروس màhrūss (*fem.* محروسه màhrūssé), *a. a.* Defended, protected; محروسه màhrūssé, *s. a.* A city, fortified city; ممالك محروسه mèmāliki-màhrūssé, (The defended dominions) The Ottoman territory.

محروم màhrūm, *a. a.* Deprived; without; disappointed. [sorrowing.

محزون màhzūn, *a. a.* Grieved, afflicted,

محسن mùhsin, *s. a.* One who confers benefits, grants favours, does kindnesses; —, mùhàsssèn, *a. a.* Approved, worthy of approbation; محسنات mùhàsssénāt, *s. pl. a.* Deeds or qualities worthy of approbation, virtues.

محسوب màhsūb, *a. a.* Counted, reckoned; محسوباً màhsūban, *ad. a.* On account of, towards the account of.

محسوس màhsūss, *a. a.* Sensible, felt, perceived.

محشر màhshèr, *s. a.* The resurrection, or place of assembly for the last judgment; an assemblage, troop, company (of people).

محصل mùhàsssil, *s. a.* Title of one class of former governors of towns or districts (*lit.* collector); محصل الكلام màhsalu-'l-kèlām, *or* mùhàsssalu-'l-kèlām, *ad. a.* In fine, in short, in one word, to sum up.

محصن mùhàsssan, *a. a.* Guarded round about, fortified; محصنات mùhàsssanāt, *s. pl. a.* Chaste, virtuous, discreet women.

محصود màhsūd, *a. a.* Reaped, mown.

محصور màhsūr, *a. a.* Bounded, confined, shut in, besieged, surrounded.

محصول màhsūl, *s. a.* Produce, fruit; محصولدار màhsūldār, *a. p.* Fruitful.

محض màhz, *a. a.* Sheer, pure; محضا màhzā, *ad. a.* Merely, purely, simply, entirely.

محضر màhzàr, *s. a.* A petition signed by all the people present (*called also* عرض محضر "àrzi-màhzar); —, mùhzir, *s. a.* An officer who cites or summons people before a court of justice.

محط màhàtt, *s. a.* A halting-place, where the baggage animals are unloaded.

محظوظ màhzūz, *a. a.* Pleased, glad; محظوظيت mùhzūzìyyèt, *s. a.* Satisfaction, pleasure, joy.

محفظه màhfaza, *s. a.* A case (for protecting anything).

محفل màhfil, *s. a.* A gallery in a mosque; any place of congregation; —همايون, màhfili-hùmāyūn, The gallery reserved for the use of the Sultan.

محفوظ màhfūz, *a. a.* Preserved; لوح محفوظ lèvhi-màhfūz, (The preserved tablet) The tablet of God's providential decrees. [temptible.

محقر mùhàkkar, *a. a.* Contemned; con-

محقق mùhàkkàk, *a. a.* Fully ascertained, verified, corroborated. [stone.

محك màhàkk (mèhènk), *s. a.* A touch-

محكم mùhkèm, *a. a.* Strong; well fortified; tight. [court of justice.

محكمه màhkémé (mèhkémé), *s. a.* A

محكوك màhkyūk, *a. a.* Scratched out (writing, with a knife); engraved.

محكوم màhkyūm, *a. a.* Subject to any jurisdiction; عليه —, màhkyūmun-"àlèyh, *a. a.* Sentenced, on whom sentence is passed.

محكى màhkī, *a. a.* Related, narrated, recounted; محكى عنه màhkìyyun-"ành, *s. a.* Him on whose authority a thing is recounted; محكى فيه màhkìyyun-fìh, *s. a.* Him about whom a narration is recounted.

محل màhàll, *s. a.* A place; the proper place for anything; a fitting place; a place in which anything occurs; اهله فى محله èhluhu-fī-màhàllihi, The right man in the right place.

محلول màhlūl, *a. a.* Dissolved; untied, loosened; vacant (a place of employ); —, *s. a.* A vacancy, vacant office.

محله màhàllé (*pl.* محلات màhàllāt), *s. a.* A parish; a quarter or locality of a town.

محلى mùhàllà, *a. a.* Adorned (with ornaments).

محمد mùhàmmed, *a. a.* Praised; praiseworthy; Muhammed (Mahomet); محمدى mùhàmmédī (*fem.* محمديه mùhàmmédìyyé), *a. a.* Muhammedan, Mahometan.

محمدت màhmédet, *s. a.* A praiseworthy point of character; praise, glory.

محمل màhmil, *s. a.* A litter for travelling on a camel; a covering for the sacred building at Mecca.

محمود màhmūd, *a. a.* Praised, glorified.

محمول màhmūl, *a. a.* Loaded (upon anything), placed upon; imputed, attributed.

محموم màhmūm, *a. a.* Attacked with fever.

محمى màhmī (*fem.* محميه màhmìyyé), *a. a.* Protected; محميه màhmìyyé, *s. a.* A city.

محنت mìhnèt, *s. a.* (*pl.* محن mìhàn), A source of grief, a trouble, affliction.

محو màhv, *s. a.* An obliterating, cancelling, demolishing; ا—, —et, *v. a.* To obliterate; to demolish; محو واثبات màhv-u-ìssbāt, A cancelling or demolishing some parts and adding or leaving others (in writings or in buildings).

محور mìhver, *s. a.* An axis.

محول mùhàvvel, *a. a.* Referred to, turned over to, left to the care or decision of (some person).

محى mùhyī, *a. a.* for محيى, which see.

محيط mùhīt, *a. a.* Encircling, surrounding; embracing, containing, comprehending; بحر محيط bàhri-mùhīt, The ocean, as surrounding the habitable earth.

محيى mùhyī, *s. a.* Who animates, gives life; who renovates, restores; who renders flourishing, populous; who reclaims (waste land).

مخا Mòkhā, *s. a.* Name of a town in Arabia.

مخابره mùkhābéré, *a. a.* Correspondence by letter or message; ا—, —et, *v. a.* To correspond, to hold communication.

مخادنت mùkhādénet, *s. a.* Friendship, amity.

مخاذيل màkhāzīl, *s. pl. a.* (*of* مخذول màkhzūl), Low wretches, rascals.

مخارج màkhārij, *s. pl. a.* (*of* مخرج màkhrèj), Places of issue, issues, outlets; the different parts of the organs of speech from whence the sounds of the several letters, or classes of letters, are derived; expenses.

مخازن màkhāzin, *s. pl. a.* (*of* مخزن makhzen), Magazines, storehouses, cellars.

مخاصمه mùkhāssamé, *s. a.* A litigating.

مخاطب mùkhātab, *a. a.* Addressed in speech by anyone; —, *s. a.* The second person of verbs and pronouns; مفرد مخاطب mùfrèd-mūkhātab, The second person singular; جمع مخاطب jèm"i-mùkhātab, The second person plural. [anyone in speech.

مخاطبه mùkhātaba, *s. a.* An addressing

مخاطره mùkhātara, *s. a.* Danger, peril.

مخالب màkhālib, مخاليب màkhālīb, *s. pl. a.* (*of* مخلب mìkhlèb, مخلاب mìkhlāb), Claws, talons.

مخالصت mùkhālésset, *s. a.* Sincerity of friendship.

مخالطه mùkhālata, *s. a.* Intercourse.

مخالف mùkhālif, *a. a.* Opposed to, contrary, adverse.

مخالفت mùkhāléfet, *s. a.* Opposition; an opposing; ا—, —et, *v.n.* To oppose, be opposed to.

مخبر mùkhbir, *s. a.* Who gives notice, communicates information, an informant.

مختار mùkhtār, *a. a.* Preferred, preferable; having the option, free to choose; —, *s.a.* Choice, election made; فاعل مختار fā"ili-mùkhtār, One who, being of age and of sound mind, is free to act according to his own discretion.

مخترع mùkhtèri", *s. a.* An inventor, introducer. [acts humbly.

مختشع mùkhtèshi", *a. a.* Humble, who

مختص mùkhtasss, *a. a.* Appropriated, dedicated.

مختصر mùkhtassar, *a. a.* Abridged, abbreviated, curtailed; short; of moderate dimensions. [self.

مختفى mùkhtèfī, *a. a.* Who hides him-

مختل mùkhtèll, *a. a.* Spoilt, deranged, injured. [site, compound.

مختلط mùkhtèlit, *a. a.* Mixed, compo-

مختلف mùkhtèlif, *a. a.* Various, divers, different, dissimilar; مختلف الاضلاع mùkhtèlifu-'l-adlā", *a. a.* Scalene (triangle).

مختوم màkhtūm, *a. a.* Sealed; طين مختوم tīni-màkhtūm (Sealed earth), *s. a.* Lesbian clay. [a narcotic.

مخدر mùkhèddir, *s.* and *a. a.* Narcotic;

مخدره mùkhàddéré (*pl.* مخدرات mùkhàddèrāt), *s. a.* A veiled woman, a chaste, retiring, modest, virtuous woman. [one serves; a son.

مخدوم màkhdūm, *s. a.* A master whom

مخذول màkhzūl, *s. a.* A miserable wretch.

مخرج màkhrèj, *s. a.* An issue, outlet; any part of the organs of speech where

the sound of a letter is formed; one of the degrees conferred upon the "*ulémā* or Doctors of Muhammedan law and divinity; —, mùkhrèj, *a. a.* Extracted, drawn out, taken out.

مخروط màkhrūt, *s. a.* A cone; مخروطی màkhrūtī, *a. a.* Conical; مخروطیات màkhrūtìyyāt, *s. pl. a.* Conics, the Conic sections.

مخزن màkhzɛn, *s. a.* A magazine, storehouse; a cellar.

مخصص mūkhàsssass, *a. a.* Appropriated, dedicated, devoted.

مخصوص màkhsūss, *a. a.* Peculiar, particular; express, special, especial; reserved, private; —, *ad. t.* Expressly; on purpose, designedly, intentionally; مخصوصیت màkhsūssìyyèt, *s. a.* Devotion, devotedness, special attachment.

مخطوب màkhtūb (*fem.* مخطوبه màkhtūbɛ), *a. a.* Sought or asked for in marriage.

مخطور màkhtūr, *a. a.* Thought of, conceived, come to one's mind; —, *s. a.* A thought, idea.

مخفف mùkhàffèf, *a. a.* Lightened, made light; not sounded as double (a letter).

مخفی màkhfī, *a. a.* Secret, secreted, hidden.

مخل mùkhìll, *a. a.* Detrimental, injurious, hurtful, which damages, destroys.

مخلاب mìkhlāb, مخلب mìkhleb, *s. a.* The clawing foot of a bird or beast of prey.

مخلد mùkhàlled, *a. a.* Lasting eternally, everlasting.

مخلص màkhlàss, *s. a.* The additional name given to young men, or assumed by them, when they become writers of any kind, either as authors, poets, or simply clerks in a government office, and by which, excepting in the case of the Sovereign, they are ever afterwards commonly known and named: رشید Rèshīd, عالی "Alī, فؤاد Fù'ād, are of this description; عمر "*Umèr*, اسماعیل Issmā'īl, محمود Màhmūd, are not; —, mùkhliss, *s. a.* A sincere and devoted friend; —, mùkhàlliss, *s. a.* A saviour, one who delivers from any evil or danger.

مخلصانه mùkhlissānɛ, *a. p.* Pertaining to a sincere and devoted friend.

مخلف mùkhàllef, *a. a.* Left behind (at death); مخلفات mùkhàlléfāt, *s. pl. a.* The effects and property of a defunct person, especially such as devolve to the crown.

مخلوط màkhlūt, *a. a.* Mixed, having some one or various ingredients mixed into itself, not pure.

مخلوع mɛ̄khlū", *a. a.* Deposed, dethroned; removed.

مخلوق màkhlūk, *a. a.* Created; مخلوقات màkhlūkāt, *s. pl. a.* All creation, all creatures.

مخمس mùkhàmmess, *s. a.* A pentagon; a small piece of poetry of five verses or hemistichs.

مخمور màkhmūr, *a. a.* Who feels and still labours under the distressing and depressing reaction consequent upon the passing off of intoxication, or, figuratively, of any elating influence.

مخنث mùkhènnèss, *s. a.* A sodomite.

مخنثلك mùkhènnèsslik, *s. t.* Sodomy.

مخوف màkhūf, *a. a.* Fearful, frightful, dreadful.

مخير mùkhàyyer, *a. a.* Optional; bought upon approval or trial; who has an option given to him.

مخيم mùkhàyyem, *a. a.* Under canvass, in tents, encamped; —, *s. a.* A camp; مخيمگاه mùkhàyyem-ghyāh, A camp, a place where an army is encamped.

مد mèdd, *s. a.* A stretching out, lengthening, prolonging; a stretching forth (the hand); the prolongation of voice in a long vowel; the sign —, which is used for marking a long initial ا, or the suppression of a long medial ا; as آفت āfet, رحمن ràhmān; high water of the sea, high tide; an additional term of office frequently given to judges at the end of the year for which alone they are always appointed; ا—, —et, *v.a.* To stretch out, lengthen, prolong; to stretch forth, put out (the hand).

مداح mèddāh, *s. a.* A public story-teller.

مداخل mèdākhil, *s. pl. a.* (*of* مدخل mèdkhàl), Entries, inlets; income, receipts; —, mùdākhil, *s. a.* An interferer, one who interferes.

مداخله mùdākhalé, *s. a.* An interference; ا—, —et, *v.n.* To interfere.

مداد mèdād, *s. a.* Writing-ink.

مدار mèdār, *s. a.* The point or place at, or about which, things revolve or turn; a centre; a tropic; مدار سرطان mèdāri-sèratān, The tropic of Cancer; مدارجدی mèdāri-jèdi, The tropic of Capricorn.

مدارا mùdārā, مدارات mùdārāt, *s. a.* A soft answer, the quiet, prudent tone and manner necessary to be used towards adversaries (it *need* not, though it *may* be *dissimulation*); ا—, —et, *v.n.* To give a soft answer, assume a quiet tone and manner (towards an adversary).

مدارج mèdārij, *s. pl. a.* (*sing. not used*), Steps, degrees of ascent.

مدارس mèdāriss, *s. pl. a.* (*of* مدرسه mèdréssé), Colleges for law and divinity.

مدارست mùdāréssèt, *s. a.* The public teaching of law and divinity.

مدافعه mùdāfa‘‘a, *s. a.* A repelling; a striving to repel (an assailant); self defence; ا—, —et, *v.a.* To repel or strive to repel.

مدام mùdām, *a. a.* Permanent, continual; —, *s. a.* Wine.

مداوات mùdāvāt, *s. a.* Medical treatment; ا—, —et, *v.n.* To treat medically.

مداوره mùdāvéré, *s. a.* A passing round, causing to circulate.

مداول mùdāvil, *a. a.* Circulating, in circulation. [(at duties).

مداوم mùdāvim, *a. a.* Assiduous, steady

مداومت mùdāvémèt, *s. a.* Constant attendance, steady application; ا—, —et, *v.n.* To be constant in attendance and steady in application.

مداهن mùdāhin, *s. a.* A flatterer, adulator.

مداهنه mùdāhéné, *s. a.* Flattery, adulation; the giving unmerited praise; or the withholding merited reproach; ا—, —et, *v.n.* To use flattery, adulation; to give false praise or to withhold merited reproach.

مدائح mèdā'ih, *s. pl. a.* (of مديحه mèdīhé), Laudable acts or qualities; praises. [mèdīné), Towns, cities.

مدائن mèdā'in, *s. pl. a.* (of مدينه

مدبر mùdbir, *s. a.* One who retrogrades; one fallen into misfortune; —, mùdèbbir, *s. a.* One who conducts business, whose mind finds plans for managing affairs.

مدبوغ mèdbūgh, *a. a.* Tanned (leather).

مدت mùddèt, *s. a.* A period, length of time; مدت عمر mùddéti-"ùmr, A lifetime.

مدح mèdh, *s. a.* A praising, speaking well of, eulogizing; ا—, —et, *v.a.* To praise, eulogize.

مدحت midhèt, *s. a.* A praiseworthy act or quality; a tribute of praise, eulogy. [(corn, &c.).

مدخر mùddakhir, *a. a.* Stored up

مدخل mèdkhal, *s. a.* An entry, inlet; participation, interest, influence, complicity.

مدخول mèdkhūl, *a. a.* Into which something has entered; (a woman) who has been deflowered, is no longer a virgin.

مدد mèded, *s. a.* Assistance, help, succour; —, *int. a.* Help! مددرس mèded-rèss, مددكار mèded-kyār, *s. p.* A helper, succourer, deliverer.

مدر mèdèr, *s. a.* A sun-dried, unbaked brick; اهل مدر èhli-mèdèr, One who dwells in a house (as opposed to اهل وبر èhli-vèber, A dweller in tents).

مدراباز mèdrabāz, *s. t.* A pedlar, huckster.

مدرس mùdèrriss, *s. a.* A public professor of law and divinity.

مدرسه mèdréssé, *s. a.* A college for the study of law and divinity.

مدرك mùdrik (*fem.* مدركه mùdriké), *a. a.* Who overtakes, comes up with; who seizes (a meaning), catches, takes; قوت مدركه kùvvéti-mùdriké, The comprehension, apprehensive faculty.

مدعا (*for* مدعى) mùdda"à, *a. a.* Contended for, pretended, maintained; —, *s. a.* A thesis; a plea; a proposition contended for and maintained.

مدعو mèd"ùvv, *a. a.* Invited.

مدعى mùddà"i, *s. a.* A contender, maintainer; a plaintiff; مدعى عليه mùdda"à-"àlèyh (mùddà"i—), *s. a.* A defendant, an accused person.

مدغم mùddàghim, *a. a.* Inserted, coalesced, comprehended in the sound of the following letter (a consonant, in Arabic grammar). [thing is buried.

مدفن mèdfèn, *s. a.* A place where any-

مدفون mèdfūn, *a. a.* Buried, interred.

مدقق mùdàkkìk, *s. a.* A person who examines minutely. [and proofs.

مدلل mùdèllèl, *a. a.* Indicated by signs

مدللی Midìlli, *s. t.* The island of Mitylene; a pony.

مدلول mèdlūl, *a. a.* Indicated by signs and proofs; —, *s. a.* The deduction, the thing, sense, or meaning indicated by any words or signs.

مدمن mùdmin, *a. a.* Who constantly practises or uses anything, who acquires a knack. [Towns, cities.

مدن mùdn, *s. pl. a.* (*of* مدينه mèdīnᴇ),

مدنی mèdénī (*fem.* مدنيه mèdénìyyᴇ), *a. a.* Living in a town or towns; civilized; not nomade; مدنيت mèdéniyyèt, *s. a.* Civilized or town life, or the abstract quality of living in towns; civilization.

مدور mùdèvvèr, *a. a.* Round, globular.

مدون mùdèvvin, *s. a.* One who collects poetry into a regular dīwān; —, mùdèvvèn, *a. a.* Collected and formed into a regular dīwān (poetry); compiled and made into a book.

مدهش mùdhìsh, *a. a.* Frightening, which causes terror.

مدهن mùddèhin, *a. a.* Oiled, greased, anointed. [scared.

مدهوش mèdhūsh, *a. a.* Terrified;

مدى mèda (mèdé *before the definite article* ال), *s. a.* As far in space or as long in time as something can reach; مدى البصر mèdé-'l-bàssar, As far as the eye can see; مدى الدهور mèdé-'d--dùhūr, As long as time lasts.

مديحه mèdīha, *s. a.* A praiseworthy quality or act; praise, eulogy, encomium.

مديد mèdīd, *a. a.* Long, extended.

مدير mùdīr, *s. a.* A manager; director; title of the petty governors of districts, who also collect the revenue, assess property, &c. [Medina in Arabia.

مدينه mèdīnᴇ, *s. a.* A town, a city;

مديون mèdyūn, *a. a.* In debt, indebted.

مديه mìdyᴇ, *s. t.* (*Greek*) A muscle (fish).

مذاب mùzāb, *a. a.* Melted, molten.

مذاق mèzāk, *s. a.* The taste.

مذاكره mùzākérᴇ, *s. a.* A conference, talking over (any subject); ا—, —et, *v.a.* To talk over, discuss.

مذاهب mèzāhib, *s. pl. a.* (*of* مذهب mèzhèb), Religious sects or peculiar creeds.

مذبح mèzbàh, *s. a.* A place for slaughtering cattle; an altar for the same (but not for fire or for burning).

مذبذب mùzèbzìb, *a. a.* A trifler who is constantly changing his fancy.

مذبوح mèzbūh, *a. a.* Slaughtered by having the throat cut; sacrificed (in like manner); مذبوحانه mèzbūhānᴇ, *a. p.* Pertaining to a slaughtered animal.

مذكر mùzèkkᴇr, *a. a.* Masculine (word

in grammar); —, mùzèkkir, *s. a.* One who repeats litanies in praise or commemoration of God or the prophet.

مذكور mèzkyūr, *a. a.* Mentioned, aforementioned, aforesaid.

مذلت mèzèllæt, *s. a.* Abjectness.

مذموم mèzmūm, *a. a.* Blamed, ill-spoken-of, detestable.

مذهب mèzhèb, *s. a.* A path; a rule of faith; a religious sect or creed; —, mùzèhbèb, *a. a.* Gilt with gold.

مذى mèzī, *s. a.* A slight seminal moisture occurring from mere lasciviousness.

مر mùrr, *s. a.* Myrrh (*generally called* مرصافى mùrri-sāfī, *Pure myrrh,* or *pure bitterness,* or *sheer gall*); —, *a. a.* [Bitter.

مرء mèr', *s. a.* A man.

مرا mìrā, *s. a.* Hypocrisy, dissimulation; —, mèrā, *s. pl. a.* (*of* مرأت mìr'àt), Mirrors, looking-glasses.

مرابحت mùrābahàt, *s. a.* A gaining, profiting in business.

مرابط mùrābit, *s. a.* One who devotes himself entirely to the service of the faith, either as a warrior to guard the frontiers against external foes, or as a man of piety to pray for the welfare of the church and combat internal enemies.

مرابع mèrābi'', *s. pl. a.* (*of* مربع mèrbà''), Houses for spring habitation; pastures for spring use.

مرأت mìr'àt, *s. a.* A mirror, looking-glass, speculum; مرات mèrrāt, *s. pl. a.* (*of* مره mèrré), Times (in succession).

مراتب mèrātib, *s. pl. a.* (*of* مرتبه mèrtébé), Grades, ranks, gradations.

مراجعت mùrāja''àt, *s. a.* A referring, having recourse (to some thing or person); ا—, —et, *v.n.* To refer, have recourse, fall back.

مراحل mèrāhil, *s. pl. a.* (*of* مرحله mèrhalé), Stations on a journey; days' journeys.

مراحلت mùrāhalèt, *s. a.* Going, starting, departing.

مراحم mèrāhim, *s. pl. a.* (*of* مرحمت mèrhàmet), Compassionate acts, graces.

مراد mùrād, *a. a.* Wished for, desired, aimed at; —, *s. a.* Wish, desire, aim, intent, intention; Murad (corrupted by ignorance into *Amurath,* proper name); ا—, —et, *v.a.* To wish, desire, aim at, intend.

مرار mìrār, *s. pl. a.* (*of* مره mèrré), Times (of repetition); مراراً mìrāran, *ad. a.* Often, repeatedly, many times.

مرارت mèrārèt, *s. a.* Bitterness.

مراسله mùrāssélé, مراسلت mùrāssélèt, *s. a.* Correspondence by letter or messages.

مراسم mèrāssim, *s. pl. a.* (*no sing.*), Ceremonies, customary usages.

مراسيم mèrāssīm, *s. pl. a.* (*of* مرسوم mèrsūm), Edicts, rescripts.

مراعات mùrā''āt, *s. a.* A careful observance (of any requisite thing); ا—,

—et, *v.n.* To observe, keep, revere, or execute, fulfil.

مرافعه mùrāfa‘‘a, *s. a.* A trial at law; —او, —ôl, *v.n.* To go through a trial at law.

مرافقت mùrāfakȦt, *s. a.* An accompanying (one) on a journey or mission; ا—, —et, *v.n.* To go in company (with someone).

مراق mèrāk, *s. a.* A whim, fancy; curiosity; taste; pleasure; anxiety, suspense; fear; monomania; hypochondria; ا—, —et, *v.n.* To be anxious, to fear; to be curious; مراقده براقمق mèrākd*a*-bràkm*a*k, *v.a.* To leave in doubt, suspense; مراقلو mèrĀkl*i*, *a. t.* Fanciful, whimsical; curious; having a taste, being an amateur. [tion and contemplation.

مراقبه mùrākaba, *s. a.* Ascetic medita-

مراقد mèrākid, *s. pl. a.* (*of* مرقد mèrkȦd), Tombs, graves.

مراكب mèrākib, *s. pl. a.* (*of* مركب mèrkēb), Things used for riding in or on, as horses, camels, mules, asses, carriages, ships, boats. [desire.

مرام mèrām, *s. a.* Intention; wish,

مرامات mùrāmāt, *s. a.* A firing, projecting, lancing (missiles at someone).

مرانقوز *or* مرانقوس *or* مرانغوس màranghoss, *s. t.* (*Italian*), A ship's carpenter; a cabinet-maker.

مرأه *or* مرئه mèr‘é, *s. a.* A woman.

مراهم mèrāhim, *s. pl. a.* (*of* مرهم mèrhèm), Ointments, salves.

مرايا mèrāyā, *s. pl. a.* (*of* مرأت mir‘ät), Mirrors, looking-glasses, specula.

مرايات mùrāyāt, *s. a.* Hypocrisy.

مرائی mùrā‘ī, *s. a.* A hypocrite, dissembler.

مربع mèrbà‘‘, *s. a.* A house for spring residence; a spring pasturage; —, mùrèbbà‘‘, *s. a.* A mathematical square (figure or number); مربعی mùrèbbà‘‘ī, *a. a.* Square.

مربوط mèrbūt, *a. a.* Connected, fastened, tied (together or to something); regular.

مربی mùrèbbī, *s. a.* One who educates; *or* مربا mùrèbbà, *s. a.* A preparation, condiment; ایوه مرباسی àyw*a*-mùrèbbàss*i*, Preserved quince.

مرتب mùrèttēb, *a. a.* Set in order, arranged, duly disposed; ready, present, existing; مرتبات mùrèttébāt, *s. pl. a.* The different things *regularly* supplied to, by, or for, any department of administration, such as money, clothes, men, arms, &c.; —, mùrèttib, *s. a.* A compositor in a printing-office.

مرتبه mèrtébé, *s. a.* A degree, gradation; a rank; كمال مرتبه‌ده kèmāli-mèrtébédé, *ad. t.* To a supreme degree, very, extremely.

مرتد mùrtèdd (mùrtȦd), *s. a.* A pervert from Mahommetanism.

مرتزقه mùrtèzik*a* (اشخاص èshkhāss, *or some similar word, being understood*), *s. pl. a.* (*of* مرتزق mùrtèzik), People who receive their pay and rations, their livelihood (from the public treasury, &c.).

مرتشی mùrtèshī, *s. a.* A man in office who accepts a bribe.

مرتضی *or* مرتضا mùrtézà, *a. a.* With whom one is well pleased; المرتضی èl-mùrtézà, "Alī, the son-in-law of Muhammed. [tree, &c.)

مرتفع mùrtèfi", *a. a.* High (hill, place,

مرتکب mùrtèkib, *s. a.* One who does, commits (any sin or crime); a corrupt bribe-taking, peculating fellow.

مرثیه mèrsìyyé, *s. a.* An elegy.

مرجان mèrjān, *s. p.* Coral; Merjan (*proper name often given to black slaves*); —بالغی, mèrjān-bālighi, *s. t.* A gold fish. [revered.

مرجب mùrèjjeb, *a. a.* Honoured,

مرجح mùrèjjàh, *a. a.* Preferable.

مرجع mèrjà", *s. a.* A place to which one returns, or has recourse.

مرجمك mèrjémek, *s. p.* A lentile.

مرجو mèrjū, *a. a.* Begged, requested, asked.

مرحبا mèrhabā! *int. a.* (In affluence!) All hail! (*said only by one Muhammedan to another*). [a station.

مرحله mèrhalé, *s. a.* A day's journey;

مرحمت mèrhàmet, *s. a.* Pity, commiseration, mercy.

مرحوم mèrhūm, *a. a.* Received into God's mercy (*said only of defunct Muhammedans*).

مرخص mùràkhkhàss, *a. a.* Having full permission; —, *s. a.* A plenipotentiary.

مرخصه mèrkhassa, *s. a.* A Christian bishop, abbot, or prior.

مرد mèrd, *s. p.* A man; a manly fellow; —, mùrd, *a. p.* Dead (*said only of non-Muhammedans, in contempt*); مردانه mèrdāné, *a. p.* Manly; brave; مردانکی mèrdānéghī, *s. p.* Manliness, bravery; مردی mèrdī, *s. p.* Manhood, manliness.

مردار mùrdār (mùndàr), *a. p.* Filthy, dirty; canonically unclean.

مردم mèrdum, *s. p.* A man; مردمك mèrdumek, *s. p. dim.* A little man; مردمك چشم mèrduméki-chèshm, *s. p.* The pupil of the eye; مردم اریکی mùrdum-èrighi, *s. t.* A damson.

مردود mèrdūd, *a. a.* Contemned, repulsed, disowned, rejected.

مرده mèrédé, *s. pl. a.* (*of* مارد mārid), Obstinate rebels; —, mùrdé, *a. p.* Dead.

مرده سنك mùrdé-sènk, *s. p.* Litharge(?).

مرز mèrz, *s. p.* A frontier, a march; مرزبان mèrzubān, *s. p.* A warden of the marches, a governor; مرزبوم mèrzubūm, *s. p.* A country, region.

مرسا (*for* مرسی) mèrsà, *s. a.* A port, harbour, anchorage-ground.

مرسل mùrsèl, *s. a.* A messenger, an apostle; سید المرسلین sèyyidu-'l-mùrsélīn, The prince of the apostles, Muhammed.

مرسوم mèrsūm, *a. a.* Delineated; drawn; written; the above-mentioned; —, *a. a.* An edict, rescript, order.

مرسی mèrsà, *s. a.* A harbour, port, anchorage-ground. [sturgeon (fish).

مرسین mèrsin, *s. t.* A myrtle (tree) ; a

مرشد mùrshid, *s. a.* A spiritual guide and preceptor ; a guide.

مرصد mèrsàd, *s. a.*, مرصدگاه mèrsàd-ghyāh, *s. p.* A place for a look-out ; a lurking-place. [precious stones.

مرصع mùràsssà'', *a. a.* Ornamented with

مرصوص mèrsūss, *a. a.* Held together firmly with cramp-irons.

مرض màraz, *s. a.* Disease, malady ; a pining sickness ; —موت, *màrazi-mèvt*, The disease of which one dies.

مرضا (*for* مرضی) mèrzà, *s. pl. a.* (*of* مریض màrīz), The sick.

مرضات mèrzāt, *s. a.* Satisfaction, the being pleased, content, satisfied.

مرضی mèrzī, *a. a.* With which one is satisfied or pleased ; —, mèrzà, *s. pl. a.* (*of* مریض màrīz), The sick.

مرطوب mèrtūb, *a. a.* Moistened, wetted.

مرعا *or* مرعی mèr''à, *s. a.* Pasture-ground.

مرعی mèr''ī, *a. a.* To which attention is paid, to which people conform ; observed, in force.

مرغ mùrgh, *s. p.* A bird ; a fowl.

مرغاب mùrghāb, *s. p.* A duck.

مرغوب mèrghūb, *a. a.* Such as is liked and desired.

مرفه mùrèffēh, *a. a.* At ease ; in good circumstances ; مرفه البال mùrèffēhu-'l-bāl, With the heart at ease. [grave.

مرقد mèrkàd, *s. a.* A sepulchre, tomb,

مرقوم mèrkūm, *a. a.* Written ; the above-mentioned.

مرك mèrgh, *s. p.* Death.

مرکب mèrkēb, *s. a.* A beast for riding, whether horse, camel, mule, or ass ; an ass, a donkey ; a carriage ; a ship or boat. (The idea of the camel being called by Arabs "the ship of the desert," is a mistaken European fable, the truth being that, if anything, they have, on the contrary, likened the ship to the camel, and called the former مرکب بحری mèrkèb-bàhrī, "*the sea-camel,*" or rather "*the marine thing for riding*") ; —, mùrèkkēb, *a. a.* Compound ; —, *s. a.* Writing ink ; —بالغی, mùrèkkēb-bàl*ighi* (The ink-fish), The cuttle-fish, the sepia ; جهل مرکب jèhli-mùrèkkēb, (Compound ignorance) The ignorance which ignores its own ignorance, presumptuous ignorance.

مرکز mèrkèz, *s. a.* A centre ; a seat of provincial government ; the head-quarters of a corps-d'armée.

مرکوب mèrkyūb, *a. a.* Ridden, mounted.

مرکوز mèrkyūz, *a. a.* Stuck in or up, planted (as a javelin in the ground).

مرلدامق mìrìldamak (*aor.* مرلدار mìrìl-dar), مرلدانمق mìrìldanmak (*aor.* مرلدانور mìrìldanir), *v.n.* To murmur, mutter.

مرمت mèrèmmet (mèrémet), *s. a.* Repairs, reparation ; ا—, —et, *v.n.* To make repairs, to repair.

مرمر mèrmèr, *s. t.* Marble ; —, mìrmìr, *s. t.* A murmuring, muttering.

مرموق mèrmūk, *a. a.* Looked at, regarded.

مرمی mèrmī (*fem.* مرمیه mèrmìyyé),*a. a.* Thrown, cast, projected ; جسم مرمی jìssmi-mèrmī, A projectile.

مرو Mèrv, *s. p.* Merv (town of).

مرواريد mèrvārīd, *s. p.* A pearl (*Greek μαργεριτη*).

مروت mùrùvvèt (*for* مروّت mùrù'et), *s. a.* Generosity, magnanimity.

مسروج mùrèvvij, *s. a.* One who promotes, advances, gives course or animation (to any business).

مرود mùrūd, *s. a.* Obstinacy, rebelliousness.

مرور mùrūr, *s. a.* A passing (over, by, or through); ا—, —et, *v.n.* To go or pass (over, by, through); —زمان, mùrūru-zàmān, The lapse of time ; —, mùrver, *s. t.* The elder tree ; —چیچکی, mùrver-chichèghi, Elder-berry-flowers.

مروی mèrvī, *q. a.* Related, handed down, told, recounted.

مره mèrré, *s. a.* A time (of repetition) ; مرةً بعد مرة mèrrétèn-bà''da-mèrrétin, *ad. a.* Repeatedly, time after time.

مرهم mèrhèm (mèlhèm), *s. a.* Ointment, salve.

مرهون mèrhūn, *a. a.* Pledged, pawned.

مريخ mèrrīkh, *s. a.* The planet Mars.

مريد mèrīd, *s. a.* An obstinate, rebellious person ; —, mùrīd, *s. a.* A follower of a religious preceptor, a novice, a disciple.

مريض màrīz, *s. a.* A sick person ; —, *a. a.* Sick, ill.

مريم mèryém, *s. a.* Mary (*proper name*) ; مريم انا mèryèm-àna, *s. t.* Mary, the mother (of Jesus) ; بخورمريم bùkhūri-mèryèm (Incense of Mary), The cyclamen, or sow-bread.

مز miz *or* miz (يمز after a consonant which will not join calligraphically) *after a vowel*, or imiz, imiz *after a consonant* ; Turkish possessive pronoun, *first pers. pl.* Our, بابامز bàbamiz, Our father, قلممز kàlèmimiz, Our pen ; برادريمز bìrādèrimiz, Our brother ; —, *or* ماز màz, *Turkish termination of the aorist participle active of every negative verb* ; كتمز ghitmàz, Who does not, will not go ; سويلمز sùwèylémàz, Who does not, will not say.

مزاج mìzāj, *s. a.* The state of a person's health ; the general constitution ; personal character, disposition ; مزاجسز mìzājsiz, *a. t.* Unwell, ill, sick ; مزاجكير mìzāj-ghīr, *a. p.* Who suits anyone's disposition, takes, and becomes liked ; مزاج شريف mìzāji-shèrīf ; مزاج شريفكز mìzāji-shèrīfingiz? (The, your, noble health?), How do you do?

مزاح mùzāh, *s. a.* Fun, a joke, a jest.

مزاحم mèzāhim, *s. pl. a.* (*of* زحمت zàhmet), Fatigues, difficulties ; —, mùzāhim, *a. a.* Impeding ; —, *s. a.* An obstacle, impediment.

مزاحمت mùzāhémèt, *s. a.* An impeding, impediment ; a crowding, thronging together.

مزاد mèzād, *s. a.* Public auction ; ا—, —et, *v.a.* To sell by auction ; مزاده ويرمك mèzāda-vèrmek, To give to be sold at auction ; مزاددن المق mèzāddan-ȧlmak, To buy at an auction ; —, mùzād, *a. a.* Increased, added to.

مزار mèzār (mèzar), *s. a.* A grave ; —طاشى, mèzar-tȧshi, A tombstone ; مزارجى mèzarji, *s. t.* A gravedigger ; مزارستان mèzarisstān, *s. p.* مزارلق mèzarlik, *s. t.* A graveyard.

مزارع mèzāri'', *s. pl. a.* (*of* مزرعه mèzra''a), Arable lands; sown fields.

مزايا mèzāyā, *s. pl. a.* (*of* مزيت mèzìyyèt), Special points, virtues, advantages ; برشيئك مزاياسنه وارمق bìr-shèy'ing-mèzāyāssina-varmak, *v.n.* To seize and appreciate the special point of anything.

مزايده mùzāyédé, *s. a.* A putting up at auction.

مزبله mèzbélé, *s. a.* مزبله‌لك mèzbélé-lik, *s. t.* A dust-heap, heap of refuse rubbish.

مزبور mèzbūr, *a. a.* Written ; the above-mentioned.

مزج mèzj, *s. a.* A mixing intimately, a blending ; ا—, —et, *v.a.* To mix, blend.

مزخرف mùzàkhrèf, *a. a.* Ornamented with false ornaments ; مزخرفات mùzàkhréfāt, *s. pl. a.* Rubbish, peccant humours.

مزد mùzd, *s. p.* A reward, recompense.

مزدحم mùzdèhim, *a. a.* In crowds, thronged (people).

مزراق mìzrȧk, *s. t.* A spear, a lance.

مزرعه mèzra''a, *s. a.* Arable land ; a sown field.

مزركش mùzèrkesh, *a. a.* Worked with gold thread.

مزروع mèzrū'', *a. a.* Sown (seed, field).

مزلت mèzèllet, *s. a.* A slip of the foot ; an error, a fault.

مزمار mìzmār, *s. a.* A pipe, a flute.

مزمن mùzmin, *a. a.* Chronic, old, long-standing.

مزور mùzèvvir, *s. a.* A lying, swindling rogue ; —, mùzèvvèr, *a. a.* Forged, made up, concocted of lies.

مزه mèzé, *s. p.* A whet before dinner, an appetizer (consisting really of dry and salt condiments, or fruit, taken with raw spirits) ; a joke, fun, raillery ; مزه‌لو mèzéli, *a. t.* Funny, joking (saying).

مزيت mèzìyyèt, *s. a.* The particular point, virtue, or advantage (of a thing).

مزيد mèzid, *a. a.* Much, increased, augmented.

مزيل mùzìl, *a. a.* Who or which causes to disappear, to vanish.

مزين mùzèyyen, *a. a.* Embellished, adorned.

مژد mùzhd, مژدكان mùzhdéghyān, مژدكانه mùzhdéghyānè, *s. p.* A present given to a bringer of good news.

مژدور mùzhdvèr, *a. p.* Rewarded, recompensed.

مژده mùzhdé, *s. p.* Good news, glad tidings of any happy event ; مژده‌جى mùzhdéji, *s. t.* Hangers-on at public offices, who, when people are appointed to any employ, carry the news to their friends, and expect a reward; مژدەرس mùzhdé-rèss, *s. p.* A bringer of good news. [an eyelash.

مژكان mùzhghyān, *s. p.* The eyelashes,

مس mèsss, *s. a.* A touching; ا—, —et, *v.n.* To touch; to happen; —, miss, *s. p.* Copper.

مسا mèssā, *s. a.* The evening.

مسابقت mùssābakàt, *s. a.* An arriving or happening before (something else); a taking the precedence; ا—, —et, *v.n.* To arrive or happen before; to take precedence.

مساجد mèssājid, *s. pl. a.* (*of* مسجد mèssjid), Small parish mosques.

مساحه mèssāha, *s. a.* A measuring, surveying (land); the measure (of a piece of land); ا—, —et, *v.a.* To measure (land).

مسارعت mùssāra''àt, *s. a.* A being quick, ready, and willing; ا—, —et, *v.n.* To hasten willingly, to be quick (about doing a thing).

مساعد mùssā''id, *a. a.* Favourable.

مساعده mùssā''adé, *s. a.* Favour shown, permission or assistance given as a favour; the admitting or allowing (anything to be done); ا—, —et, *v.n.* To show favour, to favour, to be favourable; to give permission or assistance; to admit or allow (to be done).

مساعى mèssā''ī, *s. pl. a.* (*of* سعى sà''y), Endeavours, exertions.

مساغ mèssāgh, *s. a.* Permission, toleration, indulgence. [to place.

مسافه mèssāfé, *s. a.* Distance from place

مسافر mùssāfir, *s. a.* A guest, a visitor; a sojourner; a traveller.

مسافرت mùssāférèt, *s. a.* The being a guest or visitor, quality of guest; a sojourn; a journeying; ا—, —et, *v.n.* To sojourn; to travel.

مساكن mèssākin, *s. pl. a.* (*of* مسكن mèsskèn), Habitations.

مساكين mèssākīn, *s. pl. a.* (*of* مسكين misskīn), The poor, needy.

مسالك mèssālik, *s. pl. a.* (*of* مسلك mèsslèk), Roads, paths, ways; careers.

مسالمت mùssālémèt, *s. a.* Peace, freedom from enmity or warfare.

مسامات mèssāmmāt (mèssāmāt), *s. pl. a.* (*no sing.*), Pores.

مسامحه mùssāmaha, *s. a.* A taking no notice, a not preventing; ا—, —et, *v.n.* To take no notice, not to prevent, to connive at (without corrupt motives).

مسامع mèssāmi'', *s. pl. a.* (*no sing.*), Ears.

مساوات mùssāvāt, *s. a.* Equality.

مساوى mùssāvī, *a. a.* Equal.

مسائل mèssā'il, *s. pl. a.* (*of* مسئله mèss'élé), Questions, subjects, theses.

مسبب mùssèbbib, *s. a.* He who causes or creates (needful things); —, mùssèbbeb, *a. a.* Furnished with all needful things; —الاسباب, mùssèbbibu-'l-èssbāb, (God) the creator of all needful things.

مسبوق mèssbūk, *a. a.* Precedented ; نامسبوق nā-mèssbūk, *a. p.* Unprecedented.

مست mèsst, *s. t.* A kind of light half-boot for indoor wear, and over which slippers or shoes are worn out of doors ; —, *a. p.* Drunk, tipsy, intoxicated ; مستانه mèsstāné, *a. p.* Pertaining to one who is drunk.

مستأجر mùsstè'jir, *s. a.* One who takes a thing on hire.

مستأمن mùsstè'min, *s. a.* One under safe conduct or the law of nations, to whom immunity from hostilities has been granted at his own request ; one who, being a foreigner and not a Muhammedan, goes into a Muhammedan territory or into Turkey on any peaceable mission ; any Muhammedan going abroad on any peaceable mission, and under the laws of nations.

مستبان mùsstébān, *a. a.* Clear, manifest, evident.

مستتبع mùsstètbi", *a. a.* Who or which is followed or accompanied.

مستتر mùsstètir, *a. a.* Who veils or hides himself.

مستثقل mùsstèsskàl, *a. a.* Treated as if counted a bore. [cepted, exempted.

مستثنا *or* مستثنى mùsstèssnà, *a. a.* Ex-

مستجاب mùsstéjāb, *a. a.* Answered, accepted (a prayer, request).

مستجلب mùsstèjlib, *a. a.* Which draws, attracts, causes, brings down.

مستجمع mùsstèjmi", *a. a.* Who or which contains, collects within himself.

مستحب mùsstahàbb, *a. a.* Esteemed as lovely or loving or meritorious.

مستحسن mùsstàhsèn, *a. a.* Approved of, praiseworthy.

مستحضر mùsstàhzàr, *a. a.* Of which one is informed or aware, known, understood. [risoning a fortress.

مستحفظ mùsstàhfiz, *s. a.* A soldier gar-

مستحق mùsstāhikk (mùsstahàkk), *a. a.* Deserving ; —, mùsstahàkk, *a. a.* Deserved, merited ; —, *s. a.* What one has deserved, merited ; الله مستحقکنی ویرسون àllāh - mùsstahàkkingi-vèrsin ! May God give you your deserts ! [fortified.

مستحکم mùsstàhkèm, *a. a.* Strong, firm;

مستخدم mùsstàkhdèm, *a. a.* Employed (a person), in service.

مستخرج mùsstàkhrèj, *a. a.* Extracted.

مستدام mùsstédām, *a. a.* Continual, perpetual. [Demanded, requested.

مستدعا *or* مستدعى mùsstèd"à, *a. a.*

مستدیر mùsstédīr, *a. a.* Not plane, round ; سطح مستدیر sàthi-mùsstédīr, A round surface, a non-plane superficies. [stant.

مستدیم mùsstédīm, *a. a.* Perpetual, con-

مستر mùssèttèr (*pl. fem.* مسترات mùssèttérāt), *s. a.* A veiled woman, a modest, virtuous woman. [Requested.

مسترجا *or* مسترجى mùsstèrjà, *a. a.*

مستریح mùsstérīh, *a. a.* At ease, free from care and trouble.

مستزاد mùsstézād, *a. a.* Increased, augmented, added to.

مستسقى mùsstesskī, *a. a.* Dropsical.

مستشار mùsstéshār, *s. a.* A councillor, and under-secretary of state, with whom the secretary of state advises.

مستصحب mùstasshAb (-ss-hAb), *a. a.* Taken with, made or allowed to accompany; acquired, purchased.

مستطاب mùsstatAb, *a. a.* Good, approved (book, &c.).

مستطيل mùsstatīl, *a. a.* Long, lengthened; —, *s. a.* A parallelogram.

مستظل mùsstazìll, *a. a.* Who seeks or finds protection in the shade.

مستعار mùssta''ār, *a. a.* Borrowed.

مستعان mùssta''ān, *a. a.* From whom assistance is asked; المستعان èl-mùssta''ān, *s. a.* God, from whom all ask assistance. [quired in haste.

مستعجل mùsstà''jèl, *a. a.* Pressing, re-

مستعد mùssta''ìdd (mùsstà''id), *a. a.* Prepared, ready, in readiness; ready witted, quick at learning, clever; inclined, predisposed.

مستعمل mùsstà''mel, *a. a.* Used, in use; which has been used, second-hand. [drowned.

مستغرق mùsstàghràk, *a. a.* Submerged,

مستغنى mùsstaghnī, *a. a.* Independent, not in want, able to do without (something or anything).

مستفاد mùsstéfād, *a. a.* Gathered, understood, acquired; —, *s. a.* The meaning (of a phrase or writing).

مستقبل mùsstAkbèl, *s. a.* The future time, time to come; the future tense.

مستقر mùsstakàrr, *a. a.* Firmly established, settled; a place in which one is definitively settled.

مستقل mùsstakìll (mùsstAkil), *a. a.* Independent, absolute.

مستقيم mùsstakīm, *a. a.* Straight, right; upright, honest, straightforward; خط —, khAtti-mùsstakīm, A right line, a straight line. [gust.

مستكره mùsstèkrèh, *a. a.* Held in dis-

مستلزم mùsstèlzim, *a. a.* Which causes, makes necessary. [constant.

مستمر mùsstémèrr, *a. a.* Permanent,

مستمند mùsstémènd, *a. p.* Poor, humble; مستمندانه mùsstémèndānè, *a. p.* Pertaining to a humble individual.

مستنبط mùsstènbèt, *a. a.* Deduced.

مستند mùsstènid, *a. a.* Who or which leans upon something for support; —, mùssténèd, *s. a.* A thing or person leant upon for support.

مستنير mùsstènīr, *a. a.* Deriving its light from something else.

مستوجب mùsstèvjib, *a. a.* Causing, rendering imperative.

مستور mèsstūr, *a. a.* Covered, hidden.

مستوفى mùsstèvfī, *a. a.* Sufficient, ample (salary, &c.).

مستولى mùsstèvlī, *a. a.* Overrunning, taking, occupying.

مستوى mùsstévī, *a. a.* Plane; سطح مستوى sAthi-mùsstévī, A plane superficies.

مستهزى mùsstèhzī s. a. One who ridicules others.

مسجد mèssjid, s. a. (*the original of our word* "mosque"), A place of adoration; a small parish or private mosque; —الحرام, mèssjidu-'l-hàrām, The sacred mosque at Mecca; —الاقصى, mèssjidu-'l-àksà, The temple or mosque of Omar at Jerusalem, or the heavenly temple immediately over it in paradise.

مسجع mùssèjjà'', a. a. Rhymed (prose) but not metrical.

مسجل mùssèjjèl, a. a. Inscribed in the register of a court of law.

مسجون mèssjūn, a. a. Imprisoned, incarcerated.

مسح mèssh (mèss-h), s. a. A rubbing with the inner parts of the fingers; the canonical mode of performing certain parts of the smaller ablution; ا—, —et, v.a. To rub in that particular way.

مسخر mùssàkhkhàr, a. a. Conquered, subdued, brought under subjection.

مسخره màsskh*ara*, s. a. A buffoon, tomfool; مسخره لق màsskh*aralik*, s. t. Buffoonery, tom-foolery.

مسدود mèssdūd, a. a. Closed, shut, stopped up. [mirth.

مسرت mèssèrret, s. a. Joy, gladness,

مسرف mùssrif, s. a. A spendthrift; مسرفانه mùssrifāné, a. p. Pertaining to a spendthrift. [mirthful.

مسرور mèssrūr, a. a. Joyful, glad,

مسطح mùssàttàh, a. a. Made flat; كرهٔ مسطحه kyùré'i-mùssàttaha, A planisphere.

مسطر misstàr, s. a. A machine for ruling lines on paper, consisting in a piece of cardboard with lines of hard-twisted silk sewn through it; this is placed under the paper to be ruled, and the finger being drawn along the silks, the lines are formed, raised on one side of the paper, depressed on the other; —, mùssàttàr, a. a. Having lines or writing traced upon it.

مسطور mèsstūr, a. a. Written.

مسعود mèss''ūd, a. a. Blessed with felicity and good fortune.

مسفور mèssfūr, a. a. Written; the above-mentioned (*always used as a mark of reprobation*).

مسقط màsskàt, s. a. A place where anything drops; Muscat in Arabia; —الرأس màsskàtu-'r-rè'ss, (The place where the head dropped) A birth-place, the place of one's birth.

مسقو Mòsskov (mòsskof), s. t. A Russian; Russia.

مسك missk, s. a. Musk; مسكى misskī, a. a. Musky; dark-coloured, swarthy.

مسكت misskèt, s. a. Name of a kind of grape, of a kind of apple; grape-shot; —, mùsskit, a. a. Which reduces to silence, satisfies.

مسكر mùsskir, a. a. Inebriating; مسكرات mùsskirāt, s. pl. a. Intoxicating drinks.

مسكن mèsskèn, *s. a.* A habitation, an abode.

مسكنت mèsskénèt, *s. a.* Utter poverty.

مسكوك mèsskyūk, *a. a.* Coined, struck with a die; مسكوكات mèsskyūkyāt, *s. pl. a.* Coins, medals.

مسكون mèsskyūn, *a. a.* Inhabited; ربع مسكون rùb''u-mèsskyūn, The inhabited quarter of the globe.

مسكين misskīn, *a. p.* Musky; dark-coloured, tawny; — (misskin), *s. a.* A pauper; a leper; مسكينلك miss-kinlik, *s. t.* Utter poverty, rags; [leprosy.

مسلح mùsèllàh, *a. a.* Armed.

مسلسل mùssèlsèl, *a. a.* Concatenated, continuous as the links of a chain.

مسلط mùssAllAt, *a. a.* Arrogating dominion; —اولـ, mùssAllAt-òl, *v.n.* To attack, to meddle with, to leave no peace, to pester.

مسلك mèsslèk, *s. a.* A course pursued; a path, road, way.

مسلم mùsslim, *s. a.* (*pl.* مسلمين mùss-limīn), A true Muhammedan, a follower of Islamism; —, mùssèllèm, *a. a.* Conceded; admitted; incontestable, incontrovertible; ceded, given up, delivered; —, mùssèllim (*for* متسلم mutésssèllim), *s. a.* A governor of a town; مسلمان mùsslimān, *s. pl. p.* Musslims, Isslamites, Muhammedans; (mùssulmAn, *as a Turkish singular*), A Musslim, Moslem, Muhammedan, Mahometan. [stripped.

مسلوب mèsslūb, *a. a.* Despoiled,

مسلوك mèsslūk, *a. a.* Followed, taken (a road, path, course, &c.).

مسلول mèsslūl, *a. a.* Drawn, unsheathed (a sword, &c.).

مسما (*for* مسمى) mùssèmmà, *a. a.* Named, called, bearing a name.

مسمار missmār, *s. a.* A nail.

مسمن mùssmin, *a. a.* Fat, plump.

مسموع mèssmū'', *a. a.* Heard.

مسموم mèssmūm, *a. a.* Poisoned.

مسمى mùssèmmà, *a. a.* Named, called, bearing a name.

مسن mùssinn, *a. a.* Aged, old, in years.

مسند mèssned, *s. a.* A place, post, office of high distinction; a place where one reclines on the elbow; —, mùssnèd, *a. a.* Which has been made to lean (against something), leant; imputed, attributed.

مسنم mùssènnèm, *a. a.* In profile; رسم مسنم rèssmi-mùssènnèm, A drawing or figure in profile.

مسنون mèssnūn, *a. a.* Founded on or supported by an act or saying of Muhammed.

مسواك missvāk, *s. a.* A kind of tooth-brush used in the East, made of a fibrous root; the using a tooth-brush.

مسوده mùsswèddé, mùssèvvédé, *s. a.* The rough copy of a writing; مسودهلك mùsswèddélik, *s. t.* Paper for rough copying. [gative medicine, a purge.

مسهل mùsshil (—ss-h—), *s. a.* A pur-

مسيب mùssèyyèb, *a. a.* Careless and prodigal in money matters.

مسيح mèssīh, *s. a.* The Anointed, the Messiah ; مسيحى mèssīhī, *a. a.* Christian, Messiahian.

مسير mèssīr, مسيره mèssīré, *s. a.* A place of promenade ; a journey.

مسينا Mèssīna, *s. t.* Messina, in Italy.

مسئله mèss'élé, *s. a.* A question, subject of disquisition. [swerable.

مسئول mèss'ūl, *a. a.* Responsible, an-

مش mish, mısh, Termination of the past active participle, and of the dubitative mood, of Turkish verbs. [sembling.

مشابه mùshàbīh, *a. a.* Like, similar, re-

مشابهت mùshābéhèt, *s. a.* Likeness, resemblance, similarity.

مشاتمه mùshātémé, *s. a.* A calling each other names, mutual reviling.

مشاجره mùshājéré, *s. a.* A quarrelling.

مشار mùshār, *a. a.* Shown, indicated ; مشاراليه mùshārun-ìlèyh, *s. a.* The aforementioned (only used as indicative of persons of high rank) ; مشاربالبنان mùshārun - bì -'l- bènān, *a. a.* Pointed at with the finger, distinguished, of note, of mark.

مشاركت mùshārékèt, *s. a.* Partnership ; community, participation.

مشاطه mèshāta, *s. a.* A tire-woman, a comber and decker-out of brides, a lady's-maid. [divisable (property).

مشاع mùshā'', *a. a.* Undivided, un-

مشافهه mùshāfaha, *s. a.* Verbal communication and intercourse.

مشاق mèshākk, *s. pl. a.* (*of* مشقت mèshàkkat), Fatigues, inconveniences.

مشام mèshāmm, *s. a.* The seat or organ of smelling ; the sense of smelling ; the quality of odour.

مشاوره mùshāvéré, *s. a.* Deliberation, mutual consultation ; ا—, —et, *v.n.* To deliberate, consult together.

مشاهده mùshāhédé, *s. a.* A seeing, witnessing ; ا—, —et, *v.a.* To see, witness.

مشاهير mèshāhīr, *s. pl. a.* (*of* مشهور mèshhūr), The famous, noted, celebrated.

مشائخ mèshā'ikh, *s. pl. a.* (*of* شيخ shèykh), Chief doctors of law and divinity. [net-work or trellis-work.

مشبك mùshèbbèk, *a. a.* Formed like

مشبه mùshèbbèh (*fem.* مشبهه mùshèbbéhé), *a. a.* Assimilated ; صفت مشبهه sıfatı-mùshèbbéhé, An adjective derived from a verb and assimilated to a participle. [with the fist.

مشت mùsht, *s. p.* The fist ; a blow

مشتا mèshtà, *s. t.* Winter quarters ; winter pasturage ; a conservatory, greenhouse.

مشتاق mùshtāk, *a. a.* Longing, desirous of seeing, wishing for. [ful.

مشتبه mùshtèbèh, *a. a.* Doubted ; doubt-

مشتد mùshtèdd, *a. a.* Which has become more violent. [more than one.

مشترك mùshtérèk, *a. a.* Common to

مشترى mùshtérī, *s. a.* A customer, purchaser ; the planet Jupiter.

مشتعل mùshtà''il, *a. a.* In flames, burning with a flame.

مشتق mùshtàkk, *a. a.* Derived etymologically.

مشتكا *or* مشتكى mùshtékyà, *s. a.* A subject of complaint, a thing complained of.

مشتكى mùshtékī, *s. a.* A complainant.

مشتمل mùshtèmil, *a. a.* Containing, comprising; مشتملات mùshtémélāt (mùshtémilāt), *s. pl. a.* Things contained, comprised, appurtenances.

مشتواره mùshtwārÉ, *s. p.* A handful.

مشته mùshta, *s. p.* The fist; a blow with the fist; a kind of hammer or beater used by shoemakers and bookbinders, shaped like a dumb-bell.

مشتهر mùshtèhir, *a. a.* Become famous, celebrated.

مشتها *or* مشتهى mùshtéhà, *a. a.* (*pl.* مشتهيات mùshtéhìyyāt), Desired, longed for; capable of exciting desire.

مشتهى mùshtéhī, *a. a.* Desirous, filled with desire, inflamed with desire.

مشحون mèshhūn, *a. a.* Filled, full.

مشرب mèshreb, *s. a.* Character, disposition, temperament; اچق مشرب àchik-mèshreb, *a. t.* Of a forward disposition, not sufficiently modest.

مشربه mèshrébÉ (mȦshrapa), *s. a.* A drinking-pot.

مشرف mùshèrrèf, *a. a.* Honoured, to whom or to which an honour has been paid; —, mùshrif, *a. a.* Near, bordering upon.

مشرق mèshrik, *s. a.* The place of sunrise, the east; مشرقان mèshrikĀn (oblique مشرقين mèshrikàyn), *s. a. dual,* The two places of sun-rise, *i. e.* the east and the west, since the sun is to rise in the west before the day of judgment.

مشرك mùshrik (*pl.* مشركين mùshrikīn), *s. a.* Any misbeliever who, denying verbally or practically the unity of God, treats anything else as a partner in the Godhead.

مشروب mèshrūb, *a. a.* Drunk or drinkable; مشروبات mèshrūbāt, *s. pl. a.* Drinks of the various kinds.

مشروح mèshrūh, *a. a.* Explained, commented upon.

مشروط mèshrūt, *a. a.* Stipulated, conditioned; مشروطه mèshrūta, *s. a.* A piece of property in mortmain, with the condition that, before being applied to public purposes, certain private conditions shall be carried out.

مشروع mèshrū'', *a. a.* Legal; غيرمشروع ghàyri-mèshrū'', *a. a.* Illegal.

مشعر mùsh''ir, *a. a.* Indicative, informatory. [torch, flambeau.

مشعله mèsh''àlÉ (mȦshȦla), *s. a.* A

مشغله mèshghalÉ, *s. a.* An occupation, piece of business.

مشغول mèshghūl, *a. a.* Occupied, busy.

مشفق mùshfik, *a. a.* Kind to those in trouble; مشفقانه mùshfikānÉ, Pertaining to one who is kind; kind (act).

مشق mèshk, *s. a.* A writ g copy —الموق, mèshk-Ȧlmak, To take lessons in calligraphy.

مشقت mèshàkkat, *s. a.* Trouble, inconvenience, fatigue, suffering.

مشك mùshk, *s. p.* Musk; مشكين mùshkīn, *a. p.* Musky; dark-coloured, tawny.

مشكل mùshkil, *a. a.* Difficult; —, (*pl.* مشكلات mùshkilāt), *and* مشكله mùshkilé, *s. a.* A difficulty; —, mùshèkkèl, *a. a.* Formed, figured, shaped.

مشكور mèshkyūr, *a. a.* For which thanks are given or due. [doubted.

مشكوك mèshkyūk, *a. a.* Doubtful,

مشمع mùshèmmà'', *a. a.* Waxed with wax; —(mūshàmba), *s. a.* Wax-cloth, cere-cloth, oil-cloth, tarpaulin, oiled silk.

مشمول mèshmūl, *a. a.* Comprised, contained; comprising, containing.

مشموم mèshmūm, *a. a.* Perfumed with, fragrant with, smelling of (something).

مشورت mèshvéret, *s. a.* A council; consultation; ا—, —et, *v.n.* To hold a council. [embroiled, disordered.

مشوش mùshèvvèsh, *a. a.* Confused,

مشوم mèshūm, *a. a.* Unlucky (thing or place), bringing ill-luck to the owner or holder.

مشهد mèshhèd (sh-h), *s. a.* A place where anyone was killed for the true religion, or where he is buried, a place of martyrdom. [witnessed.

مشهود mèshhūd (sh-h), *a. a.* Seen,

مشهور mèshhūr (sh-h), (mènshūr), *a. a.* Well-known, famous, celebrated, commonly known, commonly called.

مشى mèshy, *s. a.* The act of walking; مشياً mèshyan, *ad. a.* On foot, walking.

مشئت mèshi'èt, مشيت mèshìyyet, *s. a.* The will, desire, volition.

مشيخت mèshīkhàt, *s. a.* The dignity or quality of Sheykh or Shèykhu-'l-ìsslām; مشيختپناه mèshīkhàt-pēnāh, *s. p.* The Shèykhu-'l-ìsslām.

مشيد mùshèyyid, *s. a.* One who builds, lays, or erects, broadly and firmly; —, mùshèyyèd, *a. a.* Broadly or firmly built, laid, or erected.

مشير mùshīr, *s. a.* A commander, one who commands, directs, orders; the title of Pashas of the first class, who are either Ministers of State, Governors-General of provinces, or full Generals commanding armies.

مشيمه mèshīmé, *s. a.* The after-birth, the membrane which envelopes the fœtus in viviparous animals and man; *or*, that to which the fœtus is attached by the umbilical cord, the placenta; مشيمهٔ عالم mèshīmé'i-''ālem, The sun; the sky. [sheepskin, roan.

مشين mèshin, *s. a.* Leather made from

مشئوم mèsh'ūm, *a. a.* Unlucky, which brings bad luck to the owner or holder.

مشيئت mèshī'àt, *s. a.* The will, desire, volition.

مصاب mùssāb, *a. a.* Hit, struck, wounded. [of patience.

مصابرت mùssābérèt, *s. a.* The exercise

مصابح màssābih, مصابيح màssābīh,

s. pl. a. (*of* مصباح mìssbĀh), Lanterns; morning cups of drink.

مصاحب mùssāhib, *s. a.* A court functionary, whose duty it is to entertain the monarch by conversation and wit; a bosom friend; a courtier.

مصاحبت mùssāhébèt, *s. a.* A being or keeping in company or conversation; ا—, —et, *v.n.* To keep company, to converse, hold conversation.

مصاد mÀssAd, *s. t.* A steel (for sharpening knives).

مصادر mÀssādir, *s. pl. a.* (*of* مصدر mÀssdar), Issues, outlets; infinitives or verbal nouns (in grammar).

مصادره mùssĀdérÉ, *s. a.* A confiscating, escheating to the crown; ا—, —et, *v.a.* To confiscate, escheat.

مصادمه mùssĀdémÉ, *s. a.* A shock; ا—, —et, *v.n.* To knock violently (against a thing). [mÀssraf), Expenses.

مصارف mÀssārif, *s. pl. a.* (*of* مصرف

مصاف mèssĀff, *s. a.* A place where the ranks of two armies are drawn up against each other; a battle-field; a battle. [friendship, amity.

مصافات mùssāfāt, *s. a.* Friendly terms,

مصافحه mùssāfaha, *s. a.* A taking each other by the hand in token of friendship or on the conclusion of a bargain.

مصال mÀssAl, *s. t.* A tale, a fiction, story.

مصالح mÀssālih, *s. pl. a.* (*of* مصلحت mÀsslàhat), Affairs, businesses; —, mùssālih, *a. a.* At peace, not at war.

مصالحه mùssālaha, *s. a.* A making peace, a peace. [by marriage.

مصاهرت mùssāhéret, *s. a.* Relationship

مصائب mÀssāʻib, *s. pl. a.* (*of* مصيبت mùssībèt), Misfortunes, fortune's blows.

مصباح mìssbāh, *s. a.* A lantern; a torch, flambeau, a morning cup of drink.

مصبغ mùssèbbàgh, *a. a.* Dyed.

مصحح mùssàhhih, *s. a.* A corrector of the press, reader for the press; —, mùssàhhàh, *a. a.* Corrected.

مصحف mùsshàf, *s. a.* The sacred volume, the Kurʻān.

مصحوب mÀsshūb, *a. a.* Which anyone takes with or causes to accompany him, accompanied.

مصداق mìssdĀk, *s. a.* A true saying, an axiom, a trite saying; a proof of the truth of a saying; مصداقنجه mìssdĀkinja, According to the true saying that: . . . .

مصدر mÀssdar, *s. a.* An issue, outlet; a source; an infinitive or verbal noun; مصدريه mÀssdarìyyÉ, *s. a.* An old obsolete local export duty.

مصدق mùssÀddik, *a. a.* Corroborative; —, *s. a.* A corroborator or admitter of the truth of what is said; —, mùssÀddàk, *a. a.* Corroborated, confirmed, admitted.

مصدور màssdūr, *a. a.* Afflicted with a chest complaint, consumptive.

مصر mìssr (mìssir), *s. a.* A city; Egypt; Cairo; —, *or* مصر بغدايى mìssir-bòghdayi, Indian corn, maize; مصر طاوغى mìssir-tàwughu, or هند طاوغى hìnd-tàwughu, A Turkey-fowl, turkey; —, mùssìrr, a. a. Who pertinaciously sticks to any act or assertion, obstinately persisting. [poetry.

مصراع mìssrā", s. a. A hemistich in

مصرح mùssàrràh, a. a. Expressly and clearly mentioned.

مصرف mássraf, s. a. Expense, expenditure; مصرفلو mássrafli, a. t. Expensive; ايراد مصرف īrād-mássraf, Income and expenditure, incomings and outgoings.

مصروع mássrū", a. a. Struck with epilepsy.

مصروف mássrūf, a. a. Spent, expended, laid out; turned, directed (in travelling); declinable (in grammar).

مصره mássra, s. t. A small-sized pipe or measure for water in the hydraulic system.

مصطفى mùsstafà, a. a. Chosen; —, —, s. a. The chosen one, Muhammed; Mustapha or Mustafa (*prop. name*).

مصطكى másstākī, s. t. Brandy or liqueur perfumed with gum-mastic.

مصطلح mùsstalàh, a. a. Filled with hard words or with technical expressions.

مصقل másskal, مصقله másskala, s. a. A burnisher, burnishing instrument.

مصلا or مصلى mùssàllà, s. a. A place in the open air, devoted to public prayer; any place of prayer.

مصلح mùsslih, s. a. A pacificator; مصلحانه mùsslihānè, a. p. Pacificatory.

مصلحت másslahat, s. a. An affair, a piece of business; an advantage, an advantageous state of things; مصلحتكذار másslahat-ghyùzār, s. a. An agent, a chargé d'affaires.

مصلق másslak or mùssluk, s. t. A cock, tap, stop-cock, turn-cock.

مصلوب másslūb, a. a. Hung, crucified.

مصلى mussàlla, s. a. See مصلا.

مصمم mùssàmmèm, a. a. Fully intended, designed, decided upon.

مصنع mùssànnà", a. a. Made or prepared with art.

مصنف mùssànnif, s. a. An author (of a book); —, mùssànnèf, a. a. Written, composed, compiled; مصنفات mùssànnéfāt, s. pl. a. Works, compositions, compilations.

مصنوع mássnū", a. a. Made; مصنوعات mássnū"āt, s. pl. a. Things made by artificers.

مصور mùssávvir, s. a. A painter or statuary, an artist; —, mùssávvèr, a. a. Figured, drawn, painted, cut out; ornamented with figures and designs.

مصون mássūn, a. a. Protected, shielded, preserved, kept free and safe.

مصيب mùssīb, a. a. Which hits, effects the proposed object.

مصيبت mùssībèt, s. a. A calamity which befalls; —! *int. t.* You pest! the pest! [abode.

مصير mássīr, s. a. A place of being, an

مصيف màssīf, *s. a.* A summer residence. [polished.

مصيقل mùssàykAl, *a. a.* Burnished,

مضا ما مضا mÀzà-mā-mÀzà! *comp. a.* What is past is past, let bye-gones be bye-gones.

مضاربه mùzārébé, *s. a.* A mutual beating of each other, a fighting.

مضارع mùzāri'', *s. a.* The aorist of verbs which has either a present or a future signification.

مضاعف mùzā''àf, *a. a.* Doubled, *or* augmented any number of times.

مضاف mùzĀf, *s. a.* Any thing added to another, an appendix or appendage; a complement; when two nouns are in construction or *en régime* in a sentence, the governing noun is called مضاف mùzĀf, and the complement or noun governed مضاف اليه mùzĀfun-ìlèyh; مضافات mùzāfāt, *s. pl. a.* Conquered or subjected territories.

مضامين mÀzāmīn, *s. pl. a.* (*of* مضمون mÀzmūn), Things contained; contents; senses, meanings.

مضائق mÀzā'ik, *s. pl. a.* (*of* مضيق mÀzīk), Narrowed, straitened, difficult places, times, *or* circumstances.

مضايقه mùzāyaka, *s. a.* Anything which causes embarrassment or straits.

مضبطه mÀzbAta, *s. a.* A report, a protocol, a procès-verbal.

مضبوط mÀzbūt, *a. a.* Fastened, bound; subject to rule or regulation; small, handy, conveniently arranged.

مضحك mùdhìk, *a. a.* Which causes laughter; مضحكات mùdhikyāt, *s. pl. a.* Sayings which cause laughter.

مضر mùzìrr (mùzur), *a. a.* Hurtful, noxious; كل مضر يقتل kyùllu-mùzìrrin-yùktèl, Every noxious animal may be slaughtered (*prov.*).

مضراب mìzrāb, *s. a.* An instrument for striking; a musical plectrum or bow.

مضرت mÀzàrret (mÀzaràt, *pl.* مضرات mÀzàrrāt), *s. a.* Hurtfulness, noxiousness; harm, injury.

مضروب mÀzrūb, *a. a.* Struck, hit, beaten; —, *s. a.* The multiplicand (*in arith.*); مضروب فيه màzrūbun-fīh, *s. a.* The multiplier.

مضطر mùztàrr, *a. a.* Forced, obliged, constrained; in constrained circumstances.

مضطرب mùztàrib, *a. a.* Uneasy (in body or in mind), disquieted, in pain.

مضعف mùzà'''àf, *a. a.* Doubled, increased any number of times.

مضل mùdìll, *s. a.* One who leads astray; ضال مضل zĀlli-mùdìll, One in error leading others astray, the blind leading the blind.

مضمار mìzmār, *s. a.* An open plain or space for horse exercise, a racecourse.

مضمحل mùzmahìll (mùzmàhil), *a. a.* Destroyed, annihilated, disappeared.

مضمر mùzmèr, *a. a.* Intended, kept at heart.

مضمون mÀzmūn, *a. a.* Contained; —, *s. a.* The sense contained in a writing or saying; a pun, a double-entendre, bon-mot.

مضی **mŭzī** (*for* مضیء **mŭzī'**), *a. a.* Which gives light, illumines; مضی ما مضی **mʌzà-mā-mʌzā!** What is past is past! Let bye-gones be bye-gones!

مضیق **mʌzīk**, *s. a.* Any time, place, or circumstance which presses hard upon one. [cording.

مطابق **mŭtābik**, *a. a.* Conformable, ac-

مطابقت **mŭtābakʌt**, *s. a.* A conforming, a being conformable; ا—, —et, *v.n.* To follow, conform to, adapt one's self to. [difficult questions.

مطارحه **mŭtāraha**, *s. a.* A disputing on

مطاع **mŭtʌ"**, *a. a.* Obeyed; جهانمطاع **jihān-mŭtʌ"**, *a. p.* Obeyed by the whole world.

مطاف **màtāf**, *s. a.* Place or path in which people walk round in procession; —, **mŭtāf**, *s. a.* Thing round which people walk in procession.

مطالب **mʌtālib**, *s. pl. a.* (*of* مطلب **mʌtlàb**), Subjects, questions, propositions; demands; things sought or demanded.

مطالبه **mŭtālébé**, *s. a.* A demanding; ا—, —et, *v.a.* To demand.

مطالع **mʌtāli"**, *s. pl. a.* (*of* مطلع **mʌtlà"**), Points at which celestial bodies rise.

مطالعه **mŭtāla"à**, *s. a.* The studying, revolving in one's mind, carefully weighing and examining; a reading; ا—, —et, *v.a.* To study; to read.

مطاوعت **mŭtāva"àt**, *s. a.* Obedience, conformity; ا—, —et, *v.n.* To conform, act in conformity.

مطایا **mʌtāyā**, *s. pl. a.* (*of* مطیه **mʌtìyyé**), Horses.

مطبخ **mʌtbʌkh** (**mŭtfʌk**), *s. a.* A kitchen.

مطبع **mʌtbà"**, مطبعه **mʌtba"à**, *s. a.* A printing-office. [A decoction.

مطبوخ **mʌtbūkh**, *a. a.* Cooked; —, *s. a.*

مطبوع **mʌtbū"**, *a. a.* Printed; imprinted in one's nature; agreeable to anyone's taste.

مطر **mʌtār**, *s. a.* Rain.

مطرا (*for* مطری) **mŭtàrrà**, *a. a.* Made to look fresh and spruce, fresh-looking.

مطران **mŭtrān**, *s. a.* A Christian bishop.

مطرب **mŭtrib**, *s. a.* A musician, singer, or dancer; an enlivener.

مطرح **mŭtàrràh**, *a. a.* Extensive, high, and well-built (a building).

مطرز **mŭtàrrèz**, *a. a.* Ornamented; —, **mŭtàrriz**, *s. a.* One who arranges ornaments.

مطرق **mʌtràk**, *s. t.* A cudgel.

مطروح **mʌtrūh**, *a. a.* Laid, built (foundations, &c.). [cast off.

مطرود **mʌtrūd**, *a. a.* Rejected, ejected,

مطره **mʌtara**, *s. t.* A leather bottle.

مطری **mŭtàrrà**, *a. a.* Made to look fresh and spruce; fresh-looking.

مطعون **mʌt"ūn**, *a. a.* Struck, wounded by a thrust; struck with the plague.

مطفی **mʌtfī**, *a. a.* Extinguished, put out.

مطلا mùtàllà, *a. a.* Gilt; rubbed over with ointment, &c.

مطلب màtlàb, *s. a.* A subject, question, matter; a thing sought for.

مطلع màtlà", *s. a.* A place where a celestial body rises; the first distich of a poem; —, mùttali", *a. a.* Aware, informed, cognisant.

مطلق mùtlak, *a. a.* Unbound, unfettered, free, unrestrained; absolute; مطلقا mùtlakā, *ad. a.* In an absolute manner; absolutely.

مطلوب màtlūb, *a. a.* Desired, wished for; —, *s. a.* A thing desired, desideratum; an active debt, one for which payment is required by the creditor, a demand.

مطمح màtmàh, *s. a.* An object on which the eye is fixed.

مطمئن mùtma'inn, *a. a.* Feeling safe, secure.

مطوى màtwī, *a. a.* Folded up in anything, contained.

مطهر mùtahhèr, *a. a.* Cleansed, purified.

مطيه màtìyyé, *s. a.* A horse.

مطيع mùtī", *a. a.* Obedient, submissive.

مظالم màzālim, *s. pl. a.* (*no sing.*), Grievances, oppressions.

مظاهرت mùzāhérèt, *s. a.* Support, protection, a backing; ا—, —et, *v.n.* To back, support, protect.

مظروف màzrūf, *a. a.* Contained in a cover or envelope.

مظفر mùzàffer, *a. a.* Successful, attaining the end of his efforts; المظفر دائما èl-mùzàffer-dā'imā, Ever successful (*the last epithet assumed by Sultans of Turkey in the* طغرا tùghrā *or cypher of their names which is figured on coins and placed over all public buildings*, &c.).

مظلم mùzlim, *a. a.* Dark, obscure.

مظلوم màzlūm, *a. a.* Who has suffered wrong; —, *a. t.* Easy-tempered, gentle.

مظنه màzànné, *s. a.* A place where anything is supposed to be; a person on whom suspicion falls.

مظنون màznūn, *a. a.* Supposed, conjectured, suspected.

مظهر màzhàr, *s. a.* The place of manifestation, the object in or through which a thing is manifested (*practically it becomes an adjective in the sense of* "visited with"); مظهر عنايت اولدى màzhàri-"ìnāyet-òldu (He became the place of manifestation of grace, grace was manifested in him; he was an object of, or visited with, grace and favour. *N.B.*—Barker has totally misunderstood, and has, consequently, misrepresented the meaning of this word, in the notes appended to a chapter of St. John in Turkish, given in his larger Turkish Grammar); مظهريت màzhàrìyyèt, *s. a.* The quality of being the object of, or visited with, anything.

مع mà"*a*, *a. a.* With; مع هذا mà"*a*-hāzā, مع مافيه mà"-mā-fīh, *ad. a.* But notwithstanding, still; مع الكراهه mà"*a*-'l-kèrāhé, With regret; معا mà"an, *ad. a.* Together.

معابد mà''ābid, *s. pl. a.* (*of* معبد mà''-bèd), Temples, oratories, places of devotion.

معابر mà''ābir, *s. pl. a.* (*of* معبر mà''bĕr), Places or means of getting through or across a natural obstacle, as a pass, a ford, a bridge, a ferry.

معاتب mŭ''ātèb, *a. a.* Reprimanded, scolded.

معاد mà''ād, *s. a.* A place to which one returns, a resort.

معادات mŭ''ādāt, *s. a.* Enmity.

معادل mŭ''ādil, *a. a.* Equal, equivalent.

معادلت mŭ''ādélèt, *s. a.* Equity, justice.

معادله mŭ''ādélĕ, *s. a.* (*originally identic with* معادلت), An equation in algebra.

معادن mà''ādin, *s. pl. a.* (*of* معدن mà''dĕn), Mines.

معاذ mà''āz, *s. a.* A place of refuge, a refuge; معاذالله mà''āza-'llāh! God forbid! God is our only refuge (in such a case)!

معاذرت mŭ''āzérèt, *s. a.* The offering excuses.

معارج mà''ārij, *s. pl. a.* (*no sing.*), Steps by which one mounts.

معارض mŭ''āriz, *a. a.* Who squabbles, scolds, shows dissatisfaction.

معارضه mŭ''āraza, *s. a.* A squabbling, disputing; ا—, —et, *v.n.* To squabble.

معارف mà''ārif, *s. pl. a.* (*of* معرفت mà''rifet), Knowledge of various kinds, sciences; kindnesses, favours; praiseworthy acts or qualities.

معارك mà''ārik, *s. pl. a.* (*of* معركه mà''rékĕ), Battle-fields; battles.

معاركه mŭ''ārékĕ, *s. a.* A fighting; fight, battle; ا—, —et, *v.n.* To do battle.

معاش mà''āsh, *s. a.* A means of subsistence, pay, salary.

معاشرت mŭ''āshérèt, *s. a.* Living in company, getting on (with someone); حسن معاشرت ا hùssnu-mŭ''āshéret--et, *v.n.* To live on friendly terms, get on well (with someone).

معاصات mŭ''āssāt, *s. a.* Perversity, rebellion, wickedness.

معاصر mŭ''āssir, *s. a.* A contemporary.

معاصى mà''āssī, *s. pl. a.* (*of* معصيت mà''sìyyèt), Sins, wickednesses.

معاف mŭ''āf, *a. a.* Pardoned, forgiven, let off, excused; exempted; معافيت mŭ''āfìyyèt, *s. a.* Exemption, freedom.

معالجه mŭ''āléjĕ, *s. a.* A taking medicine; a curing with medicine.

معالى mà''ālī, *s. pl. a.* (*no sing.*), High qualities.

معامله mŭ''āmélĕ, *s. a.* An acting, conducting one's self (towards another); interest (upon money); ا—, —et, *v.n.* To conduct one's self (towards someone); بدمعامله bèd-mŭ''āmélĕ, Improper, unkind, disrespectful treatment; معامله يه ويرمك mŭ''āméléyĕ--vèrmek, To put out at interest; معامله جى mŭ''āméléji, *s. t.* A usurer, money-lender.

معاندت mŭ''ānédèt, *s. a.* Obstinacy.

معانى mà''ānī, *s. pl. a.* (*of* معنى mà''nà), Senses, significations, meanings.

معاودت mŭ''āvédèt, *s. a.* A returning,

coming or going back; ا—, —et, *v.n.* To return.

معاون mŭ‘‘āvin, *s. a.* An assistant.

معاونت mŭ‘‘āvénèt, *s. a.* Assistance.

معاهد mŭ‘‘āhid, *a. a.* Who has mutually entered into a treaty.

معاهده mù‘‘āhédé, *s. a.* A treaty, compact, convention; an entering into a treaty; ا—, —et, *v.n.* To enter into a treaty, make a convention.

معائب mà‘‘ā'ib, *s. pl. a.* (*no sing.*), Defects; vices.

معايده mŭ‘‘āyédé, *s. a.* A visiting and congratulating on the occasion of a religious festival.

معاينه mŭ‘‘āyéné, *s. a.* An inspecting, viewing formally; ا—, —et, *v.a.* To inspect.

معبد mà‘‘bèd, *s. a.* A place of devotion, [temple.

معبر mà‘‘ber, *s. a.* A place of passage; a pass, ferry, ford, bridge.

معبود mà‘‘būd, *a. a.* Served; —, *s. a.* An object of worship; God.

معتاد mù‘‘tād, *a. a.* To which one is accustomed; —, *s. a.* A person's custom, way, habit.

معتبر mù‘‘tèbèr, *a. a.* Esteemed, held in estimation.

معتدل mù‘‘tèdil, *a. a.* Temperate (in degree).

معترض mù‘‘tériz, *a. a.* Who objects, raises an objection; معترضه mù‘‘tèriza, *s. a.* A parenthesis; جملهٔ معترضه jùmlé'i-mù‘‘tèriza, A parenthetical phrase.

معترف mù‘‘tèrif, *a. a.* Who owns, admits, acknowledges.

معتكف mù‘‘tèkif, *a. a.* Who shuts himself up entirely for devotional purposes.

معتل mù‘‘tèll, *a. a.* Affected with some defect; (in grammar) having a و or a ى as a radical letter; معتل الفا mù‘‘tèllu-'l-fā, Whose first radical is و or ى; معتل العين mù‘‘tèllu-'l-‘‘àyn, Whose second radical is و or ى; معتل اللام mù‘‘tèllu-'l-lām, Whose third radical is و or ى.

معتمد mù‘‘témèd, *a. a.* Trusted, trustworthy; —, *s. a.* A storekeeper, or clerk of the works.

معتنا (*for* معتنى) mù‘‘ténà, *or* معتنابه mù‘‘ténà-bīh, *a. a.* Important, of importance (business), to which importance is attached.

معتوه mà‘‘tūh, *a. a.* Imbecile, in second [infancy.

معجز mŭ‘‘jiz, *a. a.* Which exceeds one's power and foils or tires out.

معجزه mù‘‘jizé, *s. a.* A miracle, what exceeds the power of man to effect.

معجل mŭ‘‘àjjèl, *s. a.* Immediate, paid down at once (any payment).

معجم mŭ‘‘jèm (*fem.* معجمه mù‘‘jémé), (A letter of the alphabet) which has one or more dots or diacritical points.

معجون mà‘‘jūn, *s. a.* Any paste-like composition; glazier's putty; any cement; an electuary; a kind of soft toffy or preparation of sugar with spices.

معده mì''dé, *s. a.* The stomach.

معدل mù''àddil, *s. a.* (A thing) which makes things equal; خطمعدل النهار khàtti-mù''àddilu-'n-nìhār, The equinoctial line.

معدلت mà''délet, *s. a.* Justice, equity.

معدن mà''dèn, *s. a.* A mine (for minerals); an ore; a metal; a metallic composition; معدنى mà''dénī, *a. a.* Mineral; معدنيات mà''déniyyāt, *s. pl. a.* Minerals, mineral substances; metals.

معدنوس mà''dénòss, *s. t.* Parsley.

معدود mà''dūd, *a. a.* Limited in number; counted (among things).

معدول mà''dūl, *a. a.* Turned out of the way, deviating. [annihilated.

معدوم mà''dūm, *a. a.* Non-existent;

معذب mù''zib, *s. a.* A tormentor, a plague; —, mù''àzzèb, *a. a.* Tormented, plagued.

معذرت mà''zérèt, *s. a.* An excuse offered; معذرتخواه mà''zérèt-khāh, *s. p.* One who offers excuses.

معذور mà''zūr, *s. a.* Excused, having a valid excuse.

معرا (*for* معرى) mù''àrrà, *a. a.* Naked, stript; free, void, exempt.

معراج mì''rāj, *s. a.* An ascension; the ascension of Muhammed into God's presence.

معرض mà''ràz, *s. a.* A cause, occasion, opportunity; —, mù''riz, *s. a.* A cause, causer.

معرفت mà''rifèt, *s. a.* Knowledge; art, cunning, dexterity; a work of art, a curious piece of workmanship; agency, intervention, instrumentality; معرفتلو ma''rifètli, *a. t.* Expert, dexterous, skilful (person); curiously or skilfully made (thing). [a battle.

معركه mà''réké, *s. a.* A field of battle;

معروض mà''rūz, *a. a.* Presented, offered, laid before; —, *s. a.* The subject of a representation or petition.

معروف mà''rūf, *a. a.* Known; favourably known; praiseworthy (acts or conduct).

معرى (*or* معرا) mù''àrrà, *a. a.* Naked, stript; free, exempt; —, mà''rà, *s. a.* Any part of the body usually exposed to view. [esteemed and honoured.

معزز mù''àzzèz, *a. a.* Held dear, highly

معزول mà''zūl, *a. a.* Displaced from office, superseded; معزولين mà''zūlīn, *s. pl. a.* Officers, or rather functionaries, who have been superseded from their places; معزولاً mà''zūlan, *ad. a.* As a superseded functionary.

معسكر mù''àsskèr, *s. a.* A camp, the assemblage-place of an army.

معشر mà''shèr, *s. a.* An assemblage, troop, body of men.

معشوق mà''shūk (*fem.* معشوقه mà''shūka), *a. a.* Beloved, the object of one's love.

معصوم mà''sūm, *a. a.* Innocent of sin; —, *s. a.* An innocent, a little child.

معصيت mà''sìyyèt, *s. a.* Sin, wickedness; rebellion.

معطر mŭ''àttàr, *a. a.* Scented, perfumed.

معطل mŭ''àttăl, *a. a.* Rendered useless and idle, inactive.

معطوف mà''tūf, *a. a.* Turned, inclined (from or towards any direction or object).

معظم mŭ''ăzzàm, *a. a.* Great, large; important; honoured, greatly respected.

معفو mà''fùvv, *a. a.* Pardoned, forgiven.

معقل mà''kĭl, *s. a.* A place of refuge, an asylum.

معقول mà''kūl, *a. a.* Intelligible, comprehensible; sage, prudent (act); معقولات mà''kūlăt, *s. pl. a.* Matters coming within the sphere of reason.

معكوس mà''kyūss, *a. a.* Inverted.

معلا (*for* معلى) mŭ''àllà, *a. a.* Exalted.

معلق mŭ''àllăk, *a. a.* Suspended, hanging; left in suspense, undecided; معلقات mŭ''àllakăt, *s. pl. a.* Ancient poems formerly suspended in the temple at Mecca before the introduction of Isslamism.

معلم mŭ''àllim, *s. a.* A teacher, instructor, trainer; —, mŭ''àllèm, *a. a.* Instructed, taught, trained.

معلوم mà''lūm, *a. a.* Known; given (in problems); —, *s. a.* A datum; ضلع معلوم dĭl''*i*-mà''lūm, A base-line (in geodesy); معلومات mà''lūmăt, *s. pl. a.* Known things; knowledge; information; معلوماتلو mà''lūmătl*i*, *a. t.* Possessed of knowledge or information.

معلى (*or* معلا) mŭ''àllà, *a. a.* Exalted.

معما (*for* معمى) mŭ''àmmà, *s. a.* A riddle, an enigma.

معمار mì''mār, *s. a.* An architect.

معمر mŭ''àmmèr, *a. a.* Long-lived.

معمور mà''mūr, *a. a.* Peopled; inhabited; cultivated; prosperous, in good estate; an epithet applied to public establishments; معموريت mà''mūrìyyèt, *s. a.* The state of being populous and prosperous (a place, a country).

معمول mà''mūl, *a. a.* Made, manufactured; artificial; معمول به mà''mūlun-bìh, *a. a.* Upon or according to which people act; in force, observed.

معمى (*or* معما) mŭ''àmmà, *s. a.* A riddle, an enigma.

معنا (*for* معنى) mà''nà, *s. a.* The literal sense, meaning (of a word or phrase), signification, import; a virtual sense, an implied sense, a real sense; a state of things; a dream; a song; معناً mà''nan, *ad. a.* In reality, virtually; in sense, logically; عالم معنا ''ālémi-mà''nà, The world of visions; a dream; معناى لغوى mà''nàyi-lŭghavī, A literal meaning; معناى اصطلاحى mà''nàyi-ìsstĭlāhī, A technical meaning; معنوى mà''névī, *a. a.* Spiritual; virtual, implied; logical.

معنبر mŭ''ànbèr, *a. a.* Perfumed with ambergris.

معنون mŭ''ànvèn, *a. a.* Bearing a title.

معنى (*or* معنا) mà''nà, *s. a.* See معنا.

معهود mà''hūd, *a. a.* Agreed upon; notorious, famous, well-known (*a sar-*

castic term for designing a person or anything). [gold or silver by.

معيار mì"yār, *s. a.* A standard for trying

معيب mŭ"àyyèb, *a. a.* Stigmatized;

معيبات mŭ"àyyébāt, *s. pl. a.* Vices.

معيت mà"ìyyèt, *s. a.* The official suite of a functionary; معيت مأمورى mà"ìyyèt - mèʻmūru, A subordinate official. [an allowance, pension.

معيشت mà"īshèt, *s. a.* Means of living,

معين mà"īn, *s. a.* A rhombus; —, mŭ"īn, *s. a.* A helper; an abettor; —, mŭ"àyyèn, *a. a.* Fixed, determined, determinate; شبه معين shìbhi-mà"īn, *s. a.* A rhomboid.

مغ mŭgh, *s. p.* A fire-priest; a wine-priest, wine-merchant, wine-shop keeper; مغ بچه mŭgh-bèché, *s. p.* A boy of either of these classes.

مغارة màghāré (mà*gh*ara), *s. a.* A cave, cavern, grotto. [mart.

مغازه mà*gh*āza, *s. t.* A shop, magazine,

مغازى màghāzī, *s. pl. a.* (*no sing.*), Warlike acts, deeds, expeditions.

مغاك màghāk, *s. p.* A ditch, a pit.

مغانم màghānim, *s. pl. a.* (*no sing.*), Booty, things captured. [formable.

مغاير mŭghāyir, *a. a.* Contrary, not con-

مغبر mŭghbèr, *a. a.* Made dusty; made turbid; discomposed, hurt (one's feelings).

مغبوض màghbūz, *a. a.* Against whom hatred and enmity are entertained.

مغبون màghbūn, *a. a.* Cheated, deceived.

مغتنم mŭghtènim, *a. a.* Who seizes or has seized booty; who takes (an opportunity).

مغرب màghrib, *s. a.* The place of setting of the heavenly bodies; the west; the west or north Africa, Morocco.

مغربلو Màghribli, *s. t.* A Moor.

مغرور màghrūr, *a. a.* Over-confident, trusting too much, vain, proud; مغروريت màghrūrìyyèt, *s. a.* Pride, over-confidence, vanity, self-esteem.

مغز màghz, *s. p.* The brain; marrow; the kernel; بيمغز bī-màghz, *a. p.* Brainless, thoughtless; سبكمغز sèbuk-màghz, *a. a.* Light-brained, foolish (person). [adulterated, false.

مغشوش màghshūsh, *a. a.* Alloyed,

مغضوب màghzūb, *a. a.* Angered, irritated; مغضوب عليه màghzūbun-"àlèyh, *s. a.* Against whom anger is felt, the object of anger.

مغفر mìghfèr, *s. a.* A helmet.

مغفرت màghfirèt, *s. a.* God's pardon of sins and admittance to a taste of the joys of Paradise.

مغفور màghfūr, *and* مغفورله màghfūrun-lèh, *a. a.* Whose sins are pardoned and who has been admitted to a taste of the joys of Paradise; deceased (*said only of a Muslim*).

مغل Mùghùl, *s. p.* The Great Mogul; the Moguls, the Tartars.

مغلطه màghl*a*ta, *s. a.* An error, confusion of ideas. [expressed, not clear.

مغلق mŭghlàk, *a. a.* Obscure, obscurely

مغلوب màghlūb, *a. a.* Vanquished, beaten; —أو, —òl, *v.n.* To be beaten, to lose (in a contest); مغلوبيت màghlūbìyyèt, *s. a.* The state or quality of one vanquished.

مغموم màghmūm, *a. a.* Afflicted, distressed in mind.

مغون mà*gh*ūn, *s. t.* Mahogany.

مغونه mà*gh*una, *s. t.* A lighter, barge.

مغيب màghīb, *s. a.* Time or place when someone is absent, absence.

مغيث mūghīss, *s. a.* One who gives aid and succour.

مغين màghin (مكين mè*ghin in soft verbs*), Turkish termination of the sixth gerund of verbs, showing a reason, or a means, or a precedent, for the occurrence of an act expressed by a following verb.

مفاتح mèfātih, *and* مفاتيح mèfātīh, *s. pl. a.* (*of* مفتاح mìftāh), Keys.

مفاخر mèfākhir, *s. pl. a.* (*of* مفخرت mèfkh*a*ret), Qualities or acts which entitle one to be proud; —, mùfākhir, *a. a.* Who glories, boasts.

مفاخرت mùfākh*a*rèt, *s. a.* A glorying, boasting; ا—, —et, *v.n.* To glory, boast.

مفارق mèfārik, *s. pl. a.* (*of* مفرق mèfr*a*k), Crowns of the heads; —, mùfārik, *a. a.* Separated (from any place or person).

مفارقت mùfār*a*kAt, *s. a.* A separation, absence (from a place or person); ا—, —et, *v.n.* To leave, quit, go away.

مفاسد mèfāssid, *s. pl. a.* (*of* مفسدت mèfsédet), Iniquities, basenesses.

مفاصل mèfāssil, *s. pl. a.* (*of* مفصل mèfsAl), Joints of the body.

مفاض mùfĀz, *a. a.* Poured out abundantly; —فيه, mùfĀzun-fīh, *a. a.* On the subject of whom much talk occurs.

مفت mùft, *s. p.* Anything acquired without trouble or payment, a windfall; the being given or acquired without any equivalent; مفتخوار mùft-khòr, *s. p.* One who looks to acquire things without an equivalent, a blood-sucker, hanger-on; مفته كتمك mùfté-ghitmek, *v.n.* To be given away for nothing. [for opening.

مفتاح mìftāh, *s. a.* A key, instrument

مفتخر mùftàkhir, *a. a.* Who feels proud, glories.

مفتش mùfèttish, *s. a.* An officer charged with scrutinizing accounts or title-deeds, &c.

مفتقر mùftàk*i*r, *a. a.* Poor, reduced to poverty, indigent; in want.

مفتوح mèftūh, *a. a.* Open, opened; conquered, taken; read with one of the vowels A, a, *a*, É, *or* é (a letter).

مفتون mèftūn, *a. a.* Subject to machinations; mad with love.

مفتى mùftī, *s. a.* A legal officer whose office it is to lay down the law on all cases submitted to him; مفتى الانام mùftìyyu-'l-ènām, The Shèykhu-'l-issalam.

مفخرت mèfkh*a*ret, *s. a.* A glorying,

feeling proud and honoured; any quality or act of which one is proud.

مفخم mŭfàkhkhàm, *a. a.* August, to whom homage is paid; متبوع مفخم mètbū‘‘i-mŭfàkhkhàmim, My august sovereign master. [spirits, cheerful.

مفرح mùfèrrih, *a. a.* Which raises the

مفرد mèfrèd, *a. a.* Large, big, enormous; —, mùfrèd, *a. a.* Single; —, *s. a.* The singular number (in grammar); مفردات mùfrédāt, *s. pl. a.* Items, single or separate things in a list. [head.

مفرق mèfrak, *s. a.* The crown of the

مفروز mèfrūz, *a. a.* Separated, divided, taken off (of anything).

مفروش mèfrūsh, *a. a.* Spread on the ground (a carpet, bed, &c.), laid, extended.

مفروض mèfrūz, *a. a.* Supposed, positively supposed, put as a supposition; essential and indispensable (in religious practices), obligatory.

مفسد mùfsid, *s. a.* A plotter, machinator, stirrer up of strife.

مفسدت mèfsédet, *s. a.* A plot, machination, evil practice.

مفسر mùfèssir, *s. a.* A commentator.

مفسوخ mèfsūkh, *a. a.* Annulled, abrogated.

مفصل mèfsàl, *s. a.* A joint of the bones, an articulation; —, mùfàsssàl, *a. a.* Detailed, long. [natural.

مفطور mèftūr, *a. a.* Created; innate,

مفعول mèf‘‘ūl, *a. a.* Which is done, or acted; which is the object of any action; اسم مفعول ìssmi-mèf‘‘ūl, The passive participle (always to be distinguished in idea from a past participle), of which there are various kinds; مفعول به mèf‘‘ūlun-bih, The accusative or direct object of an action; *also*, the instrument or object with which an act is effected; مفعول له mèf‘‘ūlun-lèh, The object for or on account of which an act occurs; مفعول عنه mèf‘‘ūlun-‘‘ành, The object from or through which an act occurs, &c. [after.

مفقود mèfkūd, *a. a.* Lost and sought

مفكوك mèfkyūk, *a. a.* Untied, loosened, unbound, dissolved.

مفلس mùfliss, *s. a.* A bankrupt.

مفلوج mèflūj, *a. a.* Paralytic, struck with palsy.

مفوض mùfèvwàz, *a. a.* Bestowed, given, delivered.

مفهوم mèfhūm, *s. a.* The purport, general sense of a writing.

مفيد mùfīd, *a. a.* Useful, advantageous.

مفيض mùfīz, *s. a.* (God) the bountiful distributor (of blessings).

مق mak (مك mek *in soft words*), Turkish termination of the infinitive.

مقابر màkābir, *s. pl. a.* (*of* مقبره màkbérē), Graves, tombs.

مقابل mùkābil, *a. a.* Opposite, facing; —, *s. a.* The place or space opposite to or facing a thing; مقابلنده mùkābilind*a*, Opposite to him (her, it); in return, as a return (for any act), as a reprisal; in answer (to anything said).

مقابله mŭkābélé, *s. a.* A facing anyone, meeting or opposing; a returning (act for act, or word for word); an answering (word for word); a comparing, collating; مقابلهبالمثل mŭkābélé-bì-'l-mìssl, A returning like for like, tit for tat; using reprisals; جبر و مقابله jèbr-u-mŭkābélé, Algebra (as a science which unites separate quantities and opposes them to each other); ا—, —et, *v.n.* To return like for like, good for good, evil for evil, act for act, word for word; —, *v.a.* To compare, collate.

مقابیح màkābīh, *s. pl. a.* (*of* مقبوح màkbūh), Detestable actions or qualities.

مقاتله mŭkātélé, *s. a.* Fight, battle, mutual slaughter.

مقادیر màkādīr, *s. pl. a.* (*of* مقدار mìkdār), Quantities. [ing, nearing.

مقاربت mŭkārébèt, *s. a.* An approach-

مقارعه mŭkāra''à, *s. a.* Fighting, battle.

مقارن mŭkārin, *a. a.* Close to, close upon, nigh, near, coming quite up to, joining in with.

مقارنت mŭkārénèt, *s. a.* A near approach; a coming close up to and touching.

مقاسمه mŭkāsséme, *s. a.* A partitioning, sharing out; ا—, —et, *v.a.* To divide, partition, share out.

مقاص màkass, *s. t.* A pair of scissors, shears, or snuffers; shears for lifting masts, &c., on board ship; مومقاصی mūm-màkassi, A pair of snuffers.

مقاصد màkāssid, *s. pl. a.* (*of* مقصد màksàd), Objects in view, designs, things sought to be accomplished or attained.

مقاطعه mŭkāta''à, *s. a.* A fief attached to an office, the tithes going to the holder of the office (*now generally abolished, salary being substituted*).

مقال màkāl, *s. a.* What is said, the words (of anyone).

مقاله màkālé, *s. a.* A book, a section (of a work) treating on a branch of the general subject (especially the "*Books*" of Euclid).

مقالید màkālīd, *s. pl. a.* (*no sing.*), Bolts, bars, locks.

مقام màkām, *s. a.* A place in which any person or thing stands; a station; a high office, department, post; a light, estimation, view (in which a thing or act is taken or intended); a time, an air (of music); قائممقام *or* قائمقام kā'im-màkām, A lieutenant, locum-tenens, alter ego, substitute; the official representative of the grand vizier at the capital while he is himself absent; a lieutenant-governor; a lieutenant-colonel (in the army); a captain of a line-of-battle ship (in the navy); a superintendant-general (of property in mortmain); قائممقام الفاعل kā'imu-màkāmi-'l-fā''il, The nominative or subject of a verb passive (*as standing in the place of the* "name of an agent").

مقاوله mŭkāvélé, *s. a.* The making an agreement; an agreement; ا—, —et, *v.a.* To covenant, agree, stipulate mutually.

مقاومت mŭkāvémèt, *s. a.* Opposition, resistance; ا—, —et, *v.n.* To resist.

مقايسه mŭkāyéssé, *s. a.* Comparing (mentally) one thing with another.

مقبره mākbéré, *s. a.* A grave, tomb, sepulchre; a burial-ground.

مقبوح mākbūh, *a. a.* Ugly, disliked, detestable.

مقبوض mākbūz, *a. a.* Taken, received; —سندى, mākbūz-sènédi, A receipt.

مقبول mākbūl, *a. a.* Liked, approved, acceptable; مقبوله كچمك mākbūla-ghèchmek, *v.n.* To be liked, appreciated, deemed acceptable.

مقت màkt, *s. a.* Hatred, enmity.

مقتدا (*for* مقتدى) mŭktédà, *a. a.* Followed, imitated (in matters of opinion and practice); —, *s. a.* A teacher, guide, ensamplar, pattern.

مقتدر mŭktèdir, *a. a.* Able, capable, powerful enough.

مقتدى mŭktédī, *s. a.* One who follows or imitates (another in matters of opinion and practice); — (*or* مقتدا) mŭktédà, *a. a.* Followed, imitated; —, *s. a.* A teacher, guide, ensamplar, pattern.

مقتضا (*for* مقتضى) mŭktazà, *s. a.* The requirement (of anything), thing required; the name of a ministerial letter generally given with a firman, addressed to the same person or persons, and indicating, in a brief way, what is ordered in the firman.

مقتضى mŭktazī, *a. a.* Needful, necessary, wanted; —, mŭktazà. See مقتضا. [to death.

مقتول māktūl, *a. a.* Killed, slain, put

مقدار mìkdār (mìktar), *s. a.* A quantity (either of bulk, number, length, duration, &c.); a portion; برمقدار bìr-mìktar, A little, some, a certain small quantity or number.

مقدر mŭkāddèr, *a. a.* Decreed by God; vouchsafed by God; duly estimated; understood (in grammar or logic), not expressed; مقدرات الهيه mŭkād-dérāti-ìlāhìyyé, The things decreed by God's providence.

مقدرت màkdérèt, *s. a.* Power, might, ability.

مقدس mŭkāddèss, *a. a.* Holy, sacred.

مقدم mākdem, *s. a.* An arrival, coming; —, mŭkdim, *a. a.* Assiduous, diligent, persevering; —, mŭkāddem, *a. a.* Placed further forward, before another thing (in space or in time); —, *s. a.* The former part (of anything); former time; a premise (in logic); an antecedent; (*and* مقدمه mŭkād-démé), the advanced guard of an army; —, *ad. t. and* مقدما mŭkād-démā, *ad. a.* Formerly; before (in time); مقدمات mŭkāddémāt,

s. pl. a. Things explained first, prefatory remarks.

مقدمه mŭkăddimé, s. a. An introduction, a preface, a peroration.

مقدور măkdūr, a. a. Predestined, vouchsafed by Providence; —, s. a. The utmost of one's power and ability.

مقر màkàrr, s. a. A place where one stays permanently; an abode, a seat, a residence; —, mŭkìrr, a. a. Who admits, confesses.

مقراض mìkrāz, s. a. A pair of scissors, shears, or snuffers. (See مقاص).

مقرب mŭkàrreb, a. a. Placed or drawn near; —, s. a. A person placed in close communication (with a sovereign).

مقرر mŭkàrrèr, s. a. Sure, certain, ascertained, beyond all doubt, confirmed, established, fully established; —, mŭkărrir, s. a. One who confirms and establishes. [pocket-handkerchief.

مقرمه màkrama (màhrama), s. a. A

مقروع măkrū", s. a. Struck; knocked at (a door).

مقرون măkrūn, a. a. Approached closely, quite touched; associated, joined, adjoined.

مقسم mŭkàsssim, s. a. A distributor.

مقسوم măksūm, a. a. Divided into portions; —, s. a. The dividend (*in arith.*); مقسوم عليه măksūmun-"àlèyh, s. a. The divisor.

مقص màkàsss, s. a. A pair of scissors, shears, snuffers. (See مقاص.)

مقصد măksad, s. a. *and* مقصود măksud, a. and s. a. Anything proposed or designed, wish, design, aim, end, intent, the thing aimed at.

مقصور măksūr (*fem.* مقصوره măksūré), a. a. Defective, wanting; shortened, abbreviated; الفـ مقصوره èlifi-măksūré, The short ا, *or* ى sounded as a short ا at the end of words.

مقضى màkzī, a. a. Accomplished, attained, granted; مقضى المرام măkzìyyu-'l-mèrām, a. a. Whose wish is attained.

مقطع màktà", s. a. A place of scission; a bone or ivory on which reed-pens are nibbed; —, mŭkăttà", a. a. Cut asunder, divided, separated; حروف مقطعه hùrūfi-mŭkătteʻ"ā, The separately written or separately named letters placed at the commencement of some chapters of the Kurʻān.

مقطوع măktū", a. a. Cut; cut off; interrupted; defined; limited.

مقعد màk"àd, s. a. The seat, breech; anus; (màkat) a small quilt used for covering the corner seats of a sofa.

مقعر mŭkà"'"àr, a. a. Concave, hollow.

مقفا (*for* مقفى) mŭkăffà, a. a. Rhymed according to the rules of prosody.

مقلب mŭkăllib, s. a. One who turns, inverts, changes (things).

مقلد mŭkăllid, s. a. One who takes on himself the yoke of submission; a mimic; an actor; —, mŭkăllèd, a. a. Whose yoke of submission is accepted.

مقلوب màklūb, *a. a.* Reversed, inverted; an anagram. [place.

مقلوع màklū'', *a. a.* Torn from its

مقناطيس mìknātīss (mìkhlàdiz), *s. a.* A magnet, loadstone.

مقند mùkànnèd, *a. a.* Candied, sugared.

مقنطره mùkàn*tara*, *a. a. fem.* Arched; supported on arches; مقنطرات mùkàn*tarā*t, *s. pl. a.* Almicanthers or circles of altitude.

مقنن mùkànnin, *s. a.* A legislator; —, mùkànnèn, *a. a.* Ordered by law.

مقوا (*for* مقوى) mùk*avwa*, *a. a.* Strengthened; —, *s. a.* Pasteboard, cardboard. [as a bow.

مقوس mùkàvvèss, *a. a.* Arched, bent

مقوله màkūlé, *s. a.* A sort, kind, species, category.

مقوى mùkàvvī, *a. a.* Corroborative, strengthening (medicine); —, mùkàvwà, *a. a.* Strengthened; —, *s. a.* Pasteboard, cardboard.

مقهور màkhūr (k-h), *a. a.* Vanquished, subjected to the overwhelming might of someone.

مقياس mikyāss, *s. a.* An instrument for measuring and comparing; a scale.

مقيد mùkàyyèd, *a. a.* Bound, tied, fastened; restricted, coupled with a restrictive complement (a word in a sentence); limited, constitutional; attentive, painstaking; registered; —او, —òl, *v.n.* To take care, take pains, pay attention.

مقيم mùkīm, *a. a.* Residing.

مقيى mùkàyyī, *a. a.* Vomitive (medicine), an emetic.

مك mek, Turkish termination of the infinitive in soft verbs.

مكابرت mùk*y*ābérèt, *s. a.* Pride.

مكاتب mèk*y*ātib, *s. pl. a.* (*of* مكتب mèktɘb), Schools; —, mùk*y*ātib, *s. a.* A covenanted slave, to whom a binding permission has been accorded to ransom himself.

مكاتبه mùk*y*ātébé, *s. a.* Correspondence by letter; ا—, —et, *v.n.* To correspond by letter.

مكاتيب mèk*y*ātīb, *s. pl. a.* (*of* مكتوب mèktūb), Letters, notes, billets, epistles. [cheat.

مكار mèkk*y*ār, *s. a.* A subtle knave and

مكارم mèk*y*ārim, *s. pl. a.* (*of* مكرمت mèkrémet), Noble or generous deeds or qualities.

مكافات mùk*y*āfāt, *s. a.* A reward, recompense, retribution; ا—, —et, *v.a.* and *n.* To reward, recompense.

مكافى mùk*y*āfī, *a. a.* Equivalent; قطع مكافى kàt''ī-mùk*y*āfī, A parabola.

مكالمه mùk*y*ālémé, *s. a.* A conference; a conferring, deliberating; ا—, —et, *v.n.* To hold a conference.

مكان mèk*y*ān, *s. a.* A place in which a thing exists, locus; مكاندن منزه mèk*y*ānd*a*n - mùnèzzèh, (God is) exempt from place (is omnipresent).

مكائد mèkyā'id, *s. pl. a.* (*of* مكيده mèkīdé), Stratagems, wiles.

مكتب mèktɘb, *s. a.* A school.

مكتفى mùktéfi, *a. a.* Who considers as sufficient what he receives, content.

مكتنى mùktènī, *a. a.* Called by a surname (كنيه kyùnyé).

مكتوب mèktūb (mèktup), *a. a.* Written; —, *s. a.* A letter, epistle, note; —سامى, mèktubu-sāmī, (High letter) A vizirial letter, an official letter written in the name of the Grand Vizier; مكتوبجى mèktupju, A secretary for official letters; مكتوبلشمك mèktuplɪshmek, *v.n. recip.* To correspond by letter.

مكتوم mèktūm, *a. a.* Hidden, concealed.

مكث mèkss, *s. a.* A staying, making a stay; a withholding, arresting; ا—, —et, *v.n.* To stay, make a stay; —, *v.a.* To withhold, arrest, stop, delay.

مكدر mùkèddèr, *a. a.* Grieved, sorry, afflicted; —, mùkèddir, *a.a.* Afflicting, vexing, annoying; مكدرات mùkèddirāt, *s. pl. a.* Afflictions, distressing things.

مكر mèkr (mèkir), *s. a.* A wile, stratagem, piece of knavery; —, mèghɪr, *c. p.* Unless; and still, and yet, and all the while.

مكرر mùkèrrèr, *a. a.* Repeated, done repeatedly; highly rectified, highly purified; مكرراً mùkèrréran, *ad. a.* Repeatedly.

مكرم mùkrim, *a. a.* Kind, courteous, affable; —, mùkèrrèm, *a. a.* Honoured, treated with respect and consideration; مكرماً mùkèrréman, *ad. a.* With great respect and with all due honours.

مكرمت mèkrémet, *s. a.* Any noble or generous act or quality.

مكروب mèkrūb, *a. a.* Sad, distressed, afflicted, sorrowful.

مكروه mèkrūh, *a. a.* Held in aversion (canonically).

مكس mèghess, *s. p.* A fly, any winged insect like a fly.

مكسر mùkèssèr, *a. a.* Broken to pieces; جمع مكسر jem"i-mukesser, An irregular plural Arabic noun.

مكسوب mèksūb, *a. a.* Gained, acquired.

مكسور mèksūr, *a. a.* Pronounced with the vowel i or *i* (a consonant).

مكشوف mèkshūf, *a. a.* Discovered, revealed.

مكعب mùkyà"àb, *a. a.* Cubical; —, *s. a.* A cube (figure, or number).

مكك mèkik, *s. t.* A weaver's shuttle.

مكلف mùkèllèf, *a. a.* Sumptuous, rich, splendid; highly adorned; resting under an obligation to do certain duties (as man is to keep the commandments of God), responsible towards God.

مكمل mùkèmmèl, *a. a.* Complete, full.

مكمون mèkmūn, *a. a.* Concealed in an ambush.

مكنوز mèknūz, *a. a.* Deposited in a treasury.

مكنون mèknūn, *a. a.* Concealed.

مكوك mèkyūk (mèkik, *see* مكك), *s. a.* A weaver's shuttle.

مكّه Mèkka, *s. a.* Mecca (the town of, in Arabia).

مكيال mìkyāl, *s. a.* A bushel or similar measuring instrument.

مكيده mèkīdé, *s. a.* A wile, a piece of deceit. [qualities, or with a quality.

مكيف mùkèyyèf, *a. a.* Endowed with

مكين mèkīn, *a. a.* Powerful, mighty, strong, firmly established; residing; abiding, dwelling; —, méghin (in soft verbs), Turkish termination of the sixth gerund. (See مغين.)

ملا mèlā, *s. a.* An assembly (of people); a plenum, space filled or occupied by matter; خلاوملا khàlā - vé - mèlā, Vacuum and plenum, void space and occupied space; على ملأ الناس "àlà--mèlāʿi-ʾn-nāss, *ad. a.* Openly, before the assembled people.

ملابسه mùlābéssé, *s. a.* A relation or connexion, a consideration; شوملابسه ايله shù-mùlābéssè-ila, From this consideration, arising out of this relation or connexion.

ملاح mèllāh, *s. a.* A sailor, a tar.

ملاحت mèlāhàt, *s. a.* Sweetness, agreeableness.

ملاحد mùlāhid (*pl.* ملاحده mùlāhidé), *s. a.* A heretic, schismatic (of a particular class).

ملاحظه mùlāhaza, *s. a.* A cautious look, examination, or consideration; caution; ا—, —et, *v.n.* To hesitate, to look before leaping.

ملاذ mèlāz, *s. a.* An asylum, refuge.

ملازم mùlāzim (mùlāzim), *a. a.* Ever accompanying and never quitting, inseparable; —, *s. a.* A constant attendant or follower; a supernumerary attached to an office, &c., without pay; a lieutenant (in the army); a mate (in the navy).

ملازمت mùlāzémèt, *s. a.* Constant attendance (about a person or place); ا—, —et, *v.n.* To attend regularly; to follow about. [attached, adherent.

ملاصق mùlāssik, *a. a.* Joining, joined,

ملاطفه mùlātafé, *s. a.* A joking, treating facetiously; kindness, treating with marked kindness; ا—, —et, *v.n.* To joke; to show kindness.

ملاعب mélā"ib, *s. pl. a.* (*no sing. used*), Games, playthings, toys.

ملاعبه mùlā"abé, *s. a.* A playing, amusing one's self; ا—, —et, *v.n.* To play, to amuse one's self; to toy.

ملاعين mèlā"īn, *s. pl. a.* (*of* ملعون mèl"ūn), Accursed ones, damned fellows. [interview, audience.

ملاقات mùlākāt, *s. a.* A meeting; an

ملاقى mùlākī, *a. a.* Who or which meets, joins.

ملال mélāl, ملالت mèlālèt, *s. a.* Sadness, vexation; fatigue, tiredness.

ملام mèlām, ملامت mèlāmèt, *s. a.* Reproach, rebuke.

ملآن mèlʿān, *a. a.* Full.

ملاهى mèlāhī, *s. pl. a.* (*no sing.*), Games, diversions; toys, playthings.

ملائك mèlāʿik, ملائكه mèlāʿiké, *s. pl. a.* (*of* ملك mèlek), Angels; (*as a Turkish sing.*), an angel.

ملايم mùlāyim, *a. a.* Mild, not severe (weather, &c.); proper, fitting.

ملايمت mùlāyémèt, *s. a.* Mildness.

ملبس mùlèbbèss, *a. a.* Clothed; confused, ambiguous (language).

ملبوس mèlbūss, *a. a.* Worn, used as raiment; ملبوسات mèlbūssāt, *s. pl. a.* Clothing, articles of dress.

ملت millèt, *s. a.* A people, community; a religious denomination or sect.

ملتبس mùltèbiss, *a. a.* Obscure, ambiguous (language).

ملتثم mùltèssèm, *a. a.* Kissed; —, *s. a.* The place kissed; —, mùltèssim, *s. a.* One who kisses.

ملتجا (*for* ملتجى) mùltéjà, *s. a.* A place of refuge, a refuge, asylum.

ملتجى mùltéjī, *s. a.* A refugee; — (*or* ملتجا) mùltèjà, *s. a.* A place of refuge.

ملتزم mùltézim, *s. a.* A farmer or contractor of the revenue.

ملتفت mùltéfit, *a. a.* Who turns his face or attention towards an object.

ملتقا (*for* ملتقى) mùltékà, *s. a.* A place of meeting, a junction.

ملتم mèltèm, *s. t.* The Etesian winds, the cooling wind from the north-east, which, during the summer, rises with the sun, blows strongly all day, and ceases at sunset.

ملتمس mùltèmiss, *a. a.* Who requests; —, mùltémèss, *a. a.* Requested; a request.

ملتهب mùltèhib, ملتهف mùltèhif, *a. a.* In flames; inflamed; in a fever; thirsting.

ملجا mèljā, *s. a.* A place of refuge, a refuge, an asylum.

ملح milh, *s. a.* Salt.

ملحد mùlhid, *s. a.* A heretic, schismatic (of some particular kinds).

ملحق mùlhàk, *a. a.* Joined on (to something), added, appended, attached; ملحقات mùlhàkāt, *s. pl. a.* Appurtenances.

ملحم mùlàhhàm, *a. a.* Corpulent, fleshy.

ملحوظ mèlhūz, *a. a.* Half expected, anticipated, thought of.

ملز mèlez, *s. t.* A mulatto.

ملزم mùlzèm, *a. a.* Convinced, silenced in argument.

ملزوم mèlzūm, *a. a.* To which something is inseparably attached.

ملس mèless, *s. a.* A mulatto.

ملعنت mèl''anèt, *s. a.* Any damnable act or quality.

ملعون mèl''ūn, *a. a.* Cursed, anathematized.

ملفوظ mèlfūz, *a. a.* Uttered, spoken, mentioned; ملفوظات mèlfūzāt, *s. pl. a.* Sayings.

ملفوف mèlfūf, *a. a.* Inclosed, enveloped; ملفوفاً mèlfūfan, *ad. a.* Inclosed, as an inclosure.

ملقب mùlàkkàb, *a. a.* Bearing a title or titles.

ملك mèlek, *s. a.* An angel; —, mèlik, *s. a.* A king, a petty ruler; —, milk, *s. a.* Dominion, sovereignty; dominions, territory; —, mùlk, *s. a.* Freehold property; ملكى mèlékī, *a. a.* Pertaining to a sovereign, or to an angel, royal, angelic; —, milkī, *a. a.* Pertaining to sovereignty, sovereign; ملكيت milkìyyèt, *s. a.* Sovereignty, sovereign rights.

ملكوت mèlékyūt, s. a. Sovereignty; God's supreme sovereignty; مالك الملك والملكوت mālikyu-'l-milki-vé--'l-mèlékyūt, Lord of all dominion and sovereignty.

ملكه mèlíké, s. a. A queen; —, mèléké, s. a. Great dexterity from constant practice.

ملل milèl, s. pl. a. (of ملت millèt), Peoples; religious denominations, sects.

ملو mali (méli *in soft words*), Turkish termination of the necessitative mood of verbs, corresponding to our *must, should, ought*.

ملوان mèlévān, s. a. *dual*, Day and night.

ملوث mùlèvvès, a. a. Dirtied, soiled, polluted.

ملوك mùlūk, s. pl. a. (of ملك mélik), Kings; ملوكانه mùlūkyāné, a. p. Royal, imperial, sovereign (*said only of the Sultan*).

ملول mèlūl, a. a. Sad, vexed; fatigued.

مله‌مك (or مه‌لمك) mèlémek (*aor.* ملر or مه‌لر mèler), v.n. To bleat.

ملهم mèlhèm (*for* مرهم mèrhèm), s. t. Ointment, salve; —, mùlhim, s. a. Who inspires, reveals; —, mùlhèm, a. a. Inspired, revealed, made known by inspiration and revelation.

ملآن mèl'ān, a. a. Full.

مليح mèlīh, a. a. Sweet, agreeable.

ملين mùlèyyin, a. a. Laxative, opening (medicine); —, mùlèyyèn, a. a. Open (the bowels).

مليون milyòn, s. t. (*French*), A million.

ممات mèmāt, s. a. Death, the state of death; مماتى mèmātī, Pertaining to the state of death.

مماثل mùmāssil, a. a. Corresponding, agreeing, like, conformable.

مماثلت mùmāssélèt, s. a. A conforming; —ا, —et, v.n. To conform.

ممارست mùmāréssèt, s. a. Experience gained by practice.

مماس mùmāsss, s. a. A tangent.

مماشات mùmāshāt, s. a. A going with the stream, obsequious compliance.

ممالك mèmālik, s. pl. a. (of مملكت mèmlékèt), Countries, territories, dominions.

ممالیك mèmālīk, s. pl. a. (of مملوك mèmlūk), Slaves; the Mamelukes of Egypt.

ممانعت mùmāna''àt, s. a. Opposition; a preventing; —ا, —et, v.n. To oppose, try to prevent.

ممتاز mùmtāz, a. a. Distinguished, pre-eminent (among others).

ممتد mùmtèdd, a. a. Prolonged, drawn out in length or duration.

ممتنع mùmtèni'', a. a. Impossible.

ممدوح mèmdūh, a. a. Praised, praiseworthy; ممدوحات mèmdūhāt, s. pl. a. Praiseworthy acts and qualities.

ممدود mèmdūd, a. a. Prolonged, extended.

ممر mèmèrr, s. a. A place of passage, a passage, path, way.

ممزوج mèmzūj, a. a. Mixed, compounded.

ممسك mùmsik, *a. a.* Tenacious, hard-fisted, grasping, avaricious.

ممشا (*for* ممشى) mèmshà, *s. a.* A place for walking; a privy, water-closet.

ممضى mùmzī, *a. a.* Signed, bearing a signature.

ممكن mùmkin, *a. a.* Possible; ممكن مرتبه mùmkin-mèrtébé, *ad. t.* As much as possible.

ممل mùmìll, *a. a.* Wearisome, fatiguing, tiring, tiresome.

مملحه mèmlaha, *s. a.* A salt-works.

مملكت mèmlékèt, *s. a.* A country; a town.

مملو mèmlū, *a. a.* Full.

مملوك mémlūk, *a. a.* Possessed, held in possession; —, *s. a.* A slave; a Mameluke; مملوكيت mèmlūkìyyèt, *s. a.* The quality of being held in possession.

مملول mèmlūl, *a. a.* Tired, wearied; vexed.

ممنوع mèmnū‘‘, *a. a.* Forbidden, prohibited; ممنوعات mèmnū‘‘āt, *s. pl. a.* Forbidden acts; prohibited things; ممنوعيت mèmnū‘‘ìyyèt, *s. a.* The quality of being forbidden, prohibited.

ممنون mèmnūn, *a. a.* Pleased, rejoiced, glad; ممنونيت mèmnūnìyyèt, *s. a.* Pleasure, gladness, satisfaction.

مموه mùmévvèh, *a. a.* Gilt or washed over; superficial, put on, false, insincere.

ممه mèmé, *s. t.* A teat, nipple; an udder, dug; any protuberance in shape of a nipple; ممه لنمك mèmélenmek, *v.n.* To acquire the form of a nipple.

ممهور mèmhūr, *a. a.* Sealed with a seal.

مميت mùmīt, *a. a.* Who causes to die (God).

مميز mùmèyyiz, *s. a.* An officer whose duty it is to examine draughts of reports, &c., and see they are properly drawn; an examiner; inspector.

من mèn, *pron. a.* Whosoever, whoever; —, mìn, *pr. a.* From, of, out of; —, mènn, *s. a.* The manna of the Israelites; من بعد mìn-bà‘‘d, *ad. a.* Henceforward.

منابر mènābir, *s. pl. a.* (*of* منبر mìnbèr), Preachers' pulpits.

منابع ménābi‘‘, *s. pl. a.* (*of* منبع mènbà‘‘), Sources, fountain-heads, springs.

مناجات mùnājāt, *s. a.* A prayer.

منادات mùnādāt, *s. a.* A proclaiming.

منادى mùnādī, *s. a.* A herald, crier.

مناره mìnāré, *s. a.* A minaret, the tower attached to a mosque, like a steeple to a church, from which the call to prayer is made.

منازع mùnāzi‘‘, *s. a.* A disputer, quarreller, contester.

منازعه mùnāza‘‘à, *s. a.* A dispute, quarrel, contest; |—, —et, *v.n.* To dispute.

منازل mènāzil, *s. pl. a.* (*of* منزل mènzil), Stations (on a road).

منازله mùnāzélé, *s. a.* A fighting, doing battle.

مناسب mùnāssib, *a. a.* Fit, fitting, proper, expedient; apt.

مناسبت mùnāssébèt, *s. a.* Fitness, propriety, expediency; aptness; relation, connexion; نه مناسبت nè-mùnāssébet! How! why! upon what grounds!

مناسبتسز mùnāssébetsiz, *a. t.* Untimely, unfitting, inexpedient, malapropos.

مناستر mʌnasstir, *s. t.* (*Greek*), A monastery, convent.

مناسك ménāssik, *s. pl. a.* (*no sing.*), Rites, ceremonies, observances used in performing the canonical pilgrimage to Mecca.

مناشير mènāshīr, *s. pl. a.* (*of* منشور mènshūr), Imperial letters-patent conferring the highest dignities.

مناصب mʌnāssib, *s. pl. a.* (*of* منصب mʌnsib), High offices of state.

مناصفت mùnāssafèt, *s. a.* Equity, justice; مناصفة mùnāssafétan, *ad. a.* In two equal shares.

مناط mùnāt, *a. a.* To which something is tacked on or suspended.

مناظر mènāzir, *s. pl. a.* (*of* منظر mʌnzàr), Aspects; —علم "ìlmi-mènāzir, The science of aspects, perspective.

مناظرت mùnāzarèt, مناظره mùnāzara, *s. a.* A disputation, discussion.

مناظم mènāzim, *s. pl. a.* (*of* نظم nʌzm), Orders, arrangements.

مناعت mènā"àt, *s. a.* Impregnability, strength, inaccessibility.

منافسه mùnāféssé, *s. a.* Spite, enmity, malevolence.

منافع mènāfi", *s. pl. a.* (*of* منفعت mènfà"*at*), Uses, advantages; interests.

منافق mùnʌfik, *s. a.* A hypocrite (canonically); a tale-bearer.

منافی mùnāfī, *a. a.* Incompatible, hindering, opposed.

مناقب mènākib, *s. pl. a.* (*of* منقبه mànkabé), Traits of character; anecdotes. [quarrelling.

مناقشه mùnākasha, *s. a.* A disputing,

مناقض mùnākiz, *a. a.* Destructive, demolishing; contrary, nugatory, contradictory. [tradiction.

مناقضه mùnākaza, *s. a.* Mutual con-

منال mènāl, *s. a.* Property, possessions.

منام mènām, *s. a.* Sleep; a dream, vision. [all good things.

منان mènnān, *s. a.* (God) the giver of

مناو mānaw, *s. t.* A dealer in fruits, a fruiterer.

مناوبه mùnāvébé, *s. a.* Alternation, a taking turn and turn about; مناوبة mùnāvébéten, *ad. a.* By turns.

مناهج mènāhij, *s. pl. a.* (*of* منهج minhèj), Roads.

مناهی mènāhī, *s. pl. a.* (*of* منهی mènhī), Forbidden things or acts.

منايا mènāyā, *s. pl. a.* (*of* منيه mèniyyé), Deaths, different kinds of death.

منبت mùnbit, *a. a.* Fertile (land).

منبر mìnber, *s. a.* A preacher's pulpit.

منبسط mùnbʌssit, *a. a.* Spread, extended; expanded; joyful.

منبع mènbà", *s. a.* A spring, source, fountain-head.

منت mìnnèt, *s. a.* A favour, grace, kindness, obligation; an averseness, backwardness from doing a favour; a reproach for favours bestowed, a throwing in one's teeth ; بيمنت bì-minnèt, *a. p.* Who is never averse from bestowing benefits ; who never hurts the feelings of those he has favoured by casting those favours in their teeth.

منتر mʌntar, *s.t.* (*Greek*), A mushroom; a toadstool, fungus ; cork ; a cork, a bung ; منتارقاوى mʌntar-kàwi, German tinder.

منتان mìntʌn, *s. t.* A short jacket.

منتج mùntij, *a. a.* Producing, resulting in. [chosen.

منتخب mùntakhʌb, *a. a.* Selected,

منتسب mùntèssib, *a. a.* Related, connected.

منتشر mùntèshir, *a. a.* Spread, scattered abroad, spread out; expanded, dilated; in a state of erection (penis).

منتظر mùntʌzir, *a. a.* In expectation, looking (for).

منتظم mùntazʌm, *a. a.* In order, arranged, regular; عساكرمنتظمهء شاهانه "ʌssākiri-mùntʌzamé'i-shāhānē, The imperial regular troops.

منتفع mùntèfi", *a. a.* Who has derived a profit or advantage.

منتقل mùntàkil, *a. a.* Who or which passes from one place to another.

منتمى mùntèmi, *a. a.* Related, connected.

منتن mùntìn, *a. a.* Putrid, stinking.

منتوى mùntèvī, *a. a.* Directed towards anything.

منتها (*for* منتهى) mùntéhà, *s. a.* The end, utmost limit.

منتهى mùntéhī, *a. a.* Who or which arrives at the end; which reaches, touches, comes quite up to; —, *s. a* A master or proficient (in science).

منثور mènsūr, *a. a.* Scattered anyhow, not arranged in order; —, *s. a.* Prose.

منجر mùnjèrr, *a. a.* Coming (to any state of things), being brought.

منجيم mùnèjjim, *s. a.* An astronomer or astrologer. [gealed.

منجمد mùnjèmid, *a. a.* Frozen, con-

منجنيق mànjénık, *s. a.* A catapulta ; a balista ; a crane (for lifting).

منح mìnàh, *s. pl. a.* (*of* منحت mìnhàt), Graces, favours, blessings.

منحرف mùnhàrif, *a. a.* Turning out of a straight path, turning aside ; —, *s. a.* A trapezium or four-sided figure, having two sides parallel but unequal; شبهمنحرف shìbhi-mùnhàrif, A trapezoid or four-sided figure having no two sides parallel.

منحصر mùnhʌssir, *a. a.* Limited, confined.

منحل mùnhàll, *a. a.* Dissolved.

منحنى mùnhànī, *a. a.* Curved ; خط منحنى khʌtti-mùnhànī, A curved line.

منحوس mènhūss, *a. a.* Ill-omened.

منخسف mùnkhàssif, *a. a.* Eclipsed (the moon).

مند mènd, Persian termination equivalent to our *ful, ish, y,* &c., as دردمند dèrdmènd, *a. p.* Sorrowful.

مندال mÀndÀl, *s.t.* A button (to a door).

مندر mìndɪr, *s. t.* A mattress; a sofa.

مندرج mùndèrij, *a. a.* Included; contained; written.

مندرس mùndèriss, *a. a.* Effaced, obliterated.

مندفع mùndèfi‘‘, *a. a.* Driven out or away.

مندوب mèndūb, *a. a.* Mourned for, wept over.

منديل mèndīl, *s. a.* A handkerchief.

منزل mènzil, *s. a.* A station-house, halting-place; a day's journey, or distance from post-house to post-house; a travelling post; the range (of a gun, &c.); a distance; a long range; a rank, degree, grade; منزلخانه mènzil-khānɛ́, *s. p.* A post-house; منزل باركيرى mènzil-(bèyghiri), A post-horse; منزل كتمك mènzil-ghìtmek, *v.n.* To travel post; منزل سورمك mènzil-sùrmek, *v.n.* To travel as fast as possible; منزل طوپى mènzil-tòpu, A gun with a very long range; سر منزل sèr-mènzil, *s. p.* The goal, the end of a journey; كوز منزلى ghyùz-mènzili, The range of vision, as far as the eye can see; منزلجى mènzilji, *s. t.* A post-master.

منزلت mènzilèt, منزله mènzilɛ́, *s. a.* A rank, grade, degree, standing; منزلتلو mènzilètlū, *a. t.* Holding a certain high rank.

منزوى mùnzèvī, *s. a.* A hermit, recluse.

منزه mùnèzzèh, *a. a.* Free, void, exempt.

منسج mùnèsssèj, *a. a.* Woven, interwoven

منسد mùnsèdd, *a. a.* Stopped up, closed.

منسدل mùnsèdil, *a. a.* Hanging down, dangling.

منسق mùnèssàk, *a. a.* Ranged in a series, or in order.

منسل mùnsèll, *a. a.* Drawn from its scabbard.

منسلب mùnsèlib, *a. a.* Taken as spoil, taken away.

منسلك mùnsèlik, *a. a.* Who follows or treads in a path.

منسوب mènsūb, *a. a.* Related, connected, pertaining; منسوبيت mènsūbìyyèt, *s. a.* Relationship, connexion, quality of pertaining; اسم منسوب ìssmi-mènsūb, An adjective showing relation, connexion, or quality of pertaining to something.

منسوج mènsūj, *a. a.* Woven.

منسوخ mènsūkh, *a. a.* Abolished, abrogated.

منسوق ménsūk, *a. a.* Ranged, placed in order.

منسى mènsī, *a. a.* Forgotten.

منش mènsh, *s. p.* Disposition, character, constitution.

منشأ mènshɛ́‘, *s. a.* A place of origin; a source.

منشار mìnshār, *s. a.* A saw; منشارى mìnshārī, *a. a.* Zigzag like the teeth of a saw in shape.

منشعب mùnshà‘‘‘ab, *a. a.* Derived (as from a family), branching out.

منشق mùnshàkk, *a. a.* Split, cleft, cloven.

منشور mènshūr, *a. a.* Dispersed, scattered, spread; —, *s. a.* A prism.

منشى mùnshī, *s. a.* A clever writer, a

practised literary or epistolary composer.

منصب mAnsib, s. a. A place where anything is set up; a post of dignity held under government; —, mùnsàbb, a. a. Poured, flowing, running (into anything).

منصبغ mùnsàbigh, a. a. Dyed; baptized.

منصرف mùnsàrif, a. a. Turned on one side, turned away; conjugated, declined (in grammar).

منصف mùnsif, a. a. Just, equitable, conscientious; منصفانه mùnsifânÉ, a. p. Pertaining to a conscientious person. [holding an office.

منصوب mAnsūb, a. a. Set up, erected;

منصور mAnsūr, a. a. Assisted by God, victorious.

منصوص mAnsūss, a. a. Established by an incontrovertible divine proof.

منصه mànAssa, s. a. A bride's throne or throne-room. [added.

منضم mùnzàmm, a. a. Added, super-

منطبخ mùntAbikh, a. a. Cooked; ripened.

منطر or منطار or منتار mAntar, s. t. A mushroom, toadstool, fungus; cork; a cork, bung; منطار قاوى mAntar-kAwi, German tinder. [out.

منطفى mùntAfī, a. a. Extinguished, put

منطق mAntik, s. a. Logic, dialectics; —, mìntAk, and منطقه mìntAka (mAntika), s. a. A zone, belt, girdle; منطقهٔ حاره (mAntika'i) - hârré, The torrid zone; منطقهٔ معتدله mAntika'i-mù"tèdilÉ, The temperate zone; منطقهٔ منجمده mAntika'i-mùnjèmidÉ, The frigid zone; منطقة البروج mAntikAtu-'l-bùrūj, The ecliptic or zodiac.

منطلق mùntàlik, a. a. Let loose; repudiated, divorced.

منطوق mAntūk, a. a. Said, spoken, expressed; —, s. a. An expression, a saying.

منطوى mùntavī, a. a. Inclosed, folded, enveloped, contained.

منظر mAnzàr, s. a. An aspect, face, countenance; a place in which anything is seen. [cleansed.

منظف mùnAzzàf, a. a. Cleaned,

منظور mAnzūr, a. a. Seen, looked at, beheld, examined; —, s. An object, aim, design.

منظوم mAnzūm, a. a. Ranged in order; ranged in metre, metrical; —, s. a. Verse.

منظومه mAnzūmÉ, s. a. A piece of poetry; a system, series, hierarchy.

منع mèn", s. a. A hindering, preventing; ا—, —et, v.a. To hinder, prevent; to prohibit, forbid.

منعدم mùn"àdim, a. a. Annihilated.

منعطف mùn"Atif, a. a. Turned on one side, turned (from or towards).

منعقد mùn"àkid, a. a. Tied; concluded, contracted (a treaty, &c.); congealed, clotted, formed. [echoed.

منعكس mùn"àkiss, a. a. Reflected;

منعم mùn"ìm, a. a. Kind, gracious, beneficent.

منغال mànghal, *s. t.* A chafing-dish for warming apartments with charcoal.

منغر *or* منقر mànghir, *s. t.* Money; copper money.

منفرج mùnfèrij (*fem.* منفرجه mùnfèrijé), *a. a.* Wide open, wide apart; obtuse (angle). [separate, isolated.

منفرد mùnfèrid, *a. a.* Alone, by itself,

منفس mènfèss, *s. a.* A breathing hole.

منفسخ mùnfèssikh, *a. a.* Abolished, abrogated. [rated.

منفصل mùnfàssil, *a. a.* Detached, sepa-

منفعت mènfà‘‘at, *s. a.* Use, utility, profit, advantage, interest. [grieved.

منفعل mùnfà‘‘il, *a. a.* Hurt in feelings,

منفك mùnfèkk, *a. a.* Detached, separated; displaced, superseded.

منفور mènfūr, *a. a.* Held in detestation, abhorred. [prehended, gathered.

منفهم mùnfèhim, *a. a.* Understood, com-

منفى mènfī, *a. a.* Exiled, banished; —, mènfà, *s. a.* A place of exile.

منقا (*for* منقى mùnàkkà), *a. a.* Cleaned, made clean. [missive.

منقاد mùnkàd, *a. a.* Obedient, sub-

منقار mìnkār, *s. a.* A bird's beak or bill.

منقال mànkāl (mànghal), *s. a.* A chafing-dish.

منقبه mànkabé, *s. a.* Any praiseworthy trait of character; an anecdote.

منقبض mùnkàbiz, *a. a.* Held tight, squeezed hard; costive, bound in the bowels; grieved, out of humour or spirits. [of defects (a writing).

منقح mùnàkkàh, *a. a.* Revised, purged

منقرض mùnkàriz, *a. a.* Extinct (a lineage, dynasty). [several parts.

منقسم mùnkàssim, *a. a.* Divided in

منقش mùnàkkàsh, *a. a.* Decorated with designs. [(a term).

منقضى mùnkàzī, *a. a.* Finished, expired

منقطع mùnkàti‘‘, *a. a.* Cut off; interrupted; withheld; ceased.

منقلب mùnkàlib, *a. a.* Inverted; changed, altered.

منقله mìnkala, *s. a.* A sector (mathematical instrument). [painted.

منقوش mènkūsh, *a. a.* Drawn, figured,

منقوط mènkūt, *a. a.* Marked with one or more diacritical points or dots (a letter).

منقول mènkūl, *a. a.* Carried from one place to another; narrated, related, handed down. [made clean.

منقى (*or* منقا), mùnàkkà, *a. a.* Cleaned,

منكر mùnkèr, *a. a.* Denied; negative; incognito; irrecognisable; bad, wicked, reprovable (act); name of one of the questioning angels who visit the dead, the other being named نكير nèkīr; —, mùnkir, *a. a.* A denier; —, mùnèkkèr, *a. a.* Incognito, irrecognisable; indefinite, indeterminate (in grammar);

منكرات mùnkérāt, *s. pl. a.* Bad, reprovable, wicked actions.

منكسر mùnkèssir, *a. a.* Broken; afflicted, grieved. [sun).

منكسف mùnkèssif, *a. a.* Eclipsed (the

منكشف mùnkèshif, *a. a.* Discovered; revealed.

منكنه mènghéné, s. t. A blacksmith's vice; a press.

منكوب mènkyūb, a. a. Fallen (in circumstances). [man; —, s. a. A wife.

منكوحه mènkyūha, a. a. Married to a

منوال mìnwāl, s. a. A manner, way, method. [or glory, aureolated.

منور mùnèvvèr, a. a. Bright with light

منوط mènūt, a. a. Depending, referred.

منوى mènvī, s. a. An intention, design, intent.

منويش mènévish, s. t. The browning on gun-barrels; the blueing on swords, watch-springs, &c.; the water on silks, &c.

منه mình, comp. a. From him (her, it).

منهاج mìnhāj, s. a. A road, way; a manner.

منهتك mùnhètik, a. a. Torn; violated.

منهدم mùnhèdim, a. a. Demolished, pulled down (a building).

منهزم mùnhèzim, a. a. Defeated, routed.

منهوب mènhūb, a. a. Taken as plunder, plundered.

منهى mènhī, a. a. Prohibited, forbidden.

منى mènī, s. a. Sperm, the seminal

منيت mènìyyèt, s. a. Death. [fluid.

منير mùnīr, a. a. Shining with its own light and giving light to other things.

منيع mènī'', a. a. Difficult, or impossible to do, to take, to get into, &c.

منيف mùnīf, a. a. Eminent, exalted.

منيه mùnyé, s. a. A wish, desire.

مو mū, s. p. A hair; سرمو sèri-mū, (A hair's-point) A hair's-breadth.

موات méwāt, s. a. Waste, unreclaimed lands.

مواجب mèwājib, a. pl. a. (no sing.), Salaries, allowances; a pension.

مواجهه mùwājaha, s. a. A being face to face with each other.

مؤاخذه mù'ākhaza, s. a. A scolding, upbraiding, reprimanding; ا—, —et, v.a. To scold, upbraid, reprimand.

مواد mèwādd, s. pl. a. (of ماده māddé), Subjects, matters; articles, paragraphs.

موارد mèwārid, s. pl. a. (of مورد mèvrid), Approaches, avenues, roads leading to.

موازنه mùwāzéné, s. a. A weighing (in the mind); ا—, —et, v.a. To weigh.

موازى mùwāzī, a. a. Parallel; —, s. a. A parallel ruler.

مواسات mùvāssāt, s. a. Kindness.

مواشى mèwāshī, s. pl. a. Cattle.

مواصلت mùwāssalèt, s. a. A coming together, being united in one place, being in each other's society.

مواضع mèwāzi'', s. pl. a. (of موضع mèvzi''), Places.

مواضعه mùwāza''à, s. a. Dissimulation, putting on a good face in respect to the acts of a superior whom we cannot control. [perseverance.

مواظبت mùwāzabèt, s. a. Assiduity,

مواعد mèwā''id, s. pl. a. (of موعده mèv''idé), Promises.

مواعظ mèwā''iz, s. pl. a. (of موعظه mèv''izé), Exhortations.

موافق mùwāfik, *a. a.* Favourable, propitious.

موافقت mùwāfakàt, *s. a.* An agreeing, consenting; ا—, —et, *v.n.* To agree, consent.

مواقع mèwāki", *s. pl. a.* (*of* موقع mèvki"), Places.

مواكب mèwākib, *s. pl. a.* (*of* موكب mèvkib), Troops, legions, armies.

موالات mùwālāt, *s. a.* Friendship, amity.

مؤالفت mù'āléfèt, *s. a.* Intimate acquaintanceship.

موالى mèwālī, *s. pl. a.* (*of* مولى mèvlà, mòlla), The higher legal dignitaries, judges.

مواليد mèwālīd, *s. pl. a.* (*of* مولود mèvlūd), Kingdoms, *in* مواليد ثلثه mèwālīdi - sèlāssé, The three kingdoms of nature, mineral, vegetable, animal.

مؤانست mù'ānéssèt, *s. a.* Familiarity [of acquaintanceship.

موانع mèwāni", *s. pl. a.* (*of* مانع māni"), Obstacles, hindrances, impediments.

مواهب mèwāhib, *s. pl. a.* (*of* موهب mèvhèb), Gifts of God.

موبد mūbèd, موبذ mūbèz, *s. p.* A fire-[priest.

مؤبد mù'èbbèd, *a. a.* Caused to last forever; مؤبداً mù'èbbèd*an*, *ad. a.* Forever, everlastingly, to all eternity.

موت mèvt, *s. a.* Death, a dying.

موتا (*for* موتى) mèvtà, *s. pl. a.* (*of* ميت mèyyit), The dead.

موتاب mū-tāb (mūtàf), *s. p.* A maker of yarns, cords, sacks, &c., of horse or other hair.

موتلو mùtlu (*corrupted from* مطلوع màtlū", *possessed of an ascendant ?*), *a. t.* Fortunate, happy, lucky; نه‌موتلو سڭا nè-mùtlu-sàng*a* (*for* نه‌مطلوعسنا nè - màtlū"sèn - ā ?) ! Lucky thou ! Lucky fellow !

موتى mèvtà, *s. pl. a.* (*of* ميت mèyyit), The dead.

مؤثر mù'èsssir, *a. a.* Efficacious, effectual, effective, productive of effect; affecting; penetrating.

موثوق mèvsūk, *a. a.* Relied upon.

موج mèvj, *s. a.* A wave, billow; موجا موج mèvj-ā-mèvj, *ad. p.* Wave upon wave.

موجب mūjib, *a. a.* Causing, requiring; —, *s. a.* A cause; —, mūjèb, *s. a.* The thing required, requirement; a ministerial letter usually given with a firman, and addressed to the same person or persons, shortly explanatory of the requirement thereof; موجبنجه mūjébinj*a*, *ad. t.* برموجب bèr-mūjèb, *ad. p.* According to the requirement, in conformity with; بلاموجب bilā-mūjib, *ad. a.* Without cause.

موجد mūjid, *s. a.* An inventor.

موجز mūjèz, *a. a.* Short, abstracted, cursory, abridged.

مؤجل mù'èjjèl, *a. a.* Postponed, deferred to a certain time.

موجود mèvjūd, *a. a.* Present, existing, inventus; in store, in stock; موجودات mèvjūdāt, *s. pl. a.* Existing things; goods or stores.

موجه mùvèjjèh, *a. a.* Approved, fit, proper, suitable.

موحد mùwàhhid (*pl.* موحدين mùwàhhidīn), *s. a.* A unitarian, a Muhammedan.

موحش mūhish, *a. a.* Which frightens, terrifies; frightful, terrific.

مؤخر mŭʿàkhkhàr, *a. a.* Posterior in time or place; postponed; retrograded; مؤخراً mŭʿàkhkharan, *ad. a.* Latterly, of late.

مؤدا (*for* مؤدى) mùʿèddà, *s. a.* The sense, purport (of a sentence).

مؤدب mŭʿèddèb, *a. a.* Well behaved, well disciplined, well educated.

مودت mèvèddèt, *s. a.* Love, affection; مودتلو mèvèddètlū, *a. t.* Friendly (person).

مودوع mèvdūʿ, *a. a.* Delivered, consigned, left in charge, entrusted.

مؤدى mùʿèddī, *a. a.* Which causes, brings about; —, mùʿèddà, *s. a.* The sense, purport (of a phrase).

مؤذن mŭʿèzzin, *s. a.* The crier who calls to prayer.

مؤذى mŭʿèzzī, *a. a.* Which gives pain, causes trouble or annoyance.

مور mòr, *a. t.* Purple, dark damask red; —, mūr, *s. p.* An ant.

موراويه Mòràvi*a*, *s. t.* Moravia.

مورث mùriss, *a. a.* Causing, producing.

مورچه mūrchè, *s. p. dim.* A little ant, an emmet; the marks on Damascus steel.

مورخ mùvèrrikh, مؤرخ mŭʿèrrikh, *s. a.* A historian, chronologist, chronicler; —, mùvèrràkh, mŭʿèrràkh, *a. a.* Dated, bearing date; مورخاً mùvèrr*a*kh*a*n, مؤرخاً mŭʿèrr*a*kh*a*n, *ad. a.* Bearing date.

مورد mèvrid, *s. a.* A way or point by which a thing is approached, an approach; a station, place, position.

موروث mèvrūss, *a. a.* Inherited, of inheritance.

مورود mèvrūd, *a. a.* Related, recited, [recounted.

موره Mòr*a*, *s. t.* The Morea.

موريته mòrin*a*, *s. t.* The tunny fish.(?)

موزون mèvzūn, *a. a.* Weighed; balanced; in metre, metrical as to the feet and syllables in it.

موزه mūzè, *s. p.* A boot.

موستار Mòstār, *s. t.* Mostar.

موسخ mùvèsssàkh, *a. a.* Filthy, dirtied.

مؤسس mùʿèsssis, *s. a.* Who founds, lays a foundation, establishes; —, *s. a.* A founder; —, mùʿèsssèss, *a. a.* Based, founded, established.

موسم mèvsim, *s. a.* A season, the particular time when anything is usually in season; (*pronounced by Arabs* mòssim: *this is the origin of our very corrupt word* monsoon, *called rather better by the French* mousson).

موسوم mèvsūm, *a. a.* Marked with a mark.

موسى mūssà, *s. a.* A razor; Moses; موسوى mūssèvī, *a. a.* Mosesian, one following the dispensation of Moses, a Jew, an Israelite, a Hebrew.

موسيقار mūssikār, *s. a.* A kind of musical instrument, a Pandean pipe; a fabulous musical bird; music; a musician.

موسيقى mūssikī, *s. a.* (*Greek*), Music as a science.

موش mūsh, *s. p.* A mouse; a rat.

موشح mùvèshshàh, *a. a.* Ornamented with a scarf or fillet.

موشكاف mū-shikyāf, *s. a.* A hair-splitter; موشكافانه mū-shikyāfānè, *a. p.* Pertaining to a hair-splitter.

موشمله mùshmula, *s. t.* A medlar.

موصل mèvsil, *s. a.* A place of junction; —, mòssil (mòssul), *s. a.* Mosul or Mosool in Mesopotamia.

موصلق mùssluk, *s. t.* A cock, a tap, a stop-cock or turn-cock.

موصوف mèvsūf, *a. a.* Possessing a quality; bearing a title; qualified by an adjective (in grammar).

موصول mèvsūl, *a. a.* To which anything is joined, or has reached; —, *s. a.* A relative pronoun (in Arabic grammar).

موضع mèvzi'', *s. a.* A place, position, situation, locality.

موضوع mèvzū'', *a. a.* Placed; used as an appellative; موضوعات mèvzū''āt, *s. pl. a.* The axioms of any science; موضوعله mèvzū''un-lèh, The thing indicated by a name, the thing treated on by a science, the subject.

موظف mùwàzzàf, *a. a.* Salaried, paid, pensioned.

موعد mèv''id, موعده mèv''idè, *s. a.* A promise.

موعظه mèv''izè, *s. a.* An admonition, exhortation.

موعود mèv''ūd, *a. a.* Promised; to which a time is fore-assigned; اجل موعود èjéli-mèv''ūd, The appointed hour of death.

موفور mèvfūr, *a. a.* Abundant, many, numerous, copious.

موقت mèvkit, *s. a.* An appointed time; —, mùwàkkit, *s. a.* A public regulator of time, an astronomer; —, mùwàkkàt, *a. a.* Temporary, ad interim;

موقتاً mùwàkkatan, *ad. a.* Temporarily, ad interim; موقتخانه mùwàkkit-khānè, *s. p.* An observatory for regulating the time.

موقر mùwàkkàr, *a. a.* Honoured, held in honour; stately, grave.

موقع mèvki'', *s. a.* A place, position, situation, locality; موقعى mèvki''ī, *a. a.* Local; —, mùwàkkà'', *a. a.* Bearing the توقيع tèvkī'' *or* طغرا tùghra, *i.e.* the Sultan's cypher.

موقف mèvkif, *s. a.* A station, halting-place.

موقود mèvkūd, *a. a.* Lighted, set fire to, burning.

موقوف mèvkūf, *a.a.* Stayed, stopped, arrested; depending, referred, referable; in mortmain, entailed; موقوفات mèvkūfāt, *s. pl. a.* Properties in mortmain; entailed estates.

موكب mèvkib, *s. a.* A camp, an army; موكب همايون mèvkibi-hùmāyūn, The imperial camp (*equivalent to our* footstool *or* throne).

مؤكد mù''èkkèd, *a. a.* Strong, express,

strongly expressed, peremptory; corroborated, strengthened.

موكل mùvèkkèl, *a. a.* Charged, appointed as agent or attorney.

مولا (*for* مولى) mèvlà, *s. a.* God, the Lord; a master; —, mòlla, *s. a.* A judge (when following a name); a student (when preceding a name). N.B. *These are merely two modifications in sound of the self-same word.* مولانا mèvlā-nā, *comp. a.* Our Lord (*said of God, Muhammed, and any high dignitary of the law*); حضرت مولانا hàzrèti-mèvlā-nā, His Holiness our Lord (Jèlālu-'d-dīni-r-Rūmī, Founder of the order of Mevlévi dervishes).

مولد mèvlid, *s. a.* A birthday; a birthplace; —, mùwèllid, *s. a.* A generator; مولد الما mùwèllidu-'l-mā, Hydrogen; مولدالحموضة mùwèllidu-'l-hùmūza, Oxygen.

مؤلف mù'èllif, *a. a.* Which consoles, accustoms, familiarizes, reconciles; —, *s. a.* An author, compiler; —, mù'èllèf, *a. a.* Consoled; accustomed, familiarized; reconciled; composed; compiled; مؤلفات mù'èllèfāt, *s. pl. a.* Works, literary productions, compilations.

مولود mèvlūd, *a. a.* Born, given birth to; a kingdom in nature, mineral, vegetable, or animal; مولودله mèvlūdun-lèh, To whom a child is born, a father; مولودلها mèvlūdun-lèhā, A mother.

مولوز mòloz, مولوس mòloss, *s. t.* Stones and brickbats, rubbish for filling in hollows, trenches, &c.

مولوى mèvlévī, *a. a.* Pertaining to the religious order founded by Molla Jelalu-'d-dini-r-Rumi.

مولى mèvlà, *s. a.* The Lord God, who is served and worshipped; بمنه المولى bì-mènni-hì-'l-mèvlà, By the grace of Him (who is) the Lord whom all worship.

موم mùm, *s. t.* A candle; بالمومى bàl-mùmu, *s. t.* Bees'-wax, wax; a wax candle; مهر مومى mùhur-mùmu, Sealing-wax; موم ياغى mùm-yàghi, Tallow.

مؤمن mù'min (*pl.* مؤمنين mù'minīn), *s. a.* One who believes in God and the prophet, a true believer.

مومى اليه mūmà-ìlèyh, *s. a.* The aforementioned (person of some, but not very high, rank).

موميا mūmiyā, مومية mūmìyyé, *s. a.* A mummy; the substance of mummified bodies (supposed to be efficacious in many diseases); an artificial compound resembling it; the state of a mummy, mashed to a pulp.

مؤنت mà'ūnèt, *s. a.* Food, feed, support, maintenance.

مؤنث mù'ènnèss, *a. a.* Feminine (in grammar).

موهبه mèvhibé, *s. a.* A gift (of God).

موهوب mèvhūb, *a. a.* Given (by God).

موهوم mèvhūm, *a. a.* Imaginary.

موى mūy, *s. p.* A hair; موىميان mūy-

-mìyān (Hair-waisted), *a. p.* Slender-waisted. [supported.

مؤيد mŭʿèyyèd, *a. a.* Strengthened,

مه mèh, *s. p.* (*contr. from* ماه māh), The moon ; —, mìh, *a. p.* Large.

مهابت màhābèt, *s. a.* Dreadness, awfulness, majesty ; مهابتلو màhābètlū, *a. t.* Dread, awful, grand, sublime, majestic (one of the special styles of the Sultan).

مهاجر mŭhājir, *s. a.* One compelled to abandon his country ; مهاجرين mŭhājirīn, *s. pl. a.* Those inhabitants of Mecca who fled to Medina and joined Muhammed.

مهاجرت mŭhājérèt, *s. a.* An abandoning one's home and country.

مهاد mìhād, *s. a.* A seat, couch, bed, sofa, throne. [snaffle.

مهار mìhār, *s. a.* A rein or kind of bit or

مهارت màhārèt, *s. a.* Skilfulness, skill, perfect experience.

مهالك màhālik, *s. pl. a.* (*of* مهلكه mèhléké), Dangerous places or enterprises.

مهام màhāmm, *s. pl. a.* (*no sing.*), Affairs of importance.

مهب mèhèbb, *s. a.* The place from whence the wind blows.

مهبط mèhbit, *s. a.* A place of descent, where one alights.

مهپاره mèh-pāré (Piece of the moon), *s. p.* A beauty, beautiful boy or girl.

مهتاب mèh-tāb, *s. p.* Moonlight, moonshine ; مهتابيه mèhtābìyyé, *s. a.* An arbour, open summer-house.

مهتدى mŭhtèdī, *s. a.* A convert to the true faith, (*called by Europeans*) a renegade.

مهتر mìhtèr (mèhtèr), *a. p.* Greater ; older, elder ; —, *s. p.* Various kinds of attendants upon pashas in the old system ; some were musicians, others tent-pitchers, &c. ; مهترخانه (mèhtèr)-khāné, *s. p.* The old feudal military band.

مهجور mèhjūr, *a. a.* Abandoned, left desolate and disconsolate.

مهچه mèhché, *s. p.* A little moon ; a little figure of a crescent.

مهد mèhd, *s. a.* A cradle ; كتخداى مهد علياى سلطنت kètkhudāyi-mèhdi-ʿùlyāyi-sàltanàt (*Steward of the high cradle of the sovereignty*), Title of the High Steward of the mother of the reigning Sultan.

مهدوم mèhdūm, *a. a.* Demolished.

مهدى mèhdī, *s. a.* A guide, conductor. Under this title a personage is expected by Muhammedans to appear, in the latter days, and to re-establish the true religion in great glory.

مهر mèhr, *s. a.* A marriage-portion, a dower given by the husband to his wife on their betrothal. It is of two kinds, one paid down and called مهر معجل mèhri-mŭʿàjjèl ; the other, deferred till their separation by his death or by divorce, is called مهر مؤجل mèhri-mŭʿèjjèl ; —, mìhr, *s. a.* Friendship, amity ; —, *s. p.* The sun ;

—, mùhr (mùhur), *s. p.* A seal; مهر ومحبت mihr-u-màhàbbèt, Friendship and affection; مهر و ماه mihr-u--māh, Sun and moon (*proper name for women*); مهر سليمان mùhri-sùlèymān, Solomon's seal; مهرلو mùhrlu, *a. t.* Sealed; سربمهر sèr-bé-mùhr, *a. p.* Of which the mouth is sealed.

مهربان mìhrbān (mìhribān), *s. p.* A friend; مهرباني mìhribānī, *a. p.* Pertaining to a friend, friendly; —, *s. p.* Friendliness, friendship.

مهردار mùhrdār, *s. p.* A seal-bearer.

مهرلمك mùhurlémek, *v.a.* To seal.

مهرو mèhrū (moon-faced), *s. p.* A beautiful girl or woman.

مهره mèhéré, *s. pl. a.* (*of* ماهر māhir), Adepts, proficients; —, mùhré, *s. p.* An instrument of agate, glass, or wood, used for polishing gold-leaf, paper, &c.; مهره‌لو mùhréli, *a. t.* Polished; glazed; مهره‌لمك mùhré-lémek, *v.a.* To polish, to glaze with a *muhré*.

مهزول mèhzūl, *a. a.* Thin, lean, emaciated. [stone.

مهك mèhèkk (mèhènk), *s. a.* A touch-

مهل mèhl, مهلت mùhlèt, *s. a.* A delay, postponement; مهلت ويرمك mùhlet--vèrmek, *v.n.* To grant a delay.

مهلك mùhlik, *a. a.* Dangerous; fatal.

مهلكه mèhléké, *s. a.* A dangerous thing, spot, or enterprise.

مله‌لمك mèlémek, *v.n.* To bleat.

مهم mùhimm (*fem.* مهمه mùhimmé), *a. a.* Important; مهمات mùhimmāt, *s. pl. a.* The most important military stores, ammunition, &c.

مهماامكن mèh-mā-èmkèn, *comp. a.* As much as possible.

مهمان mìhmān, *s. p.* A guest; مهماندار mìhmāndār, *s. p.* An officer whose duty it is to take charge of guests and attend to all their wants; مهماننواز mìhmān-nūwāz, *a. p.* Hospitable, kind to strangers; مهمانسراى mìhmān--sàrāy, *s. p.* A guest-house, hotel; the world.

مهمل mùhmèl, *a. a.* Neglected; having no dots or diacritical points (a letter).

مهموز mèhmūz (màhmuz), *s. a.* A spur; —, *a. a.* Containing a ـٔ hèmzé.

مهند mùhènnèd, *a. a.* Indian, Damascus (blade). [civil or military engineer.

مهندس mùhèndiss, *s. a.* A geometer, a

مهواره mèhwāré, *s. p.* Monthly pay.

مهوش mèhvèsh, *s. p.* A beauty, beautiful girl or boy. [equipped.

مهيا mùhèyyà, *a. a.* Ready, prepared,

مهيب mùhīb, *a. a.* Inspiring awe, awful, dreadful.

مى mi *or* mi, Turkish general interrogative particle which *must always* be used in questions if one of the special interrogatives is not introduced: it is affixed to the word on which, more especially, the question turns (see Grammar); —, mèy, *s. p.* Wine; ميخانه mèy-khāné, *s. p.* A public-house, a wine-shop.

میادین mèyādīn, *s. pl. a.* (*of* میدان mèydān), Open spaces, squares.

میال mèyyāl, *a. a.* Inclined, leaning, disposed.

میامن mèyāmin, *s. pl. a.* (*of* میمنت mèyménèt), Fortunate qualities or events.

میان mìyān, *s. p.* The middle; the midst; the waist; میان‌کوکی mìyān-kyùkyu, *s. t.* Liquorice-root; میان بالی mìyān-bāli, Spanish liquorice; میانجی mìyānji, *s. t.* A mediator.

میانه mìyāné (mèyāné), *s. p.* The midst; the relation between several things.

میاولمق mìyàwlamak, *v.n.* To mew.

میاه mìyāh, *s. pl. a.* (*of* ما mā), Waters.

میت mèyyit, *s. a.* A dead body; a dead person, dead man.

مئتین mìʿétèyn, *s. a. dual.* Two hundred.

میثاق mīssāk, *s. a.* A pact, promise, agreement.

میجو mìcho, *s. t.* A cabin-boy, sailor-boy.

میخ mìkh, *s. t.* A nail; میخلامق mìkhlamak, *v.a.* To nail; to fasten with rivets; to set (a precious stone); میخلایجی mìkhlayiji, *s. t.* A stone-setter; میخلو mìkhli, *a. t.* Nailed; rivetted; set.

میدان mèydān, *s. a.* A vacant space; a public square; an interval of time.

میدیه mìdiyé, *s. t.* A muscle or mussel (fish).

میر mīr (*contr. from* امیر èmīr), *s. p.* A commander; an officer; anyone holding the title of Begh or Bey; میر لوا mīri-lìwā, A major-general; میرمیران mīri-mīrān, A civil governor of a district, with the rank of lieutenant-general; میرالامرا mīru-'l-ùmérā, A civil governor of a district, with the rank of major-general; میرالای mīr-àlāy, A colonel (in the army); a captain of a three-decker (in the navy); میراخور mīr-àkhòr (ìmrakhòr), Master of the horse; میرکلام mīri-kèlām, An eloquent person; میری mīrī (*fem.* میریه mīrìyyé), *a. a.* Belonging to government, public.

میراث mīrāss, *s. a.* An inheritance; میراثخور mīrāss-khòr, An inheritor, one who has received an inheritance; میراث‌یمک mīrāss-yèmek, *v.n.* To receive an inheritance, to inherit; میراث‌یدی mīrāss-yèdi (Who has received an inheritance), *s. a.* A spendthrift.

میرزا mīrzā, *s. p.* A title used in three ways: when placed after a name, it signifies a *Prince of the blood;* but when placed before, it merely denotes a civilian of any grade: without a name, it means a *clerk* or *secretary*.

میزاب mīzāb, *s. p.* A canal, drain, spout.

میزان mīzān, *s. a.* A balance, pair of scales; the sign Libra; a proof (in arithmetic); an object of comparison;

ـــاورمق, mīzān-wùrmak, To compare, to draw a conclusion.

ميزبان mīzbān, s. p. A host, receiver and entertainer of guests.

ميسر mùyèsssèr, a. a. Facilitated, put into one's power or possession by God's permission; الله ميسرايليه Allāh-mùyèsssèr-èyléyé! May God facilitate it (to you). [an army.

ميسره mèyséré, s. a. The left wing of

ميشه mèyshé, s. t. An oak; oak-wood; ميشه لك mèyshélik, s. t. An oak-forest, or region bearing oaks.

ميشين mīshīn (mèshin), s. p. Leather made from sheep's skin.

ميعاد mī''ād, s. a. A place foretold, a rendezvous; the resurrection.

ميغ mīgh, s. p. A fog, a mist.

ميقات mīkāt, s. a. A time fore-appointed; a fixed or marked time, a season.

ميكده mèy-kèdé, s. p. A wine-shop.

ميل mèyl, s. a. Inclination; declination; affection; ا—, —et, v.n. To incline; to decline (north or south); to have an affection or liking; —, mīl, s. a. A pivot; a probing-needle; a mile; ميل چكمك mīl-chèkmek, To use a red-hot iron instrument for blinding state prisoners.

ميلاد mīlād, s. a. Birth; ــعيسى, mīlādi-''issà, The Nativity, the birth of Jesus; ميلاديه mīlādìyyé, a. a. (The year) reckoned from the Nativity.

ميلان mèyélān, s. a. Inclination.

ميلو Mìlo, s. t. Milo.

ميم mīm, s. a. Name of the letter م.

ميمنت mèyménèt, s. a. Any fortunate quality or event.

ميمنه mèyméné, s. a. (*Originally identic with* ميمنت), The right wing of an army.

ميمون mèymūn, a. a. Endued with felicity; fortunate, happy; —, màymūn, s. t. A monkey; ميمونجى màymunju, A monkey-leader.

مين mèyn, s. a. A lie, falsehood.

مينا mīnā, s. p. Enamel (mìné); glass; a drinking-cup; the sky; مينالو mìnéli, a. t. Enamelled; مينافام mīnā-fām, a. p. Of a sky-blue colour.

مينويش (*for* ميناوش mīnā-vèsh, s. p.), mènévish, s. t. The browning of gun-barrels; the blueing of watch-springs, &c.; the watering on silks, &c.

ميوس mèyyūss (*for* مئوس mèy'ūss), a. a. Despaired of; despairing; hopeless; ميوسيت mèyyūssìyyèt, s. a. Despair, hopelessness.

ميوه mèyvé (pl. p. ميوها mèyvéhā), s. p. Fruit; ميوه دار mèyvédār, a. p. Fruitful.

مئه mi'é, s. a. A hundred, one hundred; مئتين mi'étèyn, Two hundred.

ن

ن nūn. Twenty-eighth letter of the Turkish alphabet, having the value of *n* in English. In chronograms and astronomical tables it has the numerical value of 50, and in the dates of letters it stands for the month of Ramazan. Added to the root of a verb active or neuter, it indicates an indefinite action without exterior object; and in the case of verbs active or neuter the roots of which end in ل or in a vowel, it either takes the place of the ل which usually forms the passive, or it precedes that letter in combining the passive voice. (*See Grammar.*)

نا **nā!** *int. t.* There! There's for you! There it is! There, take that! —, Persian privative particle, preceding nouns and adjectives, and corresponding with our *un*, *in*, &c., or with our *less* at the end of words; ناامید nā-ùmīd, *a. p.* Hopeless; ناپاك nā-pāk, *a. p.* Unclean.

ناب **nāb,** *s. a.* A canine tooth, a tusk, tush; ivory; —, *a. p.* Pure, clear.

نابت **nābit,** *a. a.* Which grows, vegetates.

نابجا **nā-bé-jā,** نابهنجار nā-bé-hènjār, *a. p.* Out of time or place, unfitting, unsuitable, unseemly.

نابلس **Nābulus,** *s. a.* Samaria.

ناجی* **nājī,** *a. a.* Who escapes; who finds salvation.

ناچیز **nā-chīz,** *s. p.* A nothing, a thing of little account; a humble insignificant person; ناچیزانه nā-chīzānė, *a. p.* Pertaining to a humble, insignificant person.

ناحیه **nāhìyyė,** *s. a.* A small district, a canton, a hundred.

ناخن **nākhun,** *s. p.* A nail, claw, talon.

نادر **nādir,** *a. a.* Rare; نادراً nādiran, *ad. a.* Rarely, seldom.

نادره **nādirė,** *s. a.* A rarity, a thing seldom seen.

نادم **nādim,** *a. a.* Repenting, repentant, sorry for what he has done.

نادی **nādī,** *s. a.* A place where one is.

نار **nār,** *s. a.* Fire; hell-fire; hell; —, *s. t.* A pomegranate; ناری nārī (*fem.* ناریه nārìyyė), *a. a.* Pertaining to fire, fiery.

ناردنك **nārdènk,** *s. p.* A sharp kind of syrup, made from some fruit, either grapes(?), apples(?), plums(?), or pomegranates(?).

نارگله **nàrghìlė,** *s. t.* An instrument for smoking Persian tobacco, in which the smoke is drawn through water.

نارنج **nārinj,** *s. p.* An orange; a Seville orange.

نارين **nārin,** *a. t.* Slender, weakly made.

* It is a great mistake to suppose that this word corresponds to "Saviour." On the contrary, it means "one who escapes from peril," as Mr. Redhouse has stated. If used for "Saviour" it would be entirely misunderstood by natives, as they would take it to mean one who himself avoids or escapes from danger, and not one who saved others. This mistake was first made by Meninski, and was copied by Bianchi; and, as I find others have taken the same erroneous view of the meaning of the word, I avail myself of this opportunity of drawing attention to its real signification.—C. W.

ناز nāz, *s. p.* The conscious or unconscious self-sufficiency and graceful pride of a beautiful girl; graceful and well-founded disdain, real or pretended, for all exterior embellishment and for all admiration; the graceful playfulness and motions of a beautiful object which attract attention; the disdain of anyone for what he may consider not necessary to himself or not worthy of acceptance; نازلنمق nāzl*a*nm*a*k, *v.n.* To be disdainful of anything offered, whether homage to a beauty, or a gift of any kind to other people; نازلو nāzli, *a. t.* Who shows a real or affected disdain for offered homage or gifts; نازونیازا nāz-u-nìyàz-èt, *v.n.* To urge a request in a graceful, bashful, attractive manner.

نازك nāzik, *a. p.* Delicate (in mind, constitution, or quality).

نازل nāzil, *a. a.* Which descends; which is sent down from heaven.

نازنین nāzénīn, *s. p.* A beautiful, graceful girl, disdainful in her gracefulness, or graceful in her bashful boldness.

ناس nāss, *s. pl. a.* (*of* انسان ìnsān), Men, mankind.

ناساز nā-sāz, *a. p.* Discordant; improper; ناسازکار nā-sāz-ky*ā*r, *a. p.* Who acts improperly.

ناسوت nāssūt, *s. a.* Humanity, human nature; عالم ناسوت "ālémi-nāssūt, The world, state, or degree of human nature.

ناسور nāssūr, *s. a.* A kind of running ulcer; a fistula; —, *s. t.* A wart, a corn, the hard skin which forms on the inner parts of the hands of working men.

ناسی nāssī, *a. a.* Forgetful, who forgets.

ناشر nāshir, *s.a.* One who spreads, opens out, or disseminates.

ناشی nāshī, *a. a.* Growing, which grows; proceeding, springing, arising; —, *ad. t.* Owing to, arising from (any cause, &c.).

ناصب nāss*i*b, *s. a.* One who sets up, erects; one who appoints officers.

ناصح nāss*i*h, *s. a.* One who gives advice.

ناصر nāss*i*r, *s. a.* A helper, helper to victory; —, (*or* ناصور nĀss*i*r), *s. t.* A wart, a corn, the hard skin which forms on the inner parts of the hands of working men; ناصورلنمق nĀss*i*rl*a*nm*a*k, *v.n.* To form into a wart, corn, or hard skin.

ناصیه nāssìyyé, *s. a.* The forelock; the forehead; ناصیهٔ حال nāssìyyè'i-hāl, The appearance of circumstances.

ناطق nĀt*i*k, *a. a.* Which speaks; which reasons; which has a voice; حیوان ناطق hāywĀn*i*-nāt*i*k, Man, the speaking, reasoning animal; مال ناطق māli-nātik, Possessions in slaves, flocks, herds, &c.

ناظر nāz*i*r, *a. a.* Which looks; —, *s. a.* A spectator, looker-on; an overseer, director; a minister of state; خارجیه ناظری khārijìyyé-nāz*i*r*i*, The minister for foreign affairs; ماليه‌ناظرى māliyyé-nāziri, The minister of finance.

ناظم nāzim, *s. a.* Who puts in order, regulates.

ناف nāf, *s. p.* The navel; the middle of anything.

نافخ nāfikh, *s. a.* One who blows (a wind instrument); نافخ‌الصور nāfikhu-'ss-sūr, He who blows the trump, the angel who will blow the last trump.

نافذ nāfiz, *a. a.* Which penetrates, makes its way into or through things; (a command) which receives full execution; نافذالكلمتين nāfizu-'l-kèlimétèyn, One whose two words, yes and no, are punctually attended to.

نافع nāfi'', *a. a.* Useful, beneficial.

نافله nāfilé, *s. a.* Supererogatory prayers beyond the five canonical ones; —, *a. a.* Useless, vain; —, *ad. t.* In vain.

نافه nāfé, *s. p.* The navel; a musk-bag; the belly part of an animal's fur.

ناقص nākiss, *a. a.* Deficient, wanting; minus (in algebra).

ناقل nākil, *a. a.* Bearing, carrying about; —, *s. a.* A narrator, relater.

ناقوس nāküss, *s. a.* A bell; a piece of wood suspended in churches or monasteries in the East, and struck in lieu of a bell.

ناقه nāka, *s. a.* A female camel.

ناك nāk, One of the Persian terminations which, added to a noun, makes an adjective signifying *possessing* or *subject to*; دردناك dèrdnāk, *a. p.* Grieved; نمناك nèmnāk, Damp.

ناگاه nā-ghyāh, *a. p.* Out of time or place, untimely; sudden; suddenly.

ناكس nā-kèss (nèkess), *a. p.* Not a man, a sordid, disagreeable fellow.

ناگه nā-ghèh (*contr. from* ناگاه), *a. p.* Untimely; sudden; ناگهانى nā-ghèhānī, *a. p.* Sudden.

نالان nālān, *a. p.* Weeping, lamenting.

نالش nālish, *s. p.* A weeping, lamenting.

ناله nālé, *s. p.* Weeping, plaint, lamentation.

نام nām (nÀm), *s. p.* A name; a title, a quality; honour, reputation, repute, celebrity; —, *a. p.* Named; احمد نام كمسنه Àhmed-nām-kimèssné, A person named Ahmed; نامدار nāmdār, ناموار nāmvār, نامور nāmvèr, *a. p.* Famous, celebrated.

نامزد nām-zèd, *s. p.* One whose name has been mentioned; a betrothed person; a person named or proposed for an office.

نامكور nÀmkyūr, *a. t.* Ungrateful.

ناملو nāmli, *a. t.* Having a name or reputation; —, *s. t.* The blade of a sword or knife (*as bearing the maker's name*).

ناموس nāmūss, *s. a.* (*Greek* νομος), A law; the Kur'ān; the angel Gabriel; a person's honour; ناموسسز nāmūss-suz, *a. t.* Regardless of his honour; ناموسلو nāmūsslu, *a. t.* Careful of his honour, scrupulous as regards rectitude.

نامه nāmé, *s. p.* A letter; a royal letter; a letter of credentials; (*in composition*), a book, a treatise, or writing on any particular subject; شاهنامه shāh-nāmé, The book of kings (*name of a book*); نامه‌بر nāmé-bèr, نامه‌رس nāmé-rèss, One who brings a letter, an envoy.

نامی nāmī, *a. a.* Which grows, vegetates, flourishes.

نان nān, *s. p.* Bread; نان‌ونمك nān-u-nèmek, Bread and salt, the two sacred or essential articles of food; نانپاره nān-pāre, *s. p.* A piece of bread, a loaf or cake of bread; a subsistence, maintenance, allowance, salary, pension.

نانكور nān-kyūr, *a. p.* Ungrateful.

نانو nānū, *s. p.* A ditty sung to put children to sleep.

نانه nāné, *s. t.* Mint (herb); peppermint.

ناودان nāwdān, *s. p.* A water-pipe, canal, channel, spout.

ناورد nāvèrd, *s. p.* Battle, combat, fighting.

ناوك nāvek, *s. p. dim.* A small light arrow.

ناولون nàvlun (*from* نول nèvl, *s. a.*), *s. t.* The freight paid for carriage of goods by ship; ناولون‌ایله‌طوتمق nàvlun-ila-tùtmak, To hire (a ship).

ناوی nāvi, *s. t.* (*Italian*), A bark, three-masted vessel with only two masts full rigged.

ناهب nāhib, *s. a.* A plunderer.

ناهی nāhī, *s. a.* A prohibitor, forbidder.

ناهید nāhīd, *s. p.* A young maiden; the planet Venus.

نای nāy, *s. p.* A reed, a bamboo, a cane; a flute or flageolet; صورنای sūrnāy (zùrna), A clarion, trumpet; كره‌نای kèrré-nāy, *s. p.* A kind of long trumpet.

نائب nā'ib, *s. a.* A lieutenant, locum-tenens, substitute; a judge-substitute.

نائبه nā'ibé, *s. a.* A misfortune which befalls.

نایچه nāyché, *s. p.* A small reed; a small flute or pipe.

نائحه nā'iha, *s. a.* A woman hired or employed for screaming and weeping over the dead.

نائره nā'iré, *s. a.* Fire, flames.

نایزن nāy-zèn, *s. p.* A flute-player.

نائل nā'il, *a. a.* Who receives, acquires, attains (anything desirable); —اول, —òl, *v.n.* To receive, acquire, attain, be blessed or gratified with.

نائم nā'im, *a. a.* Sleeping, asleep.

نبات nèbāt (*pl.* نباتات nèbātāt), *s. a.* A plant; a vegetable; علم‌نباتات "ìlmi-nèbātāt, Botany; نبات‌شكری nèbāt-shèkéri (nùbèt), *s. t.* Sugar-candy; نباتی nèbātī, *a. a.* Vegetable.

نبال nibāl, *s. pl. a.* (*of* نبل nèbl), Arrows.

نبذه nèbzé, *s. a.* A small portion, a taste, an inkling.

نبرد nèbèrd, *s. p.* War, battle, fight, combat.

نبش nèbsh, *s. a.* A digging up, excavating (graves, &c.).

نبض nàbz, *s. a.* The pulse; pulsation;

نبضه‌باقمق nàbza - bàkmak, *v.n.* To feel one's pulse.

نبع nèb'', *s. a.* A springing up (water from a spring) ; ا—, —et, *v.n.* To spring up, flow from a source.

نبوت nùbùvvet, *s. a.* The quality of being a prophet or God's messenger.

نبوى nèbévī (*fem.* نبويه nèbévìyyé), *a. a.* Pertaining to a prophet. [from God.

نبى nèbī, *s. a.* A prophet, a messenger

نبيره nèbīré, *s. p.* A grandson.

نتائج nètā'ij, *s. pl. a.* (*of* نتيجه nètījé), Results, consequences.

نته‌كم nìté-kim, *ad. t.* As, even as, in like manner as.

نتيجه nètījé, *s. a.* A result, consequence; a corollary ; نتيجه‌كلام nètījé'i-kèlām, *ad. t.* In short, in fine.

نثار nìssār, *s. a.* A scattering; small money scattered at weddings ; —, *a. p.* (*in composition*), Who scatters.

نثر nèssr (nèssir), *s. a.* A scattering; prose. [(in man or horses).

نجابت nèjābèt, *s. a.* Nobility of race

نجات nèjāt, *s. a.* Deliverance, escape, salvation ; —بولمق, nèjāt - bŭlmak, *v.n.* To find a means of escape, to escape, save one's self, be saved.

نجار nèjjār, *s. a.* A carpenter.

نجاست nèjāssèt, *s. a.* Uncleanness (canonical), unfitness to be touched ; filth, dung.

نجاشى nèjāshī, *s. a.* General title for the kings of Ethiopia or Abyssinia.

نجد nèjd, *s. a.* The upper and interior part of Arabia, from whence are derived the best horses, called نجدى nèjdī.

نجدت nèjdèt, *s. a.* Courage, valour.

نجس nèjiss, *a. a.* Unclean (canonically), not to be touched.

نجم néjm, *s. a.* A star ; علم نجوم ''ìlmi-nujūm, Astrology.

نجى inji, Turkish termination of the ordinal numbers, answering to our *th* or *eth* ; —, *or* نه‌جى nèji ? Turkish interrogative of trade or occupation, سن‌نجى‌سن sèn - nèji - sin ? What is your trade or occupation ?

نجيب nèjīb, *a. a.* Of a noble race (horse or man). [bronze.

نحاس nùhāss, *s. a.* Copper ; brass ;

نحس nàhss, *s. a.* A sinister aspect or malign influence of the stars ; an unlucky star ; —, nàhiss, *a. a.* Unlucky, under an unlucky star (a day) ; نحس‌اكبر nàhsi-èkbèr, Saturn ; نحس اصغر nàhsi-àssghàr, Mars. [bee.

نحل nahl, *s. a.* Bees ; نحله nàhlé, One

نحو nàhv, *s. a.* Syntax ; نحوى nàhvī (*fem.* نحويه nàhvìyyé), *a. a.* Pertaining to syntax, syntactical ; — (*pl.* نحويون nàhvìyyūn), *s. a.* A writer on syntax.

نحوست nùhūssèt, *s. a.* The quality of possessing a malign influence, malignity. [tion, feeble.

نحيف nàhīf, *a. a.* Weakly in constitu-

نخجير nàkhjìr, *s. p.* Any animal pursued or taken in the chase as game;

نخجيركير nàkhjīr-ghīr, *s. p.* A huntsman.

نخجيل nàkhjīl, *s. p.* A kind of wood or berry of which rosaries are made.

نخست nŭkhusst, نخستين nŭkhusstīn, *a. p.* The first.

نخشب nàkhshèb, *s. p.* Name of a place near Semerkand, having a celebrated well (چاه نخشب chāhi-nàkhshèb), from whence the impostor Mukanna" (the Veiled Prophet of Khorassan) is said to have caused an artificial moon (ماه نخشب māhi-nàkhshèb) to rise.

نخل nàkhl, *s. a.* A palm-tree, a date-tree; نخلستان nàkhlisstān, *s. p.* A palm-grove.

نخوت nàkhwèt, *s. a.* Pride, haughtiness.

نخود nòkhud, *s. t.* A chick-pea; a large, white, hard-boiling pea.

ندا nìdā, *s. a.* A calling aloud; an ejaculation; ا—, —et, *v.a.* To call out aloud; to ejaculate; حرف ندا hàrfi-nìdā, An interjection, or vocative particle.

نداس nAdAss, *s. t.* A ploughing, harrowing, and cleaning land after or during a fallow; ا—, —et, *v.a.* To clean (land) by ploughing, &c.

ندامت nèdāmèt, *s. a.* A feeling of regret, repentance, penitence.

ندبه nùdbé, *s. a.* A weeping and lamenting over the dead.

ندما nùdémā, *s. pl. a.* (*of* نديم nèdīm), Companions, associates, intimate friends. [companion.

نديم nèdīm, *s. a.* An intimate friend and

نذر nèzr, *s. a.* A vow; anything sacrificed or bestowed in consequence of a vow; ا—, —et, *v.a.* To vow, to sacrifice or bestow as a fulfilment of a vow.

نر nèr, *a. p.* Male.

نرخ nèrkh (nàrk), *s. p.* The officially-taxed price of commodities.

نرد nèrd, *s. p.* Backgammon.

نردبان nèrdibān (mèrdivèn), *s. p.* A ladder, steps, a staircase; نردبان باشى (mèrdivèn)-bAshi, The top of the stairs; نردبان اياغى (mèrdivèn)-àyaghi, The foot of the stairs.

نرده nèrdé? nèrédé? Where? In what place? In whatever place?

نركس nèrghiss, *s. p.* A marigold; a beautiful eye, the eye of a mistress.

نرم nèrm, *a. p.* Soft to the touch; easy in disposition, yielding.

نره nèré? *Turkish interrogative of place,* What place? What exact spot? What place soever; نره نك nèréning? Of what place? of what place soever; نره يه nèréyé, To what place? To whatever place; نره ده nèrédé, In what place? In whatever place; نره دن nèrédan? From what place? From whatever place; نره م nèrém? What part of my body? Whatever part of my body; نره مك nèréming? Of what part of my body? &c., نره سى nèréssi, What part or spot of it? نرهسنه nèréssinė? To what part of it? &c., &c.

نريمان nèrīmān, *s. p.* A champion, a hero.

نزار nìzār, *a. p.* Thin, slender, lean.

نزاع nìzā'', *s. a.* Altercation, dispute, quarrel; ا—, —et, *v.n.* To dispute, quarrel.

نزاكت nèzākèt, *s. a.* Politeness, delicacy of manners; delicacy of taste, smell, &c.

نزال nìzāl, *s. a.* A fighting, battle, combat.

نزد nèzd, *s. p.* The immediate vicinity or proximity of anything.

نزديك nèzdīk, *a. p.* Near.

نزع nèz'', *s. a.* A tearing up, out, or away; ا—, —et, *v.a.* To tear up, tear out, tear away; حالت النزع hālétu-'n-nèz'', The agony of death, the point of death.

نزل nùzul, *s. a.* Provisions; —امينى, nùzul-èmīni, *s. t.* The commissary-general of an army.

نزله nèzlé, *s. a.* A cold in the head.

نزول nùzūl, *s. a.* A descending, going or coming down; an alighting; a stroke of apoplexy or palsy; ا—, —et, *v.n.* To descend; to alight.

نزهت nùzhèt, *s. a.* The taking a stroll for pleasure; pleasure, recreation (either by strolling or sitting in pleasant places).

نسا nìssā, *s. a.* A woman; women in general; طائفهٔ نسا tā'ifè'i-nìssā, Womankind.

نساج nèsssāj, *s. a.* A weaver.

نساجت nìssājèt, *s. a.* The weaving art.

نساق nìssāk, *s. a.* A series, arrangement, order; يكنساق yèk-nìssāk, *a. p.* Uniform; regular.

نسائج nèssā'ij, *s. pl. a.* (*no sing.*), Textile fabrics, woven articles.

نسائم nèssā'im, *s. pl. a.* (*of* نسيم nèssīm), Airs, breezes.

نسب nèsseb, *s. a.* Extraction, birth, parentage; نسبى nèssébī (*fem.* نسبيه nèssébìyyė), *a. a.* Pertaining to extraction or parentage.

نسبت nìssbèt, *s. a.* (*pl.* انساب ènsāb), Relation; ratio, proportion; a logarithm; spite; ا—, —et, *v.n.* To act in spite; (*in stating a sum in the rule of three*) as; كنسبت kè-nìssbèt, so; نسبت الى ب كنسبت ج الى د nìssbèti-èlif-ìla-bē-kè-nìssbèti-jìm-ìla-dāl (The ratio of *a* to *b* (is) as the ratio of *c* to *d*), As *a* is to *b*, so is *c* to *d*; نسبت جيبيه nìssbèti-jèybìyyė, A log. sine; نسبت ظليه nìssbèti-zìllìyyė, A log. tangent; نسبةً nìssbétan, *ad. a.* In respect, in relation, in proportion; out of spite.

نسته nèsstė, *s. t.* A thing, anything, nothing in particular (*used in humming and haing*).

نسج nèssj, *s. a.* A weaving; a texture; ا—, —et, *v.a.* To weave.

نسخ nèsskh, *s. a.* An abolishing, annulling, abrogating; ا—, —et, *v.a.* To abolish, annul, abrogate; —, nùssākh, *s. pl. a.* (*of* نسخه nùsskha), Copies (of books or writings); —, nèssikh, *s. a.* The peculiar handwriting used in copying the Kur'an and most prose books in Turkey, Syria, and Arabia.

نسخه nüsskha, *s. a.* A copy of a book or writing; (misska) an amulet or charm in writing, much used in the East, sewn to the cap, or bound round various parts of the body.

نسر nèssr, *s. a.* A bird; an eagle.

نسرين nèssrīn, *s. a.* A kind of flower; كل نسرين ghyùlu-nèssrīn, *s. p.* A kind of flower.

نسق nèssàk, *s. a.* An order, row, series, succession.

نسل nèssl (nèssil), *s. a.* Progeny, race, posterity.

نسناس nèssnāss, *s. a.* A kind of ape; a satyr.

نسنه nèssnè, *s. t.* A thing.

نسوان nisswān, *s. pl. a.* (*of* نسا nissā), Women.

نسيان nissyān, *s. a.* A forgetting; oblivion, forgetfulness; ا—, —et, *v.a.* To forget.

نسيب nèssīb, *a. a.* Belonging to a distinguished family.

نسيم nèssīm, *s. a.* A gentle air, zephyr, breeze.

نشابه nüshshābè, *s. a.* A wooden arrow; an arrow.

نشابور Nìshābūr, *s. p.* The town of Nishabur, in Khorassan.

نشادر nìshādir, *s. p.* Sal ammoniac; ammonia; —روحى, nìshādir-rūhu, Spirit of ammonia, spirit of hartshorn, sal volatile.

نشاسته nìshāssta, *s. p.* Starch; wheat fecula, used in confectionary.

نشاط nìshāt, *s. a.* Mirth, joy.

نشان nìshān, *s. p.* A mark, sign, trace, signal of any kind; an index, indication; sign-post; beacon; a mark set up to shoot at, a target; a decoration, insignia of rank or of any order of knighthood; a pledge, token (given to a girl at a betrothal); the Sultan's cypher; imperial letters-patent bearing the cypher; a sear, cicatrice; نشانگاه nìshānghyāh, *s. p.* A sight (used for pointing guns); نشانلو nìshānli, *a. t.* Marked, bearing a mark; betrothed, affianced; نشانجى nìshānji, *s. t.* Former title of a high functionary of the Ottoman Government, a kind of High Chancellor, from whose office the imperial letters-patent, firmans, &c., were issued; —, nìshān, *a. p.* (*in composition*), Who or which sits; who or which causes to sit; which calms, composes, soothes; which recalls, calls to mind; خاطرنشان khātir-nìshān, *s. p.* Anything fixed on the mind, or on which the mind is fixed.

نشانده nìshāndè, *a. p.* Planted, set up, erected.

نشانه nìshānè, *s. p.* A mark, trace, vestige.

نشر nèshr, *s. a.* A spreading out or abroad, a scattering, dispersing; a resuscitation; ا—, —et, *v.a.* To spread out or about, to scatter, disperse; to publish; to resuscitate; حشرونشر hàshr-u-nèshr, The resurrection and gathering of the dead to judgment.

نشست nìshèsst, *s. p.* The act of sitting; أ—, —et, *v.n.* To sit; نشستگاه nìshèsstghyāh, *s. p.* A seat, place for sitting.

نشسته nìshèssté, *a. p.* Seated, sitting.

نشنيده nèshinīdé, *a. p.* Unheard of; who has not heard.

نشو nèshv, *s. a.* A growing, increasing, prospering; نشوو نما nèshv-u-nèmā, A growing and prospering; نشوونمابولمق nèshv-u-nèmā-bùlm*a*k, To grow and prosper.

نشوه nèshvé, *s. a.* The hilarity caused by any stimulant; نشوه‌بخش nèshvé-bàkhsh, *a. p.* Stimulating.

نشيب nìshīb, *s. p.* A descent of ground, a declivity; low ground.

نشأت nèsh'èt, *s. a.* A springing up, shooting, sprouting; a deriving one's origin; an origin; ا—, —et, *v.n.* To spring, originate.

نشيمن nèshīmèn, *s. p.* A company, society; نشيمنگاه nèshīmènghyāh, *s. p.* A place where people meet in society.

نشين nìshīn, *a. p.* Sitting, seated.

نشئه nèsh'é, *s. a.* The hilarity caused by wine or any stimulant.

نص nʌsss, *s. a.* An irrefragable divine [proof.

نصاب nìssāb, *s. a.* The exact degree or proportion which best suits anything; rank, degree.

نصارا *or* نصارى nʌssārà, *s. pl. a.* (*of* نصرانى nʌssrānī), Christians, Nazarenes.

نصائح nàssā'ih, *s. pl. a.* (*of* نصيحت nʌssīhʌt), Counsels, advices given.

نصب nʌssb, *s. a.* A setting up, erecting; an appointing to high office; ا—, —et, *v.a.* To set up, erect; to appoint; عزل‌ونصب "ʌzl-u-nʌssb, Appointment and dismissal.

نصر nʌssr, *s. a.* Aid, help, succour; victory; —, nʌssir, *s. t.* A wart, corn, or hard skin; عزنصره "àzz*a*-nʌssruhu, (God) whose aid be powerful! (*inscribed on Turkish coins*); نصرلنمق nʌssirl*a*nm*a*k, *v.n.* To form warts, corns, or hard skin.

نصرانى nʌssrānī (*fem.* نصرانيه nʌssrānìyyé), *s. a.* A Christian, a Nazarene; نصرانيت nʌssrānìyyèt, *s. a.* Christianity.

نصرت nùssrèt, *s. a.* God's aid and suc- [cour; victory.

نصف nìssf, *s. a.* A half; half-way; the middle; نصف‌دائره nìssf*i*-dā'ìré, A semicircle; نصف‌النهار nìssfu-'n-nìhār, Noon, mid-day; نصف‌الليل nìssfu-'l-lèyl, Midnight.

نصفت nʌssafèt, *s. a.* Justice, equity, conscientiousness.

نصل nàssl? (*Turkish interrogative and exclamative of quality or manner*), How? In what way? What sort? What kind? However, howsoever; how! نصل‌سن nàssl-sin? How are you? نصل‌ايدرايسه‌ايتسون nàssl-èdèr-issa-ètsin, Let him do in any way he can.

نصيب nʌssīb, *s. a.* Whatever falls to

one's lot ; a lot, fate ; ـــاو, nAssīb-ôl, *v.n.* To fall to one's lot.

نصيكت nAssīhât, *s. a.* Advice, counsel; ـــويرمك, —vèrmek, *v.n.* To give advice ; ـــا, —et, *v.a.* To counsel.

نضارت nAzārèt *or* nAdārèt, *s.a.* Brightness, freshness, beauty, bloom.

نطاق nìtāk, *s. a.* A belt, girdle, zone.

نطع nAt'', *s. a.* A chess-board or portable leather for chess or draughts.

نطفه nùtfÉ, *s. a.* Sperm, seminal fluid.

نطق nŭtk, *s. a.* The faculty of speech ; a set speech, an oration.

نطوق nàtūk, *a. a.* Facile in speech.

نظار nùzzàr, *s. pl. a.* (*of* ناظر nāzir), Spectators.

نظارت nAzārèt, *s.a.* A view, a spectacle; direction, supervision ; a ministry, department of state, ministerial office.

نظافت nAzāfèt, *s. a.* Cleanness, cleanliness.

نظام nìzĀm, *s. a.* Order, regularity, an arrangement ; a system ; a regulation, law, bye-law ; ـــجديد, nìzAm*i*-jèdīd (New system), Name given to the general system of government introduced into Turkey by Sultan Mahmud II. in 1826, upon the suppression of the Janissaries, particularly the employment of regularly - disciplined troops ; نظام عالم nìzĀmi-''ālEm (A means of the world's being governed in an orderly manner), One of the titles given in firmans to Pashas of the highest order ; ـــعسكرى, nìzām-''Asskéri, Regular troops ; نظامه كلمك nìzĀm*a*-ghÈlmek, *v.n.* To get in order, to be put to rights ; ـــويرمك, nìzĀm-vÈrmek, *v.n.* To put in order, to regulate ; نظامسز nìzĀms*i*z, *a. t.* Irregular, disordered, disorderly ; نظامسزلق nìzĀms*i*zl*i*k, *s. t.* Disorder, want of order.

نظائر nAzā'ir, *s. pl. a.* (*of* نظيره nAzīrÉ), Similar things, parallel things ; parodies, imitations, rival pieces of composition.

نظر nAzar, *s. a.* The sight ; a looking ; the effect of an evil eye ; favour, good graces, esteem, consideration ; ـــا, —et, *v.n.* To look ; نظراً nAzar*a*n, *ad. a.* In comparison ; in respect ; نظردكمسون nAzar-dà*gh*mass*i*n ! Let not the effect of the evil eye light upon it ! (*said plainly or satirically of anything one is called upon to admire, and in the sense of,* It is beautiful ; may God preserve it from evil !) نظردن دوشمك nAzard*a*n-dùshmek, *v.n.* To fall into disgrace, get out of favour.

نظره nAzar*a*, *s. a.* A single look.

نظم nAzm, *s. a.* Verse ; a versifying ; order, regularity ; ـــا, —et, *v.a.* To put into metre, to say or write in verse, to sing.

نظير nAzīr (*fem.* نظيره nAzīrÉ), *a. a.* Similar, like ; parallel ; بينظير bī-nAzīr (bī-nāzir), *a. p.* Peerless, unequalled ; capital, very good.

نظیره nAzīrÉ, *s. a.* Any piece of composition in prose or verse, or any anecdote, told or written in imitation of some other, as a parody to it, or with a view to outrival it in excellency.

نظیف nAzīf, *a. a.* Clean, cleanly.

نعال nì‘‘āl, *s. pl. a.* (*of* نعل nà‘‘l), Pattens, slippers (for going into the street); صفّ النعال sAffu-’n-nì‘‘āl, The place near the door where the shoes are left on entering a house or room.

نعام nà‘‘ām, *s. a.* An ostrich.

نعت nà‘‘t, *s. a.* A eulogistic poem in praise of Muhammed, always to be found occupying the second place in complete collections of poetry.

نعره nà‘‘ra, *s. a.* A great noise, roar, vociferation.

نعش nà‘‘sh, *s. a.* A bier or litter with a dead body; بنات النعش bìnātu-’n-nà‘‘sh, The stars of the Great Bear.

نعل nà‘‘l, *s. a.* A patten, a slipper for going out of doors with; (nAl) a horse-shoe; نعلین nà‘‘lèyn (nAlin), A pair of pattens (one patten); نعلبند nà‘‘l-bènd (nAlbAnt), *s. p.* A farrier; نعللمك nà‘‘llèmek (nAllamak), *v.a.* To shoe.

نعلچه nà‘‘lché (nAlcha), *s. p.* An iron heel with projections, used for boots or shoes to prevent slipping in walking.

نعم nà‘‘am, *ad. a.* Yes; very good; very well; —, nì‘‘àm, *s. pl. a.* (*of* نعمت nì‘‘mèt), Comforts, blessings, benefits; ولی النعم vèlìyyu-’n-nì‘‘àm, A benefactor.

نعما nà‘‘mā, *and* nū‘‘mà (*for* نعمی), *s. a.* Any goodness, benefit, favour.

نعمت nì‘‘mèt, *s. a.* A comfort, blessing, benefit from Providence.

نعمی nū‘‘mà, *s. a.* Any benefit or favour.

نعناع nà‘‘nā‘‘, نعنع nà‘‘nà‘‘, نعنعه nà‘‘na‘‘à (nànÉ), *s. a.* Mint; peppermint.

نعوت nū‘‘ūt, *s. pl. a.* (*of* نعت nà‘‘t), Eulogistic poems on Muhammed.

نعوذ بالله nà‘‘ūzu-bì-’llAh! (We take refuge in God!) God preserve us!

نعیم nà‘‘īm, *s. a.* The state of being in possession of every blessing; جنت نعیم jènnèti-nà‘‘īm, Name of one of the subdivisions of Paradise *or* one of the names of Paradise.

نغمه nàghma (nà*gh*ma), *s. a.* A vocal time, an air in vocal music.

نفاس nìfāss, *s. a.* The condition of a woman for forty days after childbirth.

نفاست nèfāssèt, *s. a.* Goodness, excellence, superiority (of quality), delicacy, richness.

نفاق nìfāk, *s. a.* Discord, disagreement.

نفائس nèfā’iss, *s. pl. a.* (*of* نفیسه néfīssÉ), Things excellent and esteemed, precious things, valuables, delicacies.

نفت nèft, *s. p.* Bitumen; نفت یاغی nèft-yà*ghi*, *s. t.* Naphtha; spirit of turpentine; نفتی nèftī, *a. a.* Of a green-black colour.

نفح nèfh, *s. a.* A diffusion (of odour);

a blowing (of the wind or with the mouth).

نفحه nèfha, s. a. A single breath of wind or of perfume; a blast; نفحة الفزع nèfhatu-'l-fèz", The first blast of the trump at the end of time, when all living creatures will die; نفحة البعث nèfhatu-'l-bà"ss, The second blast, when all the dead shall rise.

نفخ nèfkh, s. a. A blowing with the mouth; blowing an instrument.

نفر nèfer, s. a. An individual, a person; (*pl.* نفرات néférāt), A private soldier, common sailor. (*This word is generally used after a cardinal number when followed by any word signifying man,* and is then always in the singular; برنفركمسنه bìr-nèfer-kìmèssné, One person; بش نفرچاوش bèsh-nèfer-chàwush, Five sergeants).

نفرت nèfrèt, s. a., نفرين nèfrīn, s. p. Aversion, dislike, disgust; ا—, —et, v.n. To have a dislike, aversion, disgust.

نفس nèfss, s. a. The life; the soul; the flesh (biblically speaking), the passions; the sperm or seminal fluid; one's own self, essence, or individuality; the interior of a town or country, as distinguished from the environs or dependencies; —, nèfess, s. a. The breath; one inhalation; one exhalation; a peculiar miraculous power of the breath to cure diseases, &c., believed to be possessed by many persons; نفس اماره nèfsi-èmmārè, (The commanding soul or flesh) That state of the passions when they habitually control and compel the individual to obey their exigencies; نفس لوامه nèfsi-lèvwāmè, (The upbraiding soul) That state when the passions can be controlled, though they still strive to make their voice heard; نفس مطمئنه nèfsi-mùtma'ìnnè, (The peaceful soul) That state when the passions are totally subdued; نفس الامر nèfsu-'l-(èmir), The reality of any matter; فى نفس الامر fī-nèfsi-'l-(èmir), ad. a. In reality; بالنفس bī-'n-nèfss, ad. a. Personally; بالق نفسى bālìk-nèfsi, s.t. Spermaceti; بالق نفسى ياغى bālìk-nèfsi-yàghi, Sperm-oil; نفسنه اويمق nèfsina-ǚymak, v.n. To follow or submit to one's passions; نفسنى قيرمق nèfsini-kìrmak, v.n. To subdue one's passions, to spite them; نفس المق nèfess-ālmak, v.n. To breathe, respire, to inspire; to rest; repose one's self; to have a hole, or not to be air-tight; to get air; نفس ويرمك nèfess-vèrmek, v.n. To allow breathing-time; to give rest or respite; نفسنى طيشارى ويرمك nèfessini-dìshàri-vèrmek, To expire (in breathing), to breathe out; صوك نفس sòng-nèfess, The last breath; برنفس توتون bìr-nèfess-tùtun, A whiff, a puff (in smoking).

نفسانى nèfsānī, a. a. Pertaining to the flesh or passions, carnal; نفسانيت

nèfsānìyyèt, *s. a.* Spite, a grudge, enmity, ill-will.

نفط nèft, *s. a.* Bitumen; naphtha.

نفع nèf'', *s. a.* Utility, advantage, use, benefit.

نفقه nèfaka (nàfaka), *s. a.* The allowance due to a wife and children from the husband and father for maintenance.

نفوذ nùfūz, *s. a.* A penetrating through or into; a pervading; moral influence; نفوذ صاحبی nùfūz-sāhibi, A person of influence.

نفوس nùfūss, *s. pl. a.* (*of* نفس nèfss), Persons, individuals, souls; نفوس دفتری nùfūss-dèftèri, A statistical register of births and deaths.

نفی nèfy (nèfi), *s. a.* An exiling; exile; banishment; the making an expression negative; ا—, —et, *v.a.* To banish, exile; to make negative (in grammar).

نفیر nèfīr, *s. a.* An assembling of people for political purposes; نفیر عام nèfīri-''àmm, *s. a.* A general rising, a levy in mass; —, *s. p.* A fife or kind of trumpet; also the shrill note of the same.

نفیس nèfīss, *a. a.* Good, beautiful, sumptuous, delicious, precious.

نقاب nìkāb, *s. a.* A veil.

نقابت nìkābèt, *s. a.* The office of mayor or master over a class of men; نقابت الاشراف nìkābétu-'l-èshrāf, The office of superintendent over the enregistered descendants of Muhammed.

نقاره nàkārè (nàghara), *s. p.* A kettledrum; نقاره زن nàkārè-zèn, The beater of a kettle-drum.

نقاش nàkkāsh, *s. a.* One who embellishes with designs of any material, whether embroidery, paint, &c.; a house-painter.

نقاشت nìkāshèt, *s. a.* The embellisher's [or designer's art.

نقاط nìkāt, *s. pl. a.* (*of* نقطه nòkta), Dots, diacritical points.

نقاوت nàkāvèt, *s. a.* Purity, cleanness; the select of anything.

نقائص nàkā'iss, *s. pl. a.* (*of* نقیصه nàkīssa), Imperfections, defects.

نقائض nàkā'iz, *s. pl. a.* (*of* نقیضه nàkīza), Contradictory things or sayings.

نقب nàkb, *s. a.* A hole; a subterranean way or gallery; ا—, —et, *v.a.* To work a hole or a way through a wall or underground; to tap (a person for the dropsy); to pierce (ears or noses for rings).

نقد nàkd, *s. a.* Cash, hard coin, ready money; نقداً nàkdàn, *ad. a.* In or with ready money; نقدی nàkdī, *a. a.* Pertaining to cash or ready money.

نقدر nàkadar, *Turkish interrogative and exclamative of quantity and degree of quality*, How much? How many? How ...? How much soever; how many soever; how ... soever; نقدر كوزل nàkadar-ghyùzèl, How beautiful!

نقدينه nʌkdīné, *s. p.* Cash, ready money, hard coin.

نقرس nìkriss, *s. a.* The gout.

نقره nʊkra, *s. a.* Silver.

نقش nàksh, *s. a.* An embellishing with designs or portraitures, either as writing, painting, engraving, embroidery, &c.; a design, portraiture, figure; (nàghsh) embroidery; ا—, —et, *v.a.* To draw, paint, design, portray; to write; to engrave; نقش ايشلمك (nàghsh)-ìshlémek, To work in embroidery; نقشبند nàksh-bènd (nàkshibènd), *s. p.* An embellisher in portraitures; a writer; نقشبندى nàkshibèndī, *a. p.* Name of an order of dervishes.

نقصان nòksān, *s. a.* A deficiency; a defect, fault, imperfection; —, *a. t.* Deficient, imperfect.

نقض nʌkz, *s. a.* Destroying, demolishing, pulling down, pulling to pieces; a violating, violation, deviation from; —nìkss, *s. a.* The old materials of anything pulled to pieces; ا—, nʌkz-et, *v.a.* To demolish; to violate; نقض عهد nʌkzi-àhd, A violation of treaty; a breach of allegiance or of faith.

نقطه nòkta, *s. a.* A dot, a diacritical point of a letter; a point (in mathematics); نقطه لو nòktali, *a. t.* Dotted.

نقل nʌkl, *s. a.* A transporting from place to place, removing; a changing one's residence, moving; a relating, recounting; a transferring; ا—, —et, *v.a.* To transport; to transfer; to relate; —, *v.n.* To move or change one's residence; عقلاً ونقلاً "ʌklan-u--nʌklan, According to reason and according to tradition.

نقله nʌkala, *s. pl. a.* (*of* ناقل nʌkil), Relaters, reporters, narrators.

نقم nʌkam, *s. a.* Anger; hatred, malevolence; —, nìkàm, *s. pl. a.* (*of* نقمت nìkmèt), Angers; hatreds, vengeances. [vengeance.

نقمت nìkmèt, *s. a.* Anger; hatred;

نقوت nàkvet, *s. a.* The choice, best of anything. [pieces of money.

نقود nʊkūd, *s. pl. a.* (*of* نقد nʌkd), Coins,

نقوش nʊkūsh, *s. pl. a.* (*of* نقش nʌksh), Portraitures, designs, figures.

نقول nʊkūl, *s. pl. a.* (*of* نقل nʌkl), Relations, narrations.

نقيب nàkīb, *s. a.* A special magistrate over a class of people; نقيب الاشراف nàkību-'l-èshrāf, The chief or superintendant over the registered descendants of Muhammed.

نقير nàkīr, *a. a.* Few, little; نقير و قطمير nàkīr-u-kàtmīr, *ad. t.* Minutely.

نقيصه nàkīssa, *s. a.* A defect, imperfection; a fault; a vice.

نقيضه nàkīza, *s. a.* A contradiction, contradictory fact or assertion.

نك *ning, ning, nung, nung,* Turkish prepositional particle of possession for words ending in a vowel, answering to our *'s* or *of*; بابانك bʌbʌning,

Father's ; ددەنك dèdéning, Grandfather's ; توربينك tùrpunung, Of the rasp ; قوقونك kòkunung, Of the smell.

نكات nìkyāt, *s. pl. a.* (*of* نكته nùkté), Sayings of subtle wisdom.

نكاح nìkyāh, *s. a.* An affiancing, betrothing, marrying (a girl or woman to a husband) ; the dower agreed upon as payable by the husband to the wife ; نكاحلو nìkyāhli, *a. t.* Affianced, betrothed, married ; ا—, nìkyāh-et, *v.a.* To affiance, betroth, marry (to a husband) ; —باغلامق, nìkyāh-bāghlamak, —قيرمق, nìkyāh-kìrmak, *v.a.* To assign a dower (to a wife on marriage or betrothal) ; نكاح التنده nìkyāh-āltinda, نكاح تحتنده nìkyāh-tàhtinda, Under the matrimonial pact or obligation to a husband.

نكار nìghyār, *s. p.* Any design, figure ; writing ; a statue ; a pretty woman.

نكاشته nìghyāshté, *a. a.* Drawn, figured, painted ; written. [chastisement.

نكال nèkyāl, *s. a.* Punishment, exemplary

نكاه nìghyāh, *s. p.* A look, glance ; نكاهبان nìghyāhbān, نكاهدار nìghyāhdār, *s. p.* An overseer ; a guardian.

نكايت nìkyāyet, *s. a.* Slaughter, slaying, putting to the sword.

نكبت nèkbet (nìkbet), *s. a.* The being in bad circumstances, in poverty or in disgrace, fallen circumstances ; نكبتخانه nìkbet - khāné, *s. p.* The house of one in fallen circumstances.

نكته nùkté, *s. a.* A saw, a wise saying, a fine saying which contains some piece of subtle wisdom ; نكتەدان nùkté-dān, نكتەشناس nùkté-shìnāss, *s. p.* A person up to such sayings.

نكران nìghrān (nìghérān), *a. p.* Looking, regarding, expecting ; —او, nìghérān-òl, *v.n.* To look, regard, observe, contemplate ; to be expecting, looking for.

نكره nèkré, *s. a.* A funny story ; نكرەلو nèkréli, *a. t.* Funny, witty, amusing.

نكس ا nùkss-et, *v.n.* To return in form of a relapse (a disease).

نكول nùkyūl, *s. a.* A going from a promise or compact ; ا—, —et, *v.n.* To go back (from a promise or agreement).

نكون nìghyūn, *a. p.* Reversed ; سر نكونسر sèr-nìghyūn, نكون nìghyūn-sèr, نكونسار nìghyòn-sār, *a. p.* Head-downwards, topsy-turvy.

نكه nìghèh (*contr. from* نكاه nìghyāh), *s. p.* A look, glance ; نكهبان nìghèhbān, نكهدار nìghèhdār, *s. p.* A watcher, looker, guardian. [ring.

نكين nìghīn, *s. p.* A seal, signet, signet-

نم nèm, *s. p.* Moisture, humidity, damp, dampness ; نملو nèmli, *a. t.*, نمناك nèmnak (nèmlàk), *a. p.* Damp, moist, humid ; شبنم shèbnèm (night-damp), *s. p.* Dew ; نملتمك nèmlatmek, *v.a.* To damp, moisten ; نملنمك nèmlanmek, *v.n.* To become damp or moist, become moistened.

نما nèmā, *s. a.* A growing, flourishing; interest (on moneys); —, nùmā, *a. p.* (*in composition*), Who or which shows; رهنما rèh-numā, A guide, road-shower.

نماز nȦmȦz, *s. p.* The canonical prayer; — قيلمق nȦmȦz-kılmak, *v.n.* To perform a canonical prayer; صباح نمازی sàbȦh-nȦmȦzi, The prayer of day-dawn; اویله نمازی üylé-nȦmȦzi, The noon prayer; ایکندی نمازی ikindi-nȦmȦzi, The afternoon prayer; اخشام نمازی (Ȧksham)-nȦmȦzi, The prayer of sunset; یاتسی نمازی yàtsi-nȦmȦzi, The prayer of bed-time; (there are various other special prayers).

نمای nùmāy, *a. p.* (*in composition*), Who or which shows, points out.

نمایان nùmāyān, *a. p.* Evident, manifest, visible. [ance.

نمایش nùmāyish, *s. p.* Show, appear-

نماینده nùmāyendé, *a. p.* Who or which shows.

نمچه nèmché, نمسه nèmsé (lèmsé), Germany; نمچه‌لو nèmchéli, *s. t.* A German; نمچه‌جه nèmchéjé, *s. t.* The German language. [felt.

نمد nèmed, *s. p.* A felt carpet, piece of

نمدیده nèmdīdé, *a. p.* Suffused with tears, moist, watery (eye).

نمر nèmir, *s. a.* A leopard.

نمرود Nèmrūd, *s. p.* Nimrod; a king who is said to have cast Abraham into the fire.

نمق nèmk, *s. a.* A writing, penning; —, nùmika, *v. pass. a.* It was written (used in mentioning the place where firmans, &c., were written).

نمك nèmek, *s. p.* Salt; نمکبحرام nèmek-bé-hàrām (nèmek-bùhrām), *a. p.* Ungrateful, traitor to his salt.

نمکین nèmékīn, *a. p.* Salt, saltish; —, nèmghīn, *a. p.* Moist, damp, humid.

نمل nèml, *s. a.* An ant, emmet, pismire.

نمو nùmùvv, *s. a.* Growing, vegetating, flourishing. [Which shows.

نمود nùmūd, *a. p.* (*in composition*),

نمودار nùmūdār, *s. p.* A copy, example, sample, likeness. [model.

نمودج nùmūdèj, *s. p.* A sample; a

نموده nùmūdé, *a. p.* Who or which has shown, has been shown, or to whom (something) has been shown.

نموذج nùmūzèj, انموذج ènmūzèj, *s. a.* A sample; an exemplar, model.

نمون nùmūn, *a. p.* (*in composition*), Who or which shows.

نمونه nùmūné, *s. p.* A sample, pattern.

نميقه nèmīké, *s. a.* A note, a letter.

نميمه nèmīmé, *s. a.* Detraction, slander, secret calumny.

نك nèngh, *s. p.* Name, reputation; honour; —, nèning, *compt. t.* Of what? of whatsoever.

ننوه Nìnvé, Nineveh (the city of).

ننی nìnni, *s. t.* A nurse's or mother's ditty for making a child sleep.

نو nèv, *a. p.* New; fresh; recent; young; نوبنو nèv-bé-nèv, *ad. p.* Fresh and fresh, over and over again; نوبهار nèv-bàhār, *s. p.* Early spring;

نورسيده nèv-rèssīdé, *a. p.* Newly arrived; newly come to maturity; نوايين nèv-āyīn, *a. p.* Of recent introduction; نوجوان nèv-jùwān, *s. p.* A youth, young lad; نوخاسته nèv-khāsstè, *a. p.* Newly sprung up.

نوا nùwā, *s. p.* A note, tone; خوشنوا khòsh-nùwā, *a. p.* Sweet-toned; بينوا bì-nùwā, *a. p.* Noteless, whose note is never heard; poor, friendless, who has nothing to say for himself or anyone to speak for him.

نواب nùvwāb, *s. pl. a.* (*of* نائب nā'ib), Substitutes for judges. (*The original of our word* nabob.)

نواحى nèwāhī, *s. pl. a.* (*of* ناحيه nāhìyyé), Small districts, hundreds.

نواخت nùwākht, *s. p.* A caressing; ا—, —et, *v.a.* To caress.

نواخته nùwākhté, *a. p.* Caressed.

نوادر nèwādir, *s. pl. a.* (*of* نادره nādiré), Rare things.

نواده nùwādé, *s. p.* A grandchild.

نواز nùwāz, *a. p.* (*in composition*), Who caresses, makes much of.

نوازش nùwāzish, *s. p.* A caress, a treating with kindness and consideration.

نوازل nèwāzil, *s. pl. a.* (*of* نازله nāzilé), Misfortunes which happen; —, *s. t.* A cold in the head, a fluxion.

نوافل nèwāfil, *s. pl. a.* (*of* نافله nāfilé), Supererogatory prayers.

نوال nèwāl, *s. a.* A grace, blessing, gift, favour; عم نواله "àmmé-nèwāluhu! May His blessings be made general!

نواله nèwālé, *s. a.* A single meal or blessing.

نواهى nèwāhī, *s. pl. a.* (*of* نهى nèhy), Prohibitory commands, inhibitions.

نوائب nèwā'ib, *s. pl. a.* (*of* نائبه nā'ibé), Calamities which happen.

نوباوه nèv-bāvé, *s. p.* The first-fruits; early fruits or vegetables.

نوبت nèvbèt (nùbèt), *s. a.* A turn in succession, a go, a watch, a time; a keeping watch; an access, fit, attack (of fever, &c.); each one of five times a day, corresponding more or less with the hours of prayer, when formerly the band of eastern music used to be played in the courtyards of governors, &c.; —بكلمك, (nùbèt)-bèklémek, *v.n.* To keep a watch, be on guard, stand sentry; to wait for one's turn to come; نوبتجى nùbètji, *s. t.* A man on guard, a sentry; anyone on duty when it is taken in succession; —, Nūbèt, Nūbé, *s. a.* Nubia, part of Ethiopia.

نوبر nèv-bèr, *s. p.* Fresh and early fruit.

نوبى Nūbī, *s.* and *a. a.* Nubian, a Nubian.

نوجهله nè-vèjh-la, *comp. t.* In what way? In whatsoever way.

نوح Nūh, *s. a.* The patriarch Noah.

نوحه nèvha, *s. a.* A cry of lamentation.

نور nūr, *s. a.* Light, brightness; glory, aureole; كوزيمك نورى ghyùzumung-nūru! نورديدهم nūri-dīdem! Light of my eyes! —, nèvvéré! May (God) shed glory (around it)! نورين

nūrèyn, *s. a. dual.* The two glories, *i. e.* the two daughters of Muhammed who were married to Ossman: he is therefore styled ذو النورين zū-'n-nūrèyn.

نورانی nūrānī, *a. a.* Bright, shining, glorious and incorporeal.

نورد nèvèrd, *a. p. (in composition)*, Who traverses, travels over; رهنورد rèh--nèvèrd, *s. p.* A traveller on the road.

نورس nèv-rèss, نورسته nèv-rèssté, نو رسیده nèv-rèssīdé, *a. p.* Newly arrived.

نوروز nèv-rūz, *s. p.* The day of the vernal equinox, generally called نوروز سلطانی nèv-rūzi-sùltānī, *The royal new-(year's) day.*

نوش nūsh, *s. p.* A drinking; —, *a. p. (in composition)*, Who drinks; —ا, —et, *v. a.* To drink; to smoke (tobacco); نوشانوش nūsh-ā-nūsh, Draught upon draught, cup upon cup.

نوشت nùvìsht, *s. p.* Writing.

نوشته nùvìshté, *a. p.* Written; —, *s. p.* A writing; a thing written.

نوشنده nūshèndé, *s. p.* A drinker, one who drinks. [agreeable.

نوشين nūshīn, *a. p.* Sweet, pleasant,

نوع nèv'', *s. a.* A species, sort, kind, manner; نوع بشر nèv''i-bèshèr, Mankind, the human race.

نوکر nùkèr, *s. p.* A servant, servitor.

نول nèvl, *s. a.* نولون nàvlun, *s. t.* Freight-money for carriage by ship.

نوله n'-òla (*for* نه اوله nè-òla), *comp. t.* What would happen? What may it be?

نوم nèvm, *s. a.* Sleep.

نومرو nùméro, نومره nùméra, *s. t. (French)*, Number; نومرو بر nùméro--bìr, Number one. [desponding.

نوميد nūmīd, *a. p.* Hopeless, despairing,

نون nūn, *s. a.* Name of the letter ن; a fish; ذوالنون zū-'n-nūn, Lord of the fish, *i. e.* Jonas.

نوند nèvend, *s. p.* A messenger, courier.

نوه nèvé, *s. p.* A grandson.

نويس nùwīss, *a. p. (in composition)*, نويسنده nùwīssèndé, *s. p.* Who writes, a writer; وقعه‌نويس vwàk''à-nùwīss, *s. p.* A chronicler; the official writer of the chronicles of the times at the seat of government.

نه nè, *ad. t.* Neither, nor; —, *Turkish general interrogative of matter*, What? whatever, whatsoever; (N.B. *The final* ه *being merely necessary when the word stands alone, it is generally suppressed in compound words*) ننك nèning, Of what? of whatever; نيه nèyé, To what? for what? نيچون nìchin (*for* نه ايچون) Why? What for? نره nèré (*for* نه اره) What place? ندرلو nè--(turlu), What kind? نه‌ايسه nè-issa, Whatever it may be; نه‌حال ايسه nè-hāl-issa, Never mind in what way; ندن nèdan? Why? From what (cause)? نه دكلو nè-dìnglu? What sort (obsolete); نه‌زمان nè-zàmān? نه‌وقت nè-wàkit? When? (At) what time? نه‌سی‌وار nèssi-vār? What has it? What is the matter with it? Whatever he has, whatever he may have; نه‌کوزل nè-ghyùzèl, How beautiful; how nice; how well that will be; نه‌لازم nè-lāzim, What is the use? نه‌لازم کلور nè-lāzim-ghèlir? What will have to be done? What will it be necessary to do? نه‌دیمك nè-demek? نه‌دیمك‌استر nè-demek-isstır? What does that mean? —, nùh, a. p. Nine; نهم nùhum, نهمین nùhumīn, a. p. The ninth.

نهاد nìhād, s. p. Nature, natural constitution, disposition, character; —, a. p. (*in composition*), Who places; which is placed; نیك‌نهاد nīk-nìhād, a. p. Of a good disposition; بدنهاد bèd-nìhād, a. p. Of a bad disposition; پیش‌نهاد pīsh-nìhād, a. p. Placed before; —, s. p. What one places before one as a model, a law, a custom to be followed.

نهاده nìhādé, a. p. Placed, put.

نهار nàhār, s. a. The day, day-time; لیل‌ونهار lèyl-u-nàhār, Day and night.

نهاق nìhāk, s. a. An ass's braying.

نهال nìhāl, s. a. A young shoot; a young plant or tree. [secret.

نهان nìhān, نهانی nìhānī, a. p. Hidden,

نهایت nìhāyet, s. a. The extremity, extreme limit, the end; بی‌نهایه bī-nìhāyé, a. p. بلا نهایه bìlā-nìhāyé, a. a. Endless; الی‌غیرالنهایه ìlà-ghàyri-'n-nìhāyé, ad. a. On and on without end.

نهب nèhb, s. a. A plundering, taking as pillage or booty; ا—, —et, v.a. To seize as booty, to plunder (property).

نهج nèhj, s. a. A road, path, way.

نهر nèhr (nèhir), s. a. A river.

نهضت nèhzat, s. a. A setting out, starting, marching; ا—, —et, v.n. To set out, to start, to march.

نهفته nìhùfté, a. p. Hidden, concealed.

نهم nùhum, نهمین nùhumīn, a. p. The ninth. [sword; a pen.

نهنك nèhèngh, s. p. A crocodile; a

نهی nèhy, s. a. A prohibiting, inhibiting, forbidding; a negative; ا—, —et, v.a. To prohibit, inhibit, forbid; to negative (in grammar); نهی‌الحاضر nèhyu-'l-hāzir, A negative verb in the second person of the imperative; نهی‌الغائب nèhyu-'l-ghā'ib, A negative verb in the third person imperative.

نهیق nèhīk, s. a. An ass's braying.

نی nèy (*contr. from* نای nāy), s. p. A reed, cane, or bamboo; a flute.

نیابت nìyābet, s. a. The place and functions of a نائب nā'ib, or substitute of a judge.

نیاز nìyāz, s. p. A prayer, request; ا—, —et, v.a. To request; بی‌نیاز bī-nìyāz, a. p. Who never makes or has occasion to make a request; نیازکار nìyāzkyār, نیازمند nìyāzmènd, s. p. A petitioner.

نیام nìyyām, s. p. A sheath, scabbard.

نیت nìyyèt, s. a. Intent, design, fixed purpose; ا—, —et, v.a. To intend, to resolve, to decide. [ner as.

نیته‌کم nītékim, ad. t. As, in like man-

نيچون nìchin ? *Turkish interrogative of cause, reason, motive, purpose,* Why? What for?

نيجه nïjé, *Turkish interrogative of condition or manner,* How? —, *a. t.* How much; how many; نيجه‌سن nïjé-sin? How are you? نيجه‌ادم‌واردركه nïjé-àdam-vàr-dir-ki . . . , How many men there are who . . . .

نير nèyyir, *s. a.* The sun or moon; نيرين nèyyirèyn, *s. a. dual.* The sun and moon, the two lights. [flames.

نيران nīrān, *s. pl. a.* (*of* نار nār), Fires,

نيرو nīrū, *s. p.* Strength; نيرومند nīrū-mènd, *a. p.* Strong.

نيزه nīzé, *s. p.* A dart, javelin.

نيس Nìss, *s. t.* Nice (town of, ni France).

نيسان nīssān, *s. a.* The Syro-Roman month of April.

نيست nīsst, *a. p.* Non-existent; نيست وبود nīsst-u-būd, Existent and non-existent; نيستى nīsstī, *s. p.* Non-existence, annihilation, nothingness.

نيش nīsh, *s. p.* A sting; a thorn, prickle; —, *s. t.* The town of Nish, in Servia.

نيشتر nīshtèr (nèshter), *s. p.* A lancet.

نيك nīk, نيكو nīghyū, *a. p.* Good.

نيكبولى Nìghèboli, *s. t.* Nicopolis (the town of).

نيل nèyl, *s. a.* The obtaining or attaining (what one desired); —, نيل nīl, *s. p.* Woad; indigo; —, *s. a.* The river Nile; نيلفام nīl-fām, نيلكون nīl-ghyūn, *a. p.* Blue.

نيلر nèyler (*for* نه‌ايلر nè-èyler)? What does, will, or can he do? نيلسون (*for* نه‌ايلسون nè-èyléssin)? What may or shall he do, or is he to do?

نيلوفر nīlufèr, *s. p.* The water-lily.

نيم nīm, *s.* and *a. p.* Half. [(half-body).

نيمتن nīmtèn (mintan), *s. p.* A jacket

نيه nèyé? *comp. t.* To what? For what? To whatever; for whatever.

نيورق Niūyòrk, *s. t.* New York (town of).

نيوقاستل Niūkàstel, *s. t.* Newcastle (town of).

و

و vwāw (vwòw). Twenty-ninth letter of the Turkish alphabet, being sometimes a vowel, and sometimes a consonant. As a vowel, it has each of the five values of o, u, ʊ, *u*; and as a consonant it is generally a pure *v*, often a combined sound of *v* followed by or ending in *w*, and sometimes a pure *w*. In chronograms and astronomical tables its numerical value is 6.

و vè, *c. a.* And. (*N.B.* Placed between braces of synonymous words, or between braces of words signifying different or contrary things, but which nature or the mind is accustomed to couple together, this conjunction becomes a vowel, and takes the sound of u *or* ʊ according as the preceding word of the brace is soft or hard; ليل‌ونهار lèyl-u-nàhār, Day and night;

باى وكدا bāy-u-ghèdā, Rich and poor; صلح وصلاح sùlh-u-sAlāh, Peace and concord); —, *pr. a. of asseveration,* By; والله vwA-'llāhi, By God.

وا vwā, Persian particle placed sometimes before a few words denotes a *backward motion,* or sometimes a *recurrence,* and may therefore mean *back,* or *again;* —, *int. a.* O! Oh! Alas!

وابسته vwā-bèssté, *a. p.* Tied back, attached; dependant.

واپسين vwā-pèssīn, *a. p.* The last, the hindmost. [steamboat.

واپور vàpor, *s. t.* (*Italian*), A steamer,

واجب vwājib, *a. a.* Due, incumbent, expedient, right, necessary; واجب الادا vwājibu-'l-èdā, Necessary to be paid; واجب الاذعان vwājibu-'l-iz''ān, Necessary to be obeyed.

واحد vwāhid, *a. a.* One, sole, alone; الواحد èl-vwāhid, *s. a.* The only God; واحد العصر vwāhidu-'l-''Assr, The phœnix of the age; واحدا بعد واحد vwāhidan-bà''da-vwāhidin, *ad. a.* One by one, one after another.

واخ wākh, *int. t.* O dear! Alas!

وادى vwādī, *s. a.* A valley; a stream, river, rivulet; a mode, style, manner of expression, or general sense of a writing. (*Origin of the word* "oasis.")

وار vwār, *a. t.* Existing, in being; present in person; —او, —ōl, *v.n.* To exist, to be; —, *or* واردر vwàr-dir, Exists, is, are; there exists, there is, there are. *If preceded by a noun or pronoun in the genitive, or by a possessive pronoun, this takes the incidental meaning of possession, and may be translated by the verb* to have; but it is as glaring an error as can by any possibility be conceived to call this word an impersonal verb in any case whatever: we may, according to the exigencies of our language, translate it *and some other word or words in the sentence* by our verb *to be* or *to have;* still that does not affect the essence of the original Turkish adjective; كتابم وار kìtAbim-vwàr, A book exists belonging to me, I have or possess a book; بابك وارمى bAbAng-vwàr-mi? Hast thou a father? Does there exist a father belonging to thee? وار يوق vwàr-yòk, Existing, but so little as to be accounted as not existing; ادمك وارى يوغى Adaming-vwàri--yòghu, All that a man has, *and something else besides;* واريمى يوغمى فدا ايتدم vwàrimi-yòghumu-fèdā--ètdim, I have sacrificed, forsaken, or given up all that I possessed, everything belonging to me; واريوق نه ايسه vwàr-yòk-nè-issa, Be it that there is, be it that there is not, that is as it may be; —, vār, *a. p.* (*in composition*), Like, resembling, after the form or manner of; پروانه وار pèrwāné-vār, *a. p.* Like a moth, after the manner of a moth.

وارث vwāriss, *s. a.* An inheritor, one

who has received his inheritance, or who has a right to receive it.

وارد vwārid, *a. a.* Who arrives; who attains; which is true, pertinent, applicable; which comes to one's knowledge; واردات vwāridāt, *s. pl. a.* Income, revenue (as composed of many items).

وارسته vwā-rèsstě, *a. p.* Free, exempt.

وارلق vwàrlĭk, *s. t.* Possessions, property, wealth, riches.

وارمق vwàrmak (*aor.* وارر vwàrir), *v.n.* To arrive (at a distant place), to reach; to go on further; to go close on; to go to; واردقجه vwàrdĭkja, وارەرق vwàrarak, وارەوارە vwàra-vwàra, *gerunds,* By degrees, the further it goes; —قوجەيە kòjaya-vwàrmak, To get married, to go to a husband.

وارنه Vàrna, *s. t.* Varna (town of).

واروش vwàrūsh (vwàrish), *s. t.* The suburb of a large town.

وارون vwārūn, *a. p.* Contrary, inverse, wrong; unlucky.

وارە vwārě, واری vwārī, *Persian particle placed at the end of a few words and signifying,* in order of; صرەواری sìra-vwārī, In a row, in succession.

واریت vwārìyyèt, *s. a.* (from *t.* وار vwàr), Possessions, riches, wealth; واریتلو vwārìyyètli, *a. t.* Rich, wealthy.

واریل vàril, *s. t.* A cask, a barrel, a keg; واریلجی vàrilji, *s. t.* A cooper.

واریوس vwāriyoss, *s. t.* (*Greek βαρυος*), A heavy sledge-hammer.

واز vwāz *or* wāz, *a. p.* Open, pushed back; *ad. p.* (*as a particle*), Back; again; وازکچمك vwāz-ghèchmek (*sometimes* وازکلمك vwāz-ghèlmek), *v.n.* To desist, leave off; to relinquish.

واسطه vwāssita, *s. a.* A medium, a means; intervention, mediation.

واسع vwāssi'', *a. a.* Spacious, extensive.

واصف wāssif, *s. a.* One who describes the qualities, who praises the good qualities of any person or thing; a qualifying adjective.

واصل wāssil, *a. a.* Arriving, reaching; attaining; joining (things together); —او, —òl, *v.n.* To arrive; to reach; to attain; ا—, —et, *v.a.* To join together.

واصی vwāssī, *s. a.* A testator.

واضح vwāzih, *a. a.* Evident, manifest, plain, clear.

واضع vwāzi'', *s. a.* Who puts, places; who makes or creates; واضع الامضا vwāzi''-'l-ìmzā, The (under)signed, he who signs his name.

واعظ vwā''iz, *s. a.* A preacher (title of a special functionary in a mosque).

وافتیز wàftiz, *s. t.* (*Greek*), Baptism; ا—, —et, *v.a.* To baptize.

وافد wāfid, *a. a.* Arriving.

وافر wāfir, *a. a.* Numerous, much, many.

وافی wāfī, *a. a.* Sufficient, ample.

واقع vwāki'', *a. a.* Which falls; which befalls, happens; which is, lies, is placed, is situated; which is real; —, *s. a.* The reality as it happens; —او, —ȯl, *v.n.* To happen, befall, betide, come to pass; to be, lie, be situated; واقع حال vwākiʿ'i-hāl, The truth of the matter, the reality of the circumstance; واقعا vwākiʿ'ā, *ad. a.* Truly, really, in fact.

واقف wākif, *a. a.* Aware, informed; who stops, stands still; who waits; who places property in mortmain or entails an estate; —او, —ȯl, *v.n.* To be or become aware, informed.

والا vwālā, *a. p.* High, elevated, exalted; —, vè-illā, *ad. a.* Otherwise, or if not, and if not.

والد vwālid, *s. a.* A father, a male parent; والده wālidé, *s. a.* A mother, a female parent; والدین vwālidèyn, *s. a. dual.* Both parents, father and mother; والده سلطان wālidé-sùltān, The mother of the reigning Sultan, who is an officially recognised personage in the Ottoman Court.

واله vwālih, *a. a.* Crazy, beside himself.

والی wālī, *s. a.* A governor-general. (This title is given to the Pasha of Egypt, and of Tripoli, to the Bey (as Europeans persist in calling him) of Tunis, and to the Dey (also so mis-named by Europeans) of Algiers, in exactly the same way as it is applied to the other governors-general of provinces).

وام vwām, *s. p.* Debt; وامخواه vwām-khāh, *s. p.* A creditor; وامدار vwām-dār, *s. p.* A debtor.

وامانده vwā-mändé, *a. a.* Remained behind.

وامق vwāmik, *s. a.* A passionate lover.

وانی vwānī, *a. a.* Fatigued, tired, lazy.

واو vwàw, *s. a.* Name of the letter و.

واویلا vwā-vèylā, *int. a.* O! Oh! Alas!

واه vwāh, *int. p.* O! Oh! Alas!

واهب vwāhib, *s. a.* (God) the giver of good things.

واهم vwāhim, *a. a.* Fearing, redoubting; fancying; قوت واهمه kùvvéti-vwāhimé, The creative faculty of the imagination.

واهن vwāhin, *a. a.* Feeble, weak.

واهی vwāhī, *a. a.* Baseless, unfounded.

وای vwāy, wāy, *int. t.* Holloa! Oh! Alas! وای باشمه vwāy-bàshima! Oh! the misfortune that has befallen me! (An alas for my head!)

وایه vwāyé, *s. p.* A share in any good thing; وایه دار vwāyédār, *s. p.* A sharer, participator; —او, vwāyédār-ȯl, *v.n.* To participate, share.

وبا vwèbā, *s. a.* An epidemic; the plague; the cholera. [punishment.

وبال vwèbāl, *s. a.* A crime, fault, sin; وبالت vwèbālet, *s. a.* Dangerousness, unwholesomeness, likeliness to lead to unpleasant consequences.

وبر vèbér, *s. a.* Hair of animals of which thread, string, cloth, and tents are made; اهل وبر èhli-vèbér, People who dwell in hair tents, nomades.

وتد vwèted, *s. a.* A tent-peg; a stake;

name of two kinds of elements which go to the formation of a *foot* in Arabic prosody.

وتر vwètɪr, *s. a.* The string of a bow; the chord of an arc; the diameter of a rectangular figure; the hypothenuse of a right-angled triangle; the side (of a triangle) which subtends an angle; —, vwìtr, *s. a.* A special voluntary prayer performed in addition to the five canonical.

وتيره vètīrɛ́, *s. a.* A road, path, way; a mode, manner.

وثاق vìssāk, *s. a.* A tent-rope; a rope or bond of any kind; a pact, compact.

وثائق vwèssāʿik, *s. pl. a.* (*of* وثيقه vwèssīkɛ́), Trustworthy things, assurances, securities; letters, documents.

وثبات vwèssébāt, *s. pl. a.* Assaults, attacks, flyings at. [cerity.

وثوق vwùssūk, *s. a.* Confidence; sin-

وثيق vwèssīk (*fem.* وثيقه vwèssīka), *a. a.* Firm; sincere; trustworthy.

وثيقه vwèssīka, *s. a.* A letter, a document that may be relied on.

وجاع vìjāʿʿ, *s. pl. a.* (*of* وجع vèjàʿʿ), Pains, aches.

وجاه vìjāh, *s. a.* The being face to face; وجاهاً vìjāhan, *ad. a.* Face to face.

وجاهت vèjāhèt, *s. a.* Beauty, comeliness; appositeness; fitness, seemliness.

وجد vèjd, وجدان vìjdān, *s. a.* Ecstasy, ecstatic rapture (of saints).

وجع vèjàʿʿ, *s. a.* A pain; an ache.

وجوب vwùjūb, *s. a.* The being due, incumbent, necessary, right, proper.

وجود vwùjūd, *s. a.* Existence, being; the body.

وجوه vwùjūh, *s. pl. a.* (*of* وجه wèjh), Faces; sides; considerations; ways, modes, manners; the principal people of a town, the notables; وجوه ايله vwùjūh-ila, *ad. t.* On many accounts, for many reasons, in many ways; من كل الوجوه mìn-kyùlli-'l-vwùjūh, *ad. a.* In every way.

وجه vwèj, wèjh (vwèjih), *s. a.* A face; a side; a surface; a way, mode, manner; بروجه bɛr-wèjh, *pr. p.*, على وجه ʿʿàlà-vèjh (followed by a noun with the definite article ال), *pr. a.* As, by way of; بروجه تفصيل bɛr-wèjhi-tʌfsīl, *ad. p.*, على وجه التفصيل ʿʿàlà-wèjhi-'t-tʌfsīl, *ad. a.* In detail, in a detailed manner; وجهاً من الوجوه vwèjhan-mìné-'l-vwùjūh, *ad. a.* In some one way or other; (with a negative), in no way whatever. [rection.

وجهه vwèjhɛ́, *s. a.* A side, quarter, di-

وجيع vèjīʿʿ, *a. a.* Painful.

وجيه vwèjīh, *a. a.* Beautiful, comely; apposite, fitting, seemly.

وحدانى vwàhdānī, *a. a.* Pertaining to the sole God; وحدانيت vwàhdānìyyèt, *s.a.* The divine quality of being one only God.

وحدت vwàhdèt, *s. a.* The general quality of being alone or unique.

وحش vwàhsh, *s. a.* The desert, wilderness; (*pl.* وحوش vwùhūsh), A wild animal; وحشى vwàhshī, *a. a.* Wild; avoiding the presence of man; barbarous; وحشيت vwàhshìyyèt, *s. a.* Wildness.

وحشت vwàhshet, *s. a.* Wildness, solitude (of places), voidness of man's presence; barbarity.

وحوش vwùhūsh, *s. pl. a.* Wild animals.

وحى vwàhy, *s. a.* Inspiration, revelation; امين الوحى èmīnu-'l-vwàhy, The angel Gabriel; كاتب الوحى kyātibu--'l-vwàhy, Ossman, the third Caliph, as having been Muhammed's secretary in reducing the revelations of the Kur'ān to writing.

وحيد vwàhīd, *s. a.* A unique, sole, solitary thing or person (as a phœnix).

وخامت vwàkhāmèt, *s. a.* Unwholesomeness of air or food.

وخيم vwàkhīm, *a. a.* Unwholesome, insalubrious, hurtful.

ود vidd, وداد vèdād, *s. a.* Love, affection.

وداع vwèdā'', *s. a.* A committing one to God's keeping; an adieu; a bidding farewell; —ا, —et, *v.n.* To commit to God, to take leave, to say good-bye, to bid farewell; وداعلشمك vwèdā''-lèshmek, *v.n. recip.* To bid each other farewell, commit each other to God's keeping.

ودائع vwèdā'i'', *s. pl. a.* (*of* وديعه vwèdī''*a*), Trusts, things committed to one's keeping.

ودود vèdūd, *a. a.* A loving, affectionate friend; God the loving friend of all.

وديعه vwèdī''*a*, *s. a.* A trust, anything committed to one's keeping; وديعةالله vwèdī''*a*tu-'llāh, A trust committed to one's care by God.

ودين Wìddin, *s. t.* Widdin (town of).

ور vèr (*contr. from* وار vār), *Persian termination signifying* a possessor; بهره‌ور bèhrévèr, A participator, one who has a share or part; —, (*for* بر bèr), Who carries, carries out; رهور rèh-vèr, A guide; (*for* واكر vè--èghèr), *c. p.* And if.

ورا vèrā, *s. a.* The back or hind part of anything; the space behind anything; the breech; the anus; وراده vèrād*a*, *ad. t.* Behind, in the space further back; ورايه vèrāy*a*, Behind, to the space further back; وراسنده vèrās-sind*a*, Behind him, her, it.

وراثت vìrāssèt (vèrāssèt), *s. a.* The inheriting, entering into possession of an inheritance; an inheritance. [Heirs.

ورثه vèréssé, *s. pl. a.* (*of* وارث vwāriss),

ورد vèrd, *s. a.* A rose; —, vìrd, *s. a.* Any portion of scripture or other reading which a person continually recites.

ورزش vèrzish, *s. p.* An effort, exertion, diligent application. [fearingness.

ورع vèrà'', *s. a.* Piety, devotion, God-

ورق vèr*a*k (wàr*a*k), *s. a.* A leaf (of a tree or book); leaf brass, false gold-

ورقه vèrak*a*, *s. a.* One leaf. [leaf.

ورم vèrem, *s. a.* Phthisis, consumption,

disease of the lungs; any consuming, debilitating complaint.

ورود vwùrūd, *s. a.* Arrival, coming; ا—, —et, *v.n.* To arrive, come.

ورید vèrīd (*and* حبل الورید hàblu-'l--vèrīd), *s. a.* The jugular vein.

وزارت vìzāret (vèzārèt), *s. a.* The functions and quality of vizir, viziriate; وزارت عظمی vìzārèti-"ùzmà, The Grand-Viziriate.

وزان vèzān, *a. p.* Blowing, which blows (wind); —او, —ōl, *v.n.* To blow (the wind).

وزر vìzr, *s. a.* A burden, load.

وزرا vùzérā, *s. pl. a.* (*of* وزیر vèzīr), Viziers, ministers of state.

وزن vwèzn, *s. a.* A weighing; a weight; the weight (of anything); the metre, measure (of a verse), scansion; ا—, —et, *v.a.* To weigh.

وزنه vwèzné, *s. a.* A balance; a priming-flask; وزنه‌جی vwèznéji, *s. t.*, وزنه‌دار vwèznédàr, *s. p.* A person charged with examining the weight of things.

وزیر vèzīr, *s. a.* A minister of state, one *charged with the burden* of public affairs; a pasha of the lowest subdivision of the highest class; وزیر اعظم vèzīri-à"zàm, The Grand-Vizier.

وساده vìssādé, *s. a.* A pillow, cushion.

وساطت vèssātèt, *s. a.* Intervention, medium, instrumentality.

وساوس vèssāviss, *s. pl. a.* (*of* وسوسه vwèssvéssé), Fears, alarms, anxieties; evil suggestions, infernal whisperings.

وسائد vèssā'id, *s. pl. a.* (*of* وساده vìssādé), Pillows, cushions.

وسائل vèssā'il, *s. pl. a.* (*of* وسیله vwèssīlé), Pretexts, excuses; means, occasion (for doing something).

وسخ vwèssakh, *s. a.* Filth, dirt, muck.

وسط vwàssat, *s. a.* The middle; the midst; —, *a. a.* Middling.

وسطا *or* وسطی vwùsstà, *a. a. fem.* (*of* اوسط), Middle; middling.

وسع vwùss", *s. a.* Ability, capacity, capability.

وسعت vwùss"àt, *s. a.* Spaciousness, extensiveness; space, extent; ability, extent (of pecuniary means).

وسواس vwèssvāss, *s. a.* The devil; a whisperer or suggester of evil thoughts.

وسوسه vwèssvéssé, *s. a.* An evil thought; an anxious thought, fear, care.

وسیع vwèssī", *a. a.* Spacious, extensive.

وسیله vwèssīlé, *s. a.* A means, a favourable conjuncture, opportunity, or occasion; a pretext or excuse (for doing something).

وش vèsh, *Persian particle added to words, and indicating* similarity; لاله‌وش lālé-vèsh, *a. a.* Tulip-like.

وشاح vìshāh, *s. a.* A girdle, belt, zone, baldrick.

وشاق *or* وشق vwàshak, *s. t.* A lynx or ounce (of which the fur is much esteemed).

وشناب vìshnāb, *s. t.* Syrup of morella cherries.

وشنه vìshné, *s. t.* The morella cherry; وشنه چوروکی vìshné-chùrughu, *a. a.*

The colour of a decayed morella cherry, a maroon colour.

وصاف vwàssāf, *s. a.* One who praises or describes much or well.

وصال vwìssāl, *s. a.* Union, junction; meeting, interview, tête-à-tête with one's beloved.

وصايا vwàssāyā, *s. pl. a.* (*of* وصيت vwàssìyyèt), Recommendations, exhortations, precepts, commandments.

وصايت vwìssāyet, *s. a.* Making a testament; a testament; a mandate; ا—, —et, *v.a.* To recommend, exhort; to make a testament.

وصف wàssf, *s. a.* A describing, enumerating the qualities, especially the good qualities, speaking well of, praising; an adjective; ا—, —et, *v.a.* To enumerate the qualities; to qualify with an adjective; to praise; وصف تركيبى wàssfī-tèrkībī, A compound epithet or adjective.

وصل vwàssl, *s. a.* A joining; name of the sign ــٓ, placed over the ا or ل of the definite Arabic article ال, thus آل, when the article is to be passed over in the pronunciation and the following letter doubled; بالصرور, read bì-'z-zàrūr; ا—, vwàssl-et, *v.a.* To join together.

وصلت vwùsslèt, *s. a.* A meeting, interview, tête-à-tête, bodily or carnal union with one's beloved.

وصول vwùssūl, *s. a.* Arrival, junction; —بولمق, vwùssūl-bùlmak, *v.n.* To arrive, to effect one's junction.

وصى vwàssī, *s. a.* A guardian to an orphan.

وصيت vwàssìyyèt, *s. a.* The making a testamentary bequest; a testamentary bequest; a recommendatory piece of advice; ا—, —et, *v.a.* To bequeath.

وضاعت vwàzā‘‘àt, *s. a.* Humility.

وضع vwàz‘‘, *s. a.* A placing, putting, laying, arranging; a making; a creating; a pose, gesture, attitude; a piece of conduct, an act; ا—, —et, *v.a.* To place, put, lay, arrange, make, create; وضع حمل ا vwàz‘‘i-hàml-et, *v.n.* To give birth, be confined, bring forth, be put to bed.

وضوٕ vwùz‘‘, *s. a.* The lesser or partial ablution, called also آبدست àbdesst.

وضوح vwùzūh, *s. a.* Clearness, plainness, being evident, manifest.

وضيح vwàzīh, *a. a.* Clear, plain, evident, manifest.

وضيع vwàzī‘‘, *a. a.* Low; humble.

وطن vwàtan, *s. a.* One's country, birthplace, domicile; حب الوطن hùbbu-'l-vwàtan, Love of country, patriotism; وطن غيرتى vwàtan-ghàyréti, Patriotism.

وطى (*for* وطٔ) vwàty, *s. a.* A treading under foot; a having carnal connection with a female; ا—, —et, *v.a.* To tread; to have connexion.

وظائف wàzā'if, *s. pl. a.* (*of* وظيفه

wAzīfé), Matters which concern anyone; duties, concerns; pay, salaries.

وظوب vwŭzūb, *s. a.* Assiduity, perseverance.

وظيفه wAzīfé, *s. a.* A matter which concerns anyone; a concern, duty, business; pay, salary; وظيفه خوار wAzīfé-khòr, وظيفه دار wAzīfé-dār, *s. p.* One who is in receipt of pay or salary.

وعد vwà''d, *s. a.* A promising; a promise; ا—, —et, *v.a.* To promise.

وعده vwà''dé, *s. a.* A term assigned, a set time given; وعده سی کلمش vwà''déssi-ghèlmish, Its term is come; of which the term is come, due.

وعظ vwà''z, *s. a.* An admonitory predication, a sermon; ا—, —et, *v.n.* To preach a sermon, deliver an admonitory discourse.

وغا wàghā, *s. p.* Battle, combat, fight.

وفا wèfā, *s. a.* Fidelity to an engagement, to a requirement, to a debt; ا—, —et, *v.n.* To remain faithful, act with fidelity; وفادار wèfādār, *a. p.* Faithful; بیوفا bī-wèfā, *a. p.* Faithless.

وفات wèfāt, *s. a.* Death, decease; ا—, —et, *v.n.* To die, to decease.

وفاق wìfāk, *s. a.* Concord, unanimity, agreement. [coming.

وفد wèfd, *s. a.* An arriving, arrival,

وفرت wèfrèt, *s. a.* Abundance, great number or quantity.

وفق wèfk, *s. a.* Accordance; a kind of charm consisting of a prayer or similar formula spoken or written, and believed to have the virtue of curing, &c.; بروفق bèr-wèfk, *ad. p.* According to.

وفی wèfī (*fem.* وفیه wèfīyyé), *a. a.* Amply sufficient, abundant.

وقار vwàkār, وقارت vwàkārèt, *s. a.* Gravity of appearance and demeanour.

وقاحت vwàkāmèt, *s. a.* A rude repulse, rebuff.

وقایه vwìkāyé, *s. a.* A sheltering, shielding, protecting; protection; ا—, —et, *v.a.* To shelter, shield, protect.

وقائع vwàkā'i'', *s. pl. a.* (*of* وقعه vwàk''à), Events.

وقت vwAkt (wAkit), *s. a.* Time; وقتلو vwAkitli, *a. t.* Timely; وقتلووقتنجه wAkitli-wAktinja (*or* وقتیله wàktīla), *ad. t.* Punctually, regularly in point of time; وقتسز wAkitsiz, *a. t.* Inconvenient in point of time; out of season, unseasonable; وقتلووقتسز wAkitli-wAkitsiz, *ad. t.* At all times, at any time, convenient or inconvenient.

وقس علی هذا wè-kiss-''àlà-hāzā, *comp. a.* And so forth, and thus of the rest.

وقع vwàk'', *s. a.* Gravity, stateliness of mien and behaviour.

وقعه vwàk''à, *s. a.* Any grave event; an untoward event, catastrophe; a dream; یکیچری وقعه سی yéngichéri-wàk''àssi, The destruction or insurrection of the Janissaries; وقعه نویس wàk''a-nùwiss, *s. p.* The official chronicler of passing events.

وقف wAkf, *s. a.* A staying, standing

still, halting; a pausing; the settling any property in mortmain or in tail with remainder in mortmain; (*pl.* اوقاف èvkâf), any piece of property so settled; ا—, —et, *v.a.* To settle property in mortmain or in tail with remainder in mortmain, the latter being called وقف مشروط wâkfi-mèsh-rūt, Conditional mortmain; وقفيه wâkfìyyé, *s. a.* The deed of settlement in mortmain.

وقواق wàkwāk, *s. a.* Name of a certain infernal tree, the fruit of which are said to resemble human bodies, and to cry out continually the word wàkwāk.

وقور vwàkūr, *a. a.* Grave, steady, stately in manner and demeanour.

وقوع vwùkū'', *s. a.* A happening; — بولمق, vwùkū''-bùlmak, *v.n.* To happen, to come to pass, to take place.

وقوف vwùkūf, *s. a.* A staying, halting; a pausing; knowledge, information; ا—, —et, *v.n.* To stay, halt; to pause; كسب وقوف ا kèssbi-wùkūf-et, *v.n.* To acquire information.

وقيه wàkìyyé (òkka), *s. a.* The Turkish pound weight, equivalent to nearly 2¾lbs. avoirdupois English.

وقيعه wàkī''a, *s. a.* A grave event; a battle, an affair.

وكالت vèkyālèt, *s. a.* The quality and functions of an attorney, agent, lieutenant, or *alter ego;* وكالت عظمى vèkyālèti-''ùzmà, The Grand-Viziriate, office of Sultan's *alter ego;* وكالتنامه vèkyālet-nāmé, A power of attorney.

وكلا vùkélā, *s. pl. a.* (*of* وكيل vèkīl), Agents, attorneys; ministers of state; وكلالق vùkélālik, *s. t.* The grade of a minister of state, given *ad honores* to a certain number of mushīrs.

وكيل vèkīl, *s. a.* A person entrusted to act in the absence of another, an agent, attorney, lieutenant, substitute, alter ego, locum-tenens; وكيل خرج vèkīl-khàrj, *s. t.* The servant who has charge of superintending all the ordinary household expenses.

ولا vèlā, *s. a.* Friendship, affection; allegiance.

ولات vwùlāt, *s. pl. a.* (*of* والى wālī), [Governors-general.

ولادت vìlādèt (vèlādèt), *s. a.* Nativity, birth.

ولايت vìlāyèt (wìlā'*at*), *s. a.* A country in general; a district, town, or village in particular; the quality and functions of a governor-general, or of an independent ruler; *also* of a guardian, *or* patron, *or* next of kin; *also* of a saint, saintship, sanctity; ولايتلو vìlā-yetli (wìlā'*atli*), *a. t.* Belonging to a country, a countryman; a fellow-countryman.

ولد vèled, *s. a.* (*in composition of names*), Son; (alone) a sharp fellow; احمد ولد محمد âhmed-vèlédi-Mùhàmmed, Ahmed, son of Muhammed; ولدالزنا vèlédu-'z-zìnā (vèlédiznā), A bastard.

ولكن vè-lākin, *comp. a.* But, but then.

ولو vè-lev, *comp. a.* Even, though.

ولوج vùlūj, *s. a.* Entering (into or upon anything); becoming, turning into (as night into day).

ولوله vèlvélé, *s. a.* A repeated cry; the loud noise of many voices.

وله vèlèh, *s. a.* Astonishment, amazement, stupefaction; بکا وله کلدی bànga-vèlèh-ghèldi, Amazement came over me.

ولی vèlī, *s. a.* One very near to anyone in blood, relationship, or affection; a saint; a master, patron; a servant; the next of kin; ولی الله vèliyyu-'llāh, A saint; ولی نعمت vèlī-ni''mèt, *or* ولی النعم vèlìyyu-'n-nì''àm, A benefactor; ولی عهد vèlī-''àhd, The heir-apparent or presumptive, the designated successor to the throne.

ولیمه vèlīmé, *s. a.* A marriage-feast.

ونديك Vènédik, *s. t.* Venice; a Venetian; the Venetian people or republic.

وهاب vàhhāb, *s. a.* (God) the constant giver of good things.

وهام vàhhām, *a. a.* Who fancies all manner of dangers and difficulties.

وهل vèhl, *s. a.* Fear, fright.

وهله vèhlé, *s. a. in* وهلهٔ اولاده vèhlé'i-ūlāda, *ad. t.* At first, on the spur of the moment, on first consideration (*The word itself means* an attack of fear, a sudden fright).

وهم vèhm, *s. a.* Fear, apprehension of something future; وهمناك vèhimnāk, *a. p.* Apprehensive.

ویانه Viàné, *s. t.* Vienna (town of, in Austria).

ویران vīrān, *a. p.* Ruined, in ruins, in a neglected condition, deserted and gone to ruin; ruined in pocket or in affection.

ویرانه vīrāné, *s. p.* The ruins of a house, or the empty plot of ground left after a fire has happened; ویرانه زار vīrāné-zār, A place full of ruins.

ویرش vèrish, *s. t.* A giving; a selling; الش ویرش àlish-vèrish, Trade, commerce.

ویرکو vīrghyū (vèrghi), *s. t.* A gift, present; a tax, contribution, tribute.

ویرمك vīrmek, vèrmek (*aor.* ویرر vīrir, vèrir), *v.a.* To give; to give out. Joined to the root of any verb (which is then to be augmented with the addition of a ی vowel if ending with a consonant, or the syllable یی yi, if ending with a vowel), this word forms the *verb of facility*, and has the signification of doing with facility, quickness, or offhandedness, the action expressed by the root so augmented; as, یاپیویرمك yàpi-vèrmek, To do or make with facility; سویله ییویرمك sùwèyléyivèrmek, Just to say, merely to speak.

ویره vīra, vèra, *s. t.* A capitulating, giving up; ویره ویرمك vīra-vīrmek, vèra-vèrmek, To capitulate, give up (a fortress); —, vīra, *and* ویره ویره vīra-vīra, *gerund*, By continuously giving.

giving out, giving one's self or one's strength to a thing; —, vīra! Now then, go it my boys! clap on! pull away!

ویره‌سی‌یه المق vèréssiya-àlmak, v.a. To buy upon credit, to buy on condition of paying at a future time. (This form ویره‌سی vèréssi is an obsolete verbal form, now used in only a few words, of which this is one.)

ویزلدامق wìzīldamak (aor. ویزلدار wìzīl-dar), ویزلامق wìzlamak (aor. ویزلار wìzlar), v.n. To buzz; ویزلدی wìzīldi, s. t. A buzzing noise; ویزویزاوتمك wìzz-wìzz-ùtmek, v.n. To make a buzzing, phizzing noise.

ویزیته vìzita, s. t. (Italian), A visit.

ویل vèyl, s. a. Woe; ویلا vèylā! int. a. Woe!

ویوده wàywoda, s. t. (Bulgarian), A [governor.

ه

ه hĕ or hā'i-hèwwàz. Thirtieth letter of the Turkish alphabet, having, as a consonant, the power of an aspirated h, in whatever part of a word it may occur, and, as a vowel at the end of words or syllables only, the value of one of the vowels a, ĕ, or é. In chronograms and astronomical tables, it has the numeral value of 5. Placed over letters and writings, in the middle of the very top of the page, and generally in the shape ـــه, it stands for the Arabic word هو hùwé or hū, and signifies He, God, Jehovah. At the end of Arabic compound terms, it is either the personal or possessive pronoun of the third person singular masculine, signifying his, him, it, its, and varying in pronunciation either as a final aspirate, or as the syllable hu or hi, according to the rules of Arabic grammar.

ها hā, s. a. Name of the letter ه; —, *pron. a. pers. and poss. at the end of Arabic compound terms,* Her; —, *at the end of Persian nouns,* is the sign of the plural for inanimate or irrational things; —! int. t. O! Oh! Ho!

هابط hābit, a. a. Who descends, alights; —او, —ōl, v.n. To descend, alight.

هابل hābil, s. a. Abel the son of Adam.

هاتف hātif, s. a. One who calls; a voice which calls; هاتف الغیب hātifu-'l-ghàyb, A voice from an unseen caller, a voice from heaven; an unseen, secret monitor, the heart or a guardian admonishing spirit.

هادم hādim, s. a. Who demolishes; —اللذات, hādimu-'l-lèzzāt (The demolisher of enjoyments), Death.

هادی hādī, s. a. A guide, conductor; God, the Great Guide.

هارب hārib, a. a. In flight; —او, —ōl, v.n. To take flight.

هاضم hāzim, a. a. Who digests (food); who puts up with (insults or injuries).

هالك hālik, *a. a.* Who dies, perishes; —او, —òl, *v.n.* To die, to perish (*as a wretch, never used but in a contemptuous way*).

هاله hālé, *s. a.* A halo round the moon.

هامبورغ Hàmbūrgh, *s. t.* Hamburgh.

هامون hāmūn, *s. a.* The open, uncultivated country, the wilderness.

هانى hàni, هانيا hàniya, *or* هانى‌يا hàni-yā? *ad. t.* Where? Where is it? (*for* قانى kàni).

هاوج hāwuj, *s. t.* A carrot.

هاور Hàver, *s. t.* Havre (town of, in France.)

هاوريز hàwruz, *s. t.* (*for* ابريز āb-rīz, *s. p.*), A chamber-pot, urinal.

هاون hāvèn (hàwan), *s. t.* A mortar for pounding drugs, &c., or for firing shells; هاون‌الى (hàwan)-èli, *s. t.* A pestle.

هاى hāy, *int. t.* Ho! هاى‌هاى hāy-hāy, *ad. t.* Yes, to be sure; by all means; هاى‌هوى hāy-hūy, *s. p.* The confused cries of combatants.

هايده hày-dé, هايدى hày-dì, *int. t.* Now then! Go on! Now for it! هايدى كيت hāydì-ghìt! Go along with you! Be off! هايده‌لمك hāydélémek, *v.a.* To drive forward or away.

هائل hā'il, *a. a.* Terrible, frightful.

هبا hèbā, *a. p.* Going in pure loss; —ا, —et, *v.a.* To allow (anyone's work or endeavours) to go in pure loss; —او, —òl, *v.n.* To go in pure loss, to bring in no advantage.

هبوب hùbūb, *s. a.* A blowing (of the wind); —ا, —et, *v.n.* To blow (the wind).

هبوط hùbūt, *s. a.* A descending, descent from on high, alighting; —ا, —et, *v.n.* To descend, to alight.

هبه hìbé, *s. a.* A free gift without any thing or consideration being received in exchange; —ا, —et, *v.a.* To present as a free gift.

هتك hètk, *s. a.* A tearing; a violation; —ا, —et, *v.a.* To tear, to violate.

هتمان hètmān, *s. t.* A hetman of the Cossacks.

هجأ hèjè', hèjā', *s. a.* A syllable; حروف‌هجا hùrūfu-hèjā, The letters of the alphabet; حروف‌هجا ترتيبى hùrūfu-hèjā-tèrtībi, Alphabetical order; هجالمك hèjélémek, *v.a.* To spell syllable by syllable.

هجر hèjr, هجران hìjrān, *s. a.* Exile, banishment, separation from home, family, and friends.

هجرت hìjrèt, *and* هجرت‌نبويه hìjréti-nèbévìyyé, The Hegira, the *flight*, the voluntary exile of Muhammed from Mecca, from whence dates the Muhammedan era; هجريه hìjrìyyé, *a. a. fem.* Pertaining to the era of the Hìjré or Hegira.

هجو hìjv, *s. a.* A satire; —ا, —et, *v.a.* To satirize; هجويات hìjvìyyāt, *s. pl. a.* Satires, lampoons, satirical pieces of poetry.

هجوع hùjū'', *s. a.* Sleep, slumber.

هجوم hùjūm, *s. a.* An attack, assault; ا—, —et, *v.n.* To make an attack.

هجين hèjīn, *s. a.* A half-blood Arab horse.

هدايا hèdāyā, *s. pl. a.* (*of* هديه hèdìyyé), [Presents.

هدايت hìdāyet, *s. a.* A guiding or a being guided aright, especially in matters of faith and religion; هدايته كلمك hìdāyéta-ghèlmek, *v.n.* To be brought to embrace the true religion.

هدر hèdr, *s. a.* Blood shed with impunity and going unrevenged; ا—, —et, *v.a.* To allow to go unrevenged (blood); هدراً hèdran, *ad. a.* With impunity.

هدف hèdef, *s. a.* The mark or target at which aim is taken in shooting.

هدفه hèdéfé, *s. a.* A sight (in any instrument through which one looks).

هدم hèdm, *s. a.* A demolishing, demolition; ا—, —et, *v.a.* To demolish, pull down.

هدهد hùdhùd, *s. a.* The hoopoo bird.

هدى hùdà, *s. a.* The direction or guidance which leads to salvation; السلام على من اتبع الهدى èss-sèlāmu-"àlà-mèn-èttèba"à-'l-hùdà! Salutation to whomsoever follows the true guidance!

هديه hèdìyyé, *s. a.* A present; هديه لك hèdìyyélik, *s. t.* A thing fit or intended for a present.

هذا hāzā, *a. a. mas.* (*fem.* هذه hāzihi), This.

هذيان hèzéyān, *s. a.* Nonsense, impertinence. [tinence.

هر hèr, *a. p.* Every; (*followed by any of the interrogatives*) soever; هربر hèr-bìr, Each, every one; هربريمز hèr-bìrimiz, Every one of us; هر بررلريمزه hèr-bìrerlérimiza, To each one of us; هربار hèr-bār, *ad. p.* Always, every time; هرچند hèr-chènd, How much soever, how many soever; هركز hèr-ghìz (*followed by a negation*), *ad. p.* Never; هركس hèr-kèss, All, every one, every person, every man; هركيم hèr-kìm, Whoever, whosoever; هرنه hèr-nè, Whatever, whatsoever; هرقنغى hèr-kànghi, Whichever; هرنه درلو hèr-nè-dùrlu, Whatever kind; هرنه زمان hèr-nè-zàmān, Whatever time, whenever; هرنقدر hèr-nàkadar, How much soever; هرايينه hèr-āyīné, Always, in every way.

هرات Hèrāt, *s. p.* The town of Herat.

هراس hìrāss, *s. p.* Fear, fright, terror.

هرج مرج hèrj-mèrj, *ad. a.* In confusion, in utter disorder.

هرجايى hèr-jāyī, *s. p.* A gad-about (man); a pansy, heart's-ease (flower).

هرزه hèrzé, *s. p.* Foolish talk, babble; هرزه وكيلى hèrzé-vèkīli, A person employed, as it were, to talk nonsense for someone else.

هرسك Hèrsèk, *s. t.* The Herzegovina.

هرسكلو Hèrsèkli, *s. t.* A Herzegovinian.

هرگله hèrghélé, *s. t.* A haras, establishment for breeding horses; a troop of horses brought to market fresh from the breeding establishment.

هزار hèzār, *a. p.* A thousand; هزار داستان hèzār-dāssitān, *s. p.* The nightingale, who tells a thousand tales, or of whom a thousand tales are told; هزارفن hèzār-fènn (hèzāri-fènd), *s. p.* A jack-of-all-trades.

هزبر hìzèbr, *s. a.* A lion.

هزل hèzl, *s.a.* Obscenity; هزليات hèzlìy-yāt, *s. pl. a.* Obscene poetry. [defeat.

هزيمت hèzīmèt, *s. a.* A rout, total

هست hèsst, *s. p.* Present being, actual existence; هستوبود hèsst-u-būd, What is and what has been, present and past evidence; هستى hèsstī, *s. p.* A present being, an actual existence, existence.

هشت hèsht, *a. p.* Eight; هشتم hésh-tum, هشتمين hèshtumīn, *a. p.* The eighth, هشتاد hèshtād, *a. p.* Eighty; هشتده hèsht-deh, *a. p.* Eighteen.

هضم hàzm, *s. a.* Digestion; patience, longanimity; ا—, —et, *v.a.* To digest; to bear (an insult); هضم نفس hàzm*i*--nèfss, A curbing the passions.

هفت hèft, *a. p.* Seven; هفتم hèftum, هفتمين hèftumīn, *a. p.* The seventh; هفتاد hèftād, *a. p.* Seventy; هفتده hèft-dèh, *a. p.* Seventeen.

هفته (hàft*a*), *s. p.* A week; هفته‌لك (hàft*alik*), *s. t.* A thing of a week old; a week's pay or provision.

هفوات hèfévāt, *s. pl. a.* (*no sing.*) Errors, faults.

هكبه hè*gh*bé, *s. t.* A small saddle-bag, carried on the same horse with a rider.

هكبه‌لى Hè*gh*bèli, *s. t.* Halki (one of the Princes Islands near Constantinople).

هكيم hèkīm, *s. t.* A medical practitioner (*corrupted from* حكيم hàkīm, A sage.)

هل hèl? *Arabic interrogative,* Is it or is it not so that . . . ?

هلاك hèlāk, *s. a.* Death, destruction; ا—, —et, *v.a.* To kill; او—, —ōl, *v.n.* To die, perish, be destroyed (*when said of* man, *it is always an expression of enmity*).

هلال hìlāl, *s. a.* The crescent, the moon during the first few days after new moon. [*a. a.* Deadly poisonous.

هلاهل hèlāhil, *s. a.* Deadly poison; —,

هله hèlé, *int. t.* Now! Look there! Do just look! Well! Did you ever.

هم hèm, *ad. p.* Both, also; —, *a. p.* (*in composition*), Fellow, brother, of the same —; هم كتدم هم كوردم hèm-ghìt-dim-hèm-ghy*ù*rdum, I both went and also saw; همفراش hèm-firāsh, *s. p.* A bed-fellow; همراه hèm-rāh, *s. p.* A fellow-traveller; همشهرى hèm-shèhrī, *s. p.* A fellow-townsman, fellow-countryman; —, hèmm, *s. a.* Any matter about which one troubles one's self; a single care, anxiety, solicitude; —, hìm, hùm, *pron. a. mas.* (*at the end of Arabic composites*), Their, them.

هما hùmā *and* هماى hùmāy, *s. p.* A fabulous kind of bird of paradise of good omen.

همام humām, *s. a.* A great man, a great ruler and leader; —, hèmmām, A slanderer.

همان hèmān (hèmèn), *ad. p.* Only, just, hardly, only just; in that very (time); همان‌شمدی (hèmen)-shìmdi, Just now, just this moment, this minute; هماندم hèmāndèm, همان‌ساعت hèmān-sā"*at*, *a. p.* That very moment.

همائم hèmāʿim, *s. pl. a.* (*of* همت hìmmèt), Endeavours, exertions.

همایون hùmāyūn, *a. p.* Auspicious, august, imperial (said only of the Sultan); خط همایون khàtti-hùmāyūn, An edict, being a few words in the Sultan's handwriting commanding it to be put in execution.

همت hìmmèt, *s. a.* The exertion of one's influence, authority, power, or ability; ا—, —et, *v.n.* To exert one's influence, authority, power, or ability; همتکزه محتاجدر hìmmètingiza-mùhtāj-*-dir*, It requires your kind influence.

همتا hèmtā, *a. p.* Equal; similar; بیهمتا bī-hèmtā, *a. p.* Without an equal.

همج hémej, *s. a.* An old imbecile.

همچنین hèmchùnin, همچو hèmchū, *ad. p.* As, in like manner as.

همدان Hàmàdān, *s. p.* The town of Hamadan in Persia.

همدم hèm-dèm (One breathing the same breath), *s. p.* A fellow, associate, intimate friend and companion.

همدیگ hèm-dìgher, *pron. p.* One another, each other.

همزه hèmzé, *s. a.* Name of the orthographical character ء, the various functions of which are explained in the preface.

همشهری hèm-shèhrī, *s. p.* A fellow-countryman or townsman.

همشیره hèmshīré, *s. p.* A sister.

همم hìmèm, *s. pl. a.* (*of* همت hìmmèt), Exertions of one's influence, authority, power, or ability.

هموار hèmvār, *a. p.* Equal, smooth, uniform; proper, fitting, suitable.

همواره hèmvāré, *a. p.* Continually, constantly. [Cares, anxieties, solicitudes.

هموم hùmūm, *s. pl. a.* (*of* هم hèmm),

همه hèmé, *a. p.* All. [hung at the side.

همیان hìmyān, *s. a.* A purse; a bag

همیشه hèmīshé, *a. p.* Always.

همین hèmīn, *a. p.* The very same.

هنتو *or* هنطو hìnto, *s. t.* A carriage, coach.

هنجار hènjār, *s. p.* The proper place, manner, or position of a thing; نابهنجار nā-bé-hènjār, *a. p.* Out of time, place, or position, unsuitable, unbefitting.

هند hind, هندستان hindisstān, *s.p.* India; هندی hìndī, *a. p.* An East-Indian; East-Indian, Indian; هند غربی hìndi-ghàrbī, *s. a.* The West Indies.

هندبا hìndibā, *s. t.* The dandelion, chicory, or taraxacum plant.

هندسه hèndéssé, *s. a.* Geometry; the mathematics in general. [Indian.

هندو hìndū, *s. p.* An Indian, East-

هنر hùner, *s. p.* Art; ability; talent, skill; هنرلو hùnerli, *a. t.* Skilful, talented (man); skilfully made (thing); هنرمند hùnɛrmend, هنرور hùnɛrvɛ̀r, *s. p.* A skilful, clever, talented person, a master, an artist, a genius.

هنكام hènghyām, *s. p.* Time, moment, interval, space of time; بيهنكام bī-hènghyām, *a. p.* Untimely.

هنكامه hènghyāmɛ́, *s. p.* Time, space of time; a row, confusion, tumult; a fight, conflict; هنكامه‌كير hènghyāmɛ́-ghīr, *a. p.* Filling with noise.

هنود hùnūd, *s. pl. a.* (*of* هندى hìndī), Indians, East-Indians.

هنوز hènuz (hèniz), *ad. p.* Just this moment, only just this moment; (*with a negation*) not yet.

هو hū, hùwɛ́, *pron. a.* He, it; He, God, Jehovah; ياهو yā-hū! *int. a.* (*as we should say,* O thou! *but as it means*) O He! O man! O God! O Jehovah!

هوا hèwa (hàwa), *s. a.* The air; the wind; the climate; the atmosphere; the weather; —, hèwā, *s. a.* Desire, inward inclination, taste, lust; هوا و هوس hèwā-u-hèvèss, Desires and tastes, fancies and inclinations, lusts and passions; بادهوا bàdi-hèwā (bèdāwā), *s. and a. p.* A thing got for nothing, a windfall; gratis; هوادار hàwādār, *a. p.* Open, airy.

هوام hèwāmm, *s. pl. a.* (*no sing.*), Insects, reptiles, crawling things.

هوان hèwān, *s. a.* The state of insignificancy.

هوائى hèwāʿī, *a. a.* Pertaining to the air; pertaining to the mere imagination or desire; —, *s. t.* A sky-rocket.

هودج hèvdèj, *s. a.* A kind of camel-litter, in which ladies travel; هودج نشين hèvdèj-nìshīn, *a. p.* Who sits in a camel-litter (and travels).

هوس hèvess (hàvess), *s. a.* Wish, desire, inclination; a taste, liking; ا—, —et, *v.n.* To nourish a desire, cherish a wish; هوسلو hàvessli, *a. t.* Desirous, having a wish, taste, or liking (for anything); —, *s. t.* هوسكار hàvess-kyār, *s. p.* An amateur; a candidate.

هوش hūsh, *s. p.* Mind, sense, intelligence; بيهوش bī-hūsh, *a. p.* Senseless; هوشمند hūshmènd, هوشيار hūshyār, *a. p.* Sensible, intelligent.

هول hèvl, *s. a.* Terror; هولناك hèvilnāk, *a. p.* Terrible, terrific. [manifest.

هويدا hùwèydā, *a. p.* Clear, evident,

هى hèy! *int. t.* O!

هياكل hèyākil, *s. pl. a.* (*of* هيكل hèykèl), Palaces, temples, large buildings; large colossal forms, bodies or phantoms.

هيبت hèybèt, *s. a.* Awfulness, dreadness of appearance; fear, awe; هيبتلو hèybetli, *a. t.* Awful in appearance, imposing.

هيجا hèyjā, *s. a.* Battle, combat, fight.

هيجان hèyéjān, *s. a.* The getting into motion, rising (dust or bodies of men); ا—, —et, *v.n.* To get into motion.

هيچ hìch, *a. p.* No, none, not one; —, *s. p.* Nothing; هيچ بر hìch-bìr, Not one, none.

هيخته hīkhtĕ, *a. p.* Drawn (sword).

هيزم hīzèm, *s. p.* Firewood; هيزمكش hīzèmkèsh, *s. p.* A carrier of wood.

هيكل hèykĕl, *s. a.* Any colossal thing, building, temple, image, statue, person, or phantom.

هيمه hīmĕ, *s. a.* Firewood.

هيولا hèyyūlā, *a. a.* Matter; هيولانى hèyyūlānī, *a. a.* Material.

هيهات hèyhāt, *s. a.* The open desert, wilderness, unoccupied plain; —, *int. a.* Away! Begone!

هيئت hèy'èt, *s. a.* The form, figure, appearance; the configuration (of the heavenly bodies); علم هيئت "ilmi-hèy'èt, Astronomy.

ى

ى yĕ *or* yā'i-àhtānī. Thirty-first and last letter of the Turkish alphabet, sometimes a vowel at the end or middle of words or syllables, always a consonant at the beginning: as a vowel, it has the value of ᴇ, *e*, i, or *i*, and as a consonant that of *y*. In chronograms and astronomical tables it has the numeral value of 10. In Turkish, with the sound of i or *i*, it is the sign of the definite accusative of nouns, taking, after vowels, the form يى and sound yi *or yi*; or it is the pronominal affix of the third person singular, signifying *his, her, its*. In Arabic words it is the sign of appurtenance, and changes nouns into qualifying adjectives; and in words of Persian origin it performs the like function as in Arabic, and also that of forming an abstract noun of the quality which is characteristic of the thing denoted by the original word; or sometimes it indicates a *single one* of the kind named.

يا yā, *s. a.* Name of the letter ى; —! *int. a.* O! —, *c. p.* Either, or; —? *interrog. t.* Is it so? Indeed?

ياب yāb, *a. p.* (*in composition*), Who finds or has found; found; ناقعرياب nā-kà''r-yāb, *a. p.* Bottomless, unfathomable, of which the bottom is [not found.

يابس yābiss, *a. a.* Dry.

ياپجه yàpja, *a. t.* Slowly.

ياپشقان yàpishkān, *a. t.* Sticky, sticking, adhesive; —, *s. t.* Pellitory of the wall.

ياپشمق yàpishmak (*aor.* ياپشور yàpishir), *v.n.* To stick, cleave, adhere; to take hold of; to touch, handle; to be assiduous, persevering; ياپشدرمق yàpishdirmak, *v.a.* To cause or allow to stick; to put close, quite close, to cause to touch, bring into contact.

ياپمق yàpmak (*aor.* ياپار yàpar), *v.a.* To do; to make, construct, build, manufacture.

ياپو *or* ياپى yàpi, *s. t.* A building; builder's work while in progress.

يات yāt, *s. t. in* يات و يراق yāt-u-yàrāk, Arms and accoutrements.

یاتسی yàtsi, s. t. The prayer of bed-time. [ing or sticking up.

یاتق yàtik, a. t. Lying down, not stand-

یاتمق yàtmak (aor. یاتار or یتار yàtar), v.n. To lie down; to go to bed; to keep or remain lying, keep down; یاتشمق yàtishmak, v.n. To become calm, tractable, reasonable, less virulent, less exacting; یاترمق yàtirmak, v.a. To cause or allow to lie down; to put down, lay down.

یأجوج yèʿjūj, s. a. Gog; یأجوج ومأجوج yèʿjūj-u-mèʿjūj, Gog and Magog; apparently two Scythian tribes of great antiquity, but respecting whom numerous legends are current.

یاخود yākhod, c. p. Or, or else, or otherwise.

یاد yād, s. p. Memory, remembrance; ا—, —et, v.a. To remember (in mind or by name); to mention by name; یادست yād-esst (It is remembered), s. p. Name of a game known among young people as *Josephine*; یادداشت yād-dāsht, s. p. A keepsake, souvenir, memento.

یادکار yād-kyār (yādighyār), s. p. A keepsake, souvenir, memento; a scamp, old fool, or old villain.

یار yār, s. p. (pl. یاران yārān), A friend; a lover; a mistress; یارغار yāri-ghār (A friend of the cave, *in allusion to Muhammed's companion, Èbu-bèkr, who was alone with him secreted in a cave when pursued by his enemies on his flight from Mecca*), A faithful friend in adversity; چاریارکزین chār-yāri-ghyùzīn, The four special friends (of Muhammed), Èbu-bekr, ʻʻOmar, ʻʻOssmān, and ʻʻAlī; —, yàr, s. t. A precipice, a cliff; یارانه yārānè, a. p. Friendly, pertaining to a friend; یاری yārī, s. p. Friendship; یارانلق yārānlik, Friendship, mutual friendship, acts worthy of mutual friends.

یاردم yàrdim, s. t. Help, assistance, succour, aid; ا—, —et, v.n. To give assistance, help, aid; یاردمه یتشمك yàrdima-yètishmek, v.n. To run to (anyone's) assistance; یاردمجی yàrdimji, s. t. A helper, an auxiliary.

یارش yàrish, s. t. A foot-race; ا—, —et, v.n. To have a race on foot.

یارق yàrik, a. t. Split, cracked; —, —, s. t. A split, a crack, fissure, cleft, chink.

یارلغامق yàrilghamak (aor. یارلغار yàrilghar), v.a. To pardon, forgive (*obsolete*).

یارم yàrim, a. t. That which results from splitting a thing in two, half.

یارمق yàrmak (aor. یارار yàrar), v.a. To split, cleave; to hew in pieces; یاریجی yàriji, s. t. A hewer of fire-wood.

یارمه yàrma, a. t. Split (not cut); یارمه شفتالو yàrma-shèftāli, A melting peach (not a clingstone), the cleft of which is deep.

یاره yārè (yàra), s. t. A wound; یاره‌لو

yàrali, a. t. Wounded ; یارەا yàra-et, v.n. یارەلمك yàrélémek (yàralamak), v.a. To wound ; یارەلنمك yàrélænmek (yàralanmak), v.n. and p. To be wounded.

یاری yàri, s. t. A half ; یاریسی yàrissi, Its half, half of it or of them ; یاریلری yàriléri, Half of them ; یاریمز yàrimiz, Half of us ; یاریکز yàringiz, Half of you ; یاری‌کیجه yàri-ghèyjé, Midnight ; یاری‌یری yàri-yèri, Midway, half way ; یاری‌بچوق yàri-bùchūk, About half, not half ; یاریلمق yàrilamak, v.a. To have got half way through ; —, yārī, s. p. Friendship.

یارین yàrin, s. t. To-morrow ; یارین دکل اولبرکون yàrin - dìghil - (ò) - bìr - -ghyùn (*or short* اولبرکون (ò)-bìr- -ghyùn), The day after to-morrow.

یاز yàz, s. t. Summer ; یازین yàzin, ad. t. In summer ; الك‌یاز ìlk-yàz, The first summer weather ; یازلق yàzlik, a. t. Special to summer.

یازده yāzdèh, a. p. Eleven ; یازدهم yāzdèhum, a. p. The eleventh.

یازق yàzik, int. t. Alas ! Poor thing ! What a shame ! What a pity ! —, s. t. A shame, a pity.

یازمق yàzmak (*aor.* یازار yàzar), v.a. To write, write down ; to record, to register, to enter ; to enrol (soldiers) ; —, v.n. To write (a pen) ; joined to the root of a few verbs, augmented with a vowel ة if ending in a consonant, or augmented with the syllable یه if ending with a vowel, this verb takes the sense of *being very near*, بایله‌یازدم bàyila-yàzdim, I was very near fainting ; یازلمق yàzilmak, v.p. To be written ; to be noted, entered, registered ; to be enrolled.

یازی yàzi, s. t. Writing ; handwriting ; an inscription ; یازیجی yàziji, s. t. A clerk ; the mate of a merchantman ; یازیلو yàzili, a. t. Written ; written over, bearing writing or an inscription ; یازی‌یازمق yàzi-yàzmak, v.n. To write ; to be able to write.

یأس yèʿss, s. a. Despair ; یاس yàss, s. t. Mourning ; —ا, yàss-et, v.n. To mourn, to be in mourning, wear mourning.

یاسمین yāssémīn, s. p. Jessamine.

یاش yàsh, s. t. A man's or animal's age in years ; a year of life ; wet, wetness, moisture ; —, a. t. Wet, wetted, damp, moist ; قاچ‌یاشنده‌در kāch-yàshinda-dir ? In what year of his age is he ? اون‌سکزیاشمده‌یم òn-sèkiz-yàshimda-yim, I am in my eighteenth year ; I am seventeen years old and going on for eighteen ; یام‌یاش yàm-yàsh, Very wet, quite wet ; یاشداش yàshdash, One of the same age ; یاشلق yàshlik, s. t. Wet, humidity ; یاشلو yàshli, a. t. Old in years, aged.

یاشا *or* یشا yàsha ! May he live ! (See یشامق).

یاشمق yàshmak, s. t. A lady's veil ; a kind of covering for the greater part of the face, worn by Turkish women, and showing only the eye, and part of the nose and cheeks.

یاصی yàsssi, *a. t.* Flat; squat.

یاغ yàgh, *s. t.* Any fat, oil, or unctuous substance; the fat of meat, butter, dripping, grease, tallow; ات یاغی èt-yàghi, Fat or grease of meat; بالق یاغی bàlik-yàghi, Fish-oil; ایچ یاغی ìch-yàghi, Suet; چرویش یاغی (*or* چوریش chèvrish) chèrvish-yàghi, An inferior kind of fat (butter? or dripping?) used in cooking; تره یاغی (*or* یاغ yàgh) tèré-yàghi, Fresh butter; صای یاغی sày-yàghi, Clarified butter; زیتین یاغی zèytīn - yàghi, Olive-oil; طوك یاغی dòng-yàghi, Tallow; &c. &c.; یاغلو yàghli, *a. t.* Fat; oily; greasy; —, *s. t.* Food with meat or butter in it; یاغسز yàghsiz, *a. t.* Lean; not fat; —, *s. a.* Lent diet, meagre; یاغلامق yàghlamak, *v.a.* To oil or grease. [rain.

یاغش yàghish, *s. t.* A raining, pouring;

یاغلق yàghlik, *s. t.* A handkerchief.

یاغمق yàghmak (*aor.* یاغار yàghar), *v.n.* To rain; to pour; to fall as rain does (snow, hail, dust, &c.); یاغدرمق yàghdirmak, *v.a.* To cause or allow to rain, or to fall like rain; to pour, pour out or down.

یافت yāft, *a.p.* (*in composition*), Found; —, Yāfèt, *s. a.* Japhet, the son of Noah.

یافته yāfté (yàfta), *s. p.* A ticket (stuck upon things); a placard, bill; —, *a. p.* (*in composition*), Found; which has found.

یافه Yàffa, *s. t.* Jaffa (town of).

یاقشق yàkishik, *a. t.* Seemly, fitting; suitable; —, *s. t.* The most fitting and suitable way, mode, or modification; یاقشقلو yàkishikli, *a. t.* Pretty, handsome, beautiful; یاقشقسز yàkishiksiz, *a. t.* Unseemly, unhandsome, unbecoming; یاقشق المق yàkishik-àlmak, *v.n.* To appear likely; to appear beautiful.

یاقشمق yàkishmak (*aor.* یاقشور yàkishir), *v.n.* To befit, beseem, suit, go well; to appear likely; یاقشدرمق yàkishdirmak, *v.a.* To cause (a thing) to suit; to invent (a plausible story or reason) by studying circumstances.

یاقمق yàkmak (*aor.* یاقار *or* یقار yàkar), *v.a.* To light, to set fire to; to burn; یاقلمق yàkilmak, *v.p.* To be lighted; —, *v.n.* To burn (with grief, sorrow).

یاقوت yākūt, *s. a.* A ruby; كوك یاقوت ghyùk-yākūt, A sapphire; صاری یاقوت sàri-yākūt, A topaz.

یاقی yàki, *s. t.* A cautery; a plaister, sticking-plaister; an issue; پهلوان یاقیسی pèhliwān-yàkissi, *or* انكلیز یاقیسی ìnghliz-yàkissi, A blister of cantharides; نخود یاقیسی nókhud--yàkissi, An issue kept open by the insertion of a pea; یاقی اچمق yàki--àchmak, *v.n.* To open a blister, apply a blister.

یاکز yàngiz, *a. t.* Very dark brown (colour of a horse's coat).

یاکلتماج yàngiltmàj, *s. t.* An enigma, anything difficult to pronounce or to unriddle. [—, *a.t.* Wrong, incorrect.

یاکلش yàngilish (yānish), *s.t.* A mistake;

یاکلمق yàngilmak (*aor.* یاکلور yàngilir), *v.n.* To make a mistake; یاکلتمق yàngiltmak, *v.a.* To cause or allow to make a mistake, to put out.

یال yāl, *s. p.* The mane; یال وبال yāl-u-bāl (Mane and wings), Friends, influence, power.

یالاق yàlak, *s. t.* A watering-trough.

یالامق yàlamak (*aor.* یالار yàlar), *v.a.* To lick; to lick up.

یالان yàlan, *s. t.* A lie; —, *a. t.* False (saying); یالانجی yàlànji, *s. t.* A liar; —, *a. t.* False, artificial.

یالدز yàldiz, *s. t.* Gilding; —التونی, yàldiz-àltini, Gold for gilding; a sequin of pure gold, Venetian ducat; یالدزلمق yàldizlamak, *v.a.* To gild; یالدزلو yàldizli, *a. t.* Gilt.

یالغ yàligh, *s. p.* A drinking-horn.

یالك yàling (*obsolete*), *s. t.* Flame; a flash; یالکلمق yàlinglamak, *v.n.* To flash; to flame.

یالکز yàlingiz, *a. t.* Alone, solitary; یالکزلق yàlingizlik, *s. t.* Solitude; یالکجق yàlinjak, *a. t. dim.* All alone.

یالوارمق yàlvarmak (*aor.* یالوارر yàlvarir), *v.n.* To beg and pray, to beseech.

یالی yàli, *s.t.* The beach, the sea-side, sea-shore; a waterside house; یالی کناری yàli-kènāri, The water's edge or the beginning of the beach.

یالین yàlin, *a.t.* Bare (feet); یالین ایاق yàlin-àyak, *ad. t.* Barefoot; یالینقات yàln-kàt, *a. t.* Single (flower, &c.).

یامچق yàmchik, *s. t.* A very shaggy kind of covering for the shoulders.

یامه or یما yàma, *s. t.* A patch, a piece let in on anything old.

یان yàn, *s. t.* The side; یان یانه yàn--yàna, *ad. t.* Side by side, side to side; یانم yànim, My side; یانمه yànima, To my side; یانمده yànimda, At my side, by my side; یانمدن yànimdan, From my side; یانك yàning, Thy side; of the side; &c.; یانی yàni, His (her, its) side; &c.; یانمز yànimiz, Our side; &c.; یانکز yàningiz, Your side; &c.; یانلری yànlari, Their side or sides; his (her, its) sides, &c.; یاننده قالمق yàninda--kàlmak (changing the pronominal affix), *v.n.* To remain by, or near, or with one; to remain in one's possession; یان چیزمك yàn-chìzmek, *v.n.* To get away quietly, steal away; یان باقمق yàn-bàkmak, *v.n.* To look askew; درت یانه باقمق dùrt-yàna--bàkmak, *v.n.* To look all round on every side; یان کسیجی yàn-kèssiji, *s.t.* A cut-purse, pick-pocket.

یاناشمق or یناشمق yànashmak (*aor.* یاناشور or یناشور yànashir), *v.n.* To approach, go up to, go close to, go to the side of, close with; یاناشدرمق

yànashdìrmak, *v.a.* To cause or allow (anything) to approach, go or come near; یاناشلمق yànashìlmak, *v.n.* To be such that things can approach it.

یاناشمه *or* ییناشمه yànashma, *s. t.* A farm servant on yearly wages and board.

یانغین yànghìn, *s. t.* A fire, conflagration of houses; —, *a. t.* Who has been burnt; who has been hurt, injured, deceived, or cheated; یانغین‌وار yànghìn-vàr! Fire! Fire!

یانق yànìk, *a. t.* Burnt, scorched, singed; whose feelings are hurt, or sentiments unrequited; —قوقوسی, yànìk-kòkussu, The smell of something burning or singed.

یانقو yànko, *s. t.* An echo; (*Greek*), [Jack, John.

یانمق yànmak (*aor.* یانار *or* ینار yànar), *v.n.* To burn, be on fire, be burnt; to lose (at games of chance); to burn (with heat, thirst, *or* love); یاندرمق yandìrmak, *v.a.* To cause (one) to suffer from love, &c.; (*provincial*) to light, set light to; ینارطاغ yànar-dàgh, A volcano, burning mountain.

یاور yāvèr, *s. p.* An assistant, helper; an aide-de-camp; یاوری yāvérī, *s. p.* Help, assistance.

یاوری yàvri, *s. t.* The young of any animal; یاوریم yàvrim! My boy! یاوریلمق yàvrìlamak, *v.a.* and *n.* To pup, calve, foal, kitten, &c.

یاوز yàwuz, *a. t.* Good; good-natured.

یاهو Yāhū, *s. a.* Jehovah.

یای yày, *s. t.* A bow (for shooting); a spring (of a lock, &c.); (*obsolete*) summer.

یایا yàya, *s. t.* Foot, infantry; a novice; یایان yàyan, *ad. t.* On foot; یایان کلمق yàyan-ghèlmek, To come on [foot.

یایق yàyìk, *s. t.* A churn.

یایقامق yàykamak (*aor.* یایقار yàykar), *v.a.* (*obsolete*), To wash.

یایلا yàyla, یایلاق yàylàk, یایلاغ yàylāgh, *s. t.* A summer pasturage, upland.

یایمق yàymak (*aor.* یایار yàyar), *v.a.* To spread, extend; یایلمق yàyìlmak, *v.n.* To spread of itself; —, *v.n.* To be spread; to be such that it can be spread.

یباب yèbāb, *s. p.* A desert; a ruin; —, *a. t.* Desert, deserted; خراب و یباب khàrāb-u-yèbāb, Ruined and deserted, utterly ruined and done for.

یبان yàbàn, *s. t.* The desert, wilderness, unreclaimed country; یبانی yàbānī, *a. p.* Wild, growing wild, self sown or not grafted (plant); not at all civilized, savage (man); یبان‌ادمی yàban-àdami, A wild man, an ourang-outang; یبانی‌ادم yàbāni-àdam, A savage; یبان‌اشکی yàban-èshèghi, A zebra; an onager; یبانه‌سویلمك yàbana-sùwèylémek, *v.a.* To say (a thing) without intending to apply it to anyone present; سوزم‌یبانه sùzum-yàbana, My words to the wilderness! *i.e.* my words are not intended to apply to you or to anyone here (*ex-*

pression used parenthetically whenever a term of abuse is applied to an absent person, or whenever a pig, donkey, and such like things are mentioned); يبانه كتمك yàbana-ghìtmek, *v.n.* To be expended in vain, to be spent on air (either money or some act of kindness).

يبانجى yàbanji, *s. t.* A stranger; one who is not a kinsman.

يبوست yùbūssèt, *s. a.* Dryness.

يپاغى yàpaghi, *s. t.* Wool in the fleece; a fleece.

يپراق yàprak, *s. t.* A leaf (of a plant, of paper, &c.); vine-leaves or the leaves of certain plants used for making *dolma*; يپراق طولمه‌سى yàprak-dòlmassi, Leaf dolmas, *i.e.* balls or pellets of forcemeat, &c., neatly wrapped in leaves, and so cooked, served, and eaten; يپراقلنمق yàpraklanmak, *v.n.* To put forth leaves; يپراق كوبره‌سى yàprak-ghyùbrèssi, Leaf-mould.

يتاق yàtak, *s. t.* A bed; a form, a lair (of a wild animal); a den (of thieves), or a place abounding with any noxious animal or with robbers; a secret agent of thieves, robbers, jugglers, &c.; دول يتاغى dūl-yàtaghi, The womb, uterus.

يتامى yètāmà, *s. pl. a.* (*of* يتيم yètīm), [Orphans.

يتشمك yètishmek (*aor.* يتشور yètishir), *v.n.* To come up with, overtake; to come quickly, come in time; to be sufficient; يتشدرمك yètishdirmek, *v.a.* To send quickly; to send so as to arrive in time; يتشور yètishir! That will do; it is enough.

يتمش yètmish, *a. t.* Seventy; who or which has arrived; who or which has arrived at the state of maturity, ripe; يتمامش yètmamish, *a. t.* Unripe; يتمشنجى yètmishinji, *a. t.* The seventieth.

يتمك yètmek (*aor.* يتر yèter), *v.n.* To be sufficient; to reach; يتر yèter! That will do; it is enough! برينك كوجى يتمك bìrining-ghyùju-yètmek, To be able, to be powerful enough, strong enough, have influence enough; يتورمك yètirmek (*aor.* يتورر yètirir), *v.a. caus.* (*provincial*), To cause to reach; to send.

يتيم yètīm, *s. a.* An orphan.

يخنى yàhni, *s. t.* A hash or stew of meat, fish, or fowl.

يحيا Yàhyā, *s. a.* St. John the Baptist.

يخ yàkh, *s. p.* Ice.

يد yèd, *s. a.* The hand; يد واحد yèdi-wāhid, A kind of monopoly by which the government used to give the exclusive right to a single individual to buy up some particular branch of the produce of a whole district or province, or even of the empire; يد قدرت yèdi-kùdrèt, The hand of omnipotence, or of power; يد تصرف yèdi-tàssàrruf, The hands, the possession; ذواليدين zū-'l-yèdèyn, *s. a.* One who has the power of using both hands alike, an ambidexter;

مقطوع اليد mᴀktū‘‘ᴜ-’l-yèd, *a. a.* Who has had his hand cut off.

يدك yèdek, *s. t.* A led horse; the rope or strap by which he is led; a tow-rope; the act of towing; a ship or boat in tow; a spare article kept in case of need; يدكجى yèdekji, *s. t.* A tow-man, one who tows boats; يدكلك yèdeklik, *s. t.* A spare article kept in case of need.

يدمك yèdmek (*aor.* يدر yèdᴇr), *v.a.* To lead (a horse).

يدى yèdi, *a. t.* Seven; who has eaten; who has received; يدنجى yèdinji, *a. t.* The seventh; ميراث يدى mīrāss-yèdi, *s. t.* One who has received an inheritance and cannot get through it fast enough, a spendthrift.

ير yᴇ̀r, *s. t.* The ground; the floor; place; space; room; employment; بوش ير bòsh-yᴇ̀r, An empty place; a vacant space; a vacant employ; يره قومق yᴇ̀ra-kòmak, *v.a.* To place, put, lay down on the ground or floor; يرينه قومق yᴇ̀rina-kòmak, *v.a.* To put into its proper place; بريره قومق bìr-yèra-kòmak, *v.a.* To put somewhere or other; يرطوتمق yᴇ̀r-tùtmak, *v.n.* To take, take up, or occupy space, room; to take a seat or a place (at a theatre, &c.); يرايتمك yᴇ̀r-etmek, *v.n.* To make place or room, to make a place or hole; يربولمق yᴇ̀r-bùlmak, *v.n.* To find room, to find a place or employment; يريوزى yᴇ̀r-yùzu, The face of the earth; ديكش يرى dìkish-yᴇ̀ri, A seam; عورت يرلرى ‘‘àvret-yᴇ̀rléri, The privities, privy parts; يرايله برابر yᴇ̀r-ilé-bᴇ̀rābᴇ̀r, يرايله يكسان yᴇ̀r-ila-yèksān, Level with the earth; مبارك ير mùbārek-yᴇ̀r, A holy place; يرنده yᴇ̀rinda, In its proper place; apropos, fitting, right; يرينه yᴇ̀rina, To its proper place; in place, in lieu, in stead; آدم يرينه قومق ᴀdᴀm-yèrina-kòmak (To put in the place of a man), *v.a.* To esteem and treat as a person of consideration; يرينى بولمق yᴇ̀rini-bùlmak, *v.n.* To find its proper place, its level; يرينه كلمك yᴇ̀rina-ghᴇ̀l-mek, *v.n.* To come or get into its proper place; to come true, be fulfilled; يرالماسى yᴇ̀r-èlmassi (Earth-apple), The Jerusalem artichoke; the potatoe; فرنك يرالماسى firᴇ̀nk-yᴇ̀r-èlmassi, The potatoe; يرلو yᴇ̀rli, *a. t.* Grown or born on the spot; pertaining to the proper place; يرلو يرينه yᴇ̀rli-yᴇ̀rina, *ad. t.* To its proper place; يرسز yᴇ̀rsiz, *a. t.* Out of place.

يراتمق yᴇ̀ʀᴀtmak (*aor.* يرادر yᴇ̀ʀᴀdir), *v.a.* To create, bring into existence; يرادان حقى ايچون yᴇ̀ʀᴀdan - hᴀ̀kki-itchin! By Him who creates! For God's sake!

يراسه yᴇ̀rassa, *s. t.* A bat (bird).

يراشق yèrashik, يراشقلو yᴇ̀rashikli, *a. t.* Beseeming, becoming.

يراشمق yèrashmak (*aor.* يراشور yᴇ̀rà-shir), *v.n.* To beseem, become, suit.

یراق yàrak, *s. t.* Arms, weapons; penis; یراق یمه yèrak-yèma! Hold your tongue and don't talk nonsense! (*vulgar*).

یرامق yàramak (*aor.* یرار yàrar), *v.n.* To be useful; to do good; ایشه یرامق ìsha-yàramak, *v.n.* To be useful, serviceable, of service; ایشه یرار yàrar, ìsha-yàrar, *a. t.* Useful, serviceable, of service; یرارلق yàrarlìk, *s. t.* Serviceableness, good service; یرامز yàramàz, *a. t.* Good for nothing, unserviceable, naughty; —, *s. t.* A good-for-nothing, a scamp; a naughty boy; یرامزلق yàramàzlìk, Naughtiness.

یربوع yèrbū", *s. a.* The jerboa.

یرتق yìrtìk, *a. t.* Torn, rent; —, *s. t.* A tear, rent.

یرتماج yìrtmàj, *s. t.* An opening in the skirt of a dress from the bottom upwards.

یرتمق yìrtmak (*aor.* یرتار yìrtar), *v.a.* To tear, rend; to tear to pieces; یرتلمق yìrtìlmak, *v.n.* and *p.* To be torn.

یرتیجی yìrtiji, *a. t.* Which tears (its prey); یرتیجی حیوان yìrtiji-hàywān, A wild beast, a beast of prey.

یرلشمك yèrleshmek (*aor.* یرلشور yèrlèshir), *v.n.* To become firmly or definitively settled in its place, to get into a place and remain, to settle down, to snuggle down; یرلشدرمك yèrleshdirmek, *v.a.* To cause or allow (anything) to settle itself; to put (a thing) into the place where it is to remain.

یرلیغ yèrlīgh, *s. t.* A firman, an imperial edict.

یرمك yèrmek (*aor.* یرر yèrir), *v.a. in* اش یرمك àsh-yèrmek, *v.n.* To long, to have a longing for strange things to eat (a pregnant woman).

یزد Yèzd, *s. p.* Yezd (town of, in Persia).

یزدان yèzdān, *s. p.* God.

یزید yèzīd, *s. a.* Name of the Caliph of Damascus by whose orders Husseyn, son of "Ali and grandson of Muhammed, was slain; *hence* a wretch, villain, scoundrel.

یسار yèssār, *s. a.* The left-hand side; the left wing of an army; riches, wealth.

یسارت yèssārèt, *s. a.* Riches, wealth, comfortable circumstances, comfort.

یساق yàssàk, *a. t.* Prohibited by the authorities; contraband.

یساقجی yàssàkji, *s. t.* A kind of guard or escort appointed to accompany strangers in Turkey for the purpose of seeing that no harm or insult was offered to them: they are still to be found attached to consulates and embassies, though, in the latter case, they are now more generally styled Kàwàss, the present Yassakji being quite an inferior attendant for carrying messages.

یستهلمك yèsstèhlémek (*aor.* یستهلر yèsstèhler), *v.n.* To dung, to mute.

يسر yùssr, *s. a.* Facility, ease; ease, comfort.
يسرت yùssrèt, *s. a.* Facility.
يسير yèssīr, *a. a.* Easy, not difficult; light, trifling, small, little, inconsiderable.
يشارمق yàsharmak (*aor.* يشارر yàsharir), *v.n.* To give out moisture, to run.
يشامق yàshamak (*aor.* يشار yàshar), *v.n.* To live; پادشاه يشا pādishāh-yAsha, Long live the Emperor!
يشل yèshil, *a. t.* Green; يشللك yèshillik, *s. t.* Verdure; greens, vegetables; يشللنمك yèshillEnmek, *v.n.* To become green with verdure; to make hot love to anyone, to exhibit lewdness in talk and action.
يشم yèshem, *s. t.* Jasper; بلغمى يشم bàlghàmī-yèshem, Precious jasper, looking like phlegm in colours.
يصدانمق yàssdAnmak, *v.n.* To recline by leaning on the elbow.
يصدق yàssdik, *s. t.* A pillow; a bolster; a cushion; يوز يصديغى yùz-yàssdighi, A pillow.
يعقوب Yàkūb, *s. a.* Jacob.
يعنى yà''nī, *ad. a.* That is to say.
يغما yàghma, *s. t.* Booty, plunder; sacking, plundering; ا—, —et, *v.a.* To sack, plunder; to scramble for; يغماجى yàghmaji, A plunderer.
يغمق yìghmak (*aor.* يغار yìghar), *v.a.* To pile up, heap up; to accumulate; يغلمق yèghilmak (*aor.* يغيلور yighilir), *v. p.* and *n.* To be piled or heaped up.
يغمور yàghmur, *s. t.* Rain; يغمور ياغمق yàghmur-yàghmak, *v.n.* To rain; يغمورلق yàghmurluk, *s. t.* A cloak for rainy weather.
يغندى yìghindi, *s. t.* A heap fortuitously accumulated, an accumulation.
يغيلو yìghili, *a. t.* Heaped, piled, in heaps, in a pile, stacked.
يغين yìghin, *s. t.* A heap, a pile, a stack, a mow, a hay-cock.
يقا yàka, *s. t.* The collar of any dress; the coast, sea-coast, shore (but only in the widest sense, as of a continent or whole country); يقالق yàkalik, *s. t.* A piece of stuff or fur proper or sufficient to be made into a collar.
يقالمق yàkalamak (*aor.* يقالار yàkalar), *v.a.* To collar; to seize, lay hold of; to snatch, whip up; to obtain (a good employ).
يقامق yìkamak (*aor.* يقار yìkar), *v.a.* To wash; يقانمق yìkAnmak (*aor.* يقانور yìkAnir), *v.n.* To wash, to wash one's self; —, *v.p.* To be washed.
يقظان yàkAzĀn, *s. a.* Vigilance, watchfulness.
يقظه yàkza, *s. a.* Waking, not being asleep.
يقلاشمق yàklashmak (*aor.* يقلاشور yàklashir), *v.n.* To approach, draw near; يقلاشدرمق yàklashdirmak, To cause or allow to approach; to put or bring near; يقلاشلمق yàklashilmak, *v.p.* To be such that things can approach it.
يقمق yìkmak (*aor.* يقار yìkar), *v.a.* To throw down, pull down, demolish, knock down, throw prostrate; يقلمق yikilmak, *v.n.* To fall down, tumble

down; —, *v.p.* To be thrown down, demolished, pulled down; to be cast down, knocked down; یقلەجق yìkilajak, *a. t.* Ready to fall down, in a ruinous condition.

یقندی yìkindi, *s. t.* Fallen materials of a demolished building.

یقین yàkin, *a. t.* Near, close; —, yàkīn, *s. a.* Certain knowledge, positive knowledge; یقیناً yàkīnan, *ad. a.* For certain, positively; علم الیقین "ìl-mu-'l-yàkīn, Positive knowledge; یقینیات yàkīnìyyāt, *s. pl. a.* Things positively known, known for certain.

یك yèk, *a. p.* One; sole; —, yègh, *a. t.* Preferable; —, yèng, *s. t.* A cuff, the lower parts of a sleeve.

یکا (*erroneously used for* یانه) yàna, To *or* on the side; on account of, in respect of.

یکاز yàngaz, *a. t.* Hard to please, quarrelsome.

یکاق yàngak, یناق yànak, *s. t.* A cheek.

یکانه yèghyānè, *s. p.* A sole, unique thing; یکانکی yèghyānéghī, *s. p.* Uniqueness.

یکان‌یکان yèghyān-yèghyān, *ad. p.* One by one.

یکپاره yèkpārè, *a. p.* Consisting of one single piece.

یکتا yèktā, *a. p.* Unique.

یکجهت yèk-jìhèt, *a. p.* Unanimous, accordant; یکجهتی yèk-jìhètī, *s. p.* Unanimity, accord, concord.

یکچشم yèk-chèshm, *s. p.* A one-eyed man; a person blind of one eye.

یکدیکر yèk-dìgher, *pron. p.* One another, each other.

یکرمی yìghirmi, *a. t.* Twenty; یکرمنجی yìghirminji, *a. t.* The twentieth.

یکزبان yèk-zàbān, *a. p.* Unanimous in what they say.

یکسان yèksān, *a. p.* Equal, similar; یرایله یکسان yèr-ilè-yèksān, Level with the earth.

یکشنبه yèkshènbih, *s. p.* Sunday.

یکن yèghen, *s. t.* A nephew.

یکون yèkyūn, *s. a.* A sum total.

یکه yèkè, *s. t.* The helm, bar of a rudder; —, *a. p.* (*in composition*), One; sole, unique.

یکی yèngi, *a. t.* New; یکیدن yèngidan, *ad. t.* Newly.

یکیچری yèngichéri, *s. t.* A janissary; the old Turkish embodied militia; یکیچری‌وقعه‌سی yèngichéri-wàk"àssi, The last rebellion and final suppression of the janissaries.

یکیت yìghit, *s. t.* A young man; a brave fellow, hero, champion; بابا یکیت bāba-yìghit, A full-grown young man; غریب یکیت ghàrīb--yìghit (kàripīt), A poor fellow in bad circumstances, *as though he were away from home and among strangers.*

یل yèl, *s. t.* The wind; a fart; wind on the stomach; rheumatism; a swelling; قره یل kàra-yèl, The north-west wind or quarter; یلدز قره یل yìldiz-kàra-yèl, N.N.W.; باطی قره یل bàti-kàra-yèl, W.N.W.; یللنمك yèllenmek, *v.n.* To break wind; یله ویرمك yèla-vèrmek, *v.a.* To give to the winds; —*or* ییل yìl, *s. t.* A year;

يللق yìllik, *s. t.* Annual pay or allowance; —, *a. t.* A year old; sufficient for a year. [drinking trough.

يلاغ yàlagh, يلاق yàlak, *s. t.* A trough,

يلان yìlan, *s. t.* A snake, serpent; —, yàlan, *s. t.* A lie, falsehood; —, *a. t.* False; يلان بالغى yìlan-bàlighi, An eel; يلانجى yàlanji, *s. t.* A liar; —, *a. t.* False, artificial. [Anthony's fire.

يلانجق yìlanjik, *s. t.* The erysipelas, St.

يلپازه yèlpāzé, *s. t.* A fan.

يلتاقلنمق yàltaklanmak (*aor.* يلتاقلنور yàltaklanir), *v.n.* To fawn, act fawningly.

يلتنمك yèltenmek (*aor.* يلتنور yèltènir), *v.n.* To pursue as an avowed admirer, to make love, coax, flatter, run after (women, &c.).

يلدا yèldā, *a. p.* The longest (night of winter); شب يلدا shèbi-yèldā, The longest night of winter; a period of eight days in mid-winter, when the nights are longest.

يلدرم yìldirim, *s. t.* A thunderbolt; the electric fluid; —چارپمق, yìldirim-chàrpmak, To strike (objects, the lightning).

يلدز yìldiz, *s. t.* A star; the north wind or quarter of the horizon; يلدز پويراز yìldiz-pòyraz, N.N.E.; يلدز قره يل yìldiz-kàra-yèl, N.N.W.; قويرقلو يلدز kùyruklu-yìldiz (Tailed star), a comet; اوچان يلدز ùchan-yìldiz, A shooting star; اى ايله يلدز ày-(lan)-yìldiz, The crescent and star (the arms or symbol of Turkey and the Ottomans); يلدز طاشى yìldiz-tàshi (Star-stone) The sparkling composition stone called in French "*aventurine*." [of an arrow.

يلك yèlek, *s. t.* A waistcoat; the feather

يلكن yèlken, *s. t.* A sail; يلكن بزى yèlken-bèzi, Sail-cloth, canvas; يلكن اچمق yèlken-àchmak, *v.n.* To set sail; يلكن باغلامق yèlken-bàghlamak, To furl sails; يلكنجى yèlkenji, *s. t.* A sail-maker; يلكنلو yèlkenli, *a. t.* Under sail; having sails; sailing.

يلمان yèlman, *s. t.* The sharp, curved, cutting part of a sabre's blade.

يلمك yèlmek (*aor.* يلور yèlir), *v.n.* (*Obsolete or provincial*), To run, run about.

يله yèlé, *s. t.* The mane.

يم yèm, *s. a.* A feed of corn; a bait (for a hook or trap); —, *particle placed before* يشل, *as* يم يشل yèm-yèshil, Quite green; —, yèmm, *s. a.* The sea, the ocean.

يما yàma, *s. t.* A patch; يمالو yàmali, *a. t.* Patched; —اورمق, yàma-wùrmak, *v.n.* To put in a patch.

يماق yàmak, *s. t.* An assistant, helper, mate.

يمامق yàmamak (*aor.* يمار yàmar), *v.a.* To place as an assistant; to place by the side of anything, to clap into a place; يمانمق yàmanmak, *v.n.* To clap one's self close to anything, huddle up to anything; to manage to get into service; —, *v.p.* To be clapt close up against anything;

يماندرمق yàmAndirmak, v.a. To cause or allow (anything) to huddle or be clapt, to clap close up (against something else).

يمان yàmAn, a. t. Bad; unkind; cruel; inauspicious, unlucky.

يمش yèmish, s. t. Fruit; قورو يمش kùru-yèmish, Dried fruit; —, a. t. Who has eaten; who has received or taken.

يمك yèmèk, s. t. Food, victuals; a meal; —, yèmek (aor. ير yèr), v.a. To eat; to receive or take; يمك يمك yèmèk-yèmek, v.n. To eat food, to take a meal; بوق يمك bòk-yèmek, خلط يمك khAlt-yèmek, v.n. To tell a lie; to do or say anything one has no business to do; —طياق dàyak-yèmek, v.n. To be thrashed, flogged, bastinadoed; —رشوت rìshvet-yèmek, To take bribes; قوشلق يمكى kùsh-luk - yèmèghi, Breakfast or lunch; اخشام يمكى (Aksham) - yèmèghi, Dinner or supper.

يملك yèmlik, s. t. A manger.

يملمك yèmlémek (aor. يملر yèmler), v.a. To bait (a trap or hook); to prime (a gun); to lay a train (to a mine).

يملمه yèmlémé, s. t. A train laid to a mine.

يمن yùmn, s. a. Felicity, prosperity; good augury, auspiciousness; —, Yèmen, s. a. Arabia Felix; —قهوه‌سی, yèmen-kàhwéssi, Mocha coffee.

يمنى yèméni, s. t. A handkerchief; a Turkish shoe; —, yùmnà, s. a. The right hand. [pest.

يمورجق yìmurjàk, s. t. The plague,

يمورطلمق yìmurtlamak (aor. يمورطلار yìmurtlar), v.a. To lay (eggs); —, v.n. To lay eggs.

يمورط yìmurta, s. t. An egg; egg-shaped lumps of steel from which Damascus blades are wrought; بالق يمورطه‌سی bàlik - yìmurtassi, The roe or spawn of fish; botargo, the dried roe of the grey mullet; قزل يمورطه kìzil-yìmurta (Red eggs), The Easter Eggs, prepared by boiling them with logwood; يمورطه‌نك اقی yìmurtaning - Aki, The white of an egg; يمورطه‌نك صاریسی yìmurtaning--sArissi, The yelk or yolk of an egg.

يموشاتمق yìmushAtmak (aor. يموشادر yìmushAdir), v.a. To soften; to make tender; to render mild. [mild.

يموشاق yìmushAk, a. t. Soft; tender;

يموشامق yìmushamak (aor. يموشار yìmushar), v.n. To become soft, tender, or mild.

يموشانمق yìmushAnmak (aor. يموشانور yìmushAnir), v.p. To be made soft, or tender.

يمين yèmīn, s. a. An oath; the right-hand side; the right wing of an army; —ا, yèmīn-et, v.n. To take an oath, to swear; يمينلو yèmīnli, a. t. Who has taken an oath, under an oath.

ينابيع yènābī", s. pl. a. (of ينبوع yènbū"), Springs, sources.

يناشمق yànashmak (*aor.* يناشور yàna-shir), *v.n.* To approach, to near.

يناشمه yànashma, *s. t.* A farm servant on yearly wages and board.

يناق yànak, *s. t.* A cheek.

ينبغى yènbàghī, *v.a.* Is suitable, is meet; *in* كما ينبغى kèmā-yènbàghī, *ad. a.* As is suitable, as is meet, suitable, well.

ينبوع yènbūʻ, *s. a.* A spring, source.

ينكچ yènghèch, *s. t.* A crab.

ينكه yènghé, *s. t.* The wife of an uncle, an aunt by marriage.

ينمك yènmek (*aor.* ينور yènir), *v.a.* To overcome, vanquish, conquer, beat; —, *or* ينلمك yènilmek, *v.p.* To be eaten; to be such as can be eaten; ينلمك yènilmek, *v.p.* To be beaten, vanquished, overcome, conquered.

ينه yīné (ghèné), *ad. t.* Again; once more; still, yet, but, on the other hand.

يوا yiwa, *s. t.* A nest.

يوارلاق yiwarlàk, *a. t.* Round, globular.

يوارلمق yiwarlamak (*aor.* يوارلار yiwar-lar), *v.a.* To roll; to roll over, knock over; يوارلنمق yiwarlanmak, *v.n.* To roll, roll over, roll down.

يواش yàwāsh, *a. t.* Mild; gentle; slow; —! *int. t.* Gently! Slowly! Softly!

يوالق yùwalàk, *s. t.* A ball; a bullet.

يوتمق yùtmak (*aor.* يوتار yùtar), *v.a.* To swallow, swallow up, swallow down.

يوجه yùja, *a. t.* (*obsolete and provincial*), High; tall.

يوخا yūkhā! *int. t.* Now then! Where are you driving to?

يوخسل yòkhsūl, *a. t.* Friendless.

يوخسه yòkhsa, *c. t.* Or else, otherwise, or (after or before a negative).

يورتى yòrtu, *s. t.* A Christian or Jewish festival or holiday.

يورد yùrd, *s. t.* A habitation, country, home; يوردلق yùrdluk, A fief or place special as a home; يوردلق اوجاقلق وجهيله yùrdluk-òjaklik-vèjhlé, By way of fief as a home and as an hereditary domain.

يورغان yùrghan, *s. t.* A coverlet, quilt for a bed; يورغانجى yùrghanji, A maker of upholstery, bedding, sofas, curtains, &c.

يورغون yòrghun, *a. t.* Tired, fatigued; يورغونلق yòrghunluk, *s. t.* Fatigue, tiredness; يورغونلغى المق yòrghun-lughunu-àlmak, *v.n.* To obviate or drive away fatigue, to rest one's self.

يورك yùrek, *s. t.* The heart; courage; hard-heartedness; اكا يورك استر ànga--yùrek-ìsster, For that one requires courage, or a heart of stone; يوركلو yùrekli, *a. t.* Courageous; يوركسز yùreksiz, *a. t.* Timid; يوركلنمك yùreklenmek, *v.n.* To take heart; يوركلندرمك yùreklendirmek, *v.a.* To encourage, give heart.

يورمق yòrmak (*aor.* يورار yòrar), *v.a.* To tire, to fatigue, to harass; يورلمق yòrulmak, *v.n.* To grow tired, to become fatigued, to be harassed; يورلتمق yòrultmak, *v.a.* To cause to fatigue one's self.

يوروك yùruk, *a. t.* Which goes fast,

travels fast, walks fast; nomade; —, *s. t.* A man of certain nomade tribes; a Turcoman.

يورويش yùruyush, *s. t.* A manner of walking; a charge, assault, escalade.

يوريمك yùrumek (*aor.* يورور *or* يورر yùrur), *v.n.* To walk, to go, to travel; يوريتمك *or* يوروتمك yùrutmek, *v.a.* To cause or allow to walk, go, or travel; يورينمك *or* يورونمك yùrunmek, *v.n.* To be such that one can walk it, *or* in, *or* on it; يورويبويرمك yùruyu-vèrmek, To just walk off *or* away.

يوز yùz, *a. t.* One hundred; —, *s. t.* The face; the right side (of any stuff, &c.); a side; اق يوزلو Àk-yùzlu, *a. t.* Whose face is white or clean, who has no reason to be ashamed; يوزى قره yùzu-kàra, *a. t.* Whose face is black, who has reason to be ashamed; يوز يوزه yùz-yùzé, Face to face; يوز سورمك yùz-sùrmek (To rub the face), *v.n.* To throw one's self at one's feet, and rub one's face (against the feet, the ground, skirts, &c.); يوز چويرمك yùz-chèvirmek, *v.n.* To turn the face (away, towards, &c.); يوز ويرمك yùz-vèrmek, *v.n.* To encourage one's impudence; يوز كوسترمك yùz-ghyùss-termek, *v.n.* To show itself, appear, come forth; يوزبولمق yùz-bùlmak, *v.n.* To grow bold from foolish encouragement; to put on a bold face; to dare; يوز اكشتمك yùz-èkshit-mek, *v.n.* To make a sour face; يوزى قوين yùzu-kòyun, *ad. t.* Flat on the face and belly (to lie or fall); يوزسز yùzsuz, *a. t.* Bold, impudent, shameless; كولر يوزلو ghyùlær-yùzlu, *a. t.* Having a cheerful countenance; ايكى يوزلو ìki-yuzlu, *a. t.* Two-faced, hypocritical.

يوزبك Yùzbek, *s.* and *a. t.* Uzbek, an [Usbek.

يوزك yùzuk, *s. t.* A finger-ring set with a stone or seal.

يوزلشمك yùzlæshmek (*aor.* يوزلشور yùz-læshir), *v.n. recip.* To come or be put face to face with someone; يوزلشدرمك yùzlæshdirmek, *v.a.* To bring face to face.

يوزمك yùzmek (*aor.* يوزر yùzær), *v.n.* To swim; —, *v.a.* To skin, to flay.

يوسف Yūsùf, *s. a.* The name of the patriarch Joseph; the proper name Joseph in general.

يوصمه yòssma, *a. t.* Fine, handsome-looking (young man).

يوصون yòssun, *s. t.* Moss; يوصونلو كل yòssunlu-ghyùl, A moss rose; يوصون باغلامق yòssun-bàghlamak, To gather moss, become mossy.

يوغرت yòghurt, *s. t.* A kind of sourish curds and whey.

يوغرمق yòghurmak (*aor.* يوغرر yòghu-rur), *v.a.* To knead.

يوغن *or* يوغون yòghun, *a. t.* (*obsolete or provincial*), Coarse; thick.

يوف yūf! *int. t.* Oh! (*mark of contempt*); يوف سكا yūf-sànga! Fie upon thee!

يوفقه yūfka, *a. t.* Very thin in substance; —, *s. t.* A kind of wafer-cake.

يوق yòk, *ad. t.* No; —, *a. t.* Absent; non-existent; سن يوق ايكن sèn-yòk-iken, While you are *or* were absent; يوق ا yòk-et, *v.a.* To annihilate; —, *or* يوقدر yòk-d*i*r, There exists not, it exists not; he is not here; he (she, it) is absent, *or* does not exist; يوقلق yòklυk, *s. t.* The want, the absence, the non-existence (of anything); يوق يره yòk-yèr*a*, *ad. t.* Without cause, for a reason which does or did not exist in reality.

يوقارى yŭkār*i*, *s. t.* The upper, higher part or top of anything; —, *ad. t.* Up, upwards; يوقاريده yŭkàr*i*d*a* (yŭ-kàrd*a*), Up, upstairs, at the top or upper part; يوقاريدن yŭkàr*i*d*a*n, From above, from the top; يوقاريدن اشاغى yŭkàr*i*d*a*n-àshàg*hi*, From top to bottom; from beginning to end.

يوقش yòkυsh, *s. t.* A hill, an ascent; يوقش يوقارى yòkυsh-yŭkàr*i*, *ad. t.* Up-hill; يوقش اشاغى yòkυsh - àshàg*hi*, *ad. t.* Down-hill; يوقشلو yòkυshlυ, *a. t.* Having several or many hills or ascents.

يوقلامق yòklam*a*k (*aor.* يوقلار yòklar), *v.a.* To examine, inspect, search; يوقلانمق yòklanm*a*k, *v.p.* To be examined, searched, inspected.

يوقلمه yòklam*a*, *s. t.* An examination; search, inspection; a muster; — دفترى yòklam*a*-dèftèri, A muster-roll.

يوك yùk, *s. t.* A load, burden; a cargo; luggage, baggage; a sum of a hundred thousand piastres; the number one hundred thousand; a large closet where bedding is put away in the daytime; —, yùn*g*, *s. t.* Wool; يوكلو yùklu, *a. t.* Loaded, laden; يوكلنمك yùklεnmek (*aor.* يوكلنور yùklεnir), *v.n.* To take one's load, load one's self; —, *v.p.* To be loaded, to have a load put in or on one; to be put in or on a thing or person as a load; to be imputed or charged to anyone as a fault; يوكلتمك yùklεtmek (*aor.* يوكلدر yùk-lédir), *v.a.* To load, to place as a load (in or upon anything); to load, to place a load in or upon (anything); to impute or charge (anything) as a fault (to anyone); يوك حيوانى yùk--hàywān*i*, A baggage-horse; يوك عربه‌سى yùk-‘‘àrab*assi*, A cart or waggon.

يوكسك yùksek, *a. t.* High, tall; —, *s. t.* A high position; يوكسكلك yùkseklik, *s. t.* Height, altitude; يوكسكه چيقمق yùksé*gha*-ch*i*km*a*k, To mount a high spot; يوكسك چيقمق yùksek-ch*i*km*a*k, To rise high up.

يوكسوك yùksuk, *s. t.* A thimble.

يول yòl, *s. t.* A road, way, path; a way, manner; the proper way; a career in life, a profession; a custom, usage; a habit; a way, means; a journey, a voyage; distance; a channel of any kind; communication (from place to place); the cause, sake, or love (of anything dear to one); يول امرى yòl-èmri, A kind of special passport for the interior of the country; يوليله yòlīla, *ad. t.* In the proper way (to do, to speak, &c.); يول المق yòl-àlmak, To make way, advance; يول طوتمق yòl-tùtmak, To take any particular road; بر يولدن اورمق bìr-yòldan-wùrmak, To turn into any road; يوله چيقمق yòla-chìkmak, To set out, take one's departure; يولنى بولمق yòlunu-bùlmak, To find the way; to find one's way; يوله كيرمك yòla-ghìrmek, To come right, to get right; يولنه كيرمك yòluna-ghìrmek, To get into proper order; صو يولى sù-yòlu, A conduit of water; اياق يولى àyak-yòlu, A privy, water-closet; وطن يولنه wàtan-yòluna, In the cause of one's country; دين يولنه dīn-yòluna, For the sake of religion; حق يولنه hàkk-yòluna, In the cause of truth, or of God; يولجى yòlju, *s. t.* A traveller, wayfarer; يولجيلق yòljuluk, *s. t.* Travel; يولجيلق نه زمان yòljuluk-nè-zàmān? When do you set out on your journey? When do you start? يولداش yòldash, *s. t.* A fellow-traveller; one in the same career (a term much used by the janissaries to each other, now much less used; قپو يولداشى kàpi-yòldashi, A fellow-servant under the same master; يوللو yòllu, *a. t.* Right, proper, regular, in rule; يوللو يولنجه yòllu-yòlunja, *ad. t.* In the proper and regular way; يولسز yòlsuz, *a. t.* Irregular, out of order; improper, unbecoming; sent to Coventry (a tradesman by his trade-corporation; he is then debarred from all the privileges of his order).

يولار yùlar, *s. t.* A headstall.

يولاف yùlaf, *s. t.* Oats.

يوللامق yòllamak (*aor.* يوللار yòllar), *v.a.* To send; يوللاتمق yòllatmak (*aor.* يوللادر yòlladìr), *v.a.* To cause or allow to send or be sent; يوللانمق yòllanmak, *or* يوللانلمق yòllanìlmak (*aor.* يوللانور yòllanir, يوللانيلور yòllanilir), *v.p.* To be sent; to be such as can be sent. [pluck, to strip.

يولمق yòlmak (*aor.* يولار yòlar), *v.a.* To

يوم yèvm (yùvm), *s. a.* A day; يوماً فيوما yèvman-fè-yèvmā, *ad. a.* Day by day, day after day, from day to day; اليوم èl-yèvm, *ad. a.* To-day, now, at present; كل يوم kyùllu-yèvmin, *ad. a.* Every day. In all the following terms this word signifies *the day of judgment*; يوم الدين yèvmu-'d-dīn, يوم القيام yèvmu-'l-kìyām, يوم القيامت yèvmu-'l-kìyāmèt, يوم الحساب yèvmu-'l-hìssāb, يوم الميعاد yèvmu-'l-mì''ād, يوم الميثاق yèvmu-'l-mīssāk, يوم القرار yèvmu-'l-kàrār, يوم السؤال yèvmu-'ss-sù'āl, &c. &c. &c. The following are the days of the week in order: Sunday, يوم الاحد yèvmu-'l-àhàd; Monday, يوم الاثنين yèvmu-'l-ìssnèyn; Tuesday, يوم الثلاثا yèvmu-'ss-sèlāssā;

Wednesday, يوم الاربعا **yèvmù - 'l - -èrba''ā ; Thursday,** يوم الخميس **yèvmu-'l-khàmīss ; Friday,** يوم الجمعه **yèvmu-'l-jùm''à ; Saturday,** يوم السبت **yèvmu-'ss-sèbt ;** يومى **yèvmī** (*fem.* يوميه **yèvmìyyé**), *a. a.* Daily ; يوميه **yèvmìyyé,** *s. a.* Daily pay or allowance.

يوماق **yùmak,** *s. t.* A ball (of thread, &c.).

يومرق **yùmruk,** *s. t.* The fist ; a blow with the fist.

يومرى **yùmru,** *a. t.* Round like the fist ; —, *s. t.* A large bump or swelling.

يومق **yùmak** (*aor.* يور **yùr**), *v.a.* (*obsolete or provincial*), To wash.

يوممق **yùmmak** (*aor.* يومار **yùmar**), *v.a.* To close tight (one's own eyes).

يونان **yūnān,** *s. t.* A Greek (of the little kingdom) ; an ancient Greek ; يونانى **yūnānī,** *a. a.* The ancient Greek (language).

يونانستان **yūnānisstān,** *s. t.* Greece.

يونتمق **yòntmak** (*aor.* يونتار **yòntar**), *v.a.* To make, to mend (a pen).

يونجه **yònja,** *s. t.* Lucerne, clover, sainfoin, trefoil.

يونس **Yònuss,** *s. a.* Jonah ; —, *and* يونس بالغى **Yònuss-bàlighi,** A porpoise.

يونغه *or* يونقه **yòngha,** *s. t.* A carpenter's chips and chocks.

يونمق **yònmak** (*aor.* يونار **yònar**), *v.a.* To cut or chip into shape (stone).

يه **yé, ya,** *pr. t.* (*joined only to words ending with a vowel*), To, towards ; for, on account of.

يهود **yàhūd,** *s. t.* The Jewish nation ; يهودى **yàhūdī,** *s. t.* A Jew.

يى **yi, yi.** *Termination of the definite accusative of nouns or nominal phrases, if ending in a vowel.*

ييل **yìl,** *s. t.* A year.

ييو **yìv, yìw,** *s. t.* A groove.

ييه‌جك **yèyéjek,** *s. t.* Food, victuals, eatables ; —, *a. t.* Ready to eat ; ready to be eaten.

END OF PART THE SECOND.

ERRATUM.

PAGE 55.—*For* Bosphorus, *s.* چناق قلعه‌سی chànak-kàléssi, *read* قره دكز بوغازى Kàra-dèngiz-bòghâzi, or بوغاز Bòghâz.

APPENDIX.

Ordinary geographical names which are well known to the Turks and whose orthography is settled, have been inserted in the body of both parts of this enlarged edition of the Dictionary. As, however, until the last few years the names of many important countries, towns, rivers, &c. out of the Turkish dominions were unknown to most Turks, and are still unfamiliar to the mass of the people, these could scarcely be considered as regularly received into the Turkish language, and their orthography was quite unsettled, and even now is somewhat uncertain. Several of these newly-adopted names having come under my notice in official documents too late to be inserted in the body of the Dictionary, I think it well to append them here, together with a few Turkish names of places accidentally omitted.—C. W.

ازميد **Ezmìd**, *s. t.* Ismid (town of, in Asia Minor).

ازاق **Azàk**, *s. t.* Azof (Sea of).

استوقولم **Isstòkolm**, *s. t.* Stockholm.

المانيا **Alàmānyà**, *s. t.* Germany.

انطاكيه **Antākiyà**, *s. a.* Antioch.

انقونه **Ancòna**, *s. t.* Ancona.

ايدين **Aydin**, *s. t.* Aden.

بارسلونه **Bàrsèlōna**, *s. t.* Barcelona.

باطوم **Bàtūm**, *s. t.* Batoum.

باب المندب **Bāb-u'l-Māndèb**, *s. a.* The Straits of Babelmandeb.

بايون **Bàyòn**, *s. t.* Bayonne.

برست **Brèst**, *s. t.* Brest.

برلين **Bèrlìn**, *s. t.* Berlin.

برم **Brèm**, *s. t.* Bremen.

برمنقام **Bìrmìnkām**, *s. t.* Birmingham.

بروكسل **Brùksel**, *s. t.* Brussels.

بريستول **Brìsstol**, *s. t.* Bristol.

بريندیزی **Brìndìsì**, *s. t.* Brindisi.

برەزيليا **Brèzīlyà**, *s. t.* Brazil.

بعلبك **Bà''lbèk**, *s. a.* Baalbek.

بوردو **Bordò**, *s. t.* Bordeaux.

بوستون **Bòston**, *s. t.* Boston (in America).

بومباى **Bòmbày**, *s. t.* Bombay.

بيروت **Bèyrūt**, *s. a.* Beyrout.

بيوك اطه **Bìyuk-Ada**, *s. t.* Pringipo (the island of, near Constantinople).

بيوك دره **Bìyuk-dèrè**, Buyukderé (a watering place on the Bosphorus).

پالرمو **Palèrmo**, *s. t.* Palermo.

پترسبورغ **Pètersbūrgh**, *s. t.* Petersburgh.

پشته **Pèshta**, *s. t.* Pesth.

پورتكيز **Pòrtàghìz**, *s. t.* Portugal.

ترابيه **Tàrāpiyà**, *s. t.* Therapia (on the Bosphorus, a summer residence of the European ambassadors).

تريسته **Trièsté**, *s. t.* Trieste.

تولونه **Tùlòn*a*,** *s. t.* **Toulon.**
تفلیس **Tìflìs,** *s. t.* **Tiflis.**
حاجی طرخان **Hājì-tìrkhān,** *s. p.* **Astrakhan.**
حلب **Hālèb,** *s. t.* **Aleppo.**
دانزیك **Dànzìk,** *s. t.* **Dantzic.**
درسد **Drèssd,** *s. t.* **Dresden.**
دوبلین **Dūblin,** *s. t.* **Dublin.**
دونکرك **Dùnkèrk,** *s. t.* **Dunkerk.**
دیاربکر **Dìyār-bèkr,** *s. a.* **Diarbekir.**
دیەپ **Dièp,** *s. t.* **Dieppe.**
راکوزه **Ràgūz*a*,** *s. t.* **Ragusa.**
راونه **Ravèna,** *s. t.* **Ravenna.**
روتردام **Rùterdām,** *s. t.* **Rotterdam.**
رومانیا **Rūmāniѐ,** *s. t.* **Roumania.**
ساقسونیا **Sàksōniyà,** *s. t.* **Saxony.**
سویس **Sùwèyss,** *s. a.* **Suez.**
سیام **Sìyām,** *s. t.* **Siam.**
سیلان **Sìlān,** *s. t.* **Ceylon.**
شیراز **Shīrāz,** *s. p.* **Shiraz.**
شیقاغو **Shìkāgo,** *s. t.* **Chicago (in America).**
شیلی **Shīlī,** *s. t.* **Chili.**
صور **Sūr,** *s. a.* **Tyre (in Syria).**
طمشوار **Tèmèshvār,** *s. t.* **Temesvar.**
عینتاب **Ayntāb,** *s. t.* **Aintab.**
قرتال **Kàrtàl,** *s. t.* **Kartal (in Asia Minor).**
قونیه **Kòni*a*,** *s. t.* **Koniah.**
کلکته **Kàlkùtt*a*,** *s. p.* **Calcutta.**
لیەژ **Liézh,** *s. t.* **Liége.**
مارسلا **Marsàla,** *s. t.* **Marsala.**
مالتپه **Māltepé,** *s. t.* **Maltepe (in Asia Minor).**
مانحایم **Mànhaym,** *s. t.* **Mannheim.**
مانچستر **Mànchester,** *s. t.* **Manchester.**
مرعش **Mèràsh,** *s. t.* **Merash.**
مرمره **Màrmarà,** *s. t.* **Marmora (Sea of).**
میسولونغی **Missolònghi,** *s.t.* **Missolonghi.**
میلان **Mìlān,** *s. t.* **Milan.**

THE END.

لوندره شهرنده وایمان افندینك مطبعه سنده
طبع اولنمشدر